Jesus Christ
Message to All Nations

Second Edition

I, JESUS CHRIST, SPEAKETH TO ALL WORLD, OF MY COMING SOON, TO CEASE WAR WAY ENTIRE, LEST GOD-SENT POWER JUDGMENTS SOON COME TO SWEEP MORE WICKED OF ALL LANDS, WHO UPHOLD CHILD MURDER OF UNBORN YOUTH ORDER IN OWN LIVING AMONG THE ORDER OF MEN ON WORLD, KNOWING I, GOD, HAVE WARNED ALL PEOPLES OF JUDGMENT ORDER. REPENT YE, REPENT YE, ALL NATIONS ON EARTH, LEST FULL ORDER JUDGMENT COMETH SOON ALL OVER WORLD. AMEN.

Jesus Christ
Message to All Nations

Second Edition

Printed in the United States of America
ISBN-13: 978-1-937271-17-6

Preface

Revelation of the Lord Jesus Christ
Given to President Warren S. Jeffs
Palestine, Texas
Monday, July 9, 2012

1. The coming of our Lord draweth nigh.

2. Be ready, all peoples of world.

3. Now come full power order purity holy living, for I judgeth all soon, who is of more righteousness in all lands on earth.

4. Now repent unto change to better order of pure way living. Amen.

5. Come full way order to Priesthood of God soon, all nations.

6. My order is everlasting, governing eternity duration on holy world of cleansed order; fire spiritual purifying all world in soon happening on world, of heavenly fire coming from heaven, entire world burned of power Celestial of full life-giving order preserving all things pure. Amen.

7. Now be full order of the New Era of terrestrial world of the full power of holy resurrected people living at time of my holy way order, to govern all families on world.

8. Now be ready.

9. A holy order soon cometh. Amen.

10. I, Jesus Christ, do full order holy way holy revealing through Keyholding authority of full apostle order. Thus is Warren Jeffs now my Keyholder of holy apostle power, Holy Priesthood, holy way order. Amen.

Jesus Christ
Son Ahman

Revelation of the Lord Jesus Christ
Given to President Warren S. Jeffs
Palestine, Texas
Wednesday, September 19, 2012

1. I, Jesus Christ, God over all world, do send my book of full warning to all legal order, to use as full evidence my holy religion revealed through Prophets order on earth hath legal right to live religion; also to use as proof God is head of His Church and guides His servant in the way of innocence before His God, Warren Jeffs, as he also lives pure way before all peoples.

2. He is innocent.

3. Let him go free soon, so my Church on earth hath full leadership of Keyholding Priesthood order as is found described in Proclamation I send to all peoples, describing my, even God, right to full holy legal preserving religion of heaven on world.

4. Now do full reading, to learn my

revealed truth order about religion of pure order, now of persecuted unholy way by nations on my land of my soon coming to New Order Zion. Amen.

We, the undersigned, bear testimony to all the world the Lord Jesus Christ speaketh all word of God herein, as a full now warning great happenings soon at hand before all world. Let all the earth resound with rejoicing: Thy Lord cometh! Now be holy order ready, as only the more righteous shall remain. Amen.

_11-18-2012_

Lyle S. Jeffs

Elder in the Fundamentalist
Church of Jesus Christ of Latter-day Saints

Nov 18, 2012

Ben E. Johnson

Elder in the Fundamentalist
Church of Jesus Christ of Latter-day Saints

Jesus Christ
Message to All Nations

Second Edition
Table of Contents

Chapter 1

Warning of the Lord Jesus Christ Through His Servant Warren Jeffs, to the United States of America

Warning of the Lord Jesus Christ to All Nations

Policies and General Principles of the Government of Son Ahman in the Kingdom of Ahman

Chapter 2

Continued Warnings of Son Ahman to the Leaders of the Nations of the Earth

SECTION REVELATION 84

Thus Saith Son Ahman, Who Is Jesus Christ, the God of Heaven and the Earth, by Whom All Things Exist, to the Leaders and Peoples of the Nation of Ivory Coast -- Words of Counsel and Warning Pertaining to Becoming Peaceful, and of My Glorious Appearing Soon at Hand, to Rule All Nations in a Condition of Peace, Having the Power of Heaven With Me to Rule in a Righteous Government and Dominion -- Thus Is the Word of the Lord to Thee:

SECTION REVELATION 85

Thus Saith Son Ahman, Jesus Christ, the Creator of Heaven and Earth, Who Speaketh From on High Through My Mouthpiece On Earth, to Your Understanding, Even to the Leaders of the Nation of Kazakhstan, the Leaders Thereof and the Peoples Thereof -- A Word of Warning, of Judgments to Come Upon Thee of the Cleansing Powers of an Almighty God Coming Forth, Whose Arm Shall Be Made Manifest Thereby to Your Knowing -- Thus Hear and Heed My Word, Which Saith Thus:

Chapter 3

Thus Saith Son Ahman, Even Your Lord Jesus Christ, My Own Will to All Nations on Earth of Full Power to Be Fulfilled, Unto All Knowing I, God, Have Spoken Eternal Power Upon All Nations

Now let my warning to all peoples be of my final warning in power unto confounding the wicked in a way of knowing I speak truth of their horrible crimes of moral and murdering ways.

SECTION REVELATION 86

Thus Saith Your Lord Jesus Christ, the Holy Power of Redeeming Power for All Mankind of All Nations, of All Ages of Time, to All Nations, Peoples, Kindreds, Tongues, and Governing Powers; My Own Word in Great Plainness to All Peoples, of My Own Coming; of Great Whirlwind Judgments of the Pure Way of My Holy Love Justifying Judgments of Eternity Power; Thus Giving Mine Own Word to All Peoples on Earth; a Word of Eternal Importance to All Now on the Earth, to Be of Full Receiving My Own Will Concerning All Peoples on Earth; Also to Teach Truth of Pure Way of Judging, of Holy Way of My Eternal Law of Holy Marriage Union of Eternal Union of Plural Celestial Marriage of My Holy Power Authorizing Select Few to

Thus Live; Not to Be of Interference by Any Not of My Own Authority of Holy Eternal Priesthood of My Sending; Thus Saith the Lord to This Now Generation on the Earth, My Own Will to All; Both of the Governing Powers of All Nations; Also Their Peoples: Hear Thou My Holy Message Given by My Holy Servant on Earth as My Mouthpiece, Though in Bondage; to Be in the Hands of All Peoples, to Know of My Soon Labor of Cleansing All Lands of More Wicked, to Preserve the More Righteous; Yea, Hear My Own Word Given Through My Own Power, to My Holy Servant Warren Jeffs; Though Suffering in Prison, Yet of My Order of Pure Priesthood of Holy Calling to Give My Own Will to All Peoples, by My Power, Who Will Receive My Word.

Thus Saith Jesus Christ, Your Lord and Holy Redeemer, Even the God Over All, to All Peoples, Nations, Kindreds, Tongues, Governing Powers on Earth, My Own Will Revealed From Heaven to All, to Know My Full Final Warning of Whirlwind Judgments Soon to Be on All the Earth; War, Famines, Earthquakes, Pestilences, Yea, of Every Kind, to Sweep the More Wicked Off the Earth; Preserving the More Righteous, Unto Zion Soon to Come Forth by Almighty Power of Mine Own Authority on Earth; to Be of Full Power of Heaven to Govern All Nations; Therefore, Give Heed Unto My Word, Even Saying Thus:

SECTION REVELATION 91

Thus Saith Jesus Christ, Who Is Son Ahman, to the Leader of This Nation of the United States of America, and All the Leaders of This Nation in Their Several Governing Appointments and Powers; and Thus to the Peoples of This Nation, Mine Own Word From the Heavens; Even the God of Glory Who Speaketh Thus to Your Understandings -- A Call to Heed My Word, Even I Who Am Soon to Come in the Powers of Heaven to Dwell Among Men, a Governing Power Over All Nations of the Earth -- Hear My Words:

SECTION REVELATION 92

Thus Saith Son Ahman, Even Your Lord and Savior Who Hath Redeemed All Mankind, Jesus Christ, Who Speaketh to the Leaders and Peoples of the Nation of Nicaragua Through the Revelations of My Will Coming Forth to Thine Understanding, Hear My Word Saying Thus:

Your National and World Power Soon at Hand, as You Continue in Your Ungodly and Wicked Practices. Heed My Word as I Give My Declaration Herein:

SECTION REVELATION 5

A Petition to the President of the United States of America

SECTION REVELATION 63

Thus Saith Son Ahman, Even Jesus Christ, the God Over All Creation, to the President of the United States of America

SECTION REVELATION 70

Thus Saith Son Ahman, Even Jesus Christ, Your Lord and Savior Who Hath Redeemed All Mankind, Whose Right It Is to Rule Over the Heavens and the Earth, a Just God Who Sees and Knows All Things, and Shall Recompense to Every Man That Which He Has Measured to His Fellow Man, According to the Light and Knowledge They Have Received: Thus I Speak to the President of the United States of America, Now in Power, and Also to the Peoples of This Nation -- This Message of Warning of the Doctrine of Eternal Judgment Upon Thee, Even Upon All Peoples, Being the God of Eternal Power, an Eternal God Who Shall Bring All to Justice; Whose Mercy Shall Claim Those Who Repenteth in a Manner to Earn

the Benefit of My Atoning Power -- Even Him, a God of Atoning and Redeeming Power, Who Suffered on the Cross and Was Raised From the Grave Unto Eternal Power to Judge All Mankind According as Their Works Are:

SECTION REVELATION 120

Thus Saith Jesus Christ, Son Ahman, to the Organization of Church Name, of Legal Name, Called the Church of Jesus Christ of Latter-day Saints, Now Not My Church, but of a Falling Away from My Priesthood; My Own Message to Thee of Pure Revealing, of Final Warning of Judgments Soon to Be Upon Thee and All on My Land of Zion. Thus I Bind Up the Law and Seal Up the Testimony Against All Who Are Against Me and My Holy Authority Among Men. Be Ye Now Warned of Judgments and to Be Now No More of My Name, Having Fought Against My Will and Holy Word. This Is My Message to Thee of Full Way Warning:

Thus Saith the Lord Jesus Christ, Even Son Ahman, to the Nations of the Earth, Another Final Warning: Heed My Word. Amen.

I, the Lord Jesus Christ, Say My Holy Word Unto You, the Peoples of the Earth and Leaders of Nations, I Whose Right It Is to Rule, Receive Ye My Word Saying Thus:

SECTION REVELATION 121

Chapter 4

Jesus Christ, Son Ahman, Sendeth Power-Word of Warning to All Peoples on Earth, Warning of Judgments of Full Power, to Call on All to Repent; Thus I Am Just, and of Full Authority to Render Judgment on All Nations

SECTION REVELATION 130

I, your Lord Jesus Christ, speak
to all peoples on the world of my
own creating, my holy word of full
warning; a call to Israel to be of full

power to cleanse all nations I cause
them to be of full victory over, such
as continue in sins of child murder
of unborn children, of Sodom and
adulterous immoral intentional
ways of corrupting ways of living

on earth; yea, on my earth; a just and holy God who sees and knows all things. Be ye open of mind, with prayerful way in soul-reaching hearts, to receive my full warning in this, my new revealing; causing my Priesthood on earth to send my own word unto all nations of the earth. Now read my will:

Jesus Christ, Even God Over All, Saith:

Thus Saith Son Ahman, Even Jesus Your Lord, to Present Court, That Is Not of Authority to Judge and Confine My People, Being No Authority Over Religion of Constitution Guarantee of Preserving Religious Freedom; Yet You Now Are of a Full Way of Persecuting Power Against My Innocent Obeying Order of Holy Eternal Priesthood; Hear My Own Message to Thee, Now to Be an Announcing of No Further Jurisdiction of Court in the Prosecution of My Representative; of Full Authority to Administer My Celestial Law Unto Pure Noble Sons, Unto My Holy Way Celestial Preparing for My Own Coming Among Men:

Jesus Christ, Even Jehovah, God Over All Creation

Thus I Have Redeemed My People. I Am Now Their Holy King of the Kingdom of Ahman of the Domain of Son Ahman. Amen.

Jesus Christ, Even Jehovah, God Over All Creation

Thus I Have Redeemed My People. I Am Now Their Holy King of the Kingdom of Ahman of the Domain of Son Ahman. Amen.

Thus saith your Lord Jesus Christ, the Holy Power of Redeeming Power for all mankind of all nations, of all ages of time, to all nations, peoples, kindreds, tongues, and governing powers; my own word in great plainness to all peoples, of my own coming; of great whirlwind judgments of the pure way of my holy love justifying judgments of Eternity Power; thus giving mine own word to all peoples on earth; a word of eternal importance to all now on the earth, to be of full receiving my own will concerning all peoples on earth; also to teach truth of pure way of judging, of holy way of my eternal law of holy Marriage Union of Eternal Union of Plural Celestial Marriage of my holy power authorizing select few to thus live; not to be of interference by any not of my own authority of Holy Eternal Priesthood of my sending; thus saith the Lord to this now generation on the earth, my own will to all; both of the governing powers of all nations; also their peoples: Hear thou my holy message given by my holy servant on earth as my Mouthpiece, though in bondage; to be in the hands of all peoples, to know of my soon labor of cleansing all lands of more wicked, to preserve the more righteous; yea, hear my own word given through my own power, to my holy servant Warren Jeffs;

though suffering in prison, yet of my order of pure Priesthood of holy calling to give my own will to all peoples, by my power, who will receive my word.

Chapter 5

Jesus Christ, Who Is Over All, Speaketh Strong Warning of Certain Holy Power of Judgments to Be Upon Nation of My Holy Power of New Jerusalem, Also to All Nations

I, Jehovah, God Over All, Speaketh, Even Jesus Christ, to All Nations, Give Heed. Amen.

I, Jehovah, Son of God, Even Jesus Christ, Speak My Own Way of True Holy Order of Warning to All People on Earth, Yet to Come Suddenly Unto Holy People Who Are Believing My Own Revealing, Now to Be Only Pure in Living Way on Earth, by My Way Being Lived. Now Repent. Receive My Way of How to Be of Holy Way. Let All Now Come Unto Me. Come Clean, Lest Full Order of Judgment Cometh on All Nations Who Forget God. Amen. Now Hear My Revealing of Holy Way to All:

SECTION REVELATION 149
Thus Saith Jesus Christ, Son Ahman, an Holy Will of Eternity Truth, to Be Answered on All of This Now Generation of the World, to Be Warned About the Way of Full Judgment to Come, Even to Be of Full Power as You Heed Not My Warning

I, Jesus Christ, Speak to All Nations, Peoples, Tongues, and Powers of Governing Power, to Heed My Will; for I Come to Cleanse All Nations, in Way of Delivery for My Holy Pure People on Earth; They Who Eschew Evil, Who Love Truth of Pure Holy Order of Salvation; Even Who Repent and Who Are of My Holy Way to Be of Exalting Pure Love-Peace. Amen.

SECTION REVELATION 150
Jesus Christ, Holy Lord Over All Nations of the Power to Be Nation on Earth, Speaketh Eternity Truth to All Peoples

Jesus Christ, of Holy Power of Union Order Eternal, Who Is of the Way of Full Power of Full Order of the Holy Order of God of Creation, to Now Be of Full Holy Truth, to Be Only Telling My Holy Way; Now Sendeth to All Nations My Own Will. Let All Listen. Let All Hear. Let All Awake to Reality of My Holy Power Coming to Dwell on the Holy Place of My Land of New Jerusalem, Even My Holy Zion. Let All Hear. Let My Word Go Forth in Pure Unchanged Way to All Peoples. Let All Be Holy. Let All Have Only My Will to Be the Guide in Living Pure Holy Way; Not Encumbered by Whims of Men or Women. Let All Receive My Own Will by My Authority I have Ordained on Earth, Now of

Nations. Receive My Holy Word of Full Truth Holy Way Revealing; Speaking to All Nations of Spanish Tongue, Through My Servant on Earth Who Is Ordained to Be My Mouthpiece to All Peoples. Let All Hearts Be Open, of a Prayerful Way; to Feel Truth of Holy Word Sent to All, to Be of Full Way Knowing I Cometh in Power, Celestial Power, to Let All Peoples Know I Am God, Even Jesus Christ, Over All Nations. Hear and Live My Will of Holy Revealing. Amen. Hear Thou My Message of Pure Will of God to People of Spanish Tongue, Saith God Thus:

SECTION REVELATION 158

Thus Saith Jesus Christ, Son Ahman, Unto All Nations on Earth, My Own Message of Holy Salvation, Truth Eternal Told to All, so All Peoples on Earth May Know True Way of Salvation; to Be of Preparing Order for My Coming in Glory Order Power; to Be on Earth for a Thousand Years Among Men as Ruler of Power Over All Peoples; Then to Be Thy Holy God of Redeeming Order Power, to Raise All From the Grave Unto a Judging, a Full Eternal Order Power Judging of a Just God Who Knoweth All Thy Works. Let This, My Holy Will, Be Thy Guide to Prepare for Mine Authority to Visit All Peoples; to Have My Way Known; to Be Only Pure Holy Way of Salvation. Hear Ye My Will:

SECTION REVELATION 159

Jesus Christ, Even Son Ahman, Jehovah, Speaketh to All Nations, a Holy Will Word Revealing, Even of Pure Way Truth, of Eternal Power, of Salvation, of Holy Pure Way to Be of a Holy Pure Order; to Be of My Order of Holy Dwelling on Earth; Thus a Holy Order Celestial of My Authority Come to Earth; to Prepare for My Glory Order of Celestial Order Power. I Come, Yea, in Power to All Nations of Survival Way After Cleansing Order Taketh Place on Every Nation. Hear Thou My Power Truth Order:

Thus Saith Jehovah, Even Son Ahman, Who Is Jesus Christ, God Over All, to All Nations on Earth, a Holy Revealing How to Be of Holy Pure Order of Survival

I, Jesus Christ, God Over All, Send to All Nations on Earth, to Their Peoples, Mine Own Will to Be Known; a Righteous Judge Over All, Who Revealeth Only Truth Way. I Speak, and the Very World of All Peoples Dwelling Obeyeth and Exist by My Power Celestial. I Am God That Now Sendeth Word of How to Dwell in More Holy Pure Way. Live Unto Righteous Holy Way to Be Surviving My Judgment on All Wicked Corrupt Peoples; a Cleansing to Happen of Soon Full Measure on All the Earth; to Cause My Kingdom to Come From Heaven; to Rule Among Men; to Have Full Way of Power Over All Peoples. Hear My Truth Way of How All Shall Live in Millennial Reign of Thy Lord on Earth:

Chapter 6

Jehovah, Even Jesus Christ, Warn All Nations to Repent; For I Cometh

Jesus Christ Giveth Own Writing to Supreme Court of Appeals

Nations. Let This, My Holy Will, Be Now of Worldwide Reading, so I May Preserve Innocent Ones Who Be Holy in Living When Judgment Cometh in Full Power; Yea, Even Soon at Hand Upon All the World of Corruption Way of Evil Intent, to Be Evil in Willful Harm to Innocence and Holy Way Virtue Order of All Mankind. Heed My Word, Saith Jesus Christ, Your Holy God Over All Peoples:

SECTION REVELATION 167

I, Jesus Christ, Holy Redeemer, Do Now Declare Way to Show Love Loyalty to Your Holy Lord, Jesus Christ, Sending My Holy Revealing to Be One, All Peoples on World of Thy Now Dwelling, to Be of a Holy Order to Celebrate My Holy Birthday of the Month of April on the Sixth Day of the Month; Also My Holy Revealed Will to Prepare Soon for the Judgment Order of Full Holy Power, Holy Power Judgments of God, Soon to Be Poured Forth in Full Way Order Holy Order Power on All Lands on World. Now Be Holy; Heed My Holy Revealing of Pure Love-Message, of Holy Way to Survive Judgments of God, to Soon Repent, to Be Holy Now, Lest Full Cleaning Order Cometh to All Lands.

SECTION REVELATION 168

I, Jesus Christ, Son Ahman, a Holy God Over All Peoples on World of Thy Now Dwelling, Send Full Way to Be Ready, Unto My Glory Holy Power Coming Soon, to Govern All; to Be Government of Holy Order, Heaven Come to Earth After Cleansing Evil Off Earth in Full Judge Way Power. Hear My Holy Word, Pure Revealed Way Through My Mouthpiece I Ordained on Earth; Now in Bondage; Yet to Be of My Full Witness Against Governing Order of All Who Neglect to Fulfill My Holy Way Revealed; Holy Word of God Now of Full Warning to All Peoples. Hasten to Prepare, by Hearing My Will.

SECTION REVELATION 169

Thus Saith Jesus Christ, God Over All, Warning Now to Be of Full Power Receiving Unto My Word Honored, Obeyed in Full Measure:

SECTION REVELATION 170

Thus Saith the Lord Jesus Christ, Son Ahman, to the Leaders and Peoples of the Nation of Libya, a Holy Word:

SECTION REVELATION 171

Thus Saith the Lord Jesus Christ Unto All People of Nation of Lithuania, a Holy Warning to Repent, to Be Holy as Individuals, Also to Leaders of Lithuania, My Own Word:

Jesus Christ Giveth Own Writing to Supreme Court of Appeals

Jesus Christ, Son Ahman

I, Jesus Christ, even Son Ahman, speak to Supreme Court of Texas, my own will even concerning 51st Judicial District Court Cause Numbers 990, 997, 1017, 1061, and Court of Appeals Court Case Number 03-11-00568-CR, as pertaining to legal prosecution against my servant Warren Jeffs, my own will telling truth to Supreme Court, exhibits of pure truth given; to now be means of use to Supreme Court to use powers of justice to be of freeing my servant Warren Jeffs, being held unjustly, by both intentional evil and lying ways, also by ignorance of this generation not knowing my full truth of religion being of constitutional protection for religious freedom. Uphold my will, my own word sent to thee in this full call of appeal. Let also Merril Jessop, of the way of imprisonment, be released soon. Let not my servant of pure holy religious practice linger any longer in prison, lest my own power be of full humbling of all who are of the lying way against my Holy Priesthood, a religious authority that should be protected fully by constitutional guarantee of religious freedom; the full way of my servant Warren Jeffs' conduct being my will. Let Merril Jessop,

of full name Fredrick Merril Jessop, Sen., be delivered. He was imprisoned for only doing my holy will. Now be just, saith Jesus Christ, your Lord, and God of all Creation. You shall soon feel my power, all who seek to hinder my holy will from being fulfilled; in the labor of pure holy way of salvation; a revealed religion on earth of my holy guiding daily, even to give this, my will, to you to be soon acted upon. Let this, my word, now be of my pure way of causing my holy power of pure holy way of truth, coming before Supreme Court, now be of a witness. I am soon to cleanse Zion's land. Thus is my word said further:

Chapter 7

Jesus Christ Holy Will to President of United States of America, New Word of Now Need of Just Order to Be of Full Now Labor. Now Do So. Amen.

SECTION REVELATION 175
I, Jesus Christ, Give My Own Way for United States President to Do

That Which Is Just, Honorable, Truth-Justice With Mercy Order Named; to Be a Ruler of Pure

Chapter 8

Jesus Christ Message of Only Peace
Holy Power Demonstrating to Ruler Order
to Make Peace in Holy Way Living

Chapter 9

APPENDIX

JESUS CHRIST SON AHMAN

PROCLAMATION

Proclamation Chapter 1
Administration of President Joseph Smith, Jun.

SECTION REVELATION 213

Thus Saith Son Ahman, Jesus Christ, to the Power of Governing in the Court of Prosecuting Labor, and to the Leaders of National Power -- Let My Word Be Heard in Your Several Placings of Your Influencing and Governing Power, Even This, My Warning to Not Abuse My Innocent People, But Maintain Their Rights of Governing Protecting of Religious Way of My Holy Order of Union Celestial in My Holy Church on Earth. Let There Cease to Be the Continued Way and Idea You Can Be of a Prosecuting Labor Against My Holy Way of Eternal Lives

of Celestial Union Power Above All Peoples and Their Claims of Power to Rule Over All the People in Their Lands of Man Organizing Power. Thus Am I Now Giving My Will to Be Known Among All Surviving People on Earth. Hear Thou My Way of Truth by This, My Revealing to All:

Martyrdom of Joseph Smith and Hyrum Smith in Carthage Jail -- June 27, 1844

SECTION REVELATION 214

Son Ahman Gives Truth of Eternal Power to Joseph Smith, a God of Power

President Rulon Jeffs' Testimony of the Prophet Joseph Smith

SECTION REVELATION 215

Proclamation Chapter 2
Administration of President Brigham Young

Proclamation Chapter 3
Administration of President John Taylor

Proclamation Chapter 4
Administration of President John W. Woolley

Proclamation Chapter 5

Administration of President Lorin C. Woolley

Proclamation Chapter 6

Administration of President John Y. Barlow

Proclamation Chapter 7
Administration of President Leroy S. Johnson

Proclamation Chapter 8
Administration of President Rulon Jeffs

Proclamation Chapter 9
Administration of President Warren S. Jeffs

Proclamation Appendix A
Warnings of Previous Sending to Leaders of the Nation

America, Now in Power, and Also to the Peoples of This Nation -- This Message of Warning of the Doctrine of Eternal Judgment Upon Thee, Even Upon All Peoples, Being the God of Eternal Power, an Eternal God Who Shall Bring All to Justice; Whose Mercy Shall Claim Those Who Repenteth in a Manner to Earn the Benefit of My Atoning Power -- Even Him, a God of Atoning and Redeeming Power, Who Suffered on the Cross and Was Raised From the Grave Unto Eternal Power to Judge All Mankind According as Their Works Are:

SECTION REVELATION 91

Thus Saith Jesus Christ, Who Is Son Ahman, to the Leader of This Nation of the United States of America, and All the Leaders of This Nation in Their Several Governing Appointments and Powers; and Thus to the Peoples of This Nation, Mine Own Word From the Heavens; Even the God of Glory Who Speaketh Thus to Your Understandings -- A Call to Heed My Word, Even I Who Am Soon to Come in the Powers of Heaven to Dwell Among Men, a Governing Power Over All Nations of the Earth -- Hear My Words:

SECTION REVELATION 99

Thus Saith Jesus Christ, Son Ahman, Unto the Leaders of the Nation of the United States of America, and to the Peoples Thereof, Warning and Continued Call to Prepare for Great Day of Final Judgments, Who Saith:

SECTION REVELATION 100

Thus Saith Son Ahman, Your Lord Jesus Christ, to All Peoples of the Earth Unto Your Salvation if You Heed Me, Saying Thus:

SECTION REVELATION 101

Jesus Christ Speaketh to the Nation of the United States Solemn Warning Again, Mine Own Word From the Heavens, to be Heeded Lest Judgments Follow Upon Those Who Heed Me Not, Saith the Lord, Even Son Ahman

Thus Saith the Lord Jesus Christ to the Leaders and Peoples of the United States of America, My Holy Word of Continued Warning of Final Judgments Soon at Hand, Heed My Word, Which Saith:

Proclamation Appendix B

Appendix of My New Word of Pure Power
Printed in This My Proclamation to All Peoples on All Lands
Referencing Pages to Find My Word in This Publishing

(Page 837)

Proclamation Appendix C

Documents Showing the Legal and Religious Establishing and Continuing of the Fundamentalist Church of Jesus Christ of Latter-day Saints Among Men on Earth, Thy Lord Establishing His Church April 6, 1830, Through Joseph Smith, Continued on Earth Through My Priesthood; Now a Legal Organization According to Law of Land Among Men, Saith Jesus Christ, Your Lord

(Page 842)

SECOND EDITION OF MY HOLY WARNING TO ALL NATIONS, EVEN JESUS CHRIST

Chapter 10

Word of the Lord Jesus Christ of Continued Sacred Warning to All Peoples on Earth

The Lord Jesus Christ Sendeth This, a Holy Word to All Nations, to Know I Continue to Speak From the Heavens Through My Servant on Earth, Warren Jeffs, and That You Must Heed My Word, for I Shall Send Whirlwind Judgments if There Is the Impurity of Life Continued in Nations Who Uphold Murder of Unborn Youth and Other Evils of Immoral Way. I Loveth All the Honest in Heart Who Will Purify Their Lives, Saith the Lord. Heed My Word in This Printing. Amen.

Chapter 11

Second Edition Continued Revealings

Chapter 12

Compiling Errors of First Edition
of Now Correction

**Jesus Christ
Jehovah Son Ahman**

SECTION REVELATION 1

Open Word of God to All Nations

I, Jesus Christ, Even Son Ahman, Revealeth to All World My Own Will of Pure Order Holy Way Pure Living, of My Judgment Soon Upon All Lands; to Give Counsel of No Nuclear Order War; to Do Full Order Counsel How to Prepare Thy People in Nation Order for My Glory Coming to World. Hear Thou My Own Will:

Revelation of the Lord Jesus Christ
**Palestine, Texas
Thursday, August 2, 2012**

1. Holy will of Son Ahman, who reigneth over all order of the nation order on world now inhabiting all lands, even the Lord of all, Jesus Christ, to be holy order government order soon upon world, in open order governing rule over all nation order: I, God, speak pure truth, of eternity. All shall rise from the death of the earthly order flesh order, to stand before me, your God, in resurrection order; each to be fully judged to know entire living order of own life in an holy view with me; nothing hidden.

2. Such is my rule.

3. Do no more sin at all.

4. All shall suffer for own sin way if not of truth order repentance full order. Amen.

5. Now let all people be of holy way entire, for I cometh soon. Amen.

6. Now learn truth that my holy power searcheth through all things; giveth light and holy order way living unto all living holy order on world of thy inhabiting.

7. Know the full justice against all loss of unborn youth order shall be of full order justice served to all father, mother order; to leave no one exempt from unholy purpose order murder of unborn child order.

8. I shall give no forgiveness to them of unholy intent to murder unborn child order, of medical, or medicine, even birth control unholy contraceptive order; all murder of unborn child order way; for life beginneth at the conception, or what could be holy life order conceiving; such medical or personal labor, medicine of stopping life from growing at conception, all are intentional murder against unborn child order.

9. Let all peoples on world of thy now dwelling be of repenting order. Amen.

10. Now tell physician order who administereth any birth control medicine they are murder unholy order; also, all

nurse order who knoweth they administer contraceptive order.

11. All physician order who removeth living fetus of any time of womb living are murder order unto eternal punishment by God. Amen.

12. Now hear eternity truth.

13. Righteous inherit eternal life of full happy order, to dwell in my power holy way presence in heaven holy living order.

14. All who take life in purpose order are murder order when innocent blood is shed.

15. Let all now repent of all former sin.

16. Judgment eternal cometh on all by Godhood order, who created all people.

17. Let science unholy lie order cease search for living order on other worlds.

18. I do not allow such in all eternity; and only allow thee to deceive all who love not eternity order truths order; so all wicked shall meet God in full desired loss of own salvation of way to be damned.

19. Let all repent on world soon; for fear cometh on all unholy people on world. Amen.

20. Let all wicked now repent.

21. Let all more holy people improve own lives, so more holy way of my power can come to all holy order on world.

22. A holy way is to forgive all people, to be kind forgiving order.

23. Let no armed force invade another people, save I, God, name full appointment by authority of my representative on world.

24. Let he be free soon to counsel any world leader. Amen.

25. Let my way be doing -- no war at all in world nation order.

26. Pull own military back into own borders of worldwide placing soon, so war of attrition does not take place, as evil power intendeth.

27. Now forgive.

28. Be justified before me, saith God. Amen.

29. I shall hold all world leadership accountable for any war.

30. Let the full United Nations meet to have my servant do full telling who is worthy of God's preserving when the full God-sending judgment cometh soon. Amen.

31. Let he be free of bondage.

32. He is of me, saith your Lord.

33. He receiveth my will.

34. Do no harm to they of my holy Church at all.

35. I guide them.

36. They belong to me, saith Jesus Christ.

37. Leave alone my Eternal Union Order of Full Order, Celestial Plural Marriage Order of full revealing from me.

38. Let my servant go free to administer salvation to all nations.

39. They who placed him in bondage are unholy order of full enemy to Christ order.

40. Do no harm to he of pure religious power. Amen.

41. Now do own nation cleansing order.

42. Remove all laws against my Church order of full Celestial Order Plural Marriage Order.

43. I come to earth in full power judgment power.

44. Wicked nation on Zion order New Jerusalem land shall fall. Amen.

45. Now repent, is God's will to all nation order on entire world.

46. Sea shall heave over many shores.

47. Earthquake cometh soon to full world order.

48. All shall be of full judged way holy

way judging of your Lord, who sendeth this holy word to all nation order on all lands. Amen.

49. Now turn to own holy improving own nation law order; no murder of unborn child order at all allowed when I cometh.

50. Let all be of now improving own peoples; ceasing war way preparing, for they who live by the weapon of nuclear order shall be of same order humbled entire order.

51. Use no nuclear bomb order, none of you on world.

52. Do not use such Lucifer order, who revealed to science unholy order the way of mass destruction of living order on world. Amen.

53. Now be holy, all people on world. Amen.

54. Read Isaiah chapter on full worldwide cleansing in last time of wicked way called "last days." Amen.

55. Do own study of my own holy word given during the holy order ministering of thy holy Lord's time on world, in the mortal order of living among men, coming to Israel, who crucified me; I, God, having power over death order, being a God of life of eternal power; suffering atonement order holy way of sacrifice for salvation of all people if of pure living on world.

56. Now believe my holy order, as God over all has right to rule on world today; also they I empower in heaven power holy authority on earth, to administer holy ordinance of faith, then baptism after holy order truth order repentance order.

57. Come unto me, all of pure holy salvation. Amen.

58. Let all idol order of fine carving, molten images of wood, stone, iron, copper, all precious metal order -- precious to man, not God -- all do full test: Did thy god of wood or stone make life in anything of world living?

59. Such evil is of devil order, leading all to unbelief order against me, your living God of Creation; who came to world in full living order, to prove all nations on world I liveth. Amen.

60. Go to own nation.

61. Find one who also receiveth Jesus Christ holy faith.

62. See if any claim revealing authority power of full Gospel of ordinations of Melchizedek Holy order Priesthood, who now receive word of thy Lord.

63. Even apostate Mormon church doth deny my full Gospel, changeth all order ordinations, liveth lie order, no present revelation order. Amen.

64. Go to Catholic order.

65. All profess me as their holy Lord.

66. All do only lip unholy order service, not original Gospel of full ordinating holy order in New Testament book holy scripture order.

67. Let no man give man of religion order full order obeying, only to God who guideth man of revealing full truth to all believer order; thus all are to account to thy Lord in day of judgment order in end of world, which is end of new Millennium order, thousand years of peace ending all nation order; redemption of full world unto sun-glory shining full Celestial glory power of God.

68. Let such be reality you believe, as you remember Joseph Smith holy testimony, which he sealed with own blood shed in martyrdom by wicked men.

69. Now do full own search for full Gospel of salvation. Amen.

70. Let this now be of full order published exact order to all thy peoples, so all read exact word of God now sent to all,

to only do so if a written version is sent to him of my Keyholder Priesthood power, Warren Jeffs, though in prison on false order accusing of the apostate order lying order against God. Amen.

71. Now tell all world I publish full warning in book.

72. Do purchase soon.

73. It hath all my more recent word warning all people of my judgment; also my Proclamation to all nations of world of pure religious power in law of pure abiding of Plural Celestial Order Marriage Order. Amen.

74. Now petition President of nation, thus having power to free my holy order of innocent authority, to do so. Amen.

75. Then he sendeth more salvation holy order message order to all believing God can speak from heaven to all nation order on world. Amen.

76. Such who do full nation way asking for him to be free shall survive if not of child murder unholy murder of unborn child order, or of adultery, or of Sodom evil way living order. Amen.

77. Now repent, all nation order world order.

78. I cometh, saith your Lord, soon. Amen.

79. Let also my servant do full reading of my will to all peoples of United Nation hearing as he is protected.

80. Let such voice resolve to have he of my power authority come to speak to full nation assembly of all nations on world hearing he of revealing power, whom I ordained.

81. Let all do soon petition so he doeth this in full freedom order protected order; else you are unbelieving people.

82. Know tsunami cometh to Indonesia, to Papua New Guinea, to Atlantic Ocean nation order, to Indian Ocean, Pacific Ocean in great order, sea heaving beyond bounds soon.

83. Let all know I am justified to remove all child murder order of both unborn child order, also child abuse way among many nations of such harm to born child order, evil youth prostitution evil corrupt order.

84. Let all cease over all world soon, lest full judgment of God causeth all corruptible things to be consumed by eternal order holy God power of fire from the order of power of God. Amen.

85. Let also all abuse of women cease, even the way of no family beating in religion of false authority allowing subservience of women in unholy way of force, beating, even murder by own husband.

86. Such must cease.

87. I shall cleanse all peoples of such. Amen.

88. Let government power do all law upholding against these evils. Amen.

89. Now be ready for my glory to shine on all people on world as I descend from heaven; all surviving order at the time seeing their holy Lord in power glory. Amen.

90. Now do full preparing before full order holy God-sent holy order judgment cometh soon. Amen.

91. Have all people return military order to own border holy nation order, not to do bomb order of any way of war order; nor secret executings of own people in own nation; heinous order of leaders of many force-governing power unholy murder for power way unholy force of police, military bombing, quiet executing order.

92. I, God, see all, and shall execute all force order soon in full God-sent judgment holy right to take life, by right of creation, by law eternal living, of God in holy

domain holy governing over all nations order. Amen.

93. Now let Mauritania cease murder unholy secret combination order.

94. I shall sweep thy land clean of all such murder order in coming war of evil nation order of bomb, chemical weapon order, disease, of full scourge order. Amen.

95. I, your Lord Jesus Christ, speak to nation of Botswana, a holy word to repent of evil murder order in national governing power, also among populace.

96. Do so now, lest my full cleansing remove all living in thy land. Amen.

97. Now do full law change order, to protect women, also children from slave labor, abuse evil of immoral using child order.

98. Let all murder of unborn youth cease in thy nation, lest full eternal judgment come on all murder order. Amen.

99. Let nation of Liberia hear word of God, even Jesus Christ, who is God over all lands, peoples, nations, governing order, to repent of unholy murder order of government secret order murder; also child unborn youth abortion entire way stopped, or great judgment cometh to cause land to not be of inhabitant, a judgment power of God. Amen.

100. Do also full female rights restoral, protection of virtue order; also no child sold to slave labor at all.

101. Do these purifying labor order, for I, Jesus Christ, soon cometh to all lands to govern all peoples. Amen.

102. Let Liechtenstein now do full repenting.

103. A devastating unholy power violent order of foreign nation cometh to execute justice on full nation, as a land of promoting evil on neighbor nation order. Amen.

104. The nation of the adultery capital of Europe of Amsterdam shall be swept, entire city from world, for adultery Sodom evil order of ofttime child murder order of unborn youth holy order by government permitting such evil. Amen.

105. Let France repent; full war cometh of the loss of most life in nation if of use of nuclear weapon unholy order.

106. Do not use such if you desire to survive.

107. Let all nation order never use nuclear weapon order, lest own land be depopulated by the order of unholy retaliation no-mercy in holocaust war order.

108. O ye people on world, be ye now soon way order peace order.

109. I cometh.

110. I am Governor of all nations.

111. Do only peace order now until I appear. Amen.

112. Have all people place olive branch wreath above front doorway of own home who have done my will of repenting when full God-order holy judgment power cometh, so destroying order passeth the pure who dwell there, still taking in death the order of murder. Amen.

113. Let also wreath have order of leaves of number exceeding the way of holy number of wreath holy order twelve branches, leaves attached.

114. Let no olive order be thereon, as symbol of holy love for peace holy living order.

115. Raise own olive plant soon, so you are ready, as were Israel in Egypt to paint lamb blood over doorpost, thus showing faith in God at that time.

116. Do no blood order painting at all this time.

117. Be symbol of peace holy twelve

JESUS CHRIST SON AHMAN

olive branch weaving, holy leaf present thereon holy order, so angel of judgment passeth pure holy living people there.

118. Let also child order be no more of world entertainment, evil music listening, unholy devil rock music or other way of immoral seeing, hearing evil way unholy order.

119. Such shall not be remaining, as evil way in mind shall be evil way still. Amen.

120. Let all be holy order living soon. Amen.

121. Let motherhood be protected as holy labor order in all nations.

122. Let all such nation power keep mother holy order in health way, living with child order, not to take child order to live at child-care way away from parent holy order.

123. Remove violent order from family order when knowing father male order, or violent mother or relative order, doeth harm to child physical way, or mental way order. Amen.

124. Now do full holy cleansing of all evil way entire. Amen.

125. Do so soon.

126. Let all nation order cleanse military of adultery, Sodom unholy order.

127. Such soldiery is only murder order who fight against own faith virtue order.

128. Let all people never believe Sodom is correct.

129. I, God, destroyed both Sodom and Gomorrah for such evil.

130. Do not let national government do such at all, lest full God-sending full judgment of full power come on all therein, who legalize Sodom, adultery, unborn child murder unholy murder of unborn child way order.

131. Such are unholy in the sight of thy Lord entire.

132. Government of man cannot alter God of eternal power holy governing Celestial order.

133. A holy way is to do full order removal of such from society entire in own land.

134. Only that can cleanse nation order for day of judgment of God soon to come. Amen.

135. Let also full drug lord unholy murderous order be completely removed soon.

136. Such are full murder way unholy order.

137. Let prison order for all, save for the order of the full justice of murder or Sodom order, adultery order; all other prison order be of pure training, holy schooled order, how to improve living, tested to go to work holy labor order. Amen.

138. Such is Kingdom of thy holy God order of soon coming, all judicial order of heaven-inspired holy full truth order, not deceiving lawyer craft unholy lying evil way of money-seeking to get freedom for guilty order way doing; yea, truth-justice in full way to be among all nations, as Zion is spread over all world. Amen.

139. Now clean own people.

140. Do so soon, is my now order to all government order over all nation order. Amen.

141. Let also any leader of any nation not upholding just holy law correct way, be also removed by legal way of proof-justice; also legislators who do unholy law upholding in local or national government order.

142. I shall send representative order to all nation order when I come to world,

revealing truth of all people on earth, past, now, and future; for I am God, Jesus Christ. Amen.

143. Let pure holy religion be protected by law in all lands.

144. Let also persecution of religion cease entire order. Amen.

145. These are the way of my Kingdom, saith thy holy Lord.

146. Prepare to live such way entire; no one exempt save they not of Zion holy power order; yet in future to do so; as all on world shall bow the knee in subservience to Christ, your holy Lord, and acknowledge His right to rule.

147. Let all do full holy preparing own laws, people, military, all of these orders, so my rule can easily bless all. Amen.

148. Now cleanse government of nation of all way immoral way; no Sodom nor adulterous order.

149. Gather immoral evil way of prostitution evil order; confine, and school, doing labor until they prove honorable; not to use around any who abuse such.

150. Let all such evil be strictly of no family order, lest disease of physical, immoral order, also of loss of love for living of such spiritual way order; to only allow by law isolation to own way living.

151. Do work order at the place of isolating, so such do production of the order of blessing honorable work order. Amen.

152. Now do these full cleansing order ways, so all are improving order. Amen.

153. Let male order work-labor order be of holy separate order from all female order holy living pure way order. Amen.

154. Now do holy raising of child order in pure love-service of all, so no evil of child way raiseth new generation of evil order on world of thousand years of peace.

155. Peace exists by holy law living in entire way of living. Amen.

156. Let United Nations immediate order cease abortion unholy murder of child unborn order in all policy of such a world organization.

157. Let all policy order not justify voting of any way of evil to child, woman, man orders at all, no use of the way of the use of murder of unborn child holy youth of unborn order; also no contraceptives forced, nor abortion of unborn child order of your organization promotion in poor nation order; or rich nation order.

158. Do no aggressive order military way of army weapon order.

159. Only do peace conference holy agreement order. Amen.

160. Have full meeting of all presidential order, king, dictatorial, or elected national leader of all nations come to me, by meeting my Mouth order of power eternal holy Priesthood Keyholder authority, to hear my will to each governing authority.

161. Let all come to me, your God, as I come to world in new order of my pure holy government on world. Amen.

162. Now cause a full holy general order to do full world cleansing order of small national order, not able to do own self-cleansing, by United Nation full council of military order do force of justice if child murder order continueth of unborn child order, so all have protection.

163. Only do so with my approving, saith the Lord, else you are evil aggressive nation unholy order. Amen.

Chapter 1

**Warning of the Lord Jesus Christ
Through His Servant Warren Jeffs,
To the United States of America**

**Warning of the Lord Jesus Christ
to All Nations**

**Policies and General Principles
of the Government of Son Ahman
in the Kingdom of Ahman**

The Lord Jesus Christ and His Servant Warren Jeffs Now Voice His Warning of Judgments

Let this be published to all peoples. Cause my word to be known. Now hear my servant thus deliver my message. Even so. Amen.

SECTION REVELATION 2

Final Warning to the Nation of the United States of America

Revelation of the Lord Jesus Christ
Draper, Utah
Tuesday, November 2, 2010

1. Thus saith the Lord unto you who are of the people of the earth, even so, I, your Lord, now send you my message of final warning;

2. For I, who reigns over all, have seen the wickedness of this generation.

3. And as I have spoken, so shall I fulfill.

4. Now cause your hearts to be open.

5. Now let your ears be inclined.

6. Let your minds be as a peaceful fountain.

7. Let there be silence as I thus speak my will.

8. I, the Lord, now turn the key against the leader of the nation of the United States of America.

9. Now her power shall be clipped.

10. Division and misrule will disturb the halls of Congress.

11. Officials shall fear for their lives.

12. My protection shall withdraw from your midst.

13. Unrest and violence shall spread.

14. Thy people shall fear.

15. Your strength shall be overthrown.

16. Your moneys shall not be your strength.

17. Your factories shall be stilled.

18. Your gardens and orchards shall be consumed by the overflowing scourge of desolation.

19. Your strongholds shall all be thrown down.

20. And all this because you would not heed my voice, nor the voice of my servants whom I sent.

21. Now repent, O ye people of this generation.

22. I shall now do my own work.

23. My Zion shall rise.

24. I shall preserve mine elect who abide in me.

25. I now send my word of judgment to you as unprofitable servants who rejected your Lord unto your own desolation.

26. Know that my servant Warren Jeffs has been humbled.

27. Though he feared in the day of

trial, I, the Lord, have lifted him up to be my spokesman.

28. Thus has he sent my word to the government officials of this nation of the United States of America.

29. And I, the Lord, who sees and knows all things, have seen you, the government officials, reject my word through my chosen servant.

30. You have allowed my people to be driven, and have caused persecution against them for their religion; even to incarcerate my sons of my Church and Kingdom, for abiding their sacred religious covenants.

31. Now my day of visitation is upon this nation.

32. I shall also warn, and visit the nations of the earth.

33. Let all give heed to this, my word, for as you see the Lord lay a heavy hand upon this nation of the United States of America, with judgment of destructive elements; yea, with fire, and the sword, with pestilence, and hail; with famine and with earthquake, and violent storms; and the sea heaving beyond its bounds; so shall all peoples know my judgments are upon the ungodly who have persecuted my people through the history of my restored Gospel, since the days of my servant Joseph Smith.

34. Thus shall I now avenge my saints, whose blood cries from the ground unto me for vengeance on this wicked people who have turned to evil continually.

35. For as it was in the day of Noah, so is it today, wherein all peoples are corrupting the way of the Lord.

36. Receive ye my messages of warning I now cause my servant Warren Jeffs to deliver unto you, O ye people of this nation, and the nations of the earth.

37. Cause your habitations to be prepared for the great day of the Lord.

38. Heed my warning I now send unto you, saith the Lord, even Jesus Christ, the God of the whole earth, who is the Savior of all who will repent and come unto Him. Even so. Amen.

A Proclamation to the Government Officials of the United States of America and to the Government Officials of Canada

Inasmuch as government officials have joined with those who were once members of Fundamentalist Church of Jesus Christ of Latter-day Saints, who are now apostate and determined to destroy the Church; and inasmuch as these government officials are now bringing prosecutions upon members of the said Church, and have fought to use Church records to persecute and prosecute members of said Church; and inasmuch as our religious freedoms are not upheld by these government officials, even to incarcerate them for performing their religious duties and living the revealed laws of their religion as given through the Prophet Joseph Smith -- We declare the warning of the Lord Jesus Christ, whom we serve, that all those who thus stretch forth their hands to bring prosecution and persecution upon His Church and use His sacred records to bring unjust and libelous attacks upon His people, He, the Lord, will send His judgments upon them, that they may know they are fighting against His Church and Kingdom on earth. And we give His warning, and not of man, as He has thus directed us, His servants. And let all be warned that the Lord Jesus Christ, who created all things, who sees and knows all things, and has all power, shall fulfill His word. This, through His servants, who only seek the salvation of all men, unto the glory of God.

We, the Quorum of the First Presidency of the Fundamentalist Church of Jesus Christ of Latter-day Saints, by the command of our Lord Jesus Christ, send to this nation and generation His warning, even a revelation of God to you, along with His revealed word through His Prophet, Joseph Smith, Jun., and other Prophets, including His own words. And we do this with soberness, with great yearnings unto God for the salvation of the souls of all men and their families, and peoples of the earth; for the Lord is God, and He shall fulfill all His words. And He lieth not, but is a God of truth. And this is our testimony to this generation, that the Lord will fulfill all His words revealed through all His holy Prophets. And with fear and trembling before Him, we uphold all His words, and seek His grace to attend the honest in heart of all nations, to prepare for the great day of the Lord. (October 2009)

Warnings of the Lord to the Nation of the United States of America
(Comprising Section Revelations 3-4)

SECTION REVELATION 3

Revelation of the Lord Jesus Christ
Kingman, Arizona
Friday, October 2, 2009

1. Thus saith the Lord unto the people of this nation who call themselves the nation of the United States of America, founded upon the Constitution that I, the Lord, established through those inspired men who fought for and loved liberty for all mankind:

2. I, the Lord, Jesus Christ, the Savior of the world, have looked upon the people of this nation, and have seen their abominations and gross wickedness, and their murders and secret combinations, and have seen wickedness in high places among the rulers of this nation;

3. And I say unto you, repent or be destroyed in the flesh; for I, the Lord, have weighed you in the balance and found this nation wanting; even unto their cup of iniquity full and running over.

4. I, the Lord, created this earth and preserved this land upon which this nation of the United States of America now exists, for a wise purpose in me, even to establish my Zion.

5. And I, the Lord, established my Church of Jesus Christ of Latter-day Saints upon this land through my servant

Joseph Smith, Jun., to fulfill my purposes, to gather mine elect unto the Redemption of Zion.

6. And this nation has persecuted and driven my people, and brought upon them persecutions against my people through laws that were unconstitutional;

7. For the rights of freedom of religion, I, the Lord, inspired the founders of this nation to guarantee, and preserve for all classes and lawful organizations, to maintain their rights of worship.

8. And thus saith the Lord: My judgments shall now come upon you as you continue to prosecute my people who are of my Church and Kingdom upon the earth.

9. And I say unto you, let my people go, and allow them their rights and privileges of worship, to establish my Zion upon the lands that my people have purchased and consecrated unto me.

10. For I, the Lord, am with them as they abide in their covenants with me, in living the laws of God, which are always more pure than the laws of man, unto the salvation of souls.

11. For my people only desire to fulfill my purposes of salvation for all mankind who come unto me, and this through my revealed word.

12. And I, the Lord, shall fulfill my promises and uphold my word as revealed through all my holy Prophets, as recorded in the scriptures.

13. And now I say unto this nation, uphold the rights of worship of my people of the Church of Jesus Christ of Latter-day Saints, known among you as the Fundamentalist Church of Jesus Christ of Latter-day Saints; those who have received and are abiding my Celestial laws.

14. For that branch called the Church of Jesus Christ of Latter-day Saints, known by the world, has become corrupt, and broke away from my Priesthood authority when they rejected my Celestial Law of Marriage; and I, the Lord, have rejected them.

15. And they shall be brought low, and feel the chastening hand of God for all their abominations against the laws of God.

16. And I say unto this people of this nation, repent ye, repent ye; for my judgments are already upon you, and will soon be poured out without measure, beginning at the house of God; those who have professed to know my name, and have blasphemed against me, and changed the law and ordinances of my Gospel, and submitted to the ways and persuasions of men.

17. O ye people of this nation, I, the Lord, shall soon bring upon you the overflowing scourge, and who can stay my hand?

18. For this land shall be cleansed for the rise of Zion in fulness.

19. And I say unto you, restore to my people their lands and houses, and deliver my people from the hand of their oppressors.

20. This from the Lord your God who created you, and who upholds all nations and peoples in their place. Even so. Amen.

SECTION REVELATION 4

Revelation of the Lord Jesus Christ
Draper, Utah
Thursday, October 7, 2010

1. Verily thus saith the Lord unto this nation called the United States of America, even that nation I, the Lord, have warned to let my people go, and to restore them to their lands:

2. I, the Lord, have seen you now reject my word.

3. Thus shall I fulfill my word upon you; for I am God, and have caused that my people be prepared for my coming.

4. And as I have purposed, so shall I fulfill.

5. Now be warned that the great city called Cincinnati shall be destroyed by the power of judgment.

6. And the city of Chicago shall also be as a place without inhabitant.

7. Verily I say unto you who have thus persecuted my chosen people --

8. Repent, and turn from all your wicked and perverse and abominable ways; for I am now sending forth the destroying elements upon this untoward and fallen people.

9. Thus shall I perform my work.

10. Let this nation hear this, my continued warning.

11. And cause that my word be published to the nation, and to the other nations that now inhabit this, my land.

12. And let this, my word, be sent to the leaders of the nations.

13. For I, the Lord, shall sweep all evil and corrupt men from off my chosen land, to prepare for my Zion to rise, and to be prepared for my appearing in my glory to the nations.

14. Cause that there shall be thy brethren of the First Presidency of my Church to stand with thee, as you thus deliver my word of continued warning.

15. Let my people go, saith the Lord unto this nation.

16. I shall be with them as they abide in their covenants with me.

17. Let my people receive the just remuneration for the loss of their lands.

18. And cause that my servant should be set free.

19. Cause that his brethren who are in bondage be set free.

20. Let this be as a final warning to the people on this land.

21. And cause that all who hear may know that the Lord has spoken, and will yet continue to voice His word.

SECTION REVELATION 5

A Petition to the President of the United States of America

Revelation of the Lord Jesus Christ
Draper, Utah
Thursday, October 7, 2010

1. To the honorable President of the United States of America now as standing at the head of this nation:

2. I who dwells on high, even your Lord and Savior, who redeemed all mankind by the shedding of His own blood, and who is over all and has all power, send to you my word.

3. Cause that my servant who presides over my Church now be delivered by thy hand.

4. Let my servant go, that he may perform his mission to prepare my people for my coming.

5. Cause that the prosecutors now cease their attack upon my servant Warren Jeffs.

6. Cause that this nation now restore to my people the consecrated land taken from them.

7. Cause that there be remuneration given them for the loss of the homes that are occupied illegally by the enemies of my people who are in the Colorado City, Arizona and Hildale, Utah area.

8. Cause that the attack against my people in Texas be stopped.

9. I, the Lord, shall cause my judgments to be withheld as you thus perform this work.

10. Otherwise, let this nation know I am with my people, and shall sweep the wicked from off the face of the land of America.

11. Thus shall I perform my work by my almighty power.

12. This from your Lord, even Jesus Christ, who shall subdue all His enemies under His feet.

13. Even as I have spoken, so shall I fulfill. Even so. Amen.

SECTION REVELATION 6

Continued Warning of the Lord to the Nation of the United States of America

Revelation of the Lord Jesus Christ
Draper, Utah
Monday, October 25, 2010

1. Thus saith the Lord, I am now again calling upon the leaders of the nation of the United States of America to let my people go.

2. And let these three warnings now be on record before me.

3. Now uphold my will, and free my servant Warren Jeffs.

4. Cause his people of my covenant who thus abide my Celestial Law be delivered unto the restoring of their lands and houses unto the religious trust, as was appointed by me through my servant Rulon Jeffs, as the United Effort Plan Trust.

5. Overrule the unjust court that thus robbed my people of their possessions.

6. Cause this to happen such that my people thus petitioning you as the President of the United States, may find just redress.

7. I, the Lord, shall stay my judgments as you thus uphold my word.

8. Otherwise, I shall sweep this nation off my land of Zion.

9. Even so shall I fulfill my word, saith your Lord Jesus Christ.

10. And thus shall this nation be rewarded for all her deeds against my Church of Jesus Christ, of the name "Fundamentalist Church of Jesus Christ of Latter-day Saints."

11. Let my people go.

12. Cause their leadership and possessions be restored, to dwell in safety in their rights of religious freedom.

13. The laws against my law of plural marriage are not just.

14. Cause your minds to discern that my law of plural marriage is of a higher and more pure and holy order than the ways of earthly unions of personal and government sanction.

15. For I, the Lord, am the Administrator of my holy law; and only those I name are of my holy law.

16. And I shall cause my servant to administer my law in holiness before me.

17. Thus, this is my people, and my law and government of religious motive and righteous doings.

18. Cause the government officials to cease their prosecution of my servant.

19. Cause him to be given freedom of movement, and to be allowed to perform my work.

20. Let him be given protection.

21. Cause that he shall be allowed to speak before the United Nations my word unto the nations of the earth.

22. Cause this to take place such that his life will be preserved as he delivers my messages to the nations.

23. Let my word he thus delivers be published to all peoples.

24. I am soon to come in the power of judgment upon every nation.

25. Cause your laws that allow the murder of unborn children to be overthrown.

26. Cause there to be a cleansing of this nation of all laws that allow Sodom and immoral ways to exist among you.

27. I, the Lord, shall purge you of all your corrupt ways.

28. Now cleanse your peoples, through righteous laws administered, of your sins of immoral and corrupt ways.

29. I, the Lord, have caused this nation to be preserved to allow my Church to exist as a beacon of righteousness.

30. My word shall be fulfilled.

31. Let my word of warning be sounded.

32. Let the officials in every government agency or position learn of my word of warning.

33. Now come unto me and learn of my ways of justice and purity of righteous living.

34. Receive ye the witness of my word being fulfilled as I now send a judgment upon you of the coming forth of the cleansing of the state of Illinois, and of Missouri, and of Ohio.

35. For I shall sweep these states clean to prepare for my coming.

36. Let the people be warned of war soon to come to your land.

37. I shall allow the cleansing to take place.

38. Cause your people to no longer have prostitution or the evils of immoral and licentious ways to be as a stench upon my land.

39. I see and know all things.

40. Let the state of Maine now overthrow the laws of immorality which allow the sins of Sodom, and of murder of unborn children.

41. Cause this to be a beginning place of cleansing among you, that I, your Lord, may receive your testimony of repentance of these abominations in your nation.

42. I shall cause the city of New York to be without inhabitant.

43. The city of Boston shall be swept clean.

44. The anger of the Lord is kindled against the people who dwell on my land where the Zion of our God shall be built.

45. Let there be an immediate calling forth, by the leaders of this nation, to repeal the laws permitting the killing of unborn children.

46. For this evil must not be among you.

47. I shall rather sweep this land clean than to continue your existence in licentious and immoral practices.

48. Thus shall you know I have sent my word.

49. The foreign nations shall rise up against this nation of the United States, and shall assist in the cleansing of my land.

50. How oft have I, the Lord, called upon the people of this land to repent through the mouths of my servants since the day of establishing my Church of Jesus Christ of Latter-day Saints, in the time of my servant Joseph Smith.

51. Thus shall I perform my perfect work of judgment upon the peoples who dwell upon the American continent of my choosing.

52. For my land must be cleansed to prepare for my presence among my people.

53. Come unto me, O ye people of all nations, to learn of the ways of Zion.

54. Let there be an acknowledgment sent by the leader of this nation of the United States of America, unto my servant Warren Jeffs.

55. Cause him to receive a place of safety.

56. Cause my people to go free from oppression of the courts.

57. Now fulfill my word.

58. And as you do, so shall I continue to preserve this nation.

59. This is the word of the Lord, who holds all things in obeyance unto His word, unto the judgment of eternal duration, even your Lord Jesus Christ, the Life and Light of all peoples in the creation of the Eternal God, who is as a consuming fire.

60. Let my people go.

61. Now uphold just laws.

62. Now overthrow those laws that are against my Celestial Law of Plural Marriage.

63. This law is of me.

64. Uphold the religious freedom for my people.

65. Religion includes marriage, and righteous conduct in marriage union.

66. Thus have I created male and female, to join only in pure and holy ways.

67. I have allowed the diseases against sexual impurity to be upon this wicked generation.

68. Now come clean before me, and I shall turn away the destroyer for your sake.

69. Otherwise, my anger continues against this nation; and I shall send forth earthquakes, disease, pestilence, and hail to destroy thy land and people.

70. For I am God, and nothing can stay my hand.

71. Thus it is to be also answered upon your heads in the day of recompense, when all men shall stand before me to be judged of their works.

72. Realize that your works must be of righteousness to be preserved.

73. Let the city of Albany hasten to repent, for your wickedness is great.

74. And I shall cause fire from heaven to descend upon you to sweep all wickedness from you, and to consume every corruptible thing.

75. And beginning at the house of God shall my judgments commence.

76. Let the courts of the land attend to the sins of the people, and not be used by government or by individuals to prosecute an innocent people.

77. Cause the city of my coming, even Kansas City, Missouri, be warned of the complete cleansing of my sacred place where the New Jerusalem shall be built.

78. Let the city of Independence preserve the location of my temple with the marks of permanent nature at the cornerstones.

79. Cause them to pound large stakes near each corner stone into the ground to preserve the location of my future temple.

80. I shall preserve those individuals who thus favor my Church and Kingdom upon the earth.

81. Let the people of New Jersey repent, that I may turn away my wrath against them.

82. Cause the cleansing of the nation of Mexico by sending forth the gifts of improvement upon them, to tend to the needs of the poor, to develop union and equity among them, lest their nation descend into mob rule, and pour forth violence into your nation.

83. Let my people in the Texas land of my choosing, be preserved.

84. Cause the unjust judge to be dismissed.

85. Cause my servant to be set free.

86. Cause his right of religious duty to be protected.

87. Cause the secret combination against my people to be overthrown.

88. Hasten ye to do these works.

89. Thus shall I be as a Guardian of your nation. Even so. Amen.

Warnings of the Lord to All Nations
(Comprising Section Revelations 7-10)

SECTION REVELATION 7

Revelation of the Lord Jesus Christ
Draper, Utah
Thursday, October 7, 2010

1. Thus saith the Lord Jesus Christ, who is above all, and who has all power, to the nations of the earth:

2. I, the Lord, shall soon send upon the earth the judgments I have named through the mouths of all my holy Prophets.

3. Cause there to be among you a cleansing of your peoples, to overthrow the laws of murder which allow the destruction of unborn children.

4. And cause your people within your lands to end all evils of immoral and corrupt ways.

5. For I, the Lord, shall cleanse the earth of wickedness, in preparation for my coming in the glory of my might; and shall thus have with me the just recompense of reward for all peoples.

6. Thus shall I cause my people of the House of Israel to be gathered to the lands of their inheritance.

7. Let the nation of my coming, even the United States of America, again receive my warning voice to repent, and to let my people go.

8. Cause that my servant Warren Jeffs be set free from bondage.

9. And cause my consecrated lands be returned to my people.

10. Thus shall I spare the nation of the United States as they repent, and also overthrow all laws that allow the murder of unborn children, and that allow the evils of immorality to exist among them.

11. And verily I say unto you, the nations of the earth: Come to the aid of my servant Warren Jeffs and set him free.

12. Let this, my word, be read to the nations.

13. And cause that they now petition the government of the United States of America to deal justly, and cause my servant and my people to be let go, that they may perform my work of building up my Zion.

14. For I, the Lord, shall appear; and only those who are pure in heart shall abide the day of my coming.

15. Let the petition to the President of the United States of America also be published in every nation.

16. And let the "Proclamation" and revelation I have already sent to the government officials in that nation also be published to every nation.

17. Thus shall I cause my word and will to be made known, that you will now prepare for my day of judgment, even the cleansing the earth of all wickedness, that I may dwell among men for a thousand years to be your King and Deliverer.

18. Thus shall I cause my people who abide my eternal and pure laws of Celestial Plural Marriage, and mine other laws, to be preserved at the day of my coming, those who have purified their lives, and who are abiding in their covenants.

19. Thus shall I be on earth to make known to the nations all things that shall establish peace.

20. Let the leaders of nations now be as kind fathers to their peoples.

21. Let the people on the land of North and South America now know my day of my coming is soon at hand.

22. I, the Lord, have reserved this land for my Zion to be established.

23. Let the people on these lands repent; for I shall cleanse these lands to prepare for my presence.

24. And let the people of Israel also prepare; for they must needs cleanse their people of all immoral and murderous ways.

25. I, the Lord, shall preserve those among them who also overthrow the laws that allow immorality, and the evil of destroying unborn children.

26. Let this, my word, be sent also to be read by my servant at the time he is delivered, unto the United Nations Assembly.

27. Cause that this, my word, be sent by the month of November to the nations.

28. And cause those government officials in Utah, and in Texas, be warned of my judgment to be poured out upon them as they continue to prosecute my servant and my people.

29. Thus shall I hold you, the nations of the earth, as friends of freedom, to pressure the government officials in these states of the nation to let my people go, lest I send my judgment of destruction upon those who neglect this, my word; to not assist my servant Warren Jeffs.

30. So shall I fulfill upon all who agree with the adversaries of my people.

31. Let there be a preparation in your several nations to receive the messengers I shall send to reveal my word, even my message of salvation.

32. And cause that there be laws prepared in your nation to allow freedom of worship.

33. Let there be a cleansing of your people who dwell in the borders of your nation, each one, of all ungodliness pertaining to adultery, and the evils of Sodom and of the ancient city Nineveh, wherein was the sin of the murder of unborn children.

34. Thus, as they abolished this evil among them did I spare their people.

35. Thus shall it be done upon you, the nations of the earth, as you thus cleanse your peoples, and cause there to be a greater justice and equity among your people.

36. I, the Lord, shall judge the leaders of nations, and cause any who continue the evil of murder, and of adultery, to be overthrown.

37. I shall soon cause there to be the war of cleansing among those nations who continue in the evils of crime and immorality by legal consent.

38. Now prepare ye, O ye nations of the earth, for my word I shall yet send unto you by the hand of my servant Warren Jeffs.

39. For I, the Lord, have forgiven him for his wrongs; and I am with him in establishing my cause of Zion, to the salvation of the nations who remain.

40. I am from above, and nothing can stay my hand.

41. And as I have spoken, so shall I fulfill. Thus it is. Amen.

SECTION REVELATION 8

Revelation of the Lord Jesus Christ
Draper, Utah
Thursday, October 21, 2010

1. O ye peoples of the earth, turn unto me.

2. I shall soon cause the coming of a heavenly body.

3. It shall cause the destruction of many as I bring forth a people to dwell upon my land of Zion.

4. This heavenly body shall bring forth a new people to receive my word.

5. So great shall be this event, that the greatest earthquake the world has ever known or recorded shall sweep peoples of iniquity off every land.

6. I shall also cause the War of Armageddon to take place among those peoples who continue to persecute my people.

7. Let go of the evils of child murder in the destruction of unborn children.

8. Overthrow the evils of Sodom.

9. Overthrow the unjust laws against freedom of religious worship in every nation.

10. I shall soon send forth my messengers who shall administer my work of salvation. Receive ye them.

11. Let all nations now send forth this, my word, to their peoples.

12. Let all peoples in their individual preparation purify their ways unto justice and equity.

13. Cause all wars to cease.

14. Prepare all within your borders to receive my messengers of peace.

15. I shall cause there to be a cleansing of all nations.

16. My thousand years of peace are now being established.

17. Hasten ye, O ye peoples of the earth.

18. How can you so openly fulfill my prophecies of destruction, knowing that I have preserved my people Israel?

19. I shall humble the nations.

20. I shall destroy the works of evil in every land.

21. I shall cause my people to be preserved.

22. Let your minds now turn to your eternal salvation; for I shall come to make myself known to all peoples by the power of my might.

23. Read of my coming in the record of my servant John, in the book called Revelations.

24. Know that Babylon is soon to fall.

25. I shall overthrow the economic powers that now uphold evil and corrupt ways.

26. Every nation shall feel the wrath of God who continue to uphold the powers of evil against my Gospel of salvation.

27. Let this, my word, be read upon the housetops.

28. Let this, my word, be remembered to the people at the time of my coming.

29. Let this be recorded in every nation.

30. Let the history of these events be told in truth.

31. Prepare ye, O ye peoples of the earth, and cause your lands to be of peace.

32. This is my word and will as the Lord who reigneth on high over all peoples, to bring to pass the salvation of all who will thus receive my holy word unto their deliverance.

33. Come ye unto me, and receive the everlasting and eternal salvation of your God who created you.

34. Thus you shall know me, and be exalted unto the knowledge of your Redeemer, even Him who lives. Thus it is. Amen.

SECTION REVELATION 9

Revelation of the Lord Jesus Christ
Draper, Utah
Thursday, October 21, 2010

1. Let the leaders of nations send forth letters of influence to cause the deliverance of my people who have been prosecuted and driven from their lands.

2. Cause my servant Warren Jeffs to be delivered into the hands of my people who are now preparing to build Zion upon the land called North America.

3. Let the people of all nations send forth their gold and precious things to beautify my Land and City of Holiness; and come unto me, your Lord, in sackcloth and ashes to the repentance required, to appease a just God, lest all His words be fulfilled, leaving your peoples neither root nor branch to be upon the earth of their posterity.

4. Now bring forth the works of righteousness, O ye people of every nation.

5. Cast off all corruption, and come unto Him who has all power.

6. I shall preserve those who are not overcome by the sins of murder of unborn children; and of the evils of crime in wicked and immoral conduct, who are not tainted by the sins of Sodom, and who seek to honor just laws within and among their peoples.

7. Let this warning be sounded by my servant Warren Jeffs, to be heard as my word and will.

8. Thus shall I fulfill unto the guidance of all peoples to receive my message of salvation.

9. Cause the removal from your shores all peoples.

10. I shall soon cause the seas to heave beyond their bounds.

11. I shall cause the mercantile trade between nations to be destroyed.

12. I shall now bring about the cleansing of the earth, to be prepared for my coming as your Lord and King who reigneth on high.

13. So let all peoples receive my word, to prepare, and cause your families to

repent of the corrupt and evil ways that hinder you in your progress as peoples of salvation in your Lord.

14. Come unto me, and I shall save you, even with an eternal salvation.

15. Hinder those who persecute my people on my land of Zion.

16. Let all nations beware and not come against my people upon the land of the place of my government, even Zion.

17. And let all nations prepare to receive my word of justice and righteous government.

18. For I, the Lord, created all things; and I shall rule over all nations, to their salvation, and to the establishment of peace. So shall I fulfill.

19. Cause the people who shall cleanse North and South America to not come against my people.

20. Remove your armies from my lands of Zion. Return to your borders.

21. Fulfill my word, lest destruction come upon you, and your armies be overthrown.

22. I shall cause there to be an overflow of the seas upon the nations who thus come to afflict my people who are the Kingdom of Son Ahman, who reigns over all nations.

23. Let this, my word, be published unto the peoples of the earth.

24. Now cause my servant Warren Jeffs to be freed from bondage.

25. Cause my people to be restored to their lands they have consecrated unto me.

26. Let my word go forth to the nations, that I am God, who has all power to overthrow this wicked generation now upon the earth.

27. Babylon shall be as a garment in the fire, consumed by the brightness of my glory, in power of all-consuming fire.

28. So shall I cleanse my land.

29. Therefore, prepare for my coming as unto a receiver of the pleasing word of peace.

30. Come unto your Lord, even Him who suffered to redeem all who come unto Him for salvation of eternal and righteous and pure dominion.

31. I have the salvation of all people in my hands.

32. Learn of me and know of my ways.

33. Come to my people and be as children of learning.

34. Be clean in your morals.

35. Purify thy habitations to be houses of love and kindness.

36. Let thy children be provided for, with knowledge of my coming.

37. Cause them to be raised in peace as messengers of the loving kindness of their Lord, who hath caused their deliverance from the powers of darkness.

38. It is I who speaketh, and send forth my word, even Him who is called Wonderful, Counselor, Prince of Peace, and Lord and King, over all flesh, even Him who is of eternal and everlasting life; who administers all things in truth and peace.

39. Come unto me, all ye ends of the earth who thus survive the day of my coming, to be thus delivered from the powers of darkness in the dominions of Sheol.

40. I am Salvation, Power, Glory, Truth, Righteous Judgment, and Life and the Resurrection, for all who come unto me.

41. Thus have I sent you my word.

42. Let those of my people of the

covenant, even of the people of my suffering, Judah, my chosen, now prepare to receive my messengers of salvation.

43. Overthrow the laws that cause the destruction of purity in every nation;

44. And thereby let your peoples show their Lord they will dwell in peace under His reign of peace.

45. Let all my people of the covenant of my salvation in Zion now dwell in peace, as I establish my rule throughout the nations.

46. Cause my word to be published. Let all peoples know of my word.

47. Cause them to receive my word by the messengers I send.

SECTION REVELATION 10

Revelation of the Lord Jesus Christ
Draper, Utah
Saturday, October 23, 2010

1. Thus saith the Lord, even Jehovah Christ, Him who was with the Father from before the foundations of this earth was laid:

2. Let the peoples of the earth receive the warning voice, and now prepare for my glorious coming.

3. Cause there to be an end of wars among you.

4. Let peace be among you.

5. Cause there to be a place for my servant Warren Jeffs to communicate my will unto you.

6. Cause that he receive of the people of each nation an acknowledgment of my word, to thus cleanse their people of the evils I have decried against that are in your lands.

7. And as I thus receive the testimonies of honest and prayerful repentance among the leaders of each nation, so shall I, the Lord, spare your nation unto a day of peace.

8. Thus shall I fulfill my word.

9. Cause that my people also be delivered from oppression.

10. I shall soon appear in the glory of my might and shall make known to all nations the truth of all things I have declared.

11. Let thy peoples hasten to cleanse themselves of all evil and corrupt ways.

12. For my judgments are soon to be upon you.

13. Cause the people of the earth to hear the warning voice. Thus shall I fulfill.

14. This from Him who has all power to bless the brokenhearted, and to subdue all enemies under His feet, even your Lord and Savior, Jesus Christ; who hath the Kingdom of endless lives in eternal duration of unity in peace, and who dwells in the power of endless and pure dominion of Celestial heights.

15. Come unto me, O ye people of all nations, to receive of me the greater gifts that ennoble unto eternal peace, of which the increase has no end.

SECTION REVELATION 11

Warning of the Lord to North America

Revelation of the Lord Jesus Christ
Draper, Utah
Tuesday, October 26, 2010

1. Thus saith the Lord unto the people of the land of North America, even Him who reigns on high, and has all power to fulfill His eternal promises unto the salvation of His elect who come unto Him: I, the Lord, have sent my warning of judgments.

2. And thus, my warning has not been answered by government officials in the nation of the United States of America, to deliver my servant Warren Jeffs, nor to deliver my people to receive their lands which have been taken from them.

3. Thus shall I fulfill my word as the nation of my coming thus ignores my word.

4. Let this, my word, be sent to the people of the nation of the United States of America, that I, who is above all, have weighed you, the people of the United States of America, in the balance and have seen the gross wickedness, even to partake of the evil of Sodom, and the murder of unborn children.

5. Thus shall I cause the coming forth of the powers of my justice, to be as a consuming fire of affliction upon the land.

6. And as you continue to persecute my people, so shall I cause the cleansing of the land upon which my Zion shall be built.

7. I, the Lord, shall cause there to be a cleansing of all nations as I come to prepare the earth for my coming in the glory of my might, to dwell on earth among men for a reign of righteousness.

8. I, the Lord, send to you who dwell upon the land of Zion another warning.

9. Receive ye my word. Cause my servant to be set free.

10. Deliver him from the hands of his enemies who seek the destruction of my Church and Kingdom.

11. Cause that my word be published to all peoples, that they may know I shall soon appear with power of judgment.

12. Let the nation of the United States of America receive my word of additional warning.

13. Cause that you allow my servant Warren Jeffs to stand before the people to deliver my word.

14. Thus shall you know my will and purposes as he declares my word. Thus shall I fulfill.

15. Let this be heard by the people who are in authority.

16. Let my servant now send my message of warning to all the peoples of every nation.

17. Cause him to sound my word freely.

18. Let the leader of the nation give heed wherein my people dwell.

19. Cause the leader of the nation of Canada to cease their attack upon my law of Celestial Plural Marriage.

20. Cause the unjust laws in the nation of the United States of America against my Celestial Law of Plural Marriage be overthrown.

21. Let my people go.

22. Cause them to have their religious freedom to live the laws of my Church in purity.

Warnings of the Lord to the Nation of Israel
(Comprising Section Revelations 12-14)

SECTION REVELATION 12

Revelation of the Lord Jesus Christ
Draper, Utah
Thursday, October 7, 2010

1. Let the nation of Israel now prepare to be delivered from all her enemies.

2. And let this nation purge from among them all evil and corrupt ways.

3. Overthrow the laws that allow the murder of unborn children.

4. And cause thy people to become as a nation of warriors to triumph over all thy foes.

5. For I am with you as you cleanse thy people of all wicked and perverse ways.

6. Otherwise, you shall feel the chastening hand of an Almighty God.

7. Let thy people hear this, my warning I now send to you.

8. And let there be among you a cleansing of wickedness from among thy people, lest I must send a scourging unto the purging of wickedness from your land.

9. I have preserved the nation of Israel for the purpose of the gathering of my people Israel; and to cause mine ancient city Jerusalem to be inhabited again by my people in holiness before me.

10. Therefore, let the nation of Israel be warned that my day of visitation is upon them.

11. This from Him who is above all, and who shall fulfill His word. Even so. Amen.

SECTION REVELATION 13

Revelation of the Lord Jesus Christ
Draper, Utah
Saturday, October 23, 2010

1. Let my word to the nation of Israel include my will, as I now say unto you of the nation of Israel:

2. Cause that within your borders you now establish a rule of equity; and no longer let there be religious conflict between your faith in the Lord, and those of the ways of the Arabic origin.

3. And cause that you now are of the covenant of your father Abraham, to be a standard of the rule of righteousness among your people.

4. Let there be abolished the law of misrule wherein you retaliate in violence against other peoples without evidence of intent against your nation.

5. Let there cease the secret murders in other lands that you have been guilty as co-conspirators in evil and secret combinations with the peoples who have helped preserve your nation in times of political and military attack.

6. Let these secret murders be eliminated in such a manner that I, the Lord, shall know, by sending to my servant Warren Jeffs, a representative declaring your obedience to my Proclamation to the nations wherein this communication is published to you.

7. And as you, the nation of Israel, thus abide this, my word, and bring forth the cleansing of corruption and immoral laws from thy people, so shall I preserve you as a nation.

8. Otherwise, you shall be purged as a sifting of wheat from the tares.

9. I, the Lord, who reigns on high, even Jehovah, the Great I AM, have spoken unto you, and so shall I fulfill.

SECTION REVELATION 14

Revelation of the Lord Jesus Christ
Draper, Utah
Thursday, October 21, 2010

1. Let the people of the nation of Israel now prepare to be preserved.

2. I again call upon the people to overthrow all laws in your nation that upholds murder of children unborn, and of licentious and immoral conduct.

3. Pass laws of purity preserved to the cleansing of your peoples.

4. I shall cause the nations to survive who thus prepare.

5. I, the Lord Jesus Christ, have spoken it.

SECTION REVELATION 15

Warning of the Lord to the Nation of Egypt

Revelation of the Lord Jesus Christ
Draper, Utah
Saturday, October 23, 2010

1. Let the city of Cairo build unto me a sanctuary, even a place for my power unto the preservation of thy nation.

2. Let this sanctuary be as a holy place wherein is kept the covenant of cleansing.

3. Let the people of the nation of my preservation be as an example of peace and equity.

4. Cause your laws to preserve virtue.

5. Purge from your midst all corrupt associations with the people of the land of Sudan.

6. Cause your laws to preserve innocence.

7. Cause your laws to overthrow the persecution of your people.

8. Let there be freedom of worship.

9. Prepare a place of a "covenant of peace" unto your Creator.

10. Send forth the petition of protection from thy land unto my servant to thus acknowledge my rule.

11. And cause this sanctuary to be a holy and protected temple, wherein my word I send shall be kept in a holy container of gold and silver, and of precious stones in a gopher-wood frame.

12. Cause my law I send to you to thus be preserved.

13. Let this sanctuary be a place of peace wherein I may come to witness the integrity of your people to just and righteous laws.

14. Sanctify your peoples by a continual labor of sacrifice, to feed the poor, to heal the afflicted, to cause the needy to no longer perish.

15. Thus shall I witness your works, and spare your nation as my judgment of cleansing is sent upon all peoples.

16. This is the word of Son Ahman, the God over all, who hath seen all peoples in the way of their doings; and who shall cause the end of all corrupt and abominable ways.

17. Now be a nation of noble cause.

18. Be as in former times, a people of the preservation of mine Israel.

19. Thus shall I also preserve thy people as you acknowledge me and my rule upon the earth.

20. Let this take place soon among you.

21. And bear affliction without retaliation.

22. Send up your petitions to Him who is the Creator of all things in the day of judgment.

23. Let these petitions also be kept in the holy sanctuary of the God of Peace and Union. Even so. Amen.

SECTION REVELATION 16

Warning of the Lord to the Nation of France

Revelation of the Lord Jesus Christ
Draper, Utah
Thursday, October 7, 2010

1. Verily thus saith the Lord unto the nation of France, even your Lord Jesus Christ, who hath all power, and who sees and knows all things:

2. I, the Lord, have caused that you shall soon be humbled, as I send my judgments against you.

3. For I have seen gross wickedness among you; and must needs cleanse you from all evil, to preserve those who can receive my Gospel of salvation at the time I shall deliver my servant from bondage.

4. Let this nation of France now receive my warning voice; that I, the Lord, shall sweep from their land the corrupt and abominable who are in the condition of the ancient city of Sodom; and as I caused fire from heaven to destroy that city, so shall the nation of France be consumed by the power of my judgment.

5. Let the people of France turn from all their wicked and perverse ways, lest my judgments shall leave your cities desolate.

6. Receive my warning voice, and cease to uphold those in thy nation that cause the legalizing of wickedness to prevail.

7. And cause that the laws that allow the murder of unborn children be overthrown.

8. And cause that the wickedness of immorality be done away with.

9. And let there be a mourning and lamentation among you for all your corrupt and fallen and perverse ways.

10. This from Him who reigns on high, and who has all power to fulfill His word, even the Lord, your Redeemer, who shall appear in the glory of His might to bring forth the day of redemption for all nations; and who shall dwell with men on earth for a thousand years, to reign in righteousness, and to cause all nations to live in peace.

SECTION REVELATION 17

Warning of the Lord to the
Nations of Germany and Belgium

Revelation of the Lord Jesus Christ
Draper, Utah
Thursday, October 7, 2010

1. Cause that the nation of Germany also be warned, that they are now ripened in iniquity, and many of their cities shall be left desolate, because of the murders and abominations and corruption that are among them.

2. Let them repent, and overthrow the laws that permit immorality to exist.

3. Let the nation of Belgium also be warned to overthrow all laws that permit corruption and immorality to exist.

Warnings of the Lord to the Nations of Denmark, the
Netherlands, and Those Nations of Their Descent
(Comprising Section Revelations 18-19)

SECTION REVELATION 18

Revelation of the Lord Jesus Christ
Draper, Utah
Thursday, October 21, 2010

1. Thus saith the Lord Jesus Christ, the Redeemer of all peoples, who shall descend in the power of His majesty to reveal salvation unto all peoples, and who holds all peoples in His power, to the people of the nation of Denmark, and of the Netherlands, and those nations of their descent:

2. I, the Lord, have in my hands the bow and the quiver to send forth my judgments; for you are a people as Sodom.

3. And thus shall I sweep you from off the face of the earth, for abominations shall not reign upon the earth to destroy the purity of my work and word of salvation.

4. Cause there to be overthrown, in your nation and those peoples of your power who thus visit within your borders to partake of the sins of Sodom, and of immorality and sorcery, all laws that uphold these evils.

5. And if you do not, so shall I fulfill my word, even suddenly.

6. Therefore, cause that my word be sounded among those who are thus among you; and cleanse your lands of these evils.

7. I shall send upon you a destroying angel to thus sweep thy land clean of those

who partake of these corruptions of eternal damnation, for you have sold yourselves for naught; and your lives of corruption are not to continue.

8. I, the Lord, have spoken it. So shall I fulfill.

9. Hasten to now purify thy land, lest sudden destruction come upon you.

SECTION REVELATION 19

Revelation of the Lord Jesus Christ
Draper, Utah
Saturday, October 23, 2010

1. Let the city of Amsterdam be warned of the desolation that awaits her; for she is as a stench in the earth, corrupting the inhabitants in continual degradation.

2. Let them repent and cleanse the land of Sodom and adulterous and evil performances; for I have seen the fruits of thy doings unto the damnation of your souls.

3. I shall cause your city to be as a garment in the fire, to cleanse your land of all corruption and gross abomination.

SECTION REVELATION 20

Warning of the Lord to the Nation of Switzerland

Revelation of the Lord Jesus Christ
Draper, Utah
Tuesday, October 26, 2010

1. Thus saith the Lord to the nation of Switzerland, even Him who reigns on high and causes His peace to rest upon the honest in heart:

2. Overthrow your unjust and corrupt laws of euthanasia, wherein you allow suicide.

3. Cause there to be a cleansing of your people of the immoral and evil ways.

4. Let there be in your borders a cleansing of those laws that allow murder of infants yet unborn.

5. Let this be done quickly.

6. Cause your nation to be a peacemaker among nations.

7. Let there be a cleansing of your financial practices that allow people to hide their corrupt and dishonest acquisition of wealth.

8. Cause any nation that practices the evil of murder to get gain, to not have power to use your financial institutions.

9. Let this be a warning to your people, lest I send my judgments upon you.

10. This from your Lord Jesus Christ, the Savior of all men unto salvation in eternal dominions. Even so. Amen.

SECTION REVELATION 21

Warning of the Lord to the Nation of Turkey

Revelation of the Lord Jesus Christ
Draper, Utah
Tuesday, October 26, 2010

1. Let the people of the nation of Turkey be warned of my judgment upon them.

2. They continue in the evils of genocide, in seeking the destruction of peoples not of their religious tenets.

3. Let those in government be warned that they must overthrow any laws of injustice.

4. Cause there to be religious freedom in your nation.

5. Cause there to be the cleansing of your people of all immoral and corrupt laws allowing murder of unborn children.

6. Cause the women to have protection from cruel and corrupt practices of their husbands, or other men who are of corrupt and evil practices.

7. Let there be peace made with the Kurdish people.

8. Cease your unjust pressures of force.

9. Let the people of Israel be as a friend to your nation.

10. Assist them as their enemies seek the destruction of their nation.

11. Now be as a protector of justice and moral conduct.

12. This is the word of the Lord your God, who has the power of salvation unto eternal life.

13. Receive ye my word, lest my judgments cleanse your people of evils and corruptions.

SECTION REVELATION 22

Warning of the Lord to the Balkan Nations

Revelation of the Lord Jesus Christ
Draper, Utah
Tuesday, October 26, 2010

1. Thus saith the Lord unto the people of the Balkans: Make peace among yourselves.

2. Let there be a summit held soon in the nation of your choosing, to bring about a cessation of animosity among your several cultures.

3. Let this summit be held soon to avoid bloodshed or violence.

4. Let there be an apportionment given minority cultures of people.

5. Let peace and love for justice be the spirit of your peoples.

6. Cause this to be as a warning, lest my judgment come upon your several peoples, to stop the evils of corrupt and immoral practices in your lands.

7. This is the word of the Lord to you. As I have spoken, so shall I fulfill.

8. Cause your people to now declare peace.

9. Be peacemakers unto the coming forth of my message of salvation.

10. Let there be a ceasing of violence.

11. Therefore, shall the blessings of peace cause my greater blessing of eternal salvation to be among those who will receive my word. Even so. Amen.

SECTION REVELATION 23

Warning of the Lord to the Nation of Spain

Revelation of the Lord Jesus Christ
Draper, Utah
Thursday, October 21, 2010

1. Verily thus saith the Lord unto the nation of Spain: I, the Lord Jesus Christ, have seen the evils that have corrupted you unto a cursing.

2. And thus shall you feel the judgments of destruction as you continue to persecute the innocent unborn children.

3. Thus shall I cause thy habitations to be as Sodom.

4. Thus shall you know the Lord reigneth.

5. Cause thy people to overthrow those evils in thy nation.

6. Let all immoral and licentious conduct be outlawed in thy land.

7. Cause the people to mourn before their Lord; for I shall cleanse you by the power of judgment as you continue in the corrupt and sinful way of unholy conduct.

8. Even so shall it be upon you.

9. Let the government no longer allow the use of weapons of mass destruction to be in your borders.

10. Cause there to be no more sending forth of soldiers to fight in foreign wars.

11. Cause thy people to let go of the sins of Sodom.

12. Let the unborn children be preserved by law.

13. Cause schools to be built for the poor.

14. Cause the army to be only for guarding the borders of your land, and no longer be used to persecute thy own nation.

15. Let union of peace be among your several peoples.

16. Cause all evils of usury be overthrown.

17. Let thy habitations be as peace.

18. Now cleanse thy nation so my judgments may be stayed.

19. This from Him who is above all things, who shall soon appear to all those who are pure.

20. Let thy people now receive my word.

21. Publish this, my warning, to all the people in the borders and throughout thy nation.

22. Send forth messengers to the nation of the United States on my land of America.

23. Cause that pressure be sent upon them who are in government to let my people go.

24. Cause thy influence be felt in behalf of my servant Warren Jeffs.

25. Let him be free of bondage and of prosecution.

26. Know that I shall see all your works, and bring with me the just recompense of reward.

27. Have only within your nation a continual searching of the ways of truth.

28. Prepare thy people to receive my Gospel of salvation, as I send forth my messengers of peace.

29. Receive ye my representatives of my Kingdom.

30. Throw down all opposition to my law.

31. I have the power of preservation.

32. You shall be used to establish peace again upon the continent where you dwell, as I sweep the nation of France clean.

33. You shall not invade other lands.

34. You shall not usurp authority over any other nation.

35. Thus shall you continue to survive the day of my coming.

36. Let this word be as a warning unto your preservation, as the nations of the earth feel the wrath of a just God upon them.

37. Now ready your armies to be as messengers and defenders of peace.

38. I shall thus cause your land to be preserved.

39. Now establish peace.

40. Do not be slow in this.

41. You only shall be preserved as you acknowledge my right to rule.

42. This is your final warning.

43. Now hasten to preserve your nation as a peacemaker among those nations who survive my day of judgment.

44. I shall call upon you by my messengers I send, as representatives of Son Ahman, even Jesus Christ.

45. And thus shall they make themselves known, by my power attending them.

46. So shall my whirlwind judgments be stayed within your borders.

47. I shall cause a tidal wave soon to come upon thy shores.

48. Cause thy people to soon leave those places where the waters of the sea would thus remove the inhabitants.

49. Let this be done during this next year.

50. I shall cause a sickness come among you to remove many of the more wicked among you.

51. Thus you shall know I, the Lord, have spoken.

52. And as you fulfill my word, to remove the evils of immorality, murder, and child murder of unborn infants, so shall I fulfill my word.

53. Thus it is upon you, a warning, and the call to purify thy land of wickedness.

54. I, the Lord, have spoken; and thus shall I fulfill.

55. Even so shall all things be prepared to receive the knowledge of blessings of the eternal world.

56. My Zion shall rise.

57. The covenant people of Israel shall be gathered.

58. My covenant people on my land of Zion shall be preserved.

59. I shall cause a new people to come upon my land to receive my Gospel.

60. I shall send messengers unto thy nation.

61. Pass and uphold laws of religious and social freedom within thy nation.

62. Prepare for freedom of worship in thy land.

63. Cause persecution to cease in thy land against those of unpopular faith.

64. Now be a nation of truth. Uphold truth.

65. Let go of false and evil traditions.

66. Learn of my eternal ways.

67. Cause thy people to receive my rule.

68. Let go of the traditions of evil and corrupt religion that oppresses the poor.

69. Humble your people by not allowing the sins of abortion to exist.

70. I shall thus continue my blessings upon you.

71. Have upon your habitations a wreath of olive leaves at the time I send forth the sickness among your people.

72. And as I spared ancient Israel, so shall I spare those who thus fulfill my word.

73. Let them also, in each household, renounce the evils I have named in this, my word.

74. Cause there to be your people to receive this, my message, soon.

75. Let their family relations be peaceful.

76. Cause that the infrastructure of thy government be organized to care for those injured by the war soon to come upon the nations of the earth.

77. Prepare for them to care for other peoples.

78. Listen to the message I now send.

79. I have chosen you to thus become a nation to bless other nations.

80. Let this now be fulfilled.

81. I shall only hold you guiltless as you cleanse these evils from among thy nation.

82. This from Him who has you and all peoples in His hands, to preserve the pure in heart through the day of judgment.

83. Hasten ye. Only now can you begin to fulfill my word before I send forth the judgments appointed.

84. Read my servant John's Revelation.

85. Know I shall fulfill my word I recorded through my ancient apostle.

86. I revealed to him the judgments to be sent upon the earth to prepare for my coming. Now believe.

87. Cause there to be an awakening of the people.

88. How oft I have sent my word through my messengers to the nations.

89. Let the people of all nations now realize I, the Lord, shall soon appear.

90. Thus shall this, my word, be on record to testify that I have sent my warning unto the salvation of the nations.

91. How oft my word has gone forth since I restored my Gospel of salvation.

92. My servant Warren Jeffs now is my Mouthpiece upon the earth. Listen to my word.

93. So shall I fulfill, as also my word and will sent forth by my people in the day of my suffering and resurrection.

94. This must become the foundation of your lives, to believe I am; that I, your Lord and Savior, have the power to lead all peoples to salvation.

95. Come unto me, and receive the knowledge and blessings of eternal life.

SECTION REVELATION 24

Warning of the Lord to the Nation of Iraq

Revelation of the Lord Jesus Christ
Draper, Utah
Thursday, October 21, 2010

1. Let the nation of the land of ancient record, even Iraq, now make peace within her borders.

2. Cause the fighting to come to an end.

3. Seek to uphold laws of justice.

4. No longer be a people of war.

5. Start anew to cause thy people to be of the ways of peace and equity.

6. Let there be no persecution of those who are not of your faith.

7. Let the sins of immorality be abolished among your people.

8. I shall cleanse your land of all wickedness.

9. My people shall yet dwell upon my land as I covenanted with my servant Abraham, and his son Isaac, and my servant Israel.

10. So shall I fulfill. Nothing can stay my hand.

SECTION REVELATION 25

Warning of the Lord to the Nation of Iran

Revelation of the Lord Jesus Christ
Draper, Utah
Thursday, November 4, 2010

1. Thus saith the Lord unto the nation of Iran, even Him who has all power, to cause the peoples of the earth to hear, and to bring forth the overthrow of all nations who are not founded upon righteous and equitable principles:

2. I have seen in your land the corrupt and evil way of violence against women.

3. I have all nations in my hands.

4. Cause there to be a cleansing of your people.

5. Cease the evils of immorality.

6. Cause the bringing forth of laws that provide for the protection of women.

7. Let there cease in your land the evil of child abuse.

8. Let all practice of the murder of unborn children be done away among your people.

9. Let the leader of the nation cease promoting violence in neighboring nations.

10. This is a practice of promoting evils of violence that shall be as a whirlwind

upon you, to be a return of evil upon your nation as you have done to other nations.

11. Cause that peace be established with other nations.

12. Let there be a freedom of worship.

13. Cause the people of minority to no longer be persecuted.

14. Allow representation of minorities.

15. Let there be a purging of immoral and corrupt ways from among your people.

16. Now cleanse the inside of the platter, and no longer be a people of corrupt and immoral ways.

17. This from your Lord who is the God over all peoples, and who shall come to make Himself known to all nations.

18. Even as I have spoken, so shall I fulfill.

19. I am of eternal power over all flesh.

20. Hear thou my word I send to you.

21. Now be a people of peace.

22. Set aside your evil and corrupt system of administering false justice to get gain.

23. Your corruptions of immoral and murderous ways have been your overthrow.

24. So shall I cleanse and purify thy people.

25. No longer cause unrest in Iraq.

26. Be a peacemaker.

27. Let vice in your borders no longer cause other peoples to visit your land.

28. Otherwise, I shall scourge your nation with sickness, and the judgment of desolating and unprecedented violence within your borders.

29. Hear this warning.

30. Let the leader of your religious governing power humble himself before Him who reigns over all peoples, even Jesus Christ, the King over all nations.

31. Let him now turn the people to principles of peace, virtue, equity, in the willingness to overthrow corruption and immoral ways.

32. Thus it is spoken by Him who has all power to fulfill His word.

33. Let thy people be rewarded according to their deeds.

34. So shall my judgments be upon you to cease all corruption.

35. I shall cause a cleansing by fire.

36. Prosperity shall flee from your land.

37. The poor must be delivered.

38. Provide for their needs.

39. Sell goods in an honest manner.

40. Turn the people to the ways of kindness and righteous and pure ways in their family organization.

41. Let the women be schooled.

42. Cause the freedom of religious worship to be protected.

43. Let thy name be known as Peace.

44. No longer be as a rebellion of threatening against other peoples.

45. Now cause the ceasing of contention against other nations.

46. Have upon your dwellings a wreath of olive leaves to show your willingness to repent and turn to obey my will.

47. Thus shall I turn away my judgment of desolation.

48. Hear my word! Cease these evils.

49. I, the Lord, have spoken, to be answered upon you in my day of judgment.

50. Let all things be prepared to receive my messengers of salvation.

51. Let them be preserved as they come to deliver my will.

52. Even so shall I be a God of preservation to you.

53. Let this be a warning heeded.

54. Let my will be sounded to your people.

55. Cause the holiness of my eternal and pure ways be an example of peace and righteous doing to all.

56. I, the Lord, have spoken it.

57. Thus it is unto you, to be a nation of my preservation as you fulfill my word.

58. Let it be written in your hearts that your God who created you has thus sent His word of warning unto you, to be answered upon you by the power of my might.

59. So shall it be as a day of sorrow if you turn from my word.

60. My coming in glory is nigh.

61. Nothing can stay my hand.

62. Hasten to obey as I have commanded.

63. No longer be a fallen and darkened people of a violent way.

64. Come unto me and learn of the way of peace.

65. I can heal you unto the deliverance of your people.

66. I shall cause you to no longer have power to be a nation of violence.

67. Now cause the coming forth of my will to you.

68. Seek unto my governing and guiding representatives as my Zion is fully established.

69. Thus you have been told to cleanse your land before my judgment of desolation comes.

70. I am the God of Israel, and of the whole earth.

71. No longer send violence to be against the nation of Israel.

72. Turn from this evil.

73. Now be a people that promotes peace with all nations, lest I send a greater power against you unto you being a nation no longer.

74. Thus has your people suffered through the generations.

75. Now be ye a people who seek truth and peace unto your own preservation.

76. I am now turning the key in your favor as you heed my word I send to you.

77. Otherwise, judgments will come upon you unto you no longer being a nation. Even so. Amen.

SECTION REVELATION 26

Warning of the Lord to the Nation of China

Revelation of the Lord Jesus Christ
Draper, Utah
Monday, November 8, 2010

1. Verily thus saith the Lord unto the people of the nation of China, to be sounded by the coming of the power of my might; to cause the consuming of the corrupt and evil ways of the rule of force against freedom.

2. I, who rules over all nations, who is God, even Jesus Christ, the Savior of the

world, thus call upon the nation of China to overthrow all laws of injustice of repression that are of the work of the governing class, to hold thy people in bondage in their rights of agency, to choose the holding of lands and possessions, to seek freedom to bring forth children unobstructed by government rule.

3. Overthrow all law and rule that causes the murder of unborn children.

4. Let there be no more unjust pillaging of minorities.

5. Allow religious freedom within your borders.

6. I shall cause you to learn ways of greater use of your resources as you come to me and my people of Zion, to take care of the needs of your people.

7. Let there be a preparing of your nation unto the performing a work of greater peace among the nations.

8. Prepare to be used to overthrow what is now of evil and corrupt rule among the nations.

9. Be a people who only come against other nations as I shall allow.

10. Let your armies not be used as a repression of your people.

11. Be of the Spirit of peace.

12. No longer threaten Taiwan or other nations not of your nationality of origin.

13. Be a people who are of the gift of religious freedom.

14. No longer repress religious minorities.

15. Make peace in your western borders with other peoples who are of peaceful intent.

16. No longer be a violent people of the way of force.

17. Cause your people to overthrow the laws that allow licentious and immoral ways.

18. Let there be a peace among the separate nationalities within your borders.

19. Cause there to be a sounding of my warning to your peoples.

20. Purify your laws.

21. Establish freedom.

22. Cease the murder of unborn children.

23. Allow families to bring forth children without government interference.

24. Be a nation of peaceful intent.

25. Overthrow the leaders of violence in a peaceful way, by not following the unjust policies of repression and murder of children who are yet unborn.

26. Allow the coming of my messengers.

27. Cause them to be heard by thy people.

28. Let there be an immediate ceasing of hostilities with all other nations.

29. Cause your laws of financial governing be equitable.

30. Cause a sending forth of needed support to be given the poor.

31. Let all things be prepared to receive and obey my word.

32. Now be a people of the readiness to be avengers of injustice as your Lord shall be your God and Ruler.

33. No more send your armies to the African nation of Somalia to get gain, wherein you seek to oppress freedom in other lands not of your dominion or rule.

34. Let this be corrected as a signal to your Lord of your obedience to my word.

35. Send representatives unto my servant Warren Jeffs to thus acknowledge my rule.

36. Let this be a time of not continuing

in gambling or immoral crimes within your borders.

37. Cause Hong Kong to cease those evil practices.

38. Now seek unto your Lord to guide your nation.

39. I, the Lord, have spoken it.

40. Perform the works I have named, and I shall spare your nation in my day of judgment.

41. Otherwise, I shall cause a great famine in your land to cleanse thy people.

42. I shall cause you to feel the judgment of earthquake, and the sea heaving itself beyond its bounds, and many other desolations.

43. Your economic power will be clipped.

44. You shall feel the anger of a just God upon you as you continue in these evils.

45. Now heed my word.

46. Hasten to relieve the poor.

47. Feed the starving people of thy land.

48. Hasten to set aside your unjust laws.

49. Now cause there to be an overthrow of the secret combinations with organized crime with the government officials in your land.

50. Set aside money to be used to build schools in your lands of influence.

51. Be a people who supports the labor of kind and charitable works.

52. Now cause my word to be fulfilled.

53. Thus saith your Lord who created you, the God over all nations; who dwells in the heavens; who sees and knows all things; and who will raise all to be judged for their works done in the flesh, to bring righteous judgment upon all of

every nation unto an eternal and final end, wherein wickedness will not rule.

54. Therefore, receive ye my word.

55. I am He who is Endless, who is of the dominion of Eternal Power governing all things in righteous rule.

56. Come unto me to learn of my ways of eternal peace in righteous reign of peace in the Kingdom of Zion.

57. Let this be as a final warning before I send my greater judgments upon all peoples of the earth.

58. My rule of righteousness shall soon be established as I come in my glory to make myself known to all nations.

59. All shall know of the glory of my might.

60. I am He who is the God over all creation, who shall subdue all enemies under my feet, to no more rise in the works of corrupt and evil ways.

61. Prepare thy people to receive my warning.

62. Let my word be published to all thy people.

63. Overthrow the ways of communism of unjust principles and laws of oppression in your land.

64. Let it be a republic form of government wherein rights of freedom are upheld.

65. Thus shall I cause the overthrow of your government of injustice by the judgments I shall send.

66. Therefore, do as I have named.

67. I shall cause your people to be preserved as you fulfill my word.

68. Hasten to do the work of cleansing these evils I have named from among your people.

69. Thus shall I cause you to remain as a nation, to be a people who learn of the

salvation of your God unto eternal life in my eternal domain of pure and holy laws that exalt unto a never-ending peace, as children of God, dwelling in the realms of the pure and righteous.

70. Now prepare to receive my messengers of salvation.

71. I shall send them to teach you of my Gospel of salvation.

72. Therefore, let there be religious freedom declared.

73. I shall then bless your people, to preserve them in the day of judgment.

74. Let there be no more disunion of violent nature in your borders.

75. I, the Lord, have spoken it.

76. Now fulfill my word. Even so. Amen.

SECTION REVELATION 27

Warning of the Lord to the Nation of Pakistan

Revelation of the Lord Jesus Christ
Draper, Utah
Thursday, November 4, 2010

1. Thus saith the Lord to the people of the nation of Pakistan, even Him who reigns on high; whose coming is as a fire that burneth, to appear to all nations; to make His ways known unto the salvation of all peoples; even Jesus Christ, the God over all, who speaks and fulfills His word:

2. I have seen your evil and corrupt ways of violence against women; and also your violent ways against other nations; even to join in secret combinations with those of a violent nature warring in other lands.

3. Thus shall I cause judgment to come upon your nation according to your continued evil and corrupt ways.

4. Now cause your people to receive my word, to cease violent and unjust ways among women, and against them in your false and evil ways.

5. Let there be equity among men and women in their freedoms of worship and conduct.

6. No longer allow the beating of women.

7. No longer allow abuse of women by their husband or other evil-motivated men.

8. Cause your secret combinations with the Taliban to be stopped.

9. Cause them to leave your land.

10. Cause your unjust and violent ways to be stopped.

11. Let the nation of India be approached to make peace.

12. No longer promote terror or violent ways.

13. Let thy people be a peaceful and kind people.

14. Now heed my word.

15. Let this be sounded to your people.

16. Cause representatives to be sent to him who is my spokesman.

17. Let them tell him of your repentance.

18. Let them receive my counsel.

19. Now be a nation that hears and follows the counsel of peace from Him who is the King of Peace, even Jesus Christ, the Lord over all.

20. I have seen the unjust ways of your rulers.

21. I shall soon cause their overthrow as they continue in their evil and unjust ways.

22. Now perform the work of peace.

23. Do this now, lest my judgment of desolation come upon you.

24. I have sent a warning of my power upon you, unto the displacement of millions by storm and want.

25. Now believe my power is over all.

26. I shall send help to relieve suffering as you cleanse your land of the violent who prey upon the weak and the poor among you.

27. Nothing is hidden from me.

28. I shall be a greater power in preserving you as you fulfill my will.

29. Hear this warning before my greater judgments come upon you.

30. Now be a people of pure motives of kindness and peace.

31. This from Him who is the Ruler of nations, who dwells in heaven in the power of His might, to redeem all the honest in heart unto eternal salvation.

32. I am the God of Israel, and of the whole earth.

33. In me all men have peace as they come unto me to be redeemed unto salvation.

34. Cause there to be freedom of religious worship.

35. Cause the corrupt ways of bribery and unjust ways of financial gain be stopped.

36. Now be as I have commanded, and I shall bless your people with the needed gifts of life.

37. Let this be as a final message before my greater judgments come upon the people of all nations.

38. Therefore, hasten to respond.

39. I, the Lord, shall fulfill all my words.

40. Nothing can stay my hand.

41. Let all beware how they treat my word.

42. Eternal is my name. Righteous is my name.

43. Come unto me for eternal life of peace and happiness.

44. Send forth help to the poor and needy in your land, and do not squander the blessings of life I have allowed you to receive.

45. Let there be an immediate ceasing of violence against India.

46. Send away the violent and secret organizations that terrorize other nations.

47. Do this, lest I cause your own government to be overthrown by violence and war.

48. Open your borders to receive minorities of peace from neighboring nations.

49. Cause freedom of the press, with guiding laws, to promote truth and equity.

50. Even so, cause thy people to be taught of ways of cleanliness, so sickness will not prevail.

51. Send the help needed to encourage your people to not seek violent solutions to their poverty.

52. Let these truths cause you to know I see all things.

53. Cause a coming forth of peace talks with India.

54. Let there be no more conflict over Kashmiri.

55. Settle this warring action.

56. I, the Lord, have spoken it, and shall be a Provider and Defense for your nation as you obey my will.

57. I am He who created you.

58. Obey my word unto the salvation of your nation.

59. Cause my word to be known unto the rich who abuse the system of government to get gain, subjugating the poor to suffering poverty.

60. How long shall I stay my hand against you?

61. Now receive my warning. Even so. Amen.

SECTION REVELATION 28

Warning of the Lord to the Nation of Great Britain

Revelation of the Lord Jesus Christ
Draper, Utah
Thursday, October 7, 2010

1. Let the people of the nation of Great Britain also receive my warning that I, the Lord, have weighed them in the balance and found them wanting.

2. And I shall send upon them my judgments, to cleanse the inside of the platter; to cause all wickedness to cease in their land; and to prepare them to receive my Gospel of salvation, as I shall soon send forth by the hand of my servant whom I have called to bear the keys of my Church and Kingdom.

3. Let them, therefore, repent; and now be warned that I, the Lord Jesus Christ, am soon to purify the nation of Great Britain by the power of my might; and to preserve among them those who will come clean before me in abiding in pure and holy laws that exalt man to become as their Lord.

SECTION REVELATION 29

Warning of the Lord to the Nation of Japan

Revelation of the Lord Jesus Christ
Draper, Utah
Monday, November 8, 2010

1. Verily, thus saith the Lord unto the nation of Japan:

2. I, the Lord, have seen your abominations, and send to you my word of warning, of coming desolation upon you who continue in the gross and immoral ways of vice and pornography, and of child murder of unborn children.

3. Thus cause there to be an immediate ceasing in your nation of the evils of immoral conduct in your legal and governing powers.

4. Cause that there be an equitable rule of governing power.

5. Let the immoral practice of men and women bathing together in public baths cease.

6. Let there be a change in your social structure wherein you do not allow the many immoral establishments to exist.

7. Cause thy people to now be a morally clean people.

8. Overthrow the laws that allow the existence of the secret combinations of immoral and murderous nature among your people.

9. Let there be a continual labor of providing for the poor.

10. Cause your nation to be an example of peaceful acquisition of financial and moral integrity.

11. Now be warned of judgment to be sent upon you as these evils continue.

12. Now be a people who throws off the tradition of false religions binding you to have among you the corrupt ways of immoral conduct.

13. Learn of my ways of eternal purity.

14. Send thy representatives to my people of Zion to learn of the ways of eternal truth.

15. Though you were humbled as a nation in the great war of your doing, I, the Lord, shall cause a greater judgment to come of desolation of abominatable and corrupt ways, even to know of the sorrows of great measure unto the cleansing of your nation of these immoral ways.

16. Now bring forth the purifying of your people.

17. I can only spare you as you remove the evils of corruption and unrighteous practices that destroy the virtue and natural purity that you have allowed to become your tradition.

18. I shall cause you to survive as a nation as you thus fulfill my word.

19. This is the word of the Lord to you. Even so. Amen.

SECTION REVELATION 30

Warning of the Lord to the Nation of Mexico

Revelation of the Lord Jesus Christ
Draper, Utah
Thursday, October 7, 2010

1. Verily I say unto the nation of Mexico, even the Lord Jesus Christ, who hath redeemed all men unto the resurrection of their souls:

2. I, the Lord, have visited you with judgment, even the pending revolution of unrest.

3. And now let thine ear be inclined to listen to Him who shall subdue all enemies under His feet:

4. I, the Lord, have seen the abominations of the people of the nation of Mexico.

5. And I call upon you of the nation of Mexico to be warned of my continued judgments to be poured out upon you.

6. For my hand shall not be stayed; and I, the Lord, shall cleanse my land of Zion of all wickedness.

7. Therefore, repent ye, and receive my warning to be of the people who heed my word; and come before me, thy God and Maker, as humble vessels, cleansing your lives of all evil.

8. For I shall soon send forth the fulness of my word to the generation that shall survive my judgments.

9. Let this, my warning, be published to all the people within the nation of Mexico.

10. And cause that my word of warning delivered to the nation of the United States of America also be published to all nations.

11. Therefore, let this, my warning, be sounded by you, my servant Warren, unto the people of this generation.

SECTION REVELATION 31

Warning of the Lord to the Nation of Brazil

Revelation of the Lord Jesus Christ
Draper, Utah
Thursday, October 7, 2010

1. Verily thus saith the Lord unto the nation of Brazil, even your Lord and Savior:

2. I, the Lord, have weighed you in the balance and found you wanting.

3. Therefore, I shall send my destroying angel to visit the inhabitants of that nation, to sweep them from off the face of my land of Zion.

4. Cause that the nation of Brazil

receive my warning, and to repent; for I, the Lord, shall soon send upon them the judgment of the overflowing scourge; for they are ripened in iniquity and must needs be swept off the land.

5. Let the leaders of the nation of Brazil receive this, my warning, that they must overthrow all laws that permit immorality to prevail.

6. And cause the people to humble themselves, as they see my chastening hand come upon them.

7. Let my servant Warren Jeffs also read this, my word, to the nation of Brazil.

SECTION REVELATION 32

Warning of the Lord to the Nation of Colombia

Revelation of the Lord Jesus Christ
Draper, Utah
Tuesday, October 26, 2010

1. Thus saith the Lord unto the people of Colombia, even Him who rules on high, and has all power to fulfill His word:

2. Cause your people to be a people of peace.

3. Overthrow those robbers of your land who cause violence to continue among your people.

4. Now be a people of justice and peace.

5. I shall soon send my judgments upon the nations.

6. Let there be overthrown the laws that allow murder of unborn children.

7. Overthrow laws of immorality being allowed in your land.

8. Now be a people who are as a defender of peace.

9. I shall cause your people to be preserved as you heed my word.

10. This is the word of Him who made you, and upholds all nations in their place. Even so. Amen.

Policies and General Principles of the Government of Son Ahman in the Kingdom of Ahman

(Comprising Section Revelations 33-34)

SECTION REVELATION 33

Revelation of the Lord Jesus Christ
Draper, Utah
Wednesday, October 27, 2010

1. Verily I say unto you, my servant Warren:

2. Now cause the organization of the Council of Fifty in the organization of "The Kingdom of Son Ahman in the Dominion of Ahman"; even the government of the Kingdom of our Lord upon the earth.

3. Cause the Constitution of my Kingdom to be: Thus saith Son Ahman, even your Lord Jesus Christ:

4. Obey my word.

5. Abide in purity.

6. Make peace.

7. Live righteous laws.

8. Be just.

9. Be equitable.

10. Have compassion.

11. Live unto principles of virtue and clean morals.

12. No longer allow murder.

13. No longer allow powers to exist that destroy virtue and innocence.

14. Govern in the Spirit of love.

15. Cause peace and truth to reign.

16. Let no more religious persecution be on earth.

17. Beat your swords into plows and pruning hooks.

18. Labor honestly.

19. Cast off usury of deceit.

20. No more allow prostitution.

21. Establish laws of righteous justice.

22. Cause adultery to be a capital punishment.

23. Let he who takes life, not live.

24. Cause all courts to be accountable.

25. Cause all leaders of nations be accountable.

26. Send forth representatives unto the governing Council of Fifty from every nation to submit to my rule.

27. Let all peoples know of my right to rule.

28. Let it be written in every nation:

29. The Lord is our King, He whose right it is to rule.

30. Honor Him who is above all things, who created all things, who gives place to every nation.

31. Let honor, virtue, truth, peace, light, and power be ascribed to our God -- for He is full of mercy, justice, grace, and truth and peace.

32. I, the Lord, formed the earth and stretched out the heavens and created all things.

33. I am God.

34. I have the right to rule in all the affairs pertaining to the Lord's dominions.

35. Let the nations take notice!

36. Cause the ears of all living to hear my word.

37. Thus shall my blessings descend from heaven upon them.

38. Come unto Him whose right it is to rule.

39. He ruleth in righteousness, equity, wisdom, and truth.

40. Righteous is His name.

41. Acknowledge my right to rule.

42. Come unto Zion.

43. I will show you marvelous and eternal happiness.

44. Now make peace with all other peoples.

45. Let thy people now learn truth.

46. I am He who gave you life.

47. Heed my word.

48. Let thy poor be cared for in kindness.

49. Let thy schools include religious teachings.

50. Cause freedom of worship to be given all peaceful organizations.

51. Let there be honesty in all financial dealings.

52. Rather suffer a wrong than do one against any other people.

53. Cause there to be heard the voice of the weak and poor.

54. Let the powers of darkness not reign.

55. Make laws that do not create dissension.

56. Uphold laws that promote peace.

57. Promote the general welfare of the people of your lands.

58. Cause disunity of selfishness be overthrown.

59. Bring forth the alms of the prayers of your people.

60. Let the officers of your nation be accountable.

61. Do not legalize adultery or nudity or evil practices of vice.

62. Promote sexual and moral purity.

63. Cause the mail in every nation to be free of corruption.

64. Let peace be in every family.

65. Bless one another.

66. Forgive and seek forgiveness.

67. Perform works of kindness.

68. Let the thoughts of your minds favor mercy.

69. Let justice be given.

70. Cause righteous rule to be exercised.

71. Bring forth the alteration or abolishment of unjust laws.

72. Let your governments be subject to an accounting.

73. Let the records of your doings be sent to Zion.

74. Send your wise men to be taught.

75. Let all come, who desire pure truth.

76. Send to Zion your learned to be humbled.

77. Declare on my day of birth allegiance to my rule.

78. Let this be a fast day in all nations.

79. Cause this day to be April 6th.

80. Let the place of my suffering be a sacred and quiet abode.

81. Let the arts of darkness be obliterated wherein is worship of Lucifer or his dark ways.

82. Let him be bound by the righteousness of thy people.

83. Bring forth restitution where you have transgressed.

84. Let other nations alone.

85. Allow my judgment to be upheld in all things.

86. Carry no longer animosity toward any other minority.

87. Seek the Lord for His judgment.

88. Uphold His word, and I shall show you how to govern in righteousness.

89. Let my love reign.

90. Let sacrifice be offered.

91. Release the political prisoners.

92. Purify the media.

93. Let go of all personal attacks of evil against all other peoples in their righteous pursuits.

94. Come to me, all ye peoples of the earth, to learn of righteous and equitable government.

95. Thus saith the Lord unto you.

SECTION REVELATION 34

Revelation of the Lord Jesus Christ
Draper, Utah
Wednesday, October 27, 2010

1. Cause the preamble of the Kingdom of God to read: "Holy, holy, art thou, O Lord and Ruler of all things. Thy righteous will be done.

2. Let all peoples bow the knee, and every tongue confess thou art just, and thy rule of righteousness is extant, and thy love for all is equity and truth upheld in dominions of peace. Thus, let us come under your rule."

3. Let my eternal ways be followed.

4. "Cause thy blessings of peace to be upon us.

5. Let thy wisdom triumph.

6. Let the knowledge of thy ways exalt.

7. Cause the earth to bring forth in rich abundance.

8. Let thy throne be as a light to all men.

9. Cause thy wrath to be stayed.

10. Let thy mercy attend.

11. Cause justice to be given.

12. Let light of truth overthrow all darkness.

13. Let thy power to bless rest upon all.

14. Thus, let thy rule of eternal wisdom abide over all people.

15. Thus shall your rule bring to pass salvation and peace.

16. We bow to your rule in the covenant of peace, in soberness and gratitude of soul."

17. Thus it is, even eternally, a government of purity; a Kingdom of righteous peace in the power of the God of Creation, whose right it is to rule over all flesh, by whom all exist, by whom all continue, even Son Ahman, the Creator of light and eternal duration of the government of power.

18. Thus it is, and thus it shall be unto eternal and holy dominion, worlds without end, unto those of the Kingdom of Zion.

19. Thus, let all be of the Kingdom of God.

20. As I speak, obey.

21. This is my rule.

22. Let my word be sounded in your nation.

23. Cause my word to be written in your hearts.

24. I, your Lord, have all power.

25. Let my power of peace now triumph.

26. Let there be a cleansing of your peoples.

27. Overthrow the evil of murder of unborn children.

28. Leave the punishment of other nations to me. I shall be justified.

29. Let the officers of my Kingdom now be preserved.

30. Let the officers of your nations now come to learn of peace in the Kingdom of Zion.

31. I shall reveal great truths such as you have not heard.

32. My blessing be upon the honest in heart.

33. I am no respecter of persons.

34. In every nation he who works righteousness shall be blessed of me.

35. Renounce war.

36. Promote peace.

37. I, the Lord, have spoken it, and shall bring about the humbling of nations.

38. Now cause my word to be received in your land.

39. Cause my word to be known among your people.

40. Let this be the continued call of Him who already rules the nations, and has the power of life and death in pure and holy dominions of eternal day.

41. I, the Lord, know all your hearts. Nothing is hidden from me.

42. I dwell in everlasting burnings.

43. All corruption is devoured by the fire of my glory.

44. Nothing can escape my righteous judgment.

45. My judgment is unto eternal duration.

46. Who am I that made man, that will not hold him accountable for his deeds done in the flesh?

47. I shall bring with me the just recompense of reward upon every nation, kindred, tongue, and individuals.

48. Thus is my righteous reign on high.

49. Thus shall my rule be on earth. Even so. Amen.

Warnings of the Lord to This Nation and Generation and the Nations of the Earth Through Joseph Smith and Other Prophets

Doctrine and Covenants Section 1

1. Hearken, O ye people of my church, saith the voice of him who dwells on high, and whose eyes are upon all men; yea, verily I say: Hearken ye people from afar; and ye that are upon the islands of the sea, listen together.

2. For verily the voice of the Lord is unto all men, and there is none to escape; and there is no eye that shall not see, neither ear that shall not hear, neither heart that shall not be penetrated.

3. And the rebellious shall be pierced with much sorrow; for their iniquities shall be spoken upon the housetops, and their secret acts shall be revealed.

4. And the voice of warning shall be unto all people, by the mouths of my disciples, whom I have chosen in these last days.

5. And they shall go forth and none shall stay them, for I the Lord have commanded them.

6. Behold, this is mine authority, and the authority of my servants, and my preface unto the book of my commandments, which I have given them to publish unto you, O inhabitants of the earth.

7. Wherefore, fear and tremble, O ye people, for what I the Lord have decreed in them shall be fulfilled.***

38. What I the Lord have spoken, I have spoken, and I excuse not myself; and though the heavens and the earth pass away, my word shall not pass away, but shall all be fulfilled, whether by mine own voice or by the voice of my servants, it is the same.

Book of Mormon Ether Chapter 2

8. And he had sworn in his wrath unto the brother of Jared, that whoso should possess this land of promise, from that time henceforth and forever, should serve him, the true and only God, or they should be swept off when the fulness of his wrath should come upon them.

9. And now, we can behold the decrees of God concerning this land, that it is a land of promise; and whatsoever nation shall possess it shall serve God, or they shall be swept off when the fulness of his wrath shall come upon them. And the fulness of his wrath cometh upon them when they are ripened in iniquity.

10. For behold, this is a land which is choice above all other lands; wherefore he that doth possess it shall serve God or shall be swept off; for it is the everlasting decree of God. And it is not until the fulness of iniquity among the children of the land, that they are swept off.

11. And this cometh unto you, O ye Gentiles, that ye may know the decrees of God -- that ye may repent, and not continue in your iniquities until the fulness come, that ye may not bring down the fulness of the wrath of God upon you as the inhabitants of the land have hitherto done.

12. Behold, this is a choice land, and whatsoever nation shall possess it shall be free from bondage, and from captivity, and from all other nations under heaven, if they will but serve the God of the land, who is Jesus Christ, who hath been manifested by the things which we have written.

Teachings of the Prophet Joseph Smith Page 17

And now I am prepared to say by the authority of Jesus Christ, that not many years shall pass away before the United States shall present such a scene of *bloodshed* as has not a parallel in the history of our nation; pestilence, hail, famine, and earthquake will sweep the wicked of this generation from off the face of the land, to open and prepare the way for the return of the lost tribes of Israel from the north country. The people of the Lord, those who have complied with the requirements of the new covenant, have already commenced gathering together to Zion, which is in the state of Missouri; therefore I declare unto you the warning which the Lord has commanded me to declare unto this generation, remembering that the eyes of my Maker are upon me, and that to Him I am accountable for every word I say, wishing nothing worse to my fellow-men than their eternal salvation; therefore, "Fear God, and give glory to Him, for the hour of His judgment is come." Repent ye, repent ye, and embrace the everlasting covenant, and flee to Zion, before the overflowing scourge overtake you, for there are those now living upon the earth whose eyes shall not be closed in death until they see all these things, which I have spoken, fulfilled. Remember these things; <u>call upon the Lord while He is near, and seek Him while He may be found</u>, is the exhortation of your unworthy servant.

(Signed) JOSEPH SMITH, JUN.

Doctrine and Covenants Section 65

1. Hearken, and lo, a voice as of one sent down from on high, who is mighty and powerful, whose going forth is unto the ends of the earth, yea, whose voice is unto men -- Prepare ye the way of the Lord, make his paths straight.

2. The keys of the kingdom of God are committed unto man on the earth, and from thence shall the gospel roll forth unto the ends of the earth, as the stone which is cut out of the mountain without hands shall roll forth, until it has filled the whole earth.

3. Yea, a voice crying -- Prepare ye the way of the Lord, prepare ye the supper of the Lamb, make ready for the Bridegroom.

4. Pray unto the Lord, call upon his holy name, make known his wonderful works among the people.

5. <u>**Call upon the Lord, that his kingdom may go forth upon the earth, that the inhabitants thereof may receive it, and be prepared for the days to come, in the which the Son of Man shall come down in heaven, clothed in the brightness of his glory, to meet the kingdom of God which is set up on the earth.**</u>

6. <u>**Wherefore, may the kingdom of God go forth, that the kingdom of heaven may come, that thou, O God, mayest be glorified in heaven so on earth, that thine enemies may be subdued; for thine is the honor, power and glory, forever and ever. Amen.**</u>

Doctrine and Covenants Section 43

17. Hearken ye, for, behold, the great day of the Lord is nigh at hand.

18. For the day cometh that the Lord shall utter his voice out of heaven; the heavens shall shake and the earth shall tremble, and the trump of God shall sound both long and loud, and shall say to the sleeping nations: Ye saints arise and live; ye sinners stay and sleep until I shall call again.

19. Wherefore gird up your loins lest ye be found among the wicked.

20. Lift up your voices and spare not. <u>Call upon the nations to repent, both old and young, both bond and free, saying: Prepare yourselves for the great day of the Lord;</u>

21. For if I, who am a man, do lift up my voice and call upon you to repent, and ye hate me, what will ye say when the day cometh when the thunders shall utter their voices from the ends of the earth, speaking to the ears of all that live, saying -- Repent, and prepare for the great day of the Lord?

22. Yea, and again, when the lightnings shall streak forth from the east unto the west, and shall utter forth their voices unto all that live, and make the ears of all tingle that hear, saying these words -- Repent ye, for the great day of the Lord is come?

23. And again, the Lord shall utter his voice out of heaven, saying: Hearken, O ye nations of the earth, and hear the words of that God who made you.

24. <u>**O, ye nations of the earth, how often would I have gathered you together as a hen gathereth her chickens under her wings, but ye would not!**</u>

25. <u>**How oft have I called upon you by the mouth of my servants, and by the ministering of angels, and by mine own voice, and by the voice of thunderings,**</u>

and by the voice of lightnings, and by the voice of tempests, and by the voice of earthquakes, and great hailstorms, and by the voice of famines and pestilences of every kind, and by the great sound of a trump, and by the voice of judgment, and by the voice of mercy all the day long, and by the voice of glory and honor and the riches of eternal life, and would have saved you with an everlasting salvation, but ye would not!

26. Behold, the day has come, when the cup of the wrath of mine indignation is full.

27. Behold, verily I say unto you, that these are the words of the Lord your God.

28. Wherefore, labor ye, labor ye in my vineyard for the last time -- for the last time call upon the inhabitants of the earth.

29. For in mine own due time will I come upon the earth in judgment, and my people shall be redeemed and shall reign with me on earth.

30. For the great Millennium, of which I have spoken by the mouth of my servants, shall come.

31. For Satan shall be bound, and when he is loosed again he shall only reign for a little season, and then cometh the end of the earth.

32. And he that liveth in righteousness shall be changed in the twinkling of an eye, and the earth shall pass away so as by fire.

33. And the wicked shall go away into unquenchable fire, and their end no man knoweth on earth, nor ever shall know, until they come before me in judgment.

34. Hearken ye to these words. Behold, I am Jesus Christ, the Savior of the world. Treasure these things up in your hearts, and let the solemnities of eternity rest upon your minds.

35. Be sober. Keep all my commandments. Even so. Amen.

Doctrine and Covenants Section 101

86. Let them importune at the feet of the judge;

87. And if he heed them not, let them importune at the feet of the governor;

88. And if the governor heed them not, let them importune at the feet of the president;

89. And if the president heed them not, then will the Lord arise and come forth out of his hiding place, and in his fury vex the nation;

90. And in his hot displeasure, and in his fierce anger, in his time, will cut off those wicked, unfaithful, and unjust stewards, and appoint them their portion among hypocrites, and unbelievers;

91. Even in outer darkness, where there is weeping, and wailing, and gnashing of teeth.

92. Pray ye, therefore, that their ears may be opened unto your cries, that I may be merciful unto them, that these things may not come upon them.

93. What I have said unto you must needs be, that all men may be left without excuse;

94. That wise men and rulers may hear and know that which they have never considered;

95. That I may proceed to bring to pass my act, my strange act, and perform my work, my strange work, that men may discern between the righteous and the wicked, saith your God.

Doctrine and Covenants Section 87

1. Verily, thus saith the Lord concerning the wars that will shortly come to pass, beginning at the rebellion of South Carolina, which will eventually terminate in the death and misery of many souls;

2. And the time will come that war will

be poured out upon all nations, beginning at this place.

3. For behold, the Southern States shall be divided against the Northern States, and the Southern States will call on other nations, even the nation of Great Britain, as it is called, and they shall also call upon other nations, in order to defend themselves against other nations; and then war shall be poured out upon all nations.

4. And it shall come to pass, after many days, slaves shall rise up against their masters, who shall be marshaled and disciplined for war.

5. And it shall come to pass also that the remnants who are left of the land will marshal themselves, and shall become exceedingly angry, and shall vex the Gentiles with a sore vexation.

6. And thus, with the sword and by bloodshed the inhabitants of the earth shall mourn; and with famine, and plague, and earthquake, and the thunder of heaven, and the fierce and vivid lightning also, shall the inhabitants of the earth be made to feel the wrath, and indignation, and chastening hand of an Almighty God, until the consumption decreed hath made a full end of all nations;

7. **That the cry of the saints, and of the blood of the saints, shall cease to come up into the ears of the Lord of Sabaoth, from the earth, to be avenged of their enemies.**

8. **Wherefore, stand ye in holy places, and be not moved, until the day of the Lord come; for behold, it cometh quickly, saith the Lord. Amen.**

Doctrine and Covenants Section 45

30. And in that generation shall the times of the Gentiles be fulfilled.

31. And there shall be men standing in that generation, that shall not pass until they shall see an overflowing scourge; for a desolating sickness shall cover the land.

32. But my disciples shall stand in holy places, and shall not be moved; but among the wicked, men shall lift up their voices and curse God and die.

33. And there shall be earthquakes also in divers places, and many desolations; yet men will harden their hearts against me, and they will take up the sword, one against another, and they will kill one another.***

39. And it shall come to pass that he that feareth me shall be looking forth for the great day of the Lord to come, even for the signs of the coming of the Son of Man.

40. And they shall see signs and wonders, for they shall be shown forth in the heavens above, and in the earth beneath.

41. And they shall behold blood, and fire, and vapors of smoke.

42. And before the day of the Lord shall come, the sun shall be darkened, and the moon be turned into blood, and the stars fall from heaven.

43. And the remnant shall be gathered unto this place;

44. And then they shall look for me, and, behold, I will come; and they shall see me in the clouds of heaven, clothed with power and great glory; with all the holy angels; and he that watches not for me shall be cut off.

45. But before the arm of the Lord shall fall, an angel shall sound his trump, and the saints that have slept shall come forth to meet me in the cloud.

46. Wherefore, if ye have slept in peace blessed are you; for as you now behold me and know that I am, even so shall ye come unto me and your souls shall live, and your redemption shall be perfected; and

the saints shall come forth from the four quarters of the earth.

47. Then shall the arm of the Lord fall upon the nations.

48. And then shall the Lord set his foot upon this mount, and it shall cleave in twain, and the earth shall tremble, and reel to and fro, and the heavens also shall shake.

49. And the Lord shall utter his voice, and all the ends of the earth shall hear it; and the nations of the earth shall mourn, and they that have laughed shall see their folly.

50. And calamity shall cover the mocker, and the scorner shall be consumed; and they that have watched for iniquity shall be hewn down and cast into the fire.

51. And then shall the Jews look upon me and say: What are these wounds in thine hands and in thy feet?

52. Then shall they know that I am the Lord; for I will say unto them: These wounds are the wounds with which I was wounded in the house of my friends. I am he who was lifted up. I am Jesus that was crucified. I am the Son of God.

53. And then shall they weep because of their iniquities; then shall they lament because they persecuted their king.

54. And then shall the heathen nations be redeemed, and they that knew no law shall have part in the first resurrection; and it shall be tolerable for them.

55. And Satan shall be bound, that he shall have no place in the hearts of the children of men.

56. And at that day, when I shall come in my glory, shall the parable be fulfilled which I spake concerning the ten virgins.

57. For they that are wise and have received the truth, and have taken the Holy Spirit for their guide, and have not been deceived -- verily I say unto you, they shall not be hewn down and cast into the fire, but shall abide the day.

58. And the earth shall be given unto them for an inheritance; and they shall multiply and wax strong, and their children shall grow up without sin unto salvation.

59. For the Lord shall be in their midst, and his glory shall be upon them, and he will be their king and their lawgiver.***

65. And with one heart and with one mind, gather up your riches that ye may purchase an inheritance which shall hereafter be appointed unto you.

66. And it shall be called the New Jerusalem, a land of peace, a city of refuge, a place of safety for the saints of the Most High God;

67. And the glory of the Lord shall be there, and the terror of the Lord also shall be there, insomuch that the wicked will not come unto it, and it shall be called Zion.

68. And it shall come to pass among the wicked, that every man that will not take his sword against his neighbor must needs flee unto Zion for safety.

69. And there shall be gathered unto it out of every nation under heaven; and it shall be the only people that shall not be at war one with another.

70. And it shall be said among the wicked: Let us not go up to battle against Zion, for the inhabitants of Zion are terrible; wherefore we cannot stand.

71. And it shall come to pass that the righteous shall be gathered out from among all nations, and shall come to Zion, singing with songs of everlasting joy.***

74. For when the Lord shall appear he shall be terrible unto them, that fear may seize upon them, and they shall stand afar off and tremble.

75. And all nations shall be afraid

because of the terror of the Lord, and the power of his might. Even so. Amen.

Warnings of the Lord to Those Who Fight Against the Lord's People

Doctrine and Covenants Section 121

11. And they who do charge thee with transgression, their hope shall be blasted, and their prospects shall melt away as the hoar frost melteth before the burning rays of the rising sun;

12. And also that God hath set his hand and seal to change the times and seasons, and to blind their minds, that they may not understand his marvelous workings; that he may prove them also and take them in their own craftiness;

13. Also because their hearts are corrupted, and the things which they are willing to bring upon others, and love to have others suffer, may come upon themselves to the very uttermost;

14. That they may be disappointed also, and their hopes may be cut off;

15. And not many years hence, that they and their posterity shall be swept from under heaven, saith God, that not one of them is left to stand by the wall.

16. Cursed are all those that shall lift up the heel against mine anointed, saith the Lord, and cry they have sinned when they have not sinned before me, saith the Lord, but have done that which was meet in mine eyes, and which I commanded them.

17. But those who cry transgression do it because they are the servants of sin, and are the children of disobedience themselves.

18. And those who swear falsely against my servants, that they might bring them into bondage and death --

19. Wo unto them; because they have offended my little ones they shall be severed from the ordinances of mine house.

20. Their basket shall not be full, their houses and their barns shall perish, and they themselves shall be despised by those that flattered them.

21. They shall not have right to the priesthood, nor their posterity after them from generation to generation.

22. It had been better for them that a millstone had been hanged about their necks, and they drowned in the depth of the sea.

23. Wo unto all those that discomfort my people, and drive, and murder, and testify against them, saith the Lord of Hosts; a generation of vipers shall not escape the damnation of hell.

24. Behold, mine eyes see and know all their works, and I have in reserve a swift judgment in the season thereof, for them all;

25. For there is a time appointed for every man, according as his works shall be.

Doctrine and Covenants Section 136

34. Thy brethren have rejected you and your testimony, even the nation that has driven you out;

35. And now cometh the day of their calamity, even the days of sorrow, like a woman that is taken in travail; and their sorrow shall be great unless they speedily repent, yea, very speedily.

36. For they killed the prophets, and them that were sent unto them; and they have shed innocent blood, which crieth from the ground against them.

The Lord's Warning Through the Prophet Leroy S. Johnson

Leroy S. Johnson Volume 7:352
February 12, 1984 CCA

The work of God must go on! Great

judgments are coming upon this great Church of ours. When Wilford Woodruff signed the Manifesto, he didn't only sign away his rights to the Celestial Law, but he also signed away his right to the Holy Priesthood. Now what kind of priesthood has the Church been operating under for ninety years? -- yea, ninety-four years? Is the "Coming Crisis and How to Meet It" being fulfilled right under our eyes and there is nobody here to defend the Gospel of Jesus Christ?

We will see the judgments of God poured out more and more from this time forth until this part of the earth is empty of its inhabitants -- those who are not able to say, "I am clean every whit," and have the Lord call us up. So we are working under a great handicap, my dear brothers and sisters. If this people that I am speaking to today don't hasten to lay away their sins and their wrong-doings and come clean before the Lord, they are going to find the Lord is not pleased with them, and they will have to go down with the wicked.

Leroy S. Johnson Volume 7:394
June 24, 1984 Canada

The Lord has said, "Stand ye in holy places and watch the arm of the Lord made manifest." The only holy places we have are our dedicated homes. The Lord is very angry with the Church of Jesus Christ of Latter-day Saints for the way it has acted and operated throughout the last hundred years or more. Since the days of Brigham Young, they have rejected the Celestial Law. Not only that -- when Wilford Woodruff signed the Manifesto, he not only signed away his rights to the Celestial Law, but he signed away his rights to the Priesthood, also. That being the case, what priesthood have they been operating under? They claim they have

been operating under a priesthood. Read "The Coming Crisis and How to Meet It." It will tell you exactly who they have been serving and what has transpired in the last few years.

It is our place now to clean up our minds and get the Spirit of God and keep it, because the Spirit of God is the only protection that we will have. The scriptures tell us that there will be two working at the mill; one will be taken and the other left. Two will be working in the field; one will be taken and the other left, and so forth. This is true. We will have to have the Spirit of God upon us enough to be caught up when the judgments of God go over the earth, then we will be let down again. That is the only way the Lord can protect His people. He says He will protect His saints if He has to send fire from heaven to do so; and this, He will do.

Matthew Chapter 24 [Inspired Version]

32. And again, this gospel of the kingdom shall be preached in all the world, for a witness unto all nations, and then shall the end come, or the destruction of the wicked.

33. And again shall the abomination of desolation, spoken of by Daniel the prophet, be fulfilled.

34. And immediately after the tribulation of those days, the sun shall be darkened, and the moon shall not give her light, and the stars shall fall from heaven, and the powers of heaven shall be shaken.

35. Verily I say unto you, this generation, in which these things shall be shown forth, shall not pass away until all I have told you shall be fulfilled.

36. Although the days will come that heaven and earth shall pass away, yet my word shall not pass away; but all shall be fulfilled.

37. And as I said before, after the tribulation of those days, and the powers of the heavens shall be shaken, then shall appear the sign of the Son of man in heaven; and then shall all the tribes of the earth mourn.

38. And they shall see the Son of man coming in the clouds of heaven, with power and great glory.

39. And whoso treasureth up my words, shall not be deceived.

40. For the Son of man shall come, and he shall send his angels before him with the great sound of a trumpet, and they shall gather together the remainder of his elect from the four winds; from one end of heaven to the other.

41. Now learn a parable of the fig tree: When its branches are yet tender, and it begins to put forth leaves, ye know that summer is nigh at hand.

42. So likewise mine elect, when they shall see all these things, they shall know that he is near, even at the doors.

43. But of that day and hour no one knoweth; no, not the angels of God in heaven, but my Father only.

44. But as it was in the days of Noah, so it shall be also at the coming of the Son of man.

45. For it shall be with them as it was in the days which were before the flood; for until the day that Noah entered into the ark, they were eating and drinking, marrying and giving in marriage, and knew not until the flood came and took them all away; so shall also the coming of the Son of man be.

46. Then shall be fulfilled that which is written, that, In the last days,

47. Two shall be in the field; the one shall be taken and the other left.

48. Two shall be grinding at the mill; the one taken and the other left.

49. And what I say unto one, I say unto all men; Watch, therefore, for ye know not at what hour your Lord doth come.

50. But know this, if the good man of the house had known in what watch the thief would come, he would have watched, and would not have suffered his house to have been broken up; but would have been ready.

51. Therefore be ye also ready; for in such an hour as ye think not, the Son of man cometh.

52. Who then is a faithful and wise servant, whom his Lord hath made ruler over his household, to give them meat in due season?

53. Blessed is that servant, whom his Lord when he cometh shall find so doing;

54. And, verily I say unto you, he shall make him ruler over all his goods.

55. But if that evil servant shall say in his heart, My Lord delayeth his coming; and shall begin to smite his fellow servants, and to eat and drink with the drunken; the Lord of that servant shall come in a day when he looketh not for him, and in an hour that he is not aware of, and shall cut him asunder, and shall appoint him his portion with the hypocrites; there shall be weeping and gnashing of teeth.

56. And thus cometh the end of the wicked according to the prophecy of Moses, saying, They should be cut off from among the people. But the end of the earth is not yet; but bye and bye.

Luke Chapter 17 [Inspired Version]

26. And as it was in the days of Noe; so shall it be also in the days of the Son of man.

27. They did eat, they drank, they

married wives, they were given in marriage, until the day that Noe entered into the ark, and the flood came, and destroyed them all.

28. Likewise also as it was in the days of Lot; they did eat, they drank, they bought, they sold, they planted, they builded;

29. But the same day that Lot went out of Sodom, it rained fire and brimstone from heaven, and destroyed them all.

30. Even thus shall it be in the day when the Son of man is revealed.

31. In that day, the disciple who shall be on the housetop, and his stuff in the house, let him not come down to take it away; and he who is in the field, let him likewise not return back.

32. Remember Lot's wife.

33. Whosoever shall seek to save his life, shall lose it; and whosoever shall lose his life, shall preserve it.

34. I tell you, in that night there shall be two in one bed; the one shall be taken, and the other shall be left. Two shall be grinding together; the one shall be taken, and the other left.

35. Two shall be in the field; the one shall be taken, and the other left.

36. And they answered and said unto him, Where, Lord, shall they be taken?

37. And he said unto them, Wheresoever the body is gathered; or, in other words, whithersoever the saints are gathered, thither will the eagles be gathered together; or, thither will the remainder be gathered together.

38. This he spake, signifying the gathering of his saints; and of angels descending and gathering the remainder unto them; the one from the bed, the other from the grinding, and the other from the field, whithersoever he listeth.

39. For verily there shall be new heavens, and a new earth, wherein dwelleth righteousness.

40. And there shall be no unclean thing; for the earth becoming old, even as a garment, having waxed in corruption, wherefore it vanisheth away, and the footstool remaineth sanctified, cleansed from all sin.

2 Peter Chapter 3 [Inspired Version]

8. But concerning the coming of the Lord, beloved, I would not have you ignorant of this one thing, that one day is with the Lord as a thousand years, and a thousand years as one day.

9. The Lord is not slack concerning his promise and coming, as some men count slackness; but long-suffering toward us, not willing that any should perish, but that all should come to repentance.

10. But the day of the Lord will come as a thief in the night, in the which the heavens shall shake, and the earth also shall tremble, and the mountains shall melt, and pass away with a great noise, and the elements shall be filled with fervent heat; the earth also shall be filled, and the corruptible works which are therein shall be burned up.

11. If then all these things shall be destroyed, what manner of persons ought ye to be in holy conduct and godliness,

12. Looking unto, and preparing for the day of the coming of the Lord wherein the corruptible things of the heavens being on fire, shall be dissolved, and the mountains shall melt with fervent heat?

13. Nevertheless, if we shall endure, we shall be kept according to his promise. And we look for a new heavens, and a new earth wherein dwelleth righteousness.

14. Wherefore, beloved, seeing that ye look for such things, be diligent, that

ye may be found of him in peace, without spot and blameless;

The Lord's Warnings Through the Prophet Rulon Jeffs

Rulon Jeffs Volume 7:368
December 6, 1991 SLC

I want you all to understand the continual use of the two words "keep sweet", means keep the Holy Spirit of the Lord, until you are full of it. Only those who have it will survive the judgments of God which are about to be poured out without let or hindrance upon the earth, beginning at the House of God, where the Mormons are. I mean the Mormon Church, which is now apostate completely, and will never be set in order. We have the true and living Church of Jesus Christ of Latter-day Saints under our administration. And we add the word "Fundamentalist" in order to distinguish the true Church of Jesus Christ of Latter-day Saints from the name of the one that now is a complete gentile sectarian church. The Lord has rejected it.

Rulon Jeffs Volume 7:402
December 4, 1992 SLC

So, if you will keep the grand teaching that we are trying to get over: Keep the Holy Spirit of God. KEEP SWEET! It is a matter of life or death. You have had the teaching regarding what is required in order for us to survive the judgments, sufficient of the Holy Spirit of God that we can be lifted up and then set down after it is over. That will be the remnant which will go to redeem Zion. The wicked will be swept off from the face of this land. The wicked are they who come not unto Christ. There is only one people who comes unto Christ, and that is this people under His servant.

Book of Mormon 3 Nephi Chapter 30

1. Hearken, O ye Gentiles, and hear the words of Jesus Christ, the Son of the living God, which he hath commanded me that I should speak concerning you, for, behold he commandeth me that I should write, saying:

2. Turn, all ye Gentiles, from your wicked ways; and repent of your evil doings, of your lyings and deceivings, and of your whoredoms, and of your secret abominations, and your idolatries, and of your murders, and your priestcrafts, and your envyings, and your strifes, and from all your wickedness and abominations, and come unto me, and be baptized in my name, that ye may receive a remission of your sins, and be filled with the Holy Ghost, that ye may be numbered with my people who are of the house of Israel.

The Word of the Lord Jesus Christ
Through His Holy Prophet Isaiah

Isaiah 2 [Inspired Version]
Book of Mormon 2 Nephi Chapter 12

1. The word that Isaiah the son of Amoz saw concerning Judah and Jerusalem.

2. And it shall come to pass in the last days, when the mountain of the Lord's house shall be established in the top of the mountains, and shall be exalted above the hills, and all nations shall flow unto it;

3. And many people shall go and say, Come ye, and let us go up to the mountain of the Lord, to the house of the God of Jacob; and he will teach us of his ways, and we will walk in his paths; for out of Zion shall go forth the law, and the word of the Lord from Jerusalem;

4. And he shall judge among the nations, and shall rebuke many people; and they shall beat their swords into ploughshares, and their spears into pruning hooks; nation shall not lift up sword against nation, neither shall they learn war anymore.

5. O house of Jacob, come ye, and let us walk in the light of the Lord; yea, come, for ye have all gone astray, everyone to his wicked ways.

6. Therefore, O Lord, thou hast forsaken thy people the house of Jacob, because they be replenished from the east, and hearken unto the soothsayers like the Philistines, and they please themselves in the children of strangers.

7. Their land also is full of silver and gold, neither is there any end of their treasures; their land is also full of horses, neither is there any end of their chariots;

8. Their land also is full of idols; they worship the work of their own hands, that which their own fingers have made.

9. And the mean man boweth not down, and the great man humbleth himself not; therefore forgive them not.

10. O ye wicked ones, enter into the rock, and hide ye in the dust; for the fear of the Lord and his majesty shall smite thee.

11. And it shall come to pass that the lofty looks of man shall be humbled, and the haughtiness of man shall be bowed down, and the Lord alone shall be exalted in that day.

12. For the day of the Lord of hosts soon cometh upon all nations; yea, upon everyone; yea, upon the proud and lofty, and upon everyone who is lifted up, and he shall be brought low.

13. Yea, and the day of the Lord shall come upon all the cedars of Lebanon, for they are high and lifted up; and upon all the oaks of Bashan;

14. And upon all the high mountains, and upon all the hills, and upon all the nations which are lifted up;

15. And upon every people, and upon every high tower, and upon every fenced wall,

16. And upon all the ships of the sea, and upon all the ships of Tarshish, and upon all pleasant pictures.

17. And the loftiness of man shall be bowed down, and the haughtiness of men shall be made low; and the Lord alone shall be exalted in that day.

18. And the idols he shall utterly abolish.

19. And they shall go into the holes of the rocks, and into the caves of the earth, for the fear of the Lord shall come upon them, and the glory of his majesty shall

smite them, when he ariseth to shake terribly the earth.

20. In that day a man shall cast his idols of silver, and his idols of gold, which he hath made for himself to worship, to the moles and to the bats;

21. To go into the clefts of the rocks, and into the tops of the ragged rocks, for the fear of the Lord shall come upon them, and the majesty of the Lord shall smite them, when he ariseth to shake terribly the earth.

22. Cease ye from man, whose breath is in his nostrils; for wherein is he to be accounted of?

Isaiah Chapter 3 [Inspired Version]
Book of Mormon 2 Nephi Chapter 13

1. For, behold, the Lord, the Lord of hosts, doth take away from Jerusalem and from Judah the stay and the staff, the whole staff of bread, and the whole stay of water,

2. The mighty man, and the man of war, the judge, and the prophet, and the prudent, and the ancient,

3. The captain of fifty, and the honorable man, and the counselor, and the cunning artificer, and the eloquent orator.

4. And I will give children unto them to be their princes, and babes shall rule over them.

5. And the people shall be oppressed, everyone by another, and everyone by his neighbor; the child shall behave himself proudly against the ancient, and the base against the honorable.

6. When a man shall take hold of his brother of the house of his father, and shall say, Thou hast clothing, be thou our ruler, and let not this ruin come under thy hand;

7. In that day shall he swear, saying, I will not be a healer; for in my house there is neither bread nor clothing; make me not a ruler of the people.

8. For Jerusalem is ruined, and Judah is fallen; because their tongues and their doings have been against the Lord, to provoke the eyes of his glory.

9. The show of their countenance doth witness against them; and doth declare their sin to be even as Sodom, they cannot hide it. Woe unto their souls! for they have rewarded evil unto themselves.

10. Say unto the righteous, that it is well with them; for they shall eat the fruit of their doings.

11. Woe unto the wicked! for they shall perish; for the reward of their hands shall be upon them.

12. And as for my people, children are their oppressors, and women rule over them. O my people, they who lead thee cause thee to err, and destroy the way of thy paths.

13. The Lord standeth up to plead, and standeth to judge the people.

14. The Lord will enter into judgment with the ancients of his people, and the princes thereof; for ye have eaten up the vineyard; and the spoil of the poor is in your houses.

15. What mean ye? ye beat my people to pieces, and grind the faces of the poor, saith the Lord God of hosts.

16. Moreover the Lord saith, Because the daughters of Zion are haughty, and walk with stretched-forth necks and wanton eyes, walking and mincing as they go, and making a tinkling with their feet;

17. Therefore the Lord will smite with a scab the crown of the head of the daughters of Zion, and the Lord will discover their secret parts.

18. In that day the Lord will take away the bravery of tinkling ornaments, and cauls, and round tires like the moon,

19. The chains, and the bracelets, and the mufflers,

20. The bonnets, and the ornaments of the legs, and the headbands, and the tablets, and the earrings,

21. The rings, and nose jewels,

22. The changeable suits of apparel, and the mantles, and the wimples, and the crisping pins,

23. The glasses, and the fine linen, and the hoods, and the veils.

24. And it shall come to pass, instead of sweet smell there shall be stink; and instead of a girdle a rent; and instead of well-set hair, baldness; and instead of a stomacher a girding of sackcloth; burning instead of beauty.

25. Thy men shall fall by the sword, and thy mighty in the war.

26. And her gates shall lament and mourn; and she shall be desolate, and shall sit upon the ground.

27. And in that day seven women shall take hold of one man, saying, We will eat our own bread, and wear our own apparel; only let us be called by thy name, to take away our reproach.

Isaiah 4 [Inspired Version]
Book of Mormon 2 Nephi Chapter 14

1. In that day shall the branch of the Lord be beautiful and glorious, and the fruit of the earth shall be excellent and comely to them that are escaped of Israel.

2. And it shall come to pass, they that are left in Zion, and he that remaineth in Jerusalem, shall be called holy, even everyone that is written among the living in Jerusalem;

3. When the Lord shall have washed away the filth of the daughters of Zion, and shall have purged the blood of Jerusalem from the midst thereof by the spirit of judgment, and by the spirit of burning.

4. And the Lord will create upon every dwelling place of mount Zion, and upon her assemblies, a cloud and smoke by day, and the shining of a flaming fire by night; for upon all the glory of Zion shall be a defense.

5. And there shall be a tabernacle for a shadow in the daytime from the heat, and for a place of refuge, and for a covert from storm and from rain.

The Word of the Lord Jesus Christ
Through His Holy Apostle John

Revelations Chapter 7 [Inspired Version]

1. And after these things I saw four angels standing on the four corners of the earth, holding the four winds of the earth, that the wind should not blow on the earth, nor on the sea, nor on any tree.

2. And I saw another angel ascending from the east, having the seal of the living God; and I heard him cry with a loud voice to the four angels, to whom it was given to hurt the earth and the sea,

3. Saying, Hurt not the earth, neither the sea, nor the trees, till we have sealed the servants of our God in their foreheads.

4. And the number of them who were sealed, were an hundred and forty and four thousand of all the tribes of the children of Israel.

5. Of the tribe of Juda were sealed twelve thousand. Of the tribe of Reuben were sealed twelve thousand. Of the tribe of Gad were sealed twelve thousand.

6. Of the tribe of Aser were sealed twelve thousand. Of the tribe of Nephthalim

were sealed twelve thousand. Of the tribe of Manasses were sealed twelve thousand.

7. Of the tribe of Simeon were sealed twelve thousand. Of the tribe of Levi were sealed twelve thousand. Of the tribe of Issachar were sealed twelve thousand.

8. Of the tribe of Zabulon were sealed twelve thousand. Of the tribe of Joseph were sealed twelve thousand. Of the tribe of Benjamin were sealed twelve thousand.

9. After this I beheld, and, lo, a great multitude, which no man could number, of all nations, and kindreds, and people, and tongues, stood before the throne, and before the Lamb, clothed with white robes, and palms in their hands;

10. And cried with a loud voice, saying, Salvation to our God which sitteth upon the throne, and unto the Lamb.

11. And all the angels stood round about the throne, and about the elders and the four beasts, and fell before the throne on their faces, and worshiped God,

12. Saying, Amen; Blessing, and glory, and wisdom, and thanksgiving, and honor, and power, and might, be unto our God for ever and ever. Amen.

13. And one of the elders answered, saying unto me, What are these which are arrayed in white robes? and whence came they?

14. And I said unto him, Sir, thou knowest. And he said to me, These are they which came out of great tribulation, and have washed their robes, and made them white in the blood of the Lamb.

15. Therefore are they before the throne of God, and serve him day and night in his temple; and he that sitteth on the throne shall dwell among them.

16. They shall hunger no more, neither thirst anymore; neither shall the sun light on them, nor any heat.

17. For the Lamb which is in the midst of the throne shall feed them, and shall lead them unto living fountains of waters; and God shall wipe away all tears from their eyes.

Revelations Chapter 12 [Inspired Version]

1. And there appeared a great sign in heaven, in the likeness of things on the earth; a woman clothed with the sun, and the moon under her feet, and upon her head a crown of twelve stars.

2. And the woman being with child, cried, travailing in birth, and pained to be delivered.

3. And she brought forth a man child, who was to rule all nations with a rod of iron; and her child was caught up unto God and his throne.

4. And there appeared another sign in heaven; and behold, a great red dragon, having seven heads and ten horns, and seven crowns upon his heads. And his tail drew the third part of the stars of heaven, and did cast them to the earth. And the dragon stood before the woman which was delivered, ready to devour her child after it was born.

5. And the woman fled into the wilderness, where she had a place prepared of God, that they should feed her there a thousand two hundred and threescore years.

6. And there was war in heaven; Michael and his angels fought against the dragon; and the dragon and his angels fought against Michael;

7. And the dragon prevailed not against Michael, neither the child, nor the woman which was the church of God, who had been delivered of her pains, and brought forth the kingdom of our God and his Christ.

8. Neither was there place found in heaven for the great dragon, who was cast out; that old serpent called the devil, and also called Satan, which deceiveth the whole world; he was cast out into the earth; and his angels were cast out with him.

9. And I heard a loud voice saying in heaven, Now is come salvation, and strength, and the kingdom of our God, and the power of his Christ;

10. For the accuser of our brethren is cast down, which accused them before our God day and night.

11. For they have overcome him by the blood of the Lamb, and by the word of their testimony; for they loved not their own lives, but kept the testimony even unto death. Therefore, rejoice O heavens, and ye that dwell in them.

12. And after these things I heard another voice saying, Woe to the inhabiters of the earth, yea, and they who dwell upon the islands of the sea! for the devil is come down unto you, having great wrath, because he knoweth that he hath but a short time.

13. For when the dragon saw that he was cast unto the earth, he persecuted the woman which brought forth the man-child.

14. Therefore, to the woman were given two wings of a great eagle, that she might flee into the wilderness, into her place, where she is nourished for a time, and times, and half a time, from the face of the serpent.

15. And the serpent casteth out of his mouth water as a flood after the woman, that he might cause her to be carried away of the flood.

16. And the earth helpeth the woman, and the earth openeth her mouth, and swalloweth up the flood which the dragon casteth out of his mouth.

17. Therefore, the dragon was wroth with the woman, and went to make war with the remnant of her seed, which keep the commandments of God, and have the testimony of Jesus Christ.

Revelations Chapter 20 [Inspired Version]

1. And I saw an angel come down out of heaven, having the key of the bottomless pit and a great chain in his hand.

2. And he laid hold on the dragon, that old serpent, which is the Devil, and Satan, and bound him a thousand years,

3. And cast him into the bottomless pit, and shut him up, and set a seal upon him, that he should deceive the nations no more, till the thousand years should be fulfilled; and after that he must be loosed a little season.

4. And I saw thrones, and they sat upon them, and judgment was given unto them; and I saw the souls of them that were beheaded for the witness of Jesus, and for the word of God, and which had not worshiped the beast, neither his image, neither had received his mark upon their foreheads, or in their hands: and they lived and reigned with Christ a thousand years.

5. But the rest of the dead lived not again until the thousand years were finished. This is the first resurrection.

6. Blessed and holy are they who have part in the first resurrection; on such the second death hath no power, but they shall be priests of God and of Christ, and shall reign with him a thousand years.

7. And when the thousand years are expired, Satan shall be loosed out of his prison,

8. And shall go out to deceive the nations which are in the four quarters of the earth, Gog and Magog, to gather them

together to battle; the number of whom is as the sand of the sea.

9. And they went up on the breadth of the earth, and compassed the camp of the saints about, and the beloved city; and fire came down from God out of heaven, and devoured them.

10. And the devil that deceived them was cast into the lake of fire and brimstone, where the beast and the false prophet are, and shall be tormented day and night for ever and ever.

11. And I saw a great white throne, and him that sat on it, from whose face the earth and the heaven fled away; and there was found no place for them.

12. And I saw the dead, small and great, stand before God; and the books were opened; and another book was opened, which is the book of life; and the dead were judged out of those things which were written in the books, according to their works.

13. And the sea gave up the dead which were in it; and death and hell delivered up the dead which were in them; and they were judged every man according to their works.

14. And death and hell were cast into the lake of fire. This is the second death.

15. And whosoever was not found written in the book of life was cast into the lake of fire.

Chapter 2

Continued Warnings of Son Ahman to the Leaders of the Nations of the Earth

SECTION REVELATION 5

A Petition to the President of the United States of America

Revelation of the Lord Jesus Christ
Draper, Utah
Thursday, October 7, 2010

1. To the honorable President of the United States of America now as standing at the head of this nation:

2. I who dwells on high, even your Lord and Savior, who redeemed all mankind by the shedding of His own blood, and who is over all and has all power, send to you my word.

3. Cause that my servant who presides over my Church now be delivered by thy hand.

4. Let my servant go, that he may perform his mission to prepare my people for my coming.

5. Cause that the prosecutors now cease their attack upon my servant Warren Jeffs.

6. Cause that this nation now restore to my people the consecrated land taken from them.

7. Cause that there be remuneration given them for the loss of the homes that are occupied illegally by the enemies of my people who are in the Colorado City, Arizona and Hildale, Utah area.

8. Cause that the attack against my people in Texas be stopped.

9. I, the Lord, shall cause my judgments to be withheld as you thus perform this work.

10. Otherwise, let this nation know I am with my people, and shall sweep the wicked from off the face of the land of America.

11. Thus shall I perform my work by my almighty power.

12. This from your Lord, even Jesus Christ, who shall subdue all His enemies under His feet.

13. Even as I have spoken, so shall I fulfill. Even so. Amen.

SECTION REVELATION 35

Revelation of the Lord Jesus Christ to the Peoples of the Nation of the United States of America and to the Peoples of the Earth Through My Servant Warren Jeffs

Big Lake, Texas
Saturday, February 5, 2011

1. Thus saith the Lord unto the nation of the United States of America: I, the Lord, am soon to send the shaking of the earth in a place in thy land not known as a usual place of violent shaking, unto the loss of many lives.

2. Let it be known, I, the Lord, have sent my message to government officials to free my servant Warren Jeffs, to cause my people to receive back their lands and houses, and you heed me not.

3. Thus I shall cause a great destruction in the land of Illinois, to the loss of life and to your awakening, that when I, the Lord, speak, let my word be fulfilled, lest you become as a people only worthy to be swept off my land of Zion;

4. For verily I say unto you, this earth is mine, and I have caused my people to receive a preparation work for my glorious coming on earth to establish my Zion, and they are my people. Let them go! For you shall now feel the wrath of an Almighty God in a place of my naming in a soon-to-happen event.

5. Though you deny me, know that I, the Lord, have spoken, and I send to you my word at this time, to receive my word that I shall cause my servant on earth to deliver to thee, a message of warning, that I, the Lord, will no longer uphold thee as a nation, corrupting your way before me, having in your midst legalized murder of unborn children, thus shedding innocent blood before the heavens, and allowing the sins of Sodom and immoral practices among you by legal consent; yet you persecute my people who abide by my will and my governing principles of purity, required of them by me.

6. No longer consider I shall preserve thy land as you continue to allow him whom I have chosen to receive and give my word to the peoples of the earth to remain in bondage; when he only is seeking to fulfill my will, saith the Lord, in preparing my people to establish on my holy land my Zion, a place of peace; which you know is among them, having illegally carried away innocent children, examining my people, knowing they are free from the corrupting influences of this wicked generation by your own examining.

7. Though you accuse them of corrupt practices and evil motives, they are my people, saith the Lord Jesus Christ, who sendeth this message to you: Let my people go! or you shall reap the whirlwind of judgments in near future sending, such as you have not seen; for I am God, and I speak from the heavens through him whom I have anointed.

8. Though he received testing, fearing for a time, yet I, the Lord, have raised him up and delivered him and am guiding him -- Now step forth and deliver my word to all peoples:

9. Repent ye! Repent ye! My day of judgments upon all the earth is at hand.

10. Send forth my word of warning to all peoples, beginning with this nation, and hereafter shall I cause a greater sounding of my warning voice, which, if you heed me not, shall be fulfilled in fulness; for I shall appear in the power of my might in the clouds of heaven, to make myself known to all peoples my right to rule; and nothing can hinder the progress of my Zion rising in fulness;

11. For though you stretch forth your hands to persecute mine elect on the earth, who have received exalted ways in pure religious motive and practice; yet you believe traitors who are themselves corrupt, partaking of a spirit of outward prosecution, condemning that which is holy because thine own hearts are corrupt before me; accusing mine elect of wicked motives who only receive my laws of Celestial Plural Marriage and my Economic Order of Heaven, a United Order of religious practice by my word, by the revelations of my will.

12. And this is my Church upon the earth, living laws that you know are of scriptural record among you; yet you condemn that which I, the Lord, have established for the salvation of the earth.

13. Verily I say unto you, let there be an immediate stop to the prosecution and governmental interference against my servant and against my people, lest you incur mine anger unto the fulfilling of what I have named, that I now send to you in a writing of your understanding.

14. And though false witnesses stand forth seeking to brand guilt upon innocence, I, the Lord, shall defend my people in a manner of deliverance to thine eternal regret and condemnation, as you stand before me in the day of judging, having lifted your hand against your God who created you.

15. Receive my word of warning, and know that I, the Lord, have spoken from the heavens at a needed time when you can respond to my word.

16. And as a testimony this is my word, I shall send forth a great storm in the land, crippling thy nation again, which I have been sending in increasing power since you allowed an unjust judge to confine my servant still, and other court actions in thy land against the holding of property where my people dwell; in that place in the Hildale, Utah and Colorado City, Arizona area, illegally, by your own laws, interfering with a religious trust by governmental intervention.

17. Now this country of the United States of America shall go down, as she does not defend innocence, religious organization of pure religious intent.

18. I, the Lord, have spoken it. Hasten to respond to my word, as I send my word again to you, lest mine anger be kindled unto the fulfilling of all my promises against a wicked generation in a manner you have not seen before.

19. This from your Lord and Savior, Jesus Christ, who hath redeemed all mankind, who will respond to my message of salvation; which shall go forth again to all surviving nations, they who will respond to my word and preserve my people who shall go among them to deliver my message of salvation in a day soon at hand.

20. And nothing can stay mine hand, saith the Lord, for all nations shall know I have spoken it.

21. And as my word is fulfilled, though the wicked among you deny me still, I shall preserve mine elect and

establish my Zion until all nations shall know I am doing my work on the earth as I have promised.

22. Receive ye my word to thy understanding, and I shall preserve thy land as you execute equity and justice, not allowing the persecution of an innocent people who are only seeking to do the will of their God -- a revelation of my giving in the law of Celestial Plural Marriage, and revelations of my giving in the Law of Consecration of Stewardships, called the Holy United Order among my people.

23. These laws are of me, saith the Lord, and are of ancient record, that record being in your hands, by my faithful apostles and patriarchs of old, by prophets and kings and rulers who lived laws of my revealing in their time, which must be lived in purity, with no corruption among them, or they cannot be my people, saith the Lord.

24. And though you condemn my law, my law shall triumph over all opposition, all opposing powers, though all the world combine; for these laws are of me.

25. My people know that they must needs abide these laws to be my people; thus, they have suffered persecution, lo, these many years, rather than surrender eternal exalting laws from their God.

26. And this is why they continue the living of my revealed eternal laws, seeking salvation of souls for themselves and all others who would come unto me through my authorized representative on earth, each in their time; yea, verily, my Prophets, upholding my law as revealed through my servant Joseph Smith, Jun., as he was instrument in mine hands to restore my Gospel of salvation and mine authority to administer my laws upon the earth; which authority continues in the person of my servant Warren Jeffs, whom I have

preserved, though tried; yet he continues to receive my word.

27. And verily I say unto you, my judgments are soon to be poured forth upon all nations that forget their God, who will not heed my word and purify their lives before me, in righteous principles known to all peoples, if you corrupt your ways before me, in licentious and immoral practices that lead to the shedding of innocent blood, in most nations where murder of unborn children is allowed by legal consent; and this stench can no longer continue, for I shall stretch forth mine hand and all peoples shall know I have spoken.

28. Repent ye! Cease these evil practices immediately!

29. Change your laws that allow this evil practice, and other evil immoral practices that lead to the murder of the unborn; for you shall rise in the resurrection unto a buffeting worthy only for murderers who consent to this practice, even a whole generation upon the earth led astray by wicked men of evil practice themselves among you.

30. Thus is my word boldly given to you and sent to you in a manner of thy receiving, with no confusion involved, for this is a pure giving from the heavens unto you through my Church of Jesus Christ of Latter-day Saints upon the earth, known among you -- separating themselves from that branch that broke away from my Priesthood on the earth, to be known as upholding the original revelations and principles I revealed to my servant Joseph Smith, known as the Fundamentalist Church of Jesus Christ of Latter-day Saints, of a legal Corporation Sole among you, which I, the Lord, have now set in order, revealing the name of my servant as President of

this Corporation Sole; which legal entity should be allowed by the courts to receive my consecrated lands.

31. But an unjust court illegally resolved to change the articles thereof to allow the taking away of my lands and houses belonging to me, saith the Lord, out of the hands of those appointed officers who answered you nothing because they only answer to the Lord their God for their religious responsibility before me; and you knowing the government, court, or authority in your land has no right to interfere with a religious trust of full religious intent, which I, the Lord, caused to be established to preserve my people in an organized labor, to live a law of eternal nature earning them a salvation in the Kingdom of heaven.

32. And they abide my law in a pure walk before me, which can only be administered by inspired religious leadership, not of governmental appointing.

33. And thus you have interfered in my Church; and I name this to you, O ye government officials of this nation -- Repair this, for you have sinned a sin against the God of Creation who made you, in interfering with my Church, taking away my lands and houses, consecrated by religious giving by a people baptized and confirmed as members of my Church upon the earth, and thou knowest it; and you have been convinced by apostate and wicked people who thus persecute my people, though it be by outward show of legal authority.

34. And through your own corruptions among you, then you accuse my people of wicked intent. And how can it be, when they give their all and are willing to suffer at thine hands, even imprisonment, rather than give up in their lives their religion, which I, the Lord, have commanded them

that they must live to earn a place with me in the heavens?

35. I, the Lord, reveal this much to you -- that you have interfered, through your legal procedures, with the Lord your God and His work of bringing forth a righteous people to receive Him in His glory, whose only purpose in living these exalted laws is to glorify their God and bring salvation to a corrupt world; that I shall cleanse by my power as I descend in the clouds of heaven to my land of Zion; and also to my Old Jerusalem, to gather mine Israel, which promises are in sacred writings among you.

36. I now step forth and cause my servant on earth to declare my word to you:

37. Let my people go! or suffer the judgments of a just God; and in eternity, the damnation of your souls, knowing that religious freedom should be guaranteed in every nation -- which you labor for; yea, for many, save for my people; having prejudiced your minds against them as though I, the Lord your God, was not guiding my Church.

38. Now receive my word and my promise of a judgment soon to come of thy knowing, and respond; for my almighty power shall be shown as a beginning of the cleansing of my land of Zion, known to you as North America, where my New Jerusalem shall be built, and extending to South America, saith the Lord God of heaven;

39. My land of Zion, appointed by me, before thy nation ever inhabited my land, to be the place of a glorious kingdom, revealed from heaven unto an obedient and pure people on earth, which revelations have been among you since I restored my Priesthood and my revealed word through the Prophet Joseph Smith; and this generation has rejected my word.

40. And I am a God of truth and shall fulfill my word, saith the Lord God of heaven, Jehovah Christ, the God of Abraham, and of Isaac, and of Jacob, and of mine apostles; who came to earth and suffered on the cross, that all men may be raised unto life and receive an eternal reward for their deeds and desires in the flesh.

41. And all things are known unto me, as I reveal your hearts, even this wicked generation upon my land of Zion, for you are a murderous and adulterous generation, legalizing the slaughter of innocence among you.

42. For verily I say unto you, you are like unto Herod of old, who sought to destroy my life when but a youth, in the slaughter of children in the city of my begetting through a pure virgin.

43. Thus you slaughter innocence like unto him, by legal consent, which must now be cleansed off the earth before my glorious appearing, saith the Lord God of heaven.

44. And this I reveal to you through him whom I have appointed to send my message unto all peoples.

45. Though you listen not, in the trembling of the earth, some shall begin to awake.

46. And as the storms roll forth of more violent nature in thy land, some shall begin to awaken and wonder what is taking place.

47. And now you know I have spoken it.

48. Receive ye my word; and if you heed me not, prepare for my word to be fulfilled, warning you through him whom I have appointed.

49. This is the word of the Lord thy God, who created all things, who preserves all nations in their place, until they prove themselves so corrupt before me, I cause the dissolution of the wicked; yea, they who are ripened in iniquity as you, the people on my land of Zion who persecute my Church upon the earth, have now become.

50. And though you deny my record, revealed through the Prophet Joseph Smith -- my holy record named as the Book of Mormon -- like the Jaredites and Nephites of old, ye shall be swept off my land, saith the Lord, as you continue in your corrupt ways as did they of old; who followed these same practices in their lives, until I, the Lord, could not allow it any longer.

51. This from Him who reigns on high and who shall render eternal justice upon all -- a reward of eternal life for the pure and the righteous among you, and the reward of a damnation unto suffering for the wicked; who knowingly sin away the day of grace, knowing mine own word hath been sent to all peoples as delivered by mine ancient apostles, my Gospel spreading over the earth and being restored anew through the instrumentality of Joseph Smith, my servant; who was martyred among you; whose murder is yet an event to be avenged by me, saith the Lord, upon this wicked nation; and the driving of my people, the murdering of my people since the days of the establishment of my Church upon the earth in thy land; whose innocent blood was shed, still cries from the ground for vengeance against this nation.

52. Thus shall I be justified, at thy receiving my warning, to send forth greater judgments, until justice is satisfied; for you reek in the shedding of innocent blood as a nation, allowing this great evil among you, destroying life of my sending, of perfect innocence, unable to defend themselves; for your immoral practices have led you to this murderous work which I have named

before you, as worthy to only be swept off my land of Zion.

53. This is the word of the Lord. Heed my word, lest I send my judgment upon you.

54. And in a time the more wicked step forth to further hinder my work, my judgments shall be poured forth without let or hindrance, to leave the wicked neither root nor branch of an inheritance upon my land of Zion, as I, the Lord, have foretold, my word being revealed through my servants, the Prophets.

55. And like the days of Noah, only those I preserve shall remain upon my land of Zion.

56. Thus you shall know thy God hath spoken, both on earth, and as you plead for deliverance in the day you dwell in the world of departed spirits, suffering justice until you have paid the debt for your evil ways upon her, before I can raise you up to a degree of glory, according to the law you lived on earth.

57. And those who shed innocent blood commit an unpardonable sin.

58. Though they shall be raised from the dead, they shall yet suffer for their evils, resulting from immoral practices among you.

59. How can you continue this corruption, O ye people of the earth, fighting against the laws of life, your own life preserved only by my grace and power, saith the Lord your God who created you; though you deny that gift for others through interfering with the gift of life in their coming forth?

60. Such legalized murder corrupts all peoples in your land, consenting thereto by allowing it to continue among you.

61. Yet you persecute my people, who have none of these evils among them, but are careful to preserve life that I send forth, and raise up children in principles of an exalting nature; which is known among you now as you carried away my innocent children from among my people in a raid that was unjust, having broken none of your laws that are just, accusing them of being abusive to children simply because they seek to live my high and holy and pure law, required by me, the Lord your God, for eternal exaltation to be earned; which my people know as the pure religious motive in their lives, willing to suffer at the hands of injustice to abide an eternal law and earn salvation in the Kingdom of heaven.

62. Let my people go! for my Zion shall rise from among them, notwithstanding all the opposition against my Church upon the earth.

63. I, the Lord, have caused this understanding now to be given in plain language.

64. I, the Lord, have spoken it; thus shall I fulfill to the sorrow of the wicked, to the rejoicing of mine elect.

65. Though they suffer at the hands of the wicked, they shall be delivered unto eternal salvation who stay faithful to my cause of Zion.

66. Thus, I record this on this day of giving mine own word from the heavens unto this wicked nation, which shall be known yet as I send forth more of my word, until all peoples know that I am a God of power and know all things.

67. I am a just God and a merciful God also, to those who repent and remove these evils from among them.

68. Now put it on record, saith the Lord, there shall now be a shaking in the place I have named, in a manner that government officials shall know

beforehand that it would be so, which shall awake a few, denied by most unto their eternal condemnation, knowing my word, and would not heed my word.

69. And when they find more of my word has been given, they shall be among those that curse God and die, not caring for their own lives, let alone the lives of others.

70. Thus are they a murderous and a wicked and immoral generation, adulterous in nature, having pleasure in unrighteousness unto the murder of innocence.

71. And though I cause this to be on record, they heed me not until the sign of judgments, of removing the wicked from my land of Zion, takes place.

72. Then they shall know, in the world of spirits, to a degree, some of their sin; for the evil powers there will promote lies, deceiving many, until they sin away every day of grace I have granted them.

73. And thus this record on earth is being made in a time I, the Lord, have reached for this generation to repent and earn a salvation, yet they would not; which causeth the heavens to mourn; yet they shall not mourn longer; for soon my justice shall be satisfied, and there shall be a cleansing; then mercy shall reach for those who repent and come unto me for salvation, saith the Lord Jesus Christ.

74. I shall cause a soon happening that shall humble many people to their awakening, that my word is coming forth with exactness, and I fulfill my word, to humble my Priesthood people, many of whom shall hasten to prepare, knowing I have spoken unto public knowing among this nation; for thus it shall be advertised and mocked and scorned until the time of fulfilling.

75. Then some few shall heed, while others shall mock more: "What else hath he said?" they will declare.

76. And when he steps forth to deliver more, and I thus fulfill, the mocker shall mourn, many taken in the holocaust of the several judgments I shall send; yet still in the spirit world, in their choosing darkness when my light was offered them, many will continue to deny me until every opportunity of salvation is rejected.

77. And when their memory is restored of once dwelling in a Celestial world with their Eternal God, who is their Father, that is the day of weeping and wailing and gnashing of teeth of eternal disappointment, that they turned against their Father, who only loveth them; yet they would not heed every warning given.

78. Thus is the fate of the wicked who deny me, saith the Lord, put on record on earth at a time my Gospel of salvation is among them; yet they persecute my servant and my people, and decry against them falsely; though all they desire is the salvation of souls through abiding eternal laws that exalt, even those who abide these laws in a pure way before me.

79. Let go of this wicked generation, saith the Lord.

80. Seek not after it, or you will partake of this sin of consenting to murder and adultery, to Sodom and other licentious practices.

81. Such are the people raised up in honor among the wicked, even many rulers partaking of these licentious and corrupt practices, some even of murder of the unborn, which lawmakers uphold the laws.

82. Though some publicly oppose, this wicked generation allows it, and all are tainted thereby who do not actively do battle against these unjust laws.

83. Thus I, the Lord, shall reward all according to their deeds and the desires of their heart.

84. Justice shall be satisfied, my work shall triumph, my Zion is rising as I cleanse my people, and deliver this, my word, to you.

85. Let there also be this sent to those government officials in the Canadian state, a nation also corrupted before me by their own choice of murderous and adulterous and immoral practices.

86. I shall cleanse my land Zion, and nothing can stay my hand.

87. Oh, this wicked generation and unbelieving and corrupt people who will not heed even common sense of truth, for how can you murder an unborn child and think you do right? Thus shows the corruption of their nature.

88. Thus saith the Lord Jesus Christ to this most wicked generation, guilty of child murder in the destruction of the unborn, an immoral and corrupt and adulterous generation, like unto previous generations that have inhabited my land of Zion, who were swept off the land when fully ripe in iniquity -- I, the Lord, have spoken;

89. Therefore, LET MY PEOPLE GO! And no longer allow these evil practices destroy your souls; for I am a just God and shall reward every man and woman, and children of age, according to their deeds done in the flesh.

90. Thus, I give my word to this nation as a final warning; and if you do not respond to my word, saith the Lord, I shall send the judgment named to awaken you, that when I, the Lord, speak, so do I fulfill.

91. This from your Lord and Savior, the God over all the earth, even Jesus Christ, who hath all power to discern the mind and heart of each and every son and daughter sent to mine earth, for nothing is hidden from me.

92. Let there be an awakening of this wicked generation against the day that my whirlwind judgments shall be poured forth.

93. Let there be an acknowledgment of my word sent by those of governing powers of this nation, that you will thus respond to my word -- to him whom I have revealed to thee is my Mouthpiece, even your Lord Jesus Christ calling my servant Warren Jeffs to that work upon the earth, that I may know you will now fulfill my word, lest this judgment come upon you, and mine other judgments, as I have promised through the mouths of all my holy Prophets, known to thee in sacred writ.

94. This is my word to this generation: Repent ye. I, the Lord, have spoken it, and so shall I fulfill.

95. I, the Lord God, am eternal and my judgments are just. I see and know all things.

96. Let this generation be warned, by this my message sent, that my day is at hand when wickedness must be swept off my land of Zion, and my New Jerusalem shall be built, and I shall come in my glory as I have promised, and none shall remain who are unclean before me.

97. Let there be an awakening in government officials of an eternal judgment that shall come upon them from the God who made them, if they allow the continuation of these wicked practices of the destruction of innocence; of which I shall hold you eternally accountable; desiring life thyself, yet denying it, through legal consent, to unborn children, as though thou art God.

98. Let there now be an instant repeal

of those laws that allow this wickedness among you, lest my judgments be hastened, having innocent blood upon your skirts, as it were; now having come up before your God, notwithstanding your professions of justifying nature.

99. I, the Lord, shall reveal more to this generation through my servant Warren Jeffs.

100. Hearken to my word, ye rulers of nations, lest your lands be left desolate in my day of greater judgments upon the earth; for I shall be known among all nations, and my power and righteous government shall be known, for I shall reveal to all peoples my message of salvation on earth who remain.

101. And all shall hear me; for I am God, thy Redeemer, doing the will of my Father, unto the salvation of souls of those who will receive me through my Priesthood authority upon the earth; which I have restored and preserved, which

Gospel of salvation has been among you, O ye people of the earth.

102. Seek unto Him who created you, and receive His message of salvation that I may own and bless you, yea, with an eternal salvation unto those who receive my Gospel through my authorized Priesthood authority among you.

103. And those who receive my Gospel of salvation on earth shall earn an eternal reward with me and with my Father; for mine atoning blood shall reach those who purify their lives in abiding the laws of my Church and Kingdom revealed among man on earth.

104. O ye people of the earth, repent ye, repent ye! My day of judgment is at hand and my word shall be fulfilled that I have spoken through the mouths of all my holy Prophets.

105. Attaint your wicked and corrupt ways. Come unto me, thy Lord and Savior. I, the Lord, have spoken it. Amen.

SECTION REVELATION 36

Final Warning of the Lord Jesus Christ

Revelation of the Lord Jesus Christ
Big Lake, Texas
Sunday, March 13, 2011

1. Verily, verily, thus saith the Lord Jesus Christ to this wicked generation now dwelling upon the earth, even Him who reigns on high, who has all power in heaven and on earth and rules over all peoples in the power of His might:

2. I am the Beginning and the End. Nothing can stay mine hand as I send you this warning:

3. My judgments must now be poured forth upon all who continue in the sins of Sodom and also the murder of unborn children and other licentious and immoral practices, which causes all nations to reek with impure unclean ways.

4. There shall come forth a desolating scourge.

5. It shall take hold of the inhabitants

of the earth, and many be removed from this mortal life, which you, the inhabitants of the earth, now possess.

6. And it will be such that you will know I, the Lord, have spoken.

7. There shall be war, famine, and earthquake of a hastening nature; and save you repent and remove many of these evils from your borders, many lands shall be left desolate.

8. Ye shall know I, the Lord, have spoken.

9. Cause there to be a repeal of all laws that permit these evil practices among you, for I am God, and the murder of unborn children is a most wicked practice against innocence, resulting from adultery and immoral conduct.

10. And I shall judge thee, and ye shall stand before the bar of God individually in a day to come, and many have blood on their skirts before their God.

11. Thus I have warned thee, having sent forth messages through my Priesthood authority on earth, and you heed me not.

12. I therefore send you this, my word: Repent ye! Repent ye! for my judgments shall soon be upon thee.

13. The nation of Great Britain shall be humbled severely for her immoral practices she allows through legal consent, insomuch that disease will remove many of the inhabitants thereof.

14. France shall be as a land of sparse population, so great are her iniquities before thy Lord.

15. Germany is of a reeking immorality; many places shall be left desolate in her borders.

16. Licentiousness cannot stand. Corruption shall be put away.

17. Your secret acts shall be revealed, and my Zion shall rise to purify the nations, a righteous kingdom of my governing, saith Jesus Christ, the Redeemer of all flesh, who holds all creation in His hands, and will no longer suffer these iniquities to continue among the nation on my land of Zion.

18. I have sent forth my word; therefore, repent ye!

19. Ye shall stand before an incensed God in a time to come, to be judged for your works done in the flesh and the desires of your hearts.

20. The wicked shall tremble and be sent to their own punishment until the day of retribution is fulfilled.

21. And my Zion, the righteous of all generations, shall rise to govern the earth, notwithstanding the armies of nations and their supposed power.

22. Nothing can stay mine hand, and this nation of great power of military might is corrupting from within, even the United States of America now on my land of Zion, which shall fall.

23. And I, the Lord, shall bring forth every element of cleansing and remove the wicked from my land of Zion.

24. And I shall gather those who can purify their lives in a manner of righteous living.

25. O ye people of the earth, hear my word: Cleanse your peoples of iniquity.

26. Cause peace to be in thy borders and with nations surrounding thee and afar off.

27. Overthrow laws of immoral conduct permitting corruption among you.

28. Be of an honest and equitous and just nature toward your own peoples.

29. Let rights of women be honored.

30. Let children be schooled and cared for.

31. Attend to the poor in your nation, each one, and I shall preserve that land, yea, any nation who purifies their lives to the care of innocence, a promotion of a pure walk before their God.

32. Now I, the Lord, reveal to the nations of the earth the coming War of Armageddon is soon at hand as you see unrest rise in every nation.

33. There shall come disease in a manner of no healing in many lands, removing many inhabitants.

34. Earthquake shall be rampant at a time I send a shaking of the earth in a manner you have not known before.

35. The seas shall heave beyond their bounds.

36. As I, the Lord, send you word to clear thy borders along the seas and go to high ground, against a time the seas shall sweep the people on the borders of your lands, along the seacoasts, out of your nations, you shall know I, the Lord, have spoken it.

37. Let there be in your nations peace established, a freedom of worship permitted, against the time I shall send my holy messengers of my Gospel of salvation to your peoples.

38. Let there not be persecution of religious minorities any longer in your borders, lest your nation be humbled, each one that persecutes those who cannot defend themselves against the aggression of unjust rulers.

39. Let your money practices be just.

40. Let news media be monitored and not cause unrighteous reporting that bring forth unrest among the nations.

41. Let there be proper banking principles.

42. Let the poor of every nation be cared for, saith the Lord your God.

43. And by these signs of your repentance, I, the Lord, shall spare those of your nation, wheresoever you dwell, who will repent and practice righteous and honorable principles before all men;

44. Otherwise you shall reap the just recompense of reward from a just God, who ruleth over all the earth and cometh to reign among men for a thousand years in Zion, a righteous government of heavenly inspiring, saith Jesus Christ, your Lord and Savior.

45. Let there also be assembly of the nations to hear my word, saith Jesus Christ, against a time I shall cause more of my word to be presented to thee, for nation shall rise up against nation in a soon happening.

46. You must needs be warned that I, the Lord, shall allow the falling away of unity from among you if you allow these evils of murder of unborn children and adulterous and corrupt ways of Sodom to continue on the earth.

47. Thus you shall know that I, the Lord, cleansed thee.

48. Therefore, let this assembly of the nations receive this, my word, and prepare for that which is to come among you --

49. More of my word, to be read by one appointed wherein I, the Lord, shall name my Mouthpiece on earth deliver my word to the nation that now inhabits my land of Zion, and also the nations of the earth; many of whom will receive my word and record my word and remember my word against a day where I fulfilled my word in full.

50. Thus I send this, my revealed word, to thee, the nations of the earth, as it were, a final warning:

51. Awake! Babylon the great shall fall and be no more, and my Zion shall rise

and fill the earth and govern all lands and all peoples in a righteous dominion of my giving, saith Him who dwells on high.

52. Hearken to my words, and know I am a just God who rewards the wrongdoer who will not repent of these wicked practices, and can send the soul to hell, in eternal, full damnation, not able to afflict a soul again in their corrupt ways.

53. Thus I, the Lord, shall rise and shine, your Redeemer and God over all the world.

54. I have sent forth mine word through mine ancient apostles and Prophets, and you know of my coming. It is not a mystery to thee.

55. You have persecuted mine elect, my Church and Kingdom upon the earth through the ages of time.

56. Now, as I cause these judgments to come forth, you shall know of the increase of the sweeping of the wicked from off the face of the land of Zion.

57. Then shall come forth other nations, cleansed until these evil practices I have named are swept off the earth.

58. Wickedness cannot stand against Celestial power that shall come to govern the earth, my righteous saints raised up by my resurrecting power to dwell upon the earth among men, with their Lord, and to administer salvation to all who will receive.

59. Prepare for my message of salvation, saith your Lord Jesus Christ.

60. The Father hath sent me to redeem all mankind from the grave, and also to raise up unto life eternal those who are pure in heart, who abide the ways of righteous living, my Gospel of salvation.

61. I raised up my servant Joseph Smith, Jun., restored my Gospel and Priesthood through him.

62. This nation allowed his death. His martyrdom will yet be answered upon this nation of the United States.

63. This so-called land of freedom has allowed persecution against my Celestial Law.

64. My people who receive Celestial Marriage, the plurality of wives in a pure state, live a higher law than man's ways; and I am the Governor of this holy law.

65. Overthrow your laws against my Celestial Law of Plural Marriage if you desire to remain a nation, saith the Lord.

66. Cause my people, the many ways of lost lands and houses because of unjust judges taking their lands from them -- cause these lands be restored to my people.

67. They are preparing for my appearing.

68. I, the Lord, have sent you my word to the leaders of this nation on my land of Zion, and you heed me not.

69. Ye shall be brought low, held accountable in eternity for the conduct you allowed among the peoples of this land, these terrible and corrupt ways I have named.

70. And though you deride me, the Lord your God, ye shall know I have come forth; and in the world of departed spirits shall be witnesses of happenings on earth, and ye shall know I have fulfilled my word.

71. Let there now be this warning sounded to all peoples.

72. Let all peoples know the prophecies of mine ancient apostles and Prophets are soon to be fulfilled; for I am sending forth mine own word through him who receives my word at this time, as a warning and invitation.

73. Repent! Remove these evil practices from your borders.

74. This from Him who reigns on high, who dwells in everlasting burnings, in all-consuming fire of Celestial power, who sees and knows all things and nothing is hidden from me.

75. Thus you shall individually be judged, rewarded according to your deeds done in the flesh.

76. I am the God who created you, who holds each nation in their place.

77. Send forth this warning: Hasten to prepare.

78. My cleansing power shall soon be upon the earth without measure.

79. You shall know and feel the promises of all my holy Prophets fulfilled.

80. All peoples shall reap the reward they have earned; and my governing power shall be known among all surviving nations, the Kingdom of Son Ahman in the domain of Ahman, a righteous government.

81. Let there now be no longer the holding in bondage of my servant.

82. Let him go free, to administer among my people, saith the Lord your God, else I shall send forth judgments to humble this nation.

83. Cause those of his brethren in bondage to go free.

84. They are innocent, having abided religious principles of righteous living, seeking only the will of their God in their lives, raising up pure families unto me to be part of my Zion on earth.

85. My Zion shall be redeemed and built up on Celestial and eternal principles, through authorized Priesthood authority on earth, and my law will triumph over all opposition.

86. Behold, nothing can stay mine hand. Ye shall know I, the Lord your God, have spoken.

87. Now act on correct principles. No longer be of a persecuting zeal against an innocent people.

88. Cause him who administers my word to the nation, to the peoples of all the earth, go free to be among my people to do his work I have appointed him.

89. If you heed me not, I shall cause division in your land, unrest, pestilence, famine and earthquake such as you have not known before; and ye shall know that I, the Lord, have spoken.

90. Let my people go to establish my Zion through righteous principles revealed from heaven, yea, even from you, all my Priesthood, receiving it from thy Lord; and my Priesthood is upon the earth among men.

91. I have published my works through my servant Joseph Smith and others of my Prophets.

92. Therefore, my Church and Kingdom is known among men.

93. I, the Lord, shall cause a cleansing of the land of Old Jerusalem.

94. Israel shall be gathered there, though she be humbled, many lives lost in the holocaust of violent war and destruction.

95. Her borders shall be enlarged. Neighboring nations shall submit to her rule.

96. Thus I, the Lord, have directed; so shall it be.

97. I, the Lord, shall cause a work to be performed of cleansing the land, wherein the peoples of the earth shall know that my judgments have begun where my Zion is to be built; and this shall be a sign to all nations the coming of thy Lord Jesus Christ is near at hand.

98. My Zion shall be built up in that place appointed in the revelations of my will through my servant Joseph Smith.

99. And mine elect shall be gathered from all nations to dwell therein, a New Jerusalem, a city of peace, holy and righteous and pure ways of governing powers, inspired of me, your Lord and Savior, bringing equity and justice and pure ways of living among all nations.

100. Prepare for this great cleansing, for I shall humble every nation who continues in these evil practices of murderous and immoral ways; thus I have spoken.

101. Fulfill my word, that in the day of judgment, mercy can be extended to those in thy borders who have repented of these evils I have named.

102. Be prepared for the message of salvation to all peoples throughout the whole earth.

103. All nations shall come up in judgment before me, and none shall escape the judgment of a just God against these corrupt practices and ways among men; and no power can stay mine hand.

104. I am a God over all creation. As I have spoken, so shall I fulfill.

105. There shall be poured forth the sweeping of the wicked from off the land, where the people of immoral practice in Amsterdam, such that that city will be without inhabitant in a time as the sea heaves beyond its bounds, sweeps the wicked of that place from off the earth, for great are her sins.

106. I, the Lord, shall cause the nations to feel my wrath, and this day of greater judging humble all peoples.

107. Lest you be found wanting, hasten to prepare by cleansing your lands and nations of these wicked practices, saith the Lord your God.

108. Let that nation called Iraq humble themselves.

109. Mine Israel shall triumph. War not against Israel.

110. Let Iran also humble themselves lest they cease to be a nation.

111. Let there not be victims of religious persecution in any land or religions of righteous principles.

112. Do not deride against other religious minorities.

113. Preserve right of worship to all peoples; thus you shall know the religion of peace.

114. I shall reveal the true religion of heaven to all peoples.

115. My power shall be known among all nations.

116. And peace and equity and righteous pure ways of living shall be revealed beyond what man knows on the earth today.

117. Ways of living and doing will be purified and not pollute the earth.

118. Great is my power yet to be revealed to all peoples; yet the earth itself is witness enough a great God of intelligence can guide and control all creation, an inhabitable orb for the children of men.

119. I am a merciful God also to those who will repent and turn from their sins.

120. All shall stand before me in the day of judgment and receive the just recompense of reward as I have named.

121. Therefore, fear and tremble, O ye wicked who will not repent.

122. My justice shall reach you, and nothing can stay mine hand bringing a judgment of righteousness.

123. I, who sees and knows all things, even the intent of thine hearts, judge righteously.

124. My dominion is over all and shall yet be honored.

125. Every knee shall bow to my rule, for fear shall come upon all peoples at my appearing, and all nations shall know of my coming.

126. I must first cleanse the earth of these great and terrible, corrupt sins in such a measure, the peoples in thy land will be prepared for a more righteous governing principle among you.

127. And I am just and administer righteousness in the power of Celestial glory, the power that brought forth the heavens and the earth in their present state,

128. The heavens and the earth shall be shaken at my appearing.

129. Be ye wise virgins with oil in your lamps.

130. Deal justly one with another.

131. War not against other nations. Be at peace in thy borders.

132. Prepare for my message of salvation to all peoples.

133. Seek unto me, the Lord your God, in prayerful supplication to be forgiven and spared in that day of great judgment when Babylon shall fall, the trade and commerce be overthrown.

134. Famine, pestilence will sweep across the nations to show you that when I have spoken, I fulfill my word.

135. I, the Lord your God, have spoken now from the heavens to your understanding. Deny me not.

136. All shall know I am the God over all the earth, and ruleth in righteous pure ways and reward every man his just dues.

137. Persecution must cease against my people and against all other minority religions in every land.

138. And I shall send judgment upon that nation that deals unjustly with peoples within their own borders, with minorities and the poor.

139. Repent ye of these evils, saith the Lord your God.

140. The scenes I shall bring upon this earth shall cause all people to marvel, and those who survive shall acknowledge their God hath preserved them, even your Lord and Savior, the Redeemer over all.

141. O ye nations, how can you so fully and openly fulfill my prophecies of all mine ancient Prophets?

142. My judgments shall roll forth as a whirlwind without measure.

143. There shall be a preservation of a righteous branch of my people Israel, to administer salvation to all nations of the earth.

144. Therefore, I shall preserve my Zion, the land now called America, and also Old Jerusalem, that nation called Israel, as governing places on earth, over all the nations of the earth that remain, after my judgments are poured forth.

145. You shall know of more of my prophecies and promises fulfilled when the whole world awakes to see when the Lord your God speaks, He fulfills His word.

146. Therefore, be subject to my righteous and pure ways of governing principles, that peace may be in your borders among thy peoples.

147. Yet, there shall be no war among nations at the time I come in my glory.

148. Let there be a seeking of righteous ways among all peoples, of equity and truth, justice.

149. Let there be a repeal of unjust laws that allow murder of unborn children in every nation.

150. I, the Lord, have spoken it.

151. Let this take place lest my judgments sweep your nation clean of all such who practice such evils, that

are enemies to the principles of life and corrupt innocence.

152. Verily, thus saith the Lord, wickedness shall not stand, and ye shall know I have spoken.

153. I, the Lord, have sent the proclamation to the President of the United States of America.

154. He heeds me not, even mine own word revealed from the heavens.

155. I have now sent another proclamation -- my revealed word of promised judgments.

156. I again send my word, being a just God.

157. Now you have my warnings, and I shall be justified, performing my work of cleansing the land of Zion where my New Jerusalem shall rise, and also the removal from all nations these corrupt practices that fight against life and corrupt the ways of men before their Lord.

158. And my day of vengeance is upon you soon, and if you heed me not, my judgments shall reach thee and thy peoples, and ye shall know I have spoken.

159. Prepare for more of my word, even to the nations of the earth, and heed my word when I send my word to you, O ye rulers of nations, lest I cause you to lose your place; for great is your responsibility to promote equity and virtue and purity of life, righteous governing principles in each of your lands.

160. And all rulers shall be held accountable to the Lord your God in the day of judging.

161. Let the nations of the earth send forth their riches to build my Zion, and I shall bless them with blessings unmeasured.

162. Let the peoples of the earth promote peace.

163. Let all peoples be of a pure living to prepare for my Gospel of salvation, which must needs spread over all the earth.

164. I am a just God that shall allow all peoples to know this great message of eternal life, if they will receive.

165. Thus I shall fulfill my promise that all nations, kindreds, tongues, and peoples shall hear of my Gospel of Jesus Christ, the Gospel of salvation unto eternal lives.

166. Your money systems will not save you.

167. The rich shall be laid low as great Babylon falls and as my Zion rises to triumph over all enemies and be the governing nation over all the earth.

168. Thus have I delivered my warning to you, O ye nations of the earth.

169. There cannot be any longer a continuation of these wicked practices I have named, lest my judgments sweep you off the land where you dwell.

170. Protect innocence and virtue through righteous governing principles.

171. Thus saith Son Ahman, Jehovah Christ, who came in the meridian of time, who suffered more than man can suffer, on the cross, to redeem all mankind from the grave and raise up those who live noble and pure lives unto a salvation.

172. Come unto me, your Lord and Savior, O ye peoples of the earth, that I may own and bless you unto the riches of eternity in righteous doing.

173. Have upon you a meek and quiet spirit as you consider the greatness of the Lord your God, and seek unto me diligently in a prayerful walk; because I see and know all things, your prayers can come up before mine ears.

174. The cries of widows and orphans comes up before me, saith the Lord, in many lands.

175. The poor and the hungry need attending to in every land.

176. Be diligent, for ye leaders of nations shall be held accountable before Him who created all things, by your conduct toward those in need, by just and righteous principles which should be lived in every land;

177. For if you do it not, I shall reward thee according to thy deeds in the flesh.

178. Now humble thyselves and believe my word, saith your Lord and Savior who ruleth over all.

179. Be it known, saith the Lord your God, that a day of humbling shall come upon any nation that exercises unrighteous, unjust ways in their borders and against other nations.

180. There must needs be a humbling of all peoples, to learn of my ways of union and peace.

181. I, the Lord, call upon the people of the earth to not turn a deaf ear to this, my warning, and then continue on in these evil practices, for I shall be justified by sending forth my warnings to be published in every nation, even this, my word.

182. And thereafter, they shall feel the wrath of a just God, all those who heed me not.

183. My peace shall rest upon all who practice virtue and holiness in righteous principles before their Lord.

184. I shall prosper your crops in your fields.

185. Thy prosperity shall continue under righteous rule on the land and not evil practices of fallen Babylon.

186. And there shall be a pouring forth of blessings on all peoples who respond to my word, even blessings of Zion, eternal in their nature, those who will receive, among your peoples, my message of salvation.

187. Let this suffice for the present, saith the Lord.

188. Hasten to prepare by cleansing lands of these iniquities, lest my judgments be poured forth without measure upon you.

189. I, the Lord, have spoken it, and thus shall I fulfill.

190. Even so, beware how you treat my word, to be answered upon you individually in a day of judgment, and more especially leaders of nations. Amen.

SECTION REVELATION 37

Son Ahman Speaketh to the Leaders of the Nation of the United States of America Warning of Judgments; And to Other Nations, Words of Warning and of Judgments Soon to Come

Revelation of the Lord Jesus Christ
Big Lake, Texas
Wednesday, March 23, 2011

*It Is the Will of the Lord to Send Forth a Message
to the Leaders of This Nation at This Time.*

1. Thus saith the Lord Jesus Christ: You have erred, sinning greatly before me in not receiving my word to cleanse thine own peoples, thine own laws, thine own nation; yet you continue to step forth to humble other nations, not having heeded my word of cleansing the inside of the platter among you;

2. For how can I, the Lord, uphold you as a nation when you continue the greater evils within your borders, even the murder of unborn children, of Sodom and adultery, licentious and corrupt ways; of persecuting an innocent religious minority who abide my laws of a Celestial, eternal nature; who persecute them to the taking of their lands and houses and hindering their advancement in my cause of Zion.

3. And yet you step forth and use the military might I have allowed you to receive, in your ability to organize, to defend, and to uphold principles according to the Constitution of original giving, wherein rights of freedom of religion and worship were to be maintained; rights of freedom of expression, rights of equality, of righteous judgment; yet you have changed your laws to allow persecution of my people.

4. Therefore, I, the Lord, declare unto you that you shall now feel my wrath, for you have stepped forth to rebuke other nations, yet you will not cleanse your own peoples.

5. And I send you this, my word, that there shall be, on the morrow month, a devastating sickness begin in a place in thy borders that shall cause fear to come upon the peoples in your land; and you shall know that I, the Lord, have spoken it.

6. And when this takes place, ye shall remember that I once again have spoken with clearness unto your understanding.

7. And I send this, my word, to thee, that you may know that you must fulfill my word to continue to exist on my land of Zion; and if you heed me not, more of my judgments I have promised shall be sent forth.

8. I have sent forth my publishings to you of recent sending.

9. Heed my word lest you fall and incur a judgment of eternal nature upon yourselves individually, you leaders of this nation.

10. And verily I say to the peoples

of this nation, who shall learn that I have spoken from the heavens by my judgments rolling forth upon them; for I have spoken since the days of my servant Joseph Smith restoring my Gospel through my instrumentality and power of Priesthood.

11. And there must needs be an accounting soon made, for this nation has been empowered to be free above all other nations, and has used her power unrighteously, trying to humble other nations, when this nation herself is corrupted from within in the evils I have named.

12. I cannot allow it any longer.

13. My judgments must soon sweep the wicked off this land of Zion, and my Zion shall rise.

14. Repent ye, ye leaders of this nation, and all ye peoples of this nation of the United States, and those nations that also occupy my land of Zion, wherein they shall also receive warnings according to my will.

15. I am Son Ahman, your Lord and Savior and Redeemer, who hath conquered death, who is a God of Creation and ruleth over all, and nothing can stay mine hand.

16. Hasten to correct these evils, or you shall begin to experience workings of destruction within thine own borders in a greater manner than before; for heretofore I have been merciful upon thee when thy peoples have cried for mercy, and for the purpose of mine elect to be preserved on my land of Zion.

17. Now all must stand on their own record of their lives, and only the pure in heart, who love righteousness and truth, peace, and eternal truths of light and knowledge of my Gospel of salvation -- only they can remain on my land of Zion and help establish Zion in full.

18. Oh, that you would rend from your hearts the unbelief that afflicts thee, saith Him who created all, for I shall perform a work that shall fill the earth.

19. My glorious coming is nigh at hand, and I am preparing the way by preserving a people who have received Celestial laws, which you have persecuted.

20. Therefore, my judgments shall be just, having sent my warnings, mine own voice out of the heavens through my servant on earth, giving my word.

21. Notwithstanding he is in bondage, yet my word goes forth.

22. Now receive my word and do my will.

23. Withdraw your attack from other nations.

24. Humble thyselves; and as a show and an outward sign that you will repent and cease thine illegal aggressions against other nations, destroy that which is of a destructive nature of power among you, even every armored vehicle in your land.

25. And if you will do this, and turn to your Lord to preserve your land and peoples and nation, I shall preserve thee.

26. And if thou doest it not, your great army shall fall; disease shall take hold of your inhabitants; other afflictions, pestilences, sicknesses, earthquakes, and judgments shall roll forth; and what can stay mine hand?

27. This shall be a sign that you are willing to turn to your God to be preserved as a nation.

28. Therefore, humble yourselves before me, ye nation of the United States of America, as you are called on the earth, upheld by my power, lo, these many years; yet your leaders have been corrupt to a great degree, allowing laws to persecute innocence, yea, against my Priesthood and Church upon the earth.

29. Now behold, I say unto you, there shall also come forth a work of the greater light that shall fill the earth.

30. It shall be among a people who shall be meek and lowly, and they shall be mine, even mine Israel gathered to my Priesthood on earth.

31. I tell thee this that ye may know that I shall preserve my land unto them, a new people, mine Israel gathered unto my greater light; for I am already preparing them, a new people to inhabit my land after thy nation shall be swept clean off my land of Zion.

32. I, the Lord, have spoken it, and it shall be known among all peoples and thus fulfilled in the eyes of nations, for wickedness cannot remain on my land of Zion any longer.

33. I, the Lord, have spoken it and shall fulfill by power from on high.

34. Receive ye my word, O ye leaders of this nation, and the peoples of this nation, and know that I am speaking from the heavens.

35. Let the city of San Diego know that a devastating earthquake and the waves of the sea shall come upon thee, and the ravenous and wild animals in thy borders shall be a distress to thy peoples in that day of greater trial and judgment.

36. This shall take place in a time I, the Lord, shall perform a work of greater cleansing of this land; and thus you know that you have been warned of a greater judging upon thy peoples, O this nation that inhabits a land reserved for my Zion to rise.

37. And other judgments have been and shall be named until you know I have spoken.

38. I, the Lord, also reveal that this nation inhabiting my land of Zion, having persecuted mine elect, my Priesthood and my Church upon the earth, shall not remain as a nation if they continue to do these evils against me.

39. Repent ye! Repent ye! and turn from your wicked ways, for you are filled with darkness, and my light dwelleth not in you, ye leaders of this nation; unto the upholding of unrighteous laws that permit corruption among thy people, and to the persecution of wicked laws upheld against my Priesthood.

40. Thy persecution is recorded in the heavens and on earth, and I shall be justified to send forth my full judgments.

41. Repent ye, for ye must stand before your God in a day to come, and nothing can stay mine hand.

42. Thus I have sent my warning of previous publishings to your immediate notice, ye leaders of this nation.

43. Let my word be heeded lest ye bring upon yourselves my full wrath.

44. How can you stand against the God of Creation over you, by whose power you exist, who gives you the breath of life, your food, your homes, your lands to be protected; and you heed me not.

45. I cannot allow this to continue among a people who have been blessed beyond measure, above all other lands and nations and peoples --

46. Yea, verily I say, freedoms of worship, of expression; freedoms to move and do and seek after the happiness of eternity; yet most will not, having hearkened to that evil power on earth, wherein mankind are troubled in their spirits, and will not listen to the just God and His Spirit of peace.

47. Come out of this wicked generation, O ye people who desire to repent, and show thy Lord you are for Him and His cause of Zion; and come clean

before me and persecute not mine elect, my Church and Kingdom upon the earth, even the Fundamentalist Church of Jesus Christ of Latter-day Saints; and know that I am with them, those who abide their Celestial covenants with me.

48. Now know this: There shall be a greater light come forth -- Zion, a Celestial power coming to earth at my glorious coming, beyond which man knows at this time on earth.

49. O ye unbelievers, ye shall be awakened too late as you are swept off the earth;

50. And you who will believe, await patiently my day of my coming, which shall soon come in a manner of you knowing; even all nations shall witness my power.

51. They shall know I am among my people, and can visit the nations with blessings unmeasured.

52. Come unto me, your Lord and Savior, Jesus Christ, who hath created all things, who was God before the world was made, and who is God who came to earth and redeemed all mankind in a marvelous way, through the suffering of His own spirit and body, in a Celestial justice administered; to satisfy the laws of eternity, to raise up mankind from the grave and give them the opportunity of hearing my Gospel of salvation unto eternal lives.

53. This is my message to you: I must needs come to fulfill the will of the Father concerning this earth, and all the peoples appointed thereto, to offer them the salvation of eternal life if they will receive.

54. I have sent forth messengers, even my Prophets throughout the generations of time.

55. My word of holy writ is in thine hands.

56. My messenger of this dispensation of time, Joseph Smith, hath done his work and was martyred, and sealed his testimony with his blood; and other Prophets have been sent forth to gather mine Israel from the nations.

57. And now I must step forth and cause Zion to rise and fill the earth.

58. And I am God. Receive my word to the joy of your souls everlastingly as you do obey my word; or to the sorrow of your souls eternally if you oppose me, and persecute mine elect, and seek the destruction of my work and Church and Kingdom upon the earth.

59. I have called upon you to overthrow those laws that permit the murder of unborn children, and also that permit Sodom among you.

60. Heed my word, read my warnings, perform my work, and show thy Lord you will set aside violence against other nations just to get gain; to think you would not counsel with your God while you continue in your own corrupt ways.

61. He cannot justify your power on earth any longer, wherein you are corrupt from within, and yet you step forth even in violence to bring low other nations.

62. Thy power shall diminish.

63. There shall be distress within thy borders. Pestilence and hail, famine and earthquake will sweep you off my land of Zion, all who cannot be of that Zion of our God of a pure nature.

64. Repent ye! Repent ye! is the word of a just God, who loveth His children on earth, yet will not allow the wicked to rule; for my Millennial Reign of Peace of one thousand years being among men is now a time upon you.

65. And I am sending my word to your understanding, that you will know I have spoken.

66. Receive ye my word, which is my law, and shall be held as a witness against thee by those who do receive my word upon the earth, through Priesthood authority that I have established to receive my word and give my word to all peoples.

67. For verily, I have more of my word to send forth, yet they heed me not; and I must needs send judgments to awaken thy minds that when I speak, I fulfill, even your Lord and Savior, the God over all creation, Son Ahman, who doeth the will of the Father in all things.

68. I am God. I am the Christ who hath redeemed all mankind.

69. Heed my word, that I may own and bless you on earth and into eternity; to be among mine elect, my Zion, my Priesthood, my governing power which shall rule the earth and all nations -- my power humbling all nations to cast off these great evils that dwell among them, even to the cleansing of thy people with judgment.

70. And in my justice and righteous purposes, equity shall be administered, truth shall be known, wickedness shall not rule or reign any longer.

71. I who have all power, that causes the heaven and the earth to exist, shall be among my people and govern this earth, doing the will of the Father in all things, even the God of Creation whose right it is to rule.

72. Thus I have spoken it.

73. Let this, my word, be sent forth to the leaders of this nation, the United States of America, and also to be known to other nations, that I shall humble this nation now, for they heed me not.

74. And let all nations know that when I, the Lord Jesus Christ, the God over all creation, speak, I fulfill my word.

75. And you have my word in holy writ throughout the earth.

76. Study my word and prepare for my glorious appearing in power and righteous governing principles and knowledge and truth and powers Celestial, which cannot be opposed by earthly powers; for I am God and shall fulfill my word.

77. My peace be upon all peoples who will receive my word.

78. Let your armies be rid of those armored vehicles in every nation that are used to destroy life.

79. This shall be a sign to thy God that you are repenting and will treat thy peoples with equity and not forceful means in harming thine own peoples in thine own borders, and will not persecute minorities or other nations.

80. This shall be a signal to thy God of repentance.

81. As you thus obey my word and perform this work, I, the Lord, shall know that you shall heed further of my word of cleansing thy people of these immoral and corrupt ways, these sins I have named in this, my word given you;

82. For this is a wicked and corrupt generation, destroying innocence, living in adultery and Sodom and the murder of unborn children, a practice that is as a stench unto the heavens that can no longer continue on earth, save judgments come to cleanse you, O ye people of all nations.

83. I, the Lord, declare my word, and I shall fulfill.

84. Let this, my word, be sent forth to the leaders of the nations in a manner I shall name, insomuch as they will receive my word; and if they heed me not, it shall yet be a witness on earth that I have sent forth my word.

85. Cleanse thine hands of these

iniquities, ye leaders of nations, for you shall be held accountable in the day of judgment, when I shall bring you up before the Father for your deeds done in the flesh.

86. This from an incensed God who sees these continual corruptions upon the earth.

87. Repent ye! is the word of thy Lord to this generation, that I may own and bless the pure in heart to become my Zion, and my presence dwell among men on earth for a thousand years in righteous dominion under my Father, Ahman; for I am Son Ahman, doing the will of the Father in all things.

88. Thus it is written. Amen.

SECTION REVELATION 38

Thus Saith Son Ahman to the Nations of the Earth -- Words of Warning and of Judgment; A Call to Repentance

Thus Saith Son Ahman

Revelation of the Lord Jesus Christ
Big Lake, Texas
Friday, March 25, 2011

1. Thus saith the Lord: Repent ye, O ye people of the earth, as I send forth my word anew unto thee from on high, Him who is Son Ahman, even Jesus Christ, Jehovah, the Great I AM, who ruleth over the heavens and the earth, and nothing can stay mine hands.

2. I am the Governor and Ruler of the earth and of the heavens, and you people of the earth are soon to receive a judgment because of the gross wickedness among all your nations.

3. And because ye heed me not, I, the Lord, shall humble you from judgment to judgment until there be these wicked ways removed from your borders and from among thy peoples, even the murder of unborn children and the persecution of minorities and of women and children and of the poor; and also adultery and Sodom and evil corruptions of immoral conduct and ways;

4. For I am the God of heaven, and I am pure and righteous and holy, and nothing can stand in my presence save it be holy and pure; for I dwell in an all-consuming fire, and nothing can be withheld from my hand being cleansed in the day of judging.

5. I, the Lord, declare unto you, I am sending forth my word through my servant on earth, that you may know of my soon coming, and I must cleanse my land of Zion from on high with the powers of heaven attending -- with earthquake, and pestilence, hail and famine, fire from heaven, the parts of the earth descending as fiery comets, as it were, in your understanding.

6. And you shall know that there are lands that will rise out of the ocean to

preserve my land of Zion when parts of the earth shall return.

7. And there shall be a new people come on my land of Zion, even Israel, my lost tribes that are known to me and the Father, and we shall bring them forth to my Zion to people my land of Zion after the wicked are swept off this land, for you will heed me not, though I have sent my Gospel of salvation, lo, these many years to thee to thine understanding.

8. Repent ye, that ye may receive my Gospel, that you may know that I am God, and that I must step forth and cleanse my land of Zion.

9. Now receive ye my word: The apocalypse that you prophesy of is soon at hand.

10. War without measure will sweep many lands clean without inhabitant.

11. Mine Israel shall survive, though be slaughtered in great numbers, and expand her borders to conquer the neighboring nations.

12. And those nations that have been evil to their own peoples shall be humbled and rulers overthrown;

13. And there shall be a fear come upon all peoples with the judgments of God rolling forth with a hastening --

14. Yea, the sea heaving beyond its bounds, earthquake, tornado, and pestilence of all kinds, of insects and disease, of wars and rumors of wars, until all people shall fear who are wicked and will not repent.

15. Therefore, great Babylon shall fall.

16. My Zion shall rise and rule all nations at my glorious appearing.

17. Now I say unto you, Repent ye! Turn from these ungodly and wicked ways, that I may spare some among you in the day of my coming, for fear shall take hold upon every person who does not repent.

18. And those nations which humble themselves and cleanse their governments of unrighteous and unjust laws, wherein you persecute your own peoples with unrighteous and iniquitous ways, in laws that permit adultery and Sodom and the murder of unborn children --

19. These must be done away for you to survive my judging and my power from on high sweeping the wicked off your lands.

20. Hasten to prepare, and remove these evils from among you, for I am sending forth more of my word unto thee, O ye peoples of the earth.

21. And the leaders of the nations shall be humbled who heed me not, and be removed from their place by my almighty power, and they shall know I have spoken, saith Jesus Christ, the God of the heavens and the earth; for all is in mine hands, and I shall repay all peoples according to their deeds done in the flesh.

22. And all glory to the Father who shall sanctify the earth, for the righteousness of God shall come forth upon the earth, and nothing can stay mine hand.

23. Only be pure and clean before me to survive the day of judging.

24. I, the Lord, have spoken it to all the nations of the earth.

25. Let this, my word, be heralded among the nations of the earth from this time forth, even in that assembly where nations meet, and other assemblies, to be kept as a sacred word, even your Lord and Savior who hath redeemed all mankind from the grave, and shall raise all through the resurrection to be judged of the Father.

26. Thus shall be my work continued into eternity; for you, the people of the

earth, shall come to know my Gospel of salvation, and all shall have the opportunity to receive thereof if you will humble yourselves before me.

27. Great is the wickedness of this generation.

28. I must cleanse the earth for my glorious appearing.

29. Be at peace in all things.

30. Through prayer approach your Lord, and be people that the Lord can send His message of salvation to in a time to come.

31. Let there be peace in your households.

32. Put a wreath of olive leaves and branches upon your doorpost above your door as a symbol that you are repenting in the day of judging, that the destroying angel may pass you by, if you are honest in heart.

33. And if there are any unclean among you of these terrible and wicked sins I have named, ye shall be purged anyway, and know that you cannot hide from a incensed God who hath preserved the earth for a wise purpose in Himself, until now His day of salvation must come forth and is at hand.

34. Awake, O ye peoples of the earth!

35. Put on the garments of righteousness.

36. Cast off the ways of evil, and no longer partake of the ways that decry against God.

37. I, the Lord, have spoken it.

38. Hasten to prepare as I send forth more of my word unto you.

39. Let those nations who desire peace destroy all armored vehicles in their army and in their weaponry as a sign to their Lord of repenting of their violent and evil ways, and depend upon thy Lord for preservation;

40. For who can withstand an incensed God who send forth such judgments that shall shake the earth and the heavens, and disease roll forth, an overflowing scourge, a desolating sickness, beginning at my house and on my land of Zion.

41. O ye leaders of nations, repent ye, and turn from your wicked ways, and know there is a God in heaven who seeth all things and shall reward thee according to thy deeds and desires in the flesh.

42. Hear thou my word and no longer stay yourselves.

43. Change these unjust and wicked laws that promote immorality, murder of unborn children, adultery, Sodom, and great injustice against your poor, against women, against minority religions.

44. Let there be peace in your borders, that I may send forth blessings upon your nations unmeasured in the day of peace.

45. I, the Lord, forewarn you: I shall be justified in sending forth my judgments upon all nations; and my land of Zion where the United States of America now exists shall be swept of all wickedness, and I alone shall rule over the earth.

46. And my Priesthood, my governing power on earth, shall reign triumphant under my direction, the Kingdom of God, the Kingdom of Ahman under Son Ahman, whom I am; for my Father Ahman has the right to rule, and I, His Son, hath redeemed all mankind to glorify the Father, and all who will receive my message and ordinances of salvation.

47. Hasten to prepare.

48. My word is just and true, and nothing can stay mine hand.

49. Humble yourselves before me, saith the Lord your God, speaking this to your understanding in a message sent forth through my Church upon the earth.

50. Hasten to prepare, O ye my people ordained to be my Zion, that my presence may dwell among thee, and my peace rest upon thee, and my power be known by thee.

51. All on earth, hasten to prepare, for this is the sounding voice that continues in this day where I am declaring myself from the heavens, that there can no longer be wickedness upon the earth save great judgments come upon you, the nations of the earth.

52. Heed my call, and be a more righteous people, purifying these great evils from among you, and preparing for more of my light of exalting nature; for I am a God of heaven and earth and eternal over all creation.

53. I created the earth to become an eternal habitation of the saints, glorified in Celestial power like unto the planets where I dwell and govern.

54. I am God, and you are the inhabitants of the earth sent forth to dwell in righteousness and overcome evil.

55. There shall be a people prepared for my Zion.

56. Hinder me not nor their progress, and free them from bondage.

57. Allow my servant to go free.

58. Allow my people their lands and houses with full freedom to organize in a Celestial manner of righteous living, as I have ordained among them and published to you inhabitants of the earth.

59. Hasten to prepare, and let my people go, that they may be my people to establish Zion, and my glory be upon them and among them, saith Jesus Christ.

60. Let there now be recorded on earth that I, the Lord, have spoken to the nations of the earth and the leaders of nations, and no longer shall I withhold my judgments until the earth is prepared for my glorious appearing.

61. You have seen the judgments of God poured forth in an increasing way, even as I have declared.

62. My message has gone to leaders of nations and they heeded me not.

63. And my land of Zion, where the United States of America now exists, shall be swept of all wickedness;

64. Thus I have warned them and sent forth to the leaders of that nation my warning voice.

65. Now let this, my warning voice, go to the United Nations, to every nation, to every ambassador.

66. Hear my voice, saith Jesus Christ, or you shall reap the reward of judgment for your wicked ways.

67. And if you heed me not, I have given a warning, and you shall see my judgments increase.

68. Repent ye, and turn from your wicked ways, is the voice of the God of heaven who rules over all nations and gives them their place.

69. The sounding voice has been given through mine ancient apostles and is in holy writ of my glorious appearing, and of righteousness ruling the earth for a thousand years, my presence among men.

70. Thou knowest my prophecies.

71. Hasten to prepare, and cease your pride and your fallen and corrupt ways, for you shall be detected and judged.

72. Change your laws that are wicked and unjust to be more equitous, to be more kind to the poor, the women having their rights of protection, and the children having schools and provisions for their needs.

73. Bless the peoples of other nations instead of warring one against another.

74. Let my peace rest upon you, O ye peoples of the earth.

75. Prepare for more of my word that I have already sent forth to be made known to you.

76. Seek unto me, your God, and I will preserve thee a nation, each one who removes these wicked ways from their borders and from among their wicked people; for there must be justice when wickedness is performed, or else innocence is not maintained.

77. You must maintain innocence of women and children, of your peoples in righteous ways, in your principles of financiering, in your principles of schooling, and of governing, and in every way.

78. I, the Lord, shall teach you as my Zion rises, and there shall be a people purified through power from on high, my Celestial powers descending to earth.

79. And there shall be your God to receive all nations of their oblations, their offerings and sacrifices, that He may bless you to exist on earth and prosper the works of your hands in righteousness and in truth.

80. Great shall be the day of my coming. Who will be able to stand?

81. You must purge yourselves of wickedness to abide the day of my coming.

82. Now behold, I say unto you, there are nations existing upon the earth who promote such gross immorality, they will be swept off the earth; they cannot exist.

83. Repent ye, ye individuals of those nations, that a salvation may be offered you, now or in a time to come, even when my Gospel is preached by my Priesthood, yea, in the world of departed spirits as well as on earth; for I am a God of equity and truth and justice, and all peoples past, present, and future shall hear my message of salvation.

84. And though this is a mystery to many of you, I am a God of truth and my message of salvation shall reach all.

85. Therefore, repent ye, and receive ye my word; and let this, my word, be known among your peoples, to repent and overthrow these wicked ways, that you may remain as a nation into the time of a thousand years of peace, when I shall appear in my glory, and all nations shall know my presence is upon the earth and my Priesthood has the right to rule, even the Kingdom of God sent from heaven.

86. Thus saith Son Ahman, the Beginning and the End, who rules over all things, for I am a God of Creation, and all things exist because of me and by my power.

87. I have spoken it. Amen.

SECTION REVELATION 39

Another Warning of Son Ahman to the Nations of the Earth Concerning Judgments and Destruction, and of His Coming in His Glory

Thus Saith Son Ahman to the Nations of the Earth

Revelation of the Lord Jesus Christ
Big Lake, Texas
Saturday, March 26, 2011

1. Thus saith the Lord unto this generation in which wickedness reigns over all the earth, wherein nation is rising against nation to humble nations, professing equitous and just means and purposes, yet they themselves are corrupt from within, even nations I have named to receive greater judging of the Lord their God:

2. Cease your warring; cease your contending.

3. Draw into your own nations and correct thyselves first, lest my judgments roll forth upon you, for I am God, and who art thou to judge who should live or perish, to exist or not exist?

4. You counsel not with me, nor seek my will.

5. Therefore, you are sealing your doom in greater judgments like unto what you have seen come upon a nation of great earthquake receiving.

6. And thou knowest that many thousands have perished, insomuch they have gone to their reward of their deeds done in the flesh. So shall it be on thy lands.

7. Cease this warring lest you contend unto emptying many parts of the earth of inhabitants with the great war prophesied of because of your wicked ways.

8. And though you heed me not, if you continue to contend, the evil powers shall take charge and there shall be slaughter, bloodshed, sadness and woe throughout the earth.

9. This is the voice of Jesus Christ.

10. Cease this contending or you shall grow into the great war that shall depopulate many parts of the earth, for thus it has begun.

11. Thou seest it not.

12. You justify yourselves to contend against others, being corrupt within yourselves of those sins of Sodom, and the murder of unborn children, and adulterous and immoral and licentious and corrupt ways; corrupt ways of financiering, of education, of governing, and the ways of the earth being corrupted before your Lord.

13. I must soon take a hand, and I have begun the judgments that shall sweep the wicked off the earth.

14. My land of Zion shall be depopulated until a new people that I shall bring, called Israel, shall gather, and my Zion shall rise, a righteous government revealed from heaven, and my appearing being known to all nations as I have promised in my holy writ.

15. Cease this great attack against

nations, combining against that which they call injustice.

16. Cleanse the inside of the platter in your own lands; and this is the word of Him who created all things.

17. And as you repent, I will preserve other nations and send forth what is needed to humble the wicked.

18. Hasten to prepare, for my coming shall be as a light from the east, shining forth where all people shall know I have appeared.

19. Therefore, a cleansing shall take place, even of those elements of earthquake, pestilence, hail and famine, if needs be, to humble thee if you heed me not.

20. Repent ye of these greater wrongs in your own lands, lest you bring forth these greater judgments upon your nation, each one, is the word of the Lord to you.

21. Now receive my word: Gentilism is selfish will. Israel is Priesthood and the government of God coming to earth.

22. Pure Israel is where my Church and Kingdom dwell.

23. Therefore, my Israel shall rise and shine, a Priesthood inspired from heaven, a religion that guides in righteous living and doing.

24. This shall come among you with a message of salvation to every nation in a time soon to happen.

25. Prepare thy laws and thy peoples to allow the messengers I shall send, saith Jesus Christ, with the Gospel of eternal life, that you may be prepared to receive in peace that which is of peace of me, Him who created all things; and nothing is withheld from me, from the Father, to govern in righteousness and truth to His honor and glory; for the Father and I are one, and we are here to do the will of the Council of the Gods, Eloheim, Gods

of Creation that rule over worlds from Celestial orbs.

26. Now we shall bring forth the Celestial powers to this earth, and all people shall know that I reigneth.

27. And I am sending my word to prepare the way, that there may be some prepared to receive the greater light and blessings offered to those who will repent and turn from their gentile and selfish will, and turn to their God and begin to bless other peoples and prove their worthiness to remain upon the earth in a day of righteousness and peace.

28. Violence must be done away with.

29. All corrupt and fallen and filthy ways must be obliterated from among you.

30. There must needs be a recompense sent forth upon present leaders who allow these terrible and corrupt ways among their peoples, having pleasure in unrighteousness.

31. I have sent forth mine word through mine apostles and through Prophets of old, and thou knowest of my coming.

32. Heed my word.

33. I am sending forth my word in a manner of your understanding, and I send this new message to thee:

34. Cease your war that is raised up one against another, justifying yourself in United Nations Council to humble one nation. It shall spread; and then what shall you do if my protecting care withdraws from your land and the peoples in thy borders rise up, and then another nation, and then another nation?

35. Awake and turn to your God who made you, and remove the evils from within your lands. Remove your laws that justify these evils I have named, that exists in almost all nations everywhere on earth.

36. Protect unborn children.

37. Protect the rights and virtue of women and children.

38. Care for the poor.

39. Do not allow illegality of immoral conduct, legalized by your corrupt laws to continue; for you cannot change eternal truths that wickedness corrupts.

40. Therefore, thus saith the Lord God of heaven, He who speaketh from on high: Repent ye, and know that if you do not, my judgments shall sweep the more wicked among you from off the earth and preserve the more righteous for a reign of righteousness at my glorious appearing, with all the saints of resurrected nature to come to dwell with men who are righteous on earth; and Zion, my heaven, coming to earth, rising upon my land of Zion where the United States of America now exists, which shall be swept off the land if she repent not.

41. I have sent forth my word. I fear you not.

42. I am God and shall fulfill my word, and you shall tremble at my name at a soon time to come, and all men shall know that when I speak, I fulfill my word.

43. The sea shall heave itself beyond its bounds.

44. Know that Italy and Sicily shall be mostly without inhabitant.

45. They are corrupt and ripened in destruction.

46. This nation is the same, ripened in corruption, and must be swept clean.

47. Thus saith the Lord, thus it is with that nation that dwells on my land of Zion, and the Canadian nation -- both corrupt, ripened in iniquity, and they heed me not.

48. I have sent forth messages to their leaders and they heed me not; therefore, they shall feel the wrath of a just God.

49. Now, O ye who are pure in heart, who will receive my message of salvation, I shall preserve thee in marvelous ways.

50. While the wicked around you are falling in the desolating scourge, the sickness without healing, you shall be preserved.

51. I shall heal thee; and as you turn to me in prayer, so shall you be preserved, as you live a more pure way of life and do not allow these great evils I have named in your nature.

52. Let there also be word sent forth to that nation of corruption, wherein there shall be a cleansing, even that land called the Philippines.

53. You have allowed your people to rise up in corrupt and licentious and filthy ways, and I shall cleanse your lands to a great cleansing, more than you have known.

54. And it shall take place by storm and disease and famine.

55. Hasten to repent, saith the Lord Jesus Christ.

56. And there shall be, yea, even come upon you a great cleansing, such as you have not known.

57. Therefore, repent ye.

58. You have felt my chastening hand at times, both in revolution, as well as the sea heaving beyond its bounds, and great storms.

59. Let there also be Malaysia repent, for her iniquities have come up before me, and Burma.

60. Let there also be Afghanistan repent, for I have sent my warning previously.

61. And may they receive my word by the hands of their ambassadors that I shall send to them.

62. Many nations are corrupt and ripened in iniquity.

63. I have sent forth some warnings and shall send forth more.

64. Receive ye this in United Nations Assembly as I mail it forth.

65. Hasten to prepare, O ye nations of the earth, for I will not allow you to continue in your corrupt and licentious and immoral ways that murder unborn children and are unjust to the poor, and to women and children.

66. Let your militaries only be used for defense and not to harm thine own peoples; and draw into your borders thine armies, that peace may dwell upon the earth.

67. This from Jesus Christ, the Prince of Peace, who shall reign in righteousness and truth on earth among men.

68. I, the Lord, have spoken it. Amen.

69. Thus saith the Lord to the nation of Spain, receive ye my word I have sent previous, and also this, my word:

70. There shall be a cleansing of thy land.

71. Draw to high ground. The sea shall heave itself beyond its bounds.

72. Be ye numbered among those who are peacemakers, and no longer transgress the ways of life, according to these sins I have named.

73. Be ye a people that cleanse the inside of the platter, and seek unto your Lord for delivering and for peace among all nations, and ye shall be emissaries of peace, saith the Lord.

74. Receive this word and more that I shall send.

75. Let that nation called Luxemburg holden itself to the Lord your God, lest it cease to exist out of the corruption of your hearts.

76. Let Bahrain also be warned of injustice toward her peoples, for I, the

Lord, shall humble thee and the leaders of thy land.

77. Let there be peace in all thy borders, saith the Lord, to the nations of the earth; and cease warring one against another, against my coming, that I may prosper you and send my healing message of salvation.

78. This from Him who reigns on high, Jehovah Christ, the God of all the earth.

79. And as I have spoken, so shall I fulfill.

80. Let there be a mediation between the nations in the Bosnia area of a soon happening, saith the Lord Jesus Christ, lest greater war break out among them and there be people swept off the earth.

81. Let there also be Russia humbled, lest she become an instrument of destruction unto her own humbling.

82. Therefore, I shall send more.

83. Hasten to prepare, for I, the Lord, have spoken.

84. Let this, my word, be received in United Nations Council as a general understanding that the Lord who reigneth over all shall soon intervene, and you shall know of my coming and my power above all.

85. And though you see great events taking place, I am in control and shall preserve mine elect for my Zion to rise, which Zion you shall know of, of a more perfect way, of my sending more of my word and my representatives to the surviving nations.

86. And at my coming all shall know of my power.

87. Repent ye and prepare, is the word of Son Ahman, who doeth the will of the Father, whose right it is to rule over all creation and over worlds of His creating.

88. And I do my Father's will, who is

only right and pure and true, just and holy in all things.

89. Thus, I declare to thee, a righteous government is soon to come to earth and make peace among all nations.

90. Repent ye, lest you be humbled by my almighty power, saith the Lord Jehovah, before all nations, Him who is called Jesus Christ, who redeemed all mankind from the grave through the suffering, more than man can suffer, administered to Him by Celestial powers.

91. Thus, He cometh forth in power from on high to redeem all mankind from the grave and to bring message of salvation to those in this life on the earth today, who must meet their Maker in the hereafter and be judged according to works done in the flesh.

92. Thus, I send my message of salvation, that you may be prepared to meet your God in a day of judging, being a just God.

93. And those who pass on from this life receive my Priesthood message of salvation in the world of departed spirits, giving all mankind equal privilege to learn my Gospel of salvation, that they may be prepared to meet their God in a day of judgment.

94. Thus I shall reward all according to their deeds.

95. You have your agency. Be ye believing and prepare for my glorious appearing on earth, and the nations being humbled and prepared for a righteous reign of peace, my Millennial Reign of Peace, a thousand years among men -- Zion rising, Celestial powers attending, and the great God of heaven being made known among all peoples as you visit my Zion and prepare for my presence.

96. Thus, I send my word to you:

Hasten to prepare, and draw into your own borders your armies; and stop warring one against another, lest greater judgment, beyond what you know, come upon thee, the nations of the earth.

97. I send my voice of warning to you: Humble yourselves and be of peace against the day of my coming.

98. Let those of my Priesthood, Church, and Kingdom upon the earth have all they need to promote Zion.

99. And have their lands and houses returned, and their brethren in bondage freed, for great is the evil of this nation of the United States of America, using unjust laws and ways to persecute mine elect, who seek only my will and my religion of heaven to promote unto the salvation of all mankind.

100. Great shall be the penalty upon that wicked generation who persecute my saints on earth.

101. Therefore, repent ye and restore to them their freedoms, their lands and houses, and all things they need to build up my Zion.

102. And let the nations of the earth flow forth with every gift needed to build my Zion, that I may come among you and bless you according to the blessings you offered to build my Zion; for as you give, so shall you receive in a multiplicity of blessings.

103. Hasten to respond, and free him who is my Mouthpiece on earth.

104. And allow peace in your own borders, and prepare the way for Zion to rise and you to come to know your Lord who created you.

105. This is His message of salvation, both in this life and toward a salvation in eternity, for you are of immortal souls in the resurrection and will stand before a God

who knows all things, and He shall judge thee according to works done in the flesh.

106. Now let your desires be purity, holiness, righteousness, and peace, and I will preserve thee a remnant on earth to know of Zion and of my coming among thee, to thy salvation on earth and eternally.

107. Thus, I have spoken my power, for all nature around you bespeaks my power, and nothing can withhold that justice that must come forth upon this wicked generation, having corrupted their way before their Lord all the day long and will not heed my message of salvation.

108. Your false religions, not of my Priesthood, cannot save you.

109. Only that which is of God, empowered of heaven, can exalt.

110. Therefore, come to know of me and my ways, and repent ye of these outward evils I have named, of a soon happening, in your borders.

111. And cease warring one against another, is the call of Jesus Christ, Son Ahman, Jehovah, the Beginning and the End, who rules over all with the power of Celestial power.

112. And nothing is withheld from me, for I know your thoughts and the desires of your hearts, and shall judge accordingly who shall remain upon the earth in the day of great judging and great destruction, both of elements and of wars, disease and pestilence, hail and famine and earthquake, the sea heaving beyond its bounds. This you know.

113. Hasten to prepare for my coming; and my coming is nigh, is the message of Him who created all things.

114. Let this be read in general assembly in the United Nations Assembly of a soon happening, and if you heed me, your nation shall be humble and do what is right one toward another and in your own lands.

115. If you heed me not, you shall feel my greater judgments coming forth, and there shall be nothing stay mine hand until you do humble yourselves and receive my message of salvation;

116. For thus has the Father who reigneth over all declared He has the right to rule over all nations, and you are His, and I am His, and His will is being done.

117. And Zion shall be cleansed, and my land of Zion purged, and mine Israel shall be gathered; and there shall be a clean and pure people to be my Zion on earth, to represent me to all peoples.

118. Hasten to prepare, is my word to this nation of the United States of America and the nations of the earth in this communication.

119. I, the Lord Jesus Christ, offer you salvation, happiness, peace in this life and eternal peace in the life to come.

120. Thus is my power, which I declare to thee.

121. Now receive my word: These corruptions I have named must be obliterated and not be among you to survive as a nation.

122. Let this be learned, and you shall know of my power.

123. Thus saith Son Ahman, He who reigneth over all and is a God of Creation, and nothing can stay mine hand; and thus I say. Amen and amen.

SECTION REVELATION 40

Son Ahman Speaketh Warning Again to the Nations on the Land of Zion of Judgments Soon to Come, Even a Warning From Him Who Reigneth Above

Thus Saith Son Ahman, His Own Word Given

Revelation of the Lord Jesus Christ
Big Lake, Texas
Sunday, March 27, 2011

1. I, the Lord, now declare:

2. Thus saith the Lord unto this nation of the United States of America: You heed me not.

3. I have warned you to cease these evil practices in your nation, to change your laws that are unrighteous, that allow the murder of unborn children, and Sodom, and adultery, and other unrighteous practices, and the persecution of an innocent people for their religion, even my Church and Kingdom upon the earth, that Church of Jesus Christ of Latter-day Saints upholding my full Celestial Law of Eternal and Celestial Marriage, the plurality of wives, and the Holy United Order, required to establish my Zion on the earth.

4. And you have persecuted my people, and you heed me not.

5. You protect corruption and fight against religion that is pure.

6. And thus saith the Lord: My judgments shall now come upon you, for you heed me not.

7. I have sent forth many warnings, both to the leaders of this land and the United Nation ambassadors of every nation.

8. Now I say unto you, Repent ye!

9. Turn from your wicked ways or feel the wrath of an incensed God who is just and true, for I shall shake terribly the earth, and you shall know I have spoken.

10. Why wait ye until destruction is in your borders, when I withdraw my protection from thy land -- why wait ye until death faces you before you will believe?

11. I, the Lord, have spoken, even Jesus Christ, the Redeemer of all mankind, and send to you this communication again:

12. Cease your war wherein you have invaded another nation without my directing, not justified these three times -- in Afghanistan and Iraq, and now Libya.

13. Though you claim other nations are joined with thee, you are the attacking force that all others depend upon.

14. And thus saith the Lord, these three witnesses are against thee.

15. You have attacked without justification or approval of thy God, not being attacked.

16. I, the Lord, shall repay, and you shall not use your military might to humble another nation, lest you fall from within.

17. This is the word of the Lord to you.

18. Though you claim righteous principles, your foundation is corrupt, and

you spread these wicked practices that I have named, that are in your nation, among the nations of the earth.

19. And thus, you are a stench to the heavens, for you spread wicked practices, even murder of unborn children and immorality and corruption throughout the nations of the earth, and you have military might to defend your stand oftentimes.

20. I, the Lord, shall bring you low, for you will heed me not, save I send judgment upon thee; and as I do, give heed to my word.

21. Cleanse the inside of the platter.

22. Change these wicked laws. Turn them from thee.

23. Protect innocence and the lives of unborn children.

24. Protect my people, who only desire to live their religion in holy and pure laws.

25. I, the Lord, command thee and shall be obeyed, and if you heed me not, you shall reap the results of thy choice and know that thy nation is but a garment in a fire and shall be consumed by the judgments of a just God.

26. And the leaders of this nation shall flee when no man pursueth, fearing their own peoples whom they represent.

27. And the businesses of great power shall fall as Babylon the great falls in her economic might.

28. And trade and commerce shall cease, and mob rule shall be in parts of thy land.

29. And the overflowing scourge and desolating sickness shall go forth and kill millions, because they heed me not, in their corrupt ways, and will not repent, sending them to the world of departed spirits where some may perchance receive my message of salvation, saith your Lord and Redeemer, Jesus Christ, who reigneth on high.

30. Oh, why will you heed me not? Why do you continue in your fallen ways?

31. My power is from on high, and nothing can stay mine hand.

32. And I am causing my warnings to come to your ears and knowledge, even to justify the Lord your God in the cleansing of your land, preparing for a new people -- mine Israel, to be gathered to help build my Zion, a place of peace and righteousness, purity and truth, equity and justice, every noble way inspired of heaven.

33. You know of my coming in my glory, as mine apostles of old declared, and is in holy writ in thine hands.

34. Be ye believing.

35. My time is at hand, and I must be justified by continuing to warn you that my judgments are upon the earth of greater happening, and you cannot stay my hand.

36. Hasten to repent and turn from your wicked ways, is the word of the Lord to you, again a message of warning.

37. And as you receive my warning, heed my word.

38. As you feel earthquake and storms and tempests increasingly, and disease not able to be healed, awake and learn that thy God reigneth, and you are but stewards in His hands to rule in righteousness and do good to all peoples; first cleansing thine own lives and the laws in your land which are unjust;

39. For you have overruled the laws of life in allowing the murder of unborn children, which causes you to reek with corruption in all other doings, having murderous blood on your hands; for thus you are, in mine eyes, who uphold this practice and other evils that corrupt the way of life that I, the Lord, have ordained since the creation of this earth.

40. I am a God of miracles.

41. I created the earth, and I, the Lord, sustain all peoples in their place.

42. And when I appoint, thus shall it happen, and nothing can stay mine hand.

43. Thus, repent ye, lest you no longer be a nation on my land of Zion, for I shall fulfill my word.

44. Now receive my word further:

45. That nation that you uphold in corruption, in a manner to uphold their leaders who are unjust and wicked, you are guilty of their same sins, even the nation of Turkey, wherein they allow persecution of the Kurdish people and of women within their own borders; and you are guilty of this persecution by upholding them.

46. And I shall cause a division in that nation, and you shall know not what to do as other nations of great power seek to bear influence and take control of lands under their control;

47. For in that nation of Turkey is corruption throughout their government of unrighteous rule, and when you uphold an unrighteous government of despotic rule that denies the rights of women and children and of minority religions, you are guilty; and thus you do throughout the earth for economic gain, and it will not stand longer.

48. And as you uphold corruption elsewhere, your power shall be overthrown.

49. I, the Lord, declare it.

50. There are many other nations you uphold in their corrupt and despotic ways for economic gain.

51. I, the Lord, will not sustain you further in this wicked practice.

52. Therefore, cleanse the inside of the platter -- your own laws, your own lives, you who are of ruling positions -- and stop upholding despotic regimes who harm their own people.

53. I, the Lord, have spoken it, and I shall be the Ruler of all lands and nations at my glorious appearing.

54. And I shall dwell on my land of Zion among a prepared and pure people.

55. Now hear my word:

56. I have promised earthquake and storm and disease in thy land to humble thee, and if you heed not these warnings, and if you do not clean up these evils that are among you, I shall name further greater judgments; and as you see them take place, you shall know I, the Lord, have spoken.

57. Now I have named many things, and there is more of my word to be sent forth.

58. Prepare thine hearts, for I shall name to the nations my law, and if they heed me not, judgments shall follow until they are humbled and bow to my rule, saith your Lord Jesus Christ, who reigneth over all.

59. Prepare for my word, for I shall send it unto thee in a manner that you will know of other judgments soon to come upon thy land.

60. This is the word of Son Ahman, Jehovah Christ, the Great I AM, speaking from the heavens by authority, and nothing can stay mine hand, saith Him who reigns on high.

61. Receive this communication with soberness and humility.

62. Consider these truths -- that I see and know all things, and nothing is hidden; and you shall be judged for your conduct in this mortal life unto an eternal judging.

63. Let there not be the continuation of these corruptions I have named, and heed my previous warnings I have given, is the word of the Lord to you, even Him who is called the Redeemer and Savior of all mankind, who hath in His hands eternal

salvation for those that will believe His message of truth.

64. Now, saith the Lord, let there be under thine influence and the European nations' influence a conference near the land Bosnia to bring peace to the different peoples, that there may not be war break out among them, for there has been great slaughter among them, even genocide, that must not take place.

65. If you would do well, bring a peace conference among the different factions that live in that area of Europe, that there may not be further war among them.

66. And save you do this, war will break out again among them of a desolating nature, and ye shall be held responsible, having been able to bear more influence in their lives.

67. I, the Lord, call you to do this.

68. Hasten that practice, and watch how peace will grow among them if you heed my word.

69. And if you heed not my word, war shall take place in which you shall be weakened also, in your influence and in your power of military might and economic might.

70. Thus saith the Lord, if war breaketh out in Europe, you shall be weakened as a nation, even the United States of America.

71. This I give as a warning.

72. Thus, help make peace among that people.

73. Now make peace in thine own borders.

74. Free mine elect, my people of my Church, and give them their houses and lands in return, for an unjust judge hath taken them.

75. And free my servant and his brethren from bondage, who only desire to live their religion unto their God.

76. And this shall be a testimony that you will heed my word further; otherwise, you shall feel my wrath of judgments, greater judgments pouring forth;

77. For my Zion shall rise, a religion of heaven inspired through the Prophet Joseph Smith, preserved on earth through a living Priesthood and by my power.

78. And that branch called the Church of Jesus Christ of Latter-day Saints, known on earth, is apostate and broke off from my Priesthood authority because they turned against my Celestial Law of Plural Marriage.

79. And my true Church upon the earth upholds all my laws revealed, yea, even from heaven through the Prophet Joseph Smith, preserved in this day in my Church and Kingdom.

80. Thus saith the Lord: Let my people go! lest judgments come upon this land to sweep all off this land of Zion where thy nation dwelleth, who oppose my rule.

81. I, the Lord Jesus Christ, hath spoken it, and nothing can stay mine hand, is His word to thee, the rulers of this nation and other nations on my land of Zion.

82. Prepare your minds to receive further of my word, for I shall reveal my word to the nations in this day when I shall come among men, and I am preparing the way that there may be a remnant out of every nation to receive their Lord in His glorious appearing.

83. And that nation that will not purify their own peoples and laws and ways shall be humbled, and some come to naught and remain no more upon the earth.

84. And I, the Lord, shall do this work, that I may be justified before all nations in being a righteous Ruler that does not allow wickedness to rule on the earth any longer.

85. Hasten to prepare for my coming

and my rule among you, ye nations of the earth, and repent ye of your wicked and corrupt ways; for my voice shall be heard, notwithstanding all your might and power and supposed authority as rulers over lands and nations and peoples.

86. I have the right to rule, from the God of Creation over me, even my Father, who ruleth in the heavens over worlds.

87. And thus I am here to do my will, even visiting the earth and going among the nations, and now revealing my word in an open manner to the leaders of this land, this nation of the United States of America and other nations on my land of Zion;

88. For my Zion shall be built up, a New Jerusalem, and all peoples shall come to it of surviving nations and learn of the heavenly and Celestial ways of life that exalt and ennoble mankind to a godly walk before the Lord.

89. Hasten to prepare, for my time is at hand, and my cleansing powers are upon the earth, which thou knoweth, such as you have not seen in past times, and shall come as a hastening, to you marveling at how many judgments and storms and wars and earthquakes are taking place, and diseases of unknown name coming forth to different lands.

90. Repent ye, repent ye, O ye peoples of the earth, saith God who reigneth on high, our Lord above all, as all shall declare in the day of my coming.

91. My peace shall be upon those who change their laws wherein they permit wickedness.

92. Outlaw the wickedness I have named -- the murder of unborn children, and Sodom, and adultery, and all evils that destroy innocence -- and promote laws of justice and equity and purity of life.

93. And cleanse thine own selves, you leaders of nations, lest my judgments come upon you, and you no longer be leaders of nations.

94. I, the Lord, have spoken it. Amen.

SECTION REVELATION 41

Son Ahman Speaketh to the Nations of the Earth, Warning and of His Coming, Even Jesus Christ, the God of Glory and Righteous Rule

Thus Saith Son Ahman to the Nations of the Earth

Revelation of the Lord Jesus Christ
Big Lake, Texas
Sunday, March 27, 2011

1. I, the Lord, now declare my word:

2. Thus saith the Lord Jesus Christ, who reigneth on high, who hath all power and authority from the Father to rule over nations and to bring about Zion in full to the peoples of the earth and all nations, I send you more of my word:

3. Bosnia and those surrounding

nations must have a peace conference soon.

4. Let it be held lest genocide and other violence break out, weakening the nations of Europe.

5. Perform this work: Call a peace conference.

6. Put great influence upon them of these factions and small nations that have broken away from one another, in that area of land in Europe wherein religious differences are so sharp and exceedingly great, they have been willing to slaughter one another in the name of God, which is a mockery before the God of heaven.

7. Now I, the Lord, declare: Let the European nations also repent for their ungodly and corrupt ways; for the murder of unborn children, and Sodom, and adultery, and corrupt ways are extant throughout your lands, and shall be met with judging from your God -- great judgments which shall cleanse many people from off your lands.

8. Thus, as you seek to make peace in other nations, cleanse the inside of the platter first.

9. Purify your own laws to protect innocence and virtue and life, saith the Lord.

10. Now cleanse your nations of these wicked practices that I have named; for I have now sent you more communications through United Nations ambassadors to each of your nations.

11. Heed my word.

12. I am the Lord and Savior of the earth, even Jesus Christ, and my glorious coming is nigh at hand; and you must needs cleanse your lands of these ungodly and wicked ways that I have named, even in my previous communicatings -- your receiving from Son Ahman my communications through my Church upon the earth.

13. Now heed my warning:

14. If war breaks out in Europe, many nations shall be involved with war, and Israel shall be threatened, and Turkey shall fall.

15. And there shall be great nations rise up determined to conquer other nations until war shall spread.

16. Heed my word.

17. Cleanse your lands and your peoples of these wicked ways -- of the murder of unborn children, and licentiousness and immoral ways.

18. Correct your laws. Overthrow these wicked ways, lest a just God send judgment upon you.

19. Make peace among nations, and I, the Lord, shall be with you who thus cleanse the inside of the platter in your own lands, your own peoples, your own laws; and promote equity and righteous and pure principles favorable to all mankind, and all religions having freedom of religious worship.

20. Thus saith the Lord unto the European nations who have joined against Libya:

21. Cleanse the inside of the platter first, your own nations, before you seek to subdue another nation for unrighteous practices.

22. And if you heed me not, your wars shall spread, and there shall be dismay and sadness and war in many nations.

23. Repent ye of this evil.

24. Correct thyselves first and prepare for my glorious appearing;

25. For I shall be the Ruler over all nations, and all people shall fear at my coming and tremble at the voice of their God being known.

26. Let that land called Mauritania now be upbraided for their wickedness, for they are promoting great evil on the earth.

27. And I, the Lord, declare their leaders shall fall, of a soon happening, if they do not stop their wicked ways.

28. There is among them organized crime and murder and corruption of every kind; and I, the Lord, shall cause the leaders of that land to be humbled and removed.

29. Revolution shall spread and is spreading in many lands.

30. Let that nation called Ethiopia cleanse the inside of the platter and overthrow laws that are not just, and protect innocence and purity.

31. Minority religions must be protected, and there must needs be the hierarchy of your government humbled, for there are many secret evils in their lives that I, the Lord, shall reveal to the nations, that shall cause other nations to be ashamed of their practices.

32. Cease these evils and purify your own peoples.

33. As you are now seeking to rule over other nations or bear influence in their lives, cleanse the inside of the platter first.

34. I, the Lord, declare to China: Cease the murder of unborn children.

35. Though you seem to have great power at this time, and though you may be used in future times as a battle-ax against wickedness, if you continue these great evils in your own land -- of injustice, and oppressing thine own peoples, and the murder of unborn children -- I shall bring you low, saith the Lord Jesus Christ, the God of all the earth.

36. And you shall know my judgments are just, until you learn to promote equitous and righteous laws that guarantee freedom of worship; and allow your peoples individual domain and ownership of land wherein there is not oppression against them.

37. Your government shall fall in a time to come, and I, the Lord, shall send forth messengers of salvation to promote righteous laws among you;

38. For the Kingdom of heaven is at hand, and shall come to earth at my glorious appearing.

39. And all nations, even the heathen nations, shall remain, only to promote righteousness.

40. And I shall send forth judgments upon those who continue in these most wicked practices that I have named in this communicating.

41. I, the Lord, shall humble Russia in a time to come, for there is great immorality and the murder of unborn children there.

42. And she shall cease to be a nation in a time to come, saith the Lord, for I shall humble her.

43. Though she shall be as a battle-ax for a time, and though she shall be a nation for a time, if these practices continue, her people shall be scattered and no longer be a united people.

44. I, the Lord, shall judge all peoples, and I fear you not; for you exist only by my grace and power.

45. Repent ye of your great wicked ways.

46. And I name all nations: Repent ye of your great and wicked ways, for a just God seeth all things and shall send forth great judgments upon the earth, which have begun.

47. The War of Armageddon shall roll forth; earthquake, storm, the sea heaving beyond its bounds -- all shall come forth as

I have named in the promises through my Prophets throughout the ages of time.

48. And my appearing in my glory shall cause all surviving nations to fear and tremble, for great is my power, even over all the earth and in the heavens.

49. Repent ye of these wicked practices, that I may spare some among your nations in the day of judgment, saith your Lord, Son Ahman, Jesus Christ, who reigneth over all.

50. Receive my communicating and prepare for more of my word, as I am sending forth my word to the nations, to be justified in sending judgments upon thee;

51. For thus I work among the nations since the days I sent my Gospel of salvation, restored through Joseph Smith, my Prophet, sending missionaries throughout the earth.

52. Now is my time of judgment upon the nations of the earth.

53. You can read his record and know he spoke my word to the nations.

54. Receive my word, saith the Lord, and prepare your peoples for more of my word to be sent.

55. And cleanse the inside of the platter in every land, even your own nations and your own laws, your own peoples, that I may spare some at my glorious appearing.

56. Think not that your secrets are hidden from me, for I shall reveal the secrets of all peoples in a soon time to come, and nothing can stay mine hand.

57. Thus saith Son Ahman, the Ruler of heaven and earth under His Father, Ahman; yea, even Jehovah Christ, the Savior of the world, the God of Israel who shall spare Israel after humbling her in the war of nations, and who shall spare His elect in New Jerusalem as the capital city of the earth; and Old Jerusalem also, as I cause mine Israel to come forth and rule the nations in Priesthood and a righteous government revealed from heaven at my glorious appearing.

58. Hasten to prepare, ye nations of the earth, for I shall humble all peoples who continue in wicked practices, especially these great wicked ways of murder of unborn children, and licentious and Sodom and adulterous ways.

59. Repent ye! for the God of heaven is nigh at hand and cometh in the power of His might to humble all peoples.

60. I, the Lord, have declared it, and so shall I fulfill. Amen.

Fundamentalist Church of Jesus Christ of Latter-day Saints
P.O. Box 840459
Hildale, Utah 84784

Thus Saith the Lord Jesus Christ

(Comprising Section Revelations 42, 23)

SECTION REVELATION 42

Revelation of the Lord Jesus Christ to the Nation of Spain
Big Lake, Texas
Saturday, March 26, 2011

1. Thus saith the Lord to the nation of Spain, receive ye my word I have sent previous, and also this, my word:

2. There shall be a cleansing of thy land.

3. Draw to high ground. The sea shall heave itself beyond its bounds.

4. Be ye numbered among those who are peacemakers, and no longer transgress the ways of life, according to these sins I have named.

5. Be ye a people that cleanse the inside of the platter, and seek unto your Lord for delivering and for peace among all nations, and ye shall be emissaries of peace, saith the Lord.

6. Receive this word and more that I shall send. Amen.

SECTION REVELATION 23

Warning of the Lord to the Nation of Spain

Revelation of the Lord Jesus Christ
Draper, Utah
Thursday, October 21, 2010

1. Verily thus saith the Lord unto the nation of Spain: I, the Lord Jesus Christ, have seen the evils that have corrupted you unto a cursing.

2. And thus shall you feel the judgments of destruction as you continue to persecute the innocent unborn children.

3. Thus shall I cause thy habitations to be as Sodom.

4. Thus shall you know the Lord reigneth.

5. Cause thy people to overthrow those evils in thy nation.

6. Let all immoral and licentious conduct be outlawed in thy land.

7. Cause the people to mourn before their Lord; for I shall cleanse you by the power of judgment as you continue

in the corrupt and sinful way of unholy conduct.

8. Even so shall it be upon you.

9. Let the government no longer allow the use of weapons of mass destruction to be in your borders.

10. Cause there to be no more sending forth of soldiers to fight in foreign wars.

11. Cause thy people to let go of the sins of Sodom.

12. Let the unborn children be preserved by law.

13. Cause schools to be built for the poor.

14. Cause the army to be only for guarding the borders of your land, and no longer be used to persecute thy own nation.

15. Let union of peace be among your several peoples.

16. Cause all evils of usury be overthrown.

17. Let thy habitations be as peace.

18. Now cleanse thy nation so my judgments may be stayed.

19. This from Him who is above all things, who shall soon appear to all those who are pure.

20. Let thy people now receive my word.

21. Publish this, my warning, to all the people in the borders and throughout thy nation.

22. Send forth messengers to the nation of the United States on my land of America.

23. Cause that pressure be sent upon them who are in government to let my people go.

24. Cause thy influence be felt in behalf of my servant Warren Jeffs.

25. Let him be free of bondage and of prosecution.

26. Know that I shall see all your works, and bring with me the just recompense of reward.

27. Have only within your nation a continual searching of the ways of truth.

28. Prepare thy people to receive my Gospel of salvation, as I send forth my messengers of peace.

29. Receive ye my representatives of my Kingdom.

30. Throw down all opposition to my law.

31. I have the power of preservation.

32. You shall be used to establish peace again upon the continent where you dwell, as I sweep the nation of France clean.

33. You shall not invade other lands.

34. You shall not usurp authority over any other nation.

35. Thus shall you continue to survive the day of my coming.

36. Let this word be as a warning unto your preservation, as the nations of the earth feel the wrath of a just God upon them.

37. Now ready your armies to be as messengers and defenders of peace.

38. I shall thus cause your land to be preserved.

39. Now establish peace.

40. Do not be slow in this.

41. You only shall be preserved as you acknowledge my right to rule.

42. This is your final warning.

43. Now hasten to preserve your nation as a peacemaker among those nations who survive my day of judgment.

44. I shall call upon you by my

messengers I send, as representatives of Son Ahman, even Jesus Christ.

45. And thus shall they make themselves known, by my power attending them.

46. So shall my whirlwind judgments be stayed within your borders.

47. I shall cause a tidal wave soon to come upon thy shores.

48. Cause thy people to soon leave those places where the waters of the sea would thus remove the inhabitants.

49. Let this be done during this next year.

50. I shall cause a sickness come among you to remove many of the more wicked among you.

51. Thus you shall know I, the Lord, have spoken.

52. And as you fulfill my word, to remove the evils of immorality, murder, and child murder of unborn infants, so shall I fulfill my word.

53. Thus it is upon you, a warning, and the call to purify thy land of wickedness.

54. I, the Lord, have spoken; and thus shall I fulfill.

55. Even so shall all things be prepared to receive the knowledge of blessings of the eternal world.

56. My Zion shall rise.

57. The covenant people of Israel shall be gathered.

58. My covenant people on my land of Zion shall be preserved.

59. I shall cause a new people to come upon my land to receive my Gospel.

60. I shall send messengers unto thy nation.

61. Pass and uphold laws of religious and social freedom within thy nation.

62. Prepare for freedom of worship in thy land.

63. Cause persecution to cease in thy land against those of unpopular faith.

64. Now be a nation of truth. Uphold truth.

65. Let go of false and evil traditions.

66. Learn of my eternal ways.

67. Cause thy people to receive my rule.

68. Let go of the traditions of evil and corrupt religion that oppresses the poor.

69. Humble your people by not allowing the sins of abortion to exist.

70. I shall thus continue my blessings upon you.

71. Have upon your habitations a wreath of olive leaves at the time I send forth the sickness among your people.

72. And as I spared ancient Israel, so shall I spare those who thus fulfill my word.

73. Let them also, in each household, renounce the evils I have named in this, my word.

74. Cause there to be your people to receive this, my message, soon.

75. Let their family relations be peaceful.

76. Cause that the infrastructure of thy government be organized to care for those injured by the war soon to come upon the nations of the earth.

77. Prepare for them to care for other peoples.

78. Listen to the message I now send.

79. I have chosen you to thus become a nation to bless other nations.

80. Let this now be fulfilled.

81. I shall only hold you guiltless as you cleanse these evils from among thy nation.

82. This from Him who has you and all

peoples in His hands, to preserve the pure in heart through the day of judgment.

83. Hasten ye. Only now can you begin to fulfill my word before I send forth the judgments appointed.

84. Read my servant John's Revelation.

85. Know I shall fulfill my word I recorded through my ancient apostle.

86. I revealed to him the judgments to be sent upon the earth to prepare for my coming. Now believe.

87. Cause there to be an awakening of the people.

88. How oft I have sent my word through my messengers to the nations.

89. Let the people of all nations now realize I, the Lord, shall soon appear.

90. Thus shall this, my word, be on record to testify that I have sent my warning unto the salvation of the nations.

91. How oft my word has gone forth since I restored my Gospel of salvation.

92. My servant Warren Jeffs now is my Mouthpiece upon the earth. Listen to my word.

93. So shall I fulfill, as also my word and will sent forth by my people in the day of my suffering and resurrection.

94. This must become the foundation of your lives, to believe I am; that I, your Lord and Savior, have the power to lead all peoples to salvation.

95. Come unto me, and receive the knowledge and blessings of eternal life.

Fundamentalist Church of Jesus Christ of Latter-day Saints
P.O. Box 840459
Hildale, Utah 84784

Thus Saith Son Ahman, Your Lord and Savior, Jesus Christ, the God Over All the Earth, to the Leaders of the Nation of Egypt and to the People of Egypt

(Comprising Section Revelations 43, 15)

SECTION REVELATION 43

Revelation of the Lord Jesus Christ to the Nation of Egypt
Big Lake, Texas
Wednesday, March 30, 2011

1. I who reigneth on high, even Jesus Christ, the Son of God, doing the will of Eloheim, the Council of the Gods of Creation over this earth and many worlds, declare my voice to the nation that now inhabits that place wherein I, the Lord, resided for a time of safekeeping, even Egypt.

2. Thus saith the Lord: I send my message to you.

3. I have caused that there be a delivering and an opportunity of a government of greater justice and equity in thy land;

4. Yet there are great evils among

you, and more especially violence against women because of your false traditions.

5. And I, the Lord, declare to thee: Humble yourselves lest greater war erupt in your borders and other judgments come upon you.

6. Allow the rights of women. Let there not be abuse.

7. Cease your evil practices lest you receive greater judgments.

8. I, the Lord, send to you this message through thy leadership and embassies:

9. Repent ye, for you have sought freedom, yet you do not give freedom to women, wherein they are abused by husbands or other men, based on tradition principles instead of righteous principles.

10. This abuse of women will lead to abuse of others in your borders and greater violence.

11. Let them have equal rights of voting, of choosing education, of having in the home respect, and not an overbearing husband who causes them to shrink from acting on correct principle out of fear their own family will deride them.

12. Thus, children are raised in your habitations to abuse innocence.

13. I, the Lord, call upon you to receive this, my word.

14. There shall also be more of my word sent to you -- a message of salvation for thy nation in a day of war and in a day of greater judgment upon the nations of the earth.

15. And I add this, my word, to you:

16. Though you are allowed a time to seek greater freedoms, if you thus abuse women and allow other evils in your borders, especially the murder of unborn children, or other evils of injustice toward minorities, or unjust laws that abuse for the sole purpose of getting gain --

17. Verily, thus saith the Lord Jesus Christ, who upholds all nations in their place, I shall allow greater distress in thy borders, and you shall know I have spoken.

18. Now receive this word and mine other word, sent forth as a beacon of peace, as a peacemaking nation.

19. Let rulers in thy land cease using military against their citizens.

20. Let thy people join in a governing power that is equitous and just, based on principles that promote happiness in righteous doing.

21. Let there not be the upholding of immorality or corruption in your midst.

22. I, the Lord, shall reward the leaders of nations with an overthrow if they continue to abuse their peoples.

23. And this violence among nations shall lead to war among many lands and peoples and nations, until I, the Lord, take a hand;

24. For the evil powers rage in whatsoever person, peoples, or nation turn away from the principles of life and virtue.

25. And immorality and crime and murder shall reign in your midst for a time when unrest takes hold.

26. Repent ye, and be people, O ye nations of the earth, preparing for the coming of thy Lord and Savior, who redeemed all mankind through the suffering of Celestial justice on the cross, raised from the grave to exalt all mankind who will receive my message of salvation and abide in heavenly laws that exalt mankind to a Celestial power, a heavenly power of righteous doing.

27. This you shall know as you open your borders to the messengers I send of my Priesthood, Church and Kingdom upon

the earth; and as you allow individuals freedom of worship in your borders in every nation.

28. This I will require of every nation that survives the judgments of God.

29. Repent ye, and be more willing and open-minded to correct principles of righteous doing, and be not harmful or abusive to any because of thy prejudice or ill-will.

30. You shall meet a God in the day of judgment, as you pass on from this life, who shall reward thee according to thy deeds.

31. You cannot hide from Him.

32. Therefore, I send you that portion of my message of salvation.

33. Repent ye of these great outward evils in your lands.

34. Thus let Egypt, which once was a protecting nation for my own life at a time Herod sought my death, let Egypt now be an ensample nation that will promote peace in her borders, and just and equitous and righteous laws for both men and women, and preserve and protect children in their innocence. School them and take care of the poor.

35. Hasten to prepare, and be a nation that promotes righteous laws, that I may preserve you in the day of greater judgment upon the earth.

36. This from Him who has all power, who sustains the heavens and the earth in their place, and is now speaking from the heavens to your understanding.

37. Thus I send to the leaders of your land this, my word.

38. I, the Lord Jesus Christ, the God of Israel and the God of all nations, hath spoken it, and so shall I fulfill. Amen.

SECTION REVELATION 15

Warning of the Lord to the Nation of Egypt

Revelation of the Lord Jesus Christ
Draper, Utah
Saturday, October 23, 2010

1. Let the city of Cairo build unto me a sanctuary, even a place for my power unto the preservation of thy nation.

2. Let this sanctuary be as a holy place wherein is kept the covenant of cleansing.

3. Let the people of the nation of my preservation be as an example of peace and equity.

4. Cause your laws to preserve virtue.

5. Purge from your midst all corrupt associations with the people of the land of Sudan.

6. Cause your laws to preserve innocence.

7. Cause your laws to overthrow the persecution of your people.

8. Let there be freedom of worship.

9. Prepare a place of a "covenant of peace" unto your Creator.

10. Send forth the petition of protection

from thy land unto my servant to thus acknowledge my rule.

11. And cause this sanctuary to be a holy and protected temple, wherein my word I send shall be kept in a holy container of gold and silver, and of precious stones in a gopher-wood frame.

12. Cause my law I send to you to thus be preserved.

13. Let this sanctuary be a place of peace wherein I may come to witness the integrity of your people to just and righteous laws.

14. Sanctify your peoples by a continual labor of sacrifice, to feed the poor, to heal the afflicted, to cause the needy to no longer perish.

15. Thus shall I witness your works, and spare your nation as my judgment of cleansing is sent upon all peoples.

16. This is the word of Son Ahman,

the God over all, who hath seen all peoples in the way of their doings; and who shall cause the end of all corrupt and abominable ways.

17. Now be a nation of noble cause.

18. Be as in former times, a people of the preservation of mine Israel.

19. Thus shall I also preserve thy people as you acknowledge me and my rule upon the earth.

20. Let this take place soon among you.

21. And bear affliction without retaliation.

22. Send up your petitions to Him who is the Creator of all things in the day of judgment.

23. Let these petitions also be kept in the holy sanctuary of the God of Peace and Union. Even so. Amen.

SECTION REVELATION 44

Fundamentalist Church of Jesus Christ of Latter-day Saints
P.O. Box 840459
Hildale, Utah 84784

Thus Saith the Lord Jesus Christ to the Nation of Syria

Revelation of the Lord Jesus Christ
Big Lake, Texas
Thursday, March 31, 2011

1. Thus saith the Lord unto the nation of Syria:

2. You have sinned greatly before me in oppressing thy peoples these many decades, and becoming, as it were, a nation of sore affliction against other nations.

3. And I have allowed thy people to rise up to oppose wicked rulers who will not give freedom of worship and of speech and expression, and of doing in their own nation, and you shall be overthrown.

4. Thus saith the Lord: Repent ye quickly.

5. Cast off this unrighteous rule, or I shall overthrow your rulers to no longer be a nation, but to be conquered and overthrown if you repent not.

6. If you will turn and overcome that unrighteous rule, and become equitous and more just, and give freedoms of righteousness, of expression, of worship, of women having rights and protection, I, the Lord, shall spare thee;

7. And save you do this, my judgments shall soon be upon you.

8. You have promoted violence, terrorism, and corruption among nations.

9. You have joined with Iran in promoting great evils on earth; and both nations shall be humbled, saith the Lord Jesus Christ.

10. Heed my word. Cast off from you those works of violence and injustice against your own peoples, and promote a governing power in your land that allows freedom of worship, owning of property without obstruction, the overthrow of terrorist organizations in your borders, casting off alliances with nations that are violent in nature.

11. Let your military only be used for self-defense, and not against mine Israel.

12. Let there not be aggression on thy part, but peace; and use not thy military against thine own peoples wherein they are peaceful.

13. Be at peace in thine own borders.

14. Cast off the evils of corruption of immoral ways, and hasten, for my glorious appearing is soon, and if you heed me not, being a nation of violence and oppression, I shall cause you to cease to exist as a nation.

15. This is the warning of the Lord who governs all creation, Jehovah Christ,

Son Ahman, who sends His message to you this day.

16. There are those among you who are murderous in your nature, in the leadership of this nation.

17. Secret murders are taking place, oppression of innocence. This cannot stand.

18. My appearing is soon, and all nations shall know of my glorious power, and you shall fear and tremble in a day of judgment.

19. I shall send a sickness among you, as well as a war that shall cause you to cease to be a nation.

20. As you thus oppress thine own peoples, it cannot stand;

21. For I who created all things, who cause all nations to exist by my power, shall overrule your unrighteous acts, your corrupt ways, your oppression, and your warring temperament;

22. For you can no longer be a force upon the earth against mine Israel or against a righteous governing power, called Zion, that shall come upon the earth at my glorious appearing, a righteous reign sent from heaven, that all nations shall know that I, your Lord and Savior, who redeemed all mankind from the grave and offer salvation to all who will receive my message of salvation, only I can deliver thee in a day of great judgment and war and trial.

23. Thus saith the Lord Jesus Christ to this nation: Turn away from your wickedness, your oppression, your warring nature, and only be of a peacemaking nature if you desire to survive as a nation;

24. Otherwise, you shall be overthrown, and you shall know that I, the Lord Jesus Christ, hath spoken.

25. Let the President of this nation, President Assad, know that his time of

ruling is short, for he hath oppressed his people and brought murder and misrule among them, and upholds violence among nations.

26. I, the Lord, shall not uphold him longer.

27. He shall be as a temporary leader.

28. I, the Lord, have spoken it.

29. Let all other leaders in this nation humble themselves, for I shall overrule in behalf of my Church and Kingdom upon the earth, which must send forth a message of salvation to all nations; and freedom of worship and expression must be in every land.

30. Cause thy laws to be just, and guarantee freedom of expression and worship and other freedoms that promote happiness among peoples of all nations.

31. Cease thine evil practices of oppression against thine own people, is the word of the Lord to you this day, lest judgment come upon you.

32. How can you stand against a God of Creation, who gives you your very lives day by day?

33. Thus I am the God of all the earth and of heaven, and shall make myself known in my glorious appearing as I have promised.

34. Hasten to prepare thy peoples. Thus saith the Lord. Amen.

SECTION REVELATION 45

Fundamentalist Church of Jesus Christ of Latter-day Saints
P.O. Box 840459
Hildale, Utah 84784

Thus Saith Son Ahman, the Lord Jesus Christ, to the Nations of the Earth: A Message and Warning, Mine Own Words From the Heavens

Revelation of the Lord Jesus Christ
Big Lake, Texas
Thursday, March 31, 2011

1. I, the Lord Jesus Christ, speak to the nations of the earth again on a day of warning when my judgments are soon to be poured out without measure, beginning among mine elect and my people on the earth, spreading across the land of Zion and to the nations of the earth.

2. Zion shall remain. The pure in heart are Zion, who love God with an undivided heart, who have in their hearts His law burned in constant remembrance as a living fire to their righteous doing, of my giving.

3. And only they who abide a Celestial law can be part of Zion; and Celestial means heavenly, sent from above -- the laws of a kingdom of glory, of eternal all-consuming fire, that fire being the Holy Ghost, the Spirit of God.

4. Thus saith the Lord to the nations of the earth: I am soon to come in my glory and my power, and you shall feel this power, even to consume the wicked and preserve the more righteous among you, saith Jesus Christ.

5. Now behold I say unto you, ye nations of the earth, I send my message again of warning:

6. Cease your wars against one another.

7. Draw your militaries into your own borders. Do not oppress thine own peoples.

8. Let there be a destruction of all armored vehicles as a sign that you will repent and turn to the God who made you.

9. Awake with this warning, that if you heed me not, your wars shall spread, for the evil powers shall take hold of leaders of nations unto unjust causes one against another.

10. And behold, if I withdraw from you as your protection, as the power by which your nation exists, ye shall be filled with such unrest in your borders, many nations shall be disrupted, leaders shall be removed through revolutions and wars and other judgments that I, the Lord, shall send to humble thy peoples for their wickedness.

11. I have declared the murder of unborn children in all nations of the earth is a great crime against heaven and against the principles of life, and it is centered in immorality, adultery, and Sodom, a crime of licentious behavior.

12. Thus saith the Lord: Cleanse the inside of the platter, your own nations and peoples. Correct your laws that allow these immoralities, and murder of unborn children, and other corrupt practices.

13. Cause these laws to be changed unto righteous doing, to preserve innocence and purity and life.

14. I, the Lord, declare it again: How can you withstand mine hand when I send forth judgments, that which you see happening on the earth, of great storms and flooding and earthquake and other judgments?

15. And unrest in nations depicts the time of my coming as I prophesied -- unrest in nations, wars and rumors of wars.

16. Now hasten to prepare thy peoples.

17. Pass laws that allow freedom of worship, and expression, and other freedoms that allow individual happiness in righteous and equitable and just ways.

18. Do not have men's traditions any longer as your guide, but principles of my giving, that are in my holy writ, as well as that of my soon giving; for the Kingdom of God, called Zion, shall rise and shine by my preserving hand.

19. The nation and nations that inhabit my land of Zion shall be removed as they prove unworthy to exist because they uphold these evil practices I have named.

20. My people Israel who can be converted to my Gospel of salvation shall be gathered to my land of Zion.

21. Behold, I say unto you more, ye nations of the earth.

22. Though you believe me not at this time, it shall be in your records as you shall come to know the truth thereof.

23. This earth was divided.

24. I am a God of Creation. I created this earth. And parts of this earth were separated, and a people under a great Prophet named Enoch, and another people under a great Prophet named Melchizedek, who is Shem, the son of Noah;

25. Verily, I say unto you, these two Prophets, through their faith and the faith of their righteous peoples, were removed from the earth with part of the earth, separate orbs to dwell in a more exalted condition where the heavenly powers could dwell among them.

26. They are soon to return -- Enoch and his people in the Gulf of Mexico and the Atlantic Ocean surrounding my land

of Zion; and Melchizedek and his people also, their part of the earth shall return.

27. Though you believe me not, and deny my power to create and uphold earths in their existence, I put it on record by mine own words to the nations, that when these parts of the earth return by my power, and the more righteous among you are miraculously preserved, it shall be acknowledged the God of heaven spoke of these things before they took place.

28. I have sent this word before in the revelations through my servant Joseph Smith.

29. They are in the record -- that Enoch and his people would return and meet a righteous people called Zion on earth, my Church and Kingdom now established and preparing for my glorious appearing.

30. Assist my people. Do not hinder them.

31. Send forth strength that they may help build a New Jerusalem.

32. And you, each nation that thus assists, shall be blessed with a multiplicity of blessings.

33. I, the Lord, am sending my word as a record among your nations, and those nations that seek to hinder the sending forth of my message of salvation shall be humbled by the God of Creation, Jesus Christ, who ruleth over heavens and the earth.

34. And I am causing my word to go forth to you at this needed time, to warn you of the great judgments to sweep many peoples off the earth, by war and famine, by hail and pestilence, by the sea heaving itself beyond its bounds.

35. You are already seeing my judgments hasten in their time, for the seventh period of time hath begun, and I am among my people.

36. This is the will of the Lord that it should be known that the Lord Jesus Christ is doing His work on earth, preparing all peoples for His glorious appearing.

37. And though you have the prophecies of ancient Prophets in holy writ, I am now sending forth mine own word through my servant on earth, and through my Church and Kingdom on earth, upheld by those who have witness of my Spirit that my word is verily true.

38. Receive these witnesses and these testimonies of my word, and know that more of my word shall be sent forth to the humbling of thy nation, each one, who will not heed my warning to remove these great outward evils I have named from your nations, or you shall reap sorrow and stand before a just God in a day to come when all men shall be raised from the grave and be judged according to deeds done in the flesh.

39. Awake and live, and be ye believing, for my power shall be over all nations, and my Zion shall be the ruling government over all nations of the earth;

40. And you will have to bow the knee and confess that I am the Christ, the Savior of the world, even Jehovah, the Great I AM, Son Ahman, Jesus Christ, for thus am I the Ruler over all, under my Father, who has the right to rule, a God of Creation over all.

41. Now heed my word: He who created all things declareth sodomy, those sins of Sodom, shall be done away in your land or you shall meet a great sweeping of the wicked from your midst.

42. It cannot stand. It is a principle against life.

43. Thou knowest of my record of the destruction of Sodom.

44. Thus saith the Lord: Murder of unborn children is a curse in every nation that allows this evil, whether it be hidden or outward.

45. My Spirit shall not be with you to preserve you as a people in the day of great judgments.

46. This murder of innocence is so great on the earth, that I, the Lord, shall soon take a hand, that my spirit children coming to this earth may have a place and receive their earthly tabernacles in honor, and among peoples who will thus teach these children virtuous and righteous and pure ways of abiding in God.

47. Thus saith the Lord: The sins of immoral practice are the foundation of the murder of unborn children.

48. This must be cleansed from among your peoples.

49. And I, the Lord, have spoken it.

50. And all the wicked shall mourn in the day when their riches and their wealth and their commerce cease, and they are poor in their earthly habitations; and many shall perish for want and from famine.

51. O ye peoples of the earth, come unto that God who made you, and repent ye, for my time is at hand.

52. And I am sending forth warnings to leaders of nations, who should tell their peoples of my warnings, to improve their lives and overcome these outward evils.

53. I, the Lord, have declared that if you will put off these evils and remove from your borders these corruptions, that only a people in your lands uphold life in a more virtuous and pure walk before your God, I shall preserve your nation to receive the greater light from Zion, my Celestial powers among men.

54. This is my inviting of all peoples and nations.

55. Hear thou my word thus sent to you.

56. I send it to you with a publishing I have prepared -- warnings to many nations, and some warnings to all nations; other warnings to the United States of America where my people of my Church and Kingdom dwell.

57. Thus saith the Lord: Receive my publishing as a warning voice of certain judgments to come, and also declaring my policies of governing power that you will have to follow to survive as a nation in the day of my coming, when Zion shall rise and rule over the earth, my government of righteous doing.

58. And there shall be a council organized of governing power that shall send forth representatives from Zion to deliver the law of Zion to all nations, if they desire to remain upon the earth.

59. And your Lord and Savior, Jesus Christ, even I, your Lord and God, shall be acknowledged the rightful Ruler over all the earth and over heavens, yea, over worlds, as you come to know of my marvelous powers.

60. I send to you my publishing.

61. Let all your peoples know of my word being sent forth -- warnings of judgments and policies of righteous government clearly spoken to thine understanding, even before my glorious appearing, so there may be some survive and prepare for the government of the Kingdom of heaven coming forth on earth, whose right it is to rule, through rights of creation, through rights of upholding all creation in the Spirit of life.

62. I am a God of truth and of virtue and holiness, and of peace.

63. And to promote peace among all nations and within nations, promote rights of women and children to be preserved in virtue, to bless the poor, to have honest and honorable ways of living, and no evil or licentious or corrupt ways among you.

64. Evil shall be identified by the revelations of my will that are existing

among you, and your leaders shall be called upon to cleanse the inside of the platter -- your own peoples -- and have no more war against other nations.

65. Thus, any nation who heeds me not will meet judgment, saith the Lord God.

66. I thus send my word to you, ye peoples and nations of the earth, words of warning, words of invitation, to remove from you the evils that corrupt your natures and your peoples and nations; warnings to individual nations.

67. Thus saith the Lord: If you heed me, I shall preserve your peoples, those of the more righteous among you, through the day of great judgments;

68. And if you heed me not, some nations shall cease to exist as nations, as war shall spread over the earth, and famines and disease and pestilence, and earthquakes, storms of destructive nature, the sea heaving beyond its bounds; and some lands shall be desolate that were once inhabited with great population.

69. This is the voice of the God who made you.

70. Heed my warning and receive my publishing that I have caused to be sent forth through my Church upon the earth, revealing the same through him whom I have appointed to receive my word.

71. I, the Lord, declare unto thee: Let my people go! voicing again my word to the nation of the United States of America; and hinder not my work any longer, or you shall cease to be a nation --

72. This in a time soon to come, as you see earthquake increase, and disease, and mob rule, your finances weakening and falling, to no longer be an economic power; and other tribulations in thy borders, until all nations shall know what I, the Lord, have declared is happening.

73. And they shall know the coming of their Lord Jesus Christ is nigh at hand, because you heeded me not.

74. I must send these judgments.

75. This is the will of the Lord who created you: Repent! lest these judgments come in full force, without let or hindrance, in a whirlwind, yea, suddenly, thus removing the wicked from my land of Zion and preserving mine elect by my marvelous power, who can be Zion on earth to receive me and the heavenly angels on earth in a pure condition, becoming known to all other nations by the messengers they will be called to send forth with my message of salvation.

76. And thus I, the Lord, am a God that is just and true, merciful and gracious; and yet when I speak, I must fulfill.

77. Obey my word, ye nations of the earth, for in a time to come you shall bow the knee to my rule and know that I am God, being made known in my glorious appearing as I have prophesied through mine apostles in my holy writ.

78. Receive ye the word of the God who made you, in this publishing and in this, my word, being sent forth with my publishing.

79. Ye leaders of nations, cause that my word be known to your peoples. Let it be published. Let it be sent forth.

80. I, the Lord, shall send forth more; therefore, hasten to prepare.

81. This is the word of your Lord, Son Ahman, Jesus Christ, the Great I AM, the God of Israel and over all nations, He who created all things, who is the Light and Life of all peoples and all creation through the power of my Spirit.

82. Thus, I have spoken. Amen.

SECTION REVELATION 46

Fundamentalist Church of Jesus Christ of Latter-day Saints
P.O. Box 840459
Hildale, Utah 84784

Thus Saith the Lord Jesus Christ to the Nation of Yemen

Revelation of the Lord Jesus Christ
Big Lake, Texas
Thursday, March 31, 2011

1. Thus saith the Lord unto the nation of Yemen, even Jesus Christ, who ruleth over the heavens and the earth and give all nations their place:

2. Thy unrighteous rule is soon to be overthrown.

3. Thy peoples are rising up, and because of thy wickedness of thy rulers, I, the Lord, shall give you place no longer as leaders of a wicked nation that oppress your own peoples and promote terrorism and warring among nations.

4. Repent ye of this great evil of oppressing thine own people and promoting war among nations, terrorism, and violence.

5. And promote peace in thy borders, or I shall remove you out of your place.

6. My hand is upon the nations of the earth.

7. The great War of Armageddon is soon at hand, wherein nations will not hear their Lord and promote peace.

8. Cease your evil practices. Give rights to thy people of freedom of worship, and of expression, and of peaceful seeking redress and deliverance.

9. Let your courts be just.

10. Let there be the overthrow of those violent organizations in your borders.

11. Only use your military for self-defense, and to not be used against the people of thy land.

12. Hasten to prepare, for my glorious coming is nigh at hand, saith Jesus Christ.

13. You shall be humbled if you do not stop these evil practices of unrighteous governing power.

14. I, the Lord, send you this message to promote peace if you desire to exist as a nation; otherwise, you shall be overthrown and no longer be a nation.

15. This from Him who created all things, who is preparing the way of His coming, sending forth His message to the leaders of nations, that there may be a remnant in every nation of a more righteous nature, more equitous and just, who overthrows the evils of this wicked generation in their midst, and promotes kindness and peace in their borders. Thus should governing powers be toward their peoples.

16. I shall send forth more of my word.

17. Receive this portion with a warning, that you, the leaders of this nation, have now received a communication from thy God who created all things.

18. Though you acknowledge me not in all things, I, the Lord, shall fulfill my

word, and all nations shall know of my glorious appearing.

19. Therefore, you have received a warning: Judgments shall come upon you to the overthrow of your leadership if you heed me not.

20. There shall rise a faction among you that shall have greater power than the present nation and national powers within your borders, and if you heed me not, a new leadership shall come forth; then they shall be warned to be equitous and just, and give rights of freedom of religion, of worship, and of expression, of land ownership, of seeking the principles of happiness.

21. Thus saith the Lord. Amen.

SECTION REVELATION 47

A Continued Warning of Son Ahman to the Nations of the Earth of Judgments; A Call to Prepare, for My Coming Is Nigh

Thus Saith Jesus Christ to the Nations of the Earth: Hear My Word, Heed My Word

Revelation of the Lord Jesus Christ
Big Lake, Texas
Saturday, April 2, 2011

1. Thus saith the Lord Jesus Christ, the Ruler of heaven and earth, Son Ahman, the Beginning and the End, who rules with power and glory, even the God of glory:

2. My glory shall be known among all nations.

3. All nations shall hear my word, for my power is from on high and cannot be stayed, and in the power of my coming, all nations shall be humbled.

4. Therefore, thus saith the Lord to all ye nations of the earth:

5. Repent ye, for I send my word again to you --

6. Repent ye! Hasten to prepare, for my glorious appearing is nigh.

7. And I send you my word in a manner of warning, hastening my work through judgments, wars, and pestilence, famine and earthquake and other judgings;

8. For I am God, who created the earth and sent thy nations to inhabit the earth, and you are not of your own begetting.

9. It is I who cause all to have their place, for this is a time of testing, a mortal life of probationary testing, an experience to prove you worthy of eternal lives or eternal damnation according to your agency.

10. Thus saith the Lord: My Gospel of salvation shall be proclaimed in every nation, and that nation and their leaders who resist the messengers I send, and persecute and drive them away, shall be humbled of me, even by these judgments I have named, until you open your borders and allow freedom of worship.

11. Prepare thy laws now as I send my message to you, that all may be in preparedness for justice and equity, purity and truth to be proclaimed to thy peoples to their salvation.

12. It shall not be just an earthly salvation, but an eternal salvation, for I am a God of eternal life, eternal power, Celestial glory, greater than all the earth.

13. And thus I declare my word:

14. Repent ye! Hasten to prepare thy laws for my coming.

15. You will have my word now, and when my judgments sweep many of your peoples off the earth, you will know I have spoken because you would not heed my word; and then some few among you shall awake and come visit my Zion and learn of the noble ways of righteous, equitous, pure and holy and eternal ways.

16. I, the Lord, have spoken it. Receive my word, lest thou fall.

17. There shall be a tsunami of great proportion in the manner in which lives shall be lost of great number.

18. Thus saith the Lord to the nation of Indonesia:

19. Repent ye of your unjust laws.

20. Do not allow persecution of minority religions.

21. Allow freedom of worship and rights to women and children.

22. Thus saith the Lord to other nations surrounding thee:

23. Perform this same work, for though you do not acknowledge me as your God and King, I yet rule over all and send you this, my warning.

24. Receive my warning to the nations with soberness.

25. Learn of my policies of government, and know a righteous government is coming to earth from heaven under your Lord and Savior, Jesus Christ, who hath all power of creation, who was in the beginning with the Father.

26. Hasten to prepare, O ye peoples of the earth, is my message to you again.

27. O ye unbelieving people of the earth, you shall know I have spoken.

28. Thus it shall be on record to your knowing and to the future peoples in your lands, a record made on earth before the greater judgments spread forth.

29. Africa shall be depopulated to a great degree because of their great wickedness in every land.

30. Every nation is corrupt there.

31. Their leaders are corrupt; their practices are corrupt.

32. Thus saith the Lord: Asia, wherein India, Pakistan, Bangladesh, other nations that surround them, is corrupt.

33. They are taking on the ways of those nations of great power and influence in a manner to allow the evils of this wicked generation to exist among your borders and among your peoples. This must not be.

34. You must not allow the murder of unborn children, nor Sodom, nor adultery.

35. Your laws must needs protect innocence and women and their rights to be pure and not misused.

36. Your false religious ways must be changed that take life.

37. There must be the God of glory honored, even your Lord and Savior, who hath redeemed all mankind from the grave, to be raised up in the resurrection and stand before the Father and the Son to be judged of their deeds done in the flesh.

38. This is my message of salvation, and you must heed me or be humbled as a people.

39. I send my word to you now, for my coming is nigh, and my Zion shall rise.

40. A new capital city of the earth, New Jerusalem, shall be built by heavenly powers, and nothing can stay mine hand.

41. Therefore, you shall know of my coming, for I shall make known my power among all peoples of a sudden.

42. And the wicked shall fear and flee; and my power shall be over my people, who shall govern and reign in righteousness by my authority, called Priesthood, a heavenly authority sent to earth, that is now on the earth.

43. And my people living Celestial laws in a pure abiding way shall be preserved by me.

44. Though the nation of the United States persecutes them, I shall preserve them; and that nation shall go down as they thus persecute mine elect, my people of my Church and Kingdom, and who uphold these evil practices of murder of unborn children, Sodom, and adultery, and immoral and corrupt ways that destroy life and virtue.

45. And I, the Lord, have named many nations, given them exact wording in my revealed word how to repent and what to do among their peoples, and to cease their wars against one another, even other nations and within their borders.

46. And this cometh to you, ye nations in Asia and Africa, as well as other nations on every continent:

47. Repent ye! and prepare for my message of salvation to come forth.

48. There shall be in the city of New Delhi a devastating scourge.

49. Other cities in India shall experience this and know that a judgment is coming among your peoples.

50. Pakistan will feel the anger of God, as I have named, as they continue allowing war and terrorism among nations.

51. I shall cause other tempests to come upon that nation, even of India, and of Pakistan, to humble thy government and thy peoples, until you know there is a God of glory who hath spoken.

52. And you must cease these evil practices, and allow your people right of worship, and have equitous and righteous laws that promote freedom unto their agency being honored, to honor their God and obey Him who created them, even Jesus Christ, to receive the message of salvation I shall send.

53. Let that nation called North Korea know that though you shall have power for a time to humble other nations, your wickedness has come up before me; your corruptions against your own peoples are known.

54. Your leaders shall be removed from power, even by revolution and by sickness and other judgments, and you shall know thy God hath spoken.

55. Let there be in Australia a repentance, and not allow the murder of unborn children, nor Sodom, nor adultery, nor lasciviousness.

56. Do not allow your laws to protect these evils, or you shall be humbled with a greater humbling; for I have sent many judgments of recent happening upon you, and you shall know I, your Lord Jesus Christ, hath spoken.

57. Cease your evils.

58. Overcome those things that cause the corruption of your souls.

59. Prepare for my messengers to be sent to your land, and allow full freedom of worship.

60. Let thy trade with nations be honorable.

61. Let there not be a following after the ways of usury in your financial system, degrading the poor.

62. You rich men, be fathers to the poor; nurture them. Cause your governments to be influenced to do the same.

63. And I shall heal and bless any nation that will thus bless their poor and allow rights to women and children, freedom of worship, righteous and equitous laws in governing in money systems, in allowing the freedoms given of God to all mankind, to guarantee, through righteous and equitous and pure ways, these freedoms; which my holy Kingdom, coming from heaven to earth, shall guarantee -- the Kingdom of Son Ahman in the domain of Ahman, even Jesus Christ who speaketh.

64. Darkness hath covered the earth in the minds of men and women, and you are raising children in the ways of gross immorality, the ways of corrupting.

65. And my Kingdom shall promote righteousness, a righteous rule inspired of the governing powers of heaven.

66. Satan shall be bound, and there shall be no more misrule among the nations.

67. Nations that war against nations shall be humbled of me by almighty power until peace shall be over all the earth and Zion shall rise, an example of a heavenly Kingdom, pure and holy of my making.

68. Thus you shall know the Kingdom of Zion is the Kingdom of God on the earth, and my Priesthood is my authority and power on earth to govern in Zion and over the nations of the earth.

69. And I shall cause great division to take place in your lands, where leaders shall be overthrown who are unjust.

70. And there shall be more righteous governing powers, and my Zion sending representatives.

71. Thus you shall know the government of heaven hath come to earth, as peace and prosperity accompanies any nation who bows to my rule.

72. And they shall rejoice to proclaim that Jesus is the Christ and hath the right to rule over all nations, kindreds, tongues, and peoples;

73. For I have received the right of governing power from the God of Creation, Elohim, my Father, even Him who reigns on high.

74. Receive my word, ye nations of the earth:

75. Prepare ye, for I am sending my word, that you may know of my glorious appearing, judgments first to come, sweeping many of the wicked off the face of the earth, and then a day of peace and my glorious appearing.

76. My Zion shall rise, and nothing can stay mine hand.

77. This from Him who reigns on high, declaring boldly whose right it is to rule, and that you peoples of the earth shall submit to my rule in a time soon to happen, to your being blessed from the God of Creation over you as you apply righteous and equitous, just, and pure laws that promote happiness unto eternal life by the sound of my Gospel of salvation to every peoples of the earth. Amen.

SECTION REVELATION 48

Fundamentalist Church of Jesus Christ of Latter-day Saints
P.O. Box 840459
Hildale, Utah 84784

Thus Saith Son Ahman, Even Jesus Christ, to the Nation and the Leaders of Iran

Revelation of the Lord Jesus Christ
Big Lake, Texas
Saturday, April 2, 2011

1. Thus saith Son Ahman, even Jesus Christ, to that people of ancient origin, even Iran,

2. I send you another warning:

3. Cease your violent intent toward other nations, your corrupt ways against your own peoples, against women and children, and promoting immorality in some parts of your nation.

4. Repent ye of seeking to do that which gains power over other nations, or you shall cease as a nation and no longer exist under heaven.

5. I, the Lord, send you this warning: Repent ye of this great evil, of seeking to be as a warrior nation, defiant against righteous laws.

6. Let the religious leader repent, or I shall humble him and those who follow him until they are no longer leaders of this nation.

7. There must needs be a ceasing of your inward atrocities, putting down your own peoples with violence.

8. If you continue this, I, the Lord Jesus Christ, shall send judgment against you until you are no longer a nation on earth; thus, I send my warning to you again.

9. Let this be an awakening to thee that I am judging all nations.

10. I am soon to appear on earth, and you shall no longer be a nation if you continue in the evils I have previously named.

11. Repent ye, you leaders of this nation of Iran, and turn to equitous and righteous and pure principles, allowing freedom of worship, allowing rights to women and children, and taking care of the poor, not having forceful means against your own population just to keep power.

12. I, the Lord, uphold all nations in their place; and if you continue in sin and corruption as I have named, even in my previous communicating of warning to the nations, wherein is warning to thy nation exactly and with great specific nature -- I, the Lord, declare to thee, so shall I fulfill.

13. Let this be as a letter received with rejoicing that your God would warn you beforehand to change your unrighteous and unjust laws.

14. Your despotic regime must not be bearing down on your own peoples -- taking away proper rights of worship, of

ownership of property, of business that is honorable.

15. Thus, the Lord hath spoken to this nation.

16. Though you seem to have power on earth, your power shall soon be clipped.

17. The economy of the nations shall fall, and then where is thy power?

18. Mine authority is from above, from the Father of Creation.

19. The God over all the earth speaketh to thee.

20. Repent ye, and turn from your wicked ways, is the word of the Lord Jesus Christ, the Redeemer of all mankind, to thee.

21. And I shall own and bless those of thy peoples who deal righteously one with another through equitous and just laws, through ways of moral conduct.

22. There shall be a recompense of reward come upon thee, ye leaders of this nation.

23. Thus, you shall receive my communicating; and if you heed me not, you shall know I have spoken nevertheless.

24. And you shall feel my wrath in a day of judgment, even upon the nations of the earth.

25. No longer war against mine Israel nor against other nations.

26. Do not cause unrest in neighboring nations.

27. Let there be peace in thy borders.

28. Care for the poor.

29. Do that which promotes righteous commerce and trade.

30. Cast off immoral laws, laws that promote immorality among you.

31. Be a people of peace.

32. I, the Lord, have spoken it, and I will fulfill my word notwithstanding all thy supposed power and authority;

33. For you are as grass before the rising sun, that shall wither if you oppose the word of the Lord, that God of Creation who made you.

34. I have spoken. Amen.

SECTION REVELATION 49

Fundamentalist Church of Jesus Christ of Latter-day Saints
P.O. Box 840459
Hildale, Utah 84784

Thus Saith Son Ahman, Even Jesus Christ, to the Nation and Leaders of Italy, and Those Surrounding Nations Wherein Have Similar Heritage

Revelation of the Lord Jesus Christ
Big Lake, Texas
Saturday, April 2, 2011

1. I, the Lord Jesus Christ, speak unto the nation of Italy:

2. Thou hast corrupted thy way before the Lord.

3. A great tsunami, earthquake, and volcanos shall come upon thy land and depopulate many from off thy land because of your wickedness continuing through the ages of time, and more especially now.

4. The leader of your nation is corrupt and unworthy to be a leader.

5. He promotes immoral conduct of every kind, and your peoples allow immorality to run extant in your borders.

6. And I shall depopulate your nation through judgments only from God.

7. Thus, you have derided against me and my Celestial way of life that was once delivered to thee through mine apostles.

8. And though you have your false churches in my name, you have not revelation from me and are not my true Church of God among you.

9. Thus saith the Lord Jesus Christ: Repent ye of the murder of unborn children in your borders, for there are some who do this, though you be a nation that claims to uphold life.

10. Repent ye of Sodom and of licentious and adulterous ways.

11. This runs rampant throughout your society, and your laws allow the same.

12. It must stop, or you shall not be a nation much longer.

13. I, the Lord, have power to cleanse the earth.

14. Repent ye, is my word to you, the nation of Italy.

15. And thus saith the Lord, the island nations around you shall also be mostly depopulated because they follow thy corrupt ways.

16. Repent ye! Repent ye! and cease your evil practices, for my judgments shall sweep most of you off the earth; for I will not let wickedness rule.

17. My glorious appearing is nigh at hand, and I must cleanse the earth of the more wicked, lest they continue their wickedness.

18. I, the Lord, shall bring righteousness and truth, peace, equity and

justice to the nations of the earth through the rise of my Zion on the North American continent, and there shall be my governing seat and power -- Son Ahman in the domain of Ahman, my Father, even Jesus Christ, who is Jehovah Christ, the Beginning and the End, the Ruler of the heavens and the earth.

19. I have spoken, and I shall fulfill my word.

20. Turn from your wicked ways lest you no longer be a nation on earth. Amen.

SECTION REVELATION 50

Fundamentalist Church of Jesus Christ of Latter-day Saints
P.O. Box 840459
Hildale, Utah 84784

Thus Saith the Lord Jesus Christ to the Nation of Burma and the Leadership Thereof

Revelation of the Lord Jesus Christ
Big Lake, Texas
Tuesday, April 5, 2011

1. He who reigneth on high, even your Lord and Savior, Jesus Christ, speaketh to that nation called Burma, a nation of ancient origin and of modern wickedness where the leaders of this nation oppress their own peoples, even to the murdering of their own peoples in a despotic and unrighteous rule.

2. Thus saith the Lord who made you: Judgment shall come upon you for your wickedness as leaders, and I shall humble thee through storm and disease.

3. And there shall come upon you a work that shall remove present leadership.

4. Thy people shall be delivered in a time soon to come from your despotic rule.

5. And thus saith the Lord: Great is thy wickedness, to be answered upon your heads in this life and in the day of judgment, before an eternal God, when I who redeemed all mankind raise you from the grave to stand before the Father to be judged.

6. I, the Lord, call upon thee to hear my word and respond to my word of an immediate repentance and turning from your wicked misrule, your wicked oppression.

7. And I send you my word to allow your peoples greater freedoms of expression, freedom of worship, freedom in owning of property wherein there are not oppressive measures in your governing laws and powers.

8. You leaders roll in pomp and riches, and your people are poor.

9. Attend to the poor.

10. Let freedom of expression be a beginning improving of your laws.

11. Let leaders know that their sins are

known before the Lord, and their evil ways shall be answered upon their heads.

12. I who created all things send you my word in a manner of your understanding, for I speak from the heavens, and I, the Lord, give you my word: Your nation shall not stand as a nation if you continue these oppressive ways.

13. As you see the greater judgments coming upon the nations, you shall know I am keeping my word, for I have sent to you warnings to the leaders of nations.

14. Now hear my word concerning thee: A shaking is soon to come to thy nation.

15. You shall know the God of all creation hath spoken.

16. There shall be a revolution in the degree that thy people shall know of their rights of freedom.

17. There shall be sickness and storm come upon thee, and other pestilences, until you are humbled.

18. I, the Lord, who created all things, hath spoken.

19. Repent ye of your wicked ways and allow greater freedoms for thy peoples, saith Jesus Christ, who hath redeemed all mankind from the grave, and who shall come in His glory to rule over the surviving nations in a time soon to happen to your knowing, and to all nations knowing of my word and will and my coming upon the earth;

20. For my Zion, where righteousness shall rule, shall be the governing power over the earth, and all shall bow to my rule, saith the Lord Jesus Christ, who hath all power, who giveth all nations their place.

21. Thy misrule has caused murder of innocence.

22. Let there be no state police force of secret nature going among your people destroying life and oppressing thy people.

23. Change your laws to allow freedom of worship, that you may be prepared for my message of salvation, to preserve the lives of those I send into thy borders; for all surviving nations shall know I, your Lord, reigneth and shall hear my message of salvation.

24. Repent ye, O ye leaders of this nation, and no longer oppress thy people.

25. Attend to thy poor rather than heap up riches to thine own keeping, and be a nation of peace toward all other nations, if you desire to continue as a nation on the earth.

26. The sweeping of the wicked from off the face of the earth shall take place in a great measure of soon happening.

27. Inform thy peoples to live just and equitous ways of life, preserving innocence and life.

28. Promote freedoms as I have named, if you desire to continue as a nation, saith Him, Son Ahman, even Jesus Christ, unto you, whom you shall know hath the right to rule, who rules in the heavens and gives the earth an existence and all peoples their place on earth.

29. I, the Lord, have spoken it; and as I have spoken, so shall I fulfill.

30. Hasten to prepare, for my day of great judgments is soon upon you.

31. Receive my word, and you shall know I have spoken in a time soon to come.

32. Your leadership shall be as a garment in a fire at my glorious appearing, and all peoples humbled by the power of my might.

33. There shall not be one of you to stand of this wicked government when thy

Lord appeareth, as you continue in these great evils of oppression of thine own peoples.

34. Repent ye! Repent ye! For great are my judgments; and I, the Lord, warn thee to justify myself in the heavens of sending forth humbling judgments upon those who will not respond to my word.

35. Thus I have spoken and shall fulfill. Amen.

SECTION REVELATION 51

Fundamentalist Church of Jesus Christ of Latter-day Saints
P.O. Box 840459
Hildale, Utah 84784

Thus Saith the Lord Jesus Christ to the Nation of Sri Lanka and the Leadership Thereof

Revelation of the Lord Jesus Christ
Big Lake, Texas
Tuesday, April 5, 2011

1. Thus saith the Lord Jesus Christ to the leaders of the nation of Sri Lanka:

2. I have seen your abominations and your oppressions upon your peoples;

3. And I, the Lord, declare: Repent ye! Repent ye! of your oppressions and unrighteous rule.

4. And I call upon thee to allow freedom of choice, freedom of expression, freedom of worship, and allow rights given to thy peoples that I may send my message of salvation into your borders;

5. For I, the Lord Jesus Christ, who reigneth in the heavens, shall soon come to earth in the power of my might and make myself known to all peoples.

6. And you of oppressing nature to your own peoples shall be removed out of power.

7. And I, the Lord, whose right it is to rule, shall cause thy people to be humble to receive my message of salvation.

8. Repent ye now if you desire to exist as a nation, for thy peoples shall largely be swept off thy land when the greater judgments of the sea heaving beyond its bounds, of earthquake and of storm, bringing forth pestilences, and disease come upon thy peoples. And they shall know I, the Lord, have spoken.

9. I thus sent my word to you, that if you desire to remain as a nation on earth, you must be of a more liberal and kind rule, ye in power over this nation.

10. And though you have your military might, it shall serve you nothing in the day of my judgments. And I who reigneth, who giveth all nations their place, who ruleth over the heavens and the earth, speaketh, even Son Ahman, who is Jesus Christ, having the right of rule from my Father, Ahman, even the God over all creation, He who speaketh to thee:

11. Awake! Turn from your wicked

ways, and give your peoples greater freedoms.

12. Take care of the poor.

13. Cause thy nation to have just laws, that there be happiness promoted in more righteous and pure, equitous and just laws.

14. Let there not be this oppression any longer, lest my judgments come upon you in great measure and I remove you out of your place, you leaders of this nation.

15. I, the Lord, who have created all things, by which all things are upheld and have their existence, have spoken this word to you. Amen.

SECTION REVELATION 52

Fundamentalist Church of Jesus Christ of Latter-day Saints
P.O. Box 840459
Hildale, Utah 84784

Thus Saith Son Ahman, Even Jesus Christ, to the Leaders and Peoples of the Nation of Nicaragua

Revelation of the Lord Jesus Christ
Big Lake, Texas
Wednesday, April 6, 2011

1. I who reigneth on high speak to the peoples of Nicaragua:

2. Repent ye, or an earthquake of large size shall soon come to thy borders and destroy many lives.

3. Heed my word in the warning to the nations I have sent to your leaders.

4. Let leaders of this nation make known to the peoples of this nation my warnings and my policies of governing power.

5. And prepare ye to be a people that I, the Lord, shall use as you cleanse the inside of the platter, cleansing your own nation of the wicked ways of the gentile nations, wherein they allow murder of unborn children, and Sodom, and adultery, legalized, or allowed by legal authorities in their lands.

6. Turn ye away from these wicked practices.

7. Be kind to the poor.

8. Do not give way to the influence of gentile nations that lead thee to these evils that I have named.

9. I am soon to send messengers of salvation to thy borders. Let them enter and be preserved, and allow freedom of worship in thy land.

10. You shall know of my soon coming, saith Jesus Christ, the God over all, as you see the United States of America humbled by great judgments of my sending.

11. Therefore, heed my word.

12. Do not be violent against thine own peoples.

13. Let leaders of this nation humble

themselves and correct their unjust and wicked laws.

14. Allow thy people freedom of expression and of worship.

15. Let there be no longer using of military against thine own peoples.

16. Let this nation be a nation of peace, and not have in your borders those of violent nature that would cause war in other nations.

17. There shall be those of the blood of Israel dwelling among you come forth and help build my Zion in a future day.

18. Preserve religious rights, preserve equitous and just laws, freedoms of my giving to all mankind to have their agency in freedom of worship and freedom of expression without bringing violence upon others.

19. I send this to the leaders of this nation, saith the Lord Jesus Christ, to prepare you to be a more peaceful nation among the nations that border your nation;

20. For thus saith the Lord, I shall establish peace among nations, even if needs be I humble many nations by the judgments I send, of earthquake and storm, of disease and pestilence and hail, yea, even famine if they heed me not, until they cry unto their God for deliverance.

21. And thus I, the God over all the earth, shall hear the prayer of faith in a day that a nation and a people repent, and prosper their nation and their lands in preparation for my message of salvation to be sent into thy borders and to thy peoples; for this shall happen, and nothing can stay mine hand.

22. Be a nation of peace is my command. Amen.

SECTION REVELATION 53

Thus Saith the Lord Jesus Christ: My Warning of Judgments Soon at Hand to the Nations Now Dwelling on My Land of Zion

Thus Saith Son Ahman, Even Jesus Christ, to the Nations Now Inhabiting North America, and Also Warnings to Those Nations in South America, Even He Who Reigneth on High and Hath All Power

Revelation of the Lord Jesus Christ
Big Lake, Texas
Wednesday, April 6, 2011

1. He who reigneth on high declareth: Let my people go! Let them be free and dwell on their own lands and in their own homes, that have been consecrated to the Lord God of heaven, even Jesus Christ, or you shall reap the whirlwind of judgments.

2. Cause my servant Warren Jeffs to go free from prison to do my will, and his brethren who linger in bonds and imprisonment; for I, the Lord, justified them in abiding Celestial laws, and you have caused innocence to dwell in prison.

3. And your laws and your ways are corrupt and shall fall; and I shall deliver mine elect who abide Celestial laws of purity and holiness before me.

4. Thus, the Lord says; yea, even He who created all things and upholds all things, who has all power in heaven and on earth, and who shall come in the glory of His might to deliver His people Israel, to establish Zion in fulness, even New Jerusalem on that consecrated place --

5. Verily I say unto you, the leaders of this nation of the United States of America, there shall be a shaking.

6. Your governing powers will lose strength.

7. Thy peoples shall not be united; unrest shall ensue.

8. I have warned you of my judgments soon at hand, and you heed me not; therefore, know that I, the Lord, yea, the God over all the earth, speaketh, and you shall feel my judgments of a greater degree.

9. And if you continue to heed me not, there shall be a just recompense of reward to no longer have dominion on earth as a nation -- swept clean because you deride against my Celestial laws and persecute my people who have received my true Church upon the earth, my Priesthood through revelation from heaven.

10. I, the Lord, revealed to Joseph Smith my glorious coming must be preceded by the building of a city, New Jerusalem, on the land known as North America.

11. This has gone forth to all this generation, knowing of this truth; and I shall prepare the way, and nothing can stay mine hand.

12. I declare it to thee to thy knowing, for I shall be justified in sending my judgments when you allow injustice and corruption to rule.

13. And only I, the Lord, can preserve mine elect in their covenants of righteous living, that only I, the Lord, can establish on earth by the revelations of my will through my servant.

14. Verily, I say unto you: Let my people go! Free him in bondage whom I have chosen to receive my word and to give my word to the nations.

15. Let there be a hastening of this, lest you feel my wrath.

16. I, the Lord, will be justified, and send you this warning to the leaders of this nation called the United States of America, and also to the leaders of the Canadian nation.

17. I who reigns on high hath spoken it.

18. I have called upon you to cleanse the inside of the platter, thine own laws and lives, where you permit murder of unborn children, and Sodom, and other immoralities, corrupt ways of living that destroy innocence, yea, in their youth.

19. And none doeth good who partake of the spirit of this wicked generation -- in entertainments, in governing powers, in philosophies, in religions that are false, that claim authority to bless and save mankind, yet deny revelation.

20. Thus saith the Lord: I shall appear in my glory, and my land of Zion shall be cleansed, and my New Jerusalem shall be built -- all in preparation for my glorious appearing to the nations that survive the judgments of God, removing the more wicked part of the peoples of the earth, preserving the more righteous who can receive my message of salvation within their nations.

21. Thus, I send my word again: Repent ye! and turn from your own wicked ways, and allow my people to go free to fulfill my word I have revealed to them through my servant, and through

my servant Joseph Smith, to establish my Zion.

22. You have this opportunity, which shall be the result of your receiving an eternal judgment at the hands of the Lord.

23. My word is sure and true.

24. I have published my word to the nations of the earth since the days of my servant Joseph Smith revealing my word to the nations, and thou knowest I have given my word; therefore, I shall fulfill.

25. My time is at hand; and because I love all peoples and call all to repentance, I send this, my word, to the leaders of this nation, and all the peoples of this nation where my New Jerusalem shall be built, even in Jackson County, Missouri, at that Center Place, and nothing can stay mine hand.

26. And my Zion shall be the ruling power over all nations.

27. You only exist as a nation by my grace and power; and as I withdraw my protecting hand, there shall be a cleansing of the land, and only the more righteous shall remain, who are worthy to be part of my Zion.

28. This is my revealing to you as a warning, even unto an eternal judging when you stand before your God of Creation, He who made you, your Lord and Savior, the Redeemer of all mankind, the God of all the world, who is righteous and holy, pure, upholding just, equitous and pure laws of governing power.

29. Thus I have sent my word to you, my policies of governing power;

30. And all nations that remain on earth, after my cleansing the more wicked from off the face of the earth, shall bow to my rule or cease to be a nation;

31. For wickedness shall not reign, and righteousness revealed from heaven shall ennoble all mankind unto more pure ways of living and have peace among nations.

32. My Gospel of salvation shall be heralded to all nations.

33. My messengers shall go forth, protected and prospered by mine hand, even He who reigneth on high.

34. I have revealed to you some of my judgings upon thy land and thy peoples, thy cities, thy governing powers.

35. These you can read, even my recent word sent to you and to the leaders of the nations.

36. Heed my word.

37. Call that peace conference in the Bosnia national area of the different religious tenets and followers of that which they profess is the religion of heaven, and yet they join in violence one against another, going against the will of the God of Creation over the earth, even Jesus Christ.

38. Let there be peace made among them, lest war break out and spread over all the earth.

39. Now heed my word.

40. I, the Lord, shall fulfill my word upon you according as your works shall be.

41. And though in thy pride you think you bear influence over the nations of the earth, it is only by my power you exist as a nation; therefore, heed my word.

42. Let the leaders of this nation of the United States of America humble themselves and approach the Lord your God in personal fervent prayer; and act on correct principle and heed the word of the Lord, who reigneth on high, even principles of equity and justice.

43. Do not be a nation any longer that fights against the way of God, for you have corrupted the way of the Lord and you

must be cleansed, that my coming may be in a pure revealing to those who survive the day of judgment.

44. All shall fear who oppose me; and mine elect who become recipients of my presence shall know I am, and rejoice in their Lord, and Zion shall rise.

45. This is the will of the Lord to this nation: Repent ye! and turn from your wicked ways.

46. Let there be known that Washington D.C. shall be a city overrun by thine enemies, that in the fleeing from foreign armies, disease and famine will take hold of many.

47. Mine overflowing scourge and desolating sickness shall sweep many off your land because they heed me not.

48. Many cities shall be left desolate.

49. Earthquake and storm, hail and pestilence shall come upon thee because you heed me not.

50. And you shall know by the hastening of these judgings upon thy nation and the nations on the North American continent in particular -- and also that of the South American continent -- they shall know my day of coming in my glory is nigh at hand.

51. And I have sent my Gospel of preparation since the days of my servant Joseph Smith revealing my word to the nations of the earth, in sending forth missionaries; yet few heed my word.

52. Therefore, I, the God of Creation, being a God of truth, who has spoken, shall fulfill His word.

53. And though all nations deride and deny me, I shall make known my power.

54. And the more righteous who remain shall come to Zion and know thy God reigneth, even Jehovah Christ, who is Jesus Christ, the God over all the earth.

55. My Israel shall be gathered.

56. A righteous government in Zion, in New Jerusalem, shall rule over all the nations, bringing about peace for a thousand years of my giving.

57. Wickedness must be done away with, in every land.

58. And I, who see and know all things, shall reveal what each nation must do to cleanse the inside of the platter, as it were, their own peoples and their own laws and governing powers to be of a more equitous and noble and just cause; and not allow corruption and immorality, crime to be upheld;

59. For thus many leaders of nations join with secret combinations to get gain and influence and power in their lands, and thus allow great evils to take place among their peoples.

60. It shall not be, as my rule over all the earth comes forth in power.

61. And I shall humble nations afar off by the judgments, through the power of my might; and all shall know when I speaketh, saith your Lord Jesus Christ, the Redeemer of all mankind.

62. Hasten to prepare, for my coming is nigh.

63. And do as I have commanded, or you will cease to be a nation, even this nation of the United States of America.

64. And I shall bring forth a righteous rule on thy land, and a new people, called Israel, gathered, who will do my righteous and pure and holy way and will.

65. Thus it is. Amen.

SECTION REVELATION 54

Son Ahman Speaketh, Another Warning to the Leaders of All Nations of the Earth, Even Jesus Christ Who Hath Created You, Who Is the God Over All the Earth and in Heaven

This Is the Word of Jesus Christ to the Leaders and Peoples of All Nations, a Warning -- My Call of Preparing for My Glorious Appearing in the Power of My Might

Revelation of the Lord Jesus Christ
Big Lake, Texas
Wednesday, April 6, 2011

1. I, the Lord Jesus Christ, the Ruler of heavens and the earth, who created all things, even worlds and the inhabitants thereof, speak to the nations of the earth again:

2. Draw your militaries into your own borders, every one of you, and cease your wars one against another, or you shall cause a great destruction of war.

3. Let there not be the continuation of the wars in thy borders, lest my almighty hand be exercised and humble thee with almighty power, with judgments that ye shall know the God of heaven hath sent, even in thy borders where you allow corruptions and crime and abuse of innocence.

4. I, the Lord, send my warning voice again to the leaders of nations: Heed my word, as it were a final warning before greater violence and judgments, of earthquake and storm and the sea heaving beyond its bounds, pestilence and famine and disease.

5. Verily I say, heed my word, lest my greater judgments come upon you, the nations of the earth, saith Jesus Christ. I, your Lord and Savior, speak it again:

6. Withdraw your armies and bring them into your own borders, every nation on earth, for you exist only because of my Spirit of peace upon your peoples.

7. And when you reject my word, and my Spirit of peace withdraws, darkness rules.

8. And there shall be violence in many lands, and I shall send my judgments to cleanse the more wicked out of every nation and preserve the more righteous in preparing for my glorious appearing on earth.

9. My word is given through mine apostles to the nations of the earth of my glorious appearing, and through my servant Joseph Smith, whom I caused to write the revelations of my will and publish to the nations of the earth.

10. Therefore, my time is at hand, and I speak from the heavens as a final warning, as it were; for I shall be justified in sending forth the cleansing of the earth for a righteous reign of a thousand years

where thy God, even Jesus Christ, the Savior of all, ruleth on earth among His righteous people, and over all nations; and the wicked shall fear and tremble at my coming.

11. Heed my word.

12. Prepare ye, O ye peoples of the earth, for my coming is nigh at hand.

13. This is my revealing to you at this

time, even Jehovah Christ, Son Ahman, who doeth the will of the Father in all things, whose right it is to rule over all peoples, and whose rule is a righteous and pure and holy way, eternal ways of happiness and peace.

14. There shall be peace in my message of salvation sent to all peoples.

15. I, the Lord, have spoken it. Amen.

SECTION REVELATION 55

Thus Saith Son Ahman to the Leaders of the Nations of the Earth and All Peoples: A Warning and Continued Call to Repentance

Thus Saith Son Ahman, Even Jesus Christ, to the Leaders of the Nations of the Earth, and All Peoples of the Earth:

Revelation of the Lord Jesus Christ
Big Lake, Texas
Saturday, April 9, 2011

1. Hear thou the voice of Him who dwells on high, having all power over all nations, kindreds, tongues, and peoples, speaking to the nations of the earth at this time:

2. Verily, thus saith the Lord, your Savior, Ruler, and King, who reigns on high in the heavens and over all the earth, I speak to you, the leaders of nations and the peoples of the earth:

3. Repent ye! Repent ye! and turn from your wicked and corrupt and perverse and immoral ways.

4. For thus saith the Lord, I am holy and pure, and my Kingdom dwelling in heaven is soon to come to earth as the governing power over all surviving

nations of the earth, and you must needs be ready to receive the proclamations of righteous governments; and you must have removed from among you those laws in your nation that curtail the spread of religious freedom, that hinders freedom of speech, that causes oppression upon your peoples.

5. Thus saith the Lord: Every kingdom shall be shaken.

6. Every land shall feel the power of an Almighty God in judgments of cleansing; and the more wicked shall be removed from the earth, preserving the more righteous who live more noble and equitous and just ways, who deal justly with other nations, who do not oppress the poor nor murder

unborn children, who give women and children their rights.

7. Yea, verily, thus saith the Lord: The leaders of all nations are soon to be judged.

8. And I send you this, my warning, that you hasten to correct these evils and remove them from your midst, for they cannot stand before the almighty power of a God in His glory appearing to all nations on earth, to rule in a righteous government, whose policies promote happiness on earth and unto eternal lives;

9. For I am the God of glory, a God of Creation, He who created the heavens and the earth.

10. Thus you must hear my word, even if it must needs be by the voice of thunderings and lightnings, earthquakes and tempests, the sea heaving beyond its bounds; pestilence, hail, and famine; yea, the shaking of the earth to humble all peoples to know thy God reigneth, and He is the God of life, and all life is in His hands.

11. Now bow to my rule in a manner to respond, in preparation for my glorious appearing, or you leaders of nations and the more wicked among your peoples shall not survive the great whirlwind judgments I am soon to pour forth upon the earth, yea, over all the earth, beginning at mine house and on my land of Zion, even North America, spreading to South America and the continents of the earth.

12. I, the Lord, have spoken. Do this thing lest you be removed out of your place, all ye leaders of nations, by the judgments of my power.

13. And I send you this, my word, in the power of my might, in a manner of your understanding, for my Spirit shall attend my word to the honest heart.

14. There must needs be a reconciliation among your peoples where there is unrest and factional fighting, especially between religious factions of differing philosophies and tenets, wherein they are willing to be of a violent nature one against another over religion.

15. It must not be, for the religion of thy God from heaven is peace to all, and blessings upon correct and righteous principles that ennoble mankind, that enliven the soul unto an awakening of eternal principles that can guide the governing of nations on earth unto the salvation of souls, wherein my message of salvation shall come among you, and many shall receive my great work of redeeming love.

16. I have suffered the pains of all men, saith your Lord Jesus Christ.

17. I have carried all of you on earth lo, these many generations since the creation of this earth.

18. And verily I say unto you, heed my word, for my redeeming love and power of the atonement of my suffering, though it bring you from the grave in a resurrection, yet that atoning love is for those who live a more pure and righteous life, and will condemn the wicked unto an eternal judgment; for I, the Lord, cannot allow wickedness to reign.

19. I am here to do the will of my Father in the governing of this earth, and my word is coming forth to you, the nations of the earth, to prepare you unto your understanding, that I am going to come in power -- first in judgments, removing the more wicked from all nations, and more especially from my land of Zion where New Jerusalem shall rise.

20. And then cometh the preservation of the more righteous in the gathering to Zion as I appear in my glory, and all

peoples know I am present on earth with my heavenly powers, a Priesthood of Celestial giving from heaven.

21. Thus saith the Lord who made you: Heed my word if you desire to be of a surviving nature in the great holocaust among nations, as they who reject my word turn to the powers of darkness in wars and violence, in revolutions and mob rule, even in their own borders, causing thy God to send forth famines, earthquakes, pestilence, and hail, and other desolations to sweep the more wicked off the earth, that the more righteous may be prepared and preserved for my righteous rule upon the earth in every nation under heaven of my giving;

22. For you only have place on the earth by the grace and power of God attending thee;

23. Yet I cannot uphold your wicked ways, and I must have those removed from the earth who continue in the corruptions that I have named.

24. Now receive my word, and hasten to prepare the way before me, that at my coming you may be favored to learn of the exalted ways, noble ways, pure ways of governing and of living.

25. Let any nation who will heed my word send an acknowledgment to my servant, though he be in bondage, that you are thus attending to this preparatory work of the glorious appearing of the God who made you, who carries all creation in its place, who shall cleanse the earth of wickedness and promote a righteous and pure governing principle among the nations;

26. For I am King of kings and shall rule over the nations of the earth in a righteous and heavenly power which upholds all creation.

27. Therefore, I send you my word that you may prepare for that which is soon to come.

28. Thus saith Son Ahman, the Beginning and the End, Jehovah Christ, who is Jesus Christ, He who is the God over all the earth:

29. Let there be peace among the nations.

30. Do as I have commanded. Draw your militaries back into your own borders and cease warring against other nations.

31. I, the Lord, shall know that you will heed my word as you change your wicked laws to not allow any longer the murder of unborn children, and corrupt and immoral ways of Sodom and adultery and other wickedness among your peoples.

32. And as you destroy those armored vehicles in your military, I shall know that you want to be a nation of peace, to be preserved in my day of greater judgment.

33. These have been given to you, even my words, conditions to show that you are repenting.

34. And if you heed me not, I shall fulfill what I have spoken in this, my word sent to you, to remove the more wicked from among all nations in judgments of God;

35. For who can stand against a just God who knoweth and seeth all things, who shall pluck out the wicked and preserve the more righteous?

36. Therefore, heed my word!

37. I, the Lord, have spoken it, and all peoples shall know I have spoken as they feel the power of my might in judgments, and in great glory upon the more righteous who remain, to be blessed with the gifts of eternal power and knowledge in my Zion, as they thus visit and learn of my eternal ways.

38. Let there no longer be the promoting of secret combinations to gain power among leaders of nations.

39. Let there no longer be secret murders, for great shall be the eternal sorrow and suffering of those who have murder in their hearts, willing to take life when they are not appointed.

40. Verily, thus saith the Lord, I am the Giver of life, and all life is in mine hands.

41. Promote laws that preserve life and purity and innocence.

42. Hasten to prepare, is my word to the nations of the earth, and to you leaders of nations who can bear influence unto a righteous governing principle among your peoples.

43. This from Him, even your Lord and Savior, whose dominion ruleth over all, under the Father Elohim, even Ahman; for I am Son Ahman, doing the will of my Father in all things, for He whose right it is to rule over all things, being the Creator of all things, thus I have spoken. Amen.

SECTION REVELATION 56

Son Ahman Speaketh Again to the Leaders of Nations: A Call to Repentance; Prepare for My Gospel of Salvation

Thus Saith Son Ahman to the Leaders of the Nations of the Earth:

Revelation of the Lord Jesus Christ
Big Lake, Texas
Monday, April 11, 2011

1. I who reign on high give my word.

2. Receive my word, ye nations of the earth, as I give you another warning of my glorious appearing and my judgments soon at hand.

3. I am He who created all things.

4. I have sent my warnings, mine own words to you, for I shall be justified by sending forth my word and fulfilling my word, even that of the prophecies I have given through mine ancient apostles of my glorious appearing and the sweeping of the wicked off the land of Zion; yea, verily, even among the nations where wickedness rules.

5. I deliver you this day to a greater judgment, saith the Lord, because you heed not my words I have sent to you;

6. And my judgments shall increase upon the earth until your nation feels in increasing measures my chastening hand until you repent or cease to exist as an organized nation, wherein war shall spread throughout the earth, and unrest in nations shall overthrow principalities and powers on the earth, alliances that now exist.

7. Thus saith the Lord: Repent ye of those evils that I have named -- of the murder of unborn children, and Sodom, adultery and immorality, of causing suffering in your own borders.

8. Thus saith the Lord: I am soon to perform a work as I have named, and I will be justified by sending forth my warning; and if you heed me not, your peoples shall know I have spoken by the power of judgments.

9. Let there be peace. Let there be a seeking unto thy God who made thee, in prayer seeking, and no longer be nations of unrest and warring one against another.

10. It must cease, for my righteous rule shall bring peace to all nations who will heed my word, as the governing power over all the earth; otherwise, they shall meet judgments to humble them; yea, judgments of God, until they know when I, the Lord, speak, I shall be obeyed.

11. You heed me not, ye nations of the earth.

12. Ye shall feel my wrath; and I am justified, as I have warned thee, sending mine own word to the leaders of your nations.

13. Let the nation of Bahrain, even the leaders thereof, hear my word:

14. Cease your oppression upon thy peoples.

15. Give them voice and rights that are proper for all mankind to receive, and freedom of worship and expression, of representation and privileges that promote happiness, rights to women.

16. Be not an oppressive nation any longer to thine own peoples.

17. My judgments shall be upon you if you heed me not, you leaders of this nation, and you shall know it is I that hath removed thee from power.

18. Let the nation of Saudi Arabia repent of military assistance to thee.

19. And let all peoples know that they must not uphold an oppressive regime by military might, or they will partake of the sin of that wicked way and reap the judgment of a just God upon them.

20. Let this be an ensample to all nations.

21. If you, to get economic gain or influence, uphold a regime of despotic nature that oppresses their own peoples, you are partaking of that sin and will reap the judgments of God.

22. Thus, let there not be these wicked alliances that promote oppression among the people of the earth, for many nations do this. It is a practice that must cease.

23. Let economics not rule all things, but let correct principle, and equity, and justice, and seeking the happiness of thy people in righteous doing, in ways that exalt the nature in noble ways of thinking and feeling, of living, be among thy people.

24. I, your Lord, shall reveal more, through Zion being established, to the nations of the earth, and there shall be a people that you can visit, even mine Authority on earth, who will show thee of the righteous ways of the Eternal God who created you and upholds you as a nation in your place.

25. Thus, heed my word that I send to you, as it were a final warning, lest these greater judgments come upon the earth, when I, the Lord, have offered you repentance and a cleansing, of peace, changing your wicked laws so they do not uphold these evil practices I have named, saith the Lord Jesus Christ.

26. Let there be the nations heed my warning I have previously sent, even to the leaders of all nations of the earth.

27. Heed my word, for I can only sustain that peoples who repent of these gross and wicked ways lest they fall, for they cannot stand against a just God who seeth all things, who worketh only holiness

and righteousness, who hath invited all to salvation, through repentance and the living of a godly walk.

28. I am soon to be upon the earth in power, and there shall be a remnant left to know of my glorious appearing.

29. My fire from heaven is the power of your existence and will be a power of cleansing the earth, preparing the earth through a cleansing for a more glorious way of living among all mankind -- all pollutions being done away with, all evil ways cast off, and righteousness rule throughout the nations of the earth of my inspiring;

30. For I am God, and I speak by authority, doing the will of the Father; for I am Jesus Christ, the Son of God, who hath redeemed all mankind by the suffering of the pains of all men.

31. Thus saith the Lord: Repent ye, that I may have my blessings rest upon thee, the nations of the earth.

32. There must needs be a reconciliation among the different factions of religion where peace is among you; for violence because of religion is not of God. It is of the evil powers.

33. Thereby can you discern your own lives.

34. Let these wars cease.

35. Let there be peace, if you would do the will of God who is above all.

36. My eternal ways are soon to be revealed on earth in the Zion of the New Jerusalem, built upon the American continent in the place I have designated.

37. And my glorious appearing shall come forth as New Jerusalem is built.

38. I must clean off the land of Zion of wickedness completely, and judgments shall roll forth until only those who can endure my Zion and my Celestial power shall remain, and those who can be converted thereto.

39. Thus saith the Lord: My time is at hand, and you must heed my word or meet the result of your wickedness, which will be the judgments of God removing the more wicked from the nations of the earth, preserving the more righteous who will heed my word.

40. Have compassion upon the poor in your own lands.

41. Let your laws be such that you will provide for the poor.

42. I shall throw down the strongholds of nations, even their economic power, who will not heed these warnings because of your pleasure in wickedness.

43. There cannot be these practices I have named continued for you to continue as a nation.

44. And thus, my judgment shall be upon the earth until all peoples are humbled unto a righteous living, a pure governing principle of justice and equity, and a more noble walk of peace.

45. And I shall prosper thee as a nation, and thy peoples in thy lands, if you will heed my words of peace.

46. I have with me the recompense of reward as I cometh upon the earth; and the wicked shall fear and tremble and flee;

47. And my Zion shall rise as the ruling power and governing power of the nations of the earth.

48. Heed my word and know that I shall fulfill all things as I have spoken through my servants the Prophets throughout the generations of time, found in sacred and holy records in thy midst.

49. Read the words of Isaiah and know of my coming.

50. Know the testimony of mine apostles is true -- that I shall descend in

the clouds of heaven with power, almighty power, to humble all peoples, to remove wickedness from the earth and promote righteous governing powers that exalt mankind to a greater purity and noble way of life.

51. Now you have heard and read my word, you who have received it.

52. Awake to the responsibility upon you as leaders of nations to fulfill this, my word, saith Jesus Christ, the God over all, lest you be removed out of your place by my almighty power and judgments to come.

53. No one can stay mine hand, for I am above all, and all things exist because of me; and through my power and authority do all things continue to exist for a wise purpose, even laboring for the salvation of souls eternally in the religion of heaven, to be brought forth as a message of peace to your peoples.

54. And when my missionaries and representatives thus enter thy borders, have laws of protection, of freedom of worship, that they can deliver my word and message.

55. Have this in place, that I can send to the surviving nations my word in peace;

56. For the agency of man must be honored, and my Gospel of peace and salvation shall be offered all peoples, that they may choose the God who made them, and follow His word unto their own salvation, even eternally; for I offer eternal life to those who obey eternal and exalting principles and laws.

57. Those laws are greater than the laws of man, for the laws of man only promote an earthly happiness, even righteous laws that are just.

58. My laws are eternal and lead the soul to eternal life in the presence of thy God, even the Creator of the earth and the heavens.

59. Nothing is withheld from me from the Father.

60. He hath sent me, the Savior of the world, to redeem all mankind from the grave, and to stand before Him unto an eternal judgment for deeds done in the flesh, which shall cause the wicked to mourn, not heeding the call of their Lord, having known of the Gospel of salvation of your Lord and Savior.

61. Thus, I send my word to you: Prepare the way for my message of salvation to come and for my glorious appearing being made known to all nations in the power of my might,

62. And all shall know I have come to earth with the hosts of heaven and established a righteous government in Zion to rule over the nations, to be inviting to all peoples unto peace, righteous prosperity, a blessing of other nations, that you may be blessed of me with the gifts of life.

63. Thus I have spoken it; thus shall I fulfill; for I am a God of truth and all things are in mine hands.

64. I have loved all peoples of the earth of all ages of time, and carried them; and when they ripened in iniquity and would not repent, I have swept nations off the earth, that they might repent in the world of departed spirits when my Priesthood teaches them the truth, offering salvation, even hereafter, if they will;

65. Yet, if you are offered my Gospel of salvation in this mortal existence on earth and heed me not, ye shall reap the reward of damnation in eternity, not able to progress unto eternal life.

66. This shall be taught thee, even the consequence of how you treat thy Lord and His Gospel message of salvation by

the messengers of salvation I send to your lands and peoples.

67. I, the Lord, have spoken it.

68. Heed my word, that I can own and bless all who come unto me, your Lord Jesus Christ, the power of governing power over all things.

69. I am a God of love.

70. I have loved all peoples and offered salvation to all peoples of all ages of time.

71. My Priesthood is the governing power in heaven and on earth, notwithstanding the nations do not acknowledge my right to rule.

72. Yet I am making my name known before my glorious appearing by the messages I am sending.

73. I am Son Ahman, the Savior of all mankind.

74. Heed my word. My reward is with me. Amen.

SECTION REVELATION 57

Fundamentalist Church of Jesus Christ of Latter-day Saints
P.O. Box 840459
Hildale, Utah 84784

Thus Saith Son Ahman, Even Jesus Christ, To the Peoples of the Earth:

Revelation of the Lord Jesus Christ
Eldorado, Texas
Friday, April 22, 2011

1. Thus saith the Lord Jesus Christ, the Redeemer of all mankind, the Savior of the world, to all peoples of the earth:

2. I send forth my warning of judgments nigh at hand, and the call to repentance of all peoples of every nation, to be received by the means I send, my word printed to your understanding;

3. For I am the God over all the earth, who reigneth in the heavens.

4. I have all power and right to rule by the will of the Father; for I am the Son who hath redeemed, through the suffering of His own mind and body, spirit and soul, on the cross, all mankind from the grave;

and all shall be raised by me to an eternal judgment in the resurrection.

5. I, the Lord, declare to all peoples, I have sent forth mine words of warning to the leaders of all nations, and I now send forth my word further:

6. Repent ye, for my coming is nigh at hand in the glory of my might.

7. I am a Man of Holiness, eternal in the heavens, the God over all, by the will of the Father.

8. My mission of Zion, in building a New Jerusalem on the continent of North America, shall take place.

9. I have appointed the location. It

is written in the revelations of my will revealed through my servant Joseph Smith.

10. I send forth my word to you in printed nature, accompanied by this, my word.

11. Let it be published to all nations and peoples that thy Lord hath spoken from the heavens and His coming is nigh;

12. And there cannot be the gross crimes of the murder of unborn children, and Sodom, and adultery, and the immoral ways among you, or you shall not survive the day of my judgment if these corruptions continue in your lands.

13. My word has been given to individual nations as well as the nations of the earth in general.

14. I have sent many warnings to the leaders of the United States of America to let my people go and be free to establish my Zion; and if you heed me not, nations shall cease to exist that inhabit my land of Zion, known among the earth and the peoples of the earth as the Americas.

15. I am the Creator over all.

16. You only have place by my power, and I speak from the heavens in a manner of your understanding, that can be translated into your languages, as you will, that all peoples may know I have warned of specific judgments and of my coming if they heed me not;

17. For the more wicked of every land and people and nation and tongue shall be removed from the earth who are guilty of these gross crimes of murder and immoral conduct, that corrupt the way of life and pervert innocence.

18. It shall not stand in the day of my coming.

19. The revelations of my will have been published lo, these many years, given by me during my ministry on earth, saith Jesus Christ, and through the mouths of mine apostles, well kept in holy writ to thine understanding and study, and nothing can stay mine hand.

20. I call upon those of the ability to publish my word to give my word to all peoples wherein it comes into thine hands and they know it has been published.

21. And if they will seek from the right source, from my Church and Kingdom, they can receive those publishings by a proper way, through mine authority of my Priesthood, Church, and Kingdom upon the earth.

22. Let the peoples of the earth know, on your receiving my publishings, that I am sending out warnings, to be justified as a God of Creation to cleanse the earth of wickedness, the more wicked being removed out of every nation, the more righteous preserved who will heed my word.

23. The nations of the earth have corrupted their way before the Lord.

24. My words to mine ancient apostles are being fulfilled.

25. Wars and rumors of wars, earthquakes in divers places, pestilences, hails, and famines are upon the earth to humble all peoples to awaken that in wickedness there is not happiness; but only in your Lord and Savior and His righteousness revealed from heaven can purity of life bring happiness on earth and unto an eternal salvation, which the God over thee can only give.

26. I am Son Ahman, the Beginning and the End, the righteous Judge. I am He who stood with the Father before the earth was made, as a God of Creation.

27. Thus saith the Lord to all peoples of the earth, through the communication abilities I have allowed you to have among you:

28. Receive my word of warning. My judgments shall increase.

29. Read my words of warning in my publishings of recent happening, that the leaders of every nation have received of recent sending, those nations that allow the receiving, through the mailing ability, publishings of my word.

30. Now know that thy God hath spoken from the heavens.

31. And as you see His word verified, you shall know He hath spoken; and when He speaks He fulfills His word.

32. And there cannot be a slowness any longer to prepare; for thus I sent my message of salvation during my ministry and heralded to the nations of the earth, for these many ages of time, the prophecies of my glorious appearing and of the rise of Zion, and the coming of New Jerusalem from the heavens.

33. And my people on earth, my Priesthood, my Church and Kingdom, the Church of Jesus Christ of Latter-day Saints, known among men as the Fundamentalist Church of Jesus Christ of Latter-day Saints, has been in operation, preparing mine elect to receive me in honor, who abide Celestial laws guided by my revealings through Priesthood authority.

34. And though all the world combine, nothing can reach the heavens to overthrow their God who hath created thee.

35. I shall overrule and bring forth New Jerusalem, a Zion of governing power over all the earth.

36. And in my glorious appearing in the clouds of heaven, all people shall know I have come; and the wicked shall tremble and fear, for judgment shall come upon those who seek to destroy my righteous rule.

37. Heed my word, and let all peoples receive my warnings.

38. And let my people be of a free nature to perform their work, given them of me, their Lord and Savior, to benefit all nations and peoples, kindreds and tongues, in the message of salvation I shall send; and also the rule of the Kingdom of heaven coming to earth, a righteous government of Son Ahman in the domain of Ahman, my Father, the God over all.

39. This from Him whose voice shall be heard by the shaking of the earth, by the desolating sickness, by pestilence, hail, and famine if you heed not my word of peace; for in this, my word, I have called upon all nations to make peace, and cease their corruptions and their murderous and adulterous and corrupt and immoral ways of Sodom, which are sins against life.

40. I am the God of righteous and holy works.

41. The evil powers shall be bound, and my righteous reign shall come on earth, and all who remain shall know of my right to rule.

42. And my Zion shall rise and bless all nations, kindreds, tongues, and peoples who thus visit and seek out their God in the Zion of our God, seeking Him through those I send -- my representatives on earth, my Priesthood revealed from the heavens, not of man nor of the ways of man, but of my revealing;

43. For that ancient order revealed in the days of mine apostles must be on earth to be of my Church and Kingdom.

44. The revelations of my will guided them, and the order of my Church is the same.

45. The principles of eternal life shall be delivered thee by messengers of salvation from my Zion, my New

Jerusalem that shall be built in that place I have named.

46. Read my word revealed through the Prophet Joseph Smith, and you shall know of the location of my New Jerusalem.

47. I shall also appear in Old Jerusalem to the knowledge of mine Israel there, in my glory, at a time of they being ready to receive their Lord.

48. First, there shall be the cleansing of the more wicked part of all peoples and nations from off the earth, who continued in these gross immoralities and crimes against life and against innocence, to preserve the more righteous to seek unto their God through my Kingdom upon the earth in New Jerusalem in a time soon to come, for the ways of peace, enlightenment, prosperity, in a more noble and holy walk on earth; while those who are removed from the earth shall go to the world of departed spirits to hear my message of salvation there; for this is recorded in holy writ and is the prison house where the spirits shall be visited by my Priesthood there.

49. And men on earth in Zion shall administer the ordinances in sacred houses to both the living and those in the world of departed spirits.

50. My message of salvation shall be heard by all, for I am a just God;

51. And thus my Zion shall rise and fill the earth with a righteous government, a heavenly power among man, promoting happiness in this life and in the life to come.

52. This is my revealing at this time. Heed my word of warning. Prepare for my coming.

53. Heed my word concerning the sea heaving beyond its bounds in many places.

54. Let nations heed my word, for I have addressed them individually in language you can understand.

55. Let the nation of the United States of America know that if she heed me not, her power shall be clipped. And when the nations witness greater judgments on thy land, all nations shall know my coming is nigh.

56. And I shall preserve the more righteous among all nations as my Zion shall rise, that they may visit my Zion to approach their God and know of His ways, both on earth and in eternity;

57. For I am the Eternal God, the Creator of worlds who rules in the heavens, who has sent His message of salvation through the ages of time, and sent messengers of salvation since the days I revealed and restored my Gospel of salvation through my servant Joseph Smith.

58. Now you know my word. Ye shall be held accountable before thy God, having been warned by these several publishings, now in the hands of the leaders of nations, of my glorious appearing and of my warning to cleanse your laws and your lands and your peoples of these immoral and corrupt ways.

59. Your murder of unborn children is a stench before the heavens in every land, resulting from the sins of Sodom and adultery and immoral desires.

60. Babylon the great shall fall, as I have prophesied through my servant John the Beloved; and Zion shall rise, a Holy City and a governing power over all the nations of the earth.

61. I send this to thy knowing beforehand that I may be justified in cleansing all thy lands of these gross sins that must cease; for this is the command of the God of Creation over you, even Jesus

Christ, who is Jehovah Christ, the Great I AM, the God of Israel and over all peoples of the earth, who shall gather Israel as the chosen people to administer righteous laws and eternal blessings for eternal salvation unto the peoples of all nations who will receive the same.

62. And my Prophets shall be honored of all ages in the fulfilling of my words through them, no longer to be derided or mocked, lest judgments come upon you, the nations and peoples of the earth.

63. I have called upon, saith the Lord, elders from among my people to give their names as witnesses of my word being sent to you, with the testimony of my Holy Spirit in their souls.

64. Know that there shall be a day of deliverance for mine elect who come unto their Lord and Savior to live the principles of salvation in abiding Celestial and heavenly laws.

65. And this is my warning and mine invitation to all peoples -- to prepare for my glorious appearing and for my righteous government to reign upon the earth over all peoples and nations.

66. Establish righteous laws among thy peoples.

67. Do as I have commanded and draw thy militaries into thine own borders, and promote peace among all nations.

68. Correct thy laws. Remove these evils I have warned thee about in this communicating, lest a great cleansing come in thy land, each nation of the earth, and leaders of nations be removed by powers greater than the earth, from the God of heaven, whose power is as the going forth of the mighty waters and the sounding of rejoicing from the heavens in the ears of all living at the time of His glorious appearing, to the lifting up of mine elect

into the cloud of glory, to descend with me, with the resurrected saints, to rule on earth a thousand years, Millennium of Peace, administering salvation to all nations, the words of my Prophets honored and fulfilled, mine own words through them.

69. Prepare ye! Prepare ye! O ye peoples of the earth; and receive my message and these, my warnings in my publishings.

70. Let all peoples know how they can obtain these truths.

71. Let this general warning be given through the communication abilities to all peoples of the earth; and on thy receiving my publishings, you of communicating abilities do not change my word, but let it stand as I have sent, for you to be innocent before me in the day of judgment in receiving my warning; for they that are warned are to warn others until all peoples have received the message of thy God's appearing soon at hand -- first, with judgments to remove the more wicked from the earth, and then my glorious appearing, bringing the message of salvation to the more righteous who will honor my word;

72. For the wicked in this day heed me not, though my published word be among you lo, these many years, mine own word in Doctrine and Covenants, revealed through Joseph Smith, my servant; and mine own word in New Testament through mine apostles; yet you heed me not, but continue in these corrupt and fallen and perverse ways.

73. And I, the God of Creation, have promised a day of deliverance for my saints, and those who can be my saints, unto the salvation of nations, of all ages of time;

74. For I am a God of eternal salvation, able to administer the blessings of life

eternal to the peoples of all ages on earth, in the world of departed spirits, and to prepare the way for spirits yet to be born on earth, to receive salvation in a day of peace, when corruptions are removed from the earth, that cause the soul to have no hope into eternity -- those corrupt ways that now are among all nations.

75. Man of Holiness is my name; righteous and pure are my ways; eternal is my power, saith Jesus Christ, whom all shall know hath appeared in His glory.

76. And the wicked shall tremble and stand afar off, and my Zion shall rise.

77. This is being given thee at this time to thy knowing that I am soon and shall be justified to do a work of the cleansing of the wicked off the earth, and the preserving of the more righteous for a day of glory of the God of Creation over thee coming among thee, and ruling in a reign of righteous and pure governing power.

78. I, the Lord, have spoken it.

79. Repent ye, repent ye, of these gross crimes, and begin to study my published word, both of recent giving and that through my servant Joseph Smith and mine other apostles and Prophets, my Priesthood which has continued on the earth and continues this day, as I give my word to the nations of the earth through him whom I have appointed to deliver my word to thee;

80. And you shall know this is my word well-spoken as you see my judgments roll forth, justified upon those who heed me not, having been warned to repent of these evils.

81. In the manner of communicating, leaders of nations know I have sent my word.

82. And they were called upon by me, in receiving of my words, to declare my word to the peoples in their nations and lands; yet many heed me not.

83. My word shall go forth and has gone forth, and I, the Lord, shall be justified and hold responsible those of communicating ability and the leaders of nations in a day of judgment for the warning of their peoples and the cleansing of their peoples before my glorious appearing, cleansing their peoples of these gross crimes, immoral conduct, the destruction of innocence of which unborn children are -- who have the right to live, being sent from heaven to earth to earn the approval of their God by choosing good and casting off evil, using their agency to choose my message of salvation, if they will.

84. And who art thou, leaders of nations, peoples of the earth, to decide what spirit shall dwell on earth and who shall not? Art thou God?

85. Thus is thine aspiring in allowing the murder of unborn children; and I rebuke thee openly for your corrupt ways and fear thee not, saith the God of Creation over you.

86. Cease this evil practice, lest my judgments come upon thee; for as you allow, through legal proceedings, these corrupt ways in thy lands, all thy doings become corrupt before me.

87. I am a God of truth, and when I thus speak, I shall fulfill my word.

88. And my word shall cut you to the heart in a day of judgment to come, when you realize the God of Creation hath spoken and warned thee to cease these evil practices among your nations and peoples;

89. Yet, with healing in my wings, in the power of my might, I bring the message of salvation to the more righteous who will heed my word and be preservers

of life and promoters of innocence and purity among their peoples; who will give place and rights of protection for women and children; who will take care of the poor and the needy; who will promote righteous governing powers of justice and equity and happiness on earth; who will allow freedom of worship in their lands, that my message of salvation may come among you.

90. Thus shall it be, the cleansing power so complete that every nation shall be humbled to desire counsel from thy God to preserve their lives and promote the message of salvation I shall send to come among your peoples in a day soon to happen, which must needs happen;

91. For I am a God of glory and of truth and of righteousness, and I will cause my message of salvation to be given to all peoples, this being the equity among all, both the living and among the departed spirits where my Priesthood is laboring, which world of the departed spirits I visited after I was crucified on the cross and before my resurrection, to organize my Priesthood there, to administer salvation and deliver the message that men on earth would one day be prepared in a New Jerusalem, the Zion of our God being raised up to administer eternal blessings to them by proxy, through Priesthood authority.

92. Zion shall rise and perform this work of salvation for the living and the departed spirits.

93. I am a God of equity and justice, and my message shall reach all peoples.

94. Nothing can stay mine hand.

95. And I reveal these eternal purposes, by mine own word given thee, to the nations of the earth, that you may be prepared to assist thine own peoples to receive my words of salvation, which must be given and shall be given, notwithstanding the opposition that has risen against my Church and Kingdom these many ages of time on the earth.

96. I was God before the earth was made and cause the peopling of this earth, and have upheld every nation in their place and time, and removed nations of corrupt ways and followings, and caused the rising of other nations who arose in power until they became corrupt and had to be removed from the earth because of these terrible crimes that I have named are among all the nations of the earth at this time that now must be removed.

97. And even as I destroyed Sodom and Gomorrah and great nations who promoted these corrupt ways, removing them from the earth through judgments coming upon them, so shall whirlwind judgments come upon the earth suddenly, judgments I have already prophesied through the mouths of my servants the Prophets.

98. And thus you have been warned these many hundreds of years, and I am justified as the God of Creation, a God of righteousness and truth, to send forth my cleansing powers upon thee, the nations of the earth -- all nations, kindreds, tongues, and peoples having my word sent to them, even of recent happening to the leaders of nations.

99. I now send forth this, my word of warning, authorizing this, my immediate word, to be published to all nations, kindreds, tongues, and peoples, that is addressed through thy communication ability and organization, and mine other words in published works to come into thine hands in this mailing, to tell all the peoples of thy lands how they can thus obtain my word in a pure giving, without alteration by the hands of wicked designing men and women on earth.

100. And if they desire the pure giving,

they can send forth the inquiries contained herein, which I command thee to publish, saith the Lord, for thine own good and the salvation of souls.

101. And if you heed me not, I shall hold you responsible in a day of judgment, having the power to do good to thy peoples and would not heed the God of glory who reigns over all the earth, when you had the power to bless them in the nation in which you reside.

102. You have promoted wickedness in your publishings, many of you in your organizations.

103. Some are innocent, having pure hearts and desires to promote life and protect innocence in thy lands.

104. I, the Lord, shall preserve the more righteous, as I have named, if they heed my word.

105. Now heed my word, that I can bless you to remain as a nation, addressing this message to each nation of the earth.

106. And receive my publishings, mine own word from the heavens of recent giving, well-warned; for as mine apostles saw in vision my coming in the clouds of glory, so shall it take place in a day soon to happen.

107. Let my people go, in that nation of the United States of America, to be free to dwell on their lands and live Celestial laws.

108. Study my policies of governing power in my publishings, to be well prepared to change your laws to comply with my governing power that shall come to earth from heaven;

109. And know I have spoken these things, these eternal truths, to promote happiness and righteous governmental reign in every land upon the earth, for every peoples of every color and nationality of my revealing.

110. Mine Israel shall be gathered to my Zion and to Old Jerusalem and be trained in Celestial principles of governing power, that a righteous rule, under your Lord Jesus Christ, who speaketh to you through these words, shall be given among you, the peoples of the earth.

111. I am the Authority and the Power by which the earth was made and continues to exist, and the Giver of all good and the blessings of life.

112. The evil powers shall be subdued; my righteous reign shall come forth, and nothing shall stay mine hand, is the declaration of thy God to the nations of the earth.

113. Thus saith Jesus Christ, Jehovah Christ, the Great I AM, the Beginning and the End, the eternal Judge, whose name is Endless, Eternal, Righteous; who hath all power to fulfill His word; whose power shall go before Him in judgments to cleanse the earth of wickedness before His glorious coming, preserving the more righteous for the message of salvation and the power of eternal life to be administered to the pure in heart who will receive my message of eternal life.

114. This is my eternal purpose, to bring salvation to the souls of all men who will receive my message.

115. Apply my word in obedience to eternal laws that exalt.

116. I, the Lord, have spoken it. Amen.

Word of the Lord to the Nations of the Earth -- Another Great and Final Warning and Call to Repentance

Thus Saith Son Ahman, Even Jesus Christ, to the Peoples of the Earth of All Nations:

(Comprising Section Revelations 58-59)

SECTION REVELATION 58

Revelation of the Lord Jesus Christ
Eldorado, Texas
Sunday, April 24, 2011

1. I, your Lord and Savior, Jesus Christ, who reigneth on high, was born into the flesh and suffered the pains of all men, raised by the power of the resurrection, being the Resurrection of the life, speaketh.

2. Let all nations hear; let all peoples know I have spoken.

3. Receive ye my word, even Son Ahman who saith:

4. Distress of nations is at hand -- war, famine, and earthquake, pestilence, hail, the overflowing scourge and desolating sickness.

5. I have proclaimed peace to all nations through my Gospel of peace, and you heed me not, but continue on in your war-making and your immoral and murderous and corrupt ways.

6. Heed my word and make peace among nations, lest I withdraw my protection from many lands and the great war commence, to overflow many nations, to throw down some nations that they exist no more.

7. Thus saith the Lord: The United States of America shall be left without a responsible head -- I, the Lord, allowing the government powers to be disrupted in a manner that they will not be able to fulfill any governmental duties.

8. And it shall be such a distress that the people of this nation will arise and try to join in groups for self-protection, mob rule reign in many places, trade stop.

9. There shall be sickness, even that sickness that shall pollute the air and the soil and destroy many souls, because you heed me not and would continue in your murderous and immoral ways to the destruction of your soul and the destruction of innocence, of spirits unborn yet to come to earth, and the destruction of innocence on earth;

10. Thus do your ways of living perform the corruption of souls, where my Spirit withdraws and the devil hath taken power.

11. And thus saith the Lord: The powers of darkness shall overshadow many unto the wailing of everlasting regret, even on earth, for their lost and fallen condition of corrupt and evil ways; for the wicked shall not always find happiness in unrighteous

ways, but shall mourn and some curse God and die.

12. Thus shall be the condition before my glorious coming, because you heed me not and would not prepare for my coming; for my coming shall bring forth the blessings of heaven to earth and raise up a generation on earth of a more righteous nature, who will not condone the corrupt ways of this present generation, but shall heed my word of a peaceable and moral walk.

13. Thus saith your God: Heed my word while it is yet today, for soon all this distress shall be upon thee because of the wickedness of this generation -- all nations denying their God, corrupting their way before the Lord, causing Him to send forth judgments to remove the more wicked out of every nation, kindred, tongue, and people; until all shall know that what I, your Lord, speak, it shall be fulfilled.

14. I send this to you who govern the nations, withholding not my word from going forth, for my time is at hand, and there cannot be wickedness continue on my land of Zion in a manner of unrestrained corruption that is spreading throughout thy nations who dwell on the lands of America, my lands of Zion where a righteous generation shall be raised up by me, even Israel to be gathered from every nation under heaven.

15. Thus saith the Lord: I have spoken. Heed my word.

16. Make peace among nations.

17. Remove these great corruptions of murder of unborn children, Sodom, adultery, and immorality, sanctioned in most nations by law, being led by the powers of darkness throughout the earth.

18. Great Babylon is falling.

19. Your economic powers shall fail thee.

20. Trade shall cease for a time.

21. Earthquake, pestilence, hail, and famine I have declared among those peoples who will not turn from these most wicked ways, corrupting their ways before the Lord in a manner of no redemption for many souls, holding the leaders of nations responsible in eternal judgment for their conduct among nations; seeking riches and gain and influence of power, rather than follow just and correct laws, pure and righteous governing power.

22. Thus I shall bring to earth a heavenly government, the angels attending mine elect of my Priesthood and Church and Kingdom upon the earth, to guide in the government of the Kingdom of God through a Council of Fifty, with representatives sent to every nation, and every nation able to visit my Zion -- those who remain through the great cleansing process I shall send.

23. My prophecies are extant and known among this generation in holy writ.

24. My word is sure and shall be fulfilled.

25. O ye people of the earth, hear the word of the God who made you, who has given you your agency and placed good and evil before you by allowing you to be born into this mortal existence, a time of testing to see what you will love and follow;

26. Yet, most have rejected the Lord's good, and sought after compromise after compromise with the ways of life, until you have chosen death and destruction, unto your immortal souls coming to an end;

27. For that immortality is of the spirit in its native element, and you, as an organized son or daughter, can only remain into eternity by abiding Celestial and righteous principles, laws of thy

Lord Jesus Christ, who exalteth the more righteous unto eternal lives as they are worthy.

28. Now heed my word.

29. I am merciful and gracious unto those who will repent; and to those who will not, they will have to meet the full measure of justice, even in the eternal judgment.

30. This I give to you, the peoples of the earth again, as it were, another final warning, justifying your Lord to send forth greater humbling powers upon thee, even all peoples of all nations, beginning at my house, even among the people who profess my name, of my Church and Kingdom upon the earth, who continue to compromise with this wicked generation in partaking of the spirit of darkness.

31. Thus saith the Lord: Who shall carry thee in the day of greater trial, O ye peoples of the earth?

32. Who shall preserve thy peoples and nations when I, the God of justice, administer righteous judgment?

33. Thus saith the Lord: Cease your evil practices, lest my judgments come upon you suddenly, and leave you neither root nor branch upon the earth, as individuals and families and nations.

34. I created the earth and have peopled the earth, and I alone have the right to promote life and send forth spirits to earth.

35. I take in death whom I will, to lead them to life, if they will accept my Gospel of salvation in the world of departed spirits, not heeding my word in this mortal existence.

36. I am the God of Creation who speaketh.

37. Though all the world deride and oppose, when I speak, I shall fulfill, and all shall know thy Lord and Redeemer hath

done right in the day of judgment, when your lives are revealed to you and nothing is hidden;

38. For I shall reveal all secrets of all nations in every age of the earth unto my people in Zion and to those nations who will come unto Zion to learn of eternal and righteous and holy ways of governing power, and pure abiding principles of happiness.

39. Those who receive my message of salvation, by baptism and the ordinances of my Priesthood, can earn eternal happiness through the mediation and atonement of your Lord and Master, Jesus Christ, who speaketh at this time to thee, sending this word of my warning again to your understanding.

40. Heed my word, for the work of darkness shall come to an end, and satan shall be bound, and my righteous reign shall come forth, and nothing can stop that which I have ordained.

41. Though you seem to hinder my work at this time by putting my servant and servants in bondage, and distressing my people; and though government powers follow the lies of apostate influence -- those who once upheld my word as sacred, and partook of wickedness and fell away because of their own sins -- verily I say, I shall preserve my righteous, though some may be taken as witnesses on earth and in heaven, of my doing.

42. I, the Lord, shall send the angels of preservation to the more righteous, and I shall sweep the more wicked off the land of every nation who continue to promote these gross crimes and evils I have named.

43. I give this to your understanding -- not with a single warning alone, but I have sent many now to the leaders of nations.

44. Those who heed my word and

repent, that nation shall remain, at least in part, of the more righteous among them.

45. That nation which opposes my Priesthood and fights against my Church and Kingdom shall come to naught; shall be as a garment in a fire, as my fire from heaven, like unto Sodom and Gomorrah, shall be consumed.

46. And verily, every wicked nation throughout the history of this earth that has fallen because of these gross crimes of wickedness that now exist in most nations of the earth, so shall it be to the nations of the earth today.

47. Now heed my word.

48. Leaders of nations shall fall. Armies shall clash because they heed me not.

49. I have warned thee, the nation of the United States of America, to cleanse the inside of the platter.

50. Correct your own laws which allow the murder of unborn children, gross immorality; and cease these evil practices; and free my people to establish my Zion, and I shall favor thee.

51. And if thou heed me not, you shall not be a nation much longer -- only among mine elect who survive the whirlwind judgments I send, upholding righteous principles inspired of their God who made them, even your Lord and Savior, Jesus Christ, these words being His, sent to the nations of the earth.

52. Los Angeles shall sink in the earth, the time that the earth reels to and fro.

53. Albany, New York shall burn with fire from heaven.

54. I have declared the destruction of other wicked cities who will not receive my message of truth and heed my word.

55. Distress among nations shall increase, and as a whirlwind, great judgments will sweep millions of people off the face of the earth who are the more wicked, who continue in these gross crimes that I have named.

56. Oh, that you would heed my word! for I am a God of salvation; yet I can only bring that happiness, through righteous living, into your souls.

57. And if you promote these great evils on earth, you shall have to suffer the justice of a God who is just and true in all things.

58. Justice must be satisfied that mercy may take hold.

59. And those who apply my atoning love and sacrifice to their lives through repentance can reap benefit, but I have satisfied justice to a great measure, according to their deeds, for some have committed gross crimes of the shedding of innocent blood, which they must mediate themselves in an eternal judgment, having lost the love of life, and the loss of natural affection being among many peoples of the earth, hardened by gross immorality and crime.

60. All people shall know that a righteous and holy God shall come in the power of His might, recompense to every man that which he has measured to his fellow man.

61. This is my heed unto my Father, Elohim, for I am Jehovah Christ, Son Ahman, who speaketh; as I heed my Father's word to cleanse the earth of wickedness and cause Zion, a City of Righteousness, to rise; my Priesthood sent to earth, among men now, being prepared by abiding Celestial and heavenly laws.

62. This to thy knowing, O ye people of the earth, that my Zion is rising in the minds and hearts of a few whom I shall preserve through the great holocaust and

whirlwind judgments yet coming upon the earth.

63. Hasten to prepare, for you individually will have to answer to thy God who made thee, for thy conduct in this earthly, probationary existence.

64. This I reveal to thee, for the wicked shall tremble at my coming, and nothing can stay mine hand; while the righteous of every nation shall come to Zion and learn of happy ways of earth and of heaven, of the beautifying of their lives, their habitations, their laws and governments, to willingly be subject to the government of Zion, an eternal government revealed from heaven that shall rule the earth for a Millennium.

65. Rio de Janeiro, repent ye! for you are nigh unto destruction.

66. Colombia, as a nation, is corrupt with violence within.

67. Many shall lose their lives if they repent not of their gross crimes, many having murder in their hearts, of violence one against another.

68. I have warned many nations.

69. My word is to all nations.

70. Heed my word, lest thou fall and be a nation no more, in a time soon to happen, when the God of Creation stretches forth His hand and sweeps the more wicked off the earth, preserving the more righteous who can receive my message of salvation unto their eternal joy, who receive my word and obey my word.

71. The secret combinations among nations shall be revealed to all peoples, and nothing shall be hidden, O you who work in darkness, and you shall tremble at the revealing of thy works upon the housetops.

72. The power of my righteous government shall come to earth, and

nothing shall stay mine hand, as I rebuke wicked nations afar off and humble them to know wickedness cannot continue among them.

73. I am the God of life and light and truth, of mercy and justice, of righteous judgment.

74. I have spoken, and I hold not back, fearing no man; for as I have spoken, so shall I fulfill, saith the God of glory, the God of Abraham, Isaac, and Jacob, the God of Noah and Enoch and Adam, the God over all the earth today, guiding my servant and my servants in my Church and Kingdom to promote righteousness, Celestial laws of heavenly giving, to continue in that mission, notwithstanding the pressures of persecution and prosecution.

75. Thus my word is spoken, by authority that I have appointed on earth to receive and give my word to the peoples of the earth, now to thy knowing, through him who is in bondage at this time; yet my word is going forth; and thus saith the Lord, I shall fulfill my word.

76. Repent ye! Repent ye! is the word of the God who made you, to the peoples all over the earth, lest sudden judgments and destruction come upon you and leave you neither root nor branch of posterity on the earth, among many nations and families of the earth.

77. I must stop the horrible, murderous ways in many nations -- slaughtering innocence, abusing and adulterating innocence.

78. The God of glory cometh, and all people shall know and fear and tremble who would not heed His word.

79. Let those government officials who are fighting against my Priesthood, Church, and Kingdom beware, lest the justice of a righteous God come upon you

in ways you have not expected; for it shall come upon you in a manner, knowing that the God of heaven hath done a work to humble thee, not by man nor the ways of men; for I have given thee life, even the breath of life.

80. Fight not against my Priesthood, Church, and Kingdom upon the earth, lest righteous judgment come upon you suddenly, to thy knowing that a heavy hand of thy God hath been laid upon thee.

81. Let the honest in heart everywhere resound: We are for life and for truth and justice!

82. Let the honest in heart everywhere open their hearts unto the God of heaven to receive the glad message of salvation as I send my messengers in a soon time to happen, as Zion rises and New Jerusalem is built at the appointed place.

83. Heed my word. Thus saith Jesus Christ. Amen.

SECTION REVELATION 59

Revelation of the Lord Jesus Christ
Eldorado, Texas
Monday, April 25, 2011

1. Thus saith the Lord Jesus Christ, your Lord and Redeemer over all; who, by the shedding of His own blood by wicked men, brought forth the redemption of all mankind from the grave and to stand before Him, of the Father, to be judged for works and deeds and desires done in the flesh:

2. Thus saith Him who reigns on high, judgments shall soon come upon this land, and nothing can stay mine hand; for it is decreed in heaven to cleanse my land of Zion and purify mine elect, even through tribulation, sending forth mine angels, mine heavenly powers upon them, preserving them for the fulness of Zion;

3. And thus the rise of New Jerusalem is at hand in the minds and hearts of those who stay constant unto their God and will not turn from Him for anything, but are converted unto a continual increase of my holy light always abiding in them, through the prayer of faith extant, always exercising

my holy love extant, which guides and rules and beautifies all pertaining to Zion and to all creation.

4. You see the order, even in what mankind calls nature -- an intelligent God guiding all creation -- that all things work together in the form of life increasing and continuing, giving life to the seeds, to the animal life, to the microbes that can purify, and even sending forth a destroyer to purge out ungodliness from among the people until my Holy Spirit takes hold and purifies and gives life again.

5. Thus is the will of the Lord to be understood:

6. That city called Austin shall be covered by a great mountain, having become a capital city of opposition against my Zion.

7. This is a promise of the Lord, for they heed me not.

8. Even those who dwell therein have my message given of warning to let my people go.

9. I shall cause a scourging to come upon this state where my Land of Holiness is located on the earth, where my house is built.

10. People shall feel the chastening hand of a just God, for they have agreed with lawmakers against my Priesthood and my Zion rising -- lawmakers who have heard lies and given way to the influence of apostates, who were darkened by their own craftiness and corrupt ways, desiring only darkness rather than light; who declare ungodly talk against Celestial and pure ways of living of my Priesthood.

11. Thus saith the Lord: It shall not stand, though mine elect shall be tried.

12. Though all people shall know of their labors in the cause of Zion, there shall be a cleansing of all until only purity abides on my Land of Holiness and among mine elect in every stake of Zion where my people are taught the Order of Enoch, the United Order covenant by ordinance, well received in a pure way, through Priesthood, of my revealing.

13. I am the Author of these eternal ways, saith your Lord and Master, Jesus Christ, who is Jehovah Christ, the God over all creation.

14. Thus shall the states of Utah and Arizona also be humbled, capital cities left desolate in a time of great judgment; and they shall know that I, the Lord, have spoken, that those who fight against my Priesthood and the rise of Zion shall come to naught.

15. Their habitations shall be empty and left desolate.

16. And my people shall be humbled to know that when their God speaketh, they obey, if they desire the continued blessings of righteousness in their lives.

17. There shall be witnesses on earth who thus hear this, my word, who remain and go forward unto New Jerusalem being built, and bear witness to future generations that those who opposed my Zion's rise came to naught, and their habitations were left desolate.

18. Thus are the prophecies of Isaiah, that all the world can study, and know that I, the Lord, dictated to him mine own word to nation of Israel of ancient time, yet talking of gentile nations of future time, which now are upon the earth;

19. And mine Israel is scattered by them, my Priesthood even now being persecuted by gentile powers; the gentile nations not being of my Priesthood in their nature and desire, nor their organization, but being of the traditions of men for selfish will to be fulfilled, seeking power and authority not of their God.

20. Thus saith the Lord: My righteous rule shall come to earth soon.

21. Celestial powers of governing authority shall descend to earth, mine angels with me; mine elect on earth used as vessels of honor to assist in the governing of the nations that survive the whirlwind judgments I shall send.

22. And thus I reveal to all peoples that I, the Lord your God, have spoken from the heavens; so shall I fulfill.

23. This wicked generation, perverse and corrupt in the spirit of murder, even the murder of innocence in most nations of the earth -- the taking of life of the unborn, hindering the progress of the work of God in giving spirits the opportunity to come to a probationary earth to prove themselves in a mortal body, whether they will serve the God of Creation --

24. Thus saith the Lord: I must cleanse all peoples of this ungodly way, lest there be none left on earth at my glorious appearing.

25. And I shall preserve the more righteous who set aside these wicked ways now engendered as tradition among all nations in their daily practices and conduct of immoral ways, which is the motive of this murderous disposition among the nations.

26. The more pure way of life shall be required through righteous laws in every land as the government of the Kingdom of heaven comes forth on earth to rule in righteousness of thy Lord Jesus who reigneth.

27. Thus saith Him who reigneth: Repent ye, all ye nations of the earth, and hasten to prepare, for the time of my coming is at hand, and there cannot be the opposition to my Zion and you remain as a nation.

28. Thus shall it be to your knowing of soon events of greater power being shown forth -- of earthquake and tornado, storms of great capacity paralyzing the population in their doings at times; pestilences, the overflowing scourge and desolating sickness, hail and famine.

29. Thus saith the Lord: You only exist, ye peoples of the earth, by my grace and power, allowing you the gifts of life and any degree of peace in thy borders and in thine hearts.

30. It is my Holy Spirit sent forth from the Father to all creation that brings order, even to what you call nature around you;

31. And when that Holy Spirit withdraws from an individual or a people, darkness reigns, violence easily ensues, and thereafter comes sadness and woe.

32. There are, in some nations, government powers murdering their own peoples secretly, to retain their government power.

33. Thus saith the Lord: I shall bring justice on all those leaders who perform these secret combinations of murder, until it is removed from the earth, this gross wickedness of the shedding of blood to get gain; which corrupts most nations of the earth, where they are determined to render violence rather than promote peace -- many who have power on the earth in their several nations as leaders.

34. I, the Lord, have created man for a purpose of salvation, an eternal salvation; for I am a God eternal, and you are my sons and daughters on earth, sent to prove your worth where good and evil are present, and to choose the good; for I send my Spirit as a light into your minds to know right, choose the right -- that which promotes life and peace and well-doing toward your fellow man; kindness -- that which is of a noble nature; for as you bless others, so I, the Lord, shall bless you as an individual, as families, and as nations.

35. Those nations that promote war shall meet a destruction great, of the Lord's sending, to cease violence in the earth.

36. Those peoples that promote peace, many shall remain to assist other nations in need in the time of great whirlwind judgments, which shall suddenly appear, not having to be of long duration because of the power of my might of cleansing the earth of ungodly ways.

37. Heed my word, O ye nations of the earth, and receive this word also, well-prepared, to your understanding in language and wording that you can comprehend;

38. For the God of heaven hath spoken by His authority on earth, whom He hath ordained by His own power to deliver His word to all peoples.

39. Now heed my word.

40. That ancient land of Mesopotamia

and those nations thereon must needs repent who now inhabit that area.

41. That ancient land of Greece, those lands to the north, wherein there is violence in their nature one against another -- yea, some over religious differences -- shall be a place of great warmongering, erupting the nations round about into unrest.

42. There must needs be a peace conference for these lands, of Bosnia and the neighboring lands, of a soon nature.

43. Do away with violence, or many other nations shall be involved in a great war.

44. I, the Lord, reveal this.

45. There must not be the promotion of war of nations by any nation, for I am a God of peace.

46. And though I have almighty power and carry you day by day, and allow my sun, the light of heaven, to shine on the righteous and the wicked, give them time to prove their worth, what they will choose in this life of testing, I am a just God and shall repay all peoples according as their works are.

47. Therefore, knowing I have called for peace, if the nations promote war, they shall receive as they desire, until they are humbled and the more wicked population in every land be removed, both by war and famine and earthquake, hail and pestilence, the sea heaving beyond its bounds, which I have warned thee shall happen in many lands, and told thee, that you may be prepared and not have large population along the sea coasts;

48. Yet you heed me not, loving the philosophies of fallen man in their ignorance and darkness, who only express unbelief when thy God speaketh; and government powers turn to learned men of no faith in God, but only faith in the ways

of man, a blindness of life that corrupts the soul; listens to the dark powers of that evil one that has led mankind into gross sensuality and murder and secret combinations throughout the ages of time.

49. And as I, the Lord, would see this would not be repented of in any nation, I have brought that nation to an end and raised up another in its stead.

50. Thus shall I do in this day, especially on my land of Zion where New Jerusalem shall rise; for my word has been spoken throughout the ages of time through my Prophets, and every word shall be fulfilled.

51. Thus I, your Lord Jesus Christ, send forth my word to the nations again:

52. Awake! My time is at hand.

53. In my loving kindness, I am sending forth my invitation of peace to all nations.

54. You only exist by my power and grace, and if you continue in your violent natures and corrupt ways, I must needs remove those from power in every nation; and the more corrupt among your peoples who promote the ways of corrupt secret combinations, the ways of murder and immorality that destroy innocence.

55. Let there be a promotion of virtue among your peoples, even in your laws and your government powers.

56. Let there be practices promoted among thy youth to retain their virtue.

57. And prepare all nations, saith the Lord, ye government officials of every land and nation, for freedom of worship, to allow my message of salvation to be sent forth from Zion as Zion rises in full power.

58. My Zion shall be built by the powers of heaven attending mine elect; this to thy knowing, even beforehand; for thus it is in holy writ -- the powers of

heaven descending with the resurrected saints to rule on earth a thousand years among men.

59. Thy Lord and Savior, whose words these are, speaking to your understanding, He shall rule in righteous governing power, a heavenly government.

60. He who knoweth and seeth all things shall judge all, and all shall know He hath done right, even your Lord and Master over all.

61. Thus every knee shall bow, and every tongue shall confess that Jesus is the Christ, whose right it is to rule, from the Father, the God over all Creation.

62. I do the Father's will.

63. In me is life and the light of all peoples.

64. Heed my word, ye leaders of nations and ye peoples of the earth.

65. Let this, my word, go forth, that all may hear;

66. And he who receives this, my word, give it to another, to know that my glorious appearing is nigh at hand.

67. My Zion shall rise, and the more wicked of every nation shall be swept off the earth by the eternal powers of God coming forth in judgments, which no man can resist, for it shall be of God, who is just, whose word is true.

68. I am the God of peace. Make peace among yourselves, in your nations and between nations in your relationship.

69. Do as I have spoken in my warnings I have sent forth of recent doing.

70. Heed my words, saith your God, who created you, and who can promote the happiness of all peoples through the blessings of life as you promote peace, and just and equitous laws.

71. Violence against minorities must cease.

72. Promotion of terrorism among nations must cease.

73. Using your militaries against your own peoples must cease, where you promote violence to retain power.

74. Thus saith the Lord: My word shall go forth, and when I speak through righteous governing powers as Zion rises, you shall heed my word or be humbled by an almighty power, until you know that the God of righteous and endless ways of eternal life hath spoken;

75. And you are subject to a greater power than that of the voice of man -- even the God of Creation, who shall come to earth soon, to the knowing of all peoples, and rule in a righteous domain in the name of the Father, the God over all earth, and the God over worlds, to perform a labor of salvation.

76. You know not your origin before your birth, ye peoples of the earth.

77. I, who knoweth all things, ordained that this earth should be created for you, as sons and daughters of God, to be born on a probationary earth of testing, in a mortal existence where good and evil are present.

78. And I send my Spirit upon you, even at birth, to know good from evil, to grow up in your young years innocent, if there would be a protection around you;

79. Yet most children of the earth are raised in the traditions of men, now corrupt before their Lord, promoting unrighteousness even in their youth.

80. Your amusements and entertainments are corrupt, promoting immorality and murder in every way, even to the youth of all the earth.

81. In many nations adultery is promoted, even by legal consent.

82. The sin of Sodom has become rampant throughout the earth because of the

loss of my Spirit, choosing evil rather than good, having pleasure in unrighteousness.

83. Thus saith the Lord: You shall meet the result of your choice; for I am the Eternal God, and I give you these truths to your understanding at this time, against a day when my judgments shall come; and you shall know that my word is true and my purposes fulfilled in the lives of all men and women.

84. Let there be in those nations that abuse the rights of women greater protection; where in some lands, even under legal authority, husbands abuse, in a brutal manner, their own wives. This must cease.

85. In many lands the youth are abused, both in secret and some openly, in immorality and corrupt ways.

86. Thy schools are against the Lord your God, and many lands do not teach freedom of worship.

87. Their promotion of commerce often, in many lands, is by bribery and usury of an abusive nature.

88. Government powers in many nations are used to get gain and make rich those in power, keeping thy peoples poor and in need.

89. The abuse of thy people by leaders of nations shall be answered upon the heads of leaders of nations at my coming, and beforehand; for before I come in my glory, there shall be sent forth judgments to cleanse the more wicked population of every nation from off the face of the earth, and preserve the more righteous who will uphold the more pure ways of noble and equitous and just living in their lands.

90. My Zion shall rise and teach all nations how to abide in peace, through righteous governing powers inspired of heaven -- all by your agency, choosing the good, seeing that there is no happiness in wickedness in the end of that way of life which does not lead to principles of eternal progression.

91. There shall be a binding of satan, the rise of Zion, and a dwelling on earth of the heavenly powers in a Millennial Reign of Peace, under your Lord Jesus Christ, whose words are herein spoken, my own message to the leaders and peoples of the earth of every nation.

92. Hasten to prepare.

93. Make peace is the call of thy God, who fears thee not.

94. I am the God of power and the God of glory. Righteous and Holy is my name.

95. I shall promote righteousness upon the earth, eternal ways unto eternal happiness for those who receive my Gospel of salvation and abide pure laws that exalt the nature into a more godly way of life.

96. Let the governing powers in the city of Austin cease their attack upon my people.

97. Let those governing powers in Utah and Arizona, and other states in the nation of the United States of America, heed my warning to let my people go, and provide for them the return of their houses and lands, through an unjust court taking those lands and promoting the ways of their enemies to afflict them, even among them.

98. If you heed me not, the judgments I have pronounced herein shall be of full measure upon you, saith the God of Creation.

99. I forgive all men who repent and come unto me and turn from their unrighteous ways, so often promoted by the lies of apostate influence from my Church and Kingdom, those who were once numbered as faithful members; and then, through their own sinning, false

and corrupt ways, turning traitor against the plans of salvation, promoted through my Church and Kingdom -- those plans of eternal life, the Gospel of salvation -- through their sin and influence, unjust laws have been promoted against my Celestial Law, which is religious.

100. This nation of supposed guaranteed religious freedom is using legal and illegal means, as they call it, to promote a prosecution that persecutes mine elect, my Church and Kingdom upon the earth.

101. My Celestial Laws of Plural Marriage and the United Order are of my revealing. They are of God and are in holy writ, restored through the Prophet Joseph Smith by thy God of Creation to promote peace and purity of life, where none can enter therein save those whose names I reveal through my Priesthood authority on earth, and it is not for mankind in general.

102. Therefore, thus saith the Lord: Let my people go!

103. I give this to your understanding that I may be justified in sending my judgments if you heed me not;

104. Yet, if you will heed my word, free my servant and my servants in bondage; let my people go to dwell on their lands in peace to promote my cause of Zion by living the more noble and heavenly laws that I have named.

105. Those who have fallen away from my Priesthood are covenant breakers and liars, and the truth is not in them.

106. They shall be of the greatest condemnation by their God in the day of judgment, knowing the light of truth and turning from truth.

107. Now receive my word, ye leaders of nations:

108. At my glorious appearing you shall fear and tremble at my power; yet I shall send forth messengers of salvation to your knowing they are from thy God, for my power shall attend them, and they shall bring forth the policies and rules of my governing power to be promoted in thy nations;

109. And if you heed me not, and promote wickedness and corrupt ways, I, the God of Creation, having the right over life and death -- because I have made thee and am the power by which you exist -- behold, I say unto you, I shall send humbling judgments until you bow the knee to my righteous rule, and promote peace rather than war and violence among your peoples or against other nations.

110. I am beginning to send forth my right to rule and this, my word.

111. Begin now to be of peace, and more equitous and just ways, and promote the protection of innocence and of life.

112. The city of New Orleans is a most corrupt place, and I sent forth a great judgment upon her; and she shall be swept off the earth by the sea as that iniquity continues, even of legal consent among you.

113. Let those who are honest in heart remove themselves therefrom if they would turn to their God and be of a believing nature.

114. Remember the ancient city of Nineveh, that Jonah was sent to preach repentance and warn them of a coming judgment, for in their borders and in their city they promoted the murder of unborn children, and licentious and immoral ways;

115. And when they received my word, they repented and I spared them for the time that they thus turned to their God, casting off that most wicked way;

116. Thus I, the Lord, have spoken to the nations of the earth:

117. Cast off the murder of unborn children, and your immoral and licentious and wicked ways that promote the murder of unborn children, that I may spare thee a nation at the time of my coming, the more righteous among you able to receive the presence and knowledge of God in His glory, to your understanding and capacity, through my governing powers visiting you; and my messengers of salvation coming to your peoples, and you allowing freedom of worship.

118. The God of glory hath spoken.

119. Heed my word. Amen.

SECTION REVELATION 60

Fundamentalist Church of Jesus Christ of Latter-day Saints
P.O. Box 840459
Hildale, Utah 84784

Thus Saith the Lord, Son Ahman, to the Leaders of the Nation of Mauritania

Revelation of the Lord Jesus Christ
Eldorado, Texas
Sunday, April 24, 2011

1. Thus saith the Lord to the leaders of the nation of Mauritania, even Jesus Christ, the governing power over all the earth and in the heavens, speaking to you, the leaders of that nation:

2. I know of your secret murders and your slaughter of innocence.

3. I know of your corrupt ways, and I shall bring judgment upon you; for I declare it by the mouth of my servant on earth to your understanding, to reveal to you your sins and wickedness of gross crimes, even against thine own peoples, is known by the God of heaven; and you shall find yourselves without power in a time soon to come.

4. Judgment shall come upon thee because of your murderous ways in seeking power and influence and gain. I, the Lord, have declared it.

5. Your crimes have come up before me, and I, the true God of heaven, shall show you I have almighty power and shall overthrow thy rule at a time you continue in these gross crimes.

6. Though I have sent warning to the leaders of all nations, you heed me not; and I hold you responsible for great wickedness in your nation.

7. Thus saith the Lord Jesus Christ, even He who loves the salvation of all men and women who would heed my message of salvation; but when your crimes are of a murderous and corrupt nature, great shall be your condemnation, even in eternity.

8. This I declare to you -- that my

mercy can only reach those who repent and turn from their wickedness, if they have not sinned unto death, in the murder of unborn children or of innocence among your own peoples, which you are guilty of.

9. I give this revealing, for your sins shall be shouted upon the housetops in a time soon to come, and you shall be ashamed before thy God in such a humbling of eternal duration to that soul who is of a murderous nature.

10. I declare this openly, for I am the God of all the earth and will serve justice upon all who do not deal righteously and justly, even with their own peoples, O ye leaders of nations.

11. You exist by my power attending you, with the breath of life and the gifts of life; yet you have promoted corruption and murder among your peoples, even in secrecy, and I shall make these secrets known.

12. Let the rulers of this nation take heed, for surely as I have spoken, so shall I fulfill. Amen.

SECTION REVELATION 61

Fundamentalist Church of Jesus Christ of Latter-day Saints
P.O. Box 840459
Hildale, Utah 84784

Thus Saith Son Ahman, Even Jesus Christ, to the Leaders of the Nation of Turkey

Revelation of the Lord Jesus Christ
Eldorado, Texas
Sunday, April 24, 2011

1. Thus saith the Lord Jesus Christ to the nation of Turkey and the leaders thereof:

2. I, the Lord, have sent you warnings, even Jesus Christ who reigneth on high, and you heed me not; and you continue the injustice toward women and minority religions.

3. Thus saith the Lord: Your power shall soon be clipped. You shall lose possessions of those strategic straits from the Black Sea to the Mediterranean Sea.

4. You shall find yourselves a tributary nation.

5. You shall find yourselves unable to control your population in a time soon to come, because you heed me not.

6. And through your weakness of power, there shall arise other nations willing to clip thy power.

7. Oh, that you would heed my word and deal proper justice, equity, kindness to women and children, and not of a false religious tradition that abuses innocence and oppresses women.

8. Thus saith the Lord: Your traditions cannot save you in a time of greater judgment.

9. Heed my word and correct these evils!

10. Cause that there be no murder of unborn children in thy borders, nor Sodom, nor adultery.

11. Do not apply the traditions of corruption to present philosophy of laws and governing.

12. Heed my word.

13. I have called upon you to be a friend to that nation called Israel, and also to be just and equitous toward your own peoples and minority religions.

14. Cease to destroy the Kurdish people.

15. Promote peace in thine own borders.

16. Let there not be secret combinations in government power to get gain and power.

17. I, the Lord, send you this warning -- that your power shall soon be clipped as a nation, and leaders shall be overthrown.

18. And you shall find yourselves in the midst of war, wanting peace, even in thine own borders;

19. And there shall be other judgments of pestilence and famine come upon thee, because you heed me not, because you remove not those evils I have named to be overthrown among your people.

20. I am the Lord Jesus Christ who speaketh, who shall soon make His presence known among all nations, wherein my Kingdom of Zion shall send forth representatives, and you shall know that I have come in my glory; and all nations shall know when I speak, I fulfill, as the God of glory in heaven and over all the earth.

21. My presence goes where I will, reading the minds and hearts of all men and women, and nothing is hidden from me.

22. And thy sins shall be shouted on the housetops, thy secret acts revealed, you who are leaders of corrupt ways among this nation.

23. Thy corruptions shall be known, and eternal shall be a judgment on those of a murderous disposition.

24. There shall be a great earthquake also humble parts of thy land.

25. Thy God hath spoken.

26. Repent ye of these evils, that I may spare some among your nation, the more righteous, in the day of greater judgments soon at hand, before I appear in my glory to make myself known among all nations.

27. I, the Lord, have spoken it. Heed my word, for my word is sure and true.

28. Let that work of darkness -- of military agreement, wherein you promote the secret evil of murder in secret to maintain government power -- cease among this governing power now in the nation of Turkey.

29. Those of a murderous disposition shall find themselves removed from the earth through the judgments of a just God.

30. If the leaders of this nation uphold those of secret combination of a murderous doing among your own peoples to keep in power, thus saith the Lord, it shall fall, and be shouted on the housetops, and known by all peoples to your eternal shame.

31. I fear thee not, for I am the God over all the earth, who dwells in the heavens and seeth and knoweth all things.

32. Repent ye of these great evils, for I have detected them, and will not uphold thee as a nation of greater power, even in thine own borders, if you continue to pursue these evil acts among ruling power.

33. I am a God of mercy to those who will repent and turn from their wicked ways, who have not sinned unto death in a murderous spirit.

34. Thus saith the Lord who is over all: Heed my word. Amen.

SECTION REVELATION 62

Fundamentalist Church of Jesus Christ of Latter-day Saints
P.O. Box 840459
Hildale, Utah 84784

Thus Saith Son Ahman, Even Jesus Christ, to the Leaders of the Nation of Israel

Revelation of the Lord Jesus Christ
Eldorado, Texas
Tuesday, April 26, 2011

1. Thus saith the Lord to the nation and leadership of Israel, even Jesus Christ, the God of all creation, of heaven and over all nations of the earth, who hath all power, even Jehovah Christ, who reigneth, who doeth the will of the Father, who is guiding the events of nations toward the redemption of Old Israel and Jerusalem, which shall be rebuilt after the war of great destruction comes among you.

2. Thus saith the Lord: Call a peace conference. Cease your murderous intent among nations of secret combination doing.

3. Use your military only for self-defense; and when neighboring nations seek your destruction, I shall allow you to defend yourself to the conquering of nations;

4. Nevertheless, I shall not prosper you if you continue the sin of Sodom in your borders, and the murder of unborn children, and the secret murder among thy peoples, among the Arabian or Moslem people, or among the peoples of the earth by your secret organization.

5. A great war, and famine resulting, shall remove many of your leadership who promote these murderous ways, and the more wicked of your people; yet I shall cause the more righteous to remain and my Judah to be gathered before my glorious appearing, in a manner of receiving my message of salvation.

6. In my scripture, the naming of two witnesses to be in Old Jerusalem shall come forth as a witness to thy people that the God of heaven has His Zion growing on the North American continent, my Church and Kingdom upon the earth, mine Israel there.

7. And there shall be gathered the lost tribes of Israel to that land first;

8. And you who are in power in Old Israel and Old Jerusalem are preparing the way for the return of the tribes of Israel to their chosen land.

9. And you must be justified before your God, else I shall cause many of your peoples to be swept off the earth in the great holocaust of warring nations coming against thee; yet I shall empower thee to conquer neighboring nations as the more wicked are removed from among you.

10. This is the will of the Lord, who created all things and holds all nations in their place, even Son Ahman, Jehovah Christ, who is Jesus Christ; for these are

my words, spoken through mine authority on earth.

11. Thus I speak: Cease your murderous ways, or you shall not be justified in the great war ahead.

12. And many of your people shall be swept off the earth; nevertheless, a remnant shall survive, whom I shall empower to be a governing body over neighboring nations in Old Jerusalem, as my Prophets have declared, even Isaiah and Jeremiah, and many other Prophets; and mine own words given during my ministry on earth, and the words of mine apostles, who sent forth my Gospel of salvation from Jerusalem to the nations of all the earth.

13. Verily I say unto you: Heed my word, and cease your murderous practices, even those in secret, for all secrets are known to thy God, and nothing is hidden from me.

14. And I shall bring you to judgment if you heed me not, and an eternal judgment in the day you stand before your God to be judged for deeds done in the flesh.

15. Thus I have spoken to the leaders of this nation of Israel; and you shall know I have spoken, as the great events are soon to take place that I prophesied in the record of John, my Beloved, in New Testament record, which thou hast in thine hands.

16. Therefore, heed my word, for I shall gather mine Israel unto Zion, unto Old Jerusalem, and I shall be the Ruler over the nations, a righteous government inspired of heaven;

17. And my Church and Kingdom shall triumph over all who oppose them, and you shall know it is I who reigneth.

18. Therefore, heed my words, that there may be a remnant preserved among you to redeem Old Israel.

19. Let there be a law passed allowing freedom of worship in your borders to show you will heed the word of your God, who created you and upholds all peoples in their place, is the voice of Jesus Christ, the Great I AM, the God of Abraham, Isaac, and Jacob, even Jehovah.

20. You only exist by the grace of your God, even I who speaketh to you at this time in this, my message, sent to warn you to cleanse the inside of the platter in your nation, that you may survive as a people and a nation, and be as a ruling power among bordering nations;

21. For I shall fulfill the promise given to Abraham, thy father, that the lands appointed him and his posterity shall be settled by the gathering of Israel by my power.

22. But you must receive my Priesthood and my eternal Gospel to be in Israel, of gathered condition, unto righteous government and rule upon earth.

23. Promote peace with those of the Moslem religion in your borders.

24. Let the Lord settle the controversy concerning Jerusalem and the temple site. Leave it in mine hands.

25. Promote peace among your peoples and among nations, and I shall preserve you a nation as you heed my words, and lay low thine enemies to have no power over thee any longer; for a day of righteous reign, the heavenly inspired government of thy Lord and Savior, Jesus Christ, who speaketh at this time in this message, is soon at hand.

26. You must be a nation of peace and turn to thy God for deliverance and protection to justify thee in the labor of defense, raising an ensign of peace to neighboring nations and those in your borders, that you may be justified in your Lord fighting your battles.

27. Two prophets are soon to be known among you who shall testify that Jesus is the Christ, the Messiah -- righteous men of my raising up to testify to the peoples of your land that I am God who shall show forth mighty works among your people to prepare the honest in heart among you to believe that I am God.

28. And when my message of salvation comes to your nation, open your borders to those I send, lest greater judgments come upon you to humble you as a people, until you know that when your Lord speaketh, He fulfills His word.

29. Thus I send my message to you to prepare the way for the Gospel of salvation revealed from heaven, administered by an authorized Priesthood from heaven, now on earth, who shall administer the ordinances of salvation to the honest in heart; and nothing can stay mine hand, for I am a just God, who shall offer all people salvation through my Gospel of peace and righteous rule.

30. I ascended on high, and reign under my Father, Ahman.

31. Verily I say unto you, the earth shall shake, the sea heave beyond its bounds.

32. The whirlwind judgments shall come to prepare the earth for my glorious appearing by removing the more wicked and preserving the more righteous in every nation, that they may come to Zion, mine Eternal City of governing power over all nations of the earth, to learn of God and His ways; which shall come to Old Jerusalem, to the believing among you, mine Israel, and establish my government of power as a governing nation among nations.

33. These are my purposes soon to be fulfilled, having allowed this nation to rise and have a place on earth to prepare for the gathering of Israel and of my glorious appearing.

34. I sent my Priesthood to thy land in the days of my servant Joseph Smith, to dedicate thy land for the gathering of Israel, which is now happening.

35. And you, the leaders of this nation, are called upon by the God of Creation over you, even Jehovah, to justify thy God in preserving thee as a nation by performing these works of cleansing the inside of the platter, even thine own peoples and laws and ways from these corruptions and murderous ways I have named that are among you.

36. Only your God can sustain you as a people in the day of great judgments and the great war and holocaust soon at hand.

37. And my Judah and mine other tribes shall be gathered unto the Gospel of salvation.

38. Truth shall prevail. All secrets shall be revealed among all nations and peoples of every age of time.

39. The words of all the ancient Prophets shall be fulfilled; and my promise to Abraham, Isaac, and Jacob shall be of full measure fulfilled, as I have promised, even through the mouths of all the holy Prophets throughout the ages of time.

40. You, mine Israel, were scattered because of thy sins against your God.

41. Now my arm of mercy is stretched out to bring about the gathering of a righteous branch of Israel unto the Gospel of salvation, to be a ruling power on earth.

42. Send forth food and provisions to the Palestinian people, that area of Gaza, of a soon nature, to promote peace; and cease sending war among them, notwithstanding their threats.

43. Pour forth the blessings of life upon

them, of food and raiment and provisions of need.

44. Do this of a soon doing to promote peace.

45. Use your military in self-defense and not aggression, until the time when the nations shall rise.

46. Out of necessity, defend thyself.

47. Thus be leadership promoting peace; and if thou wilt do this, you shall see the blessings of thy God upon thy peoples and nation.

48. And thus you shall be believed at a peace conference -- not giving away any of thy lands, only to promote peace as a nation of peace, of all peoples who enter thy borders.

49. This from Him who is the God of peace, the God of eternal life, the God who led your forefathers out of Egypt through the Red Sea on dry ground, and preserved thee a people on earth; though scattered among all nations, yet to be gathered to fulfill my promises of salvation -- Israel being a governing family of Priesthood and heavenly authority to bless all peoples of the earth through your Lord and Savior's atoning power unto salvation.

50. Let there be sent forth a peace delegation to the nation of Iran, representatives of thy government;

51. And if they repulse thee and reject thy offers of peace -- sending forth offers of trade and to prosper their land through legal commerce, of that which is of peaceful intent, and of food and raiment -- verily I say unto you, justify thy God in fighting the battles of thy nation by promoting peace.

52. And if they repulse thee once, send again. If they repulse thee twice, send a third time, to justify thy God in fighting thy battles and empowering thee

to triumph over thine enemies in a day where you need to defend thyself against thine enemies.

53. I shall prosper thee, if, with honest hearts, ye seek peace through righteous and just principles.

54. I have sent my warning to the leaders of all nations to promote peace or meet the judgments of a just God, the God of Creation over all the earth.

55. Receive my warnings of previous sending.

56. Study my policies of righteous government, and know that Zion shall rise as the governing power over all nations; and your Lord and Savior, Jesus Christ, whose right it is to rule, even Son Ahman, who is Jehovah Christ, shall be as a God to you to preserve you as you promote righteous and just and equitous principles of governing power, and come under my governing rules, for they promote peace among all nations.

57. Heed my word, that I may preserve you a nation and a people, is the word of the Lord who made you and sustains you in your place.

58. Even so shall I fulfill, as I have spoken;

59. And according as your deeds shall be, so shall I send judgments upon the wicked among you, and deliverance for those who are of a peaceful and more righteous nature.

60. My judgments are just. I am the God of life that gives you the breath of life moment by moment.

61. And though Israel is scattered among all nations under heaven, Israel shall be gathered to my Zion and to the land of thy Father, Abraham.

62. As I have spoken, so shall I fulfill, for I am the God of Abraham, that led him

to that promised land, and he rejoiced to see this day when his posterity would be gathered, as I showed him in vision the gathering of Israel.

63. And though nation rise against nation, I shall preserve thee, mine Israel, as you cleanse your own peoples.

64. Promote peace and cease all murderous ways, which leaders have promoted in secret for many years.

65. This must cease, that your God, who is over all the earth, can preserve you as mine Israel, to prosper you on earth a chosen people of righteous government power, allowing my message of salvation

to be sounded to thy people, being instruments in mine hands to promote peace and salvation to other nations.

66. You shall soon know of my righteous reign coming to earth through my glorious appearing, making my presence known on earth to all peoples of all nations.

67. Heed the words of warning I have sent to you previously; and heed this word, and perform these works to show thy God that you are men and women of righteous principles, ye leaders of this nation -- principles that promote peace.

68. I, the Lord, have spoken it. Amen.

SECTION REVELATION 63

Fundamentalist Church of Jesus Christ of Latter-day Saints
P.O. Box 840459
Hildale, Utah 84784

Thus Saith Son Ahman, Even Jesus Christ, the God Over All Creation, to the President of the United States of America

Revelation of the Lord Jesus Christ
Eldorado, Texas
Tuesday, April 26, 2011

1. Thus saith the Lord Jesus Christ unto you, the leader of the nation of the United States of America, even the President of this nation:

2. I address you, as the God of Creation, even Jesus Christ, who gave His life for the salvation of all mankind and is able to raise all in the resurrection and judge all for their deeds done in the flesh.

3. Righteous is my name; Endless and Eternal is my name.

4. When I speak, I fulfill.

5. I have sent to you mine own word to let my people go, and release my servant from bondage, and allow them freedom of worship in Celestial laws of my revealing.

6. I have warned this nation and the leaders of this nation by sending mine own word to overthrow those laws that allow murder of unborn children, the gross immorality of Sodom and adultery; promotion of which is allowed by legal

consent, even in entertainments and music and social ways throughout your land.

7. As the leaders of this nation allow these great evils to continue, I shall bring you to judgment.

8. Thou sayest you promote peace among nations and religious freedom, the freedom of expression; yet, since the days of my servant Joseph Smith receiving my Gospel of salvation, restored from heaven to earth, upholding my word in Old and New Testament, the words of all the ancient Prophets, my people have been a driven people.

9. And government powers of this nation of the United States of America have used their civil powers to prosecute and persecute my people of my Church of Jesus Christ of Latter-day Saints; which Church has continued under my Priesthood eternal authority revealed from heaven to Prophets since Joseph Smith's time, now known among men as the Fundamentalist Church of Jesus Christ of Latter-day Saints, known as upholding all the laws of my Gospel revealed through Joseph Smith, of their Lord.

10. But I will support and sustain and preserve my people, even through great whirlwind judgments that I prophesied of, as you can read in New Testament record.

11. I refer you to Matthew 24 specifically, one of mine apostles of old who heard my word and recorded my word.

12. I send you this, my word, calling upon you who leads this nation to promote true justice and religious freedom for my people; for they are of peaceful nature and only desire the salvation of all peoples.

13. They are seeking to build my Zion, prepare for my glorious appearing;

14. And if you will heed my word,

blessings shall come upon this nation; else there shall come judgments to make room for the rise of Zion on this, the American continent, which is my land of Zion where New Jerusalem shall be built, as described by John the Beloved in the Book of Revelations in New Testament record; and I refer this to your reading, knowing of my Bible record.

15. My servant on earth is in bondage through unjust laws aimed to destroy my Priesthood, Church, and Kingdom upon the earth;

16. For I am the God of eternity, and the laws of my Church are revealed from heaven and guided by your Lord; and my people in thy land, of my Church and Kingdom, have rights of religious worship and religious freedom; and my Celestial Law is pure and only promotes happiness and salvation among the pure in heart.

17. My Zion shall rise through the principles of the laws of my Church and Kingdom upon the earth, revealed from heaven.

18. You can peruse these laws in my sacred writings through Joseph Smith in Doctrine and Covenants.

19. You can read of my coming among a former people that dwelt on this land, and my prophecies to them concerning these days -- of this nation coming upon this land.

20. My record is extant and witnesses of my glorious coming, both ancient scripture and modern revelation, as is known among men.

21. And these are the motives of my Priesthood and my servant and my servants in my Church and Kingdom, who seek to live pure and eternal laws of salvation, which I require of them in this

mortal existence on earth to prove worthy of an eternal salvation;

22. And this is the motive of their lives, notwithstanding the persecuting zeal of those who come against them, promoted by the lies of former members who have apostatized because their own lives were full of sin, accusing my Priesthood, Church, and Kingdom of unrighteous domain.

23. Come to understand the truth of these realities among you, and free my servants who are in bondage because of their religious beliefs and practices in obedience to my eternal laws, the revealed religion from heaven.

24. As I spoke concerning the destruction of Jerusalem and the scattering of the Jews, and thus fulfilled my word, so have I spoken concerning the judgments of God -- even of your Lord who sendeth this word to you -- upon this nation and the nations of the earth, if you continue to promote these great evils among your peoples, and allow the persecution and prosecution, which is an injustice against my Church, people, and Kingdom upon the earth.

25. And if you heed me not, you leaders of this nation of the United States of America, you shall feel the chastening hand of a just God; and all my promises and prophecies of judgments upon the gentile nations shall be fulfilled in full measure.

26. Heed my word, that the more righteous among you may be preserved; and if you do not, and the peoples of this nation oppose the rise of Zion, I must needs come out in judgment to cleanse my land of Zion.

27. I shall come in my glory to establish righteous domain, a just and equitous government of eternal power, to rule over all nations, and nothing can stay mine hand, being the God of all creation over all nations.

28. Thus I send my word to you again, according to the understanding of men, in simple language, that you may see truth revealed by your God, which truth you can understand by simple perusal of the scriptures revealed through Joseph Smith, my servant, continued on earth in my Church and Kingdom.

29. I have declared to you that if these evils continue among your people and this nation, that I have named in many messages I have sent, the judgments I have promised shall take place, for wickedness shall not reign.

30. There shall be a thousand years of peace under my righteous rule, saith Jesus Christ, the Beginning and the End, who has all power and authority and right to rule, in heaven and on earth.

31. As you see a great storm of paralyzing nature over many parts of thy nation, and also an earthquake of damaging nature and the loss of lives in a place of unusual happening, as I have named, let your heart be touched that thy God hath spoken; and when He speaks, He fulfills His word.

32. My coming in glory is nigh.

33. I send you my word through my authority of Priesthood on the earth.

34. I, the Lord, reveal to you, the leader of this nation, the formation of that which is of a secret combination among rich businessmen and some leaders of this nation, disturbed by thy policies of economic practices, using government powers, some of whom have joined with organized crime, plotting thy destruction.

35. This I reveal to you, to be careful in thy movements.

36. There are some of them determined to overthrow your influence, thinking your policies are destroying this nation in economic power, fearing that political means may not be sufficient in their power to bring another into that presidential position in future election.

37. Let there be an investigation, of careful means and ways, into the organization of business leaders of banking industry combining with the political arm that is promoting free trade, opposing thy policies of increased debt that are joined with authorities from China, to which this nation has depended on investment into treasury and other stocks to bolster this economy, which organization is of the policy of free trade without restrictions, wanting to set aside governmental restrictions to allow economic growth without government hindrance, wherein the policies of this nation presently limit some exports to nations considered in human rights violations; yet this organization desires free trade, notwithstanding the policies of this government today.

38. Look well into organized crime in Chicago connecting with rich businessmen of an organization seeking free trade, and also having made some connections with foreign powers who also seek economic benefit by changing of laws and rules, in trade and commerce, the laws of this nation, seeking to get gain thereby.

39. I, the Lord, reveal this much, that the fears of this secret combination are, they will lose their wealth if you promote certain policies in government concerning economic development.

40. I give you this, my word, saith the Lord, that you may know I see and know all things; can reveal my word and preserve life as I will.

41. I have named judgments to come upon this nation if they continue these most wicked practices of murder of unborn children, and Sodom, and the immoral wickedness that promotes these sins against innocence and against life;

42. Yet, if you will heed my word and now promote the repeal of those practices now upheld by law, I, the Lord, shall cause this nation to continue as they allow freedom of religion of my Church and Kingdom.

43. And if the leaders of this nation heed me not, my full judgment shall come to thy knowing; for I am the God of glory and fear no man, and shall come to earth in my glory to reign a thousand years in righteous dominion and government over all nations.

44. This is my word to you. Heed my word and promote principles of righteous government.

45. And thus this message is to the leaders of all bodies of government over this nation, to promote righteous principles that preserve life and purity and religious freedom.

46. I tell you these things beforehand for thy good.

47. Do not be taken in a snare by rich businessmen in promoting thy attending a business conference in Chicago of soon naming.

48. Excuse thyself that you may be preserved, is the word of the Lord to you.

49. Promote no longer war against other nations, save for self-defense.

50. Do not be the originator of attack against any nation, that this nation may be justified before your God as you also remove these great evils I have named from among thy peoples, which are allowed by legal consent in this day.

51. I, the Lord, have spoken it. Give

heed to my word, and know that I shall repay all peoples according to the measure they have measured to their fellow men, an eternal judgment, being the God over all creation, who came to earth among mortal men and suffered more than man can suffer, conquering death, hell, and the grave, to raise all peoples up in the resurrection to stand before the judgment bar of God, which tribunal shall render an eternal judgment upon all peoples -- happiness and eternal life for those who measured justice, righteousness and equity, and purity of life toward their fellow men and in their own lives; and promoting a great and eternal punishment upon those who would seek the destruction of life and of innocence, whether openly by legal means, or in private.

52. I have warned the leaders of nations to remove these great sins from among their peoples before my glorious appearing by sending forth my word.

53. And I shall be justified in cleansing the more wicked out of every nation on earth before my glorious appearing, preserving the more righteous who will receive my message of salvation and a righteous government power, even of thy Lord, on earth for a thousand years, a Millennial Reign of Peace, as I have promised.

54. My coming is nigh at hand. Let my people go, to worship me in the freedom guaranteed by the laws of thy nation, my revealed religion from heaven promoting pure and holy principles unto eternal life for those who obey my religious laws, that should be protected by the laws of thy land, yet have not been protected for many years -- legal prosecution and persecution coming against my people in many ways in this nation.

55. I send you my word to help you overcome the inward prejudice held by many lawmakers against my true Church and religion upon earth.

56. Peruse my policies of government in my recent sending of my publishing to thee, with the warnings to this nation and other nations.

57. I say to you lawmakers and government officials in this nation and in every state: My time of coming is at hand.

58. Turn to righteous principles that promote life and virtue and innocence, and protect the same, for I shall hold you accountable, saith the Lord God of heaven and over the earth.

59. Righteous and Holy is my name. Endless is my name. Eternal is my name, even Jesus Christ.

60. This earth is mine.

61. I have given man his agency to choose. Both good and evil are present before all peoples.

62. Choose to promote righteousness.

63. A heavenly power is coming to earth to govern the nations of the earth on my land of Zion, and my power shall be among them; and this is revealed in the scriptures of holy writ in thine hands.

64. I am a God of truth, and I have spoken my word through all the holy Prophets, and shall fulfill. Amen.

SECTION REVELATION 64

Fundamentalist Church of Jesus Christ of Latter-day Saints
P.O. Box 840459
Hildale, Utah 84784

Thus Saith Son Ahman, Even Jesus Christ, to the Leaders of the Nation of Syria

Revelation of the Lord Jesus Christ
Eldorado, Texas
Tuesday, April 26, 2011

1. Let it be known that your Lord Jesus Christ, who reigns on high, and has all power and sees and knows all things, by whom all creation exists, hath seen thy sin against thine own people; for the leaders of your nation are guilty of murder of your own peoples, repressing them in their rights and privileges of freedom.

2. And I send to you my word, that you shall soon not be a nation, as you continue this great evil among you, in secret combinations and using military power to the destruction of souls who only desire freedom of speech and worship, and those rights belonging to all mankind of thy God, by which they can pursue the happiness, even unto eternal life, if they seek unto their Lord who hath redeemed them;

3. For I am the God of Creation, and of redeeming and atoning power, that speaketh, and you shall yet stand before me to be judged, even of the secrets of your life; for thy sins shall be shouted on the housetops, even all mankind, men and women of all nations and generations, to be judged unto an eternal judgment for their deeds and desires in the flesh, in this mortal state that you now dwell.

4. Thus saith the Lord: Cease this evil, for those of violence shall be removed from power by the judgments of a just God.

5. And I send you my word, to be soon verified in the great war at hand, of which thy nation shall cease to be a nation; thy lands go to thine enemies, whom you have fought against, even mine Israel, because you heed me not.

6. Promote peace. Repent ye of this great evil. Bring to justice those leaders in your land and nation who have promoted this murder of your own citizens to keep power and get gain.

7. Your corruptions have come up before the heavens. You stand judged unworthy before me, the leaders of this nation of Syria, at this time, and I shall cause you to cease to be a nation.

8. You shall know well my word is fulfilled.

9. My judgments shall pour forth, and present leaders shall feel the weight of the wrath of a just and equitous and righteous God, who knoweth and seeth all things.

10. And if any of you, of your nation -- both leaders and peoples who dwell therein -- would seek deliverance of thy God, bring these leaders to justice who

have allowed murder of your own citizens and continued as a warring nation against neighboring nations, desiring power and gain, pleasure in unrighteousness.

11. Your conscience is seared, you leaders of this nation, with the shedding of innocent blood among thine own peoples.

12. The God of heaven and earth hath spoken to your understanding through mine authority on earth, who receives my word and gives my word to all peoples as I will.

13. My coming in glory is soon at hand, and you shall feel the weight of great judgments in your land as you continue this murderous practice among your own peoples.

14. I who reign on high and over all nations, even Jesus Christ, who holds all people in His hands through almighty power, shall bring you low; and you know, in time to come, that when I speak, so shall I fulfill, through the witness of judgments upon the more wicked among you, who destroy innocence and shed innocent blood.

15. Your secret combinations with nations and organizations of murderous and warring nature are known by your God, and I shall lay you low, and remove your power of government and influence in the earth because of your great sins and corruptions.

16. Let any of my believers who will heed my word in thy land, who will heed the word of the God of Creation over you, be of the nature of turning to your God who made you, in fasting and prayer in your habitations, to approach Him for mercy and deliverance, lest His wrath come full measure upon all your peoples in the day of a great war, and pestilence and famine among you, to remove the more wicked from the earth.

17. Cry unto your God, even now, that He may know, by your repentance in turning to Him for deliverance from oppression, that you will be of the more peaceful among your peoples, that I may preserve some among you to know of my coming and of my Zion rising as the governing power over the earth, of a soon happening; for nothing can stay mine hand.

18. I am He who was crucified, and suffered for all mankind to be raised from the grave.

19. I am sending forth my message of salvation to the honest in heart everywhere, saith the Lord.

20. I shall send mine angels to pluck out the more wicked from your nation, and spare those of the peaceable nature who can receive my message of Priesthood and of Zion sent from heaven, the righteousness of your God dwelling on earth at His glorious appearing to all nations.

21. I send you my word now, that you may know that you shall be held accountable for this great wickedness taking place in your land, the leaders of this nation, by the God of Creation, through whom all peoples exist and have a being upon earth;

22. For the mocker shall mourn when the power of my might is revealed and you are laid low.

23. Heed my word and cease this atrocity of government power against your own citizenry.

24. No longer consider that your deeds done in secret are hidden from the God of Creation over you.

25. Let President al-Assad know that he has been weighed in the balance of eternal judgment and found wanting, he and those who support him in power as leader of this nation of Syria.

26. Thus has spoken the God of heaven and earth, and none can stay mine hand.

27. When my righteous and just decrees are spoken, so shall I fulfill.

28. And I shall send mine Israel to overthrow you as a nation, and you shall know I have spoken; though they also shall be humbled in the great war and holocaust of many lives lost.

29. If you would repent and do the will of the God of Creation who made you, promote a peace conference, and turn from your war and violent nature wherein you promote terrorism against mine Israel.

30. Bear influence with the Palestinian authorities to make peace.

31. Let there be peace in my land of Jerusalem, for my coming is nigh.

32. I shall appear on that Mount of Olivet, and in my Zion on the land of America; touch the mighty ocean and bring to pass the restoration of Israel as a power on earth in righteous government, inspired by the powers of heaven coming to earth.

33. Let your governing body gather together and vote for peace among nations, and send forth messages of peace; and only use thy military for defense and not aggression.

34. And more especially, cease the murder of your own citizens.

35. I am the God of peace and of power eternal; I am the God of glory, and nothing can stay mine hand.

36. When I decree a just decree of judgment, then you shall feel my wrath, removing those from power who promote this great wickedness that I have named that is among you, saith your Lord and Savior, Jesus Christ, who reigneth on high. Amen.

SECTION REVELATION 65

Fundamentalist Church of Jesus Christ of Latter-day Saints
P.O. Box 840459
Hildale, Utah 84784

Thus Saith Son Ahman, Even Jesus Christ, The Creator of Heaven and Earth, by Whose Power All Things Exist and Continue, to the Leaders of the Nation of Afghanistan

Revelation of the Lord Jesus Christ
Eldorado, Texas
Thursday, April 28, 2011

1. Thus saith the Lord Jesus Christ to the leaders of the nation of Afghanistan, even He who creates all things and holds all things in their place, a God over all the earth who reigns in heaven and looks down upon the earth and sees and knows all things by His almighty power:

2. I have seen your gross wickedness, in murder, in secret combinations to get gain, in using religious justification to

destroy souls, abusive to women and children, the territorial warlords seeking power through murder, joining with that former organization that governed that nation in secret, which was most corrupt.

3. Thus saith the Lord: Though foreign nations have come to thy land, thy government is corrupt, abusing thine own people, leaders in secret combinations to get gain, even to the murdering of your own peoples.

4. And though you outwardly maintain some civil rights for thy peoples, requiring foreign powers to maintain thy government in power, there are elements in your government secretly in collusion with the enemy, that those foreign powers are battling, to get gain and power in corrupt ways.

5. You have become a land as a warring nation for generations, a gathering place for the beginning of great wars.

6. You are of ancient heritage of mixed nations that have often conquered thee.

7. And though thy religious traditions upheld by your civil laws permit abuse of women and children, of murder in secret, not bringing leaders to justice, I, the Lord, shall stretch forth mine hand and humble thee.

8. There shall be the increase of violence in thy borders, and in a time to come, soon at hand, such a measure of my judgments that leaders shall not be in power who are presently in power.

9. There shall be a cleansing of the more wicked of thy peoples who thus abuse innocence, carrying on traditions that do not bring forth righteous justice and judgment among thy peoples.

10. I shall fulfill my word, saith the Lord Jesus Christ, the God over all creation, who rules in the heavens, and nothing can stay mine hand.

11. I send you my word, that you have been weighed in the balance and found wanting, and my judgments shall be upon you to a greater degree.

12. There shall be a famine, the destruction of trade of your illegal and corrupt drug practices; and also, you shall see your land controlled by another nation for a time, which nation shall also be overthrown by the wars that shall come upon thy land and in their own borders.

13. I shall humble all nations and remove the more wicked from all nations, for my glorious coming is nigh at hand, and all peoples of all nations shall know that the God who made you has come to earth to rule over all nations with a righteous dominion, even Son Ahman, who is Jesus Christ, the God of Israel and the God of all nations.

14. Through thy corrupt ways of governing powers -- of those in office of power in your governing powers -- thus saith the Lord, you promote the violence by not taking care of your poor, which, if you do, they would not turn to thine enemies that swell into thy borders administering death through war and violence, wherein they continue to seek power also, that former regime of violent nature, also abusive to thy peoples.

15. And how can you stand if the God of heaven withdraws His protection from thee?

16. Thus, great violence is in thy borders to the loss of many lives of thine own citizenry.

17. And you should promote peace and care for the poor in a manner that they will not seek after thine enemies for support.

18. Because the leaders of this nation

of Afghanistan continue in their corrupt ways, violence continues in your nation.

19. If you would seek peace, you would bring to justice those leaders who are corrupt in secret combinations to get gain and power, even to the murdering of your own peoples and joining with thine enemies in secret.

20. This is known to thy God, and He revealeth it that there may be a just recompense upon thee, both in this, your present existence, and also the hereafter, when you stand before your God to be judged with an eternal judgment.

21. This I reveal to you, that I am the God of eternity. Eternal and Endless is my name. Righteous and holy and pure are my ways of governing power to preserve virtue and innocence.

22. Such shall my righteous reign be as my government of heaven comes to earth, descending in the clouds of glory, all nations knowing of my appearing.

23. My coming is nigh.

24. Repent ye of these great evils, and remove from power those wicked rulers who abuse thine own people and join in these wicked ways, lest all of you be removed in judgments that shall be as a thief in the night appearing, removing thee from thy place.

25. There shall be a happening in thy borders, called by man as a natural disaster, the power of God exercised to reveal that I, your Lord, hath spoken, and you shall feel a humbling.

26. Thus you shall know the God of heaven hath spoken to thee, the rulers of this nation, sending my word to your understanding through my servant on earth, whom I have appointed to be my Mouthpiece to all peoples.

27. And thus saith the Lord: Repent ye, and bring to justice those wicked rulers who will not turn from their murderous and corrupt ways, wherein innocent lives are lost because you will not perform works of righteous government in your land.

28. My righteous rule shall promote justice and equity, prospering all peoples of peace.

29. And those nations that heed me not shall be humbled by my almighty power until they bow the knee to your Lord and Savior, even Jesus Christ, whose words these are, sent to you, the leaders of this nation; for you are responsible for the condition of your nation.

30. Promote righteous principles of governing power among you, for you shall be a tribute nation for a time to another national power for a time, which power shall also be overthrown in the greater wars that shall take place soon at hand.

31. O all ye peoples of the earth, heed my word! Promote peace, for my righteous rule shall bring peace to all nations as they follow my righteous governing power, saith the God who seeth and knoweth all things, and shall make Himself known in power and might to all peoples.

32. There shall be foreign nations in your land for a time; then cometh greater events that shall cause them to focus their power elsewhere, leaving thee weak in a manner that another nation shall make you a tribute nation, removing those from power who are presently leaders of this nation of Afghanistan.

33. I, the Lord, will cause it to happen because of your wicked and corrupt ways of murder and to get gain.

34. This is the will of the Lord.

35. Bring to justice those who are corrupt leaders among you; and cleanse the inside of the platter of your governing

authority and powers, else I shall cause these greater judgments to come upon you and remove you from your place.

36. I, the Lord Jehovah, even Jesus Christ, hath spoken and shall fulfill my word.

37. Let there be among your peoples schools that protect also the female portion of your population to be educated, that those equal rights will be in place.

38. Let there be a reining in of the power of warlords spread throughout your land who do not come under government rule.

39. Let there not be a using of them who abuse women and children and promote corruption and murderous ways among your peoples in order to govern thy land.

40. Bring them to justice and I will spare your nation and prosper your land to be peaceful and have war no more among you; and save you do this, my full judgment shall come to remove those in power, both of national government and those spread throughout your land.

41. This from Him who reigns on high and fulfills all His words. Amen.

SECTION REVELATION 66

Fundamentalist Church of Jesus Christ of Latter-day Saints
P.O. Box 840459
Hildale, Utah 84784

Thus Saith Son Ahman to the Leaders of the NATO Nations, Even Jesus Christ, Your Lord, His Own Word to Thee

Revelation of the Lord Jesus Christ
Eldorado, Texas
Saturday, April 30, 2011

1. Thus saith the Lord Jesus Christ, your Redeemer and God over all, who reigns on high in the heavens and has all power of government, who sees and knows all things, and nothing is hidden; whose Spirit goeth forth to give life to all creation, who can take whom He will and raise up whom He will to power; to the leaders of the NATO nations:

2. You have committed a great sin in seeking the assassination of other leaders by military might, even in that nation of Libya.

3. And behold, I say unto you, you have turned to violence, when I, the Lord, have commanded to withdraw your military into your own nation, each nation, to make peace.

4. And behold, I say unto you, if thou heed me not, your alliance shall weaken at a break-out of a war on the European continent; and you shall be divided and

no longer be of a defensive nature, which your alliance was intended to be; but now you have attacked a nation in an aggressive nature.

5. I, the Lord, did not send thee to do this work, and you are not justified.

6. When you are aggressive, you shall weaken your own power in time, for thy God shall not sustain thee.

7. Let this alliance labor in defense of your nations, and not be of a secretive, murderous nature at all.

8. I, the Lord, justify defense when petitions of peace have been raised many times to an aggressive nation.

9. And I am the God over all, of a soon appearing in the glory of my might; and I am causing mine own word to be revealed in a manner of your understanding, that your Lord Jesus Christ cometh in the power of His might, sending before Him whirlwind judgments to depopulate many nations of the more wicked part of their population, preserving the more righteous; and to remove from the earth the scourge of the murder of unborn children among your nations, sanctioned by most nations by law and by practice; and also Sodom, as well as adultery and licentious and immoral ways that promote the murder of unborn children, that fight against the principles of life and virtue.

10. I, the Lord, shall bring all to an accountability, even a judgment, to remove leaders of nations from power, even from this mortal life of a probationary earth, of which you now dwell; a life where I sent you to be tested, as children of God, where both good and evil are present;

11. And I send my Spirit to touch minds and hearts of every son and daughter born on earth, to choose the good and know good from evil;

12. And thou knowest that murder is a capital crime.

13. And murder of unborn children is an offense against the God of life, and against the most innocent portion of mankind, who cannot defend themselves -- spirits seeking to be born on a probationary earth to be proved worthy of salvation.

14. I shall come in my glory.

15. All nations shall fear and tremble.

16. My Zion shall rise on the American continent at the appointed place, after the wicked are swept off my land of Zion, by earthquake and pestilence, hail and famine, wars, the overflowing scourge and desolating sickness.

17. And many of these judgments, including the sea heaving beyond its bounds, shall continue to come upon many nations.

18. Thus, I have warned thee to get thy people away from the coastlines of low elevation in your nations, in my published word I have sent to the leaders of all nations of the earth, warning some individual nations to do so.

19. Thus saith the Lord: Italy shall suffer, being of a most immoral and corrupt nature, being mostly depopulated by those judgments I have named in previous warnings; as will Sicily and Sardinia, and island nations in the Mediterranean Sea.

20. When the sea heaves itself beyond its bounds, and volcanoes and earthquakes come forth, disease shall result, and many shall perish who will not repent of these gross, immoral, and murderous ways.

21. Thus saith the Lord: All nations shall feel the justice of an Almighty God who continue in these evils that are a stench before the heavens, of which a God of eternal power and justice, of perfect righteousness and peace in His eternal

domain, shall visit the earth with these judgments of cleansing.

22. I shall cause peace to reign in the nations at my coming, and my Zion shall be the capital city of governing power of the whole earth.

23. And those nations that continue these corrupt ways of injustice upon their own peoples or minorities, or abuse of women, or murder of unborn children, that do not give equal rights in education, in protections of law, they shall be visited with judgments of their God until they are humbled.

24. Let all nations allow freedom of worship of religion, of peaceful intent, in every land of the earth.

25. I, the Lord, am soon to send my messengers of salvation from Zion; and every nation shall heed my word; for every knee shall bow and every tongue confess that Jesus is the Christ, even Him who speaketh these words through mine authority on earth.

26. Though he be in bondage, my word shall be sent to you to thine understanding.

27. Awake! My coming is nigh, and you shall be humbled.

28. And cease your murderous intentions against peoples of other nations, when I, the Lord your God, have not been consulted by mine authority on earth receiving your message.

29. And thus I have made him known to thee.

30. And save you do this -- only going to battle against other nations by permission of thy God, for justice to be met and meted out, and as you have promoted peace continually -- if you perform these aggressive actions, my judgments shall be upon you and your peoples, of the more wicked portion among them;

31. For I am able to pluck out the more wicked and preserve the more righteous in every nation under heaven.

32. I am a God of almighty power who has all knowledge.

33. I am the Redeemer and Savior of all mankind, and shall raise them from the grave to be judged for their deeds done in the flesh with an eternal judgment.

34. And you leaders of nations must know my warning voice -- that I, the Lord, who created all things, shall make myself known, removing those from power who continue to rule in an unjust and wicked and a murderous way.

35. Cleanse the inside of the platter in your nations.

36. Cease this practice of aggression when you now know I have my representative and Mouthpiece on earth, to whom you can counsel before you are an aggressive nation at all, only laboring for self-defense.

37. You claim to be of a peaceful nature, of defense organization; and now you have stepped forth in aggression against a nation who attacked thee not.

38. And you must not go against a nation, though they are unjust in their own borders, save I, the Lord, command; for thus shall it be during my reign of righteousness, to your knowing;

39. For all people shall see I have appeared in my glory, and the wicked of all nations shall fear and tremble and stand afar off, as New Jerusalem is built and Zion rises.

40. Let that nation of the United States of America again receive my warning to let my people go! and free my servant and my servants in bondage, for your laws are unjust!

41. They are living my Celestial laws,

of plural marriage, wherein I, the Lord, have revealed this law; and it is of me, and only for my Church and Kingdom on earth, and none others.

42. They are not aggressive on any people.

43. They are of the most pure motive.

44. And I, the Lord, reveal this; for my coming is nigh at hand, and I shall hold all government officials accountable for their aggression against my Church and Kingdom upon the earth;

45. For I have sent my message to the leader of this nation, and the leaders of this nation, to let my people go, of more than one correspondence and publishing, and you heed me not.

46. And though you have but little time to repent, and seem to be of a peaceful nature in many ways, my judgments shall come as a thief in a night against thy nation, and the nations of the more wicked of the earth who have these terrible crimes among them, upheld by consent of law in most nations -- the murder of unborn children, and Sodom, and adultery, and immoral ways that corrupt the way of life and destroy virtue.

47. These I will remove from the earth by judgment if the peoples of the earth repent not.

48. Repent ye! all ye peoples of the earth, saith the God who made you.

49. And come unto me through my Priesthood, and my Church and Kingdom, which hath already been in operation on earth since I restored my Gospel of salvation and my eternal Priesthood from heaven, through my servant Joseph Smith; continued through a true and faithful Priesthood on the earth unto this day.

50. And though apostates and the wicked accuse my servant and my faithful of my Church and Kingdom, they are liars, having broken their Church and Priesthood covenants of sacred and holy walk, being corrupt themselves.

51. Examine their lives, for many are guilty of the sins they accuse my Priesthood and mine authority on earth of being guilty of in their daily walk.

52. Yea, these apostates, in their lives, are most often guilty of what they accuse others of.

53. I, the Lord, declare it to your understanding.

54. Examine the lives of witnesses accusing innocent people, and you will see they are often guilty of that immoral conduct and evil intent that they accuse mine innocent people.

55. Thus saith the Lord: I shall hold you accountable, the leaders of this nation and of the nations of the earth, to pass laws that are just and equitable, and preserve my Church and Kingdom upon the earth.

56. And save you do this, if you come against my people more, there shall be great judgments as they are threatened with destruction at thine hands.

57. And thus saith the Lord: The nations of the earth must open their border, each one, to allow freedom of worship and my messengers of salvation to come in thy lands, to deliver my message of salvation to thy peoples without violence upon them.

58. Let the nation of Israel heed my word:

59. Let there be a law allowing freedom of worship in thy borders and among thy people;

60. And do that peaceful work of sending food and clothing and provisions to those of the Palestinian people in the Gaza area, of soon doing;

61. And you shall have more power

in peace negotiations, and I shall prosper your peace effort, that thy nation not suffer what shall come upon them if you heed me not, by the violence of other nations against thee.

62. And though I spare thy nation at a future time when a great battle shall come, the more wicked part of your population shall be removed by destructive elements and by war, and by judgments of your God, and only leave the more righteous;

63. For I have declared to thee, by a correspondence, that there are two prophets among you now who shall bear witness of the rise of my Zion and the coming of thy Lord Jesus Christ in His glory.

64. And though they meet violent means among thy people, they shall be known; and their testimonies shall be held among your people by those who hear their testimony, as a preparation to receive my messengers of salvation to thy nation.

65. I, the Lord, have spoken it.

66. Let NATO be a defensive organization, and let it not be an aggressive organization at all.

67. You shall not prosper in the nation of Afghanistan because you were aggressive without that nation attacking thy borders.

68. And though you justified, on accusations of terrorism, your attack, thus saith the Lord: That government that was in power attacked thee not, and you were not justified.

69. Now I, the Lord, reveal this to thee:

70. During my reign of righteousness, a thousand years among men on this earth, I shall rule in peace and promote peace among all peoples.

71. And though war be at the beginning of my Millennial Reign of Peace, I shall send judgments to humble all nations until peace rules the earth for a time --

72. This to thine understanding, that I am the God of peace, and have commanded all leaders of all nations to draw their militaries into their own borders and their own nation to make peace;

73. And if they heed me not, my judgments shall humble your nation and remove those leaders from power in a time soon to come; for my coming is nigh at hand, and I must needs be justified in sending my judgments upon the earth, by my word of warning going forth again to your understanding.

74. Thus I send my word to NATO nations, another word of warning of an immediate heeding needed on your part:

75. Cleanse the inside of the platter!

76. Cleanse your own nations of these evils I have named, and I will preserve the more righteous of your people at my glorious appearing, and through judgments sent beforehand, of a soon nature, coming upon the earth, some of which you have seen increasing;

77. For those storms in the United States of America, of recent happening, I warned the leaders of that nation I would do so to humble this nation, to show them when I, the Lord, speak, my word shall be fulfilled, for they were judgments of a just God upon a wicked generation who will not heed my word.

78. Thus, the leader of this nation beheld with his own eyes, even the United States of America leader, the President of the United States, the damage done that a just God can perform, as an example that when He speaketh, He keepeth His word.

79. I am the God of love.

80. My reign of righteous dominion extends beyond this mortal existence

into the world of departed spirits, where I send my Priesthood; where I, your Lord and Savior, visited for three days while my body laid in the grave, and organized my Priesthood to spread my message of salvation to the spirits in the world of departed spirits, that I may be a just God to deliver my salvation message to all peoples of every nation, kindred, tongue, and people of every age of the earth.

81. And they are awaiting for Zion's rise in the ordinances in sacred temples to be performed for their salvation, those believing spirits awaiting the resurrection for these blessings to be given by proxy.

82. Thus saith the Lord: My work of salvation shall be performed, and all nations shall know that I am the God over all the earth, saith Jesus Christ, who is Jehovah Christ, Son Ahman, doing the will of the Father, Ahman, in all things. Amen.

SECTION REVELATION 67

Fundamentalist Church of Jesus Christ of Latter-day Saints
P.O. Box 840459
Hildale, Utah 84784

Thus Saith Son Ahman, Even Jesus Christ, to the Leaders and Peoples of the Nation of Bosnia -- A Word of Warning to Make Peace With Neighboring Nations. Hear My Word, Yea, the Eternal Judge and God Over All Peoples, Who Ruleth in the Heavens and Over All the Earth:

Revelation of the Lord Jesus Christ
Eldorado, Texas
Tuesday, May 3, 2011

1. I who reign on high, Jesus Christ, speaketh to the nation, even the leaders thereof, which is called Bosnia:

2. There are elements in your land seeking to harm other peoples of neighboring nations now surrounding thee, thy leaders partaking of that spirit also.

3. I, the Lord, call upon thee as a nation to repent of using violent means to further your claims of governing independence or authority and power over any peoples, even of a minority religion among you, or a religion opposite to thy faith.

4. Thus saith the Lord Jesus Christ, who created all peoples, the Great I AM who reigneth on high, who sees and knows all things: Repent ye of your murderous and warlike tendencies, and know that if you heed me not, war shall break out to absorb thee, to no longer be a nation.

5. This is my warning; for justice shall be met by a God of justice and eternal power, even I who speaketh through mine authority on earth -- which leaders shall know I have spoken when removed from power, if they perform violence upon

minorities or other nations, save it be for self-defense.

6. Thus saith the Lord God of heaven: Cease this idea and philosophy and way of living, of resorting to violence to fulfill your purposes, even oftentimes of hatred against other peoples of other religions.

7. It must not stand and will not stand on earth; and if you heed me not, a war shall commence to absorb thee as I have named.

8. Hasten to prepare for my glorious appearing, saith Jesus Christ, your Lord, who suffered the pains of all men, that they may be raised from the grave and be judged before the Eternal God for their deeds and desires done in the flesh.

9. Thus, I have spoken to thee, sending you my message of peace; for I am the God of peace of righteous and holy ways, a God of life that created this earth and caused the peopling thereof to take place; who upholdeth all peoples and nations in their place by His almighty power, and shall bring all to a righteous judgment; and justice shall be met upon those who would murder and kill to get gain and power; and it must not be any longer;

10. For of a soon happening, my appearing shall come, and the more wicked of every nation shall be swept off the earth by eternal judgments of an Eternal God, meaning being swept off this earth and not being in this life -- sent to the world of departed spirits where they will receive my message of salvation, if they have not committed the sin unto death, even willing murder against their fellow men, women, or children.

11. I, the Lord, declared a warning of an eternal judgment coming upon leaders of nations who use murder to get gain or power on the earth.

12. Be ye of a peaceful nature. Seek peace among the nations that surround thee, lest a great war erupt and absorb thee. Amen.

SECTION REVELATION 68

Fundamentalist Church of Jesus Christ of Latter-day Saints
P.O. Box 840459
Hildale, Utah 84784

Thus Saith Son Ahman, Even Jesus Christ, to the Leaders of the Nation of Greece, and Thus the People of Greece -- the God Over All, Who Speaketh Thus, Even a God of Glory, Whose Coming Is Nigh at Hand, Who Shall Make Himself Known to All Peoples -- Hear Ye My Word:

Revelation of the Lord Jesus Christ
Eldorado, Texas
Tuesday, May 3, 2011

1. I, the Lord, speak now to the leaders of the nation of Greece, that ancient land where my Gospel and message of salvation, saith Jesus Christ, was delivered by mine ancient apostles:

2. There is violence in the hearts of thy peoples and the leaders of thy nation.

3. And there must needs be a repentance of the leaders of this nation in seeking power through secret combinations with the rich, thus causing thy people to be of a poor nature.

4. And if you would heed my word and be preserved as a nation in a time of a great war soon to happen, let there be a greater equity in the raising up of the poor in thy nation, saith the Lord Jesus Christ.

5. Through the forces of thy government being oppressive, thy citizenry has the spirit of revolution in their nature; and if you would be wise, promote those policies that are more equitous among thy peoples.

6. Heed my word, and join not in aggression against any nation.

7. Only use thy military for self-defense, and not against thine own peoples; for this is a grave sin in the leadership of nations, even resorting to murder to get gain or power.

8. I am the God of Creation that speaketh.

9. I have sent my warning to the leaders of all nations, including this nation of Greece; and you are bordering nations that shall erupt into a great war if they heed not my peace-keeping command and counsel that I have sent to them, and to the nations of the earth.

10. And your nation shall be embroiled in war if you heed me not, that shall absorb many of your population in violence and death.

11. And this I warn thee, to be of a peaceful nature, not use thy military in any aggressive manner, only for self-defense if need be.

12. Oppress not thine own peoples any longer, and attend to the poor, as I have named.

13. This is the word of the Lord to the leaders of this nation, as I reveal further:

14. My glorious appearing, saith Jesus Christ, is nigh at hand.

15. I shall make all peoples of all nations know of my coming and my right to rule, the government of heaven coming to earth under my rule as King of kings and Lord of lords, a righteous reign of a thousand years of peace established on earth, my Zion rising on the American continent, of a soon happening, and nothing can stay mine hand.

16. And thus saith the Lord: The leaders of every nation shall be brought to an accounting by thy God; and those of wicked intent, of injustice, of violence and murderous intent to keep power, or get gain and power, shall be brought to judgment by a just God, and shall not remain as leaders of nations;

17. For the more wicked of every nation shall be swept off the earth, and the more righteous preserved to know of my glorious appearing, and of my Zion rising as the governing power over all the earth.

18. Prepare thy peoples with this announcement -- that I shall soon send my message of salvation to all nations that remain on the earth, for I shall send judgments of a whirlwind nature, of great power.

19. I am a just God and shall answer upon the wicked of every nation a righteous judgment; and thus justice shall be met.

20. And in eternity I am the God of Creation who hath conquered death, and all men and women and children shall be raised in the resurrection and stand before their God to be judged with an eternal judgment.

21. And I shall cause you to be witnesses against thyself, wherein you have sinned, by unlocking your mind and revealing the truths of thy life; for in my Millennial Reign of Peace, in Zion, shall all things be revealed that are secret.

22. And those secret works of corruption and murder, of robbery and usury, of all leaders of all nations, shall be revealed, and nothing shall be hidden.

23. Thus thy Lord speaketh. Heed my word.

24. Make peace within thine own borders.

25. Be of a more equitous nature in thy laws, and let religious freedom and religious worship in a free and peaceable manner be allowed in thy land.

26. Thus saith Jesus Christ, even Son Ahman, who is Jehovah Christ, the God of Israel and of all peoples, who ruleth on high, and nothing can stay mine hand;

27. And as I speak, so shall I fulfill.

28. Heed my word. Amen.

SECTION REVELATION 69

Fundamentalist Church of Jesus Christ of Latter-day Saints
P.O. Box 840459
Hildale, Utah 84784

Thus Saith Son Ahman, Even Jesus Christ, the God of Glory Who Created All Things and Upholds All Nations and Peoples of the Earth in Their Place, Who Is the Redeemer and Savior of All Mankind, to the Leaders and Peoples of Japan, Through Mine Authority on Earth: Awake! and Heed My Word, Which Saith Thus -- Even a Word of Final Warning Before Greater Judgments Come Upon Thee, From a Just God Who Hath Warned Thee Beforehand the Greater Judgments of Destructive Power Would Come Upon Thee if You Heed Me Not -- Hear Ye My Word Herein:

Revelation of the Lord Jesus Christ
Eldorado, Texas
Tuesday, May 3, 2011

1. Thus saith the Lord unto the nation and the leaders of the nation of Japan:

2. I, the Lord, have humbled thee, even Jesus Christ, the God of heaven and earth, by sending forth a rebuke because of thy wickedness; showing my power, able to fulfill mine own word to the leaders of all nations, that when I call upon a nation to repent and turn from their corrupt and immoral ways, if they heed me not, my judgments of great power shall be poured forth.

3. I have sent warnings to you, even published it to the leaders of the nations, and to thy knowing -- the leaders of thy nation thus receiving my word.

4. Heed my word.

5. Repent ye of your corrupt and immoral ways, for thy peoples tend toward immorality through your traditions of your fathers carrying on in your lives.

6. And change thy laws to not allow immorality, pornography, Sodom, or the murder of unborn children to take place at all, lest my greater judgments come upon thee.

7. I have allowed you to exist as a nation still, and you shall become a tributary nation to a greater power in a time to come if you heed me not.

8. And your leaders shall be removed from power if they do not cleanse the inside of the platter -- thine own peoples and thine own laws; laws that allow corrupt ways, murder of innocent unborn children, corruption of your peoples, not protecting virtue.

9. Thus saith your God who created you: Repent ye! is a final warning to the nation of Japan and the leaders of Japan; and turn from these most wicked practices, that you may remain a nation; for I shall

send my judgments to sweep the more wicked part of every nation from off the earth, and preserve the more righteous, at my glorious appearing, by my almighty power;

10. For you shall see more tidal waves, earthquakes, and volcanos and great storms, and disease spread across thy nation if you heed not the God of glory, the God who created all things, who upholds all nations and all peoples upon the earth in their place, and who shall humble all peoples if they continue in their wicked and corrupt ways.

11. I have favored thee, after thy great war of thy starting, with prosperity, and then humbling.

12. I reveal further, thus saith Jesus Christ, the God over all things, who suffered on the cross, laid in the grave, even His body, for three days, His spirit in the world of departed spirits, organizing His Priesthood authority to teach the spirits in the world of departed spirits, then resurrected unto great power over heaven and the earth -- it is I who speaketh:

13. My glorious appearing to all peoples and nations is soon at hand, even to Zion, which is soon to be raised up on the American continent, even New Jerusalem, to be the governing city and power over all nations of the earth, the powers and governing authority of heaven coming to earth, of thy Savior's giving.

14. Thus saith the Lord: My coming is soon at hand.

15. Hasten to prepare, and cause thy peoples to be of a more pure walk through righteous, equitous, and virtuous laws that promotes life and virtue among thy peoples.

16. And cause the influence, through law, to cease your immoral practices among thy people, that I have named in a previous warning.

17. Heed my word, saith the God of glory over all creation, to the nation and leaders of Japan. Amen.

SECTION REVELATION 70

Fundamentalist Church of Jesus Christ of Latter-day Saints
P.O. Box 840459
Hildale, Utah 84784

Thus Saith Son Ahman, Even Jesus Christ, Your Lord and Savior Who Hath Redeemed All Mankind, Whose Right It Is to Rule Over the Heavens and the Earth, a Just God Who Sees and Knows All Things, and Shall Recompense to Every Man That Which He Has Measured to His Fellow Man, According to the Light and Knowledge They Have Received: Thus I Speak to the President of the United States of America, Now in Power, and Also to the Peoples of This Nation -- This Message of Warning of the Doctrine of Eternal Judgment Upon Thee, Even Upon All Peoples, Being the God of Eternal Power, an Eternal God Who Shall Bring All to Justice; Whose Mercy Shall Claim Those Who Repenteth in a Manner to Earn the Benefit of My Atoning Power -- Even Him, a God of Atoning and Redeeming Power, Who Suffered on the Cross and Was Raised From the Grave Unto Eternal Power to Judge All Mankind According as Their Works Are:

Revelation of the Lord Jesus Christ
Eldorado, Texas
Tuesday, May 3, 2011

1. Let there be written my word, saith the Lord, in a manner of correspondence to the leader of this nation of the United States of America, a word of warning and counsel -- even Jesus Christ, who reigneth over all, empowering this nation to be a free nation since its creation, I guiding forefathers of the revolutionary battles wherein they broke away from the mother gentile nation from which they emanated.

2. And I, your God, inspired leaders of this nation to establish the Constitution of the United States, and the Bill of Rights, as it is called, guaranteeing religious freedom, even freedom of worship in a land of plenty at that time.

3. Thus saith the Lord to those who thus murdered Osama bin Laden:

4. You have transgressed greatly, turning to murder in a manner of seeking to retaliate against one in another land, not using the government powers where he dwelt to apprehend him safely, which could have easily been accomplished had you thus stepped forth and acted on correct principles.

5. But in thy glory-seeking and in thy violent nature, yea, to the celebration of millions in thy nation, you hath murdered a man who could have been apprehended peacefully, were attempts made therein by the governing power of the nation

where he dwelt, being near the capital city and power of authority of that nation in Pakistan.

6. I, the Lord, rebuke thee for thy murderous intent, turning to violence when peaceful means, or the governing powers over that place of residence, could have been used to apprehend and take in custody one accused of crimes.

7. And if you continue this practice, your murderous intentions shall turn upon thine own peoples, and mob rule shall ensue throughout thy land; murder and rapine, robbery and violence one against another, showing thy murderous intent and nature of the people of this nation, proving to thy God you are not worthy to remain on my land of Zion, but would have to be swept clean by just, yea, by justified judgments of God, to send thee to the world of departed spirits where you transgress no more in this mortal existence of probationary testing; which I, the Lord your God, have sent all mankind to be tested, allowing good and evil to be placed before all, sending my Spirit -- which is only good, of the inspiring unto good -- to the mind and heart of every man, woman, and child who would receive and listen to what they call their conscience unto righteous works, choosing good, eschewing and casting off evil.

8. And thus all have their agency, as they come to mature years more especially, even the age of accountability; yea, even by the age of eight years old, a child knows good from evil.

9. Thus saith the Lord: As you continue in the spirit of murder of unborn children, and then become aggressive when peaceful means could be used -- I command thee to repent!

10. I am the God of Creation.

11. Cease these murderous ways.

12. Cease your military actions in nations who have not thus attacked thee.

13. I, the Lord, command thee to repent unto a bringing forth of a change of policy and intent, and even justice served upon leaders of nations, thus saith the Lord, within each nation by their lawmaking bodies, and not think that you can transgress the borders of another nation aggressively and perform murder -- thine own pride satisfied, and not correct principle of law-abiding and just ways being followed.

14. Thus I send this corresponding of mine own words to the leader of this nation, to his Cabinet, to lawmakers of high standing.

15. I reveal my word to thee: Repent of thy murderous and immoral ways, the leaders of this nation as well as the peoples of this nation, for you have offended thy God, the great numbers in millions celebrating in their hearts the murder of a soul who could have been taken peaceably, and tried before the courts in the jurisdiction appointed, and of justice, by the nation that could have apprehended him.

16. Thus saith the Lord: Let this wicked generation repent speedily, lest my cleansing process sweep them off my land of Zion and leave them neither root nor branch -- in earthquake, tornado, storm and windstorms, pestilence, hail, and famine, the overflowing scourge and desolating sickness promised this wicked generation if they repent not.

17. For I am the God that made you. You are sons and daughters of God sent to a probationary earth to be tested what you will choose.

18. And when leaders of nations

choose wickedness, I, the Lord, execute judgment upon them through righteous justice administered, even overthrowing leaders of nations, removing them from power, and, at times, sweeping the wicked of a nation off the earth, where they can further repent, if they will, in the world of departed spirits; I being a God of love, laboring for the salvation of all, whether on earth, whether they be spirits yet unborn who shall be sent to this probationary earth, preserving their lives unto those who can beget them unto correct principles, just and righteous, to earn an eternal salvation; and also among those in the world of departed spirits.

19. My Gospel message shall go to all on this earth and in the world of departed spirits, now and in the future giving.

20. And I shall be called justified as every knee bows and every tongue confesses that Jesus is the Christ, a God over all creation, and He ruleth righteously, and He hath done right toward all peoples, nations, kindreds, and tongues.

21. This shall be declared in future time as truth is revealed and all secrets are made known.

22. And thus saith the Lord to the leaders of this nation and all nations: All your secret acts and intentions of the heart shall be revealed in the Millennial Reign of Peace, in the government of God in Zion, and sent forth to the nations, and in the day of judgment when you stand before a just God in the resurrection;

23. For I am the Resurrection and the Life, and the God that shall judge thee, appointed by my Father, Elohim, even Ahman; for I am Son Ahman, to perform that work of judging all mankind.

24. Ye shall stand before me.

25. I shall unlock thy mind, which shall reveal all the secrets of thy life, and nothing hidden; and you shall be judged by a just and holy God, even your Lord and Redeemer, Jesus Christ, who speaketh these words to the leaders of this nation through mine authority on earth.

26. Thus saith your God to thee: You shall be judged, and wickedness shall be punished with that degree of buffetings and suffering requisite for justice to be satisfied upon every person who repenteth not, even a full justice;

27. For my atoning power and suffering can only be a benefit to those who repent and accept my Gospel of salvation; yea, my message of salvation I shall soon send to every nation of the earth, both before my glorious appearing, to prepare many peoples, and a greater degree after my glorious coming to New Jerusalem, which shall rise in this generation.

28. This is my revealing to you at this time of a needed message to be given to the leaders of this nation of the United States of America, for you have offended your God in following wicked and unjust and corrupt principles, even unto murder, not having placed the accused before a tribunal, which you do in your own land for any criminal thus apprehended, of general policy, save those secret combinations which the leaders of this nation have sometimes followed in destroying life secretly in murderous intent.

29. Thus have the people of this nation offended their God, in glorying in murder, which could have been avoided.

30. The wicked shall slay the wicked, even in mob violence in thy land, if you heed me not; if this spirit of glorying in the loss of life, instead of mourning when one who is wicked passes on unprepared for salvation -- thus should all peoples do, understanding the purposes of thy God of Creation over thee, in bringing thee forth

in this life of probationary and testing time to prove thy characters, whether or no you will love life and eternal principles that exalt, or transgress against the principles of life and earn a never-ending judgment of sorrow, not being exalted to be with the God who made thee.

31. And in the resurrection there shall be added to your mind the memory of having been born to a God of Creation, well-prepared; to know the purpose of this mortal life, forgetting previous existence as a test, yet having my Spirit of light and life in thee at birth, and in thy growing years, to teach you good from evil, prompting you in what you call your mental conscience unto better works.

32. I am the God of Creation whose Spirit of light and life shineth upon all creation, to give all creation its existence.

33. I am a God of love that blesseth all.

34. And as death passeth on all, sending their spirits inhabiting their mortal bodies, the body lying in the grave, the spirits going to a world of living, a place of departed spirits where my Priesthood labors to administer the message of my salvation to all of every nation, kindred, tongue, and peoples; verily, I reveal to you, murderers hath no forgiveness.

35. If you take on the spirit of that sin and consent to this evil in the conduct of any person, you shall also have the same degree of judgment according to thy crimes in the flesh -- crimes against thy God, and eternal, exalting principles; crimes against thine own knowledge; for all shall be judged according to the light they received in this mortal existence, saith the Lord God, who administers life unto eternal life to those who love and obey laws that exalt, ways to their greatest ability to understand according to the light

they receive; yea, even a God who can exalt thee unto eternal life, those who live laws of progression unto eternal life, of my message, and Priesthood, Church and Kingdom, of salvation powers that are now on the earth, preparing the way for the rise of Zion in fulness, a New Jerusalem built on the continent where the United States of America dwells at this time; and nothing can stay mine hand;

36. For I shall sweep the more wicked off the earth and preserve the more righteous unto my reign of righteousness, which shall be for a thousand years of my dwelling among men, to their knowing, in my power and glory in Zion; and the Kingdom of heaven coming forth to earth as the governing power over all nations.

37. Heed my word.

38. Repent of your murderous and immoral ways, which leads thee to a murderous way;

39. For thus are the corrupt in heart not able to govern themselves, being blinded by their own corruptions, justifying their murderous ways.

40. I, the Lord, shall bring them to justice, even in the eternal duration of time, feeling the wrath of a just God, who hath given them His Spirit in their minds and hearts as a conscience to know good from evil.

41. Let the policies of thy government cease this practice, is the command of thy Lord in this correspondence of needed message to thee. Amen.

42. Thus saith your Lord and Savior, Jesus Christ, further, to the people of the nation of the United States of America:

43. Repent ye! Repent ye! for my day of my glorious coming is nigh at hand.

44. Heed my word.

45. I have sent many warnings to the

leaders of this nation, and to the peoples of this nation, of recent doing.

46. You must heed my words, lest there be upon you a greater judgment than you can bear, to leave you neither root nor branch of posterity upon the earth.

47. There are the sins of the shedding of innocent blood of unborn children legalized in this nation; the sins of corruption, of secret combinations to get gain by evil means, even of murder, upon this land and among your peoples, even among the leaders of this nation, which I, the Lord, reveal openly, and shall reveal more in a time soon to come;

48. For you cannot hide from a God who seeth all things, and is just and holy and righteous, who shall judge all men according to their deeds done in the flesh.

49. Thus saith the Lord: Let there not be a celebration of thy peoples again of any man's being murdered, yea, his death.

50. Mourn over the loss of life when they go to the world of departed spirits, not having my message of salvation, unprepared for a glorious salvation, losing the same because they would not hear my word sent forth by testimony and holy writ.

51. Let not this people of this nation again glorify themselves in murder, wherein a man whose known location in another nation could have been apprehended by the authorities of that nation and placed before a tribunal, and not taken in death.

52. Thus saith the Lord: Let this cease in your natures.

53. Violence covereth this land, even in the spirit of the people of this nation.

54. Thus saith the Lord: I am the God of peace.

55. I will sweep those off the land where thy nation resides, in every nation on that continent, yea, on the North American continent who have violence in their nature.

56. For Zion is a place of peace, and my Zion shall rise, even New Jerusalem in the Center Stake of Zion, in Jackson County, Missouri, as I have proclaimed; and nothing can stay mine hand.

57. Thus I have sent this warning to the leader and peoples of this nation to repent, and know that my coming is nigh at hand. Amen.

SECTION REVELATION 71

Fundamentalist Church of Jesus Christ of Latter-day Saints
P.O. Box 840459
Hildale, Utah 84784

Thus Saith Son Ahman, Even Jesus Christ, to the Leaders of the Nation of Serbia -- A God of Glory Who Ruleth Over All Peoples, Dwelling in Heaven, Soon to Come to Earth in a Glorious Appearing, Who Shall Make Himself Known as a God of Power -- Hear My Word to Thee:

Revelation of the Lord Jesus Christ
Eldorado, Texas
Tuesday, May 3, 2011

1. Thus saith the Lord unto the nation of Serbia:

2. I, the Lord, warn thee and send you this, my word, even Jesus Christ who reigneth, Him who has all power and sees and knows all things, who speaks from the heavens through His authority on earth:

3. Repent ye of your warlike and jealous ways against other nations, even of your vengeful and revenging ways.

4. Forgive, and offer peace to the neighboring nations, to Bosnia and others that surround thee, and be of peaceful intent.

5. I call upon your leaders, even the leaders of Serbia, to cease your warlike and hateful ways, where you are willing to use violence against other peoples, and to get gain and power. Let it not be.

6. And treat minority religions in thy borders, in thy land, with freedom of worship and kindness; and promote peace with other nations around thee, that you may remain a nation;

7. For those of violent nature, willing to use aggressive means of violence against other nations, shall cause a war to erupt that shall absorb thee, to no longer be a nation.

8. This I warn thee, that the leaders of this nation may know that thy God hath spoken, who is the God of peace, of righteousness and truth and holy walk, who requireth all men, yea, and their families, to be of the nature of peace.

9. For I am a God of truth and shall cause all men to be raised from the grave -- a God of glory, who suffered on the cross and bore the weight and sins of all peoples to conquer death, to raise in the resurrection, unto eternal judgment, all peoples;

10. Yea, I shall stand as a Judge of your deeds done in the flesh.

11. Those who are of a murderous and violent nature shall reap the reward of sorrow in an eternal judgment.

12. Make peace. Repent ye of your warlike tendencies, lest your nation be absorbed in a war that shall crush thee, to be a nation no longer.

13. Now hear my word:

14. I, your Lord and Savior, Jesus Christ, speaketh, that my appearing is soon at hand, and all nations and all people shall know of my glorious appearing.

15. And I shall send, of necessity, a cleansing power over the earth, yea, to cleanse the more wicked out of every nation and every land of the earth, and preserve the more righteous.

16. For my message of salvation, even mine eternal message unto eternal life, of thy Holy Savior, must be sent forth to all peoples, nations, kindreds, and tongues.

17. And those who pass on to the world of departed spirits from this mortal life, of a probationary testing time, shall hear my Gospel of salvation through my Priesthood authority now laboring among the spirits in the world of departed spirits.

18. And I am a just God who shall bring forth my message of salvation to all peoples.

19. And my Zion, even New Jerusalem on the American continent, shall rise of a soon happening, and nothing can stay mine hand;

20. For I shall cleanse all wickedness off that land also, to prepare for my glorious appearing.

21. And all people shall know of my glory, and the wicked shall fear and stand afar off, and I shall send my message of salvation, my love-giving message of peace to all surviving peoples of every land and nation, kindred, tongue, and people.

22. Thus saith the Lord: Prepare ye, and allow freedom of worship in thy borders and in thy land, by legal proceedings and laws well-kept; and do not persecute minority religions at all.

23. And I shall bless thy nation if you heed my words.

24. Only use military force for self-defense, and not aggression, that you may be honored by thy God as a people -- who are more righteous among you -- to remain on earth and know of my glorious appearing, which is nigh at hand.

25. I, the Lord, have spoken it, and am the God of glory and of all power.

26. All nations exist only by my grace, and there are none who have power greater than their God who created them.

27. Therefore, humble yourselves before me, lest you be humbled and no longer remain as a nation on earth, is the word of thy God, who upholds all peoples and nations in their place, by His grace and power. Amen.

SECTION REVELATION 72

Fundamentalist Church of Jesus Christ of Latter-day Saints
P.O. Box 840459
Hildale, Utah 84784

The God of Glory, Even Jesus Christ, Who Is Son Ahman, Speaketh to the Leaders of the Nation of Bahrain, to Be Known by Their Peoples, Also, That the God of Heaven Hath Spoken Concerning What Shall Come Upon Thee, of a Soon Happening -- Judgments, That Are Just, Upon the Leaders of This Nation:

Revelation of the Lord Jesus Christ
Eldorado, Texas
Friday, May 6, 2011

1. I, the Lord Jesus Christ, even Son Ahman, the Creator of heaven and earth, who uphold all peoples and nations in their place, sendeth further word to the leaders of Bahrain:

2. Repent ye! And cease your aggressive nature against your own citizenry, the peoples in thy land.

3. Though you be a nation of small size, yet your leaders are enriched in the economic ability of moneymaking; and having that blessing of thy God upon thee, having preserved thee, do not use your military nor police force against thine own citizens in a violent nature.

4. And do not accept compromise in thy lawmaking ability, wherein immorality and crime is upheld.

5. Be of a just and equitous governing power, and not oppressive, or you shall cease to be a nation, as another nation shall conquer thee and remove your leaders from power if you heed me not.

6. I have sent you a warning, even a warning to the leaders of all nations, of my glorious appearing -- a just and merciful God, who shall soon sweep the more wicked of the earth from off the face of the earth in great judging powers, cleansing powers, and preserve the more righteous in every nation.

7. Thus I will do, as the God of glory, as I descend to earth, making myself known to all peoples of surviving nature in every nation of the powers of heaven, to dwell on earth among men in my Zion, a New Jerusalem, soon to be built up in fulness on the American continent in the place I have appointed, having sent my word to the nations of the earth of my glorious appearing in sacred and holy writing of mine apostles of old, who were with me in my ministry on earth, saith Jesus Christ; and also through my servant Joseph Smith, and my messengers of salvation to the nations of the earth, well published to the peoples of the earth.

8. Thus saith the Lord: Cease your aggression against your own peoples.

9. Do not allow the murder of unborn

children in thy nation at all, nor adulterous or immoral ways sanctioned by law.

10. And cease using force to get gain or power, but be of a more equitous and inviting nature to your people; of peace; for if you use the shedding of blood, even murder against thine own people through military action, my blessings of protection shall withdraw, your wealth shall wither away in your hands and not be present, and the leadership shall be removed and be a tributary people to another nation.

11. This is my warning to you.

12. If you heed my word, I shall preserve thee as a blessing to other surrounding nations in a time of great need and trouble in their borders, and call upon thee to be a strength of righteous doing, and kindness, and peacemaking.

13. Heed my word; for as I have spoken, even the Lord over all -- who created and upholds all things as I have named, who seeth and knoweth all things, and looketh down from the heavens seeing the unjust ways of thy governing powers, thine oppressive ways -- send you this, my warning, through mine authority on earth, through whom I speak as my Mouthpiece to all peoples of the earth.

14. Prepare thy people for my message of salvation when I send my messengers to thee, whom you shall know are from Zion; Son Ahman, even Jesus Christ, sending them forth by my almighty power to warn and teach all peoples.

15. Hasten to prepare, and cleanse thine own borders and nation and peoples of corrupt and immoral and murderous ways within thy borders, saith the Lord, the God over all. Amen.

SECTION REVELATION 73

Fundamentalist Church of Jesus Christ of Latter-day Saints
P.O. Box 840459
Hildale, Utah 84784

Thus Saith the Lord Jesus Christ, Even Son Ahman, the Creator of Heaven and Earth, Who Has All Power to Govern Worlds, Who Came to Earth and Suffered for All Mankind, to Redeem Them From the Grave and Raise Them Up to the Resurrection to Be Judged of a Just God -- Yea, I, Your Lord and Savior, the God of Creation Over You, Speaketh to the Leaders of China and the Peoples of China, Who Shall Fulfill All His Words as a God of Truth -- Hear Ye My Word, Which Saith Thus:

Revelation of the Lord Jesus Christ
Eldorado, Texas
Friday, May 6, 2011

1. Thus saith the Lord unto the nation of China, even Jesus Christ, who reigneth on high, the God of heaven and over all nations of the earth, who has all power:

2. You heed me not.

3. You continue in a practice of murder of unborn children, and oppression to thine own peoples in great measure.

4. And though you become as a warring nation in future time, seeking to conquer other nations, I shall humble thee because you heed me not.

5. And you shall feel a great depopulation of thy people in great judgments of God, removing the more wicked, preserving the more righteous in thy land, that they may know the God of glory hath spoken.

6. And thus saith the Lord: Those of political power shall be removed from power at a time soon at hand, when I, your God, come in my glory, even Jesus Christ, with all the righteous saints from heaven coming to earth to establish a dominion on the American continent called Zion, a New Jerusalem of almighty and eternal power, becoming the governing power over all nations of the earth.

7. And you shall heed me, or receive the judgments of a just God for your wickedness among your own peoples, and against other peoples of other nations, which is now in the intent of thy military build-up and in the hearts of thy leaders.

8. And though I, the Lord, may allow a humbling of other nations by thine hand, I shall reward thee according to thy deeds if you heed me not, corrupting the way of the Lord before thee.

9. Thus saith the Lord: The murder of unborn children is a great crime against thy God, who sendeth forth the spirits of the children of men to inhabit mortal tabernacles of the flesh.

10. And when you thus perform this most wicked crime of destroying unborn children before they can take the breath of life, you are fighting against the plan of your God, who hath promised His spirit children in heaven to receive an earthly tabernacle of mortal existence on that probationary earth upon which you dwell.

11. And who art thou to dictate thy God, saith the Lord, in deciding what spirit shall be born and which children shall not be born on the earth that thy God hath made, who gave thee life?

12. Thy murders shall canker thy soul into eternity, seeking power and gain through corruption and this most wicked form of murder that exists among the children of men, inspired by the dark powers that seek to destroy the purposes of God in the advancement of the children of men unto eternal life.

13. And I, the Lord, rebuke thee, this nation of China, for your practice of corruption, of the murder of unborn children.

14. Thus saith the Lord: Your form of government shall fail in a time soon to come, as I shall cause the more wicked of your nation to be swept off the earth in the judgments of a just God to cease this crime.

15. For verily I say unto you, in the day of eternal judgment, when you stand before your God, a murderer shall not have happiness, but shall have to receive of thy God a just punishment, a punishment so great, thy minds cannot comprehend;

16. For thy life and the secrets of thy life shall be revealed before all peoples, and nothing shall be hidden, unlocking thine own mind and you being your own accuser of that which you have done in the flesh; and you shall be judged for the deeds done in the flesh.

17. And I give you this strong word that perchance some among you may be of an awakening nature, your hearts touched with truth eternal, that there shall be an eternal judgment for your actions done in the flesh, for the desires of your heart that you sought after.

18. And if you would do well, cease this practice among your peoples of the murder of unborn children; and seek unto thy God how to supply the needs of your peoples without murder of the innocence.

19. Thus it is -- the most innocent forms of life, unable to defend themselves, the unborn children, destroyed by thee who have darkened minds and will not consider there is a God of glory who can supply the needs of life to every nation if they will but seek unto Him.

20. And I am that God of glory, saith Jesus Christ, and speaketh to thee in plain, understanding language, revealed from the heavens through my servant on earth, appointed by me to be my Mouthpiece to all nations, kindreds, tongues, and peoples; that I, the God of glory, even Jesus Christ, am soon to come to earth in the power of great glory and make myself known to all nations, all who remain;

21. For first must come the cleansing of the more wicked of every nation from off the earth, in a just judgment I shall send; having sent my words of warning, yea, my publishing of mine own word of recent giving, into your own hands.

22. Thus saith the Lord: I shall be justified in removing the more wicked from off the earth through the cleansing processes of eternal powers -- through earthquake, tornado, windstorms, floods, pestilence, hail, famine; through overflowing scourges

and diseases; through wars of thine own begetting, because of the darkness of thine hearts, not responding to the God of peace when He calleth upon all nations to be at peace one toward another.

23. The time of my coming is soon at hand; and thus I send my word, by mine authority on earth, to the nations of the earth, and, in this communication, a strong warning unto an eternal judgment to the leaders of the nation of China; yea, in this communication warning thee that though your mortal flesh may lie in the grave, your spirit continues to live, and goes to the world of departed spirits wherein I still govern; and you cannot escape the vengeance of a just God.

24. And in the day of judgment, when your body is raised from the grave, with your spirit entering therein, in a more exalted nature, you shall stand before your God of glory, even Jesus Christ, who shall judge thee, and all secrets be revealed of thy life.

25. And there shall be a punishment and a suffering for those of a murderous nature, all according to the degree of their crimes; for I shall recompense to every man, woman, and child what they have measured to their fellow man.

26. And this is the word of the God of glory.

27. Though you deny me, even Jesus Christ, and my message of salvation, yet I am just and equitous and shall allow all peoples, either on earth or in the world of departed spirits, to hear my message of salvation.

28. And during this thousand years, after my appearing to the nations of the earth, shall I reign on earth among men, a reign of righteous governing peace, the powers of heaven coming to earth, and

my authority on earth being the governing power over all nations that survive the great judgments of a just God upon the more wicked of every nation now upon the earth.

29. And so great is this event of cleansing, I, the Lord, am justified by sending forth my word of warning in language to be understood, and calling upon thee, leaders of nations, and the peoples of all nations, to repent of these most wicked practices;

30. For the eternal duration of judgment shall be woeful unto thee, of extreme sorrow and suffering, for the guilty crime of murder.

31. Thus saith the Lord: Do not consent to this murdering crime of the destruction of children unborn, and of other crimes of violence upon the living, just to get gain and power; for all corruption shall be answered with a just judgment by an Eternal God of glory, whose works are only righteous, pure, and holy;

32. For all mankind, in the day of judgment, yea, eternal judgment, when raised from the grave by the resurrection of the power of thy Savior, shall declare thy God hath done right as they acknowledge their sins before Him, those who would not repent and turn to a righteous way of doing in their mortal existence on this probationary earth where you now dwell.

33. Though you be a nation that shall yet be used to humble other nations, the continuation of wicked aggression, the oppression of thine own peoples, and the murder of unborn children shall cause a just God to come out in judgments against thee and remove those from power who now hold power as leaders of this nation if they continue in wicked practices.

34. They have partaken of philosophies

of men, which have been influenced by the dark powers of Lucifer to destroy life before life comes forth, and to use military and forceful means to oppress thine own peoples.

35. And there are secret murders taking place by the direction of the leaders of the nation of China, even within your nation, of those you call dissident or unfavorable.

36. And you oppress many in jails of oppression because they agree not with thy wicked ways of ruling, of governing, and concerning the ways of life which are unjust.

37. I have allowed your nation to become rich and prosper thy peoples in commerce and trade well-prepared; yet you continue in these crimes against mankind in your own nation, and would oppress other nations likewise if I allowed thee to expand thy power elsewhere over other nations on the earth.

38. I, the Lord, call thee to repent, and be equitous and just, and give proper rights of freedom of speech and of worship to the peoples in thy land.

39. Prepare thy peoples for my message of salvation by allowing freedom of worship of religion of choice, wherein they harm no one, only seeking a salvation in an eternal existence that the God of Creation, who made this earth and sent thee forth as sons and daughters of God to people this earth, can thus exercise His powers of Godhood to exalt the more righteous unto eternal life.

40. This is in language to thine understanding, that thy God, yea, the God of Creation, even Jesus Christ, who reigns over the earth, hath eternal purposes to fulfill, upon this earth and in behalf of all mankind.

41. Search your hearts and repent, and

cease these evil practices of oppression and murder and violence, of immorality, even organized crime, often joining with leaders of the nation to get gain; for all these secret combinations are known by thy God, who shall reward all mankind as I have named.

42. I am the God of glory.

43. My Zion, a New Jerusalem, shall be built on the American continent, to be the governing city over all nations that survive my whirlwind judgments of eternal power upon all nations, soon to take place.

44. Thus I am justifying this cleansing power coming forth by sending forth my word of warning;

45. For any nation who continues in these sins -- of the murder of unborn children, and Sodom, and adultery, and immorality -- and any leaders that oppress their people and murder their own people, a just God shall send judgments to remove those more wicked individuals from off the land where they dwell, to depart this life through the destructive and cleansing process coming among you.

46. Prepare ye for my eternal glory coming to earth, and my righteous reign of a Millennium over all nations, and for my messengers of salvation to come among your peoples;

47. For I shall send cleansing powers to remove those from power who thus would oppress the freedom of worship and of speech and of representation;

48. For the Kingdom of heaven is coming to earth, even the God of glory, thy Lord and Savior, with the heavenly powers to establish peace among all nations, prospering all peoples in a more righteous and pure way of living; just to all, equitous in rights and privileges to pursue the ways of happiness.

49. Thus saith the Lord to the leaders of

the nation of China, and to all thy peoples: Repent ye! Repent ye! lest you receive a judgment hard to bear, beyond what you can consider, even in this mortal lifetime of suffering, if you are of a murderous spirit as I have named.

50. I, the Lord, will forgive whom I will forgive.

51. The God of glory cometh. Prepare ye for my glorious appearing, saith Son Ahman, Jehovah Christ, even Jesus Christ, coming in the clouds of heaven as a power to cleanse the earth of wickedness and bring forth a righteous reign, and build a city, New Jerusalem, of governing power.

52. And all nations shall flow to that city to learn of the eternal and happy ways of the God of glory, who dwells in eternal happiness through righteousness and a pure and holy walk with those who can be sanctified unto eternal lives.

53. My message of salvation shall be delivered to thy peoples. Prepare ye for the receiving thereof; and preserve my messengers when they are sent into thy borders, lest judgments come upon you.

54. Be of a peacemaking nature toward neighboring nations, is the command of thy God; and I shall prosper thee and thy people as you repent and remove these evils, and even cause leaders guilty of secret murders and of crimes of oppression to be brought to justice.

55. I, the Lord, have spoken it; so shall I fulfill, and nothing shall stay mine hand;

56. For so great are thy crimes in the policy of thy government to destroy unborn children and oppress thine own people, I must needs warn thee that after you become a nation that oppresses other nations, a cleansing power shall remove the more wicked from thy borders and on thy land, and preserve the more righteous for my message of salvation, the Gospel of Jesus Christ unto eternal life. Amen.

SECTION REVELATION 74

Fundamentalist Church of Jesus Christ of Latter-day Saints
P.O. Box 840459
Hildale, Utah 84784

Your Lord and Savior, Jesus Christ, Speaketh, Even Son Ahman, to the Leaders and Peoples of the Nation of France, Saying Thus:

Revelation of the Lord Jesus Christ
Eldorado, Texas
Friday, May 6, 2011

1. Thus saith the Lord Jesus Christ unto that nation and the leaders of the nation of France, having promoted, yea, of a beginning nature, an attack against the nation of Libya, when I sent you warning to cleanse the inside of the platter.

2. I am the God of glory and shall soon come in the glorious apparel of the

clouds of heaven, the powers of an eternal governing nature to earth, to govern all nations, to dwell among my people Zion in New Jerusalem, on the land of America, as it is known among men.

3. I, the Lord, speaketh to thee:

4. Withdraw thy military from aggressive ways against another nation that did not attack thy borders at all.

5. And set an example to be of a peaceful nature, of soon happening.

6. And cleanse the inside of the platter, your own peoples, before you seek to thus discipline other nations; for the crimes of Sodom and Gomorrah, and of the murder of unborn children, and of adultery and licentious and corrupt ways are rampant in thy land; and if you heed me not, my greater judgments shall sweep most of your population off the earth, only a few remaining;

7. And your power shall be clipped, and not be a power upon earth, only to have a record kept that the word of thy God who made thee and allows thee a place on earth, and time and agency and the gifts of life to prove what thou lovest most, whether it be good or evil, yea, a God of justice shall render thee an accounting, a rendering of a just judgment upon thee if you heed me not.

8. Thou knowest my message of my coming in the writings of mine apostles, who were with me in the day of my ministry, saith Jesus Christ.

9. Thou knowest of my word I have recently sent, of warning to the leaders of the nations of the earth, to be of a peacemaking nature.

10. Glory not in violence.

11. I, the Lord, am able to hear prayers and answer prayers of the honest in heart in every nation.

12. And those leaders of nations who become aggressive against other nations shall be humbled, and their power clipped, and they removed from power.

13. And if their peoples continue in those most corrupt ways and heinous crimes of murder and immorality, yea, even murder of unborn children -- the most innocent, unable to defend themselves -- declaring unto thee:

14. Who art thou, the leaders of nations, and of this nation of France, to allow the murder of unborn children, even by legal consent, to decide who shall have life and who shall not have life, of the spirits I send to earth to inhabit mortal and earthly tabernacles, to prove themselves whether they will choose good and eschew and cast off evil through their agency?

15. And thus your national laws must be changed, and justice administered to remove these corrupt ways among thee;

16. For wickedness shall not rule during my thousand years of peace as I dwell among men on earth, as the governing power over all the earth.

17. And all peoples shall be humbled, I removing the more wicked from off the earth, preserving the more righteous, preparing them for my glorious appearing.

18. And I am God, the God of Creation, who rules in the heavens and over all nations of the earth that speaketh, who sees and knows all things, and nothing is hidden.

19. Hear my words:

20. Repent ye! yea, even the leaders of this nation.

21. Promote peace among the nations, for all these judgments I have named, even whirlwind and disease and famine, earthquake, hail -- and violent wars, if you continue in violence, of thine own make

because you heed me not -- these shall sweep the more wicked off thy land and out of thy nation.

22. I am a God of truth, of righteous and holy and pure ways, and know all things, and am able to judge a righteous judgment upon all peoples.

23. Let the leaders of this nation realize the eternal truth that a just God, who hath conquered death and can raise all mankind from the grave through the resurrection powers -- you shall be raised from the grave to stand before me and be judged for your deeds done in the flesh.

24. And if you allow these murderous ways to continue, that most heinous and corrupt crime of the murder of unborn children shall corrupt thy souls unto a woeful and just existence against thee in the realms of Sheol, even the buffetings and powers of distress upon thy soul for committing such crimes on earth.

25. And the more righteous shall inherit salvation unto happiness by a just God as they perform works of righteousness and promote virtue and life in just laws upheld.

26. Cleanse thy people.

27. Humble thyselves, and set an example of peace by withdrawing thy military from attacking another nation, which did not attack your nation, you becoming an aggressive nation in this action against Libya.

28. It will not stand, as you have proved your nature to be a violent nation, and yet will not cleanse your own peoples of their corrupt ways.

29. Set thyselves in order first.

30. Overthrow any laws that advance the murder of unborn children and immorality.

31. Perform the works I have named if you desire to be a preserved nation in the time of my greater judgments, else all my promises shall be fulfilled concerning thee, both in this warning and my previous warnings I have sent, saith your Lord and Savior, Jesus Christ, who ruleth over all, who bringeth with Him the reward of a just recompense to all men, according to the measure they have given toward their fellow man. Amen.

SECTION REVELATION 75

Fundamentalist Church of Jesus Christ of Latter-day Saints
P.O. Box 840459
Hildale, Utah 84784

Thus Saith Son Ahman, Even Jesus Christ, the Creator of Heaven and Earth, the God of Glory and of Power, to the Leaders of the Nation of Germany -- My Warning Voice of Judgments Soon to Come, and of My Glorious Appearing to Reward Thee According to Thy Deeds, Yea, to Both Leaders and the Peoples of This Nation, Saying Thus, Mine Own Word, to Your Understanding -- Mine Authority on Earth, My Mouthpiece Thus Sending Forth My Word by Mine Authority and Command, and Who Shall Come in Great Power to Govern the Nations of the Earth From New Jerusalem, Built Upon the American Continent as My Zion -- Thus Saith the Lord:

Revelation of the Lord Jesus Christ
Eldorado, Texas
Friday, May 6, 2011

1. I who reigneth on high, even your Lord and Savior, Jesus Christ, the Governor and Ruler of the heavens and the earth, having all power, soon to come to earth in His glory to make Himself known to all surviving nations on the earth, soon to send forth whirlwind judgments to cleanse all nations of the more wicked of their population, preserving the more righteous among them, speaketh; being the God of glory and of all creation, unto the people of Germany:

2. You have become corrupt before me.

3. Your open immorality and the murder of unborn children is a stench on earth before the heavens, of gross corruption and evil ways.

4. I have called upon thee in former communications, of mine own word to thee, to repent of these gross crimes, of the murder of unborn children, and of Sodom and adultery, and open nakedness allowed by rule of law, promoting wickedness and corruption in thy nation.

5. Thus saith the Lord: You shall become a mostly depopulated nation and land as you continue in these wicked practices, only a remnant of thy peoples remaining, even the more righteous, for you heed me not.

6. I have called upon thee, along with leaders of all nations of the earth, to do away with these outward crimes against humanity, against thine own peoples and thine own nature.

7. I am the God that created thee, and upholds all nations and peoples in their place, and my glorious appearing is nigh at hand.

8. I shall bring with me the powers of heaven in my great glory to dwell in Zion, a New Jerusalem built on the American continent, soon to happen; and shall make myself known, and my righteous governing power rule over all remaining nations, cleansed by earthquake and windstorm, pestilence, hail, and famine, and wars of their own choosing wherein they heed me not, when I have declared unto all nations and leaders of all nations to be of peace toward all nations, and within thine own borders and among thine own peoples.

9. I suffered on the cross and conquered death in the resurrection; and I shall raise all men, women, and children in the resurrection and judge all peoples according to their works done in the flesh.

10. And murder and consent to murder is a gross crime, unto an eternal judgment of suffering, greater than you know, for sins.

11. I send the light of my Spirit upon all peoples, called by the children of men as their conscience, to touch them to promote righteous and pure ways of living.

12. And as you heed me not and follow the enemy of your souls, even the powers of darkness, Lucifer, who promoteth wicked men to perform murder and secret combinations to get gain and power, thus saith the Lord, it shall not stand.

13. I am the God of all power, and shall reward all peoples according to their deeds done in the flesh.

14. I shall send my message of salvation from my Zion to all surviving nations.

15. Prepare ye thy peoples, and remove these most wicked ways and heinous crimes that I have named from among your people, and no longer uphold them by legal consent, or you shall cease to be a great nation of power, and only have a remnant scattered that shall know that the God of heaven hath spoken and hath fulfilled His word, as I have named.

16. There hath been among thy people great wars in the last century, humbling thee for aggression.

17. Now humble yourselves, and remove these great sins from among thy people, and have laws upheld by legal legislative bodies and governing powers among thee, removing these evils, punishing even leaders who perform secret murders and uphold immorality and crime in any way; for it is a great crime before the heavens -- the murder of unborn children, and your immoral and corrupt ways of adultery and Sodom.

18. There is among your people the blood of Israel, and my message of salvation shall gather out the believing blood to my Zion.

19. And I shall preserve, by my almighty power, the more righteous among your peoples, removing the more wicked through the judgments I have named.

20. Heed my word, and repent ye of these most wicked crimes, lest my full judgments come upon you and you no longer be a nation of power on the earth, is the word of thy God who made thee, and who shall judge thee according to thy deeds. Amen.

SECTION REVELATION 76

Fundamentalist Church of Jesus Christ of Latter-day Saints
P.O. Box 840459
Hildale, Utah 84784

Thus Saith Son Ahman, Even Jesus Christ, the God of Creation Who Dwells in the Heavens, Who Created the Earth -- A God of Glory of Eternal Power, Who Sees and Knows All Things, to the Leaders of the Nation of Iran and the Peoples Thereof, Even the God Who Made You, Speaking Words of Warning Unto Eternal Consequences Resting Upon Thee -- Receive Ye My Word, Which Saith Thus:

Revelation of the Lord Jesus Christ
Eldorado, Texas
Friday, May 6, 2011

1. Thus saith the Lord, the Great I AM, even Jehovah, your Lord and Redeemer, who dwells on high and has all things in His power to redeem mankind, unto eternal lives for the obedient, and an eternal judgment upon the disobedient, unto a place according as their works are; unto that people residing in the nation and kingdom of Iran, wherein you continue to not heed my word, saith Jesus Christ:

2. I shall fulfill my word, and nothing can stay mine hand; and the leaders of this nation shall no longer be in power in a time soon to come, as a revolution shall take place;

3. And other warring nations, because of thy violent nature, shall come upon thee in a manner to humble thee;

4. For great shall be thy humbling and the loss of life among thy peoples, because you heed me not.

5. I commanded that ye be of the peacemaking nature, and be more liberal and kind in allowing freedoms to women, and protection from abusive husbands and abusive men, which abuses are harbored by tradition among thy peoples; and also the gross immorality that is among thy nation, overlooked by leaders, allowed to continue because leaders' hearts are corrupt.

6. I am the God of Creation, who seeth and knoweth all things, and nothing is hidden from mine eyes.

7. And I reveal that there shall be a great war to remove thee from power, saith the Lord.

8. I am the Lord over all, a God of redeeming and atoning power, who has conquered death and shall raise all mankind unto life in the resurrection and judge all peoples according as their works have been in the flesh;

9. Therefore, beware how you conduct your lives before me, for I am the God over all, and have all power to fulfill my word.

10. Heed my word.

11. Remove these evils of corruption and abuse, even among thine own people;

12. And this warlike and violent tendency to oppose other nations, let it cease, and be of a peacemaking nature.

13. Allow worship, of free agency applied, to whatsoever religion people choose, to be of a legal standing in thy land, yea, the free exercise of choice, that my message of salvation may come forth among thee.

14. And be of the nature of righteousness and truth; establishing, in the lives of individuals, hope of a glorious resurrection unto thy God who created thee.

15. A time of great distress and trial is soon to come upon all nations.

16. Heed my word, ye leaders of this nation of Iran, lest perils come upon you and remove you out of your place for not heeding the word of the God who created you and sustains all peoples in their place.

17. This, an additional message, that I will be justified in sending judgments upon thee to remove the more wicked from thy land, even the leadership that now stands as a governing power over this nation, preserving the more righteous against the time of my coming and the rise of New Jerusalem on my land of Zion, the American continent;

18. For I shall bring forth the powers of heaven as the governing power over the earth, over all nations, and all shall hear my voice and acknowledge my right to rule as the God over all.

19. This is my revealing and also my warning, that I will be justified in performing these works of cleansing of the earth, and also of this nation that I have sent forth my own word of warning to, in previous publishings, in corresponding revealings of mine own word through mine authority on earth.

20. Hasten to prepare, for I am the God of glory that cometh to earth in the clouds of heaven, the angels attending.

21. And all shall know of the coming of thy Lord. Amen.

22. Thus saith the Lord unto that nation, Iran, in my continued word:

23. Thy folly blindeth thee as you heed me not.

24. In a day as a thief in the night cometh, my judgments shall suddenly awake you that thy God hath spoken, and you shall know, of a surety, every word I have given thee shall be fulfilled.

25. Let the leader of this nation repent of his secret combinations to get gain and power, not attending to the protecting of innocence and purity, having used police and military power to subjugate thy people, wherein they desire freedom of expression and of worship and equal rights, and women desire rights of protection.

26. Thus saith the Lord: Thy nation shall cease to be, and thy peoples be part of other nations and earthly powers not now in power in thy land, if you continue in your warlike and unpeaceful ways;

27. For I am the God of peace over all creation, and my Millennial Reign of Peace is nigh at hand.

28. I send you my warning continued, that I may be justified before the Councils of the heavens, who send forth a just God, even Jehovah, who am Jesus Christ, which giveth these words at this time, through him whom I have chosen to be my Mouthpiece on earth.

29. And thus, by authority shall the key be turned against thee, and any conflict you seek against other nations shall bring thy nation to its knees.

30. Heed my word, for I am seeking to preserve those on earth who will be of the

more righteous among all nations at my glorious appearing in the clouds of glory, as written in my record through mine apostles;

31. And mine Israel shall be preserved and gathered to the sacred lands of promise, as I promised to Abraham of old.

32. I, the Lord Jesus Christ, declare to this nation: Cease your warlike intentions, and be of a peacemaking nature to the nations around you, that I may preserve you a nation still, as you purify the inside of the platter, even your own peoples, overcoming unjust laws in your land, being of a nature to give voice to thy people wherein their rights of freedom are upheld.

33. This from a just God, who shall come in a day with great power soon at hand to establish Zion on the continent of America, a Celestial city, New Jerusalem, the powers of heaven attending; which shall rise and be the ruling city and governing power over all the earth, and I, your Lord Jesus Christ, being King and Ruler by appointment of my Father, Elohim, the Creator of this earth, doing the will of the Father in all things, whose right it is to rule by right of creation.

34. And though you acknowledge me not, many of you, yet my eternal truth stands that there shall come forth the God of glory, even Jesus Christ, to earth, even He who speaketh and sendeth you this message, and shall establish, through the heavenly powers, a righteous government.

35. And the wicked shall fear and stand afar off, yea, fear to oppose me, for I am a God of almighty power who sees and knows all things.

36. And it is I who speaketh to thee, to repent and turn from your wicked ways of oppression and usury, of abuse of women, of immoral ways in thy nation.

37. And there must not be allowed the murder of unborn children in thy land at all.

38. Thus, let the rights and protection of innocence be maintained by all, is the counsel of thy God, who shall hold thee responsible for thy conduct, and shall come to recompense to every man the measure he has measured to his fellow man.

39. There must not be aggression against my Israel any longer, for I shall preserve my people Israel.

40. Let thy religious intent be of peace, saith the God of glory, and of blessing the nations of the earth, and not of aggression nor oppression at all.

41. I have sent forth my previous word to you in my publishing to the leaders of the nations of the earth.

42. Heed my word, saith the God of heaven, who ruleth over all nations of the earth unto a day of judgment soon at hand, is the word of thy God to thee. Amen.

SECTION REVELATION 77

Fundamentalist Church of Jesus Christ of Latter-day Saints
P.O. Box 840459
Hildale, Utah 84784

I, the Lord and Savior, Son Ahman, Even Jesus Christ, Speaketh to the Leaders of the Nation of Iraq and to the Peoples Thereof, a Word of Warning of Events Soon to Come Upon Thee, According as Your Works Shall Be, Saying Thus -- Mine Own Words Revealed From the Heavens to a Manner of Your Understanding:

Revelation of the Lord Jesus Christ
Eldorado, Texas
Friday, May 6, 2011

1. He who reigns on high, even Jesus Christ, the Lord and Redeemer over all peoples, past, present, and future, the Governor and Ruler in heaven who shall soon come to earth in His power and glory to make Himself known to the peoples of all nations, sendeth His word.

2. Thus saith the Lord, even Jesus Christ, the Savior and Redeemer of all mankind, who sees and knows all things, who shall reward a just recompense to every man, woman, and child according to the measure they have given their fellow man; I am the God of glory, and when I speak, so shall I fulfill, as I speak to the people of the nation of Iraq:

3. Make peace.

4. Cease your warring tendencies, or you shall cease to be a nation, and shall be absorbed by mine Israel in a devastating war if you heed me not.

5. And though many in that nation of Israel shall lose their lives in the devastating war and in other judgments I shall send upon the nations of the earth, you shall cease to be a nation, as I have given my land to the descendants of Abraham, Isaac, and Jacob, even Israel, in a future happening.

6. And if you would have a place on earth in the land you dwell, make peace. Let your religious factions not war one against another.

7. This is the word of the God who made thee, who has all power to fulfill His word.

8. And though you have had a war in your borders for many years, through the aggression of a foreign nation attacking thee, and because thy leadership was corrupt, thus saith the Lord, uphold laws that promote peace, that protect women from abuse but do not allow the murder of unborn children, but allows religious freedom in thy nation, and freedom of expression.

9. And do not join with any nation against mine Israel, or you shall be consumed, not having power to defend thyself against foreign nations that shall come against thee who also seek the destruction of mine Israel.

10. And though Jerusalem be mostly

destroyed, it shall be rebuilt against the time of my coming, for I shall appear in the clouds of heaven as the God of glory in my almighty power, descending to earth, making myself known as dwelling among men, among all nations of surviving nature; and the peoples of thy land of the more wicked nature shall be swept off the earth, preserving only the more righteous by my almighty power, though they be few in number; for great wickedness is in thy traditions, causing thee to be a warring people.

11. Be of a peaceful nature, for those who justify murder, suicide bombings, murder of unborn children, aggression against other nations, and violence among thine own people and government powers, violent against your own people -- it must not be.

12. For I shall bring to justice, knowing all things, all who thus are of a violent nature, humbling all peoples of all nations by greater judgments of war and famine, earthquake, hail, and pestilence, who heed not my message of salvation.

13. I have sent my words of warning to you and other nations of the earth, yea, to all the nations of the earth, in my recent word given, published to all peoples, and commanded the leaders of all nations to publish my word of warning to them, among all their peoples who inhabit their nations; and as I have spoken, so shall I fulfill.

14. My time of coming in my glory is soon at hand.

15. My Zion shall rise.

16. New Jerusalem shall be built on the American continent.

17. The heavenly powers shall come to dwell on earth, to be the governing power and city, even New Jerusalem, over all surviving nations of the earth, and nothing can stay mine hand.

18. I shall send forth messengers to proclaim my message of salvation, my Gospel of Jesus Christ, even thy Lord who speaketh this message to thee, through mine authority and my Mouthpiece on earth, to thine understanding.

19. Thus saith the Lord: Repent ye! Repent ye! of your violent ways, lest you cease to be a nation, and many lives be lost because of your violent nature and warlike ways.

20. This must not be if you desire to survive that which is coming upon earth -- the judgments of a just God removing the more wicked from the earth, preserving the more righteous to learn of my ways of eternal progression, of life eternal earned by obeying the God who made you, in the Gospel and plan of salvation of saving nature unto eternal life.

21. I do the will of the Father, Elohim, even Ahman, for I am Son Ahman who speaketh, the God of Israel and over all nations of the earth, a just God who shall reward every man according to the deeds done in the flesh, who hath conquered death, suffering on the cross eternal justice, yet being innocent and free from sin; being raised from the dead unto eternal power, being the Resurrection and the Life, who shall resurrect all peoples from the grave to be judged before a just God, even thy Lord and Savior, unto an eternal judgment wherein the more righteous shall earn an eternal salvation.

22. And the wicked, not heeding the light of heaven that shines upon all men in the conscience of their mind, turning to violence and murder, they shall receive a judgment of suffering in Sheol, until all their sins and corrupt ways receive of their

just God a just punishment unto great woe and sorrow.

23. Heed my word, and be of a peacemaking nature, even toward Israel, my people, and with the nations round about thee.

24. And make peace among religious factions of a soon nature, lest war break out and the more violent take control of thy nation, and you humbled by other nations again.

25. For thus saith the Lord: When the kings of the east come against Israel, the great War of Armageddon shall take place, because the nations of the earth heed not my warning I have sent to make peace, even in their own lands among their own peoples.

26. I am able to fulfill my word.

27. And my message of salvation shall go to all nations from New Jerusalem, and you shall know thy God reigneth, saith Jesus Christ to the leaders and peoples of the nation of Iraq at this time, having been a nation of violence for many years; which violence shall be overthrown in a manner of thy humbling by a just God, and in the wars and power of cleansing powers I shall send forth against any people of evil and violent intent; to preserve the innocence of the more righteous and their lives against the time of coming to my Zion, and learning of more noble and exalted ways of governing power and of living, and learn of my message of salvation that I have promised to be sent forth to all peoples of the earth; being the Creator of the heavens and earth, having come to earth and suffered more than man can suffer, conquering death; being the Resurrection and the Life of all peoples, wherein all shall be raised from the grave and receive that judgment according as their works have been in the flesh.

28. Thus the God of glory over heaven and earth, who has all power, has spoken to thee. Amen.

SECTION REVELATION 78

Fundamentalist Church of Jesus Christ of Latter-day Saints
P.O. Box 840459
Hildale, Utah 84784

Thus Saith Son Ahman, Even Jesus Christ, the Creator of Heaven and Earth, Through Mine Authority Whom I Have Appointed as My Mouthpiece on Earth, to the Leaders of the Nation of Pakistan and the Peoples Thereof, Even the People of Pakistan, to Receive My Word and Message of Warning, to Know of My Glorious Coming to Earth, Yea, the God of Glory Who Created You and Has All Power and Knows All Things, for Nothing Is Hidden From Me; Verily I Say to You Thus -- Mine Own Words Revealed From the Heavens to Your Understanding:

Revelation of the Lord Jesus Christ
Eldorado, Texas
Friday, May 6, 2011

1. I, the Lord, speak thus -- mine own word, even Jesus Christ, the Creator of all, who reigneth in heaven and over all peoples of the earth; who shall subdue all enemies under His feet and shall come in the clouds of heaven in glory, making Himself known to all peoples of every nation, first sending forth the cleansing judgments to remove the more wicked from the earth, preserving the more righteous unto a day of righteousness when my Zion shall be established, yea, New Jerusalem, the heavenly powers descending to earth with thy God to dwell among men --

2. Speaking unto the people and nation and leaders of Pakistan, again sending my word of warning that my judgments are nigh at hand, and you must not have within your borders those of a terrorist or violent nature in their organizations, who try to destroy life in violent means against other nations, or in thine own borders and thine own peoples.

3. Bring them to justice, and do not let them dwell in thy borders.

4. And let the leaders of this nation again receive my warning, that you shall be removed from power by a just God sending judgments, yea, a righteous judgment upon thee, if you continue in your secret combinations to get gain and power, and also to oppress women and the poor.

5. Cease your war with India.

6. Use military only for self-defense, and not to oppress thy people at all.

7. I am the God of glory.

8. I have sent you my word previous.

9. You have allowed leaders of violent organizations to dwell in thy borders, and

you brought them not to justice, knowing the same;

10. And yet, through thine own corrupt ways and motives for gaining power, you allowed these murderers to continue among your peoples, which must not be if you are to remain as a nation and leaders of nation, this nation of Pakistan.

11. And if you heed me not, my judgments shall come upon you as I have named.

12. Let this, my warning, be heralded to the peoples of your nation, that my coming is nigh at hand in my glory, and my governing powers shall be a city, New Jerusalem, built upon the American continent, to rule over all nations, even my Zion, a righteous government of heavenly powers coming to earth, the God of glory known among all peoples as dwelling among men on earth.

13. I, the Lord Jesus Christ, speaketh, and my words shall be fulfilled, both in this warning and my previous warnings to this nation, that if you heed me not, I shall send my cleansing powers to remove the more wicked from your nation, and preserve the more righteous, who shall be preserved unto my coming, to know of the greater ways of noble and exalted and pure living and governing power, promoting happiness.

14. Let there be freedom of speech and expression, and freedom of worship in thy land, without oppressing minorities of religion or of political ideas.

15. And let there not be any longer the secret combinations of murder, of your leaders and military against thine own peoples.

16. And let there be peace made with India.

17. Do not allow that Taliban organization to be in thy borders at all; for you are becoming a nation promoting violence, and I, the Lord, shall bring judgment upon any nation of a violent nature, with judgments of God which no man can resist or overthrow -- of disease and famine, earthquake and pestilence, hail, yea, and as you choose, even wars among thy peoples, being of a violent nature of governing power, not heeding my warning to make peace with neighboring nations, which shall erupt in a war that shall consume thy nation, as I have said before.

18. Hasten to prepare for my coming, and be a peacemaking nation among nations, especially those that border thy land.

19. Murder is in the hearts of some of thy leaders who seek to get power and gain through that corrupt and most heinous crime.

20. Let there not be the murder of unborn children allowed by law in your land at all, and let equal rights to women -- for education and protection, even to be protected against abusive husbands and other men -- be put in place.

21. Let there be a promoting of equity and justice in thy land.

22. There shall be a preservation of thy nation by the God of Creation over thee, saith your Lord and Savior, who hath redeemed all mankind from the grave, and shall bring forth all peoples in the resurrection to stand before a just God, to be judged for works done in the flesh.

23. Thus shall leaders of nations be brought to account.

24. And if they have promoted oppressive or murderous or harmful ways in their governing, even against their own peoples or other nations, they shall be

held to an accounting of a judgment that is eternal, from a just God who seeth and knoweth all things; for all your secrets shall be revealed in that day of judgment.

25. Prepare thy peoples to receive my message of salvation, is the warning I again send; for I am a just God, who created the heavens and the earth, and have sent forth the children of men to the earth and given all nations and peoples their place as a testing in a probationary testing life of mortal existence, which you now dwell in, placing good and evil before them, sending my Spirit of gentle peace, prompting the mind in what is known as the conscience among mankind to choose good and eschew and discard evil.

26. Thus saith the Lord who made you: Govern through righteous principles of equity and justice.

27. Preserve innocence and virtue.

28. Protect the women in their rights, and do not allow organizations of violent nature to be in thy borders at all.

29. And as you make these works of more pure living, even bringing to justice leaders that have thus abused their own people, or continued the practice of murder to get gain or power; yea, as you show by your works you will heed my word, I shall preserve this nation in the day of my coming. And if you heed me not, all my words concerning thee shall be fulfilled. Amen.

SECTION REVELATION 79

Fundamentalist Church of Jesus Christ of Latter-day Saints
P.O. Box 840459
Hildale, Utah 84784

The Lord Jesus Christ, the God of Heaven and Earth, Speaketh to the Leaders of Russia and the Peoples Thereof -- I, Who Am Son Ahman, Who Has All Power to Fulfill His Word, the Creator of Heaven and Earth, Revealing My Word From the Heavens, a Word of Warning and Eternal Importance to Thine Understanding -- A Just God, Yea, the God of All Creation Speaking Thus:

Revelation of the Lord Jesus Christ
Eldorado, Texas
Friday, May 6, 2011

1. I, the Lord Jesus Christ, who reigneth on high, having all power over all nations of the earth, who sees and knows all things, speaketh to the nation of Russia, to the leaders of that nation and the peoples thereof, a word of warning unto an eternal judgment from a just God, who seeth and knoweth all things, in a manner to reward all men, women, and children according to their deeds done in the flesh -- the God of

glory, even Son Ahman, Jehovah Christ, who is Jesus Christ, who shall come to earth in His glory in a soon happening, making myself known as present on earth among men to all peoples of the earth.

2. Thus I declare to thee again: Cease the murder of unborn children with legal consent in thy nation.

3. It must not be, for I shall sweep the wicked, yea, the more wicked out of your nation in whirlwind judgments in a time when thou thinkest thou art a powerful nation.

4. And there shall be earthquake, windstorm, disease and famine, pestilence and hail, even the sea heaving itself beyond its bounds to humble thy peoples, preserving only the more righteous against a time my message of salvation shall be sent to thy peoples; when Zion, even New Jerusalem, is built up in full on the American continent, and become the capital and ruling governing city over all peoples of the earth, over every nation, kindred, tongue.

5. Yea, thus saith the Lord Jesus Christ to you, the rulers of this nation:

6. Your corruptions of bribery, of murder, yea, even secret combinations of secret murders, are known by me, your Lord, who seeth all things.

7. And you shall receive the just recompense of reward for your murderous ways.

8. And though you shall yet stretch forth thine hand to use your military to conquer other nations, humbling them, there shall come a humbling of these greater judgments upon thee; because there are among your peoples, even the leaders of this nation, and neighboring nations of similar descent, to commit that heinous crime of murder against unborn children;

and some of your peoples being of Sodom, and of adulterous and licentious ways.

9. Thus saith the Lord: Corruptions and wickedness will not stand at my glorious appearing.

10. Heed my warning.

11. Be a nation of peace among nations.

12. And if you do it not, though you may be allowed to humble other nations before thy Lord appeareth, you shall not harm my Zion; for I shall send greater judgments to any nation that steps forth, and I shall fight the battles for Zion, even New Jerusalem, that shall be raised up on the American continent in that place I have revealed in the center of the land.

13. I am the God of glory, who conquered death by suffering on the cross, raised in the resurrection; and shall raise all men, women, and children in the resurrection to stand before your God, even Him who speaketh these words to thee through mine authority on earth.

14. And ye shall be judged unto an eternal judgment in the resurrection.

15. Your minds shall be unlocked and you shall be your own accusers, revealing what you hath done in the flesh.

16. There cannot be a continuation on earth of these great crimes and sins, of murder, of immorality that promotes the murder of unborn children at my glorious appearing, for all shall be cleansed off the earth of this nature, save they have the gift of my delivering, for the murderer hath the greatest judgment in eternal judgment in the resurrection.

17. Promote virtue and life.

18. Who art thou, the leaders of this nation, that allow the murder of unborn children as though thou wert God to decide which children should be born of

the spirits I send to earth to inhabit earthly bodies, wherein they are brought to the test, knowing good from evil, what they will choose, to earn what they will in eternal judgment, the righteous, those who promote justice and purity of life, unto eternal salvation; and the more wicked unto an eternal judgment -- even the buffetings of Lucifer in the realms of Sheol, wherein all must pay the price of sins unrepented of?

19. For I, a God of glory and of redeeming and atoning power, have suffered on the cross to redeem all mankind from the grave, and who can forgive sins, and wash away sins, and make your garments white before me in the resurrection of the just, who receive my message of salvation and the ordinances and blessings of my eternal Priesthood.

20. Thus saith the Lord God of heaven, the warning voice to the nation and leaders of Russia:

21. Repent ye! for my coming is nigh.

22. And I will be justified, by giving these words of warning to thee, of sending whirlwind and great destructive powers against thee if you heed me not -- removing the more wicked from thy lands, preserving the more righteous to know of the ways of Zion, and of the eternal heavenly powers coming to earth, which I will perform for the good of all mankind, and promote peace, happiness, and eternal salvation among all peoples, earned by them receiving my message and Gospel of salvation.

23. I send you this, my communication, to your understanding that the God of heaven hath spoken; and as He speaks, so shall He fulfill, being the God of truth, holding you leaders of this nation responsible, even unto an eternal judgment in the day of the resurrection for what thou doest on earth.

24. Let there also be in your borders the ceasing of murdering your own peoples by many of the leaders, in secret combinations and secret murder, an oppressing dissidence in those who oppose your oppressive ways, in prisons, some even unto taking of their lives.

25. Thus saith the Lord, I see all.

26. Fear and tremble in the day of my coming.

27. And if you will, cease these wicked ways, for I shall recompense to thee the measure you have given to your fellow man; being the God that is just, righteous and holy, having all power, yea, a righteous governing power that shall come to earth to rule over all nations in a time soon to happen, being justified to send my cleansing, eternal power judgments; a just God who knows your works, rewarding thee according to thy deeds, having with me powers greater than anything on earth to thus administer righteous judgment; which powers shall administer that righteous judgment, notwithstanding the claims of men in their military might, and their ability to oppress and destroy other peoples to get gain and power, which is in the hearts of thy leaders, of thy nation, even in Russia; for you shall be an avenging nation for a time, yet you shall become a humbled nation when thy God reigneth, if you heed me not -- to withdraw thy military into thine own borders from among other nations, and only use your military for defensive principles and not of aggression at all.

28. And as the day of my coming shall be as a thief in the night, surprising all peoples -- for no man knows the day or the hour of my coming, only my Father who dwells in the heavens -- yet I shall come of a soon happening, and there shall be with me powers eternal to administer righteous

judgment; and the cleansing of the earth of all those who have murder in their nature to get gain or power.

29. Thus are the leaders of this nation corrupted in their nature.

30. And this is my revealing to you.

31. Though you remain in power for a time, and become a conquering nation for a time, humbling other nations, there shall yet come a just judgment upon thee, and your power shall be clipped; and your aspiring, violent nature shall not bear the fruit of the victories you had hoped, in a time to come.

32. And you shall be looked upon with disdain by other nations, as not having heeded the word of thy God in the day of His coming, and beforehand, before He appeareth in His glory.

33. And thy peoples will seek for peace from other nations, being humbled by the God of heaven.

34. This is my revealing to thee, even the Lord God of heaven who holds all nations in their place; and as I have spoken, so shall I fulfill.

35. And there shall be a day soon to come when you will fear and tremble at my appearing.

36. Heed my word.

37. And if you would do well, be of a peaceful intention toward all nations and not of a warlike nature at all.

38. Yet, it is in thine hearts, even the hearts of the leaders of this nation, and many of thy peoples -- a hardness of heart through the murder of unborn children allowed in thy nation, being of a violent nature in seeking for gain and power, willing to attack other nations.

39. Thus saith the Lord: I shall reward thee according to thy deeds.

40. I am the God of peace and of all power, the God that has promoted the reign of Zion unto the salvation of all nations, kindreds, tongues, and peoples who would heed my message of salvation.

41. And having all power, and being a God of truth, of justice and mercy, according as men's works shall be, so shall I fulfill my word. Amen.

SECTION REVELATION 80

Fundamentalist Church of Jesus Christ of Latter-day Saints
P.O. Box 840459
Hildale, Utah 84784

Thus Saith Son Ahman, Jesus Christ, Your Lord and Savior, Who Redeemed All Mankind From the Grave Unto a Resurrection, to Be Judged by a Just God for Deeds Done in the Flesh; Speaking to the Leaders of the Nation of Saudi Arabia and the Peoples of Saudi Arabia, to Their Knowing, That I, Your God, Who Created You and Who Upholds All Peoples in Their Place, Has Spoken From the Heavens, Speaking to Thee Thus:

Revelation of the Lord Jesus Christ
Eldorado, Texas
Friday, May 6, 2011

1. I, the Lord Jesus Christ, speak to the leaders of Saudi Arabia again.

2. Even the Creator of heaven and earth speaketh unto thee, saying thus:

3. Repent ye! Repent ye! and heed the warnings I have sent, and assist no nation that adds to the violence against other nations for the sake of economic gain; for this covetousness and wickedness among thee shall be answered with judgments to the removing of your riches;

4. For Babylon the great shall fall, as you have partaken of the spirit of great Babylon, the nations of the earth joining in the ways of immorality and crime, the murder of unborn children, oppressive measures of governing powers, oppressing women and the poor.

5. And though you be a nation of wealth at this time, if you assist other nations who are violent in their nature -- even one nation I have warned you about assisting, which is oppressive to its own people, even Bahrain -- heed my word lest my greater judgments come upon you and you become weak, and the more wicked among you swept off the earth in the power of eternal judgments and the power of destructive elements I can send upon any land.

6. For you have witnessed the heaving of the sea beyond its bound against another nation, taking life in a quick manner.

7. I, the Lord, shall send forth the humbling powers against all nations who promote these crimes and oppressive measures against their own peoples or against peoples of other nations.

8. Heed my word.

9. I am the God of glory that shall appear and make myself known to the peoples of all nations in a time soon to come; establish a New Jerusalem on the American continent -- my Zion, which shall be the governing city over all nations, a governing power from heaven come to earth.

10. There must be in your borders laws passed allowing freedom of worship, freedom of expression, rights toward women.

11. And there must needs be the continuation of thy works of caring for the poor.

12. And as you heed my word, I shall preserve your nation to be as a healing power among nations.

13. Join not with any nation in violence against another nation.

14. Use your military for defensive means only.

15. Be of a peacemaking nature among the nations that surround thee, and the nations of the earth; and know that I am a God who seeth and knoweth all things, and shall reward the leaders of nations and all men, women, and children with a just recompense for the deeds done in the flesh, as their works have been toward their fellow man and in their own lives.

16. Thus, I reveal my word to you again.

17. Heed my warning, and repent ye of those practices that are oppressive, or that join with other nations of more violent nature against other nations, or against their own peoples, is the word of the Lord to you, and His promise that He will fulfill -- giving blessings upon thee of preservation and to prosper thee to bless other nations of surviving nature, who are humbled by my almighty power; or to my judgments of destructive nature to remove the more wicked from thy land, preserving the more righteous, who shall yet learn of my Zion and my governing power, and my exalting and noble and pure and holy ways that shall be revealed to all mankind as New Jerusalem rises and Zion is established in fulness as the governing power over all nations of the earth. Amen.

SECTION REVELATION 81

Fundamentalist Church of Jesus Christ of Latter-day Saints
P.O. Box 840459
Hildale, Utah 84784

Thus Saith Jesus Christ, the Creator of Heavens and the Earth, Who Ruleth Over All Peoples, Who Shall Come in the Power of His Might, and Build New Jerusalem Upon the American Continent, to Reign as King Over All Nations, Bringing a Righteous Government from Heaven to Earth, Making Himself Known to Be on Earth Among Men, to Peoples of All Nations, Kindreds, and Tongues, Speaking to the Leader of Libya, Muammar Qaddafi, Making the Same Known to the Peoples of His Land Where He Thus Rules, Saying Thus:

Revelation of the Lord Jesus Christ
Eldorado, Texas
Saturday, May 7, 2011

1. Thus saith the Lord Jesus Christ, the Great I AM, who dwells in the heavens and rules over all nations of the earth, to the leader of Libya, even Muammar Qaddafi:

2. Thou hast transgressed greatly in oppressing and murdering many of thine own people, and being of a violent nature toward other nations, wherein you have sought to get gain and bear influence and promote war for aspiring to power, even over thine own people. And your reign shall soon be ended, and you brought to justice before a just God.

3. Though I, the Lord, have reprimanded foreign nations for attacking thy nation, yet you are meeting a just judgment of a just God. Cease your aggression against thine own peoples.

4. Repent ye! Repent ye! is the word of the God who made you, for you shall stand before Him in the day of judgment and receive according to the deeds done

in the flesh, for thou art a corrupt and murderous and immoral man, and I, the Lord God, declare it to thee.

5. Great shall be thy punishment in Sheol for performing these crimes, when you could have been a just and kind and equitous leader toward your peoples.

6. And you have sought riches through secret combinations with other nations. And you have sought after that which is unhallowed -- immorality in your life -- justifying the same because of your dictatorial powers.

7. Nothing is hidden from your God, even Jesus Christ who speaketh, for these are my words. As I speak, so shall I fulfill.

8. If you would do right the remainder of thy days, give thy people representative government, and step down, and no longer be the leader of this nation of Libya; but other leaders of an elected nature be in place who will heed their God's word, for

there is among thy people and among thy military of force, great corruptions and murderous ways, and it shall not stand.

9. I, the Lord, have declared it -- that though you remain in power a short time, I, the Lord God, shall cause thee to be removed from power. And then cometh the time of thy passing soon after, wherein you shall stand before a just God for a just judgment.

10. Perform kind and benevolent works among thy peoples, and cease this attack amongst thine own people. Declare to them you will step down from power, and it shall be to thy good in the hereafter; for when thy body lies in the grave, thy spirit yet liveth that dwells in thy mortal earthly body, and shall go to the world of departed spirits and there suffer a punishment.

11. And in the resurrection, when I bring forth your spirit and body to unite, you shall stand before me, a just God, and be rewarded according to thy deeds in the flesh. Thus, while thy life yet remaineth on earth, do good. Give way, and cease this war of aggression against thine own peoples, for you have caused them, through thine own oppressive ways, to seek relief of foreign nations.

12. Thy corruptions have come up before heaven. You are weighed in the balance and found wanting. Heed my word, saith God over all, who has all power to fulfill His word. Amen.

SECTION REVELATION 82

Fundamentalist Church of Jesus Christ of Latter-day Saints
P.O. Box 840459
Hildale, Utah 84784

Thus Saith Son Ahman, Even Jesus Christ, the Creator of Heaven and Earth, the Redeemer of All Mankind, Suffering the Pains of All Men Who Would Repent and Apply Unto Their God, Who Created Them, for a Salvation -- His Message of Salvation Soon to Be Sent to Thee; Yea, Thus I Speak to the Leaders and Peoples of Rwanda, the Message of My Glorious Appearing and of Great Warning Against Those Who Have Committed Gross and Heinous Crimes Among Thy Peoples; Yea, Your Lord and Savior Speaketh Thus to You, the People of This Nation, Concerning a Just Judgment Soon to Come Upon Thee, Yea, Upon the More Wicked Among Thee. Hear My Word --

Revelation of the Lord Jesus Christ
Eldorado, Texas
Saturday, May 7, 2011

1. I, who have created all things, even Jesus Christ, the God of all eternity in heaven, who reigns over the earth, and all nations subject to my power, who giveth life to all peoples, who is the God of Creation who made thee, speak to the leaders of the nation and the peoples of the nation of Rwanda:

2. I, the Lord, have weighed thee in the balance and found thee wanting.

3. The genocide and the murders that have been in thy nation, and the cries of the innocent, even women and children, whose virtue and lives were destroyed, even at a young and infant age, by murderous and immoral government powers and tribal powers seeking gain and power; even justifying your genocide and murders against one another as political or religious groups, based on your religious profession, or your political effort to gain power --

4. Thus saith the Lord: I shall send a judgment upon this nation to destroy the more wicked from among you, for murder and through rapine and abuse.

5. Thus saith the Lord: You who have been guilty of these great crimes, both leaders and military and evil tribal factions, shall meet the just recompense of reward of a just God upon you; for as you have measured to your fellow man, so shall your God who created you measure to thee.

6. I, the Lord God of heaven, who suffered on the cross for the salvation of all mankind, to raise them from the grave unto a resurrection to stand before a just God to be judged, speaketh to thee:

7. Your works done in the flesh, in your earthly and mortal tabernacle that you now possess, shall be rewarded unto thee unto an eternal judgment.

8. Many hearts have been hardened among thy peoples because of these murders; and the spirit of corrupt ways, of immorality and crime, continue among you.

9. I send you my word, that my glorious appearing is nigh at hand, when I shall make myself known, yea, even the God of glory coming in almighty power with the angels of heaven to earth, yea, known to all peoples, nations, and kindreds and tongues; first sweeping the more wicked of every nation off the earth who are guilty of murderous and immoral crimes of Sodom and adultery, of abuse and violence, preserving the more righteous in every nation who can thus learn of my ways of Zion at my coming, and as I send messengers of salvation.

10. I, the Lord, send this warning to the leaders and peoples of this nation -- to cease these most corrupt and abominable and heinous crimes, causing you to know that I have spoken from the heavens.

11. Let those who are innocent be preserved by rule of law, and by any military or police force in self-defense against aggressors; not to be aggressors themselves against any, whether they be men, women, or children.

12. And wherein you have stolen the lands, tribes or peoples, families or individuals, return the same and make reparation fourfold for thy wicked aggressions against others, or I shall bring forth a judgment hard to bear, even an eternal judgment;

13. For I am the God of eternity; and though, when you pass on from this mortal life of earthly existence and your body lies in the grave, your spirit yet lives and must give an accounting to the God of heaven for what you have done, according to your works in the mortal flesh.

14. And He shall reward thee with an eternal judgment -- blessings of happiness and salvation for those of the more righteous and pure, who have dealt justly and kindly to their fellow man, blessing the widows and orphans and the poor; and then also rendering a judgment of punishment of suffering, of great nature, to murderers and those who abuse innocence and destroy virtue, who pillage and rob to get gain.

15. Great shall be your woeful moaning in severe punishment, in an eternal judgment, in the day I raise thee from the grave to stand before a just God.

16. And I give you this portion of my message of salvation -- that all peoples will meet the judgment of a just God for their deeds and desires in the flesh.

17. Heed my word, and let these aggressive and criminal practices cease among your peoples.

18. And let leaders of this nation send forth my word;

19. And let leaders and all peoples of this nation repent and turn from their most wicked practices; and prepare for my message of salvation, which shall come at a time to thy land, of my sending, as I thus offer my Gospel first to mine Israel, and, in my time, to those of thy nationality and origin.

20. Yet you shall know of the governing powers of righteous and pure and equitous and just ways of Zion as I send messengers of my governing powers to teach your peoples and leaders of nations, even thy nation, these ways of more exalting and noble nature;

21. For I shall appear and dwell among mine elect, my people in New Jerusalem on the American continent, and there shall my Zion rise.

22. I shall rule over all nations, a God of heaven coming to earth, making myself

known, bringing to justice all leaders of all nations who thus are criminal and murderous and immoral in their conduct.

23. I, the Lord Jesus Christ, who reigneth over all, have spoken it, and I am a God of truth.

24. Let those tribal factions make peace among themselves, who have warred one against another, slaughtering and maiming, abusing and adulterating innocence, which crime is so grievous to the God of heaven.

25. I shall sweep the more wicked of your nation off the earth in a day soon at hand, who have committed these terrible and heinous crimes, and preserve the more righteous among you to know of my ways of Zion, yea, the God of heaven coming to earth with a righteous and eternal power; whose right it is to rule, for He hath created all peoples and sent them to this earth for a life of testing to prove them, knowing good from evil.

26. I have sent my light of heaven into the minds and hearts of men, women, and children at birth, to carry with them that which is called among men as personal conscience, to choose good and eschew and discard the evil;

27. Yet when you choose to follow the dark powers of Lucifer and the evil ways among men, committing these heinous, immoral, and terrible crimes, knowing principles of justice, I, the Lord God of heaven, shall reward thee according to the light you have received on earth.

28. And being an informed nation of thy Lord and Savior Jesus Christ's mission, even by religions among men coming among thee, and by publishings, and by school and other information facilities, I am He who speaketh these words through my Mouthpiece on earth, appointed of

God to deliver my word to the peoples of all nations.

29. And as I have spoken, so shall I fulfill;

30. For the wicked shall tremble at my appearing, to know I have sent forth my word.

31. For I am Son Ahman, who is Jehovah, even Jesus Christ, that speaketh.

32. And there shall come my messengers of salvation, at a time in the future, to thy posterity who survive the great whirlwind judgments that cleanse many nations of the earth, yea, even all nations, before my glorious appearing, which is soon at hand.

33. This is the reason I have sent forth my word of warning, that your crimes will cease, that innocence will be preserved in your land and your nation, and you will not be aggressive toward any other nation, or peoples of other nations.

34. Let there be laws upheld that are just and that protect innocence and virtue and life.

35. Let there be the rising up of honorable men to govern, who will defend innocence and virtue and life, as just and equitous and noble leaders.

36. Let the population uphold the same, for this shall be the rule of government at my glorious appearing among all nations.

37. I have sent forth, to the leaders of this nation and all nations, my publishings of my word of warning, yea, even your Lord Jesus Christ, of recent receiving and sending.

38. Heed my words of warning.

39. And read my policies of government of eternal power, even of King of kings, even Jesus Christ who speaketh; and know of His rule of government of righteous dominion.

40. Thus saith Son Ahman. Amen.

SECTION REVELATION 83

Fundamentalist Church of Jesus Christ of Latter-day Saints
P.O. Box 840459
Hildale, Utah 84784

Thus Saith Jesus Christ, the God of Heaven and Earth, Speaking Through My Servant and Mouthpiece on Earth, Mine Own Words to the Warring Factions and Leaders and Peoples of Sudan, a Word of Warning That Must Be Heeded, Lest My Greater Judgments of a Sudden Nature Come Upon Thee. Heed My Word, Saith the God Who Made Thee, Which Saith Thus:

Revelation of the Lord Jesus Christ
Eldorado, Texas
Saturday, May 7, 2011

1. I, the Lord Jesus Christ, speak to the peoples of the nation of Sudan, who have been in wars, abuse of women and children, murderous practices of rapine, of robbery and plunder, having had warring factions against one another for years.

2. I, your Lord and Savior, Jesus Christ, send my word: Repent of these evils, for this is my word of warning -- that I am soon to send forth judgments of great power to cleanse the more wicked of thy peoples from off the earth, and preserve the more righteous who deal just and equitous one with another, of a kind and noble way of living.

3. And though nations have come to the aid of the poor to a great degree, I, the Lord, send forth my word that there shall come forth a great dearth, of starving nature in thy land, to empty the land of the more wicked, to stop this war of destruction.

4. And those who have been guilty of murder, to get gain and power by force, destroying virtue of women, and the innocence of children being destroyed by your murderous and warlike practices, I, the God of heaven, who made all peoples, who created the heavens and the earth, speaketh:

5. The vengeance of a just God cometh upon thee.

6. And that I may be justified in performing this work of cleansing my land and thy peoples, removing the more wicked from this life, which you dwell as peoples of the earth at this time, I am sending my word of warning, for I am the God of heaven, soon to come to earth with the powers of heaven, and build a governing capital city called New Jerusalem on the American continent, where my Zion shall rise and be the governing power over all nations of the earth; and I shall bring to justice all peoples who thus perform these heinous and terrible crimes.

7. Repent ye! Repent ye! is the call of thy God who made thee.

8. And know that I am soon to send

forth these great cleansing powers, justified now by sending forth my warning to you, a nation of violence;

9. For I am the God of peace, and my almighty power shall humble all peoples to convince them to be of peace, and cease their fighting and contending, and evil and immoral and corrupt ways.

10. Let there not be the abuse of women in thy borders.

11. Attend to the poor.

12. This is thy God who speaketh, who has eternal power, and who shall make Himself known to all peoples of the earth as coming to earth and establishing a government of righteous and just and equitous and noble ways.

13. I am He who suffered on the cross, a God of eternity coming to earth, dwelling in the mortal flesh, taking upon me the pains of all men who would thus repent; conquering death, being raised in the resurrection unto eternal power and glory, reigning in heaven over all the earth, yea, even over all nations of the earth.

14. I am He who shall raise all men, women, and children from the grave, their spirit and body reuniting in the resurrection to stand before me, a just God, to be judged according to their works done in the flesh, of this earthly existence where you now dwell.

15. Thus saith the God of heaven: Cease your war, cease your abuse, cease your evils that I have named, or I shall be justified in sending this, my warning to your peoples, of the sending forth of a greater judgment to stop your fighting and to cleanse thy peoples of the more wicked who dwell among you.

16. I am Son Ahman, the Beginning and the End, even Jehovah Christ, who is Jesus Christ, that speaketh; and as I have spoken, being a God of truth and of all power, so shall I fulfill.

17. Heed my word, lest a greater judgment come upon thee in this mortal and earthly life, and a greater judgment of punishment upon the wicked the day I raise thee from the grave in the resurrection, rewarding the more righteous unto a salvation, and the more wicked to that punishment requisite to meet the crimes done in the flesh.

18. This is the word of a just and holy God, who only doeth right to all peoples. Amen.

19. I, the Lord, say further to the leaders and peoples of Sudan:

20. I have sent forth mine word, mine own word revealed from the heavens of recent giving, to the leaders of all nations, and my policies of governing power.

21. Read these policies, and heed these policies, for this shall be my rule when I reign in righteousness in New Jerusalem on the American continent over all nations and peoples of the earth.

22. Allow there to be peace in thy borders and among thy peoples. This is the command of the God who made thee. Amen.

SECTION REVELATION 84

Fundamentalist Church of Jesus Christ of Latter-day Saints
P.O. Box 840459
Hildale, Utah 84784

Thus Saith Son Ahman, Who Is Jesus Christ, the God of Heaven and the Earth, by Whom All Things Exist, to the Leaders and Peoples of the Nation of Ivory Coast -- Words of Counsel and Warning Pertaining to Becoming Peaceful, and of My Glorious Appearing Soon at Hand, to Rule All Nations in a Condition of Peace, Having the Power of Heaven With Me to Rule in a Righteous Government and Dominion -- Thus Is the Word of the Lord to Thee:

Revelation of the Lord Jesus Christ
Eldorado, Texas
Tuesday, May 10, 2011

1. I, the Lord Jesus Christ, the God of heaven and earth, who created all things and uphold all things, speaketh to the nation and peoples of Ivory Coast, a warring nation of unrest.

2. I am the God of heaven and earth, by whom all things were created and made, and I am the God who controllest the destiny of nations, which speaketh to the leaders of this nation, Ivory Coast, yea, and the peoples thereof:

3. Cease your wars. Promote peace. Care for the poor.

4. Do not be of a violent nature any longer, for my day of my appearing is nigh at hand, and there must needs be in your borders freedom of worship of any peaceful, religious, and rightful way.

5. And there must be freedom of speech and expression, kindness toward women established in your laws, and peace among nations.

6. There must not be a joining with any who promote the murder of unborn children, as leaders of this nation, for this is a grievous sin among my dominion of this earth in all nations.

7. And I shall cleanse the earth of this most heinous and corrupt crime -- the murder of unborn children.

8. You have received my publishings of a recent sending, wherein mine own word has been sent to the leaders of all nations who would thus receive, and they shall be held accountable unto an eternal judgment by thy God who made thee.

9. I am Christ who suffered on the cross, conquering death, being raised in the resurrection unto eternal power, who seeth and knoweth all things, and nothing is hidden, past, present and future.

10. I am soon to come in my glorious appearing, to dwell among men on earth in my New Jerusalem on the American continent, even my Zion, to be the ruling city and governing power of the earth over

all remaining nations after my greater judgments cleanse every nation of the more wicked of their nation, preserving the more righteous.

11. And thus I am the God of glory who cometh. It is I who speaketh to thee through my Mouthpiece on earth.

12. Cease your war. Make peace.

13. Let there not be the sins of the murder of unborn children, nor of Sodom, nor of adulterous nor licentious ways, for I shall cleanse the earth of these corrupt practices, which promote the murder of unborn children.

14. And I shall hold the leaders of nations accountable.

15. I am the God of eternal life. Endless is my name.

16. I have sent forth my Gospel of salvation to be learned by the nations of the earth, and there is a day of eternal judgment;

17. For when your mortal body, yea, your earthly body lays down in the grave, your spirit yet lives, and goes to the world of departed spirits where I still govern.

18. And my message of salvation shall be presented to those who dwell in the world of departed spirits also, their blessings unto eternal life given in New Jerusalem.

19. This you shall learn more of in future time when my Gospel of salvation cometh to thy borders and thy peoples.

20. Thus saith the Lord Jesus Christ: The wicked shall fear at my power and glory when I appear.

21. I am the God of peace, and also the God of life, who willeth whom He shall take or whom He shall preserve, who deals righteously and justly with all peoples, and is equitous and pure and holy toward all.

22. And as you remain on mine earth in the nation you have thus claimed as your habitation and nationality, thus saith the Lord, I shall hold the leaders of this nation, whether they be new in power or long time standing, unto an eternal judgment -- the righteous, of more pure nature, in the resurrection from the grave, raised up to be judged by this, your just God, who sendeth these words to your understanding, raised up to a salvation; yea, verily, those of the more wicked part raised up to a judgment of punishment in Sheol, requisite and mete for their sins that they have committed on earth, for all shall be judged for their deeds done in the flesh.

23. Let the leaders of this nation publish my word to the peoples of this nation, to know of my soon appearing in glory in New Jerusalem on that American continent, the appointed place I have named, mine own word being sent forth to this generation through Joseph Smith, my Prophet.

24. Thus I have continued my Priesthood, my Church and Kingdom upon the earth until this day for the salvation of all mankind, in preparing for my glorious appearing in power to establish a reign of peace for a thousand years upon the earth among men, mine own presence on earth in my Zion, in New Jerusalem.

25. Now receive my word and heed my word, is the message of the Lord, that there may be peace among nations at my appearing.

26. For only those of peace can be preserved, of the nature of not being violent nor aggressive toward their own peoples or other nations.

27. Let there be a preservation of virtue and innocence, of youth, especially the female portion of thy population, by law and by proper monitoring and practice; and I shall preserve the more

righteous among you, and you yet remain a nation.

28. And save you do this, there shall come upon other national powers against thee, and you shall be a tributary nation to another, no longer leaders in power, saith the Lord Jesus Christ to thee.

29. Let there be honesty in economic developing.

30. Do away with the bribery that exists in thy government and in secret combinations of murder that leaders hitherto have committed; for I, the Lord, knoweth all things and shall fulfill my word as I have spoken.

31. The sea shall heave itself beyond its bounds in the waters that border thy land.

32. Let there be a moving of thy population to higher ground if you would heed the word of the Lord.

33. Thus I say to all nations who border thee, if you desire to preserve life in the day of greater judgment soon at hand, to cleanse the more wicked off the earth, preserving the more righteous to know of my glorious appearing and my Zion being the governing power over the earth. Amen.

SECTION REVELATION 85

Fundamentalist Church of Jesus Christ of Latter-day Saints
P.O. Box 840459
Hildale, Utah 84784

Thus Saith Son Ahman, Jesus Christ, the Creator of Heaven and Earth, Who Speaketh From on High Through My Mouthpiece On Earth, to Your Understanding, Even to the Leaders of the Nation of Kazakhstan, the Leaders Thereof and the Peoples Thereof -- A Word of Warning, of Judgments to Come Upon Thee of the Cleansing Powers of an Almighty God Coming Forth, Whose Arm Shall Be Made Manifest Thereby to Your Knowing -- Thus Hear and Heed My Word, Which Saith Thus:

Revelation of the Lord Jesus Christ
Eldorado, Texas
Tuesday, May 10, 2011

1. Thus saith the Lord God of heaven, Jesus Christ, the Creator of heaven and earth, in whose hands is the right to rule over all peoples of the earth, He who redeemed all mankind by the suffering of His own body and the spilling of His own blood by wicked men, on the cross of affliction, being raised from the grave unto eternal power in the realms of the sanctified in the eternal heavens, who

looketh down from heaven upon earth, and nothing is hidden, who sees and knows all things; yea, verily, being the Light and Life of all peoples and all creation, giveth my word at this time to that nation Kazakhstan, formerly part of the Soviet Republic, a nation who has opened your borders to receive the transfer of armies and military equipment, even from the United States of America and the NATO nations, to supply the war in Afghanistan; and a people who also, and the leadership thereof, that have condoned, even by legal consent, the murder of unborn children, and adulterous and immoral ways in your borders, of Sodom; and also guilty, as leaders of this nation, of receiving bribery to get gain and power.

2. And among some of your leaders, I, the Lord, have seen secret murders through secret combinations to get power.

3. And I, the Lord, declare to thee: Close thy borders to the invading nations of another nation, and do not allow violence to continue at thine hand in thine own borders, or assisting other nations in a warlike action against another nation.

4. Now turn to peace.

5. Control thy borders in a manner to not allow this transfer of military power.

6. I am the God of peace. I shall bring all leaders to an accounting for their conduct, and there shall be removed from power those leaders who allow the continuation of war-making, and also these most corrupt and abominable ways -- the murder of unborn children, and the immoral ways I have described that are among thee, that promote the murder of unborn children. This must not be in thy nation.

7. I, your Lord Jesus Christ, am soon to come in my glory and power, and build a city of governing power, New Jerusalem, on the American continent, even my Zion; and I shall rule over all nations.

8. Let this nation of Kazakhstan hear my word and heed my word, saith the God who made you, as a witness on earth that I can speak through my servant on earth to your understanding, against a time when, if you do not do as I command, in becoming a people of peace and ceasing your warring effort and your murders, even of unborn children, and of secret murders by governing powers among you, and immoral and corrupt and violent ways against your own peoples and in connection with Russia, to whom you shall join in time soon to come again, to make war upon other nations --

9. Thus it shall be answered upon your own heads if you become a warring nation.

10. And I shall send judgments to sweep the more wicked out of thy land, preserving the more righteous, yet a humbled and sparse people remaining as I send forth earthquake and storms and disease, the wars that thou engendered and sought after, and other pestilences I shall send -- all to prepare every nation on earth, leaving the more righteous among them, through great judgments of God, to come to Zion and know of my eternal ways from heaven as I descend to earth and establish my righteous reign.

11. Let there no longer be the permitting of NATO nations and the United States of America to use thy facilities for air transportation of military into that nation of Afghanistan, where they invaded without being attacked themselves by that nation.

12. Thus, they are invading nations, having promoted the principle of violence instead of peace against a people that was

not warring against themselves, and thus you have assisted them at this time.

13. I, the Lord, have warned the NATO nations about their transgressions against their God in promoting violence instead of peace;

14. And I warn this nation and those nations that will join with Russia in a time soon to come, in wars that they will promote; that though you seem to be conquering nations at a time when other nations are weak, I, the Lord, shall cause the sword to be met by the sword, as it were; yea, the sword of eternal justice falling upon thee in the judgments I have named if you heed me not.

15. This is my love-giving warning, for I am the God of peace and love and righteousness and truth, holiness and purity, that speaketh to thee, that if you would have peace in your land and be preserved through the great day of judgments thy God is soon to send upon all nations of the earth, as a whirlwind suddenly, be peacemakers.

16. Do not join with other nations at war.

17. And cleanse the inside of the platter, yea, even your own rulers being brought to justice who have performed secret works of murder as well as allowing the policy of murder of unborn children and immoral ways to be among your peoples.

18. Prepare the way for my message of salvation to come forth, my Gospel of Jesus Christ.

19. Allow freedom of worship, freedom of speech, guided and proper freedom of press, not persecuted by government powers; freedom to own property wherein government powers are not oppressive in taxation or harsh laws to limit that which could promote happiness among thy people.

20. I, the Lord, have spoken it.

21. Be a nation of peace, is the call of the God over all, yea, Jehovah Christ, who is Jesus Christ, Son Ahman.

22. Heed my word, for as I have spoken, so shall I fulfill.

23. There are among you peoples of the blood of Israel, mine ancient people who shall yet be gathered to my Zion.

24. Prepare the way for the messengers of salvation from my New Jerusalem to enter thy land in peace and be preserved, to gather out those who can be part of thy God in Zion, a people of peace and purity, holiness and righteous doing; and I shall preserve your nation for acting in righteousness toward mine Israel and heeding my word. Amen.

Chapter 3

Thus Saith Son Ahman, Even Your Lord Jesus Christ, My Own Will to All Nations on Earth of Full Power to Be Fulfilled, Unto All Knowing I, God, Have Spoken Eternal Power Upon All Nations

Now let my warning to all peoples be of my final warning in power unto confounding the wicked in a way of knowing I speak truth of their horrible crimes of moral and murdering ways.

SECTION REVELATION 86

Thus Saith Your Lord Jesus Christ, the Holy Power of Redeeming Power for All Mankind of All Nations, of All Ages of Time, to All Nations, Peoples, Kindreds, Tongues, and Governing Powers; My Own Word in Great Plainness to All Peoples, of My Own Coming; of Great Whirlwind Judgments of the Pure Way of My Holy Love Justifying Judgments of Eternity Power; Thus Giving Mine Own Word to All Peoples on Earth; a Word of Eternal Importance to All Now on the Earth, to Be of Full Receiving My Own Will Concerning All Peoples on Earth; Also to Teach Truth of Pure Way of Judging, of Holy Way of My Eternal Law of Holy Marriage Union of Eternal Union of Plural Celestial Marriage of My Holy Power Authorizing Select Few to Thus Live; Not to Be of Interference by Any Not of My Own Authority of Holy Eternal Priesthood of My Sending; Thus Saith the Lord to This Now Generation on the Earth, My Own Will to All; Both of the Governing Powers of All Nations; Also Their Peoples: Hear Thou My Holy Message Given by My Holy Servant on Earth as My Mouthpiece, Though in Bondage; to Be in the Hands of All Peoples, to Know of My Soon Labor of Cleansing All Lands of More Wicked, to Preserve the More Righteous; Yea, Hear My Own Word Given Through My Own Power, to My Holy Servant Warren Jeffs; Though Suffering in Prison, Yet of My Order of Pure Priesthood of Holy Calling to Give My Own Will to All Peoples, by My Power, Who Will Receive My Word.

Revelation of the Lord Jesus Christ
Palestine, Texas
Monday, December 12, 2011

1. Let all peoples be of a listening; to be of full pure receiving; to have my own will manifest unto the way of pure holy eternal truth being sent to all nations on earth.

2. Let now my holy will be known.

3. Let all render honor, obeying, and pure holy living unto your Holy Redeemer, even I who speaketh, Jesus Christ, who is of eternity unto eternity in full Godhood power over all peoples, both on earth; also departed spirits who are of salvation unto my Priesthood eternal power among all nations of the way of teaching my plan of eternal salvation to all, past, and now on the earth in the flesh.

4. Now receive my final power-word warning:

5. You are only of the earth; I am of Eternal Power Celestial over all creation.

6. Now be of full obeying my will, to repent, lest sudden eternal holy power full judgments cometh on all nations.

7. Let all be humble.

8. Let all be ready.

9. I soon cometh in holy power of heavenly governing holy authority, to rule on earth for a thousand years with the heavenly hosts, come with my holy authority to be among all peoples, a Millennial Reign of Peace; pure governing power Celestial.

10. Thus I send mine own will to all -- Repent, and be of pure living Celestial way of holy power; a government of pure knowing all things, nothing secret.

11. Verily I say unto all nations -- be ye ready.

12. Make peace, both among thine own peoples and with all other peoples of every land, kindred, tongue; yea, be of my peace-loving forgiveness; for I, God, am the Judge of all peoples, with eternal knowledge Celestial to be my power of knowing all things, nothing hidden.

13. Therefore, fear ye, all ye wicked peoples who are not of belief of my power eternal Celestial; for you shall be of a sudden awaking unto fear when my hand of eternal holy way is stretched forth in judgments of eternal power, such as earthquake, tornado, the sea heaving beyond its bounds unto many swept away; yea, the desolating sickness, the overflowing pestilence of new diseases, of insects, animals, of crops destroyed, famine -- all to humble all people who will not give heed to my holy will, the God of all the earth, even Son Ahman, who is Jesus Christ, the Righteous Judge, the Holy Governor, your Eternal Ruler as King over all peoples.

14. Let now my published Proclamation be of full giving, even to all thy peoples; now of full mailing to libraries all over the world in all nations.

15. Let my other revealings of holy word of my sending, published to all, warning all of my soon power of cleansing; let these go to all thy peoples, having been mailed to the libraries of the earth; so common, and high, and they of power way can read my holy revealing of events of judgments soon to happen on earth; to cleanse off the face of the earth the more wicked; to preserve the more righteous.

16. Let my word cause all to be of sober way, to change from wickedness of violent way, of immoral, murder of unborn children way of living, and be more holy and pure of motive also of living.

17. Let all be more of peace.

18. I soon come to be of a revealing all secrets, past, present, and many eternal future happenings of God's dealings with the nations.

19. Let all now be receiving my holy will. Amen.

20. Let all peoples now give heed.

21. Let my holy power be upon thee through prayer; through noble, humble

forgiving all; for the love-peace kindness toward all.

22. Let my holy peace dwell in thy heart, each one, by choosing my holy power Celestial; by receiving my holy Gospel; by knowing all thy works cannot establish peace without God and His eternal power. Amen.

23. Let also all peoples dwell in holy peace of my governing power I send among you when I come; to have Zion my Capital Governing Authority; to have Old Jerusalem a governing power; for my people Israel shall be gathered from among all nations under heaven.

24. Read Isaiah in Old Testament.

25. He telleth thee mine own will concerning Israel being my Holy Priesthood Celestial authority, to rule all nations under thy Lord and His Celestial power extant, over all the world.

26. Now be of full power to correct these heinous crimes upheld by your national laws in many lands, the murder of unborn children, some full term, of soon delivery, murdered by legal consent.

27. Thus it is among all peoples -- lustful immoral ways cause many to shed innocent blood, thus becoming nations of murder of innocent, and of unholy doing against innocence.

28. Let all be of my way to uphold virtue, purity of living as honorable, to provide for the raising of children in peace, in a virtuous way; not of hindering the bringing forth of life.

29. Let all cease this most eternal damning sin.

30. Let all know I cometh to bring to an end these horrible evils on earth, to provide new peoples sent by my power Celestial to earth.

31. Let all be my people of pure motive of virtue and life-giving way; to protect unborn children.

32. I shall provide thy peoples with sufficient, to provide food, raiment, housing; all life-needed elements to give to all born on earth; to govern in peace; for the nations on earth shall prosper unto the plenteous gifts of life without covetous way; which leadeth to war and violence among nations, and among peoples of nations one against another.

33. My rule is sure, and true, and of peace, of righteous holy way of living.

34. Come unto me, your Lord.

35. Your earthly governing powers cannot exalt any to eternal life.

36. Only I, your Holy Redeemer, can bring salvation eternal to all who live eternal pure holy way of my holy power of the heavenly powers come to earth.

37. I send you my new publishing of final warning to all nations.

38. Let this be a final word, before whirlwind eternal power judgments cometh on all nations; more especially on my land of Zion, even North and South America, soon to happen;

39. For my holy warning is my justification to sweep the wicked off my land Zion, and from all lands who heed me not, but continue in the sins of spiritual Babylon, which shall fully be removed from the nations, even the corrupt unholy people that inhabit all lands, who have fallen into temptation as entire nations corrupt themselves before the Lord, saith He, even Jesus Christ, who shall recompense to all people the measure they measured to their fellow man on earth; unto a full judgment hereafter;

40. For you are each a son or daughter of God, sent to earth by my power, to be of full way proving thy life, whether you

would choose evil or good; the good being of me and my eternal plan of salvation, even the Gospel of life unto eternal life.

41. I am Eternal, my power is eternal.

42. I see all things.

43. Tremble, all ye nations, at my power soon to be fully felt as I remove the righteous unto safety, and the wicked slay the wicked in wars; also, by my eternal power, swift judgments need to come in order that the wicked do not slay all mine elect who can be of my holy Zion; a chosen pure holy people; my holy people who will receive me and my Gospel in full power Celestial.

44. Let these eternal truths touch honest hearts and minds everywhere.

45. Let only my holy way be thy way, saith God over all, your Lord and Just Holy King; yea, King of kings and Lord of lords. Amen.

46. I, your Lord, now reveal through my servant on earth my holy will, even him whom I have preserved to cause my holy will to go forth before my glorious appearing, to justify thy God to send full cleansing powers to the whole earth, soon to take place.

47. I have him in mine hands. Harm him not.

48. Be of a more sure way of preserving his life while in hands of the present governing powers on my land of my soon coming; for evil and unholy people are seeking to be of a full way removing him from the earth.

49. I, your Lord, tell you of governing powers this truth, so he may be of protecting to do my will.

50. Hinder not my will from coming to all people, lest a swift judgment cometh.

51. I am God.

52. I have all peoples in mine holy hands of eternal power.

53. Cease thy wicked attacks, ye government authorities in the United States of America, against my people and my Church.

54. Do not be of the way like they who crucified your Lord, believing false witnessing against my servant and my people on earth.

55. Let all my servants in bondage go free.

56. Merril Jessop, an aged ailing pure holy man of my Church, of eternal holy way of pure holy living, is now also unjustly held in prison by an unjust court; an evil tribunal who combined with lying apostate witnesses of evil combination with government prosecuting power, to put innocent and obeying sons of my Priesthood authority behind the prison walls.

57. Now let them all go free, lest the nation prove only to be of the way of persecuting innocence; destroying life of unborn children; of taking away my people's homes by court unjust rulings in the way of false witnesses believed; a holy Church under government attack, not protected in religious practice in a land boasting of religious freedom; yet denying my people freedom to live my holy religion revealed from heaven by your Lord, through the instrumentality of my holy Prophet Joseph Smith in previous century in thy nation of the United States.

58. Behold my Proclamation recently mailed to all nations, to all leaders of nations, to governing authorities in every state in thy nation of the United States; yea, to all religious societies and libraries -- all receiving my own holy will of pure truth; telling all of my holy religion being of persecuted way since Joseph Smith's

time; he also suffering a martyr's death in a nation of supposed freedom; leaders not willing to step forth and protect an unpopular people; who, at many instances, aided in the drivings, persecutions, and prosecuting labor lo, these many years, yea, even one hundred and eighty years since my Church was organized in the nation of constitutional guarantee of religious freedom, of pure freedom, to voice beliefs, without harm coming upon them; yet you protect not my people and my Church, because you claim they are law-breaking people for living my holy Eternal Union Marriage Law of Celestial Plural Holy Union.

59. Let my people be free to live my holy law, lest judgments come in full way, to you no longer being a power to oppose me and my Zion, to no longer be a land of persecution, to no longer be a people of pure government of freedom powers, because leaders do not uphold constitutional law.

60. Let this truth be heeded by judges, President, Congress, all branches of governing power on thy land.

61. Let Canada be warned to not persecute my holy law and Church among you.

62. I shall turn on your own heads pure judgment of thy own intent against my people and Church; to humble all with the war soon coming on thy own land; verily it shall be so.

63. Let all be preparing for thy God to intervene, by correcting thyselves, thy rulers, thy evil ways now no longer followed.

64. Thy pride as a nation is of over-towering height, soon to fall by my power eternal.

65. Let all beware.

66. Let all become more pure, more holy, more of upholding virtue and innocence, of preserving life, even of unborn children;

67. Thus, evil of unborn children being murdered, even by government consent, bringeth a judgment of a just God of Creation on all peoples.

68. This causes you to be nations of murdering way.

69. Thus it is. Amen.

70. Let this be my final full way of pure truth, telling all peoples to repent, to aid my servant to go free, to allow my Church freedom of religion, as guaranteed to all religions by governing pure principled powers of the nation on my holy land of Zion; a New Jerusalem soon to rise without opposition, because I, your God, provide full power of deliverance, and no one can stay my hand.

71. You are all my creations.

72. Nothing can stay my hand from taking whom I will in death.

73. Let all beware, lest you corrupt the way before yourselves, bringing eternal damnation upon you, even a punishment of suffering for sins of thy knowing.

74. Now my own will has been made known to all nations.

75. Let this be thy now full awakening to eternity truth, that all will have to answer for deeds and desires done on the earth, before a just and holy God, who has all things pure, holy, noble, righteous in His power, to judge a pure, holy, noble righteous way, all peoples of all generations.

76. Now receive this, my holy will, to let my servant Warren Jeffs, also Merril Jessop and their innocent brethren in prison, in a country now proving no religious free way is in thy land; to be of a

letting go unto freedom, unto my right to rule; even more so than the rule of man's governing power.

77. Let pure religion alone, ye rulers and judges.

78. Let my holy religion be full free to live Celestial laws of pure holy revealed pure holy laws only pertaining to those of my Church, who seek to live those eternal laws, who only are of peace, pure way of living.

79. The lies of apostates are believed by wicked powers in power, and by people of juries who listen.

80. Let it now be of truth telling: The false witnesses are of lying way; they once having been of truth living the very eternal laws of holy religion, then turned therefrom because of their own corrupt way.

81. Thus it is now. They are guilty of now being unjust persecuting power using governing powers in way of prosecuting power to harm my people of my Church.

82. No victims are harmed, thus not being a victim; yet courts sentence innocent men to full lifetime sentence in prison for only living their holy religion, is the pure truth.

83. I, Jesus Christ, am the Author of this holy religion.

84. I am the God of Abraham, Isaac, and Jacob, mine Israel.

85. They also lived these eternal ways.

86. Now this nation seeks to hinder my people from earning full Celestial power salvation.

87. How can you be justified when I, God, have commanded them to live this holy eternal law, which can only be guided and governed by your Lord, through His appointed and ordained holy authority on earth?

88. This earth is mine, saith the Lord.

89. Believe principles of pure truth; that marriage is of pure religion, since the time I put Adam and Eve together to people the earth; a religious principle eternal.

90. You are breaking thine own national laws when you hinder a religion from obeying righteous holy way.

91. Let this be a full reversing; these unjust laws against my holy law Celestial Union Law of Marriage, a holy law of my revealing, of my holy authority being full authority to bless unions to be eternal; all of me, even your Lord.

92. This is my holy way to call on all powers of governing to be of protecting religious freedom in the nation of guarantee of religious freedom.

93. Now heed my word.

94. I shall soon sweep this unholy, most wicked generation off my land of Zion with the besom of whirlwind judgments, soon of full power.

95. Thy people have seen me send tornados of full destructive power show to all complete judgment, nothing but rubble remaining.

96. How can your puny arm of flesh withstand my almighty power?

97. The whirlwind power is an ensample of all my cleansing powers eternal.

98. Let all see this life of earthly existence is temporary, and of my power to tell length of living on earth for every individual.

99. Now be repenting unto more pure works.

100. Let all be of holy way.

101. Let all be pure in heart, that my holy people can be also of an example of Zion, my own holy power on earth from

heaven, come to redeem all mankind of all ages of time.

102. Let this truth tell all I can administer eternal life gifts, even to people of past ages and nations now as organized spirit people awaiting the holy resurrection, by first receiving eternal blessings of my own revealing to my authority on earth, who is worthy for blessings Celestial, unto eternal lives.

103. Thus, thy God is Just, Eternal, Holy, Pure, Noble, Righteous, Peace and Pure Way of Eternal Power of Governing Way over all nations.

104. Thus, I have now given full way justification to let my servant and my servants in prison house go free; also to let my people of my holy revealed religion on earth be of full free way.

105. Let all now be warned: Those places of prosecuting zeal against my holy religion shall be of no power to do so again.

106. Let them cease such unholy way of persecuting innocent people, when thy nation reeks in the blood of innocence of murder of unborn children through adultery and Sodom rampant on the land among all other peoples and religions.

107. Now cleanse thine own households of thine own begetting, of thy schools and governing powers; thy laws of corrupt way allowing immoral way to go unchecked; yet my innocent people are imprisoned for pure way of living; no crime, no corrupt way, no evil way among those who are of my Celestial Law, who are holy in practice of my holy law of my own holy power among them, judging each person who is of full way receiving my Celestial Law, unfettered by evil powers, governing powers and persecuting powers; to be of full freedom of religious living their only motive.

108. Now be of truth: Prosecutors lie. Witnesses lie.

109. My people go to prison because of lies told and believed in court of unjust way.

110. I caused my own word to be read in open court, telling these truths when my servant stood alone to voice the truth of unjust way of court proceedings, of the power to stop religious pure holy way being of ignoble attack in open court, defiling sacredness of my holy religion.

111. Thus, court shall be of full receiving my judging of eternal power in day to come, when all shall stand before me, even your Holy Redeemer, to be judged.

112. All shall know unobstructed truth then, when they stand before a just holy God to be of full way power to render true justice.

113. Let all be careful how they are of a way of believing lying court and prosecuting power; for my law is only holy, pure, noble, and of Celestial power; not of man, nor of the world; only to be of full way holy knowledge to obedient sons and daughters to my eternal law of Celestial Plural Union Marriage; my own way in heaven.

114. Thus I revealed this to my servant Joseph Smith over one hundred seventy years ago.

115. Let this truth be told: My law is of pure religious motive, no evil intent nor practice.

116. All must be pure to live my law, to be of receiving my Celestial Law and gifts of happiness therein.

117. This truth apostate lying witnesses know, who themselves sinned against my holy Celestial Law, to follow practices of immoral way of this wicked generation.

118. You who dwell in corrupting ways and unholy practices set up yourselves as judges of the most holy pure way of living my Celestial Law of eternal exalting authority for obedient sons and daughters.

119. Now receive my full warning.

120. My coming is soon to take place.

121. I shall reward all for deeds and desires done in the flesh on earth.

122. You cannot escape my all-seeing eye.

123. I know all things.

124. I am to bring all to full power judging of their individual lives.

125. Be ye pure, to stand before a holy God, to be of happiness on earth, and hereafter, in eternal world of glory, my heaven coming to earth to build New Jerusalem, my Zion, prophesied of by all holy Prophets of my sending; whose record is in Bible to thy easy reading; which gift I preserved through mine Israel; a people soon to be gathered to Zion, notwithstanding all opposition.

126. Be ye ready.

127. Great changes on my land of my holy New Jerusalem, on the surface thereof, soon cometh; even present cities, many to be of full cleansing, to be without inhabitant; yea, great and notable cities now on my land of Zion shall be sunk in the earth, or covered by mountains; or sunk in the sea; some destroyed by my eternal fire; some of the destruction by war, mob rule rising in many places; leaders of governing power without power to govern; armies left desolate; places of more wicked way destroyed in full.

128. Such shall be where they of full hatred against my holy law of Celestial Eternal Union of my eternal order of marriage of plural living in holy order of pure noble way; yea, those who thus seek to destroy my holy law and authority shall be of full receiving of my judgment.

129. Let all these truths settle on the mind of each; even to awake all people unto full way power to repent; unto my holy way becoming the way of salvation to all honest in heart everywhere.

130. Let this be my holy word eternal, to be of full weight on each who is of this present generation, to be of full authority to judge all; yea, all now on my land of Zion having within reach my holy word; both my word of generations past in Bible recording, also my word in Book of Mormon, Doctrine and Covenants, Pearl of Great Price; now my new published word mailed of recent time to all peoples in all nations.

131. Thus I am doing my work of pure holy justice, unto full power judgments, being the God of Creation, whose right it is to rule.

132. Thus am I doing all things righteous and holy, to be of full power justified to render full judgment here and hereafter.

133. Be ye pure. Be ye clean in morals.

134. No one need destroy themselves.

135. All can choose to do good, and eschew evil, even now.

136. Let all religions be of truth.

137. Let all tell truth, they receive not mine own revealed word for thy Lord unto the people of their religious group or order.

138. None can name my will; only my holy power attending my Mouthpiece.

139. Let all be of truth; they have not authority from God to administer eternal salvation unto any on earth.

140. Such was the first revealing to my holy servant Joseph Smith, Jun., in 1820, when God, the Father, and His Only Begotten Son, Jesus Christ, appeared to

him in a sacred grove, after he was of full faith.

141. I gave him my eternal authority called Priesthood.

142. I caused him to know of Celestial Plural Eternal Union of pure living marriage, a most holy law requiring purity of living entire.

143. Let this most wicked generation be of receiving truth: You of corrupt way persecute my pure way of pure revealed holy way of my Church.

144. Now cease thy folly.

145. Your laws against my Celestial Law of Eternal Union Marriage of Celestial Plural Union are unjust from the beginning.

146. Congress and President in each time of passing these unjust rulings of man's law were purposeful attacks against my holy law and religion.

147. I am of full way power to set all right; even by removing from the earth all wicked and evil-practicing immoral people; to preserve mine elect who do abide my holy law in full way Celestial power. Amen.

148. Now let these truths go before appeals courts as my own will, saith Jesus Christ, to be of full way considered, as pure truth; sufficient to reverse all unjust court rulings against my servant and his brethren prosecuted because they live my Celestial Law, which only I, the Lord, can rightly govern.

149. Let also this be published to all peoples in every land and nation, to learn truth of my glorious coming as both a Holy Redeemer, also the Righteous Judge over all peoples; soon to send, before my coming in full power glory eternal Celestial authority, full judgments of cleansing power on all nations; which promise I gave in the New Testament, even in Matthew 24; also in Doctrine and Covenants, also in my holy true book called Book of Mormon; all telling same truth of my coming; first sending whirlwind judgments.

150. Let all know I am God who speaketh, who tells only truth; who is of full power Celestial to do all as I have spoken.

151. Now receive my word.

152. Obey my will, to abide the day of my coming. Amen.

Thus Saith Jesus Christ, Your Lord and Holy Redeemer, Even the God Over All, to All Peoples, Nations, Kindreds, Tongues, Governing Powers on Earth, My Own Will Revealed From Heaven to All, to Know My Full Final Warning of Whirlwind Judgments Soon to Be on All the Earth; War, Famines, Earthquakes, Pestilences, Yea, of Every Kind, to Sweep the More Wicked Off the Earth; Preserving the More Righteous, Unto Zion Soon to Come Forth by Almighty Power of Mine Own Authority on Earth; to Be of Full Power of Heaven to Govern All Nations; Therefore, Give Heed Unto My Word, Even Saying Thus:

(Comprising Section Revelations 87-90)

SECTION REVELATION 87

Revelation of the Lord Jesus Christ
Palestine, Texas
Monday, December 5, 2011

1. Verily, verily, thus saith the Lord Jesus Christ, Redeemer of all, who hath power eternal; yea, Eternal Judge over all nations, peoples, tongues, kindreds of all ages of the world:

2. I, who am God over all, speak to all peoples of the earth, by my Mouthpiece on earth whom I have ordained, and is of my Order Eternal, notwithstanding all evil reporting and unjust attacks against him.

3. I speak thus to all peoples my own will, to show all I am God; who is God over all and is of eternal power; who created the earth; who reigns over all in the heavens eternal.

4. Let now my will be given. Let all know I speak, who hath the true governing power over all peoples.

5. I, your Lord, who soon cometh in power to be the Holy One of Israel, the God over all nations, whose right it is to rule over all peoples, from the Father, whose servant I am eternally, in redeeming all mankind by the suffering of my own body and soul on the cross of holy, eternal, infinite, atoning and holy love power for the salvation of all who will be of receiving my holy Gospel of salvation unto eternal life; yea, verily, all who obey my holy laws of eternal life;

6. Thus I speak mine own will to all peoples; to reveal truth, eternal truth; to judge all of mankind unto full eternal duration of final judging worthiness for delivering from death, hell, and the grave.

7. I am He, Jesus Christ, your Lord, who hath conquered death, who hath been thine only power from the beginning, to redeem all.

8. Let all give ear to my holy will concerning all peoples, nations, tongues, kindreds of the earth; yea, even spirits of the order of having dwelt on earth awaiting

my message of salvation through my eternal Priesthood.

9. I now reveal full truth, eternal truth, to all peoples, now sent to all nations, to be known as a final holy word, a full warning of eternity importance to all peoples, more than your fleeting way of attending a religion.

10. Let all be of full awakening.

11. Let all hear the God of Glory over all creation, by whom all things exist, that have been created by my eternal power Celestial.

12. Thus saith the Lord: My holy way hath been trampled upon from the day of Adam until now.

13. Noah was my servant of saving all mankind to continue on earth.

14. The peoples in his day were ripe in iniquity, unto violence continually, evil only in their thinking; acts of gross immoral way unto murder of unborn children practiced openly on earth in all then nations.

15. I sent the flood upon all the earth, only sparing a few souls who were of me in the way of eternal salvation; yea, who were of the way of Jesus Christ, your Lord, who now revealeth that the present generation on the earth is more wicked in immoral way and in murder and violence, in evil thinking and living, than the people in Noah's time.

16. Now receive my judging of you, all rulers of nations who allow open way of immoral practices of adultery and Sodom, which is the foundation of murder of unborn children, spirits I send to earth to receive earthly tabernacles to prove themselves worthy, by choosing my Gospel of salvation, to earn life eternal.

17. You rob them of opportunity to be eternal in my holy dominion of Son Ahman in the Kingdom of Ahman, my Eternal Father.

18. Let all be known as murderers who practice any form of restricting life from coming forth through natural process of birth.

19. National leaders, now being warned by my continual sending of mine own will to thee, now reek in blood of innocent children murdered before birth; yea, millions in some nations since I sent my own will to thee, to cease this way of murder now; yet you trample my word upon the ground as a thing of naught.

20. Verily I say unto you, both leaders of nations, also ye peoples who destroy life in immoral practices of your nations allowing such atrocities against life and virtue, innocent children unborn; you now are guilty against knowing mine own will hath been sent to thee.

21. You shall be of millions of years, as it were, paying in suffering for the multitudes of lives you have destroyed; for I am Eternal; Eternal is my name.

22. My habitation shall be on earth.

23. Nothing can overthrow my rule.

24. I shall reach thee, notwithstanding your armies of power. Your folly is of greatest height.

25. Your self-indulgent ways of sin reek now with blood of innocence.

26. You are adulterous in way of living your unions.

27. You justify murder for sake of saving what you name as needed resources for the living.

28. You justify murder even as a full-term unborn child is about to come forth in many nations.

29. Doctors who abort children are of murder of innocence.

30. I shall repay in full measure unto

untold suffering for such murderous sins in the day I called on all peoples to cease such corruption against my holy way of life and salvation.

31. Now be of pure holy way.

32. Cleanse this evil from thy nation, each one.

33. Overthrow all immoral ways upheld by law in your lands.

34. Prosecute adultery, Sodom, and licentious way.

35. Let not these crimes that promote murder of unborn children go unpunished.

36. You promote this in medical profession worldwide, in all nations.

37. Now let my holy way be thine only way.

38. Capital punishment for both Sodom and adultery shall be my rule on earth in the day of my coming to my people of pure holy way of eternal life.

39. Let it be known I am angry at this evil, perverse, adulterous, murderous and fully ripened in iniquity generation.

40. I shall sweep many more wicked off the earth, even soon, who heed me not.

41. I have earthquake, tornado, hurricane, the pestilences of disease, of insects, of animals; of the heavenly armies of vengeance to command; and no army of man can oppose my power.

42. All shall feel my holy way Celestial power sweep entire areas clean off the earth, to prepare for my reign of holy peace, a Millennium of Peace.

43. I am God.

44. I have right to rule; and I rule in holy righteous way of justice, equity, peace, love for truth, eternal truth; that wickedness shall not reign longer, but shall be overcome by my holy power of Celestial heavenly power.

45. Know ye, I have not been silent through the generations of time.

46. I have sent holy Prophets to warn nations, leaders of nations; which rejected my will, and now are only of the history of old, no longer a nation on earth; because they practiced immoral ways of Sodom and adultery, of murder of unborn children; yea, Egypt and Babylon, Greece and Rome, all corrupted and defiled by sinning against life and eternal ways of life; yea, my way, saith the Lord.

47. Let all peoples learn that I have spoken again.

48. My Gospel of pure holy way is in thine hands in Bible, in Book of Mormon, also in my holy revealings of Joseph Smith in Doctrine and Covenants.

49. Verily I say unto all, you are left without excuse.

50. Your leaders and peoples are of violent ways.

51. You persecute my Church, lo, these many years since Joseph Smith was of full Priesthood eternal authority to restore my true Church of Jesus Christ of Latter-day Saints on the earth.

52. Now know I have rejected that organization of that legal name, because they also persecuted my Priesthood, and now have become like the world in these immoral and unholy ways; even to fight against mine own Celestial laws of progression of holy way eternal, of my Celestial power administering my law of Celestial Plural Union Marriage by the revelations of my will; yet national powers of government do not defend religion to be free in land of so-called freedom.

53. My law overthrows all immoral ways of adultery, Sodom, and never has murder of unborn children.

54. You prosecute my holy way; yet

your nation reeks in blood of innocence shed for licentious immoral way of living for lust, not for salvation nor for thine own future generations that could rejoice in the forefathers of their generations.

55. Now behold, I reveal a new era of full justice against all immoral practices in every nation remaining on earth after judgments of whirlwind suddenness and power sweep the more wicked off the earth.

56. Let all tremble at my name.

57. Let all be awake to the judgment of eternal power now resting upon all peoples of the earth, for a great desolation of scourging, of war and disease, of tempest, sea heaving beyond its bounds. Verily I say unto all peoples, be ye awake.

58. I shall fulfill all my will.

59. No one can oppose my power of eternal Celestial might.

60. I am God. I am the Holy One of Israel.

61. I come to gather the pure in heart of every nation, of all lands, unto a holy and righteous governing power called Zion; a Kingdom of my own authority from heaven dwelling on earth, bringing my governing authority to all surviving nations.

62. You are all of my creating, to earn a place with me, your God of full power, of full creation power; to raise therefrom the grave in the holy power of my redemption, to stand before me to be judged of the Father for all thy doings on earth, nothing hidden.

63. No false religion of man can save you from pure truth justice, of which I am in fulness.

64. Now be ye ready. I come.

65. Cleanse thy peoples of these horrific terrible corruptions.

66. Let all now be warned of my judgment on earth; also of eternal judgment.

67. Let all be my holy way.

68. Let all come unto me, your Holy Redeemer.

69. I have done my work.

70. I have conquered death.

71. I am the Resurrection and the Life.

72. I come to teach, to save, to establish peace of eternal power over all the earth.

73. My coming is of thy own knowing.

74. My name, though of thine defiling, is holy.

75. I shall not be mocked without just recompense on all who offend me or my little ones of pure holy living of eternal happiness of my giving life eternal to pure souls who are of my holy Gospel.

76. Let all know your churches cannot save you in eternal life.

77. You must come to me, your Redeemer, through my authorized representative, to be of the Gospel of salvation, even of faith on the Lord Jesus Christ, of holy sincere repentance unto change of life from sin unto purity of living laws of pure exalting holy way;

78. Then be baptized by my legitimate authority of Priesthood, unto receiving my Holy Spirit gift of the Priesthood eternal power that changes all unto holy loving peace way of living.

79. My holy way is simple, pure, noble, godly, and of eternal power and duration of salvation.

80. I am He, the Author of salvation.

81. I am God over all.

82. Heed my word.

83. I fear no man; I am your Creator of Eternal Power.

84. My Holy Spirit shines forth on all creation.

85. All things came by me, and of my holy will.

86. All things exist by my power.

87. I am the God over all that speaketh.

88. Now learn of me and my way of salvation.

89. In thy minds is a recording of all thy life.

90. I shall raise thee from the grave unto the resurrecting both spirit and body together as a living soul, like unto my resurrection of full power over death eternally; and you shall each one stand before me; and I shall unlock thy mind; and you shall be thine own accuser in the day of eternal judgment.

91. I shall show each one truth of their lives, and wherein they sinned against knowledge willingly, they shall be damned in a realm of suffering for sin for a duration appointed according to their crimes against their own existence and harm and evil toward all others;

92. Thus leaders of nations shall reap a full condemnation of all murders they allowed of unborn children in the resurrection, now that I have fully warned them with many warnings through my Priesthood and people on earth, who follow me and obey my Celestial laws of progression.

93. Now be believing.

94. Death is of sure coming on all on earth.

95. All shall be knowing I have spoken.

96. I come as an all-consuming fire, to consume all corruptible things, to purge my own people of all ungodly ways, and remove from all nations the more wicked.

97. Now repent, and come unto me.

98. My servant still lingers in unjust bondage.

99. He is innocent, only living as I command him.

100. He hath been attacked by evil combination of wicked powers, both in this world and by evil powers seeking his destruction of spiritual darkness.

101. I have him in my hands.

102. He speaketh my own will, and is faithful to my Gospel of salvation as I have revealed to man on earth, as far as mankind have been willing to learn truth, eternal truth unto eternal life.

103. Now free him and his brethren, all unjustly held in bondage in unjust court way.

104. Let all my people have their lands and houses where unjust court stole from me my consecrated land.

105. Verily I say, wicked is this governing power over my land of Zion, the land of New Jerusalem soon to rise in glorious Celestial majesty unto the Eternal King Emmanuel, even your Lord Jesus Christ, coming in power Celestial eternal, of legitimate holy governing power, to rule over all nations in a holy righteous pure government of God.

106. I am your King.

107. I am Ruler over all that cometh.

108. I send my love-message to all, so all may prepare.

109. Believe not lies against mine authority on earth.

110. Wicked combination joined with governing powers to defame in an unholy wicked combination, to deceive any who would believe a lie and be of no truth telling of my holy Gospel and Priesthood.

111. Hear them not.

112. They are of evil themselves, both the false witnesses who hath perjured themselves knowingly until they glory in their lies of affliction upon my people, my

servant and Church; now to be answered upon their heads by a just God who knows all things; who shall be of full measure sweeping them off the earth; declaring to such in my day of judgment: Where is thy glory and happiness now?

113. Thy folly is eternal damnation earned.

114. You sinned away my day of mercy.

115. You knowingly perjured thine own children to lie against my servant; to tell world he is guilty; when you yourselves practice immoral ways, having fallen from my Church, having rejected salvation for the world's ways of no salvation; to wallow in pure corruption increasingly daily, until you are no more a full truth teller; thine own power now of the devil, the father of lies.

116. Now shall come the day of thy calamity.

117. The Dan Fischer secret combination shall be of full overthrow, as they are revealed as liars from the beginning; having once upheld my Gospel, then falling away, until they convince false witnesses to join in the unjust attack against my holy servant Warren Jeffs, and to influence government authority to prosecute, to cause unjust attack to seek overthrow of my Priesthood on earth.

118. Such has been their works.

119. Now what shall they do when my hand takes them unto eternity of justice?

120. They reek in the spirit of murder and immoral way themselves, having lost all pure way of living.

121. They love evil for evil's sake.

122. They should never be trusted.

123. They are traitors.

124. They are of evil intent naturally now, having lost the Spirit of peace forever; a vessel of dishonor, each one.

125. She who once loved my servant as a holy man, fell also to disgrace her own family as a false witness.

126. She hath caused many families to suffer, only to seek her own way of seeking world's way; no promise; only eternal judgment.

127. My servant silently witnessed the open lies.

128. She is of a way of personal immorality.

129. She accuses others for her own evil way being justified.

130. She is motivated by pride and person favor of evil combination.

131. Look into the lives of false witnesses to know my word is truth;

132. And I shall repay in full, both in this life, and eternally in the world to come; even my eternal power of Celestial power reigning forever over all peoples of resurrected state; all standing before a just God of Creation; the wicked then shrinking from before my power in suffering of soul unquenchable; as their sins were willful and against knowledge.

133. Such is the condition eternally of the wicked who persecute my people.

134. Let these eternity truths rest upon all.

135. I shall do my own will.

136. I shall not bow to courts and change my eternal Gospel according to the ways of man, of fallen, unholy, carnal, sensual ways of the world.

137. I am holy.

138. My way is only pure.

139. I have Celestial power of eternal fire that destroys all corruption and preserves and exalts all things pure.

140. Be pure in heart and soul in living on earth to survive the day of my holy power coming among men on earth.

141. Let these, my holy words, touch hearts everywhere, while any time remaineth to repent, all ye ends of the earth.

142. My voice is to all peoples.

143. Live unto me, thy Lord and Savior.

144. My Gospel plan is of eternal power, Celestial power.

145. I speak by authority.

146. I shall humble all leaders, judges, governing powers, to know I am the Ruler over all.

147. You shall feel the weight of my power.

148. Already some who have prosecuted him, my servant in bondage, have felt my hand of justice touch their lives.

149. All such shall know soon they have fought against their Holy Lord Eternal, in following their evil intent to afflict an innocent people, even my Church on earth, called the Fundamentalist Church of Jesus Christ, even of the Latter-day Saints as members thereof.

150. The former church of my naming hath fallen, and has no authority to administer unto eternal life.

151. The ordinances they perform, in what is called the Church of Jesus Christ of Latter-day Saints, are of no efficacy or of enduring value, not having my eternal authority called Priesthood; no, not one in that now apostate gentile church.

152. Verily I say to all peoples, I reveal this so you do not join with that lost branch that hath withered; first fighting against me after giving up Celestial Plural Union Marriage, my holy law of eternal lives for the faithful; a pure law only for the faithful of my Church on earth, and into eternity of increase, for they whole are of pure abiding my Celestial laws.

153. Let my people go free, is the word of God to the nation of affliction against my Church, my holy eternal Priesthood authority; a nation boasting of freedom, yet will not protect my Church in holy pure revealed religion from heaven, to live without evil attack.

154. Thus they are in prison only for obeying my Celestial Law of Eternal Union Marriage, because of false tradition that the nation follows, and because government powers believe lies of false witnesses.

155. I shall make free my people by my almighty power, known to all nations soon at hand, to become a full governing power of Zion over all peoples remaining on earth after whirlwind judgments cleanse my land of Zion; also the more wicked out of every nation.

156. Let all be holy to survive.

157. This from the God who made you, now speaking pure unobstructed truth from the heavens, through mine holy Mouthpiece, who only seeks my way eternally.

158. Let all come unto me;

159. Let all seek thy God diligently in prayer, in holy sacrifice of all evil in thy individual lives.

160. Behold, the leaders of nations, many themselves follow immoral ways; many herald immoral way as righteous in this day of perversion.

161. It is more wicked, even this generation on earth, than all former peoples and generations on earth.

162. I, who is God over all, who was God before the earth was made, and the

God over all now, am soon to come to earth to the knowing of all peoples, nations, tongues, and governing powers.

163. Now repent and prepare, for your very life's and eternal life's sake, is the word and will of thy Lord to all peoples. Amen.

SECTION REVELATION 88

Revelation of the Lord Jesus Christ
Palestine, Texas
Tuesday, December 6, 2011

1. Thus saith Jesus Christ, your Lord, in a further holy way of my will manifest to all peoples of the earth: Repent ye, repent ye.

2. I am soon to come in full eternal power.

3. Let all peoples be of full repenting now, lest you go down with the wicked in every nation being cleansed of more wicked people being destroyed from off the earth; by my eternal power of judgments; to be known as my time of full visitation of judgments.

4. Now be ready, lest my power only sweep you off the earth; is my holy word to all. Amen.

SECTION REVELATION 89

Revelation of the Lord Jesus Christ
Palestine, Texas
Thursday, December 8, 2011

1. Thus saith Jesus Christ, God over all, who hath overcome all things, and sits with His Father on eternal power throne forever, saying to all peoples on earth:

2. I now reveal soon happening, a great tempest of powerful storm over Northern Europe of devastating result.

3. Repent ye, for I shall fulfill my word.

4. Also a Turkey national power broken up; also Liechtenstein as a country humbled; let all be repenting.

5. Let all be ready for my glorious coming, saith Jesus Christ. Amen.

6. Now let Asia feel my wrath for their continued sins; floods, earthquake in populated area of great power; sea swallowing up coastal cities; tsunami of power on East Asia coasts; great hailstorms destroying crops; disease to greater degree in areas of the land of Europe, in Thailand, Singapore, in Burma and Laos; war throughout the earth; mob rule in Moslem nations; the Latin American nations of new scourge of insects, also diseases; all nations in great upheaval of war, famine, earthquake, diseases also.

7. Let all peoples repent lest few remain at my coming. Amen.

8. Let people of North America

now feel great devastating storm; also earthquake in major city and population area; soon war; also new diseases, and pestilences of famine, also insects, plant diseases; trade and commerce of an overthrow; hunger, mobs, leaders of nations fearful in their own lands; all things in commotion, to prepare the way of my glorious appearing, saith God, even Jesus Christ, Son Ahman to all peoples.

9. You continue in gross heinous crimes.

10. You have of murder of unborn children, of sorcery of drug of degrading way among all nations; adultery, fornication, Sodom; also many secret combinations of violent powers in many nations.

11. These evils must be blotted out from among your peoples, or I shall send my own judgments to sweep the wicked off the earth.

12. O that ye would repent, is the call of thy God to all peoples. Amen.

13. Let Spain be humbled for not heeding my word.

14. Let also Italy be mostly empty.

15. Let the Netherlands be as a desolate place in many areas.

16. Let all peoples feel my anger of just holy way, to humble all nations.

17. Let all peoples come unto me, your Lord, through my holy authority on earth, my Priesthood, Church, and Kingdom among men.

18. Let there be the great War of Armageddon take place if nations will not cease murder of unborn children and immoral ways.

19. When I appear, such things shall be of capital punishment, as my Zion rises to rule over all nations.

20. Let also China and Russia be humbling nations against other nations, then be humbled themselves.

21. Let United States of America feel full weight of judgments of God upon them if they heed not my own word sent to you; yea, my many warnings I have sent to leaders and peoples of all nations.

22. Let thy walk center around my coming, also obedience to my Gospel plan of salvation, to purify your lives through faith unto repentance.

23. Let my glorious appearing startle the wicked, and cause the more righteous to rejoice.

24. Let holy power Celestial descend to earth with your Lord and Just King of Eternal Power come upon all peoples to prepare the way before me. Amen.

SECTION REVELATION 90

Revelation of the Lord Jesus Christ
Palestine, Texas
Sunday, December 11, 2011

1. Verily thus saith the Lord to all peoples of all nations: My holy way of eternal power Celestial is the Holy Priesthood of Melchizedek, the Priesthood of eternal power.

2. All of the earth; yea, all nations past, present, future, into eternity, must bow to this eternal power legitimate holy government over all peoples, to be of full way holy exalting gift unto eternal lives.

3. This is the love-power of God toward all of His children who will receive my holy power unto perfect obedience to Celestial holy eternal law, of the revelations I give, even Jesus Christ, your Eternal God, who giveth this holy and pure revealing of my Eternal Union with my Father, who is over all, even Ahman, saith Son Ahman, Jesus, your Lord of Eternity Authority over all. Amen.

4. Now believe you cannot advance in eternal progression save you hold the eternal authority called the Holy Priesthood, of my Eternal Union power with my Holy Eternal Order as the way of progression eternal.

5. Let all be holy who bear my Holy Priesthood.

6. Let all repent unto purity of life to receive this holy power by the holy order of receiving eternal power, even by my power of the Priesthood. Amen.

SECTION REVELATION 91

Fundamentalist Church of Jesus Christ of Latter-day Saints
P.O. Box 840459
Hildale, Utah 84784

Thus Saith Jesus Christ, Who Is Son Ahman, to the Leader of This Nation of the United States of America, and All the Leaders of This Nation in Their Several Governing Appointments and Powers; and Thus to the Peoples of This Nation, Mine Own Word From the Heavens; Even the God of Glory Who Speaketh Thus to Your Understandings -- A Call to Heed My Word, Even I Who Am Soon to Come in the Powers of Heaven to Dwell Among Men, a Governing Power Over All Nations of the Earth -- Hear My Words:

Revelation of the Lord Jesus Christ
Eldorado, Texas
Thursday, May 26, 2011

1. Thus saith the Lord Jesus Christ, Son Ahman, the Creator of heaven and earth, who is Jehovah Christ, the Great I AM, even the Beginning and the End, who reigns in the heavens eternal, Creator over this earth, sending forth the children of the Father to this probationary world for their time of testing, being given their agency to know good from evil, left to choose, yet being born with enough of my holy light to know good from evil from birth, yea, to be agents to themselves --

2. I who created all things speaketh from on high as one crying in the wilderness, a light that reigns over all, yet the inhabitants of the earth, dwelling in gross darkness, discern not the light that came among them in the meridian of time as the sacrifice of atoning power to conquer death and raise all in the resurrection to be judged by a just God for the deeds and desires in the flesh;

3. Yea, I speaketh, saith your Lord who created you, again, to the leader of the nation that now inhabits my land of Zion where my New Jerusalem shall be built, that you have heeded me not.

4. Though I have sent mine own word, my revealed word to thee, and have spared thy life as the God of Creation over thee, who giveth life to all who dwell upon the earth, who enlightens the mind to more noble thoughts and works; thus have I sent my words to you.

5. And you have gloried in thy doings wherein I have reproved thee and this nation, of which you, the President of the United States of America, officiate over by my grace, in that executive branch of earthly governing power, having influence over many peoples.

6. And how shalt thou stand in the day of judgment when the resurrection is brought forth in thy behalf before a just

God, knowing the word of God has been given you, warning thee to bear influence to cease the murder of innocent unborn children in this nation, and bear influence in other nations to do the same?

7. And I have reproved thee and the leaders of this nation by mine own words revealed from the heavens for thy aggressive acts toward other nations who have not attacked thee, not being justified in thine aggressions, which shall clip thy power; as I have weighed thee in the balance and found you and the leaders of this nation wanting.

8. And as I have spoken judgments against thee and this nation, if you heed me not, so shall I fulfill.

9. And you have witnessed, even by personal traveling to see the destruction of the windstorms I have sent, that I warned thee of in my previous communicating, saith the Lord Jesus Christ;

10. Thou hast seen the power of thy God humble this nation in allowing windstorms and flooding, as an example that when He speaketh, He fulfilleth His word.

11. My word is sure, unto an eternal duration of the consequence of the choices made in every man's life being returned upon them -- a just recompense of reward -- that as they measure to their fellow man, so shall I, their God, measure an eternal judgment upon each one favored to come to the age of accountability.

12. Thus saith the God of heaven: My time is at hand.

13. My chastening hand is upon this nation and upon the nations of the earth, and I have sent forth mine own word through my servant, my Mouthpiece I have appointed and ordained on earth.

14. And my word has now gone forth to the leaders of all nations to cease their wars and draw their military and armies into their own borders, to only be used for defensive needs, save I, the Lord, shall command; for in my glorious appearing, I, your Lord and King, shall be the governing power known among all nations to humble all peoples who continue in a violent nature and in murderous and immoral ways.

15. I am the God of glory who giveth and taketh life as I will; and I doeth the will of the Father, performing a work to bring forth a thousand years of peace under the reign of a governing power sent from heaven, known among men as the Kingdom of God, yea, the Kingdom of Ahman, my Father;

16. For I am Son Ahman and doeth the will of the Father in all things, to the redeeming of all mankind from the grave and judging all in the resurrection.

17. And nothing shall be hidden, and all secrets shall be revealed, and the wicked shall tremble before me, a just and holy God who must soon send forth His message of salvation to all surviving nations; for this murder of unborn children, and Sodom, and violent and unjust ways, and immoral and corrupt ways cannot stand.

18. And I have sent forth my word to be justified before the heavens to send forth the cleansing powers to sweep the more wicked out of the lands of every nation on earth, to preserve the more righteous, who shall know of my ways of Zion and of New Jerusalem, that shall be built in that Center Stake appointed, of Jackson County, Missouri; and nothing can stay mine hand.

19. I have caused you to be warned of an assassination plot among the rich of this nation. Heed my word and I shall preserve thy life, to the performing of the works of overcoming these great outward evils I have named -- of legal consent in

thy nation, upholding those evils to exist among thy people.

20. I have allowed you to know of mine own words coming forth, showing thee and the leaders of this nation, and the leaders of all nations, that I, the God of Creation, who brought forth this earth and caused the peopling thereof, am able to speak from the heavens; yet few will heed my words and accept my Gospel of salvation, having pleasure in unrighteousness;

21. Yet I, the God of glory, who am just and holy, shall reward all, and wickedness cannot reign.

22. A righteous government of heavenly power cometh to earth as I caused mine apostles in the meridian of time to preach the same; which record, known as the Bible, though it has been altered by wicked men in parts, yet it testifieth many truths of my coming, and the building of New Jerusalem, which is on the land known as North America, as I have named -- my land of Zion -- as I shall cleanse, as a whirlwind coming upon them, which example you have recently seen in the sweeping of life off certain places of thy land with the whirlwinds, of such destructive nature that should humble all peoples that the God of power and of glory speaketh.

23. Yet they heed me not, in overcoming their own evils, needing to cleanse the inside of the platter, as it were, in your own nation; for your laws are corrupt that uphold these great sins I have named, which sins shall be swept off the earth, saith the Lord Jesus Christ, out of every nation in the great judgments of a just God soon at hand.

24. And if you would seek the blessings of thy God who created thee, act on these true and correct principles to favor life, virtue and purity, honesty, lest

my judgments humble you to the dust, and thy power be so clipped, you rise not again as leaders of a nation that could have done the works of righteousness, yet only promote the justifying of thy peoples in ways opposing the plan of life established by the God who created thee; which the murder of unborn children and sodomy and adultery and immoral ways promote that sin of corruption of immoral ways that promotes the destruction of life of unborn children.

25. How canst thou not be touched by the flagrant and outward attack on the principle of life?

26. Yea, thy God speaking to the leader of this nation and all the leaders within this nation:

27. Awake! This sin of gross darkness shall blight thy soul unto an eternal damnation, you having been warned in this mortal and earthly existence by thy God sending His own word unto thine understanding, and you heed me not; I being justified now to send forth more judgments upon this nation -- earthquake, more storms of destructive nature, to thy knowing I have warned thee.

28. And as thou continuest warring against nations and supporting other nations in their wars against other nations, when those nations that are attacked by thee and thine allies, yea, thy NATO allies, not having attacked thee first, you become the aggressors in the sight of heaven and are promoting violence and war among nations, that if you do not withdraw, your violent ways shall erupt in a conflict that shall absorb nations in that prophesied war that my servant John my Beloved recorded, seeing in vision these last days before my glorious appearing, to establish peace once again upon earth among all nations, by establishing my New Jerusalem,

my Zion on my land of Zion in full power from heaven.

29. Thus I send my word again to the leaders of this nation, and I fear thee not; for thy power can only exist of governing ability by the grace of God who created thee.

30. And as I predicted, during my ministry among mine apostles, the destruction of the Jewish nation and the scattering of that people, so shall it be with this nation -- a sweeping of this nation clean who oppose my Zion and my righteous rule soon to come, by opposing my Priesthood, Church, and Kingdom upon the earth, imprisoning and persecuting my people who are established by the revelations of their God, even Jesus Christ, who speaketh these words unto thee and sendeth them to thee by my Priesthood and eternal authority now dwelling upon the earth, my people being prepared for my glorious appearing, to build my Zion, even New Jerusalem, to receive their Lord in His glory.

31. Thus my people have been a persecuted people since the days of Joseph Smith, my servant and Prophet, whom I used, saith Jesus Christ, to restore my Church, Priesthood, and Kingdom upon the earth.

32. I have sent forth my policies of governing power in my publishings, mine own word revealed from heaven, that the governing power in New Jerusalem and in Zion shall administer justice and equity, and pure and noble ways of living.

33. Study the same, correct thy laws, and remove these greater outward evils from being upheld by legal consent.

34. Warn thy people of coming judgments soon at hand -- the sea heaving beyond its bounds, great cities swallowed up in the earth, disease, the overflowing

scourge with no cure being sent forth upon this people who will not heed my word, but continue in their gross wickedness and corrupt ways.

35. Oh, that you would heed my word!

36. For the heavens weep over the wickedness now dwelling in the hearts of the children of men in this nation and in all the nations of the earth; yet I must do my will, declared from the heavens, the will of the Father, whose perfect way and will I do, saith Son Ahman.

37. And this earth shall know one thousand years of peace, my Zion the ruling city, the capital city of governing power over the earth, raised up by the visitation of the heavenly powers to earth.

38. As recorded in holy writ, verily it shall be so.

39. And because you are my children on earth, having your agency, I, your just and holy God, who loveth all, send forth the warning voice that you shall reap as you have sown.

40. And my day of greater judgments are soon at hand.

41. And I loveth the salvation of souls through righteous works, who promote life and purity of life unto their own salvation and the salvation of the generations ahead.

42. There shall not be a prolonging much further in my merciful hand of warning.

43. My judgments have begun to cleanse my land of Zion, to preserve mine elect who will heed my words.

44. Mine Israel shall be gathered from all nations under heaven unto New Jerusalem and inherit their promised lands -- both my land of Zion and that land of Old Jerusalem.

45. I shall humble this nation through a judgment they have not expected -- of

a large city mostly destroyed, which city the inhabitants thereof have continued in gross wickedness for many years, having been warned since the days of my servant Joseph Smith, yet they will not repent.

46. And I being a just God, shall fulfill my word.

47. I have allowed my servant to be in the hands of bondage, and now make known that my word is coming forth to the leaders of all nations, and to thy peoples in every nation, that you may know I, a just God, am able to speak from the heavens and deliver my word, to be justified to cleanse wickedness off the earth and preserve the more righteous, who uphold the ways of life and virtue, justice and equity.

48. With blessings unmeasured shall the more righteous be favored -- with knowledge from heaven and the blessings of a just and holy God upon them, who sees and knows all things, and nothing is hidden.

49. And verily, upon the ungodly who delight in violent ways, in murder, in immoral and in corrupt ways, sudden judgment and a sweeping off the earth shall take place.

50. And I send you my warning voice again, that I may be justified, as a just and holy God, to perform this work of cleansing the earth and my land of Zion, to prepare the way for a righteous government of heavenly power coming to earth to rule over all nations, even by their consenting, seeing the noble and exalting ways of a Celestial heavenly power, and desiring the ways of Zion in their own lives, yea, those who remain upon the earth.

51. Now heed my word:

52. If you would reap the blessings, through repentance, from thy Lord, to preserve thy peoples in more righteous ways, and to receive my Zion without

obstruction, without persecuting zeal against them -- neither by prosecution nor by mob rule, as has been done against my people in days gone by, even in this nation that professed religious freedom, driving my saints from that Center Stake of Zion in Missouri, never having made reparation to my Church and my Kingdom, which testimony cometh up before the heavens, justifying thy God to clip the power of this nation and bring them low, as I have done other wicked nations in ages gone by, when they rose to the height of corruption; for this nation is ripened in iniquity to overflowing in the eyes of heaven.

53. And I have declared that this land of Zion shall be reserved for a righteous people who serve the God of the land, even Jesus Christ.

54. I am He, your Lord and Savior, that speaketh these words, which you shall know in the day of judgment and resurrection that thy God hath spoken, and shall hold thee accountable, the leader of this nation and the leaders of this nation, in the several offices and government positions, for your conduct; for the judge on earth shall be judged of a just Judge in heaven.

55. Behold the earth, the heavens, the perfection of the bringing forth of life upon earth in every form and nature, the mysteries of which are only known by a God of Creation.

56. I am He who created this earth and peoples this earth by sending forth spirits to dwell in earthly bodies, giving them their life.

57. And this gross crime of the murder of innocence, of unborn children, is the powers of darkness working on the selfish will of those of immoral nature, to have pleasure in unrighteousness and not meet the responsibility of their own actions,

thus destroying life before it is born, depriving spirits appointed this earth from the heavens to come to this earth and prove themselves, through their agency, whether or not they would choose good and eschew and cast off evil;

58. For my plan of salvation is extant, and shall reach all mankind -- past, present and future.

59. And I am the God of heaven that shall cause my Gospel of salvation to spread to every nation on earth in the day of the thousand years of peace, as I come to earth in my glory and cause my Kingdom of God, Council of Fifty, to be the ruling body over all nations, having representatives therein sufficient to maintain the rights of religious freedom and other freedoms thy God bestoweth upon His children to work out their salvation, without intrusion upon other peoples and their religious ideas and ways and tenets.

60. Therefore, know that the God of glory cometh, and hath warned the people of this nation and the leaders of this nation of greater judgments soon at hand, such that you have not witnessed before in your lifetimes nor in thine history as a nation;

61. For I have preserved this land to be a land of freedom where religion would be protected by law, yet my people have been a persecuted people by the falsehoods promoted by those of aspiring power and apostate and wicked intent, darkened by their own sins to persecute an innocent people.

62. And only by the grace of the God of heaven has my Church and Kingdom continued on earth;

63. Yea, verily, only by my grace do all nations keep their place; and all leaders of all nations shall soon be held accountable to the God of heaven, who cometh to earth

in His glory, to their knowing I have come to earth.

64. And in that accounting, justice shall be satisfied where murderous and immoral ways have been promoted to gain power and to increase in power of governing nature.

65. Great Babylon, yea, spiritual Babylon, of which this nation is a part, soon falleth; and my Zion shall rise; and I shall preserve those who can be representatives of righteous living in the Zion of our God coming forth in fulness.

66. I, the Lord, have spoken it; and as I have spoken, so shall I fulfill.

67. And though the heavens weep over this most wicked generation that has ever been on my land of Zion, I must fulfill my word; for I am a God of truth, and nothing is hidden from before mine eyes.

68. And though I have been long-suffering, I shall send my fire from heaven to purify my land of Zion of all wickedness, and raise up a more righteous generation of mine Israel, and other peoples that shall be brought to my land of Zion, and receive my message of salvation unto their eternal lives being earned, and the blessing of many souls upon the earth unto eternal life; and also, the blessing of many souls who dwell in the world of departed spirits awaiting the blessings and ordinances of salvation through the Redemption of Zion;

69. For I, the Lord, have organized this earth to fulfill the purpose of its creation, and I send forth children to earth to prove themselves.

70. And there is a day of judgment beyond this life that pertains to this life of your earthly existence, when all secrets shall be known and nothing hidden from all.

71. Thus, awake! Awake!

72. Repent ye! Repent ye! is the call of thy just God, even your Lord and Master, who ruleth over all things, soon to come in the clouds of heaven in the power of His might to visit the righteous and to sweep the wicked off this land of Zion and in many lands of the earth. Amen.

73. I who reigns on high speaketh further -- He who has all power:

74. Though no man knoweth the hour or the day of my glorious appearing, it is nigh at hand.

75. And these, my words, being sent to the leaders of this nation, and mine other words revealed to the leaders of all nations, sent forth by my Church and Kingdom upon the earth, the sending forth of my word is witness that my coming is nigh at hand, to justify thy Lord in what He must do to preserve Zion -- a city of righteousness, of peace and holiness, wherein all who dwell therein shall be called holy.

76. Let none oppose my Zion, or I shall send forth the judgments of a just God upon thee, saith the Lord to this nation and all peoples of the earth.

77. And that nation that raises their hand against my Zion shall be laid low and lose power and influence on earth;

78. For my judgments are just, and all peoples shall stand before me in the day of the resurrection and know that thy God who created thee, who redeemed thee from the grave, hath done right.

79. And the wicked shall tremble at my appearing and stand afar off.

80. How oft would I have gathered you into the arms of my redeeming love, O ye peoples of the earth, and you heed me not.

81. Yet those who mock their God shall mourn and know that He fulfilleth His word, all being accountable to a just

God for the conduct through their agency on earth.

82. I, your Lord Jesus Christ, call upon the leader of this nation and those who are of influence in Congress to heed my word:

83. Be peacemakers among nations.

84. Overthrow these wicked laws that allow murder of unborn children, and of Sodom and adultery in thy land; for you are like the people in the days of Noah, with evil continually in your minds, and violence throughout thy land and in thy natures; and of a sudden, my whirlwind judgments shall come upon thee, even this nation on my land of Zion, and other nations on this land where my New Jerusalem shall rise.

85. While the governing powers are in thine hands, O ye leaders of this nation, do well.

86. Let deliverance and protection come for my people, for my servant and my servants in bondage.

87. And as my servant Daniel of old saw the destruction and upheaval of nations until Michael, mine Archangel, shall be sent to give the governing powers into the hands of my saints, there shall be unrest and overthrow of nations until only my Zion remaineth on my land of Zion.

88. War shall come to thy borders. Millions shall flee to the center of thy land and fill the mountains.

89. A great famine shall be among those who flee, and where the war taketh place on thy borders, because you heed me not.

90. How can I favor thy nation above others in continued protection if you allow these gross evils to exist among you, and allow the persecution of my Church and Kingdom upon the earth, whether by persecuting zeal of outward prosecution

of government powers against my Church and Kingdom, or whether it be persecuting zeal of a secret nature, seeking the lives of mine elect in a day of greater violence soon to come among the people of this land? -- which shall disrupt governing powers, unable to control thine own peoples, the unrest increasing, notwithstanding your supposed military might in the world today; a day when all people shall fear, when brother shall rise up against brother, mother against daughter, and daughter against mother, father against son, as I predicted, revealing these truths of coming events to mine apostles of old, which shall take place in this nation, being a nation of supposed freedom, which I have favored with great power and influence on earth; yet, if you continue in these most wicked ways, my justice and full judgment shall fall upon thee.

91. Oh, that you would heed my words and turn thy lives to righteousness, and turn thy governing powers to justice and equity.

92. You depend upon thy God who created thee for the breath of life, for health, for the preservation of all you have, for the sun that shineth, and the rains that bringeth water of life to thy crops and fields and orchards, that allows peace in thy borders and in the hearts of the children of men, mine own heavenly Spirit sent forth to touch people's minds and hearts to be of a peaceful way if they would receive the impressions of good, of kindness and peace in their souls.

93. And as I labor with the children of men, giving them their agency, I am a just God who intervenes in the lives of those who do what is right in the sight of their God.

94. And my Gospel of salvation has been published and sent to the nations of the earth lo, these many years, both in that holy writ known as Bible printing, and also in the revelations of your God, even Jesus Christ, through my servant Joseph Smith, Jun., which has been published to all peoples, nations, kindreds, and tongues.

95. And therein my word declares of my glorious appearing to preserve the righteous, who remembereth thy Lord in His ways, who rejoice in His coming and glory in His redeeming love, applying His Gospel of salvation of righteous principles, yea, eternal principles revealed from heaven to their individual lives.

96. Thus shall be the favored lot of those who heed my word.

97. In my holy love, I send forth these words of warning to the leaders of this nation of the United States of America in plain, understanding language; a God of eternal power speaking, inviting thee, the leaders of this nation and the peoples of this nation, to be of an influence of more righteous ways, and preserving my people in their freedoms to establish Zion in their midst;

98. For I shall reward all peoples according to the blessings offered, yet, through their own actions and words and desires, reject blessings that could promote life, yea, and also eternal life for those who would receive my message of salvation, saith your Lord.

99. And in my glory coming to earth, I shall heal the surviving nations and make known to them the mysteries of all ages of time; and truth shall be told concerning every nation, people, tongue of every age of time. Even so. Amen.

SECTION REVELATION 92

Fundamentalist Church of Jesus Christ of Latter-day Saints
P.O. Box 840459
Hildale, Utah 84784

Thus Saith Son Ahman, Even Your Lord and Savior Who Hath Redeemed All Mankind, Jesus Christ, Who Speaketh to the Leaders and Peoples of the Nation of Nicaragua Through the Revelations of My Will Coming Forth to Thine Understanding, Hear My Word Saying Thus:

Revelation of the Lord Jesus Christ
Eldorado, Texas
Friday, May 27, 2011

1. Thus saith the Lord Jesus Christ, the Redeemer of mankind who suffered on the cross, conquering death, bringing forth the resurrection of all mankind, wherein all shall be judged of a just God for their deeds done in the flesh, of their earthly mortal existence:

2. I who reigneth on high speaketh, and there cannot be anything stay mine hand, for I am Eternal and the God of Creation, and have brought forth the earth; and I dwell in the heavens in the dominion of my Father, Ahman;

3. For I am Son Ahman, even Jesus Christ who speaketh, sending forth mine own word revealed from the heavens to that nation called Nicaragua, wherein there are evils among thee; sending forth mine own word to the leaders of this nation and the peoples of this nation to repent of your corrupt and immoral ways, lest my judgments come upon thee;

4. For I shall preserve those among thy nation who are of the more righteous.

5. And I send my word of warning, that there must not be murderous ways, nor murder of unborn children, nor injustice and corrupt ways to gain power among you;

6. For I am the God of glory soon to come in power and make myself known to all nations, and bring forth a government of heaven to earth to reign on earth among men for a thousand years in my Zion, and build a New Jerusalem on that land known as North America.

7. And you, the people of this nation, must needs be ready to be useful to thy Lord.

8. Take care of thy poor.

9. Have laws that allow freedom of religion, and also freedom of speech without obstruction.

10. And let there be, in the leaders of this nation, an honest labor to seek after the interest of thy peoples and not be oppressive at all, as has been done in the past by many leaders of this nation.

11. It must not be, for I shall remove leaders from nations who deal unjustly with their own peoples, or are of a violent nature to gain power and influence.

12. And verily, I am a just God, who cometh soon, and sendeth my word to thee that you may know this, my word, being received into thine hands and among thy people by my sending, shall justify thy God to cleanse thy nation of the more wicked who dwell therein, and preserve the more righteous against the day of my coming.

13. For I am the God of glory who hath created all things, who upholds all peoples in their place, to give them time and opportunity to prove what they will love and follow;

14. For good and evil are placed before you on this earth of testing time, a probationary existence; for you are sons and daughters of God, sent to earth by thy Lord through birth.

15. Though you forgot all of your previous existence, I am able to send forth my message of salvation, which is soon to dawn upon all nations of the earth as Zion rises and New Jerusalem is built as the governing city and authority over all nations of the earth.

16. And I am the King that rules over all, yea, the God of heaven who cometh.

17. Repent ye, ye leaders of this nation and ye peoples of this nation, of your immoral and murderous and corrupt ways.

18. And know that I shall reveal the secrets of all men's lives, and judge all men, women, and children in the day of resurrection power; and nothing shall be hidden, and all secrets shall be known.

19. There cannot be secret combinations of murderous and immoral intent, for it shall be answered upon your heads unto an eternal judgment.

20. Improve thy laws.

21. Guarantee proper freedoms, that agency may be maintained without oppression and fear of government intervention, whether it be in civil or religious matters.

22. And let there be peace in thy land in preparation for my messengers of salvation to come among thy people;

23. For I am sending you this warning, that a judgment of sweeping destruction shall render many no longer part of this life, a judgment of thy God upon those who continue in these wicked ways, and preserving the more righteous unto a greater light of Zion shining forth upon all nations.

24. This is the word of the Lord thy God. Amen.

SECTION REVELATION 93

Fundamentalist Church of Jesus Christ of Latter-day Saints
P.O. Box 840459
Hildale, Utah 84784

Thus Saith the Lord Jesus Christ, Even Son Ahman, Who Ruleth in the Heavens and Over All Nations, to the Leaders of Venezuela and the Peoples Thereof, Mine Own Words of Warning and a Call to Prepare for My Glorious Appearing, Saying Thus:

Revelation of the Lord Jesus Christ
Eldorado, Texas
Friday, May 27, 2011

1. Thus saith the Lord Jesus Christ, the God of heaven and earth, who created all things, who hath redeemed mankind from the grave by the suffering upon the cross and the shedding of His own blood by wicked men, conquering death, bringing forth the resurrection of all peoples to stand before a just God to receive an eternal judgment for their works done on earth;

2. And thus I speak, saith Him who sees and knows all things, who is the Great I AM, even Jehovah, the Beginning and the End, to that people of the nation of Venezuela and the leaders thereof;

3. For thus saith the Lord to the leaders of Venezuela: Turn from your wicked ways of seeking power among nations, of being oppressive to thine own peoples.

4. And let there not be the evil practices of murder of unborn children, nor of Sodom, nor of immoral and adulterous ways among thy people by consent of law.

5. And seek to benefit the poor.

6. And give freedom of religion and free expression.

7. And promote just and equitous laws that promotes the happiness of thy peoples;

8. For I, the Lord Jesus Christ, send you mine own word from the heavens through my servant on earth, to your understanding, that my glorious appearing is nigh at hand.

9. And those leaders of nations, even of this nation who continue in their wicked ways, in seeking power by unjust means and by secret combinations, by military and police might, I shall handle them and remove them from power, to no longer be leaders of nations, even those who oppress their own peoples and promote these gross immoral crimes, even murderous ways;

10. For I, the Lord, shall cleanse all peoples in the whirlwind judgments I shall send.

11. And if you heed me not, you shall know that I, the Lord, your Savior Jesus Christ, hath spoken, who hath all power and authority to render to every person, men, women, and children; yea, measure to them as they have measured to their fellow men.

12. New Jerusalem, even my Zion, shall rise and be the governing city of eternal, heavenly power, come to earth

with thy Lord to govern all nations of the earth that survive the great judgment of God, of wars and pestilence, hail and famine and earthquake, the sea heaving beyond its bounds.

13. Great is the day of my coming, and you must be prepared.

14. Let there be in thy borders of thy land, among thy people who dwell in this nation of Venezuela, a preparation for thy Lord's coming.

15. Cease to fight among yourselves.

16. Let freedom of religious worship be proclaimed in thy land, without obstruction of government powers.

17. Attend to the poor in a manner to promote peace among thy peoples.

18. There must needs be in your nation an awakening, lest my almighty power, in judgments sent, humble thee.

19. Awaken, and repent ye, repent ye, of these greater evils in thy land, saith the Lord who reigns in the heavens, and by whose grace and power all peoples and nations have their place on earth, who can raise one up and cast one down at His pleasure, being the God of eternity, looking upon all peoples as children of the Father, sent to earth in a probationary testing existence to prove their characters and their worth, having good and evil placed before them, and having agency to choose; therefore, choose good principles.

20. I have sent to you mine own publishings of recent giving, my warning to the leaders of nations, wherein is published my policies of governing power, which shall be the law of Zion over all nations.

21. Study these policies of governing power of Son Ahman, who reigneth under His Father, Ahman, even Elohim.

22. I am the God of glory and of power, and bringeth with me the just recompense of reward to reward every man, woman, and child according as they have measured to their fellow man, and their deeds and desires in the flesh upon the earth.

23. Heed my word, and prepare ye, for a great day of cleansing is nigh at hand.

24. And I am justified, having sent forth my warnings to the leaders of the nations of the earth, to cleanse every land of the more wicked of their peoples from off the earth with great judgments of God, and nothing can stay mine hand.

25. Heed my word and prepare ye.

26. Repent ye, repent ye! is the word of the Lord thy God to the peoples of the earth and to this nation, that must not turn to a warlike desire or way, and must not use their own military and police force to oppress your own peoples.

27. It must not be, lest judgment suddenly come upon the leaders of this nation and others who will not turn from their most wicked practices that I have named;

28. For these evils cannot be in your nation in the day of my coming, lest great destruction take place among thee.

29. I, the Lord, have spoken it, and send forth my word to your understanding; and as I have spoken, so shall I fulfill, saith the God of glory. Amen.

30. The Lord saith further in His message to that nation, yea, the leader of that nation of Venezuela:

31. Humble thyself, lest my judgments come upon thee and remove thee from power.

32. Promote good in thy borders, and be no longer an oppressive leader to thine own peoples; for I have seen the secrets of thine administration and shall cleanse your

land and your governing officials, even to the removing from power those who reign in this nation at this time.

33. Heed my word, and promote justice and the freedoms I have named, that there may be peace in thy land in the day of my coming in my power; for I shall promote the peace and happiness of all mankind through the redemption and building up of my Zion in New Jerusalem.

34. I, the Lord, have spoken it, and so shall I fulfill. Amen.

SECTION REVELATION 94

Fundamentalist Church of Jesus Christ of Latter-day Saints
P.O. Box 840459
Hildale, Utah 84784

Thus Saith the Lord Jesus Christ, Even Son Ahman, the God of All Creation, to the Leaders of the Nation of Latvia and to the People Thereof. Amen. Thus Hear My Word:

Revelation of the Lord Jesus Christ
Eldorado, Texas
Monday, May 30, 2011

1. Thus saith the Lord Jesus Christ, the Beginning and the End, the God over all creation, who reigns in the heavens above and over all nations of the earth, who is known as Jehovah Christ, even Son Ahman; who shall appear in His great glory in the power of His might to all surviving nations, and build up New Jerusalem in fulness as the governing city of heavenly power to rule over all nations for a thousand years, as thy Lord descends with the resurrected saints and the saints on earth who are lifted up into the cloud of His glory, to descend with Him to earth to be the governing power over the earth --

2. I, the Lord, speak to the nation of Latvia:

3. Repent ye! yea, the leaders thereof more especially, and do not allow contention among thee, lest violence come upon thy borders and you be a conquered nation again, as you hitherto have been.

4. And let there be peace proclaimed toward other nations.

5. And repent ye of the murder of unborn children in thy legal allowance, and also allowing Sodom and adultery and immorality to be rampant among thy peoples;

6. And have laws that forbid these evils; and prosecute those who are guilty, and do not allow even leaders to continue in this wickedness in thy borders and in thy nation.

7. I, the Lord, am the God of truth, and see and know all things, and shall judge all peoples, and am soon to appear in my glory.

8. And whirlwind judgments shall first remove the more wicked of all nations from the earth, preserving the more righteous.

9. And I shall be justified in sending whirlwind judgments upon thee and other nations who heed not my word.

10. Thus I give you my warning, for the appearing of thy God hath been published to thee, and I have sent to your leaders, yea, and to common man, my publishings of my warnings to the leaders of nations, that the peoples of the earth may know I have spoken from the heavens.

11. And these great evils, these heinous crimes of murder of unborn children, and of secret combination murders by many leaders of nations, must be done away, or they will be removed from power unto an eternal judgment as I remove them from the earth in the judgments of a just God coming upon a wicked generation.

12. Thou knowest my word through Isaiah, and through John the Beloved, mine apostle, saith Jesus Christ, whose words these are, through His servant on earth, given to your understandings, O ye leaders and peoples of the nation of Latvia;

13. For you shall be consumed as a nation and be a nation no more if you continue in these sins, when you have had time of self-governing nature to purge these evils from your nation.

14. And if ye heed me not, I shall remove that ability to be an independent people from you, and you shall be a tributary people to a greater power on earth until I, the Lord, free thee when my message of salvation comes to thy people and the peoples of those, the nations that surround thee, that bring thee under their subjection, and they also feel the love-giving message of thy Lord, a message of salvation, of eternal worth.

15. Thus saith the Lord: Repent ye of these evils, that I may preserve you as a people against the time of my coming to New Jerusalem, yea, the place appointed on the land of America.

16. My Zion shall rise, and there shall be a New Era of Peace and Righteous Government, equity and justice served, nobleness of purpose lived, an exalted way of life, of my revealing.

17. I have already sent my publishings to you leaders of the nations, and this nation of Latvia, containing my policies of government.

18. Study these policies, that you may be well prepared with your own laws already amended and corrected to preserve virtue, innocence, and life, yea, even the lives of unborn children, which murder shall be the shedding of innocent blood, judged in an eternal judgment in the day of the resurrection.

19. I am the Resurrection and the Life; and as I raised Lazarus from the grave, to the knowing of the Jewish nation, so do I raise all people from the grave according to their worthiness and time appointed; for it is in my scriptures that the first resurrection is for the righteous.

20. Thereafter cometh the second resurrection, where even all the wicked shall stand before thy God and be judged for deeds done in the flesh while on earth.

21. And none can escape my eternal eye, yea, my all-seeing eye; and you shall be your own accusers as your mind is unlocked in the day of judgment in the resurrection, when thy Lord standeth to judge all.

22. Be ye believing to that degree that you will correct your lives and your laws of

national government and local government to be of a justice and a kindness to your people.

23. Let there not be oppression or tyranny by those in authority toward thy population.

24. Let there be freedom of worship allowed, that my message of salvation may come to thy peoples and you be blessed of thy God to be a surviving nation through great judgments that will sweep many nations clean of all wickedness.

25. I, the Lord, have spoken it.

26. And if you will thus clean the inside of the platter, even your own peoples and laws and governing ways, I shall preserve thee against the oppression of other neighboring nations.

27. And if thou heed me not, it shall be fulfilled even as I have said. Amen.

SECTION REVELATION 95

Fundamentalist Church of Jesus Christ of Latter-day Saints
P.O. Box 840459
Hildale, Utah 84784

Thus Saith Your Lord and Savior, Jesus Christ, Who Is Son Ahman, to the NATO Nations, to the Leaders of NATO Nations, to the Commanders of NATO Military -- Mine Own Word of Prophecy and Warning Because You Heeded Me Not, Becoming an Aggressive Organization, No Longer of a Defensive Nature Alone; Yea, I Send My Word That You May Know of That Which Is to Come Upon Thee if You Continue to Be an Aggressive Organization, and Also as You Continue the Great Evils I Have Previously Named to Be in Your Nations -- Thus Saith the Lord:

Revelation of the Lord Jesus Christ
Eldorado, Texas
Tuesday, May 31, 2011

1. I who reigns on high, even Jesus Christ, the God of Creation over this earth, who dwells in the heavens, having all power over all nations and peoples, speaketh to the NATO nations:

2. Yea, thus saith the Lord: You have transgressed greatly against my word, and I shall now bring judgment upon thee, for you are not as you have professed -- a defensive organization -- but you have become an aggressive, violent organization against other nations who have not attacked any of thee.

3. Therefore, thus saith the Lord, I shall cause you to have all power clipped, and you fall short of your intentions of

present doing, thinking you will free a people in Libya or other nations where you have your military might thus in an aggressive attacking nature.

4. Thus saith the Lord, you have heeded me not; therefore, this organization shall be weakened until that nation of greater power comes forth and sweeps across your lands in Europe as a conquering nation, because you heeded me not.

5. You shall be weakened, broken up, and become tributary nations to another power.

6. And thus saith the Lord, you shall be cleansed by other judgments until you know I, your God, have spoken.

7. And you shall know that in the day I clip the power of that mighty nation who conquers thee, then is the time my land of Zion shall be completely cleansed, as a whirlwind of judgments, sweeping that nation of great power that now inhabits my land of Zion from off the earth for her transgressions against my Church and Kingdom, against my Zion.

8. And then is the time, as New Jerusalem is built up and my Zion rises as the governing power on the earth, that you shall be free from bondage, from that greater nation and power that shall conquer thee to make your nations tributary nations.

9. And as you allow my message of salvation to come into your borders, and I drive back that conquering nation over thee, thus saith the Lord, you shall know that I have done this work, telling thee beforehand of these events.

10. My time is nigh at hand of my glorious appearing, but first must come the cleansing of the more wicked of every nation from off the earth, preserving the more righteous.

11. Because you heed me not and have become aggressive nations, no longer of a defensive way only, as you have professed, you shall not prosper as a defensive organization.

12. War shall break out.

13. There shall be a fear come upon thy peoples.

14. The judgment of a just God shall come upon thy nations, and also upon the nation that inhabits, yea, a nation of great power today that inhabits my land of Zion shall be swept off the earth because she heeds me not, notwithstanding I have sent many warnings to the leaders thereof.

15. And now I have caused my word to be sent forth to all nations of the earth, my word of warning of soon-to-happen judgments.

16. I have called upon all peoples and all leaders of every nation to make peace, lest that great war of sweeping the wicked off the earth takes place, that great war to remove one third part of the earth of population now inhabiting this orb.

17. I, the Lord, have spoken it and shall be justified in allowing thee to receive as you have sown.

18. Yea, the harvest is upon you, and as you have sown, so shall you reap.

19. And as you sow violence, corruption, murder of unborn children, Sodom, and licentious and adulterous and immoral ways, even by legal consent in most nations of the earth, I, the Lord, shall sweep this off the earth.

20. And it shall be on record that I have spoken and warned thee that I would have saved thy nations if you had heeded my word.

21. And now, that the more righteous may be spared at the day of my coming, there shall be war and pestilence, famine, hail, and earthquake, and many

desolations; yea, an overflowing scourge and desolating sickness beginning upon my land of Zion, where a nation of great wickedness dwells who will not heed my word of warning, notwithstanding mine own word hath gone forth.

22. I send you this word, that there will be a day of deliverance after you are humbled by a greater power, sweeping NATO's alliance off the earth because you heed me not and would not make peace.

23. In the day I warned thee was the time to make peace, lest violence erupt in your own borders, an invading nation come against thee when you are weakened by internal strife, economic disaster, other pestilences and judgments weakening thy power as an alliance, no longer able to defend itself because of in-striving among you.

24. Therefore, thus saith the Lord God of heaven: Repent ye!

25. And in a day when you are humbled, and I remove power from that conquering nation over thee, then is the time you shall know I am sending my message of salvation among you;

26. To prepare thy peoples at that time for my deliverance;

27. For Zion shall rise, and New Jerusalem shall be the governing capital city of the earth; and Old Jerusalem shall also be a governing capital city over neighboring nations.

28. I, the Lord, have spoken it; so shall I fulfill.

29. Let there also be known that Belarus must be humbled, for therein is great wickedness among her leaders and her people.

30. And I, the Lord, send this warning to that nation and people: Repent ye, lest you be no longer a people on earth.

31. I, the Lord, have spoken it.

32. Thus let Belarus know that when a conquering nation cometh against thee, it is because of your own wickedness, in a manner of promoting among you licentious and immoral ways, even by leaders knowing it is so among thy people, and you would not correct the evils among you that would destroy innocence and purity; and also because you would join with another power to gain influence, economic advantage and desires for power among your leaders, unknown to your peoples, which would bring about a delivering thee over to another nation, wherein you will not seek unto principles of equity and justice among your own peoples.

33. Your sins shall be made manifest in a time to come, and there shall be a humbling of thee because of your wickedness and not turning to correct principle of governing power.

34. I have sent forth my policies of governing power to the leaders of all nations of the earth to prepare them for Zion's rise and New Jerusalem to be the heavenly powers come to earth, governing all nations of the earth, yea, thy Lord Jesus Christ, who speaketh these words through mine authority on earth to you.

35. He shall come in His glory and empower His elect, even mine Israel, gathered to New Jerusalem to be His Church and Kingdom, well prepared to guide the nations of the earth to peace and equity and justice among themselves.

36. They shall marvel at the power of God and declare: Yea, verily, God is among His people Israel in Zion.

37. This shall be acknowledged by all people when they see my power at my glorious appearing.

38. And as I humble any nation that

allows these corrupt practices, yea, these heinous crimes and corruptions that I have named, by legal consent, they shall be humbled by my judgments until the more wicked are removed and the more righteous remain to search unto their God who created them, for more noble, exalting, and pure ways of abiding on earth in laws that are righteous, acting on principles of equity and justice, that all peoples may have freedoms of worship and expression without becoming a distress of unrighteous oppression on other peoples.

39. For I am God and have the right to rule by right of creation, and because I have suffered and conquered death, doing the will of the Father, saith Jesus Christ, whose suffering hath atoned for all mankind to be raised from the grave and stand before thy God, even Jesus Christ, who speaketh this message of warning and a call of repentance to thee.

40. And you shall be judged in the resurrection for your works and deeds done in the flesh on earth, and it shall be fulfilled as I speak.

41. Oh, that you would heed my word, for now I am expressing a judgment against NATO nations, that European nations of this now aggressive coalition of nations shall be humbled by a conquering power;

42. And then cometh the overthrow of that greater nation, by my power of judgments on the continent of North America, because she heeds me not and has corrupted her way, yea, ripened in iniquity, worthy only to be swept off the earth in a day of greater evils and violence and distress in her borders.

43. And invading nations shall attack her, even that nation that boasts to be the great world power at this time, yet not acting on correct principle when invading

other nations who have not attacked her. It will not stand.

44. And I, the God over all, can guide the events of nations, giving life and judging all who is worthy to continue upon the earth unto New Jerusalem's rise and my glorious appearance being known among you, yea, among all nations of the earth.

45. I, the Lord, shall appear in my glory, and nothing can withstand my power.

46. And I am justified in sending my judgments to humble all nations, now having sent forth my warning to the leaders of all nations.

47. I am able to fulfill my word.

48. Thus, as you see my words fulfilled in European nations, becoming tributary nations, in general, to a greater power, humbled; which conquering nation shall oppress them until they realize the God of heaven hath spoken, and they are humbled by other judgments of my sending because they heed me not and continue in these wicked ways, having taken upon them pleasure in unrighteousness, destroying innocence, which the murder of unborn children is -- the most helpless of creations -- yet you heed me not, and judgments shall follow as you continue in these gross crimes, saith the Lord, until thy nations are cleansed of all who uphold such evil practices in their lives.

49. For I am able to remove the more wicked and preserve the more righteous in every land, nation, kindred, and tongue, against the time of my coming.

50. Therefore, heed my words, lest my full judgments come upon you.

51. Let France know you have sinned greatly against your God in being an aggressive nation now, heretofore careful

to not attack any other nation, save you were attacked first.

52. I allowed your military to be strong. Now it shall be broken up and not of a strong nature, even to defend thine own borders.

53. And you shall tremble when a greater power steps forth to conquer other nations on the European continent; for there shall be pestilences weaken thee to remove many of the wicked from thy land, humbling thy peoples.

54. And I have named other judgments in my words sent to thee.

55. Italy shall be of a sparse population after many judgments come upon her for her gross wickedness.

56. I, the Lord, have spoken to Spain to be of a peaceful intent, and not join with any nation in promoting war and violence against other nations. Heed my word.

57. Let Bosnia and Serbia make peace, lest a war break out on the European continent that cannot be contained, justifying a greater power to come against other nations in their own mind and thinking, even the leaders of that greater power who shall boast of military might;

58. Yet, when she attacks my land of Zion, though she progress in battle, she shall be driven back.

59. I shall send judgments upon that conquering nation over the European nations that comes against my land of Zion, until her power is clipped.

60. That is the day European nations will awake and see thy God hath spoken these truths, when you will begin to lend a listening ear, after you have been humbled to the dust in bondage as tributary nations, and by other judgments removing the more wicked from your lands.

61. And then is the day I shall send my message of salvation from Zion, my New Jerusalem in the center place appointed on the American continent, my Church and Kingdom being preserved by my almighty power on earth to be messengers of salvation to the surviving peoples in every nation on earth as I send them.

62. Hasten to prepare!

63. Humble yourselves by fervent repentance.

64. Some of my judgments can be stayed if you will cleanse the inside of the platter and destroy those laws that promote the murder of unborn children in your nations, and that promotes Sodom and adultery, and licentious and immoral ways that leads to the murder of unborn children and other evil practices.

65. I, the Lord, have spoken it.

66. And if you would have the survival of your nation through great judgments from God and from invading nation coming against thee, heed my words, lest the full measure of justice must be poured out upon thee for thy crimes and corrupt ways, and in some nations few remain.

67. I, the Lord, have foreseen these events, promoted by the powers of darkness among you, my pure word now being sent forth unobstructed; yea, the Lord God of heaven speaking to the peoples of the earth:

68. Repent ye! Repent ye! for the day of great judgments is upon you.

69. Turn from your wicked ways that corrupt and destroy life, that destroys virtue and innocence.

70. Oh, that you would heed my word, for I, the Lord your God, gave His life, suffering more than man can suffer, to conquer death and bring about the resurrection, giving all mankind the opportunity to earn eternal life if they

would heed my message of salvation and obey my laws and commandments.

71. And though men and the peoples of the earth in many places may profess my name, if they obey not my words, they are not my people, many deceiving themselves that mere profession that I am God is sufficient for them to earn salvation, and it is not so;

72. For I, the Lord, have declared: If you love me, keep my commandments. Do the works of righteousness that I have revealed.

73. And verily I say unto you, I restored my Gospel and my Priesthood from heaven through the instrumentality of Joseph Smith, my servant; and he sealed his testimony with his blood as a witness against this wicked generation, and for my Church and Kingdom rising.

74. And I have continued my Priesthood, Church, and Kingdom upon the earth to this day through Prophets I have called and preserved, and some few peoples who would heed my warning through them.

75. And now my Church and Kingdom continues, and I am preparing the way for my more pure people to receive me in the clouds of heaven, and descend with me to earth again, to New Jerusalem, being established in fulness as the governing heavenly power, the government from heaven come to earth to reign over all nations and peoples.

76. And by my judgments upon you shall you know I have spoken, because you heed me not in a day of offered peace.

77. Thus saith the Lord to those nations who seek to invade my land of Zion in a day soon to come:

78. Though you may be permitted to help cleanse my land of Zion of wickedness, you must withdraw and not remain upon my land of Zion, or I shall send judgments upon you to weaken you and clip your power, and humble you to no longer be an invading nation.

79. And there shall be come upon you pestilence and famine, earthquake, and other judgments, even removing thine armies from my land of Zion by great destructive elements coming upon you, of thy God, to your knowing it has happened by the power of God, until you withdraw your invading armies from my land of Zion.

80. And thus I have spoken and will fulfill, telling all peoples of every nation through this, my word given, what is soon to happen upon the earth.

81. NATO nations have now caused thy God to withdraw His preservation and protecting hand from thee.

82. Inward strife and fear of an invading nation against thee shall cause many to succumb to her power, yea, even an invading nation that has boasted world conquest in past times.

83. Her leaders shall be professing peace, yet promoting war, preparing for aggressive actions against other nations.

84. One of those among their leadership shall rise, of a more aggressive nature, to come against the European nations now united as NATO.

85. And NATO shall be weakened and not able to defend herself, causing certain nations to become tributary nations, and others to be invaded with military might; and other nations on European continent humbled by pestilence and famine and economic disaster as great Babylon, yea, spiritual Babylon falleth.

86. And there shall be sorrow in every land and nation of this alliance as your

disunity causes even economic breakup among you, and your prosperity be clipped.

87. Thus I send forth my word that it may be on record in every nation I have spoken of, yea, until all peoples of the earth shall know the word of the Lord hath been given of what is soon to come to pass because you would heed not my warning that I have sent to the leaders of all nations, even mine own word of recent giving, publishing the same to the peoples of the earth, directing my corresponding letters and publishings to the leaders of every nation of the earth, through my Church and Kingdom performing that work in my behalf; which Church and Kingdom I shall preserve, though they be a persecuted people by a wicked nation, and by the hands of traitors who turn against them, which traitors are corrupt themselves, accusing mine elect of evils.

88. Yet, I shall preserve mine elect who obey my laws, and prove them worthy of mine own presence and representatives of your God, soon to be sent as messengers of salvation to every surviving nation after I appear in my glory, known to all nations as I have prophesied.

89. I, being a just God, send forth these warnings to the leaders of nations and the peoples of all nations, to be justified in that which must take place to humble thee, to cease these gross evils.

90. For I am the God of salvation and know how to redeem mankind to a greater state of pure abiding and holy ways of righteous governing powers that are noble and that exalt mankind to that higher state of intelligence and peace.

91. I have given my life for the salvation of all mankind, saith your Lord and Savior, Jesus Christ, if they would but heed my message of salvation.

92. And I shall promote my Kingdom upon the earth to be the governing city and nation, even the Kingdom of Son Ahman, who is Jesus Christ, which Kingdom is Zion, of my revealing from heaven, and I and the angels dwelling on earth, guiding my Church and Kingdom upon the earth to be the governing power over all peoples.

93. Thus shall I fulfill my word, and thus my word is sent to you, the leaders of nations and the peoples of the earth, that you may know my time is at hand.

94. And I shall heal the brokenhearted, and raise up the poor, and comfort the needy, and bless those who labor with their might to make peace and bless mankind through righteous principles.

95. The earth shall reel to and fro as a drunken man in great earthquakes and other distress.

96. The peoples of all nations shall fear, yet I shall cause the more righteous to survive by my matchless power, a power eternal in the heavens that holds the earth in its orbit with exactness, that you might exist on earth by my grace, that you may learn my message of salvation if you will; and heed my warnings and repent, and come unto your God who made you, who can save you unto an eternal salvation.

97. And this is my purpose in the creation of this earth, in allowing nations to rise; yet, it is I who have the right to rule by right of creation.

98. And I have the governing power of the heavens to bring to earth among men, to promote a thousand years of peace among all peoples in my Zion being established in fulness, where thy God liveth and reigneth from on high and dwelleth among His people, His elect, who love truth and righteousness, a revealing of thy God to the salvation of souls.

99. I speak with boldness to the leaders of nations: Heed my word!

100. Cleanse your lands. Remove these evils I have named.

101. Awake! Your power is soon to be clipped, until I alone am heralded as the rightful Ruler of the earth, the King of glory, descending from heaven in the clouds and power of my might and glory, to be known among all peoples as dwelling among His people Zion, and sending forth His message of salvation to all surviving nations.

102. I, the Lord, have spoken it. Amen.

SECTION REVELATION 96

Fundamentalist Church of Jesus Christ of Latter-day Saints
P.O. Box 840459
Hildale, Utah 84784

Thus Saith Son Ahman, Even Jesus Christ, to the Leaders of Somalia, Word of Prophecy and Warning and Judgment to Come Upon Thee

Revelation of the Lord Jesus Christ
Eldorado, Texas
Tuesday, May 31, 2011

1. I, the Lord, speak to the nation of Somalia, my word to be sent to what leadership remains there, and to their ability to let their people know my word, even Jesus Christ who speaketh:

2. Repent ye of your violent ways, or you shall no longer be a nation, conquered by other nations and humbled, not only by war, but by pestilence and famine in thy borders.

3. Let this, my word, be sent forth to the leaders of Somalia of a soon happening, those who can be found; and if needs be, through United Nations representatives, other nations who go therein to deliver food and clothing and are of a defensive nature in behalf of United Nations, to tell leaders of Somalia I, the Lord, have spoken.

4. I am Son Ahman, the Creator of heaven and the earth, sending my word through my servant on earth to your understanding.

5. And I have redeemed all mankind by suffering on the cross more than man can suffer, yea, redeemed all peoples from the grave to be resurrected and brought forth to stand before me to be judged for their works done in the flesh on this earth.

6. I am a just God.

7. Because of your corruption in government, taking of bribes, giving way to the desires of other nations to come into your borders, wherein you sought to get gain and power thereby, now you have revolution and great corruptions in your own government.

8. Thus saith the Lord: Do a work of peace negotiation with neighboring nations

of soon happening, and be of a peaceful intent, even upon thine own peoples.

9. I shall cause a healing to take place; otherwise revolution shall sweep through thy land and you no longer be a nation of sovereign power, other nations conquering thee.

10. And they also shall be humbled by my judgments as they continue in wickedness.

11. And though you heed me not, my word shall be known in future times that I warned thee, and my word has been fulfilled. Amen.

SECTION REVELATION 97

Thus Saith Jesus Christ, Even Son Ahman, To the Leaders of the Nations of the Earth A Great Call of Warning

Thus Saith Son Ahman, Even Jesus Christ, to All the Leaders of All Nations of the Earth, and Thus All Peoples of the Earth -- A Great Warning to Make Peace, and Prepare for My Glorious Appearing to All Peoples Who Survive the Great Judgments of God Nigh at Hand -- Hear Ye My Word:

Revelation of the Lord Jesus Christ
Eldorado, Texas
Wednesday, June 15, 2011

1. I, your Lord, even Jesus Christ, who is Son Ahman, the Beginning and the End, the Creator of heavens and earth, who upholds all people in their place, who has all power, who seeth and knoweth all things, and nothing is hidden; who dwells in the eternal vision of the power of Celestial Godhood over all creation, who hath redeemed all mankind from the grave, by whose power all things exist and continue -- I, the Lord, speaketh to the people of the earth, to the leaders of all nations:

2. You have not heeded my word in the warning I have sent forth, saith the Lord, to make peace among nations and not use your militaries in aggressive ways against your own peoples, nor against other nations, especially those nations who have sought, in a violent way, attacks upon nations who have not attacked them in kind.

3. This is the will of the Lord. If you heed me not, as my Spirit withdraws from those of darkened nature who will not heed their God, the powers of darkness shall lead the leaders of nations and the peoples of nations unto the great war mine apostle John my Beloved testified of in that book of New Testament recording, yea, one-third part of the earth, of the population thereof, destroyed by their own violent ways.

4. And I, your God, have declared that if you will heed my word, your nation can be a surviving nation, by drawing into your lands your militaries, destroying your armored vehicles, as a witness you will make peace; and becoming a more pure and noble nation, not allowing those in power to uphold laws of the murder of unborn children, of Sodom, and of adultery, and licentious and corrupt ways.

5. And as you remove those outward evils, I have promised the more righteous of your peoples shall be of a surviving nature in the day of greater judgments soon at hand; yet you heed me not.

6. The great war shall take place if you heed me not, though I, a God of love and peace, who shall reign among the children of men personally, with the powers of heaven coming to earth with me in my glory and mighty power, to the knowing of all surviving nations; I, the God of heaven, shall establish a thousand years of peace upon the earth, binding satan through the righteousness of the people responding to my word, yea, a righteousness revealed of thy God and joyfully lived through agency.

7. Thus is the will of the Lord to hear my warning again:

8. You see the upheaval in nations, leaders fearing their own peoples, and now unrest spilling into other nations.

9. I, the Lord, foretold this in my word I have sent, and you heed me not.

10. Hear my word, and make peace, lest you invite the dark powers to inhabit your souls and lead you to bloodletting, not justified, but out of the darkness of hate one against another, which shall envelop the soul who continues to uphold the ways of corruption, of the murder of unborn children, of immoral ways of Sodom and adultery, not considering the word of thy God, who hath declared that He will be a preserver of eternal power over any nation who will clean up themselves, the inside of the platter.

11. Remove these wicked laws that allow these heinous crimes, for many leaders have joined in secret combinations with the rich, with those of illegal practices, seeking riches and powers to gain and keep power; and it will not stand as a just God executes full justice upon any peoples who continue in these terrible sins that cannot be in any nation in the day of great peace when I shall reign on earth.

12. And the wicked shall fear and tremble at my coming, for I have sent mine own word through my servant on earth, and through mine own words preserved and published throughout the earth in that Bible of sacred keeping, even the testimonies of the prophets and apostles of old; and I am a God at hand.

13. Darkness covereth the minds of the people of the earth, because when I send my word, they heed me not, thus turning away from the God of glory who created you and the earth and gives you life -- all things -- both in what is termed nature, even in your own organization, and all things in heaven and on the earth testify of an intelligent God, creating all things; establishing laws of governing, of kingdoms, in plant life, animal life, and among the children of men;

14. For the children of men are children of God, sent to earth to receive an earthly body for their spirits, to purify and to prove they will choose good and overcome evil;

15. And my Spirit is sent forth to touch the hearts of all peoples on the earth to give them enlightenment and knowledge of good from evil.

16. And according to the laws of

righteousness they have received, in their mortal lives and in their present enlightened way of laws of principles of righteousness, so shall they be judged, even eternally, in the day of the resurrection.

17. And I, a God of eternal power, have declared my word through my servant Joseph Smith in the day of his being on earth, now published in Book of Mormon, Doctrine and Covenants, Pearl of Great Price, and other writings of my servant Joseph Smith of my sacred revealing -- that I am a God who revealeth Himself from the heavens to a living representative on earth; and my Priesthood, Church, and Kingdom hath continued through a true and faithful line of Priesthood authority I have authorized on earth, giving you the names, that you may know my Priesthood continues:

18. My servant Joseph Smith; then Brigham Young continued my work; John Taylor thereafter; then John W. Woolley, and Lorin C. Woolley after him; John Y. Barlow; Leroy S. Johnson after him; and my servant Rulon T. Jeffs;

19. And my servant on earth continues my work, though in bondage, though accused by those who are of wicked intent in their own lives, who do not see truth of the beauty of the Everlasting Gospel of Jesus Christ; who fighteth against my Church and Kingdom, even those of apostate influence, who have turned from my Gospel, Church, and Kingdom.

20. Yet I am the God of glory, who hath preserved my Church and Kingdom upon the earth.

21. And now you know, saith the Lord, that I am with my servants; and their testimonies are recorded on earth in the many sermons and teachings of authorized publishings through my Church and Priesthood.

22. Verily, thus saith the Lord: The Book of Mormon is true. My Doctrine and Covenants is mine own word, that which was revealed through my servant Joseph Smith, Jun., and my servant Brigham Young contained therein; and my testimony of Zion's mission is upon the earth and among the children of men, well published.

23. Missionaries were sent forth in the day my revelations were received, and lo, these many years have been in the hands of the peoples of the earth who would seek the same, and you heed me not.

24. And I have caused mine own word to be received and sent to the leaders of nations and the peoples of the nations of the earth, of recent receiving and sending, and you heed me not.

25. And thus saith the Lord: A day of the shaking of the earth is nigh at hand; and the overthrow of nations, and the sweeping of the more wicked out of every nation is soon to take place by war and pestilence, hail, and famine, and earthquake, and windstorms, and that which is of disease, of the overflowing scourge and desolating sickness, because you will continue in wickedness to the destruction of your souls.

26. And I am the God of eternal life; Endless is my name. And I labor with the peoples of the earth according to their understanding; and I speak in the language of men to my servant to your understanding, and to the understanding of any who will seek the interpretation thereof, in your own tongue, as you thus seek unto eternal truths from your Eternal God, your Creator, saith Jesus Christ.

27. I have called upon you to make peace and be prepared for the rise of New Jerusalem as my Zion on earth, on the continent of North America.

28. I created the earth. You know even the revolutions and movements of the earth and the planets follow a regular time, showing the order of my creating, an almighty power.

29. Awake! Repent ye, repent ye, before the day of greater judgments cometh.

30. And I shall be justified, saith your God, because I have sent my word of warning.

31. And if you heed me not, I, a God of truth and righteous and holy and perfect way, shall fulfill my word.

32. This is the word of the Lord. As I have spoken, so shall I fulfill.

33. The heavens weep over the peoples of the earth, though my word is given to plain language and understanding, being used to enlighten thy minds of that which is nigh at hand.

34. Nevertheless, a day of righteousness shall soon dawn upon all the earth in the rise of Zion and New Jerusalem; and Old Jerusalem shall be rebuilt after the devastating war in the land of Old Israel.

35. And mine Israel shall be gathered; and my Zion shall be the governing city and power over all the earth, and nothing can stay mine hand;

36. For any nation opposing my Zion shall be humbled by great judgments, until they humble themselves to bow to my righteous rule, saith the God of Creation, even Jehovah Christ, the Beginning and End.

37. Your very breath of life is of my free love-giving, saith the Lord to all peoples, nations, kindreds, and tongues.

38. Life and death are before you, and I offer you eternal life through obedience to my commandments in my Gospel of salvation through my authorized Priesthood on the earth.

39. Therefore, hear my word:

40. Make peace. Prepare for my messengers of salvation to come into your nations and lands, that I may preserve your peoples against a day of my coming, being known by the power of the shaking of the earth;

41. For before my glorious appearing, the sun shall be darkened and the moon be turned to blood, and parts of the earth will return, seeming to be the stars falling from heaven.

42. For I, the Lord, have all things in hand, in the heavens and the earth, and speaketh to my children on earth to hasten to prepare, being justified by sending forth my Gospel of salvation lo, these many years, and preserving my Church and Kingdom upon the earth; and soon to restore the full work of Zion's mission; of earning, each one who will receive my message of salvation, their eternal salvation; for my Priesthood, revealed from heaven, restored to earth, shall continue administering blessings and ordinances of everlasting life.

43. And thus I send my word to the peoples of the earth, that you may know, in a day when my word is fulfilled, that Zion is rising.

44. I shall preserve mine elect, as I have named in those prophecies of mine own speaking when in my ministry, as recorded in New Testament record -- they who receive my Gospel of salvation in fulness and obey my word.

45. And though with persecuting zeal the wicked have fought against my Church and Kingdom since the days of my restoring my Priesthood upon the earth, through the instrumentality of my

servant Joseph Smith, I have preserved my Priesthood on the earth, and my Priesthood shall continue unto my glorious appearing in the powers of heaven coming to earth to govern the earth.

46. I am King of kings and Lord over all creation, saith Jesus Christ.

47. My day of peace shall be a marvel to all peoples of every land, nation, kindred, and tongue.

48. Mine elect will become the Saviors on Mount Zion, administering blessings unto eternal life through my Priesthood.

49. Oh, that ye would hear my word; for I shall fulfill that which I have spoken, to the salvation of many souls yet unborn, to come forth in a day of righteousness and peace.

50. Men's hearts shall fail them who continue in these wicked practices I have declared you must not perform in your nations and peoples and lands, and among them.

51. It cannot be continued in my day of my coming, for I shall remove all such wicked practices from the earth, saith the God of heaven, through my judgments, which are just, because I have warned thee lo, these many years.

52. Now seek unto thy God in a prayerful walk.

53. Heed my published word I have sent forth.

54. Read my Policies of Governing Power published therein to know how your laws must be of a more righteous way, for justice and equity to be served on all peoples, for happiness to be reachable, obtainable in every nation; because thy God shall reign, and all shall willingly acknowledge my right to rule, being the God of Creation over all things.

55. And I, the Lord, send this, my word, as it were a final warning, that I may be justified in sending forth my judgments if you heed me not, to preserve the more righteous in every nation, and to clean my land of Zion of all wickedness, that Zion, the New Jerusalem, may rise unopposed by any earthly power.

56. For I shall be with mine elect, and they shall heed my voice and do my will, saith your God, the God over all peoples -- Jehovah Christ, who is Son Ahman, even Jesus Christ, who hath redeemed you from the grave, who will raise you up in the resurrection, even all peoples of every time of the earth, to answer for their deeds done in the flesh before a just God, who shall reward thee according as your works have been.

57. And nothing is hidden from me, causing the wicked to tremble in the day of judgment, knowing of their evils.

58. Little children I have redeemed, who pass on to the world of departed spirits in their young years; and they shall have an everlasting salvation; for I am just -- having died before the age of accountability, and their reward shall be glorious.

59. Yet those who knew my Gospel of salvation was among the children of men, who would not heed my word, having opportunity to receive of the same, great shall be their mourning and lamentation in the day of judgment, in the day they are raised from the grave to stand before your Lord to be judged according to the measure they have measured to their fellow man.

60. And this message of salvation shall go forth, and nothing can stay mine hand. Amen.

61. I, the Lord, direct further:

62. The NATO nations must cease their attack, having become aggressors,

now three times in coalitions of unity against nations who did not attack thee.

63. And these three witnesses come up before the heavens of your violent and unjust ways; when I, the Lord, have commanded you to cleanse the inside of the platter, your own peoples and laws, to not permit the murderous spirit to be among you, of the murder of unborn children; and the corrupt, immoral ways of Sodom and adultery; many leaders of the nations joining in secret combinations, with secret crime syndicates, to keep and maintain and gain power and influence on the earth; and nothing is hidden from thy God.

64. And I shall reveal your secrets in a day to come, which shall be spoken upon the housetops; for you are promoting -- you who have military power to keep peace among nations and within your borders of righteous ways -- as you use that power to attack nations who have not attacked thee, you are not justified before the heavens, and you shall be broken up in your coalition, not being a defensive organization, but now becoming an offensive attacking organization.

65. And because of this, you are promoting war to break forth in other nations; and unrest is rising in many nations, which shall bring about the great desolating war upon all the earth, and sweeping the wicked off my land of Zion;

66. For I shall send forth other judgments as violence erupts in the nation where my Zion is to be built, because they heed me not, and they seek the destruction of my Church and Kingdom lo, these many years.

67. My word is true and cuts to the heart of those who thus are liars, and among the wicked, who will not heed my word after knowing my word is true;

68. And my word is in Bible, and in those scriptures I have named in this communicating.

69. Thus, awake! and be a repenting nature against the day of judgments nigh at hand, that I may preserve the more righteous among your peoples, of any nation who will turn to your God and overthrow these gross crimes I have named in this communication, that dwell in most nations of the earth.

70. I, the Lord, have spoken it. Amen.

SECTION REVELATION 98

Fundamentalist Church of Jesus Christ of Latter-day Saints
P.O. Box 840459
Hildale, Utah 84784

Thus Saith Son Ahman, Even Jesus Christ, to the Leaders of All Nations Through Ambassadors in United Nations:

Revelation of the Lord Jesus Christ
Eldorado, Texas
Friday, July 22, 2011

1. Thus saith Son Ahman, even Jesus Christ, Jehovah, the First and the Last, the Beginning and the End, He who was of the full power before this earth was created to bring forth worlds, even the God over all peoples:

2. I have caused my word to be of a legal filing, calling on leaders of the nation of where my Church is now of an attack by governing powers, to make all know that I have carried that nation of the United States and will carry her no longer, and shall increase my judgments upon that nation; which will continue until my holy land of Zion is cleansed of all evil.

3. Let all nations now bear influence with the leaders of the United States of America to let my Priesthood authority on earth go free; for my holy law of Celestial Power of Eternal Union is of me, even your Lord Jesus Christ, who is over all peoples, nations, kindreds, tongues, and governing powers.

4. I am fulfilling my will sent to you in previous publishings, even to leaders and ambassadors of every nation now represented in the United Nations Assembly; and now I shall fulfill my will.

5. I have allowed the events to commence leading to war among all nations; as you witness great unrest among many nations, even in their own borders.

6. If you will survive the day of my glorious appearing, even the judgments of whirlwind nature before my coming in the holy power of eternal Celestial Glory, repent ye, repent ye, and be peacemakers among your own peoples, and among nations.

7. If the nation of the United States of America does not heed my warning, that nation shall feel my chastening hand in the judgments I have pronounced upon them, and they shall know thy God hath spoken.

8. Let all nations now read my word sent to you, calling on the deliverance of my people in a land of freedom yet being as persecutors to my people.

9. Let laws be just.

10. My Celestial Law of Eternal Union in the holy pure Marriage Law is of me, your Lord, only to be received by my word through my servant, among my Church on earth.

11. Be of diligent cleansing of thy own nation, each one.

12. Let just laws of religious and civil freedoms be upheld in every nation.

13. Overthrow those evils I have named are in most nations in my previous publishings; even the murder of unborn children, as also Sodom and adultery and immoral ways, lest a just God come out of His hiding place and humbles all peoples in every land on earth.

14. I see all things; nothing is hidden from me.

15. Your secret acts shall all be revealed.

16. Repent ye, is the will of your Lord, who hath redeemed you from death unto a resurrection; to stand before me to be judged for deeds done in the flesh.

17. None can escape. All must account for their time and blessing upon the earth.

18. I have the right to rule by reason of creation; for none could exist except by my grace and mercy.

19. Now bear influence with the United States of America, lest my judgment cleanse the land, and all lands, of wicked men and women, though they deride their Creator;

20. I shall bless the obedient in this world and with eternal life in the next.

21. Let all beware how they treat this, my word; and now be ye believing unto my word and will being done.

22. Let all parents look deep. Some children, when with other children, still forget their Lord and turn to light-minded ways, thus losing the Spirit of God, and getting the spirit of that evil one, who tried before to get the Kingdom of God to compromise with ways of the world.

23. Hasten to prepare, O ye my people of my Church, and also all ye people on earth in every nation, lest my judgments come to leave you individually with neither root nor branch.

24. I love all, and call upon all men everywhere to repent. Amen.

SECTION REVELATION 99

Fundamentalist Church of Jesus Christ of Latter-day Saints
P.O. Box 840459
Hildale, Utah 84784

Thus Saith Jesus Christ, Son Ahman, Unto the Leaders of the Nation of the United States of America, and to the Peoples Thereof, Warning and Continued Call to Prepare for Great Day of Final Judgments, Who Saith:

Revelation of the Lord Jesus Christ
Huntsville, Texas
Thursday, August 18, 2011

1. Verily, verily, thus saith the Lord, even Jesus Christ, the Great Power over all peoples; who is the power of Eternal Union of all other powers; who spake, and the

world was made; who came in the day of the way of redemption; who suffered and atoned for all peoples; who hath conquered death; who is Resurrection and Life to all;

2. Verily I say to all peoples of the entire world, by the Mouthpiece of my sending: Ye are of fully ripening in iniquity.

3. Soon, yea, very soon cometh the entire cleansing I have given in many warnings, and by Isaiah, Jeremiah, and other Prophets, as testimony of my holy word being fulfilled.

4. The evil powers are as a blinding power over all mankind, though my language is given to your understanding; though you can read in a worldwide accepted language; yet you heed me not.

5. I, the Creator over all things, have not been silent.

6. I have given to national powers what must be done to survive my day of full cleansing power of whirlwind and destructive power.

7. My holy scriptures are full.

8. My time is nigh.

9. I shall burn my holy land of Zion of all evil, to prepare for a holy city to rise, even Zion, New Jerusalem; telling all peoples before what I shall do; that all may know thy God hath fulfilled His word, and shall continue to speak and fulfill.

10. Let now the storm of great power soon come to be as a full measure to humble this nation.

11. Know I held off this judgment to see if you would heed my word, in preparing for my coming; in cleansing thy evil laws of evil power, to be just; to preserve virtue, life; and also to send forth deliverance for my Mouthpiece; yet you heed me not.

12. Does not the loss of life mean anything to the rulers of this land?

13. Do they not see wickedness rules over the land -- putting innocence in prison now, even mine elders of obedient doing to Celestial Law of religion of my own revealing?

14. I am God, and all shall know my will.

15. Now cometh a shaking on thy land to humble thousands; yea, all the nation shall feel the result.

16. Let the people of my Church go free, lest I needs continue to pour out judgments on the land, like I did unto Pharaoh and the Egyptians, until they no more could oppose my right to rule.

17. I am Jehovah, even Jesus Christ, Son Ahman, the Full Governing Power of Celestial Priesthood power over the earth; yea, over the nation boasting great power on earth; yet now being but a waning power, none to console her, as nations turn from thee in the great fall of power of money system.

18. I alone have held thee in place.

19. Only I, your Lord, can preserve any of all peoples.

20. Let it be known a great heavenly body cometh, unseen by your technology; I able to blind your way until I take away the covering.

21. Know it shall be of a happening within new year's coming; an event of such magnitude, all peoples shall wonder.

22. I tell not exact time, whether one or two years of my giving a warning; yet some heavenly bodies of larger size shall soon strike the earth to the amazing thoughts of many; which shall begin to disturb the protective atmosphere layer, to cause men on earth to not be of my protecting; to suffer greater burnings on their bodies, as my servant John Beloved recorded; caused by heavenly bodies increasing to disturb the protective atmosphere layer.

23. Judgments shall be felt in the rising up of the people of Turkey, and cause many other people to falter in European stability.

24. NATO has lost credibility; has become spread far; is now an aggressive alliance.

25. Let all know I warned all of the fall of earthly powers.

26. Now know Israel shall step forth and be of an aggressive way when threatened.

27. Then shall my people know I have spoken, as I preserve the nation; though many perish because they also heed me not; do not cleanse their own peoples; nor do the peace labor I have named.

28. Libya is now a full way of aggression by countries never attacked by that nation.

29. Example of fear of aggression shall unite other nations to fight NATO nations.

30. Disunity shall absorb thee.

31. The economy of your lands shall wither. United States is a power of soon instability in own economic instability.

32. The holy law of retribution for aggression is upon her.

33. I am God. I hath spoken truth. She will not free him, my servant.

34. She shall feel my wrath soon. Then shall come to pass mine elect be preserved, while the wicked shall tremble and be no more a power against Zion rising.

35. O ye people of my earth, awake to catastrophe you are bringing upon yourselves.

36. I must fulfill the purpose of this earth.

37. Your temporary ways cannot overrule the eternal purposes of a God of power.

38. You are my creation.

39. Humble thyselves, to be of a receiving of some degree of life and salvation, from your Lord, Jesus Christ, who speaketh, as a voice from the wilderness -- from the wilderness because you seeth me not; my voice being my Spirit of truth, which toucheth every pure, honest mind with a witness of truth, in a gentle peace.

40. My holy way shall soon be known unto all peoples.

41. Receive ye my next warning; from thy God who loveth all, yet despiseth evil; to guide all here and hereafter to repentance, lest full eternal judgment cometh upon the soul who dies in their sins; to rise in never-ending sorrow for turning from me, your Redeemer; thus choosing death.

42. I am the Light, Life, Happiness, Peace, Truth, and Hope of all peoples.

43. I am your Savior, which speaketh.

44. Seek unto me through my Priesthood to receive my will; to benefit nations, peoples, individuals in soul-raising powers unto earthly and eternal salvation; through the full way of pure holy religion being my authority of heaven, now on earth.

45. Let the wicked of false testifying have one soon reveal their lying; to now show the world prosecuting power followed a scheme of lying combination of years of maturing; to imprison my servant.

46. Their falsehoods shall become a blot on their lives not able to be borne, even before all peoples.

47. Let the governing powers cause the illegal governing work of fighting a holy religion, clouded over by blinding legal and unjust attack of falsehoods, now to be a catalyst to be of a fulfilling all my will concerning my own word to leaders of this nation, and other nations.

48. I am God who lendeth you breath;

who upholds all powers of every kingdom to exist; to test all; to now be judged.

49. Let all receive my will, and hasten to be repenting, lest all my full judgments of full power of pure way be sent forth, to be testimony of my almighty power to all peoples of every nation.

50. I cometh quickly. Amen.

SECTION REVELATION 100

Fundamentalist Church of Jesus Christ of Latter-day Saints
P.O. Box 840459
Hildale, Utah 84784

Thus Saith Son Ahman, Your Lord Jesus Christ, to All Peoples of the Earth Unto Your Salvation if You Heed Me, Saying Thus:

Revelation of the Lord Jesus Christ
Huntsville, Texas
Friday, August 19, 2011

1. Verily, saith your Lord, come unto me, all ye people who have the power to repent, lest sore affliction soon overtake you, in a manner you think not; in an awakening the soul from deep sleep spiritual; in bringing all to hear my way of salvation eternal, saith Jesus Christ.

2. I am your Advocate with the Father.

3. I have overcome, and sit at the right hand of the Father to bring all unto Him who will receive the message of salvation of souls.

4. Let all hear my will.

5. I am now to send a sickness upon the land of my coming, even in power upon all the earth, to be known of all peoples thy God of glory reigneth!

6. Let all now be of the order of endless and eternal lives, of the people of the promise of Israel being gathered unto Zion, as I confided in Peter, James, and John would take place in power in the days of wickedness, when I would be of the power of gathering all who have the blood of Israel of the pure seed of my holy family of the flesh, when I was on earth; with eternal power as thy Lord.

7. I was with men with the full power of Priesthood.

8. I could raise the dead, heal and bless by the power of Godhead in my own possession, of the Father, doing His will in all things.

9. Thus, am I your Advocate with the Father, to bring all unto salvation to all who heed my word unto character of God becoming your natural way, of my Spirit; through thy faith always exercised.

10. Let all be of the way of improving.

11. Let all be of truth.

12. Let all be of receiving my own way, saith the Light of all men.

13. Let my light of pure holy way enlighten thy daily walk unto overcoming evil.

14. I am only Just, Holy, True, Righteous; Governing Power; Equitous, Noble, Exalting, and the Rock of Salvation for all to build on.

15. Let all come unto me, your Lord, who saith to all nations of the earth -- come to me.

16. Be ye clean to survive my holy power of cleansing judgments upon all nations.

17. Let my love shine in you. Forgive all peoples.

18. I shall repay in a just judgment.

19. Let the Holy Priesthood be purged.

20. Let my Church be cleansed.

21. Let all now live my Gospel of peace. Amen.

SECTION REVELATION 101

Jesus Christ Speaketh to the Nation of the United States Solemn Warning Again, Mine Own Word From the Heavens, to Be Heeded Lest Judgments Follow Upon Those Who Heed Me Not, Saith the Lord, Even Son Ahman

Thus Saith the Lord Jesus Christ to the Leaders and Peoples of the United States of America, My Holy Word of Continued Warning of Final Judgments Soon at Hand, Heed My Word, Which Saith:

Revelation of the Lord Jesus Christ
Tennessee Colony, Texas
Sunday, September 25, 2011

1. I who reign on high speaketh, even Jesus Christ, through my servant on earth to the nation of the United States of America: You have transgressed and not kept my word, though I have sent mine own word unto you in sacred revealings and publishings, yea, to leaders of nations.

2. My warning voice has been sounded. I am the God of Creation which speaketh. My servant is in bondage. You yet hold him from my people.

3. My Zion shall rise, and I shall intervene in a judgment that you shall soon feel, and it shall continue until opposition is removed.

4. Thus saith the Lord to the leaders and peoples of this nation: Though my voice has been sounded often to you and sent forth, and you heed me not, I shall fulfill my word, and you shall know at the removing of those in power to their everlasting regret for not heeding my word when sent to them.

5. And I give my word to you as a

witness that thy God can speak from the heavens and communicate in preparing those who will heed my word for my coming; for I shall have a people in every nation that survives to come to Zion and receive of the greater light coming forth of my revealing.

6. And I, the Lord, give to this nation and this people the warning, to be justified in the cleansing that must take place if they heed not the God who created them;

7. For I am God, Son Ahman, and I do the will of the Father, who is Ahman.

8. And thus saith the Lord: The will of the Father is being done, for you have seen increased storms, flooding, even more than you have witnessed before in areas where it has not taken place before.

9. Ye shall witness further, as I have named, until you are humbled.

10. O that you would heed my word and receive my word; and I send my word to you again, that hearts can be touched who will heed my word, both of the leaders of this nation, of states, counties, places of governing power, and also among the population of thy people, for the cleansing shall be of such a nature that only that which can be of a purification remain.

11. I have named many places that shall be cleansed entire, and as you witness this, the memory of my word shall hearken in your souls that thy God reigneth; and if you are of the ability to repent, your hearts shall be touched.

12. Yet my word shall be fulfilled, as I spoke before I was taken upon the cross to be sacrificed, saith the Lord Jesus Christ, even that word that among the wicked in the last days, when judgments come, many would lift up their voices against me, cursing God and perishing because they would not heed my word, having their hearts set on wickedness and pleasure in unrighteousness.

13. Repent ye of the great sins I have named that are among your people, for the murder of unborn children is a stench of corruption that causeth all thy works to be of the way of ignoble shame, the very heavens seeing your works limiting the coming forth of spirits to earth, appointed to receive tabernacles and prove their worthiness before the Lord.

14. Your practice of this murder of children yet unborn shall be answered upon thy souls in the day of eternal judgment, with a suffering of soul that you would be of an assenting or agreeing to this sin and would not stop it among your peoples.

15. Your adulterous ways are the motive for this sin that must be obliterated of my judgments coming upon all who will not receive my word and change their ways from this terrible crime against innocence, purity, and life.

16. I, your God, have spoken it.

17. Let the laws be changed if you would be of a repentance, else full judgment shall come upon thy peoples, and you shall know it.

18. You have also persecuted my Church and Kingdom and allowed my leadership to be in bondage, when I have called upon thee to let my people go to their worshiping and laboring, having their houses and lands restored to them of legal appointing, being of an illegal way in removing them from their homes, who have thus been ruled against in courts of law.

19. Heed my word: Let my servant go.

20. And let there be a changing of your laws to purify thy peoples, lest there be full judgment of the removing of this nation from this land, of whirlwind nature, that

I have promised in all my holy scriptures through my servants, the Prophets, whom I have sent -- in particular, Joseph Smith, Jun., in revealing my word to this generation.

21. There shall come upon the nation that inhabits this land, yea, each nation, a full judging, a cleansing, to only allow there to remain those who can endure the presence of God in Zion, New Jerusalem being built in that Center Stake appointed on the land called United States of America; that Center Stake being Jackson County, Missouri, well-appointed, and nothing can stay mine hand; for I shall claim my lands purchased by my Priesthood in former times, taken from them by mobocracy and driving and killing in the days of my servant Joseph Smith.

22. Heed my word: I shall recover what belongeth to me, and New Jerusalem shall rise, and nothing can stay mine hand.

23. Though you oppose me, and pass laws, and have thy people rise up against innocence, against my Church, I shall be of a defending nature, and you shall know that I have preserved my people against the day of my coming in my glory, as I have promised mine apostles in the meridian of time when I was upon the earth and after I was resurrected, angels revealing to them my glorious coming in power in the clouds of heaven.

24. This is in sacred holy writ, which you can peruse.

25. My coming is soon, and there cannot be these sins and corruptions on my land where I shall appear unto an elect people who have kept Celestial laws, holy laws of eternal revealing.

26. My law is pure, and you have attacked my Law of Celestial Plural Marriage and other laws of my Priesthood as though it was of a corrupt way. It is not so.

27. My law is pure and of my governing through my revealed authority, my Priesthood, my servant on earth, not to be given to general populous among your peoples, only to those who are pure and holy.

28. Thus you have imprisoned men who are holy and pure, of pure religious motive, not desiring harm to anyone; and your prosecuting zeal is of a crime against my Priesthood, Church, and Kingdom that shall be answered upon thy people and governing powers if you heed me not.

29. Let them go, saith the Lord. Amen.

SECTION REVELATION 102

Fundamentalist Church of Jesus Christ of Latter-day Saints
P.O. Box 840459
Hildale, Utah 84784

Thus Saith Jesus Christ, Your Holy Power of Eternal Holy Power of Union Power Celestial Over All Creation; the God Over All, to All Peoples of the Earth; Who Now Dwell on Earth, Even to All Nations, My Word of Pure Holy Revealing Who to Come to as My Holy Servant of My Priesthood Authority on Earth, to Receive My Holy Gospel in Pure Holy Truth Way to Be of Full Way to Earn Holy Life on Earth, to Also Be of Eternal Holy Life of Full Power of Salvation. Come Unto Me Through My Holy Power on Earth, All Ye Ends of the Earth, Even to Be of a Pure Power of My Kingdom Celestial. Hear Thou My Will:

Revelation of the Lord Jesus Christ
Palestine, Texas
Sunday, October 2, 2011

1. As one who is over all things in His glorious majesty, who is above all things, and is in all things by His Holy Spirit, which is my power of Godhood in fulness increasingly; thus do I speak, and give my own will to all peoples of the earth; a holy way of pure governing; to be Zion in full coming forth unto a full power over all nations, peoples, and all holy and noble power of Celestial revealing.

2. I, Jesus Christ, your Holy Advocate of redeeming power, reveal to all people my soon Advent, my presence being known on the land of my coming, even North and South America in a power of eternal might; even New Jerusalem being revealed from Celestial eternal realms, unto mine holy people prepared by living my Celestial Law and eternal way of full power of exaltation.

3. I who has all things of eternal power to govern saith:

4. Let all nations now bow to my holy rule as your Holy and Eternal King.

5. Let all now be of a full preparation of their individual characters; to be like the fountain of righteous dominion; even like your Lord, in holy ways; that I may be known as your King, which has all power of heaven in Him; to bring forth truth of exalting power to all who will come unto my Holy City of the domain of my government of Celestial holy order eternal.

6. Let all nations now be of a humbling before me, even Jesus Christ, who is called Jehovah Christ.

7. Let all now have my law unto them being governed by my authority of eternal power, my Holy Priesthood revealed from heaven, through the ministering of my holy

sons of keys and powers thereof, Peter and my son John, called Beloved, with James; my quorum of key power, sent to ordain my chosen servant Joseph Smith in his time on earth; which Priesthood keys of power, even in full power of authority to be the holy governing power over all peoples, unto me, your God and Savior, being the Ruler over all, through the power of Celestial revelations of my own will coming forth; guiding my Holy Priesthood to guide all peoples.

8. Thus do I reveal that my holy power is on earth, and continues to be that eternal authority unto whom all peoples must come to receive my word and holy way eternal; to be governed by my holy revealings.

9. Thus shall all nations learn my way of holy power; to be of a way of greater power that is recognized by the God of Creation over thee; who alone prospers all peoples in good gifts of earth and of sacred ways of eternal power unto the earning eternal salvation, my Gospel of Priesthood authority revealed since the earth was inhabited by man, even Adam and his posterity.

10. I, your Lord, soon cometh; in power of eternal pure holy way of light and pure holy revealings of truths that raise your minds above the evil surmisings of mortal fallen ways.

11. I shall send my Spirit upon all who come unto my authorized agent of key position; unto my holy representative of the order of pure holy Priesthood power, even my servant Warren Jeffs on earth.

12. Let all now know he is of my whole power of governing, and able to reveal my will to every governing power on the earth; for I lead him unto my way being revealed to all who come unto me in faith and good works.

13. Now let all peoples receive my own revealings of pure truth unobstructed by the ways of evil, which have combined against my Priesthood, to prosecute and to seek to hinder the progress of my holy way of a prepared people of Celestial holy laws lived.

14. I shall cause a humbling of the nation which is now persecuting my holy governing authority, by the power of my sending judgments of destructions so great, that only my holy people who are of my Celestial Law shall be of a pure and full delivering unto New Jerusalem being built on my Center Stake of Zion; which is in the now named place of Jackson County, Missouri; which place I revealed as the holy locating of my City of Holiness since Joseph Smith's time on earth.

15. Now I am soon to cleanse my land of Zion, to cause my way to be the way of governing authority, to come to the full and legitimate ruling power over all nations.

16. Let my holy and pure revelations be received by all peoples of every nation on the present lands of your dwelling; which shall be of a great change, as my revealings have named; unto new peoples soon to come forth to join in my government of pure holy authorized Priesthood power, of eternal holy power Celestial; sent to the earth by the holy powers of heaven; mine Holy Priesthood of heaven to dwell on earth among men; to be as my continual power of true authority among men.

17. Joseph Smith with the Keyholders of my holy eternal power of Holy Priesthood to this time shall also be revealed to be among my pure people, as governing powers of Priesthood authority, guiding my Priesthood on earth how to be of Celestial power and exalting way of pure governing authority.

18. Now be ready, all ye peoples of

the earth; for judgments of cleansing power already goeth forth upon the land of Zion, and other lands; such as you are just beginning to awake to the greater way of nature, as is called among men; my powers of life or of judgment, according to the heed the children of men render to my revealings.

19. I have caused my word to be sent to all peoples since the day I revealed my holy will through Joseph Smith; and now have sent my own will through my Mouthpiece on earth unto you, the leaders of nations, and to be known among man; as a final warning authority, that thy God, even Son Ahman, who is Jesus Christ, hath spoken to you, and caused my own will to be sent to all peoples; to make known my holy will, and to call on all to be of peace, to be of pure ways of living, to do away with murder and adulterous and Sodom ways; yet you heed me not.

20. Therefore, you shall reap the full measure of my power felt as a cleansing of all wicked, perverse ways in every land.

21. I shall soon be known to be on earth.

22. When the greater powers of cleansing come upon my land of Zion, and on many nations, know that my holy Advent of power and Celestial powers of governing power has been exercised, to prepare for the God of glory to be on earth; to be your Lord and King of eternal power; to be the Righteous Holy One of Israel; to be the only power of Celestial and eternal holy power on earth; bringing forth the truths of eternity to man; to exalt man to a more holy noble way of abiding this earthly life of probationary testing.

23. I, your Lord, am causing my own will to be known to all peoples of the earth by causing my word to be as a sending forth my new and holy and noble pure governing truths; and by authority not of man, but of me, your Holy Power of Government Celestial, sent by Ahman, my Father, a God of holy Celestial power.

24. I am your Holy and Eternal King, even Jehovah Christ, Jesus Christ, who was slain by wicked men on a cross of atoning and pure power of justice satisfied, unto you able to earn salvation on the earth; which shall be of a Celestial power of eternal life unto those who live my Celestial and holy laws of Eternal Union power of my Holy Priesthood.

25. Thus do the powers of evil follow the dark revealings to evil minds from that fallen and corrupt son, Lucifer; who goeth up and down through the earth deceiving the people of the way of unrighteousness; who delight in sin and in their evil and fallen ways more than in principles and ways of God.

26. I, your Lord, have the right to rule; and I rule by almighty power and authority given me by my Father, Ahman, even Him who is my Holy and Eternal King, whom I serve as the Son of God.

27. Let all nations now be ready.

28. Let all now be of a full preparing.

29. I send this, my holy revealing, to you through my authority on earth; making this an eternal word unto you of all peoples, nations, tongues, and powers on earth, accountable to God; for my word is eternal; for I am Eternal; and none can escape my eternal judgment on their souls for their works done in the flesh.

30. Now know that through my holy love do I send my holy will as an eternal warning voice; that you, each son or daughter of men on earth, shall be of an accounting to me, your King and Eternal Father in heaven, for your doings, desires, and works on earth; and also to know I

shall rule over all surviving peoples on every land during this new Millennium of my power coming to earth to govern all peoples.

31. This is my holy way of justifying my judgments to be sent upon all peoples.

32. Let my will be published to all peoples; to know of my purposes of eternal duration in your lives; your life on earth being a testing time to your souls, as a witness of what you desire and love.

33. I shall recompense to each son or daughter as they measured to their fellow men, and to their God according to the light they were given, or what was within their reach.

34. Heed my word. Cause my servant to go free.

35. Let all peoples know I have spoken, and am soon to fulfill my word upon nations, peoples, and governing authorities.

36. Now receive and give heed to my will, lest full powers of the order of cleansing all wickedness from thy borders of all peoples cometh as a whirlwind, suddenly, to humble all to know thy God speaketh and fulfilleth His word. Amen.

SECTION REVELATION 103

Fundamentalist Church of Jesus Christ of Latter-day Saints
P.O. Box 840459
Hildale, Utah 84784

Thus Saith Son Ahman, Even Your Lord Jesus Christ, to All Peoples on Continents Called the Americas, Warning and Call to Prepare:

Revelation of the Lord Jesus Christ
Palestine, Texas
Wednesday, October 5, 2011

1. Thus saith Jesus Christ, even the Great I AM, the Beginning and the End, Jehovah, unto all peoples of the land of my holy and soon coming; more especially the nation of my restoring my Gospel and Church on earth:

2. Verily I say unto all peoples on my land of Zion, even to all the noble and high positioned leaders of the Americas: I am soon to make my coming known by a great tsunami, of the sea heaving beyond its bounds upon the east coast.

3. Let all now be of a full way of preparing, and remove thy habitation of personal and work labor staying to be inland.

4. This I send as a warning, for great and notable cities on the coast shall be swept off the land.

5. I reveal this to be of a delivering to believing souls.

6. Let also Arizona know that my judgment cometh; that earthquake and the sinking in the earth shall be on the capital

city there; also volcano and earthquake take power in many inhabited and large populated places in Utah and Arizona. As took place in the meridian of time in days of the Nephite cleansing of my land, preparing for my coming among them, so shall it be in this time.

7. Idaho shall be as a melting fire of such powers to cleanse my land of all evil.

8. Let also Seattle know there cometh a shaking and tidal wave upon her.

9. Also cometh the shaking of the land where New Zion, even Jerusalem of New Holy Way is to rise on my land of Zion.

10. Tempests, earthquakes, even war and famine cometh upon the land; all to cleanse my land for my appearing in holy power of pure Celestial power.

11. Let this be known by all peoples, to know I am God, having all right to rule over all nations, soon to happen, in the rise of Zion, and Celestial powers coming to earth to reign among men as the governing powers over all nations.

12. Let also the honorable lawmakers in this nation's capital city know that place of government powers is to be the target of attack of an invading power.

13. Let all know my judgments are soon at hand and shall be felt by all people; and only the pure in heart shall remain to be witness to my coming on this land of Zion, even to establish a city of holy way of heavenly powers coming to earth after corruption and evil are swept off the earth by whirlwind judgments roll forth.

14. Now learn of my holy way.

15. Be of diligent learning of way of righteous governing of my power among men.

16. I have published to every nation my "Policies of Governing."

17. Let all study the same, to know of a holy and righteous power eternal coming among all peoples in every land on earth; to be the governing authority over all nations; to be the Millennial governing power over all the earth.

18. Such is my righteous holy power to be over all; to bring peace to all peoples of the inhabitable earth; as some places shall at first be made desolate by wicked national leaders using weapons of lasting harm against populations of other nations in their blinding anger of war waged.

19. Let the nation of professed freedom look well to their own conditions; having persecuted my Church over a century of time, yet still doing that evil against me and my Church in placing my servant and servants in prison, seeking to criminalize my holy eternal Celestial Law of Plural Marriage; yet having the greatest crimes of immoral ways and murderous ways among themselves, even the nation of great power now inhabiting my land of Zion.

20. Thus saith the Lord: This nation shall be laid low, having proven she is a war nation, attacking other nations who never attack her.

21. Thus saith your Lord: As you again attack another nation, so shall your power be clipped, and other nations of military powers shall be of a combining attack upon thee.

22. O that you would heed my will; to only be of a defending power, not of aggression.

23. Three testimonies of thy aggression of unprovoked attack on other nations has come up before the heavenly authority to now humble thee.

24. Now beware, lest you openly fulfill my promises; to cease being of aggression, lest my full cleansing power be upon thy nation, even the United States of America,

as it is called among men on earth; a nation of most corrupt ways among men, to soon no longer be a power against my Zion being established on earth; unto a full rewarding the nation for shedding the blood of my people, and hindering my Priesthood from fulfilling my holy purposes of salvation being administered to obedient sons and daughters on earth unto earning eternal salvation.

25. Now receive my warnings sealed in your hearts, to know that I, the God over all, hath spoken beforehand, when you see and witness these and other great cleansing powers sent upon thee; for all shall be humbled. Amen.

SECTION REVELATION 104

Fundamentalist Church of Jesus Christ of Latter-day Saints
P.O. Box 840459
Hildale, Utah 84784

Thus Saith Jehovah, Son Ahman, Even Your God of Creation, Jesus Christ, to the Leaders of the Nation of Israel; Firm Commandment to Be Now Heeded for Your Preservation:

Revelation of the Lord Jesus Christ
Palestine, Texas
Sunday, October 9, 2011

1. Thus saith the Lord, even Jesus Christ, who is the Eternal God over all creation, doing my Father's will, to the land and people of Israel, a nation being preserved by my power:

2. Do not attack the now nation of Jordan at the time enemy influence of Palestinian Arab Moslem peoples incite unrest there.

3. Seek to make peace, to be justified before your God, lest a war of great desolation take place, which will remove many of thy own people from this life.

4. When a greater power threatens thee and shows continued attacks against thee, then shall be the time to fully defend thyself, unto other nations becoming subject to thee.

5. Heed my will.

6. Be not the first to attack. Be of a defending practice, until the greater power of enemy is prepared to seek your overthrow.

7. Then I shall inspire your leadership to be of full way of conquering thy foes. Amen.

SECTION REVELATION 105

Fundamentalist Church of Jesus Christ of Latter-day Saints
P.O. Box 840459
Hildale, Utah 84784

Thus Saith Son Ahman, Even Jesus Christ, to Nation of Egypt, My Will as God of All Creation, to Now Be of Peace, Saying Thus:

Revelation of the Lord Jesus Christ
Palestine, Texas
Friday, October 21, 2011

1. Now saith your Lord to the people of Egypt --

2. I, your Lord, even Son Ahman, Jesus Christ, give my own will to the leaders and also to the populace of Egypt --

3. Now be at peace.

4. Do not continue fighting.

5. Let all be peace; and labor in peace to be a preserved land of a nation still existing after my greater judgments are felt.

6. You are not to fight against Israel in any way.

7. You can only survive if you do not join in an attack on Israel.

8. Let all thy preparing be to store food, clothing, medical supplies, household supplies, in abundance; so thy people may be cared for; for a war cometh, a battle that will be sore and devastating.

9. Be at peace among your populace.

10. Let leaders be at peace.

11. Remember my previous word I sent to you to prepare a sacred house to be a sanctuary of a covenant of peace and obedience to your Lord; to be people of greater peace among nations.

12. Now be rid of sins of Sodom, also adultery, and child murder.

13. Let thy peoples raise up my right to rule over all peoples as the God of Creation over all.

14. Let also peace rule thy nation, and not be at war in your own nation.

15. Be at peace. Amen.

SECTION REVELATION 106

Fundamentalist Church of Jesus Christ of Latter-day Saints
P.O. Box 840459
Hildale, Utah 84784

Thus Saith Son Ahman, Even Jehovah, Your Lord, Who Is Jesus Christ, to All Peoples in Israel, to the Leadership of Israel, a Word of Full Call to Prepare for Greater Powers of Violence Coming Against Your Nation. Heed My Word:

Revelation of the Lord Jesus Christ
Palestine, Texas
Friday, October 21, 2011

1. Verily I, your Lord Jesus Christ, speak again to nation of Israel:

2. Be of preparation of defending thy nation in full way soon at hand, to have your peoples supplied with provisions of food, clothing, other needs, water purifying devices; also bandaging and medicines in greater abundance; for soon thy army shall be of full power to defend thyself.

3. Let not thy way be of provocation of enemy powers; but always be of peacemaking without compromising thy lands.

4. Let thy pure holy way be of peace seeking, by emissaries of peace sent to enemy powers.

5. Let the call to be ready be of a full way.

6. Soon you shall be attacked, or of a full power of enemy combining against you.

7. United powers shall ready themselves against you.

8. Let all soon preparing be of people's needs.

9. Let water be of a soon storing by your governing power, and your people in preparing wells.

10. Let thy whole way be to be ready. Amen.

11. Now let all in Israel know my will, saith Jehovah, even Jesus Christ, who reigneth over all peoples, nations, kindreds and tongues, to be aware of my will. Amen.

SECTION REVELATION 107

Fundamentalist Church of Jesus Christ of Latter-day Saints
P.O. Box 840459
Hildale, Utah 84784

Thus Saith Jesus Christ, Son Ahman, God Over All Nations and of Heavenly Eternal Powers Soon to Descend to Earth, to Govern All Nations for a Thousand Years of Righteous Pure Way of Governing Authority, to Nation of Germany; Also to Netherlands, My Own Revealing to You to Heed Immediately Unto Thy Deliverance if You Do My Will, to Be Answered on Thee of Soon Coming Powers, Celestial, to Cleanse All Peoples of Their Ungodly Ways:

Revelation of the Lord Jesus Christ
Palestine, Texas
Monday, October 24, 2011

1. I, your Lord Jesus Christ, speaketh to the nation of the sins of heightening corruption, of continual display of immorality, thus of the way of full judgments of a just God upon them, even the country of now economic Europe strength; now be humbled by me, saith Jesus Christ, God over all, unto a full cleansing of all who will thus continue in sins of destruction of purity, innocence, and against principles of life in murder of unborn children through legal upholding of the practice in infanticide --

2. Now let Germany be known as a past-time strength.

3. Let her power of economic wealth fall.

4. Let her peoples be of a full cleansing of all her capital sins, unto a full way of only more righteous to remain.

5. I have sent mine own word to you, yea, to the high-minded governing authorities of your nation; and you heed me not.

6. Correct these sins.

7. Let them be of a capital crime, punishable by a capital punishment; no longer sympathizing with wealthy, who guide nation to great sins and capital crimes before me; for I shall punish such of full judging into a full eternal duration if they heed not my holy word unto a ceasing these ungodly practices now, saith your God and Redeemer; who only suffered for repented sins, then wrongdoers ceasing sin.

8. Your existence as a nation is only by my power, to cause you to be tested what you will do in your earthly existence.

9. Now heed my word; for I am soon to appear, unto a cleansing of the wicked ways from all nations; and preserving pure holy people, law, government, and practices of righteous noble way. Amen.

10. I, your Lord, speak thus to Germany; also Netherlands, also of most corrupt ways; both to meet great judging of removing the more corrupt from among thee. Amen.

SECTION REVELATION 108

Fundamentalist Church of Jesus Christ of Latter-day Saints
P.O. Box 840459
Hildale, Utah 84784

Thus Saith Jesus Christ, Even Jehovah, Son Ahman, God of All Peoples of All Lands on Earth; a God Over All in Full Power to See and Hear, Yea, Know All Things; to Albania Leadership and the People of Albania -- My Word of Final, Full Warning, to Prepare for My Glorious Coming in Power of Full Authorized Power of the Father, Over All Kingdoms, Now Heralding My Power Soon at Hand to Reign Over All Nations for a Millennium -- Hear My Word of Pure Giving to Thee:

Revelation of the Lord Jesus Christ
Palestine, Texas
Thursday, October 27, 2011

1. Thus saith your Lord and Holy One of My Eternal Domain of Son Ahman, Jesus Christ, unto the people of Albania, a nation now of great way of corruption:

2. I, your Lord, am soon to give my full way of plan of salvation.

3. Let repenting now be thy offering unto me, your Redeemer, of immoral, licentious way of corrupting thy people.

4. Let child murder of unborn, yet of living gift, be done away among laws of tolerance for such corrupt way.

5. Now prepare to be of a more pure way; for my glory shall cause fear to take hold of the wicked of every land and nation, so great shall the power of my coming be. Amen.

Your Lord and Redeemer Jesus Christ Speaketh Warning and Word of Cleansing Power to Soon Come Upon Brazil and Other Nations of America

(Comprising Section Revelations 109, 31)

Thus Saith Son Ahman, Jesus Christ, to the Leaders and Peoples of Brazil, Warning and Message to Prepare Unto Purity of Living:

SECTION REVELATION 109

Revelation of the Lord Jesus Christ
Palestine, Texas
Thursday, October 27, 2011

1. Thus saith your God over all creation, Jesus Christ, to nation of Brazil, another word of warning to your leaders, and all thy peoples, to now know I continue to behold from the heavens the corrupt, murderous, immoral way of thy living; a nation of full corrupting power unto crime being of heightening increase, soon to burst forth as warring and violent organizing power against governing powers and each other; thus promoting the dissolution of thy government:

2. Repent ye, repent ye, for my glorious appearing is soon at hand, in Celestial power of my eternal domain; to be among men for a Millennium of Peace; to judge all peoples; to be a removing power of gross, wicked way; of full power to remove the more wicked, to preserve the more righteous.

3. Know I have now given mine own word to all nations of my holy Advent in eternal power.

4. Cause this, my word, to be published to all peoples in thy nation, even exact.

5. Let it also tell of mine other recent revealings of pure truth, of holy writing.

6. Let all now be of a full stop of organized crime and Sodom and licentious adultery way; of dwelling as peoples of knowing corrupting way, pleasures being of evil, not being of holy way.

7. Let murder of unborn children cease in thy nation now; for I, your Lord, send forth children through birth to earth, to be their holy way of gaining happy crowns of salvation by receiving earthly body; to know good from evil, to choose good.

8. I can discern all thy lives. Nothing is hidden.

9. Let all beware.

10. I shall reward all according to their deeds done in this earthly existence unto an eternal judgment.

11. Let all be ready for my coming.

12. Now heed this, my will; also my other revealing of pure truth of new, also recent sending to all nations.

13. Let all know libraries have received my revealings, to peruse my word in their ability to gain true knowledge. Amen.

SECTION REVELATION 31

Warning of the Lord to the Nation of Brazil

Revelation of the Lord Jesus Christ
Draper, Utah
Thursday, October 7, 2010

1. Verily thus saith the Lord unto the nation of Brazil, even your Lord and Savior:

2. I, the Lord, have weighed you in the balance and found you wanting.

3. Therefore, I shall send my destroying angel to visit the inhabitants of that nation, to sweep them from off the face of my land of Zion.

4. Cause that the nation of Brazil receive my warning, and to repent; for I, the Lord, shall soon send upon them the judgment of the overflowing scourge; for they are ripened in iniquity and must needs be swept off the land.

5. Let the leaders of the nation of Brazil receive this, my warning, that they must overthrow all laws that permit immorality to prevail.

6. And cause the people to humble themselves, as they see my chastening hand come upon them.

7. Let my servant Warren Jeffs also read this, my word, to the nation of Brazil.

Message of God Over All, Even Jesus Christ, Unto Nation of France, My Word of Warning to All of My Soon Appearing. Let My Holy Word of Now Sending a New Revealing, With My Previous Revealing to Thee, Be of a Hearing by All Thy Peoples.

(Comprising Section Revelations 110, 16, 74)

Thus Saith Jesus Christ, God Over All Nations, Kindreds, Tongues, and Governing Powers, to Nation of France, My Own Will Concerning Thee, of Warning to Repent, or Be of Few Populace Soon, of Cleansing Powers Celestial. Amen.

SECTION REVELATION 110

Revelation of the Lord Jesus Christ
Palestine, Texas
Thursday, October 27, 2011

1. The God of all creation speaketh unto the nation of France, even Jehovah, who is Jesus Christ, to know your peoples are of a stench to the very heavenly powers, being of a corrupting, immoral way; that you heed me not in beridding your nation of infanticide, even murder of unborn children; a practice promoted by immorality of heightened way among you as a nation.

2. My time is soon, of my glorious coming in eternal power; first of cleansing all nations of the more wicked, preserving the more righteous, then sending forth my eternal plan of salvation to all the earth; verily I say, my own Gospel of eternal life.

3. Let your peoples repent; for you are soon to reap the depopulation of most of your land; for your sins corrupt even thy youth.

4. O repent, and turn from Sodom and adulterous ways of corrupting evils.

5. Now heed my will sent to thee.

6. Also, never again let thy NATO alliance convince thee to attack another land of national independent power not of thy own domain, when they never attacked thee first.

7. Let all thy military be of home staying, to not be aggressive; to not rely on leaders who seek vain glory in military attack on a nation not a threat to you nor your interests worldwide.

8. Be of peace.

9. Let all now learn my will, lest full judgments of my full power of cleansing cometh upon you. Amen.

SECTION REVELATION 16

Warning of the Lord to the Nation of France

Revelation of the Lord Jesus Christ
Draper, Utah
Thursday, October 7, 2010

1. Verily thus saith the Lord unto the nation of France, even your Lord Jesus Christ, who hath all power, and who sees and knows all things:

2. I, the Lord, have caused that you shall soon be humbled, as I send my judgments against you.

3. For I have seen gross wickedness among you; and must needs cleanse you from all evil, to preserve those who can receive my Gospel of salvation at the time I shall deliver my servant from bondage.

4. Let this nation of France now receive my warning voice; that I, the Lord, shall sweep from their land the corrupt and abominable who are in the condition of the ancient city of Sodom; and as I caused fire from heaven to destroy that city, so shall the nation of France be consumed by the power of my judgment.

5. Let the people of France turn from all their wicked and perverse ways, lest my judgments shall leave your cities desolate.

6. Receive my warning voice, and cease to uphold those in thy nation that cause the legalizing of wickedness to prevail.

7. And cause that the laws that allow the murder of unborn children be overthrown.

8. And cause that the wickedness of immorality be done away with.

9. And let there be a mourning and lamentation among you for all your corrupt and fallen and perverse ways.

10. This from Him who reigns on high, and who has all power to fulfill His word, even the Lord, your Redeemer, who shall appear in the glory of His might to bring forth the day of redemption for all nations; and who shall dwell with men on earth for a thousand years, to reign in righteousness, and to cause all nations to live in peace.

SECTION REVELATION 74

Fundamentalist Church of Jesus Christ of Latter-day Saints
P.O. Box 840459
Hildale, Utah 84784

Your Lord and Savior, Jesus Christ, Speaketh, Even Son Ahman, to the Leaders and Peoples of the Nation of France, Saying Thus:

Revelation of the Lord Jesus Christ
Eldorado, Texas
Friday, May 6, 2011

1. Thus saith the Lord Jesus Christ unto that nation and the leaders of the nation of France, having promoted, yea, of a beginning nature, an attack against the nation of Libya, when I sent you warning to cleanse the inside of the platter.

2. I am the God of glory and shall soon come in the glorious apparel of the clouds of heaven, the powers of an eternal governing nature to earth, to govern all nations, to dwell among my people Zion in New Jerusalem, on the land of America, as it is known among men.

3. I, the Lord, speaketh to thee:

4. Withdraw thy military from aggressive ways against another nation that did not attack thy borders at all.

5. And set an example to be of a peaceful nature, of soon happening.

6. And cleanse the inside of the platter, your own peoples, before you seek to thus discipline other nations; for the crimes of Sodom and Gomorrah, and of the murder of unborn children, and of adultery and licentious and corrupt ways are rampant in thy land; and if you heed me not, my greater judgments shall sweep most of your population off the earth, only a few remaining;

7. And your power shall be clipped, and not be a power upon earth, only to have a record kept that the word of thy God who made thee and allows thee a place on earth, and time and agency and the gifts of life to prove what thou lovest most, whether it be good or evil, yea, a God of justice shall render thee an accounting, a rendering of a just judgment upon thee if you heed me not.

8. Thou knowest my message of my coming in the writings of mine apostles, who were with me in the day of my ministry, saith Jesus Christ.

9. Thou knowest of my word I have recently sent, of warning to the leaders of the nations of the earth, to be of a peacemaking nature.

10. Glory not in violence.

11. I, the Lord, am able to hear prayers and answer prayers of the honest in heart in every nation.

12. And those leaders of nations who become aggressive against other nations shall be humbled, and their power clipped, and they removed from power.

13. And if their peoples continue in those most corrupt ways and heinous crimes of murder and immorality, yea,

even murder of unborn children -- the most innocent, unable to defend themselves -- declaring unto thee:

14. Who art thou, the leaders of nations, and of this nation of France, to allow the murder of unborn children, even by legal consent, to decide who shall have life and who shall not have life, of the spirits I send to earth to inhabit mortal and earthly tabernacles, to prove themselves whether they will choose good and eschew and cast off evil through their agency?

15. And thus your national laws must be changed, and justice administered to remove these corrupt ways among thee;

16. For wickedness shall not rule during my thousand years of peace as I dwell among men on earth, as the governing power over all the earth.

17. And all peoples shall be humbled, I removing the more wicked from off the earth, preserving the more righteous, preparing them for my glorious appearing.

18. And I am God, the God of Creation, who rules in the heavens and over all nations of the earth that speaketh, who sees and knows all things, and nothing is hidden.

19. Hear my words:

20. Repent ye! yea, even the leaders of this nation.

21. Promote peace among the nations, for all these judgments I have named, even whirlwind and disease and famine, earthquake, hail -- and violent wars, if you continue in violence, of thine own make because you heed me not -- these shall sweep the more wicked off thy land and out of thy nation.

22. I am a God of truth, of righteous and holy and pure ways, and know all things, and am able to judge a righteous judgment upon all peoples.

23. Let the leaders of this nation realize the eternal truth that a just God, who hath conquered death and can raise all mankind from the grave through the resurrection powers -- you shall be raised from the grave to stand before me and be judged for your deeds done in the flesh.

24. And if you allow these murderous ways to continue, that most heinous and corrupt crime of the murder of unborn children shall corrupt thy souls unto a woeful and just existence against thee in the realms of Sheol, even the buffetings and powers of distress upon thy soul for committing such crimes on earth.

25. And the more righteous shall inherit salvation unto happiness by a just God as they perform works of righteousness and promote virtue and life in just laws upheld.

26. Cleanse thy people.

27. Humble thyselves, and set an example of peace by withdrawing thy military from attacking another nation, which did not attack your nation, you becoming an aggressive nation in this action against Libya.

28. It will not stand, as you have proved your nature to be a violent nation, and yet will not cleanse your own peoples of their corrupt ways.

29. Set thyselves in order first.

30. Overthrow any laws that advance the murder of unborn children and immorality.

31. Perform the works I have named if you desire to be a preserved nation in the time of my greater judgments, else all my promises shall be fulfilled concerning thee, both in this warning and my previous warnings I have sent, saith your Lord and Savior, Jesus Christ, who ruleth over all, who bringeth with Him the reward of a just recompense to all men, according to the measure they have given toward their fellow man. Amen.

SECTION REVELATION 111

Fundamentalist Church of Jesus Christ of Latter-day Saints
P.O. Box 840459
Hildale, Utah 84784

Thus Saith Jehovah, Even Son Ahman, Your Lord and Savior, Jesus Christ, to the Leaders of Israel -- A Word of Calling on Thee to Now Prepare for Coming Attack of Enemy Powers, to Also Cleanse Thine Own People to Be of a Pure Way to Earn My Power of Full Conquering Power Over Unjust Attack

Revelation of the Lord Jesus Christ
Palestine, Texas
Thursday, October 27, 2011

1. Thus is my will of holy pure authority, of the Order of Union Power of pure power over all, in Celestial Kingdom of my abiding, now, saith your Lord, Son Ahman, even Jesus Christ, to all people of the land of my origin, Israel --

2. Now be ready for war.

3. Let all be of a ready power only to defend thy land, if needs be conquering of neighboring nations must be part of thy defending.

4. Soon riseth a power to join, even unite together, thine enemies.

5. When this takes place, know thy full time of self-defending is nigh, needing full power of defending.

6. Let all thy people now be preparing, to have little provision.

7. Let thine way of war be ultimate defending, to be of a full power of conquering, to subjugate enemy powers to thy full reign as conquering power.

8. Let all be of a full power of thy honorable way to defend; first petitioning for peace, not of compromise to thy lands being given to enemy hands, nor of allowing my holy site of temple future building, yea, that place known to all, to not be compromised, but to hold control over my sacred site.

9. Now be of full power, to know thy God is with thee, as you cleanse your peoples through just, righteous, pure way of ruling in governing power; to overthrow law of allowing infanticide, murder of unborn children; also to prosecute sin of Sodom and also adultery, not to be allowed nor upheld by legal consenting.

10. Now prepare by purifying thine own land.

11. Let all be more holy, pure, noble of purpose, saith thy God, Jehovah Christ, even Jesus Christ. Amen.

I, Jesus Christ, Send Word to Leadership and Peoples of Japan, of Full Warning of Judgment of a Greater Power Than You Have Before Received, Save You Repent

(Comprising Section Revelations 112, 29, 69)

SECTION REVELATION 112

Thus Saith Son Ahman, Even Jesus Christ, to the Nation and Leadership of Japan, My Own Way of Revealing My Purposes Soon to Be of a Full Measure Upon Thee if You Continue in Evil and Immoral Ways, of Thy Way Being a Stench in the Earth of Immoral Ways; Heed My Word Which Saith:

Revelation of the Lord Jesus Christ
Palestine, Texas
Thursday, October 27, 2011

1. Let Japan hear my holy word:

2. I, your Lord Jesus Christ, Son Ahman, who ruleth over all, give my holy word to the rulers and peoples of the nation of Japan.

3. I have sent a humbling of earthquake and tidal wave upon thee, your nation still feeling the effects of that power of judgment.

4. Now repent as I have before called upon you to do, lest a invading power subjugate your nation in a war and bondage not yet experienced by the present generation of your nation.

5. You are to repent of evil immoral ways, of any infanticide of murder of unborn children, of your licentious ways.

6. Yet you continue to not heed my word.

7. A great and full power of my judgment soon cometh to remove the wicked from thy nation, preserving the more pure of more noble way.

8. Let leaders be of a full convincing way to teach need of thy people of entire land of Japan to go away from traditions of bathing men and women together in public; from being of immoral upholding of laws allowing evil, licentious, immoral publishings.

9. Let all be of a way of the more holy noble living.

10. I am God. I am over all.

11. Nothing is of a hiding from my view. All things past, present, future are known of me.

12. I can be of righteous, holy, eternal power of judging.

13. I shall raise all from the grave, to each be judged for deeds in the fleshly earthly existence, according to the light they have received in this life.

14. You are soon to be a people of tribute to a conquering power as you continue to heed not my word.

15. Let the people of Japan receive my new writing of testimony of thy God concerning my Church on earth; and of publishing warnings to nations of my soon coming in almighty power.

16. Let all heed my word. Amen.

SECTION REVELATION 29

Warning of the Lord to the Nation of Japan

Revelation of the Lord Jesus Christ
Draper, Utah
Monday, November 8, 2010

1. Verily, thus saith the Lord unto the nation of Japan:

2. I, the Lord, have seen your abominations, and send to you my word of warning, of coming desolation upon you who continue in the gross and immoral ways of vice and pornography, and of child murder of unborn children.

3. Thus cause there to be an immediate ceasing in your nation of the evils of immoral conduct in your legal and governing powers.

4. Cause that there be an equitable rule of governing power.

5. Let the immoral practice of men and women bathing together in public baths cease.

6. Let there be a change in your social structure wherein you do not allow the many immoral establishments to exist.

7. Cause thy people to now be a morally clean people.

8. Overthrow the laws that allow the existence of the secret combinations of immoral and murderous nature among your people.

9. Let there be a continual labor of providing for the poor.

10. Cause your nation to be an example of peaceful acquisition of financial and moral integrity.

11. Now be warned of judgment to be sent upon you as these evils continue.

12. Now be a people who throws off the tradition of false religions binding you to have among you the corrupt ways of immoral conduct.

13. Learn of my ways of eternal purity.

14. Send thy representatives to my people of Zion to learn of the ways of eternal truth.

15. Though you were humbled as a nation in the great war of your doing, I, the Lord, shall cause a greater judgment to come of desolation of abominatable and corrupt ways, even to know of the sorrows of great measure unto the cleansing of your nation of these immoral ways.

16. Now bring forth the purifying of your people.

17. I can only spare you as you remove the evils of corruption and unrighteous practices that destroy the virtue and natural purity that you have allowed to become your tradition.

18. I shall cause you to survive as a nation as you thus fulfill my word.

19. This is the word of the Lord to you. Even so. Amen.

SECTION REVELATION 69

Fundamentalist Church of Jesus Christ of Latter-day Saints
P.O. Box 840459
Hildale, Utah 84784

Thus Saith Son Ahman, Even Jesus Christ, the God of Glory Who Created All Things and Upholds All Nations and Peoples of the Earth in Their Place, Who Is the Redeemer and Savior of All Mankind, to the Leaders and Peoples of Japan, Through Mine Authority on Earth: Awake! and Heed My Word, Which Saith Thus -- Even a Word of Final Warning Before Greater Judgments Come Upon Thee, From a Just God Who Hath Warned Thee Beforehand the Greater Judgments of Destructive Power Would Come Upon Thee if You Heed Me Not -- Hear Ye My Word Herein:

Revelation of the Lord Jesus Christ
Eldorado, Texas
Tuesday, May 3, 2011

1. Thus saith the Lord unto the nation and the leaders of the nation of Japan:

2. I, the Lord, have humbled thee, even Jesus Christ, the God of heaven and earth, by sending forth a rebuke because of thy wickedness; showing my power, able to fulfill mine own word to the leaders of all nations, that when I call upon a nation to repent and turn from their corrupt and immoral ways, if they heed me not, my judgments of great power shall be poured forth.

3. I have sent warnings to you, even published it to the leaders of the nations, and to thy knowing -- the leaders of thy nation thus receiving my word.

4. Heed my word.

5. Repent ye of your corrupt and immoral ways, for thy peoples tend toward immorality through your traditions of your fathers carrying on in your lives.

6. And change thy laws to not allow immorality, pornography, Sodom, or the murder of unborn children to take place at all, lest my greater judgments come upon thee.

7. I have allowed you to exist as a nation still, and you shall become a tributary nation to a greater power in a time to come if you heed me not.

8. And your leaders shall be removed from power if they do not cleanse the inside of the platter -- thine own peoples and thine own laws; laws that allow corrupt ways, murder of innocent unborn children, corruption of your peoples, not protecting virtue.

9. Thus saith your God who created you: Repent ye! is a final warning to the nation of Japan and the leaders of Japan; and turn from these most wicked practices, that you may remain a nation; for I shall

send my judgments to sweep the more wicked part of every nation from off the earth, and preserve the more righteous, at my glorious appearing, by my almighty power;

10. For you shall see more tidal waves, earthquakes, and volcanos and great storms, and disease spread across thy nation if you heed not the God of glory, the God who created all things, who upholds all nations and all peoples upon the earth in their place, and who shall humble all peoples if they continue in their wicked and corrupt ways.

11. I have favored thee, after thy great war of thy starting, with prosperity, and then humbling.

12. I reveal further, thus saith Jesus Christ, the God over all things, who suffered on the cross, laid in the grave, even His body, for three days, His spirit in the world of departed spirits, organizing His Priesthood authority to teach the spirits in the world of departed spirits, then resurrected unto great power over heaven and the earth -- it is I who speaketh:

13. My glorious appearing to all peoples and nations is soon at hand, even to Zion, which is soon to be raised up on the American continent, even New Jerusalem, to be the governing city and power over all nations of the earth, the powers and governing authority of heaven coming to earth, of thy Savior's giving.

14. Thus saith the Lord: My coming is soon at hand.

15. Hasten to prepare, and cause thy peoples to be of a more pure walk through righteous, equitous, and virtuous laws that promotes life and virtue among thy peoples.

16. And cause the influence, through law, to cease your immoral practices among thy people, that I have named in a previous warning.

17. Heed my word, saith the God of glory over all creation, to the nation and leaders of Japan. Amen.

SECTION REVELATION 113

Fundamentalist Church of Jesus Christ of Latter-day Saints
P.O. Box 840459
Hildale, Utah 84784

Thus Saith Jesus Christ, Who Is Son Ahman, Jehovah Christ, Alpha and Omega, the Beginning and the End, to the Catholic Church Leaders and Members; Mine Own New Revealing, to Now Be of Open Way to Know, in Willing Minds and Hearts, My Truths. Amen.

Revelation of the Lord Jesus Christ
Palestine, Texas
Thursday, October 27, 2011

1. The word of the Lord of all, even your Redeemer Jesus Christ, Jehovah, Son Ahman, the Beginning and the End, Alpha and Omega; to the Vatican, even that worldwide church claiming to represent me to all peoples: Now be of a warning of all peoples to be of a purity of life; to full do away with murder of unborn children; to cast off Sodom and adulterous way.

2. Though thy way appeareth holy, yet your church is of no eternal Priesthood power.

3. You are of the way of no power to bless unto eternal lives.

4. You are not my full true Church among men.

5. My soon coming shall be to my true Church.

6. Receive my new writing of Proclamation of pure unobstructed truth into thine hands, to know of my true Priesthood power among men.

7. Let thy hearts be open.

8. Let truth be sought.

9. I am a God of immediate revealing of my holy will.

10. I do not dwell in idols.

11. I am of holy power eternal, soon to come to all peoples in all full glory and might on earth, for a Millennium of Peace of true abiding governing power.

12. I shall make known to thy surviving membership my true order of pure truth of salvation.

13. Let the way of priests of immoral way be curtailed in thy organization, immediately casting away any of immoral way.

14. Let also all be as humble people unto a cleansing of lives to be of more pure way, unto my presence able to be endured; for I shall judge all peoples according to the light they have received.

15. My coming is as a Man, an exalted Man of Godhood eternal power; for as I was in the flesh, now raised to heavenly eternal authority as King Emmanuel over all, so shall people know a God of glory was sacrificed on the cross for sins repented of.

16. Therefore, be of a pure way of open minds, unto receiving my own word to you, to know pure truth eternal. Amen.

17. Now let thy church know of my other publishing of recent and of new holy power writing, my own word through my Mouthpiece on earth, Warren Jeffs; a word of my revealing truth of my authority of Priesthood authority of revealed holy gift.

18. Let my Proclamation to all peoples also be read by members of thy church, to learn of truth, to be of a more ready way for power Celestial to dwell among men in Zion, even New Jerusalem, a City of Holiness, a people of holiness, a dwelling of God. Amen.

Message of Jesus Christ of Warning, and Blessing on the More Pure in the Order of Preparing for My Glorious Coming, in Nation of Peru, a New Word of My Own Way to Come Forth in Power Celestial
(Comprising Section Revelations 114, 103)

SECTION REVELATION 114

Thus Saith Son Ahman, Even Jesus Christ, Who Cometh in Glorious Power Eternal to All Nations Soon at Hand, to the Peoples of Peru, More Especially to the Pure Bloodline of Israel Living Among You, and to All Thy Peoples, of Ability to Purify Thy Lives unto Surviving My Full Cleansing Powers of Judgments, Also to Precede and Prepare the Way of My Glorious Appearing:

Revelation of the Lord Jesus Christ
Palestine, Texas
Friday, October 28, 2011

1. Thus saith your Holy Lord and Ruler over all nations, even Jesus Christ, Jehovah, the Creator of all things, the Life of all men and the Light of all men, to the people of the nation of Peru --

2. I, your Lord, am soon to appear on earth.

3. I shall come in glorious Eternal Godhood power to govern all nations, peoples, lands, governing powers.

4. Let thy people prepare.

5. Cast off all sin of thy way of immoral ways of destroying virtue and innocence;

also to cast off murder of unborn children, for this sin corrupteth all peoples who uphold such gross evil.

6. I, your Lord, shall send cleansing powers of eternal power, to remove the more wicked from the earth in every land.

7. Thus shall you know my coming is nigh.

8. All judgments of the order of full cleansing shall combine to cleanse my land of Zion, which is North and South America, the land of my coming in power

Celestial eternal; to be the ruling, guiding power over all nations; to be the purifier of Israel, of which many of thy nation are a part of Israel of ancient coming; for my record of Book of Mormon is true, telling of the coming of thy forefathers to this land by my guiding them daily.

9. Let all thine holy way be of more pure way.

10. Do not allow destruction of children unborn who are defenseless. Amen.

11. Now receive my word, you of Israel bloodline, of pure way of not mingling thy bloodline with gentile nor wicked corrupt way.

12. I shall soon bestow upon the more righteous a power to be of the cleansing power among nations.

13. Be pure.

14. You shall be visited by one who is knowing my way of holy cleansing power Celestial.

15. Thine ancient fathers are also among thee, prompting many to be ready.

16. Now know my land of Zion shall be cleansed.

17. Be of ready pure way in having your lives pure, holy, and not tainted with corrupting gentile way of immoral nor murderous practicing in family nor associating doings.

18. Now be my holy people of soon hearing of my coming, to gather to my Center Place of Zion in the now place called Missouri.

19. Let all be full of righteous will and living, to be of a survival when great cleansing judgments are poured out as a whirlwind upon all nations; when the nation of my coming shall no longer be a nation of power over all nations; even United States of America in their present power and short power glory over all.

20. Let my people now be pure.

21. I shall cause the removal of all who are not of my Zion preparing people of Israel, and in every nation.

22. Let Peru be a land of preparing for holy temples to be built to administer to Israel of gathering authority.

23. Let all be my holy nation Israel, of Zion. Amen.

SECTION REVELATION 103

Fundamentalist Church of Jesus Christ of Latter-day Saints
P.O. Box 840459
Hildale, Utah 84784

Thus Saith Son Ahman, Even Your Lord Jesus Christ, to All Peoples on Continents Called the Americas, Warning and Call to Prepare:

Revelation of the Lord Jesus Christ
Palestine, Texas
Wednesday, October 5, 2011

1. Thus saith Jesus Christ, even the Great I AM, the Beginning and the End, Jehovah, unto all peoples of the land of my holy and soon coming; more especially the nation of my restoring my Gospel and Church on earth:

2. Verily I say unto all peoples on my land of Zion, even to all the noble and high positioned leaders of the Americas: I am soon to make my coming known by a great tsunami, of the sea heaving beyond its bounds upon the east coast.

3. Let all now be of a full way of preparing, and remove thy habitation of personal and work labor staying to be inland.

4. This I send as a warning, for great and notable cities on the coast shall be swept off the land.

5. I reveal this to be of a delivering to believing souls.

6. Let also Arizona know that my judgment cometh; that earthquake and the sinking in the earth shall be on the capital city there; also volcano and earthquake take power in many inhabited and large populated places in Utah and Arizona. As took place in the meridian of time in days of the Nephite cleansing of my land, preparing for my coming among them, so shall it be in this time.

7. Idaho shall be as a melting fire of such powers to cleanse my land of all evil.

8. Let also Seattle know there cometh a shaking and tidal wave upon her.

9. Also cometh the shaking of the land where New Zion, even Jerusalem of New Holy Way is to rise on my land of Zion.

10. Tempests, earthquakes, even war and famine cometh upon the land; all to cleanse my land for my appearing in holy power of pure Celestial power.

11. Let this be known by all peoples, to know I am God, having all right to rule over all nations, soon to happen, in the rise of Zion, and Celestial powers coming to earth to reign among men as the governing powers over all nations.

12. Let also the honorable lawmakers in this nation's capital city know that place of government powers is to be the target of attack of an invading power.

13. Let all know my judgments are soon at hand and shall be felt by all people; and only the pure in heart shall remain to be witness to my coming on this land of Zion, even to establish a city of holy way of heavenly powers coming to earth after corruption and evil are swept off the earth by whirlwind judgments roll forth.

14. Now learn of my holy way.

15. Be of diligent learning of way of righteous governing of my power among men.

16. I have published to every nation my "Policies of Governing."

17. Let all study the same, to know of a holy and righteous power eternal coming among all peoples in every land on earth; to be the governing authority over all nations; to be the Millennial governing power over all the earth.

18. Such is my righteous holy power to be over all; to bring peace to all peoples of the inhabitable earth; as some places shall at first be made desolate by wicked national leaders using weapons of lasting harm against populations of other nations in their blinding anger of war waged.

19. Let the nation of professed freedom look well to their own conditions; having persecuted my Church over a century of time, yet still doing that evil against me and my Church in placing my servant and servants in prison, seeking to criminalize my holy eternal Celestial Law of Plural Marriage; yet having the greatest crimes of immoral ways and murderous ways among themselves, even the nation of great power now inhabiting my land of Zion.

20. Thus saith the Lord: This nation shall be laid low, having proven she is a

war nation, attacking other nations who never attack her.

21. Thus saith your Lord: As you again attack another nation, so shall your power be clipped, and other nations of military powers shall be of a combining attack upon thee.

22. O that you would heed my will; to only be of a defending power, not of aggression.

23. Three testimonies of thy aggression of unprovoked attack on other nations has come up before the heavenly authority to now humble thee.

24. Now beware, lest you openly fulfill my promises; to cease being of aggression, lest my full cleansing power be upon thy nation, even the United States of America, as it is called among men on earth; a nation of most corrupt ways among men, to soon no longer be a power against my Zion being established on earth; unto a full rewarding the nation for shedding the blood of my people, and hindering my Priesthood from fulfilling my holy purposes of salvation being administered to obedient sons and daughters on earth unto earning eternal salvation.

25. Now receive my warnings sealed in your hearts, to know that I, the God over all, hath spoken beforehand, when you see and witness these and other great cleansing powers sent upon thee; for all shall be humbled. Amen.

SECTION REVELATION 115

Fundamentalist Church of Jesus Christ of Latter-day Saints
P.O. Box 840459
Hildale, Utah 84784

Thus Saith Jesus Christ, Who Is Son Ahman, Even God Over All in Heaven and Earth, to All Peoples of Every Nation, to Be Warned of Full Judgments Soon to Be of Full Power of Full Purging of All Wickedness of Greater Degree Than Heretofore Taking Place; Hear Thou My Holy Will:

Revelation of the Lord Jesus Christ
Palestine, Texas
Friday, October 28, 2011

1. Thus saith the Lord, even Jesus Christ, Redeemer and Holy One of Israel, to all people of the earth:

2. My coming is nigh.

3. Now prepare for my cleansing judgments of greater and more destructive life-taking power; for the nations will not hear nor heed my word.

4. Only greater judgments can turn the determined, more wicked-desiring mind to repentance.

5. Thus shall all soon feel my wrath,

as you continue in the sins of immorality, murder of unborn children in nearly every nation now inhabiting my world; to now be of the full knowing that I have spoken, and I fulfill all my will and revelations given through him appointed as my Mouthpiece on earth, even my servant Warren Jeffs.

6. Now heed my word.

7. You cannot be of these gross crimes and survive my soon to be on earth greater cleansing and preparing judgments of an Eternal God; who is to soon appear to all peoples in glory and majesty Celestial; bringing with me the powers of heaven to rule over all peoples for the thousand years of peace.

8. Oh, hear my will --

9. Prepare ye, for I shall recompense all according to the measure they have measured to their fellow man; to be a full Judge over all through eternal power of full Godhood of holy and Eternal Power. Amen.

SECTION REVELATION 116

Fundamentalist Church of Jesus Christ of Latter-day Saints
P.O. Box 840459
Hildale, Utah 84784

Thus Saith Jesus Christ, Your Lord and Savior, to the Nation of Finland, a Word of Sacred Calling, to Be More Pure in Ways of Living, So as to Be a Surviving People in My Soon Day of Full Power of Judgments Upon All Nations; Hear Ye My Will:

Revelation of the Lord Jesus Christ
Palestine, Texas
Monday, October 31, 2011

1. Thus saith your Lord, even Son Ahman over all, who is Jesus Christ, the full Savior power of Eternal Holy Order of Redeeming Authority for all mankind, to the peoples of the nation of Finland:

2. I, your Lord, am soon to appear in great power on earth, to know you are called to overcome sins of Sodom and immorality among you, to cast out of your traditions and present practice the infanticide, of murder of unborn children.

3. Let thy land become an example of more pure way of dwelling on earth than the power nation that has subjected you many times, to be of their ways.

4. Let all in thy nation be of more pure way than other surrounding nations.

5. There are events in your near future that will bring about full freedom of religion in your nation; to allow freedom of choice, of which religion you will choose to follow; to allow all to choose thy God in my new revealed power Celestial.

6. Let all be of a more pure way; for

soon you shall be tested by judgments who is of pure way of dwelling in law of pure way of preserving innocence, virtue, and life.

7. Let all in thy land be of more pure living, so as to do away with child murder of unborn children; also licentious, corrupt ways.

8. Let now thy laws make Sodom and adultery capital crimes.

9. Let thy nation be example of more holy pure way of living. Amen.

10. Let Finland also send to my servant a corresponding reply to tell of new improvings in thy national law to do away with these evils; and I will spare your peoples unto being my nation of caring for other nations who are without order, in need of law and order, you providing neighboring nations with help to restore order; for there shall be war seen in most lands; and you can use your weapons only for defending, lest my blessings cease of preserving your peoples for my Zion to be among you.

11. Let thy peoples be told to be ready for my eternal pure plan of salvation to be among you without obstruction, to be a nation of surviving my day of visitation; for there shall be a remnant survive.

12. I shall be your power of a governing authority over all thy people.

13. Let also all be told my Israel dwelling in thy land to gather to Zion if pure way of living is like Zion; to have full power to join in eternal power of blessings unto salvation, saith Jesus Christ, your Eternal Ruler, Redeemer, Guide, and Power of resurrecting gift. Amen.

SECTION REVELATION 117

Thus Saith Jesus Christ, Son Ahman, Who Is Jehovah Christ, to All Peoples of All Lands, Nations, and Governing Powers on Earth, Warning of Final Cleansing Soon to Be Upon My Land of Zion; There Also Coming Same Cleansing Upon All Nations

Thus Saith God Over All, Even Jesus Christ, My Holy Will Revealing My Soon Coming Events Upon My Land of Zion; Also Upon All Peoples of Every Nation; A New Revealing, to Know I Have Warned All, and Will Be of Full Power of Cleansing:

Revelation of the Lord Jesus Christ
Palestine, Texas
Monday, October 31, 2011

1. I who is over all things, by whom all things were created, and by whom all continue in organizing power of existing in present personal sphere of action; even Jesus Christ, Son Ahman, the Beginning and the End, speak to all peoples on the earth, now to learn of a judgment of full power of my sending; a storm of great destructive power upon the nation of United States in America, even my nation of my coming to build New Jerusalem.

2. This shall paralyze many parts of thy nation for a time, causing great distress, to show thee I have spoken warnings of recent sending; and that as I speak, so shall I fulfill.

3. Such shall be the result of this devastating storm.

4. You shall know it is of my power sent to humble my nation of soon removal if they continue in murder of unborn children, and Sodom and immoral ways not of the pure way of my coming; for I must cleanse all nations of these sins to allow them knowledge of my presence on earth as Ruler and Eternal Power. Amen.

5. Thus is the Lord's will, to be of full knowing of my coming soon at hand.

6. Let all in this nation of my New Jerusalem to rise, be ready.

7. Only they who are of purity of living can survive my full measure of purifying cleansing; leaving only my Order Eternal of Zion on the land of the Zion of our God, even North and South America; a land that will be of righteousness after all wicked inhabitants are swept off by my eternal power, they who no longer care for pure holy way of your Lord, who commanded to not kill, neither commit adultery, nor anything immoral like unto that sin of personal defiling.

8. Let all be full of pure noble desire.

9. Leave alone my people.

10. Let my servant go.

11. Let all men of my Priesthood in prison go free. Amen.

12. Thus is the revealing of the God of Creation over all; to know my time is soon to be on earth with cleansing powers; to govern all peoples in a Millennium of Pure Holy Peace.

13. Let all know they shall be judged, who is of purity of living, to be worthy of preservation by my grace and power.

14. Let all nations be warned again.

15. Let only thy will be to do as I have said, to purge the gross contagious crimes of murder of unborn children and of Sodom and adulterous ways from among thy nation, each one; lest great and full power of cleansing cometh.

16. Know when North America is of full judging that my time is soon; also when Israel is a people gathering unto my land.

17. Let all be my Israel who would be of pure way of holy walk before Him who is your Lord, Savior, Judge, and Holy Advocate unto redeeming power eternal.

18. Let this, my word, be as another full warning and call to final preparing; and to cause the full way of my Holy Priesthood to be free to do my will on earth, to build up my Zion.

19. Let Zion now be the way of governing power over all peoples.

20. I am with them, my Church and people of the way of salvation.

21. Let them, even my Church, be of full freedom to serve their Lord in full Celestial Plural Marriage Law unobstructed.

22. Let my United Order law no longer be under attack, as my consecrated lands and homes in the court's ruling have been taken from my holy Order.

23. Let all now be of a full way of pure holy way of giving to all pure, true, noble ruling of delivering my people.

24. Let now there be only my people to dwell on my consecrated lands where they have been removed out of the hands of my Priesthood, now of tribute to ungodly ruling board by court appointment; unjust court interfering in my true religion; thus breaking the law of Constitution religion freedom guaranteed.

25. Let also my Priesthood in prison go free, as they only have done my will in abiding Celestial Plural Marriage by my own will revealing my law to be lived by them.

26. No governing power on earth of authority, especially where religious freedom is of constitutional guarantee, can be of an interfering power in religion of my guiding.

27. Let the nation humble themselves who are thus of a persecuting zeal against my holy Celestial Law of Celestial Marriage of Plural revealing; only to be of my Church, not for the world. Amen.

28. Now be of hastening to prepare for my great power to soon be of judgment upon the land. Amen.

29. This holy will of God is to now be of a full warning to the people over all the earth, wherever they reside; that when they see United States in America humbled by great power of my causing many to be of a life-taking, then they shall be aware I, your Lord, fulfill all my will.

30. Now be of full way of full cleansing on part of leaders and peoples of nations to remove the greater sins I have named that are among you. Amen.

31. Jesus, your Lord, hath spoken, and shall fulfill unto full knowing my coming in power of my might in the clouds of heaven, which hideth many things from the seeing of mankind, until I cause my coming in full power to be known among

you, to be of full way Celestial in governing authority over all surviving nations.

32. Let Australia know population on low lands shall be of a tsunami tidal wave.

33. Many shall perish who will not move to higher lands of elevation.

34. Let China also be warned to only cleanse my land of wickedness, not my people.

35. Let also all nations leave alone my Zion, lest great whirlwind judgments speak the justice of an offended God. Amen.

36. Thus is the will of Jesus, your Lord, to the sure knowing of all peoples; so that when they see my will fulfilled, they know I have spoken beforehand; and are thus fully aware I shall fulfill all my will as I have revealed through my servants, the Prophets; and mine own word found in New Testament record. Amen.

37. The Lord also revealeth to Russia to not remain on my land of Zion, lest full powers of whirlwind judgment come upon thee.

38. Though you believe me not, my judgments shall convince all they must not come against my people Israel.

39. Let the nation of Iran cease all aggressive power against neighboring lands and peoples, lest you become a nation no more; only to be of subjugation to a foreign power, to no longer be of aggression; for I shall reward thee with full cleansing judgments as you promote violence against my Israel or other neighboring nations. Amen.

40. Let Turkey aid Israel in day of great attack against my Israel, lest you also fall and become a subject nation. Amen.

41. Let also my holy land of New Jerusalem only be for my Church and Priesthood people of Zion's preparation in their lives, my Celestial Law of holy Eternal Union lived. Amen.

42. Thus have I been warning all peoples to prepare, I already in the midst of my people, notwithstanding full persecuting powers coming against my Church.

43. Read fully my new publishing of Proclamation of full giving my history by my own word sent to teach all about my Priesthood and my Celestial Plural Marriage Law continuing among men on earth since I revealed my Priesthood and my Celestial laws in the day of my holy Prophet Joseph Smith; continuing these gifts through a faithful order of full Celestial authority from heaven, my Keyholders well honored by me in my own word given; now printed and sent forth to all nations.

44. Let my Keyholder of full authority go free, my now Prophet, Mouthpiece, and pure sealing authority unto sealing blessings unto eternal life.

45. Let all know, how they treat my Priesthood on earth, so shall I be to them a Savior, if faithful, or a Judge of whirlwind almighty power if they reject me by hindering the progress of my Church on earth.

46. Let all murderous secret combinations in every nation be punished and overthrown.

47. Let secret agencies of violent ways of managing your people's behavior be no longer in your governing powers.

48. Let truth, justice, purity of living, equity of opportunity of freedom of living and of worship be of a full upholding by all governing powers on earth; for I shall cause the waters to boil, volcanoes, earthquakes, storms, the desolating sickness of an overflowing scourge, also pestilences

of disease, and other destructive powers shall soon be felt by all peoples, nations, tongues, kindreds, and governing powers.

49. Let my people be my people, not to be cast out nor driven.

50. Let my people also hasten to prepare to be worthy of greater Celestial powers; to assist in governing the earth in full power and Priesthood authority.

51. Now come full measure to be among my full law of Zion. Amen.

52. Let the people of Central America, also pure bloodline of Lamanite and Nephite people in Americas, be ready to be as a full power of helping thy God cleanse all wickedness off my lands of Zion; a battle-ax in mine hands to the fear of all the nations and their peoples on my holy lands of Zion; to have my heavenly powers assist you of pure line of Israel to be an army of cleansing power against the wicked on my land of Zion. Amen.

53. Let also Bolivia with Ecuador hear my word, to cleanse their own nation, each one, of the gross evils among the gentile nations of murder of unborn children, also Sodom and immoral ways, to then be of a cleansing authority of other peoples.

54. I shall cause my holy power to be on thee. Amen.

55. Let also Nicaragua be of a humbling, as her leaders have tried to be of oppressive way on her own peoples.

56. Let all peoples be at peace when I appear; for my full power shall soon be felt by neighboring nations of more pure way, humbling wicked nations; also to receive my full gifts of blessings of life, of food, clothing, shelter, to remain intact and with you, each nation or peoples who thus receive this, my word, and heed my will, saith Jesus Christ, your Lord. Amen.

57. I am soon to use whom and what I will, saith God over all, to cleanse all nations.

58. Be ye ready. Amen.

SECTION REVELATION 118

Fundamentalist Church of Jesus Christ of Latter-day Saints
P.O. Box 840459
Hildale, Utah 84784

Thus Saith Jesus Christ to the Leaders in Governing Powers, Also to All Peoples of the Nation of United States of America, My Own Word of Full Power Soon to Take Full Way of Cleansing Power Upon All in This Nation if You Repent Not. I Shall Send the Promised Judgments if You Do Not Let My Servant and People Go Free. I Speak Thus to All:

Revelation of the Lord Jesus Christ
Palestine, Texas
Tuesday, November 1, 2011

1. Thus saith the Lord Jesus Christ to the nation of my coming, the United States of America:

2. I have now enlightened all thy rulers by my Proclamation History and revelation writing, of pure unobstructed truth, not to be of a light way of receiving; to be my holy truth, that no governing power of man on earth hath any jurisdiction to judge my authority of Celestial authority and eternal keys of power I cause to be my Keyholder on earth.

3. He shall be thy judge of me. I am Judge, Ruler, Deliverer, God and Holy Eternal Power over all, and none can stay my hand.

4. Though I have allowed my servant to be in bondage to prove the people of the land of my coming, I shall send power of pure cleansing, to leave neither root nor branch of thine own household of present nation.

5. There shall be complete besom of destructive power come forth, O ye people of the land of New Jerusalem rising unto full governing power.

6. Let this be an awakening -- I have commanded my servant to no longer be of an answering to court of persecuting power; to now silently witness thy God send forth the greater humbling of nation of persecution against my Church and my Priesthood; to be of full way of knowing you are fighting me, your Lord; who shall be of full power to overthrow thy minuscule might, to cause the sea to heave beyond its bounds, to bury and wash away cities of corruption on borders of land; to shake the earth unto cities becoming of no existing; mountains found where cities were.

7. O ye people, repent ye, for my time is soon to do the full cleansing labor of my Zion land of North and South America.

8. Let all be of full repenting, lest judgments come in full power. Amen.

Thus Saith the Lord Jesus Christ to the President of the United States of America, to the Members of Congress, Both Senate and House of Representatives, to the High Leaders of This Nation in Every State, and the Peoples of This Nation, a Declaration of Judgment Upon Thee for Thy Continued Wicked Representation Against Innocence, Against Life, Against Purity. Amen.

(Comprising Section Revelations 119, 5, 63, 70)

SECTION REVELATION 119

Thus Saith the Lord Jesus Christ, Son Ahman, the Ruler of Heaven and Earth, the God Over All Nations, to the President of the United States of America, to the Senators and Congressmen, of Federal National Governing Power, to State Governors, to Governing Powers in Every State in This Land of Freedom, So-called -- Another and Final Warning and a Declaration That I Have Weighed You in the Balance and Found You Wanting, and Shall Overthrow Your National and World Power Soon at Hand, as You Continue in Your Ungodly and Wicked Practices. Heed My Word as I Give My Declaration Herein:

Revelation of the Lord Jesus Christ
Palestine, Texas
Saturday, November 5, 2011

1. Now the Lord speaketh, even Jesus Christ, your God and Ruler over all, Son Ahman, the Beginning and the End, Alpha and Omega, the Righteous Judge, a God of truth who hath all power to be of a sending forth of His own word to the leaders of nations and all peoples, that I may be justified in sending forth judgments of whirlwind power, eternal power of cleansing upon all peoples, until the more righteous only remain in every land, and they of corrupting ways of murder and immoral ways to be removed entire, wherein they would govern their peoples in this corrupting way.

2. I speak a holy word to the leader of the nation of my coming, a President of world power, as it were, to influence many nations:

3. Had you heeded my word and cast off from thy land the immoral ways upheld by legal consent, and the murderous ways of unborn children that governing powers even promote oftentimes, fighting against my plan of life of salvation eternal, hindering the sending forth of spirits to this earth, which is my earth of probationary testing; wherein my children are sent forth to receive earthly tabernacles, to prove themselves what they will choose, whether

good or evil in the conduct of their lives; to be rewarded with an eternal judgment and reward, according as their works may be, whether good or evil -- the righteous, who choose good, unto salvation; and the wicked, who loved evil and take pleasure in that which is corrupt, in that which destroys innocence, purity, and holiness, and destroying life; behold, an eternal suffering cometh upon them, having my Spirit upon all mankind, sent forth as the light of intelligent thoughts of noble and holy walk and purity of life desired, that monitor within every person born on earth saying that evil is evil and to come away therefrom, and to seek after the good.

4. Behold, I say unto you, the God of glory shall hold you, the leader of this nation, eternally accountable for what you have done in not heeding my word, the word of a just God, who has sent forth many messages through my servant on earth, and you left it unnoticed as though it was not my word;

5. Yet if you had done what I had declared, to go in prayer and ask thy God: "Is this verily your word?" an impressing would come upon you; yet you of a darkened mind heeded me not, and now the murder of many unborn children hath taken place, even since my correspondence has come to thee and the leaders of this land -- members of Congress, judges, others of important governing positions having received my word in Proclamation.

6. Therefore, I declare thee unfit for leadership, and there shall come forth a deposing of thee from power in a manner you knew not; being of national prominence, yet you shall be no longer of that power; sending this, my word, to thee that you may know the cause of thy losing grace before thy God, and Him not upholding thee in that greater gift of influencing peoples of the nation and of the earth; for you could have done well, and heeded me not, saith Jesus Christ, your God and King, who ruleth over heavens and earth and worlds, and nothing can stay mine hand.

7. Oh, that you had heeded my word, and that this nation would heed my word even still, that some few may be of a repentance before whirlwind judgments of cleansing power come upon thy land, which you shall soon know.

8. Remember what I declared to thee -- I would send storms of destructive power -- and you visited the locations, saith the Lord, even you, the President of this nation, saying you have never seen such destruction before, in public declaring.

9. Therefore, I kept my word, saith the Lord, to your witnessing, and you still heed me not.

10. Now I have sent more of my word of more judgments soon to come; and as they take place, the people on this land shall know I, the God of glory, hath spoken beforehand, as I did to my servant Isaiah and other Prophets, who then went and told kings of nations what would take place and in future times, and it took place to their knowing.

11. I am the God of heaven. My word is sure and true. Nothing can stay mine hand.

12. Heed my word, if you would do well; otherwise, in the day you face thy Lord, the blood of innocence shall be upon thee, thy God having personally sent His word through His Mouthpiece on earth, a servant of God in bondage, yet able to send forth my declaring; behold, I say unto you, a holy word of eternal importance to thine own self, and to many others in thy land and the peoples of the earth, if you

would begin to be of a cleansing of these wicked practices from among thy nation, and set an example to other peoples of other nations.

13. Behold, this is the will of God; therefore, they would follow likewise through thy influence of righteousness, a righteous walk if you would be of a sacred doing, saith the Lord God of heaven. Amen.

14. I, the Lord, speak to the members of Congress, both Houses who represent the peoples in the United States of America:

15. You have not heeded my word.

16. I have sent my own word through my Mouthpiece on earth in corresponding mail, in Proclamation, in publishings of recent sending, your Lord Jesus Christ, Son Ahman, the Beginning and the End, a righteous Judge, yea, the God over all Creation giving His own name, declaring His own word to the leaders of this nation, and you heed me not.

17. You have power in your hands to influence even the leader of the nation to sign and pass laws that would deliver innocence, penalize the murder of unborn children by those who thus practice that infanticide, that evil practice that destroyeth nations heretofore;

18. For I say unto you, this was the fall of Rome.

19. This was the fall of Babylon and of the Greek Empire, the Sodom ways taking charge; and they deriding against the plan of life by the murder of unborn children for licentious, immoral, adulterous purposes.

20. Thus the people of the whole earth are after this same spirit and practice.

21. I have caused my own word to be sent forth as a warning to all nations and leaders of nations, and the peoples of every land, to heed my word and speedily repent of these most wicked practices.

22. And you, the leaders of this nation in power, able to adjust your laws and cause judges to uphold those laws, verily I say unto you, I am the God of glory. Eternal is my name.

23. What you do on earth, in the day of the resurrection shall come up before thee in full view.

24. And the blood of innocence already rests upon your skirts, as it were, in allowing the continued practice, known in thy land as abortion, even the murder of full term unborn infants in some places, by choosing of darkened parents or others who would kill a living soul by legal consent;

25. Verily I say unto you, great is the stain upon your skirts for having allowed this corrupting way to continue in this land of supposed freedom -- not free to the unborn child to be born free from attack. Amen.

26. Now I, the Lord, declare further: If you continue, as leaders of this nation, to allow these evil practices, you shall be thrown from power, and your nation shall cease to be a world power, and there shall not be enough among you to herald the cause of freedom;

27. And only my Priesthood, my Church and Kingdom, will step forth to herald religious freedom in the day I give full power unto Zion's mission. Amen.

28. Now I, the Lord, have spoken to the leaders of this nation, to be known also to the peoples of this land. Amen.

SECTION REVELATION 5

A Petition to the President of the United States of America

Revelation of the Lord Jesus Christ
Draper, Utah
Thursday, October 7, 2010

1. To the honorable President of the United States of America now as standing at the head of this nation:

2. I who dwells on high, even your Lord and Savior, who redeemed all mankind by the shedding of His own blood, and who is over all and has all power, send to you my word.

3. Cause that my servant who presides over my Church now be delivered by thy hand.

4. Let my servant go, that he may perform his mission to prepare my people for my coming.

5. Cause that the prosecutors now cease their attack upon my servant Warren Jeffs.

6. Cause that this nation now restore to my people the consecrated land taken from them.

7. Cause that there be remuneration given them for the loss of the homes that are occupied illegally by the enemies of my people who are in the Colorado City, Arizona and Hildale, Utah area.

8. Cause that the attack against my people in Texas be stopped.

9. I, the Lord, shall cause my judgments to be withheld as you thus perform this work.

10. Otherwise, let this nation know I am with my people, and shall sweep the wicked from off the face of the land of America.

11. Thus shall I perform my work by my almighty power.

12. This from your Lord, even Jesus Christ, who shall subdue all His enemies under His feet.

13. Even as I have spoken, so shall I fulfill. Even so. Amen.

SECTION REVELATION 63

Fundamentalist Church of Jesus Christ of Latter-day Saints
P.O. Box 840459
Hildale, Utah 84784

Thus Saith Son Ahman, Even Jesus Christ, the God Over All Creation, to the President of the United States of America

Revelation of the Lord Jesus Christ
Eldorado, Texas
Tuesday, April 26, 2011

1. Thus saith the Lord Jesus Christ unto you, the leader of the nation of the United States of America, even the President of this nation:

2. I address you, as the God of Creation, even Jesus Christ, who gave His life for the salvation of all mankind and is able to raise all in the resurrection and judge all for their deeds done in the flesh.

3. Righteous is my name; Endless and Eternal is my name.

4. When I speak, I fulfill.

5. I have sent to you mine own word to let my people go, and release my servant from bondage, and allow them freedom of worship in Celestial laws of my revealing.

6. I have warned this nation and the leaders of this nation by sending mine own word to overthrow those laws that allow murder of unborn children, the gross immorality of Sodom and adultery; promotion of which is allowed by legal consent, even in entertainments and music and social ways throughout your land.

7. As the leaders of this nation allow these great evils to continue, I shall bring you to judgment.

8. Thou sayest you promote peace among nations and religious freedom, the freedom of expression; yet, since the days of my servant Joseph Smith receiving my Gospel of salvation, restored from heaven to earth, upholding my word in Old and New Testament, the words of all the ancient Prophets, my people have been a driven people.

9. And government powers of this nation of the United States of America have used their civil powers to prosecute and persecute my people of my Church of Jesus Christ of Latter-day Saints; which Church has continued under my Priesthood eternal authority revealed from heaven to Prophets since Joseph Smith's time, now known among men as the Fundamentalist Church of Jesus Christ of Latter-day Saints, known as upholding all the laws of my Gospel revealed through Joseph Smith, of their Lord.

10. But I will support and sustain and preserve my people, even through great whirlwind judgments that I prophesied of, as you can read in New Testament record.

11. I refer you to Matthew 24 specifically, one of mine apostles of old who heard my word and recorded my word.

12. I send you this, my word, calling upon you who leads this nation to promote true justice and religious freedom for my people; for they are of peaceful nature and only desire the salvation of all peoples.

13. They are seeking to build my Zion, prepare for my glorious appearing;

14. And if you will heed my word, blessings shall come upon this nation; else there shall come judgments to make room for the rise of Zion on this, the American continent, which is my land of Zion where New Jerusalem shall be built, as described by John the Beloved in the Book of Revelations in New Testament record; and I refer this to your reading, knowing of my Bible record.

15. My servant on earth is in bondage through unjust laws aimed to destroy my Priesthood, Church, and Kingdom upon the earth;

16. For I am the God of eternity, and the laws of my Church are revealed from heaven and guided by your Lord; and my people in thy land, of my Church and Kingdom, have rights of religious worship and religious freedom; and my Celestial Law is pure and only promotes happiness and salvation among the pure in heart.

17. My Zion shall rise through the principles of the laws of my Church and Kingdom upon the earth, revealed from heaven.

18. You can peruse these laws in my sacred writings through Joseph Smith in Doctrine and Covenants.

19. You can read of my coming among a former people that dwelt on this land, and my prophecies to them concerning these days -- of this nation coming upon this land.

20. My record is extant and witnesses of my glorious coming, both ancient scripture and modern revelation, as is known among men.

21. And these are the motives of my Priesthood and my servant and my servants in my Church and Kingdom, who seek to live pure and eternal laws of salvation, which I require of them in this mortal existence on earth to prove worthy of an eternal salvation;

22. And this is the motive of their lives, notwithstanding the persecuting zeal of those who come against them, promoted by the lies of former members who have apostatized because their own lives were full of sin, accusing my Priesthood, Church, and Kingdom of unrighteous domain.

23. Come to understand the truth of these realities among you, and free my servants who are in bondage because of their religious beliefs and practices in obedience to my eternal laws, the revealed religion from heaven.

24. As I spoke concerning the destruction of Jerusalem and the scattering of the Jews, and thus fulfilled my word, so have I spoken concerning the judgments of God -- even of your Lord who sendeth this word to you -- upon this nation and the nations of the earth, if you continue to promote these great evils among your peoples, and allow the persecution and prosecution, which is an injustice against my Church, people, and Kingdom upon the earth.

25. And if you heed me not, you leaders of this nation of the United States of America, you shall feel the chastening hand of a just God; and all my promises and prophecies of judgments upon the gentile nations shall be fulfilled in full measure.

26. Heed my word, that the more righteous among you may be preserved; and if you do not, and the peoples of this nation oppose the rise of Zion, I must needs come out in judgment to cleanse my land of Zion.

27. I shall come in my glory to establish righteous domain, a just and

equitous government of eternal power, to rule over all nations, and nothing can stay mine hand, being the God of all creation over all nations.

28. Thus I send my word to you again, according to the understanding of men, in simple language, that you may see truth revealed by your God, which truth you can understand by simple perusal of the scriptures revealed through Joseph Smith, my servant, continued on earth in my Church and Kingdom.

29. I have declared to you that if these evils continue among your people and this nation, that I have named in many messages I have sent, the judgments I have promised shall take place, for wickedness shall not reign.

30. There shall be a thousand years of peace under my righteous rule, saith Jesus Christ, the Beginning and the End, who has all power and authority and right to rule, in heaven and on earth.

31. As you see a great storm of paralyzing nature over many parts of thy nation, and also an earthquake of damaging nature and the loss of lives in a place of unusual happening, as I have named, let your heart be touched that thy God hath spoken; and when He speaks, He fulfills His word.

32. My coming in glory is nigh.

33. I send you my word through my authority of Priesthood on the earth.

34. I, the Lord, reveal to you, the leader of this nation, the formation of that which is of a secret combination among rich businessmen and some leaders of this nation, disturbed by thy policies of economic practices, using government powers, some of whom have joined with organized crime, plotting thy destruction.

35. This I reveal to you, to be careful in thy movements.

36. There are some of them determined to overthrow your influence, thinking your policies are destroying this nation in economic power, fearing that political means may not be sufficient in their power to bring another into that presidential position in future election.

37. Let there be an investigation, of careful means and ways, into the organization of business leaders of banking industry combining with the political arm that is promoting free trade, opposing thy policies of increased debt that are joined with authorities from China, to which this nation has depended on investment into treasury and other stocks to bolster this economy, which organization is of the policy of free trade without restrictions, wanting to set aside governmental restrictions to allow economic growth without government hindrance, wherein the policies of this nation presently limit some exports to nations considered in human rights violations; yet this organization desires free trade, notwithstanding the policies of this government today.

38. Look well into organized crime in Chicago connecting with rich businessmen of an organization seeking free trade, and also having made some connections with foreign powers who also seek economic benefit by changing of laws and rules, in trade and commerce, the laws of this nation, seeking to get gain thereby.

39. I, the Lord, reveal this much, that the fears of this secret combination are, they will lose their wealth if you promote certain policies in government concerning economic development.

40. I give you this, my word, saith the Lord, that you may know I see and know all things; can reveal my word and preserve life as I will.

41. I have named judgments to come

upon this nation if they continue these most wicked practices of murder of unborn children, and Sodom, and the immoral wickedness that promotes these sins against innocence and against life;

42. Yet, if you will heed my word and now promote the repeal of those practices now upheld by law, I, the Lord, shall cause this nation to continue as they allow freedom of religion of my Church and Kingdom.

43. And if the leaders of this nation heed me not, my full judgment shall come to thy knowing; for I am the God of glory and fear no man, and shall come to earth in my glory to reign a thousand years in righteous dominion and government over all nations.

44. This is my word to you. Heed my word and promote principles of righteous government.

45. And thus this message is to the leaders of all bodies of government over this nation, to promote righteous principles that preserve life and purity and religious freedom.

46. I tell you these things beforehand for thy good.

47. Do not be taken in a snare by rich businessmen in promoting thy attending a business conference in Chicago of soon naming.

48. Excuse thyself that you may be preserved, is the word of the Lord to you.

49. Promote no longer war against other nations, save for self-defense.

50. Do not be the originator of attack against any nation, that this nation may be justified before your God as you also remove these great evils I have named from among thy peoples, which are allowed by legal consent in this day.

51. I, the Lord, have spoken it. Give heed to my word, and know that I shall repay all peoples according to the measure they have measured to their fellow men, an eternal judgment, being the God over all creation, who came to earth among mortal men and suffered more than man can suffer, conquering death, hell, and the grave, to raise all peoples up in the resurrection to stand before the judgment bar of God, which tribunal shall render an eternal judgment upon all peoples -- happiness and eternal life for those who measured justice, righteousness and equity, and purity of life toward their fellow men and in their own lives; and promoting a great and eternal punishment upon those who would seek the destruction of life and of innocence, whether openly by legal means, or in private.

52. I have warned the leaders of nations to remove these great sins from among their peoples before my glorious appearing by sending forth my word.

53. And I shall be justified in cleansing the more wicked out of every nation on earth before my glorious appearing, preserving the more righteous who will receive my message of salvation and a righteous government power, even of thy Lord, on earth for a thousand years, a Millennial Reign of Peace, as I have promised.

54. My coming is nigh at hand. Let my people go, to worship me in the freedom guaranteed by the laws of thy nation, my revealed religion from heaven promoting pure and holy principles unto eternal life for those who obey my religious laws, that should be protected by the laws of thy land, yet have not been protected for many years -- legal prosecution and persecution coming against my people in many ways in this nation.

55. I send you my word to help you overcome the inward prejudice held by

many lawmakers against my true Church and religion upon earth.

56. Peruse my policies of government in my recent sending of my publishing to thee, with the warnings to this nation and other nations.

57. I say to you lawmakers and government officials in this nation and in every state: My time of coming is at hand.

58. Turn to righteous principles that promote life and virtue and innocence, and protect the same, for I shall hold you accountable, saith the Lord God of heaven and over the earth.

59. Righteous and Holy is my name.

Endless is my name. Eternal is my name, even Jesus Christ.

60. This earth is mine.

61. I have given man his agency to choose. Both good and evil are present before all peoples.

62. Choose to promote righteousness.

63. A heavenly power is coming to earth to govern the nations of the earth on my land of Zion, and my power shall be among them; and this is revealed in the scriptures of holy writ in thine hands.

64. I am a God of truth, and I have spoken my word through all the holy Prophets, and shall fulfill. Amen.

SECTION REVELATION 70

Fundamentalist Church of Jesus Christ of Latter-day Saints
P.O. Box 840459
Hildale, Utah 84784

Thus Saith Son Ahman, Even Jesus Christ, Your Lord and Savior Who Hath Redeemed All Mankind, Whose Right It Is to Rule Over the Heavens and the Earth, a Just God Who Sees and Knows All Things, and Shall Recompense to Every Man That Which He Has Measured to His Fellow Man, According to the Light and Knowledge They Have Received: Thus I Speak <u>to the President</u> of the United States of America, Now in Power, and Also to the Peoples of This Nation -- This Message of Warning of the Doctrine of Eternal Judgment Upon Thee, Even Upon All Peoples, Being the God of Eternal Power, an Eternal God Who Shall Bring All to Justice; Whose Mercy Shall Claim Those Who Repenteth in a Manner to Earn the Benefit of My Atoning Power -- Even Him, a God of Atoning and Redeeming Power, Who Suffered on the Cross and Was Raised From the Grave Unto Eternal Power to Judge All Mankind According as Their Works Are:

Revelation of the Lord Jesus Christ
Eldorado, Texas
Tuesday, May 3, 2011

1. Let there be written my word, saith the Lord, in a manner of correspondence to the leader of this nation of the United States of America, a word of warning and counsel -- even Jesus Christ, who reigneth over all, empowering this nation to be a free nation since its creation, I guiding forefathers of the revolutionary battles wherein they broke away from the mother gentile nation from which they emanated.

2. And I, your God, inspired leaders of this nation to establish the Constitution of the United States, and the Bill of Rights, as it is called, guaranteeing religious freedom, even freedom of worship in a land of plenty at that time.

3. Thus saith the Lord to those who thus murdered Osama bin Laden:

4. You have transgressed greatly, turning to murder in a manner of seeking to retaliate against one in another land, not using the government powers where he dwelt to apprehend him safely, which could have easily been accomplished had you thus stepped forth and acted on correct principles.

5. But in thy glory-seeking and in thy violent nature, yea, to the celebration of millions in thy nation, you hath murdered a man who could have been apprehended peacefully, were attempts made therein by the governing power of the nation where he dwelt, being near the capital city and power of authority of that nation in Pakistan.

6. I, the Lord, rebuke thee for thy murderous intent, turning to violence when peaceful means, or the governing powers over that place of residence, could have been used to apprehend and take in custody one accused of crimes.

7. And if you continue this practice, your murderous intentions shall turn upon thine own peoples, and mob rule shall ensue throughout thy land; murder and rapine, robbery and violence one against another, showing thy murderous intent and nature of the people of this nation, proving to thy God you are not worthy to remain on my land of Zion, but would have to be swept clean by just, yea, by justified judgments of God, to send thee to the world of departed spirits where you transgress no more in this mortal existence of probationary testing; which I, the Lord your God, have sent all mankind to be tested, allowing good and evil to be placed before all, sending my Spirit -- which is only good, of the inspiring unto good -- to the mind and heart of every man, woman, and child who would receive and listen to what they call their conscience unto righteous works, choosing good, eschewing and casting off evil.

8. And thus all have their agency, as they come to mature years more especially, even the age of accountability; yea, even by the age of eight years old, a child knows good from evil.

9. Thus saith the Lord: As you continue in the spirit of murder of unborn children, and then become aggressive when peaceful means could be used -- I command thee to repent!

10. I am the God of Creation.

11. Cease these murderous ways.

12. Cease your military actions in nations who have not thus attacked thee.

13. I, the Lord, command thee to repent unto a bringing forth of a change of policy and intent, and even justice served upon leaders of nations, thus saith the Lord, within each nation by their lawmaking bodies, and not think that you can transgress the borders of another nation aggressively and perform murder -- thine own pride satisfied, and not correct principle of law-abiding and just ways being followed.

14. Thus I send this corresponding of mine own words to the leader of this nation, to his Cabinet, to lawmakers of high standing.

15. I reveal my word to thee: Repent of thy murderous and immoral ways, the leaders of this nation as well as the peoples of this nation, for you have offended thy God, the great numbers in millions celebrating in their hearts the murder of a soul who could have been taken peaceably, and tried before the courts in the jurisdiction appointed, and of justice, by the nation that could have apprehended him.

16. Thus saith the Lord: Let this wicked generation repent speedily, lest my cleansing process sweep them off my land of Zion and leave them neither root nor branch -- in earthquake, tornado, storm and windstorms, pestilence, hail, and famine, the overflowing scourge and desolating sickness promised this wicked generation if they repent not.

17. For I am the God that made you. You are sons and daughters of God sent to a probationary earth to be tested what you will choose.

18. And when leaders of nations choose wickedness, I, the Lord, execute judgment upon them through righteous justice administered, even overthrowing leaders of nations, removing them from power, and, at times, sweeping the wicked of a nation off the earth, where they can further repent, if they will, in the world of departed spirits; I being a God of love, laboring for the salvation of all, whether on earth, whether they be spirits yet unborn who shall be sent to this probationary earth, preserving their

lives unto those who can beget them unto correct principles, just and righteous, to earn an eternal salvation; and also among those in the world of departed spirits.

19. My Gospel message shall go to all on this earth and in the world of departed spirits, now and in the future giving.

20. And I shall be called justified as every knee bows and every tongue confesses that Jesus is the Christ, a God over all creation, and He ruleth righteously, and He hath done right toward all peoples, nations, kindreds, and tongues.

21. This shall be declared in future time as truth is revealed and all secrets are made known.

22. And thus saith the Lord to the leaders of this nation and all nations: All your secret acts and intentions of the heart shall be revealed in the Millennial Reign of Peace, in the government of God in Zion, and sent forth to the nations, and in the day of judgment when you stand before a just God in the resurrection;

23. For I am the Resurrection and the Life, and the God that shall judge thee, appointed by my Father, Elohim, even Ahman; for I am Son Ahman, to perform that work of judging all mankind.

24. Ye shall stand before me.

25. I shall unlock thy mind, which shall reveal all the secrets of thy life, and nothing hidden; and you shall be judged by a just and holy God, even your Lord and Redeemer, Jesus Christ, who speaketh these words to the leaders of this nation through mine authority on earth.

26. Thus saith your God to thee: You shall be judged, and wickedness shall be punished with that degree of buffetings and suffering requisite for justice to be satisfied upon every person who repenteth not, even a full justice;

27. For my atoning power and suffering can only be a benefit to those who repent and accept my Gospel of salvation; yea, my message of salvation I shall soon send to every nation of the earth, both before my glorious appearing, to prepare many peoples, and a greater degree after my glorious coming to New Jerusalem, which shall rise in this generation.

28. This is my revealing to you at this time of a needed message to be given to the leaders of this nation of the United States of America, for you have offended your God in following wicked and unjust and corrupt principles, even unto murder, not having placed the accused before a tribunal, which you do in your own land for any criminal thus apprehended, of general policy, save those secret combinations which the leaders of this nation have sometimes followed in destroying life secretly in murderous intent.

29. Thus have the people of this nation offended their God, in glorying in murder, which could have been avoided.

30. The wicked shall slay the wicked, even in mob violence in thy land, if you heed me not; if this spirit of glorying in the loss of life, instead of mourning when one who is wicked passes on unprepared for salvation -- thus should all peoples do, understanding the purposes of thy God of Creation over thee, in bringing thee forth in this life of probationary and testing time to prove thy characters, whether or no you will love life and eternal principles that exalt, or transgress against the principles of life and earn a never-ending judgment of sorrow, not being exalted to be with the God who made thee.

31. And in the resurrection there shall be added to your mind the memory of having been born to a God of Creation, well-prepared; to know the purpose of this

mortal life, forgetting previous existence as a test, yet having my Spirit of light and life in thee at birth, and in thy growing years, to teach you good from evil, prompting you in what you call your mental conscience unto better works.

32. I am the God of Creation whose Spirit of light and life shineth upon all creation, to give all creation its existence.

33. I am a God of love that blesseth all.

34. And as death passeth on all, sending their spirits inhabiting their mortal bodies, the body lying in the grave, the spirits going to a world of living, a place of departed spirits where my Priesthood labors to administer the message of my salvation to all of every nation, kindred, tongue, and peoples; verily, I reveal to you, murderers hath no forgiveness.

35. If you take on the spirit of that sin and consent to this evil in the conduct of any person, you shall also have the same degree of judgment according to thy crimes in the flesh -- crimes against thy God, and eternal, exalting principles; crimes against thine own knowledge; for all shall be judged according to the light they received in this mortal existence, saith the Lord God, who administers life unto eternal life to those who love and obey laws that exalt, ways to their greatest ability to understand according to the light they receive; yea, even a God who can exalt thee unto eternal life, those who live laws of progression unto eternal life, of my message, and Priesthood, Church and Kingdom, of salvation powers that are now on the earth, preparing the way for the rise of Zion in fulness, a New Jerusalem built on the continent where the United States of America dwells at this time; and nothing can stay mine hand;

36. For I shall sweep the more wicked off the earth and preserve the more righteous unto my reign of righteousness, which shall be for a thousand years of my dwelling among men, to their knowing, in my power and glory in Zion; and the Kingdom of heaven coming forth to earth as the governing power over all nations.

37. Heed my word.

38. Repent of your murderous and immoral ways, which leads thee to a murderous way;

39. For thus are the corrupt in heart not able to govern themselves, being blinded by their own corruptions, justifying their murderous ways.

40. I, the Lord, shall bring them to justice, even in the eternal duration of time, feeling the wrath of a just God, who hath given them His Spirit in their minds and hearts as a conscience to know good from evil.

41. Let the policies of thy government cease this practice, is the command of thy Lord in this correspondence of needed message to thee. Amen.

42. Thus saith your Lord and Savior, Jesus Christ, further, to the people of the nation of the United States of America:

43. Repent ye! Repent ye! for my day of my glorious coming is nigh at hand.

44. Heed my word.

45. I have sent many warnings to the leaders of this nation, and to the peoples of this nation, of recent doing.

46. You must heed my words, lest there be upon you a greater judgment than you can bear, to leave you neither root nor branch of posterity upon the earth.

47. There are the sins of the shedding of innocent blood of unborn children legalized in this nation; the sins of corruption, of secret combinations to get gain by evil means, even of murder, upon

this land and among your peoples, even among the leaders of this nation, which I, the Lord, reveal openly, and shall reveal more in a time soon to come;

48. For you cannot hide from a God who seeth all things, and is just and holy and righteous, who shall judge all men according to their deeds done in the flesh.

49. Thus saith the Lord: Let there not be a celebration of thy peoples again of any man's being murdered, yea, his death.

50. Mourn over the loss of life when they go to the world of departed spirits, not having my message of salvation, unprepared for a glorious salvation, losing the same because they would not hear my word sent forth by testimony and holy writ.

51. Let not this people of this nation again glorify themselves in murder, wherein a man whose known location in another nation could have been apprehended by the authorities of that nation and placed before a tribunal, and not taken in death.

52. Thus saith the Lord: Let this cease in your natures.

53. Violence covereth this land, even in the spirit of the people of this nation.

54. Thus saith the Lord: I am the God of peace.

55. I will sweep those off the land where thy nation resides, in every nation on that continent, yea, on the North American continent who have violence in their nature.

56. For Zion is a place of peace, and my Zion shall rise, even New Jerusalem in the Center Stake of Zion, in Jackson County, Missouri, as I have proclaimed; and nothing can stay mine hand.

57. Thus I have sent this warning to the leader and peoples of this nation to repent, and know that my coming is nigh at hand. Amen.

SECTION REVELATION 120

Fundamentalist Church of Jesus Christ of Latter-day Saints
P.O. Box 840459
Hildale, Utah 84784

Thus Saith Jesus Christ, Son Ahman, to the Organization of Church Name, of Legal Name, Called the Church of Jesus Christ of Latter-day Saints, Now Not My Church, but of a Falling Away from My Priesthood; My Own Message to Thee of Pure Revealing, of Final Warning of Judgments Soon to Be Upon Thee and All on My Land of Zion. Thus I Bind Up the Law and Seal Up the Testimony Against All Who Are Against Me and My Holy Authority Among Men. Be Ye Now Warned of Judgments and to Be Now No More of My Name, Having Fought Against My Will and Holy Word. This Is My Message to Thee of Full Way Warning:

Revelation of the Lord Jesus Christ
Palestine, Texas
Wednesday, November 9, 2011

1. I, your Lord, send my word to the Church of Jesus Christ of Latter-day Saints, by name in legal way, to give you my own word of full warning, of full truth of true Priesthood authority in my Proclamation of Priesthood history and doctrine of Celestial Law still among men on earth.

2. You have been of a persecuting power for over one hundred years against my Priesthood.

3. Now know you are the fulfilling of Isaiah's words, of having made a covenant with death and an agreement with hell, when you upheld, and still uphold, action of Wilford Woodruff in signing away your rights to my Priesthood and my Celestial Law.

4. I now tell thee, you were rejected in full by God as any virtue being in thy organization when you allowed the so-called giving of Priesthood to those not yet to receive until I, the Lord, appointed, even to that race of people forbidden to hold Priesthood.

5. Be it known you were then fully rejected.

6. Let my warning be to you, as Isaiah prophesied, that the covenant with death and agreement of evil, with the doing away of my Celestial Plural Marriage Law and you fighting against my Priesthood, all shall come to an end, when I cause my judgments to cleanse Zion, even all North and South America, to prepare for my glory in New Jerusalem.

7. You have broken my Celestial covenant.

8. And by my warning coming to thee, and my Proclamation of true

Priesthood power and authority, and my own word of the continuing of my Celestial Law of Eternal Plural Marriage, is as a binding up the law and sealing up the testimony against thee; to leave neither root nor branch of any who stand up the wall of opposition against my Priesthood and against my Celestial Law of Plural Celestial Marriage; which can never be done away; for my law is eternal and cannot be done away by any; for I, God, am eternal, and I have guided my Priesthood to continue my law of Eternal Celestial Plural Union.

9. Now be of full repenting.

10. Now be of awakening.

11. You are of the world, of spiritual Babylon.

12. I shall cleanse my land of Zion. My warnings have now gone forth.

13. Now is my full warning to you.

14. Repent. Fight not against my Church, Priesthood, nor against my Celestial Law of Plural Celestial Marriage, lest full judgments come upon thee, is the word of your Lord Jesus Christ to your now unholy branch of falsehood doctrine, having compromised with the world, having fought against my Holy Priesthood.

15. Now know I shall reward all according to their doings; and preserve my Church, my Priesthood, my Celestial Law on earth, being fully justified to cleanse all nations now my Proclamation of pure unobstructed truth has been sent to all peoples, and to all leaders of nations, with my many recent warnings to all peoples and governing powers on earth.

16. Oh that ye would repent, and cease your false representing of my holy way; having lost your way; not able to offer salvation to any; not having my Holy Priesthood in your lives at all; yea, none in your current membership now hold Priesthood; therefore, your administrations are false and of no authority; not unto eternal salvation.

17. I am God, and shall cleanse all falsehoods from my land of Zion, is the word of the Lord to you. Amen.

Thus Saith the Lord Jesus Christ, Even Son Ahman, to the Nations of the Earth, Another Final Warning: Heed My Word. Amen.

(Comprising Section Revelations 121, 122, 123, 97, 115, 117)

I, the Lord Jesus Christ, Say My Holy Word Unto You, the Peoples of the Earth and Leaders of Nations, I Whose Right It Is to Rule, Receive Ye My Word Saying Thus:

SECTION REVELATION 121

Revelation of the Lord Jesus Christ
Palestine, Texas
Friday, November 4, 2011

1. Now, saith your Lord, come to me, all ye people of the earth.

2. I am God.

3. I have spoken.

4. Now be of preparing.

5. Now be ready, as I declared my word to mine apostles on earth in the day of my ministering among men.

6. Now be pure.

7. Let all peoples be my holy way exemplified.

8. Let all peoples only do right. Amen.

9. Thus saith Jesus Christ, your Lord and Ruling Power over all peoples: I am soon to cleanse all nations.

10. My time is soon.

11. Let all be ready.

12. Let this be as a final warning.

13. Let thy nation each be of repenting; for I come with power Celestial to purge all peoples. Amen.

SECTION REVELATION 122

Revelation of the Lord Jesus Christ
Palestine, Texas
Monday, November 7, 2011

1. Now let my word, even of Jehovah, be heralded to all peoples: My time is now upon all nations.

2. I am Jesus Christ, Son Ahman, God of all Creation.

3. I come to earth to rule during time of Millennium of Peace.

4. Celestial powers come to rule all nations that survive my eternal power of judgments.

5. I am God.

6. Heed my word, all ye peoples of the earth.

7. Now be more pure.

8. Be of holy noble way.

9. No longer be of spiritual Babylon.

10. Let all receive my Proclamation of historical and doctrine writing of my own pure word of pure revelation.

11. Let all be of a delivering my servant.

12. Let all be upholding my will; for I come as a refiner of gold and silver in eternal fire coming on all nations.

13. My holy Gospel shall be preached to every nation by my Priesthood.

14. All shall know I have spoken, and thus shall fulfill all my words.

15. Let nations make peace, lest my almighty power be upon aggressors. Amen.

SECTION REVELATION 123

Revelation of the Lord Jesus Christ
Palestine, Texas
Wednesday, November 9, 2011

1. Come to me, all ye peoples of the earth, saith Jesus Christ, before my overflowing scourge taketh thee in a never-ending death of full power, save ye should repent.

2. I am of the Celestial all-consuming fire cleansing power.

3. Let all beware how they treat my servant Warren Jeffs and my Priesthood and Church, for I shall bring full power to recompense to every person what they have chosen. Amen.

SECTION REVELATION 97

Thus Saith Jesus Christ, Even Son Ahman, To the Leaders of the Nations of the Earth A Great Call of Warning

Thus Saith Son Ahman, Even Jesus Christ, to All the Leaders of All Nations of the Earth, and Thus All Peoples of the Earth -- A Great Warning to Make Peace, and Prepare for My Glorious Appearing to All Peoples Who Survive the Great Judgments of God Nigh at Hand -- Hear Ye My Word:

Revelation of the Lord Jesus Christ
Eldorado, Texas
Wednesday, June 15, 2011

1. I, your Lord, even Jesus Christ, who is Son Ahman, the Beginning and the End, the Creator of heavens and earth, who upholds all people in their place, who has all power, who seeth and knoweth all things, and nothing is hidden; who dwells in the eternal vision of the power of Celestial Godhood over all creation, who hath redeemed all mankind from the grave, by whose power all things exist and continue -- I, the Lord, speaketh to the people of the earth, to the leaders of all nations:

2. You have not heeded my word in the warning I have sent forth, saith the Lord, to make peace among nations and not use your militaries in aggressive ways against your own peoples, nor against other nations, especially those nations who have sought, in a violent way, attacks upon nations who have not attacked them in kind.

3. This is the will of the Lord. If you heed me not, as my Spirit withdraws from those of darkened nature who will not

heed their God, the powers of darkness shall lead the leaders of nations and the peoples of nations unto the great war mine apostle John my Beloved testified of in that book of New Testament recording, yea, one-third part of the earth, of the population thereof, destroyed by their own violent ways.

4. And I, your God, have declared that if you will heed my word, your nation can be a surviving nation, by drawing into your lands your militaries, destroying your armored vehicles, as a witness you will make peace; and becoming a more pure and noble nation, not allowing those in power to uphold laws of the murder of unborn children, of Sodom, and of adultery, and licentious and corrupt ways.

5. And as you remove those outward evils, I have promised the more righteous of your peoples shall be of a surviving nature in the day of greater judgments soon at hand; yet you heed me not.

6. The great war shall take place if you heed me not, though I, a God of love and

peace, who shall reign among the children of men personally, with the powers of heaven coming to earth with me in my glory and mighty power, to the knowing of all surviving nations; I, the God of heaven, shall establish a thousand years of peace upon the earth, binding satan through the righteousness of the people responding to my word, yea, a righteousness revealed of thy God and joyfully lived through agency.

7. Thus is the will of the Lord to hear my warning again:

8. You see the upheaval in nations, leaders fearing their own peoples, and now unrest spilling into other nations.

9. I, the Lord, foretold this in my word I have sent, and you heed me not.

10. Hear my word, and make peace, lest you invite the dark powers to inhabit your souls and lead you to bloodletting, not justified, but out of the darkness of hate one against another, which shall envelop the soul who continues to uphold the ways of corruption, of the murder of unborn children, of immoral ways of Sodom and adultery, not considering the word of thy God, who hath declared that He will be a preserver of eternal power over any nation who will clean up themselves, the inside of the platter.

11. Remove these wicked laws that allow these heinous crimes, for many leaders have joined in secret combinations with the rich, with those of illegal practices, seeking riches and powers to gain and keep power; and it will not stand as a just God executes full justice upon any peoples who continue in these terrible sins that cannot be in any nation in the day of great peace when I shall reign on earth.

12. And the wicked shall fear and tremble at my coming, for I have sent mine own word through my servant on earth, and through mine own words preserved and published throughout the earth in that Bible of sacred keeping, even the testimonies of the prophets and apostles of old; and I am a God at hand.

13. Darkness covereth the minds of the people of the earth, because when I send my word, they heed me not, thus turning away from the God of glory who created you and the earth and gives you life -- all things -- both in what is termed nature, even in your own organization, and all things in heaven and on the earth testify of an intelligent God, creating all things; establishing laws of governing, of kingdoms, in plant life, animal life, and among the children of men;

14. For the children of men are children of God, sent to earth to receive an earthly body for their spirits, to purify and to prove they will choose good and overcome evil;

15. And my Spirit is sent forth to touch the hearts of all peoples on the earth to give them enlightenment and knowledge of good from evil.

16. And according to the laws of righteousness they have received, in their mortal lives and in their present enlightened way of laws of principles of righteousness, so shall they be judged, even eternally, in the day of the resurrection.

17. And I, a God of eternal power, have declared my word through my servant Joseph Smith in the day of his being on earth, now published in Book of Mormon, Doctrine and Covenants, Pearl of Great Price, and other writings of my servant Joseph Smith of my sacred revealing -- that I am a God who revealeth Himself from the heavens to a living representative on earth; and my Priesthood, Church, and Kingdom hath continued through a true and faithful line of Priesthood authority I have authorized on earth, giving you the

names, that you may know my Priesthood continues:

18. My servant Joseph Smith; then Brigham Young continued my work; John Taylor thereafter; then John W. Woolley, and Lorin C. Woolley after him; John Y. Barlow; Leroy S. Johnson after him; and my servant Rulon T. Jeffs;

19. And my servant on earth continues my work, though in bondage, though accused by those who are of wicked intent in their own lives, who do not see truth of the beauty of the Everlasting Gospel of Jesus Christ; who fighteth against my Church and Kingdom, even those of apostate influence, who have turned from my Gospel, Church, and Kingdom.

20. Yet I am the God of glory, who hath preserved my Church and Kingdom upon the earth.

21. And now you know, saith the Lord, that I am with my servants; and their testimonies are recorded on earth in the many sermons and teachings of authorized publishings through my Church and Priesthood.

22. Verily, thus saith the Lord: The Book of Mormon is true. My Doctrine and Covenants is mine own word, that which was revealed through my servant Joseph Smith, Jun., and my servant Brigham Young contained therein; and my testimony of Zion's mission is upon the earth and among the children of men, well published.

23. Missionaries were sent forth in the day my revelations were received, and lo, these many years have been in the hands of the peoples of the earth who would seek the same, and you heed me not.

24. And I have caused mine own word to be received and sent to the leaders of nations and the peoples of the nations of the earth, of recent receiving and sending, and you heed me not.

25. And thus saith the Lord: A day of the shaking of the earth is nigh at hand; and the overthrow of nations, and the sweeping of the more wicked out of every nation is soon to take place by war and pestilence, hail, and famine, and earthquake, and windstorms, and that which is of disease, of the overflowing scourge and desolating sickness, because you will continue in wickedness to the destruction of your souls.

26. And I am the God of eternal life; Endless is my name. And I labor with the peoples of the earth according to their understanding; and I speak in the language of men to my servant to your understanding, and to the understanding of any who will seek the interpretation thereof, in your own tongue, as you thus seek unto eternal truths from your Eternal God, your Creator, saith Jesus Christ.

27. I have called upon you to make peace and be prepared for the rise of New Jerusalem as my Zion on earth, on the continent of North America.

28. I created the earth. You know even the revolutions and movements of the earth and the planets follow a regular time, showing the order of my creating, an almighty power.

29. Awake! Repent ye, repent ye, before the day of greater judgments cometh.

30. And I shall be justified, saith your God, because I have sent my word of warning.

31. And if you heed me not, I, a God of truth and righteous and holy and perfect way, shall fulfill my word.

32. This is the word of the Lord. As I have spoken, so shall I fulfill.

33. The heavens weep over the peoples of the earth, though my word is given to plain language and understanding, being used to enlighten thy minds of that which is nigh at hand.

34. Nevertheless, a day of righteousness shall soon dawn upon all the earth in the rise of Zion and New Jerusalem; and Old Jerusalem shall be rebuilt after the devastating war in the land of Old Israel.

35. And mine Israel shall be gathered; and my Zion shall be the governing city and power over all the earth, and nothing can stay mine hand;

36. For any nation opposing my Zion shall be humbled by great judgments, until they humble themselves to bow to my righteous rule, saith the God of Creation, even Jehovah Christ, the Beginning and End.

37. Your very breath of life is of my free love-giving, saith the Lord to all peoples, nations, kindreds, and tongues.

38. Life and death are before you, and I offer you eternal life through obedience to my commandments in my Gospel of salvation through my authorized Priesthood on the earth.

39. Therefore, hear my word:

40. Make peace. Prepare for my messengers of salvation to come into your nations and lands, that I may preserve your peoples against a day of my coming, being known by the power of the shaking of the earth;

41. For before my glorious appearing, the sun shall be darkened and the moon be turned to blood, and parts of the earth will return, seeming to be the stars falling from heaven.

42. For I, the Lord, have all things in hand, in the heavens and the earth, and speaketh to my children on earth to hasten to prepare, being justified by sending forth my Gospel of salvation lo, these many years, and preserving my Church and Kingdom upon the earth; and soon to restore the full work of Zion's mission; of earning, each one who will receive my message of salvation, their eternal salvation; for my Priesthood, revealed from heaven, restored to earth, shall continue administering blessings and ordinances of everlasting life.

43. And thus I send my word to the peoples of the earth, that you may know, in a day when my word is fulfilled, that Zion is rising.

44. I shall preserve mine elect, as I have named in those prophecies of mine own speaking when in my ministry, as recorded in New Testament record -- they who receive my Gospel of salvation in fulness and obey my word.

45. And though with persecuting zeal the wicked have fought against my Church and Kingdom since the days of my restoring my Priesthood upon the earth, through the instrumentality of my servant Joseph Smith, I have preserved my Priesthood on the earth, and my Priesthood shall continue unto my glorious appearing in the powers of heaven coming to earth to govern the earth.

46. I am King of kings and Lord over all creation, saith Jesus Christ.

47. My day of peace shall be a marvel to all peoples of every land, nation, kindred, and tongue.

48. Mine elect will become the Saviors on Mount Zion, administering blessings unto eternal life through my Priesthood.

49. Oh, that ye would hear my word; for I shall fulfill that which I have spoken, to the salvation of many souls yet unborn,

to come forth in a day of righteousness and peace.

50. Men's hearts shall fail them who continue in these wicked practices I have declared you must not perform in your nations and peoples and lands, and among them.

51. It cannot be continued in my day of my coming, for I shall remove all such wicked practices from the earth, saith the God of heaven, through my judgments, which are just, because I have warned thee lo, these many years.

52. Now seek unto thy God in a prayerful walk.

53. Heed my published word I have sent forth.

54. Read my Policies of Governing Power published therein to know how your laws must be of a more righteous way, for justice and equity to be served on all peoples, for happiness to be reachable, obtainable in every nation; because thy God shall reign, and all shall willingly acknowledge my right to rule, being the God of Creation over all things.

55. And I, the Lord, send this, my word, as it were a final warning, that I may be justified in sending forth my judgments if you heed me not, to preserve the more righteous in every nation, and to clean my land of Zion of all wickedness, that Zion, the New Jerusalem, may rise unopposed by any earthly power.

56. For I shall be with mine elect, and they shall heed my voice and do my will, saith your God, the God over all peoples -- Jehovah Christ, who is Son Ahman, even Jesus Christ, who hath redeemed you from the grave, who will raise you up in the resurrection, even all peoples of every time of the earth, to answer for their deeds done in the flesh before a just God, who

shall reward thee according as your works have been.

57. And nothing is hidden from me, causing the wicked to tremble in the day of judgment, knowing of their evils.

58. Little children I have redeemed, who pass on to the world of departed spirits in their young years; and they shall have an everlasting salvation; for I am just -- having died before the age of accountability, and their reward shall be glorious.

59. Yet those who knew my Gospel of salvation was among the children of men, who would not heed my word, having opportunity to receive of the same, great shall be their mourning and lamentation in the day of judgment, in the day they are raised from the grave to stand before your Lord to be judged according to the measure they have measured to their fellow man.

60. And this message of salvation shall go forth, and nothing can stay mine hand. Amen.

61. I, the Lord, direct further:

62. The NATO nations must cease their attack, having become aggressors, now three times in coalitions of unity against nations who did not attack thee.

63. And these three witnesses come up before the heavens of your violent and unjust ways; when I, the Lord, have commanded you to cleanse the inside of the platter, your own peoples and laws, to not permit the murderous spirit to be among you, of the murder of unborn children; and the corrupt, immoral ways of Sodom and adultery; many leaders of the nations joining in secret combinations, with secret crime syndicates, to keep and maintain and gain power and influence on the earth; and nothing is hidden from thy God.

64. And I shall reveal your secrets in a day to come, which shall be spoken upon

the housetops; for you are promoting -- you who have military power to keep peace among nations and within your borders of righteous ways -- as you use that power to attack nations who have not attacked thee, you are not justified before the heavens, and you shall be broken up in your coalition, not being a defensive organization, but now becoming an offensive attacking organization.

65. And because of this, you are promoting war to break forth in other nations; and unrest is rising in many nations, which shall bring about the great desolating war upon all the earth, and sweeping the wicked off my land of Zion;

66. For I shall send forth other judgments as violence erupts in the nation where my Zion is to be built, because they heed me not, and they seek the destruction of my Church and Kingdom lo, these many years.

67. My word is true and cuts to the heart of those who thus are liars, and among the wicked, who will not heed my word after knowing my word is true;

68. And my word is in Bible, and in those scriptures I have named in this communicating.

69. Thus, awake! and be a repenting nature against the day of judgments nigh at hand, that I may preserve the more righteous among your peoples, of any nation who will turn to your God and overthrow these gross crimes I have named in this communication, that dwell in most nations of the earth.

70. I, the Lord, have spoken it. Amen.

SECTION REVELATION 115

Fundamentalist Church of Jesus Christ of Latter-day Saints
P.O. Box 840459
Hildale, Utah 84784

Thus Saith Jesus Christ, Who Is Son Ahman, Even God Over All in Heaven and Earth, to All Peoples of Every Nation, to Be Warned of Full Judgments Soon to Be of Full Power of Full Purging of All Wickedness of Greater Degree Than Heretofore Taking Place; Hear Thou My Holy Will:

Revelation of the Lord Jesus Christ
Palestine, Texas
Friday, October 28, 2011

1. Thus saith the Lord, even Jesus Christ, Redeemer and Holy One of Israel, to all people of the earth:

2. My coming is nigh.

3. Now prepare for my cleansing judgments of greater and more destructive life-taking power; for the nations will not hear nor heed my word.

4. Only greater judgments can turn the determined, more wicked-desiring mind to repentance.

5. Thus shall all soon feel my wrath, as you continue in the sins of immorality, murder of unborn children in nearly every nation now inhabiting my world; to now be of the full knowing that I have spoken, and I fulfill all my will and revelations given through him appointed as my Mouthpiece on earth, even my servant Warren Jeffs.

6. Now heed my word.

7. You cannot be of these gross crimes and survive my soon to be on earth greater cleansing and preparing judgments of an Eternal God; who is to soon appear to all peoples in glory and majesty Celestial; bringing with me the powers of heaven to rule over all peoples for the thousand years of peace.

8. Oh, hear my will --

9. Prepare ye, for I shall recompense all according to the measure they have measured to their fellow man; to be a full Judge over all through eternal power of full Godhood of holy and Eternal Power. Amen.

SECTION REVELATION 117

Thus Saith Jesus Christ, Son Ahman, Who Is Jehovah Christ, to All Peoples of All Lands, Nations, and Governing Powers on Earth, Warning of Final Cleansing Soon to Be Upon My Land of Zion; There Also Coming Same Cleansing Upon All Nations

Thus Saith God Over All, Even Jesus Christ, My Holy Will Revealing My Soon Coming Events Upon My Land of Zion; Also Upon All Peoples of Every Nation; A New Revealing, to Know I Have Warned All, and Will Be of Full Power of Cleansing:

Revelation of the Lord Jesus Christ
Palestine, Texas
Monday, October 31, 2011

1. I who is over all things, by whom all things were created, and by whom all continue in organizing power of existing in present personal sphere of action; even Jesus Christ, Son Ahman, the Beginning and the End, speak to all peoples on the earth, now to learn of a judgment of full power of my sending; a storm of great destructive power upon the nation of United States in America, even my nation of my coming to build New Jerusalem.

2. This shall paralyze many parts of thy nation for a time, causing great distress, to show thee I have spoken warnings of

recent sending; and that as I speak, so shall I fulfill.

3. Such shall be the result of this devastating storm.

4. You shall know it is of my power sent to humble my nation of soon removal if they continue in murder of unborn children, and Sodom and immoral ways not of the pure way of my coming; for I must cleanse all nations of these sins to allow them knowledge of my presence on earth as Ruler and Eternal Power. Amen.

5. Thus is the Lord's will, to be of full knowing of my coming soon at hand.

6. Let all in this nation of my New Jerusalem to rise, be ready.

7. Only they who are of purity of living can survive my full measure of purifying cleansing; leaving only my Order Eternal of Zion on the land of the Zion of our God, even North and South America; a land that will be of righteousness after all wicked inhabitants are swept off by my eternal power, they who no longer care for pure holy way of your Lord, who commanded to not kill, neither commit adultery, nor anything immoral like unto that sin of personal defiling.

8. Let all be full of pure noble desire.

9. Leave alone my people.

10. Let my servant go.

11. Let all men of my Priesthood in prison go free. Amen.

12. Thus is the revealing of the God of Creation over all; to know my time is soon to be on earth with cleansing powers; to govern all peoples in a Millennium of Pure Holy Peace.

13. Let all know they shall be judged, who is of purity of living, to be worthy of preservation by my grace and power.

14. Let all nations be warned again.

15. Let only thy will be to do as I have said, to purge the gross contagious crimes of murder of unborn children and of Sodom and adulterous ways from among thy nation, each one; lest great and full power of cleansing cometh.

16. Know when North America is of full judging that my time is soon; also when Israel is a people gathering unto my land.

17. Let all be my Israel who would be of pure way of holy walk before Him who is your Lord, Savior, Judge, and Holy Advocate unto redeeming power eternal.

18. Let this, my word, be as another full warning and call to final preparing; and to cause the full way of my Holy Priesthood to be free to do my will on earth, to build up my Zion.

19. Let Zion now be the way of governing power over all peoples.

20. I am with them, my Church and people of the way of salvation.

21. Let them, even my Church, be of full freedom to serve their Lord in full Celestial Plural Marriage Law unobstructed.

22. Let my United Order law no longer be under attack, as my consecrated lands and homes in the court's ruling have been taken from my holy Order.

23. Let all now be of a full way of pure holy way of giving to all pure, true, noble ruling of delivering my people.

24. Let now there be only my people to dwell on my consecrated lands where they have been removed out of the hands of my Priesthood, now of tribute to ungodly ruling board by court appointment; unjust court interfering in my true religion; thus breaking the law of Constitution religion freedom guaranteed.

25. Let also my Priesthood in prison go free, as they only have done my will

in abiding Celestial Plural Marriage by my own will revealing my law to be lived by them.

26. No governing power on earth of authority, especially where religious freedom is of constitutional guarantee, can be of an interfering power in religion of my guiding.

27. Let the nation humble themselves who are thus of a persecuting zeal against my holy Celestial Law of Celestial Marriage of Plural revealing; only to be of my Church, not for the world. Amen.

28. Now be of hastening to prepare for my great power to soon be of judgment upon the land. Amen.

29. This holy will of God is to now be of a full warning to the people over all the earth, wherever they reside; that when they see United States in America humbled by great power of my causing many to be of a life-taking, then they shall be aware I, your Lord, fulfill all my will.

30. Now be of full way of full cleansing on part of leaders and peoples of nations to remove the greater sins I have named that are among you. Amen.

31. Jesus, your Lord, hath spoken, and shall fulfill unto full knowing my coming in power of my might in the clouds of heaven, which hideth many things from the seeing of mankind, until I cause my coming in full power to be known among you, to be of full way Celestial in governing authority over all surviving nations.

32. Let Australia know population on low lands shall be of a tsunami tidal wave.

33. Many shall perish who will not move to higher lands of elevation.

34. Let China also be warned to only cleanse my land of wickedness, not my people.

35. Let also all nations leave alone my Zion, lest great whirlwind judgments speak the justice of an offended God. Amen.

36. Thus is the will of Jesus, your Lord, to the sure knowing of all peoples; so that when they see my will fulfilled, they know I have spoken beforehand; and are thus fully aware I shall fulfill all my will as I have revealed through my servants, the Prophets; and mine own word found in New Testament record. Amen.

37. The Lord also revealeth to Russia to not remain on my land of Zion, lest full powers of whirlwind judgment come upon thee.

38. Though you believe me not, my judgments shall convince all they must not come against my people Israel.

39. Let the nation of Iran cease all aggressive power against neighboring lands and peoples, lest you become a nation no more; only to be of subjugation to a foreign power, to no longer be of aggression; for I shall reward thee with full cleansing judgments as you promote violence against my Israel or other neighboring nations. Amen.

40. Let Turkey aid Israel in day of great attack against my Israel, lest you also fall and become a subject nation. Amen.

41. Let also my holy land of New Jerusalem only be for my Church and Priesthood people of Zion's preparation in their lives, my Celestial Law of holy Eternal Union lived. Amen.

42. Thus have I been warning all peoples to prepare, I already in the midst of my people, notwithstanding full persecuting powers coming against my Church.

43. Read fully my new publishing of Proclamation of full giving my history by my own word sent to teach all about my Priesthood and my Celestial Plural

Marriage Law continuing among men on earth since I revealed my Priesthood and my Celestial laws in the day of my holy Prophet Joseph Smith; continuing these gifts through a faithful order of full Celestial authority from heaven, my Keyholders well honored by me in my own word given; now printed and sent forth to all nations.

44. Let my Keyholder of full authority go free, my now Prophet, Mouthpiece, and pure sealing authority unto sealing blessings unto eternal life.

45. Let all know, how they treat my Priesthood on earth, so shall I be to them a Savior, if faithful, or a Judge of whirlwind almighty power if they reject me by hindering the progress of my Church on earth.

46. Let all murderous secret combinations in every nation be punished and overthrown.

47. Let secret agencies of violent ways of managing your people's behavior be no longer in your governing powers.

48. Let truth, justice, purity of living, equity of opportunity of freedom of living and of worship be of a full upholding by all governing powers on earth; for I shall cause the waters to boil, volcanoes, earthquakes, storms, the desolating sickness of an overflowing scourge, also pestilences of disease, and other destructive powers shall soon be felt by all peoples, nations, tongues, kindreds, and governing powers.

49. Let my people be my people, not to be cast out nor driven.

50. Let my people also hasten to prepare to be worthy of greater Celestial powers; to assist in governing the earth in full power and Priesthood authority.

51. Now come full measure to be among my full law of Zion. Amen.

52. Let the people of Central America, also pure bloodline of Lamanite and Nephite people in Americas, be ready to be as a full power of helping thy God cleanse all wickedness off my lands of Zion; a battle-ax in mine hands to the fear of all the nations and their peoples on my holy lands of Zion; to have my heavenly powers assist you of pure line of Israel to be an army of cleansing power against the wicked on my land of Zion. Amen.

53. Let also Bolivia with Ecuador hear my word, to cleanse their own nation, each one, of the gross evils among the gentile nations of murder of unborn children, also Sodom and immoral ways, to then be of a cleansing authority of other peoples.

54. I shall cause my holy power to be on thee. Amen.

55. Let also Nicaragua be of a humbling, as her leaders have tried to be of oppressive way on her own peoples.

56. Let all peoples be at peace when I appear; for my full power shall soon be felt by neighboring nations of more pure way, humbling wicked nations; also to receive my full gifts of blessings of life, of food, clothing, shelter, to remain intact and with you, each nation or peoples who thus receive this, my word, and heed my will, saith Jesus Christ, your Lord. Amen.

57. I am soon to use whom and what I will, saith God over all, to cleanse all nations.

58. Be ye ready. Amen.

SECTION REVELATION 124

Jesus Christ, Son Ahman, Speaketh His
Full Warning of Judgments to All Nations

Thus Saith Jesus Christ, God Over All Creation, to All Nations, Peoples, Kindreds, Tongues, and Governing Powers on Earth; My Own Holy and Eternal Power Authority of Truth and Holy Power of My Bringing Full Power to Earth, to Rule Over All Peoples Who Survive Judging Powers Soon to Come in Full Power; Thus Calling on All to Heed My Word, Saying Thus:

Revelation of the Lord Jesus Christ
Palestine, Texas
Saturday, November 12, 2011

1. Thus saith your Lord of Power over all nations, to all people on the earth: I have heralded my own word to all nations.

2. I am God.

3. I have spoken.

4. I shall fulfill. Amen.

5. Now repent.

6. You are now soon to be purified by fire and my whirlwind judgments of eternal power.

7. O ye fallen and perverse generation, how long I have called thee to repentance, and you heed me not.

8. I shall be as a full purifier of all nations, peoples, tongues, kindreds, over all powers of every land.

9. Now herald my will to all thy people in thy land; that the God of glory cometh, to be Ruler over all people, to have all accountable for deeds done in the flesh; to know I am, and to have all thy works known that are hidden; yea, all secrets revealed to all people.

10. Now heed my word:

11. I have sent my Proclamation to all people on earth, of my holy authority on my land of my coming.

12. My Proclamation is of your awaking to eternal truth, that I have commenced years and also ages ago to send forth my message of my coming.

13. I am the Creator over all.

14. I shall fulfill all my purposes of eternal and Celestial authority of the Father.

15. I am to soon be your Judge.

16. I shall be only the way of pure cleansing soon to all peoples.

17. My word is power of truth.

18. My way is holy.

19. My purposes are eternal.

20. No one can stay my hand.

21. Heed my word, lest full judgment come upon thee, each one, in the full giving of my power of the cleansing of thy land. Amen.

22. Thus shall all feel my wrath, for your murder of unborn children, for your

Sodom and licentious corrupt way of destroying innocence, virtue, life of the most innocent of all peoples, the very spring of life in unborn children; an evil practice in most nations.

23. Now let it be known murder is the unforgivable sin.

24. Let this cause all to be of a ceasing of this most heinous crime, upheld by most nations by legal consent.

25. I shall cause rulers to be judged for allowing this most horrible evil to continue; innocent blood on thy skirts.

26. Let all be awake to thy plight in eternity of judgment of a just God, who favors purity to be of pure way.

27. Let children be of most favored protecting, innocent of sin; only learning ways of parents, of peoples they are among.

28. Now know thy sin is so great, I must cleanse all nations by judgments to prepare for my coming; a glory eternal from heaven; a power of pure fire of all-consuming power, to consume every corruptible thing.

29. My holy word has been among you for many generations.

30. Now be ready for my coming.

31. Let all be my holy people, a people ready to receive Zion in full way.

32. I am soon to be their Deliverer.

33. Nothing can stay my hand in gathering mine elect from all nations, unto New Jerusalem, a holy city of my making.

34. All shall be my full way of pure holy power who dwell therein. Amen.

35. Now let my message go forth to all thy peoples, ye rulers of nations.

36. I shall be the Holy Power Celestial that comes among all peoples to your knowing.

37. Thus I, God, am justified to purge all nations.

38. I am the God of Power.

39. I am thy Advocate with the Father unto you earning eternal salvation if you repent.

40. I shall judge all in the day of resurrecting power.

41. I have conquered death.

42. I am over all.

43. Nothing is hidden.

44. I know your whole and personal lives in the secrets of thought, of desire, of intent; of true way of full truth known without lies of thy making hindering truth to be revealed by me in day of judging thee.

45. I shall reward thee for deeds done in this life.

46. I am the God of Creation.

47. I shall fulfill all my will concerning thy creation as a son or daughter of my creating.

48. Thus shall all things be put right; and evil shall be overthrown in total. Amen.

49. Let this holy word now go forth, saith Jesus Christ, God over all, to thy peoples.

50. Let all be of ready power of purity in their lives, lest sudden destruction come.

51. Let all have this published.

52. Let all heed my will.

53. I am the only way of salvation.

54. I shall come to declare my way eternal.

55. Now be ready, is the call of thy God. Amen.

SECTION REVELATION 125

Jehovah, Your Lord, Even Jesus Christ, Son of God, the Beginning and the End, Speaketh Full Warning to National Leaders and Peoples of United States of America, Even My Own Word

Jehovah, Even Jesus Christ, Speaketh to High and Local Leaders in Governing Positions, Also to All People of United States of America, My Own Will of Warning in Full Measure, Even of My Holy Will Revealed from Heaven:

Revelation of the Lord Jesus Christ
Palestine, Texas
Sunday, November 13, 2011

1. A word of full warning from God, even Jesus Christ, through mine authority on earth, Warren; to be of my full power to deliver my will, even eternal power bequeathed to do a labor of my Holy New City of holy power rising as land of my full power is of a cleansing in full.

2. For this is my word to all high and local leaders of governing power on the land of the now peoples of present nation of United States of America:

3. I, God, have spoken.

4. I have sent my many warnings to show all I am speaking to all nations, to prepare for my coming in full almighty power of eternal power, even to cleanse my land of Zion in full way of fire Celestial consuming every corrupt and evil thing on my land.

5. All shall know I have previously spoken, when full cleansing power is in full way happening.

6. Receive ye my word.

7. I am God.

8. I speak. I tell only truth.

9. I raise up one nation and throw down another.

10. All are subject to my authority on earth for their continued existence.

11. All must bow to my rule.

12. All must be cleansed to dwell among my Celestial powers coming to earth.

13. All will be judged.

14. All will know I am of full power over all the earth.

15. This is my earth of probationary testing.

16. I am Ruler over all.

17. I have full authority from the Father to do full cleansing before my full appearing.

18. Now learn of my holy way to cleanse all off my land of Zion.

19. New Jerusalem shall rise after present wicked and perverse peoples now dwelling on my holy land are of full removing by destructive powers; unto no one left that is of unclean ways of the present generation.

20. Let all know I speak, to be justified.

21. I am now of full way justified.

22. I have sent many warnings, even to all on my earth.

23. Now be warned.

24. You must not be of immoral nor evil intent ways of living.

25. You must be pure in heart to remain, unto my glory preserving the holy people, of my raising up, unto New Holy City of my holy power.

26. Let all now be holy.

27. Let all repent.

28. Let immoral, licentious way of present peoples be no longer.

29. Let all my way of pure abiding more holy way be lived.

30. Now learn of my full cleansing.

31. My earth has had parts removed heretofore in bygone days.

32. Parts of my earth soon returneth, causing great and full shaking.

33. Many shall perish.

34. Also sea shall heave beyond its bounds;

35. Also pestilence of disease, also insects, animals, and the weather power used in full, as a sudden whirlwind of full power of cleansing.

36. I am God, and have full power to do my will of a sudden.

37. Mountains shall be raised up to cover most wicked cities.

38. Some shall be sunk in the earth;

39. Others be shaken in full way, leaving no inhabitants remaining therein.

40. War shall come. An invading power on east coast cometh; also another on west coast; some from the south, to destroy many of this most wicked nation ever to dwell on my land of Zion.

41. Now heed my word.

42. All this is of soon happening.

43. All things are ready.

44. All my people of pure holy living are ready.

45. Be ye ready. Amen.

46. Now be believing.

47. All my people of pure holy living are not now gathered.

48. My Spirit labors with honest minds to be believing.

49. Some in many lands are of full way believing.

50. Some are of repenting gift of my answering prayers.

51. I also have a new people coming.

52. They are on a part of my earth, the lost tribes of Israel, who shall also help cleanse my holy Zion land.

53. Let believing Israel hearken.

54. Know I have all power to cleanse all nations.

55. Know I am God, and my power Celestial from heaven cometh to govern all people.

56. Let this solemn reality facing all be as an holy warning.

57. My people know of my power being their guide.

58. My servant must now go free.

59. Let my people have full possessing of land and of homes.

60. Let prisons release my sons of pure living.

61. Let Texas now be of true way of justice.

62. Let my servant go.

63. He is innocent.

64. He doeth my will.

65. He is not of the order of bowing to governing powers of man when I, his Lord, am the power of authority to guide my Church and people, in living Celestial

holy laws of pure religious way; supposed to be of protection by the law of the order of constitutional protection of religious freedom.

66. My law of Celestial Union of eternal and of pure holy motive of marriage plural, in my Church only, is of me.

67. I am God.

68. They only seek to obey my Celestial eternal power law of a holy authority revealed from heaven.

69. Now let them go free, lest I send my judgment of full cleansing.

70. I have spoken.

71. Heed my word, all governing powers on nation where my Church now is on earth, even the nation of United States of America. Amen.

72. Now heed my full warning.

73. Celestial powers cometh to fully cleanse the land of New Jerusalem.

74. None shall remain who are not pure before me, saith the Lord, to this wicked, perverse, corrupt people now ripened in full way in iniquity; upholding, by legal consent, murder of unborn children; also of Sodom and of immoral ways.

75. Let nation cleanse these evils from among them to be of survival. Amen.

76. Now learn of Zion's rising.

77. My Celestial powers cometh to cleanse, then they bring Celestial way of living in holy pure way, in ways of governing, in holy purity of plant and animal life; in ways of only dwelling in peace on earth; my holy power Celestial made known to all surviving peoples on earth.

78. Babylon the great whore of all the earth falleth at my appearing; unto full way no longer being on earth.

79. I send my representatives of authority power from New Jerusalem.

80. I shall send my holy salvation ordinance of pure holy religion to all peoples remaining on earth after whirlwind power judgments sweep the more wicked from the face of the earth.

81. Then riseth in all nations my Church of salvation, eternal power.

82. Then cometh a Millennial Reign of Peace; Christ, your Lord, ruling all nations unto peaceful dwelling among all men.

83. Let this be the full warning.

84. Let all be of my way of more pure holy dwelling.

85. Let no one say I hath not sent my word.

86. I have done so to all nations.

87. My holy writing of Proclamation, of naming my Priesthood authority restored to earth, hath gone to all nations.

88. Now believe unto doing; even as I command all peoples everywhere to repent, lest full cleansing powers come on them.

89. Let United States of America leaders repent of their most wicked unholy ways, most of immoral personal way.

90. Let also all peoples bow to my rule.

91. Let all be my holy nation on my land of Zion; for by cleansing authority powers, so shall it be.

92. I have now spoken. Now know as I speak, so shall I do. Amen.

93. Now hear more of my will:

94. Let secret combination seeking to destroy my servant now be of full way of removal, lest you seek to be against thy God in full way of eternal judgment.

95. I see all things.

96. Secret combining of evil design

hath put him in the place of bondage, and still seek to destroy my servant in way of violence.

97. This is of my detecting.

98. Let his life be protected, is my word to all governing powers in place of his unjust and fully innocent holding, unjust governing powers holding my innocent representative on earth, who only seeks my holy way eternal, for salvation of all who would seek salvation of their Lord; even I, Jesus Christ, who sendeth this, my own revealing, to all peoples on my land of soon rising New Jerusalem, an Holy City of my building through revealing Celestial gifts. Amen.

SECTION REVELATION 126

The Kingdom of God, of Zion
2420 County Road 300
Eldorado, Texas 76936

I, Jehovah, Even Jesus Christ, the Great I AM, Send My Own Word to Nation of Israel, a Counsel and Warning to Prepare for War Soon Upon Thee, Saying Thus:

Revelation of the Lord Jesus Christ
Palestine, Texas
Monday, November 14, 2011

1. I who reigns on high, your Lord and Redeemer, Jesus Christ, call on the nation of Israel to be of full power to defend thy nation, and to have my preserving powers.

2. Let thy nation cause all her people to now prepare, for war of greatest way soon shall be upon thee.

3. Believe you must be ready of a soon way.

4. Prepare to be rationing.

5. Be of building up supplies of military and of civil powers, providing emergency food, blankets, medical supplies, clothing, all necessaries of life.

6. Also cleanse thy laws to absolute upholding of principle of life, not allowing unborn children to be murdered.

7. Let immoral media be stopped.

8. Let there be a stop to the gaining power by secret murders authorized by leaders, so thy God Jehovah can be fully justified in preserving you as a nation; else many of your peoples shall be taken in the holocaust.

9. Yet thy nation shall be of my preserving, unto Israel being preserved for salvation labor among nations who are of peace.

10. Let Israel believe.

11. Let Israel no longer be of joining with any immoral nor murderous ways.

12. Be ye of an open mind.

13. These are eternal principles of life.

14. Let also leadership be sought who upholds virtue and purity of the law of life upheld; for unborn children are most innocent of all, not able to be protected of themselves.

15. Be a protector of life.

16. Let also all my other warnings of my judgments on nations be heeded.

17. I am Jehovah, Jesus Christ, your Lord. Amen.

SECTION REVELATION 127

Jesus Christ, God Over All, Sendeth a Final Warning to All Peoples of Every Land on Earth, to Be Heeded Now by All Peoples

Thus Saith Your Lord and Righteous Judge, Even Jesus Christ, to All Peoples on Earth, to All Leaders of Nations, to All Religious Societies, to All Common People, and All Governing Powers, the Word of Your Lord, to Be Heeded Now, Who Saith:

Revelation of the Lord Jesus Christ
Palestine, Texas
Sunday, November 20, 2011

1. I, even Jesus Christ, your holy Redeemer over all flesh, even unto the giving life eternal to pure holy sons and daughters; also to be Judge of all in the holy resurrection, speaketh to the whole earth, even all peoples; that I am soon to come in glory of full heavenly power; to be the Governing Authority over all peoples; to be of a full cleansing of all nations; to show that righteousness is of me, to be holy unto full way eternal.

2. Let all now repent, to be holy as I am holy.

3. Let all be pure as I am pure.

4. I can be your loving Father as you become pure in living my law of holy pure way eternal; even my whole law of my holy love extant becoming thy way extant. Amen.

5. Now be ye believing.

6. I am soon to cause all my promises to be fulfilled.

7. All need to be of me to survive the day of my coming; even Judah, my driven persecuted people soon to rise in full power of my giving, saith Jehovah, who am Jesus Christ, the Great I AM; the Holy Redeemer of Israel spoken of in Isaiah.

8. Let all read my revealed word through my servant in Bible writ of ancient revealing, even Isaiah, to know of my coming revealed to Israel; not to all peoples, lo, these many years of earth's history.

9. My name is of holy way.

10. I only do right, judge right, labor in righteous power.

11. None can be above me, nor dictate me, only my Father of all creation, Ahman; I being Son Ahman.

12. Now behold, I say unto all, be ye clean and pure, holy, noble, godly in all conversing and dwelling on earth, in the Gospel of salvation as contained in Bible of true holy translating; for many precious parts of my word have been altered or removed by evil powers in Bible.

13. I have caused my servant of holy calling in his time on earth, even my Prophet, Seer, Revelator, and Prophet authority among men, Joseph Smith, Jun., to reveal my own full Gospel in sacred receiving.

14. I have caused my own revealed word to now be published to all nations in my now publishing of Priesthood succession on earth among men in my Proclamation; my own revealing to all peoples of the Priesthood power revealed from heaven by ministering of angels, the same principle of ministering as recorded in my holy scripture in New Testament; showing I am of the way of continuing offering salvation to all peoples through a living power of eternal authority; even through my servant on earth now among you, now in bondage through the conspiring of wicked men and women, seeking to hinder my holy word from being fulfilled.

15. Notice how original charges are all of an overthrow in first cases arresting him.

16. Now my servant is of life sentence to be confined by a power of no just way; not preserving my right to rule as God among mine elect people who have received my holy law of Celestial Holy Eternal Union of Plural Union Marriage, a law of Bible upholding, to the knowing of all religious societies.

17. Now I have my authority of full power among you, and you show your evil and ungodly way as a nation of now persecution power against a religion -- a religion revealed from me, your Lord and Master, Jesus Christ.

18. Now I have revealed thy hearts, to be justified to be of whirlwind judgments upon wicked powers in a land of professed freedom.

19. Evil powers combined with the power of governing power man-attack against mine authority and mine holy pure law of my own Priesthood power of eternal power, Celestial Plural Marriage; a law confined only to my authority, to only be lived by my holy will revealing who is of pure noble way; to be of only pure holy living in raising up unto me a holy people of full faith and holy love of my inspiring.

20. Now receive my revealed holy will to all peoples --

21. I cometh; and with me ten thousand of the saints of resurrected Priesthood power of Celestial world, of heaven coming to earth, soon to happen.

22. Let all prepare.

23. I shall cause all who imprisoned my holy authority to soon feel my wrath.

24. You shall know I have tested all, to reveal hearts unto full cleansing my land of Zion, unto a holy power Celestial soon to come; to first cleanse my land by whirlwind judgments; then cometh thy Lord in eternal power of legitimate governing authority.

25. I shall be as a burning fire, consuming every corruptible thing, as spoken of in my scriptures; even in Isaiah, also Ezekiel, and other of my servants, the Prophets; causing my own word to be on earth for all peoples to know of my

glory, power, of holy power, coming to all peoples.

26. A legitimate administrator is among you, yet held in unrighteous captivity by a nation of now murder ways; all to be of a way to be persecuting my chosen.

27. Let all know I have been merciful to all.

28. Now be of full awakened way of knowing death overtaketh the wicked suddenly, in full judging powers.

29. Let all be of learning how my word was fulfilled, recorded in Matthew chapter 24 in New Testament, of the destruction of Jerusalem, also Judah being scattered to all nations.

30. Let my holy word be of full power resting on thy soul as I spake, as recorded in this chapter, of my latter-day coming in full judging and holy cleansing power, to be among men a thousand years until all of all peoples have heard my plan of salvation.

31. Let all be aware I am God. I have spoken; and as I speak, I also fulfill.

32. Let this holy revealing prompt all honest in heart to be now preparing through humble repentance for my coming.

33. This from thy God who created all; who is as a Judge Eternal over all peoples.

34. I am soon to deliver mine elect unto Zion being redeemed.

35. Let all be of a hastening to be ready soon. Amen.

36. I, even God, have thus spoken to all nations.

37. Receive my holy will, of eternal life earning by all of holy pure way eternal in their receiving mine holy power through my holy authority on earth; yea, my servant Warren Jeffs, now in bondage, needing true just courts of appealing power to heed my own word to release him and my other holy servant Merril Jessop, a son of pure holy way; yet court of unjust way allowed him in his aged and poor health condition to linger in prison for only doing my will.

38. Thus another testimony against this nation lingereth in prison house, to be as a sounding voice against nation of corruption that seeks to be of a full power to destroy my Priesthood and my Celestial Eternal Union Law.

39. Now be of heralding my will -- I shall be as a flaming fire to consume all wickedness of Zion's land, even North and South America.

40. Be ye ready.

41. Be pure, is the word of the Lord to all. Amen.

42. Now let nation know truth, that the apostate enemy witness against all these of my holy people now in prison in Texas unjust rulings and prejudiced jury assembled in each trial, even she who was once pure, has become an full power of corruption in her own life; of a unholy way of living; having been of Celestial Eternal Plural Union in Marriage living, then becoming as an adulterous woman; even so it is, as she is upheld by all as reliable, yet corrupt in all ways of living, like unto this wicked, unholy and adulterous and Sodom generation now on my land.

43. You uphold immoral ways of living, yet fight against the most holy way of Eternal Union; not believing in the order of eternal lives yourselves; yet you set yourselves up as judges of my Eternal Union law, a way of the God of Creation, living this law in Celestial power Himself, to create all peoples through a law of progression in heaven and on earth.

44. Behold, my holy law exalts to pure living.

45. All must be of my Holy Priesthood

in pure holy faith living to enter into and live my holy law.

46. Yet among you, even all nations, adultery is common to never be of a prosecuted way of living; which evil destroyeth souls and breaketh up families entire.

47. Verily I say unto the nation, your sins are a stench before God and angels, soon to be wiped off the earth by the besom of judgment power. Amen.

48. I have thus reasoned with you, this now generation on my land of Zion, where I must raise up Israel to build New Holy Jerusalem in the place named, even Jackson County, Missouri.

49. Learn of my holy way.

50. Come full measure to live pure way, lest cleansing power showeth all I have thus spoken. Amen.

51. Let all peoples know I have again spoken from heaven to earth concerning my holy way coming to earth in full power, to govern all nations in laws of pure holy ways of dwelling before thy Lord of Glory.

52. Let all be of full ready power to be held of full way upholding Celestial powers of governing soon to be known among all peoples.

53. Let my servant Warren Jeffs go, to be among mine elect, lest you bring my full cleansing of the land where he is in bondage, unjustly held. Amen.

54. Now be of great concern a war cometh to nation holding him.

55. He of my holy power standeth before me continually as a holy testifying power against all people of this nation, I having caused him to travel much before unholy way of imprisonment took place.

56. Now the law is of a binding upon this nation by my power, the testament is sure against you, and I am justified to send greater whirlwind power judgments against present unjust nation.

57. My Zion is rising in way of eternal power.

58. You cannot stop the God over all from fulfilling my own will of eternity purpose of salvation for all believing peoples. Amen.

59. Now receive more of my truth:

60. I am Jesus of the holy order of Christ, who suffered on cross by hands of Judah of old in conspiring way with government powers.

61. I was heralded as most wicked by the then peoples on earth among whom I dwelt.

62. My way was eternal.

63. Their way was of lusts of the flesh.

64. This conflict brought upon all a full judgment, a nation of Israel destroyed for evil.

65. I now tell all, my servant is pure, and he doeth my will, and liveth my Eternal Union power law.

66. This is an immoral, unjust and wicked generation, fighting for over one hundred eighty years against my eternal authority of Priesthood in the nation I restored my Gospel.

67. Now I must cleanse all wickedness from my holy land, to prepare for Zion's rise, a Holy City; a people pure.

68. Learn that the nation of power on my land, though you have prospered unto world power, shall soon be at war, and lose all.

69. I shall send whirlwind power, in famine, a desolating scourge, a sickness of no cure at first; earthquake, windstorms, pestilence, famine by mob rule; all to sweep quickly this most wicked generation that has ever been on my holy land where my

Holy City and people shall be established for an eternity.

70. I am of full holy power.

71. I send my own word, to be justified to sweep all evil off my land.

72. Repent ye, repent ye, is the word of the Lord to all on earth, for my judgments shall cleanse all nations; and this nation of United States of America shall only be of my pure and holy Zion remaining on my holy land after whirlwind judgments sweep all off my holy land. Amen.

73. O ye people of the earth, heed my voice, my holy warnings.

74. Let all read my holy Proclamation of my own writing.

75. Let all be of pure holy intent who are not of the way of pure holy laws, but of upholding wicked, corrupt, Sodom and immoral ways.

76. All ye of pure holy way, come unto me through my authority on earth; and learn of my holy way of my New Zion Order Eternal Power way Celestial.

77. Come to your Lord, by righteous holy laws of my holy Gospel, lest all be as a dream in the night, gone forever, even thy posterity from earth, to not be of salvation into eternal life of my holy power Celestial, of pure holy exalting power; even eternal life, the greatest of all gifts of God. Amen.

78. Now let this, my will, be printed exact.

79. Let all who touch my word treat my word holy.

80. All shall soon know I have again spoken eternal words of pure holy power Celestial from heaven to earth by my Mouthpiece, who is of pure receiving of my word, to all peoples, nations, kindreds, tongues, and powers on my earth; soon to be redeemed by my holy power Celestial, as I have all power to fulfill my will.

81. Let leaders of nations care for poor, for needy, for orphans, widows, the aged; against a time of judgment.

82. Food shall be scarce.

83. Store food in abundance in all nations, lest famine sweep multitudes off the earth.

84. Let weapons of great power be all removed from among all nations.

85. Let all armies withdraw from foreign lands into their own borders, save I, the Lord, command defense of poor or weak nations needing protection.

86. Let only self-defense justify war of foreign lands coming against thee.

87. When United States nation of America again is of aggression, all world shall see my hand raised against this nation of evil way, which hold power to destroy other nations; which power shall be clipped to preserve my Zion land for New Jerusalem, by heavenly armies cleansing land.

88. I have spoken it. Amen.

89. Now be believing, as I now send my own word to your understanding.

90. Present nation leader of nation on my holy land shall fall from power, not heeding my will.

91. Also many in Congress shall not be of power to oppose my Church and Zion from rising.

92. Yet mobs shall erupt in many parts of this present powerful nation, to bring all to their knowing I have spoken and fulfill all my word.

93. Let the unholy nation let my people be free to worship and serve me, the God over all, lest I cause all on my Zion land to feel my wrath of eternal power. Amen.

94. I now reveal my holy way:

95. There shall be no adultery nor Sodom in any land during my holy reign as King of kings on earth.

96. All ways of spiritual Babylon shall be swept off all lands.

97. All peoples shall be of a purifying cleansing, removing the more wicked from off the earth in all nations.

98. Only the more righteous shall remain, to learn of my Zion, my own presence on earth among men.

99. My Zion shall be capital city of world governing power, of eternal heavenly power come to earth; over all nations of a surviving power by my grace preserving some, to come to learn of Zion and pure holy ways of dwelling on earth.

100. Now be ye ready.

101. I can cleanse all peoples by sending mine angelic armies of heaven of eternal judgment authority among your peoples; to pluck out the more wicked, even among rulers of nations.

102. I am soon to do this, to you knowing nothing can stay my hand.

103. Eventually all peoples shall bow the knee and their tongues confess my rule is righteous legitimate authority. Amen.

104. I also reveal to all peoples that satan shall be bound, to not be great power during Millennial Time of Peace, because more wicked shall be removed by my judgments; and surviving people will live more holy way of my giving holy way by revealings I shall send to all surviving national powers.

105. I shall be seen by all.

106. I shall be of great eternal power that consumes all wickedness.

107. Let all be of my way of Zion, in law principles, in family principles, in building ways, in farming, and ways of honest trade among nations.

108. All shall know my Celestial eternal authority reigneth over all nations.

109. Some nations shall be humbled by judgments of my sending if they heed me not; until all shall fear the God of Zion.

110. Let all be my chosen people of eternal and holy principles of my revealing when I come to make myself known.

111. Pray always unto your Lord, to be of a full power of survival, and live pure lives unto preserving virtue, purity, innocence, and life of peaceful way.

112. Let murder of unborn children be of no longer being among you.

113. Stop allowing evils of the wicked, lustful ways of legal consent to licentious, immoral ways among you, fostering other heinous crimes. Amen.

114. Let also peoples of warring nations now make peace, lest my humbling power be felt in removing more violent peoples from your lands and powers of leadership. Amen.

115. Now I have spoken to all.

116. Preserve virtue and innocence of children, of women, of all.

117. Let all be of a more holy way, to be of full power Celestial unto purifying your own lives in living my eternal plan of holy progression unto eternal life.

118. Let also holy authority be of a freedom to do my will, to establish my holy Zion in full power of my revealing all needed ways of full redemption.

119. I am God. Heed my will, saith Jesus Christ, your Redeemer and Holy One of Israel, Ruler over the nations. Amen.

SECTION REVELATION 128

The Kingdom of Zion
Holy One of Israel
2420 CR 300
Eldorado, Texas 76936

Jesus Christ, Son Ahman, God Over All, Even Power Eternal Speaketh

Thus Saith Jesus Christ, Son Ahman, to Leaders of National Power, and to All of Governing Power in Nation of the United States of America, a Word of Holy Deliverance for the Nation, to Be a Continued Nation of Noble Pure Way on Earth. Heed My Will, Even Thus:

Revelation of the Lord Jesus Christ
Palestine, Texas
Wednesday, November 23, 2011

1. Thus saith the God of all peoples on earth, Jesus Christ, your Holy Redeemer, the Resurrection and the Life; to the nation of power on the holy land of my coming, even United States of America, to now prepare to be of war.

2. You must not attack any other country that has not attacked you.

3. You must be only of self-defense to be favored in war, unto my preserving thee at all as a nation of power.

4. You must also release my people in bondage, my servant Warren Jeffs, to have my preserving gift continue with you.

5. Draft none who are of my people into armed forces.

6. Do not be of forcing any to go battle.

7. Let army cleanse itself.

8. Let laws allowing Sodom and immoral ways in ranks of military be no longer of upholding, lest you lose all power over military and organizing governing unity in your national organized way to guide armies of power.

9. I shall be a Judge.

10. You must prepare righteously for coming great war.

11. Nevertheless, if you heed me not, your power shall be as the loss of all.

12. Let this be a warning, to now be a nation that is peace in readiness, so thy God, who is only pure and holy, can preserve thee. Amen.

SECTION REVELATION 129

Fundamentalist Church of Jesus Christ of Latter-day Saints
P.O. Box 840459
Hildale, Utah 84784

Thus Saith Your Lord and Holy Savior, Jesus Christ, Who Is Son Ahman, to the Leaders and Peoples of the Nation Called the Philippines, Mine Own Word of Warning, Even Word of God Over All to You. Hear My Word:

Revelation of the Lord Jesus Christ
Palestine, Texas
Sunday, November 27, 2011

1. Your Lord Jesus Christ speaketh to the people of the land and kingdom on earth called among men as Philippines:

2. I, your Lord, call upon you as a people to be of prepared way to move to high grounds, as a great tidal wave cometh to sweep clean thy shores; also to be of proving thee, whether you will believe unto further obeying.

3. You have been a people of corrupt ways, allowing traditions of European gentile nations to be of a following.

4. Repent of the gross crime of murder of unborn children, of licentious, immoral Sodom ways of adulterous practices often sanctioned by legal consent.

5. Let thy peoples hear my word:

6. A great judgment cometh to cleanse the more wicked from among your land.

7. Let also selling of children cease.

8. Let also prostitution of young or old daughters and women cease.

9. Let all be more holy, pure, and caring.

10. Let thy governing powers be of purifying their laws and upholding just laws.

11. Let all be a people who can be called the more righteous, who can be preserved in a day of whirlwind judgments.

12. Let also practice of slave labor cease.

13. Let all thy unholy ways cease, lest full cleansing powers come against thee.

14. Study my Policies of the Kingdom of Son Ahman.

15. I am He, even Jesus Christ, your holy Lord and Redeemer, who has conquered death, who is the Resurrection and the Life, the Light of all men, who shall raise all from the grave to judge all for the deeds done in the flesh.

16. I am Eternal, Righteous, Pure Holy Governing Power Celestial Power over heaven and earth.

17. Nothing can stay my hand.

18. As I speak, so do I fulfill.

19. Repent ye of these evils of greater crimes against life, against purity and virtue, innocence and holy ways.

20. Repent of your immoral and murderous ways.

21. The murder of unborn children doth corrupt all peoples.

22. Be ye ready, for judgments of great power soon cometh.

23. I, your Lord, am justified to cleanse all peoples, my warnings being sent to all nations.

24. Now come to me in the day I send my holy messengers as missionaries of salvation to your land.

25. Receive them, and be prepared to believe that I, the God of glory over all nations, hath spoken, and hath fulfilled His own word to all nations.

26. Let the leaders of the Philippines be of pure way of governing, and repent of the evil of bribery, and thus unjust rulings.

27. Let your system of governing be of helping the poor, the orphans, widows, and aged.

28. Be ye a nation that I can preserve because of you being more pure. Amen.

Chapter 4

Jesus Christ, Son Ahman, Sendeth Power-Word of Warning to All Peoples on Earth, Warning of Judgments of Full Power, to Call on All to Repent; Thus I Am Just, and of Full Authority to Render Judgment on All Nations

SECTION REVELATION 130

Jesus Christ
Son Ahman

I, your Lord Jesus Christ, speak to all peoples on the world of my own creating, my holy word of full warning; a call to Israel to be of full power to cleanse all nations I cause them to be of full victory over, such as continue in sins of child murder of unborn children, of Sodom and adulterous immoral intentional ways of corrupting ways of living on earth; yea, on my earth; a just and holy God who sees and knows all things. Be ye open of mind, with prayerful way in soul-reaching hearts, to receive my full warning in this, my new revealing; causing my Priesthood on earth to send my own word unto all nations of the earth. Now read my will:

Revelation of the Lord Jesus Christ
Palestine, Texas
Tuesday, January 3, 2012

1. Jesus Christ, your Lord, of all peoples, nations, kindreds, tongues and powers over nations; yea, God over all speaketh to all on earth:

2. My time is soon to dwell on earth among men; to be thy Holy Governing Power of holy way of equity, justice, holy peace of heavenly origin, pure abiding in my way eternal.

3. Let all prepare.

4. Let all be ready.

5. Let all be pure. Amen.

6. Now receive my own will:

7. Let nation of Brazil be destroyed.

8. Let it no longer be a nation on my land of my coming -- corrupt in murderous, adulterous, Sodom way of corrupting all in thy land.

9. Only my Israel in more mountainous land are of some virtue.

10. Now shall they of greater virtue render the evil in thy land as cut off from the earth extant. Amen.

11. Now know such a nation fostering crime by governing powers shall end. Amen.

12. Thus I have spoken. Amen.

13. Now let Argentina be warned:

14. Thy sin against innocence yet riseth as a stench unto the heavens, murdering in yesteryears thine own youth who would not give way to unjust governing powers.

15. There are yet some of governing authority in thy land who were of participating in such murder.

16. Let all leaders now in power in thy nation now be brought to full justice.

17. Let this show thy Lord you will no longer uphold murder by governing powers. Amen.

18. Now let nation of Somalia hear my will:

19. Violence stalks thy streets in open day.

20. Your leaders are powerless.

21. Tribes of an invading way rule haphazardly, not caring for virtue, life, nor of innocence.

22. Let thy military send forth and now drive out tribes of violence, and I shall spare thy people; else a great dearth cometh to humble all in thy land, more than heretofore. Amen.

23. Now let Nicaragua hear my will:

24. You are of Israel, of the original people on thy land.

25. You have a mission to assist in cleansing the land of my coming, you of pure bloodline of my servant of old, even my Prophet Lehi of Book of Mormon first history.

26. You are of Israel, sent to assist in establishing holy Zion on North America.

27. Some pure bloodline of Lehi is yet among you.

28. Come forth. Cleanse my Zion land.

29. Cleanse thy leadership first; for they have joined with gentile nation of violent way, to render thy land as subservient to the rule of a nation of the conquering spirit over the earth.

30. Thy land is mine, saith Jesus Christ, unto my holy power resting on Israel in thy land to become of full power to cleanse my land of Zion.

31. Be ye ready.

32. I speak to Israel in thy land. Amen.

33. Let nation of Paraguay be told, much of bloodline of Lehi of Book of Mormon history, of first recording therein, is in thy land.

34. You shall help cleanse my land of my Zion, soon to come, even pure Israel, of the original inhabitants of thy land.

35. Do my work.

36. I send heavenly powers to guide leaders of tribes in mountainous, more isolated areas.

37. Let them heed my messengers of translated way, powers of heaven sent to earth.

38. They shall lay hands on thy sick and the sick shall be healed of my power Celestial Eternal Order; thereby showing tribes of more pure bloodline of Israel my word is true.

39. My servant Warren Jeffs is led by my power to address the pure Israel among thy land, to be of ready way soon; to cleanse first thy own land, then neighboring nation of Brazil, which is ripened for full overthrow as a corrupt land of the criminal way of living in all manner of corrupting power; destroying the youth, the women's virtue lost, all in commotion in violent way, with crime rampant in a land of plenty; yet the poor suffer in that nation because of rich men hoarding to themselves, by the labor of the poor, riches of that land, taking no thought for welfare of future generation. Amen.

40. Now let Ecuador receive my will, saith Jesus Christ, your Lord over all nations:

41. Be ye also of a cleansing my Zion land, as you also have pure bloodline of my Lehi of old in Book of Mormon first writing, Israel of the calling to cleanse Zion land where you dwell; mostly of original inhabitants not of mixed bloodline.

42. Now be ye ready to first cleanse thy own people of corrupting way of child murder of unborn children; also of Sodom and adulterous immoral ways.

43. Let thy army of pure men go forth to cleanse thy land; then go into Brazil and destroy the people of the sin of corrupting way of governing who promote licentious immoral ways that destroy virtue and innocence; that destroy life of innocent children unborn; to gratify lustful desires of fallen man and women of earthly selfish way.

44. Let such practices be abolished entire, saith the Lord over all peoples; yea, the God over heaven and earth; who sees all things; who shall render a full accounting upon all who are guilty of these most heinous crimes. Amen.

45. Now let Israel, the land of my birth on earth, be ready.

46. A coalition of Moslem nations shall combine soon to attack thy land, to drive you off the chosen land of Old Jerusalem.

47. I shall be with thy nation as you first cleanse your own peoples of child murder of the unborn, yet having full right to life of thy God who created all things; to be a God of full justice in the day of judging in the time of my coming; also into eternity on all such as think they can hide their crimes from me; for I shall take them in their own snare, and publish to all their sin of the way of immorality, crime, murderous licentious way.

48. Teach thy children to be of the holy way; to cover their bodies, not of inviting immoral conduct, so I may preserve your people as a more righteous holy Israel on the earth; among nation of surrounding order, to make you victorious over coalition of Moslem and other arming nation, who is arming Moslem nations to attack thee; also United States of America being soon attacked.

49. Let all be of a more holy way of living; to justify thy God to preserve thee, giving thee victory from Euphrates River to the Nile River, over neighboring peoples, of the time they join together to attack thy nation in a unity of power.

50. Be of full force. Do not hold back.

51. I shall give you victory, to make neighboring peoples serve thee, as Isaiah my holy Prophet saw and recorded concerning triumph of Israel in the latter days.

52. Know I shall then send missionaries of my own saving Gospel Salvation Order, to teach remaining people of thy land, my Gospel of Saving Redeeming power.

53. All must be pure, for I am only pure, holy, righteous; inspiring all to better works.

54. Let peace be thy labor; only going to battle after three honest attempts to make peace, not giving up Jerusalem nor Israel's full right to possess my land of promise; a covenant with thy fathers Abraham, Isaac, and Jacob in time of yesteryears.

55. Now be more holy pure way of living to be preserved, many of pure Israel. Amen.

56. Let now this be of a sending.

57. Let it be sent to all nations of Israel blood.

58. Let all nations learn I am now cleansing their land of all ungodly, murderous, adulterous way of corrupting principles of virtue, holiness, love of God, from among all peoples. Amen.

59. Now let all nations be more pure holy way of living laws even revealed through Moses, my holy historian and Prophet of old; the record of sacred writing in Bible.

60. Let all be holy to survive the day of judgment. Amen.

61. Thus saith the Lord to the nation of Laos:

62. Be ye more concerned with the

care for thine own people; and care for the poor and needy.

63. Do not let gentile nations take away freedom of holy religion in thy nation.

64. Let all be rid of child murder of the unborn.

65. Let murder not be of thee at all; that I may cleanse all nations from Sodom, child murder of unborn children; also licentious, immoral, adulterous ways of living.

66. Rid thy peoples of such soul-destroying crimes; also usury; and secure thy way of surviving by being more pure in every way.

67. Let all be of keeping my holy way of purity. Amen.

68. Now let nation of my coming, United States of America, hear my will:

69. Stop shedding innocent blood, all of you, in the now legal way in thy nation, to abort children, even up to full term.

70. This is as Herod of old cleansing Bethlehem of purity, becoming a murderer of children outwardly, to promote higher way of purity standards, punishable by law on any who corrupt away their own existence.

71. Let this be of full way of final warning. Amen.

72. Now let all peoples on earth repent of these same soul-destroying sins that corrupt the way of all nations.

73. Now be of surety the armor light yet perfecting thy lives in pure way of my own holy revealing in time soon of a full way coming on all peoples. Amen.

74. Now let nation of United States of America receive full warning: If you continue to heed me not, full judgment cometh --

75. Storms, windstorms, earthquakes, pestilences, hail, famine, mob rule, governing powers made helpless; invading nations of soon attacking when thou art not ready.

76. Thus with besom of destruction cometh end to thy power, my Zion rising on the land I have named.

77. Now be of releasing him, my servant, from bondage, lest you become unable to control thine own future at all; I taking all in hand to sweep wicked ruling powers off my land of Zion. Amen.

78. Let all nations now repent.

79. My full power that is over all the earth cometh on earth to cleanse all nations.

80. I give to you reason:

81. The earth hath been visited by heavenly powers throughout the ages of time.

82. The nation of Israel was my people for a thousand years, yet proved wicked, and were destroyed and scattered throughout all nations.

83. Though many nations have been on earth and then fallen, my Israel yet is upon the earth by my preserving tribes of Israel.

84. Let it be known there cometh a full gathering of Israel.

85. They shall be the full Twelve Tribes.

86. All shall know I have ordained this to take place.

87. Let Isaiah in Old Testament be read by all, to learn my own will through him in writing future of Israel and of gentile non-Israel nation of my coming; even in Isaiah of old telling of the judgment of God on a people of immoral corruption of the way of Sodom; of the fall of nations even in times past; all of which took place.

88. History records fall of mighty kingdoms.

89. They were warned by Prophets to repent of the same evil among them, as I, even God, have now warned all nations on earth.

90. Let it be known that when a nation is of a full warning, I, God over all, am full justified to throw down the nation of continued sinning in the way of destroying way of life, virtue, innocence, pure holy way being persecuted and corrupted, even by governing powers.

91. When a nation is fully ripened in iniquity, I then reserve all power to cleanse such.

92. Now know I have been of a flow of my own will revealed to all peoples, through my own word sent to all leaders of all nations on earth, to ambassadors of all nations, in the United Nations Organization, to libraries in all lands among common man to read; also to church organizations, to media of communication ability, to other ways of sending to all peoples my own will; all to be answered upon all peoples on earth.

93. My will is known.

94. It is not hidden.

95. I am God over all peoples.

96. I speak, I shall be obeyed, or full judgments of whirlwind power cometh as I have promised.

97. Now know tsunami in Asia soon cometh, of many more souls lost; like previous tidal wave of many nations afflicted.

98. An earthquake shall devastate a city in the nation of the United States of America, to humble that people, now an over-proud people, soon to be fully humbled.

99. There shall be a devastating storm cripple that nation for a length of time, to feel my power.

100. All this because they heed me not; in calling upon all peoples to cleanse themselves for my glorious coming on earth with heavenly power; a warning now fully given.

101. Thus my Israel shall rise and help cleanse my Zion land before New Jerusalem is built in full.

102. Let all beware.

103. I send my will of full warning, to tell truth of thy fallen way.

104. All must know my way is for peace, kindness, love-joy in righteous way of purity of living on earth with all other nations.

105. Be ye ready.

106. I shall destroy all peoples of the practice of unholy child murder of unborn children; also sins of adultery and Sodom completely. Amen.

107. Now let all peoples read this, my will, to be ready.

108. Let all be warned.

109. My holy way is to be justified.

110. I am now justified to cleanse all peoples.

111. I am God who speaketh.

112. My word cometh to all nations on earth. Amen.

113. Now receive more warning:

114. The nation of violence, even of Libya, also Egypt in upheaval of rebellion, shall both fall.

115. Both shall be of full judgment, not heeding my will to give greater freedom to common man and women in these Moslem nations, after they have tasted freedom.

116. Abuse of women in such nations claiming worship of God is proof enough of unholy way of such religions of abusing women and daughters; to not give full rights of freedom, of education, of labor

and caring for the needy among your peoples.

117. These are evils needing to be no longer among peoples and nations; to be of full way warned of God what He is soon to do on earth, now known by all. Amen.

118. Now let Russia, and the other nation of power to humble the nation on my land of Zion, fear not the nation of seeming power.

119. She teeters on precipice of full fall from power on earth; notwithstanding supposed might.

120. I shall cause the land to be in chaos; then invasion cometh; thus my word being fulfilled.

121. Let invading armies withdraw, lest they also meet my full judgment powers while on Zion's land of my coming.

122. They cannot remain. Amen.

123. Now the Kingdom of God goeth forth in power, to triumph on earth; to be prepared to meet the holy order of my coming to the land of New Jerusalem on the North American continent; yea, a full Celestial new governing righteous pure holy power Celestial, soon. Amen.

124. Let the nation of Mexico gain control soon of robbers and drug cartels, lest you be laid waste.

125. Your government reeks with corruption in bribery received from crime organizations that destroy virtue, life, openly before all thy people.

126. It will be of my full judgment soon, as Mexico is on my Zion land. Amen.

127. Let all Central American nations also be warned; my judgments of power cometh on thee.

128. The more pure shall survive.

129. Disease shall take many; also a devastating sickness shall sweep across North and also South America, to remove millions off the land of such corrupt ways. I cannot uphold thy nation, United States of America, any longer, as a power of influence over many nations.

130. You are of Lucifer.

131. You are of evil.

132. I am of purity and holiness.

133. I am all power to judge.

134. All shall bow before me, even Jesus Christ, soon, who remains; for I shall appear in mighty power to make afraid all peoples, to not come against my New Jerusalem; my holy power on earth of revealed authority from heaven.

135. This is my power-word to all -- repent or be swept off my land of Zion, and other lands.

136. Let Australia repent as a people; having background historical ties to England, a nation of Israel blood, of my way of preserving Israel on earth by making Great Britain a conquering nation in the centuries she prospered worldwide.

137. Yet she hath fallen from power she once held because of her unjust force way on many nations who sought freedom.

138. Even because England was Israel, did I preserve power in that land; yet that people now are of debilitating sins of corruption of Babylon, even most immoral ways, of allowing murder of unborn children, immorality flowing rampant through all levels of social way, even in royal family in many lives, as supposed examples of right way to live on earth my religion of the Gospel of salvation; yet having no religious authority among them from me, even your Savior, Jesus Christ.

139. All religions on earth, save my true holy revealed religion through the holy labor of my servant Joseph Smith in the nineteenth century on my land of my

coming to build my Zion -- I say unto all peoples on earth, he is my servant to restore all to the knowledge of God coming again to earth in glory power Celestial Order governing power. Amen.

140. Now read my Proclamation, even of Son Ahman, Jesus Christ, sent to all nations on earth of recent sending, to learn of truth of my Priesthood eternal authority on earth, continued through a pure holy authority of Keyholders of my own power on earth; thus all peoples have salvation in their reach, by coming to my authority.

141. Thus my warning includeth my invitation to be receiving my truth, of full salvation to be of a full love-power unto eternal life.

142. You are a vain, adulterous, murderous, unholy, wicked, and licentious generation now upon the earth; and in your full ripened iniquity, you misjudge my holy Eternal Union Holy Marriage Order of Plural Holy Union Marriage.

143. You depict my holy way as evil; yet all nations are reeking in immoral way unto murder of unborn children; and gross abuse of women, also children, even in corrupt family ways now common among nation of prosecuting way against my people, placing in prison innocent men who only seek to perform righteous holy way of my Celestial Order of holy way; and you who thus afflict my people, being of full corrupt way, such that you reek in bloodshed of unborn children in most nations, even some euthanasia practice of self-murder legalized; thus of the way of being against thy Lord in many gross heinous crimes against principles of life; all being of a religion of falsehood who would uphold such immoral, murderous ways of living; yea, living unto my full power of judgment, both on earth in whirlwind-power cleansing of all nations; also eternal judgment when all stand before me in the resurrection of my raising up all from the grave; spirit and body joining in an immortal state, to be judged by me, God over all; yea, all thy ways known, nothing hidden.

144. This is eternal truth all face; as I, God, speak truth, to make known all thy sins now, so some perchance will choose to repent in this day of final way of preparing for my own Reign of Righteousness on earth in Zion, New Jerusalem, soon to rise in full Celestial power. Amen.

145. Now let this be heralded.

146. Let all peoples give ear.

147. Let all rulers of nations know I cometh to judge you all.

148. You cannot escape in this life, nor in the life to come when you are taken in death, then resurrected to stand before me, God and Holy Redeemer over all nations of all generations.

149. These terrible and soul-destroying sins of the murder of unborn children, immoral Sodom and adulterous ways, are the full cause I destroyed ancient nations.

150. I am the same God today as in all former generations on earth.

151. I created you all, and the earth, to send you here to prove each soul, allowing you to choose good and cast off evil way.

152. Most have rejected me and my Gospel in a pure way delivered by inspired Priesthood on earth, lo, these many years and generations of past. Amen.

153. Now be receiving with prayerful hearts my own word; to now be of full way repenting, so you may be of salvation; not of damnation in eternal world; where all shall know I am God, who hath sent His own way of salvation.

154. Receive ye, therefore, my own word; and repent unto change of living more holy way before me, a God of all

creation who is able to be of discerning power, even to know thy thoughts and desires; for all things are known by me, a just God of mercy and truth. Amen.

155. I, even God, who am Jesus Christ, speak to all my Church: Now be clean before me.

156. Be ye one in Celestial holy bond of Priesthood.

157. Let love of God and pure holy way be thy only way, coming out of the world entirely, to be of pure holy way Celestial love-power for thy God and Eternal Union of Celestial power. Amen.

Fundamentalist Church of Jesus Christ of Latter-day Saints
P.O. Box 840459
Hildale, Utah 84784

Jesus Christ, Even God Over All, Saith:

Thus Saith Son Ahman, Even Jesus Your Lord, to Present Court, That Is Not of Authority to Judge and Confine My People, Being No Authority Over Religion of Constitution Guarantee of Preserving Religious Freedom; Yet You Now Are of a Full Way of Persecuting Power Against My Innocent Obeying Order of Holy Eternal Priesthood; Hear My Own Message to Thee, Now to Be an Announcing of No Further Jurisdiction of Court in the Prosecution of My Representative; of Full Authority to Administer My Celestial Law Unto Pure Noble Sons, Unto My Holy Way Celestial Preparing for My Own Coming Among Men:

(Comprising Section Revelations 131-132)

SECTION REVELATION 131

Revelation of the Lord Jesus Christ
Palestine, Texas
Monday, October 24, 2011

1. Verily, thus saith the Lord, even Son Ahman, unto court of persecution against my Church, of the way of not being of pure ruling; using governing power unjustly; even unto a wrong ruling of penalizing my Priesthood power of my own eternal power on earth unto bondage keeping, as it were, for a life sentencing --

2. I, your Lord, have seen the conspiring and evil combining, in mind and word also now in full way of fulfilling, to put my holy servant in prison unto a full lifetime.

3. Let all now know I shall be my full administering justice on all of the power of dark intent, who have judged my holy way

to be of evil, when my appointed servant and Keyholder of the full power of Eternal Power of thy God on earth, only has done my holy appointed guiding, ordaining, administering, of a holy Celestial Law; not to be interfered with by earthly and civil governing powers; my Order being of full religious protecting by Constitution guarantee; thus you have been told by my own will sent to you of thy full sin.

4. Now reverse all rulings of unjust, and now imprisoning way.

5. Now let my servant be free.

6. I shall have all be of an accounting, unto Eternal Judgment, saith your God. Amen.

SECTION REVELATION 132

Revelation of the Lord Jesus Christ
Palestine, Texas
Thursday, October 13, 2011

1. I, even Jesus Christ, speak to the present judge over court proceedings against my servant Warren Jeffs: I cause him to no longer be of an answering of your unjust and corrupt and unauthorized rulings; as I, the Lord, even Jesus Christ, am above all, and my law is religious and of me, a heavenly power over all creation.

2. Your judging is not based on truth.

3. I cause him to not answer to the court.

4. Let thy rulings against him cease.

5. I shall soon lay a heavy hand on all who fight against my Priesthood and Church, saith the Lord.

6. Now know I am God, even above all, and court of persecution shall be of a ceasing in my way of eternal power taking a hand if you will continue unjust way. Amen.

The Lord Jesus Christ
Author

Warren S. Jeffs

President Warren S. Jeffs, President of Church of Jesus Christ
Representative of our Lord and God who is Jesus Christ

Kingdom of Zion
2420 CR 300
Eldorado, Texas 76936

Jesus Christ, Even Jehovah, God Over All Creation

(Comprising Section Revelations 133-136)

Thus I Have Redeemed My People. I Am Now Their Holy King of the Kingdom of Ahman of the Domain of Son Ahman. Amen.

Thus saith the Lord to Appeals Court in consideration of Appeal Number 03-11-00568-CR:

SECTION REVELATION 133

Revelation of the Lord Jesus Christ
Palestine, Texas
Saturday, November 12, 2011

1. I, Jesus Christ, over all, even God over all, speak to appeals court:

2. Let my servant and his brethren in prison go free.

3. Reverse unjust court's rulings.

4. Do not uphold unjust way.

5. My religion of my own revealing has constitutional protection of freedom of religion.

6. Now be of just power.

7. Receive my holy will.

8. My word is truth.

9. I am now of full power to reverse all courts.

10. Be ready to do justly on following cause numbers:

51st Judicial District Court Cause No. 990

51st Judicial District Court Cause No. 997

51st Judicial District Court Cause No. 1017

51st Judicial District Court Cause No. 1061

11. I, your Lord, am soon to drive all evil from my land of Zion, even America.

12. I shall be of full way of cleansing.

13. Now deal justly, and order case dismissed; reversing unjust life sentence on foundation truth my religion of my own giving among men is not being protected by law of constitutional freedom. Amen.

14. Hear now my revealing in thy souls.

15. Let my own appeal document of my own revealing touch truth-loving hearts. Amen.

Kingdom of Zion
2420 CR 300
Eldorado, Texas 76936

Jesus Christ, Even Jehovah, God Over All Creation

Thus I Have Redeemed My People. I Am Now Their Holy King of the Kingdom of Ahman of the Domain of Son Ahman. Amen.

Thus saith your Lord Jesus Christ, the Holy Power of Redeeming Power for all mankind of all nations, of all ages of time, to all nations, peoples, kindreds, tongues, and governing powers; my own word in great plainness to all peoples, of my own coming; of great whirlwind judgments of the pure way of my holy love justifying judgments of Eternity Power; thus giving mine own word to all peoples on earth; a word of eternal importance to all now on the earth, to be of full receiving my own will concerning all peoples on earth; also to teach truth of pure way of judging, of holy way of my eternal law of holy Marriage Union of Eternal Union of Plural Celestial Marriage of my holy power authorizing select few to thus live; not to be of interference by any not of my own authority of Holy Eternal Priesthood of my sending; thus saith the Lord to this now generation on the earth, my own will to all; both of the governing powers of all nations; also their peoples: Hear thou my holy message given by my holy servant on earth as my Mouthpiece, though in bondage; to be in the hands of all peoples, to know of my soon labor of cleansing all lands of more wicked, to preserve the more righteous; yea, hear my own word given through my own power, to my holy servant Warren Jeffs; though suffering in prison, yet of my order of pure Priesthood of holy calling to give my own will to all peoples, by my power, who will receive my word.

SECTION REVELATION 134

Revelation of the Lord Jesus Christ
Palestine, Texas
Monday, December 12, 2011

1. Let all peoples be of a listening; to be of full pure receiving; to have my own will manifest unto the way of pure holy eternal truth being sent to all nations on earth.

2. Let now my holy will be known.

3. Let all render honor, obeying, and pure holy living unto your Holy Redeemer, even I who speaketh, Jesus Christ, who is of eternity unto eternity in full Godhood

power over all peoples, both on earth; also departed spirits who are of salvation unto my Priesthood eternal power among all nations of the way of teaching my plan of eternal salvation to all, past, and now on the earth in the flesh.

4. Now receive my final power-word warning:

5. You are only of the earth; I am of Eternal Power Celestial over all creation.

6. Now be of full obeying my will, to repent, lest sudden eternal holy power full judgments cometh on all nations.

7. Let all be humble.

8. Let all be ready.

9. I soon cometh in holy power of heavenly governing holy authority, to rule on earth for a thousand years with the heavenly hosts, come with my holy authority to be among all peoples, a Millennial Reign of Peace; pure governing power Celestial.

10. Thus I send mine own will to all -- Repent, and be of pure living Celestial way of holy power; a government of pure knowing all things, nothing secret.

11. Verily I say unto all nations -- be ye ready.

12. Make peace, both among thine own peoples and with all other peoples of every land, kindred, tongue; yea, be of my peace-loving forgiveness; for I, God, am the Judge of all peoples, with eternal knowledge Celestial to be my power of knowing all things, nothing hidden.

13. Therefore, fear ye, all ye wicked peoples who are not of belief of my power eternal Celestial; for you shall be of a sudden awaking unto fear when my hand of eternal holy way is stretched forth in judgments of eternal power, such as earthquake, tornado, the sea heaving beyond its bounds unto many swept away; yea, the desolating sickness, the overflowing pestilence of new diseases, of insects, animals, of crops destroyed, famine -- all to humble all people who will not give heed to my holy will, the God of all the earth, even Son Ahman, who is Jesus Christ, the Righteous Judge, the Holy Governor, your Eternal Ruler as King over all peoples.

14. Let now my published Proclamation be of full giving, even to all thy peoples; now of full mailing to libraries all over the world in all nations.

15. Let my other revealings of holy word of my sending, published to all, warning all of my soon power of cleansing; let these go to all thy peoples, having been mailed to the libraries of the earth; so common, and high, and they of power way can read my holy revealing of events of judgments soon to happen on earth; to cleanse off the face of the earth the more wicked; to preserve the more righteous.

16. Let my word cause all to be of sober way, to change from wickedness of violent way, of immoral, murder of unborn children way of living, and be more holy and pure of motive also of living.

17. Let all be more of peace.

18. I soon come to be of a revealing all secrets, past, present, and many eternal future happenings of God's dealings with the nations.

19. Let all now be receiving my holy will. Amen.

20. Let all peoples now give heed.

21. Let my holy power be upon thee through prayer; through noble, humble forgiving all; for the love-peace kindness toward all.

22. Let my holy peace dwell in thy heart, each one, by choosing my holy power Celestial; by receiving my holy

Gospel; by knowing all thy works cannot establish peace without God and His eternal power. Amen.

23. Let also all peoples dwell in holy peace of my governing power I send among you when I come; to have Zion my Capital Governing Authority; to have Old Jerusalem a governing power; for my people Israel shall be gathered from among all nations under heaven.

24. Read Isaiah in Old Testament.

25. He telleth thee mine own will concerning Israel being my Holy Priesthood Celestial authority, to rule all nations under thy Lord and His Celestial power extant, over all the world.

26. Now be of full power to correct these heinous crimes upheld by your national laws in many lands, the murder of unborn children, some full term, of soon delivery, murdered by legal consent.

27. Thus it is among all peoples -- lustful immoral ways cause many to shed innocent blood, thus becoming nations of murder of innocent, and of unholy doing against innocence.

28. Let all be of my way to uphold virtue, purity of living as honorable, to provide for the raising of children in peace, in a virtuous way; not of hindering the bringing forth of life.

29. Let all cease this most eternal damning sin.

30. Let all know I cometh to bring to an end these horrible evils on earth, to provide new peoples sent by my power Celestial to earth.

31. Let all be my people of pure motive of virtue and life-giving way; to protect unborn children.

32. I shall provide thy peoples with sufficient, to provide food, raiment, housing; all life-needed elements to give to all born on earth; to govern in peace; for the nations on earth shall prosper unto the plenteous gifts of life without covetous way; which leadeth to war and violence among nations, and among peoples of nations one against another.

33. My rule is sure, and true, and of peace, of righteous holy way of living.

34. Come unto me, your Lord.

35. Your earthly governing powers cannot exalt any to eternal life.

36. Only I, your Holy Redeemer, can bring salvation eternal to all who live eternal pure holy way of my holy power of the heavenly powers come to earth.

37. I send you my new publishing of final warning to all nations.

38. Let this be a final word, before whirlwind eternal power judgments cometh on all nations; more especially on my land of Zion, even North and South America, soon to happen;

39. For my holy warning is my justification to sweep the wicked off my land Zion, and from all lands who heed me not, but continue in the sins of spiritual Babylon, which shall fully be removed from the nations, even the corrupt unholy people that inhabit all lands, who have fallen into temptation as entire nations corrupt themselves before the Lord, saith He, even Jesus Christ, who shall recompense to all people the measure they measured to their fellow man on earth; unto a full judgment hereafter;

40. For you are each a son or daughter of God, sent to earth by my power, to be of full way proving thy life, whether you would choose evil or good; the good being of me and my eternal plan of salvation, even the Gospel of life unto eternal life.

41. I am Eternal, my power is eternal.

42. I see all things.

43. Tremble, all ye nations, at my power soon to be fully felt as I remove the righteous unto safety, and the wicked slay the wicked in wars; also, by my eternal power, swift judgments need to come in order that the wicked do not slay all mine elect who can be of my holy Zion; a chosen pure holy people; my holy people who will receive me and my Gospel in full power Celestial.

44. Let these eternal truths touch honest hearts and minds everywhere.

45. Let only my holy way be thy way, saith God over all, your Lord and Just Holy King; yea, King of kings and Lord of lords. Amen.

46. I, your Lord, now reveal through my servant on earth my holy will, even him whom I have preserved to cause my holy will to go forth before my glorious appearing, to justify thy God to send full cleansing powers to the whole earth, soon to take place.

47. I have him in mine hands. Harm him not.

48. Be of a more sure way of preserving his life while in hands of the present governing powers on my land of my soon coming; for evil and unholy people are seeking to be of a full way removing him from the earth.

49. I, your Lord, tell you of governing powers this truth, so he may be of protecting to do my will.

50. Hinder not my will from coming to all people, lest a swift judgment cometh.

51. I am God.

52. I have all peoples in mine holy hands of eternal power.

53. Cease thy wicked attacks, ye government authorities in the United States of America, against my people and my Church.

54. Do not be of the way like they who crucified your Lord, believing false witnessing against my servant and my people on earth.

55. Let all my servants in bondage go free.

56. Merril Jessop, an aged ailing pure holy man of my Church, of eternal holy way of pure holy living, is now also unjustly held in prison by an unjust court; an evil tribunal who combined with lying apostate witnesses of evil combination with government prosecuting power, to put innocent and obeying sons of my Priesthood authority behind the prison walls.

57. Now let them all go free, lest the nation prove only to be of the way of persecuting innocence; destroying life of unborn children; of taking away my people's homes by court unjust rulings in the way of false witnesses believed; a holy Church under government attack, not protected in religious practice in a land boasting of religious freedom; yet denying my people freedom to live my holy religion revealed from heaven by your Lord, through the instrumentality of my holy Prophet Joseph Smith in previous century in thy nation of the United States.

58. Behold my Proclamation recently mailed to all nations, to all leaders of nations, to governing authorities in every state in thy nation of the United States; yea, to all religious societies and libraries -- all receiving my own holy will of pure truth; telling all of my holy religion being of persecuted way since Joseph Smith's time; he also suffering a martyr's death in a nation of supposed freedom; leaders not willing to step forth and protect an unpopular people; who, at many instances, aided in the drivings, persecutions, and prosecuting labor lo, these many years,

yea, even one hundred and eighty years since my Church was organized in the nation of constitutional guarantee of religious freedom, of pure freedom, to voice beliefs, without harm coming upon them; yet you protect not my people and my Church, because you claim they are law-breaking people for living my holy Eternal Union Marriage Law of Celestial Plural Holy Union.

59. Let my people be free to live my holy law, lest judgments come in full way, to you no longer being a power to oppose me and my Zion, to no longer be a land of persecution, to no longer be a people of pure government of freedom powers, because leaders do not uphold constitutional law.

60. Let this truth be heeded by judges, President, Congress, all branches of governing power on thy land.

61. Let Canada be warned to not persecute my holy law and Church among you.

62. I shall turn on your own heads pure judgment of thy own intent against my people and Church; to humble all with the war soon coming on thy own land; verily it shall be so.

63. Let all be preparing for thy God to intervene, by correcting thyselves, thy rulers, thy evil ways now no longer followed.

64. Thy pride as a nation is of over-towering height, soon to fall by my power eternal.

65. Let all beware.

66. Let all become more pure, more holy, more of upholding virtue and innocence, of preserving life, even of unborn children;

67. Thus, evil of unborn children being murdered, even by government consent, bringeth a judgment of a just God of Creation on all peoples.

68. This causes you to be nations of murdering way.

69. Thus it is. Amen.

70. Let this be my final full way of pure truth, telling all peoples to repent, to aid my servant to go free, to allow my Church freedom of religion, as guaranteed to all religions by governing pure principled powers of the nation on my holy land of Zion; a New Jerusalem soon to rise without opposition, because I, your God, provide full power of deliverance, and no one can stay my hand.

71. You are all my creations.

72. Nothing can stay my hand from taking whom I will in death.

73. Let all beware, lest you corrupt the way before yourselves, bringing eternal damnation upon you, even a punishment of suffering for sins of thy knowing.

74. Now my own will has been made known to all nations.

75. Let this be thy now full awakening to eternity truth, that all will have to answer for deeds and desires done on the earth, before a just and holy God, who has all things pure, holy, noble, righteous in His power, to judge a pure, holy, noble righteous way, all peoples of all generations.

76. Now receive this, my holy will, to let my servant Warren Jeffs, also Merril Jessop and their innocent brethren in prison, in a country now proving no religious free way is in thy land; to be of a letting go unto freedom, unto my right to rule; even more so than the rule of man's governing power.

77. Let pure religion alone, ye rulers and judges.

78. Let my holy religion be full free to

live Celestial laws of pure holy revealed pure holy laws only pertaining to those of my Church, who seek to live those eternal laws, who only are of peace, pure way of living.

79. The lies of apostates are believed by wicked powers in power, and by people of juries who listen.

80. Let it now be of truth telling: The false witnesses are of lying way; they once having been of truth living the very eternal laws of holy religion, then turned therefrom because of their own corrupt way.

81. Thus it is now. They are guilty of now being unjust persecuting power using governing powers in way of prosecuting power to harm my people of my Church.

82. No victims are harmed, thus not being a victim; yet courts sentence innocent men to full lifetime sentence in prison for only living their holy religion, is the pure truth.

83. I, Jesus Christ, am the Author of this holy religion.

84. I am the God of Abraham, Isaac, and Jacob, mine Israel.

85. They also lived these eternal ways.

86. Now this nation seeks to hinder my people from earning full Celestial power salvation.

87. How can you be justified when I, God, have commanded them to live this holy eternal law, which can only be guided and governed by your Lord, through His appointed and ordained holy authority on earth?

88. This earth is mine, saith the Lord.

89. Believe principles of pure truth; that marriage is of pure religion, since the time I put Adam and Eve together to people the earth; a religious principle eternal.

90. You are breaking thine own national laws when you hinder a religion from obeying righteous holy way.

91. Let this be a full reversing; these unjust laws against my holy law Celestial Union Law of Marriage, a holy law of my revealing, of my holy authority being full authority to bless unions to be eternal; all of me, even your Lord.

92. This is my holy way to call on all powers of governing to be of protecting religious freedom in the nation of guarantee of religious freedom.

93. Now heed my word.

94. I shall soon sweep this unholy, most wicked generation off my land of Zion with the besom of whirlwind judgments, soon of full power.

95. Thy people have seen me send tornados of full destructive power, show to all complete judgment, nothing but rubble remaining.

96. How can your puny arm of flesh withstand my almighty power?

97. The whirlwind power is an ensample of all my cleansing powers eternal.

98. Let all see this life of earthly existence is temporary, and of my power to tell length of living on earth for every individual.

99. Now be repenting unto more pure works.

100. Let all be of holy way.

101. Let all be pure in heart, that my holy people can be also of an example of Zion, my own holy power on earth from heaven, come to redeem all mankind of all ages of time.

102. Let this truth tell all I can administer eternal life gifts, even to people of past ages and nations now as organized spirit people awaiting the holy resurrection, by first receiving eternal blessings of my

own revealing to my authority on earth, who is worthy for blessings Celestial, unto eternal lives.

103. Thus, thy God is Just, Eternal, Holy, Pure, Noble, Righteous, Peace and Pure Way of Eternal Power of Governing Way over all nations.

104. Thus, I have now given full way justification to let my servant and my servants in prison house go free; also to let my people of my holy revealed religion on earth be of full free way.

105. Let all now be warned: Those places of prosecuting zeal against my holy religion shall be of no power to do so again.

106. Let them cease such unholy way of persecuting innocent people, when thy nation reeks in the blood of innocence of murder of unborn children through adultery and Sodom rampant on the land among all other peoples and religions.

107. Now cleanse thine own households of thine own begetting, of thy schools and governing powers; thy laws of corrupt way allowing immoral way to go unchecked; yet my innocent people are imprisoned for pure way of living; no crime, no corrupt way, no evil way among those who are of my Celestial Law, who are holy in practice of my holy law of my own holy power among them, judging each person who is of full way receiving my Celestial Law, unfettered by evil powers, governing powers and persecuting powers; to be of full freedom of religious living their only motive.

108. Now be of truth: Prosecutors lie. Witnesses lie.

109. My people go to prison because of lies told and believed in court of unjust way.

110. I caused my own word to be read in open court, telling these truths when my servant stood alone to voice the truth of unjust way of court proceedings, of the power to stop religious pure holy way being of ignoble attack in open court, defiling sacredness of my holy religion.

111. Thus, court shall be of full receiving my judging of eternal power in day to come, when all shall stand before me, even your Holy Redeemer, to be judged.

112. All shall know unobstructed truth then, when they stand before a just holy God to be of full way power to render true justice.

113. Let all be careful how they are of a way of believing lying court and prosecuting power; for my law is only holy, pure, noble, and of Celestial power; not of man, nor of the world; only to be of full way holy knowledge to obedient sons and daughters to my eternal law of Celestial Plural Union Marriage; my own way in heaven.

114. Thus I revealed this to my servant Joseph Smith over one hundred seventy years ago.

115. Let this truth be told: My law is of pure religious motive, no evil intent nor practice.

116. All must be pure to live my law, to be of receiving my Celestial Law and gifts of happiness therein.

117. This truth apostate lying witnesses know, who themselves sinned against my holy Celestial Law, to follow practices of immoral way of this wicked generation.

118. You who dwell in corrupting ways and unholy practices set up yourselves as judges of the most holy pure way of living my Celestial Law of eternal exalting authority for obedient sons and daughters.

119. Now receive my full warning.

120. My coming is soon to take place.

121. I shall reward all for deeds and desires done in the flesh on earth.

122. You cannot escape my all-seeing eye.

123. I know all things.

124. I am to bring all to full power judging of their individual lives.

125. Be ye pure, to stand before a holy God, to be of happiness on earth, and hereafter, in eternal world of glory, my heaven coming to earth to build New Jerusalem, my Zion, prophesied of by all holy Prophets of my sending; whose record is in Bible to thy easy reading; which gift I preserved through mine Israel; a people soon to be gathered to Zion, notwithstanding all opposition.

126. Be ye ready.

127. Great changes on my land of my holy New Jerusalem, on the surface thereof, soon cometh; even present cities, many to be of full cleansing, to be without inhabitant; yea, great and notable cities now on my land of Zion shall be sunk in the earth, or covered by mountains; or sunk in the sea; some destroyed by my eternal fire; some of the destruction by war, mob rule rising in many places; leaders of governing power without power to govern; armies left desolate; places of more wicked way destroyed in full.

128. Such shall be where they of full hatred against my holy law of Celestial Eternal Union of my eternal order of marriage of plural living in holy order of pure noble way; yea, those who thus seek to destroy my holy law and authority shall be of full receiving of my judgment.

129. Let all these truths settle on the mind of each; even to awake all people unto full way power to repent; unto my holy way becoming the way of salvation to all honest in heart everywhere.

130. Let this be my holy word eternal, to be of full weight on each who is of this present generation, to be of full authority to judge all; yea, all now on my land of Zion having within reach my holy word; both my word of generations past in Bible recording, also my word in Book of Mormon, Doctrine and Covenants, Pearl of Great Price; now my new published word mailed of recent time to all peoples in all nations.

131. Thus I am doing my work of pure holy justice, unto full power judgments, being the God of Creation, whose right it is to rule.

132. Thus am I doing all things righteous and holy, to be of full power justified to render full judgment here and hereafter.

133. Be ye pure. Be ye clean in morals.

134. No one need destroy themselves.

135. All can choose to do good, and eschew evil, even now.

136. Let all religions be of truth.

137. Let all tell truth, they receive not mine own revealed word for thy Lord unto the people of their religious group or order.

138. None can name my will; only my holy power attending my Mouthpiece.

139. Let all be of truth; they have not authority from God to administer eternal salvation unto any on earth.

140. Such was the first revealing to my holy servant Joseph Smith, Jun., in 1820, when God, the Father, and His Only Begotten Son, Jesus Christ, appeared to him in a sacred grove, after he was of full faith.

141. I gave him my eternal authority called Priesthood.

142. I caused him to know of Celestial Plural Eternal Union of pure living marriage, a most holy law requiring purity of living entire.

143. Let this most wicked generation be of receiving truth: You of corrupt way persecute my pure way of pure revealed holy way of my Church.

144. Now cease thy folly.

145. Your laws against my Celestial Law of Eternal Union Marriage of Celestial Plural Union are unjust from the beginning.

146. Congress and President in each time of passing these unjust rulings of man's law were purposeful attacks against my holy law and religion.

147. I am of full way power to set all right; even by removing from the earth all wicked and evil-practicing immoral people; to preserve mine elect who do abide my holy law in full way Celestial power. Amen.

148. Now let these truths go before appeals courts as my own will, saith Jesus Christ, to be of full way considered, as pure truth; sufficient to reverse all unjust court rulings against my servant and his brethren prosecuted because they live my Celestial Law, which only I, the Lord, can rightly govern.

149. Let also this be published to all peoples in every land and nation, to learn truth of my glorious coming as both a Holy Redeemer, also the Righteous Judge over all peoples; soon to send, before my coming in full power glory eternal Celestial authority, full judgments of cleansing power on all nations; which promise I gave in the New Testament, even in Matthew 24; also in Doctrine and Covenants, also in my holy true book called Book of Mormon; all telling same truth of my coming; first sending whirlwind judgments.

150. Let all know I am God who speaketh, who tells only truth; who is of full power Celestial to do all as I have spoken.

151. Now receive my word.

152. Obey my will, to abide the day of my coming. Amen.

SECTION REVELATION 135

Revelation of the Lord Jesus Christ
Palestine, Texas
Tuesday, November 8, 2011

1. I, your Lord Jesus Christ, speak to appeals court, my own will, to have true justice administered; to have unjust imprisonment of my servant reversed, he of free way; also to release my other servants in the unjust holding in prison who only obey my will in abiding Celestial Law of my holy Order Eternal.

2. Now receive my own word; also appendix of my own will of Proclamation to governing powers as testimony of my own right to rule over all nations; thus court of prosecuting power is of no jurisdiction in cases brought before court; also unjust ruling to cause no religious protection.

3. Let appeals court now consider my will:

SECTION REVELATION 136

Revelation of the Lord Jesus Christ
Palestine, Texas
Thursday, October 13, 2011

1. I, even Jesus Christ, speak to the present judge over court proceedings against my servant Warren Jeffs: I cause him to no longer be of an answering of your unjust and corrupt and unauthorized rulings; as I, the Lord, even Jesus Christ, am above all, and my law is religious and of me, a heavenly power over all creation.

2. Your judging is not based on truth.

3. I cause him to not answer to the court.

4. Let thy rulings against him cease.

5. I shall soon lay a heavy hand on all who fight against my Priesthood and Church, saith the Lord.

6. Now know I am God, even above all, and court of persecution shall be of a ceasing in my way of eternal power taking a hand if you will continue unjust way. Amen.

Holy Power Celestial of the Domain of Ahman in my own Kingdom Son Ahman

In behalf of Jesus Christ, Warren Jeffs is to sign for court to know I represent our Lord.

President Warren S. Jeffs, President of Church of Jesus Christ Servant of Jesus Christ

Appendix of Exhibits

SECTION REVELATION 137

Jesus Christ, Son Ahman
Savior of All Peoples on Earth

Thus Saith Jesus Christ, Son Ahman, Ruler Over All, Who Discerns the Souls of All Men, Who Is of Holy Pure Dwelling in Eternal Holy Power Over All Creation; Now Hear My Final Warning:

Revelation of the Lord Jesus Christ
Palestine, Texas
Sunday, December 11, 2011

1. Thus saith Jesus Christ, Son Ahman, God over all nations; who ruleth in the heavens; who hath conquered death; and who is full of eternal power, speaketh to all nations:

2. Now be full of more holy pure living to be surviving my Eternal Power come to earth.

3. Let all peoples hasten to repent.

4. I have sent my final warning.

5. I am doing my will in cleansing the earth.

6. I am now sending promised cleansing power of the way of full removing of wicked peoples from the earth; also overthrowing of evil rulers through both war, also my sending my cleansing judgment of purifying power.

7. Let all be humble.

8. Let all be knowing as I speak, so do I fulfill.

9. This from Him who is over all, who is of full authority to cleanse ungodly way of unborn child murder, also of immoral way of adultery and of Sodom. Amen.

SECTION REVELATION 138

Jesus Christ, Son Ahman
Savior of All Peoples on Earth

God Over All Creation of All Peoples

Thus Saith Jesus Christ to All Peoples on Earth, and to All Nations on My Land of New Jerusalem, Even Where I Shall Appear in Full Power Glory of the Holy Celestial Governing Powers Soon to Come on Earth, My Holy Power of Governing All Nations, to All on Earth:

Revelation of the Lord Jesus Christ
Palestine, Texas
Thursday, December 15, 2011

1. Thus saith Jesus Christ, your Holy Redeemer, unto all nations on earth, even to be of a full way of truth-telling to all people; to know I am your Lord Eternal; to know I am of a way of fulfilling all my will I have of recent time sent to all peoples, in my several holy revelations through him I have ordained to be my Keyholding authority on earth, to be of full ordination as an holy apostle; a full power of my eternal power on earth to administer Celestial blessings, eternal gifts of salvation; yet you heed not my word.

2. Now cometh dearth, famine in land where I am to appear, even in nation of power.

3. Let all now be of food preserving in the land of my soon coming, to be of full way ready way, unto full preserving of life.

4. Famine shall be enhanced by mob rule in many parts of the land where formerly wealth of food hath been raised; a mob rule of violence beyond measure; of murder extant; of full way of the fall of national authority.

5. You shall be then of invasion by two foreign powers.

6. Then cometh more judgments of my sending as many seek to destroy my people off the land of violent way.

7. I am God.

8. I have sent all to earth.

9. I have power eternal.

10. Repent ye, repent ye, all ye people on the American full continents, my land of Zion.

11. Your armies and navies cannot save you.

12. From among your own people cometh unrest of entire land becoming a full way of the wicked slaying one another in desperate struggle that only leads all to death, not life of happy way any longer; for I will not allow you of the American land to continue in pleasure in unholy wicked way; of child murder of unborn children, of Sodom extant spreading through all thine peoples of every clime and social order in nation of once freedom of law and peace-living together.

13. Let all repent.

14. You shall be a people of full way of no order nor peace.

15. Thy nation falleth from evils of corruption within, then outside and other powers of judgment cometh.

16. Thy full way of evil surpasses all former generations.

17. Satan worship is extant among thy nation in the way of sacrificing.

18. Let it be of full way knowing full way of idol sacrifice of human life soon shall be in land of former free way; then to be swept off the earth by my judgments.

19. Your violent way is ingrained even in thy youth, in wicked picture and other unholy time-wasting folly of the idolatrous way of self-entertaining.

20. Thus thy people worship man and man's creations of designing possessions, of way of technological advancings of my own inspiring; yet used to corrupt thy way before thy Lord, who has openly declared I am soon to appear to mine elect; yet you heed me not.

21. Now cometh full power of cleansing.

22. Now cometh my holy judgment power of removing all wickedness off my holy land of New Jerusalem.

23. O that ye would hear my word, all ye peoples on Zion's land of North and South America.

24. Canst thou stand against earthquake, storm, pestilence, famine, windstorms, even almighty powers I soon send; to destroy all who are of ignoble corrupt way of violence and immoral way of destroying virtue and innocence, of destroying life-way by aborting your developing child, all ye of the way of child murder in the eyes of God?

25. I am He, even Jesus your Lord, who speaketh to all on Zion's land, and to all peoples of every land, nation, kindred, tongue, and governing power on earth.

26. Your leaders reek in blood.

27. Your peoples live in wickedness and corrupt ways of Babylon of spiritual free-fall of unholy way eternal.

28. I shall fulfill this now you have shown you reject all my holy revelations I have recently sent to you and all leaders and peoples of all nations; my own Proclamation revealing my holy Keyholding Power of authority on earth; also my several warnings.

29. Let now this awake thee.

30. Cincinnati shall soon be a destroyed city.

31. Now hear my will.

32. Withdraw from the violent way in your gaming and wicked entertaining, lest thy people quickly turn to idol worshiping human sacrifice openly in many places in your nation; such as peoples of ancient times have followed whom were the powers on earth in leadership way; yet descended to state of satanic worship of self, in destroying life for pleasure.

33. Such shall soon be the conditions on my land of New Jerusalem soon in the fall of freedom in a nation of former free way. Amen.

34. Now hear my will, saith Jesus, your Lord and Redeemer: If thou wilt repent and cease these wicked ways I named are leading your peoples to violent mob rule and human sacrifice like former days, if you will cause my servant to go free, also his brethren held in prison houses; also make law to cease such child murder of unborn children; also cause Sodom to be a crime of punishment, not of a social way but of wicked way answered by law to be of full punishing; verily I say, cease such

life-corrupting way; then I shall spare the nation of free way if true justice is on the land.

35. Otherwise, there cometh soon full power of judgments of full power to cleanse all wickedness off my land of New Jerusalem.

36. I, the Lord, have spoken it. So shall it be full way cleansing if you heed me not, saith Jesus Christ, God over all; who cometh with Celestial power of full power to do all things I have revealed.

37. Now know my holy way is life, peace, justice against corrupting way of living of degradation way of immoral way of life-destroying way in thy social corrupt way of dwelling in unions not of purity, but of a flood of adulterous way extant; even thy youth dwelling in sexual sins extant.

38. Verily I say, all such shall be swept off my land, and off the earth. Amen.

39. Now behold my holy power send forth storm of devastating power, to cause serious damage through part of land of great and wicked places of the population.

40. Let all supply themselves with heating ability of wood or other way, as storm shall be of damaging electrical system in many places in United States of America.

41. Also supply thyselves and the poor with food, as thy way of transport shall soon be hindered for a time of my shaking nation of freedom for not giving my holy way freedom.

42. Thus I tell you before my judgment cometh.

43. Tell all people to be of the way of sharing, for short time of want cometh.

44. Also earthquake shall destroy part of a major city in the nation.

45. Thus you shall know I have spoken, saith Jesus Christ, God over all peoples; who is thy Holy Power of Life, who is your Holy Power to bring salvation to all peoples who would be of salvation. Amen.

46. Now let this word awake all peoples, as you see my very word fulfilled.

47. When there cometh mob rule, fall of nation is soon thereafter; as economic power fails, government will lose control of many in large population places; violence shall cause whole areas of greater population to flee, mostly west from the eastern part of land, also east to mountains from west coast larger population areas.

48. Great shall be the suffering of millions, who could have been of peaceful prosperity if they had been pure of the sin of immorality and child murder of an open practice in the nation, and in most nations of the earth.

49. The governing peoples now reek in blood unto the eternal judgment of God, for allowing murder of unborn children to continue by legal ruling of wicked way to destroy life for immoral way to continue among thy people.

50. Let all know such is murder in mine eyes, and shall be of full force judgment in the day of resurrection.

51. Now heed my word, and seek salvation, all ye peoples of the whole earth; for judgment of cleansing shall be in all nations.

52. Let my holy word be heralded in every land.

53. Let all people be of full hearing.

54. Let none be unbelieving. Amen.

SECTION REVELATION 139

Jesus Christ, Son Ahman
Savior of All Peoples on Earth

Jesus Christ, Who Is Son Ahman, Speaketh to the Nation and Leaders of Sierra Leone, a Holy Word From Your Eternal God, Who Is of Power Over Life and Death; Who Ruleth in the Heavens: Hear My Word of Eternal Authority and Power. Amen.

Revelation of the Lord Jesus Christ
Palestine, Texas
Saturday, December 17, 2011

1. Let my full way of warning be given nation of Sierra Leone.

2. Thus saith the Holy God over all peoples, Jesus Christ, God of all creation, who suffered on the cross, who rose the third day unto resurrected full Eternal Godhood power; conquering death, to bring all peoples from the otherwise eternal death, unto life, even eternal living with God in Celestial heavenly power who obey my holy Gospel; speaking now to the nation of Sierra Leone:

3. Your way of unholy way of murder of prisoners, also of unborn children, bringeth a full judgment on thee, soon to be of full power Celestial eternal power.

4. Let all thy evil ways of immoral way, also of the evil that caused God to destroy Sodom and Gomorrah by fire and brimstone, evils of slave trade also from among thy people -- behold, cease such evils, lest I cleanse you unto not being a people on earth.

5. Let this my warning be of a now obeying; to be of freedom of religion, also of free expression; to not imprison unpopular cause, of people not agreeing with leaders of thy nation.

6. Be of surety, I shall sweep all wicked out of thy land, unto the world of spirits, where all peoples await the holy resurrection unto the degree of glory happiness they earn.

7. I call on you to cease government injustice against they who disagree with the governing power being in prison, to be of no true justice.

8. Repent ye, all leaders and peoples in this nation. Amen.

SECTION REVELATION 140

Jesus Christ, Son Ahman
Savior of All Peoples on Earth

Thus Saith Jesus Christ, Son Ahman, to the Leaders of the Nations, to the Governing Powers in Every Land; to the Peoples of Every Nation, My Own Word to You of Warning of Declaring Eternal Truth of Judgments for Deeds Done on Earth; From the God of All Creation, Even I, Your Holy Redeemer, Jesus Christ, Jehovah, the Great I AM to All; to Now Awake, and Receive Unto Heeding My Revealed Word From the Heavens to All Peoples on Earth.

Revelation of the Lord Jesus Christ
Palestine, Texas
Monday, December 19, 2011

1. Now let my servant Warren Jeffs herald to all peoples my own will as I declare through him I have appointed; yea, ordained to hold sealing holy full powers of Priesthood Celestial, unto all peoples coming unto my holy authority to be of receiving my holy Gospel of salvation by pure authority revealed from heaven;

2. Thus I speak to all nations: Now cometh full retribution on all wicked of every nation who continue in child murder of unborn children; in practices of immoral way of Sodom and adulterous way.

3. I shall cleanse off this, my land of Zion, all who are of spiritual wicked way, not of my holy way.

4. Repent ye, all ye peoples on my land of Zion, for the cleansing powers shall be full measure suddenly, as you continue in degrading practices of immoral and murderous way.

5. Your lives are full measure being corrupted by continued way of child murder of unborn children before the God over all, even I, Jesus Christ.

6. Hear my full judgment into eternity on all such, knowing my own word of warning hath been heralded to all ends of the earth --

7. You who shed innocent blood shall suffer the pain of spirit and resurrected body until full debt of sin against my holy eternal plan of life is paid; a full measure of the way of full reward eternal damnation of suffering for willful sinning against knowledge.

8. Thou knowest my judgment on city of Sodom, also on city of Gomorrah; also on nations of power; Rome, Greece, Babylon. All were reeking in these sins; thus they are no more nations of earth, possessing power no more among men.

9. I cleansed them unto full loss of their governing other peoples.

10. Now heed my word, as you see my word begin to be fulfilled in the storms, earthquakes and other judgments of power.

11. I have warned of war soon on my land of Zion; telling nation of United States of America to prepare proper way --

free my servant Warren Jeffs, also Merril Jessop and their brethren from unjust holding in confinement; also to cleanse thy laws and uphold moral purity, doing away with legalized Sodom, and of horrible sin of child murder of unborn children.

12. I can shake you by my almighty power.

13. Be humble.

14. Awake to need to cleanse thy laws of these ways of allowing these heinous life-destroying crimes.

15. Now let it be known I shall hold all accountable, saith God, even Jesus Christ, for all deeds done in the flesh on earth.

16. None can escape my all-seeing eye and power of Divine Justice.

17. You deceive yourselves to think forgiveness for murder and immoral-crime sins of Sodom and adultery can be forgiven just on the asking; when sacred writ clearly decries against such sins, especially murder of children unborn; yet you go on in sins that shall be upon you eternally.

18. You are of full darkness who follow such an unhallowed wicked practice.

19. Children are of my sending, saith the Lord.

20. You are not the deciding authority to choose who shall live, of unborn children.

21. Must full destruction come before any surviving my judgments begin to believe a just holy God speaketh, and renders exact full measure justice into eternity?

22. My way is eternal.

23. I am Celestial Heavenly Governing Power over all creation who speaketh.

24. I am for life, life eternal.

25. Your way of justifying this heinous sin is to corrupt all in your nation who does not rise up to stop such evil.

26. Thus all shall be judged for individual works in the flesh. Amen.

27. Now come unto thy Lord by more righteous works; unto your Holy Lord who reigneth; who is of full power to preserve the innocent among you, to remove the wicked by full judgments of war, earthquake, famine, pestilences of nature, of war and hunger, also windstorms, the world in commotion.

28. O all ye peoples of the earth, thy God speaketh.

29. Heed my word.

30. Deny not eternal truth that murder is a full sin unto eternal death of thy spirit in a suffering untold for such as sin against knowledge. Amen.

31. Now let this, my word, touch honest hearts everywhere.

32. Let the pure, noble, and seekers of eternal truth come unto me, your Lord.

33. My Zion soon riseth in eternal power.

34. Your leaders are now of the full receiving of eternal judgment, after my own warnings have been sent to all peoples, to receive justice judgment reward for blood upon them, for allowing child murder of the unborn to continue by legal consent.

35. If you uphold them in power, you are against God and eternal holy way of life, virtue, purity, innocence, and of the way of holy walk.

36. Let all well consider who they uphold in governing power.

37. Many leaders in power turn blind eye, even though public expressions are made against these wicked ways; yet leaders of the nation of the United States of America now are of full receiving just recompense of reward by your Lord over all, in full judgments coming to cleanse thy people of all such wicked practices.

38. Let this, my full warning, finally be heeded. Amen.

39. Now I reveal coming war.

40. The nation of attacking power shall first be of a subduing other nations.

41. Then cometh war on the land of America in full power.

42. Only I, your Lord, can cause war to not sweep all off the land.

43. Yet I shall send whirlwind judgments when no other way of stopping bloodshed is of a full power.

44. Let all beware and touch not my people, my Church, my holy authority.

45. Let all be of knowing they belong to me, your Lord.

46. Give my servant freedom; give my Church freedom to live my holy Eternal Union Marriage Law of my own Kingdom Celestial, to be of pure way of my holy power dwelling among them on earth.

47. Thus is my call of full way, to repent and be of honoring thy own laws of religious freedom guaranteed, a holy religion of my revealing.

48. Let all be holy who would be of my Zion. Amen.

49. Verily thus saith the Lord to all nations on earth: Heed my will.

50. I have spoken.

51. Do all to make holy what you have made of evil intent in thy way of pleasure in evil way. Amen.

SECTION REVELATION 141

Jesus Christ, Son Ahman
Savior of All Peoples on Earth

Thus Saith the Lord Jesus Christ, Even Son Ahman, to the People of the Earth of all Nations, Mine Own Word Sent Forth as a Continued and Final Warning of My Great Powers of Judgment Upon Thee. Hear Thou My Word:

Revelation of the Lord Jesus Christ
Palestine, Texas
Saturday, December 24, 2011

1. I, the Lord, speak through my servant Warren Jeffs to all peoples on earth a message of warning, mine own word revealed from the heavens, my holy love reaching for all honest in heart who will purify their lives and be of a receiving of thy Lord at His glorious appearing, prophesied of by ancient apostles, and thy Lord's own words, recorded by them in sacred Bible, known to this generation of my coming soon at hand.

2. Verily thus saith the Lord, Jesus Christ, who is Jehovah Christ, Son Ahman, the Beginning and the End, who hath all power over all nations, who ruleth in the heavens above and governeth all things unto Zion of New Jerusalem coming forth as the ruling governing power on earth; a New

Jerusalem of Celestial power and authority sent from heaven, thy Lord appearing with ten thousand of saints and more, who shall come from heaven of governing authority of my Holy Priesthood now prepared, a people who shall go among surviving nations who survive the great whirlwind judgments of my sending because you heed me not;

3. Thus saith the Lord to this wicked and perverse and immoral generation: You must be purged of the sins of murder, of child murder of unborn children, of Sodom and adulterous ways, before my glorious appearing.

4. This is my revealing to you:

5. That if I came this day, all-consuming fire would leave your lands without inhabitants.

6. I send my word that perchance some honest in heart will be touched by the power of my Spirit and repent, for some lands shall be left desolate because these sins pervade entire throughout the population in some wicked places on earth.

7. And I shall purge, yea, pluck out the wicked from among the righteous, by judgments of power, by disease, by earthquake, by pestilence, hail, and famine; by wars that shall remove the more violent from the earth.

8. Verily thus saith the Lord: My word shall be performed and fulfilled.

9. Hasten, lest there be none in your lands remain, for these gross and heinous crimes must be obliterated from among all peoples of the earth;

10. For my glorious appearing shall bring Celestial power of governing power throughout the earth, sent forth by representatives from New Jerusalem on Zion's land, called now North America; also South America, having Zion places established of mine Israel gathered to those lands unto Old Jerusalem, even Judah and other tribes gathering to that former land of their possessing, as I, the Lord, have caused mine Israel to be gathered in latter days from every nation under heaven. Amen.

11. Now receive my word, ye peoples of the earth: Repent ye, repent ye, for my time is at hand.

12. And I have not been silent.

13. And I have sent forth my word; and I have given my word in great plainness, even declaring new windstorms and earthquakes, and other cities to be swept off the earth if they heed me not;

14. And you must be of a prepared way, even to be preserved as my scriptures declare, mine angels preserving the more righteous, catching them up, yea, lifting them up off the earth, if needs be, by power of Celestial power.

15. This is in sacred writ, in the book of Luke, if you would be of believing, 17th chapter and 18th, declaring that mine elect would be spared, though they would be few in number.

16. I, your Lord, concerned, seeing in vision that few would remain on the earth in the latter days, who are of the purity of Zion; therefore my Zion land, North America, South America also, shall be swept of these heinous and corrupt and most horrible crimes of child murder, of Sodom and adultery, of other murdering ways that many leaders of nations use to force their power upon other nations or upon their own population.

17. It must not be, for my reign in the Millennial time of a thousand years among men shall be a time of great peace, of Celestial established peace-power of governing nature.

18. This is the word of the Lord to all peoples. Amen.

SECTION REVELATION 142

Jesus Christ, Son Ahman
Savior of All Peoples on Earth

I, Jesus Christ, Jehovah, Even Son Ahman, Speak to All Peoples on Earth, My Own Will to Be Known Among All Nations. I Am Soon to Come in Mighty Power Celestial, to Be the Holy Power Over All Peoples Who Are of the Purity of Life to Be of Survival When My Full Power of the Judgments I Send Cometh on All Nations. Hear Ye My Will:

Revelation of the Lord Jesus Christ
Palestine, Texas
Tuesday, December 27, 2011

1. The Lord Jesus Christ, even God over all, speaketh to all peoples on earth, even to be the Holy Power of Salvation unto all who cometh unto me, in holy pure living on earth.

2. My Gospel of salvation has been sounded.

3. You are of full way without excuse, all ye peoples on earth.

4. I have been of full revealing my holy way to all leaders of all nations, thus to the people of all nations, kindreds, tongues; peoples of every land to know of my coming in Glory Power Celestial Order of pure holy power over all nations; to rule as King of kings over all peoples.

5. Thus I am sending my own holy will to all; to repent; to be pure in way of my holy way; to be only loving, peaceful, full of pure holy power, through my grace attending the pure in heart, who only live to do good to all people.

6. Let this be my full warning of holy receiving by all people on the earth, to now be only of holy pure living, only seeking good toward all on earth.

7. You must be of way of preserving the way of life, of virtue, purity way of life-giving way eternal; to not be of sin of immoral way; to be of life-power, preserving life of unborn children no longer murdered.

8. Let this be a way to show thy God, even Jesus Christ, who seeth and knoweth all things, to cleanse thyselves, thy laws of nations; cleansing this murderous way from thy peoples entire; to be nation, each one, of more life-preserving way.

9. I shall soon cleanse all off the earth who are of guilty way of child pre-birth murderous practice; even to be plucking out the more wicked among all peoples.

10. Thus I am God; I give life.

11. I take whom I will.

12. I shall purge all nations of the immoral corruption way of murder for lustful and immoral way; even to be holy people who dwell in the love of God and

my eternal power way of pure holy living, in thy being only of my way of pure living, being of my holy love-peace shining over all nations; as my Zion rises in full power over all peoples, nations, tongues, kindreds, governing powers.

13. I have spoken.

14. All shall be mine, the God of full holy power over all the earth. Amen.

15. Now let this be my final holy way to show all peoples I have spoken.

16. My way is of witnessing.

17. My way is of truth-holy way, telling all peoples on earth I speak through him whom I have ordained; though in bondage.

18. Let all be my holy order of delivering him of my pure holy order of Priesthood; to be of my order of administering salvation to all who desire my Gospel of pure holy living; a plan of eternal power, Celestial power, of the way eternal, of my plan eternal. Amen.

(DECEMBER 26, 2011   PALESTINE, TEXAS)

The Lord Jesus Christ speaketh, even Him who is over all who hath all power unto full power to exalt all who are of the order of obedience to My holy way of salvation. Let my holy power be thy only power, all ye who are of My church on earth. Let all now be of My Holy United Order who are of My church. amen.

Warren S Jeffs

WARREN S. JEFFS   PRESIDENT OF THE CHURCH
OF JESUS CHRIST OF LATTER-DAY SAINTS

SECTION REVELATION 143

Jesus Christ, Son Ahman

I, Your Lord Jesus Christ, Even Son Ahman, Speak to All Nations on Earth, My Own Revealing of My Soon Coming. Let All Hear My Will:

Revelation of the Lord Jesus Christ
Palestine, Texas
Tuesday, December 27, 2011

1. Let now all people on earth be told my holy will.

2. I, who am of full Godhood power over world, even of my Father, Elohim, who is my Eternal Father, saith Jesus Christ, your Lord and Holy Savior, Son Ahman; who redeemed all mankind from the grave, to lift each up by my power over death unto life in the holy resurrection; I say to all nations --

3. Repent ye; now be of full humbling; all peoples shall be humbled in full way; as I send full judgments.

4. Now repent, so I may own and bless all who come unto me; even to be my people of Zion. Amen.

SECTION REVELATION 144

Jesus Christ, Son Ahman
Savior of All Peoples on Earth

Thus Saith Jesus Christ, God Over All, to the President of the United States, a Word of Judgment for Not Giving Heed to My Own Will Revealed to Deliver You and the Nation You Lead Unto Full Power Continued; Now to Not Be of Full Power, Even I, God, Saying Thus:

Revelation of the Lord Jesus Christ
Palestine, Texas
Tuesday, December 27, 2011

1. Thus saith the Lord to the President of the United States of America, to the leader of national power, who heedeth not the God over all: Now know you hath been of a way of full neglect.

2. You are of the way of my judgment soon to happen.

3. Be ye aware that I, God, have spoken my own will.

4. I am soon to be of full power Celestial in sending full judgments upon my land of my holy power of Zion.

5. You are of the order of falling from power.

6. I shall be of full way to humble thee, unto no influence in national power, soon to be of fall in full way; no longer to be of full authority in political way of power.

7. You shall feel a way of darkening in thy soul, causing you not to be of full deciding way in many of thy doings, being of confusion in many items needing national power to be of certain way of deciding.

8. Then cometh thy downfall.

9. I have spoken it.

10. Let all thy whole soul now be of full humble way before me, your Lord Jesus Christ; who only can redeem the soul from darkness unto light eternal.

11. Let all now hear my will; that you, the President of the power to do well, now shall lose power, to no longer have full way of support in many issues in thy caretaking. Amen.

SECTION REVELATION 145

Thus Saith Son Ahman, Jesus Christ, Your Lord, a Warning of Judgments on All Nations to Be Heard by All Peoples

Jesus Christ
SON AHMAN

I, Jesus Christ, God of All the Heavens and Earth, Speak to All Peoples on Earth, to Leaders of Nations, My Own Will and Holy Message of Full Warning of Future Soon Happenings on Earth; That if You Believe and Obey My Will, You May Be Preserved. Amen. Thus Do I Speak Holy Will of My Holy Order of Mercy and Justice, My Own Way to Be Justified to Send My Full Judgments of Cleansing Power Celestial on All Inhabitants on Earth; for This Is My Word, Saith Your Own God Who Made You. Thus Saith the Lord to All Peoples of All Nations: Heed My Holy Will, Lest Sudden Powers of Whirlwind Judgment of Almighty Holy Power Having the Power of Leaving on Earth Whom I Will. Now Read My Holy Warning of Pure Holy Truth of Soon Happening.

Revelation of the Lord Jesus Christ
Palestine, Texas
Thursday, December 29, 2011

1. I who reigns on high, even Jehovah, the Beginning and the End, who reigneth, even Jesus Christ, speaketh to all people of the world, to hasten to prepare; for I am soon to come in power, a holy reign on earth for a thousand years among men.

2. Come to me through my Holy Priesthood to receive the Gospel of salvation.

3. Come to me through my holy Apostle Warren Jeffs, to be of full power of the holy Gospel.

4. Let all be aware I am now of the power to cleanse all peoples of the heinous, most wicked crime of child murder of unborn children; also Sodom and adulterous way.

5. Let the law of thy nation be to overthrow evil practices that destroy life, virtue, innocence; and be more pure in living way of holy conduct.

6. Let all leaders of nations again hear my word; to change laws in every nation; to be more pure and of virtue protected by law; even death penalty for such outward evils.

7. Let this be a soon happening, lest my

full judgment of the way of full cleansing power.

8. Now heed my many warnings sent by my holy order of authority to deliver my own will. Amen.

9. Now I reveal to all the world a coming full way to be of believing I have spoken, even your God over all; when I send a full tidal wave tsunami judgment upon Asia again; also to be of a way to be felt on many other island lands near the center of earthquake.

10. This is to show my power is of sure way of the sending full judgment upon all peoples of all nations soon, at a time you think I am of silent way.

11. My voice is being heralded.

12. My will is being made known.

13. Let all be of pure way, lest an holy God send all needed judgment of full cleansing way.

14. Let all be of holy way; casting out of their lives all evil they know is of full way wrong; even the murder of unborn children, the moral crimes that bring this evil about; also drunkenness, the sin of outward abuse of woman, also family abuse of both the woman and of children.

15. Care for the poor in thy land, all ye who seek a blessing of thy God, who shall reward all peoples for all deeds done in this earthly existence of my own giving life to all. Amen.

16. Now let leaders of all nations bear influence to free my servant, an act which shall be thy acknowledgment of my own will of the rightful Ruler over all the earth, over all nations; and to be acknowledging mine own authority I have ordained on earth to be as a legal administrator of mine own will.

17. Let all be of way of sending a delegation to the land he is held in bondage, to demand his freedom; to be of inquiry unto me, your Eternal God, for all things necessary for thy survival.

18. Let also all people on earth be of holy way in daily living; to be of full preserving.

19. Let my holy people who are of my order of Zion be pure.

20. Let all be holy, noble, godlike, in all thy own way of doing, in family, business, religious way of loving God over all; to be of more pure holy way.

21. Let all people now come unto me, your Holy Redeemer, even Jesus Christ, who speaketh to your understanding.

22. Now come before me in my day of judging, to be pure as you have light and truth of eternal way; of my holy order of holy living, as is recorded in New Testament; also in my Book of Doctrine and Covenants, the revelations of my own will to all peoples of the earth.

23. Read and follow my own will in holy writ, to be prepared for all my holy way coming forth. Amen.

24. Now receive more witness I am speaking from the heavens to all people on earth through my holy Mouthpiece; to be of sure way I am God speaking.

25. The nation of Syria shall be overthrown.

26. They shall lose war.

27. My holy people Israel shall conquer.

28. They shall only be a tributary nation to my Israel, which also shall be cleansed by my allowing the full way of humbling them for evils I have told must be no longer among their nation.

29. Let this be a full way to know I have spoken before my full judgment cometh. Amen.

30. Let now this be my full way to show I know all things.

31. Let all on seashore of the lands of Asia be of moving.

32. Let them not be in low level areas for the season of my sending tidal wave to humble many peoples; even to be of full warning by me, your Lord.

33. Let they who move also clean up their moral ways, lest greater judgments of my power come by war, earthquake, even my power almighty in various ways of judgments of God upon all nations, soon to be the preparatory work for my coming, saith your Most Holy Lord, whose holy way

of purifying all lands shall be so full, that all peoples everywhere shall witness their own land receiving whirlwind judgments.

34. Let all be of sure way to have full power to be of receiving this, my holy word, in every nation, to publish with exactness this, my word sent to all peoples on earth; to be of leaders of nations' receiving.

35. Let my word of previous sending to libraries all over the earth be read. My more recent will of God, published in several pamphlets of my pure holy way of truth-telling, can be of thy receiving.

36. The honest in heart shall know I am speaking. Amen.

SECTION REVELATION 146

Jesus Christ
Son Ahman

I, Jesus Christ, Speak to All Peoples of the Earth; to Hear My Will of Salvation; to Set Aside War and Violent Ways of Evil Intent by Force to Promote Injustice, Unrighteous Ways. Now Be of Holy Way and Hear My Word Saying Thus:

Revelation of the Lord Jesus Christ
Palestine, Texas
Sunday, January 1, 2012

1. Now behold my own will to the whole world, even Jesus Christ, Son Ahman, Creator over all things that are of the dominion of my Holy Father Elohim; to be Ruler as Christ, the Savior of Redeeming Atoning Power; to raise all peoples from the grave, to be the power of life, even as I am to all creation:

2. Hear thou my warning, sent to all peoples on the earth. I am to be a fire

eternal of all-consuming power, leaving neither root nor branch of the wicked nor their posterity, as they are of Sodom and murder of unborn children.

3. I am above all.

4. Nothing can stay my hand.

5. I hold all nations in my power.

6. All ye proud and fallen-way peoples on the earth, heed my word, lest you die.

7. I am God of salvation over all

peoples, holding the scepter of holy eternal authority over all; to come soon to earth; to be the Deliverer of the innocent; of virtue, purity; yea, of every good thing.

8. Be ye of sure way to know you please me in all thy ways.

9. Now come unto me, saith Jesus Christ, God over all.

10. Let now leaders of nations make peace.

11. Let armies be of no aggression.

12. Let navies only guard shores, not of attack.

13. Let policing be of protecting innocence, not of aggression.

14. Let militaries only be used by they who are of noble giving, to preserve peace, not promote violent way.

15. Let all be of more pure holy way of living.

16. I, God, have all power.

17. I can see all things.

18. All is of open view before me, a God of all creation.

19. Heed my holy will to continue on earth. Amen.

20. Now let truth prevail. I am all Truth.

21. All truth is full reality way of eternal existence.

22. I am God of eternal power, Celestial authority power; able to exalt all obeying children to receive my glory, happy way of salvation.

23. Now come unto me.

24. I have power to overcome all evil and make holy all that is obeying heavenly laws of progression.

25. My way is not man's way.

26. My way is eternal.

27. I am a God of eternal power, always there to be Giver of all good.

28. Heed my word.

29. Do not be slow to be about full repenting, is the call of thy Lord. Amen.

30. Let all the world receive this call to repentance.

31. Let all peoples beat swords into pruning hooks; and thy weapons become of no use.

32. Let peace be thy covenant, to be established entire on earth among all peoples.

33. Let all ways of harsh law enforcing cease now.

34. Be equal at law, not forgetting the poor who have not wherewithal to pay for representation, to be free to do all they can to be of noble way unto them having equal rights.

35. Let all now be ready to come to a full peaceful dominion of Christ. Amen.

36. Now let all peoples hear truth.

37. If thou heed me not, I come first to sweep wickedness off the earth, to preserve the more righteous of every nation.

38. Now be subject to my rule, even to inherit eternal life when I come to reward every man with the power of eternity, to make holy eternal power Celestial love-power of my inspiring all who remain on earth, to greater, more holy way of living. Amen.

39. I shall also be vengeance in behalf of the innocent who come unto me.

40. The virtuous and holy way of truth eternal shall be taught by my governing and holy power to all surviving peoples on earth; so all may share in the holy order I am establishing on earth, to be a full power of pure holy love-power over all; that shall quench the violent way with love-joy and joyful love-peace, a love for God that shall plant in each heart a pure holy way of holy pure living.

41. Now awake, ye spirits in the world

of departed spirits; to be ready to receive thy ordinances of eternal peace through my holy way lived among all holy peoples in the day of my coming.

42. Let these sobering truths be on thy souls as an awakening.

43. Let all consider well my eternal holy word. Amen.

Chapter 5

Jesus Christ, Who Is Over All, Speaketh Strong Warning of Certain Holy Power of Judgments to Be Upon Nation of My Holy Power of New Jerusalem, Also to All Nations

I, Jehovah, God Over All, Speaketh, Even Jesus Christ, to All Nations, Give Heed. Amen.

(Comprising Section Revelations 147-148)

Jesus Christ
Son Ahman

I, Jehovah, Son of God, Even Jesus Christ, Speak My Own Way of True Holy Order of Warning to All People on Earth, Yet to Come Suddenly Unto Holy People Who Are Believing My Own Revealing, Now to Be Only Pure in Living Way on Earth, by My Way Being Lived. Now Repent. Receive My Way of How to Be of Holy Way. Let All Now Come Unto Me. Come Clean, Lest Full Order of Judgment Cometh on All Nations Who Forget God. Amen. Now Hear My Revealing of Holy Way to All:

SECTION REVELATION 147

Revelation of the Lord Jesus Christ
Palestine, Texas
Sunday, February 5, 2012

1. I who is over all speak through my order of holy power of holy order revealing, unto all on the earth, of full way of knowing I speak, then am of the holy order of full way fulfilling all, as I say to all, I soon come unto all holy people on the world of my holy way of creating.

2. I say unto all, be of pure holy way, even my full holy way now of you having my way of holy preparing; unto all knowing my way.

3. I am now of holy order power Celestial, to be only of readiness; to have full order of government order over all nations.

4. Now let only my holy way be lived, lest full judgment come on all you who labor not in holy way extant; for now cometh my wrath upon all who are of evil way; of the order of unholiness.

5. Let all be holy, pure, of the way of true holy way; not of man, but of my power; to give unto God full way obeying way, lest none be of a remaining on the earth of the mortal way; for I come in Celestial power of heaven.

6. Now be holy, so you who are of mortal way are also pure, to be a holy people on my world of probationary testing of all in the earth, now of the way to be only wicked, because you heed my message of my holy power of my way to be holy, yet continue in sin and debauchery way of the unholy immoral way of the adulterous and Sodom unholy way among men, as though you could change God from doing all as He listeth to all men on the earth.

7. Such sons and daughters of unbelieving order shall suddenly be

surprised as I am soon to be of full power revealing all truth to all peoples.

8. Let all be holy, so you can abide the day of my holy Advent, even of full holy order power Celestial order holy power, of full way Celestial glory mighty power. Amen.

9. Thus saith the Lord, a full and final warning, telling all nations soon cometh full way order power, to be of my way of full holy order, of the holy way to lift up all more holy righteous out of all lands, as I declared in my holy New Testament holy writing, found in Book of Luke of your chaptering number 17, telling of last days of vengeance of my full way power of preserving the more holy people unto my holy power of angelic order from heaven attending more pure people.

10. Let all do the now needed holy repenting, so all may be lifted up, to have my power to be preserved when whirlwind sudden power cometh soon, to cleanse all nations of more wicked peoples from among you.

11. Let this be of thy now receiving, believing, and doing, saith God, even your Holy God, Jesus Christ; soon to appear to all nations suddenly. Amen.

12. Now let rulers be of full way preparing for my holy way.

13. Let all read new publishing; my holy way of holy preparing of all nations, now to be judged by me, your Holy Lord, by angelic labor among all nations coming at time great judgment cometh.

14. As it was in the time of Father Noah, so shall it be in the latter-day coming of thy Lord.

15. Be ye full of peace order, in knowing you are now of repenting order.

16. Now love peace, holy way of kindness, moral pure holy way; to be of the holy order of preserving, thus to be my holy order of full love-order preserving way order, to be of my holy way of the coming of God among you; to have full witness I am dwelling on the very way of man among you on the world of thy now dwelling.

17. My message of full holy justifying hath now been fully sent to all nations.

18. War is soon to take place, as prophesied by my holy apostle of the writ in holy order of my New Testament holy order preserved in worldwide publishing; which many religionists quote in continual, also way of repeated concern, yet not of my way of full way to be holy; fearing man more than my way, even to change to more holy way of pure holy living; unto compromising with sinful way.

19. Thus do I judge all unholy way of false way of warning; they who do not purify themselves unto my holy named way in my holy scripture of being purity living now on earth; not of self-righteous way of joining in unholy conduct of this most, of all former generations, now more corrupt in murderous, adulterous, Sodom way worldwide than all former times I sent cleansing powers upon the world.

20. Now be holy, lest full judging power descend in full power order upon all not of holy way on earth.

21. This from God, even your Holy Lord, Jesus Christ; who is soon of full power holy order of full holy way of cleansing all peoples off the earth, who do not be of my holy order; all to soon be judged extant; none remaining who continue in sin, knowing I am soon to be Judge of all peoples; both on the now world you are of full living upon; to be of the deciding holy power to decide who remaineth on the world, now of the way of a unholy living in all lands, nations,

peoples, kindreds, tongues, governing authorities now on this world; also eternal judging in resurrection of all peoples; I having conquered the devil, hell; the way of death having been overcome by God through holy way of Eternal Atonement. Amen.

22. Now let all peoples have this, my will: Repent ye, repent ye, all nations, peoples, way of kindreds of same way of family living; also the way of law of nations no longer of allowing unholy murder of unborn children by thy legal consenting; also cleanse immoral way out of every people now on the world you inhabit together, by my holy will; yet most deny me, your holy Lord, even He who made all unto a living, breathing soul on the present world of my testing all what thou art in character, developed by using agency on world where my holy order of full testing taketh place, so I may judge all.

23. Let all be holy, lest my full judgment of eternal way of the duration of eternal power in the God shall give unto punishing for sin; now of thy knowing my holy way is published to all nations now on earth; a time of the full judgment of my sending on all full power, in my time, to be holy power extant; to have all of full judging order; to have my holy way known; to be only of the order of living as you are holy unto me, Jesus Christ, your holy and loving Lord of all, even God over all now peoples; also my whole way of full way of judging reaching all now in world of spirits, a full order of all peoples of all generations knowing I have come to this now world upon which all on earth now dwell; yea, even the world around you of invisible order to earthly way of now living on world of physical order; to be of they of the way of departed spirits from physical order you now have in mortal living, as pertaining to my holy order of people needing salvation teaching before the holy time of resurrecting power is of my holy labor entire; to grant all, both now on my world you now live on, also all who formerly dwelt on this world, you of the order of dwelling now on this world; yea, all shall be offered salvation; as my holy Priesthood power dwells there also, to be of administering to all they who believe my holy way of holy salvation; yea, to all nations of the earth of all time, to be of hearing my holy way of sure holy saving order unto living with thy holy order of the way of God; to be my way of salvation, thus of me.

24. Let all peoples hear my message of saving order; to be holy, as I am holy, saith God, Jesus Christ, in all holy way of dwelling among men on present world of present living; to be judged in eternal holy order of my Eternal Godhood holy order of pure all-knowing, all-seeing power, over all who are born on the world you now dwell on.

25. I send my own word to all.

26. Repent, repent, is my call to all.

27. Now learn full judging soon to happen.

28. Nation of the way of my New Era holy way, even of my Holy City of New Holy Way Jerusalem, is to be of full cleansing; also more wicked in all lands of the world you now dwell upon; to be no longer of this life, nor to be able to hinder my holy Zion order of holy order of pure living unto the way of holy way being only governing holy order way order of pure redeeming way of all mankind.

29. Let all be of holy order to be delivered unto life everlasting way order. Amen.

SECTION REVELATION 148

Revelation of the Lord Jesus Christ
Palestine, Texas
Monday, February 6, 2012

1. Thus saith the Lord to all peoples on earth: A day of wrath of God is soon at hand.

2. Repent ye, repent ye, is the word of God to all peoples, to now repent, for time is soon to be of great violent way among nations, within nations, bringing economic way to not be of full way of thy power to feed thy peoples; mob rule in many places; evil way of the order of sacrifice of the way of ancient peoples in many places, even in nation of power, when people fall into disorder unto violent way soon at hand.

3. Oh that ye would do my will, saith the Lord, to be of peace-loving order.

4. You heed me not.

5. Murder and rapine shall be of full way of the evil power destroying many through the wicked being of no unity; only of violent order of life-taking evil unholy way.

6. I, God, have sent my way to be of surviving in the great day of visiting all nations on earth with justice, judgment; also thy own sins be upon you of murder of unborn children, in thy immoral way of living unholy way on earth.

7. Soon my word shall be verified; that I have fully warned all of my power coming to cleanse of the earth more wicked out of every land, people, kindred, tongues; even nations being no longer nation of existence on now world of great and unholy way of full iniquity ripened unto full judgment of God to soon be poured forth on all peoples; especially on holy Zion continent of North America, also all lands.

8. Now repent; be ye holy, is the continued and full warning I send to all peoples. Amen.

SECTION REVELATION 149

Thus Saith Jesus Christ, Son Ahman, an Holy Will of Eternity Truth, to Be Answered on All of This Now Generation of the World, to Be Warned About the Way of Full Judgment to Come, Even to Be of Full Power as You Heed Not My Warning

Jesus Christ
Son Ahman

I, Jesus Christ, Speak to All Nations, Peoples, Tongues, and Powers of Governing Power, to Heed My Will; for I Come to Cleanse All Nations, in Way of Delivery for My Holy Pure People on Earth; They Who Eschew Evil, Who Love Truth of Pure Holy Order of Salvation; Even Who Repent and Who Are of My Holy Way to Be of Exalting Pure Love-Peace. Amen.

Revelation of the Lord Jesus Christ
Palestine, Texas
Monday, January 9, 2012

1. I, Jesus Christ, Holy God over all, to all nations, kindreds, peoples; nations of power over all the earth; to step forth and cleanse thy hands entire of murder of unborn children, a heinous crime against me, your Lord, who is over all things; even the Creator of heaven and earth, and all things thereon:

2. Hasten now, ye people of all lands on earth, to cleanse thyselves. Amen.

3. Listen, saith the Lord, to Eternity Truth.

4. I am Celestial Eternal Holy Governing Order of Ahman, who is Father over all creation; Son Ahman, even Jesus Christ, sent to redeem all from the grave; which witness of my holy resurrection is in New Testament, also Book of Mormon.

5. I caused Joseph Smith to be my holy Seer, Revelator, and holy Prophet, to be my holy instrument of restoring my pure holy Gospel.

6. Let all peoples be ready.

7. My testimony hath gone forth.

8. Nothing can stay my hand.

9. I am Endless.

10. My name is Jesus Christ, Holy One of Israel.

11. I shall bequeath to all my salvation who are obeying my revealed truths. Amen.

12. Now be ready, is the call of thy Lord.

13. Let only pure holy men rule in national government authority; who

preserve way of life; also who allow religious freedom.

14. Let all be of ready way to be judged.

15. I send whirlwind cleansing power.

16. I am the Power of Eternal Truth.

17. I send my will forth; then nations rise or fall as they choose whether to heed my word or reject my holy revealing. Amen.

18. Now receive Eternity Truth, that all born on earth are my sons and daughters from Celestial glory world, sent to earth to have full trial.

19. You are able to know good from evil at an age of accountability, yea, even by the time you would hear and receive baptism by immersion in holy blessed water of my holy authority called Priesthood; which age is of the appointed ability of choosing with understanding of eight years old.

20. Children are innocent.

21. They can be taught truth, to love truth in young years; so they have opportunity to be baptized into my Church at eight years old.

22. Let parents bequeath upon family of their raising, my own will; to repent of fallen way of the world, and come unto me as little children, young and old of full knowledge I am speaking, I can redeem.

23. All things are before me;

24. Nothing hideth.

25. Only I remain above all, to be the power of all holy truth that can exalt to heaven.

26. All must be pure to dwell in Celestial full glory.

27. All must have baptism after faith unto me, in full repentance.

28. All can earn this. Amen.

29. Now learn separation of bloodlines.

30. All of race of color of the land of Cain, even Africa, shall be of separate line of progenity.

31. All others shall be of my Gospel.

32. The people of the order who give full Priesthood gifts to them are not of me.

33. I have in holy scripture, through Joseph Smith, revealed such can only be of baptism, not of Priesthood holding.

34. I reveal to all that the race of Cain cannot receive all Priesthood gifts in the way of now receiving, until after all other races, for their salvation, have been offered my eternal plan in full.

35. Thereafter cometh opportunity for Cain's posterity, he having been cursed by his own continual corrupt way.

36. Now know I forgive all sins save murder against innocent blood shed, by evil intent.

37. All such of all peoples cannot be of my Gospel. Amen.

38. Thus let the murder of innocence cease in all nations; for all people shall know I have sent my own will forth; to cleanse all peoples of an eternal damnation of murder guiltiness.

39. Thus all must cleanse themselves, even all nations, of murder, lest I cease thy dominion on earth, as an evil unworthy vessel. Amen.

40. I am God.

41. I am Truth.

42. I fear not all peoples.

43. Be receiving Truth Eternal from God over all. Amen.

44. Now let all be repenting.

45. Ignorance is forever gone when truth cometh forth.

46. Now my holy word hath been published to all nations.

47. I have required my Holy Priesthood

to now reveal more truth to save all nations, so people are not deceived.

48. Let Eternity Truth hold full power in lives of all.

49. Rulings of man cannot overthrow God and His eternal way of salvation.

50. Time changeth not Truth of Eternal Power unto exalting way power over all creation.

51. All things testify of my power of creation, even earth and heaven.

52. I have not been of a silent way.

53. I have spoken, sent forth my own revealings, lo, these many generations since thy father Adam was on earth teaching his posterity.

54. He is my Son, a God of Creation sent to earth to people this probation and testing world; for a God had to come to people the world.

55. He repented and is with me eternally as a Son of God of holy way.

56. His son Abel was also of holy way, and was murdered by his brother Cain; which brought my way of peopling a land not of my holy way; a people who were not to have more than one holy way companion throughout history; a tradition among them usurping authority of my own Order, not of Eternity Authority.

57. Such should have only one companion to be of purity on earth. Amen.

58. Now learn that I judge according to knowledge.

59. My Celestial Law of Plural Union is only to be received by Keyholding authority on earth, having my own will.

60. Let all who claim authority cease.

61. Let all who say revealing from my own holy order is in them be no longer heeded by the people on my now soon to be of full cleansing world.

62. Let all heed my will; to cease immoral way of your many connections of illicit intercourse not of pure holy way.

63. Adultery is an eternal damnation sin in all religion of pure way teaching.

64. Sodom is also an eternal damning sin of immoral way.

65. It is of a witness to pure mind on earth by my holy power of life, light, truth of the holy way God speaketh to the soul that will be enlightened through my answer to prayerful honest heart; to know sins of immoral and also murderous way are most destructive to thee, and to nations, in way of living ways of destructive way.

66. I have now left all peoples without excuse; my own word having been sent to all nations, leaders of nations; to prepare the way for my holy appearing to all remaining peoples on earth.

67. Thus I, God, am justified to now cleanse all peoples.

68. Hearken to my will.

69. Be ye pure, lest sudden judgment remove thy way of existing on my earth, unto you still of a spirit way of living go to my world of the peoples who were on earth in the flesh, now in spirit world, of full way knowing judgment cometh in resurrection of all peoples to be of standing before me, Jesus Christ, God of life and salvation, to be judged for deeds done in the flesh. Amen.

70. Now be ye ready, all ye peoples of the earth. Amen.

71. I who reigns on high, whose way of pure truth is over all the earth, speak to my people of holy way, to now be holy. Amen.

72. Let all peoples hear my will; to now be of sure way to know I am of the order of the way of holy power.

73. Only I can be thy Deliverer, thy only Friend of the holy way of salvation.

74. Come unto me, thy Lord, the Redeemer over all mankind; to be thy holy way of the power of peace, love, joy; to be the full way of pure holy power Celestial.

75. Let all people be of holy power; to be my Zion, a holy way of full way to eternal living with all the holy angels. Amen.

76. I, your Lord, speak. Let all listen.

77. Let all have open hearts, to hear my love-power as a pure holy law unto the whole world.

78. Be ye of the way of holy power, a law of eternity, a power Celestial; my holy love bonding all people of all nations to live in peace; a Millennial Reign of holy order of pure power.

79. I am He who is of the order of holy power, dwelling in my Kingdom over the whole heavens, to come in power unto all on earth; to make myself known as the God of all creation unto all people on earth; to be thy holy power of pure love.

80. I speak, and worlds come into existence.

81. My hand is over all.

82. Nothing can stay my holy power.

83. I am the Life and the Way of salvation.

84. Come unto me, all ye ends of the earth, to be of holy salvation, that I may own and bless you, to be holy as I am holy; to have life eternal unto full love-power Celestial flowing as a full holy way of salvation in continual blessings of life, of joy everlasting.

85. Such is the inheritance of the people who abide in my holy power of Eternal Union.

86. Now have thy lives be purified by full repenting, is the word of the Lord to all nations of all lands on earth, even to all peoples, saith God, even Jesus Christ, your Holy King over all nations, unto thy holy way being of my power of eternal lives.

87. Let all now bow to my rule, an eternal holy governing authority.

88. Let all be of pure holy way to be of the full blessing of preservation in the soon time of full power cleansing of wicked way of all peoples off the world, of the way of holiness being established forever.

89. Let these truths of my holy way be of full power in thy lives; to be only of pure holy way, is my will to all peoples; to be answered upon all peoples in the day of my coming unto full power of heaven descending to earth; to rule a holy and pure way on my land of Zion; to send to all who remain in every nation my full power to govern, in a holy power of pure holy way; to be the way of truth everlasting.

90. Thus it is. Amen.

91. Let all be of my holy peace. Amen.

92. Now be holy as I am holy.

93. I can heal all wounds; to be of full exalting. Amen.

SECTION REVELATION 150

Jesus Christ, Holy Lord Over All Nations of the Power to Be Nation on Earth, Speaketh Eternity Truth to All Peoples

Jesus Christ
Son Ahman

Jesus Christ, of Holy Power of Union Order Eternal, Who Is of the Way of Full Power of Full Order of the Holy Order of God of Creation, to Now Be of Full Holy Truth, to Be Only Telling My Holy Way; Now Sendeth to All Nations My Own Will. Let All Listen. Let All Hear. Let All Awake to Reality of My Holy Power Coming to Dwell on the Holy Place of My Land of New Jerusalem, Even My Holy Zion. Let All Hear. Let My Word Go Forth in Pure Unchanged Way to All Peoples. Let All Be Holy. Let All Have Only My Will to Be the Guide in Living Pure Holy Way; Not Encumbered by Whims of Men or Women. Let All Receive My Own Will by My Authority I have Ordained on Earth, Now of Bondage; Yet to Be of My Full Way Truth Telling. Hear My Holy Will:

Revelation of the Lord Jesus Christ
Palestine, Texas
Wednesday, January 11, 2012

1. Thus saith the Lord to all people of the earth, a holy word of pure Eternity Truth, to be of holy power unto my holy Order of Eternal Power, Celestial glory of full power to be given all who are pure:

2. I, God, am Endless.

3. My love-power is forever increased by righteous holy way abided.

4. All who are of me come to my authority I send, even my servant on earth.

5. The way to me on earth is to seek my power of Priesthood of the order of my own power I send, to be administrator of all ordinances that exalt the soul into my own power presence.

6. I am Jesus Christ, Son of God.

7. My holy way is to redeem my holy Church.

8. I am of Eternal Order of Endless Lives.

9. Believe all the earth was made by me.

10. I am God over all.

11. I can make all become pure if they have not sinned unto death, the sin of murder in the shedding of innocent blood.

12. Do not again do the evil of child murder of unborn children, lest you shed innocent blood.

13. This heinous evil is rampant among all peoples on earth not of my holy order of Priesthood power.

14. Know I soon take full measure to stop this evil practice; if needs be I send full judgment on all peoples to cleanse thy nation.

15. Let this be your awakening, to cease child murder, by purity of living.

16. Learn there is an eternal judgment on all who promote this evil.

17. Let all medical people know to destroy unborn children is a heinous crime of murder, the shedding of innocent blood.

18. Now understand why I have been sending forth my own word to all nations; a loving God over all is calling on all to be of pure way.

19. Great shall be the eternal way of atoning suffering for they who shed innocent blood, even fighting against way of life; thy Lord's way to people an world of probationary testing.

20. The governing powers in all nations are immoral.

21. They allow this ignoble heinous practice of child murder of unborn children.

22. This evil caused me, even your Lord, to sweep former nations off the earth, when ripened in this sin, unto violence being a continual way of living.

23. Violence now fills the world, because the people follow their lustful way, not acting on pure way of holy living to preserve virtue, life, innocence; the necessary power of purity of bringing forth children to earth.

24. Let all now be of remembering I am Eternal.

25. I shall resurrect all from the grave.

26. You all shall stand before me, a just God, to be judged, all deeds done in the flesh on earth.

27. Nothing is hidden from me.

28. All can feel right from wrong.

29. Legislative power of man's governing authority cannot be of a way of eternal judgment, yet to come on all, whether they be lawmaking authority, or people in every nation.

30. Receive these Eternity Truths.

31. You are each a son or daughter of God.

32. He created you, and has sent you to this probation existence to be tested, having both good and evil before you.

33. Now choose good.

34. Come away from this horrible sin of eternal weight of responsibility; to be of pure holy way. Amen.

35. Now let all remember I, God, have spoken.

36. All who do not heed my will shall soon be of full receiving my own cleansing power on earth.

37. All nations shall know I am He who is God over all the earth that speaketh to all on earth, eternal truth, that truth all must be aware of to be accountable to God for conduct on earth.

38. I now have sent my own will to all nations.

39. Uphold my will in thy individual lives.

40. Seek out my holy authority to be forgiven of sins not unto death; even the shedding of innocent blood. Amen.

41. Now let my holy will be of holy giving to all nations.

42. Let the leaders of nations, of religious societies, of governing powers

who communicate the way of governing to your peoples, tell them God hath spoken.

43. Tell them He shall judge all for this sin of murder who partake thereof, even the aborting of unborn children.

44. Let all know I gave thee this gift to bring spirits to earth by birth as a holy order of life; to be giving life, not death, to your posterity.

45. Be of pure holy way.

46. Be promoting life way in all thy living.

47. Sin of Sodom, also immoral adulterous way, taketh away love for way of living in pure way of bringing children into the earth.

48. All must account for their conduct on earth.

49. Let this Eternity Truth sober all peoples. Amen.

50. Now let my eternal truth be told to the rising generation, so they do not dwell in practice of holding the way of life as a light event or practice.

51. Let young and also middle-aged of childbearing gift honor their own purity way.

52. Let it be for the blessing of new people born through you who now have gift of life on earth.

53. Now be of pure way.

54. Live to bless future posterity. Amen.

55. Let peace be in thy habitations.

56. Let go of evil way of the learning corruption.

57. Let all media be cleansed.

58. Let not youth learn of evil in youth.

59. Let them learn pure way eternal. Amen.

60. All who are subject to be of light are of the way of life, of learning truth of God, who shall be soon of a holy appearing to all peoples remaining on earth.

61. Now be ye clean in all holy way of living, lest innocent blood be upon you, even in marriage conduct, where your way destroys life when life is in mother of new life coming forth. Amen.

62. Let this be the way of establishing love for truth eternal, to preserve life in all way of living pure. Amen.

63. Now let this generation hear more eternity truth: I, God, am of holy way.

64. I dwell in all-consuming eternal fire of the Holy Spirit, guarding the way before my presence. Only that which is pure can dwell in my holy presence.

65. All must have my power to be pure.

66. My power is given by the laying on of hands of my Priesthood authority after one who believes is of full repenting and is baptized by Priesthood authority of my holy order of pure holy power.

67. I have caused my holy message of my holy plan of salvation to go forth to all peoples; my Gospel of Jesus Christ, who now speaketh this, my will, to all; to be of full way able to come unto me by proper authority.

68. Now learn that this life is to test all, through hearing Eternity Truth, then being of a choosing.

69. Let all choose way of eternal life, through my holy order of salvation.

70. This is my holy word to all peoples, nations, kindreds, tongues, governing authorities among men; to know I have spoken Eternity Truth; now of full force on all to hearken.

71. My holy will is now being heralded to all nations.

72. Be of full way pure, lest judgment eternal cometh upon you, each one of every land on earth.

73. Let go of evil.

74. Cleave unto good.

75. Guard virtue of mind and body of thy children.

76. Parents have an eternal and full responsibility to teach children.

77. Let all be holy in thy heart.

78. Let only pure way be lived. Amen.

79. I can purify all who have not sinned unto death.

80. Let all repent, so my holy Order of Eternal Union, an holy way of salvation, can be administered to thee, each during my Millennial Reign of Peace, soon to burst forth in power, Celestial holy power eternal, to govern all remaining people on earth, after my full power of cleansing taketh place; as I told mine apostles in the time I was in my ministry.

81. Let all read New Testament record, to know of my holy Gospel.

82. Therein have I caused all to know to live pure holy way, of love for God, for life, of pure holy way. Amen.

83. Now I have done my will, to tell all people I am soon to come.

84. Let all prepare.

85. Let all repent.

86. Let all be of the holy pure way of living.

87. Come away from all things that corrupt thy lives. Amen.

88. Now be of holy conduct. Thy life is but a moment of time in the eternity you dwell in on earth.

89. Now be of holy way to be of my holy redeeming power unto eternal life, that thy soul may be saved in heaven, to dwell with me, your holy God; to be of a full way delivered from death, hell, the devil, and way of the order of suffering for sin of shedding innocent blood. Amen.

90. Let also all peoples labor for my servant to be set free from bondage.

91. Thy nation can bear influence with unjust governing power that holds him in the way of the keeping him from administering life of my holy power.

92. Let all call on leader of nation of his imprisonment to set him free. Amen.

93. Now also free my other servants in prison bondage, of my Church, all of innocent way of living; to be of full way free to live my Gospel. Amen.

94. Let also my aged son of now unjust imprisonment, Fredrick Merril Jessop, of unhealthy way of poor health, be freed.

95. Let government power set him free soon, so his life may be with his family and my Church, to be of full free way, not to be prosecuted for my Gospel.

96. He is of full way innocent.

97. Let him go. Amen; yea, even to return to his home in the time of life they need a loving holy father to guide them in pure way of living.

98. Thus unjust court hath done another gross crime against my holy religion, in separating man of holy way from a family of pure way.

99. Let all know he is example of holy pure way of living on earth; as are also many of my Holy Priesthood who are of my holy order of my Church on earth; examples of pure way of living; of Zion, of my holy Eternal Union Order of Celestial Union Marriage, a holy order under my own directing by keys of power I have conferred on my holy Prophet Warren Jeffs, now in bondage by conspiracy of wicked men.

100. Let him go.

101. Let all be upholding my holy way, to allow my Zion to rise unmolested by governing powers on earth.

102. Thus shall I intervene, with almighty power, if no one cometh to the full way of delivery.

103. Let all be of my holy way, to deliver innocence; to be of holy way in Eternity Truth abided on earth. Amen.

104. Now receive this, my power-word of Eternity Truth.

105. Let all peoples now come unto me, your Lord over all peoples, saith Jesus Christ. Even so. Amen.

106. Thus saith the Lord unto all nations: Be ye ready for full judgment of whirlwind way if ye heed me not, is the will of God to all peoples, soon to stretch forth His holy arm of full power over all on the earth.

107. Why will ye not hearken before I needs send full cleansing powers upon all of the world of evil way?

108. I am able to bless all peoples.

109. My sun shines on all.

110. My holy way is eternal.

111. I am God. I can do the will of my Father in blessing all His children on earth.

112. Repent ye, repent ye, one and all on earth, now; for my great and full power cometh as blessings on the more righteous; power of cleansing on the more wicked of every nation.

113. Now heed my holy way of pure holy warning; to be only of pure way of living in all way of thy lives being now of my holy teachings, as is in New Holy Testament record.

114. I have caused Joseph Smith to retranslate my Bible, as more of truth told.

115. Use the way of pure revealing in my Inspired Version of Bible.

116. Men of modern time taketh away meaning of my holy word in changing Bible to mean what they, in fallen nature, think of me and my eternal way.

117. Joseph Smith, my inspired Seer and Prophet, wrote Bible to be of restoring some portions to my original word given by mouth of thy Holy Lord, as recorded by my Prophets and apostles at the day of my holy ministry on earth.

118. I am he, Jesus Christ, which speaketh.

119. Do as I have left on record for all mankind to learn more holy way of living.

120. I also left in my record of Bible, promise of my coming to earth again, as Ruler and King over all.

121. This is common knowledge on earth among all peoples, my record of pure way in Bible, more especially Inspired Version of Bible.

122. Now read more accurate version of Bible, to not change my word, all ye denominations of religious way, thinking you can improve my word according to your present living way.

123. My way of Eternal Union of full salvation is the same yesterday, today, and forever.

124. I change not.

125. Receive my word entire; for all can apply present Eternity Truths contained in more holy accurate Bible to themselves in a holy way of living. Amen.

126. Now read Matthew chapter of my judgment, chapter 24.

127. Read in Luke of my coming being in a day like unto day of Noah, a generation of wickedness now upon the earth.

128. This is my time of final warning, to tell all peoples of my holy Advent, of Glory Power Revealing Authority over all nations, peoples, dominions, governing powers on the earth.

129. Heed my will, saith Jesus Christ.

Even so, be ye ready, as I told my disciples as recorded in New Testament.

130. Only pure in heart peoples shall remain on earth, to be of Zion. Amen.

131. I shall also preserve my authority on earth, as I promised Joseph in Egypt of old, to have his posterity build a New Jerusalem; prophecy found in Book of Mormon record of my seeing truth to be preserved.

132. Let all honest in heart be receiving and living my holy way on earth.

133. This from Him, your Holy Lord, who hears prayers of all pure in heart, and all of true repenting power unto betterment of living. Amen.

134. Thus saith God over all, unto nation of unholy way of the way of attack when no one of other nation power attacked thee, only of verbal attack -- repent ye of such folly; for you are starting war of world involvement.

135. You must be of a more way of peace-seeking before force is used.

136. Be ye ready for full war.

137. Soon cometh power of unrest in nation of Syria, such that only restraint can accomplish full peace by negotiation this time; as all national powers are not ready for full caring of their peoples in time of need.

138. I, Jesus Christ, speak to nation of United States, also Israel; to now be of full power to prepare properly for war, in land of Old Jerusalem wherein my Israel shall gather.

139. Let all be of full way preparing thy own peoples in thy nation, each one, to be independent in needed supplies of live-giving gift. Amen.

SECTION REVELATION 151

Jesus Christ
Son Ahman

I, Jesus Christ, God of All Creation, Speak Truth to All Governing Powers in Present Nation on Land of Zion, of My Soon Coming, of Full Judgments of Full Order on the Wicked Who Are of the Way of Life-Destroying; Who Consider Not Rights of the Unborn Children; to Heed My Holy Will Saying Thus:

Revelation of the Lord Jesus Christ
Palestine, Texas
Thursday, January 12, 2012

1. I, Jesus Christ, Redeemer of all, speak to Congress --

2. Repeal all laws allowing child murder of unborn children in this so-called nation of freedom, lest innocent blood be upon thee in day of resurrection judging, unto full eternal punishing, to be of God as Judge over all.

3. Now live unto holy way; protect life way, to be of higher standard of example-living than people of nation, so my holy light may dwell in you, each one, unto a oneness among you.

4. If you heed me, I shall prosper you and this nation, as nation ceases such murder; yea, in my eyes as an eternal crime against my holy order of life.

5. If you be against my life-giving order on earth, you only inherit eternal suffering in eternal resurrection; a just God of full eternity power over all, rewarding all for deeds and desires in the flesh on earth.

6. Heed my many warnings sent to show all I am speaking from the heavens through him whom I ordained to be my holy Mouthpiece on earth; I commanding him to send my full order of warning, to now be for life.

7. If ye be not for life, ye are for death-way, a traitor against God, even I, your Lord Jesus Christ, who is over all.

8. As I spoke eternal salvation truth on earth during my ministry, now enthroned in heavenly power Eternal Order Power in the domain of my Father, who is God over all, my Father Ahman, even Elohim; I, Jesus Christ, being Son Ahman of the ruling Godhead over this world upon which you stand; I thus having the right of Governing Authority over all peoples on the earth; as I spoke salvation truths on earth, now exalted in heaven; surely you can reason I, of Eternity Holy Power, can speak to all peoples on earth to be of believing seriousness of eternal result of my judging all ye of governing authority over nation.

9. Receive my warnings, all of legislative power, lest great full judgment flow forth, to cut off all from this existing order who sin unto death, to no longer be of way to have power over the unborn children in being against life order.

10. Know life is proper way to legislate; not death of children unborn; is the word of the Lord to all of authority on earth over nations, saith God over all, even Jesus Christ, your Lord of Redeeming Holy Power, soon to come on earth to govern all peoples. Amen.

SECTION REVELATION 152

Jesus Christ
Son Ahman

Jesus Christ, God Over All, Sendeth His Own Will to Leaders of Nation Called Indonesia, a Word of Peace. Hear My Will:

Revelation of the Lord Jesus Christ
Palestine, Texas
Friday, January 13, 2012

1. Thus saith God over all, to nation of Indonesia, hear my word, saith Jesus Christ:

2. Unrest cometh into thy borders among thy people.

3. It shall cause great suffering among you.

4. Let peace reign over your peoples. Make peace.

5. Do not use military to harm thy own people when of peace. Amen.

SECTION REVELATION 153

Jesus Christ
Jehovah Christ, Son Ahman

Jesus Christ, God Over All Nations, Who Made the Earth, Who Upholds All Peoples in Their Place, Speaketh to Nation of Israel; Hear My Will:

Revelation of the Lord Jesus Christ
Palestine, Texas
Friday, January 13, 2012

1. Thus saith the Lord unto nation of Israel, my own will to thee; even Him, Jehovah, over all; to cease your way of open murder of they you consider, of thy enemy nations, a open threat to you.

2. Do not assassinate. Do not secret murder, as I, your God, shall first cleanse you if this evil is followed by military of Israel; a humbling so great, few shall remain. Amen.

3. Now hear my will:

4. Cleanse thy own nation to overthrow evil of immoral motive way.

5. Let there be my way of no immoral

way, nor murder of unborn children in thy land, lest the humbling depopulate most of thy land.

6. I am God who hath all power.

7. You exist because I have caused you to have power over enemy nations.

8. Now do not assassinate officials nor other peoples in secret murders, lest it turn against you, and you go down as a governing authority in my Israel, even present secret combination, which considers murder of whom you will as a national interest of preservation.

9. Now learn I, Jehovah, am Judge, and that vengeance is mine.

10. I shall cause thee to win battles as you first cleanse thyselves and thy people of these most horrible crimes against principle of life, even child murder of the unborn, also Sodom and adultery.

11. Cleanse thyselves.

12. Do not use the way of self-justifying of pleasing allied nations to allow such evils to be among you.

13. Prepare also for my Gospel of salvation to be as a holy message to all thy people. Amen.

14. Now let Israel watch for alliance of the nation of power nearby Syria faltering, also the land of Iraq being taken in influence by Iran.

15. Let the authorized of thy God power be when all nations of Moslem faith system combine against thee, and are gathering to destroy thee.

16. Three times put toward these wicked nations a petition of peace, to be justified of God.

17. Be of self-defense when the enemy openly prepareth for war.

18. Now hear the will of God and do His will, saith your Lord Jesus Christ, even Jehovah, Son of God, to soon come in Celestial power to govern all peoples on earth, and be thy Holy Creator of love-kindness power; even Jehovah, the Great I AM, who led thy fathers through the Red Sea on dry ground, so shall fight the battles for my Israel as she doeth as I command. Amen.

19. Now let my will go forth to the leaders of the nation of United States, to be of no attack against another nation, save I, your Lord, direct.

20. Cleanse thy nation of gross sin of murder against unborn children, also sin of legalizing Sodom, and also adultery.

21. Let nation be of full warning I cometh, saith Jesus Christ, to cleanse nation of power if she heed me not.

22. Now receive this, ye leaders of this nation; that when Israel goes against all surrounding enemy nations that surround her, assist only, not sending full army into battle; only supplying Israel in her full way of self-defense. Amen.

23. Now let President of nation heed my word; do not go out to battle save I command.

24. I can communicate with thee through my servant on earth.

25. Be ye aware that you only exist by my power.

26. Now do as I have declared: Let my holy order of Priesthood held in bondage go; and also cleanse thy peoples, to be of more pure way; that I may preserve, in day of cleansing, the more righteous among you. Amen.

27. Now let not Israel be of full way of way of battle until I have first named. Amen.

SECTION REVELATION 154

Jesus Christ
Son Ahman

I, Jesus Christ, God Over All the World, Speak to All People of Samoa, Also to Western Samoa, to All Pacific Islands, My Own Strong Warning That Great Sweeping Tidal Waves of Great Power Cometh; Thus Hear My Will to Be of Surviving Way:

Revelation of the Lord Jesus Christ
Palestine, Texas
Friday, January 13, 2012

1. Thus saith the Lord to the nation of the ocean way of island dwelling of the order of soon consuming by full tidal wave, even land of the people of Israel of Samoa, also Western Samoa:

2. There cometh, saith your Lord Jesus Christ, a large way of flooding all unto nothing remaining on island nations' land.

3. You needs begin relocating to another higher ground continent entire.

4. I tell thee this, to let all be accountable.

5. I am soon to use the earth itself as a giving power of judgment upon the inhabitants.

6. Let thy holy peace be my peace.

7. Let all who dwell on island nations in Pacific Ocean beware.

8. Be believing, tidal waves of great magnitude shall sweep low-lying lands clean entire.

9. Relocate to a higher land.

10. Let the place of the land of Zion be thy gathering land, as original inhabitants of Samoa, also Western Samoa, are of Israel. Amen.

SECTION REVELATION 155

Jesus Christ
Son Ahman

Thus Saith Jesus Christ, Even Son Ahman, to the People of the United States of America, and the Leaders and Peoples of All Nations, My Own Word of Warning Again, Lest You Be in Any Way Continuing in Such Gross Crimes as I Have Named to Repent of, and My Judgments Come in Full. Hear Thou My Word:

Revelation of the Lord Jesus Christ
Palestine, Texas
Sunday, January 15, 2012

1. Thus saith the Lord Jesus Christ to the nation of the United States of America: I shall soon send judgment upon thee if you heed not my many warnings, for there must needs be a humbling of this nation to know I, your God, have spoken of a whirlwind judgment nature soon at hand. And I shall cause thy people to feel my chastening hand day by day until you heed my word or are humbled to the dust unto full cleansing of the land for my Zion to rise.

2. I am a God of eternal truth, and when I speak, I uphold my word; and you are a nation of gross immoral wickedness and a murderous way of unborn children, a sin that is blighting your eternal way before me; for I must judge you, even with a complete judging after you have received my sacred warning of this gross crime among you.

3. You must change your laws and cease this evil practice of child murder of unborn children, lest many of you arise in the morning of the resurrection so unclean you have no salvation.

4. Thus saith the Lord to you. Amen.

5. Now I speak to the leaders of the world: Repent ye quickly, for I have spoken mine own word.

6. Overcome the child murder called abortion in a manner of unborn children being taken in death.

7. Thus saith the Lord, this is a gross crime that hindereth you from progressing as people on earth in the way of salvation.

8. And thus you shall reap sorrow in the hereafter and on earth for such a terrible crime among you.

9. Now receive my word: Change your laws and cause this to cease, lest my full judgments come upon the world, and I shall fulfill my word entire. Amen.

SECTION REVELATION 156

Jesus Christ
Son Ahman

Thus Saith Jesus Christ, Even Jehovah Over All, to All Peoples on Earth, a Holy Revealing of Pure Holy Way to Be of Full Power to Be of Surviving Power on the Way of Judgments of Power Coming on All Nations. Let This Be a Way to Know How to Be of Survival. Amen. Let Also All Be Pure, by Heeding My Own Way, Saying Thus:

Revelation of the Lord Jesus Christ
Palestine, Texas
Monday, January 16, 2012

1. Come ye to thy Lord, all peoples on earth; to be fed word of life eternal; to have my Gospel of salvation; to be mine holy elect; yea, a holy Zion on earth.

2. Come ye, all Israel, to be gathered home.

3. I make a way of your escape.

4. Be ye clean from the wicked generation on the earth, even to be of holy way of my holy pure people of full order of Celestial power, to administer my blessings of eternal power on all nations.

5. Let all be holy.

6. Let all have pure hearts; only of the holy order of Celestial holy union of my holy way; to have only purity of soul; to only bring forth pure sons of God, daughters of holiness.

7. Let now all be only of my order of salvation, even all my holy people of the order of my Church on earth. Amen.

8. Let all nations now hear the Gospel plan.

9. I, Jesus Christ, have conquered death.

10. I am the Life of all men on earth.

11. All are my sons and daughters of the way of the order of Godhead right to rule over all peoples.

12. I am the Holy One of Israel prophesied of to come on earth, to rule Israel.

13. Let Israel be pure of the way of not mixing with they not of Israel.

14. Let thy way be holy, to honor God; to be of Israel of pure holy descent. Amen.

15. Now let all Israel come from among all nations, to dwell on my holy land of Zion, until Judah is converted; thereafter to go dwell on promised land of Old Jerusalem; even land promised to my servant Liahoni, Father of faithful, Abraham; who hath been of my holy sons of eternal progression, by abiding Celestial Law of probationary pure holy governing Godhood law of my Eternal Order; a son of pure and noble order of faith unto my full order of holy way.

16. Let all peoples honor God and the holy way of Eternal Union unto my way of full exalting order of marriage; the holy way of pure living in my Order of Eternal

Order of pure holy family way of Eternal Union, of my own order, saith Jesus Christ.

17. I am of the power to exalt all men unto Godhood who abide Celestial holy Law of Plural Union Marriage by my appointing.

18. Let not any deride.

19. Let all humble themselves.

20. My servant on the earth can administer the holy way to all peoples.

21. Let all be only pure, holy, of noble way.

22. Let all repent of immoral way of the sin of that which caused thy God to send fire and brimstone to destroy Sodom of old; even the illicit way of immoral corrupt way, an unholy corruption that destroys the way of life.

23. Let now my way be upheld, to cause Sodom to be of full removing.

24. Let adultery be no longer a way of the nations.

25. Let all be pure of motive, to consider flow of pure intelligence is of greater value than immoral decadence of loss of love of life, even to destroy unborn children to be of following lustful way of immoral way.

26. Let all be of cleansing thy nation, each to be of pure holy way. Amen.

27. Now let this be of Jesus Christ, your Holy Lord's way to know nation of full repentance seeks deliverance in day of whirlwind judgments on earth.

28. Only pure in heart shall remain. Amen.

29. Now let all nations receive this as a way to know you are repenting.

30. Let this be guide, to have laws of nation of repenting way be of full enforcement by governing powers therein; to show thy Lord thy full way holy pure holy way of cleansing thy land, each to be of full accounting soon on earth, for all thy way of governing. Amen.

31. Now let all nations attend to cleansing of thy laws and peoples of all immoral way; to be surviving judgment of power, soon to sweep all evil off earth; to be my way of holy appearing to pure in heart of all lands on earth; to be of my holy way. Amen.

32. Let also children be of pure upbringing, to not be of an unholy way; to be more guarded; to have love for pure way of holy order of children brought through the way of holy order of marriage; not any of illicit way of immoral union.

33. Let all be only taught to live pure way, to be of surviving judgment of holy power, eternal power of my Godhood Order Celestial Power, which shall cleanse all by full power of judgment. Amen.

34. Now let all children have a way of education, of way to learn moral holy way; to not be of unholy connecting, of the pure way of innocent mind being kept innocent.

35. Let all be holy on earth, to be of my order of pure holy way.

36. Let all be only holy, to be of me, saith Jesus Christ, God over all nations, a God of holy pure way eternal power of holy union Celestial power. Amen.

37. Now know my holy way includeth full way justice, to judge a holy pure way of eternal holy order; to be of full way just; to restore to all men the just way of pure holy order of instituting justice of full revealing; where everyone shall be their own accuser; to have mind unlocked; to reveal all secrets to all.

38. Let all be of repenting way, to overcome evil, to be of holy way eternal. Amen.

39. Let my holy order of Eternal Power

descend to my holy order of the way of the full way of pure holy power; to be my holy way on the full order of Celestial way; to have only pure holy order in Church of my name. Amen.

40. Now be holy, is the word of God to all peoples, to be of way of surviving on earth as whirlwind judgments roll forth to cleanse all nations. Amen.

41. Let also schools change from unbelieving way to belief in God.

42. I am He who made all things, who cometh.

43. I have all things as proving way that a Great Intelligence hath made all creation on earth, in heaven; to be governing power, Celestial power, of full Godhead rule over this world. Amen.

44. Now let there be only holy way. Amen.

45. Come unto my holy power on the order of earth way holy labor among men; to be learning my holy way eternal.

46. Let Gospel of my own order, even Jesus Christ, be of free way living.

47. Let all peoples be of free way of religious order abiding, to be never of a persecuted way because religion. Amen.

48. Now have this heralded to all thy people in every land.

49. Let my way be holy, honored by you, even my holy way of eternal exalting order. Amen.

50. Let also all be holy of the way of the order of the way of the power of the way of the power of a faith labor over peoples, to only be the holy labor to believe in God, even I, your Lord; lest you be of idolatry order.

51. Let all be of a full faith, that God speaketh in this thy day, as well as in days of old, to all peoples through a Prophet. Amen.

52. Come ye, to reason with the God of all power, to feel truth, of the holy order of pure holy power; to know all way of inhabiting earth is of a way of holy power, not of man, nor of the way of unbelief of the way of denying me.

53. I have all power Celestial, to know all the way of holy order of creating all things by my power; to have all my holy way in Godhead governing authority over all nations; of the holy way to people an world of the order of worlds of living power. Amen.

54. The order of living is of me, your Lord, who is God over many worlds, even your God of Creation over thee, all ye peoples on the earth, that ever have been, and are, and shall be; to be the holy order of holy begetting in heaven; in spirit form, of children of the holy way of the God of Creation begetting all, unto a family order of Adam on earth; to whom all are accountable for all they perform on this world of testing power, where both good and evil are placed in reach of all of my family.

55. Let this real and true way of understanding show all I am Father over all the human family; to be thy Judge also, as a just God, who is of full power to record all happenings; to have all things revealed when all are of full power of the way of resurrection.

56. Let all be holy.

57. Let all repent.

58. Let all raise your own family up to be holy on earth; for you will be accountable to me, saith your Lord. Amen.

59. Learn also to be of pure way toward all.

60. Learn you shall be of a way of receiving as you send; to be recompensed as you measure to your fellow men in all way of full way.

61. Let this be sobering real truth to all. Amen.

62. Let governing authority in all peoples and nations be humble, to govern to bless, not to seek of the way of gain of self-aggrandizement; to be governing power to uphold way of pure way, of holy way; to be responsible for what thou doest among men on earth.

63. Let schools be purified.

64. Cast out all immoral way of teaching to be unclothed before one another, for such promoteth evil in youth from youngest years.

65. Thy holy way is to teach body is sacred, to not display body; to be of more pure way.

66. Let this be my way, saith God over all.

67. Let all be holy, therefore, to be of my holy way of pure power, soon to be on earth over all nations; as the holy power of governing order over all lands, peoples, nations, holy way of all eternity coming among men.

68. Let this awake all, to know I am soon to come in full power, all peoples on all lands knowing I am on earth, to reign as the Ruler of all nations as your Holy Lord over all. Amen.

69. Now have all peoples receive this.

70. Let leaders over peoples have all my pure will of pure holy way of giving to their peoples, unchanged, of exact holy way as I have caused all to receive.

71. Let this holy will of my own word be of full way of publishing to all thy peoples. Amen.

72. Now come to me, ye nations.

73. Time is of soon way to humble all nations unto judgment of full power. Amen.

74. Thus am I of full power, of holy order of salvation to all peoples who come unto me, through my order of holy way of Gospel of salvation. Amen.

75. Now repent, all ye ends of the earth, unto a full way holy order of my holy power being of full power of my plan of the way of salvation; of Eternal Power Celestial coming unto a pure people who are mine holy order of the way of Eternal Order Power, Celestial Power. Amen.

76. I cometh with the heavenly order. I am God.

77. Heed my will.

78. Let all be of pure holy power of my Order of Eternal Union Power Celestial Order. Amen.

79. Let all people on my world of testing be of pure way, to prepare for my coming to my holy order of the elect of God on earth, who do abide love of God in full power order. Amen.

80. Now let all be holy who are of a surviving power on earth, to be more of my way of the order of learning of Zion; for only my pure in heart shall remain on land of Zion. Amen.

81. Now have thy whole soul seek for truth by prayer, all ye peoples on earth, so I can be your full delivering order unto continued living on earth, so I can visit all by my order of messengers sent, messengers of truth unto salvation. Amen.

82. This is my way.

83. This shall be my order of pure order of holy delivery of word of salvation, my Priesthood coming to thy people after cleansing of wicked way from among all peoples; so only they of more holy way remain in all lands and peoples of holy way being more receptive to holy will of thy God. Amen.

84. Now be of my way of more holy

power of pure holy love of God, through sacrifice, a sacrifice of thy evil, which only brings blessings of living pure, in holy way of happiness; no vice, no evil of power among any nation; only equity, truth, holy peace of my giving; blessings of life on earth unto happy way; yea, even to eat the fruit of thy labors of orchard, of the way of preparation to live on earth in blessings of life. Amen.

85. Now heed all my will, to be holy on the land where you dwell.

86. All my will shall be sent, so all may be of full way of holy power, because I, God, hear prayers of the honest in heart in all lands; to have gift of pure holy blessings of life in all way of pure holy truth that can be given, until my Gospel of salvation is administered to all peoples.

87. Zion is government power over all nations during my holy Reign of Peace for a holy and pure Peace Reign of one thousand years on earth among men. Amen.

88. Such is my will, holy, pure, noble, godly in all way of pure holy power that cannot be overthrown; I, the God of all, ruling all, by righteous eternal duration law of God, a holy power of full power Celestial. Amen.

SECTION REVELATION 157

Jesus Christ, Who Is Jehovah, of Full Power of Godhood Power Over All Nations, Sendeth His Own Will to Mexico; Also to Be Known by All Spanish Speaking Nations on the Land Called America; North and South Are My Holy Land of Zion, Central Also. Let All Be Holy. Amen.

Thus Saith Jesus Christ, Son Ahman, to All Peoples of Mexico, Also to All Spanish Speaking Peoples on America Lands of North and South America, a Holy Will of God Over All, to Know of My Holy Way of Surviving Coming Power of Cleansing Judgment on All Nations. Receive My Holy Word of Full Truth Holy Way Revealing; Speaking to All Nations of Spanish Tongue, Through My Servant on Earth Who Is Ordained to Be My Mouthpiece to All Peoples. Let All Hearts Be Open, of a Prayerful Way; to Feel Truth of Holy Word Sent to All, to Be of Full Way Knowing I Cometh in Power, Celestial Power, to Let All Peoples Know I Am God, Even Jesus Christ, Over All Nations. Hear and Live My Will of Holy Revealing. Amen. Hear Thou My Message of Pure Will of God to People of Spanish Tongue, Saith God Thus:

Revelation of the Lord Jesus Christ
Palestine, Texas
Monday, January 16, 2012

1. The Lord speaketh, your Holy Redeemer, Jesus Christ, the Alpha and Omega over all, Beginning and End of probationary way of exalting; your All-in-All Power of full salvation; to people of Mexico.

2. Let all hear my will to know my full order of holy cleansing coming to all in thy land; to be a holy way; to first send cleansing of power over living on earth; to be of holy way to have only power to be more peaceful, not of war, nor of violent way.

3. Let order of crime cartels cease, lest thy full household no longer be on earth, by my own cleansing power of power of God being on all; earthquake, windstorm, pestilence, famine, hail, even salvation for all to be lost who are of murderous way.

4. Let all learn peace.

5. Let all be motivated by my inspiring holy love-peace, to no longer be of way of unholy way.

6. Let all now come unto your Lord by prayerful way lived in all thy way of living; to now be of holy way.

7. Now let also cleansing of thy people include a holy way.

8. Let it be open minds, to hear salvation revealed from heaven.

9. Let all be hearing my own full Gospel of salvation.

10. Let the governing power over nation of Mexico now allow full freedom.

11. Allow my holy way to be of full way abided; not to be of way of limit.

12. Let full freedom of Celestial Order of Marriage Order Plural Union be of holy living.

13. Let it be only for my people of my holy Church; to know religious freedom is of full protecting way for my Celestial Law to be abided by they of my revealing unto them by my Keyholder on earth, my holy way unto worthy sons and daughters; not for any others, save I reveal through my Prophet the names of who is of worthiness.

14. Let not governing power limit this holy way in an unholy attack.

15. Let all my Church live pure.

16. Let all my holy way be only my revealing. Amen.

17. Now let this be my holy message -- repent, ye people of Mexico.

18. Now be holy.

19. Read New Testament.

20. It is my holy way.

21. Let all read Joseph Smith translating of Bible to have more exact word of thy holy Bible; a holy way to know thy Redeemer cometh soon to be known to all nations.

22. Let also my holy way be to make a holy contact with my servant by governing powers in thy land; to show thy God you will cleanse thy people of gross crime of unhallowed child murder of order of unborn children being of way of abortion before birth.

23. This is shedding innocent blood, a sin of damnation eternally.

24. Let men and women be more holy in moral way.

25. Cease the way of adultery, also of Sodom.

26. Be of life-preserving way.

27. Let sin of robbery, also of illicit drug trafficking cease.

28. Let none use illegal drugs.

29. It is sorcery among unholy partakers thereof; to invite evil way of thinking, of feeling false way.

30. Let all be humble, so I can spare more holy people in day of full power cleansing on land of Zion -- North and South America, Central America also; all Zion land to God; to be of full way cleansed, to be of ready way for my power to dwell among mine holy people who dwell on Zion land. Amen.

31. Now let army only be used to promote peace in thy land; not to oppress thy people; also police.

32. Let all be free way.

33. Let not war be thy way at time United States is of unrestful way in her borders.

34. Be of peace.

35. Be only of cleansing the violent from thy land; to be of peacemaking to all peoples, if you are to be of survival way.

36. Let all be ready; for I soon send full power of my judgments of full cleansing order. Amen.

37. Now let thy way be my holy way, all ye people of Mexico. Amen.

38. Let also leaders of Mexico allow this, my will, to be of full publishing in the way all thy people uphold my will in day

of cleansing Zion land in full power; that all may learn how to survive. Amen.

39. Now let Savior, Lord of all, be honored.

40. Call forth all priests of the way of religion to only teach by word of God in holy Bible, not of tenet of way of man's way of law of unjust way upheld to prosecute the pure.

41. Let all be pure, noble, godlike.

42. Let all learn habit of clean way of living, both in mind-thinking, and in earthly habit of cleanly way of living; so my holy power may deliver pure holy peoples from the disease of immoral way being of judgment on a whole generation on earth.

43. Such immoral-way diseases depict an immoral way people. Amen.

44. Forgive all.

45. Be pure to be forgiven of me, your Lord.

46. Let all do only pure holy living way toward all people; fair, just, kind love-power unto favoring noble holy order of peace among thy people.

47. Let also poor have needs like unto they with plenty; governing authority ceasing evil of bribery to king to get personal gain; an unholy way rampant in governing powers in Mexico.

48. Let priests also labor to raise food for poor.

49. Let all labor, to be of better living condition in family way; in all way of living.

50. Let also government authority only be of kind way, to be preserving youth in innocent pure holy living. Amen.

51. Now let Mexico hear truth:

52. I come to cleanse land of thy dwelling.

53. Only pure people shall remain, of bloodline of the original order of inhabitants on Zion land, of pure bloodline.

54. All others of gentile descent must repent to become holy, part of Israel bloodline by my holy power, else not be of holy way of surviving judgments of God on all nations on Zion land of North, Central, also South America.

55. Be holy.

56. Repent.

57. Receive my Gospel through my own power of authority on earth to be Zion people.

58. Let this sober all.

59. Let all know I have sent my own Gospel to thy people since the time I appeared to a Prophet, even Joseph Smith; who, with Keyholders of same power of heaven, following Joseph Smith, sending my message to thy people, lo, these many years, even over one hundred eighty years since my holy Church was restored. Amen.

60. Now let all be holy.

61. Let all be of pure motive in all way of abiding more holy way of living, is the call of thy Holy God, Jesus Christ; who speaketh now through a Prophet, holy way; as in all past times. Amen.

SECTION REVELATION 158

Jesus Christ
Son Ahman

Thus Saith Jesus Christ, Son Ahman, Unto All Nations on Earth, My Own Message of Holy Salvation, Truth Eternal Told to All, so All Peoples on Earth May Know True Way of Salvation; to Be of Preparing Order for My Coming in Glory Order Power; to Be on Earth for a Thousand Years Among Men as Ruler of Power Over All Peoples; Then to Be Thy Holy God of Redeeming Order Power, to Raise All From the Grave Unto a Judging, a Full Eternal Order Power Judging of a Just God Who Knoweth All Thy Works. Let This, My Holy Will, Be Thy Guide to Prepare for Mine Authority to Visit All Peoples; to Have My Way Known; to Be Only Pure Holy Way of Salvation. Hear Ye My Will:

Revelation of the Lord Jesus Christ
Palestine, Texas
Tuesday, January 17, 2012

1. Come, all ye peoples on earth, unto me, Jesus Christ, God over all, to be of holy way.

2. Be all of my holy way, not of evil any longer.

3. Thy way of every nation is in spiritual Babylon; none doeth good of the way of the world, not of me, saith God.

4. I am over all.

5. I intervene.

6. I make truth known by my holy way of holy revealing.

7. I am over thy path unto eternity living.

8. All are subject to my rule.

9. Now hearken to Him who is thy way unto life in happiness Celestial presence of God.

10. He is over all.

11. None escape His notice.

12. All are subject to judgment of God.

13. All are only of my full power, to be thy God of all power eternally.

14. Now heed my will.

15. I shall soon send cleansing power on earth.

16. No one shall escape my judgment.

17. Be pure. Repent. Have only thy way be my will done; He who hath right to rule over all people on earth. Amen.

18. Now be ready.

19. My holy will hath been made known to all nations.

20. Wicked men of intent to fight truth are in power.

21. My holy way is truth, to only be of way of love of truth, holy exalting true way of salvation eternal.

22. My way is to live on earth in holy power of faith living.

23. I have power to know all things.

24. I am Giver of all blessings of eternal life.

25. I am He who conquered death, who hath key to resurrecting power, of raising all from grave, to be a soul exalted as you live law of progressive way unto eternal life.

26. Now be holy in daily living.

27. Be a person, each one, who is of me, who is thy holy power of good through choosing good.

28. Know I have power to overthrow all evil.

29. I am Holy Power Celestial order of Godhood power over all.

30. Let this true way be thy way. Amen.

31. Let now truth reasoning come to thee, all ye ends of the earth; to reason by light truth, not dark way of denying eternity truth.

32. Light is peace.

33. Peace is my way of life everlasting.

34. Now be of peace, prayerful in all way of living; for I read thy mind continually.

35. I send my power of Spirit called the Holy Power Celestial, like the ray of the sun shining on all creation; to be light of truth in mind of all on my world of testing what all love most -- truth or evil of lies lived.

36. Let all know I have preserved eternity truth in my holy Bible of the common way among men to know I am God come to earth, to redeem all peoples from the grave; to be thy Judge of Eternal Power; to raise all from death to life; to judge all to the end of personal reward according to thy works on earth.

37. This is my eternity truth.

38. I am God. I speaketh.

39. I am to be thy only way of pure truth of life eternal, all ye peoples on earth.

40. Now be ye of belief.

41. Believing includes listening to peace-truth I send to be as a light of truth in thy mind, telling thy intelligence I am, I speak, I govern, I bless all peoples with good.

42. Now be of me, your Holy Lord, even Redeemer of all.

43. Let all be holy, of pure way.

44. Let all have only my way in living pure way; not to be partly of evil way.

45. This is my way to tell all I am soon to come to the earth in glory power, Celestial glory power, of heaven come to earth.

46. This is my holy revealing by authority I have established among men, to be witness of holy way of my holy power.

47. Let all come to me through my authority of power I have sent. Amen.

48. Thus is my holy way, more pure than man's way of dwelling on my world of probationary testing; an earth of good and evil present to choose what thou wilt, in daily thought and doing as you choose.

49. Let all be choosing only good.

50. Let all read my will of my holy order of sacred word, Bible; also my new revealed word of my Prophet I sent in the way of seeing God the Father, and His Son; even I, your Lord Jesus Christ, in New York in spring of 1820, in a sacred grove, where we taught him my own way of eternal life.

51. Now read my word revealed through him in Book of Mormon, also Doctrine and Covenants, of holy word revealing my will to the generation now

on earth; a holy word that tells of my own holy order of Priesthood authority -- Prophets as angels, from former times, even Peter, James, John; also my holy Prophet of old, Elijah, as a translated son of Priesthood, coming to bestow all keys of holy power unto eternal life being administered by Priesthood ordinance, of all needed gifts of life in my holy Gospel order of salvation; even fulness of gift of salvation on earth; continued through a pure line of Keyholders of same authority until this time; to have on earth my own authority from heaven; to bestow blessings upon pure men and women; to have all be my holy order of Holy Priesthood from on high dwelling among men on earth.

52. Such is my holy plan of holy Gospel of salvation; an holy way of my own order Celestial; to continue on earth unto my coming in glory power soon at hand. Amen.

53. Now receive my order of holy power.

54. Let my people go to my holy place.

55. Let my holy way be upheld by governing authority, lest I send judgment to cleanse my land of Zion on earth by almighty power of Celestial order of justice, of my own Kingdom on earth being preserved by my power, eternal power.

56. You cannot join together without mine own holy plan of salvation, nor with thine own way of earthly power.

57. I am from on high, a holy order of heavenly power come to earth, as my holy apostle John spoke.

58. Let his word be read.

59. I am God, who came to earth to suffer more than man can suffer, to redeem all. Amen.

60. Now be ye of full receiving my Gospel.

61. I shall send my Prophet to reveal to thy people all needed truth to be of my Gospel of saving eternal order power.

62. Be ye pure, ready to receive my own will; a living God who reveals only truth, to all who love truth, eternal truth that exalteth the soul unto heavenly domain of God. Amen.

63. Let now my way be no longer hindered.

64. Free my servant from bondage, all of the way of truth-loving order of governing power.

65. President over nation can easily sign his return to my holy people of my way of establishing my Zion on earth among thy nation.

66. Let all beware how they treat my servant; for I shall be Judge, to render full eternal power over all in eternal judgment.

67. Let this be sobering truth.

68. This nation is yet guilty of having Joseph Smith martyred in prison, by the way of governing power allowing violence to come upon he and his fellows in prison.

69. It was a conspiracy of government authority with mob of violent way attending the most wicked attack against my holy power on earth.

70. I, God, am of all power.

71. I preserved my key power on earth.

72. I caused my servant Brigham Young to receive keys of power of eternal power, to bless believing saints of God unto eternal lives, who were faithful on earth to the end of living in time of probation testing order in this now earthly way of dwelling where good and evil existeth; to test all men who are born here; to see what they will do when left to themselves; I, God, also prompting all peoples with good desires to do good on earth.

73. Now you are proving yourself,

each one, whether you will choose good or evil.

74. Now choose good, now knowing of my Gospel plan, and my holy purpose of sending all to earth.

75. Know I can prepare a way, through living faith, for all to receive my holy order of eternal life salvation.

76. Desire good, to be of good.

77. Love my way of pure holy way eternal order of salvation. Amen.

78. Now be of full power through approaching me, your Holy Lord, in personal prayer in private order of honesty lived; to be of pure holy motive to only want God's will in thy living on earth.

79. Be of holy motive to only desire my good, my holy way and will of truth Celestial power order, sent to thee by thy living pure way of faith prayer.

80. Let all then stay clean from the sins of men, of thy knowing evil is evil, to stay away from immoral impurity, of the way of order of my holy will known in Bible holy way reading.

81. Let all study whole portion of my holy revealing will you now have in thy hand.

82. Be ye of full purpose of heart, not of compromise with any of the evil way of Babylon, of the world's way of thinking, wherein they deny God and His eternity truth of Him redeeming all from the grave to be a living soul, to be judged for all deeds on the earth.

83. Let this sober all to well be of sure way pure, against time I raise all up to be judged.

84. Let my holy pure order of Church holy way on earth come away from evil, and dwell in law of eternal lives; to be a holy people.

85. I can own and bless in the day of my holy appearing in the power of God manifest on earth. Amen.

86. Now be ye ready, all ye peoples on earth.

87. My word is true, power of God of eternal power.

88. No one is to escape my all-seeing eye.

89. I can see into thy soul.

90. I know all things.

91. I have my servant of pure holy way of the way of blessing any who come to me in prayer faith unto good works; who remain on earth after judgment of power remove more wicked from earth; preserving more righteous in all nations by almighty power, Celestial power. Amen.

92. Let all follow my way of love for light, truth, holy way of pure holy way Celestial order power; to have only peace in thy soul, by knowing you please thy Lord in all way of dwelling on earth.

93. Let all be Spirit of peace.

94. Let all be my holy way of guiding elder; not of evil any longer.

95. Now come to me, Jesus Christ, your God of Redeeming Order of Celestial Order of Power of my revealing life eternal, to all who come to me by my Holy Priesthood power authority on earth. Amen.

96. Thus saith God over all, to all nations, my holy will, even to know I cometh in power on earth; to learn I am of full order of holy power of governing all on earth; to be of the light of all men; to have holy power of full love-power order of peace; to know I am God by all who obey.

97. I shall be telling my stories of Godhood order over world, the way of pure holy power.

98. Let all humble themselves to be of pure holy way. Amen.

SECTION REVELATION 159

Jehovah
Jesus Christ
Son Ahman

Jesus Christ, Even Son Ahman, Jehovah, Speaketh to All Nations, a Holy Will Word Revealing, Even of Pure Way Truth, of Eternal Power, of Salvation, of Holy Pure Way to Be of a Holy Pure Order; to Be of My Order of Holy Dwelling on Earth; Thus a Holy Order Celestial of My Authority Come to Earth; to Prepare for My Glory Order of Celestial Order Power. I Come, Yea, in Power to All Nations of Survival Way After Cleansing Order Taketh Place on Every Nation. Hear Thou My Power Truth Order:

Revelation of the Lord Jesus Christ
Palestine, Texas
Sunday, January 22, 2012

1. I, God, Jesus Christ, over all, speak to all nations, word of holy eternal order of my holy will; a full order of warning to all; to now be holy; for I am He who judgeth; yea, a righteous holy way of judging all according to works, nothing of a way to be unknown; for all my power is of full order of full Godhood order over all my way of creating order; even all things that do exist; also all that shall exist on the world of thy habiting; even my earth of holy way of full test; of a holy probation way; to prove all; to be my holy order of pure testing unto thy whole future determined by thy choice-making, unto eternal result of full order of being placed to be of a glory of thy earning; unto life of full way order of a power of pure giving of God to each, after punishing order is fulfilled.

2. Let this create in all a full power of holy pure awakening, to know I reward the soul for deeds, also any full desires of the heart -- what you would do had you the power -- all as a full revealing when brought to my own judgment of Godhead authority as thy Holy Redeemer.

3. Now be of holy way, lest full punishing order of suffering for the sin of being of evil knowingly; for my Spirit is light, and is given all at birth, to grow unto full accountability by age of eight years of age on earth, to know good; to be of wanting truth; yet many do not heed my holy order of thy way of hearing true way of purity; a conscience order of my giving; so even young and growing youth can feel to do good, not evil.

4. Now be honorable according to truth-light I have given thy peoples of the way of pure holy way, to choose the kind way one toward another, to be holy in pure moral way; to now be of considering I shall be a Judge of all, nothing hidden. Amen.

5. Let fathers treat family kindly. Let

mothers be loving toward all in family; cease unholy divorces.

6. Be ye of full family love-peace of pure holy love-power, in all way of my holy order of family dwelling; love-kindness order of heaven on earth; for family of pure raising involveth holy connection, not immoral lustful way of deriding against pure way of honorable marriage.

7. Let all holy way be followed in social way of knowing thy companion in marriage hath holy motive; to be father or mother of holy way; not to be with another.

8. Let it be a holy way, to have marriage holy in thy lives, as my holy way of Celestial order is only for holiness of living. Amen.

9. Let also all be holy in business labor; paying labor, of full honorable labor, a just recompense for labor; to raise up all to higher way of honest labor; to have no poor; to pay for wanting poor in food need, by government of holy order of pure caring; not to get a way of bribery-giving to select peoples, causing starvation to be among some.

10. Let all be holy, even as I, Jesus Christ, your Holy Lord, am holy, pure, and of my order of just way. Amen.

11. Now awake, all ye ends of the earth.

12. My love-message of my holy Advent is of full sending by mine holy Prophet on earth sending to all nations mine own will; to be holy, ready for my coming.

13. Now be holy, ready unto pure way of family dwelling in all society way of thy order of marrying only one woman to one man, save I, God, shall be of my Eternal Union Order of Celestial order of revelation way of uniting holy men with holy wives of full Order of Union Power

of Plural Union Order; all only by my holy word revealed to my servant on earth.

14. Let all be holy in conduct.

15. Judge not my Order of Eternal Plural Union by thy evil way of joining.

16. Let all be only of pure way of marriage.

17. Let no illicit connecting be allowed by law in any land, nor of adultery upholding.

18. Let pure way of holy family way be lived.

19. Let this be my holy way to train all how to be ready for my judgment soon of full power on all nations. Amen.

20. Now let all peoples hear my full judgment on murder of unborn children.

21. My Spirit is the power of life.

22. I give life to all of my order of children of spirit living in heaven; sent to earth through way of birth, my giving unto men and women the gift of bringing to earth sons and daughters of my own way of begetting spirit children.

23. Let it be of my way, of pure begetting; no adulterous way, no Sodom way, only pure holy way of my way taught in the order of pure honorable marriage union, even in every religious holy way; a union of holy way of my own doing, for I lived holy way on earth with holy order of Union of Celestial Marriage; my family of the order of my Union Plural Celestial being of full order.

24. I am of pure way.

25. You are not of pure way as you join with any who are not of honorable marriage union of single way, not of my holy Eternal Union Order of Plural Celestial Order of Marriage Order of pure holy revelation from God.

26. Let all now be of knowing my

order is holy pure way of Eternal Order. Amen.

27. Let my holy will now be of full knowing.

28. I had many wives during my holy way of ministry on earth, which was a reason leaders of Jews wanted me to be of a way of not dwelling among men on earth.

29. They learned I was of full living Celestial Plural Marriage Union.

30. I was husband on earth to wives pure, holy, noble, of only pure holy way.

31. Let this be to thy knowing that my Eternal Union Order is holy, of me, thy Lord.

32. Though men revile against my holy order, and prosecute my servant of holy order on earth, I am the way of eternity truth, that my holy order is pure, holy, and of me, Jesus Christ.

33. I caused Joseph Smith to write conditions of full abiding my Eternal Union Order in a holy revealing, now printed in scripture book called Doctrine and Covenants, of thy way of language receiving.

34. It is my holy revealing to all to be knowing this Plural Union Order is only of my revelation power through Keyholder of Priesthood on earth; to only be of pure holy religion way; not common among men.

35. Let men cease the way of many wives not appointed by my holy revealing.

36. Let single unions be holy; never with any not appointed them in adulterous connectings; which corrupteth the way of all peoples, unto the now common way of aborting unborn, of the now fully understood way of murder.

37. It must be of a stop in all nations now, lest my full power of judgment cometh forth upon all not of holy way. Amen.

38. Now let governments do full enforcement against unholy way of illicit union not of my holy law of pure marriage way; to even be defending my law, not of persecuting unholy way of trying by legal court unjust way of prosecution way used to separate holy men from their family of Eternal Union Order of my own holy way.

39. I am God.

40. I speak. I shall be obeyed, else just judgment cometh. Amen.

41. My holy way is in New Testament; to not be of immoral way; a tradition upheld since my full Gospel was among men.

42. Let all read. Let all abide pure way.

43. Legal government way is no eternal justifying order.

44. All shall be held accountable for my holy way printed among you, known to all peoples, even Bible holy way, of pure union.

45. Let Joseph Smith, Jun's., version of Inspired Version of Holy Bible be of thy reading, being of more truth way.

46. Let also Doctrine and Covenants with Section 132 on Eternal Plural Union Marriage be read; even as I cause such to be of an addition to this revealing, so all peoples can read my holy way, Eternal Order way. Amen.

47. Let all peoples on earth know I am soon to appear in Glory Power; to be thy God of Government Full Power Order. Amen.

48. Now let all be ready to believe; for by power shall all learn all my holy word hath been sent to this now most wicked of all former way of immoral murderous generations previously on earth; yea, more so than even Noah's time, when earth was filled with immoral way as thou art,

even murder of unborn children as way of limiting populating; as though I would bow to man's unholy order of murder to stop populating the world.

49. I am God.

50. My purposes are eternal.

51. I speak with eternity truth of purpose of my creating all nations; to allow, according to capacity from previous spirit order of heavenly residing, all to be of accounting to me, the Holy Lord, Jesus Christ, for all things done in mortal flesh.

52. I am to be Judge alone.

53. None need command God.

54. I am of way to only raise from the bond of being in punishment order in world of spirits of earth dwelling around mortal people; which spirits of forefathers are subject to suffering in spirit world after death; until I, your Redeemer, resurrect all from grave to be judged.

55. I shall raise up more righteous first, in the first resurrection.

56. I shall leave more wicked where spirit of justice rules, as a punishment on all of knowing evil, choosing evil, not repenting on earth; to allow many not having heard my plan of salvation opportunity to hear Gospel by my order of holy authority laboring in spirit world; believers there to receive my order of holy salvation by men of authority in holy way among men on earth in earthly existence; holding keys of power, to be of way of blessing all spirits believing Gospel; so I am of just way to all peoples past, present, also future yet to be born on earth.

57. Thou art of an unholy way who hinder birth of children.

58. Contraceptive way of limiting ability to bring forth children is unholy way, of being of way against honorable holy living of bringing to honorable marriage union noble pure spirits to be born.

59. I shall judge all who limit birth-life, especially they of full destroying unborn children, to accounting; an eternal judgment of full justice power.

60. You prosecute my pure people of moral holy begetting in honorable marriage union; yet your government authority reeks with blood on your skirts, as it were, of unborn children; in the eyes of Eternal Power Godhood, of the holy life-giving order of Eternal Power, a rending against God and His holy way.

61. Now be of full awaring; I cometh.

62. I judge. I reward.

63. I give the full judgment of punishing order to evil; full deliverance to more pure order in every nation. Amen.

64. Let now my holy order be pure, holy, not of Babylon way of immoral murderous way.

65. Thy man-made order of governing over daily living is only of this way of earthly dwelling.

66. My way is of eternal way.

67. Now be of full way awakening to truth now sent to all peoples; I shall judge all. Amen.

68. Let this holy way of pure new revealing reach all peoples for salvation of eternal duration sake in lives of all on earth.

69. Let all be aware I sendeth this through him appointed by me, on earth, to be my mouth to all peoples; a voice, as it were, crying in wilderness; for my voice is Spirit; my Spirit is truth; truth shineth through the darkness to touch all honest of mind; to reason in eternity truth now sent to all, both men, women; also to be of children full learning as they earn intelligence of truth way, to guide youth to better, more pure way of living.

70. Let children be holy in my way, to not be unclothed in way of world.

71. Be ye clothed in daily living; not of evil way now of thy false way of tradition, allowing gazing on body to be of legal way.

72. Dress thyselves, as I commanded Adam and Eve, to be clothed.

73. Let all nations do all possible way of purifying from thy midst immoral way of prostituting way; also preserve youth in pure way, to no longer be subject to parading of immoral way on your instrument of visual communicating; nor in music, or printed way of evil order of pictures or adultery way of story reading.

74. Let youth have advantage of full pure upbringing, protected from evil way of vice and immoral order of evil.

75. Let also all peoples know I shall cause all such evil to be done away at my Glory Power coming on the earth.

76. I shall be of full revealing pure holy way.

77. Nation of evil shall be humbled by my power of full judgments of cleansing order; to remove from earth of evil way or intent of immoral or murder way.

78. I shall be of sending full message of Eternal Order of full salvation soon, as government order of nation of thy dwelling is first cleansed; which cleaning cometh by my power judgment. Amen.

79. Now let this be my will known to all peoples; to be holy, pure; noble of living on earth in more holy pure way.

80. Let all be of pure way, as I send judgment to be of my way of my coming among all nations.

81. Let this now be of a full way order of exact publishing to all thy peoples.

82. Let no one be of any way changing my word; lest sins of people not of pure hearing this my will with exactness; you who thus send my word to thy peoples of printing way to do so exactly as my holy revealing cometh into thy hands. Amen.

83. This is your Lord, Jesus Christ, speaking to all my order of earthly dwelling, to be holy. Amen.

84. Now let all peoples learn now I cometh to purge from all nations the murderers of unborn children; also Sodom; also adultery of moral corrupt way of dishonoring God and pure way of dwelling on the world of testing order.

85. Now let all be of the way of repenting; change to more pure way.

86. Let all repent in open way of bettering thy daily living as I have herein named to all peoples.

87. Treat wives kindly.

88. Treat girls as sacred vessels.

89. Let sons be moral.

90. Let all my Order of Eternal Union of Plural Order be pure, lest greater judgments cometh on you of Eternal Union Order Celestial Power Order.

91. Let also my Holy Priesthood be holy on earth; not of Babylon, lest you reap the whirlwind of justice in full way power of judgment.

92. I have spoken.

93. Now be clean, ye that bear my holy authority, lest you receive the greater punishment for compromising my Celestial Order unto traitor way.

94. Let all such be cursed. Amen.

95. Now let also the way of full deliverance come from government power.

96. Let my servant and his fellow order of imprisoned way go free.

97. Let all such evil prosecuting way cease in nation itself so corrupt; it teetereth on precipice of self-destruction

from in the government order, now so evil, they themselves delve into Sodom and adulterous way; many already of the child murder of the unborn. Amen.

98. Such judge my order of holy Eternal Union way; and shall be of full judged way by me, your Holy God over all creation.

99. Let now truth be of full way knowing by this, my holy word sent to all peoples, soon to be of governing authority as my holy Zion on New Era of Peace is of full power over all surviving peoples on earth.

100. Holy, holy art thou, Lord God of all the earth, Jesus Christ, our Holy God of Eternal Order of full Godhood holy power. Amen.

101. Now let United States of the land of my holy order of my power in holy order of Priesthood held in bondage, hear my Supreme Court, of the state of his holding, appeal of full reason way my holy order in the way of full order of my own power is of suffering in bondage, to set them free now.

102. Let this be of a holy message.

103. Let court use authority to dismiss all such way of unjust way.

104. He is innocent.

105. Lying witness is the unholy one.

106. Let truth be told. Amen.

107. Let also my son of aged way, Fredrick Merril Jessop, go free.

108. Let him be known as a holy son.

109. He is only pure, of holy way of Eternal Union way of pure holy living.

110. Let him now go free.

111. He languisheth in prison house by evil judge of the lower court not considering at all his age and poor health way.

112. I shall be of full judgment on all who unjustly treated him. Amen.

113. Now know my servant can be set free on religious freedom of constitutional guarantee of religious way freedom, of law of land upholding the way of constitutional guarantee of religious way freedom on land professing freedom; yet of full way attack on my Church.

114. Let all such be of a reversing, so my holy law of Church governing order only be of free exercise of living on land of professing freedom. Amen.

115. Let also all who are of prosecution way first examine lives of false witness who is adulterer way of living; also betrayed own eternal order of former living herself; Becky Wall; of evil intent; open lying as her way, with aim to only destroy family way of Eternal Union Order; herself a full way immoral adultery way.

116. Let such never be trusted.

117. All such are called apostates.

118. Let such be of the way of fear. Amen.

119. I am the Judge.

120. My people are peace.

121. I am telling all government order to be just; to no longer prosecute my Church order, of pure way open living of eternal holy pure power. Amen.

122. Let also my holy way be upheld, to allow appeal to be heard; to not allow the way of the dismissing be in court; to be of truth learning; lower court not allowing constitutional freedom of religion order as defending my holy order; my authority on earth judged by one not of full way of the power to free him. Amen.

123. Let also my son, Fredrick Merril Jessop, be now of free way.

124. He is attacked.

125. He was of not hearing one of the guarding way.

126. He was attacked, innocent of any error.

127. Now let governing order investigate his injury. Amen.

128. Let also son of Fredrick Merril Jessop be of full free way, Raymond Jessop; also his other son, Leroy Jessop.

129. Let also Michael Emack, Lehi B. Jeffs, Keith William Dutson, Jun.; also Allan Keate; also Abram Jeffs; also LeRoy Steed; all my sons of holy Order of Eternal Union; separated by unjust way from family; to be a way of the wicked attack, to be innocent of all such way of false way of law misused; when thy own way of monogamous way is of full immoral way on the land of professed virtue; now not of justified way to continue as long as you as a nation uphold the way of unholy living, then attack my order of holy living.

130. Such is the guilt way of this present governing power.

131. I shall be Delivering Power of mine elect.

132. The other way of evil is soon to be of full judging power of God upon all.

133. I have allowed sons of pure way to prove present governing power.

134. Let state of them held in the way of their unjust prison holding let them go by my appeal to the Supreme Court of that state, Texas; to be of true way understanding; reading my appeal and exhibit of documents of my own will to the present government on land; to be knowing I cometh; to have true justice upheld.

135. Now learn truth of religious motive of living Celestial holy Plural Eternal Union, in Proclamation I have of my own will revealed truth to all nations.

136. Let this be of evidence; as lower court did not allow full religious freedom of constitutional guarantee of my order to be presented; only warned such would bring my power of judgment.

137. I am God speaking to present government court power, who can release sons of pure innocent way of religious freedom order.

138. Unions of their living were of my order of pure way.

139. Apostate and evil way governing authority plotted this long ago, after my servant was of full way doing my holy way.

140. Let all be of full truth knowing government power gave way to false witnessing way of no pure way.

141. Let it be that not pure way never judge pure way of living; lest own impure way be foundation of evil way of the wrong way of judging.

142. Such was prosecution way; to attempt to present holy way as evil way; when only way of my holy presenting was to tell truth, that I, your Lord Jesus Christ, speak through a Prophet to my Church on earth; to be only holy pure order of Celestial Power Order.

143. I shall cause all such unholy way to be of full receiving of my judgment. Amen.

144. Let now my holy Order be holy, so I may be of full way power of delivery unto innocence. Amen.

145. Let also all of government first be pure themselves, before attempting prosecution judging of my pure holy order of Eternal Union Order, of holy way Celestial; my own way Eternal Union Order. Amen.

146. Let also full Order of Eternal Union have full religious free way in all nations when I come.

147. Pass law for religion to be of free way in all lands, so I can establish holy pure way among all peoples of holy pure way; mine Israel being my Priesthood order of full way order of holy order among nations

on the world now of evil way, yet to be changed to my holy way, those of Israel lineage of pure descent order being of my holy order when converted by my holy way being only eternal life way of salvation.

148. Let Israel now be of full gathering to my holy land as Zion, New Era of Peace, riseth to rule over all nations, soon to happen; as I, God over all, have sent my own will to all nations of earthly government authority to know I cometh.

149. This is also a full warning to all peoples, how to be pure holy way; unto Zion of full way order being governing order of full Eternal Order Celestial Order Power over all lands, peoples, nations; even the way of the governing order to be the full power over all peoples. Amen.

150. Also let this all be reprinted in pure translating order in every tongue, so all peoples read my will in own language; all of reading gift in every land.

151. Send thy copy to my servant, so I may be of full way approving thy translation. Amen.

152. Now let my order of full holy union be holy. Amen.

153. I, Jesus Christ, am God.

154. I have conquered death, hell, the devil, even now Ruler over heaven and earth.

155. I am to reveal secrets of all nations.

156. I reveal as faith is of full way abiding in you.

157. All not of faith, who are of full way of the order of not upholding my word, shall know truth by my holy way of full judgments on the earth; thereby all shall know I, God, your Lord, hath been of sending my own revealed way, how to be preparing for my holy Advent, my Zion government authority coming to the earth from heaven; yea, my own presence, power, authority; even to be of seeing by all in my Glory Power in all nations; so all may learn my eternal way of holy order of holy living on earth; unto holy way of earning eternal holy living on earth, as it becomes a holy earth of full power of heaven on earth. Amen.

158. Now hear my will: I come with ten thousand angels of power authority to rule over all nations.

159. All must be more of the way of holy pure way to be on earth.

160. This is of sacred way of former revealing.

161. All know my prophecy of returning to earth in power in Bible record of holy Prophets, with my own revealing in Matthew 24 of New Testament record.

162. I am soon to be among surviving nations.

163. I shall descend as I declared.

164. I shall be Celestial Government order of Eternal Order Power of Son Ahman, Jesus Christ, your Holy King Emmanuel.

165. Though all nations deny my Order of Celestial Power, I shall do as I promised.

166. All of evil way shall hide.

167. I shall be of sudden appearing; no one of evil of the way to oppose me.

168. I come soon; thus I send this full warning.

169. Let all be of faith, so you may have more eternity truth revealed to all nations.

170. I can speak all languages.

171. I hear prayers of thy heart, desiring truth.

172. Be prayer order lived now.

173. Be holy, so prayers can be of my fulfilling by almighty power, the power that gives you life of mind, body, and unto eternal life. Amen.

Thus Saith Jehovah, Even Son Ahman, Who Is Jesus Christ, God Over All, to All Nations on Earth, a Holy Revealing How to Be of Holy Pure Order of Survival

(Comprising Section Revelations 160-161)

Jehovah
Son Holy Ahman
Jesus Christ

I, Jesus Christ, God Over All, Send to All Nations on Earth, to Their Peoples, Mine Own Will to Be Known; a Righteous Judge Over All, Who Revealeth Only Truth Way. I Speak, and the Very World of All Peoples Dwelling Obeyeth and Exist by My Power Celestial. I Am God That Now Sendeth Word of How to Dwell in More Holy Pure Way. Live Unto Righteous Holy Way to Be Surviving My Judgment on All Wicked Corrupt Peoples; a Cleansing to Happen of Soon Full Measure on All the Earth; to Cause My Kingdom to Come From Heaven; to Rule Among Men; to Have Full Way of Power Over All Peoples. Hear My Truth Way of How All Shall Live in Millennial Reign of Thy Lord on Earth:

SECTION REVELATION 160

Revelation of the Lord Jesus Christ
Palestine, Texas
Friday, January 27, 2012

1. I, your Holy God, speak; yea, even your God of the full power of judgment; who hath all power of my holy Godhead authority, unto all nations being of the way to be of the order of way to be of a cleansing; yea, even in full measure, unto all peoples being humbled, unto my holy will of full way, to have all people on the holy way of my order of pure love-order becoming holy in all way of my Eternal Order of Zion on my holy land of the New Era of my New Holy City of the holy power of my governing order Celestial over all nations.

2. Now let all hear my holy way, even Jesus Christ, my will of the order of pure principle, a holy power eternal, of full Godhead authority over all the world; to have full power to be my holy order of pure way to be my holy power of Celestial oneness among the holy order of my way being to have place among men as governing authority over all peoples on earth.

3. Now be holy, so I may ordain all according to principles of eternal power; to be the only power over whole world, unto a full way power, to be government of peace, of pure way; to overthrow all evil; a way of Celestial holy order, unto all power of pure governing order being upheld by the voice of all nations, to have all sound with rejoicing my rule is of the way of purity, holiness, righteous way.

4. Verily I say, I am the way of light eternal, life everlasting, who speaketh to all peoples; a holy light of never-ending joy.

5. I have been thy holy way of the way of eternal power.

6. I am Lord of all, a Holy Power Eternal, who dwells on high; whose coming is soon; yea, to be of full governing order over all who shall remain.

7. I have with me a sure holy order.

8. My order is pure.

9. No one is of the order of my holy order save they are pure.

10. Be pure. Be holy, saith Jesus Christ, your Lord. Amen.

11. Now learn of my holy order.

12. Men and the way of holy order of the pure way is to have no way of unholy power to let passion riot in way of the corrupting of the female purity, nor to be of the unholy power of force on another.

13. Thus, I shall allow only pure way of the order of holy union of marriage; also in general social way; not to be of unholy connecting of male and woman in way of the unholy who are of the moral evil of the intimacy, both of outward connecting, also of mind pure way not kept.

14. Therefore, in my order, men do not dwell in full way with women in the order of labor.

15. Men will be of my way of pure labor separate, in general, from women; in workplace, in the way of gathering, in schooling; all in a moral way.

16. I, God, shall cause this to be way of social living; thus, all connecting of men and wives of moral holy order of marriaging shall be both of no previous of way of intimacy with another, save previously of a married way of one who is deceased; new union performed by law of righteous way, honoring all in moral clean holy union.

17. Children shall not have connection in union of male and girls, save of age for married order.

18. Thus, all evil pertaining to connection of intimate way shall be by law, not by the licentious order of present generation on earth.

19. Law in all lands shall guard virtue, unto a more holy way of dwelling as families.

20. Children shall have separate way according to the gender.

21. Also, sons shall not be of the way of the connecting of the intimate order before married union order is of lawful order.

22. Woman shall not be of a order of evil connecting at all, nor used by the way of gain in the way of any immoral usury, nor children, in all nations.

23. Under my Holy Reign, all peoples who are of the way of immoral force on youth or others shall be of death way administered by government authority; no way of living of the way of the forcing of intimacy. Amen.

24. Now be clean, holy, pure, noble of pure holy way in thy moral conduct; for I am God; I can send the fulfilling of law in full authority, knowing all things; revelation followed by pure men

in judging; no women of judging of the power of government; my order being to have my holy power of Priesthood, only held by men of pure holy living, administer law by my inspired holy order of only truth upheld in all things; I able to reveal secrets of mind, desire, action; all knowing I can be approached by prayer, and honest pure living, to learn truth.

25. I shall govern by law, not by evil of gain or violent way of army.

26. I shall teach all to rely on the order of government power to be of safety; no violent way of weapons of violence in any land among the people.

27. All shall have love-peace, safety in own home always, a love-peace order of pure holy way.

28. Let all now know my holy order is of revealing truth; to punish men, or the way of learning truth by holy confessing, also witnessing of truth way of self-living, so no falsehood is upheld --

29. I able to reveal truth in all cases of judging in my pure holy way. Amen.

30. Thus, by Godhood holy power, sons of my authority power shall govern in truth; righteous way of holy way of full order of truth of all involved in any case of misconduct. Amen.

31. Now know the way of God, who shall uphold pure holy way that will preserve virtue, also innocence of youth all their lives.

32. All shall be held accountable for conduct.

33. All shall be of open knowing of truth of lives shown by revealing order of governing authority.

34. My rule shall be of the way of true holy love of forgiving; prisons being changed to have the way of converting wayward people to honor and upright

dwelling through repentance, unto seeking a holy way order of renewed dwelling; thus a reformation order shall labor with wrongdoers of the order of still living on earth; not of crime worthy of full life-taking punishment; even murder, also immoral way of destroying innocence in self, or another; as all shall be known by my power eternal order of governing order on earth; the heavenly authority dwelling among men in all places that the people are under my holy power.

35. Let all now learn Catholic order of priests not married is unholy; they not of governing family; thus not of experience to guide others of the congregation in religious way of the way of truth-telling how to be of moral family way.

36. My holy religion shall be over all religion law in the governing order of nations; having pure law, my law, saith Jesus Christ; all religions of freedom of religious way; yet none being of harm to another;

37. Thus I shall guarantee agency of holy faith order of religious order; none forced to be of my revealed order of pure holy order of true religion from Celestial holy domain of thy Lord.

38. Though I have true religion, men shall be choosing; no force involved in moral and pure faith order in lives of all peoples on earth.

39. You can be free in all lands under my rule, saith Jesus Christ; unto no violent nor immoral way lived, even all thy lifetime on earth.

40. Let all peoples prepare, for I shall be of power to judge all; to be of order of cleansing by judgments of order of cleansing all peoples of murder, of vice, of immoral way in all way of the governing order doing labor to be of truth in all

principles of holy revealed order of law-living order; all law honest and of equity administered.

41. The way of usury, of evil way shall not be.

42. All shall labor in honest way.

43. All shall be taught my way to care for the sick, the poor, the aged -- none of a neglect.

44. Lives shall be of longer dwelling in mortal earthly living as way of pure living is followed. Amen.

45. Thus, New Era of Peace of holy power on earth soon cometh.

46. Prepare ye, all ye peoples on earth, who are of more holy way, to be of way of Zion, a holy inspired way, taught to all nations. Amen.

47. Now be of the way to cease practice of evil of any way against order of virtue; or pure preserving of innocence of youth, of women and men, in social living purified by legal guarding way of governing order in all lands being my holy order of inspiring order of full holy revealing truth in all cases; nothing hidden --

48. Thus all shall abide truth, with no evil deceiving in any way upheld; true justice upheld by governing power, so all are of truth.

49. Let all learn to be of truth, in innocence and virtuous way of all thy living.

50. Let all be honest, of virtue and more holy way, to be among they who are of full dwelling, yet on earth; for I, the Eternal King, hath eternal authority order of full order of the holy power of truth, righteousness, of holy order of all things known by me, God over all.

51. My power is with me always.

52. Such shall be known in all lands, among all peoples; that God hath come,

and is in His holy way among men in daily governing; all to promote holy pure way.

53. I shall bring all authority power to maintain my holy way; to be of influence to purify all peoples in all way of living; no order of evil; nor of the corrupt way of the power of my order purifying all holy order power of the way of religion truth living; not to be of the way to deceive minds unto evildoing in falsehood, lived by ministers not of pure truth on earth; who seek gain of earthly power more than salvation of souls.

54. Women shall be treated as honorable, not used to be of the way of men's unholy desires abused, not of immoral way.

55. Let all, therefore, hear my holy way; to be of full governing authority, my holy order of governing having sons of Priesthood of eternal authority sent to teach thy peoples how to dwell in my way of peace-order in daily doing. Amen.

56. Now be ye ready, is the will of God to all peoples surviving my whirlwind judgments on all nations.

57. Let sober holy way be thy way, to prepare for mighty power of my Godhood authority on earth from heaven; to rule over all nations on earth; all having way to be accounting for own living unto governing pure authority on earth; no one forced to do right; yet all being trained in holy way of living; therefore, be more holy way of pure holy living in all way of purity abided in my order of truth peace.

58. Let all holy ones of the way of loving truth be of sure way ready; for when I appear, all peoples shall see me together; a holy revealing of almighty order power, all at once suddenly of my knowledge, causing the wicked to fear.

59. I am holy. Be ye holy. Amen.

SECTION REVELATION 161

Revelation of the Lord Jesus Christ
Palestine, Texas
Monday, January 30, 2012

1. The great power over all speaketh, Jesus Christ, your Lord, Holy One of Israel; yea, the Beginning and the End, Alpha and Omega, all in all for all nations, peoples, orders of governing power on the world of my holy power creating; yea, He who is over all now is of telling all my holy way to be pure, even to dwell on my world during my Millennial Reign of Power, Peace Order of all men having only pure way of dwelling on my world of renewal power unto Celestial world coming to the world upon which you dwell.

2. I have all power.

3. I am Christ, the Holy Power of all being redeemed; to be of full way order of Judge of all; to have my power Celestial Governing Order among men; verily I say, eternal power of an Eternal God cometh.

4. Be ye ready, for only they of pure way shall remain on my world of my creation for all to have given holy order of the way of progress, even to obtain an earthly body for thy progression into eternity; a body necessary to be of Godhood power, like unto me, even God over all; for you were of my holy order on another world of spirit way in exact form as present body on earth; yet of matter of spirit that is eternal pure intelligence of mind.

5. Let all know spirit of thy first holy existing is thy soul in thy earthly body; taking the way of my coexisting order, eternal spirit matter that is alive to feel all thy body of an earthly way feels; to make thee a living soul; a soul of my creating. No other could make such. Amen.

6. Now know I, God, speaketh to be justified to cleanse all lands of the way of outward evil that destroys way of living pure holy way on the earth.

7. There is nothing greater than I, your Lord, who is just, holy order of eternal salvation of all who dwell in holy pure way on the world of thy now dwelling; a full way eternal reward, of the way of punishing for sin of evil intent, and of power of eternal holy happy way for saints who dwell in holy pure way during earthly existence now of thy testing, according to what they on earth choose.

8. Let all now choose to do all good way of blessing, in pure way, all thy way of doing allows.

9. Let all my holy power be acquired by obeying my holy power Gospel plan of saving power on earth.

10. Let all be holy on earth to be of earning holy palaces of eternal domain on earth, as I can do the work of Celestializing world on which you dwell by fire of heaven coming to convert all to high order of heavenly order power; a holy way to transfigure all creation unto Celestial power on present world of now corruption order; yet to be changed by heavenly order returning.

11. Verily I reveal this to all, so all may know why I cometh; to change earth to heavenly order for the holy order of pure holy Godhood to dwell; to continue on the world of thy present dwelling, full power of heavenly power; to be world of heavenly happiness unto all of holy happy salvation order.

12. This is my revealing to present generation on earth; to learn of thy Lord His purpose to descend to this earth, to change this world of evil way into world of heavenly order.

13. Let all therefore be of full way right in living full Gospel of salvation, as all shall inherit what is of earned order of thy choosing.

14. Any who dwell in evil shall be cast off to another orb of sinning way, not of full way of heavenly way.

15. This is according to my holy order of holy way eternal order plan of salvation of my holy order Celestial way of holy order of my plan Celestial coming to be among all my whole domain on this earth, to all peoples knowing I have appeared.

16. Let all now learn eternity truth of thy saving, unto a holy order to be yet revealed by my order of revealing holy saving intelligence of truth-way only; even my authority on earth now sending to all nations my own will by the order of being in language of men.

17. Let all be holy to remain on world of thy present dwelling.

18. Let all be of holy way.

19. Let my holy way be as I have revealed; to not allow mingling of social way before marriage, men and female order among thy social group.

20. Let men be separate, in that they dwell in a way to not be among women in workplace.

21. Let women be of separation of workplace, to not mingle among men.

22. Let this be in all thy way of labor; to be holy on earth; only of connecting by holy principle of the order of the way of marriage union; to be of the pure holy way on my world of more pure order during Millennial Reign of pure holy way. Amen.

23. Now be holy according to this pattern in general way, as some way of holy labor is done by men guiding women.

24. Let this be in family order, not workplace order.

25. Let all be some of my holy ones of holy order of pure way; so when I come among thee in every land, moral way is followed. Amen.

26. Now let children be separate in schooling of gender order, so boys and girls are separate in school labor.

27. Let this be so moral way is followed by all who are of a way of pure holy way on earth to prepare for my holy order of pure salvation way. Amen.

28. Let also men not be of my condemning them of immoral way of usury of female way, lest they die.

29. I am of full order of pure holy way, saith thy God.

30. I shall suffer no man to be of immoral way on earth as I am Ruler over all.

31. Let this be known by all; for such a unholy way of immoral way shall be of a full punishing. Amen.

32. Let now order of child delivery be told to be as a holy way.

33. Let no man be doctor to woman of delivery.

34. Let man be only there if of husband pure order.

35. Let all be delivered of child-way delivery by midwife way, to be holy pure way.

36. This is my way during Millennial Reign of my holy way on the world upon which you now dwell; when I come to be as a burning fire to consume every corruptible thing not of my pure way order I bring from heaven to dwell among men on this earth. Amen.

37. Now learn of business banking way of my holy way: All belongs to God; as He is holy order of creation order holy power order over all.

38. There shall be no poor on earth. All shall have my blessing of need.

39. All shall be only of the way of donation to a full storehouse of needing order of the way of the daily needs of all. All shall build up a storehouse.

40. All shall be of full holy way giving. All shall be of love-kindness order. All shall have holy motive who remain. All shall be my holy way of blessing all. Amen.

41. Now learn about my holy way to be of peace: All nations shall destroy all weapons. All shall turn to the Lord for protecting from all of violent way.

42. I shall humble the wicked nation that declareth war or violent way on any other with no way justified order of war, save for self-protecting order.

43. I shall be of full way order of sending humbling judgment of my power, unto humbling violent people with death order of judgment, of my order of Godhood authority to give or take life by way of the natural way of mortal existence being ended by my life or life-taking order; even by disease, earthquake, nature-way of giving or taking life order on they who are violent.

44. Thus I have told all nations to destroy armored vehicles as a way to show me you will be of peace, not war among nations, nor in thy own land of dwelling in force way.

45. Let peace be now. Let all be holy way. Amen.

46. My holy power of holy government cometh among all peoples when I send first destroying angels of power to remove more wicked from all peoples, nations, governing order of warning way.

47. Now learn to make peace, lest my great power be of full way upon all of wicked order of harm to other nations.

48. I have caused my own way of order to be of a published order in print to all peoples.

49. You heed me not.

50. I shall now tell thee what cometh if you are to be of evil unholy way continued, I being holy pure way eternal order way of peace-power through Godhood order power.

51. I soon send tsunami upon Asia lands.

52. Cause all along low-level land by sea to go to high area, lest many perish who could have been of a holy way believing God would humble order of judgment on wicked who continue to dwell in moral degradation way on earth.

53. China shall be humbled. She shall be of a way of internal way of strife in starvation time after she attends order of humbling nation of my coming.

54. There is also a way to be of pure order of surviving, if nation of my coming ceaseth child murder of unborn children, also immoral adulterous Sodom way.

55. Let also my holy servant of holy authority be freed.

56. Let his brethren be freed, to be with my elect, to prepare them for my holy coming; to have full religious freedom to dwell in my law of pure holy marriage plural order on land of claimed religious freedom.

57. Let also the way of lands and houses taken by illegal court way be of full return to my religion leadership among my people on the order of my holy way of Zion rising among people who are of my order

of pure religious motive in living Celestial Marriage Order in plural marriage way order, Celestial order, of my eternal way of pure holy family living.

58. Let my people go.

59. Let all be of only leaving them to my way of government of pure holy way among them; my holy power of Priesthood authority. Amen.

60. Now let the people of the nation of my holy way be of more holy way themselves, obliterating out of their lives all immoral corrupt way; not to judge my people from basis of their own evil way, being of governing by world of government of man in way to stop immoral order that destroys life and innocence, virtue and holiness of pure holy revealed way of my religion.

61. Such was attempt by prosecution order in present unjust attack of court.

62. They took my innocent pure holy order youth, sent them out to all places corrupt; many abused in immoral way by government power of child-caring way; to return in fear they would be harmed by police or other of the way of government way power, as they were. Amen.

63. Now let such unhallowed way of corrupt judging cease.

64. It is an abomination among you of a so-called free preservation order of purity preserved by law order; yet promoting attack against my holy way of pure childbearing and raising in holy way, not of world wicked way of evil continually of the giving youth.

65. Let it be of my order, to tell truth of evil performed on my people of raid of government order of evil intent against my holy religion of revealed eternal salvation order.

66. Let all peoples know child was molested in many of the places of holding by government authority labor.

67. Many have scars on their minds against this wicked generation; my youth who were wickedly of a scattering out among the wicked world being of a way of knowing they were of my delivering, they being only delivered as I touched mind of higher court.

68. Let not any take glory to themselves.

69. Only God can deliver. Only He gives free way. Only He is of holy way free to deliver all of pure way.

70. Let all now assemble truth of raid against my youth by wicked government power in Texas.

71. Let my record show truth.

72. Let it be of naming any who are such wicked way, to cause youth to be of abuse way, to be themselves evil, thinking my order of plural order union marriage way order was not of pure holy motive and practice order way.

73. I caused all to know my way is pure in child holy raising and birthing in holy conduct of Family Order of Heaven.

74. Let all be holy. Let all be pure.

75. Let all know my order hath no immoral order, lest they be expelled from my order of holy way.

76. Such are accusing way of they who now persecute my holy order, even apostate former order of living my holy way, then turning away from my holy way, to dwell in evil way of world; they to be used by government prosecution order to be of imprisoning my innocent ones of fatherhood order in my holy order.

77. Let such wicked way be no longer of a unholy way doing against my holy order of pure holy way, saith Jesus Christ, God over all nations; soon to come in holy

power order of full governing power order. Amen.

78. Now hear my way to punish government order who are such crimes themselves to corrupt youth.

79. They shall be no longer of power.

80. They shall be of way to know of sin they did.

81. They shall be of a dishonor to their called authority.

82. They shall never rise again to influence.

83. I shall also send judgment upon all who did abuse way of my innocent youth, to feel result of their own way of corrupt way; to never find happy way; all to know of my judgment in day of power of my coming.

84. Let such repent, and cease corrupt way.

85. Let all such cease being of child-caring way now. Amen.

86. Such should be my way when I come to govern all people on earth. Amen.

87. Now learn of way to heal youth of abuse way of such evil way order of government corrupt way.

88. Let my holy way be to tell them of pure holy living way of God; to set example of parents, and all who labor with them, of moral way; to be of holy power by my power of governing family.

89. Let my people heal.

90. Let all be of holy order.

91. Let all be one in my pure religion. Amen.

92. Now let all nations be told truth.

93. My holy order is under attack because apostate corrupt men and unholy women fight against their own former way of pure way of my holy religion of revealed order.

94. Let all know I shall leave such hypocrites a way no longer on the earth, neither their posterity.

95. They shall be of full power of judging by God in the hereafter.

96. Let all be holy, lest such full judging come upon you by me, God over all. Amen.

97. Now let all people be of full way preparing for my holy Advent in Godhood glory power extant over all peoples.

98. I cometh, saith Jesus Christ, your Holy God of full order power.

99. I am He who reigneth.

100. My holy way is to do the will of my Father, who is God over all creation; who is my Holy Father Eternal, of the way of Godhead order over this world.

101. Let all know God is of full way order power to be governing power of just holy order. Amen.

102. Thus saith the Lord to all ends of the earth: Calamity soon cometh on all lands.

103. Be ye pure to abide the way of judgment of my pure way of judging all on earth; is my will to be published to all nations on earth, even now to know war of full order of full way power cleansing order soon cometh, because man of unholy way over nation of power is soon to fall from his power; then to have another who is soon to be of way of war.

104. He shall use weapons of great order way of destructive way.

105. He shall be of a way to be only in power for a short time of rule over land of my coming.

106. Then cometh the order of full way judgment on holy Zion land.

107. This is my holy order of truth-telling to all peoples on earth.

108. Now know my holy way to send

truth is of an expense of needing my word to be of continued sending.

109. Assist my religious order to be of continued way sending truth to all peoples. Amen.

110. Now let all peoples be of the way to be holy pure order of the way to be of ready way.

111. Let all not be of unbelieving way on earth; to be of sudden surprise at my power of shaking; also of government order from heaven coming to my world upon which you now dwell.

112. Let all be holy, lest judgment be of full way order cleansing order power, of just way served on all wicked.

113. Let all such repent now, lest their sins be answered eternally in day of my holy judging power over all peoples.

114. Let the Lord's way be thy only way, to now repent, all ye ends of the world. Amen.

Jesus Christ
Son Ahman

I, Jehovah, Even Son Ahman, Who Is Your God of All Creation, Jesus Christ, Now Send My Own Way of Holy Eternal Salvation; Also Warning of Coming Full Judgments of God. Let All Take Heed to Be of Eternal Wise Order. Hear My Will of the Order of Eternal Power:

(Comprising Section Revelations 162-163)

SECTION REVELATION 162

Revelation of the Lord Jesus Christ
Palestine, Texas
Thursday, February 9, 2012

1. God who reigneth over all, by power, Eternal Order Power, saith to all this wicked and ungodly generation, you hear me not.

2. I weep over thee, ye unbelieving peoples of all nations; for your calamity is of your own bringing; my love-light having been sent; to warn how to be of full way order of being of holy way, to survive destructive way of whirlwind judgment; and even send signs of earthquake, sea heaving beyond bounds of her keeping; hail, famine, wars of more destructive force soon at hand; and ye will not be of a holy way worthy to be delivered from all lost, of thyselves and thy peoples continuing on the earth.

3. Hear thou my call!

4. Be ye holy!

5. No longer delve into satanism nor sorcery, nor a moral way of iniquity way.

6. Be ye sure of thy holy way pleases God, by comparing lives to holy writ of my own Gospel of saving power in scriptures; not in one doctrine only, but in all my will being holy way extant. Amen.

7. Thus shall a doomed way inhabit nation of persecution way against my people; none to be thy shield and provider, none to stay storm or earth shaking down thy dwellings entire, in places of full doing of evil against my holy call to repent of such gross immoral crimes of adultery, an unholy way of no fruitful unions in the corrupt Sodom order of no way saving of thyself, nor of bringing forth pure posterity; corrupting your way before your Holy God, who seeth all thine wicked abominations of full way of sure judgment soon to roll forth, to cleanse all off this holy land of Zion, my Zion soon to rise. Amen.

8. Now be ye holy, to remain on land of New Era Government Order of New Holy City of Eternal Order Heavenly Power of Ahman, yea, Son Ahman coming, even I, your Holy God, Jesus Christ, who is Jehovah of all Godhead order now of the holy power governing all way order of nations all over present world.

9. Let all now know I have sent my power to earth, to be witness of personal way experience, son of witnessing way who holdeth my full power of Power Eternal Order of full order of the Holy

Priesthood from my Eternal Dominion; a continued holy authority; that as you thus do to him, my servant of Keyholder authority, so you do to me, your Lord.

10. As you thus do to my representative on this world, so do you have in your minds to do to my Kingdom of Peace Power, Celestial way Order Authority Order Holy Power, Eternal Power of Jesus Christ, Emmanuel, God who redeemed all by His own suffering. Amen.

11. Now receive my holy peace way, all ye nations on earth order of now existing on my way of testing all peoples, to see whether you shall be hearing my will or no.

12. Now learn my order is above the power of man to resist.

13. Any way of fighting against my authority on earth, I, who is Power Eternal, shall turn what thou doest upon thine own way of not surviving. Amen.

14. Hear, O hear my plea to all, to repent of sin of immoral way of murder of unborn children, of Sodom way.

15. O ye peoples, how can you so openly deny my word, when I speak by Spirit power accompanying my holy will to all honest-in-heart susceptible receiving minds who yet have degree of pure way living, not of full evil intent; who desire to prayerfully be of a holy way unto the God of Creation, even I, your Lord; who seeth all things; who is of Eternal Order, of Everlasting Lives Order, of Power Celestial of holy way of pure way Eternal Order Authority over worlds? Amen.

16. Now receive a prophecy, to know I speak, to know God seeth all, to be of sure knowing I told thee before what taketh place; so all who are of more holy way may awake and repent while still in time of living on earth.

17. Verily I say to you, a hinderment to prosperity to United States of America concerning money system soon riseth; by unholy way alliance of foreign powers to overthrow thy power of economic power, on the way of nations no longer of trust of the nation who sold power for nothing; by selling manufacturing might to go overseas to other growing economic power nations.

18. Now thy dependence on their money power shall soon be of the way of them no longer needing you as a nation to police them; as a way to show they are of power of economic order of withdrawing money support of national power of the nation now the largest debtor nation among economic powers of full debt of public and personal business way debt or people of personal debt; brought to economic crisis; such as no longer having credit way among powers of wicked moneymen and people of power in the way of lending; no longer of lending way power, as money system faileth; thus thy trade and travel order hindered; thy way to feed nation becoming a stopped way of no travel of goods; thus mob rule when starvation in population of large city dwelling; such unholy riot way and violence increasing suddenly, to cause government order distress untold heretofore; thus only unrest on land of once civil order.

19. A unholy way then riseth, of city against city, of neighborhood against neighborhood, in land of once peaceful outward order.

20. A unholy unrighteous way ariseth soon as enough of the banking way organizing order of money handling fails; unto no trust in paper system.

21. Verily I say, you are on brink of disaster; of no food, nor way of trade; until population is of no way of the peaceful order of a nation who would not believe

your Lord, to be soon of a way to pour forth food storage unto population; yea, war shall come as nation proves weakness of power.

22. A holy way shall rise among my people, as wicked are of degenerate way of full mob rule, of life-taking way in many way order of city way across land.

23. Then cometh my full judgment as unholy way seeketh to destroy my holy way.

24. I am God over all, that holdeth all things in my power.

25. Heed my holy way to be pure, holy way of sure living law of moral pure holy way, as I have named, both in my holy Bible record, also in Holy Scriptures, of revelation and teachings of Prophets on land you now national order existence on land of Zion, soon to rise, a Holy City, New Jerusalem.

26. All peoples shall know I have spoken, as New Era of Peace cometh after violent order in nation of violent way is of spent way to no longer be violent order.

27. A way of peace cometh to all nations, my holy order of Celestial Order Power, saith your God, Jesus Christ, in language of thy understanding.

28. Now be holy, lest thine own works condemn thee.

29. You are an unholy people mostly, of way to uphold corrupt way; also of the belief of lie against my holy order of holy governing authority on earth; my holy power I established through a way of heavenly revealing to chosen Prophet Joseph Smith, Jun., in land of professed religious freedom; which holy way has not been of freedom for my holy religion in nation boasting religious freedom.

30. Now let my holy servant go free, lest I allow nation to feel my judgments.

31. I have been of a holy revealing through him, my Mouthpiece on earth; also my holy revelation of New Testament, Old Testament order; also Joseph Smith as a Seer, Prophet, Revelator, recording my own will to this wicked generation; calling on all to repent, lest judgment of full way order power sweep wicked off land of Zion, a City of Holiness soon to shine forth unto a more holy people preserved by my almighty power.

32. Let my word be heard.

33. Open your hearts through believing prayer, to have my peace-Spirit witness to your soul, to know these warnings and call to holy way repenting order are of me, thy Holy Lord Eternal Order Governing Power, Son Ahman, who is God over worlds. Amen.

34. Let President of nation sign release way of my Holy Priesthood, held by illegal persecuting way against holy revealed religion, not of freedom to live my religion, not to be of government power of men to abuse living my holy revealed order of eternal order of saving way of holy way dwelling on earth; all to be of a holy soon way delivery by signing of highest authority of government order; also my other sons of needed free way of religious persecuted way by unjust court order; all only living my holy religion by my own way revealed; none of own way to live a way of only God guiding, establishing; upholding my own way eternal saving order of Celestial way Marriage of Plural Order.

35. Verily I say to all, let my servants go, to be free to have religious order of living a protection under thy heaven-inspired Constitution of religious freedom guarantee order, now broken by own court not upholding own freedom law ability; to soon be of no religion fully free if nation continues in evil way.

36. Let all awake, for if you do not do right, thy wrong way bringeth full order of disannulling unjust way by the coming of misrule, lawlessness; order of mob rule; war, pestilence, diseases of great harm of overflowing scourge, of earthquake, in divers places; all because you continue in degradation practices of corrupt immoral way, murder way of the abortion evil way; contraceptive way to hinder life coming forth; all of man, not of God.

37. I have shown my way to be of a holy way ready; how Zion shall be of holy way over all nations; no evil in the Zion Kingdom; no evil law of my holy Zion, of soon full power appearing on earth, suddenly; to surprise all wicked; so they are of fear, to be of humbled way, saith your Lord. Amen.

38. Let Congress pass law to be now holy order to abolish law of being a way to persecute my holy order of religion, to have all now be of true upholding of religion free way on present nation power land of United States of America national power way; to uphold my own holy revealed order having free way to live holy Plural Order Marriage; also to provide deliverance for my Holy Priesthood in bondage way, by you being influence for freedom.

39. I have sent my own revealed Proclamation of my own revealed order to all lawmaking national, local authority of recent mailed order, even to high office of President of nation.

40. I shall see to my holy will fulfilled, according to thy choosing way, you do or not do my holy way of freedom of religion preservation order or no.

41. Let all be humble, purify own selves, as I, God, shall reveal thy secrets, even of personal way in time of judgment of an all-knowing just God over all.

42. Be ye holy.

43. Be ye of pure holy just governing law, not of corrupt immoral way, which is of whole land of my Zion land now, of both North and South America. A New Era cometh.

44. Repent ye; be clean morally to be of Zion order, which shall fill the earth entire as holy Celestial power way order of pure holy government power over all land, peoples, nations, tongues, governing powers now on all lands.

45. A way soon cometh to be only holy pure people in all lands.

46. A new power, not mankind known at present, is of heaven coming to earth to rule.

47. Let all be holy to survive, is God's own will to all peoples of all lands on earth. Amen.

48. I, God, even Son Ahman, Jesus Christ, Redeeming Power over death, the Resurrection and the Life, speak not of earthly judgment alone, of the way of the living now on earth; also I tell all I am Eternal Judge of all peoples.

49. You are of way of both spirit son or daughter of same way image of man or woman of flesh order on earth, you alive by my marvelous power of life-giving way of your spirit body in the way of dwelling in your physical earthly body, to make each a living soul on earth, to be of way of testing; to know at age of intelligent way of maturing in agency to know good from evil, having power to choose good.

50. Let all be aware, I judge all in after-death resurrection order to be of reward of all you chose to perform on earth.

51. I judge all.

52. I am God over all.

53. Spirit of the way of departing from earthly body at death is yet alive in the

way of still being same intelligence as in body of earthly way, of the order to yet feel, learn, know, to be of agency there in my world of departed spirits of they who lived on earth, still on earth in sphere of dwelling, unseen by mortal eye, save I enlighten vision.

54. A way of full dwelling exists among the departed spirits who are of a way of holy living; of the way to dwell in peace-joy love-power of my power of holy light.

55. They are of preserved way of happiness who do good on earth, my love-light shining in such honorable souls who loved the right while on earth in earthly body; continuing to love good, do good, in world of departed spirits of my own creating as sons and daughters of God.

56. Now know when death cometh, spirit leaves body of earthly order, and is still of full intelligence of loving, of understanding, thinking, doing order of living in sphere of action around present mortal earthly peoples; to be as a full living son or daughter of intelligence; able to associate; all being of way to dwell among their own way of spirit order, evil with evil, good with good; all who never heard my Gospel salvation plan to hear my full Gospel plan of saving order by my holy Eternal Authority of pure Holy Priesthood authority of a way of still awaiting resurrection; yet laboring among spirits who never heard my holy Gospel order of saving power unto the way of joining my holy way among spirits.

57. Let all know I shall give repentance order to they who never heard my holy Gospel on earth, to all in world of departed spirits, to give all peoples equal opportunity to hear and receive, and live pure way of my Gospel of salvation.

58. They who learn on earth, in their earthly body, my holy Gospel salvation plan, who rejected or fought against my holy Gospel and Priesthood authority on earth in mortal flesh, shall be of a suffering punishment in spirit world equal to sins committed; then cometh the resurrection, when my holy way rewardeth all eternally according to law lived on earth, pertaining to eternal living in a kingdom of my glory if worthy.

59. Let all realize I am thy Father in heaven, who loveth all, who offers same plan of salvation I abide in my Godhood eternal order, full glory order, holy power order of eternal power of holy heavenly way order.

60. I give eternal happiness to pure-in-soul peoples of all way order of eternal living in increase of holy happy order of full salvation, if pure of way on earth.

61. Let all who reject me and my holy plan of salvation, both on earth, and when in world of departed spirit-dwelling after this life, you shall be of a way of bringing all from grave as a living soul, I of Godhood full power, to bring all flesh and sinew, all full physical order of earthly way physical body to join spirit of your existence, as a spirit son or daughter, joined as a living soul of both spirit and earthly body together; to receive just eternal holy reward of eternal living with me and the Father, if holy; else an eternal shutting out of heaven way of not being of full Celestial glory order with thy Holy Lord, to be of way to dwell in lesser glory way if of lesser degree of holy dwelling; all to receive physical body again in an immortal condition; yet able to die second death of the way of thy spirit and body not being an eternal union; dwelling in lesser glory until you reach full ability of law of progression you chose to live on earth; a holy reward labor of thy Holy God upon

all, recompensing to all according to the measure they meted to all others on earth.

62. Let all be of pure holy way in all thy dwelling in the flesh of this life, so you may be of full reward in heaven, according to thy works of your own agency living order on earth; this mortal earthly life having an eternal duration result, of never-ending consequence way in the way of sure living in resurrection order of my power giving all full restoring in full stature way; for as you lay your body down in the earth, so shall it rise again, to become a living soul.

63. Let all know I see all things, and shall give a just judgment upon all peoples.

64. Do right.

65. Live holy way.

66. Be pure in heart, only desiring good, so I may own and bless you unto happiness eternal. Amen.

67. As you send out, so shall I cause to return to you eternally, of result of thy choice to be of receiving blessing or cursing, according to your own choosing on earth.

68. Let this eternal sobering reality awaken all to better works.

69. Let all peoples repent now, and be always only doing good to all peoples.

70. Let not any think you can hide from God.

71. I can reveal the minutest detail of thy feeling, thinking, unto you in the day of full judging all on earth; to show all I have done right according to justice and truth.

72. Let all awake to shortness of the time to repent, for I must stop gross wicked way on earth, and establish reign

of righteousness and pure truth of holy way, the only true eternal living order in only good way.

73. Thus I shall have full power to bring all to me to be judged of the Father; you then placed in a world of the order of thine own condition -- Celestial, terrestrial, or telestial.

74. For apostates who fight against my holy Church and governing authority, they are of full punishment eternal order, to have no glory nor happy way eternal, because they seek my destruction and to destroy my holy order of Church and of salvation of the way to seek to bring harm or affliction on my people.

75. Let all such beware, for no reward of happiness is for they who once receive my salvation plan by holy baptism law, then reject me and fight against me and my holy authority on earth; shall be of most evil wicked way, now to be of the order of being of evil eternally. Amen.

76. Now come unto me, all ye ends of the earth, through my holy authority of pure holy power of Priesthood power Celestial order authority now on earth, to be of salvation unto eternal living in resplendent increasing glory holy bliss way; I, your Lord, giving all their reward of holy deliverance if of righteous way; a punishment of personal suffering equal to thy sin, if at all choosing evil on earth; to reap reward of eternal bliss if holy obeying order while on earth.

77. Hasten to repent, is the word of a just God over all, a holy God of pure truth, knowing all the full way of revealing truth power that never varies; always same Gospel plan eternal way order.

78. Be sober. Amen.

SECTION REVELATION 163

Revelation of the Lord Jesus Christ
Palestine, Texas
Sunday, February 12, 2012

1. I, your Lord Jesus Christ, Son Ahman, speaketh to nation of present inhabiting of Zion's land:

2. Hear thou my word, yea, ye rulers of this nation, and all peoples thereof.

3. There is coming a scourging of famine, earthquake, hail, governing powers overcome by mob rule because of unrest and economic collapse, all because you heed me not, and continue to promote Sodom and immoral ways unto murder of unborn children; which rendereth you, who perform such wicked ways, murderers in thy God's eyes.

4. In eternal judgment you shall meet thy Lord in shame, having been warned that this must cease, else judgment come upon thee, and you shall have to be of the buffetings of punishing powers until you pay the uttermost price that you have rendered upon thee; my redeeming love not able to reach thee because you have shed innocent blood, a sin that you must answer for yourself.

5. And this is my revealing to this nation and the peoples of the earth, that this sin must be answered by thine own suffering in eternal judgment of a just God; for the shedding of innocent blood cannot be of my redemption.

6. Though I forgive sins repented of, this repentance can only be by thy own atoning and suffering.

7. This from a just God who will not uphold murder at all, which cannot be of a forgiven way when it is of an intended way.

8. Thus saith the Lord: Repent ye, for I am your Redeemer, to save you from sin, and not in your sins; and your sins that continue prove that you mock thy Lord's redeeming power.

9. And you will have to answer in full judgment-suffering manner of full punishment way in the resurrection if you continue in a non-repented way, where you heed not thy Lord message given.

10. Thus saith the Lord: Be ye a more holy and pure and noble way, not of a murderous immoral way, that in the day of judgment on earth, and eternal judgment in the resurrection, I can own and bless you and deliver you from the sins of this wicked generation, and from the powers of evil that shall seek to overthrow you, even in the hereafter if you be not of a pure way.

11. Now let my servant know that you will do this, by sending message to him, though in bondage, that you will make changes in your laws of the land to not allow child murder, and to seek the overthrow of the ways of Sodom and immoral ways.

12. And if you heed me not, I shall bring full judgment upon this land, and cleanse this land of wickedness; and there shall be a people raised up of my Zion, of my preserving; yea, by the power of my Godhood shall I raise up a people who have kept themselves pure, gathering mine Israel as I have promised in ancient writ.

13. This is the word of God. Be ye clean and pure that I may own and bless you.

14. Repent ye, and cease these evil ways of great corruption that are now in thy nation and the nations of the earth. Amen.

SECTION REVELATION 164

Jesus Christ
Holy Son Ahman

I, Jesus Christ, Your Holy God Over All Creation, Speaketh Message of Continued Full Final Warning of Holy Revealed Will of God to All Nations, How to Be Ready, Holy, for My Holy Advent in Glory, Might, Power, Governing Order Power. Hear, All Ye Peoples on Earth, Mine Own Will:

Revelation of the Lord Jesus Christ
Palestine, Texas
Sunday, February 19, 2012

1. The great God of Creation speaketh. He is over all, hath all power; goeth here unto a full coming on earth soon, of full Celestial order governing power; over all peoples who now dwell on world of His creating.

2. Hear my will, all ye peoples of all lands, who shall soon witness mighty changes on earth, such as you have not seen.

3. Alive are they, in the spirit of love-light, who live for truth only; who are of upholding virtue complete, not selling eternity for temporary earthly vanity pleasure of momentary lust-love of self-will performed, committing knowingly sin of grievous weight on soul, such that I, God, withdraw my power of truth-love-light.

4. Such say darkness is light, and light is darkness, who love a lie rather than eternal daylight dwelling in the honest heart soul.

5. A way of full cleansing cometh.

6. All such an one as loving evil because learning to have pleasure in unrighteousness, deeds being evil continually, even in wicked imaginations, shall all be visited soon by thy Lord with consuming fire of full judgment, to remove such darkness.

7. I am God which speaketh to all the ends of the earth; a light hid from darkness of mind because you reject my love-light shining brighter than the sun at noonday in clear sky.

8. Now be humble. Seek truth.

9. Repent unto a broken heart of inspired love for truth, eternity truth; that this life of mortal earthly now dwelling is only a testing on earth, to listen through a prayer of faith, a prayer of honest seeking unto God, for wisdom from Him, to be a shining light to thy soul within, by my grace, by my power, saith Jesus Christ; to guide you to wisdom's path of salvation, not to earthly vain way of temporary lust fulfilled; but to eternal power of overcoming evil with good works, earning love for truth thereby; yea, eternal God-loving truth, that enlivens thy living soul unto my eternal power of vision of eternal duration, greater than earthly cares; to the choosing to pray; to seek after God in thy heart, to be sons of pure holy motive

of my truth-love power in all purity of living; daughters on earth also, who listen to monitor within of sacrifice of selfish fleshly vain unholy desire, unto a lively power of love-giving order, to bless others as a philanthropist of peace-serving order to all around ye who listen to peace whisperings in your soul of my uplifting love-joy power; a power Celestial; a love-light I send to honest seeking souls on earth, no matter what nation or peoples they are among on earth.

10. Now listen to thy God over all creation, who am Jesus Christ, a God who made all things, who is Life and Light of all things; who is your Advocate with the Father; who came and suffered a holy way of righteous power of no sin, for all who sin who can and will repent; I, God, intervening for all peoples, to conquer death, to raise all from the grave in holy resurrection power.

11. It is I who speaketh love-message for all on earth, to now put away evil; to seek unto me, your Holy God, to be holy pure sons or daughters of more pure holy living; so I can preserve such at time I must needs cleanse all peoples of all nations of wickedness, which wickedness hath risen to an over-towering height, soon to fall, even by own empty souls not of pure light, groping for a nothingness of consequence of evil lust-love for moral degradation now over all nations.

12. Look to me, your Light of Peace, truth-love power over all creation.

13. I hear honest prayers accompanied by honest pure living, coming away from all corrupting evils of this most wicked generation ever to inhabit the earth; worldwide spreading of immoral murderous way of unborn child murder, licentious adulterous corrupt ways of unnatural and false love, even unto sin of Sodom, which I, God, destroyed openly, now on sacred writ holy accounting.

14. Such is soon to happen on any who continue in open degradation.

15. I can lift up my elect, also leave wicked to remain in judgments of cleansing order power, heavenly power, which controlleth the earth and all things pertaining to continuation of the living on earth.

16. I am He who is All in All.

17. Nothing exists but by my eternal power; Celestial God of Creation order power.

18. Hear my final and continued message, of a God of truth, of holy love for all who love truth by living pure law of moral holy way, who will not sell virtue nor love for life of pure way, all for things that perish of world lust-love vain way.

19. O ye people of all nations, come unto me, Jesus Christ, God over all, lest all be of damnation of eternal power judgment.

20. My own Gospel is now of full open reading in New and Old Testament Bible holy record, though changed through last millennium by wicked priests of false representation, of need for more holy translation; yet sufficient truth therein that all feel truth when of prayer faith.

21. Now awake, all ye of this generation, to be holy, ready for my holy coming in full power, is the call of a holy and just God over all; to warn and prepare all for my holy power to govern in Zion, even a New Jerusalem on my land of Zion; also Old Jerusalem to be rebuilt after the war of great destruction in that land taketh place; yet Israel of mastery nation over other nations who come against my people Israel; I shall fulfill my will revealed in sacred prophetic writ of Old and New Testament in full soon.

22. I declare my word through mine authority on earth, to all ends of the earth at time of preparing soon to end in full whirlwind power judgments.

23. A why is asked by doubtful thinking of earthly judgment alone, why God would intervene in all nations.

24. I created the earth to people the earth, to be tested, having both good and evil to choose from; to influence every mind by my eternal love-light power shining like the brilliant sunlight on clear day; yea, upon all people born on earth, to guide all to do good, an inborn conscience of love for right and just ways of caring.

25. Such feelings of holy way are my holy inspiring order of heavenly light shining in all, if not of love for sin knowingly.

26. Be ye now repenting, and now seeking to pray in all you do, to be sensitive to my eternal light that can awaken thy soul to better, more holy way, heavenly eternal power within thy mind and heart; to give exalting way of love for truth, eternal truth, that God lives and is a God at hand, able to hear and answer prayers of honest hearts seeking His truths of eternal life; not of man's ways alone that do not bring increase of love, peace, joy, uplifting feeling, as a witness of peace guiding the soul to perfect good in lives, not to do evil.

27. Such is my instant-giving power to all peoples when they choose good, unto kindness toward all; unto pure holy living; unto my power of love-peace joy dawning in soul, to be holy sons or daughters on earth.

28. Be ye ready.

29. I soon cometh, saith God, Jesus Christ, your Holy Lord. Amen.

Chapter 6

Jehovah, Even Jesus Christ, Warn All Nations to Repent; For I Cometh

---

Jesus Christ Giveth Own Writing to Supreme Court of Appeals

SECTION REVELATION 165

Thus Saith Jesus Christ, Jehovah, Son Ahman, to All Nations, Rulers of All Lands, to All People on World, My Own Full Warning Sent to All Nations as Witness I Come Soon. Now Let All Read My Own Will:

Revelation of the Lord Jesus Christ
Palestine, Texas
Tuesday, May 1, 2012

1. The Lord Jehovah speaketh to all nations, even God over all, a holy will for all to hear, to be of full warned order, to be on earth only way of the soon passing if of evil way.

2. Hear the will of God of all, Jesus Christ, Holy Lord, who atones for sin of mankind calling from eternal way of holy revealed truths of righteousness; thus able to deliver the faithful out of all nations who are my elect according to the holy way living Gospel of salvation.

3. Now be of pure holy living; to forever forsake wicked way; to be my disciple of pure obeying holy living on earth; to have my peace dwell in thy soul, thy habitations, many turned to righteousness.

4. Now heed my will through my holy Priesthood Keyholder on earth, my own holy authority I have on earth in my servant Warren Jeffs, of holy order of the full way holy power of Priesthood power of sealing keys, a continuation of my own authority given to Joseph Smith, Jun., in 1829 by Peter, James, John; quorum of my Keyholder power sent to restore full way power of heavenly power to earth; so ordinances of salvation would be valid into eternity under God.

5. Now be of truth knowing, no other authority on earth among man is of me, saith the Lord.

6. All peoples, to receive me, my Gospel, my holy power unto salvation, must come to my authorized authority on earth, to be blessed eternally of God; for I am Eternal; my Priesthood authority is power everlasting, without end; thus all can receive my approbation, even full exaltation; all able to learn truths that exalt the soul unto eternal life; to change thy way to be holy by my power, which shineth on all as the light of the sun shineth on all creation.

7. I am God, Jesus Christ, which giveth this holy word: You needs now prepare for my coming; changing to more holy way of holy living pure way; coming out of world way of unholy corrupt way, immoral murderous way; even murder of innocence of unborn children.

8. Now learn eternity truth so all may overcome sin way, unto holy living.

9. Know I am over all; all things are subject unto my rule, my power only able to uphold all creation.

10. I am Judge of all.

11. All shall be of full knowledge of conduct, desires, ways of doing on earth when raised from grave by my power of the holy resurrection; for I am the Resurrection and the Life; I reveal all truth at judgment day of all standing before me.

12. Let all be holy, for I am holy.

13. Let all be pure, for only purity can

stand in holy pure order of eternal salvation; who can dwell with God in eternal burnings of eternal life.

14. Come unto me, thy Holy Redeemer, all ye ends of the earth; to be saved from death, hell, the power of darkness in individual lives.

15. Come out of the way of Babylon, even spiritual darkness, unto life, thy Lord Jesus Christ, who speaketh truth, eternal truth of salvation.

16. I come. I am power eternal.

17. Nothing can hinder my word being of full way fulfilling holy word.

18. All shall be judged. All shall come out of grave.

19. All shall be of full knowing own guilt at day of full resurrection time of judgment of thy Lord.

20. Let this eternity reality awaken thy soul unto repentance now; to be holy, more holy daily.

21. Let all be pure, for only they can dwell in my power presence in Zion, New Jerusalem, soon to be of full building by heavenly powers come to world on which you now dwell; this world being an eternal order of the way of future full glory like unto the sun in the heavens.

22. Now do only good; make peace; cast out all of way of the unhallowed sin of murder of unborn children, of immoral way.

23. My Gospel changeth not.

24. New Testament truths of pure reading are of me, of eternity truth.

25. I can only uphold righteous way of my way living on earth.

26. I came to earth in flesh tabernacle, did no sin; as sacrifice for sin repented of, where sin no more is done; full confession way as truth-telling for honest repentance to be lived and accepted.

27. Let all thus be holy, so I can, of correct eternal law principles, uphold repenting souls in day of judgment; that you may be found on my right hand, obedient to eternity truth law principles of God.

28. Let all be holy, lest soon whirlwind judgments cometh on world you dwell on, such as has not been before; of earthquake, storm, tornado, pestilence, desolating sickness, famine, sea heaving beyond its bounds, cleansing off earth more wicked out of all lands, nations, kindreds, tongues, peoples.

29. All shall soon know I cometh.

30. Wicked of violent way shall slay the wicked; I only able to preserve you in day of whirlwind judgment coming on all the earth.

31. Let rulers now govern in holy peace, caring for the people they govern in kind peace holy order of governing.

32. Let fathers be holy kind peace-love to households, to servants, to family.

33. Let contention cease.

34. Let all military forces now be only in own land.

35. Destroy all armor vehicles.

36. Do not attack other nation of no aggression against other nations.

37. Let only self-defense be order, after peace-seeking of the labor of full pure motive of peace holy labor is of other aggressive nation returning unholy violent way.

38. Let all be of now raising food in plenteous way order, as war, famine cometh.

39. All shall be in need.

40. Let all make peace, so war ceaseth; else your own will of loving violent way be of unholy doing, leaving thee and thy people in thy land of desolate way, because you heed me not.

41. I can bless all the world with increase of crops, of healthy way.

42. I have all things in full governing order power.

43. Come to me in faith prayer, of good works, to be preserved in the time of full order cleansing wicked way off the earth. Amen.

44. Come, ye heavy laden. Let holy way be lived.

45. I can lift thy soul to eternity holy way.

46. Come be fed word of Eternal Union living of thy Lord, who soon cometh to dwell on earth.

47. Let all assist Zion rising.

48. Send forth your treasures to build Zion, New Jerusalem, that you will honor your Holy Lord, Jesus Christ; to then receive His protection in day of judgments of God on all nations; to now help free my holy servant from the way of illegal bondage, by influencing the governing power holding him and his brethren in bondage to let him go free to do my will.

49. I shall reward such bounteously if of pure way living law of purity, of life preserving, of holy way to overthrow corruption immoral way living in thy own lives, and in thy land; law of preserving purity of preserving life upheld in thy nation.

50. This is the Lord over all, calling upon all peoples on world of my creating; having given you your agency, to be answered upon you individually in eternal judgment, in day of resurrection; all works to be rewarded; punishment for evil; blessings eternally if of holy order of righteous holy living on earth in the flesh.

51. This is my plan of salvation.

52. Live as I revealed when in the flesh during ministry among nation of Israel, my chosen; who rejected me, crucifying their Lord after knowing the works of thy Lord; yet aspiring against God to take the worldly kingdom to themselves, even the wicked, who persecuted their King Emmanuel, the Jews of meridian of time; yet to be fully gathered, to receive Him whom they pierced, at the glorious appearing in Celestial heavenly order holy governing power.

53. Now be holy order well-obeying way in thy individual living, lest justice be of full judgment on all unholy wicked people on world of thy now living.

54. Let all humble themselves.

55. Few honored my holy April 6th birthday in fasting prayer order on earth, as I sent my will to be done, as a holy believing pure love-giving to thy Lord, of self to be more holy, unto prepared order in time of holy power coming to world of now corrupt order, soon to be cleansed in holy judgment of God on all.

56. Now be ready, all ye peoples of the world, in all lands, among all nations, is the will of the Lord to all on earth; my own word sent by authority of my holy order of Priesthood Keyholder authority power.

57. Pray as you read these, my word to all peoples, to feel witness of my peace on thee; reading my word also in Matthew of Sermon on the Mount, to feel same peace-love power of me, the Creator and Ruler over heaven and world of thy now dwelling.

58. Be holy.

59. Be pure.

60. Be peace holy living on earth.

61. Now come to full awake order.

62. Judgment is of now cleansing earth in increase of judgment of thy God, in tornado storms, earthquake, other ways of my power shown to all, that time is now to repent and prepare for my glorious appearing. Amen.

63. Let all my people of my Church be holy to survive day of visitation, to be Zion here on world of my soon appearing in love-peace holy order power.

64. Let all who persecute my people know I cometh to reward all according to their works.

65. Let government power officials do justice right order to now let my servant go free, now with appeal of the Lord's own will written to State Supreme Appeal Court there, of state of him, my servant Warren Jeffs, holding in bondage for only doing my will in religion freedom living; my law of Celestial Marriage of plural order my holy way, only to be governed by religious leadership of my holy inspiring; not to have men's governing authority interfere at all; thus no religion is of full free order in professed free land of religious guarantee of holy freedom of choice dwelling.

66. They of legislative power have made my holy law as though it is unholy way living; now of persecution way against my Church in several states.

67. I shall reward all according to justice eternal for such unhallowed wicked unjust way.

68. Let lawmaking authority cease such evil, lest nation of United States of America feel full order justice judgment on peoples professing freedom of religion; yet now against such holy needed freedom for all people.

69. Let order be signed by President of that land to give free way dwelling to my servant Warren Jeffs, also to his brethren held in prison for only living their religion, revealed from God to man on earth by pure religious law, not of carnal motive at all; my holy order of Celestial Order Union only governed by me, your Lord Jesus Christ, to lawmaking, judge order also, over land

of professed freedom of religion order; not now fully free.

70. Let all just-minded people send own call to release my servant and servants in my Church from unholy bondage; to bear public influence on unjust judges, rulers, legislative and executive lawmakers, to now allow full freedom order.

71. Let Supreme Court of Appeals release them from prison now, thy Lord's own writing of appeal order calling on court to accept my own will of pure holy truth-telling; not to allow prosecution unholy order to use lie of the way of false witness way of court of unjust no religious freedom defending way.

72. Let all nations call on nation of the holding Keyholding authority in bondage, send forth emissaries to call on leader authority to let them go.

73. Let all peoples be holy themselves.

74. Let my Church on earth be holy, cleansed, purified individually, to prepare for my holy Advent on world of soon full order of holy power from the Celestial world of heaven, to dwell among men on earth soon, as the holy governing holy power over all nations.

75. I have caused my word to be published to all leaders of nations; to all peoples.

76. I now send copy of appeal filings with this holy word as filed in Texas Supreme Appeals Court for their now ruling in pure principle of truth-knowing, truth-upholding my own word, witness order in every writing sent to Supreme Court of Appeals.

77. Read; to be knowing I have petitioned governing order; yet all such heed me not, bringing whirlwind God-sending order cleansing closer to full sending; for my word shall be full way fulfilling all

prophecies of all my holy order of Prophets throughout time order; I being same holy Lord over all peoples of all ages of time.

78. I created man, Adam, and peopled this world through holy marriage order.

79. They lived Celestial Eternal Marriage order of God, as did Abraham, Isaac his son, Jacob, and Israel peoples of old time; my own word guiding administering this holy law of eternal holy union of plural wife order, holy order.

80. Let all uphold right to live as Bible record of revealed holy religion order, as I, your holy Lord, lived on earth during time of my ministry among men; Jewish order seeing I had faithful plural order bearing children, not of their false authority; thus they in fear of no authority losing their earthly influence and earthly power among men, persecuted their Lord unto fulfilling the crucifixion redeeming law.

81. Let all hear my Eternity Truth that God has family in heaven, begetting in my pure holy law of Plural Celestial Order Marriage pure spirit children in heaven; of which all people on world of thy now dwelling are sons or daughters of God.

82. Thus scripture teacheth to call God "Father in Heaven," for thus I, God, am Father over all peoples on earth.

83. Let Eternity Truth be honored.

84. Let my holy revealed religious marriage law of holy marriage revealed concerning only pure people in my Church, not of world way at all; thus only governed by revealing of God through Keyholder holy power.

85. Let government cease unholy attack against their Lord, lest full judgment cometh upon land of my coming, soon.

86. Let all on American continent, of both North, also South America, know such is called land of Zion.

87. Zion shall soon rise, heavenly agents to come with thy Lord to world of soon cleansing, to do labor of salvation.

88. Now know holy power greater than any earthly man power weapon power of man can oppose.

89. Angel labor cometh with heavenly order to cleanse all evil off land of my coming, Zion land, soon.

90. Thus I, God, send to all peoples my message of pure revealing eternal truth of my way of saving mankind in Millennial Reign of Holy Peace Order, love of God and of truth prevailing.

91. I, God over all, sent my Prophet Joseph Smith in eighteen hundred five, year of his birth on earth, to be my Prophet to restore full Gospel of salvation.

92. He did His work faithfully.

93. Keyholder power has continued on world of thy dwelling to this time, keeping Zion mission of full labor among my Church of full Gospel living plural order of Eternal Union of Plural Order Marriage, even through continual prosecution of unjust way through year of full attack many times; now of partial telling in holy Proclamation of Priesthood defending publishing to all the nations, sent in recent times to all peoples in all lands, to media of news reporting, to library order in all lands on world; to religious societies of all names in all lands known to be such.

94. Let all know I am now justified, even God, to send forth whirlwind storm of great destructive order on nation of unjust holding servant of Keyholder authority, if they heed me not; also other promised judgment order, if heinous sin of murder of unborn child order continueth on Zion land, to cleanse my land for my coming.

95. I have now told only truth to all peoples on world.

96. Now cometh full order of judgment on all nations that deny my word when my power sendeth my will to all people on world.

97. Now repent, all ye people on world of my creating; thus all belongeth to me, God over all.

98. Let not time pass before all now humble themselves before me, saith the Lord. Amen.

99. Now tell thy own peoples in every land to hear this, to read at library order, to go to governing power in own land to read thy God's own holy power-word, holy revealed order word.

100. Now be holy governing way order, all ye national, also local leader holy calling order; to tell God's own truth order unchanged to thy own peoples in all nations.

101. Tell all to repent by the holy call of God, to be ready for His holy Advent; for New Reign of Peace holy way law lived by all surviving peoples; some lands to become desolate when full judgment of God cometh, because none listened, nor obeyed, like unto Sodom.

102. Let all such of same sin of immoral unnatural evil way as Sodom be cleansed from every nation, so such evil doth not corrupt thy people longer, lest full judgment cometh upon all who continue in Sodom way.

103. Let adultery be abolished; unclean immoral order, which now corrupts all ways of living throughout world in governing power; in media showing evil continually; in school way, in family order; all corrupt.

104. Let all now be of repenting holy way, and seek thy way of holy order of God soon, is thy Lord's own will to all nations, peoples, orders of dwelling as organized living; all to be of my judging soon; heavenly power coming to world openly, as scripture of New Testament, Old Testament revealeth; my own word to Isaiah and other holy Prophets of Israel descent; a holy family of the order of plural union of old, now to be gathered to Zion, as promised in Old Testament when they were scattered by my judgment power, allowing gentile peoples to conquer all Israel when Israel also murdered as gentile idolatrous nations at the time did; they rejecting God.

105. Let this Bible holy order record witness that the same God of the Old and New Testament now speaketh through Prophet of now order, my own way to survive judgment power promised as wicked way is followed by all people on earth, save a few who believe my word and do my holy way of prayer pure way holy living on world.

106. Now be holy, is my now holy word to all on world of my soon visiting personally; dwelling among pure people of my order of holy living; now preparing for my coming soon to them of holy living according to my Gospel Order of Eternal Holy Union. Amen.

107. Even now, let all people be of pure holy living before I come, is the will of the Lord to all peoples on earth. Amen.

108. The holy coming shall be like a holy power shining all minds on earth at once, also a holy star of great size shall be in the night sky as Millennium of Peace is in progress.

109. This star shall shine as a power for earth to be of full work of paradisiacal glory power purifying the earth.

110. Now know a planet of size cometh to join this portion of world, that shall fulfill scripture, that the earth shall reel to and fro as a drunken man; also the earth shall roll together as a scroll, unfolded, then portion of returning earth absorb into this portion

as two scrolls are unrolled; then rolled back together as one; all creation experiencing greatest earthquake world has ever seen; such as was at time I removed Enoch's portion.

111. Now know he and his portion returneth as part of Millennial Reign of Christ on world.

112. Now be ready, for great power of God shall be manifest, of sure way to unite all peoples under rule of Jesus Christ, your Holy King and Holy Power of life eternal, saith your Lord to all.

113. Be ye believing my warning goeth to all peoples, so all may be ready for whirlwind judgment eternal power; such as shall remove more wicked from the earth, to preserve the innocent and more holy peoples in all nations.

114. Let Isaiah be read by all; for he saw in visions my glorious coming, even Christ, your Lord; who speaketh word of inviting order of repentance to all peoples of earth; the very heavens being shaken, unto parts of the earth returning by my holy power; fulfilling the scripture, the stars shall fall from heaven; thus I fulfill all my word.

115. Repent ye, repent ye, all peoples on earth.

116. I am God that speaketh power-word of sure fulfilling.

117. Do as I call on officials of governing power to do -- publish in perfect exact order this, my word, to the peoples in thy land, each of receiving this publishing.

118. Now herald to all to hear eternal truth unobstructed by evil designing men on earth.

119. Now let my people have my consecrated lands, taken by unjust court rulings, even United Effort Plan lands; to be upholding just way; for judge is not principled in truth, who hath taken my lands unto the taking land from Church.

120. Let all such apostate enemies, lying to court, taking Priesthood lands, be of full knowing they shall be they whom shall be of full judgment in day of my coming to earth.

121. Let also President of United States of America hasten to do as I, Jesus Christ, hath commanded; to make holy order of saving unborn children from murder a way of executive order; not allowing such heinous crime against living to exist in nation on my land of Zion.

122. Now also sign order to release my servant Warren Jeffs from unjust holding, for religious freedom pure principle sake, to bear influence with thy Lord to hold back whirlwind judgments unto more repenting before I, God, cometh to judge all nations on world for their conduct.

123. Let my people be given back all lands and houses taken from them by governing power. Amen.

124. I, God, speak also to federal government officers, Senators, Congress holy calling governing responsibility order, to be just, equitous, pure in lawmaking holy way doing; to preserve life, to not allow murder of unborn children; to preserve virtue, to be self-pure in the way of moral purity; all being example of better way of living pure holy living.

125. Let also all my portion of pure people of Church of holy Order of Eternal Order be more pure, holy, for my coming among you soon.

126. Let Priesthood rise and set royal noble uplifting holy way example of pure holy living; so I can dwell among you in soon time to come on earth.

127. I shall bring my reward with me.

128. Let all people be holy, is the full

call of repentance of a just holy God unto all peoples on world.

129. Now accept my will by doing my will, is the word of the Lord Jesus Christ, God over all creation, soon to appear in glory order holy governing power; to administer justice upon all; to reward all peoples for deeds on earth, to have dominion forever over all nations remaining on world after cleansing taketh place.

130. Such is Eternity Truth spoken to all peoples to thy understanding.

131. Let all be holy. Amen.

SECTION REVELATION 166

Jesus Christ
Son Ahman

I, Jesus Christ, Your Holy Lord, Send My Own Will to All Nations, Even a Holy Way of Pure Holy Revealed Word, Unto All Peoples in Every Land, to Now Awake, to Now Be Holy, to Learn of My Own Way, to Be Ready to Dwell With God on Earth in Holy Living; Lest You Not Remain After My Full Cleansing Order Sweep Through All Lands, to Remove More Wicked Peoples Off the Earth; Yea, Whirlwind Full Celestial Power Holy Judgment Against a Wicked Generation, Who Continue to Be Unbelieving I Cometh to All Nations; to Be Thy Power of Full Government Order, Celestial Power; to Be Peace-Love Order Over All Peoples; to Have Full Way Power Over All Nations, Soon to Happen Among All Nations. Let This, My Holy Will, Be Now of Worldwide Reading, so I May Preserve Innocent Ones Who Be Holy in Living When Judgment Cometh in Full Power; Yea, Even Soon at Hand Upon All the World of Corruption Way of Evil Intent, to Be Evil in Willful Harm to Innocence and Holy Way Virtue Order of All Mankind. Heed My Word, Saith Jesus Christ, Your Holy God Over All Peoples:

Revelation of the Lord Jesus Christ
Palestine, Texas
Tuesday, March 6, 2012

1. The way of my coming soon is to be manifest in full order among wicked peoples of the fulfilling all my word, saith Jesus Christ, to all nations, peoples, kindreds, tongues, governing authorities on earth.

2. I have spoken, so shall I fulfill in might and power, Celestial Order Power, Eternal Power, soon to be poured forth in full measure on all offending peoples; for thy wicked way of full measure of iniquity of unholy abominating corrupting order

of Babylon shall be consumed entire, unto no one left on my holy land of New Jerusalem; even America, save they who are holy Order of Zion; my pure in heart sons of Priesthood authority; with all who have cleansed their lives by obeying my covenant of Eternal Power Union Celestial order authority power; a heaven-sent authority; not a dead-letter religious farcity of man's doing of false religions among all peoples.

3. Now be ready, all ye peoples on earth.

4. My coming shall awaken all to be holy who remain, from the least to the greatest. I have spoken it. Amen.

5. Now be of holy way, all peoples of all nations, to survive whirlwind judgments of Celestial order power, of pure Godhood power soon to be sent forth, first upon my land of holiness; then on all nations; for the people of my holy land, America of the North continent, have been preserved since my revealed Constitution was ratified by founding fathers of United States of America, to be a holy land, to be people of my faith in most early settling of the land where my coming shall be unto the Zion of our Lord shall rise in fulness.

6. Now be holy, all of my Church, to be of full trustworthiness order; to be of lifted-up order of my marvelous power over elect, who have been purifying lives, coming away from spiritual Babylon entire; so they can be whole, pure entire.

7. Now purify all who should elect to be my holy Zion.

8. A way to be holy is to let go of all evil desire of world way in the full measure of moral pure way; to not view evil, nor seek evil way of music, nor of unholy unmarried way.

9. Let governing order in all lands on earth be now requiring married order for children to be of a bringing forth; also to punish all who are immoral, or of a way of adultery or of Sodom, both punishable by the law of every nation if truth of virtue is lived by rules of each nation.

10. I, God, have the power to establish holy way when I cometh.

11. Be now of holy way, lest no one in thy land remain; for I cleanse off the earth all such sin.

12. Now be holy, ye peoples of religion way, to never be of claiming authority of Eternal Union Law of Marriage separate from mine holy Priesthood authority.

13. When have any of you of religion way of minister way in all Christendom had thy Lord visit thee to establish my order of full authority, to bless on earth eternal blessings of Eternal Union?

14. Even so-called Church of Jesus Christ of Latter-day Saints authorities of leadership have no order of revealed holy way to appoint marriage union as my revelation names.

15. They have turned from my Eternal Union Celestial Plural Marriage Law, to grovel in apostasy; to be like the world in love-lust unions not of God at all; all to please government powers of man on earth, which governing authority can never exalt the soul to eternal life, as I, your holy God, even Jesus Christ, can do to all pure holy order of my Church; which is now of full preparing order to be cleansed entire; yea, to only be of holy order of Celestial Law.

16. Now be holy, all ye so-called Christian ministers, and know I, Jesus Christ, now send my own will to all nations; to be holy, pure way of moral pure holy way, lest judgment cometh in full power.

17. Let all peoples be more pure now, so I can heal the brokenhearted, and renew all souls who are of pure way; both in this life of thy earthly living way, also in eternity living; for all born on earth shall be raised from the grave; to be judged by me, your Holy Lord, Jesus Christ, even I who now send my own way to all peoples; having sent my own word of Proclamation to all peoples of all lands on earth; to know my authority dwelleth among men on earth; yet few hearken to my will on earth; all because their deeds are evil, and they take a pleasure in unholy way, to be of a full way preparing for damnation in the life hereafter, according to the light they received on earth.

18. Be ye holy, all peoples of the world, lest all full judgments roll forth unto full cleansing powers sweeping wicked way out of all nations on earth, even soon.

19. Let all be my order of pure way, so everlasting death be not thy portion in full day of full judgment on thy soul; which shall be of sure way in eternity.

20. Now be clean of sin of murder of unborn children, which is the shedding of innocent blood.

21. Do not such evil; for such have no forgiveness of sin in this world, nor in the world to come; knowing I can reveal truth, even in thy mind, unto all peoples; for I see and know all things; yea, even the intent of every heart who dwells on earth; all to be brought to my full accounting for deeds done in the world you now dwell upon; yea, also for desires you would have performed had you the power.

22. Now know I can forgive according to repentance, as they who knew no law shall be judged with no law condemning such who were of ignorance; who were of way to know not truth of eternal way truth on earth; yet to have some truth; also

my power of the Holy Spirit resteth on all when born on earth to grow unto age of accountability; to guide the mind to do good; to cast off evil; yea, even wicked people knowing they do evil unto the full condemnation in eternal judgment, according to the circumstances of living on earth; a Just Judge, even I, your Lord Jesus Christ, now leaving all peoples without excuse; having warned all peoples by missionary authority sent to all nations through my Priesthood Keyholding power authority since the nineteenth century in Joseph Smith, Jun's., time upon the earth; when he received God the Father, and His Son Jesus Christ in full power visitation; called to be my Witness and holy Testator on earth to all peoples on the world you now dwell upon.

23. This is my continued authority on earth I now work through, to send my own word to all nations, kindreds, tongues, peoples of all lands on earth; now a holy revealing of God to be my full way holy warning; now incumbent upon all to heed my will, lest they be of neglecting truth that God speaketh, and is able to communicate in language easily understood by all people on world of testing holy order, of God proving all on this world since mankind was born here, to be tested in all way of pure way of living; this being my purpose of creating a world of probationary testing order, of temporary dwelling in world of both good and evil present.

24. Now be advised by my authority on this world you now inhabit, even my own will, saith the Lord, that I cometh to cleanse all nations of ungodly murderous immoral way; to be Judge over all nations, to be now the way of pure holy way; to know I cometh, even as I revealed to mine ancient apostles; kept in Bible holy writ; now in all nations knowing I cometh; even

ministers of Christendom naming of my holy Advent soon at hand; many not of inspired order, only of man's reasoning way.

25. Now be holy, is the call of God of Creation, even Jesus Christ; though you deny me; yet my word goeth forth, unto all nations.

26. Be ye clean that do have witness of my holy order of governing order of heaven coming to earth.

27. You publish my name, ye uncalled unholy ministers of Christendom religious way, not by mine authority; only on belief in Bible, yet of no way power to benefit anyone in a ministerial order, not of Eternal Power, nor professing to have such power, ye of the order of Catholic and Protestant order of false religion order not of me, your Lord; yet still continue to teach people of the world as though I authorized you to teach; yet you deny my true order of revealed religion of power from on high.

28. Let all such false ministers cease claiming they can lead a soul unto salvation at all, lest they deny me while professing to uphold my holy eternal order of salvation.

29. Now cease persecution of my true authority, if you would be of honorable way; also government authority to be just; to never persecute my servant, nor my servants on earth for the living my holy law of Celestial Order of Eternal Union; a Plural Order as Abraham and Isaac, also my servant Israel of old lived in holy order faithful; who dwell with thy God in realms Celestial order power now for having lived law of holy way of God; eternal way order not of man, nor of man's government order on earth; my holy order revealed through my holy authority of revelation received by Joseph Smith, my Prophet of power in last dispensation of God coming among

men to rule through His eternal order of Priesthood revealed from heaven.

30. Now awake, all ye peoples on earth, to be ready, to be pure, to have oil in your lamps of the parable of the wise virgins in New Testament record, well published throughout the world.

31. Now be pure, is my holy revealing to all now peoples dwelling on my world of probationary testing, an eternal order of Gods of Creation, to test their children; to be proved what they choose to follow in a test of both good and evil present in all peoples' minds; yet given intelligence to choose to obey the way of pure way; not of unclean way.

32. Let all awake to feel my power accompany these, my own word to all peoples.

33. Turn to me through prayer.

34. I will witness peace to any honest heart these are my own words sent by my holy power through mine authority I have ordained on the world you now are of full living, to prove way of thy salvation or damnation, as you choose.

35. Though the wicked persecute and slay my Prophets throughout history of all nations born on the world you now dwell upon, my Eternal Truth remains -- I am God, and have redeemed all peoples from the grave, to be raised in resurrection in time soon at hand; yea, before most are preparing in full way to meet full way consequence resulting from agency followed on world of full way order of holy probation way of test of what thou, each one on earth, desire in time you did not receive my own message of holy way power; not of man, but of me, your Savior, calling as a voice in the wilderness to all, though you cannot see me; yet my power is of full way power to reveal to every son

or daughter on the world you now live upon, truth power witness order to thy soul, that I speak; that Gospel of salvation is truth eternal; even to know I am, that I came in meridian of time to atone on the cross for all mankind, to be Savior and Redeemer over all nations; to be Holy Lord of Redemption Holy Eternal Life order over all.

36. Let my word of now receiving order be holy to all my order of children now on the earth.

37. Let all be holy to be of continuing way on world now of full way to be cleansed of wicked way entire.

38. A way to be holy is to be my order of faith prayer; to test all thy way by a gentle peace witness I send to accompany truth I reveal on earth by authority.

39. Let not eternal salvation be lost by neglect to petition God for way to go on world of probation way holy order of holy testing order of God.

40. Let all be of my holy order. Amen.

SECTION REVELATION 167

Jesus Christ
Jehovah Son Ahman

I, Jesus Christ, Holy Redeemer, Do Now Declare Way to Show Love Loyalty to Your Holy Lord, Jesus Christ, Sending My Holy Revealing to Be One, All Peoples on World of Thy Now Dwelling, to Be of a Holy Order to Celebrate My Holy Birthday of the Month of April on the Sixth Day of the Month; Also My Holy Revealed Will to Prepare Soon for the Judgment Order of Full Holy Power, Holy Power Judgments of God, Soon to Be Poured Forth in Full Way Order Holy Order Power on All Lands on World. Now Be Holy; Heed My Holy Revealing of Pure Love-Message, of Holy Way to Survive Judgments of God, to Soon Repent, to Be Holy Now, Lest Full Cleaning Order Cometh to All Lands.

Revelation of the Lord Jesus Christ
Palestine, Texas
Saturday, March 17, 2012

1. Holy, holy art thou, O Lord over all, who is Jehovah Ahman Holy Christ; Son of Ahman, even Elohim.

2. Now come to eternal power of Priesthood eternal power, governing authority over all the world; none to be of independent dwelling on earth as separate from Zion, saith Christ Jehovah Ahman Holy Lord.

3. Now have all peoples hear my holy will to celebrate my Holy Day of my birth, even April 6th, with fasting rejoicing holy

prayer; offering national prayer by leaders over all lands of separate nations, all at time I came forth, at thy clock time of 7:18 a.m.

4. Let all peoples bow the knee, confessing Jesus is the Christ, the Son of God, Jehovah Christ Ahman Holy Lord over all peoples. Amen.

5. Love begets love.

6. I am love, saith thy Lord and Holy Redeemer, Jesus Christ.

7. I have the birthright to rule all nations, kindreds, tongues, peoples on earth.

8. Holy way of Celestial Eternal Authority shall descend to earth; Celestial Eternal Authority from the holy world government authority over the earth; to be holy power, Celestial, like God on earth seeing unto the holy order of eternal full power of knowing all things on earth; to be government eternal for the thousand years of a Millennium of heavenly pure dwelling of the Kingdom of my power come among men; a holy reign of the King of kings; all my power coming to change this earth to fiery heaven Celestial power; my one hundred forty-four thousand sons of power of the way of Eternal Union holy power, governing holy order of pure holy way Celestial order authority; yea, a full exaltation of the world now under a fall of man now dwelling thereon; yet soon to be cleansed by fire from the Celestial earth now shining heavenly light-life-giving light on the now temporal world.

9. Let all know my purpose to forming this world and peopling the same is to be a full order of Celestial orb of governing power; to be of eternal holy way holy governing authority; to have holy sons of holy Godhood full creation power redeem all mankind unto each of my sons of holy Godhood authority as Saviors of

men under Christ, thy God over all; yea, a holy domain of Ahman, my Eternal Holy Beloved Holy Father God over all; a realm of only righteousness and pure holy sons and daughters exalted on heavenly order holy world of thy now habitation; changed by Celestial fire power to shine like the holy sun of governing authority.

10. Now learn full cleansing of present world is at end of Millennial Reign of pure holy power peace-holy-love power of Christ on this now probationary earth; to be heavenly orb of heavenly holy power holy authority.

11. Now cleanse thy lives, all peoples on this now temporal mortal existing world, to be Celestial holy way holy power; to be raised unto a kingdom of glory holy way full happy-way order of glory-peace-love-joy on this earth, with I, your Holy Lord, among pure holy people resurrected unto full order of Celestial holy eternal life.

12. Now be holy, so all such can dwell on this eternity world.

13. Be knowing different degrees of happiness of glory unto my full order of salvation shall include telestial temporary happiness glory portion of separated world of light telestial of lower order of love-power-peace love-joy power, like unto the light of the stars of distant dim shining at night on this world; also a higher terrestrial order of power-love-joy power, like the borrowed light of the order of the moonlight on clear night; to be holy way holy glory of salvation for they of greater righteous holy way power, holy way glory-love-holy-order of peace-love-holy-way eternal happiness order of lesser righteous happy way than that of Celestial highest glory of exaltation holy glory-love power of eternal duration order.

14. Let all know the way of telestial holy glory saved way; also terrestrial lesser

glory than full Celestial holy order; yea, both shall dwell for a time in resurrection glory, each of their order of degree of righteousness on earth while in the mortal earthly present temporal order; yea, both my kingdoms of lesser glory, also kingdom of full way evil order of full darkness who are traitors against God and murderers of shedding innocent blood.

15. All these shall only exist in their order in resurrected order for a time; then be of second death of dissoluting order; to return both spirit and resurrected earthly body into native original dissolution element, that which is the order of condition before such were organized before birth, on Celestial world of God's begetting as sons and daughters of God, His own spiritual offspring.

16. Let all awake to truth, that all shall meet thy Lord in the judgment day after raised from grave, through the power of holy Godhood redeeming holy way holy resurrection holy order power of Jesus Christ; when all shall be judged; when all thy secrets shall be fully revealed; to be placed in a kingdom of thy earning while on the world of probationary mortal existence while in the earthly world of both good and evil present, by which all are tested.

17. Let all be soon prepared to be of the way of judgment of full order of cleansing on earth, soon to happen; whirlwind holy eternal holy Godhead governing holy order power to remove wicked from earth; to be a way of more pure way of pure holy way of pure people on the world now of great evil order in all nations.

18. Let all peoples now prepare.

19. Let all now repent, to be of holy living.

20. Now be sons and daughters of my holy way to dwell on New Era Holy Order Zion-Order world, of the order of pure holy way order of heavenly order come to world now of full need of holy order of cleansing order; to have more holy people preserved; to be holy way of New Era of Zion, governing over all survival order of mortal earthly peoples left in every land after whirlwind full order holy eternal holy power judgments come on all nations. Amen.

21. Let this be of full world published order soon.

22. Let all peoples see my will done, of full labor on my day of birth; yet of full single day of fasting and gratitude way prayer unto thy Holy God, Jesus Christ; to show love-loyalty to Him who hath conquered death; to raise all unto judgment, each before your holy God.

23. Now be more holy, all ye peoples on world of my creating; for all things do testify of God's workmanship of pure eternal holy power.

24. Now hear these truths, eternal order truths; for none can be of hiding way of own way of no judging way of God if next life.

25. All shall answer for deeds done in world you now dwell in; yea, my world, saith Jesus Christ, Son of Man, Eternal Father under my Holy Father Ahman, Father Eternal over all creation.

26. Be publishing my holy revealing of holy celebration, all ye nations on world of my creating and holy atoning holy suffering as Savior of all mankind of all ages of time.

27. A way to be of full order of acceptable order of full worship of God, even of I, your Holy Redeemer Lord over all, is to have only thy family home; all others in their own home; to be family of

holy order of holy way praise-worship of thy holy Lord; to be acceptable, worthy to survive the soon whirlwind full eternal power order holy way order of cleansing order of full power judgments of God on world you now inhabit.

28. Sea soon heaveth beyond its bounds in Asia area.

29. Move to higher order of no shore-way dwelling, all Asian lands, if you would be of life-caring way order.

30. Also windstorm of great destructive force power cometh upon nation of the holy land of Zion, North America land, as called among mortal earthly powers.

31. Let Europe also plan a way to survive all my diseasing and earth-shaking way holy cleansing judgment against all of murder-way of abortion way of infanticide evil corrupt way; also against Sodom and adulterous immoral evil corruption order in all lands on earth.

32. Such shall not remain. Amen.

33. Let also Europe be of cleansing the evil of promiscuity of immoral evil way; to be survival way, holy living order; to remove all such of prostituting way, of Sodom way from all lands; for my power shall be full search power of cleansing all nations of these corrupting way order from the earth soon; by whirlwind judgments of my holy way order of eternal order holy eternity governing holy order power against such as they who love a lie; who corrupt themselves; also who love not truth, but believe a lie because their deeds are knowingly sin.

34. Now be holy way dwelling on world now of thy dwelling.

35. Spirit world shall also be of full shaking; separating wicked from righteous among all deceased, yet living people of spirit way of original created form of same form spiritual as earthly form of earthly body; yet not of death order of spirit organization nor of loss of identity; of full way holy order of God's sons and daughters of God's own children sent to world of my holy order of creating.

36. Let all such be holy way of living so my holy Priesthood order dwelling among spirit children way order may hear and obey my way of salvation; for I only am God and holy power of holy life and holy resurrection unto life everlasting.

37. Be holy, all peoples on earth, and in spirit existence world on earth, for such dwell in sphere of present earth of more pure holy order of pure way of the more pure way of the organization of sons and daughters of spirit refined element holy order of living. Amen.

SECTION REVELATION 168

Jesus Christ
Jehovah Son Ahman

I, Jesus Christ, Son Ahman, a Holy God Over All Peoples on World of Thy Now Dwelling, Send Full Way to Be Ready, Unto My Glory Holy Power Coming Soon, to Govern All; to Be Government of Holy Order, Heaven Come to Earth After Cleansing Evil Off Earth in Full Judge Way Power. Hear My Holy Word, Pure Revealed Way Through My Mouthpiece I Ordained on Earth; Now in Bondage; Yet to Be of My Full Witness Against Governing Order of All Who Neglect to Fulfill My Holy Way Revealed; Holy Word of God Now of Full Warning to All Peoples. Hasten to Prepare, by Hearing My Will.

Revelation of the Lord Jesus Christ
Palestine, Texas
Monday, April 9, 2012

1. He who is over all, Jesus Christ, saith: Holy way Celestial is soon to be full power on earth.

2. Repent, all ye peoples of the world; to now prepare for my coming in glory power, eternal holy power, to rule all nations soon.

3. Let only peace be thy whole way of just and equitous labor toward all, to be of remaining way on world of my holy purpose of salvation fulfilled; for this is my earth, my children sent from first estate in my Celestial holy power presence, to dwell on probationary world of full way good and evil present holy testing, of all who are born in the earth as telestial holy testing is of full way in each son or daughter's life.

4. Now receive my own way to be holy; to cease fleshly selfish unholy way; to not be of the world; to not be of immoral way at all; not to have unholy connecting with any in immoral corrupting way.

5. Let go of evil communications; also evil governing powers that lead thee to justify child murder of unborn children, which is an eternity punishable crime by God upon evil-minded people.

6. Let thy way be holy pure moral way entire; so I, your Lord, Redeemer, and King of glory power of eternal holy power can redeem thy soul unto everlasting resurrection salvation power only He can give.

7. Let all be sons of pure way, to not abuse women, to be kind to all; to have pure way of my Gospel as your way to be of flesh way living in pure holy motive to please thy Lord in all way of holy living; so I can preserve thy household unto Millennial Reign of joy-love peace, a Holy Spirit power even now upon honest souls worldwide dwelling wherever they inhabit my earth.

8. Now receive my will, to soon declare

peace in all nations; to be withdrawing military of thy nation back to thy own borders; only of self-defense; all of peace holy order; that I may preserve pure people in all nations by Celestial heavenly power.

9. Now do this, lest you be aggressors against innocence, even in own nation.

10. Let Syria leadership cease wicked attack on own peoples to be preserved as a nation, else I withdraw my power of holy power from thy land; war being full way thy choosing by usurpation of man's ability to do evil on own peoples in thy own land.

11. Cease such, lest my power withdraw of preserving all in their present lands by peace-love power enjoyed by peace-loving people everywhere.

12. Let leader of Angola bring rebel unholy leader to full justice, lest entire land be of war.

13. Let China cease aggressive preparing, lest unholy way of attack on neighbor land be fulfilled, leading to world conflict of thy making neighbor nation of North Korea able to incite conflict; you, in private dealing, empowering the North Korean power to launch way of bombing distant lands of weapon of great now destructive way.

14. I shall return on China a just holy judgment as though China was first aggressor if China cease not evil attack preparation; a cleansing of thy land entire in future time.

15. Thus, I send my own will, as you continue murder of unborn children; thus a nation of murderous order of judgment in full Godhood power of thy Lord Jesus Christ in day to come.

16. Now cease these most horrid evils that corrupt the way of thy nation before me, saith the Holy God over all peoples.

17. Now let all nations seek honest way of peace, to cease sending to other lands thy way of abortion evil order of child murder; to be preserving virtue, pure way of family honorable way of day-by-day dwelling in pure holy power I send as Holy Spirit holy power on all of pure way dwelling on earth.

18. Babylon is Babylon by choice way, not by God's will.

19. All evil is of choosing evil, not by my will at all.

20. Be ye repenting order; turn to prayer, for I, God, shall bless they who use their holy way of prayer unto better way works, unto guiding them to be more holy.

21. Now be of the full way holy way order of cleansing own peoples of adultery-Sodom way, of child murder of unborn children evil way; to be of holy lawmaking, not to steal by government power from thy own peoples their just way of possessing needs of living.

22. I shall hold all leaders accountable for conduct of how they governed.

23. Now repent, all ye rulers of all nations, is my word to all; for I, God over all nations, soon cometh to rule personally on world of thy now dwelling; sending my own will in understandable word given; so all may know I speak and fulfill my word entire.

24. Now repent, is my now way to continue as a nation only by thy repentance. Amen.

25. Thus saith Jesus Christ, Lord Redeemer, Holy God over all, my own holy will to all leaders of all nations: Repent now of war way of unhallowed most evil way of inciting evil violence corrupt motive way to gain influence; yea, even nation of the most power in military way on earth needing also to cease secret

way of being interfering way in another land not of immediate attack against any other nation, to let all such evil aggressive secret way of sending such way to other lands, to not do so, lest war of full way come on all lands and peoples; to not do this, for war shall be of full desolating way on many lands if of now doing, save I, God, intervene for sake of more righteous among all nations on earth.

26. Soon cometh my full way governing order to survival order. Amen.

27. Let also United Nations be now of being a way to cease the evil way of upholding child murder of abortion way, lest entire order of full judgments cometh, saith your Holy Lord to all peoples on earth.

28. Now cease all such evil promoting murder in secret, or in open abortion wicked evil corrupt soul-destroying and damning way among all peoples by United Nations evil organizing way among way of child aborting wicked way nations.

29. Let my way be done, to punish all of such murder way, lest no one be of full surviving order when thy Lord appeareth suddenly to all nations, a holy power Celestial holy order power of all minds opened by Spirit of God, to behold heaven come full order holy order power. Amen.

30. Let my holy way be done to send thy upholding my word to my Holy Priesthood holy message giving full power of holy word of God giving, to be of survival; to do honorable welcoming of thy Lord, of way to be holy order to show thy Lord you be of faith of His power, holy order holy way full order power come to earth.

31. Let my Priesthood receive thy acknowledging by mail or visit soon, to show me, your Holy Lord, Jesus, of my holy will received by government powers; to send thy humble full way of the holy receiving my holy messaging sent by a way of sure way holy receiving in all lands, of the confiding full way holy power order, of ambassador appointed order; to come not in fear, only in holy reverence to thy God of power; even to acknowledge thy way to do as I have revealed, to be a surviving people on world of thy dwelling; yea, by my holy power only, even the way of life of my giving all mortal existing to test all; for death is of sure way order unto all born on my world; death only of flesh, not of mind holy order of spirit of thy inward self.

32. All shall be accountable in resurrection for all thy dwelling on world; all to feel my almighty power soon.

33. Now repent, all ye of order of mortal dwelling among men.

34. Know only they who acknowledge the Lord soon cometh, preparing now; even to more holy way order of living, shall survive soon whirlwind judgments.

35. Come unto me, your Lord and Savior, Jesus Christ, who liveth, who conquered death; who is the Life, Light, and Love-order to all of the inhabitants of the earth, of the way to learn my holy way by revealed order, holy way revealing power, to be my power on world of now soon full judgment of full power, extant power, eternal order power of God. Amen.

SECTION REVELATION 169

Jesus Christ
Jehovah Son Ahman

Revelation of the Lord Jesus Christ
Palestine, Texas
Tuesday, April 24, 2012

1. I, Jesus Christ, send holy revealing of soon full power judgement upon Italy, Sardinia, Corsica, Crete, neighboring nations of isle order, of this holy date being day of the martyrdom of my holy order of Keyholder of apostle order, Peter, by nation of Rome in year Rome proved herself murder order against Priesthood, Paul also of martyr order by emperor Nero, most wicked murder order, Paul being first of torture way seeking to cause denial, then beheaded.

2. Let it be a day of holy way remembered, that as Peter was of crucified way hanging upside down for time of suffering while soldier order tortured him unto death by stabbing slight wounds until bled to death; thus Rome condemned to destruction.

3. Let all know I, Jesus Christ, cause Italy to now be judged; as land of immoral way entire; to no longer have church of false way Catholic order, a church which, in time of Protestant religion holy division from false church, tortured many for religion free worship holy right order.

4. Let all Italy mourn for great wicked way in land of supposed church of my name; not of me at all; only ripened to destruction in full order.

5. Let Italy and nations of her way of national way of the bloodline of Italy order among them, repent, to be holy order of survival order of now coming to my Holy Priesthood with remorse for unholy way among thee in ancient land professing religion of my order, not of God at all; only a church of former political order force order power over Europe in time past; now only a false church.

6. Let all read of my will now sent to you:

Thus Saith Jesus Christ, God Over All, Warning Now to Be of Full Power Receiving Unto My Word Honored, Obeyed in Full Measure:

1. Thus saith the Lord, even God over all to all nations:

2. Repent unto full power of full order of holy order of salvation, to be of full power preserved in the day of my glorious appearing.

3. Now feel my power as sudden judgement cometh, a full order of pure cleansing power on nation of unholy living, even Italy, also Sardinia, Crete, neighboring isles on sea of shores of Italy.

4. Be now humble; for great power of soon judgement is upon the land of Catholic deceptive order of world corrupt

order, not of me, your Lord Jesus Christ, who sendeth His own word to all, to be of full order of repenting.

5. Let people also send love repenting message to my servant, to acknowledge thy Lord, to be now repenting, holy order of holy living as true revealed order in Bible record declareth; to be holy pure way entire, overcoming dross, corrupt order of immoral way, of murder of unborn children by legal consent.

6. Now be for life and pure holy order, unto full declaring national way of governing is of holy order to be of my order of pure holy order extant, is thy Lord's own will to peoples of soon full judgement receiving, unto full knowing I warned all of my coming. Amen.

JESUS CHRIST SON AHMAN

HOLY REVEALING
APRIL 24, 2012

THUS SAITH JESUS CHRIST
GOD OVER ALL, WARNING
NOW TO BE OF FULL POWER
RECEIVING UNTO MY WORD
HONORED, OBEYED IN FULL MEASURE:

THUS SAITH THE LORD, EVEN GOD OVER ALL TO ALL NATIONS: REPENT UNTO FULL POWER OF FULL ORDER OF HOLY ORDER OF SALVATION, TO BE OF FULL POWER PRESERVED IN THE DAY OF MY GLORIOUS APPEARING. NOW FEEL MY POWER AS SUDDEN JUDGEMENT COMETH, A FULL ORDER OF PURE CLEANSING POWER ON NATION OF UNHOLY LIVING, EVEN ITALY, ALSO SARDINIA, CRETE, NEIGHBORING ISLES ON SEA OF SHORES OF ITALY. BE NOW HUMBLE; FOR GREAT POWER OF SOON JUDGEMENT IS UPON THE LAND OF CATHOLIC DECEATIVE ORDER OF WORLD CORRUPT ORDER, NOT OF ME, YOUR LORD JESUS CHRIST, WHO SENDETH HIS OWN WORD TO ALL, TO BE OF FULL ORDER OF REPENTING. LET PEOPLE ALSO SEND LOVE REPENTING MESSAGE TO MY SERVANT, TO ACKNOWLEDGE THY LORD, TO BE NOW REPENTING, HOLY ORDER OF HOLY LIVING AS TRUE REVEALED ORDER IN BIBLE RECORD DECLARETH; TO BE HOLY PURE WAY ENTIRE, OVERCOMING DROSS, CORRUPT ORDER OF IMMORAL WAY, OF MURDER OF UNBORN CHILDREN BY LEGAL CONSENT. NOW BE FOR LIFE AND PURE HOLY ORDER, UNTO FULL DECLARING NATIONAL WAY OF GOVERNING IS OF HOLY ORDER TO BE OF MY ORDER OF PURE HOLY ORDER EXTANT, IS THY LORD'S OWN WILL TO PEOPLES OF SOON FULL JUDGEMENT RECEIVING, UNTO FULL KNOWING I WARNED ALL OF MY COMING. AMEN.

Warren S. Jeffs

SECTION REVELATION 170

Jesus Christ
Jehovah Christ, Son Ahman

Thus Saith the Lord Jesus Christ, Son Ahman, to the Leaders and Peoples of the Nation of Libya, a Holy Word:

Revelation of the Lord Jesus Christ
Palestine, Texas
Saturday, April 28, 2012

1. I, the Lord Jesus Christ, speak a holy word unto the people of the nation of Libya:

2. Repent ye, for there cometh war to sweep thee off the earth if you continue in any corrupt way of child murder immoral way, corrupt way, wherein you are of oppression to women and children, abusive in your ways of family living.

3. And I, the Lord, shall see that you receive full just recompense for corrupt way in thy land, having in admiration the ways of men more than correct principles of pure living.

4. Murder way of unborn children is done in secret through thy land, though many decry against it.

5. And I shall be of a full justice sending whirlwind judgments upon thee that none remain.

6. And it shall be known in this generation that none remain in thy land if you continue in this corrupt way. Amen.

7. Now hear my word:

8. Repent ye, you lawmakers of that nation, and do not allow legal consent or private consent of doctor way, of physician way, in murder of unborn youth wherein life is taken before birth.

9. Let there be women's rights carefully given, education to daughters as well as sons without obstructing.

10. And let there be kindness in your homes if you would be of a surviving way of whirlwind judgments soon at hand.

11. This from the Lord who created all, even Jehovah, who is Jesus Christ, who ruleth over the heavens and the earth, soon to appear to give justice toward all who would be of the Millennial Reign of my righteous rule. Amen.

SECTION REVELATION 171

Jesus Christ
Jehovah Son Ahman

Thus Saith the Lord Jesus Christ Unto All People of Nation of Lithuania, a Holy Warning to Repent, to Be Holy as Individuals, Also to Leaders of Lithuania, My Own Word:

Revelation of the Lord Jesus Christ
Palestine, Texas
Sunday, April 29, 2012

1. Thus saith the holy Lord Jesus Christ to nation of Lithuania:

2. You are not of pure order as a nation, murder both of unborn children, also secret government murder of they of disagreeing way against government officials now rampant in governing power order in thy nation.

3. I, God, even Jesus Christ, who sees all thy works in secret, shall reward all such openly who are of secret way of unholy government way in Lithuania.

4. Be ye now of removing official over secret police, lest he do more murder; also do all law cleansing labor to preserve life, so people of thy land murder unborn child order no longer.

5. Let this warning be heeded; for your sin is great, of murder order, to be answered upon all of such corruption. Amen.

6. Let also thy land be peace keeping, not to join at all with unholy aggressive nation of the order of conquering in way to harm other nation power order in future way of violent order, is thy Lord's will to land of soon power of my holy cleansing, God-power order; to fulfill my will; to cleanse off earth all of unholy murder way extant; not of pure holy order of free way living in peace way.

7. Let Lithuania repent as individuals, as a nation of repenting of murder order now.

8. A holy way to show God you do receive my will is to change law of Lithuania to protect unborn child way order; also to remove official of secret police from power in Lithuania, investigating him for crime of murder of own citizen order.

9. Let also all read this, my will, in land of thy dwelling on earth, so all know judgment is of soon way on nation if murder order continueth in Lithuania. Amen.

10. Now let all people of Lithuania personally repent of child murder abortion wicked order, to be surviving way in the way of own lives unholy in the way of immoral unholy adulterous evil order, Sodom way of most unholy way.

11. Let all be for pure way, to know holy way hath the purifying order of the preparing for my holy glorious hallowed coming to world in power, insomuch as to reward all for doings on world of thy habiting.

12. A way to cleanse nation is individual labor to be personally holy in thy life.

13. Now repent, is the will of thy God, Jesus Christ, God over all nations. Amen.

Jesus Christ Giveth Own Writing to Supreme Court of Appeals

(Comprising Section Revelations 172-174)

Kingdom of Zion
2420 CR 300
Eldorado, Texas 76936

Jesus Christ, Son Ahman

I, Jesus Christ, even Son Ahman, speak to Supreme Court of Texas, my own will even concerning 51st Judicial District Court Cause Numbers 990, 997, 1017, 1061, and Court of Appeals Court Case Number 03-11-00568-CR, as pertaining to legal prosecution against my servant Warren Jeffs, my own will telling truth to Supreme Court, exhibits of pure truth given; to now be means of use to Supreme Court to use powers of justice to be of freeing my servant Warren Jeffs, being held unjustly, by both intentional evil and lying ways, also by ignorance of this generation not knowing my full truth of religion being of constitutional protection for religious freedom. Uphold my will, my own word sent to thee in this full call of appeal. Let also Merril Jessop, of the way of imprisonment, be released soon. Let not my servant of pure holy religious practice linger any longer in prison, lest my own power be of full humbling of all who are of the lying way against my Holy Priesthood, a religious authority that should be protected fully by constitutional guarantee of religious freedom; the full way of my servant Warren Jeffs' conduct being my will. Let Merril Jessop, of full name Fredrick Merril Jessop, Sen., be delivered. He was imprisoned for only doing my holy will. Now be just, saith Jesus Christ, your Lord, and God of all Creation. You shall soon feel my power, all who seek to hinder my holy will from being fulfilled; in the labor of pure holy way of salvation; a revealed religion on earth of my holy guiding daily, even to give this, my will, to you to be soon acted upon. Let this, my word, now be of my pure way of causing my holy power of pure holy way of truth, coming before Supreme Court, now be of a witness. I am soon to cleanse Zion's land. Thus is my word said further:

SECTION REVELATION 172

Jehovah Speaketh, Who Is Jesus Christ

Revelation of the Lord Jesus Christ
Palestine, Texas
Wednesday, November 16, 2011

1. Thus saith the Lord to Supreme Court of Texas, my own revealed word from heaven, addressing this court of appealing power, to uphold freedom rights of my holy religion.

2. Let all be true justice.

3. Let all be firm in pure freedom protection.

4. Let freedom of worship protect all of true religion.

5. My holy Church, called among men the Fundamentalist Church of Jesus Christ of Latter-day Saints, is true religion, being my true Church of revealed and holy power.

6. I am of the soon coming to cleanse all peoples who oppose the rise of my Church and Zion, from off the land of Zion, even North and South America.

7. Your high court is able to reverse completely my servant's prison sentence of lower court.

8. Now know my Proclamation to all peoples, to all governing powers, is sent to you to read, and know I, God, have sent my own revealing of history, of persecution of United States Government against my Church since days I revealed my Church through my servant Joseph Smith, and of mine authority from heaven, called Priesthood, carried through faithful walk by Prophets ordained by me to officiate in the Gospel Plan of Salvation.

9. My people have endured persecution by government powers since Joseph Smith's day on earth; and this nation is ripened for my full judgments, living in corruption.

10. Let my servant and his brethren of my Church in Texas prisons be released, for they are prosecuted for abiding my law of Celestial Eternal Marriage of Plural Marriage Celestial; my most holy pure law of salvation, necessary for them and all others to receive full salvation.

11. This is my appeal to the Texas Supreme Court, calling on the court to know of my Proclamation, to know I, God, am over all; to allow thee to intervene;

to also tell all courts my people are pure, noble, holy, righteous people, only desiring to live Celestial Law of pure religion, even Celestial Plural Marriage by my revealing.

12. This Order of Eternal Union is of me, and I, Jesus Christ, your Lord, hath caused this law and my holy Keyholder power to continue among men on earth.

13. I tell thee these truths to cause you to release my servant and his brethren on pure principle of constitutional freedom guarantee of religion.

14. Let this be my own will fulfilled by you, to show all of true justice, protecting innocence of pure religion, being full and only motive of these, my sons in Priesthood, to live the law of Celestial Plural Marriage in a holy way.

15. Let them be of full freedom.

16. They are innocent by religious worship guarantee of freedom.

17. Let also my people be undisturbed by governing powers, is the word of the Lord Jesus Christ to Supreme Court in Texas.

18. Now be enlightened by my holy writing in Proclamation of thy Lord to governing powers in the nation of United States of America, also my revealing court of prosecution did not uphold freedom of religion protection; heralding my sacred holy house and sacred marriage and holy ways before world, not protecting my full religion of Eternal Power truth.

19. Now be of true justice.

20. Let my servants go. Amen.

21. Now be a court of true justice equitable way of full pure righteous power; to protect innocence, even my obedient Priesthood sons on earth, whose only motive in receiving Celestial Plural Marriage is for religious worship of God, who revealed this law through Joseph Smith.

22. I am fully able to defend my people.

23. You are under a sacred trust to uphold righteous religion of pure holy way.

24. My holy word in my published Proclamation to governing powers on earth dispels all falsehood, as it is mine own eternal truths, all new revealings therein, telling courts of prosecution way they do not have jurisdiction over my Church; my holy religion being from heaven, guided and governed by me, your Lord, only accountable to me, your God and Eternal Ruler.

25. I shall preserve my holy religion and Eternal Law of Marriage Union, and my Priesthood on the earth.

26. If you do well, reverse ruling of lower courts, and let my servant Warren Jeffs go free. Amen.

27. Read my Proclamation, the exhibit with this, my own revealed appeal of naming I am above your jurisdiction, and thus you only have authority to fully dismiss the present cases now before prosecuting court and past court actions, thus preserving thy nation from full whirlwind judgments.

28. Now obey my will, and on constitutional protecting principles alone, be justified to dismiss all charges. Amen.

SECTION REVELATION 173

Revelation of the Lord Jesus Christ
Palestine, Texas
Wednesday, November 30, 2011

1. I, your Lord, speak to full power Court of Appeals, even Texas Court having full power to cause justice to be given, Texas Court of the way of no other court save national highest court being of higher appeal power, State Supreme Court of Texas, a word of calling on you to reverse all cases against my people in Texas, holding my servant Warren Jeffs, also Merril Jessop, also others of unjust holdings; to now set them free.

2. Let thy justification in law be to protect constitutional religious freedom guarantee by First Amendment.

3. Thus I send my own word, saith Jesus Christ, Son Ahman, to you, to now release them from unjust court, and be of full freedom to do my will.

4. They are of me, and innocent.

5. Let the new holy revealing of my holy proclaiming in a publishing, as an exhibit to this appeal to the Texas Supreme High Court, to be of full witness I am of my holy way to be of full truth, to show all my holy revealing of my Church and Priesthood are a holy religion, to have full protection of law, to be free to live my revealed eternal religion.

6. Let no one judge not having right to judge, where pure holy religion from my holy revealing since day of Joseph Smith in the nineteenth century did a labor of my revealing laws Celestial; to be of full holy religion; now of an abuse by governing powers in the court system of the nation of United States of America; an evil combination of governing powers joining with wicked former members of my Church, now turned to evil, forming

lies to be of the use of prosecuting powers.

7. Verily I say unto you, I am God, and a God of truth.

8. Receive my own word: Let them go free, as they are of my holy pure Church; of Celestial Law of holy religious intent, practice, and pure way of the Eternal Plan of Salvation; Celestial Eternal Marriage Union by my own guiding my servant on earth, to administer my holy law to only members of my Church who are living moral pure holy lives.

9. I am the holy power over my Church, not government of man on earth.

10. I established Constitution of this nation through noble-minded founding fathers of pure holy freedom principles that all men of all nations could come under, to enjoy freedom of religion, of expression, of rights of way of enjoying life in pursuit of happiness, not intrusive on others' rights of free way of living.

11. Let court be of now considering this need of justice served, lest I, God over all nations, see unjust ways upheld by higher governing powers, and then send greater power of humbling to present nation and governing powers; a humbling of eternal power of cleansing more wicked off my land of Zion, which land is North and South America.

12. Receive my Proclamation as evidence.

13. Let it be thy way of receiving my pure word of truth, unobstructed by lying witnesses.

14. Let it be my holy will, to be of full truth telling, that my servant is only doing my holy will, saith Jesus Christ, sending my own will to you.

15. I have also called on the holy order of pure way of truth, to send my word of Proclamation to all nations, all governing powers on earth; to know I soon cometh, with almighty power, to sweep wickedness off all lands.

16. Let thy only way be to uphold truth, as I, your God of truth, who is over all eternally; who shall reward all for deeds done in this life unto an eternal judgment in the resurrection, speak my will to now be just; giving high court the way of truth, to deal justly in releasing men of my Church now held in prison houses for the truth of living by my own revealed word; my Celestial holy law of holy Eternal Union in Marriage; all by my will.

17. Now learn that I shall prove all.

18. I shall be justified to send cleansing powers upon all.

19. Let thy court receive my appeal.

20. Let it now be of full considering.

21. Send forth order to release him and his brethren, even all prosecuted by an unjust court, using the law of my holy way as though it were of evil and of the way of courts being dictating religion.

22. It must not be allowed to have government of man dictate a religion in religious law. Amen.

23. Now be of soon delivering of my servant Warren Jeffs, also Merril Jessop, others of the same court prosecution against them for being of my Church and of my holy law of Celestial Marriage Plural Union; a law of my revealing.

24. My Proclamation telleth all of my holy way and eternal purposes.

25. Also receive books of my revealing; even scriptures showing my law was of antiquity; even in thy own national history my Doctrine and Covenants scripture tells of Celestial Plural Marriage.

26. It tells of doctrine of three degrees of heavenly glory; the highest earned by

those who abide my Celestial Law of Celestial Plural Marriage Union a pure holy way; all through my revealing through my holy authority on earth, whom I have appointed and ordained by my own power, to administer my Eternal Union law only to pure members of my Church.

27. Thus it is religion you are interfering with, when courts of governing bodies or officials among the way of man's governing order, to be illegal by thy own laws of pure truth justice, even constitutional holy law of my establishing.

28. Let this court be of truth.

29. You are not ignorant of unjust prosecuting court action.

30. Judge Walther, even the judge who rules against my law in every way of the court powers bestowed on a judge of trial court ability, was the unjust judge taking away children unjustly from my people; which this court ordered reversal of judge's way of taking innocent children away from pure holy parents, who raise their children according to my holy Church on earth.

31. Let it be evidence to you, even to know I shall cleanse all nations who seek to destroy innocence.

32. Thus unjust Judge Walther tried to destroy the family relationship of pure children.

33. Let this be testimony to you, Judge Walther is not of pure holy ruling; but seeks to be of a full way against my Celestial holy law of religion.

34. Let also court be of full returning all the government powers unrighteously seized from my holy Church and people; coming on my holy land; entering, by Judge Walther's unjust ruling, my holy temple and other sacred religious buildings, to take whatsoever they desired; then, not being of pure justice, allowed my holy temple to be defiled before all peoples, both by illegal entry and defiling my sacred temple by they of governing powers, and also allowing prosecution to display my temple's sacred and holy places unto all peoples.

35. It is open defiling of pure holy religious sacred place.

36. Let all this be witness enough to show unjust Judge Walther erred in continued rulings.

37. Let my holy religion be protected.

38. Let all my holy Church be protected, to not be of attack by governing powers.

39. They were of believing a lie when first entering my holy land and temple, thinking the report was true, when they had sufficient grounds to wait and investigate.

40. Let it be of full way investigated, why the power of man's government has trampled on sacred religion without any governing power in this once free land, to stop unrighteous attack.

41. Let this court now be of full power, to return all my sacred and holy items illegally and in a forceful way that were taken from my people and from my holy religious power of Priesthood; a holy authority on earth only subject to God, even I, your Lord Jesus Christ, who sendeth these words to you.

42. You are ignorant of truth about my religion revealed from heaven since days of Joseph Smith, who was my holy Prophet, Seer, and Revelator.

43. He was martyred.

44. He was also pure.

45. He was also my holy messenger to all peoples of the earth of my revealed religion of eternal salvation.

46. He continued to be so until he was murdered.

47. He is a holy Prophet that dwelt in your nation.

48. Now my holy revealing of my Proclamation is in hands of all leaders of nations.

49. Let it be your justifying holy truth of pure holy order of revealing my truth, to release my people from present unjust court ruling of imprisonment.

50. Now be just.

51. Do what I command, as the God of all the earth; to be justified as a nation; to be of a preserving of your peoples at my glorious coming; else I shall intervene and fulfill all my words of warning I have published to you of governing powers, also of religious receiving my own Proclamation throughout thy land; also other warning of recent sending, of which copies I have caused to be included in publishings also recently sent to all nations.

52. My official warning has now been sent to all peoples.

53. Now I am fully justified to be of full power of my judgments of cleansing power to cleanse all peoples who continue in wicked ways.

54. I shall be heard above all opposition.

55. I am the God of Power.

56. All creation exists because of my power.

57. Let all peoples now tremble at my holy power.

58. The word of thy Lord is sure and true. As I speak, so do I fulfill.

59. Repent ye, all ye peoples of every land; and of the land of the United States of America, the land of my holy Advent, my holy coming in almighty power; first cleansing off my Zion land all outward and secret wickedness. Amen.

SECTION REVELATION 174

Revelation of the Lord Jesus Christ
Palestine, Texas
Wednesday, December 14, 2011

1. Thus saith the Lord Jesus Christ to the Supreme Court of Texas, highest court in the state where my servant Warren Jeffs is of the imprisonment by unjust court:

2. Let my holy Proclamation be thy full witness to court of pure holy religion being of government persecution since the nineteenth century in present nation.

3. Let it be known I have preserved my holy authority; also my Celestial Law of pure holy Marriage Eternal Union of Plural Marriage Union Celestial, my holy law revealed through Joseph Smith.

4. Let court be firm in truth seeking; to not hear of the way of not admitting truth because prosecution uses reasons not of truth seeking.

5. I have let my appeal wait until Appeals Court received my own appeal; to be of the way of true holy justice being given in court of man on earth.

6. Let all be just, seeking full truth.

7. I send my Proclamation as an exhibit; yea, my new full truth power of my holy Keyholder authority; also truth of Celestial Law of my Eternal Union Plural

Holy Marriage Law being of me, your Lord; of pure religion, of holy sacred truth of salvation earned by living my holy law through my Holy Priesthood authority on earth, inspired of me, even your Lord Jesus Christ.

8. Let appeal be to release my servant; also Merril Jessop and their brethren in prison; to be free to live on my land of Zion, to live my holy law; to be free to practice and abide Celestial revealed law, not subject to governing powers, who are not lawful in attacking a religion of pure holy revealing from heaven; even from I, your Lord.

9. Let all these truths be of full justifying power to be of pure holy way justice; to have nation overthrow all unjust past law rulings against my holy law and pure marriage authority on earth.

10. Let also all be of full way honest, to allow my own word to be of court receiving; as I only speak through One Man, my Keyholder on earth, to all peoples on the earth.

11. Let it be thy full way to honor God, and true holy principles of religious freedom guaranteed by Constitution.

12. Now let my servant be free.

13. Let his brethren, prosecuted for abiding my Celestial Law of Eternal Union Marriage Holy Plural Union, also go free.

14. Let this also be a way this persecution against my authority on earth, also the prosecuting power against my Celestial Law of Plural Marriage of my holy religion, cease.

15. Let all be truly just.

16. Let all be responding to mine own word; to be honorable toward all religion; to have place in history as they who would defend rights of freedom for an unpopular people and religion.

17. Let all be noble, of pure thought, of truth seeking.

18. My holy law hurts no one.

19. This is the Lord God of heaven speaking to the Texas Supreme Court, telling you only truth. Amen.

Jesus Christ

Holy Power Celestial of the Domain of Ahman in my own Kingdom Son Ahman

In behalf of Jesus Christ, Warren Jeffs is to sign for court to know I represent our Lord.

President Warren S. Jeffs, President of Church of Jesus Christ Servant of Jesus Christ

Appendix of Exhibits

Exhibit 1 Letter to the 51st Judicial District Court of Schleicher County, Texas

Exhibit 2 Proclamation -- Published November 2011

Exhibit 3 Book of Mormon -- Doctrine and Covenants -- Pearl of Great Price

Exhibit 4 Warning to the Nations -- 2010-10-31

Exhibit 5 Proclamation to the Nation -- 2010-07-17

Exhibit 6 Continued Warnings of Son Ahman to the Leaders of the Nations of the Earth

Exhibit 7 Appeal to Court of Appeals for the Third District of Texas

Exhibit 8 Thus Saith Son Ahman, Even Your Lord Jesus Christ, My Own Will to All Nations on Earth of Full Power to Be Fulfilled, Unto All Knowing I, God, Have Spoken Eternal Power Upon All Nations

Chapter 7

Jesus Christ Holy Will to President of United States of America, New Word of Now Need of Just Order to Be of Full Now Labor. Now Do So. Amen.

SECTION REVELATION 175

Jesus Christ
Jehovah Son Ahman

I, Jesus Christ, Give My Own Way for United States President to Do That Which Is Just, Honorable, Truth-Justice With Mercy Order Named; to Be a Ruler of Pure Honorable Correct Principle Order; Unto Defending Innocence, Life of Unborn Children; of Religion Being of Truth Free to Live in Nation of Professed Religious Freedom Order. Now Read My Own Way to Do That Which Shall Preserve Nation Unto Good Example, How to Do Right Way of Such Order to Be Holy Way Living at My Glorious Coming, Saith Jesus Christ. Amen.

Revelation of the Lord Jesus Christ
Palestine, Texas
Sunday, May 27, 2012

1. I, Jesus Christ, the Maker of heaven and earth, God of creating power eternal, even Jehovah, speaketh to, by my authority I have anointed on earth, to President of nation of the United States of America; a holy will, to make ruler of nation of my way to be just, holy, of honest governing power to all, lest God speaketh a way to not be ruler at time transgressing holy way is of full order of turning unto evil.

2. Let President now do labor of full prayer, to have heart open to read my way, even God over all, to be holy, way of pure peace living; to do governing order by principle of truth order; not for self-aggrandizing order of seeking own order to be pleasing unto way of other order of evil self-serving intent, which lobbying order constantly doeth.

3. Now consider all things are of my holy way to exist on earth by almighty power.

4. All thy way of governing, though of united way entire of all governing order, if of voting as united power, cannot change truth to error, nor to be overthrowing God.

5. All fools of mankind order who aspire to overthrow eternal power of God are fool order.

6. Remember my judged way on Nebuchadnezzar in Daniel's time.

7. Though ruler over nation, by my word he was humbled to know only I, God, rule; and man is of full accounting to thy Lord.

8. Be humble order of only desiring to do good according to my holy way, even Jesus Christ, who loveth truth, who reigns in heaven, who is Light and Life of all men; who conquered death, to give eternal life to they who obey my salvation Gospel, as I caused apostle witness order to record in New Testament holy record.

9. Now know I cometh to land of Zion, land where New Jerusalem shall be built.

10. Know I come with my governing order, of heavenly power.

11. All surviving order in all nations shall see me at once, to know I have come to rule over all peoples on world.

12. Now be awake to coming unholy attack against nation you govern.

13. A way of money order manipulating the money order, to cause economic collapse, when they who own the debt order of nation do work to allow rich order of debt-spending to collapse, you will then know folly of such; as it is a folly to place thy order of economic prosperity in hand of foreign power who are of full intent to overthrow government in thy land.

14. Thus, thy way needs be to ready military in own land; for thy way to take conflict to other lands shall only cause weak way in own national defending.

15. Let thy wise order be to not do a way of unholy way aggression after you cleanse own nation of murder of unborn child order; to do so as sign of national humbling; you standing for living order.

16. Let this be now presidential order, to have such cease.

17. Let also thy way be presidential order to free my holy authority from jail, held by governing power.

18. Let thy mind be open.

19. Read my own appeal I sent to state Supreme Order Appeals Court.

20. I spake. Man heeded not God.

21. Therefore I doeth my own way to establish freedom.

22. As nation rose from oppression of European mother land of England, so shall I cause Zion to rise above oppression of present nation on land of my holy coming; to build capital city of my governing order, New Jerusalem; a city eternal order to be capital governing order over all lands, peoples, nations, governing powers, soon to be full power as I descend from the abode of holy power in heaven order, to dwell among men on earth to they all knowing I am on world of thy now dwelling.

23. My time is soon to come.

24. No man knoweth exact time I descend; thus my warning voice hath sounded I cometh soon.

25. Do the honorable order of releasing my servant, along with his other brethren held unjust way in bondage, for they live higher more pure way holy Celestial Law of my Church, not to be given to world; only to obedient order to Celestial exalting law of eternal holy order of God.

26. Now cease unholy aggression on other land, nation who never attacked thy peoples.

27. Withdraw from the land of military involvement entire; bring military home.

28. Strengthen own home military, to repel the unholy attack of the nation now holding economic power over thy own nation.

29. Russia and China have private agreement to attack thy land.

30. Release my servant.

31. Stop child unborn youth order murder.

32. Bring military home.

33. Do so soon, if nation is to continue order of example of truth-order justice; mercy-governing power order; a nation I established by sending to world such forefathers who loved freedom principles more than their earthly life order.

34. Do these works to prove thy willing order to do truth justice to all. Amen.

SECTION REVELATION 176

Jesus Christ
Jehovah Christ, Son Ahman

I, Jesus Christ, Speak Warning to Leaders and Peoples of Nation of Mauritania, Word to Heed Now, Lest Judgment Come Soon on Thy Peoples and the Leaders of Mauritania.

Revelation of the Lord Jesus Christ
Palestine, Texas
Tuesday, May 1, 2012

1. I, the God over all, give word to land of Mauritania, nation of wicked order: Cease violent order in thy land lest I, God over all creation, send forth my judgments upon thee in full measure, for murder of unborn child order is of thy way, no longer to continue, save God's judgment come on you.

2. Now heed my will.

3. Murder is unforgivable sin unto God rendering eternal judgment come on all violent order people in thy land.

4. Government of thy nation practices much evil, even immorality, adultery, Sodom, upon people by force in prison way.

5. It is not hidden from me, your God who made you, and shall be restored on such as practice immoral way.

6. Now be warned, lest none remain in thy nation, which is ripened in evil.

7. Now be more holy, pure government order, is the will of God to leaders of a land of unholy way, of murder, of licentious order, soon to be of full judged way by your Lord, even Jesus Christ. Amen.

SECTION REVELATION 177

Jesus Christ
Jehovah Son Ahman

I, Jesus Christ, Jehovah, Speak Love-Joy-Peace Love Message to All Peoples on World. Now Heed My Word, so to Be Ready for My Soon Holy Power Dwelling on Earth Among Surviving Peoples, in Zion City of New Jerusalem; Old Jerusalem Also, Mine Ancient Abode of Final Witness Order Unto Crucifixion of Me, Thy God; Now a Living Order of Heaven Governing All Peoples, Though They Do Not Now Acknowledge Your Lord as God Over All at This Time; Time Soon to Be That Every Knee Shall Bow to My Rule; Every Tongue Confess Jesus Christ, Even I Who Speaketh, Is the Literal Son of God. Now Hear My Holy Love-Peace-Joy Order Love Message to All Peoples on Orb of Earth You Now Dwell Upon, by My Grace.

Revelation of the Lord Jesus Christ
Palestine, Texas
Sunday, May 13, 2012

1. O ye people of all the world, repent ye, repent ye, is the call of your holy Lord, Jesus Christ; for I cometh; and ye must needs be holy to remain.

2. Be now peace-giving power, ye nations, ye leaders of nations, lest great war among you come, even a day of sorrow, running over, in thy ability to endure.

3. Cleanse ye, all people, murder of unborn children, adultery, Sodom, as a full measure who shall be of full judgment of God receiving.

4. I know all things, see hidden order of mind over all peoples, to reveal truth of individual life of each person at the day of resurrection justice judgment in full.

5. This is my world.

6. I created the earth for eternity dwelling of pure children of thy Lord, who are receivers of salvation.

7. Now repent, that I, God, can heal you, is my message; yea, my love-message to all peoples on world of soon judgment of God receiving in all lands, such that only the more righteous remain.

8. A holy way to live is to send full order of peace tidings among your own land, peoples of fighting order; to have peace thy full labor, not of evils of murder, nor youth slavery, nor abuse of thy own family.

9. Let women be free, to be educated, to have full law protection from abuse, ye nations.

10. All shall be holy peace-love-joy when, I, your Lord, cometh; angel order

of governing authority on world in judging order.

11. Let this truth awaken all to have life, yea, individual lives, in order, a holy way of living my law of love for all, through pure way living on world.

12. Now come to me in prayer.

13. Let thine oblations rise to heaven, even love-devotion to the God who created all things, who is over all things; who hath all power to discern the intent of each heart-order of soul.

14. Now be of faith love kindness way, so I can spare such in holocaust of war and whirlwind judgments.

15. Give a holy love offering to my name by this day praying, all ye peoples of world, for peace, then make peace among family, nation, and between nations over full world order of nations.

16. Cease gross crimes of child murder before their birth, abortion of any fetus a murder in God's eyes, lest ye be murderer of own child order.

17. Discipline moral personal living so you harm not unborn.

18. Let thy way be to honor God and way of preserving life order of unborn children unto peace-love family of thy prayerful living unto me, your Lord; who is Jesus Christ, Jehovah, the Great I AM, the Redeemer of all mankind of all ages of time on world you now dwell upon; all ye peoples of my own giving you life, hope everlasting, love gifts of living peace-love holy prayer order.

19. Be ye ready. A holy preparing for my coming, both on this world, and they who are of spirit world of passing on to next spirit world, is to have own life in love-peace order of blessing all people in kind order, giving to poor, blessing they of youth, the aged attend to; all in need not of thy neglect; for what you individually give, shall I, your Lord, cause you to receive unto an eternity of like unto like, blessing those who are pure love-power-giving in all honorable order of caring; also full suffering for sin of murder, also suffer for knowing sin is sin, and living evil way by choosing evil.

20. Now choose to do good to all, so I may be your Savior, Redeemer, Eternal Friend Holy God of Creation; to raise you up to my heaven power order. Amen.

SECTION REVELATION 178

Jesus Christ
Jehovah Son Ahman

Jesus Christ, Your God and Ruler, Speaketh Eternity Truth, Also Warning of Traitor Against Nation of United States of the Land of My Holy Advent Soon; to Know I Cometh to Preserve Holy Pure Order in All Nations; This, My Word to All People on Earth Now Inhabiting All Lands. Hear My Holy Will Unto Full Way of Holy Observance:

Revelation of the Lord Jesus Christ
Palestine, Texas
Saturday, May 19, 2012

1. I, God of all the full order of worlds, who saw the end from the beginning, even Jesus Christ, speak to all people of world, of the way I am bringing forth a thousand years of my holy power on world, of governing power over all nations; for I shall appear unto all people suddenly, to fear coming on all the evil of all nations.

2. Now know in United States of America a traitor shall cause enemy armies to come on land where he was of the causing armies of the nation to not be of a full ready order; even now doing this.

3. He is in the way of the organizing military placing in nation.

4. Military is of going where sent in land; and large area is now of the way to be weak on both the eastern, also southern shores of United States.

5. I shall call on leader of nation to be of search way such large space of no military defending way, such as is now of traitor way, knowing foreign power organizing a way to overthrow nation on my land of Zion; to make organized military unusable soon when force cometh against nation.

6. Now awake.

7. Look at own organization of armies present on nation of my Zion of soon power over all peoples.

8. You are clamoring over the way of riches, not aware of soon attack.

9. Let nation continue in search for usual riches seeking, disregarding my warning, even thy Lord Jesus Christ, to the people on Zion land of United States of America; to question leaders of nation.

10. Now be of sure way, enemy intends to come on nation suddenly, to be on land of own soil, so nation doth not use weapon of greatest way of destroying, lest own people are of great harm.

11. Be ye of search for who organizes military locating in own land.

12. If you would be prepared, do so; for I, your holy Lord, have long defended thy nation for my people's sake, even to prosper thee above all nations for century of full way preparing in holy peace on own land since Civil War was of finish.

13. Now learn you transgress when I, God over all, send my own will and you heed me not.

14. Enemy country holding debt of great overabundant order of the nation of United States soon cause economic way of harm to thy economy such as to disrupt international balance, a way to do such unrest way in all financial way of nation of thy now most power way of money influence, to then bring present leadership to condition of confused disunity way, so as to not have order in all governing departments of nation.

15. Thy civil force of militia shall not have the way to be of full defense when powerful alien army of other coalition of nation of enemy power cometh on land.

16. You shall flee; then band together in south, also mid-eastern, then mid-west area, not of full power to repulse enemy.

17. Thus, I, your holy God, speaketh: Rid yourselves of heinous crime of child, unborn child unholy most wicked way murder of legal now consent; also let my servant in bondage go, to organize my people, as spiritual power with the God over all, to preserve more righteous on land.

18. Now be diligent, leaders of nation of United States of America, lest you, in unbelief, though these signs of present way are even now upon you as a nation; yet you join in secret governing agreeing with foreign power of economic power, so as to fulfill my word given, that you shall cease to be a nation of world power if evil traitor way continueth; also thy own evil of murder and of immoral evils continuing among nation that was freest nation on world, now not of giving religious full freedom.

19. I shall intervene for mine elect's sake at time nation is cleansed, as you do own way, not God over all of holy way doing of repentance of such gross evil way as shedding innocent blood of unborn child holy order.

20. Be ye preparing for the promised humbling of destructive order of storm; of need of food, clothing, temporary blanket warmth need; to feed people in need at time I show I have spoken; also earthquake in the nation of my coming.

21. Now be aware I can only preserve among the people of all nations on world.

22. Let thy study be to do home emergency military organizing.

23. You as a nation have offended thy Lord in the attack of other nation not of attack against you at all in most recent war of Libya, also Iraq and Afghanistan; three unholy aggressive attacks against other nations, for pride sake, when you suffer new attack on own soil.

24. Now be of own self-way preparing.

25. Also let him, my servant Warren Jeffs, and his brethren in prison for living their holy religion in land of professed freedom of religion; to go to their holy way of living; for when the more obeying people are of a way of unjust way unholy attack in nation, great judgment cometh.

26. Look at time of greatest attack of nation against my Church, and war of nation cometh to humble all; also disease, thereafter; even my holy Church feeling judgment on nation.

27. Now be holy.

28. I have sent my own will to all lands of recent holy sending.

29. Heed my will lest thy nation is humbled in full way of storm, earthquake, sudden disease, also fulfilling promise of God to overthrow all such who are against purity of living, against life of unborn child order.

30. All ancient nations were destroyed when of this evil of murder of unborn child order, because they were of immoral living, even this present generation all over the earth now of this sin in all lands, notwithstanding my own now recent word going forth to warn all nations.

31. Do no more against law of life in your immoral living, else judgment of eternal order cometh; yea, of an eternity of loss of life for they of evil of murder, Sodom, adultery unholy living.

32. My law of Celestial order holy eternal union is pure holy law of moral way.

33. Now come to me, you of professing moral way; yet in your order of living the self order of judging my holy order, you put my servants in prison; yet crime of murder of unborn youth order is replete throughout nation.

34. Now do true cleansing.

35. Let murder of unborn youth be punished, not to be of own living if not innocent in preserving own child order in birth way right to live; for such shall be when thy Lord cometh on earth; to do full justice to all such evil practice; even to do the full order of true justice to they against life holy preserving way; also against open immoral way.

36. England did a work with young nation when virtue queen punished adultery of any, no matter who, in nation.

37. Then I, God, prospered that people.

38. When they became evil way of immoral way of both kings, people, then their empire was of full way lost forever, not of world power now.

39. United States was of defending more pure order during time nations of attack in last century were violent, immoral way; thus this nation I, your God, prospered to protect virtue, law-keeping peace way on all lands.

40. Now this nation hath become ripened in evil way of murder, of immoral way unto now promised judgment of thy God upon you, so a new people, even Israel from among all nations under heaven, soon to be gathered by my holy order of my Church, my holy way of full eternal salvation; to go to all lands, peoples, nations, tongues, governing power.

41. Now be humble, all nations, as judgment of great power of God cometh; a sudden appearing of a large orb striking earth, at angle coming toward world, a holy orb of people of Israel descent, not polluted by present generation of murder unholy order.

42. Such is fulfilling my word that Ten Tribes of Israel come from north country.

43. I am God. I made this earth.

44. I separated portion with such of faith of tribe of Ephraim, also other tribes after taken captive by Assyria in old time, Prophet leading few faithful to place of them being of planetary separation.

45. Let all be knowing I, God, have preserved that orb to return suddenly at angle no telescope detects.

46. Now do full order repentance; for such shall cause present world to reel to and fro as a drunken man, as Isaiah declared.

47. Read his prophecy to know I shall bring together all parts of world, including Enoch and his city, also a portion of world taken in separation order; to return to place I named of removal, even Gulf of Mexico; to be a holy people of Zion.

48. My Zion cometh soon.

49. Repent ye, repent ye, is thy Lord Jesus Christ own word to this generation, is my full holy word to all. Amen.

50. I, Jesus Christ, God over all, give my eternity truth, I come with ten thousand saints from Celestial realm to rule earth for a thousand years, dwelling in Zion, visiting nation of repentance, each one, with blessings; nations of wicked order with humbling, more wicked swept off the world, soon to be full measure.

51. Hear my will, and do my way of holy living on world, lest you cease to be a nation at all; for my holy way is to send fire from heaven to cleanse all world of wicked way.

52. A holy order shall rise in full power of righteous saints to govern all peoples remaining on earth.

53. Repent now, or lose opportunity to prepare for my holy Advent on world.

54. Now learn truth of eternity holy living.

55. Your spirit dieth not at death on earth.

56. You are son or daughter of my begetting in Celestial world, and you must not dwell only on earthly way to see present living is test unto eternal way of full order of God, testing what thou lovest; good, evil both before all of age who can be accountable, of sure record made of all thy doing.

57. It is spirit of my holy order power that records all things, so in day of judgment all things of individual living are presented to thy holy way of truth knowledge being of thy understanding.

58. Now awake.

59. Thou knowest thy memory can recall instantly experience from yesteryears.

60. Now this is example how I review thy individual living in day of full eternity power, Godhead power of right to judge all, yea, day of all raised from the holy order of spirit world living unto holy power raising all to life in immortality of spirit, body of risen particles of flesh apportioned thee, not of any other, only thy identity full restored by holy Godhood of atoning authority, to resurrect all; to be judged for all done on world of probation test way, now of thy dwelling on world.

61. Now be holy, so all will draw near to me, thy Lord Jesus Christ, who is the hope of saints of righteous of all generations of time, none lost, save traitor order.

62. Let all be holy now.

63. Judgment cometh.

64. Nothing is hidden.

65. I reveal secret of traitor to thee in government power to show all I can awake nation of power to truth, as you behold my word soon fulfilled.

66. Traitor is bought with aspiring promise of power when nation is subdued as enemy supposed; yet I, God over all, hold all in my power, and guide, by correct holy established eternal holy order, all increase.

67. Let not such be established who seeketh power by traitor order.

68. Now that I reveal this, do look at military placing at land where invading enemy could come to thy easy way to land as invading force.

69. Look at acquired communicatings of such that has China in admiration power in personal way order in government order.

70. Such plan to harm leader of nation if able; which I, your Lord, already warned him in previous corresponding message.

71. If he would do well, do not attend any business assembly hosted by representative of that enemy people of China; a land of gross way murder of unborn children order of unholy oppression; yet money order of nation upholds China as

financial power, having done own way of weakening thy own financial order by greed of business leaders with nation desiring thy overthrow.

72. Now look at truth, not just at diplomatic expression.

73. I know all things, and as I revealed to king of Israel of old, through my holy Prophet Isaiah, conspiracy against Judah by king of Syria, also tribe of Ephraim in secret unholy combining; so do I now reveal truth of present time evil conspiring among own governing power, easy to identify if of any pure holy motive to learn truth.

74. Now do so, lest my holy will go unheeded and all nation soon suffer.

75. Country of Cuba, also of Panama and Venezuela, are to be of conspiring with such enemy in time attack cometh.

76. Now be ready, is thy Lord's own word to nation of United States of America.

77. This from thy holy Lord, leaving government authority on own responsibility to do right, to free my holy order of pure Mouthpiece of God to this now world, of all people now of knowing I speak through him as my authority on world now of thy dwelling.

78. He speaketh truth.

79. He is of order of true way of no fear of world leader order in telling truth to all people on world.

80. Be apprised enemy of bitter way, blinded by apostate unholy lying order, now seeks his, my servant in bondage, harm.

81. I tell thee, to know he is of the way of harm by traitor order also.

82. Be of sure order to keep him safe from traitor order.

83. Now be of true justice. Examine motive of unholy witness order against government power dealing just way toward my Church in all courts.

84. Government of free nation hath wronged own governing law order, by not providing preserving way of religious holy order; thus you destroy principle of religious freedom for all.

85. Now do truth way -- my Church is revealed religion opposed by all religion of man way not of present order of revelation from God.

86. Now reflect on martyrdom of my Prophet Joseph Smith, why he was opposed from youth for telling true order of my visiting him as witness that I, God, am an immortal God in same way of man, of same form as man, yet of eternity holy order Godhead power over all creation.

87. My Celestial holy order includeth a world of my dwelling, as Moses described I dwell in all-consuming fire of eternal holy order of full creation governing order.

88. I speak to thy way of communication, so thy way of learning truth is not of confusion.

89. My power brought forth world of thy present now living.

90. All nature of organized natural living testifies of God being supreme intelligence order; not anything existing save by my holy power.

91. I speak, and all creation obeyeth, of more obedient holy obeying holy order of the order of nature, as you name such.

92. I can move mountain at a command, even the movement of the earth, unknown to you, altered, as I did in day earth was moved back to show Hezekiah my power.

93. Now believe Bible holy word, and know as I spoke to Prophet order then in day of faith among Israel, so do I speak today to Prophet holy called, holy ordained holy order.

94. Now be ye ready, is the will of thy Lord unto present generation on world.

95. Be holy, is the word of thy Lord; yea, thy holy Lord who is of soon coming to all pure people on world.

96. Be one in manner to receive word of salvation to thy land, when I send messenger of salvation soon to every peoples from Zion on land of my coming, Jackson County, Missouri, a place of the full order of Celestial power dwelling on world soon to come with thy Lord, unto all people on world knowing I am God, of my power, of true order of salvation to all people of all generations.

97. Know Zion is eternal power come to world, to rule surviving order in all lands on world.

98. Now be holy, lest thy own way be as a branch withered; broken off tree unto only of fire-consumed order at my holy Advent.

99. Repent ye, repent ye, all ye people on world, for the way of men shall not save you, only Godhead holy power of your Lord Jesus Christ, is my message to all nations on earth. Amen.

100. Now receive my will, to let my holy order of Priesthood holy authority go unto my Church; free to move and do without hindrance, telling nation to let my people go free to establish Zion on land of my coming.

101. Nation on land of Zion stole my land by government unholy persecution in my order of buying land through consecrating order in my Church.

102. Now my land shall again be in my hand, to do as I revealed; to build a new City of Holiness, New Jerusalem.

103. Now read Prophet Isaiah, of Zion rising in the last days of wicked people removed by judgment of God, to learn how I shall do so.

104. Read chapter 20, also all of Isaiah, to know promise of God to be of full way order fulfilling, as I spoke to him and also to all my Prophet order through ages of time, Joseph Smith my witness of seeing Godhead of Father and Son, as two exalted Gods in man's image, man created as Adam testified, written in holy writ of Bible.

105. Now believe exalted God speaketh true order of cleansing world you dwell on now, all ye people of world of telestial earthly order, probation way of testing all born on world of test order; you now knowing my purpose of each born on world, a holy calling for all peoples from their Father God.

106. Now receive my revealing, is the holy will of the order of God, who hath right to rule over all men, of all generations; who rules only in righteous order eternal power holy order.

107. Now receive more truth of holy way:

108. When I cometh, full Godhood power shall lift up faith order, as I named in New Testament record; lifting up pure holy peoples when earth rolls together as a scroll in power return of parts of world.

109. Know scripture is of full order in thy hand in Bible, also Doctrine and Covenants, Book of Mormon, Pearl of Great Price; my holy new revelation order now among all nations; my new revelings also recently sent to all leaders of national power of all peoples; to library way order for all to read holy warnings of God; to county government order throughout nation of United States of my land of my order of free exercise of holy speech, religion, privacy of living holy order of revealed religion.

110. Now let him, my servant on

world, go free, to show appreciation for this revealing coming to be a deliverance, if governing powers of noble motive do work of removing traitor unholy way order among military positioning authority among civil government hired order among military higher authority on national level of apportionment; not to be done by economic justification in this now danger period of time when weak way is being established in nation; to govern placing of military at easy location order to land military force on nation of my coming to world on earth order, of full knowing I am among you, all ye people of world, good or evil, all knowing I have appeared.

111. Let this be sober time to reflect, on eternity living, not just temporary pleasure-seeking of evil desires of unholy living of immoral way order, destructive to thy individual soul if following most corrupt way of adultery, Sodom, murder of unborn children holy order.

112. Now repent, to be of salvation eternally, is the will of God, who reigneth over all eternally; a holy God of full order power, to govern in holy order forever; I, your Redeemer, eternal power, atoning authority power forever present to bless all pure holy sons, daughters of holy living. Amen.

113. I, Jesus Christ, Son Ahman, the Beginning and the End, sent of my Father to redeem all who receive Gospel of salvation, do speak to entire way of all nations a holy word warning; to now be of holy way order of holy living, to survive judgment of power soon at hand.

114. Now repent to be surviving holy order.

115. Now learn my way to be holy order of full survival way through judgment order soon upon all nations; to repent, to be moral living holy life-preserving holy order; to never fight against God nor against His authority of holy revealed order of Priesthood.

116. Let all be holy order now.

117. Do so for salvation, also for life in this earthly existence sake.

118. This from thy God, who reigneth on high, in heaven, over world entire order, even now.

119. Let all be holy order of moral pure living; no longer of the life-taking of unborn youth; to never sin against life holy giving order. Amen.

SECTION REVELATION 179

Jesus Christ
Jehovah Son Ahman

Jesus Christ Speaketh Now Warning of Nuclear Terror Attack Within Borders of United States of America, Also in Nation of Israel, for Governing Authority in These Lands to Now Do Preventive Labor. Heed My Will, Saith Your Lord Jesus Christ, for Sake of Innocence Protected All Over World From Such Attack Resulting in War of Desolation if You Heed Me Not. Hear My Will:

Revelation of the Lord Jesus Christ
Palestine, Texas
Friday, May 25, 2012

1. Now let government over present nation of power on Zion land take my warning; to know enemy power shall do full way attack of nuclear order.

2. Let all do most holy humbling.

3. Nuclear way is to be not of use, lest entire world be destroyed.

4. Nation of Islamic power hath bomb.

5. They are soon to be of such aggressive way, United States is to be object.

6. Let this nation do diligent search through all boxes of freight order, the order of shipping off cargo freight source from land of Pakistan, not of knowing to present authority as threat. Missile organized to be of assembly on United States soil will be covered as freight for embassy of named land of source of the order of danger to government of United States; enemy power thinking when bomb of much destructive order power is on United States soil, then nation will think traitor order in own military exists, bringing military to temporary standstill by they of such way

to think own nation caused great nuclear destructive way on own land; enemy then poised to attack nation of my holy Jerusalem, Israel in old land.

7. Let military be to do full investigation on such freight as named; as you will learn I see all things.

8. Nuclear use will devastate nation of first use.

9. Do not be first aggressive using such unhallowed weapon that would also destroy many souls.

10. Now think of innocent many children I can preserve in all lands on earth if life is of full preserving.

11. Now, for government to prove to themselves I speak truth, go to the city of the capital of the land of the way of Asian nation Pakistan where freight is of usual way of United States receiving, to look there for such as shall soon be of freight order to a connection in my Zion land on port of the state of the most active foreign receiving in United States.

12. Let it be followed to order of

receiving to learn actual wicked organized traitor order in thy land. Nuclear weapon cometh by way of hiding in other machine of more peaceful deceiving, parts hidden in the way of no detecting as unseen, as though other peaceful-type machinery is encasement for disassembled portion of nuclear weapon, able to assemble parts, not of missile way; only of transport order from receiving wicked evil traitor way order, to city of their naming as population center to destroy much of city on United States soil, as distraction to also do this to Israel nation at same, after United States attack, near-time.

13. Now go search, ye government officials, to watch such as freight machinery of peaceful use from Pakistan to United States, to learn of unusual amount shipped at place of the usual receiving of peaceful machinery of large equipment type, equipment of contractor use of making large order of usual tractor large equipment order.

14. Now know source was of other Islamic nation to Pakistan; that allied nation to United States of the way to take any government inspecting off fervent guard way, thinking friendly allied land is of peaceful order still. Amen.

15. Now let United States do close watch, lest my warning go unheeded, and war come on thee of destructive order soon by formed coalition of now seeming economic peaceful trade; yet to, of way of trade, already place weapon order on American land soon of seeming usual freight as other peaceful order, even using second named peaceful allied nation to send order of weapon of destructive way unknown to government order; to do such as they would have done through Pakistan.

16. Now be of sure way watching all Pakistan freight to United States.

17. Do so for sake of life-saving holy order; for innocence sake of many not of evil intent in world; as conflict would spread throughout the order of military lands.

18. A holy way is to find such before wicked violent order has such in hand. Amen.

19. Let nation of Israel also be of government holy inspecting of all freight from nation of allied way, of equipment of construction way order hiding missiles, also bomb of nuclear means of placing in population city.

20. Let it be only examined; then follow to who is of such wicked destroying of innocence. Amen.

21. Now let this be of careful order holy done mail way; if government power doeth quiet watch way, they findeth who is of wicked way to destroy innocence.

22. If of way of no watching, all nation shall be disturbed, confounded, not of organized defending if of no heed to this, my word about aggression against United States, also against land of Old Jerusalem; some Islamic secret violent way in old order of martyrdom way, shall disrupt both nations unto great war of many nations.

23. Now awake.

24. Do investigation labor as I named, to find such attack of soon happening if not heeded by government order. Amen.

Chapter 8

**Jesus Christ Message of Only Peace
Holy Power Demonstrating to Ruler Order
to Make Peace in Holy Way Living**

SECTION REVELATION 180

Jesus Christ
Jehovah Christ

Revelation of the Lord Jesus Christ
Palestine, Texas
Sunday, June 10, 2012

1. Thus saith God, Jesus Christ, to all peoples on world:

2. Repent ye, repent ye -- my day of eternal power vengeance cometh in full power.

3. Thy earthly weapons are of no defense against armies of God of heaven order now on land.

4. O, be ye holy, for disease unhindered cometh; also storm of great power cometh, to cast down strength of nation for a time; to humble all to know thy Lord hath warned this world.

5. Now repent. Amen.

6. I, God, speaketh.

7. Zion order is rising.

8. Cleansing of world way taketh place in labor of true Church of thy God on earth.

9. Revelation cleanseth evil from my holy Church.

10. Thy Lord revealeth truth alone, not of deceived way.

11. All other way not of God hath murder of unborn child order among uninspired priestcraft order, of not revealed to leader way of all religions on world not of God.

12. Thus, all can know only where my holy will governeth entire, is my Church on world.

13. Come to me, all you of purity motive, by coming to my Priesthood; else judgment cometh onto false prophets and religion labor not of God. Amen.

14. Now come to him who holds Holy Priesthood authority of apostle order of full keys of holy power holy order; to receive truth unadulterated; else go down with the wicked forever.

15. Now let all church order to be truth-telling to their congregation, if they in church holy truth calling among all religion order who seek truth.

16. Let holy motive for eternal salvation be in all peoples who love free order of holy religion, that all may hear my solemn ruling order of pure intent; to be holy as I am holy. Amen.

17. Let full truth be God is truth, only truth.

18. Now be ye true youth of Christ, all of religious intent.

19. Be holy living according to scripture of my holy apostles.

20. Now learn truth order: Religion of all Protestant churches broken off from Catholic connection are also not holy original doctrine of Christ holy revealing --

21. All not of principle of now revelation from God; all lip-service way, not actual holy power of holy revealed order.

22. Now awake! If thy leader of thy religion hath not the oracles of God, they are not of me, your Lord.

23. My truth cometh by my appointment; not according to men or church congregation power of earthly power. In will of God coming to all my Church, holy revealings guide, administering of law of Church.

24. Now learn my servant is of the way as I was on world; the world derideth my word through him of pure motive to labor only for holy way of Christ's salvation.

25. All other religions only repeat word of former-time Prophets; all true Prophet order persecuted by false religion way in all time on world.

26. Thus he languisheth in unholy hands of evil world power.

27. Now learn he is witness against world rejecting my new and old word given, by my power, witnessing to all evil is rampant among all religions on earth; thus I prophesied evil would rise in persecuting true saints in John righteous holy writing, in Book of New Testament. Amen.

28. Let truth be followed; and revealed religion of my, Jesus Christ, your Lord's own revealing, hath always been of world rejected way.

29. Now see who is persecuted, everywhere spoken evil of; who is receiving new full truth revealings for all mankind, unto Christ coming as He foretold.

30. A holy religion is only holy, not of man only; as man steps forth to judge religion of revealed order by they openly denying gift of revealed order in authority.

31. Now judge. Who is thus persecuted?

32. Who is of no power of world power stepping forth to do my holy way of full truth telling?

33. Come to me through holy authority.

34. Do not persecute revealed holy religion at all; to be honest order of freedom of religion on land of holy freedom.

35. Let all come to me, your holy God, to earn salvation; not by lip-service of belief only, but by works of holy religion living.

36. A holy way is to analyze truth by comparing new revelation with former revealing of Christ and apostolic order.

37. Do so, and all agree, of true translation order of Bible. Amen.

38. Now do all thou canst to cause all national ruler order to stop murder of unborn youth from earliest time of holy conception, so such ceases by thy holy labor; lest all world be tainted by murder spirit of immoral way living.

39. Let all consider eternity ahead.

40. Do not do murder of own unborn child, lest innocent blood be on you in eternal judgment come on you hereafter; even of standing before God, who seeth all thy way of secret motive, such as to know willful order of such heinous murder of innocence.

41. Let all such know at my holy Advent, true order justice cometh by my revealing hearts of all.

42. Let not any be unholy from this time after reading my way, to not allow nation child murder of unborn youth legally at all from this time forth, lest all in nation reap full order holy God-sent holy judgment power, to cleanse earth entire, all save they who are innocent.

43. Be pure, to survive the day of whirlwind judgment of the Lord soon to take place; my warning now sent to all peoples on world of thy inhabiting.

44. Now repent, is my call to all authorities of national power of all lands. Amen.

45. Now call on thy peoples to overthrow all leaders of murder order, who

come to power by unholy bloodshed way order.

46. Let peace way to demonstrate be entire way; not descending to like violent order, both of shedding innocent blood in conflict.

47. Do not evil when seeking to overthrow evil governing authority.

48. Go direct to them in population power, as I inspired Gandhi in India to do.

49. Let all true order of pure living do so. Amen.

50. Thus be peace-loving, ye who are political persecuting object of unholy national power order.

51. Let all people thus establish peace in own land.

52. I, God, can remove evil order when justified by people repenting of their wrong way, unto full obeying order of law of pure holy living; giving all people their God-given rights of freedom of holy order of religion freedom.

53. Now come forward in peace holy demonstrating way as population of thy land shows leaders of thy land you all want peace in holy living way; not to continue innocent bloodshedding by order of terror way.

54. Now be holy. Amen.

55. Now be my holy order, saith Jesus Christ, of peace.

56. Let all populations of all nations rise to peaceful holy no-violence, no order of weapons on hand at all in own possessing; to do as Egypt was inspired in part; for some were of rock, brick throwing, not of peace; thus bloodshed ensued.

57. Now do only order of holy peace-loving and doing. Amen.

58. Now let all be holy, is the God over all nations' word. Amen.

59. I, your Lord, now tell all peoples on earth, dearth is soon.

60. Be of full storing food now in all national powers, lest untold untimely death cometh because leader order neglected my word.

61. Remember Joseph in Egypt warned, storing seven years of food extra; now do so, as I shall humble all nations that forget God. Amen.

SECTION REVELATION 181

Jesus Christ
Jehovah Son Ahman

Thus Is My Holy Will, Saith Jesus Christ, God Over All Nations, to Nation of Korea, Both North Aggressive Land of Evil Combining With the Rulers of China, Against South Korea, Then United States and Asian Allies of Taiwan, Japan -- My Holy Order of Full Way to Be of Now Peace Dwelling on World; Not Aggressive of Either First Order Attack, Nor of Second Order of Retaliation, if South Korea and Allies Desire God Over All the Earth to Preserve Them of Innocence Order, Not of Murder Nor Aggressive Order. Hear My Way of Peace-Establishing Holy Love-for-Life Order Between Nation of Separate Border From Aggressive Way of Fighting in Way of Full Conflict, Unhallowed Order in Early 1950 Decade. Hear My Will. Amen.

Revelation of the Lord Jesus Christ
Palestine, Texas
Thursday, May 31, 2012

1. The God of glory speaketh, Jesus Christ, Jehovah, the Beginning and the End; even He who was God before the earth was of existence -- I speaketh strong warning to the Korea nation of allied to United States of America: North Korea is in alliance with China to bring United States into conflict in Korea, causing China to aid North Korea, weakening United States ability to defend own land.

2. Know South Korea, no matter what aggressive assault cometh, forbear. Retaliate not this attack.

3. They would then use greater bombing, to overthrow South Korea, then invade land of Japan; thereafter, world will be in unholy conflict.

4. Now hear my will, saith God over all nations, to not be offense first strike for thy Lord to be of defending you.

5. Let a holy order of forbearance rule governing power in both South Korea, Taiwan, also United States; as Taiwan would easily be of conquered order.

6. Now let North Korea and China of unholy organized attack know if they do so of first full aggression, I, God, interveneth, and shall eventually completely destroy thy nation, each in order of unhallowed life-taking order of the aggression way to seek power on world over other peoples.

7. Now let all hear me, Jesus Christ, God of holy power --

8. I soon cometh in full glory power, to rule all peoples on world now of full way wicked.

9. Cleanse own peoples of sin of murder of unborn youth in own lands; also overthrow immoral way of adultery, of

money earning by immoral way living, of Sodom, of adultery way of selling women and youth to people for evil way abuse way.

10. Let thy governing power in all nations do this national cleansing, else my almighty power cometh; to cleanse way before me; for Man of Holiness is my name; righteous judgment and holy order of pure justice is my way.

11. Do all holy cleansing to be surviving people.

12. Now beware, North Korea standeth in personal way to help aggression of China, by being first unholy aggressing power.

13. This is well awaring in recent island and military ship order unprovoked aggressive attacks against South Korea in recent year.

14. Now do full holy life-saving way order of talk with North Korea, showing in way of truth-telling they cannot attain south land of Korea and survive conflict.

15. Do so in peace-seeking, forgiving recent North Korean aggressive unholy attacks; so much as to send food, clothing to North Korea to feed their order of poor, of the way of humanitarian good done; and to show thy God you would forgive, returning good deed to aggressive nation; so you may be justified for God to defend thy people in large conflict.

16. Now do this, soon, to show peaceful intent, even before peace order is fully of holy order done.

17. Now show no military aggressive return force.

18. Thou hast nuclear bomb order.

19. Thou art of power to destroy all of North Korea from full defense order.

20. Do not be offensive order.

21. Only be true order of peace-living toward all peoples;

22. Yet if unholy murder against unborn child order, other evil of immoral order, you shall not be a nation when I cometh, thine own evil answered upon thyself.

23. Let all nations be of holy order of cleansing child unborn youth order murder from own nation; to survive conflict soon on world, also God-sent whirlwind judgments soon to cleanse these sins off all lands. Amen.

24. Thus saith the holy Lord to all my Israel: Gather to land of Zion; Judah to Old Jerusalem; to receive thy Lord soon, is my holy call to Israel; knowing this holy order of God coming to world soon; prepare ye, all of pure Israel, to know lineage by patriarchal order blessing; of now in my Church.

25. Now come, to assist my order of holy Order Eternal Union holy way Celestial order; to be of holy temple ordinance receiving soon by hand of holy Keyholding authority already on world, yet held in unjust order of persecution bondage these years of world now knowing he is of me, Jesus Christ, and Eternal Union Order, Celestial power order extant.

26. All who seek salvation through thy Lord and atoning power of Godhead authority over all peoples of every nation, past, present, and on to eternity order, come to my authority who receiveth this, my will; to obey Eternal Union holy law. Amen.

27. Now come, all holy people on earth, to receive my will, through my son of Keyholding holy power, Warren Jeffs known on earth; whom I have placed full eternal holy order of Apostleship and full keys of sealing order.

28. Now come to me through Priesthood.

29. Free him.

30. Do so now, if any on earth desire salvation.

31. Let governing powers be petitioned by all honest in heart.

32. My order Celestial power holy order governs all world, all creation.

33. Feel my truth-peace in soul of they who are more pure order of personal living, the witness of these, my eternity truths, saith your holy power redeeming Lord, Jesus Christ. Amen.

SECTION REVELATION 182

Jesus Christ
Jehovah Son Ahman

I, Jehovah, Even Your Holy God, Speak to Israel, Holy Word, to Now Heed, Lest Thy Land Be of No People Soon. I Give Way for Victory Order Holy Way of God Defending Israel if They Be More Holy Than Enemy; Else All Alike Be of No People in Own Land. Use Not Any Nuclear Weapon as First Aggression Against Any Nation. Hear My Will to Israel:

Revelation of the Lord Jesus Christ
Palestine, Texas
Monday, June 4, 2012

1. I, your holy Lord, Jesus Christ, speaketh to all people of nation of present day Israel, to go to other land soon, not of thy land, in a way to do full labor with governing power, to show full way disagreeing of present governing power using nuclear weapon order on foreign nation in first strike unholy order; which retaliation from angry order of allied nation on Israel shall destroy most of Israel nation.

2. All leave now, if life is to be of holy life-saving for self and family.

3. Deterrent use of no-use will not be usual order if leader useth such aggressive force of full nuclear weapon unholy life-taking way, lest none remain.

4. Let all population go into other allied land of now more freedom way of Egypt, taking own food, clothing stored, holy way preparing order, where I, God, Jehovah, shall deliver Israel again.

5. If leader useth nuclear weapon of soon way order, after a terrorist order explodeth nuclear bomb in large order Israel city if government power of Israel ignoreth my recent world-order message sent; if terror order doeth such, then strike not with nuclear way of full power; to use still as deterrent way defending order.

6. I, God, seeth world conflict soon to be all nation of full nuclear power unholy use way, if such way of hasty retaliation happeneth.

7. Now use usual weapon order if other combinating nation of the way of Moslem uniting of nation of Iran, all order of such who combine against thee, when aggression causeth thee, Israel, to defend, then use no nuclear war way, only usual defending weapon order, to conquer all land near thy nation, to make Syria subservient, Moslem land of Jordan, Iraq and other combined against thee way of Moslem attack way; to subdue all at same time, as I see you first remove, now, child murder unholy murder of unborn child order from thy nation; else full cleansing cometh to thee, Israel, few remaining if unholy way is of thy doing against unborn youth holy order.

8. Now learn God doth speak.

9. Learn from scripture to Moses, thy Lord speaketh to Prophet order on earth, to guide Israel to victory if of holy way justified.

10. Remember scattering of Jew order after they persecuted apostle order of my Church, in Old Jerusalem being full way destroyed, not one stone of original temple left on another, as I, your Lord, told nation of Israel before they crucified their Lord, as Isaiah said in telling a child would be born among them to be governing power in last days of world.

11. I am He that speaketh this order of holy message way holy will of God of all nations on world; telling all to have no aggressive way at all, lest aggressive unholy nation cease to exist.

12. Do not use nuclear weapon way to defend, lest all thy land not be of use until I, God, burn land with fire from heaven as Ezekiel, my Prophet, named.

13. Now be holy order of defending original Israel land so I may come where I ascended, Mount of Olives near Old Jerusalem, to do full cleansing of Israel nation, to be converted that the promised Messiah hath already been on world.

14. Now repent, all nations on earth today.

15. I, Jesus Christ, Jehovah holy Redeemer, reveal terror group planneth nuclear bomb of hidden way through nation of Pakistan trade way; yea, Iran trade order through another terror group of sympathy with Palestine order; to use in large way city of Israel way soon if not of examining heavy earth-moving equipment order of import order.

16. Follow such to destination to capture terror order of nuclear way attack.

17. Heed my full previous sent holy word, to do full attack of defending order, not first attack unholy aggressive way.

18. Let all nations on world hold back when nuclear weapon is of full way use, to not be murder in mass order.

19. Great is evil order on world.

20. Evil doeth not good.

21. Do not let leader use nuclear weapon of first attack. Amen.

Chapter 9

SECTION REVELATION 183

Jesus Christ
Jehovah Christ, Son Ahman

I, Jesus Christ, Speak Eternity Truth to All Peoples on World: Now Be for Life, Unto Eternal Order Judgment, Saith God.

Revelation of the Lord Jesus Christ
Palestine, Texas
June 2012

1. Come to pure truth, saith God, to all nations, to learn of God eternity holy way full truth; life of unborn child order beginneth at concepting holy way order, not after weeks of development; for all element order of life is present at conceiving hour, not at time only when breath of life is of first taking.

2. Living child outside womb needs be of own breathing way to be living soul on earth, to be of spirit order receiving own tabernacle.

3. They who do procedure on early expecting order are full guilt order eternal way before me, saith God, even Jesus Christ, thy eternal Judge; yea, all shall be of guilt eternally for child unborn youth murder of unborn even to have that which is of life at concepting order, as full intent to destroy life, such are guilty before heaven of the sin unforgivable, if of harm way intent to harm life order of such unforgivable sin way.

4. Therefore, repent all nations.

5. My revealing here shall stand as full testimony against all nations, people, tongues, kindreds, governing order in all lands, my word sent to all nations of sure knowing my word, of from order of judge of thy now order of no ignorance of such heinous sin as taking of life of innocent order of unborn youth order.

6. I shall judge all such purposeful murder of unborn child order as eternal full power punishing power, as though taking life of any of full term birth-living order.

7. Let no one be of the believing evil false order of medical order who get gain at doing such life removal order in women of expecting holy order.

8. Guard unborn child living order as with thy own life, nourishing and caretaking entire, to preserve life of such as could be born and grow to be of good on world.

9. Now learn my eternal way, all riseth from grave by God power atoning power of thy holy God, Jesus Christ.

10. Nothing is hidden from all people.

11. Now do self-cleansing.

12. If of guilt way, do no more order of murder of unborn child order at all, which bringeth even greater eternal punishment after knowing such is of guilty order.

13. Repent!

14. Cease destroying life order entire, if of any repentance. Amen.

SECTION REVELATION 184

Jesus Christ
Jehovah Son Ahman

Revelation of the Lord Jesus Christ
Palestine, Texas
Monday, June 11, 2012

1. Your holy Lord is of full order of governing power to nation of Bosnia, a holy will of thy holy Lord to now make peace order of full diplomatic order as war is soon to be in way of Europe in full order way.

2. Do full negotiating with neighboring order nation of order of unholy conflict of past history order.

3. A holy order is to not attack first order, nor retaliate in next attack, showing desire for peace order.

4. Do so now, lest world order war is of full order.

5. Do not retaliate save full destructive order is upon nation.

6. A holy order is to do full negotiating to be of thy Lord's holy way doing.

7. Now be peace loving, not to destroy enemy.

8. All are mine, saith God, even your holy order holy Redeemer, Jesus Christ, of holy power over all nations on world extant.

9. Now do peace order in own nation to do full order life-saving peace order.

10. Do this now, is thy God's own will to nation of Bosnia. Amen.

SECTION REVELATION 185

Jesus Christ
Jehovah Son Ahman

I, Jesus Christ, Holy One of Israel, Speak Word of Military Counsel to Leader Order of Nation of Israel, to Never Be First Aggressor in Large Conflict. Hear My Holy Will:

Revelation of the Lord Jesus Christ
Palestine, Texas
Monday, June 11, 2012

1. Let nation of Israel receive my holy will concerning war of great force of Moslem nation combining other Moslem order.

2. When thou seest unholy gathering to nation of thy border, Jordan, know full order conflict is soon, as combined nation order shall attack from all sides of thy now border order.

3. Do not be first aggressor.

4. Take care to not attack first order.

5. Do defensive way, no nuclear order, and I, Jehovah, shall intervene and spare thy land.

6. If you attack of first unholy aggression order, you shall be defeated to only be shadow governing order subserving order to other nation order enemy of harsh governing way order.

7. Do not be first to attack, to justify God to intervene for Israel's gathering sake.

8. This from God, even Jehovah, Jesus Christ, your Lord, who is all power unto survival order nation who does also full order cleansing of legal consent order of murder of unborn child unholy way of child murder unborn order.

9. You guard youth who are full term born, yet not youth unborn order, who could come to full living order in mortal life on world I am soon to come in full order power.

10. Now attend to these, my will, to nation of Israel, to survive full combined attack soon to come. Amen.

SECTION REVELATION 186

Jesus Christ
Jehovah Son Ahman

I, Your Lord Jesus Christ, Speaketh to All Peoples of the Earth, Another Great Final Warning of My Coming and to Repent of Unborn Child Youth Murder, Yea, the Aborting Murder of Unborn Youth and Also Other Immoral Sins. Hear My Word of Great Warning, for I Cometh.

Revelation of the Lord Jesus Christ
Palestine, Texas
Sunday, June 24, 2012

1. Thus saith the Lord Jesus Christ to the nation of the United States of America: I cometh soon to that holy land where Zion, New Jerusalem, shall be built, and you must be pure to endure the day; for my coming shall be as the clouds of heaven, eternal fire to cleanse land of all impurities, every corruptible thing removed from land; and there shall be whirlwind judgments sent of the nature that there will be full cleansing of the wicked off this land, other nations also being cleansed of the sin of child murder of unborn youth, wherein the shedding of innocent blood taketh place in the heart and the soul of parent order, of immoral conduct order.

2. Thus saith the Lord God of heaven, I shall cleanse the entire nation if needs be,

if they continue in this corrupt way; and ye shall know I have spoken in my day of vengeance upon such heinous crime as shedding of innocent blood, which your nation allows by rule of law at this time, yet persecutes my Church and Kingdom upon the earth of the pure living.

3. I am cleansing my Church of this most heinous crime, that any who have been of such order are removed from Church, that my Church will become pure.

4. Know this, that apostate order are generally of this sin, who went to world way of removing of unborn youth way, willingly, knowingly, and are of apostate way, no longer member of Church or of my Holy Priesthood.

5. Therefore when apostates speak to thee, they are of murder order against unborn youth order, and have lost the Spirit of God entire.

6. Believe them not. Their report is lie against the pure in heart of my Church and Kingdom; and you, if you accept their word and sympathize with them, would be of similar sin by assent by joining with them against my Priesthood, not able to be preserved against the whirlwind judgments I shall send.

7. Therefore, I give this sacred revealing.

8. Repent ye, repent ye, all ye people who dwell on the American continents, my land of Zion where New Jerusalem shall be built, Enoch's city of a full New Jerusalem visit and way; more to be revealed in future time.

9. Hear my word: Cleanse thine own nations, ye peoples of the earth, of the sin of the shedding of innocent blood of unborn child youth and the immoral way that leads to that great sin, lest you be no surviving order in the great holocaust of whirlwind judgments and great war soon at hand, for you heed me not, that war cometh.

10. I have called on all nations to make peace and withdraw their military from attacking ability, and to only guard their own borders and to not be of attacking nuclear warfare way.

11. Therefore, hasten to prepare. I cometh, saith Jesus Christ, even God over all creation. Even so. Amen.

12. Now hear my word further.

13. There cometh a dearth of great cleansing of all wicked of unbelief.

14. Store food if you would be of a believing way in thy different lands throughout the earth.

15. And it shall be a dearth not just by weather causing, but because trade and commerce ceaseth in most places on earth during war time and other judgment time.

16. Be of diligence in storing clothing, food, and proper medicine way that is not of the harm way of unborn youth.

17. I, the Lord, cometh. Amen.

SECTION REVELATION 187

Jesus Christ
Jehovah Son Ahman

I, Your Lord and Redeemer, Jesus Christ, Sendeth Own Word to the Full Indian Tribe Order to Be of Knowing Thy Future Calling to Cleanse Zion Order Holy Land. Do So, as Full Order Holy Power Holy Full Way Full Cleansing Order as Book of Mormon Declares Mine Own Will. Do Full Preparing Order Now. A Holy Way Is to Do So as My Other New Will Cometh Through Visit Holy Order of Holy Angel Order Soon. Amen.

Revelation of the Lord Jesus Christ
Palestine, Texas
Sunday, June 24, 2012

1. The holy way of Lamanite holy nation on land of Zion must cease usury money order of unholy gambling order, lest they go down and no longer exist in place of such unholy order.

2. Let my will go to all tribes now, to know Jesus Christ, God over all national powers of world, speaketh.

3. Lamanite tribe of power, when nation goeth to no power to defend self, must then do full power holy cleansing, as Book of Mormon holy record of my own will therein printed in Third Nephi.

4. Now do holy living, else other holy Israel people of Ten Tribes cometh in holy power to do full holy order cleansing of thy nation of Indian peoples, with all people Zion land. Amen.

SECTION REVELATION 188

Jesus Christ
Jehovah Son Ahman

I, Jesus Christ, Send Own Will to President Order of National Power of United States, Also China and to the President of Russia, My Will.

Revelation of the Lord Jesus Christ
Palestine, Texas
Sunday, June 24, 2012

1. I, the Lord of all the earth, speak to leaders of United States of America, also of China and Russia main leader who is supreme authority: I, God, even your Redeemer, God over all creation, who sees the full world all at same instant, now tells all three supreme order leader-president order ruling order of all three power lands, I behold thy own conduct is adulterous order, you all of murder of unborn child order abortion order in own living evil murder of unborn youth order.

2. Now know thy example leadeth each land of people of thy personal life example being evil murder of unborn youth order.

3. I, God, declare thy own life each shall be of only the way of short time on world of thy now living, as the way of evil is among they of own way of power, to remove each from power, because you do unholy way of murder of unborn youth of aborting way, a practice of immoral living.

4. Now repent, lest full opposing power of own way political national order remove thee in full way from all way of living on world; God causing enmity in own house; also friendless soon, as to world not of thy staying after own political order removeth each; history showing my word of full order fulfilling. Amen.

SECTION REVELATION 189

Jesus Christ
Jehovah Son Ahman

I, God, Speak Purity Word to All World, to Prepare for My Coming. Amen.

Revelation of the Lord Jesus Christ
Palestine, Texas
Thursday, June 28, 2012

1. Love order in world is of sin way.

2. Love order in God is of pure holy way living.

3. Now come, all nation of land of my coming, to be holy unto God, not of murder of unborn youth order of no care for unborn child holy order of my sending.

4. Now come to full order of repenting, all nations on earth.

5. Now be pure order entire in holy living to pure order of living.

6. Both saint and they not of Church of Jesus Christ must be of no murder of innocent blood of unborn youth holy order to survive judgment of God on world now of thy dwelling. Amen.

SECTION REVELATION 190

Jesus Christ
Son Ahman

Jesus Christ, God Over All World, Sendeth Sure Will of Judgment of the Holy Order Godhead Power to Do Full Order Holy Repenting Order, for Full Ceasing Child Unborn Youth Murder. Hear My Word to All Lands, Nations, Peoples, Tongues, Governing Order of All Lands:

Revelation of the Lord Jesus Christ
Palestine, Texas
Sunday, July 15, 2012

1. Thus saith the Lord to all nations on world: Go to thy homes now to mourn, as murder of unborn child order sickeneth the heavens.

2. You are of full iniquity in full order murder, shedding the most innocent blood.

3. Now repent, all order of physician, government unholy way doing.

4. Life begins at the time of conception, not after growth time.

5. Now be awake; my full cleansing of world soon cometh. Amen.

6. The full order of Godhead over this world shall meet soon on world in New Era of Peace; no murder of innocent bloodshed can exist among surviving nation order on world.

7. Do full ceasing of legal way of such heinous crime, else full order pure Godhood of my power cometh to end all such evil on earth in full power judgment of God. Amen.

8. Now tell all thy nation population in all nation order, I, Jesus Christ, God over all, soon cometh. Amen.

9. Let my people of my holy name Church on world do full cleansing, no murder of unborn youth, to have all such no-member forever. Amen.

10. Now cleanse full order of physician rules order, to not allow the removal of the unborn in any land on world by physician order.

11. I, God, have seen full murder of full term unborn child order, even in some heathen lands; removed child hath its head smashed unto full taking of youth-born life undesired by anyone. Amen.

12. Now do full cleansing in own land, lest eternity judgment cometh on individual of such upholding child murder.

13. This also includeth harlot prostituting unholy way in all lands, who do immediate aborting by pill of contraceptive pill order, removing life conceived order immediate way done unholy immoral order.

14. Such also have only murder of unborn child order in heart, both men and unholy female harlot way, way of full murder clinic hospital way, pill order, or herbal evil intent to remove life order.

15. All such are of murder intent of innocent child unborn order.

16. Know ye not, all people on world, I, God, am the Giver of life, not of death order?

17. Such is my creation power, to bring life to soul.

18. Now know God is just.

19. All such shall be of full order holy judgment of God in time of resurrection judgment; for nothing is hidden. Amen.

20. Tell all thy people I cometh to judge all.

21. Let no murder of living order also be of thy legal way of innocent order where you defend murder of purpose way order unto no capital punishment order.

22. Such purposeful way of murder of anyone not of own call to be of life loss is such an unholy premeditated order of murder.

23. Eternal law is required of nation of any land to take life of murder order who do purpose order murder.

24. Now learn God shall come to do full justice, knowing all.

25. Let wicked tremble at my appearing. Amen.

26. Now do full cleansing of law order so no nation allows any legal order murder. Amen.

27. Let also all physician/nurse order be now ceasing all removal of fetus of any way save God should train justified care order of mother life order, tubal pregnancy order not of full ability to grow.

28. Thus sure way knowing such is case must be in place, else you do unholy way interfering with God of Creating order.

29. Do no more unholy removal of living able to grow unborn child order, lest murder of shedding innocent blood be upon all such physician/nurse order,

none exempt from eternal justice of God. Amen.

30. Let national leaders set example to personally live pure life-saving way of no abortive of unborn child order full murder in sight of the order of Godhead over present world. Amen.

31. Let all thy hospital order learn this, my will, saith God, to all nation order on world. Amen.

32. As physician unholy way order murdereth unborn child order, such break oath of life-saving covenant. Amen.

33. Let thy youth in all nation order be of the way to respect life of unborn for own eternity sake. Amen.

34. Now do full truth-telling.

35. Government order that is upholding this order of unholy way murder of unborn child holy order shall come to end. Amen.

36. This is God's own will. Amen.

SECTION REVELATION 191

Revelation of the Lord Jesus Christ
Palestine, Texas
Monday, July 9, 2012

1. To all order of full murder of unborn child order:

2. You are guilty of shedding innocent blood, God speaking to all such; as are of full knowing with intent to harm unborn youth order.

3. Do not continue such heinous crime to hide immoral order of all such as murder unborn order to hide immoral sin way unholy order. Amen.

4. Now know such was sin of ancient Babel when tower was of height of three miles, of such sin, to do aborting at top to hide sin from justice of power of God.

5. They thought to offer blood sacrifice to Lucifer to deliver them from God's judgment for doubt to spread over world to populate after flood.

6. Do not sin same way any longer.

7. Such shall be thy full way judgment.

8. Only a small portion at Babel survived, most of this damning evil of murder of unborn child order.

9. Now be holy order child preserving order, all people on world of my soon coming. Amen.

SECTION REVELATION 192

Revelation of the Lord Jesus Christ
Palestine, Texas
Monday, July 9, 2012

1. Thus saith God, Jesus Christ, to all nations, my power resteth over all lands to preserve all who are of pure innocent holy living.

2. Come to God through prayer soon, in time He sendeth full judgment way sending.

3. Prayer of any guilty of aborting, thus of murder of unborn youth order, shall be in vain.

4. Do not such sin way, all peoples on world.

5. I only hear prayer order of innocent order entire, who do not hypocritical way of destroying unborn child life, seeking own life to be of preserved order.

6. Such shall meet end. Amen.

7. Now repent, all leaders of nations.

8. Come away from legal consent to abortion of unborn child order.

9. When nation is of euthanasia of self-murder unholy order, soon to be considered legal death order, nation is ripe for destructing power of God; for other violent mob rule shall soon be on such who legalize self-destroying order.

10. Now repent, any nation allowing euthanasia of self-murder order, not even for terminally ill medical order of doctor naming no way healing order for such who suffer illness order.

11. Do not this evil, for lawmaker order who legalize further way of murder shall be accountable to me, your God over all, in day of holy resurrection. Amen.

SECTION REVELATION 193

Message to Russia, China by Jesus Christ

Revelation of the Lord Jesus Christ
Palestine, Texas
Monday, July 9, 2012

1. Now come to me, all nations of sure order of way to do full cleansing of Zion land if all are of Israel. Amen.

2. Now tell Russia, China, they shall be cleansed if use of nuclear weapon anywhere on world.

3. Let this be God's warning to both if of nuclear weapon use at all, to cease such, else full God-given judgment come to such as use the Luciferian weapon at all. Amen.

SECTION REVELATION 194

Revelation of the Lord Jesus Christ
Palestine, Texas
Sunday, July 15, 2012

1. I, God, over all world, dwelling on earth soon among men, cometh soon in power to cleanse all nations.

2. Do full order no war preparing in own nation to survive; as war nation shall have full judgment of God. Amen.

SECTION REVELATION 195

Revelation of the Lord Jesus Christ
Palestine, Texas
Wednesday, August 1, 2012

1. Thus saith Jesus Christ, God of all the earth, to all inhabitants thereof: I come as a holy order of Celestial order holy power, to cause all evil to be consumed entire, of the way to purify all nations. Amen.

2. Come to me, all peoples of all lands.

3. Come to He who giveth life to all, who conquered the grave for all to rise resurrected in immortal flesh, raised to be judged what degree of happiness they earned on world of probationary mortal flesh. Amen.

4. Let all now be holy on all lands.

5. Now come to me, your Lord, lest sudden judgment come.

6. France is near full wicked order; few to remain on earth if of nuclear weapon use; also let England not use any nuclear weapon to be a surviving nation.

7. Amsterdam repenteth not; sudden full judgment covereth such with sea heaving beyond bounds.

8. Also Liechtenstein is corrupt total, worthy for full judgment.

9. Now repent.

10. Germany is immoral order entire.

11. Few shall be remaining after full judgment. Amen.

12. Indonesia with Brunei lieth in path of my full judgment, total loss of living entire.

13. Japan, China repenteth not of heinous abortion sin way, immoral order causing full judgment to come on both after war. Amen.

14. Now know I reward into eternity, all men, women, child order. Amen.

15. Come full repenting order of humbling thyself, all on world.

16. My glorious coming is a holy event, of heaven power come to world to govern.

17. Joseph Smith, my latter-day Prophet is third member of Godhead over this world under God the Father, and His holy Son of God the Redeemer. Amen.

18. Now know Celestial power shall bind all power order of evil, so devil is bound.

19. Let all who sin, repent; for no sin can dwell on world of Zion holy order, save cast out of Zion order to own place, to be subjugated by the Kingdom of God on world, all peoples acknowledging my right to rule as Creator of this world, even Jesus Christ, Son Ahman.

20. Though many deride against my holy name, I shall be feared by the wicked nations on earth, to the way of they all submitting to my holy governing order. Amen.

21. Now come to me, to Zion, to God's rule, to enjoy Eternal Union power of God.

22. Come to my order now of Keyholding power of Celestial governing power called Priesthood after the order of the holy Son of God. Amen.

23. The nation of Mauritania is most corrupt, also Libya, as all North Africa nation order, all to be such way cleansed to have none remain if people in such nations are murder of unborn child order, other evil violent order, by great war soon to come.

24. Repent, repent, all nations of world.

25. Day of sorrow cometh on all nations. Amen.

26. Let also Mali, Botswana, South Africa, neighboring nations all cease child slavery, murder of child order, of women.

27. Now do so, lest full cleansing take place of thy nation power entire. Amen.

28. Now tell own peoples I, God, cometh on world of thy inhabiting.

29. Believe Bible message of my own word, saith Jesus Christ, through apostle holy witness order during my time on world. Amen.

SECTION REVELATION 196

Jesus Christ
Son Ahman

I, Your Lord, Jesus Christ, Speak Through My Holy Servant on World, a Holy Order of Full Military Counsel to Leader Order of United States, to Preserve All From Tragedy Planned by Evil Power Over Enemy Order, Both Other Power of Nation Order Coalition Against United States; Also Internal Evil Planning of Harm to Nation if Largest Bomb of Any Time Previous Is Assembled. Do Not This Evil. Amen. Now Read My Full Now Warning. Amen.

Revelation of the Lord Jesus Christ
Palestine, Texas
Tuesday, August 21, 2012

1. I, your holy Lord, come.

2. Let all now be holy Order Union Eternal. Amen.

3. Now come to Priesthood.

4. Free my servant from prison, ye leader power over land of so-called freedom.

5. Now show you have true love for justice and truth.

6. He is of me, your God.

7. I guide him daily in truth knowing.

8. All he is of the way of truth telling.

9. Come to me, your God, Jesus Christ, soon, through my servant Warren Jeffs, my Keyholding power of full holy order governing authority, to bless of God Eternal Union Order unto eternal lives.

10. Now learn eternity truth.

11. All not of me, your Lord, shall be damned unto no glory happy way.

12. Now come to God who already revealeth truth about judgment order on world.

13. Syria shall be of internal way to harbor weapon of great destruction from the communist realm soon; unto keeping my holy seed of Israel at bay from full attack.

14. Know this is time Israel shall attack, not to wait for Syria to use nuclear weapon.

15. Also Iran to not use nuclear power in bombing way against the other power she now calleth satan order, United States of America.

16. Let no package of large order come to nation through Pakistan, lest nuclear weapon come among United States.

17. Do full examining of all such hiding of nuclear weapon, under the label of farm equipment.

18. Now use full investigating, so all is secure; for if weapon is used, full war cometh to entire world of arming selves.

19. Let not this happen, ye power over nation of United States of America. Amen.

20. Let also President of nation learn CIA hath a plan to assassinate him if he

causeth any order of disrupting economic order according to power of money order over banking industry.

21. I reveal this happened to President John F. Kennedy, a CIA agent sent by the power that had the control over agency secret murder order; Oswald was pawn.

22. Now be only careful with trust order of secret service alone around thee. Amen.

23. Let also all Senate and House of Representatives be honest labor for freedom, and write to the President to free my son of religious persecuted order for teaching eternity truth. Amen.

24. Let President of nation also beware nation of China alliance.

25. Venezuela is of harm to south border of nation.

26. Place sufficient defense in southern shores. Amen.

27. Let also nation set aside the law allowing child murder of unborn child order, lest whole land receive promised judgment of God named in Doctrine and Covenants -- of war, famine, earthquake, windstorms, mob rule at time of no power to govern in peace power when economy faileth through the order of the nation under rule of one who is neglectful of national order of preserving own economy in time world banking order is of faltering power again; which I, God, allowed in part at the first of present President's office holding.

28. Now believe bank order shall crumble. Amen.

29. Let also Senate do full investigation of rule of House Armed Forces Committee for order of the assigning funds for weapon of full power over a full loss of living order of largest magnitude, a secret weapon not now in full order ready way, that could be of drop on a land, and millions of people die.

30. Such is Luciferian weapon, to be of use if war against the united power of large order coalition nations opposing United States as world power order. Amen.

Jesus Christ

SECTION REVELATION 197

Jesus Christ
Son Ahman

Revelation of the Lord Jesus Christ
Palestine, Texas
Wednesday, September 19, 2012

1. Thus saith the Lord to all nations, my coming draweth nigh.

2. Now do full order holy repenting. Amen.

3. Send an emissary to my servant Warren, to know my will of thy land in now war coming, lest I humble all to no war, by greater God-sending judgment order.

4. Now repent of way of war.

5. Do no aggressive war labor at all. Amen.

Jesus Christ

SECTION REVELATION 198

Jesus Christ
Son Ahman

I, Jesus Christ, Send All-Important Order Call to Leader of United States of America, for Defense on Land of Nation. Amen.

Revelation of the Lord Jesus Christ
Palestine, Texas
Monday, August 27, 2012

1. I, Jesus Christ your Lord, speak to the ruler of the nation of United States of supreme authority over all other order of the enforcing of word of government order; to let the order of no nuclear first strike happen, to be only self-defending order if you desire thy God to intervene in war soon to take place.

2. Navy shall have full attack of missile way, to hinder national holy defense order.

3. Now know I, God, control all; and according to pure holy order motive of

any leader, notwithstanding thy many sin way against unborn youth order, I, God, am to come to more pure on world soon, and declare Gospel order to all who remain after more of the evil of man is fully of removal from world. Amen.

4. Now learn in Italy among NATO military are the traitor order revealing to Russia all NATO defense order of command; to do full way order hinderment of all such self-defending of Europe allies order.

5. The two are high in own nation military, already of traitor, giving all NATO secret organizing of communication.

6. Herdigo, with other traitor order, are now of no way with united order of NATO.

7. Learn what they have revealed, so no one is of Italy in high NATO trust at all, even to not use Italy force in any defense order.

8. I do this so you can trust my will is for peace, for the suffering of innocence shall be great if traitor order in NATO causeth full war among Serbia area nation order, that is soon to break forth if no peace order conference order happeneth.

9. Do full order peace-seeking in Bosnia-Herzegovina area. Amen.

10. Now do full order search in own nation.

11. There is plot to send small order nuclear bomb of the size of inside farm equipment on flight of airline of cargo way selling farm equipment.

12. Do full order seeking, so no such is harm order in thy land. Amen.

13. Let also full military be changed to defending own land soon if thou desirest to dwell as a nation of repenting unto me, your holy Redeemer, who seeth war soon over economic change.

14. Let own way be to let my servant

Warren Jeffs receive full holy order freedom by executive order.

15. I do all this for innocence order sake. Amen.

16. Now let him go free to do my will in Church of my restoring.

17. I have book of warning to send to all, all nation order of recent sent messaging from God.

18. Now dwell on my will, so you are holy order doing what God over all declareth; else nation shall fall into chaos, which shall cause the God over all to intervene, according to worthy order of preserving more holy repentant peoples in all land of full world order, judgments of God in full Godhood power; to fulfill all prophecies of all my holy order Prophets. Amen.

19. The Lord revealeth enemy order invading nation to President of United States.

20. We, thy God and my servant, tell thee, when Europe falleth, not by ship alone cometh enemy, but unholy invasion by many commercial airline planes seized by enemy.

21. Do full international airport closing so foreign troop order, unholy life-taking full order weapon order not distributed to entire nation.

22. One nation with coalition invadeth east coast; other nation with own military first subdueth the Philippine land order, then Taiwan, to do full subjugating Japan; then cometh to thy land if no organized defending is in place by unrest in nation from loss of power from storm I sendeth; also earthquake in central nation state order.

23. Do full preparing nation for war needs of medical; also store blanket order as time of storm soon cometh of devastating power, to be remembered by all as my promised beginning order

humbling of nation if continue to allow murder of unborn child order.

24. Let also all nation conserve food, fuel order, as trade shall be only military return way, navy helpless after major organized missile sinking of many coalition order of unholy attack way.

25. Do no nuclear bomb order, or retaliation endeth life on world.

26. Do not think I, God, allowed such to be made for holy purpose.

27. Own evil aggression on Japan brought such to use.

28. Now do full control of no use of nuclear bomb order, lest no life remain on world, save God taketh hand to remove many who designed such. Amen.

29. Come to me, your holy Lord, all nations on world, to do full holy order repentance, to be preparing for full order judgments of my order eternal power order, saith Jesus Christ. Amen.

30. Let nation of my Israel be told also, by holy way revealing, two Prophets come among population in Old Jerusalem, of Jehovah sending, to prove record of my holy order of redeeming order, New Testament, is true; to Judah, to all Israel, as spoken in Isaiah, who shall both be as witness order to God. Amen.

Jesus Christ

Matthew 24 (Inspired Version)

1. And Jesus went out, and departed from the temple; and his disciples came to him for to hear him, saying, Master, show us concerning the buildings of the temple; as thou hast said; They shall be thrown down and left unto you desolate.

2. And Jesus said unto them, See ye not all these things? And do ye not understand them? Verily I say unto you, There shall not be left here upon this temple, one stone upon another, that shall not be thrown down.

3. And Jesus left them and went upon the mount of Olives.

4. And as he sat upon the mount of Olives, the disciples came unto him privately, saying, Tell us, when shall these things be which thou hast said concerning the destruction of the temple, and the Jews; and what is the sign of thy coming; and of the end of the world? (or the destruction of the wicked, which is the end of the world.)

5. And Jesus answered and said unto them, Take heed that no man deceive you.

6. For many shall come in my name, saying, I am Christ; and shall deceive many.

7. Then shall they deliver you up to be afflicted, and shall kill you; and ye shall be hated of all nations for my name's sake.

8. And then shall many be offended, and shall betray one another, and shall hate one another.

9. And many false prophets shall arise, and shall deceive many.

10. And because iniquity shall abound, the love of many shall wax cold.

11. But he that remaineth steadfast, and is not overcome, the same shall be saved.

12. When ye therefore, shall see the

abomination of desolation, spoken of by Daniel the prophet, concerning the destruction of Jerusalem, then ye shall stand in the holy place. (Whoso readeth let him understand.)

13. Then let them who are in Judea, flee into the mountains.

14. Let him who is on the housetop, flee, and not return to take anything out of his house.

15. Neither let him who is in the field, return back to take his clothes.

16. And woe unto them that are with child, and unto them that give suck in those days!

17. Therefore, pray ye the Lord, that your flight be not in the winter, neither on the Sabbath day.

18. For then, in those days, shall be great tribulations on the Jews, and upon the inhabitants of Jerusalem; such as was not before sent upon Israel, of God, since the beginning of their kingdom until this time; no, nor ever shall be sent again upon Israel.

19. All things which have befallen them, are only the beginning of the sorrows which shall come upon them; and except those days should be shortened, there should none of their flesh be saved.

20. But for the elect's sake, according to the covenant, those days shall be shortened.

21. Behold these things I have spoken unto you concerning the Jews.

22. And again, after the tribulation of those days which shall come upon Jerusalem, if any man shall say unto you, Lo! here is Christ, or there; believe him not.

23. For in those days, there shall also arise false Christs, and false prophets, and shall show great signs and wonders; insomuch that, if possible, they shall deceive the very elect, who are the elect according to the covenant.

24. Behold, I speak these things unto you for the elect's sake.

25. And ye also shall hear of wars, and rumors of wars; see that ye be not troubled; for all I have told you must come to pass. But the end is not yet.

26. Behold, I have told you before, Wherefore, if they shall say unto you, Behold, he is in the desert; go not forth. Behold, he is in the secret chambers; believe it not.

27. For as the light of the morning cometh out of the east, and shineth even unto the west, and covereth the whole earth; so shall also the coming of the Son of man be.

28. And now I show unto you a parable. Behold, wheresoever the carcass is, there will the eagles be gathered together; so likewise shall mine elect be gathered from the four quarters of the earth.

29. And they shall hear of wars, and rumors of wars. Behold, I speak unto you for mine elect's sake.

30. For nation shall rise against nation, and kingdom against kingdom; there shall be famine and pestilences, and earthquakes in divers places.

31. And again, because iniquity shall abound, the love of men shall wax cold; but he that shall not be overcome, the same shall be saved.

32. And again, this gospel of the kingdom shall be preached in all the world, for a witness unto all nations, and then shall the end come, or the destruction of the wicked.

33. And again shall the abomination of desolation, spoken of by Daniel the prophet, be fulfilled.

34. And immediately after the tribulation of those days, the sun shall be darkened, and the moon shall not give her light, and the stars shall fall from heaven, and the powers of heaven shall be shaken.

35. Verily I say unto you, this generation, in which these things shall be shown forth, shall not pass away until all I have told you shall be fulfilled.

36. Although the days will come that heaven and earth shall pass away, yet my word shall not pass away; but all shall be fulfilled.

37. And as I said before, after the tribulation of those days, and the powers of the heavens shall be shaken, then shall appear the sign of the Son of man in heaven; and then shall all the tribes of the earth mourn.

38. And they shall see the Son of man coming in the clouds of heaven, with power and great glory.

39. And whoso treasureth up my words, shall not be deceived.

40. For the Son of man shall come, and he shall send his angels before him with the great sound of a trumpet, and they shall gather together the remainder of his elect from the four winds; from one end of heaven to the other.

41. Now learn a parable of the fig tree: When its branches are yet tender, and it begins to put forth leaves, ye know that summer is nigh at hand.

42. So likewise mine elect, when they shall see all these things, they shall know that he is near, even at the doors.

43. But of that day and hour no one knoweth; no, not the angels of God in heaven, but my Father only.

44. But as it was in the days of Noah, so it shall be also at the coming of the Son of man.

45. For it shall be with them as it was in the days which were before the flood; for until the day that Noah entered into the ark, they were eating and drinking, marrying and giving in marriage, and knew not until the flood came and took them all away; so shall also the coming of the Son of man be.

46. Then shall be fulfilled that which is written, that, In the last days,

47. Two shall be in the field; the one shall be taken and the other left.

48. Two shall be grinding at the mill; the one taken and the other left.

49. And what I say unto one, I say unto all men; Watch, therefore, for ye know not at what hour your Lord doth come.

50. But know this, if the good man of the house had known in what watch the thief would come, he would have watched, and would not have suffered his house to have been broken up; but would have been ready.

51. Therefore be ye also ready; for in such an hour as ye think not, the Son of man cometh.

52. Who then is a faithful and wise servant, whom his Lord hath made ruler over his household, to give them meat in due season?

53. Blessed is that servant, whom his Lord when he cometh shall find so doing;

54. And, verily I say unto you, he shall make him ruler over all his goods.

55. But if that evil servant shall say in his heart, My Lord delayeth his coming; and shall begin to smite his fellow servants, and to eat and drink with the drunken; the Lord of that servant shall come in a day when he looketh not for him, and in an hour that he is not aware of, and shall cut him asunder, and shall appoint him his portion with the hypocrites; there shall be weeping and gnashing of teeth.

56. And thus cometh the end of the wicked according to the prophecy of Moses, saying, They should be cut off from among the people. But the end of the earth is not yet; but bye and bye.

APPENDIX

SECTION REVELATION 199

Revelation of the Lord Jesus Christ
Palestine, Texas
Monday, July 9, 2012

1. The Holy God of Creation, even Jesus Christ, cometh soon to world, to govern all flesh.

2. Do repentance in full labor.

3. Do no sin.

4. I come in full power to judge all people on earth.

5. Now do full cleansing of own people in all nations order. Amen.

6. Now come to me, all nations on world.

7. Do so soon, that I may save thee of repenting holy living unto godly way order. Amen.

8. Do so now, for my time is soon at hand to appear in glory power order to all peoples, as I personally said to Twelve Apostles as is in record of holy Bible of full inviting all peoples to be also ready, as found in Book of Matthew of chapter of my coming in great power order. Amen.

9. God sendeth own will to all world -- to now repent, lest full order holy judgment of God cometh on all world. Amen.

SECTION REVELATION 200

Revelation of the Lord Jesus Christ
Palestine, Texas
Thursday, August 23, 2012

1. To all nations on world, Jesus Christ, Holy One of Israel, sendeth His own word concerning now soon holy way of sure way power to subdue all nations under His rule.

2. I, God, speaketh, and shall be obeyed, is the law of God to all peoples on world.

3. Now know when I do reveal my will, though I be of long-suffering to test all peoples, my word shall be fulfilled. Amen.

4. Tell thy nation, each leader, to repent unto purity of living; for soon the earth shaketh, and reeleth to and fro like a drunken man, to waste away the ungodly. Amen.

5. Now do full order repentance, all people on world, before full judgment cometh in soon full judgment power of God on all nations. Amen.

6. Now come full order to my Holy Priesthood, each leader of all nations, to learn my will concerning thy peoples, to know government of Celestial love power, planting love for peace, for lovely power

of kind peace governing all peace order, so no evil exists.

7. Fire from heaven shall destroy all who are not with me. Amen.

8. Now cleanse out all in thy nation of murder of unborn child order.

9. Know I shall send full judgment of full power on all peoples who delight in sin, evil order. Amen.

10. Now do full obeisance to Jesus Christ, your holy Lord, to prepare for my full power in world on the holy Zion order land. Amen.

11. Tell thy nation Christ Jesus is God, who hath full order power extant, to see and know all secret works world over, nothing hidden.

12. Let truth of God be thy full way, so I can heal all unto saving order, eternal power order. Amen.

SECTION REVELATION 197

Jesus Christ
Son Ahman

Revelation of the Lord Jesus Christ
Palestine, Texas
Wednesday, September 19, 2012

1. Thus saith the Lord to all nations, my coming draweth nigh.

2. Now do full order holy repenting. Amen.

3. Send an emissary to my servant Warren, to know my will of thy land in now war coming, lest I humble all to no war, by greater God-sending judgment order.

4. Now repent of way of war.

5. Do no aggressive war labor at all. Amen.

Jesus Christ

SECTION REVELATION 201

Revelation of the Lord Jesus Christ
Palestine, Texas
Wednesday, September 19, 2012

1. Come all people of world to your full order only way of salvation of your holy Lord, even Jesus Christ, to be holy unto my coming.

2. A holy way of my order of pure living is to abstain from all unholy immoral way at all, in mind or body order.

3. Now cease child murder of unborn youth who are of conception.

4. Do not use removal method of physician order, both parent and doctor of removing order of such way of eternal loss of own salvation.

5. Now do no more unholy child murder of unborn child order, lest full judgment come on all who doeth this heinous evil. Amen.

6. Now learn truth; God is all-knowing, who controllest all heaven and earth way living.

7. Now be holy. Amen.

8. Let all people hear warning again.

9. Let this, my will, be published to all thy people on world.

10. My servant Warren Jeffs is held illegal way entire.

11. All proof was hearsay of no way tape order of sound only of full proof order, no witness order at all.

12. Let court of appeals reconsider such overthrow of illegal way judging.

13. Do no further order of unholy murder of unborn child order, nation holding my Prophet in prison order, lest full eternal judgment of my power, saith the Lord Jesus Christ, even God over all. Amen.

14. Thus saith God, Jesus Christ, to all world, my holy word: Insect plague cometh soon of overthrow of crop order.

15. Now store all excess food in own land. Amen.

16. Also do full repentance, no murder of unborn child holy order in own nation if desiring to survive. Amen.

SECTION REVELATION 202

Revelation of the Lord Jesus Christ
Palestine, Texas
Wednesday, September 19, 2012

1. Thus saith the Lord above all to all world: I come to show all world God liveth, and fulfills all His word.

2. Now repent, repent, unto pure living in my holy order of my holy power. Amen.

3. Now be holy, all nations, lest own land become a unholy battle ground, as was during United States of America Civil War. Amen.

4. Now learn I come in holy power fire from heaven.

5. Let all prepare; find way to my holy Prophet, though in bondage.

6. He can tell thee my will in nation, or individual life way. Amen.

7. Now be pure holy people, is the will of the Lord. Amen.

PROCLAMATION

PROCLAMATION OF SON AHMAN, EVEN JESUS CHRIST, TO ALL PEOPLES OF THE EARTH, EVEN MY HOLY WILL TO WARN ALL OF MY JUDGMENT UPON ALL PEOPLES

PREFACE

SECTION REVELATION 203

Revelation of the Lord Jesus Christ
Palestine, Texas
Sunday, October 2, 2011

1. Come ye, all ye people of the whole earth, unto me, and be ye ready for the coming of your Lord.

2. I send my own word to you to know I soon shall appear, making myself known to all people.

3. Let all now read of my coming in New Testament record.

4. Read Doctrine and Covenants of my holy word given through my holy Prophet and messenger of salvation, Joseph Smith; to know I have warned the people of the earth these many years to be ready.

5. Read Matthew chapter 24, to know I revealed of my return to earth in glory and power, to save mine elect who obey my Gospel of holy power.

6. I, your Lord Jesus Christ, now, in my loving power of my holy way being known on earth, send this, my Proclamation of my own revealing, to know my Holy Priesthood and my holy way of eternal marriage of my holy power of Celestial Plural Marriage has continued on earth, by my grace, attending my Holy Priesthood.

7. Let this Proclamation be known to all people of the earth.

8. I have caused my own word to go forth as a testimony I speak from the heavens, in plain language, to your understanding, to all people of every nation, having sent my own word to you; to be within reach to all people in your library book places; to be of a reading to any who will seek truth.

9. My Spirit shall witness to all honest and praying hearts and minds my word is only pure, true, peaceful, and of authority.

10. I shall fulfill my will in full as you, the people of every nation, prove your lives, whether you choose my ways or choose the way of evil; for my way is only pure, holy, noble, exalting, righteous, and is from Celestial eternal realm of my abiding.

11. Let this holy Proclamation be as a final message of a call to prepare, before I, your Lord Jesus Christ, your Redeemer and Savior over all appear in power.

12. Let all people hear and obey my will to survive my time

of judgments upon all nations; to be ready for my coming, is my revelation to all; for I have named in my Proclamation the way to know my plan of salvation that continues on earth.

13. I, your Lord, have spoken, and shall fulfill all my will. Amen.

HOLY WORD OF JESUS CHRIST TO ALL GOVERNING POWER OF CIVIL GOVERNING POWER OF THE LAND OF THE UNITED STATES OF AMERICA

INTRODUCTION

Thus Saith Jesus Christ, Even the Ruler Over All, Who Hath Now Sent You His Word of Judging and Cleansing Power, Who Now Declareth Judgment Upon Present Judge and Law Officials of Present Persecution Against My Fundamentalist Church of Jesus Christ of Latter-day Saints; to Know I Am Soon to Judge All in Government Positions of Unrighteous Prosecution Against My People, to Show My Will Concerning Present Court Persecuting Power; Which Judge Is Now to Be of My Holy Judging Upon Her and Others Who Have Mocked My Holy Religious and Pure Holy Law of Celestial Plural Marriage in Open Court: Let All Such Proceedings Cease Now!

SECTION REVELATION 204

Revelation of the Lord Jesus Christ
San Angelo, Texas
Thursday, July 28, 2011

1. I send this, my own word of defending authority, to be as a full understanding of my holy power of holy authority, and of principles of eternal life; and to show how governing power of both local and national power in the days of my Church coming forth until now has been named; to know of my people always being the object of attack, in the many tasks of government interference against my holy revealed religion, saith Jesus Christ, the God over all peoples.

2. Let my writing be examined by all government authorities in the nation, as from my own mouth, even my judging of peoples and lawmaking and court authority.

3. Let all now hear your Lord's will, to now release my servant Warren Jeffs and his brethren from imprisonment.

4. Read my will herein, and obey, saith your Lord, lest judgments, acute and keen, come upon Texas and the nation of the United States of America.

5. No longer be of a way of attacking my true Priesthood authority I have ordained, though he be in bondage.

6. I shall deliver my people, and leave their enemies who sought

their destruction with neither root nor branch of posterity, which time is soon at hand; for I shall not allow my Celestial Law to be destroyed by ungodly power of governing power, unto the governing power that thus persecute my elect shall be brought low unto dissolution if they heed me not.

7.   Be ye ready for my word to be fulfilled, and be of a pure holy way of living in your own families, communities, and this nation.

8.   Let my people be no longer persecuted nor prosecuted.

9.   Now read my own will to the people of present court prosecution of religious way of my holy will and revealing, and history of governmental attacks; and also naming Keyholders of my Holy Priesthood until now. Amen.

SECTION REVELATION 205

Thus Saith Jesus Christ to All of the People of the Nation, to Government Authorities of Every Place and Calling in Civil Power of Man's Governing, by the Grace of God Who Speaketh:

**Revelation of the Lord Jesus Christ
Eldorado, Texas
Thursday, July 21, 2011**

1.   I am to be now recognized as the power of eternal authority on earth, to be honored as the Ruler over my world of my creating; to have my servant known to be my spokesman to all nations of all lands on the earth.

2.   Hear my message of warning, to be of a full understanding of my eternal purpose of creating; to be known as soon to come in my glory unto my chosen people who live the law of holy pure intent, principle, and practice; even to be of a holy way of Celestial revealing of pure and sacred keeping of laws of Eternal Power, unto the salvation of my Church.

3.   Let all be of an awake and pure doing, to now receive my holy will; to know of the intent of thy Eternal Father, the Creator of all, in preparing a people for my coming.

4.   Let all now be ready to learn my holy purpose of creation, as unto a labor of pure holy living in my holy Church.

5.   Let my Celestial Law of Eternal Union of Eternal Plural Marriage now be protected by government power.

6.   Let all now be of a delivering of my holy way, to be protected by the power of governing authority, according to the principle of religious and holy and sacred law of Celestial Union, guided by my own voice through my servant, revealing

who is worthy of Eternal Marriage in my Church.

7. Let no one think those outside my Church can receive this, my holy law of pure sacred motive; to only be lived by he who is pure in moral doing and feeling, and she who is virtuous and of a motive of pure holy religion; to attain a salvation unto my Kingdom of Eternal Authority of a Celestial power of eternal and holy pure living.

8. Let all now see I have spoken my will, and shall soon call to accounting they who persecute through governing power of legal action, or by violent effort, or combination of those who oppose my revealed faith and Priesthood authority, Church of Jesus Christ of Latter-day Saints, known among men as the name of Fundamentalist Church of Jesus Christ of Latter-day Saints.

9. Let my people be of freedom of religious and pure living.

10. My Celestial Law of Union in Marriage is of holy way; to be a principle not of any evil nor false nor of a work of men only, but of thy Lord who is over all people; who is to be soon appearing to all nations in the power of my might; to be known as Ruler over all; who shall be as a flaming fire unto all people in my glory.

11. Now let my people be of free exercise of my holy law of Eternal Power; soon to be my elect who dwell in my eternal place of Celestial power on the land of America, a Zion to be of my creating, even new and holy power of Celestial Eternal Authority.

12. Let my people be as free to be my holy laboring agents for the salvation of all nations; for I am God, who is the Framer of the earth, and who is the full power of holy and Celestial governing power.

13. Let all now be my whole and full warning of awake and preparing children; to know I am to be a holy revealing of all secrets of all peoples of all generations, as my holy revealing is sent forth from the city New and Holy Jerusalem, a power of full governing power over all peoples.

14. Let my people have all their free religious rights protected.

15. Let the present attack against my people through government interfering be stopped.

16. I am the God over all.

17. Let my word be conveyed to governing power on my land of my coming, even to dwell among men on earth for a Millennial Reign of Peace.

18. Let all now be of a preparing, to be of a surviving the judgments of my power on all wicked, corrupt, and violent peoples in every nation; to be preserving the more righteous

unto my holy way of salvation of eternal life.

19. Let my will now be fulfilled, unto you who do my holy will being blessed, unto my giving preserving of your people and nation, each one.

20. Let no one be of violent way, to bring harm on other nations or people, even in thy own nation.

21. Let leaders be of a fatherly kind way, to lift up the needy, to be just and equitous unto all in the governing power you hold, by my grace.

22. I have sent you my own will.

23. Let all be of full preparing for my holy will to be manifest.

24. Receive my previous will revealing my holy way.

25. Let my Church be pure in all holy conduct, in all my law of sacred giving.

26. Let the court release my servant.

27. Let his brethren also be set free.

28. They only abide my Celestial Law of a more pure holy conduct and religious love for God and my purpose of preparing for my holy power of Zion to come forth on the land of Zion, even America.

29. Let my whole way be learned.

30. Judge my people no more as of evil way.

31. Let them be of free exercise of religion.

32. I, your Lord, have preserved this land for my Zion to rise.

33. Do not obstruct Zion.

34. Let all be peace.

35. Now hear my will: Learn of my law and of the labor of my servants, the Prophets, in establishing my Kingdom of pure holy way.

36. Let my truths be honored.

37. Let my holy walk be your way.

38. Let no aggressive way be exerting to destroy my people, who have been called by my revealing Celestial eternal laws that do not alter.

39. My law of Eternal Union is an holy pure law, only to be my Church preparing for my own will in their lives.

40. Let my people be free to have their lands and houses, to be of a work of pure living; no hindering of my Church by powers of governing power; to be of free labor, as is guaranteed by the law of original power of the full religious freedom.

41. Let my people now have all their pure holy way be protected, to have my law their way. Amen.

TABLE OF CONTENTS

Chapter 1
Administration of President Joseph Smith, Jun.

SECTION REVELATION 213

Thus Saith Son Ahman, Jesus Christ, to the Power of Governing in the Court of Prosecuting Labor, and to the Leaders of National Power -- Let My Word Be Heard in Your Several Placings of Your Influencing and Governing Power, Even This, My Warning to Not Abuse My Innocent People, But Maintain Their Rights of Governing Protecting of Religious Way of My Holy Order of Union Celestial in My Holy Church on Earth. Let There Cease to Be the Continued Way and Idea You Can Be of a Prosecuting Labor Against My Holy Way of Eternal Lives of Celestial Union Power Above All Peoples and Their Claims of Power to Rule Over All the People in Their Lands of Man Organizing Power. Thus Am I Now Giving

My Will to Be Known Among All Surviving People on Earth. Hear Thou My Way of Truth by This, My Revealing to All:

SECTION REVELATION 214

SECTION REVELATION 215

Chapter 2
Administration of President Brigham Young

Chapter 3
Administration of President John Taylor

Chapter 4

Administration of President John W. Woolley

Chapter 5

Administration of President Lorin C. Woolley

Chapter 6

Administration of President John Y. Barlow

Chapter 7

Administration of President Leroy S. Johnson

Chapter 8

Administration of President Rulon Jeffs

Chapter 9
Administration of President Warren S. Jeffs

Appendix A

Warnings of Previous Sending
to Leaders of the Nation

America, Now in Power, and Also to the Peoples of This Nation -- This Message of Warning of the Doctrine of Eternal Judgment Upon Thee, Even Upon All Peoples, Being the God of Eternal Power, an Eternal God Who Shall Bring All to Justice; Whose Mercy Shall Claim Those Who Repenteth in a Manner to Earn the Benefit of My Atoning Power -- Even Him, a God of Atoning and Redeeming Power, Who Suffered on the Cross and Was Raised From the Grave Unto Eternal Power to Judge All Mankind According as Their Works Are:

SECTION REVELATION 91

Thus Saith Jesus Christ, Who Is Son Ahman, to the Leader of This Nation of the United States of America, and All the Leaders of This Nation in Their Several Governing Appointments and Powers; and Thus to the Peoples of This Nation, Mine Own Word From the Heavens; Even the God of Glory Who Speaketh Thus to Your Understandings -- A Call to Heed My Word, Even I Who Am Soon to Come in the Powers of Heaven to Dwell Among Men, a Governing Power Over All Nations of the Earth -- Hear My Words:

SECTION REVELATION 99

Thus Saith Jesus Christ, Son Ahman, Unto the Leaders of the Nation of the United States of America, and to the Peoples Thereof, Warning and Continued Call to Prepare for Great Day of Final Judgments, Who Saith:

SECTION REVELATION 100

Thus Saith Son Ahman, Your Lord Jesus Christ, to All Peoples of the Earth Unto Your Salvation if You Heed Me, Saying Thus:

SECTION REVELATION 101

Jesus Christ Speaketh to the Nation of the United States Solemn Warning Again, Mine Own Word From the Heavens, to be Heeded Lest Judgments Follow Upon Those Who Heed Me Not, Saith the Lord, Even Son Ahman

Thus Saith the Lord Jesus Christ to the Leaders and Peoples of the United States of America, My Holy Word of Continued Warning of Final Judgments Soon at Hand, Heed My Word, Which Saith:

Appendix B

**Appendix of My New Word of Pure Power
Printed in This My Proclamation to All Peoples on All Lands
Referencing Pages to Find My Word in This Publishing**

(Page 275)

Appendix C

**Documents Showing the Legal and Religious Establishing
and Continuing of the Fundamentalist Church of Jesus
Christ of Latter-day Saints Among Men on Earth, Thy
Lord Establishing His Church April 6, 1830, Through
Joseph Smith, Continued on Earth Through My
Priesthood; Now a Legal Organization According to
Law of Land Among Men, Saith Jesus Christ, Your Lord**

(Page 280)

Chapter 1

Administration of President Joseph Smith, Jun.

SECTION REVELATION 206

Joseph Smith, "Revelator of My Holy Will to All Nations"

Revelation of the Lord Jesus Christ
San Angelo, Texas
Tuesday, July 26, 2011

1. Thus saith the Lord, who is Jesus Christ, to all people of holy way of living my holy way:

2. Now be of rejoicing.

3. My Holy Priesthood shall be with you, for nothing can stay my holy will from being fulfilled.

4. I shall have my holy will manifest, to have full way of Joseph Smith, my holy Revelator of pure giving to the generation in which my holy will has to be fulfilled.

5. Now be of an open mind, and no longer be of a slow preparing, for all I have revealed shall be fulfilled, given through my servant Joseph.

6. He shall yet be among you, the people of my holy way, and he shall be the One Mighty and Strong sent to set in order my house; even my Priesthood, Church, and Kingdom on earth.

7. Let all give heed to my holy way being fulfilled, to Zion being established in full.

8. Let my believing pure vessels be purified by the Holy Spirit.

9. Receive ye my holy will in full purpose of heart, that all may be done according to my revealing power. Amen.

Joseph Smith's First Visitation

President Joseph Smith, Jun.
Pearl of Great Price, Joseph Smith 2

5. Some time in the second year after our removal to Manchester, there was in the place where we lived an unusual excitement on the subject of religion. It commenced with the Methodists, but soon became general among all the sects in that region of country. Indeed, the whole district of country seemed affected by it, and great multitudes united themselves to the different religious parties, which created no small stir and division amongst the people, some crying, "Lo, here!" and others, "Lo, there!" Some were contending for the Methodist faith, some for the Presbyterian, and some for the Baptist.

6. For, notwithstanding the great love which the converts to these different faiths expressed at the time of their conversion, and the great zeal manifested by the respective clergy, who were active in getting up and promoting this extraordinary scene of religious feeling, in order to have everybody converted, as they were pleased to call it, let them join what sect they pleased; yet when the converts began to file off, some to one party and some to another, it was seen

that the seemingly good feelings of both the priests and the converts were more pretended than real; for a scene of great confusion and bad feeling ensued -- priest contending against priest, and convert against convert; so that all their good feelings one for another, if they ever had any, were entirely lost in a strife of words and a contest about opinions.

7. I was at this time in my fifteenth year. My father's family was proselyted to the Presbyterian faith, and four of them joined that church, namely, my mother, Lucy; my brothers Hyrum and Samuel Harrison; and my sister Sophronia.

8. During this time of great excitement my mind was called up to serious reflection and great uneasiness; but though my feelings were deep and often poignant, still I kept myself aloof from all these parties, though I attended their several meetings as often as occasion would permit. In process of time my mind became somewhat partial to the Methodist sect, and I felt some desire to be united with them; but so great were the confusion and strife among the different denominations, that it was impossible for a person young as I was, and so unacquainted with men and things, to come to any certain conclusion who was right and who was wrong.

9. My mind at times was greatly excited, the cry and tumult were so great and incessant. The Presbyterians were most decided against the Baptists and Methodists, and used all the powers of both reason and sophistry to prove their errors, or, at least, to make the people think they were in error. On the other hand, the Baptists and Methodists in their turn were equally zealous in endeavoring to establish their own tenets and disprove all others.

10. In the midst of this war of words and tumult of opinions, I often said to myself: What is to be done? Who of all these parties are right; or, are they all wrong together? If any one of them be right, which is it, and how shall I know it?

11. While I was laboring under the extreme difficulties caused by the contests of these parties of religionists, I was one day reading the Epistle of James, first chapter and fifth verse, which reads: *If any of you lack wisdom, let him ask of God, that giveth to all men liberally, and upbraideth not; and it shall be given him*.

12. Never did any passage of scripture come with more power to the heart of man than this did at this time to mine. It seemed to enter with great force into every feeling of my heart. I reflected on it again and again, knowing that if any person needed wisdom from God, I did; for how to act I did not know, and unless I could get more wisdom than I then had, I would never know; for the teachers of religion of the different sects understood the same passages of scripture so differently as to destroy all confidence in settling the question by an appeal to the Bible.

13. At length I came to the conclusion that I must either remain in darkness and confusion, or else I must do as James directs, that is, ask of God. I at length came to the determination to "ask of God," concluding that if he gave wisdom to them that lacked wisdom, and would give liberally, and not upbraid, I might venture.

14. So, in accordance with this, my determination to ask of God, I retired to the woods to make the attempt. It was on the morning of a beautiful, clear day, early in the spring of eighteen hundred and twenty. It was the first time in my life that I had made such an attempt, for amidst all

my anxieties I had never as yet made the attempt to pray vocally.

15. After I had retired to the place where I had previously designed to go, having looked around me, and finding myself alone, I kneeled down and began to offer up the desire of my heart to God. I had scarcely done so, when immediately I was seized upon by some power which entirely overcame me, and had such an astonishing influence over me as to bind my tongue so that I could not speak. Thick darkness gathered around me, and it seemed to me for a time as if I were doomed to sudden destruction.

16. But, exerting all my powers to call upon God to deliver me out of the power of this enemy which had seized upon me, and at the very moment when I was ready to sink into despair and abandon myself to destruction -- not to an imaginary ruin, but to the power of some actual being from the unseen world, who had such marvelous power as I had never before felt in any being -- just at this moment of great alarm, I saw a pillar of light exactly over my head, above the brightness of the sun, which descended gradually until it fell upon me.

17. It no sooner appeared than I found myself delivered from the enemy which held me bound. When the light rested upon me I saw two Personages, whose brightness and glory defy all description, standing above me in the air. One of them spake unto me, calling me by name and said, pointing to the other -- *This is My Beloved Son. Hear Him*!

18. My object in going to inquire of the Lord was to know which of all the sects was right, that I might know which to join. No sooner, therefore, did I get possession of myself, so as to be able to speak, than

I asked the Personages who stood above me in the light, which of all the sects was right -- and which I should join.

19. I was answered that I must join none of them, for they were all wrong; and the Personage who addressed me said that all their creeds were an abomination in his sight; that those professors were all corrupt; that: "they draw near to me with their lips, but their hearts are far from me, they teach for doctrines the commandments of men, having a form of godliness, but they deny the power thereof."

20. He again forbade me to join with any of them; and many other things did he say unto me, which I cannot write at this time. When I came to myself again, I found myself lying on my back, looking up into heaven. When the light had departed, I had no strength; but soon recovering in some degree, I went home. And as I leaned up to the fireplace, mother inquired what the matter was. I replied, "Never mind, all is well -- I am well enough off." I then said to my mother, "I have learned for myself that Presbyterianism is not true." It seems as though the adversary was aware, at a very early period of my life, that I was destined to prove a disturber and an annoyer of his kingdom; else why should the powers of darkness combine against me? Why the opposition and persecution that arose against me, almost in my infancy?

21. Some few days after I had this vision, I happened to be in company with one of the Methodist preachers, who was very active in the before mentioned religious excitement; and, conversing with him on the subject of religion, I took occasion to give him an account of the vision which I had had. I was greatly surprised at his behavior; he treated my communication not only lightly, but with

great contempt, saying it was all of the devil, that there were no such things as visions or revelations in these days; that all such things had ceased with the apostles, and that there would never be any more of them.

22. I soon found, however, that my telling the story had excited a great deal of prejudice against me among professors of religion, and was the cause of great persecution, which continued to increase; and though I was an obscure boy, only between fourteen and fifteen years of age, and my circumstances in life such as to make a boy of no consequence in the world, yet men of high standing would take notice sufficient to excite the public mind against me, and create a bitter persecution; and this was common among all the sects -- all united to persecute me.

23. It caused me serious reflection then, and often has since, how very strange it was that an obscure boy, of a little over fourteen years of age, and one, too, who was doomed to the necessity of obtaining a scanty maintenance by his daily labor, should be thought a character of sufficient importance to attract the attention of the great ones of the most popular sects of the day, and in a manner to create in them a spirit of the most bitter persecution and reviling. But strange or not, so it was, and it was often the cause of great sorrow to myself.

24. However, it was nevertheless a fact that I had beheld a vision. I have thought since, that I felt much like Paul, when he made his defense before King Agrippa, and related the account of the vision he had when he saw a light, and heard a voice; but still there were but few who believed him; some said he was dishonest, others said he was mad; and he was ridiculed and reviled.

But all this did not destroy the reality of his vision. He had seen a vision, he knew he had, and all the persecution under heaven could not make it otherwise; and though they should persecute him unto death, yet he knew, and would know to his latest breath, that he had both seen a light and heard a voice speaking unto him, and all the world could not make him think or believe otherwise.

25. So it was with me. I had actually seen a light, and in the midst of that light I saw two Personages, and they did in reality speak to me; and though I was hated and persecuted for saying that I had seen a vision, yet it was true; and while they were persecuting me, reviling me, and speaking all manner of evil against me falsely for so saying, I was led to say in my heart: Why persecute me for telling the truth? I have actually seen a vision; and who am I that I can withstand God, or why does the world think to make me deny what I have actually seen? For I had seen a vision; I knew it, and I knew that God knew it, and I could not deny it, neither dared I do it; at least I knew that by so doing I would offend God, and come under condemnation.

26. I had now got my mind satisfied so far as the sectarian world was concerned -- that it was not my duty to join with any of them, but to continue as I was until further directed. I had found the testimony of James to be true -- that a man who lacked wisdom might ask of God, and obtain, and not be upbraided.

27. I continued to pursue my common vocations in life until the twenty-first of September, one thousand eight hundred and twenty-three, all the time suffering severe persecution at the hands of all classes of men, both religious and irreligious, because I continued to affirm that I had seen a vision.

Visitation of Angel Moroni to Joseph Smith; The Book of Mormon a Revealed Work

President Joseph Smith, Jun.
Pearl of Great Price, Joseph Smith 2

28. During the space of time which intervened between the time I had the vision and the year eighteen hundred and twenty-three -- having been forbidden to join any of the religious sects of the day, and being of very tender years, and persecuted by those who ought to have been my friends and to have treated me kindly, and if they supposed me to be deluded to have endeavored in a proper and affectionate manner to have reclaimed me -- I was left to all kinds of temptations; and, mingling with all kinds of society, I frequently fell into many foolish errors, and displayed the weakness of youth, and the foibles of human nature; which, I am sorry to say, led me into divers temptations, offensive in the sight of God. In making this confession, no one need suppose me guilty of any great or malignant sins. A disposition to commit such was never in my nature. But I was guilty of levity, and sometimes associated with jovial company, etc., not consistent with that character which ought to be maintained by one who was called of God as I had been. But this will not seem very strange to any one who recollects my youth, and is acquainted with my native cheery temperament.

29. In consequence of these things, I often felt condemned for my weakness and imperfections; when, on the evening of the above-mentioned twenty-first of September, after I had retired to my bed for the night, I betook myself to prayer and supplication to Almighty God for forgiveness of all my sins and follies, and also for a manifestation to me, that I might know of my state and standing before him; for I had full confidence in obtaining a divine manifestation, as I previously had one.

30. While I was thus in the act of calling upon God, I discovered a light appearing in my room, which continued to increase until the room was lighter than at noonday, when immediately a personage appeared at my bedside, standing in the air, for his feet did not touch the floor.

31. He had on a loose robe of most exquisite whiteness. It was a whiteness beyond anything earthly I had ever seen; nor do I believe that any earthly thing could be made to appear so exceedingly white and brilliant. His hands were naked, and his arms also, a little above the wrist; so, also, were his feet naked, as were his legs, a little above the ankles. His head and neck were also bare. I could discover that he had no other clothing on but this robe, as it was open, so that I could see into his bosom.

32. Not only was his robe exceedingly white, but his whole person was glorious beyond description, and his countenance truly like lightning. The room was exceedingly light, but not so very bright as immediately around his person. When I first looked upon him, I was afraid; but the fear soon left me.

33. He called me by name, and said unto me that he was a messenger sent from the presence of God to me, and that his name was Moroni; that God had a work for me to do; and that my name should be had for good and evil among all nations, kindreds, and tongues, or that it should be both good and evil spoken of among all people.

34. He said there was a book deposited, written upon gold plates, giving an account of the former inhabitants of

this continent, and the source from whence they sprang. He also said that the fulness of the everlasting Gospel was contained in it, as delivered by the Savior to the ancient inhabitants;

35. Also, that there were two stones in silver bows -- and these stones, fastened to a breastplate, constituted what is called the Urim and Thummim -- deposited with the plates; and the possession and use of these stones were what constituted "seers" in ancient or former times; and that God had prepared them for the purpose of translating the book.***

42. Again, he told me, that when I got those plates of which he had spoken -- for the time that they should be obtained was not yet fulfilled -- I should not show them to any person; neither the breastplate with the Urim and Thummim; only to those to whom I should be commanded to show them; if I did I should be destroyed. While he was conversing with me about the plates, the vision was opened to my mind that I could see the place where the plates were deposited, and that so clearly and distinctly that I knew the place again when I visited it.

43. After this communication, I saw the light in the room begin to gather immediately around the person of him who had been speaking to me, and it continued to do so until the room was again left dark, except just around him; when, instantly I saw, as it were, a conduit open right up into heaven, and he ascended till he entirely disappeared, and the room was left as it had been before this heavenly light had made its appearance.

44. I lay musing on the singularity of the scene, and marveling greatly at what had been told to me by this extraordinary messenger; when, in the midst of my meditation, I suddenly discovered that my room was again beginning to get lighted, and in an instant, as it were, the same heavenly messenger was again by my bedside.

45. He commenced, and again related the very same things which he had done at his first visit, without the least variation; which having done, he informed me of great judgments which were coming upon the earth, with great desolations by famine, sword, and pestilence; and that these grievous judgments would come on the earth in this generation. Having related these things, he again ascended as he had done before.

46. By this time, so deep were the impressions made on my mind, that sleep had fled from my eyes, and I lay overwhelmed in astonishment at what I had both seen and heard. But what was my surprise when again I beheld the same messenger at my bedside, and heard him rehearse or repeat over again to me the same things as before; and added a caution to me, telling me that Satan would try to tempt me (in consequence of the indigent circumstances of my father's family), to get the plates for the purpose of getting rich. This he forbade me, saying that I must have no other object in view in getting the plates but to glorify God, and must not be influenced by any other motive than that of building his kingdom; otherwise I could not get them.

47. After this third visit, he again ascended into heaven as before, and I was again left to ponder on the strangeness of what I had just experienced; when almost immediately after the heavenly messenger had ascended from me for the third time, the cock crowed, and I found that day was approaching, so that our interviews must have occupied the whole of that night.

48. I shortly after arose from my bed, and, as usual, went to the necessary labors of the day; but, in attempting to work as at other times, I found my strength so exhausted as to render me entirely unable. My father, who was laboring along with me, discovered something to be wrong with me, and told me to go home. I started with the intention of going to the house; but, in attempting to cross the fence out of the field where we were, my strength entirely failed me, and I fell helpless on the ground, and for a time was quite unconscious of anything.

49. The first thing that I can recollect was a voice speaking unto me, calling me by name. I looked up, and beheld the same messenger standing over my head, surrounded by light as before. He then again related unto me all that he had related to me the previous night, and commanded me to go to my father and tell him of the vision and commandments which I had received.

50. I obeyed; I returned to my father in the field, and rehearsed the whole matter to him. He replied to me that it was of God, and told me to go and do as commanded by the messenger. I left the field, and went to the place where the messenger had told me the plates were deposited; and owing to the distinctness of the vision which I had had concerning it, I knew the place the instant that I arrived there.

51. Convenient to the village of Manchester, Ontario county, New York, stands a hill of considerable size, and the most elevated of any in the neighborhood. On the west side of this hill, not far from the top, under a stone of considerable size, lay the plates, deposited in a stone box. This stone was thick and rounding in the middle on the upper side, and thinner towards the edges, so that the middle part of it was visible above the ground, but the edge all around was covered with earth.

52. Having removed the earth, I obtained a lever, which I got fixed under the edge of the stone, and with a little exertion raised it up. I looked in, and there indeed did I behold the plates, the Urim and Thummim, and the breastplate, as stated by the messenger. The box in which they lay was formed by laying stones together in some kind of cement. In the bottom of the box were laid two stones crossways of the box, and on these stones lay the plates and the other things with them.

53. I made an attempt to take them out, but was forbidden by the messenger, and was again informed that the time for bringing them forth had not yet arrived, neither would it, until four years from that time; but he told me that I should come to that place precisely in one year from that time, and that he would there meet with me, and that I should continue to do so until the time should come for obtaining the plates.

54. Accordingly, as I had been commanded, I went at the end of each year, and at each time I found the same messenger there, and received instruction and intelligence from him at each of our interviews, respecting what the Lord was going to do, and how and in what manner his kingdom was to be conducted in the last days.***

59. At length the time arrived for obtaining the plates, the Urim and Thummim, and the breastplate. On the twenty-second day of September, one thousand eight hundred and twenty-seven, having gone as usual at the end of another year to the place where they were deposited, the same heavenly messenger

delivered them up to me with this charge: that I should be responsible for them; that if I should let them go carelessly, or through any neglect of mine, I should be cut off; but that if I would use all my endeavors to preserve them, until he, the messenger, should call for them, they should be protected.

Priesthood Authority Restored to the Earth

President Joseph Smith, Jun.
Pearl of Great Price, Joseph Smith 2

66. On the 5th day of April, 1829, Oliver Cowdery came to my house, until which time I had never seen him. He stated to me that having been teaching school in the neighborhood where my father resided, and my father being one of those who sent to the school, he went to board for a season at his house, and while there the family related to him the circumstances of my having received the plates, and accordingly he had come to make inquiries of me.

67. Two days after the arrival of Mr. Cowdery (being the 7th of April) I commenced to translate the Book of Mormon, and he began to write for me.

68. We still continued the work of translation, when, in the ensuing month (May, 1829), we on a certain day went into the woods to pray and inquire of the Lord respecting baptism for the remission of sins, that we found mentioned in the translation of the plates. While we were thus employed, praying and calling upon the Lord, a messenger from heaven descended in a cloud of light, and having laid his hands upon us, he ordained us, saying:

69. *Upon you my fellow servants, in the name of Messiah, I confer the Priesthood of Aaron, which holds the keys of the ministering of angels, and of the gospel of repentance, and of baptism by immersion for the remission of sins; and this shall never be taken again from the earth until the sons of Levi do offer again an offering unto the Lord in righteousness.*

70. He said this Aaronic Priesthood had not the power of laying on hands for the gift of the Holy Ghost, but that this should be conferred on us hereafter; and he commanded us to go and be baptized, and gave us directions that I should baptize Oliver Cowdery, and that afterwards he should baptize me.

71. Accordingly we went and were baptized. I baptized him first, and afterwards he baptized me -- after which I laid my hands upon his head and ordained him to the Aaronic Priesthood, and afterwards he laid his hands on me and ordained me to the same Priesthood -- for so we were commanded.

72. The messenger who visited us on this occasion and conferred this Priesthood upon us, said that his name was John, the same that is called John the Baptist in the New Testament, and that he acted under the direction of Peter, James and John, who held the keys of the Priesthood of Melchizedek, which Priesthood, he said, would in due time be conferred on us, and that I should be called the first Elder of the Church, and he (Oliver Cowdery) the second. It was on the fifteenth day of May, 1829, that we were ordained under the hand of this messenger, and baptized.

73. Immediately on our coming up out of the water after we had been baptized, we experienced great and glorious blessings from our Heavenly Father. No sooner had I baptized Oliver Cowdery, than the Holy Ghost fell upon him, and he stood up and prophesied many things which should

shortly come to pass. And again, so soon as I had been baptized by him, I also had the spirit of prophecy, when, standing up, I prophesied concerning the rise of this Church, and many other things connected with the Church, and this generation of the children of men. We were filled with the Holy Ghost, and rejoiced in the God of our salvation.

74. Our minds being now enlightened, we began to have the scriptures laid open to our understandings, and the true meaning and intention of their more mysterious passages revealed unto us in a manner which we never could attain to previously, nor ever before had thought of. In the meantime we were forced to keep secret the circumstances of having received the Priesthood and our having been baptized, owing to a spirit of persecution which had already manifested itself in the neighborhood.

75. We had been threatened with being mobbed, from time to time, and this, too, by professors of religion. And their intentions of mobbing us were only counteracted by the influence of my wife's father's family (under Divine providence), who had become very friendly to me, and who were opposed to mobs, and were willing that I should be allowed to continue the work of translation without interruption; and therefore offered and promised us protection from all unlawful proceedings, as far as in them lay.

Restoring Melchizedek Priesthood on Earth

President Rulon Jeffs
Rulon Jeffs' Sermons 1:249 Dec. 16, 1962 SLC
Now brethren and sisters, we read in Section 110 that all of the heads of previous dispensations came and gave their keys to Joseph Smith; Elias delivering the gospel of Abraham to him, Moses the keys of the gathering, and Elijah the keys of the sealing powers of the holy Priesthood. Peter, James, and John had previously come and given him their keys of the meridian dispensation of the Kingdom of God -- Peter, James, and John, not just John alone. We read in many places in the Doctrine and Covenants where Joseph has these keys, the fullness of the keys of the holy Priesthood, and of the last Dispensation of the Fullness of Times, never to be taken from him in heaven or in earth. And he holds them today.

We testify that Joseph Smith is the third member of the Godhead, and in this last and great dispensation, he holds all of the keys, and is still directing the affairs of this dispensation under the direction of Jesus and Father Adam. He stood by directing the proceedings when this special dispensation of the Priesthood was given under John Taylor in 1886; and he is still directing this work in the same way.

President Brigham Young
JD 1:134 April 6, 1853 SLC
Joseph was ordained an Apostle -- that you can read and understand. After he was ordained to this office, then he had the right to organize and build up the kingdom of God, for he had committed unto him the *keys* of the *Priesthood*, which is after the order of Melchizedec -- the *High Priesthood*, which is after the order of the Son of God. And this, remember, *by being ordained an Apostle.****

I know that Joseph received his Apostleship from Peter, James, and John, before a revelation on the subject was printed, and he never had a right to organize a Church before he was an Apostle.

Revelation of the Lord Jesus Christ
Given to President Joseph Smith, Jun.
August 1830
Doctrine and Covenants, Section 27

12. And also with Peter, and James, and John, whom I have sent unto you, by whom I have ordained you and confirmed you to be apostles, and especial witnesses of my name, and bear the keys of your ministry and of the same things which I revealed unto them;

Revelation of the Lord Jesus Christ
Given to President Joseph Smith, Jun.
September 6, 1842
Doctrine and Covenants Section 128

20. And again, what do we hear? Glad tidings from Cumorah! Moroni, an angel from heaven, declaring the fulfilment of the prophets -- the book to be revealed. A voice of the Lord in the wilderness of Fayette, Seneca county, declaring the three witnesses to bear record of the book! The voice of Michael on the banks of the Susquehanna, detecting the devil when he appeared as an angel of light! The voice of Peter, James, and John in the wilderness between Harmony, Susquehanna county, and Colesville, Broome county, on the Susquehanna river, declaring themselves as possessing the keys of the kingdom, and of the dispensation of the fulness of times!

President John Taylor
Mediation and Atonement, Page 159

We read that Moses and Elias came to administer to Jesus, on the Mount, while Peter, James and John were with him. Who were this Moses and this Elias? Moses was a great Prophet, appointed by the Lord to deliver Israel from Egyptian bondage, and lead them to the promised land; and he held the keys of the gathering dispensation, which keys he afterwards conferred upon Joseph Smith in the Kirtland Temple.

Who was Elias? Elijah; which name in the old Scriptures is made synonymous with Elias; and who held, according to the testimony of Joseph Smith as elsewhere stated, the keys of the Priesthood. These men, who held those keys and officiated upon the earth, having left the earth, now come, associated with Jesus, to administer to Peter, James and John, and confer upon them the Priesthood which they hold; and these three ancient Apostles conferred the Priesthood upon Joseph Smith and Oliver Cowdery in this dispensation.

President Joseph Smith, Jun.
Teachings of the Prophet Joseph Smith, Page 346

Here, then, is eternal life -- to know the only wise and true God; and you have got to learn how to be Gods yourselves, and to be kings and priests to God, the same as all Gods have done before you, namely, by going from one small degree to another, and from a small capacity to a great one; from grace to grace, from exaltation to exaltation, until you attain to the resurrection of the dead, and are able to dwell in everlasting burnings, and to sit in glory, as do those who sit enthroned in everlasting power.

Revelation of the Lord Jesus Christ
Given to President Joseph Smith, Jun.
November 1, 1831
Doctrine and Covenants, Section 1

1. Hearken, O ye people of my church, saith the voice of him who dwells on high, and whose eyes are upon all men; yea, verily I say: Hearken ye people from afar; and ye that are upon the islands of the sea, listen together.

2. For verily the voice of the Lord is unto all men, and there is none to escape; and there is no eye that shall not see, neither ear that shall not hear, neither heart that shall not be penetrated.

3. And the rebellious shall be pierced with much sorrow; for their iniquities shall be spoken upon the housetops, and their secret acts shall be revealed.

4. And the voice of warning shall be unto all people, by the mouths of my disciples, whom I have chosen in these last days.

5. And they shall go forth and none shall stay them, for I the Lord have commanded them.

6. Behold, this is mine authority, and the authority of my servants, and my preface unto the book of my commandments, which I have given them to publish unto you, O inhabitants of the earth.

7. Wherefore, fear and tremble, O ye people, for what I the Lord have decreed in them shall be fulfilled.

8. And verily I say unto you, that they who go forth, bearing these tidings unto the inhabitants of the earth, to them is power given to seal both on earth and in heaven, the unbelieving and rebellious;

9. Yea, verily, to seal them up unto the day when the wrath of God shall be poured out upon the wicked without measure --

10. Unto the day when the Lord shall come to recompense unto every man according to his work, and measure to every man according to the measure which he has measured to his fellow man.

11. Wherefore the voice of the Lord is unto the ends of the earth, that all that will hear may hear:

12. Prepare ye, prepare ye for that which is to come, for the Lord is nigh;

13. And the anger of the Lord is kindled, and his sword is bathed in heaven, and it shall fall upon the inhabitants of the earth.

14. And the arm of the Lord shall be revealed; and the day cometh that they who will not hear the voice of the Lord, neither the voice of his servants, neither give heed to the words of the prophets and apostles, shall be cut off from among the people;

15. For they have strayed from mine ordinances, and have broken mine everlasting covenant;

16. They seek not the Lord to establish his righteousness, but every man walketh in his own way, and after the image of his own God, whose image is in the likeness of the world, and whose substance is that of an idol, which waxeth old and shall perish in Babylon, even Babylon the great, which shall fall.

17. Wherefore, I the Lord, knowing the calamity which should come upon the inhabitants of the earth, called upon my servant Joseph Smith, Jun., and spake unto him from heaven, and gave him commandments;

18. And also gave commandments to others, that they should proclaim these things unto the world; and all this that it might be fulfilled, which was written by the prophets --

19. The weak things of the world shall come forth and break down the mighty and strong ones, that man should not counsel his fellow man, neither trust in the arm of flesh --

20. But that every man might speak in the name of God the Lord, even the Savior of the world;

21. That faith also might increase in the earth;

22. That mine everlasting covenant might be established;

23. That the fulness of my gospel

might be proclaimed by the weak and the simple unto the ends of the world, and before kings and rulers.

24. Behold, I am God and have spoken it; these commandments are of me, and were given unto my servants in their weakness, after the manner of their language, that they might come to understanding.

25. And inasmuch as they erred it might be made known;

26. And inasmuch as they sought wisdom they might be instructed;

27. And inasmuch as they sinned they might be chastened, that they might repent;

28. And inasmuch as they were humble they might be made strong, and blessed from on high, and receive knowledge from time to time.

29. And after having received the record of the Nephites, yea, even my servant Joseph Smith, Jun., might have power to translate through the mercy of God, by the power of God, the Book of Mormon.

30. And also those to whom these commandments were given, might have power to lay the foundation of this church, and to bring it forth out of obscurity and out of darkness, the only true and living church upon the face of the whole earth, with which I, the Lord, am well pleased, speaking unto the church collectively and not individually --

31. For I the Lord cannot look upon sin with the least degree of allowance;

32. Nevertheless, he that repents and does the commandments of the Lord shall be forgiven;

33. And he that repents not, from him shall be taken even the light which he has

received; for my Spirit shall not always strive with man, saith the Lord of Hosts.

34. And again, verily I say unto you, O inhabitants of the earth: I the Lord am willing to make these things known unto all flesh;

35. For I am no respecter of persons, and will that all men shall know that the day speedily cometh; the hour is not yet, but is nigh at hand, when peace shall be taken from the earth, and the devil shall have power over his own dominion.

36. And also the Lord shall have power over his saints, and shall reign in their midst, and shall come down in judgment upon Idumea, or the world.

37. Search these commandments, for they are true and faithful, and the prophecies and promises which are in them shall all be fulfilled.

38. What I the Lord have spoken, I have spoken, and I excuse not myself; and though the heavens and the earth pass away, my word shall not pass away, but shall all be fulfilled, whether by mine own voice or by the voice of my servants, it is the same.

39. For behold, and lo, the Lord is God, and the Spirit beareth record, and the record is true, and the truth abideth forever and ever. Amen.

The Articles of Faith of the Church of Jesus Christ of Latter-day Saints

President Joseph Smith, Jun. Pearl of Great Price, Page 64 [1978 Ed.]

1. We believe in God, the Eternal Father, and in His son, Jesus Christ, and in the Holy Ghost.

2. We believe that men will be punished for their own sins, and not for Adam's transgression.

3. We believe that through the Atonement of Christ, all mankind may be saved, by obedience to the laws and ordinances of the Gospel.

4. We believe that the first principles and ordinances of the Gospel are: first, Faith in the Lord Jesus Christ; second, Repentance; third, Baptism by immersion for the remission of sins; fourth, Laying on of hands for the gift of the Holy Ghost.

5. We believe that a man must be called of God, by prophecy, and by the laying on of hands, by those who are in authority, to preach the Gospel and administer in the ordinances thereof.

6. We believe in the same organization that existed in the Primitive Church, namely, apostles, prophets, pastors, teachers, evangelists, etc.

7. We believe in the gift of tongues, prophecy, revelation, visions, healing, interpretation of tongues, etc.

8. We believe the Bible to be the word of God as far as it is translated correctly; we also believe the Book of Mormon to be the word of God.

9. We believe all that God has revealed, all that He does now reveal, and we believe that He will yet reveal many great and important things pertaining to the Kingdom of God.

10. We believe in the literal gathering of Israel and in the restoration of the Ten Tribes; that Zion (the New Jerusalem) will be built upon the American continent; that Christ will reign personally upon the earth; and, that the earth will be renewed and receive its paradisiacal glory.

11. We claim the privilege of worshiping Almighty God according to the dictates of our own conscience, and allow all men the same privilege, let them worship how, where, or what they may.

12. We believe in being subject to kings, presidents, rulers, and magistrates, in obeying, honoring, and sustaining the law.

13. We believe in being honest, true, chaste, benevolent, virtuous, and in doing good to all men; indeed, we may say that we follow the admonition of Paul -- We believe all things, we hope all things, we have endured many things, and hope to be able to endure all things. If there is anything virtuous, lovely, or of good report or praiseworthy, we seek after these things.

JOSEPH SMITH.

One Man on the Earth at a Time Holds the Sealing Power to Seal Blessings Unto Eternal Life

SECTION REVELATION 207

Revelation of the Lord Jesus Christ San Angelo, Texas Tuesday, July 26, 2011

1. The revelations on my Holy Right to Rule, in my holy will manifested through my Seer and Prophet, Joseph Smith, are in Doctrine and Covenants as my guide to all people, to know that my authority has been restored among men to govern my holy law of plural marriage in my stead, as I reveal through my representative I have

named, to be known now as Warren Jeffs, my Prophet, who is now of the full authority to administer all blessings of my holy Church on earth.

2. Let all now know that my holy authority to seal eternal blessings upon men of my Church, and also women of my Church, is Warren Jeffs, the One Man I place the full power of sealing keys of my Melchizedek Priesthood, to administer lives of pure abiding to receive endless lives through Priesthood sealing keys.

3. The sealing keys are of my guiding, empowering; presenting my will as Mouthpiece of God on earth; being the power of eternal power, of Celestial eternal power now upon earth.

4. Let all know I have set upon my Prophet the gift to know me by the revelations of my will in a flow of holy revealing, to know my will, to give to my people the way of truth of holy and eternal way unto life eternal.

5. Let all be of a full way of receiving my will as I reveal my authority to be on earth; to honor thy God, to be of my holy power, to have life given through authorizing power now on earth, to guide all people of faith unto saving principles of eternal truths.

6. Let my Church now be of a full believing to be of my holy way; to be of the New Era of Peace; to have full way of coming to my holy place of receiving eternal gifts of love, light, peace, knowledge, justice, truth, power eternal; to be of my holy Order of Union Power.

7. Let all people know I have given my will, to be of a full power of pure light, knowledge, and truth; to be of a full way of pure holy guiding to all people who desire truth, unto them having all things being my Kingdom, all to be made holy and of eternal way of life everlasting.

8. Such does my eternal power of holy authority perform, by my holy power attending the administering power of Priesthood.

9. Receive ye my servant to receive me, saith your Lord, even Jesus Christ, who reigneth over all, justified by my holy sacrifice; redeeming all people of every time of the world from the grave, to stand before my holy presence to be judged according to the deeds done in the flesh.

10. Now receive ye my will, even Son Ahman, who is Jesus Christ: I am He who ruleth, who has all power, who sees and has knowing of all things in each person's life.

11. I am the rightful and true King over all.

12. Hear my holy word, will, and purposes in bringing all peoples of the earth on this globe of probationary testing.

13. I give my holy will and must be obeyed.

14. Now learn my holy will, to be obedient to my law of righteous dominion on earth and in Celestial worlds, even being my holy will to all peoples of the earth:

15. Let my servant go free to do my will.

16. He is in bondage because corrupt men have joined with a combination of several branches of earthly governing power in several places on the land of Zion, even known now as America, both North and South.

17. I have the right to rule.

18. No one has any authority to dictate God who made them.

19. Now be of good cheer, as I cause my dominion of Zion to soon take the reign of governing power over all peoples of the earth.

20. Let all now acknowledge me having the right to rule over all nations, kindreds, tongues, and governing powers.

21. And if present nations of the earth seek to overthrow my Church and Kingdom, even Zion, they shall be brought low, to no longer be a nation, nor a people; who will now be of a full accounting, having knowledge now of my revealed power and divine authority on earth.

22. You "come unto me" through obedience to my law and Gospel. Amen.

Revelation of the Lord Jesus Christ Given to President Joseph Smith, Jun. July 12, 1843 Doctrine and Covenants, Section 132

7. And verily I say unto you, that the conditions of this law are these: All covenants, contracts, bonds, obligations, oaths, vows, performances, connections, associations, or expectations, that are not made and entered into and sealed by the Holy Spirit of promise, of him who is anointed, both as well for time and for all eternity, and that too most holy, by revelation and commandment through the medium of mine anointed, whom I have appointed on the earth to hold this power (and I have appointed unto my servant Joseph to hold this power in the last days, and there is never but one on the earth at a time on whom this power and the keys of this priesthood are conferred), are of no efficacy, virtue, or force in and after the resurrection from the dead; for all contracts that are not made unto this end have an end when men are dead.

Revelation of the Lord Jesus Christ Given to President Joseph Smith, Jun. September 1830 Doctrine and Covenants, Section 28

1. Behold, I say unto thee, Oliver, that it shall be given unto thee that thou shalt be heard by the church in all things whatsoever thou shalt teach them by the

Comforter, concerning the revelations and commandments which I have given.

2. But, behold, verily, verily, I say unto thee, no one shall be appointed to receive commandments and revelations in this church excepting my servant Joseph Smith, Jun., for he receiveth them even as Moses.

3. And thou shalt be obedient unto the things which I shall give unto him, even as Aaron, to declare faithfully the commandments and the revelations, with power and authority unto the church.

4. And if thou art led at any time by the Comforter to speak or teach, or at all times by the way of commandment unto the church, thou mayest do it.

5. But thou shalt not write by way of commandment, but by wisdom;

6. And thou shalt not command him who is at thy head, and at the head of the church;

7. For I have given him the keys of the mysteries, and the revelations which are sealed, until I shall appoint unto them another in his stead.

SECTION REVELATION 208

Revelation of the Lord Jesus Christ
San Angelo, Texas
Tuesday, July 26, 2011

1. I, your Lord, have only One Man at a time on earth to be my holy Revelator of my new word.

Revelation of the Lord Jesus Christ
Given to President Joseph Smith, Jun.
February 1831
Doctrine and Covenants, Section 43

1. O hearken, ye elders of my church, and give ear to the words which I shall speak unto you.

2. For behold, verily, verily, I say unto you, that ye have received a commandment for a law unto my church, through him whom I have appointed unto you to receive commandments and revelations from my hand.

3. And this ye shall know assuredly -- that there is none other appointed unto you to receive commandments and revelations until he be taken, if he abide in me.

4. But verily, verily, I say unto you, that none else shall be appointed unto this gift except it be through him; for if it be taken from him he shall not have power except to appoint another in his stead.

5. And this shall be a law unto you, that ye receive not the teachings of any that shall come before you as revelations or commandments;

6. And this I give unto you that you may not be deceived, that you may know they are not of me.

7. For verily I say unto you, that he that is ordained of me shall come in at the gate and be ordained as I have told you before, to teach those revelations which you have received and shall receive through him whom I have appointed.***

12. And if ye desire the glories of the kingdom, appoint ye my servant Joseph Smith, Jun., and uphold him before me by the prayer of faith.

13. And again, I say unto you, that if ye desire the mysteries of the kingdom, provide for him food and raiment, and whatsoever thing he needeth to accomplish the work wherewith I have commanded him;

14. And if ye do it not he shall remain unto them that have received him, that I may reserve unto myself a pure people before me.

SECTION REVELATION 209

Revelation of the Lord Jesus Christ
San Angelo, Texas
Tuesday, July 26, 2011

1. In my holy will concerning Celestial Law of Plural Eternal Union --

2. My power is described as the only way to receive plural marriage.

3. Let all know the true power of governing power over my Church on earth is the Holy Melchizedek Priesthood, of the full order of Prophet, Seer, and Revelator.

4. Be of the way of knowing, by prayerful walk, and by my grace attending you, who is my Prophet, Seer, and Revelator to give my will to all people.

5. I have given to my Keyholder in the Melchizedek Priesthood the full key and knowledge of God to bring a people into the presence of your Lord.

6. Such is the call of our Lord, to now cease present proceedings of unjust attack in a court, not having power to be judge over my Celestial authority; even to be subservient to my Holy Priesthood authorized servant on my land of the full Kingdom of God ruling over all nations; which is the holy Order of Union Power of the dominion of my coming eternal power of Zion on earth.

7. Now hear my will: Be ye my holy will fulfilling --

8. Let my servant be free to do my will on earth; to let freedom of religion be your justification.

9. Let all now learn my holy will concerning the power of eternal authority of keys of holy power of my holy Order of Eternal Priesthood, that I have given my power of full and eternal authority to my servant on earth, to be of full power of my holy eternal authority.

10. Let all be of my eternal Kingdom, as you are my son or daughter on earth sent to do thy Lord's will.

Revelation of the Lord Jesus Christ
Given to President Joseph Smith, Jun.
July 12, 1843
Doctrine and Covenants, Section 132

7. And verily I say unto you, that the conditions of this law are these: All covenants, contracts, bonds, obligations, oaths, vows, performances, connections, associations, or expectations, that are not made and entered into and sealed by the Holy Spirit of promise, of him who is anointed, both as well for time and for all eternity, and that too most holy, by revelation and commandment through the medium of mine anointed, whom I have appointed on the earth to hold this power (and I have appointed unto my servant Joseph to hold this power in the last days, and there is never but one on the earth at a time on whom this power and the keys of this priesthood are conferred), are of no efficacy, virtue, or force in and after the resurrection from the dead; for all contracts

that are not made unto this end have an end when men are dead.***

45. For I have conferred upon you the keys and power of the priesthood, wherein I restore all things, and make known unto you all things in due time.

46. And verily, verily, I say unto you, that whatsoever you seal on earth shall be sealed in heaven; and whatsoever you bind on earth, in my name and by my word, saith the Lord, it shall be eternally bound in the heavens; and whosesoever sins you remit on earth shall be remitted eternally in the heavens; and whosesoever sins you retain on earth shall be retained in heaven.

47. And again, verily I say, whomsoever you bless I will bless, and whomsoever you curse I will curse, saith the Lord; for I, the Lord, am thy God.

48. And again, verily I say unto you, my servant Joseph, that whatsoever you give on earth, and to whomsoever you give any one on earth, by my word and according to my law, it shall be visited with blessings and not cursings, and with my power, saith the Lord, and shall be without condemnation on earth and in heaven.

49. For I am the Lord thy God, and will be with thee even unto the end of the world, and through all eternity; for verily I seal upon you your exaltation, and prepare a throne for you in the kingdom of my Father, with Abraham your father.***

58. Now, as touching the law of the priesthood, there are many things pertaining thereunto.

59. Verily, if a man be called of my Father, as was Aaron, by mine own voice, and by the voice of him that sent me, and I have endowed him with the keys of the power of this priesthood, if he do anything in my name, and according to my law and

by my word, he will not commit sin, and I will justify him.

60. Let no one, therefore, set on my servant Joseph; for I will justify him; for he shall do the sacrifice which I require at his hands for his transgressions, saith the Lord your God.

Obedience to Priesthood Is Obedience to God

President Rulon Jeffs
Rulon Jeffs' Sermons 3:504 April 4, 1976 CCA

The first law of heaven goes through my mind, which I feel to speak upon with the help of the Lord here today. The first law of heaven is obedience. Jesus said, "The first and greatest commandment, or law, is that we love our Father in heaven with all our heart, might, mind, and strength." These two are the same, brothers and sisters. Jesus said, "If you love Me, obey My commandments." That Being whom we love, we list to obey, and so it is indeed part and parcel of the first and great commandment and law of God, both in heaven and in earth.

If we love God, we love His Priesthood, because He is Priesthood. In fact, the holy Priesthood is God with us, if we understand Priesthood. It has been said, and truthfully, that -- and I am sure if you will trace the history, you will find it is true -- that man who apostatizes from this work, the work of the Priesthood, the work of God, has done so because he did not understand Priesthood. So we have, by the mercy and blessing of God, delegated to His chosen servants, and particularly I mention the keyholder, the keys of the holy Priesthood, from which we obtain the blessings of salvation. Therefore, it is necessary, if we take it to its correct and ultimate conclusion, that we obey Priesthood, which is the same as obeying God.

Some men who do not understand seem to feel that obedience is giving up our free agency. On the contrary; to enjoy our free agency, we must obey God. Disobedience to the law will bring about an abridgement of our agency, ***

So, brethren and sisters, President Johnson and those of the same order of Priesthood which holds that same Priesthood with him, are called of God. They belong to God, and as I have said many times in rather strong terms, hands off! It is for us to obey the principles of truth which is given us by that Priesthood and the keys thereof. If we will obey His servants, we will be obeying God. God cannot be here personally, and He has delegated His power and authority in the very highest that is given to man to President Johnson in this day and time. Brothers and sisters, if we do not draw near to him and be subject to his direction, when the time of visitation and of judgments come, we may not be in the right place, standing in holy places.

You brethren holding the holy Melchizedek Priesthood, heads of families, should have your families rallying around you in such a way that they would move as by a hair, that they might stand in holy places, and make your homes a temple. Those are the holy places that we must stand in, unless our head calls for us to go some place while the overflowing scourge passes over, for it is coming in soon.

I try to liken our condition, brothers and sisters, to that of the Zion's camp. God called upon Joseph to gather five hundred men to go up and redeem Zion. The least He would be satisfied with would be one hundred, but he gathered two hundred. Now, I am sure that God knew by His foreknowledge that this would not be accomplished, the redemption of Zion, though the set time had been given, September of 1836.

The conditions of this great work and mission that was given these men was that they should go and follow their head as by a hair, and go without murmuring, walking in perfect obedience, being one with him, walking as one man; so perfect in their unity and their oneness that they would have put to flight all of the mobs and the armies and the aliens and could have redeemed Zion. Had they complied with all of the conditions of that great commandment that was given them, they could have done it, because there was a set time, had they complied.

We have heard many, many times in recent years and times that the Gospel of preparation is upon us. We will not become prepared, brothers and sisters, short of this thing that I am speaking of here today; and that is obedience to Priesthood, obedience to President Johnson, our head, and the medium through which the word of God comes, and thus we will be obeying God. He is giving us these instructions and commandments by reason of the revelations of God with him, therefore this law of obedience is upon us; which, if we do, we will obey the law of sacrifice and come to know that our course is pleasing to God. And by the power of faith, the power of the Holy Ghost, through the Priesthood, we will accomplish this great work of preparation and be raised up as a people, out of the heart's core of this people. Not everyone under the sound of my voice will be called up, I can promise you that, or else God never spoke by the mouth of His Prophets.

So, where do we stand, brothers and sisters? Are we walking in perfect obedience, in perfect love? Love and obedience are the same thing. Whom we love, we list to obey, as Jesus said. Now let us, therefore, love God, love His Priesthood, love the truth, the true and correct principles that are expounded and given to us by that Priesthood, and become one, that we may have power with God through faith. Faith is power with God, in the application of these principles of obedience and love.

Erastus Snow
JD 24:159 June 24, 1883 Parowan

Brother Cannon speaks of President Young and President Taylor, and other good men, our leaders, being led, as it were, by a hair in obedience to the Priesthood, which implies simply obedience to truth and to correct doctrine, and to righteousness. This is the explanation the Prophet Joseph Smith gave to a certain lawyer in his time who came to see him and his people and expressed astonishment and surprise at the ease with which he controlled the people, and said it was something that was not to be found among the learned men of the world. Said he: "We cannot do it. What is the secret of your success?" "Why," said the Prophet, "I do not govern the people. I teach them correct principles and they govern themselves."

Power of Priesthood

Revelation of the Lord Jesus Christ Given to President Joseph Smith, Jun. May 6, 1833 Doctrine and Covenants, Section 84

17. Which priesthood continueth in the church of God in all generations, and is without beginning of days or end of years.

18. And the Lord confirmed a priesthood also upon Aaron and his seed, throughout all their generations, which priesthood also continueth and abideth forever with the priesthood which is after the holiest order of God.

19. And this greater priesthood administereth the gospel and holdeth the key of the mysteries of the kingdom, even the key of the knowledge of God.

20. Therefore, in the ordinances thereof, the power of godliness is manifest.

21. And without the ordinances thereof, and the authority of the priesthood, the power of godliness is not manifest unto men in the flesh;

22. For without this no man can see the face of God, even the Father, and live.*

35. And also all they who receive this priesthood receive me, saith the Lord;

36. For he that receiveth my servants receiveth me;

37. And he that receiveth me receiveth my Father;

38. And he that receiveth my Father receiveth my Father's kingdom; therefore all that my Father hath shall be given unto him.

39. And this is according to the oath and covenant which belongeth to the priesthood.

40. Therefore, all those who receive the priesthood, receive this oath and covenant of my Father, which he cannot break, neither can it be moved.

41. But whoso breaketh this covenant after he hath received it, and altogether turneth therefrom, shall not have

forgiveness of sins in this world nor in the world to come.

42. And wo unto all those who come not unto this priesthood which ye have received, which I now confirm upon you who are present this day, by mine own voice out of the heavens; and even I have given the heavenly hosts and mine angels charge concerning you.

43. And I now give unto you a commandment to beware concerning yourselves, to give diligent heed to the words of eternal life.

44. For you shall live by every word that proceedeth forth from the mouth of God.

45. For the word of the Lord is truth, and whatsoever is truth is light, and whatsoever is light is Spirit, even the Spirit of Jesus Christ.

46. And the Spirit giveth light to every man that cometh into the world; and the Spirit enlighteneth every man through the world, that hearkeneth to the voice of the Spirit.

47. And every one that hearkeneth to the voice of the Spirit cometh unto God, even the Father.

48. And the Father teacheth him of the covenant which he has renewed and confirmed upon you, which is confirmed upon you for your sakes, and not for your sakes only, but for the sake of the whole world.

49. And the whole world lieth in sin, and groaneth under darkness and under the bondage of sin.

50. And by this you may know they are under the bondage of sin, because they come not unto me.

51. For whoso cometh not unto me is under the bondage of sin.

52. And whoso receiveth not my voice is not acquainted with my voice, and is not of me.

53. And by this you may know the righteous from the wicked, and that the whole world groaneth under sin and darkness even now.***

63. And as I said unto mine apostles, even so I say unto you, for you are mine apostles, even God's high priests; ye are they whom my Father hath given me; ye are my friends;

Priesthood to Be of Pure Love

Revelation of the Lord Jesus Christ Given to President Joseph Smith, Jun. March 20, 1839
Doctrine and Covenants, Section 121

41. No power or influence can or ought to be maintained by virtue of the priesthood, only by persuasion, by long-suffering, by gentleness and meekness, and by love unfeigned;

42. By kindness, and pure knowledge, which shall greatly enlarge the soul without hypocrisy, and without guile --

43. Reproving betimes with sharpness, when moved upon by the Holy Ghost; and then showing forth afterwards an increase of love toward him whom thou hast reproved, lest he esteem thee to be his enemy;

44. That he may know that thy faithfulness is stronger than the cords of death.

45. Let thy bowels also be full of charity towards all men, and to the household of faith, and let virtue garnish thy thoughts unceasingly; then shall thy confidence wax strong in the presence of God; and the doctrine of the priesthood

shall distil upon thy soul as the dews from heaven.

46. The Holy Ghost shall be thy constant companion, and thy scepter an unchanging scepter of righteousness and truth; and thy dominion shall be an everlasting dominion, and without compulsory means it shall flow unto thee forever and ever.

Sealing Powers Restored
(My Will of Holy Celestial Power)

SECTION REVELATION 210

Revelation of the Lord Jesus Christ
San Angelo, Texas
Tuesday, July 26, 2011

1. I, your Lord, appearing to Joseph Smith in my holy temple, declared eternal power to rest upon my people.

2. I sent the Keyholders of keys and powers to deliver to my One Man holding full Priesthood authority, to also hold keys of Priesthood in full, which is the keys of Elijah, to seal Celestial unions of marriage, even plural marriage upon faithful sons and daughters of my holy Church on earth.

Revelation of the Lord Jesus Christ
Given to President Joseph Smith, Jun.
April 3, 1836
Doctrine and Covenants, Section 110

1. The veil was taken from our minds, and the eyes of our understanding were opened.

2. We saw the Lord standing upon the breastwork of the pulpit, before us; and under his feet was a paved work of pure gold, in color like amber.

3. His eyes were as a flame of fire; the hair of his head was white like the pure snow; his countenance shone above the brightness of the sun; and his voice was as the sound of the rushing of great waters, even the voice of Jehovah, saying:

4. I am the first and the last; I am he who liveth, I am he who was slain; I am your advocate with the Father.

5. Behold, your sins are forgiven you; you are clean before me; therefore, lift up your heads and rejoice.

6. Let the hearts of your brethren rejoice, and let the hearts of all my people rejoice, who have, with their might, built this house to my name.

7. For behold, I have accepted this house, and my name shall be here; and I will manifest myself to my people in mercy in this house.

8. Yea, I will appear unto my servants, and speak unto them with mine own voice, if my people will keep my commandments, and do not pollute this holy house.

9. Yea the hearts of thousands and tens of thousands shall greatly rejoice in consequence of the blessings which shall be poured out, and the endowment with which my servants have been endowed in this house.

10. And the fame of this house shall spread to foreign lands; and this is the beginning of the blessing which shall be poured out upon the heads of my people. Even so. Amen.

11. After this vision closed, the heavens were again opened unto us; and

Moses appeared before us, and committed unto us the keys of the gathering of Israel from the four parts of the earth, and the leading of the ten tribes from the land of the north.

12. After this, Elias appeared, and committed the dispensation of the gospel of Abraham, saying that in us and our seed all generations after us should be blessed.

13. After this vision had closed, another great and glorious vision burst upon us; for Elijah the prophet, who was taken to heaven without tasting death, stood before us, and said:

14. Behold, the time has fully come, which was spoken of by the mouth of Malachi -- testifying that he [Elijah] should be sent, before the great and dreadful day of the Lord come --

15. To turn the hearts of the fathers to the children, and the children to the fathers, lest the whole earth be smitten with a curse --

16. Therefore, the keys of this dispensation are committed into your hands; and by this ye may know that the great and dreadful day of the Lord is near, even at the doors.

The Government of God

President Joseph Smith, Jun.
Teachings of the Prophet Joseph Smith, Page 248

An Editorial by the Prophet On the Failure of Man-made Governments and the Right of God to Rule

The government of the Almighty has always been very dissimilar to the governments of men, whether we refer to His religious government, or to the government of nations. The government of God has always tended to promote peace, unity, harmony, strength, and happiness; while that of man has been productive of confusion, disorder, weakness, and misery.

Man's Government Brings Misery and Destruction

The greatest acts of the mighty men have been to depopulate nations and to overthrow kingdoms; and whilst they have exalted themselves and become glorious, it has been at the expense of the lives of the innocent, the blood of the oppressed, the moans of the widow, and the tears of the orphan.

Egypt, Babylon, Greece, Persia, Carthage, Rome -- each was raised to dignity amidst the clash of arms and the din of war; and whilst their triumphant leaders led forth their victorious armies to glory and victory, their ears were saluted with the groans of the dying and the misery and distress of the human family; before them the earth was a paradise, and behind them a desolate wilderness; their kingdoms were founded in carnage and bloodshed, and sustained by oppression, tyranny, and despotism. The designs of God, on the other hand, have been to promote the universal good of the universal world; to establish peace and good will among men; to promote the principles of eternal truth; to bring about a state of things that shall unite man to his fellow man; cause the world to "beat their swords into plowshares, and their spears into pruning hooks," make the nations of the earth dwell in peace, and to bring about the millennial glory, when "the earth shall yield its increase, resume its paradisean glory, and become as the garden of the Lord."

Failure of the Governments of Men

The great and wise of ancient days have failed in all their attempts to promote eternal power, peace and happiness. Their nations have crumbled to pieces; their thrones have been cast down in their turn, and their cities, and their mightiest works of art have been annihilated; or their dilapidated towers, or time-worn monuments have left us but feeble traces of their former magnificence and ancient grandeur. They proclaim as with a voice of thunder, those imperishable truths -- that man's strength is weakness, his wisdom is folly, his glory is his shame.

Monarchial, aristocratical, and republican governments of their various kinds and grades, have, in their turn, been raised to dignity, and prostrated in the dust. The plans of the greatest politicians, the wisest senators, and most profound statesmen have been exploded; and the proceedings of the greatest chieftains, the bravest generals, and the wisest kings have fallen to the ground. Nation has succeeded nation, and we have inherited nothing but their folly. History records their puerile plans, their short-lived glory, their feeble intellect and their ignoble deeds.

Has Man Increased in Intelligence?

Have we increased in knowledge or intelligence? Where is there a man that can step forth and alter the destiny of nations and promote the happiness of the world? Or where is there a kingdom or nation that can promote the universal happiness of its own subjects, or even their general well-being? Our nation, which possesses greater resources than any other, is rent, from center to circumference, with party strife, political intrigues, and sectional interest; our counselors are panic stricken, our legislators are astonished, and our senators are confounded, our merchants are paralyzed, our tradesmen are disheartened, our mechanics out of employ, our farmers distressed, and our poor crying for bread, our banks are broken, our credit ruined,

and our states overwhelmed in debt, yet we are, and have been in peace.

Man Not Able to Govern Himself

What is the matter? Are we alone in this thing? Verily no. With all our evils we are better situated than any other nation. Let Egypt, Turkey, Spain, France, Italy, Portugal, Germany, England, China, or any other nation, speak, and tell the tale of their trouble, their perplexity, and distress, and we should find that their cup was full, and that they were preparing to drink the dregs of sorrow. England, that boasts of her literature, her science, commerce, &c., has her hands reeking with the blood of the innocent abroad, and she is saluted with the cries of the oppressed at home. Chartism, O'Connelism, and radicalism are gnawing her vitals at home; and Ireland, Scotland, Canada, and the east are threatening her destruction abroad. France is rent to the core, intrigue, treachery, and treason lurk in the dark, and murder, and assassination stalk forth at noonday. Turkey, once the dread of European nations, has been shorn of her strength, has dwindled into her dotage, and has been obliged to ask her allies to propose to her tributary terms of peace; and Russia and Egypt are each of them opening their jaws to devour her. Spain has been the theater of bloodshed, of misery and woe for years past. Syria is now convulsed with war and bloodshed. The great and powerful empire of China, which has for centuries resisted the attacks of barbarians, has become tributary to a foreign foe, her batteries thrown down, many of her cities destroyed, and her villages deserted. We might mention the Easter Rajahs, the miseries and oppressions of the Irish; the convulsed state of Central America; the situation of Texas and Mexico; the state of Greece, Switzerland and Poland; nay, the world itself presents one great theater of misery, woe, and "distress of nations with perplexity." All, all, speak with a voice of thunder, that man is not able to govern himself, to legislate for himself, to protect himself, to promote his own good, nor the good of the world.

The Design of Jehovah

It has been the design of Jehovah, from the commencement of the world, and is His purpose now, to regulate the affairs of the world in His own time, to stand as a head of the universe, and take the reins of government in His own hand. When that is done, judgment will be administered in righteousness; anarchy and confusion will be destroyed, and "nations will learn war no more." It is for want of this great governing principle, that all this confusion has existed; "for it is not in man that walketh, to direct his steps;" this we have fully shown.

If there was anything great or good in the world, it came from God. The construction of the first vessel was given to Noah, by revelation. The design of the ark was given by God, "a pattern of heavenly things." The learning of the Egyptians, and their knowledge of astronomy was no doubt taught them by Abraham and Joseph, as their records testify, who received it from the Lord. The art of working in brass, silver, gold, and precious stones, was taught by revelation, in the wilderness. The architectural designs of the Temple at Jerusalem, together with its ornaments and beauty, were given of God. Wisdom to govern the house of Israel was given to Solomon, and the Judges of Israel; and if he had always been their king, and they subject to his mandate, and obedient to his laws, they would still have been a great and mighty people -- the rulers of the universe, and the wonder of the world.

Government Established by God

If Nebuchadnezzar, or Darius, or Cyrus, or any other king possessed knowledge or power, it was from the same source, as the Scriptures abundantly testify. If, then, God puts up one, and sets down another at His pleasure, and made instruments of kings, unknown to themselves, to fulfill His prophecies, how much more was he able, if man would have been subject to His mandate, to regulate the affairs of this world, and promote peace and happiness among the human family!

The Lord has at various times commenced this kind of government, and tendered His services to the human family. He selected Enoch, whom He directed, and gave His law unto, and to the people who were with him; and when the world in general would not obey the commands of God, after walking with God, he translated Enoch and his church, and the Priesthood or government of heaven was taken away.

Abraham was guided in all his family affairs by the Lord; was conversed with by angels, and by the Lord; was told where to go, and when to stop; and prospered exceedingly in all that he put his hand unto; it was because he and his family obeyed the counsel of the Lord.

When Egypt was under the superintendence of Joseph it prospered, because he was taught of God; when they oppressed the Israelites, destruction came upon them. When the children of Israel were chosen with Moses at their head, they were to be a peculiar people, among whom God should place His name; their motto was: "The Lord is our lawgiver; the Lord is our Judge; the Lord is our King; and He shall reign over us." While in this state they might truly say, "Happy is that people, whose God is the Lord." Their government was a theocracy; they had God to make their laws, and men chosen by Him to administer them; He was their God, and they were His people. Moses received the word of the Lord from God Himself; he was the mouth of God to Aaron, and Aaron taught the people, in both civil and ecclesiastical affairs; they were both one, there was no distinction; so will it be when the purposes of God shall be accomplished: when "the Lord shall be King over the whole earth" and "Jerusalem His throne." "The law shall go forth from Zion, and the word of the Lord from Jerusalem."

Universal Peace to Come from God

This is the only thing that can bring about the "restitution of all things spoken of by all the holy Prophets since the world was" -- "the dispensation of the fullness of times, when God shall gather together all things in one." Other attempts to promote universal peace and happiness in the human family have proved abortive; every effort has failed; every plan and design has fallen to the ground; it needs the wisdom of God, the intelligence of God, and the power of God to accomplish this. The world has had a fair trial for six thousand years; the Lord will try the seventh thousand Himself; "He whose right it is, will possess the kingdom, and reign until He has put all things under His feet;" iniquity will hide its hoary head, Satan will be bound, and the works of darkness destroyed; righteousness will be put to the line, and judgment to the plummet, and "he that fears the Lord will alone be exalted in that day." To bring about this state of things, there must of necessity be great confusion among the nations of the earth; "distress of nations with perplexity." Am I asked what is the cause of the present distress? I would answer, "Shall there be evil in a city and the Lord hath not done it?"

Earth Now Groaning Under Corruption

The earth is groaning under corruption, oppression, tyranny and bloodshed; and God is coming out of His hiding place, as He said He would do, to vex the nations of the earth. Daniel, in his vision, saw convulsion upon convulsion; he "beheld till the thrones were cast down, and the Ancient of Days did sit;" and one was brought before him like unto the Son of Man; and all nations, kindred, tongues, and peoples, did serve and obey Him. It is for us to be righteous, that we may be wise and understand; for none of the wicked shall understand; but the wise shall understand, and they that turn many to righteousness shall shine as the stars for ever and ever.

It Behooves Us to Be Wise

As a Church and a people it behooves us to be wise, and to seek to know the will of God, and then be willing to do it; for "blessed is he that heareth the word of the Lord, and keepeth it," say the Scriptures. "Watch and pray always," says our Savior, "that ye may be accounted worthy to escape the things that are to come on the earth, and to stand before the Son of Man." If Enoch, Abraham, Moses, and the children of Israel, and all God's people were saved by keeping the commandments of God, we, if saved at all, shall be saved upon the same principle. As God governed Abraham, Isaac and Jacob as families, and the children of Israel as a nation; so we, as a Church, must be under His guidance if we are prospered, preserved and sustained. Our only confidence can be in God; our only wisdom obtained from Him; and He alone must be our protector and safeguard, spiritually and temporally, or we fall.

We have been chastened by the hand of God heretofore for not obeying His commands, although we never violated any human law, or transgressed any human precept; yet we have treated lightly His commands, and departed from His ordinances, and the Lord has chastened us sore, and we have felt His arm and kissed the rod; let us be wise in time to come and ever remember that "to obey is better than sacrifice, and to hearken than the fat of rams." The Lord has told us to build the Temple and the Nauvoo House; and that command is as binding upon us as any other; and that man who engages not in these things is as much a transgressor as though he broke any other commandment; he is not a doer of God's will, not a fulfiller of His laws.

The Saints Subject to Divine Counsel

In regard to the building up of Zion, it has to be done by the counsel of Jehovah, by the revelations of heaven; and we should feel to say, "If the Lord go not with us, carry us not up hence." We would say to the Saints that come here, we have laid the foundation for the gathering of God's people to this place, and they expect that when the Saints do come, they will be under the counsel that God has appointed. The Twelve are set apart to counsel the Saints pertaining to this matter; and we expect that those who come here will send before them their wise men according to revelation; or if not practicable, be subject to the counsel that God has given, or they cannot receive an inheritance among the Saints, or be considered as God's people, and they will be dealt with as transgressors of the laws of God. We are trying here to gird up our loins, and purge from our midst the workers of iniquity; and we hope that when our brethren arrive from abroad, they will assist us to roll forth this good work, and to accomplish this great design, that "Zion may be built up in righteousness; and all nations flock to her standard;" that as God's people, under His direction, and obedient to His law, we may grow up in righteousness and truth; that when His purposes shall be accomplished, we may receive an inheritance among those that are sanctified. (July 15, 1842.) D.H.C. 5:61-66.

Plural Marriage Established; Reward of Those Who Abide Their Covenants Unto the End

SECTION REVELATION 211

Revelation of the Lord Jesus Christ San Angelo, Texas Tuesday, July 26, 2011

Celestial Plural Marriage Established by Revelation of God

1. Thus saith the Lord, even your Savior over all flesh, to all peoples of every nation on earth; and to governing authority on my land of Zion where I am to soon come to dwell among men a thousand years; to govern all peoples as your God and King, all to my right to rule:

2. I have been your Lord all your eternal existence as a son or daughter of God.

3. I am a God of eternal power.

4. I have all knowledge, light, truth eternal, Priesthood power and authority from my Father, the God of Holy Priesthood power over all.

5. I am Son Ahman, even Jesus Christ, whose holy will and atoning and perfect way hath caused you to

have hope eternal, to be of such a way to learn of eternal way of life everlasting.

6. I have instituted eternal laws of progression of pure holy conduct and of faith, to bring children on earth to be of my holy order of eternal lives.

7. Celestial Marriage is a law and principle of eternal life of my holy power of Priesthood, to exalt pure sons to Godhood; daughters to a Celestial, eternal, happy life of mothers of children in eternal union of my guiding, perfecting, and exalting; unto a mother of creating sons and daughters of spirit power on an eternal earth of high Celestial power; to be eternal parents, to be of pure begetters of children eternally.

8. Let all know this law is of me and is eternal, unchangeable, and is a holy, pure, exalting law of salvation, and must be lived by my revealing; and by my holy revealing, appointing unions eternal as I reveal all truth, of pure truth, who is of worthy condition to be a God of Creation.

9. Such is this law of pure religious and holy intent, practice, and eternal result of my power guiding all in this law by my Holy Priesthood.

10. Thus, I reveal to all people of the earth that I shall uphold my Priesthood power I cause to reveal my will; and I shall be the holy power to perfect my people who abide faithfully my law.

11. Let my holy will now be of a way to understand I revealed my law of Celestial Union of Plural Marriage to my servant on earth, even my servant who held all the powers of Priesthood authority in the beginning of this time of preparing for my holy power coming to earth from Celestial realms of my eternal domain, which rules over all people and shall be of my whole and holy power.

12. Let all now be receiving my word as given through Joseph Smith, my holy Seer of the time of final preparing for my coming, to be my law under my revealing, not to be given to any outside my Holy Priesthood.

13. All must be of my true faith and Kingdom to be receiving my holy law.

14. No one can enter into this law who is not of my Church and Kingdom.

15. Therefore, this law is of religion of heaven revealed by your God to His Prophet of full Priesthood authority and power eternal, to be my law, not of any government power among men to be of a way of justice power over my Church, for it is mine, not of man.

16. Therefore, thy Lord revealeth all needed truth, that my law will be preserved on earth, to prepare my Church for my coming; which law is Celestial and is not to be of earth only.

17. I am God. I have my eternal law to reveal, guide, and preserve.

18. Let my truth be upheld by my Priesthood.

19. Let all government powers of man not interfere in the religious free living of my holy way; to no longer be of a prosecuting power against my holy religion.

20. Receive ye my will on the truths revealed through my servant Joseph Smith, and as I caused others of my servants of Priesthood power to continue on earth; to have a pure people raised unto your God for His coming.

Revelation of the Lord Jesus Christ Given to President Joseph Smith, Jun. July 12, 1843 Doctrine and Covenants, Section 132

1. Verily, thus saith the Lord unto you my servant Joseph, that inasmuch as you have inquired of my hand to know and understand wherein I, the Lord, justified my servants Abraham, Isaac, and Jacob, as also Moses, David and Solomon, my servants, as touching the principle and doctrine of their having many wives and concubines --

2. Behold, and lo, I am the Lord thy God, and will answer thee as touching this matter.

3. Therefore, prepare thy heart to receive and obey the instructions which I am about to give unto you; for all those who have this law revealed unto them must obey the same.

4. For behold, I reveal unto you a new and an everlasting covenant; and if ye abide not that covenant, then are ye damned; for no one can reject this covenant and be permitted to enter into my glory.

5. For all who will have a blessing at my hands shall abide the law which was appointed for that blessing, and the conditions thereof, as were instituted from before the foundation of the world.

6. And as pertaining to the new and everlasting covenant, it was instituted for the fulness of my glory; and he that receiveth a fulness thereof must and shall abide the law, or he shall be damned, saith the Lord God.

7. And verily I say unto you, that the conditions of this law are these: All covenants, contracts, bonds, obligations, oaths, vows, performances, connections, associations, or expectations, that are not made and entered into and sealed by the Holy Spirit of promise, of him who is anointed, both as well for time and for all eternity, and that too most holy, by revelation and commandment through the medium of mine anointed, whom I have appointed on the earth to hold this power (and I have appointed unto my servant Joseph to hold this power in the last days, and there is never but one on the earth at a time on whom this power and the keys of this priesthood are conferred), are of no efficacy, virtue, or force in and after the resurrection from the dead; for all contracts that are not made unto this end have an end when men are dead.

8. Behold, mine house is a house of

order, saith the Lord God, and not a house of confusion.

9. Will I accept of an offering, saith the Lord, that is not made in my name?

10. Or will I receive at your hands that which I have not appointed?

11. And will I appoint unto you, saith the Lord, except it be by law, even as I and my Father ordained unto you, before the world was?

12. I am the Lord thy God; and I give unto you this commandment -- that no man shall come unto the Father but by me or by my word, which is my law, saith the Lord.

13. And everything that is in the world, whether it be ordained of men, by thrones, or principalities, or powers, or things of name, whatsoever they may be, that are not by me or by my word, saith the Lord, shall be thrown down, and shall not remain after men are dead, neither in nor after the resurrection, saith the Lord your God.

14. For whatsoever things remain are by me; and whatsoever things are not by me shall be shaken and destroyed.

15. Therefore, if a man marry him a wife in the world, and he marry her not by me nor by my word, and he covenant with her so long as he is in the world and she with him, their covenant and marriage are not of force when they are dead, and when they are out of the world; therefore, they are not bound by any law when they are out of the world.

16. Therefore, when they are out of the world they neither marry nor are given in marriage; but are appointed angels in heaven, which angels are ministering servants, to minister for those who are worthy of a far more, and an exceeding, and an eternal weight of glory.

17. For these angels did not abide my law; therefore, they cannot be enlarged, but remain separately and singly, without exaltation, in their saved condition, to all eternity; and from henceforth are not gods, but are angels of God forever and ever.

18. And again, verily I say unto you, if a man marry a wife, and make a covenant with her for time and for all eternity, if that covenant is not by me or by my word, which is my law, and is not sealed by the Holy Spirit of promise, through him whom I have anointed and appointed unto this power, then it is not valid neither of force when they are out of the world, because they are not joined by me, saith the Lord, neither by my word; when they are out of the world it cannot be received there, because the angels and the gods are appointed there, by whom they cannot pass; they cannot, therefore, inherit my glory; for my house is a house of order, saith the Lord God.

19. And again, verily I say unto you, if a man marry a wife by my word, which is my law, and by the new and everlasting covenant, and it is sealed unto them by the Holy Spirit of promise, by him who is anointed, unto whom I have appointed this power and the keys of this priesthood; and it shall be said unto them -- Ye shall come forth in the first resurrection; and if it be after the first resurrection, in the next resurrection; and shall inherit thrones, kingdoms, principalities, and powers, dominions, all heights and depths -- then shall it be written in the Lamb's Book of Life, that he shall commit no murder whereby to shed innocent blood, and if ye abide in my covenant, and commit no murder whereby to shed innocent blood, it shall be done unto them in all things whatsoever my servant hath put upon them, in time, and through all eternity; and shall

be of full force when they are out of the world; and they shall pass by the angels, and the gods, which are set there, to their exaltation and glory in all things, as hath been sealed upon their heads, which glory shall be a fulness and a continuation of the seeds forever and ever.

20. Then shall they be gods, because they have no end; therefore shall they be from everlasting to everlasting, because they continue; then shall they be above all, because all things are subject unto them. Then shall they be gods, because they have all power, and the angels are subject unto them.

21. Verily, verily, I say unto you, except ye abide my law ye cannot attain to this glory.

22. For strait is the gate, and narrow the way that leadeth unto the exaltation and continuation of the lives, and few there be that find it, because ye receive me not in the world neither do ye know me.

23. But if ye receive me in the world, then shall ye know me, and shall receive your exaltation; that where I am ye shall be also.

24. This is eternal lives -- to know the only wise and true God, and Jesus Christ, whom he hath sent. I am he. Receive ye, therefore, my law.

25. Broad is the gate, and wide the way that leadeth to the deaths; and many there are that go in thereat, because they receive me not, neither do they abide in my law.

26. Verily, verily, I say unto you, if a man marry a wife according to my word, and they are sealed by the Holy Spirit of promise, according to mine appointment, and he or she shall commit any sin or transgression of the new and everlasting covenant whatever, and all manner of blasphemies, and if they commit no murder wherein they shed innocent blood, yet they shall come forth in the first resurrection, and enter into their exaltation; but they shall be destroyed in the flesh, and shall be delivered unto the buffetings of Satan unto the day of redemption, saith the Lord God.

27. The blasphemy against the Holy Ghost, which shall not be forgiven in the world nor out of the world, is in that ye commit murder wherein ye shed innocent blood, and assent unto my death, after ye have received my new and everlasting covenant, saith the Lord God; and he that abideth not this law can in nowise enter into my glory, but shall be damned, saith the Lord.

28. I am the Lord thy God, and will give unto thee the law of my Holy Priesthood, as was ordained by me and my Father before the world was.

29. Abraham received all things, whatsoever he received, by revelation and commandment, by my word, saith the Lord, and hath entered into his exaltation and sitteth upon his throne.

30. Abraham received promises concerning his seed, and of the fruit of his loins -- from whose loins ye are, namely, my servant Joseph -- which were to continue so long as they were in the world; and as touching Abraham and his seed, out of the world they should continue; both in the world and out of the world should they continue as innumerable as the stars; or, if ye were to count the sand upon the seashore ye could not number them.

31. This promise is yours also, because ye are of Abraham, and the promise was made unto Abraham; and by this law is the continuation of the works of my Father, wherein he glorifieth himself.

32. Go ye, therefore, and do the works of Abraham; enter ye into my law and ye shall be saved.

33. But if ye enter not into my law ye cannot receive the promise of my Father, which he made unto Abraham.

34. God commanded Abraham, and Sarah gave Hagar to Abraham to wife. And why did she do it? Because this was the law; and from Hagar sprang many people. This, therefore, was fulfilling, among other things, the promises.

35. Was Abraham, therefore, under condemnation? Verily I say unto you, Nay; for I, the Lord, commanded it.

36. Abraham was commanded to offer his son Isaac; nevertheless, it was written: Thou shalt not kill. Abraham, however, did not refuse, and it was accounted unto him for righteousness.

37. Abraham received concubines, and they bore him children; and it was accounted unto him for righteousness, because they were given unto him, and he abode in my law; as Isaac also and Jacob did none other things than that which they were commanded; and because they did none other things than that which they were commanded, they have entered into their exaltation, according to the promises, and sit upon thrones, and are not angels but are gods.

38. David also received many wives and concubines, and also Solomon and Moses my servants, as also many others of my servants, from the beginning of creation until this time; and in nothing did they sin save in those things which they received not of me.

39. David's wives and concubines were given unto him of me, by the hand of Nathan, my servant, and others of the prophets who had the keys of this power; and in none of these things did he sin against me save in the case of Uriah and his wife; and, therefore he hath fallen from his exaltation, and received his portion; and he shall not inherit them out of the world, for I gave them unto another, saith the Lord.

40. I am the Lord thy God, and I gave unto thee, my servant Joseph, an appointment, and restore all things. Ask what ye will, and it shall be given unto you according to my word.

41. And as ye have asked concerning adultery, verily, verily, I say unto you, if a man receiveth a wife in the new and everlasting covenant, and if she be with another man, and I have not appointed unto her by the holy anointing, she hath committed adultery and shall be destroyed.

42. If she be not in the new and everlasting covenant, and she be with another man, she has committed adultery.

43. And if her husband be with another woman, and he was under a vow, he hath broken his vow and hath committed adultery.

44. And if she hath not committed adultery, but is innocent and hath not broken her vow, and she knoweth it, and I reveal it unto you, my servant Joseph, then shall you have power, by the power of my Holy Priesthood, to take her and give her unto him that hath not committed adultery but hath been faithful; for he shall be made ruler over many.

45. For I have conferred upon you the keys and power of the priesthood, wherein I restore all things, and make known unto you all things in due time.

46. And verily, verily, I say unto you, that whatsoever you seal on earth shall be sealed in heaven; and whatsoever you

bind on earth, in my name and by my word, saith the Lord, it shall be eternally bound in the heavens; and whosesoever sins you remit on earth shall be remitted eternally in the heavens; and whosoever sins you retain on earth shall be retained in heaven.

47. And again, verily I say, whomsoever you bless I will bless, and whomsoever you curse I will curse, saith the Lord; for I, the Lord, am thy God.

48. And again, verily I say unto you, my servant Joseph, that whatsoever you give on earth, and to whomsoever you give any one on earth, by my word and according to my law, it shall be visited with blessings and not cursings, and with my power, saith the Lord, and shall be without condemnation on earth and in heaven.

49. For I am the Lord thy God, and will be with thee even unto the end of the world, and through all eternity; for verily I seal upon you your exaltation, and prepare a throne for you in the kingdom of my Father, with Abraham your father.

50. Behold, I have seen your sacrifices, and will forgive all your sins; I have seen your sacrifices in obedience to that which I have told you. Go, therefore, and I make a way for your escape, as I accepted the offering of Abraham of his son Isaac.

51. Verily, I say unto you: A commandment I give unto mine handmaid, Emma Smith, your wife, whom I have given unto you, that she stay herself and partake not of that which I commanded you to offer unto her; for I did it, saith the Lord, to prove you all, as I did Abraham, and that I might require an offering at your hand, by covenant and sacrifice.

52. And let mine handmaid, Emma Smith, receive all those that have been given unto my servant Joseph, and who are virtuous and pure before me; and those who are not pure, and have said they were pure, shall be destroyed, saith the Lord God.

53. For I am the Lord thy God, and ye shall obey my voice; and I give unto my servant Joseph that he shall be made ruler over many things; for he hath been faithful over a few things, and from henceforth I will strengthen him.

54. And I command mine handmaid, Emma Smith, to abide and cleave unto my servant Joseph, and to none else. But if she will not abide this commandment she shall be destroyed, saith the Lord; for I am the Lord thy God, and will destroy her if she abide not in my law.

55. But if she will not abide this commandment, then shall my servant Joseph do all things for her, even as he hath said; and I will bless him and multiply him and give unto him an hundredfold in this world, of fathers and mothers, brothers and sisters, houses and lands, wives and children, and crowns of eternal lives in the eternal worlds.

56. And again, verily I say, let mine handmaid forgive my servant Joseph his trespasses; and then shall she be forgiven her trespasses, wherein she has trespassed against me; and I, the Lord thy God, will bless her, and multiply her, and make her heart to rejoice.

57. And again, I say, let not my servant Joseph put his property out of his hands, lest an enemy come and destroy him; for Satan seeketh to destroy; for I am the Lord thy God, and he is my servant; and behold, and lo, I am with him, as I was with Abraham, thy father, even unto his exaltation and glory.

58. Now, as touching the law of the priesthood, there are many things pertaining thereunto.

59. Verily, if a man be called of my Father, as was Aaron, by mine own voice, and by the voice of him that sent me, and I have endowed him with the keys of the power of this priesthood, if he do anything in my name, and according to my law and by my word, he will not commit sin, and I will justify him.

60. Let no one, therefore, set on my servant Joseph; for I will justify him; for he shall do the sacrifice which I require at his hands for his transgressions, saith the Lord your God.

61. And again, as pertaining to the law of the priesthood -- if any man espouse a virgin, and desire to espouse another, and the first give her consent, and if he espouse the second, and they are virgins, and have vowed to no other man, then is he justified; he cannot commit adultery for they are given unto him; for he cannot commit adultery with that that belongeth unto him and to no one else.

62. And if he have ten virgins given unto him by this law, he cannot commit adultery, for they belong to him, and they are given unto him; therefore is he justified.

63. But if one or either of the ten virgins, after she is espoused, shall be with another man, she has committed adultery, and shall be destroyed; for they are given unto him to multiply and replenish the earth, according to my commandment, and to fulfil the promise which was given by my Father before the foundation of the world, and for their exaltation in the eternal worlds, that they may bear the souls of men; for herein is the work of my Father continued, that he may be glorified.

64. And again, verily, verily, I say unto you, if any man have a wife, who holds the keys of this power, and he teaches unto her the law of my priesthood, as pertaining to these things, then shall she believe and administer unto him, or she shall be destroyed, saith the Lord your God; for I will destroy her; for I will magnify my name upon all those who receive and abide in my law.

65. Therefore, it shall be lawful in me, if she receive not this law, for him to receive all things whatsoever I, the Lord his God, will give unto him, because she did not believe and administer unto him according to my word; and she then becomes the transgressor; and he is exempt from the law of Sarah, who administered unto Abraham according to the law when I commanded Abraham to take Hagar to wife.

66. And now, as pertaining to this law, verily, verily, I say unto you, I will reveal more unto you, hereafter; therefore, let this suffice for the present. Behold, I am Alpha and Omega. Amen.

SECTION REVELATION 212

On My Way of Revealing Necessity of Revelation Being Needed to Be My True Religion of Heaven --

Revelation of the Lord Jesus Christ San Angelo, Texas Wednesday, July 27, 2011

1. Let all now be of a holy way.

2. Let my way be of a pure holy way of revealing marriage unions, to be my law of holy eternal revealing;

not of man, but of me, your Lord Jesus Christ; He who is over all and who dictates and guides His servant to administer my holy way, not to others not in my Church and Priesthood law.

3. Let my people quietly abide the sacred covenants they have received to be as an example to guide souls to see as God sees in all things.

4. No longer live in prejudicing the people of the world who do not understand eternal law.

5. Let no one set on my servant and Keyholder on earth, as he is my vessel of holy power to bless pure holy vessels on the way of my giving increase in salvation power eternal.

6. Let my servant Warren Jeffs be free to conduct my affairs in my Church as I shall name, without government interference or persecution, for I shall preserve the faithful in the way unto eternal life. Amen.

President Joseph Smith, Jun.
Teachings of the Prophet Joseph Smith, Page 257

Our heavenly Father is more liberal in His views, and boundless in His mercies and blessings, than we are ready to believe or receive; and, at the same time, is more terrible to the workers of iniquity, more awful in the executions of His punishments, and more ready to detect every false way, than we are apt to suppose Him to be. He will be inquired of by His children. He says, "Ask and ye shall receive, seek and ye shall find;" but, if you will take that which is not your own, or which I have not given you, you shall be rewarded according to your deeds; but no good thing will I withhold from them who walk uprightly before me, and do my will in all things -- who will listen to my voice and to the voice of my servant whom I have sent; for I delight in those who seek diligently to know my precepts, and abide by the law of my kingdom; for all things shall be made known unto them in mine own due time, and in the end they shall have joy.

Celestial Plural Marriage Established by the Revelations of God

Testimony of President Brigham Young

President Brigham Young
JD 16:166 August 31, 1873 Paris, Idaho

After this doctrine was received, Joseph received a revelation on celestial marriage. You will recollect, brethren and sisters, that it was in July, 1843, that he received this revelation concerning celestial marriage. This doctrine was explained and many received it as far as they could understand it. Some apostatized on account of it; but others did not, and received it in their faith. This, also, is a great and noble doctrine. I have not time to give you many items upon the subject, but there are a few hints that I can throw in here that perhaps may be interesting.***...the people of God, therefore, have been commanded to take more wives. The women are entitled to salvation if they live according to the word that is given to them; and if their husbands are good men, and they are obedient to them, they are entitled to certain blessings, and they will have the privilege of receiving certain blessings that they cannot receive unless they are sealed to men who will be exalted.

President Brigham Young
JD 11:239 June 3, 1866 SLC

We are told that if we would give up polygamy -- which we know to be a doctrine revealed from heaven, and it is God and the world for it -- but suppose this Church should give up this holy order of marriage, then would the devil, and all who are in league with him against the cause of God, rejoice that they had prevailed upon the Saints to refuse to obey one of the revelations and commandments of God to them. Would they be satisfied with this? No; but they would next want us to renounce Joseph Smith as a true prophet of God, then the Book of Mormon, then baptism for the remission of sins and the laying on of hands for the reception of the Holy Ghost. Then they would wish us to disclaim the gift of prophecy, and the other gifts and graces of the Holy Spirit, on the ground that they are done away and no longer needed in our day, also prophets and apostles, etc.

President Brigham Young
JD 13:239 February 20, 1870 SLC

Well, I need not talk about this; but I will say that the principle of patriarchal marriage is one of the highest and purest ever revealed to the children of men. I do not say that it will not injure a great many. I heard brother Joseph Smith say a number of times, "There is no question but it will be the means of damning many of the Elders of Israel; it is nevertheless true and must be revealed; and the Lord designs that it shall be revealed and go forth, and that this people must receive the oracles of truth, and they must receive this holy ordinance, and that that pertains to the celestial world; and they will retrograde if they do not embrace more of the celestial law than they have yet."

I say, with regard to this principle, if it was good in the days of Abraham and

of the Patriarchs and Prophets, or at any other period of the world's history, and the fact that the Lord commanded His servants anciently to observe it, is conclusive proof that it was so considered by Him, why is it not good now?

Testimony of Heber C. Kimball

Heber C. Kimball
JD 5:203 October 12, 1856 SLC

Let the Presidency of this Church, and the Twelve Apostles, and all the authorities unite and say with one voice that they will oppose that doctrine, and the whole of them would be damned. What are you opposing it for? It is a principle that God has revealed for the salvation of the human family. He revealed it to Joseph the Prophet in this our dispensation; and that which he revealed he designs to have carried out by his people.

Heber C. Kimball
JD 4:224 February 8, 1857 SLC

Do you suppose that Joseph and Hyrum and all those good men would associate with those ancient worthies, if they had not been engaged in the same practices? They had to do the works of Abraham, Isaac, and Jacob, in order to be admitted where they are; -- they had to be polygamists in order to be received into their society. God knows that I am not ashamed of those good men now, and how much more I shall prize my associate polygamists, when I am further advanced in knowledge, I do not know. I am talking in earnest, and from the experience I have had.

Testimony of President John Taylor

President John Taylor
JD 24:230 (Unknown Date) Trip to Bear Lake

This you will see is strictly in accordance with what I have told you Joseph Smith told the Twelve -- that if this law was not practiced, if they would not enter into this covenant, then the kingdom of God could not go one step further. Now, we did not feel like preventing the kingdom of God from going forward. We professed to be the Apostles of the Lord, and did not feel like putting ourselves in a position to retard the progress of the kingdom of God. The revelation, as you have heard, says that, "all those who have this law revealed unto them must obey the same." Now, that is not my word. I did not make it. It was the Prophet of God who revealed that to us in Nauvoo, and I bear witness of this solemn fact before God, that He did reveal this sacred principle to me and others of the Twelve, and in this revelation it is stated that it is the will and law of God that "all those who have this law revealed unto them must obey the same."***

Now, as I have already said, the reason was very obvious why a law of this kind should be had. As a people we professed to be Latter-day Saints. We professed to be governed by the word, and will, and law of God. We had a religion that might do to live by, but we had none to die by. But this was a principle that God had revealed unto us, and it must be obeyed. I had always entertained strict ideas of virtue, and I felt as a married man that this was to me, outside of this principle, an appalling thing to do. The idea of my going and asking a young lady to be married to me, when I had already a wife! It was a thing calculated to stir up feelings from the innermost depth of the human soul. I had always entertained the strictest regard for chastity. I had never in my life seen the time when I have known of a man deceiving a woman -- and it is often done in the world, where notwithstanding the crime, the man is received into society, and the poor woman is looked upon as a pariah and an outcast -- I have always looked upon such a thing as infamous, and upon such a man as a villain, and I hold to-day the same ideas. Hence, with the feelings I had entertained, nothing but a knowledge of God, and the revelations of God, and the truth of them, could have induced me to embrace such a principle as this. We seemed to put off, as far as we could, what might be termed the evil day. Some time after these things were made known to us, I was riding out of Nauvoo on horseback, and met Joseph Smith coming in, he, too, being on horseback. Some of you who were acquainted with Nauvoo, know where the graveyard was. We met upon the road going on to the hill there. I bowed to Brother Joseph, and having done the same to me he said; "Stop;" and he looked at me very intently. "Look here," said he, "those things that have been spoken of must be fulfilled, and if they are not entered into right away, the keys will be turned." Well, what did I do? Did I feel to stand in the way of this great, eternal principle, and treat lightly the things of God? No. I replied: "Brother Joseph, I will try and carry these things out," and I afterwards did, and I have done it more times than once; but then I have never broken a law of the United States in doing so, and I am at their defiance to prove to the contrary.

Testimony of William Clayton

William Clayton
The Historical Record Volume 6, Page 224

The following statement was sworn to before John T. Caine, a notary public, in Salt Lake City, Feb. 16, 1874:

"Inasmuch as it may be interesting to future generations of the members of the Church of Jesus Christ of Latter-day Saints to learn something of the first teachings of the principle of plural marriage by President Joseph Smith, the Prophet, Seer, Revelator and Translator of said Church,

I will give a short relation of facts which occurred within my personal knowledge, and also matters related to me by President Joseph Smith.

"I was employed as a clerk in President Joseph Smith's office, under Elder Willard Richards, and commenced to labor in the office on the 10th day of February, 1842. I continued to labor with Elder Richards until he went east to fetch his wife to Nauvoo.

"After Elder Richards started east I was necessarily thrown constantly into the company of President Smith, having to attend to his public and private business, receiving and recording tithings and donations, attending to land and other matters of business. During this period I necessarily became well acquainted with Emma Smith, the wife of the Prophet Joseph, and also with the children -- Julia M. (an adopted daughter), Joseph, Frederick and Alexander, very much of the business being transacted at the residence of the Prophet.

"On the 7th of October, 1842, in the presence of Bishop Newel K. Whitney and his wife Elizabeth Ann, President Joseph Smith appointed me Temple Recorder, and also his private clerk, placing all records, books, papers, etc., in my care, and requiring me to take charge of and preserve them, his closing words being, 'When I have any revelations to write, you are the one to write them.'

"During this period the Prophet Joseph frequently visited my house in my company, and became well acquainted with my wife Ruth, to whom I had been married five years. One day in the month of February, 1843, date not remembered, the Prophet invited me to walk with him. During our walk, he said he had learned that there was a sister back in England, to whom I was very much attached. I replied there was, but nothing further than an attachment such as a brother and sister in the Church might rightfully entertain for each other. He then said, 'Why don't you send for her?' I replied, 'In the first place, I have no authority to send for her, and if I had, I have not the means to pay expenses.' To this he answered, 'I give you authority to send for her, and I will furnish you with means,' which he did. This was the first time the Prophet Joseph talked with me on the subject of plural marriage. He informed me that the doctrine and principle was right in the sight of our Heavenly Father, and that it was a doctrine which pertained to celestial order and glory. After giving me lengthy instructions and informations concerning the doctrine of celestial or plural marriage, he concluded his remarks by the words, 'It is your privilege to have all the wives you want.' After this introduction, our conversations on the subject of plural marriage were very frequent, and he appeared to take particular pains to inform and instruct me in respect to the principle. He also informed me that he had other wives *living* besides his first wife Emma, and in particular gave me to understand that Eliza R. Snow, Louisa Beman, Desdemona W. Fullmer and others were his lawful wives in the sight of Heaven.

"On the 27th of April, 1843, the Prophet Joseph Smith married to me Margaret Moon, for time and eternity, at the residence of Elder Heber C. Kimball; and on the 22nd of July, 1843, he married to me, according to the order of the Church, my first wife Ruth.

"On the 1st day of May, 1843, I officiated in the office of an Elder by marrying Lucy Walker to the Prophet Joseph Smith, at his own residence.

"During this period the Prophet Joseph took several other wives. Amongst the number I well remember Eliza Partridge, Emily Partridge, Sarah Ann Whitney, Helen Kimball and Flora Woodworth. These all, he acknowledged to me, were his lawful, wedded wives, according to the celestial order. His wife Emma was cognizant of the fact of some, if not all, of these being his wives, and she generally treated them very kindly.

"On the morning of the 12th of July, 1843, Joseph and Hyrum Smith came into the office in the upper story of the 'brick store,' on the bank of the Mississippi River. They were talking on the subject of plural marriage. Hyrum said to Joseph, 'If you will write the revelation on celestial marriage, I will take and read it to Emma, and I believe I can convince her of its truth, and you will hereafter have peace.' Joseph smiled and remarked, 'You do not know Emma as well as I do.' Hyrum repeated his opinion and further remarked, 'The doctrine is so plain, I can convince any reasonable man or woman of its truth, purity or heavenly origin,' or words to their effect. Joseph then said, 'Well, I will write the revelation and we will see.' He then requested me to get paper and prepare to write. Hyrum very urgently requested Joseph to write the revelation by means of the Urim and Thummim, but Joseph, in reply, said he did not need to, for he knew the revelation perfectly from beginning to end.

"Joseph and Hyrum then sat down and Joseph commenced to dictate the revelation on celestial marriage, and I wrote it, sentence by sentence, as he dictated. After the whole was written, Joseph asked me to read it through, slowly and carefully, which I did, and he pronounced it correct. He then remarked that there was much more that he could write, on the same subject, but what was written was sufficient for the present.

"Hyrum then took the revelation to read to Emma. Joseph remained with me in the office until Hyrum returned. When he came back, Joseph asked him how he had succeeded. Hyrum replied that he had never received a more severe talking to in his life, that Emma was very bitter and full of resentment and anger.

"Joseph quietly remarked, 'I told you you did not know Emma as well as I did.' Joseph then put the revelation in his pocket, and they both left the office.

"The revelation was read to several of the authorities during the day. Towards evening Bishop Newel K. Whitney asked Joseph if he had any objections to his taking a copy of the revelation; Joseph replied that he had not, and handed it to him. It was carefully copied the following day by Joseph C. Kingsbury. Two or three days after the revelation was written Joseph related to me and several others that Emma had so teased, and urgently entreated him for the privilege of destroying it, that he became so weary of her teasing, and to get rid of her annoyance, he told her she might destroy it and she had done so, but he had consented to her wish in this matter to pacify her, realizing that he knew the revelation perfectly, and could rewrite it at any time if necessary.

"The copy made by Joseph C. Kingsbury is a true and correct copy of the original in every respect. The copy was carefully preserved by Bishop Whitney, and but few knew of its existence until the temporary location of the Camps of Israel at Winter Quarters, on the Missouri River, in 1846.

"After the revelation on celestial marriage was written Joseph continued his instructions, privately, on the doctrine, to myself and others, and during the last year of his life we were scarcely ever together, alone, but he was talking on the subject, and explaining that doctrine and principles connected with it. He appeared to enjoy great liberty and freedom in his teachings, and also to find great relief in having a few to whom he could unbosom his feelings on that great and glorious subject.

"From him I learned that the doctrine of plural and celestial marriage is the most holy and important doctrine ever revealed to man on the earth, and that without obedience to that principle no man can ever attain to the fulness of exaltation in celestial glory.

(Signed)   WILLIAM CLAYTON
"Salt Lake City, February 16th, 1874."

Testimony of Eliza R. Snow

Eliza R. Snow
The Historical Record Volume 6, Page 224
The following was also published in the *Deseret News* (weekly) of Oct. 22, 1879:

"Recently, to my great astonishment, I read an article headed 'Last Testimony of Sister Emma,' published in the *Saints' Advocate*, a pamphlet issued in Plano, Ill.

"In the article referred to, her son Joseph reports himself as interviewing his mother on the subject of polygamy, asking questions concerning his father. Did his father teach the principle? Did he practice or approve of it? Did his father have other wives than herself? To all of these and similar inquiries, Sister Emma is represented as answering in the negative, positively affirming that Joseph, the Prophet, had no other wife or wives than her; that he neither taught the principle of plurality of wives, publicly or privately.

"I once dearly loved 'Sister Emma,'

and now, for me to believe that she, a once highly honored woman, should have sunk so low, even in her own estimation, as to deny what she *knew* to be true, seems a palpable absurdity. If what purports to be her 'last testimony' was really her testimony, she died with a libel on her lips -- a libel against her husband -- against his wives -- against the truth, and a libel against God; and in publishing that libel, her son has fastened a stigma on the character of his mother, that can never be erased. It is a *fact* that Sister Emma, of her own free will and choice, gave her husband four wives, two of whom are now living, and ready to testify that she, not only gave them to her husband, but that she taught them the doctrine of plural marriage and urged them to accept it. And, if her son wished to degrade his mother in the estimation of her former associates, those familiar with the incidents of the period referred to, he could not do it more effectually than by proving her denial of any knowledge of polygamy (celestial marriage), and its practice by her husband. Even if her son ignored his mother's reputation for veracity, he better had waited until his father's wives were silent in death, for now they are here living witnesses of the divinity of plural marriage, as revealed by the Almighty, through Joseph Smith, who was commanded to introduce it by taking other wives.

"So far as Sister Emma personally is concerned, I would gladly have been silent and let her memory rest in peace, had not her misguided son, through a sinister policy, branded her name with gross wickedness -- charging her with the denial of a sacred principle which she had heretofore not only acknowledged but had acted upon -- a principle than which there is none more important comprised in the Gospel of the Son of God.

"It may be asked, Why defend plurality of wives, since the United States government forbids its practice? The action of the executors of this government can neither change nor annihilate a fundamental truth; and this nation, in preventing the practice of plural marriage, shoulders a heavier responsibility than any nation has ever assumed, with one exception -- that of the ancient Jews. If the government can afford it, we can. The controversy is with God -- not us.

ELIZA R. SNOW
A wife of Joseph Smith, the Prophet.

Testimony of Eliza Partridge

The Historical Record Volume 6, Page 223
"Eliza M. Partridge's Affidavit.

"Territory of Utah, } ss.
County of Millard. }

"Be it remembered that on the first day of July, A.D. 1869, personally appeared before me, Edward Partridge, probate judge in and for said county, Eliza M. (Partridge) Lyman, who was by me sworn in due form of law, and upon her oath saith, that on the 11th day of May, 1843, at the City of Nauvoo, County of Hancock, State of Illinois, she was married or sealed to Joseph Smith, President of the Church of Jesus Christ of Latter-day Saints, by James Adams, a High Priest in said Church, *** in the presence of Emma (Hale) Smith and Emily D. Partridge.

(Signed)   ELIZA. M. (P.) LYMAN.

"Subscribed and sworn to by the said Eliza Maria Lyman, the day and year first above written.

[SEAL.]   EDWARD PARTRIDGE,
Probate Judge.

Testimony of Lucy W. Kimball

Lucy W. Kimball
The Historical Record Volume 6, Page 229

"When the Prophet Joseph Smith first mentioned the principle of plural marriage to me I became very indignant, and told him emphatically that I did not wish him ever to mention it to me again, as my feelings and education revolted against any thing of such a nature. He counseled me, however, to pray to the Lord for light and understanding in relation thereto, and promised me if I would do so sincerely, I should receive a testimony of the correctness of the principle. At length I concluded to follow this advice, and the consequence was that the Prophet's promise unto me was fulfilled to the very letter. Before praying I felt gloomy and downcast; in fact, I was so entirely given up to despair that I felt tired of life; but after I had poured out my heart's contents before God, I at once became calm and composed; a feeling of happiness took possession of me, and at the same time I received a powerful and irresistible testimony of the truth of plural marriage, which testimony has abided with me ever since. Shortly afterwards I consented to become the Prophet's wife, and was married to him May 1, 1843, Elder William Clayton officiating. I am also able to testify that Emma Smith, the Prophet's first wife, gave her consent to the marriage of at least four other girls to her husband, and that she was well aware that he associated with them as wives within the meaning of all that word implies. This is proven by the fact that she herself, on several occasions, kept guard at the door to prevent disinterested persons from intruding, when these ladies were in the house.

LUCY W. KIMBALL."

Testimony of Lydia Knight

Lydia Knight
Lydia Knight's History, Page 95

"I had always believed in the principle of celestial marriage, since I received a testimony of its truth in an early day from the Prophet Joseph's teachings. I have heard him teach it in public as well as in private; have heard him relate the incident of the angel coming to him with a drawn sword, commanding him to obey the law, or he should lose his priesthood as well as his life if he did not go forward in this principle; and I had received a strong testimony of its truth when under the Prophet's teachings."***

"It may be some will enquire of me, 'how do you like plurality after living in it and getting the experience you desired? What are your feelings now?' I will say I like it first-rate; my belief is strengthened; I do believe it is a principle that if not abused, will purify and exalt those that enter into it with purity of purpose, and so abide therein."

Persecutions of the Priesthood, Church, and Kingdom of God by the People of the Nation of the United States of America

Persecutions in the State of New York

Joseph Smith Receives the Plates; Persecution Becomes Severe by Enemies Seeking to Destroy the Prophet Joseph Smith

President Joseph Smith, Jun.
Pearl of Great Price, Joseph Smith 2

59. At length the time arrived for obtaining the plates, the Urim and Thummim, and the breastplate. On the twenty-second day of September, one thousand eight hundred and twenty-seven, having gone as usual at the end of another year to the place where they were deposited, the same heavenly messenger delivered them up to me with this charge: that I should be responsible for them; that if I should let them go carelessly, or through any neglect of mine, I should be cut off; but that if I would use all my endeavors to preserve them, until he, the messenger, should call for them, they should be protected.

60. I soon found out the reason why I had received such strict charges to keep them safe, and why it was that the messenger had said that when I had done what was required at my hand, he would call for them. For no sooner was it known that I had them, than the most strenuous exertions were used to get them from me. Every stratagem that could be invented was resorted to for that purpose. The persecution became more bitter and severe than before, and multitudes were on the alert continually to get them from me if possible. But by the wisdom of God, they remained safe in my hands, until I had accomplished by them what was required at my hand. When, according to arrangements, the messenger called for them, I delivered them up to him; and he has them in his charge until this day, being the second day of May, one thousand eight hundred and thirty-eight.

61. The excitement, however, still continued, and rumor with her thousand tongues was all the time employed in circulating falsehoods about my father's family, and about myself. If I were to relate a thousandth part of them, it would fill up volumes. The persecution, however, became so intolerable that I was under the necessity of leaving Manchester, and going with my wife to Susquehanna county, in the State of Pennsylvania.

The Prophet Joseph Arrested and Tried Twice -- 1830

President Joseph Smith, Jun.
Documentary History of the Church 1:88

We had appointed a meeting for this evening, for the purpose of attending to the confirmation of those who had been the same morning baptized. The time appointed had arrived and our friends had nearly all collected together, when to my surprise, I was visited by a constable, and arrested by him on a warrant, on the charge of being a disorderly person, of setting the country in an uproar by preaching the Book of Mormon, etc. The constable informed me, soon after I had been arrested, that the plan of those who had got out the warrant was to get me into the hands of the mob, who were now lying in ambush for me; but that he was determined to save me from them, as he had found me to be a different sort of person from what I had been represented to him. I soon found that he had told me the truth in this matter, for not far from Mr. Knight's house, the wagon in which we had set out was surrounded by a mob, who seemed only to await some signal from the constable; but to their great disappointment, he gave the horse the whip, and drove me out of their reach.

Whilst driving in great haste one of the wagon wheels came off, which left us once more very nearly surrounded by them, as they had come on in close pursuit. However, we managed to replace the wheel and again left them behind us. He drove on to the town of South Bainbridge, Chenango county, where he lodged me for the time being in an upper room of a tavern; and in order that all might be right with himself and with me also, he slept during the night with his feet against the door, and a loaded musket by his side, whilst I occupied a bed which was in the room; he having declared that if we were interrupted unlawfully, he would fight for me, and defend me as far as it was in his power.

On the day following, a court was convened for the purpose of investigating those charges which had been preferred against me. A great excitement prevailed on account of the scandalous falsehoods which had been circulated, the nature of which will appear in the sequel.***

At length the trial commenced amidst a multitude of spectators, who in general evinced a belief that I was guilty of all that had been reported concerning me, and of course were very zealous that I should be punished according to my crimes.***

Several other attempts were made to prove something against me, and even circumstances which were alleged to have taken place in Broome county, were brought forward, but these my lawyers would not admit of as testimony against me; in consequence of which my persecutors managed to detain the court until they had succeeded in obtaining a warrant from Broome county, which warrant they served upon me at the very moment that I was acquitted by this court.

The constable who served this second warrant upon me had no sooner arrested me than he began to abuse and insult me; and so unfeeling was he with me, that although I had been kept all the day in court without anything to eat since the morning, yet he hurried me off to Broome county, a distance of about fifteen miles, before he allowed me any kind of food whatever. He took me to a tavern, and gathered in a number of men, who used every means to abuse, ridicule and insult me. They spit upon me, pointed their fingers at me, saying, "Prophesy, prophesy!" and thus did they imitate those who crucified the Savior of mankind, not knowing what they did.

We were at this time not far distant from my own house. I wished to be allowed the privilege of spending the night with my wife at home, offering any wished for security for my appearance; but this was denied me. I applied for something to eat. The constable ordered me some crusts of bread and water, which was the only food I that night received. At length we retired to bed. The constable made me lie next the wall. He then laid himself down by me and put his arm around me, and upon my moving in the least, would clench me fast, fearing that I intended to escape from him; and in this very disagreeable manner did we pass the night.

Next day I was brought before the magistrate's court at Colesville, Broome county, and put upon my trial. My former faithful friends and lawyers were again at my side; my former persecutors were arrayed against me. Many witnesses were again called forward and examined, some of whom swore to the most palpable falsehoods, and like the false witnesses which had appeared against me the day previous, they contradicted themselves so plainly that the court would not admit their testimony. Others were called, who showed by their zeal that they were willing enough to prove something against me, but all they could do was to tell something which somebody else had told them.***

Mr. Seymour now addressed the court, and in a long and violent harangue endeavored to blacken my character and bring me in guilty of the charges which had been brought against me.***

Mr. Davidson and Mr. Reid followed on my behalf. They held forth in true colors the nature of the prosecution, the malignancy of intention, and the apparent disposition to persecute their client, rather than to afford him justice.*** In fact, these men, although not regular lawyers, were upon this occasion able to put to silence their opponents, and convince the court that I was innocent. They spoke like men inspired of God, whilst those who were arrayed against me trembled under the sound of their voices, and quailed before them like criminals before a bar of justice.

The majority of the assembled multitude had now begun to find that nothing could be sustained against me. Even the constable who arrested me, and treated me so badly, now came and apologized to me, and asked my forgiveness for his behavior towards me; and so far was he changed, that he informed me that the mob were determined, if the court acquitted me, that they would have me, and rail-ride me, and tar and feather me; and further, that he was willing to favor me and lead me out in safety by a private way.

The court found the charges against me not sustained; I was accordingly acquitted, to the great satisfaction of my friends and vexation of my enemies, who were still determined upon molesting me. But through the instrumentality of my new friend the constable, I was enabled to escape them and make my way in safety to my wife's sister's house, where I found my wife awaiting with much anxiety the issue of those ungodly proceedings, and in company with her I arrived next day in safety at my own house.

President Joseph Smith, Jun.
Documentary History of the Church 1:97

Thus were we persecuted on account of our religious faith -- in a country the Constitution of which guarantees to every man the indefeasible right to worship God according to the dictates of his own conscience -- and by men, too, who were professors of religion, and who were not backward to maintain the right of religious liberty for themselves, though they could thus wantonly deny it to us. For instance, Cyrus McMaster, a Presbyterian of high standing in his church, was one of the chief instigators of these persecutions; and he at one time told me personally that he considered me guilty without judge or jury. The celebrated Dr. Boyington, also a Presbyterian, was another instigator of these deeds of outrage; whilst a young man named Benton, of the same religious faith, swore out the first warrant against me. I could mention many others also, but for brevity's sake, will make these suffice for the present.

Persecutions in the State of Ohio

Mob Violence at Hiram, Ohio -- 1832

President Joseph Smith, Jun.
Documentary History of the Church 1:261

On the 24th of March, the twins before mentioned, which had been sick of the measles for some time, caused us to be broken of our rest in taking care of them, especially my wife. In the evening I told her she had better retire to rest with one of the children, and I would watch with the sicker child. In the night she told me I had better lie down on the trundle bed, and I did so, and was soon after awakened by her screaming murder, when I found myself going out of the door, in the hands of about a dozen men; some of whose hands were in my hair, and some had hold of my shirt, drawers and limbs. The foot of the trundle bed was towards the door, leaving only room enough for the door to swing open. My wife heard a gentle tapping on the windows which she then took no particular notice of (but which was unquestionably designed for ascertaining whether or not we were all asleep), and soon after the mob burst open the door and surrounded the bed in an instant, and, as I said, the first I knew I was going out of the door in the hands of an infuriated mob. I made a desperate struggle, as I was forced out, to extricate myself, but only cleared one leg, with which I made a pass at one man, and he fell on the door steps. I was immediately overpowered again; and they swore by G—, they would kill me if I did not be still, which quieted me. As they passed around the house with me, the fellow that I kicked came to me and thrust his hand, all covered with blood, into my face and with an exulting hoarse laugh, muttered *"Ge, gee, G— d— ye, I'll fix ye."*

They then seized me by the throat and held on till I lost my breath. After I came to, as they passed along with me, about thirty rods from the house, I saw Elder Rigdon stretched out on the ground, whither they had dragged him by his heels. I supposed he was dead. I began to plead with them, saying, "You will have mercy and spare my life, I hope." To which they replied, "G— d— ye, call on yer God for help, we'll show ye no mercy;" and the people began to show themselves in every direction; one coming from the orchard had a plank; and I expected they would kill me, and carry me off on the plank. They then turned to the right, and went on about thirty rods further; about sixty rods from the house, and thirty from where I saw Elder Rigdon, into the meadow, where they stopped, and one said, "Simonds, Simonds," (meaning, I supposed, Simonds Ryder,) "pull up his drawers, pull up his drawers, he will take cold." Another replied: *"Ain't ye going to* kill 'im? ain't ye going to kill 'im?'" when a group of mobbers collected a little way off, and said: "Simonds, Simonds, come here;" and "Simonds" charged those who had hold of me to keep me from touching the ground (as they had done all the time), lest I should get a spring upon them. They held a council, and as I could occasionally overhear a word, I supposed it was to know whether or not it was best to kill me. They returned after a while, when I learned that they had concluded not to kill me, but to beat and scratch me well, tear off my shirt and drawers, and leave me naked. One cried, "Simonds, Simonds, *where's the tar bucket?*" "I don't know," answered one, *"where 'tis, Eli's left it."* They ran back and fetched the bucket of tar, when one exclaimed, with an oath, *"Let us tar up his mouth;"* and they tried to force the tar-paddle into my mouth; I twisted my head around, so that they could not; and they cried out, *"G— d— ye, hold up yer head and let us give ye some tar."* They then tried to force a vial into my mouth, and broke it in my teeth. All my clothes were torn off me except my shirt collar; and one man fell on me and scratched my body with his nails like a mad cat, and then muttered out: *"G— d— ye, that's the way the Holy Ghost falls on folks!"*

They then left me, and I attempted to rise, but fell again; I pulled the tar away from my lips, so that I could breathe more freely, and after a while I began to recover, and raised myself up, whereupon I saw two lights. I made my way towards one of them, and found it was Father Johnson's. When I came to the door I was naked, and the tar made me look as if I were covered with blood, and when my wife saw me she thought I was all crushed to pieces, and fainted. During the affray

abroad, the sisters of the neighborhood had collected at my room. I called for a blanket, they threw me one and shut the door; I wrapped it around me and went in.***

My friends spent the night in scraping and removing the tar, and washing and cleansing my body; so that by morning I was ready to be clothed again. This being the Sabbath morning, the people assembled for meeting at the usual hour of worship, and among them came also the mobbers;...

Persecutions in the State of Missouri

Mob Violence Against the Saints in Jackson County, Missouri -- 1833

President Joseph Smith, Jun.
Documentary History of the Church 1:390

ON the 20th of July, the mob collected, and demanded the discontinuance of the Church printing establishment in Jackson county, the closing of the store, and the cessation of all mechanical labors. The brethren refused compliance, and the consequence was that the house of W. W. Phelps, which contained the printing establishment, was thrown down, the materials taken possession of by the mob, many papers destroyed, and the family and furniture thrown out of doors.

The mob then proceeded to violence towards Edward Partridge, the Bishop of the Church, as he relates in his autobiography:

I was taken from my house by the mob, George Simpson being their leader, who escorted me about half a mile, to the court house, on the public square in Independence; and then and there, a few rods from said court house, surrounded by hundreds of the mob, I was stripped of my hat, coat and vest and daubed with tar from head to foot, and then had a quantity of feathers put upon me; and all this because I would not agree to leave the county, and my home where I had lived two years.

Before tarring and feathering me I was permitted to speak. I told them that the Saints had suffered persecution in all ages of the world; that I had done nothing which ought to offend anyone; that if they abused me, they would abuse an innocent person; that I was willing to suffer for the sake of Christ; but, to leave the country, I was not then willing to consent to it. By this time the multitude made so much noise that I could not be heard: some were cursing and swearing, saying, "call upon your Jesus," etc.; others were equally noisy in trying to still the rest, that they might be enabled to hear what I was saying.

Until after I had spoken, I knew not what they intended to do with me, whether to kill me, to whip me, or what else I knew not. I bore my abuse with so much resignation and meekness, that it appeared to astound the multitude, who permitted me to retire in silence, many looking very solemn, their sympathies having been touched as I thought; and as to myself, I was so filled with the Spirit and love of God, that I had no hatred towards my persecutors or anyone else.

Charles Allen was next stripped and tarred and feathered, because he would not agree to leave the county, or deny the Book of Mormon. Others were brought up to be served likewise or whipped.***

In the course of this day's wicked, outrageous, and unlawful proceedings, many solemn realities of human degradation, as well as thrilling incidents were presented to the Saints. An armed and well organized mob, in a government professing to be governed by law, with the Lieutenant Governor (Lilburn W. Boggs), the second officer in the state, calmly looking on, and secretly aiding every movement, saying to the Saints, "You now know what our Jackson boys can do, and you must leave the county;" and all the justices, judges, constables, sheriffs, and military officers, headed by such

western missionaries and clergymen as the Reverends McCoy, Kavanaugh, Hunter, Fitzhugh, Pixley, Likens, and Lovelady, consisting of Methodists, Baptists, Presbyterians, and all the different sects of religionists that inhabited that country, with that great moral reformer, and register of the land office at Lexington, forty miles east, known as the head and father of the Cumberland Presbyterians, even the Reverend Finis Ewing, publicly publishing that "Mormons were the common enemies of mankind, and ought to be destroyed" -- all these solemn realities were enough to melt the heart of a savage; while there was not a *solitary offense* on record, or proof, that a Saint had broken the law of the land.

Expulsion of the Saints from Jackson County, Missouri -- 1833

President Joseph Smith, Jun.
Documentary History of the Church 1:426

THURSDAY night, the 31st of October, gave the Saints in Zion abundant proof that no pledge on the part of their enemies, written or verbal, was longer to be regarded; for on that night, between forty and fifty persons in number, many of whom were armed with guns, proceeded against a branch of the Church, west of the Big Blue, and unroofed and partly demolished ten dwelling houses; and amid the shrieks and screams of the women and children, whipped and beat in a savage and brutal manner, several of the men: while their horrid threats frightened women and children into the wilderness. Such of the men as could escape fled for their lives; for very few of them had arms, neither were they organized; and they were threatened with death if they made any resistance; such therefore as could not escape by flight, received a pelting with stones and a beating with guns and whips. On Friday, the first of November, women and children sallied forth from their gloomy retreats, to contemplate with heartrending anguish the ravages of a ruthless mob, in the lacerated and bruised bodies of their husbands, and in the destruction of their houses, and their furniture. Houseless and unprotected by the arm of the civil law in Jackson county, the dreary month of November staring them in the face and loudly proclaiming an inclement season at hand; the continual threats of the mob that they would drive every "Mormon" from the county; and the inability of many to move, because of their poverty, caused an anguish of heart indescribable.

On Friday night, the 1st of November, a party of the mob proceeded to attack a branch of the Church settled on the prairie, about twelve or fourteen miles from the town of Independence. Two of their number were sent in advance, as spies, viz., Robert Johnson, and —— Harris, armed with two guns and three pistols. They were discovered by some of the Saints, and without the least injury being done to them, said mobber Robert Johnson struck Parley P. Pratt over the head with the breech of his gun, after which they were taken and detained till morning; which action, it was believed, prevented a general attack of the mob that night. In the morning the two prisoners, notwithstanding their attack upon Parley P. Pratt the evening previous, were liberated without receiving the least injury.

The same night, (Friday), another party in Independence commenced stoning houses, breaking down doors and windows and destroying furniture. This night the brick part attached to the dwelling house of A. S. Gilbert, was partly pulled down, and the windows of his dwelling broken in with brickbats and rocks, while a gentleman, a stranger, lay sick with fever in his house. The same night three doors of the store of Messrs. Gilbert & Whitney were split open, and after midnight the goods, such as calicos, handkerchiefs, shawls, cambrics, lay scattered in the streets. An express came from Independence after midnight to a party of the brethren who had organized about half a mile from the town for the safety of their lives, and brought the information that the mob were tearing down houses, and scattering goods of the store in the streets. Upon receiving this information the company of brethren referred to marched into Independence, but the main body of the mob fled at their approach. One Richard McCarty, however, was caught in the act of throwing rocks and brickbats into the doors, while the goods lay scattered around him in the streets. He was immediately taken before Samuel Weston, Esq., justice of the peace, and complaint was then made to said Weston, and a warrant requested, that McCarty might be secured; but Weston refused to do anything in the case at that time, and McCarty was liberated.

The same night some of the houses of the Saints in Independence had long poles thrust through the shutters and sash into the rooms of defenseless women and children, from whence their husbands and fathers had been driven by the dastardly attacks of the mob, which were made by ten, fifteen, or twenty men upon a house at a time. Saturday, the 2nd of November, all the families of the Saints in Independence moved with their goods about half a mile out of town and organized to the number of thirty, for the preservation of life and personal effects. The same night a party from Independence met a party from west of the Blue, and made an attack upon a branch of the Church located at the Blue, about six miles from the village of Independence. Here they tore the roof from one dwelling and broke open another house; they found the owner, David Bennett, sick in bed, and beat him most inhumanly, swearing they would blow out his brains. They discharged a pistol at him, and the ball cut a deep gash across the top of his head. In this skirmish a young man of the mob, was shot in the thigh; but by which party the shot was fired is not known.

The next day, Sunday, November 3rd, four of the brethren, viz., Joshua Lewis, Hiram Page, and two others, were dispatched for Lexington to see the circuit judge, and obtain a peace warrant. Two other brethren called on Esquire Silvers, in Independence, and asked him for a peace warrant, but he refused to issue one on account, as he afterwards declared, of his fears of the mob. This day many of the citizens, professing friendship, advised the Saints to leave the county as speedily as possible; for the Saturday night affray had enraged the whole county, and the people were determined to come out on Monday and massacre indiscriminately; and, in short, it was commonly declared among the mob, that *"Monday would be a bloody day."*

Monday came, and a large party of the mob gathered at the Blue, took the Ferry boat belonging to the Church, threatened lives, etc. But they soon abandoned the ferry, and went to Wilson's store, about one mile west of the Blue. Word had been previously sent to a branch of the Church, several miles west of the Blue, that the mob were destroying property on the east side of the river, and the sufferers there wanted help to preserve lives and property. Nineteen men volunteered, and started to their assistance; but discovering that fifty or sixty of the mob had gathered at said Wilson's they turned back. At this time two small boys passed on their way to Wilson's who gave information to the mob, that the "Mormons" were on the road west of them. Between forty and fifty of the mob armed with guns, immediately started on horseback and on foot in pursuit; after riding about two or two and a half miles, they discovered them, when the said company of nineteen brethren immediately dispersed, and fled in different directions. The mob hunted them, turning their horses meantime into a corn field belonging to the Saints. Corn fields and houses were searched, the mob at the same time threatening women and children that they would pull down their houses and kill them if they did not tell where the men had fled. Thus they were employed in hunting the men and threatening the women, when a company of thirty of the brethren from the prairie, armed with seventeen guns, made their appearance.

The former company of nineteen had dispersed, and fled, and but one or two of them returned in time to take part in the subsequent battle. On the approach of the latter company of thirty men, some of the mob cried, "Fire, G— d— ye, fire." Two or three guns were then fired by the mob, which fire was returned by the other party without loss of time. This company is the same that is represented by the mob as having gone forth in the evening of the above incident bearing the olive branch of peace. The mob retreated immediately after the first fire, leaving some of their horses in Whitmer's corn field, and two of their number, Hugh L. Brazeale and Thomas Linvill dead on the ground. Thus fell Hugh L. Brazeale, who had been heard to say, "With ten fellows, I will wade to my knees in blood, but that I will drive the 'Mormons' from Jackson county." The next morning the corpse of Brazeale was discovered on the battle ground with a gun by his side. Several were wounded on both sides, but none mortally among the brethren except Andrew Barber, who expired the next day. This attack of the mob was made about sunset, Monday, November the 4th; and the same night, runners were dispatched in every direction under pretense of calling out the militia; spreading every rumor calculated to alarm and excite the uninformed as they went; such as that the "Mormons" had taken Independence, and that the Indians had surrounded it, the "Mormons" and Indians being colleagued together.***

On the morning of the 5th of November, Independence began to be crowded with individuals from different parts of the county armed with guns and other weapons; and report said the militia had been called out under the sanction or at the instigation of Lieutenant Governor Boggs; and that one Colonel Pitcher had the command. Among this militia (so-called) were included the most conspicuous characters of the mob; and it may truly be said that the appearance of the ranks of this body was well calculated to excite suspicion of their horrible designs.

Very early on the same morning, several branches of the Church received intelligence that a number of their brethren were in prison, and the determination of the mob was to kill them; and that the branch of the Church near the town of Independence was in imminent danger, as the main body of the mob was gathered at that place. In this critical situation, about one hundred of the Saints, from different branches, volunteered for the protection of their brethren near Independence, and proceeded on the road towards Independence, and halted about one mile west of the town, where they awaited further information concerning the movements of the mob. They soon learned that the prisoners were not massacred, and that the mob had not fallen upon the branch of the Church near Independence, as had been reported. They were also informed, that the militia had been called out for their protection; but in this they placed little confidence, for the body congregated had every appearance of a mob; and subsequent events fully verified their suspicions.

On application to Colonel Pitcher, it was found that there was no alternative, but for the Church to leave the county forthwith, and deliver into his hands certain men to be tried for murder, said to have been committed by them in the battle, as he called it, of the previous evening. The arms of the Saints were also demanded by Colonel Pitcher. Among the committee appointed to receive the arms of the brethren were several of the most unrelenting of the old July mob committee, who had directed in the demolishing of the printing office, and the personal injuries inflicted on brethren that day, viz., Henry Chiles, Abner Staples, and Lewis Franklin, who had not ceased to pursue the Saints, from the first to the last, with feelings the most hostile.

These unexpected requisitions of the

Colonel, made him appear like one standing at the head of both civil and military law, stretching his authority beyond the constitutional limits that regulate both civil and military power in our Republic. Rather than to have submitted to these unreasonable requirements, the Saints would have cheerfully shed their blood in defense of their rights, the liberties of their country and of their wives and children; but the fear of violating law, in resisting this pretended militia, and the flattering assurance of protection and honorable usage promised by Lieutenant Governor Boggs, in whom, up to this time, they had reposed confidence, induced the Saints to submit, believing that he did not tolerate so gross a violation of all law, as had been practiced in Jackson county. But as so glaringly exposed in the sequel, it was the design and craft of this man to rob an innocent people of their arms by stratagem, and leave more than one thousand defenseless men, women and children to be driven from their homes among strangers in a strange land to seek shelter from the stormy blast of winter. All earth and hell cannot deny that a baser knave, a greater traitor, and a more wholesale butcher, or murderer of mankind ever went untried, unpunished, and unhung -- since hanging is the popular method of execution among the Gentiles in all countries professing Christianity, instead of blood for blood, according to the law of heaven. The conduct of Colonels Lucas and Pitcher, had long proven them to be open and avowed enemies of the Saints. Both of these men had their names attached to the mob circular, as early as the July previous, the object of which was to drive the Saints from Jackson county. But with assurances from the Lieutenant Governor

and others that the object was to disarm the combatants on both sides, and that peace would be the result, the brethren surrendered their arms to the number of fifty or upwards.

The men present, who were accused of being in the battle the evening before, also gave themselves up for trial; but after detaining them one day and a night on a pretended trial for murder, in which time they were threatened and brick-batted, Colonel Pitcher, after receiving a watch of one of the prisoners to satisfy "costs of court," took them into a corn field, and said to them, *"Clear!"* [Meaning, of course, clear out, leave.]

After the Saints had surrendered their arms, which had been used only in self-defense, the tribes of Indians in time of war let loose upon women and children, could not have appeared more hideous and terrific, than did the companies of ruffians who went in various directions, well armed, on foot and on horseback, bursting into houses without fear, knowing the arms were secured; frightening distracted women with what they would do to their husbands if they could catch them; warning women and children to flee immediately, or they would tear their houses down over their heads, and massacre them before night. At the head of these companies appeared the *Reverend Isaac McCoy*, with a gun upon his shoulder, ordering the Saints to leave the county forthwith, and surrender what arms they had. Other pretended preachers of the Gospel took a conspicuous part in the persecution, calling the "Mormons" the "common enemy of mankind," and exulting in their afflictions.

On Tuesday and Wednesday nights, the 5th and 6th of November, women and children fled in every direction before the merciless mob. One party of about one hundred and fifty women and children fled to the prairie, where they wandered for several days with only about six men to protect them. Other parties fled to the Missouri river, and took lodging for the night where they could find it. One Mr. Barnet opened his house for a night's shelter to a wandering company of distressed women and children, who were fleeing to the river. During this dispersion of the women and children, parties of the mob were hunting the men, firing upon some, tying up and whipping others, and pursuing others with horses for several miles.

Thursday, November 7th, the shores of the Missouri river began to be lined on both sides of the ferry, with men, women and children; goods, wagons, boxes, chests, and provisions; while the ferrymen were busily employed in crossing them over. When night again closed upon the Saints, the wilderness had much the appearance of a camp meeting. Hundreds of people were seen in every direction; some in tents, and some in the open air, around their fires, while the rain descended in torrents. Husbands were inquiring for their wives, and women for their husbands; parents for children, and children for parents. Some had the good fortune to escape with their families, household goods, and some provisions; while others knew not the fate of their friends, and had lost all their effects. The scene was indescribable, and would have melted the hearts of any people upon earth, except the blind oppressor, and the prejudiced and ignorant bigot. Next day the company increased, and they were chiefly engaged in felling small cottonwood trees, and erecting them into temporary cabins, so that when night came on, they had the appearance of a village of wigwams, and the night being clear, the occupants began to enjoy some degree of comfort.

Lieutenant Governor Boggs has been represented as merely a curious and disinterested observer of these events; yet he was evidently the head and front of the mob; for as may easily be seen by what follows, no important move was made without his sanction. He certainly was the secret mover in the affairs of the 20th and 23rd of July; and, as will appear in the sequel, by his authority the mob was converted into militia, to effect by stratagem what he knew, as well as his hellish host, could not be done by legal force. As Lieutenant Governor, he had only to wink, and the mob went from maltreatment to murder. The horrible calculations of this second Nero were often developed in a way that could not be mistaken. Early on the morning of the 5th, say at 1 o'clock a.m., he came to Phelps, Gilbert, and Partridge, and told them to flee for their lives. Now, unless he had given the order to murder no one would have attempted it, after the Church had agreed to go away. His conscience, however, seemed to vacillate at its moorings, and led him to give the secret alarm to these men.

The Saints who fled from Jackson county, took refuge in the neighboring counties, chiefly in Clay county, the inhabitants of which received them with some degree of kindness. Those who fled to the county of Van Buren were again driven, and compelled to flee, and these who fled to Lafayette county, were soon expelled, or the most of them, and had to move wherever they could find protection.

The Prophet's Description of the Renewed Missouri Persecutions -- 1838

President Joseph Smith, Jun.
Documentary History of the Church 3:67

There is great excitement at present among the Missourians, who are seeking if possible an occasion against us. They are continually chafing us, and provoking us to anger if possible, one sign of threatening after another, but we do not fear them, for the Lord God, the Eternal Father is our God, and Jesus the Mediator is our Savior, and in the great I Am is our strength and confidence.

We have been driven time after time, and that without cause; and smitten again and again, and that without provocation; until we have proved the world with kindness, and the world has proved us, that we have no designs against any man or set of men, that we injure no man, that we are peaceable with all men, minding our own business, and our business only. We have suffered our rights and our liberties to be taken from us; we have not avenged ourselves of those wrongs; we have appealed to magistrates, to sheriffs, to judges, to government and to the President of the United States, all in vain; yet we have yielded peaceably to all these things. We have not complained at the Great God, we murmured not, but peaceably left all; and retired into the back country, in the broad and wild prairies, in the barren and desolate plains, and there commenced anew; we made the desolate places to bud and blossom as the rose; and now the fiend-like race is disposed to give us no rest.

Government Militia Comes Against Far West -- 1838

President Joseph Smith, Jun.
Documentary History of the Church 3:76

This day [September 12, 1838] also a communication was sent to Governor Boggs, dated Daviess county, containing all the falsehoods and lies that the evil genius of mobocrats, villains, and murderers could invent, charging the "Mormons" with every crime they themselves had been guilty of, and calling the "Mormons" impostors, rebels, Canadian refugees, emissaries of the prince of darkness, and signed, "The Citizens of Daviess and Livingston Counties."

Under this date, General Atchison informed the Governor, by letter from headquarters at Richmond, that on the solicitation of the citizens and the advice of the judge of the circuit, he had ordered out four companies of fifty men each from the militia of Clay county, and a like number from Ray; also four hundred men to hold themselves in readiness if required, all mounted riflemen, except one company of infantry. The troops were to proceed immediately to the scene of excitement and insurrection.

Expulsion of the Saints From De Witt, Missouri

President Joseph Smith, Jun.
Documentary History of the Church 3:156

Under the same date, [October 6th] from the mob camp near De Witt, eleven blood-thirsty fellows, viz., Congrave Jackson, Larkin H. Woods, Thomas Jackson, Rolla M. Daviess, James Jackson, Jun., Johnson Jackson, John L. Tomlin, Sidney S. Woods, Geo. Crigler, William L. Banks, and Whitfield Dicken, wrote a most inflammatory, lying and murderous communication to the citizens of Howard county, calling upon them as friends and fellow citizens, to come to their immediate rescue, as the "Mormons" were then firing upon them and they would have to act on the defensive until they could procure more assistance.

A. C. Woods, a citizen of Howard county, made a certificate to the same lies, which he gathered in the mob camp; he did not go into De Witt, or take any trouble to learn the truth of what he certified. While the people will lie and the authorities will uphold them, what justice can honest men expect?***

The messenger, Mr. Caldwell, who had been dispatched to the governor for assistance, returned, but instead of receiving any aid or even sympathy from his Excellency, we were told that "the quarrel was between the Mormons and the mob," and that "we might fight it out."

About this time a mob, commanded by Hyrum Standly, took Smith Humphrey's goods out of his house, and said Standly set fire to Humphrey's house and burned it before his eyes, and ordered him to leave the place forthwith, which he did by fleeing from De Witt to Caldwell county. The mob had sent to Jackson county and got a cannon, powder and balls, and bodies of armed men had gathered in, to aid them, from Ray, Saline, Howard, Livingston, Clinton, Clay, Platte counties and other parts of the state, and a man by the name of Jackson, from Howard county, was appointed their leader.

The Saints were forbidden to go out of the town under pain of death, and were shot at when they attempted to go out to get food, of which they were destitute. As fast as their cattle or horses got where the mob could get hold of them, they were taken as spoil, as also other kinds of property. By these outrages the brethren were obliged, most of them, to live in wagons or tents.

Application had been made to the judge of the Circuit Court for protection, and he ordered out two companies of militia, one commanded by Captain Samuel Bogart, a Methodist minister, and one of the worst of the mobocrats. The whole force was placed under the command of General Parks, another mobber, if his letter speaks his feelings, and his actions do not belie him, for he never made the first attempt to disperse the mob, and when asked the reason of his conduct, he always replied that Bogart and his company were mutinous and mobocratic, that he dare not attempt a dispersion of the mob. Two other principal men of the mob were Major Ashly, member of the Legislature, and Sashiel Woods, a Presbyterian clergyman.

General Parks informed us that a greater part of his men under Captain Bogart had mutinied, and that he would be obliged to draw them off from the place, for fear they would join the mob; consequently he could offer us no assistance.

We had now no hopes whatever of successfully resisting the mob, who kept constantly increasing; our provisions were entirely exhausted, and we were worn out by continually standing on guard, and watching the movements of our enemies, who, during the time I was there, fired at us a great many times. Some of the brethren perished from starvation; and for once in my life, I had the pain of beholding some of my fellow creatures fall victims to the spirit of persecution, which did then, and has since, prevailed to such an extent in Upper Missouri. They were men, too, who were virtuous and against whom no legal process could for one moment be sustained, but who, in consequence of their love of God, attachment to His cause, and their determination to keep the faith, were thus brought to an untimely grave.

In the meantime Henry Root and David Thomas, who had been the soul [sole] cause of the settlement of our people in De Witt, solicited the Saints to leave the place. Thomas said he had assurances from the mob, that if they would leave the place they would not be hurt, and that they would be paid for all losses which they had sustained, and that they had come as mediators to accomplish this object, and that persons should be appointed to set a value on the property which they had to leave, and that they should be paid for it. The Saints finally, through necessity, had to comply, and leave the place. Accordingly the committee was appointed -- Judge Erickson was one of the committee, and Major Florey, of Rutsville, another, the names of others are not remembered. They appraised the real estate, that was all.

When the people came to start, many of their horses, oxen and cows were gone, and could not be found. It was known at the time, and the mob boasted of it, that they had killed the oxen and lived on them. Many houses belonging to my brethren were burned, their cattle driven away, and a great quantity of their property was destroyed by the mob. The people of De Witt utterly failed to fulfill their pledge to pay the Saints for the losses they sustained. The governor having turned a deaf ear to our entreaties, the militia having mutinied, the greater part of them being ready to join the mob, the brethren, seeing no prospect of relief, came to the conclusion to leave that place, and seek a shelter elsewhere. Gathering up as many wagons as could be got ready, which was about seventy, with a remnant of the property they had been able to save from their ruthless foes, they left De Witt and started for Caldwell county on the afternoon of Thursday, October 11, 1838. They traveled that day about twelve miles, and encamped in a grove of timber near the road.

That evening a woman, of the name of Jensen, who had some short time before given birth to a child, died in consequence of the exposure occasioned by the operations of the mob, and having to move before her strength would properly admit of it. She was buried in the grove, without a coffin.

During our journey we were continually harassed and threatened by the mob, who shot at us several times, whilst several of our brethren died from the fatigue and privation which they had to endure, and we had to inter them by the wayside, without a coffin, and under circumstances the most distressing. We arrived in Caldwell on the twelfth of October.

Governor Boggs' Exterminating Order

Documentary History of the Church 3:175

HEADQUARTERS MILTIA, CITY OF JEFFERSON,
October 27, 1838.

SIR: -- Since the order of the morning to you, directing you to cause four hundred mounted men to be raised within your division, I have received by Amos Rees, Esq., and Wiley C. Williams, Esq., one of my aids, information of the most appalling character, which changes the whole face of things, and places the Mormons in the attitude of open and avowed defiance of the laws, and of having made open war upon the people of this state. Your orders are, therefore, to hasten your operations and endeavor to reach Richmond, in Ray county, with all possible speed. The Mormons must be treated as enemies and *must be exterminated* or driven from the state, if necessary for the public good. Their outrages are beyond all description. If you can increase your force, you are authorized to do so, to any extent you may think necessary. I have just issued orders to Major-General Wallock, of Marion county, to raise five hundred men, and to march them to the northern part of Daviess and there to unite with General Doniphan, of Clay, who has been ordered with five hundred men to proceed to the same point for the purpose of intercepting the retreat of the Mormons to the north. They have been directed to communicate with you by express; and you can also communicate with them if you find it necessary. Instead, therefore, of proceeding as at first directed, to reinstate the citizens of Daviess in their homes, you will proceed immediately to Richmond, and there operate against the Mormons. Brigadier-General Parks, of Ray, has been ordered to have four hundred men of his brigade in readiness to join you at Richmond. The whole force will be placed under your command.

L. W. BOGGS,
Governor and Commander-in-Chief.
To General Clark.

Great excitement now prevailed, and mobs were heard of in every direction, who seemed determined on our destruction. They burned the houses in the country, and took off all the cattle they could find. They destroyed corn fields, took many prisoners, and threatened death to all the Mormons.

President Joseph Smith, Jun.
Documentary History of the Church 3:178

LILBURN W. BOGGS had become so hardened by mobbing the Saints in Jackson county, and his conscience so "seared as with a hot iron," that he was considered a fit subject for the gubernatorial chair; and it was probably his hatred to truth and the "Mormons," and his blood-thirsty, murderous disposition, that raised him to the station he occupied. His exterminating order of the twenty-seventh aroused every spirit in the state, of the like stamp of his own; and the Missouri mobocrats were flocking to the standard of General Clark from almost every quarter.

Clark, although not the ranking officer, was selected by Governor Boggs as the most fit instrument to carry out his murderous designs; for bad as they were in Missouri, very few commanding officers were yet sufficiently hardened to go all lengths with Boggs in this contemplated inhuman butchery, and expulsion from one of the should-be free and independent states of the Republic of North America, where the Constitution declares, that *"every man shall have the privilege of worshiping God according to the dictates of his own conscience;"* and this was all the offense the Saints had been guilty of.

President Joseph Smith, Jun.
Documentary History of the Church 3:182

The mob began to encamp at Richmond on the twenty-sixth, and by this time amounted to about two thousand men, all ready to fulfill the exterminating order, and join the standard of the governor. They took up a line of march for Far West, traveling but part way, where they encamped for the night.

Tuesday, October 30. -- The advance guard of the mob were patrolling the country and taking many prisoners, among whom were Brother Stephen Winchester, and Brother Carey, whose skull they laid open by a blow from a rifle barrel. In this mangled condition, the mob laid him in their wagon and went on their way, denying him every comfort, and thus he remained that afternoon and night.

General Clark was in camp at Chariton under a forced march to Richmond, with about a thousand men, and the governor's exterminating order.

For the history of this day at Haun's Mills, on Shoal creek, I quote the following affidavit of Elder Joseph Young, First President of the Seventies:

Haun's Mill Massacre

Joseph Young's Narrative of the Massacre at Haun's Mill

On Sunday, twenty-eighth October, we arrived about twelve o'clock, at Haun's Mills, where we found a number of our friends collected together, who were holding a council, and deliberating on the best course for them to pursue, to defend themselves against the mob, who were collecting in the neighborhood under the command of Colonel Jennings, of Livingston county, and threatening them with house burning and killing. The decision of the council was, that our friends there should place themselves in an attitude of self defense. Accordingly about twenty-eight of our men armed themselves, and were in constant readiness for an attack of any small body of men that might come down upon them.

The same evening, for some reason best known to themselves, the mob sent one of their number to enter into a treaty with our friends, which was accepted, on the condition of mutual forbearance on both sides, and that each party, as far as their influence extended, should exert themselves to prevent any further hostilities upon either party.

At this time, however, there was another mob collecting on Grand river, at William Mann's, who were threatening us, consequently we remained under arms.

Monday passed away without molestation from any quarter.

On Tuesday, the 30th, that bloody tragedy was acted, the scene of which I shall never forget. More than three-fourths of the day had passed in tranquility, as smiling as the preceding one. I think there was no individual of our company that was apprised of the sudden and awful fate that hung over our heads like an overwhelming torrent, which was to change the prospects, the feelings and the circumstances of about thirty families. The banks of Shoal creek on either side teemed with children sporting and playing, while their mothers were engaged in domestic employments, and their fathers employed in guarding the mills and other property, while others were engaged in gathering in their crops for their winter consumption. The weather was very pleasant, the sun shone clear, all was tranquil, and no one expressed any apprehension of the awful crisis that was near us -- even at our doors.

It was about four o'clock, while sitting in my cabin with my babe in my arms, and my wife standing by my side, the door being open, I cast my eyes on the opposite bank of Shoal creek and saw a large company of armed men, on horses, directing their course towards the mills with all possible speed. As they advanced through the scattering trees that stood on the edge of the prairie they seemed to form themselves into a three square position, forming a vanguard in front.

At this moment, David Evans, seeing the superiority of their numbers, (there being two hundred and forty of them, according to their own account), swung his hat, and cried for peace. This not being heeded, they continued to advance, and their leader, Mr. Nehemiah Comstock, fired a gun, which was followed by a solemn pause of ten or twelve seconds, when, all at once, they discharged about one hundred rifles, aiming at a blacksmith shop into which our friends had fled for safety; and charged up to the shop, the cracks of which between the logs were sufficiently large to enable them to aim directly at the bodies of those who had there fled for refuge from the fire of their murderers. There were several families tented in the rear of the shop, whose lives were exposed, and amidst a shower of bullets fled to the woods in different directions.

After standing and gazing on this bloody scene for a few minutes, and finding myself in the uttermost danger, the bullets having reached the house where I was living, I committed my family to the protection of heaven, and leaving the house on the opposite side, I took a path which led up the hill, following in the trail of three of my brethren that had fled from the shop. While ascending the hill we were discovered by the mob, who immediately fired at us, and continued so to do till we reached the summit. In descending the hill, I secreted myself in a thicket of bushes, where I lay till eight o'clock in the evening, at which time I heard a female voice calling my name in an under tone, telling me that the mob had gone and there was no danger. I immediately left the thicket, and went to the house of Benjamin Lewis, where I found my family (who had fled there) in safety, and two of my friends mortally wounded, one of whom died before morning. Here we passed the painful night in deep and awful reflections on the scenes of the preceding evening.

After daylight appeared, some four or five men, who with myself, had escaped with our lives from the horrid massacre, and who repaired as soon as possible to the mills, to learn the condition of our friends, whose fate we had but too truly anticipated. When we arrived at the house of Mr. Haun, we found Mr. Merrick's body lying in the rear of the house, Mr. McBride's in front, literally mangled from head to foot. We were informed by Miss Rebecca Judd, who was an eye witness, that he was shot with his own gun, after he had given it up, and then cut to pieces with a corn cutter by a Mr. Rogers of Daviess county, who keeps a ferry on Grand river, and who has since repeatedly boasted of this act of savage barbarity. Mr. York's body we found in the house, and after viewing these corpses, we immediately went to the blacksmith's shop, where we found nine of our friends, eight of whom were already dead; the other, Mr. Cox, of Indiana, struggling in the agonies of death and soon expired. We immediately prepared and carried them to the place of interment. The last office of kindness due to the remains of departed friends, was not attended with the customary ceremonies or decency, for we were in jeopardy, every moment expecting to be fired upon by the mob, who, we supposed, were lying in ambush, waiting for the first opportunity to despatch the remaining few who were providentially preserved from the slaughter of the preceding day. However, we accomplished without molestation this painful task. The place of burying was a vault in the ground, formerly intended for a well, into which we threw the bodies of our friends promiscuously. Among those slain I will mention Sardius Smith, son of Warren Smith, about nine years old, who, through fear, had crawled under the bellows in the shop, where he remained till the massacre was over, when he was discovered by a Mr. Glaze, of Carroll county, who presented his rifle near the boy's head, and literally blowed off the upper part of it. Mr. Stanley, of Carroll, told me afterwards that Glaze boasted of this fiend-like murder and heroic deed all over the country.

The number killed and mortally wounded in this wanton slaughter was eighteen or nineteen, whose names as far as I recollect were as follows: Thomas McBride, Levi N. Merrick, Elias Benner, Josiah Fuller, Benjamin Lewis, Alexander Campbell, Warren Smith, Sardius Smith, George S. Richards, Mr. William Napier, Augustine Harmer, Simon Cox, Mr. [Hiram] Abbott, John York, Charles Merrick, (a boy eight or nine years old), [John Lee, John Byers], and three or four others, whose names I do not recollect, as they were strangers, to me. Among the wounded who recovered were Isaac Laney, Nathan K. Knight, Mr. [William] Yokum, two brothers by the name of [Jacob and George] Myers, Tarlton Lewis, Mr. [Jacob] Haun, and several others, [Jacob Foutz, Jacob Potts, Charles Jimison, John Walker, Alma Smith, aged about nine years]. Miss Mary Stedwell, while fleeing, was shot through the hand, and, fainting, fell over a log, into which they shot upwards of twenty balls.

To finish their work of destruction, this band of murderers, composed of men from Daviess, Livingston, Ray, Carroll, and Chariton counties, led by some of the principal men of that section of the upper country, (among whom I am informed were Mr. Ashby, of Chariton, member of the state legislature; Colonel Jennings, of Livingston county, Thomas O. Bryon, clerk of Livingston county; Mr. Whitney, Dr. Randall, and many others), proceeded to rob the houses, wagons, and tents, of bedding and clothing; drove off horses and wagons, leaving widows and orphans destitute of the necessaries of life; and even stripped the clothing from the bodies of the slain. According to their own account, they *fired seven* rounds in this awful butchery, making upwards of sixteen hundred shots at a little company of men, about thirty in number. I hereby certify the above to be a true statement of facts, according to the best of my knowledge.

JOSEPH YOUNG.***

A younger brother of the boy here killed, aged eight, was shot through the hip. The little fellow himself states that seeing his father and brother both killed, he thought they would shoot him again if he stirred, and so feigned himself dead, and lay perfectly still, till he heard his mother call him after dark.

Nathan K. Knight saw a Missourian cut down Father McBride with a corn-cutter, and also saw them stripping the dying, and heard the boys crying for mercy. Brother Knight made his escape across the mill-dam, after receiving wounds through his lungs and finger. After the massacre was over, he was led to a house by a woman, and whilst lying there wounded he heard Mr. Jesse Maupin say that he blew one of the boys' brains out. Some time later whilst walking the streets of Far West Brother Knight was met by three Missourians who threatened to butcher him, and one of them by the name of Rogers drew a butcher knife, and said that he had not got his corn-cutter with him, that he cut down McBride with, "but by —— I have got something that will do as well;" but by a great chance Brother Knight made his escape from the ruffian.

General Atchison withdrew from the army at Richmond as soon as the governor's extermination order was received. Up to this time we were ignorant at Far West of the movements of the mob at Richmond, and the governor's order of extermination.

On the 30th of October a large company of armed soldiers were seen approaching Far West. They came up near to the town, and then drew back about a mile, and encamped for the night. We were informed that they were militia, ordered out by the governor for the purpose of stopping our proceedings, it having been represented to his excellency, by wicked and designing men from Daviess that we were the aggressors, and had committed outrages in Daviess county. They had not yet got the governor's order of extermination, which I believe did not arrive till the next day.

Joseph Smith and Other Leading Men Are Taken Prisoner

Wednesday, October 31. -- The militia of Far West guarded the city the past night, and arranged a temporary fortification of wagons, timber, etc., on the south. The sisters, many of them, were engaged in gathering up their most valuable effects, fearing a terrible battle in the morning, and that the houses might be fired and they obliged to flee. The enemy was five to one against us.

About eight o'clock a flag of truce was sent from the enemy, which was met by several of our people, and it was hoped that matters would be satisfactorily arranged after the officers had heard a true statement of all the circumstances. Colonel Hinkle went to meet the flag, and secretly made the following engagement: First, to give up their [the Church's] leaders to be tried and punished; second, to make an appropriation of the property of all who had taken up arms, for the payment of their debts, and indemnify for the damage done by them; third, that the remainder of the Saints should leave the state, and be protected while doing so by the militia; but they were to be permitted to remain under protection until further orders were received from the commander-in-chief; fourth, to give up their arms of every description, which would be receipted for.

The enemy was reinforced by about one thousand five hundred men today, and news of the destruction of property by the mob reached us from every quarter.

Towards evening I was waited upon by Colonel Hinkle, who stated that the officers of the militia desired to have an interview with me and some others, hoping that the difficulties might be settled without having occasion to carry into effect the exterminating orders which they had received from the governor. I immediately complied with the request, and in company with Elders Sidney Rigdon and Parley P. Pratt, Colonel Wight and George W. Robinson, went into the camp of the militia. But judge of my surprise, when, instead of being treated with that respect which is due from one citizen to another, we were taken as prisoners of war, and treated with the utmost contempt. The officers would not converse with us, and the soldiers, almost to a man, insulted us as much as they felt disposed, breathing out threats against me and my companions. I cannot begin to tell the scene which I there witnessed. The loud cries and yells of more than one thousand voices, which rent the air and could be heard for miles, and the horrid and blasphemous threats and curses which were poured upon us in torrents, were enough to appall the stoutest heart. In the evening we had to lie down on the cold ground, surrounded by a strong guard, who were only kept back by the power of God from depriving us of life. We petitioned the officers to know why we were thus treated, but they utterly refused to give us any answer, or to converse with us. After we arrived in the camp, Brother Stephen Winchester and eleven other brethren who were prisoners, volunteered, with permission of the officers, to carry Brother Carey into the city to his family, he having lain exposed to the weather for a show to the inhuman wretches, without having his wound dressed or being nourished in any manner. He died soon after he reached home.

The Prophet and Others
Condemned to Be Shot

Thursday, November 1. -- Brothers Hyrum Smith and Amasa Lyman were brought prisoners into camp. The officers of the militia held a court martial, and sentenced us to be shot, on Friday morning, on the public square of Far West as a warning to the "Mormons." However, notwithstanding their sentence and determination, they were not permitted to carry their murderous sentence into execution. Having an opportunity of speaking to General Wilson, I inquired of him why I was thus treated. I told him I was not aware of having done anything worthy of such treatment; that I had always been a supporter of the Constitution and of democracy. His answer was, "I know it, and that is the reason why I want to kill you, or have you killed."

The City of Far West Plundered

The militia went into the town, and without any restraint whatever, plundered the houses, and abused the innocent and unoffending inhabitants and left many destitute. They went to my house, drove my family out of doors, carried away most of my property. General Doniphan declared he would have nothing to do with such cold-blooded murder, and that he would withdraw his brigade in the morning.

Governor Boggs wrote General Clark from Jefferson City, that he considered full and ample powers were vested in him [Clark] to carry into effect the former orders; says Boggs:

Excerpt from Governor Boggs' Communication to General Lucas -- 1838

The case is now a very plain one -- the "Mormons" must be subdued; and peace restored to the community; you will therefore proceed without delay to execute the former orders. Full confidence is reposed in your ability to do so; your force will be amply sufficient to accomplish the object. Should you need the aid of artillery, I would suggest that an application be made to the commanding officer of

Fort Leavenworth, for such as you may need. You are authorized to request the loan of it in the name of the state of Missouri. The ringleaders of this rebellion should be made an example of; and if it should become necessary for the public peace, the "Mormons" should be exterminated, or expelled from the state.

This morning General Lucas ordered the Caldwell militia to give up their arms. Hinkle, having made a treaty with the mob on his own responsibility, to carry out his treachery, marched the troops out of the city, and the brethren gave up their arms, their own property, which no government on earth had a right to require.

The mob (called Governor's troops) then marched into town, and under pretense of searching for arms, tore up floors, upset haystacks, plundered the most valuable effects they could lay their hands on, wantonly wasted and destroyed a great amount of property, compelled the brethren at the point of the bayonet to sign deeds of trust to pay the expenses of the mob, even while the place was desecrated by the chastity of women being violated. About eighty men were taken prisoners, the remainder were ordered to leave the state, and were forbidden, under threat of being shot by the mob to assemble more than three in a place.***

Joseph Bids Farewell to His Family

Myself and fellow prisoners were taken to the town, into the public square, and before our departure we, after much entreaty, were suffered to see our families, being attended all the while by a strong guard. I found my wife and children in tears, who feared we had been shot by those who had sworn to take our lives, and that they would see me no more. When I entered my house, they clung to my garments, their eyes streaming with tears,

while mingled emotions of joy and sorrow were manifested in their countenances. I requested to have a private interview with them a few minutes, but this privilege was denied me by the guard. I was then obliged to take my departure. Who can realize the feelings which I experienced at that time, to be thus torn from my companion, and leave her surrounded with monsters in the shape of men, and my children, too, not knowing how their wants would be supplied; while I was to be taken far from them in order that my enemies might destroy me when they thought proper to do so. My partner wept, my children clung to me, until they were thrust from me by the swords of the guards. I felt overwhelmed while I witnessed the scene, and could only recommend them to the care of that God whose kindness had followed me to the present time, and who alone could protect them, and deliver me from the hands of my enemies, and restore me to my family.

Defense Witnesses Threatened and Imprisoned; Judge Austin A. King Is an Unjust Judge

President Joseph Smith, Jun.
Documentary History of the Church 3:210

We were called upon for our witnesses, and we gave the names of some forty or fifty. Captain Bogart was despatched with a company of militia to procure them. He arrested all he could find, thrust them into prison, and we were not allowed to see them.

During the week we were again called upon most tauntingly for witnesses; we gave the names of some others, and they were thrust into prison, so many as were to be found.

In the meantime*** [six] volunteered, and were sworn, on the defense, but were prevented as much as possible by threats from telling the truth. We saw a man at the window by the name of Allen, and beckoned him to come in, and had him sworn, but when he did not testify to please the court, several rushed upon him with their bayonets, and he fled the place; three men took after him with loaded guns, and he barely escaped with his life. It was of no use to get any more witnesses, even if we could have done so.

Thus this mock investigation continued from day to day, till Saturday, when several of the brethren were discharged by Judge King.***

Our Church organization was converted, by the testimony of the apostates, into a temporal kingdom, which was to fill the whole earth, and subdue all other kingdoms.

The judge, who by the by was a Methodist, asked much concerning our views of the prophecy of Daniel: "In the days of these kings shall the God of heaven set up a kingdom which shall break in pieces all other kingdoms, and stand forever." * * * * "and the kingdom and the greatness of the kingdom, under the whole heaven, shall be given to the Saints of the Most High." As if it were treason to believe the Bible.***

The remaining prisoners were all released or admitted to bail, except Lyman Wight, Caleb Baldwin, Hyrum Smith, Alexander McRae, Sidney Rigdon, and myself, who were sent to Liberty, Clay county, to jail, to stand our trial for treason and murder. Our treason consisted of having whipped the mob out of Daviess county, and taking their cannon from them; the murder, of killing the man in the Bogart battle; also Parley P. Pratt, Morris Phelps, Luman Gibbs, Darwin Chase, and Norman

Shearer, who were put into Richmond jail to stand their trial for the same "crimes."

During the investigation we were confined in chains and received much abuse. The matter of driving away witnesses or casting them into prison, or chasing them out of the county, was carried to such length that our lawyers, General Doniphan and Amos Rees, told us not to bring our witnesses there at all; for if we did, there would not be one of them left for final trial; for no sooner would Bogart and his men know who they were, than they would put them out of the country.

As to making any impression on King, Doniphan said, if a cohort of angels were to come down, and declare we were innocent, it would all be the same; for he (King) had determined from the beginning to cast us into prison. We never got the privilege of introducing our witnesses at all; if we had, we could have disproved all the evidence of our enemies.

President Joseph Smith, Jun.
Documentary History of the Church 3:242

After we were cast into prison, we heard nothing but threatenings, that, if any judge or jury, or court of any kind, should clear any of us, we should never get out of the state alive.

President Joseph Smith, Jun.
Documentary History of the Church 3:306

Thursday, April 4. -- Brothers Kimball and Turley called on Judge King, who was angry at their having reported the case to the governor, and, said he, "I could have done all the business for you properly, if you had come to me; and I would have signed the petition for all except Joe, and he is not fit to live."

President Joseph Smith, Jun.
Documentary History of the Church 3:308

Saturday, April 6. -- Judge King

evidently fearing a change of venue, or some movement on our part to escape his unhallowed persecution (and most probably expecting that we would be murdered on the way) hurried myself and fellow prisoners off to Daviess county, under a guard of about ten men, commanded by Samuel Tillery, deputy jailer of Clay county. We were promised that we should go through Far West, which was directly on our route, which our friends at that place knew, and expected us; but instead of fulfilling their promise, they took us around the city, and out of the direct course some eighteen miles; far from habitations, where every opportunity presented for a general massacre.***

[In Daviess County] *Tuesday, April 9.* -- Our trial commenced before a drunken grand jury, Austin A. King, presiding judge, as drunk as the jury; for they were all drunk together. Elder Stephen Markham had been dispatched by the committee to visit us.*** Brother Markham brought us a written copy of a statute which had passed the legislature, giving us the privilege of a change of venue on our own affidavit.

Judge Morin arrived from Mill Port, and was favorable to our escape from the persecution we were enduring, and spent the evening with us in prison.

The State of Missouri Rewards the Mobbers

President Joseph Smith, Jun.
Documentary History of the Church 3:243

The state appropriated two thousand dollars to be distributed among the people of Daviess and Caldwell counties, the "Mormons" of Caldwell not excepted. The people of Daviess thought they could live on "Mormon" property, and did not want their thousand, consequently it was

pretended to be given to those of Caldwell. Judge Cameron, Mr. McHenry, and others attended to the distribution. Judge Cameron would drive in the brethren's hogs (many of which were identified) and shoot them down in the streets; and without further bleeding, and half dressing, they were cut up and distributed by McHenry to the poor, at a charge of four and five cents per pound; which, together with a few pieces of refuse goods, such as calicoes at double and treble prices soon consumed the two thousand dollars; doing the brethren very little good, or in reality none, as the property destroyed by them, [i.e. the distributing commission] was equal to what they gave the Saints.

The proceedings of the legislature were warmly opposed by a minority of the house -- among whom were David R. Atchison of Clay county and all the members from St. Louis and Messrs. Rollins and Gordon, from Boone county, and by various other members from other counties; but the mob majority carried the day, for the guilty wretches feared an investigation -- knowing that it would endanger their lives and liberties. Some time during this session the legislature appropriated two hundred thousand dollars to pay the troops for driving the Saints out of the state.

The Prophet Escapes From Imprisonment in Missouri

President Joseph Smith, Jun.
Documentary History of the Church 3:319

Monday, April 15. -- Having procured a change of venue we started for Boone county, and were conducted to that place by a strong guard.***

This evening our guard got intoxicated. We thought it a favorable opportunity to make our escape; knowing that the only object of our enemies was our destruction; and likewise knowing that a number of our brethren had been massacred by them on Shoal Creek, amongst whom were two children; and that they sought every opportunity to abuse others who were left in that state; and that they were never brought to an account for their barbarous proceedings, which were winked at and encouraged by those in authority. We thought that it was necessary for us, inasmuch as we loved our lives, and did not wish to die by the hand of murderers and assassins; and inasmuch as we loved our families and friends, to deliver ourselves from our enemies, and from that land of tyranny and oppression, and again take our stand among a people in whose bosoms dwell those feelings of republicanism and liberty which gave rise to our nation: feelings which the inhabitants of the State of Missouri were strangers to. Accordingly, we took advantage of the situation of our guard and departed, and that night we traveled a considerable distance.

Redress Denied by the President of the United States

George Q. Cannon
Life of Joseph Smith the Prophet, Page 328

Some time after the Saints had completed their exodus [from Missouri] Hyrum Smith epitomized the awful events in the following words:

Governor Boggs and Generals Clark, Lucas, Wilson and Gilliam, also Austin A. King, have committed treasonable acts against the citizens of Missouri, and did violate the Constitution of the United States and also the constitution and laws of the state of Missouri, and did exile and expel, at the point of the bayonet, some twelve or fourteen thousand inhabitants of the state, and did murder some three or four hundred of men, women and children in cold blood, in the most horrid and cruel

manner possible. And the whole of it was caused by religious bigotry and persecution, and because the Mormons dared to worship Almighty God according to the dictates of their own conscience, and agreeably to His divine will, as revealed in the scriptures of eternal truth.

President Joseph Smith, Jun.
Documentary History of the Church 4:80

During my stay I had an interview with Martin Van Buren, the President, who treated me very insolently, and it was with great reluctance he listened to our message, which, when he had heard, he said: *"Gentlemen, your cause is just, but I can do nothing for you;"* and *"If I take up for you I shall lose the vote of Missouri."* His whole course went to show that he was an office-seeker, that self-aggrandizement was his ruling passion, and that justice and righteousness were no part of his composition. I found him such a man as I could not conscientiously support at the head of our noble Republic. I also had an interview with Mr. John C. Calhoun, whose conduct towards me very ill became his station. I became satisfied there was little use for me to tarry, to press the just claims of the Saints on the consideration of the President or Congress, and stayed but a few days, taking passage in company with Porter Rockwell and Dr. Foster on the railroad and stages back to Dayton, Ohio.

Persecutions in the State of Illinois

Joseph Smith Arrested on False Accusations; Attempt to Forcibly Take Him to Missouri; Abuses by the Officers Upon Joseph

(Compiled By Church Historian)
Documentary History of the Church, Introduction 5:24

A second attempt of Missouri to drag the Prophet from the state of Illinois by extradition procedure, was even more infamous than the first. No sooner was Joseph released from arrest and departed from Springfield than John C. Bennett arrived there and wrote some of his friends in Nauvoo his intention to leave immediately for Missouri and obtain a new indictment by a grand jury on the old charge of "murder, treason, burglary, theft," etc., brought against the Prophet, Hyrum Smith, Lyman Wight, Parley P. Pratt *et al.,* in 1838, hoping that upon this charge he might succeed in getting out extradition papers on the ground that the Prophet was a fugitive from the justice of the state of Missouri. It will be remembered that a former attempt was made under this same charge, in June, 1841, when the Prophet was tried on writ of *habeas corpus* at Monmouth, Warren county, Illinois, before Judge Douglas and set at liberty. It was on this occasion that Esquire O. H. Browning declared that to ask Joseph Smith "to go to Missouri for a trial was adding insult to injury" (Vol. IV, chapter XX)

An indictment on these old charges was finally obtained, supposedly at the instance of Bennett and the Prophet's old Missouri enemies, at a special term of the Circuit Court of Daviess county, Missouri, on the 5th of June, 1843. Governor Reynolds, of Missouri issued a requisition on Governor Ford for Joseph Smith, and appointed J. H. Reynolds as agent of Missouri to receive the Prophet from the authorities of Illinois.

President Joseph Smith, Jun.
Documentary History of the Church 5:439-456

I sent William Clayton to Dixon at ten a.m., to try and find out what was going on there. He met Mr. Joseph H. Reynolds, the sheriff of Jackson county, Missouri, and Constable Harmon T. Wilson, of Carthage, Illinois, about half way, but they being disguised, they were not known by him; and when at Dixon they represented themselves as Mormon elders who wanted to see the prophet. They hired a man and team to carry them, for they had run their horses almost to death.

They arrived at Mr. Wasson's while the family were at dinner, about two p.m. They came to the door and said they were Mormon elders, and wanted to see Brother Joseph. I was in the yard going to the barn when Wilson stepped to the end of the house and saw me. He accosted me in a very uncouth, ungentlemanly manner, when Reynolds stepped up to me, collared me, then both of them presented cocked pistols to my breast, without showing any writ or serving any process. Reynolds cried out, "G— d— you, if you stir I'll shoot; G— d— if you, stir one inch, I shoot you, be still, or I'll shoot you, by G—." I enquired "What is the meaning of all this?" "I'll show you the meaning, by G—; and if you stir one inch, I'll shoot you, G— d— you." I answered, "I am not afraid of your shooting; I am not afraid to die." I then bared my breast and told them to shoot away. "I have endured so much oppression, I am weary of life; and kill me, if you please. I am a strong man, however, and with my own natural weapons could soon level both of you; but if you have any legal process to serve, I am at all times subject to law, and shall not offer resistance." Reynold replied, "G— d— you, if you say another word I will shoot you, by G—." I answered, "Shoot away; I am not afraid of your pistols."

By this time Stephen Markham walked deliberately towards us. When they saw him coming, they turned their pistols from me to him, and threatened his life if he came any nearer; but he paid no attention to their threats, and continued to advance nearer. They then turned their pistols on me again, jamming them against my side, with their fingers on the triggers, and ordered Markham to stand still or they would shoot me through. As Markham was advancing rapidly towards me, I said, "You are not going to resist the officers, are you, Brother Markham?" He replied, "No, not if they are officers: I know the law too well for that."

They then hurried me off, put me in a wagon without serving any process, and were for hurrying me off without letting me see or bid farewell to my family or friends, or even allowing me time to get my hat or clothes, or even suffer my wife or children to bring them to me. I then said, "Gentlemen, if you have any legal process, I wish to obtain a writ of habeas corpus," and was answered,-- "G— d— you, you shan't have one." They still continued their punching me on both sides with their pistols.

Markham then sprung and seized the horses by the bits, and held them until my wife could bring my hat and coat. Reynolds and Wilson again threatening to shoot Markham, who said, "There is no law on earth that requires a sheriff to take a prisoner without his clothes." Fortunately at this moment I saw a man passing, and said to him, "These men are kidnapping me, and I wish a writ of habeas corpus to deliver myself out of their hands. But as he did not appear to go, I told Markham to go, and he immediately proceeded to Dixon on horseback, where the sheriff also proceeded with me at full speed, without even allowing me to speak to my family or bid them good bye. The officers held their pistols with the muzzles jamming into my side for more than eight miles, and they only desisted on being reproached by Markham for their cowardice in so brutally ill-treating an unarmed, defenseless prisoner. On arriving at the house of Mr. McKennie, the tavern-keeper, I was thrust

into a room and guarded there, without being allowed to see anybody; and fresh horses were ordered to be ready in five minutes.

I again stated to Reynolds, "I wish to get counsel," when he answered. G— d— you, you shan't have counsel: one word more, G— d— you, and I'll shoot you."

"What is the use of this so often?" said I. "I have repeatedly told you to shoot; and I now tell you again to shoot away!" I saw a person passing and shouted to him through the window, "I am falsely imprisoned here, and I want a lawyer." Lawyer Edward Southwick came, and had the door banged in his face, with the old threat of shooting him if he came any nearer.

Another lawyer (Mr. Shepherd G. Patrick) afterwards came and received the same treatment, which began to cause considerable excitement in Dixon.

A Mr. Lucien P. Sanger asked Markham what was the matter, when he told him all, and stated that the sheriff intended to drag me away immediately to Missouri, and prevent my taking out a writ of habeas corpus.

Sanger soon made this known to Mr. Dixon, the owner of the house, and his friends, who gathered around the hotel door, and gave Reynolds to understand that if that was their mode of doing business in Missouri, they had another way of doing it in Dixon. They were a law-abiding people and Republicans, and gave Reynolds to understand that he should not take me away without giving me the opportunity of a fair trial, and that I should have justice done me; but that if he persisted in his course, they had a very summary way of dealing with such people.

Mr. Reynolds finding further resistance

to be useless, allowed Mr. Patrick and Mr. Southwick to come into the room to me, (but Wilson was inside guarding the door, and Reynolds guarded the outside of the door,) when I told them I had been taken prisoner by these men without process; I had been insulted and abused by them. I showed them my flesh, which was black for about eighteen inches in circumference on each side, from their punching me with their pistols; and I wanted them to sue out a writ of habeas corpus, whereupon Reynolds swore he should only wait half-an-hour to give me a chance. A messenger was immediately sent by Mr. Dixon to Mr. Chamberlain, the Master-in-Chancery, who lived six miles distant, and, another message to Cyrus H. Walker, who happened to be near, to have them come down and get out the writ of habeas corpus.

A writ was sued out by Markham before a justice of the peace against Reynolds and Wilson for threatening his life. They were taken into custody by the constable. He sued out another writ for assault and threatening my life, whereupon they were again arrested.

At this time Markham rushed into the room and put a pistol (unobserved) into my pocket, although Reynolds and Wilson had their pistols cocked at the same time and were threatening to shoot him.

About midnight he sued out a writ for a violation of the law in relation to writs of habeas corpus, Wilson having transferred me to the custody of Reynolds, for the purpose of dragging me to Missouri, and thereby avoiding the effect and operation of said writ, contrary to law, which was put over to be heard at ten o'clock tomorrow morning; and I was conducted back to the room and guarded through the night.***

About eight, the master-in-chancery arrived and issued a writ of habeas corpus returnable before the Hon. John D. Caton, Judge of the 9th Judicial Circuit at Ottawa, which was duly served on Reynolds and Wilson.

Mr. Cyrus Walker, who was out electioneering to become the representative for Congress, told me that he could not find time to be my lawyer unless I could promise him my vote. He being considered the greatest criminal lawyer in that part of Illinois, I determined to secure his aid, and promised him my vote. He afterwards went to Markham and joyfully said, "I am now sure of my election, as Joseph Smith has promised me his vote, and I am going to defend him."

President Joseph Smith, Jun.
Documentary History of the Church 5:466

If our enemies are determined to oppress us and deprive us of our constitutional rights and privileges as they have done and if the authorities that are on the earth will not sustain us in our rights, nor give us that protection which the laws and constitution of the United States, and of this State guarantee unto us, then we will claim them from a higher power -- from heaven -- yea, from God Almighty.

George Q. Cannon
Life of Joseph Smith the Prophet, Page 497

Under advice of the lawyers, Joseph with his captors was brought before the municipal court at Nauvoo, and all the writs and other papers were filed there. The case was heard upon its merits, and the Prophet was discharged. The lawyers concurred that in all the transactions since the day of his arrest Joseph had held himself amendable to the law and its officers; and that the decision of the municipal court of Nauvoo was not only legal and just but was within the power of this tribunal under the city charter.

SECTION REVELATION 213

Thus Saith Son Ahman, Jesus Christ, to the Power of Governing in the Court of Prosecuting Labor, and to the Leaders of National Power -- Let My Word Be Heard in Your Several Placings of Your Influencing and Governing Power, Even This, My Warning to Not Abuse My Innocent People, But Maintain Their Rights of Governing Protecting of Religious Way of My Holy Order of Union Celestial in My Holy Church on Earth. Let There Cease to Be the Continued Way and Idea You Can Be of a Prosecuting Labor Against My Holy Way of Eternal Lives of Celestial Union Power Above All Peoples and Their Claims of Power to Rule Over All the People in Their Lands of Man Organizing Power. Thus Am I Now Giving My Will to Be Known Among All Surviving People on Earth. Hear Thou My Way of Truth by This, My Revealing to All:

Revelation of the Lord Jesus Christ
San Angelo, Texas
Saturday, July 30, 2011

1. I who is over all peoples, your Lord Jesus Christ, declare to my present nation on the land of Zion, even the power of governing over the people of the nation of United States of America: I, your Lord, have caused history truth to be as a full seeing into abuse of governing power against my servant Joseph Smith, because he testified of my holy appearing and guiding to the people of my land of Zion, even to the nation.

2. Let my people now find true peace and preserving of religious freedom, as I, your Lord, ordained, in raising up nation of free religious exercise of the founding of my Constitution of inspiring power I caused to guide founding authorities.

3. Let all now be of a giving an accounting soon at hand, where I shall be the God over all my holy Zion, and over all remaining nations on earth.

4. You shall see my holy Zion is of a preserving, not of government prosecution, where you are defiling innocence and sacred trust in present court.

5. Let all now be of a stop! of the prosecuting power.

6. I shall send my will to you of my holy way to establish peace on my land as you uphold my will.

7. Let my servant go, to do my will with my people of the Fundamentalist Church of Jesus Christ of Latter-day Saints; to establish my holy way upon which

Zion must be built; even laws of my holy revealing, and abiding by my power.

8. It is now time to be of a ceasing of thy prosecuting power against members of my Church now under attack for religious practice, which is of a freedom guaranteed by constitutional and governing law of pure principle of rights and freedoms, of national power, over state power now afflicting my servant and my holy law of Celestial Marriage, requiring my own guiding.

9. You are now in a way of opposing God.

10. I am He who bore the sins of all who will repent and turn to a way of pure holy way of living.

11. Let all now know I shall send a judging on all of the people who combine against my holy way of pure power of Eternal Union of my revealing.

12. Let all people now be knowing of my coming to give reward to all people.

13. Let the court dismiss all counts against my servant.

14. Let my people be of free living my law of pure holy way.

15. Let it now be a new way of governing, to be as caring and protecting power over innocent peoples, who only live for God and His holy way to build up my holy place of my coming, even New Jerusalem, soon to be of full power over all people.

16. Let my will be sounded to this nation.

17. Let all now be forewarned.

18. Let all now have my will known, to be of full exercise of their choosing to do right toward my people who abide higher religious revealing law of family way; yea, as more holy, as is the heavens holy more than the earth and false ways of governing and living on earth.

19. Let all be holy among my holy way.

20. Let all be a full preparing; to be of the Zion of my making soon at hand, even my pure holy way being known to all people.

21. Let this, my will, be of a presenting.

22. Let it now be my will above your way of governing, saith God over all, to uphold my right to rule, lest my cleansing power Celestial is as a whirlwind upon the nation of my coming, to cleanse the gross evils off my land; to be a pure and holy way remaining on the land of holiness, even Zion, my Chosen.

23. Let all now be of a full repenting; for I am God; and now am causing my will to be known to all people on earth; warnings justifying me to send forth judgment upon all who are of wicked intent

against life, innocence, purity, holy way of my revealing; even to purge every peoples of the more wicked; preserving my people of purity of living if they abide their covenant of Celestial purity with me, their Lord, who is Jesus Christ, even the God of the Resurrection; bringing life, salvation, happiness on earth, and happiness eternal in the heavens, unto souls well preparing for Eternal Union power of eternal life, through my Holy Priesthood of my sending all needful way of holy and revealed truth, blessings of Priesthood revealing power, which is my authority in heaven, now bestowed on my servant on earth by my own way; to be a holy vessel of administering my holy will to all nations, peoples, and tongues; to be as a voice to the people of this generation; yet not acknowledged as being my Holy Priesthood power among men on earth; being all my power sent from heaven to earth; that my obedient children are blessed by their Lord with eternal power to be exalting in my holy power of Godhood.

24. Let my people be above reproach.

25. Let all be to me as a son or daughter of obedient way.

26. I am Jehovah Christ, even Son Ahman, Jesus Christ; the Holy Power over all creation.

27. Let all people in the nation of government power of constitutional guarantee of freedom of religion, now be of a voice to please God in preserving my obedient, peaceful people in religious rights of free living pure holy way of abiding in family and Church governing; private and sacred to me and to my people of a Celestial way of heavenly power on earth in their individual lives, by my revealing who is worthy of Celestial Union Eternal.

28. Let it be a law in the land by constitutional preserving power, to allow my Celestial Law of Plural Marriage be of a new way of pure justice, freedom; preserving religious rights of a peaceful and holy way of life on earth of thy God's sending Priesthood power on earth; to be my authority of law above the changing law of man, to preserve to my people my way to earn salvation eternal.

29. This is the will of God to the leader of the nation and to all government powers on this land of United States of America.

30. Let my people be free now, is my call to all governing powers on the land of Zion, where I shall appear in my power of pure holy power over all things.

31. I am He who created all things, is above all things, the Life

and Light of all peoples, tongues, kindreds, nations on earth.

32. I am God over all, saith your Lord, who is Jesus Christ, even I who send this holy will to court, and to leaders of governing power, as my own will revealing truth, that shall be as a foundation of pure holy way of my Kingdom soon to rise and be the governing power over all nations; New Jerusalem being the city of power, governing all peoples by my holy power.

33. I am to soon cleanse all peoples of evil practices of murder of unborn children, as well as secret combinations in nations and between national leaders of murder and combinations of evil to get gain by evil, immoral, licentious way of corrupting innocence and virtue.

34. Let all beware.

35. I come suddenly.

36. Be ye ready.

37. I am above all, and have the right to rule over all flesh, saith Son Ahman, your Lord and Holy Redeemer. Amen.

Martyrdom of Joseph Smith and Hyrum Smith in Carthage Jail -- June 27, 1844

(Compiled by Church Historian)
Documentary History of the Church 6:602

5:30 a. m. -- Arose. Joseph requested Dan Jones to descend and inquire of the guard the cause of the disturbance in the night. Frank Worrell, the officer of the guard, who was one of the Carthage Greys, in a very bitter spirit said, "We have had too much trouble to bring Old Joe here to let him ever escape alive, and unless you want to die with him you had better leave before sundown; and you are not a damned bit better than him for taking his part, and you'll see that I can prophesy better than Old Joe, for neither he nor his brother, nor anyone who will remain with them will see the sun set today."

Joseph directed Jones to go to Governor Ford and inform him what he had been told by the officer of the guard. While Jones was going to Governor Ford's quarters, he saw an assemblage of men, and heard one of them, who was apparently a leader, making a speech, saying that, "Our troops will be discharged this morning in obedience to orders, and for a sham we will leave the town; but when the Governor and the McDonough troops have left for Nauvoo this afternoon, we will return and kill those men, if we have to tear the jail down." This sentiment was applauded by three cheers from the crowd.

Captain Jones went to the Governor, told him what had occurred in the night, what the officer of the guard had said, and what he had heard while coming to see him, and earnestly solicited him to avert the danger.

His Excellency replied, "You are unnecessarily alarmed for the safety of your friends, sir, the people are not that cruel."

Irritated by such a remark, Jones urged the necessity of placing better men to guard them than professed assassins, and said, "The Messrs. Smith are American citizens, and have surrendered themselves to your Excellency upon your pledging your honor for their safety; they are also Master Masons, and as such I demand of you protection of their lives."

Governor Ford's face turned pale, and Jones remarked, "If you do not do this, I have but one more desire, and that is if you leave their lives in the hands of those men to be sacrificed --

"What is that, sir?" he asked in a hurried tone.

"It is," said Jones, "that the Almighty will preserve my life to a proper time and place, that I may testify that you have been timely warned of their danger."

Jones then returned to the prison, but the guard would not let him enter. He again returned to the hotel, and found Governor Ford standing in front of the McDonough troops, who were in line ready to escort him to Nauvoo.

The disbanded mob retired to the rear, shouting loudly that they were only going a short distance out of town, when they would return and kill old Joe and Hyrum as soon as the Governor was far enough out of town.

Jones called the attention of the Governor to the threats then made, but the Governor took no notice of them, although it was impossible for him to avoid hearing them.

Jones then requested the Governor to give him passports for himself and friends to pass in and out of the prison, according to his promise made to the prisoners. He refused to give them, but he told General Deming to give one to Dr. Willard Richards, Joseph Smith's private secretary.

The Prophet's Life Is Threatened

While obtaining this, Jones' life was threatened, and Chauncey L. Higbee said

to him in the street, "We are determined to kill Joe and Hyrum, and you had better go away to save yourself."

At 7 a. m., Joseph, Hyrum, Dr. Richards, Stephen Markham and John S. Fullmer ate breakfast together. Mr. Crane ate with them, and wanted to know if the report was true that Joseph fainted three times on Tuesday, while being exhibited to the troops. He was told it was a false report.***

Dr. Southwick was in the meeting, seeing what was going on. He afterward told Stephen Markham that the purport of the meeting was to take into consideration the best way to stop Joseph Smith's career, as his views on government were widely circulated and took like wildfire. They said if he did not get into the Presidential chair this election, he would be sure to the next time; and if Illinois and Missouri would join together and kill him, they would not be brought to justice for it. There were delegates in said meeting from every state in the Union except three. Governor Ford and Captain Smith were also in the meeting.

Captain Dunn and his company were ordered to accompany the Governor to Nauvoo. The Carthage Greys, who had but two days before been under arrest for insulting the commanding general, and whose conduct had been more hostile to the prisoners than that of any other company, were selected by Governor Ford to guard the prisoners at the jail; and other troops composed of the mob whom the Governor had found at Carthage, and had mustered into the service of the State and who had been promised "full satisfaction" and that they should be marched to Nauvoo, were disbanded and discharged in Carthage; yet Governor

Ford suffered two or three hundred armed men to remain encamped about eight miles off on the Warsaw road, apparently under the control of Col. Levi Williams, a notoriously sworn enemy to Joseph, and who had on many occasions threatened the destruction of Nauvoo and the death of Joseph. Moreover it was the duty of the Governor to dismiss the troops into the hands of their several officers in order to be marched home and there disbanded, and not to have disbanded them at a distance from home, and at a time and place when they were predisposed to acts of lawless violence, rapine and murder.

Cyrus H. Wheelock, states that previous to leaving Carthage he said to the Governor, "Sir, you must be aware by this time that the prisoners have no fears in relation to any lawful demands made against them, but you have heard sufficient to justify you in the belief that their enemies would destroy them if they had them in their power; and now, sir, I am about to leave for Nauvoo, and I fear for those men; they are safe as regards the law, but they are not safe from the hands of traitors, and midnight assassins who thirst for their blood and have determined to spill it; and under these circumstances I leave with a heavy heart."

Ford replied: "I was never in such a dilemma in my life; but your friends shall be protected, and have a fair trial by the law; in this *pledge* I am not alone; I have obtained the *pledge* of the whole of the army to sustain me."

The Martyrdom

(Compiled By Church Historian)
Documentary History of the Church 6:617

Immediately there was a little rustling at the outer door of the jail, and a cry of surrender, and also a discharge of three

or four firearms followed instantly. The doctor glanced an eye by the curtain of the window, and saw about a hundred armed men around the door.

It is said that the guard elevated their firelocks, and boisterously threatening the mob discharged their firearms over their heads. The mob encircled the building, and some of them rushed by the guard up the flight of stairs, burst open the door, and began the work of death, while others fired in through the open windows.

In the meantime Joseph, Hyrum, and Elder Taylor had their coats off. Joseph sprang to his coat for his six-shooter, Hyrum for his single barrel, Taylor for Markham's large hickory cane, and Dr. Richards for Taylor's cane. All sprang against the door, the balls whistled up the stairway, and in an instant one came through the door.

Joseph Smith, John Taylor and Dr. Richards sprang to the left of the door, and tried to knock aside the guns of the ruffians.

Hyrum was retreating back in front of the door and snapped his pistol, when a ball struck him in the left side of his nose, and he fell on his back on the floor saying, "I am a dead man!" As he fell on the floor another ball from the outside entered his left side, and passed through his body with such force that it completely broke to pieces the watch he wore in his vest pocket, and at the same instant another ball from the door grazed his breast, and entered his head by the throat; subsequently a fourth ball entered his left leg.

A shower of balls was pouring through all parts of the room, many of which lodged in the ceiling just above the head of Hyrum.

Joseph reached round the door casing, and discharged his six shooter into the passage, some barrels missing fire. Continual discharges of musketry came into the room. Elder Taylor continued parrying the guns until they had got them about half their length into the room, when he found that resistance was vain, and he attempted to jump out of the window, where a ball fired from within struck him on his left thigh, hitting the bone, and passing through to within half an inch of the other side. He fell on the window sill, when a ball fired from the outside struck his watch in his vest pocket, and threw him back into the room.

After he fell into the room he was hit by two more balls, one of them injuring his left wrist considerably, and the other entering at the side of the bone just below the left knee. He rolled under the bed, which was at the right of the window in the south-east corner of the room.

While he lay under the bed he was fired at several times from the stairway; one ball struck him on the left hip, which tore the flesh in a shocking manner, and large quantities of blood were scattered upon the wall and floor.

When Hyrum fell, Joseph exclaimed, "Oh dear, brother Hyrum!" and opening the door a few inches he discharged his six shooter in the stairway (as stated before), two or three barrels of which missed fire.

Joseph, seeing there was no safety in the room, and no doubt thinking that it would save the lives of his brethren in the room if he could get out, turned calmly from the door, dropped his pistol on the floor, and sprang into the window when two balls pierced him from the door, and one entered his right breast from without, and he fell outward into the hands of his murderers, exclaiming, "O Lord, my God!"

Announcement of the Death of Joseph and Hyrum Smith

President John Taylor
Doctrine and Covenants, Section 135

1. To seal the testimony of this book and the Book of Mormon, we announce the martyrdom of Joseph Smith the Prophet, and Hyrum Smith the Patriarch. They were shot in Carthage jail, on the 27th of June, 1844, about five o'clock p.m., by an armed mob -- painted black -- of from 150 to 200 persons. Hyrum was shot first and fell calmly, exclaiming: *I am a dead man!* Joseph leaped from the window, and was shot dead in the attempt, exclaiming: *O Lord my God!* They were both shot after they were dead, in a brutal manner, and both received four balls.

2. John Taylor and Willard Richards, two of the Twelve, were the only persons in the room at the time; the former was wounded in a savage manner with four balls, but has since recovered; the latter, through the providence of God, escaped, without even a hole in his robe.

3. Joseph Smith, the Prophet and Seer of the Lord, has done more, save Jesus only, for the salvation of men in this world, than any other man that ever lived in it. In the short space of twenty years, he has brought forth the Book of Mormon, which he translated by the gift and power of God, and has been the means of publishing it on two continents; has sent the fulness of the everlasting gospel, which it contained, to the four quarters of the earth; has brought forth the revelations and commandments which compose this book of Doctrine and Covenants, and many other wise documents and instructions for the

benefit of the children of men; gathered many thousands of the Latter-day Saints, founded a great city, and left a fame and name that cannot be slain. He lived great, and he died great in the eyes of God and his people; and like most of the Lord's anointed in ancient times, has sealed his mission and his works with his own blood; and so has his brother Hyrum. In life they were not divided, and in death they were not separated!

4. When Joseph went to Carthage to deliver himself up to the pretended requirements of the law, two or three days previous to his assassination, he said: "I am going like a lamb to the slaughter; but I am calm as a summer's morning; I have a conscience void of offense towards God, and towards all men. I SHALL DIE INNOCENT, AND IT SHALL YET BE SAID OF ME -- HE WAS MURDERED IN COLD BLOOD." -- The same morning, after Hyrum had made ready to go -- shall it be said to the slaughter? yes, for so it was -- he read the following paragraph, near the close of the twelfth chapter of Ether, in the Book of Mormon, and turned down the leaf upon it:

5. *And it came to pass that I prayed unto the Lord that he would give unto the Gentiles grace, that they might have charity. And it came to pass that the Lord said unto me: If they have not charity it mattereth not unto thee, thou hast been faithful; wherefore thy garments are clean. And because thou hast seen thy weakness, thou shalt be made strong, even unto the sitting down in the place which I have prepared in the mansions of my Father. And now I....bid farewell unto the Gentiles; yea, and also unto my brethren whom I love, until we shall meet before the judgment-seat of Christ, where all men shall know that my garments are not spotted with your blood.* The testators are now dead, and their testament is in force.

6. Hyrum Smith was forty-four years old in February, 1844, and Joseph Smith was thirty-eight in December, 1843; and henceforward their names will be classed among the martyrs of religion; and the reader in every nation will be reminded that the Book of Mormon, and this book of Doctrine and Covenants of the church, cost the best blood of the nineteenth century to bring them forth for the salvation of a ruined world; and that if the fire can scathe a green tree for the glory of God, how easy it will burn up the dry trees to purify the vineyard of corruption. They lived for glory; they died for glory; and glory is their eternal reward. From age to age shall their names go down to posterity as gems for the sanctified.

7. They were innocent of any crime, as they had often been proved before, and were only confined in jail by the conspiracy of traitors and wicked men; and their *innocent blood* on the floor of Carthage jail is a broad seal affixed to "Mormonism" that cannot be rejected by any court on earth, and their *innocent blood* on the escutcheon of the State of Illinois, with the broken faith of the State as pledged by the governor, is a witness to the truth of the everlasting gospel that all the world cannot impeach; and their *innocent blood* on the banner of liberty, and on the *magna charta* of the United States, is an ambassador for the religion of Jesus Christ, that will touch the hearts of honest men among all nations; and their *innocent blood*, with the innocent blood of all the martyrs under the altar that John saw, will cry unto the Lord of Hosts till he avenges that blood on the earth. Amen.

SECTION REVELATION 214

Son Ahman Gives Truth of Eternal Power to Joseph Smith, A God of Power

Revelation of the Lord Jesus Christ
San Angelo, Texas
Friday, July 29, 2011

1. I who am Endless, even your Lord Jesus Christ, declare that my servant Joseph Smith, my holy Prophet, Seer, and Revelator, performed a work that is now to soon burst forth in my holy power still on him as the third member of the Ruling Power over this world; to be my holy Son of God who is to be of the full and ordained Gods in Celestial and eternal Priesthood authority in heaven; to come to earth to rule on my land and place of power, of Celestial governing power over all peoples, under Christ; to be a holy power of governing authority; to subdue all powers to be of my Kingdom on earth.

2. Let all people revere the holy name and perfect mission of Joseph Smith; restoring my Gospel, Priesthood, and Kingdom of God, Church and holy order of power Celestial to earth.

3. Such is his mission to yet be done on earth; all peoples learning of his grandeur and eternal power of my giving him dominion over all peoples; to be the power of eternal authority over all peoples; as I have ordained upon him to be an holy Celestial God over all peoples on earth, as a God of pure governing power.

4. Not one law was of a leaving out.

5. All was restored through this great Prophet of God, unto my full Kingdom being restored on earth; he being my Messenger of the power of life and holy way, unto being a full God of Eternal Union Power.

6. Let all rejoice in the God of all for Joseph Smith, and the grand mission performing now, to be of a fulfilling of the promise of my coming, even Jesus Christ, to all nations knowing of my power.

7. Let all now be my Zion on earth to receive more eternal truths.

8. Let all be my pure holy way of Eternal Union, in my holy way of my New Jerusalem soon to come forth in fulness. Amen.

President Rulon Jeffs' Testimony of the Prophet Joseph Smith

Joseph Smith Is the Third Member of the Godhead and the Witness and Testator

President Rulon Jeffs
Rulon Jeffs' Sermons 2:8 August 7, 1966 SLC

I testify to you that Joseph Smith, the Prophet, the Witness and Testator, is the One Mighty and Strong who shall come and set in order His House. And we should be so ordering our lives, brothers and sisters, that we will be found worthy to meet him and be instructed of him; for he will come, under the direction of the Holy One of Israel, and he will speak to His servants first, and then to those who are worthy.

President Rulon Jeffs
Rulon Jeffs' Sermons 2:42 Feb. 5, 1967 SLC

TPJS Page 190
The Three Personages

Everlasting covenant was made between three personages before the organization of this earth, and relates to their dispensation of things to men on the earth; these personages, according to Abraham's record, are called God the first, the Creator; God the second, the Redeemer; and God the third, the witness or Testator.

It is a wonderful thing to contemplate who this Witness and Testator is, and that it is not beneath the place and the dignity of Joseph Smith to class him among the grand Presidency of this earth, the Godhead: the Father, the Son, and the Holy Ghost. This great man who witnessed the Father and the Son together as a fourteen-year-old boy, and undoubtedly subsequent to this, stood in Their presence, and was indeed Their Witness and Testator, standing in the office of the Holy Ghost. Heber C. Kimball made the statement on one occasion: "Let me tell you, the Holy Ghost is a man." Now who is that man? Joseph Smith. The Holy Ghost is also that great spiritual power and essence, the foundation of all things, that emanates from the Father and issues forth from Himself throughout all His creations, and is the instrument of God in creating this earth and all of His dominions, and is

the power and gift by which we are able to come back to Him. There is another very important thing that I think might be called to our attention, and that is something that the Prophet Joseph said himself, of himself, although he did not give it in so many words.

TPJS Page 364

The last time I spoke on this stand it was on the resurrection of the dead, when I promised to continue my remarks upon that subject. I still feel a desire to say something on this subject. Let us this very day begin anew, and now say, with all our hearts, we will forsake our sins and be righteous. I shall read the 24th chapter of Matthew, and give it a literal rendering and reading; and when it is rightly understood, it will be edifying.

I thought the very oddity of its rendering would be edifying anyhow -- "And it will be preached, the Gospel of the kingdom, in the whole world, to a witness over all people: and then will the end come." I will now read it in German [which he did, and many Germans who were present said he translated it correctly].

The Savior said when these tribulations should take place, it should be committed to a man who should be a witness over the whole world: the keys of knowledge, power and revelations should be revealed to a witness who should hold the testimony to the world. It has always been my province to dig up hidden mysteries -- new things -- for my hearers. Just at the time when some men think that I have no right to the keys of the Priesthood -- just at that time I have the greatest right. The Germans are an exalted people. The old German translators are the most nearly correct -- most honest of any of the translators; and therefore I get testimony to bear me out in the revelations that I have preached for the last fourteen years. The old German, Latin, Greek and Hebrew translations all say it is true: they cannot be impeached, and therefore I am in good company.

All the testimony is that the Lord in the last days would commit the keys of the Priesthood to a witness over all people. Has the Gospel of the kingdom commenced in the last days? And will God take it from the man until He takes him Himself? I have read it precisely as the words flowed from the lips of Jesus Christ. John the Revelator saw an angel flying through the midst of heaven, having the everlasting Gospel to preach unto them that dwell on the earth.

The scripture is ready to be fulfilled when great wars, famines, pestilence, great distress, judgments, &c., are ready to be poured out on the inhabitants of the earth. John saw the angel having the holy Priesthood, who should preach the everlasting Gospel to all nations. God had an angel -- a special messenger -- ordained and prepared for that purpose in the last days. Woe, woe be to that man or set of men who lift up their hands against God and His witness in these last days: for they shall deceive almost the very chosen ones!

Joseph Smith is that Witness. It is my testimony to you that everyone who has stood in his place since he was taken, has been able to speak with the same authority. They are not that Witness as he is; no one can take his place, or his kingdom, or his Priesthood. But this is the authority that we are dealing with, brothers and sisters. Joseph Smith stands next to Jesus Christ, Himself, as John Taylor wrote, as we have recorded in Section 135; and I thought it might even be well to read that if it be edifying to us today. Sometimes we have some of these scriptures before us that we never think to read, and we need to have them read to us from this stand occasionally, I think; learn to appreciate what we have and who these men are that God has raised up.

President Rulon Jeffs
Rulon Jeffs' Sermons 2:138 May 19, 1968 SLC

Joseph later corrected this to say, "Again, this Gospel of the kingdom shall be preached in all the world, to a witness over all nations." That witness is Joseph the Prophet, that great Witness and Testator who filled the office of the Holy Ghost and stands in that office as to the Godhead -- the Father, the Son, and the Holy Ghost, the Godhead of this earth. How blessed we are to have the message and the testimony and the witness of this great man in our day and time.

President Rulon Jeffs
Rulon Jeffs' Sermons 2:173 Nov. 17, 1968 SLC

I appreciate my brethren, President Johnson who presides over us, his great faith and love for this work and this people. It reminds me, as I contemplate Brother Johnson, the great love of the Prophet Joseph Smith for all men and especially the saints, desiring nothing but their salvation and exaltation. He was sent at the head of the last dispensation to do the great work of the gathering, the bringing together of Israel, and to bring together all the former dispensations under the Lord Jesus Christ, preparatory to the coming of the Lord in glory, so that the great Millennium might be ushered in after the redemption of Zion. I desire, brothers and sisters, to read some of the words of Joseph, which I think might help us to appreciate him more as the One Mighty and Strong and the great Witness and Testator.

Testimony of President Brigham Young Concerning the Calling and Mission of the Prophet Joseph Smith

President Brigham Young
JD 5:332 October 7, 1857 SLC

What is the nature and beauty of Joseph's mission? You know that I am one of his Apostles. When I first heard him preach, he brought heaven and earth together; and all the priests of the day could not tell me anything correct about heaven, hell, God, angels, or devils: they were as blind as Egyptian darkness. When I saw Joseph Smith, he took heaven, figuratively speaking, and brought it down to earth; and he took the earth, brought it up, and opened up, in plainness and simplicity, the things of God; and that is the beauty of his mission. I had a testimony, long before that, that he was a Prophet of the Lord, and that was consoling. Did not Joseph do the same to your understandings? Would he not take the Scriptures and make them so plain and simple that everybody could understand? Every person says, "Yes, it is admirable; it unites the heavens and the earth together;" and as for time, it is nothing, only to learn us how to live in eternity.

President Brigham Young
JD 7:289 October 9, 1859 SLC

Joseph Smith holds the keys of this last dispensation, and is now engaged behind the vail in the great work of the last days. I can tell our beloved brother Christians who have slain the Prophets and butchered and otherwise caused the death of thousands of Latter-day Saints, the priests who have thanked God in their prayers and thanksgiving from the pulpit that we have been plundered, driven, and slain, and the deacons under the pulpit, and their brethren and sisters in their closets, who have thanked God, thinking that the Latter-day Saints were wasted away, something that no doubt will mortify them -- something that, to say the least, is a matter of deep regret to them -- namely, that no man or woman in this dispensation will ever enter into the celestial kingdom of God without the consent of Joseph Smith. From the day that the Priesthood was taken from the earth to the winding-up scene of all things, every man and woman must have the certificate of Joseph Smith, junior, as a passport to their entrance into the mansion where God and Christ are -- I with you and you with me. I cannot go there without his consent. He holds the keys of that kingdom for the last dispensation -- the keys to rule in the spirit-world; and he rules there triumphantly, for he gained full power and a glorious victory over the power of Satan while he was yet in the flesh, and was a martyr to his religion and to the name of Christ, which gives him a most perfect victory in the spirit-world. He reigns there as supreme a being in his sphere, capacity, and calling, as God does in heaven. Many will exclaim -- "Oh, that is very disagreeable! It is preposterous! We cannot bear the thought!" But it is true.

I will now tell you something that ought to comfort every man and woman on the face of the earth. Joseph Smith, junior, will again be on this earth dictating plans and calling forth his brethren to be baptized for the very characters who wish this was not so, in order to bring them into a kingdom to enjoy, perhaps, the presence of angels or the spirits of good men, if they cannot endure the presence of the Father and the Son; and he will never cease his operations, under the directions of the Son of God, until the last ones of the children of men are saved that can be, from Adam till now.

Should not this thought comfort all people? They will, by-and-by, be a thousand times more thankful for such a man as Joseph Smith, junior, than it is possible for them to be for any earthly good whatever. It is his mission to see that all the children of men in this last dispensation are saved, that can be, through the redemption. You will be thankful, every one of you, that Joseph Smith, junior, was ordained to this great calling before the worlds were. I told you that the doctrine of election and reprobation is a true doctrine. It was decreed in the counsels of eternity, long before the foundations of the earth were laid, that he should be the man, in the last dispensation of this world, to bring forth the word of God to the people, and receive the fulness of the keys and power of the Priesthood of the Son of God. The Lord had his eye upon him, and upon his father and upon his father's father, and upon their progenitors clear back to Abraham, and from Abraham to the flood, from the flood to Enoch, and from Enoch to Adam. He has watched that family and that blood as it has circulated from its fountain to the birth of that man. He was foreordained in eternity to preside over this last dispensation, as much so as Pharaoh was fore-ordained to be a wicked man, or as was Jesus to be the Saviour of the world because he was the oldest son in the family.***

Joseph Smith, junior, was foreordained to come through the loins of Abraham, Isaac, Jacob, Joseph, and so on down through the Prophets and Apostles; and thus he came forth in the last days to be a minister of salvation, and to hold the keys of the last dispensation of the fulness of times.

President Brigham Young
JD 15:138 August 24, 1872 Farmington

I am going to stop my talking by saying that, in the millennium, when the kingdom of God is established on the earth in power, glory and perfection, and the reign of wickedness that has so long prevailed is subdued, the Saints of God will have the privilege of building their temples, and of entering into them, becoming, as it were, pillars in the temples of God, and they will officiate for their dead. Then we will see our friends come up, and perhaps some that we have been acquainted with here. If we ask who will stand at the head of the resurrection in this last dispensation, the answer is -- Joseph Smith, Junior, the Prophet of God. He is the man who will be resurrected and receive the keys of the resurrection, and he will seal this authority upon others, and they will hunt up their friends and resurrect them when they shall have been officiated for, and bring them up. And we will have revelations to know our forefathers clear back to Father Adam and Mother Eve, and we will enter into the temples of God and officiate for them. Then man will be sealed to man until the chain is made perfect back to Adam, so that there will be a perfect chain of priesthood from Adam to the winding-up scene.

This will be the work of the Latter-day Saints in the millennium.

Joseph Suffered Because He Is the Messenger to the People of the Entire Earth

President Brigham Young
JD 9:366 August 31, 1862 SLC

This whole people were cast out for believing that God spake to Joseph Smith and chose him to be his messenger -- his Apostle -- to this generation. I testify to you that we were not cast out for teaching and practising the Patriarchal doctrine, as our enemies now declare, for at that time it [had] not been published to the world, but it was for believing, preaching and practising the doctrines of the New Testament; for believing in the events to take place in the latter days, as foretold by the ancient Prophets; and, for believing the declarations of Joseph Smith, that Jesus was indeed the Christ and the Saviour of all men, but especially of them that believe, and that he had set to his hand the second time to gather his people, to establish his kingdom, to build up Zion, redeem Jerusalem, empty the earth of wickedness and bring in everlasting righteousness.

SECTION REVELATION 215

Revelation of the Lord Jesus Christ
San Angelo, Texas
Saturday, July 30, 2011

1. Thus saith the Lord Jesus Christ to all nations, kindreds, tongues, peoples of all the earth:

2. I have sent Joseph Smith as my great Prophet, Seer, and Revelator, to restore my revealings of the Gospel of preparation in my holy order of restoring to earth all Priesthood authorities, powers, retributions, powers eternal; to now be among men with thy Lord as he who is under Christ, to be Governor over all.

3. Let my will be known, that Joseph Smith is the third member of the Godhead that now rules over this earth.

4. Let all now know that every nation in this now present earth, that you mock God when you deride against His labor through Joseph Smith.

5. He who opposes any labor I called upon Joseph to perform, you are then deriding against me, saith your Lord Jesus Christ, to this generation, knowing I, your God, that I speak as to be understood, saith:

6. Let my people go who have received my Celestial Law of Eternal Union of Celestial Power of Marriage Eternal.

7. Let all beware to not treat lightly my holy way of Priesthood power, authority, and dominion; for my holy way is to only be of eternal power Celestial.

8. Thus, you who are not acquainted with my Church and Kingdom, come learn of me eternal truths that exalt the mind to be of a full-hearted way of obeying my will of Eternal Union law of Celestial authority, power, and dominion; not to be slow in final preparing, but to now be ready to receive Joseph Smith again among you, now soon at hand.

9. Let all now be of resounding rejoicing, that you know Joseph Smith shall be on earth, among my Priesthood; to direct my will to the people of the earth in all lands,

languages, isles of the sea, as well as parts of earth returning.

10. Great is the day of my coming in glory.

11. No evil again can remain on my land of Zion.

12. Let only pure way of doing be of my whole labor of preparing, among all people of the earth; for my holy coming in eternal power is nigh and must be met in a pure way of living.

13. Repent ye, Repent ye, all ye peoples of every nation, lest you fall short of any blessing needful for eternal progression, in the eternal realm of Ahman, even God over all creation.

14. I am Son Ahman, Jesus Christ, over all the earth, as my Father hath appointed.

15. I am the Holy One of Israel who speaketh, who shall gather mine Israel unto Zion to live Eternal Power of truth Celestial.

16. Let all now realize without Joseph Smith's mission being fulfilled, all peoples would be lost unto never-ending sadness and despair, for his work is my will and way done in full organizing of Eternal Union power over all people.

17. Let my will now be known, to realize I am now speaking from my own eternal home through my Mouthpiece of pure receiving and revealing holy truth, eternal truth;

that exalts the soul unto Godhood or Goddesshood in Celestial realms of everlasting burnings of heavenly power.

18. Let all now heed my will, and now be ready for more of my word, even concerning the other Israel soon to return to this globe.

19. I am the Creator of the earth, and all flesh on the earth.

20. I am a God of Creation power eternal.

21. You cannot escape from a God who sees and knows all things, who has all power to accomplish every good thing of my Father's naming; to bring immortality and eternal lives to a few who will listen and obey my every word I send through my servant on earth, even my holy servant now in bondage by the land of governing power, which power is over all the earth; I being your God and King, even Jesus Christ, by my holy Priesthood authority given me of my Father.

22. Let all be holy, pure, righteous, in spirit and in truth, to be of a full preparing against the time of my glorious appearing, prophesied of by my holy Prophets.

23. Let United States governing power of just and holy preserving of religious freedom, now deliver my holy servant Warren Jeffs from bondage, to now dwell freely among my Church; to have all

needed things be of a full ready way, to allow my elect to be gathering unto my appointed gathering place, New Jerusalem; to have all things fully ready for my glory to be their deliverance for mine Israel, my chosen; to be of Celestial eternal power in my Kingdom.

24. Let all now be aware of coming power of cleansing the earth.

25. Let all have only my will to be done; then do my will, and not be hearers only, being as hypocrites, professing to know my name, yet you do not know me, because you have a form of godliness, but you deny the power thereof; even my Priesthood authority I have ordained to dwell among you, even my Keyholder and Mouthpiece, holding the sealing power of Elijah in full Priesthood power over all people; to deliver Israel unto the Zion of pure governing power; to bless all peoples of every nation, to have all being of a revealing of my truths Celestial unto holy, pure, noble, exalting, inspiring ways, being upheld by every power on earth, because they heed my will.

26. I will own anyone, whether they be national power or individual personal devotion, who come unto me, your Lord Jesus Christ, through my authority on earth; to be an administering authorized agent, to perform labor of holy and pure way of my revealing.

27. Let all people now rejoice in thy God who created you, and for Him now making Himself known to all people, to be preparing for my coming unto all people, to them knowing, in fear of transgressing my right to rule; unto all who remain shall know your Lord.

28. Be ye clean and pure.

29. Cease the attack against my Holy Priesthood and people.

30. Now be truly just, and honored as governing power that preserves purity and pure religious and constitutional power of preserving freedoms; who will cleanse people of your ruling of murder, and Sodom, of immoral ways, which afflicts your very inward workings as a people, corrupting all you do by the corrupt way allowed by governing power over this present people now dwelling on my Zion, a land of future cleansing in full, even soon at hand; is the will of thy God who now revealeth truth without interfering of governing powers; who seek to prosecute an innocent religion of pure revealing from my own will being manifest.

31. My love shines over all peoples, holding them in their place.

32. Come unto me, your Savior, O ye people of the world, and come

out of Babylon; which evil power shall soon be subdued by my holy arms stretched out all the day long for salvation to be your eternal power as you abide in me.

33. Let Judge recuse herself for honor's sake, for truth is she is of a way of pride, defending her rulings of unrighteous way, afflicting my Church; to be of an affliction that sought to destroy my Celestial and Eternal Law by seeking to be as God over my Church to declare policy of way of doing in my holy way of pure Celestial Law of Priesthood governing power yesterday; when I caused my servant to voice my will, to call on you to not be of a Judge over religion, when it was in your ability to stop the attack of government against a religious and holy way constitutionally guaranteed in religious practice freedom; a freedom for all peoples to enjoy in pure way of a revealed Priesthood and religious authority God, that rules over all, hath ordained, and shall yet be the Eternal Head of my Church, in heaven and on earth.

34. O ye who afflict my Church, sorrowful shall you be in days to come if you repent not of your wicked, perverse ways of ignoble corrupt way; to allow evil of immoral practice in every way of living in this nation, in politics, in governing power, in social evils, and in allowing murder of innocence, yea, the most helpless of creations, the unborn children; a sin that corrupts your very way of life, before a just God, who shall now no longer uphold your nation as a power over other nations, lest you corrupt the way of all the earth.

35. Thus, my promises concerning your overthrow as a nation of corruption shall be fulfilled by the Almighty power of Eternal Power.

36. Let these evils cease, saith God, lest you go to a judging of thy God, unto you not having place on earth anymore, is the warning voice of God over all. Amen.

Chapter 2

Administration of President Brigham Young

SECTION REVELATION 216

Let Brigham Young Be Upheld as a Prophet of Power, Who Also Sought Celestial Power of Holy Way of Union Celestial

Revelation of the Lord Jesus Christ
San Angelo, Texas
Saturday, July 30, 2011

1. I, your Lord Jesus Christ, reveal truth of my servant Brigham Young as a holy son of my sending, to continue my Priesthood on earth; having received my holy Order of Eternal Power by the hand of my servant Joseph Smith; and having proved pure as a man of holy way, to be of full Priesthood power of Keyholder and Mouthpiece of my sending; even as Moses.

2. Let all rejoice in your God for the mission of Brigham Young; as he continues to labor in my holy Order of Holy Union, a holy angel sent to do my bidding among my holy way of governing all my pure way of Priesthood in every department of my domain, to be of my order of Priesthood power to sons of God who are worthy to be receiving angelic visiting.

3. Let my holy way be known, that Priesthood is eternal; and faithful sons of Celestial Power in my Priesthood are ministering power of Celestial Priesthood power, in eternal labor of advancing my Kingdom.

4. Let my Priesthood be pure, to increase unto the gift of becoming like me in full power of Eternal Priesthood; to be as God in the inherited dominion they earn, by faith and obeying my every will and way of pure and holy increase, worlds without end.

5. Let all know he is with me in all power of Priesthood power, by my holy way abiding in him.

6. Let my Priesthood be of great power in mortal life, so as to be of greater power in Celestial realm of pure holy power of Priesthood; as my son, Brigham Young, now is; as an holy pure son of God, able to disseminate truth eternal to worthy men in my holy Order of Eternal Union; Gods of Creation in everlasting lives.

7. Let all know Brigham Young was faithful unto the end, and is with me in Celestial power of my Godhood-giving power in lives of my pure in heart, who are constant unto me.

8. Let all, every one, be of full power of pure obeying, to magnify Priesthood, like unto this faithful son of Priesthood, holding the keys of Elijah, and having proved humble and holy, worthy to be with his Lord in all-consuming power of fire of heaven as a power of continual heavenly authority; to administer to chosen vessels in the world of departed spirits, and also to those on earth who love God with an undivided heart, with all their soul and might, in increasing power Celestial; to be Gods of holy Order of Union Power; to govern domain of my appointing.

9. Let all my people rejoice in His continuing the keys of sealing power on earth through chosen sons of Priesthood and holy power, who abide in me, through the gift of revealing my will; which is the way of my holy way of governing authority; always abiding in my holy will, unto full confidence bestowed as a God in Celestial realms of eternal gift, of my Celestial holy way of my holy power extended to men, to give full glory of pure exalting; to be holy men of pure eternal Priesthood authority of Holy Priesthood revealing my truths unto the way of union eternal.

10. Let all now be of holy way. Amen.

Saints of God Were Driven West

Battle of Nauvoo -- 1845

President Brigham Young
Documentary History of the Church 7:439

Thursday, [September] 11, -- I received a letter from Sheriff J. B. Backenstos announcing the death of General Miner R. Deming, who died at half past ten o'clock yesterday of congestive fever; during his illness his life was repeatedly threatened by the mob, he was prevented from sleeping at night by their yells and hideous screams, as they kept up a continual row in the streets of Carthage near the general's residence which greatly aggravated his fever, and doubtless caused his death.

I answered Sheriff Backenstos' letter assuring him of our regret at the loss the cause of liberty, law, and order had sustained in the unexpected death of General Deming, and informed him of the burning of the houses of the citizens of Morley Settlement by the mob yesterday, and requested him to take immediate steps to suppress the mob, advised him to inform the governor that he may take the necessary measures to protect the lives and property of the people in this country.

A messenger from Lima reports eight houses burned.***

SOLOMON HANCOCK'S ANSWER TO
BRIGHAM YOUNG

By letter from Solomon Hancock, Yelrome, we learn that the mob have burned all the houses on the south side of the branch [brook], and left last evening for Lima, said they would return this morning as soon as light, and swear they will sweep through and burn everything to Nauvoo. Colonel Levi Williams is at the head of the mob.

President Brigham Young
Documentary History of the Church 7:443

Sunday, 14. -- *** I said, in relation to the mob burning houses, I was willing they should do so, until the surrounding counties should be convinced that we were not the aggressors, peradventure they may conclude to maintain the supremacy of the law by putting down mob violence and bringing offenders to justice.

I counseled the brethren to bring their families and grain here, and called for volunteers with wagons and teams to aid in removing the saints to this place; one hundred and thirty-four teams were procured and started forthwith. The brethren agreed to continue until they had brought in all their families, effects and grain of the saints in the settlements attacked by the mob.***

Monday, 15. -- Seven a. m., the police met at my house and put me up a stable.

Sheriff Backenstos went to Warsaw and tried his best to summon a posse to stop the burning but could not raise one.

Forty-four buildings have been burned by the mob. Several houses have been burned in the Prairie branch, Green Plain precinct.

Michael Barnes a constable from Carthage, and his brother came into Nauvoo with writs for H. C. Kimball, Willard Richards, John E. Page, Daniel Garn, Wm. and George A. Smith, and myself, issued by Captain Smith of the Carthage Greys, on the complaint of _____ Backman. The charges were for aiding and abetting Joseph Smith in treasonable designs against the state, for being officers in the Nauvoo Legion, for building an arsenal, for keeping cannon in times of peace, for holding a private council in Nauvoo, and for holding correspondence with the Indians.***

I received a letter from J. B. Backenstos, dated, Carthage, September 15th, in which he stated his inability to raise law and order citizens to quell the mob and requested us to hold two thousand well armed men in readiness for immediate service at any hour that he may call for them and added: that if we will not defend our own lives and property that we cannot reasonably expect any considerable support from those citizens commonly called 'Jack-Mormons'. 'Colonel Levi Williams has ordered out his brigade of militia, I am certain the turnout will be slim, we must whip them.'

In reply I advised him to wait a few days and see if there are any law and order citizens in the county that are not Mormons, and if it proved there were none else to stand up for the Constitution and laws of the state, it would then be time enough for us, as the old citizens had heretofore advised us to 'hold still'! 'Keep cool'! 'Be quiet'! etc., etc., we were determined to do so.

The first regiment, second cohort of the Nauvoo Legion met and organized, choosing the old officers, to place themselves in readiness to act at the sheriff's call.***

Tuesday, 16. -- Sheriff Backenstos arrived in great haste and somewhat excited, said that the mob had driven him from his house in Carthage yesterday, and he went to Warsaw and stayed over night. He soon ascertained that the people were so enraged at him for trying to stop the house-burning that there was little probability of getting away alive, but finally prevailed on an influential mobocrat to escort him out of Warsaw this morning, who came with him about three and a half miles and on leaving cautioned him that if he saw two men together to avoid them for there were deep plans laid to kill him. Soon after he was pursued by a party of the mob on horseback, three of whom took the lead, one of the three had a swifter horse and gained a hundred yards in advance of his party in a short time when his horse stumbled and threw his rider. Backenstos maintained his speed, driving as fast as his horse could go.

The mob took the nearest road to cross his track and on his arrival at the old railroad crossing, the mob were within about 200 yards, they being on horseback and he in a buggy, they had gained on him considerably.

Orrin P. Rockwell and John Redding were refreshing themselves near the crossing as they had been out to bring in some of the burnt-out families who were sick, and on looking up saw Backenstos coming down the hill at full speed, and asked what was the matter. Backenstos replied the mob were after and determined to kill him and commanded them in the name of the people of the state to protect him, Rockwell replied, fear not, we have 50 rounds (two fifteen-shooter rifles besides revolvers).

Sheriff Backenstos then turned to the mob and commanded them to stop, and as they continued to advance raising their guns, he ordered Rockwell to fire; he did so aiming at the clasp of the belt on one of the mob, which proved to be Frank Worrell, who fell from his horse and the rest turned back and soon brought up a wagon and put his body into it. ***

Tuesday, 30. -- *** I went with the Twelve to Elder Taylor's and saw Judge Douglas and Sheriff Backenstos.

They said it was hard to make the people, the other side of the Illinois river, believe that it was not the Mormons that were burning houses in Hancock county.

They wished us to go and see General Hardin. In company with H. C. Kimball, W. Richards, John Taylor, George A. Smith and Amasa M. Lyman, I went on to the hill and met General Hardin and staff surrounded by his troops, four hundred in number. He read us his orders from the governor to come here and keep the peace if he had to keep the county under martial law: said he wished to search for the bodies of two dead men who were last seen in Nauvoo and it was supposed they had been murdered.

I told him he was welcome to search for dead bodies or anything else he pleased. He inquired if I knew anything about them or of crimes having been committed in Nauvoo. I replied I knew nothing of the kind, but that I had reliable information that some hundred houses had been burned in the south part of the county and probably if he would go there, he would find the persons who had done it.

I tendered him the hospitality of the city and a home at my house, to which he replied drily, 'I always stay in camp.'

General Hardin marched his troops to, and searched the Temple, Masonic Hall, Nauvoo House, and the stables of the Mansion.***

President Brigham Young
Documentary History of the Church 7:481

General Hardin has pledged himself to the mob that he will come to Nauvoo with his troops and either arrest Orrin P. Rockwell and some others of the brethren or he 'will unroof every house in Nauvoo'. Three hundred of our enemies have volunteered to come with him from

Quincy and they expect to be joined by others on the way.

There seems to be no disposition abroad but to massacre the whole body of this people, and nothing but the power of God can save us from the cruel ravages of the bloodthirsty mob.***

Bishop Miller, Sheriff Backenstos, and those who went with them to Quincy, have all returned safely.

Backenstos is bound over to court in three thousand dollar bonds. General Hardin has gone to Springfield.

Tuesday, 14. -- Major Warren came into the city with a detachment of the troops.

President Brigham Young
Documentary History of the Church 7:486

Saturday, 25. -- 4 p.m., A. W. Babbitt arrived from Carthage and stated that when the brethren went in yesterday as witnesses of the house-burning the grand jury refused to hear their testimony, or to admit any of them into the jury room, which effectually shields the house-burners from justice and blockades the way for the sufferers to obtain redress.***

This morning Hosea Stout and John Scott stationed themselves at the mound, seven miles east of Nauvoo, and extended a few men for miles north and south to ascertain and express any hostile movements which might be made towards Nauvoo.

Major Warren, Judge Purple, J. B. Backenstos, Judge Ralston and Mr. Brannan with a detachment of troops came into town and Warren demanded an explanation in relation to seeing some fifteen or twenty of our express men on the prairie.

I went to the Mansion and in plain but mild language stated the reason why our men were there. Warren in a great rage declared he would issue his manifesto on Monday morning and put the county under martial law. After this Elder John Taylor made some very just and spirited remarks in relation to the foul treachery or criminal imbecility of the governor's protection, telling Mr. Warren that we had placed our express men in a position to communicate the earliest intelligence should any mob violence be attempted upon our brethren while at Carthage and further said: 'We lack confidence in the governor's troops under your command while hundreds of murderers, robbers and house-burners roam at large unwhipped of justice. We shall take measures to protect ourselves. I, Sir, have been shot all to pieces under the 'protection' of the governor's troops. Our leading men have been murdered in Carthage and we shall not trust ourselves unprotected again until the state gives some evidence more than it has done of its justice and humane intentions to enforce its laws.'

President Brigham Young
Documentary History of the Church 7:510

Saturday, November 1, 1845. -- ***
The following editorial appeared in the Times and Seasons:

GREAT PERSECUTION OF THE CHURCH
OF JESUS CHRIST OF LATTER-DAY SAINTS
IN ILLINOIS

'After we had begun to realize the abundance of one of the most fruitful seasons known for a long time, and while many hundreds of saints were laboring with excessive, and unwearied diligence to finish the Temple and rear the Nauvoo House, suddenly in the forepart of September, the mob commenced burning the houses and grain of the saints in the south part of Hancock county. Though efforts were made by the sheriff to stay the torch of the incendiary and parry off the deluge of arson, still a 'fire and sword' party continued the work of destruction for about a week, laying in ashes nearly two hundred buildings and much grain.

Nor is this all: as it was in the sickly season, many feeble persons, thrown out into the scorching rays of the sun, or wet with the dampening dews of the evening, died, being persecuted to death in a Christian land of law and order; and while they are fleeing and dying, the mob, embracing doctors, lawyers, statesmen, Christians of various denominations, with the military from colonels down, were busily engaged in filching or plundering, taking furniture, cattle and grain. In the midst of this horrid revelry, having failed to procure aid among the 'old citizens', the sheriff summoned a sufficient posse to stay the 'fire shower of ruin', but not until some of the offenders had paid for the aggression with their lives.

This, however, was not the end of the matter. Satan sits in the hearts of the people to rule for evil, and the surrounding counties began to fear that law, religion, and equal rights, in the hands of the Latter-day Saints, would feel after iniquity or terrify their neighbors to larger acts of 'reserved rights', and so they began to open a larger field of woe. To cut this matter short they urged the necessity (to stop the effusion of blood), to expel the church, or as they call them, the Mormons, from the United States, 'peaceably if they could, and forcibly if they must', unless they would transport themselves by next spring. Taking into consideration the great value of life, and the blessings of peace, a proposition upon certain specified conditions was made to a committee of Quincy, and which it was supposed from the actions of conventions was accepted. But we are sorry to say, that the continued depredations of the mob and the acts of a few individuals, have greatly lessened the confidence of every friend of law, honor and humanity, in everything promised by the committees and conventions, though we have already made great advances towards outfitting for a move next spring.

A few troops stationed in the county, have not entirely kept the mob at bay: several buildings have been burned in the month of October.

We shall, however, make every exertion on our part, as we have always done, to preserve the law and our engagements sacred, and leave the event with God, for he is sure.

It may not be amiss to say, that the continued abuses, persecutions, murders, and robberies practiced upon us by a horde of land pirates with impunity in a Christian republic, and land of liberty, (while the institutions of justice, have either been too weak to afford us protection or redress, or else they too have been a little remiss) have brought us to the solemn conclusion that our exit from the United States is the only alternative by which we can enjoy our share of the elements which our heavenly Father created free for all.

We can then shake the dust from our garments, suffering wrong rather than do wrong, leaving this nation alone in her glory, while the residue of the world, points the finger of scorn, till the indignation and consumption decreed, make a full end.

In our patience we [will] possess our souls and work out a more exceeding and eternal weight of glory, preparing, by withdrawing the power and priesthood from the Gentiles, for the great consolation of Israel, when the wilderness shall blossom as the rose, and Babylon fall like a millstone cast into the sea. The just shall live by faith; but the folly of fools will perish with their bodies of corruption: then shall the righteous shine: Amen.'"

President Brigham Young
Documentary History of the Church 7:523

Saturday, 15. -- ***

DEATH OF EDMUND DURFEE -- SHOT BY A MOB
OF HOUSE-BURNERS

A considerable party of the mob set fire to a stack of straw near Solomon Hancock's barn and concealed themselves. Hancock and others went out to put out the fire which was the only way to save the building, when they were fired upon by the burners, and Elder Edmund Durfee killed on the spot, many balls flew around the rest of the brethren, but none of the rest were hurt.***

Sunday, 16. -- *** I received the following:

BACKENSTOS' NOTE TO THE TWELVE

'To the Twelve: On last night Elder Edmund Durfee was basely murdered by the mob in the Green Plains precinct, what shall be done to avenge his blood? the troops afford us no protection.

Yours etc.,

NOVEMBER 16TH, 1845 J. B. BACKENSTOS.'

President Brigham Young
Documentary History of the Church 7:527

Tuesday, 18. -- The Twelve met in council at Dr. Richards'.

Mr. Brayman, attorney for the state, wrote a letter to the council desiring witnesses against the murderers of Durfee to be sent to Carthage, also affidavits; forwarded in relation to the burning of Rice's house, and advising us of the arrest of George Backman, Moss and Snyder, who were charged with the murder of Elder Edmund Durfee, Sen.

The council replied immediately and requested the witnesses to start in the morning for Carthage to perform their part in another judicial farce.***

NAUVOO NEIGHBOR -- EXTRA

Nauvoo, November 19th, 1845

MURDER AND ARSON
EDMUND DURFEE SHOT--TWO HOUSES BURNED

'As may be seen by the affidavits below, it falls to our painful lot to chronicle two more outrages upon the lives and rights of the Latter-day Saints, since they have been using all diligence to secure their crops, build wagons, and leave next spring.

Mr. Durfee was one of the most industrious, inoffensive and good men that could be found, and having his house burnt in September last, moved to Nauvoo and went on Saturday last for a load of grain, was shot dead in cold blood, at midnight while striving with others to save property from the flames by an armed mob!

As to the destruction of the houses and property, and the treatment on that occasion---let the affidavit speak for itself.

We have nearly two thousand five hundred wagons commenced for our Pacific journey next spring, but such outrages certainly are not calculated to aid us in getting ready. We have borne the Missouri persecution; we have mourned the loss of the Prophet and Patriarch, Joseph and Hyrum Smith; we feel the destruction of one or two hundred houses the present season, and our hearts are pained at the murder of Edmund Durfee, because he was a good man; but, we, as in all cases of the saints, leave the disposition of these matters in the care of a wise God, and the perpetrators, to the mercy of (as they say), a country of laws, and be those laws honored or disgraced we cannot be charged with revenge; and we do beseech the people and the authorities not to impute crime to us, to raise excitement, when we see our accusers wiping the blood of innocent men, women, and children, from their garments, as though this was the realm of Nero.

If thieves and robbers escape to Nauvoo, our rule is to deliver them up to the law of the land, and that is all that we can do.

We believe there is virtue and humanity among high-minded men, that know what honor is, and we appeal to them to lend a helping hand, while we are outfitting for our intended removal in the spring. Give us peace, for you that hold the balances of power can! And when we have settled on the other side of America you will know of a truth that we were friends and not enemies to life, law, and liberty! That we were good men, engaged in a good cause, and will receive the meed of praise we deserve for universal benevolence, and everlasting friendship to goodness.

The jealousy of the present generation is so great against the saints, that we have deemed it our duty to give this and the accompanying affidavits, that the world may know the continued ravages, and bloody outrages of a midnight mob; and for another important reason, that as Major Warren has pledged himself to use every exertion in his power to allay excitement, prevent the destruction of property, and stop the shedding of blood, we cannot feel anything better than that he will exhibit his honor and clemency in our behalf, that we may prepare for our exodus in peace henceforth.'

President Brigham Young
Documentary History of the Church 7:541

ACQUITTAL OF SHERIFF BACKENSTOS FOR
THE KILLING OF FRANK A. WORRELL

News has arrived that Sheriff Backenstos, who went to Peoria in charge of Henry W. Miller, coroner of Hancock county, and was tried before Judge Purple on the charge of the 'murder' of Frank A. Worrell, was acquitted. The moral atmosphere around the judge was so different, than when at Carthage, that in all his charges and rulings, he appeared like another judge, and as though he had never been afflicted with mobocratic mania.

The jury said if there had been no witnesses only on the part of the state, it would not have required more than two minutes to have made up their verdict. There are two of the mob witnesses in jail for perjury and Backenstos is gone to Springfield to request the governor to withdraw his troops.

Story of Bogus Brigham

President Brigham Young
JD 14:218 July 23, 1871 Logan

While brother George A. Smith was referring to the circumstance of William Miller going to Carthage, it brought to my mind reflections of the past. Perhaps to relate the circumstance as it occurred would be interesting.

I do not profess to be much of a joker, but I do think this to be one of the best jokes ever perpetrated. By the time we were at work in the Nauvoo Temple, officiating in the ordinances, the mob had learned that "Mormonism" was not dead, as they had supposed. We had completed the walls of the Temple, and the attic story from about half way up of the first windows, in about fifteen months. It went up like magic, and we commenced officiating in the ordinances. Then the mob commenced to hunt for other victims; they had already killed the Prophets Joseph and Hyrum in Carthage jail, while under the pledge of the State for their safety, and now [they] wanted Brigham, the President of the Twelve Apostles, who were then acting as the Presidency of the Church.

I was in my room in the Temple; it was in the south-east corner of the upper story. I learned that a posse was lurking around the Temple, and that the United States Marshal was waiting for me to come down, whereupon I knelt down and asked my Father in heaven, in the name of Jesus, to guide and protect me that I might live to prove advantageous to the Saints. Just as I arose from my knees and sat down in my chair, there came a rap at my door. I said, "Come in," and brother George D. Grant, who was then engaged driving my carriage and doing chores for me, entered the room. Said he, "Brother Young, do you know that a posse and the United States Marshal are here?" I told him I had heard so. On entering the room brother Grant left the door open. Nothing came into my mind what to do, until looking directly across the hall I saw brother William Miller leaning against the wall. As I stepped towards the door I beckoned to him; he came. Said I to him, "Brother William, the Marshal is here for me; will you go and do just as I tell you? If you will, I will serve them a trick." I knew that brother Miller was an excellent man, perfectly reliable and capable of carrying out my project. Said I, "Here, take my cloak;" but it happened to be brother Heber C. Kimball's; our cloaks were alike in color, fashion and size. I threw it around his shoulders, and told him to wear my hat and accompany brother George D. Grant. He did so. I said to brother Grant, "George, you step into the carriage and look towards brother Miller, and say to him, as though you were addressing me, 'Are you ready to ride?' You can do this, and they will suppose brother Miller to be me, and proceed accordingly," which they did.

Just as brother Miller was entering the carriage, the Marshal stepped up to him, and, placing his hand upon his shoulder, said, "You are my prisoner." Brother William entered the carriage and said to the Marshal, "I am going to the Mansion House, won't you ride with me?" They both went to the Mansion House. There were my sons Joseph A., Brigham, jun., and brother Heber C. Kimball's boys, and others who were looking on, and all seemed at once to understand and partake of the joke. They followed the carriage to the Mansion House and gathered around brother Miller, with tears in their eyes, saying, "Father, or President Young, where are you going?" Brother Miller looked at them kindly, but made no reply; and the Marshal really thought he had got "Brother Brigham."

Lawyer Edmonds, who was then staying at the Mansion House, appreciating the joke, volunteered to brother Miller to go to Carthage with him and see him safe through. When they arrived within two or three miles of Carthage, the Marshal with his posse stopped. They arose in their carriages, buggies and waggons, and, like a tribe of Indians going into battle, or as if they were a pack of demons, yelling and shouting, they exclaimed, "We've got him! we've got him! We've got him!" When they reached Carthage the Marshal took the supposed Brigham into an upper room of the hotel, and placed a guard over him, at the same time telling those around that he had got him. Brother Miller remained in the room until they bid him come to supper. While there, parties came in, one after the other, and asked for Brigham. Brother Miller was pointed out to them. So it continued, until an apostate Mormon, by the name of Thatcher, who had lived in Nauvoo, came in, sat down and asked the landlord where Brigham Young was. The landlord, pointing across the table to brother Miller, said, "That is Mr. Young." Thatcher replied, "Where? I can't see any one that looks like Brigham." The landlord told him it was that fat, fleshy man eating. "Oh, hell!" exclaimed Thatcher, "that's not Brigham; that is William Miller, one of my old neighbors." Upon hearing this the landlord went, and, tapping the Sheriff on the shoulder, took him a few steps to one side, and said, "You have made a mistake, that is not Brigham Young; it is William Miller, of Nauvoo." The Marshal, very much astonished, exclaimed, "Good heavens! and he passed for Brigham." He then took brother Miller into a room, and, turning to him, said, "What in hell is the reason you did not tell me your name?" Brother Miller replied, "You have not asked me my name." "Well," said the Sheriff, with another oath, "What is your name?" "My name," he replied, "is William Miller." Said the Marshal, "I thought your name was Brigham Young. Do you say this for a fact?" "Certainly I do," said brother Miller. "Then," said the Marshal, "why did you not tell me this before?" "I was under no obligations to tell you," replied brother Miller, "as you did not ask me." Then the Marshal, in a rage, walked out of the room, followed by brother Miller, who walked off in company with Lawyer Edmonds, Sheriff Backenstos, and others, who took him across lots to a place of safety; and this is the real pith of the story of "Bogus" Brigham, as far as I can recollect.

The Saints Begin Their Exodus in Freezing Weather

President Brigham Young
Documentary History of the Church 7:552

Friday, 26. [1846] --***Sheriff Backenstos informed me that the United States deputy marshal was in town with writs for the Twelve and Brother George Miller.

President Brigham Young
Documentary History of the Church 7:567

Sunday, 11. [1846] -- The General Council met and arranged to make an early start west.***

The captains of fifties and tens made reports of the number in their respective companies, who were prepared to start west immediately, should the persecutions of our enemies compel us to do so: one hundred and forty horses and seventy wagons were reported ready for immediate service.

President Brigham Young
Documentary History of the Church 7:577

Sheriff Backenstos has returned from Springfield, and says, that Governor Ford has turned against us, and that Major Warren is making calculations to prevent our going away.

I received a letter from Josiah Lamborn, Esq., Springfield, stating that Governor Ford was decidedly in favor of General J. J. Hardin's policy, which is, that of suspending all civil offices, the collection of taxes, and placing the county under martial law.***

Thursday, 29. -- ***Quite a number of the governor's troops are prowling around our city; I am informed that they are seeking to arrest some of the leading men of the church.***

Monday, [February] 2. [1846] -- *** Ten a. m., the Twelve, Trustees and a few others met in council, to ascertain the feelings of the brethren that were expecting to start westward. We agreed that it was imperatively necessary to start as soon as possible. I counseled the brethren to procure boats and hold them in readiness to convey our wagons and teams over the river, and let everything for the journey be in readiness, that when a family is called to go, everything necessary may be put into the wagon within four hours, at least, for if we are here many days, our way will be hedged up. Our enemies have resolved to intercept us whenever we start. I should like to push on as far as possible before they are aware of our movements. In order to have this counsel circulated, I sent messengers to notify the captains of hundreds and fifties to meet at 4 p. m. at Father Cutlers'.

At four o'clock, I met with the captains of hundreds and fifties, and laid my counsel before them, to which they all consented, and dispersed to carry it into execution.

President Brigham Young
Documentary History of the Church 7:585

Sunday, 15. [1846] -- I crossed the river with my family accompanied by W. Richards and family and George A. Smith. We traveled on four miles, when we came to the bluff. I would not go on until I saw all the teams up. I helped them up the hill with my own hands. At dusk started on, and reached Sugar Creek about 8 p. m., having traveled nine miles. The roads were very bad.

President Brigham Young
Documentary History of the Church 7:592

Thursday, 19. -- From Dr. Richards' *Camp Journal:*

'The wind blew steadily from the northwest accompanied by snow which fell to the depth of seven or eight inches, but much thawed as it fell, the storm was unceasing, and the evening was very cold, which caused much suffering in the camp, for there were many who had no tents or any comfortable place to lodge: many tents were blown down, some of them were unfinished and had no ends.'

President Brigham Young
Documentary History of the Church 7:596

Tuesday, 24. -- ***The cold has been severe the past night, a snowstorm this morning which continued during the forenoon, blowing from the northwest, which prevented Captain Bent's Company from moving; the cold was severe through the day and increased as night approached.***

Wednesday, 25. -- The morning was colder than any one since the encampment, but the sun rose clear, the whole camp appeared cheerful and happy.

Nine a. m., the blast of the bugle and the raising of the flag called the brethren together.

Persecution Against Leaders of Priesthood

President Brigham Young
JD 19:61 July 24, 1877 SLC

We lived in the State of Illinois a few years; and here, as elsewhere, persecution overtook us. It came from Missouri, centering itself upon Joseph, and fastened itself upon others. We lived in Illinois from 1839 to 1844, by which time they again succeeded in kindling the spirit of persecution against Joseph and the Latter-day Saints.*** They took Joseph and Hyrum, and as a guarantee for their safety, Governor Thomas Ford pledged the faith of the State of Illinois. They were imprisoned, on the pretense of safe keeping, because the mob was so enraged and violent. The Governor left them in the hands of the mob, who entered the prison and shot them dead.*** After the mob had committed these murders they came upon us and burned our houses and our grain. When the brethren would go out to put out the fire, the mob would lie concealed under fences, and in the darkness of the night, they would shoot them. At last they succeeded in driving us from the State of Illinois.

Orson F. Whitney
The Life of Heber C. Kimball, Page 359 ©1888

It soon became evident to the enemy that the death of the Prophet, so far from destroying, or even impeding Mormonism, had only given it fresh impetus, an energy which they feared, if allowed to increase, might prove irresistible. They therefore renewed the attack, Brigham, Heber and the Twelve now being the especial objects of their animus.***

The chief inciters of the opposition were the Laws, the Fosters, and the Higbees, apostates who had betrayed and sacrificed Joseph and Hyrum, with others who now joined them in their warfare against the Twelve. The most strenuous efforts were made, generally under cover of law, to get President Young into their power; and even his life, it is said, was attempted by the midnight assassin. Knowing their fell purpose, and remembering the fate of the martyrs, Joseph and Hyrum, who had tested the virtue of official pledges and the protecting majesty of the law in Illinois, Brigham and Heber wisely determined not to be taken.

President John Taylor
Life of John Taylor, Page 164

[Speaking to Major Warren] "I will touch upon the things of the present in a moment -- You may think this outrage was an outbreak -- a sudden ebullition of feeling that the governor could not control; but who was it that did this deed? The governor's troops, sir, were among the foremost of that bloody gang. And where, sir -- tell me where is our redress? You talk about the majesty of the law! What has become of those murderers? Have they been hung or shot, or in any way punished? No, sir, you know they have not. With their hands yet reeking in blood, having become hardened in their deeds of infamy, knowing that they will not be punished, they are now applying the torch to the houses of those they have already so deeply injured. What has been done to them under your administration? Have they been brought to justice, have they been punished for their infamous proceedings? No, sir; not one of them. They are still burning houses under your supervision; and you have either been unwilling or unable to stop them. Houses have been burned since your arrival here; men have been kidnapped, cattle stolen, our brethren abused and robbed when going after their corn. Are we to stand still and let marauders and house-burners come into our city under the real or assumed name of "governor's troops," and yet offer no resistance to their nefarious deeds? Are we to be held still by you, sir, while they thrust the hot iron into us? I tell you plainly for one I will not do it. I speak now on my own responsibility, and I tell you, sir, I will not stand it. I care nothing for your decrees, your martial law or any other law, I mean to protect myself; and if my brethren are to be insulted and abused in going after their own corn, and pursuing their lawful business -- if nobody else will go to protect them I will. They shall not be abused under pretext of law or anything else; and there is not a patriot in the world but what would bear me out in it.

"Where is the spirit of '76? Where is the fire that burned in the bosoms of those who fought and bled for liberty? Is there no one who will stand up in defense of the oppressed? If a man had the least spark of humanity burning in his bosom -- if he were not hardened and desperate, he would be ashamed to oppress a people already goaded by a yoke too intolerable to be borne, and that, too, in a boasted land of liberty. Talk about law! Sir, I stand before you as a victim of law. I feel warm on this subject -- who would not? I have seen my best friends shot down while under legal protection. What is our governor? These scenes have been enacted under his supervision. What are our generals and judges? They have aided in these matters. If an honorable jury is legally selected, a house-burner or perhaps a murderer makes affidavit that he has reason to believe they are partial and the judge will order a mobocratic sheriff and jury for the purpose of acquitting the guilty and condemning the innocent. What are all these legal men but a pack of scoundrels? And you will talk to us of law and order, and threaten us with punishment for disobeying your commands and protecting our rights! What are we? Are we beasts? I tell you for one, sir, I shall protect myself, law or no law, judge or no judge, governor or no governor. I will not stand such infernal rascality, and if I have to fight it out, I will sell my life as dearly as I can."

Government of the United States Rejects My People of Priesthood, Saith Jesus Christ

President Brigham Young
JD 19:62 July 24, 1877 SLC

Three congressmen came in the Fall of 1845, and had a Conference with the Twelve and others; they were desirous that we should leave the United States. We told them we would do so, we had staid long enough with them; we agreed to leave the State of Illinois in consequence of that religious prejudice against us that we could not stay in peace any longer. These men said the people were prejudiced against us. Stephen A. Douglass, one of the three had been acquainted with us. He said "I know you, I knew Joseph Smith; he was a good man," and this people was a good people; but the prejudices of the priests and the ungodly are such that, said he, "Gentlemen, you cannot stay here and live in peace." We agreed to leave.*** We left Nauvoo in February, 1846. There remained behind a few of the very poor, the sick and the aged, who suffered again from the violence of the mob: they were whipped and beaten, and had their houses burned.

Orson F. Whitney
The Life of Heber C. Kimball, Page 360

The anti-Mormons were clamoring for the removal of the entire community of Latter-day Saints from the state, and they, seeing no alternative but to comply with this outrageous demand, or experience a repetition of the murderous scenes of Missouri, had resolved to again sacrifice their homes and seek a land of peace and liberty in the wilds of the savage west.

Before coming to the conclusion to thus expatriate themselves, the Saints, through their leaders, had petitioned the President of the United States, James K. Polk, and the Governors of all the states excepting Missouri and Illinois, for aid and protection from the efforts of those who were plotting their destruction. But the appeal was in vain.

President Brigham Young
JD 11:17 December 11, 1864 SLC

The Lord has thrown his people on several occasions, into circumstances of destitution and dependence, to try the leaders of the nation, and has thus said unto them, what will you now do for my poor and afflicted people; and their reply has been, "We will destroy them, if we can." They think they will destroy us yet. In this, however, they are mistaken, "for God hath not appointed us to wrath, but to obtain salvation by our Lord Jesus Christ."***

When we were driven from Nauvoo, our Elders went to the East to lay our case before the judges, governors, and rulers of the different States to ask for an asylum; but none was offered us. We sent men through the Eastern country to try and raise some means for the destitute women and children, whose husbands, fathers and brothers had gone into the Mexican war at the call of the General Government, leaving their wives and children and aged fathers and mothers upon the open prairies without home or shelter, and the brethren who went East hardly got enough to bear their expenses. The great men of the nation were asked if they would do anything for the Lord's people. No; not a thing would they do, but hoped they would perish in the wilderness. "Therefore," saith the Lord, "behold, the destroyer I have sent forth to destroy and lay waste mine enemies: and not many years hence they shall not be left to pollute mine heritage, and to blaspheme my name upon the lands which I have consecrated for the gathering together of my saints." In the year 1845 I addressed letters to all the Governors of States and Territories in the Union, asking them for an asylum, within their borders, for the Latter-day Saints. We were refused such privilege, either by silent contempt or a flat denial in every instance. They all agreed that we could not come within the limits of their Territory or State. Three members of Congress came to negociate with us to leave the confines of the United States, and of the public domain. It was understood that we were going to Vancouver Island; but we had our eye on Mexico, and here we are located in the midst of what was then northern Mexico. Fears have been entertained that we shall again be meddled with; but you will find that the enemies of the cause of God will have plenty of business besides digging gold and silver and fighting the Saints, and I trust Utah will be left as unnoticed as it is in the President's message. I thank them for what they have done and for what they have not done. I thank the Lord that He has led this people, and suffered them to be driven from place to place. I thank the Lord that we have the words of eternal life; and if we live by them, our feet are as sure and as fast as these everlasting hills. I know where the Saints will dwell.

George A. Smith
JD 6:87 November 29, 1857 SLC

We petitioned the several States and also the United States for an asylum where we could enjoy ourselves; and all our petitions were answered with coldness and indifference, and there was not a place in the United States where a man that professed to be a Latter-day Saint could have peace. There was nothing but to be mobbed, driven, his houses burned, wherever he might be; and no governor, no legislature, no authority would extend any better prospect than the repetition of the murder, robberies, and persecution we had suffered in Missouri, and that we were then enduring in Illinois.

Holy Temple in Nauvoo Defiled

President Brigham Young
JD 2:32 April 6, 1853 SLC

While these things were transpiring with the Saints in the wilderness, the Temple at Nauvoo passed into the hands of the enemy, who polluted it to that extent the Lord not only ceased to occupy it, but He loathed to have it called by His name, and permitted the wrath of its possessors to purify it by fire, as a token of what will speedily fall on them and their habitations, unless they repent.

Government Demand for Troops on My Driven People of Priesthood, Saith the Lord

Orson F. Whitney
The Life of Heber C. Kimball, Page 369 ©1888

Word was brought to head-quarters on the Missouri, that a United States army officer with a squad of soldiers had arrived at Mt. Pisgah, with a requisition for five hundred men, to be furnished by the Mormons, to enter the army and march to California to take part in the war against Mexico.

Imagination can alone picture the surprise, almost dismay, with which this startling news was received. What! the nation whose people had thrust them from its borders, robbed them of their homes and driven them into the wilderness, where it was hoped they might perish, now calling upon them for aid? And this in full face of the fact that their own oft reiterated appeals for help had been denied?

It was even so. Five hundred able-bodied men, the flower of the camp, were wanted. And this in the heart of an Indian country, in the midst of an exodus unparalleled for its dangers and hardships, when every active man was needed as a bulwark of defense and a staff for the aged and feeble. For even delicate women, thus far, had in some instances been driving teams and tending stock, owing to the limited number of men available.

Government Conspiracy to Destroy the People of God

President Brigham Young
JD 8:335 February 17, 1861 SLC

Did Thomas H. Benton aid in gathering the Saints? Yes, he was the mainspring and action of governments in driving us into these mountains. He obtained orders from President Polk to summon the militia of Missouri, and destroy every "Mormon" man, woman, and child, unless they turned out five hundred men to fight the battles of the United States in Mexico. He said that we were aliens to the Government, and to prove it he said -- "Mr. President, make a requisition on that camp for five hundred men, and I will prove to you that they are traitors to our Government." We

turned out the men, and many of them are before me to-day; among whom is father Pettigrew -- a man that ought to have been asked into the Cabinet to give the President counsel; but they asked him to travel on foot across the Plains to fight our country's battles against Mexico. We turned out the men, and Mr. Benton was disappointed.

President Brigham Young
JD 10:106 March 8, 1863 SLC

This is the outside pressure. It forced us from Ohio to Missouri, from Missouri to Illinois, and from Illinois into the wilderness. We were accused of disloyalty, alienation, and apostacy from the Constitution of our country. We were accused of being secessionists. I am, so help me God, and ever expect to be a secessionist from their wickedness, unrighteousness, dishonesty and unhallowed principles in a religious point of view; but am I or this people secessionists with regard to the glorious Constitution of our country? No. Were we secessionists when we so promptly responded to the call of the General Government, when we were houseless and friendless on the wild prairies of Pottowattamie? I think not. We there told the brethren to enlist, and they obeyed without a murmur.***

I knew then as well as I do now that the Government would call for a battalion of men out of that part of Israel, to test our loyalty to the Government. Thomas H. Benton, if I have been rightly informed, obtained the requisition to call for that battalion, and, in case of non-compliance with that requisition, to call on the militia of Missouri and Iowa, and other States, if necessary, and to call volunteers from Illinois, from which State we had been driven, to destroy the camp of Israel. This same Mr. Benton said to the President of the United States, in the presence of some other persons, "Sir, they are a pestilential race, and ought to become extinct."

I will again urge upon this people to so live that they will have the knowledge they desire, as we have knowledge not of all, but only of that which is necessary. Have we not shown to the world that we love the Constitution of our country and its institutions better than do those who have been and are now distracting the nation? You cannot find a community, placed under the circumstances that we were, that would have done as we did on the occasion of furnishing the Mormon Battalion, after our leading men had been slain and we had been compelled to leave our farms, gardens, homes and firesides, while, at the same time, the general Government was called upon in vain to put a stop to such a series of abuses against an innocent people.

Brigham Young Arrives in Salt Lake, Late, After Pioneers on July 24, 1847

Orson F. Whitney
History of Utah, Volume 1 Page 303

On April 16th, at about 2 p. m., the pioneers broke camp and traveled three miles.***

During the next few days the camp was thoroughly organized under the direction of President Young. In addition to the captains of tens, already named, there were captains of hundreds and fifties appointed.***

Thus organized, equipped and instructed, the pioneers proceeded on their way, slowly traveling up the north bank of the Platte.***

Orson F. Whitney
History of Utah, Volume 1 Page 323

The rear wagons, with the sick President, were at the same time approaching East Canyon. On the 22nd they encamped there, and on the 23rd crossed Big Mountain. The President, reclining in Apostle Woodruff's carriage, requested to have it turned upon the summit so that he might see those portions of the Valley that were now visible. Gazing long and earnestly at the prospect, he exclaimed: "Enough. This is the right place. Drive on."***

It was late in the forenoon of the day following -- the memorable 24th -- that the rear wagons rolled through the mouth of Emigration Canyon, and Brigham Young, the founder of Utah, looked his first upon the full glory of the Valley by the Lake.

George A. Smith
JD 13:85 June 20, 1869 SLC

After the death of Joseph Smith, when it seemed as if every trouble and calamity had come upon the Saints, Brigham Young, who was President of the Twelve,*** ... sought the Lord to know what they should do, and where they should lead the people for safety, and while they were fasting and praying daily on this subject, President Young had a vision of Joseph Smith, who showed him the mountain that we now call Ensign Peak, immediately north of Salt Lake City, and there was an ensign fell upon that peak, and Joseph said, "Build under the point where the colors fall and you will prosper and have peace." The Pioneers had no pilot or guide, none among them had ever been in the country or knew anything about it. However, they travelled under the direction of President Young until they reached this valley. When they entered it President Young pointed to that peak, and said he, "I want to go there." He went up to the point and said, "This is Ensign Peak."

Missionaries Sent to the Nations of the Earth to Gather Israel to the Mountains

SECTION REVELATION 217

Son Ahman, Your Lord, Speaketh of the Pure Governing Power of All Nations of Millennial Time of Holy Pure and Authoritative Governing of Celestial Power; My Holy Power of Eternal Celestial Authority:

Revelation of the Lord Jesus Christ Galveston, Texas Thursday, September 8, 2011

1. Thus saith God, over all, to all nations: My holy way shall be the Millennium of holy pure noble righteous power.

2. Let all know the holy way shall be known by the holy word of my testimony of the holy Prophets being of a fulfilling; even to gather to my Zion.

3. Let all know my time is soon at hand, to cleanse all peoples of every nation; leaving the way of pure power of Zion to be of your holy power of my sending.

4. Let all know I am soon to be of a full power to be among all people of every nation.

5. Let all come to my New Jerusalem as I establish my governing power over the whole earth.

6. Let all be of a hearing my doctrine of civil governing authority.

7. Let my holy will be thy way of the power to govern. Amen.

Isaiah 2 (Inspired Version)

1. The word that Isaiah the son of Amoz saw concerning Judah and Jerusalem:

2. And it shall come to pass in the last days, when the mountain of the Lord's house shall be established in the top of the mountains, and shall be exalted above the hills, and all nations shall flow unto it.

3. And many people shall go and say, Come ye, and let us go up to the mountain of the Lord, to the house of the God of Jacob; and he will teach us of his ways, and we will walk in his paths; for out of Zion shall go forth the law, and the word of the Lord from Jerusalem;

4. And he shall judge among the nations, and shall rebuke many people; and they shall beat their swords into plowshares, and their spears into pruning hooks; nation shall not lift up sword against nation, neither shall they learn war any more.

President Joseph Smith, Jun.
Teachings of the Prophet Joseph Smith, Page 92

Much has been said and done of late by the general government in relation to the Indians (Lamanites) within the territorial limits of the United States. One of the most important points in the faith of the Church of the Latter-day Saints, through the fullness of the everlasting Gospel, is the gathering of Israel (of whom the Lamanites constitute a part) that happy time when Jacob shall go up to the house of the Lord, to worship Him in spirit and in truth, to live in holiness; when the Lord will restore His judges as at the first, and His counselors as at the beginning; when every man may sit under his own vine and fig tree, and there will be none to molest or make afraid; when He will turn to them a pure language, and the earth will be filled with sacred knowledge, as the waters cover the great deep; when it shall no longer be said, the Lord lives that brought up the children of Israel out of the land of Egypt, but the Lord lives that brought up the children of Israel from the land of the north, and from all the lands whither He has driven them. That day is one, all important to all men.

In view of its importance, together with all that the prophets have said about it before us, we feel like dropping a few ideas in connection with the official statements from the government concerning the Indians. In speaking of the gathering, we mean to be understood as speaking of it according to scripture, the gathering of the elect of the Lord out of every nation on earth, and bringing them to the place of the Lord of Hosts, when the city of righteousness shall be built, and where the people shall be of one heart and one mind, when the Savior comes: yea, where the people shall walk with God like Enoch, and be free from sin. The word of the Lord is precious; and when we read that the veil spread over all nations will be destroyed, and the pure in heart see God, and reign with Him a thousand years on earth, we want all honest men to have a chance to gather and build up a city of righteousness, where even upon the bells of the horses shall be written *"Holiness to the Lord."*

The Book of Mormon has made known who Israel is, upon this continent. And while we behold the government of the United States gathering the Indians, and locating them upon lands to be their own, how sweet it is to think that they may one day be gathered by the Gospel!

President Joseph Smith, Jun.
Teachings of the Prophet Joseph Smith, Page 183

The greatest temporal and spiritual blessings which always come from faithfulness and concerted effort, never attended individual exertion or enterprise. The history of all past ages abundantly attests this fact. In addition to all temporal blessings, there is no other way for the Saints to be saved in these last days, [than by the gathering] as the concurrent testimony of all the holy prophets clearly proves, for it is written -- "They shall come from the east, and be gathered from the west; the north shall give up, and the south shall keep not back." "The sons of God shall be gathered from afar, and his daughters from the ends of the earth."

It is also the concurrent testimony of all the prophets, that this gathering together of all the Saints, must take place before the Lord comes to "take vengeance upon the ungodly," and "to be glorified and admired by all those who obey the Gospel." The fiftieth Psalm, from the first to the fifth verse inclusive, describes the glory and majesty of that event. (Jan. 8, 1841.) DHC 4:272.

President Joseph Smith, Jun.
Teachings of the Prophet Joseph Smith, Page 254

In regard to the building up of Zion, it has to be done by the counsel of Jehovah, by the revelations of heaven; and we should feel to say, "If the Lord go not with us, carry us not up hence." We would say to the Saints that come here, we have laid the foundation for the gathering of God's people to this place, and they expect that when the Saints do come, they will be under the counsel that God has appointed. The Twelve are set apart to counsel the Saints pertaining to this matter; and we expect that those who come here will send before them their wise men according to revelation; or if not practicable, be subject to the counsel that God has given, or they cannot receive an inheritance among the Saints, or be considered as God's people, and they will be dealt with as transgressors of the laws of God. We are trying here to gird up our loins, and purge from our midst the workers of iniquity; and we hope that when our brethren arrive from abroad, they will assist us to roll forth this good work, and to accomplish this great design that "Zion may be built up in righteousness; and all nations flock to her standard;" that as God's people, under His direction, and obedient to His law, we may grow up in righteousness and truth; that when His purposes shall be accomplished, we may receive an inheritance among those that are sanctified. (July 15, 1842.) DHC 5:61-66.

President Joseph Smith, Jun.
Teachings of the Prophet Joseph Smith, Page 308

It was the design of the councils of heaven before the world was, that the principles and laws of the priesthood should be predicated upon the gathering of the people in every age of the world. Jesus did everything to gather the people, and they would not be gathered, and He therefore poured out curses upon them. Ordinances instituted in the heavens before the foundation of the world, in the priesthood, for the salvation of men, are not to be altered or changed. All must be saved on the same principles.

President Joseph Smith, Jun.
Teachings of the Prophet Joseph Smith, Page 310

The doctrine of baptism for the dead is clearly shown in the New Testament; and if the doctrine is not good, then throw the New Testament away; but if it is the word of God, then let the doctrine be acknowledged; and it was the reason why Jesus said unto the Jews, "How oft would I have gathered thy children together, even as a hen gathereth her chickens under her wings, and ye would not!" -- that they might attend to the ordinances of baptism for the dead as well as other ordinances of the priesthood, and receive revelations from heaven, and be perfected in the things of the kingdom of God -- but they would not. This was the case on the day of Pentecost: those blessings were poured out on the disciples on that occasion. God ordained that He would save the dead, and would do it by gathering His people together.

President Brigham Young
JD 11:125 June 18, 1865 SLC

It is through the proclamation of the gospel that this great people have been gathered from their homes in distant parts of the earth. It is not in the power of man to accomplish such a work of gathering thousands of men, women, and children from different nations to a distant inland country, and unite them together and make of them a powerful nation. They heard the sound of the gospel, they repented of their sins, and were baptized for the remission of them, and received the Holy Ghost by the laying on of hands; this Spirit caused them to gather themselves together for the truth's sake; they came here because the voice of the Lord called them together from the ends of the earth. They needed not to be persuaded to gather themselves together, for they knew it was the will of God by the power of the Spirit which they had received through the ordinances of the gospel. Here sits brother George D. Watt, our reporter, who was the first man to receive the gospel in a foreign land; there had not been a word spoken to him about gathering to America; but he prophesied that the land of America was the land of Zion, and that the Lord would gather His people to that land in the last days, and thus he prophesied by the Spirit of prophecy which he had received by embracing the gospel.

Law of Eternal Marriage Made Known to All People as a Holy Way of Pure Holy Law of Exaltation

SECTION REVELATION 218

Son Ahman Saith Thus to the People of the Earth, of Full Way of Knowing I Am Continuing My Law of Celestial Union on the Land of Zion. Amen.

Revelation of the Lord Jesus Christ Galveston, Texas Thursday, September 8, 2011

1. Thus saith the Lord unto the people who are of holy and noble cause; unto a full and pure living my holy law of Eternal Power: My holy way is holy, pure, of Celestial Power of Eternal Union in holy marriage.

2. Let all know I sent my servant Brigham Young to reveal to the people of all nations my holy law must be lived to gain eternal exaltation. Thus did I cause all people to learn my holy way.

3. I am the Author of this holy law.

4. Let my people be of a full way of religious and of a pure living of this, my holy law of Eternal Power.

5. I am the God over all.

6. I shall fulfill my way of eternal and holy laws of Priesthood, not to be controlled by man's governing.

7. Thus do I give my way to all, that you may let alone my Celestial way, to be of a pure power of my revealing, unto the holy law of the government of heaven being a law of progress eternal. Thus do I reveal my holy law as a pure way eternal.

8. Let governing power of civil law not be of a way of being of a governing my holy law.

9. I am the Giver of all my holy way Celestial.

10. Let my people be of a way of Eternal Union of holy religious living of constitutional guarantee of freedom of worship. Amen.

The Celestial Law Is Summarized as Perfect Christlike Obedience

President John Taylor
JD 26:350 February 20, 1884 SLC

That is taking this nation as an example, all laws that are proper and correct, and all obligations entered into which are not violative of the constitution should be kept inviolate. But if they are violative of the constitution, then the compact between the rulers and the ruled is broken and the obligation ceases to be binding. Just as a person agreeing to purchase anything and to pay a certain amount for it, if he receives the article bargained for, and does not pay its price, he violates his contract; but if he does not receive the article he is not required to pay for it. Again we ask, what is this celestial law? The celestial law above referred to is absolute submission and obedience to the law of God. It is exemplified in the words of Jesus, who, when He came to introduce the Gospel said, "I came not to do my will but the will of the Father that sent me;" and His mission was to do the will of the Father who sent him, or to fulfill a celestial law.

The Celestial Law to Be Lived in a Pure and Holy Way

President John Taylor
JD 24:295 October 7, 1883 SLC

We have embraced the Gospel. We have placed ourselves in another position from that of the world. We have entered into sacred covenants with the Lord, and He expects us to fulfill our covenants, and those who do not fulfill them will be condemned. There are certain rules and regulations that exist in the heavens, as well as on the earth. We are told that before we can enter into the celestial kingdom of God, we shall have to pass by the angels, and the Gods, and if the Latter-day Saints aim at a celestial exaltation, they must live and abide by the celestial law, or they will not get it, any more than the Gentiles will. Hear it, ye Latter-day Saints! God expects you to be pure, virtuous, holy, upright, prayerful, honest, obedient to His law, and not to follow the devices and desires of your own hearts. God has revealed many things to you, and He will reveal many more. He expects you to abide His law, and those who do not want to abide it, had better quit to-day, the sooner the better, for God expects us to do His will in all things.

Joseph F. Smith
Gospel Doctrine, Page 272

I desire to emphasize this. I want the young men of Zion to realize that this institution of marriage is not a man-made institution. It is of God. It is honorable, and no man who is of marriageable age is living his religion who remains single. It is not simply devised for the convenience alone of man, to suit his own notions, and his own ideas; to marry and then divorce, to adopt and then to discard, just as he pleases. There are great consequences connected with it, consequences which reach beyond this present time, into all eternity, for thereby souls are begotten into the world, and men and women obtain their being in the world. Marriage is the preserver of the human race. Without it, the purposes of God would be frustrated; virtue would be destroyed to give place to vice and corruption, and the earth would be void and empty.

President Brigham Young
JD 13:272 July 24, 1870 SLC

Should we not obey the requirements of Heaven? Certainly we should. Would it be the least injurious to the human family to receive the Gospel of the Son of God, and to have the man Christ Jesus to rule over them? Not at all; but, on the contrary, it would fill them with peace, joy, love, kindness, and intelligence. Would the principles of the Gospel, if obeyed, teach us to control ourselves? They would. They will teach men and women to govern and control their own passions.

President Brigham Young
JD 13:239 February 20, 1870 SLC

...I will say that the principle of patriarchal marriage is one of the highest and purest ever revealed to the children of men.

Orson F. Whitney
History of Utah, Volume 1 Page 490

In the summer of 1852 the tenet of celestial or plural marriage -- commonly called polygamy -- which was destined to become in after years the leading question of the so-called "Utah Problem," was for the first time publicly proclaimed by the Church of Jesus Christ of Latter-day Saints. It had been practiced, as seen, at Nauvoo, and subsequently at Winter Quarters and in Utah; but up to this time the Church had never enunciated it. The practice, however, had long been evident, even to strangers visiting Utah; little or no effort being made by the Saints to conceal it. It had also been much commented upon, not only by such critics as Judge Brocchus and his colleagues, and others equally inimical to the Mormons, but by friendly visitors as well.***

It was during a special conference of the Church, held at Salt Lake City on the 28th and 29th of August, that the public avowal of plural marriage was made. The conference convened in the building which afterwards became known as the "Old Tabernacle," though it was then quite new, having been completed for dedication on the 6th of the preceding April.***

There on the 29th of August, 1852, the revelation on Celestial Marriage, first recorded from the lips of the Prophet Joseph Smith on July 12th, 1843, was read to the assembled Saints and sustained by the uplifted hands of the large congregation as a doctrine of their faith and a revelation from the Almighty. The same day Apostle Orson Pratt preached to the conference the first authorized public discourse on the subject of plural marriage. Thousands of copies of the revelation were published and circulated throughout the Union and carried by missionaries to various parts of the world. One of these is preserved in the Deseret Museum. It is the proof revised by Editor Willard Richards, and authenticated by

James McKnight, at that time foreman of the *Deseret News*.

Temples Built by Priesthood for the Work of Holy Ordinances of Salvation

President Brigham Young
JD 18:262 October 8, 1876 SLC

Now, I will make a proposition, and you may have five years to do the work I am about to assign you. To the people of the Sevier Valley, Millard County, Iron County, Piute County, Beaver County, with Juab, Kane, Washington, and Sanpete Counties, I will say, Go to work and build a Temple in Sanpete. As soon as you are ready to commence, I will provide the plan. The ground is already selected. We do not ask whether you are able to do this; but ask yourselves if you have faith sufficient to do it, for we know that you are perfectly able to do it if you are willing, and do it inside of three years from next April. Then to the people of Box Elder County, the Malad Valley, Cache Valley, Soda Springs, and Bear Lake Valley, Rich County, and the people on Bear River, I say, unite your labor and commence as soon as you can to build a Temple in Cache Valley. Again, to the people of Weber County, Davis County, Morgan and Summit Counties, Salt Lake County, Tooele and Utah Counties, with the people east and west, I will say, Go to work and finish the Temple in this city forthwith. Can you accomplish the work, you Latter-day Saints of these several counties? Yes, that is a question I can answer readily, you are perfectly able to do it, the question is, Have you the necessary faith? Have you sufficient of the Spirit of God in your hearts to enable you to say, Yes, by the help of God our

Father, we will erect these buildings to his name. There will be little money comparatively needed, it is nearly all labor, such as you can perform. If the people had paid their Tithing, and paid the hands employed on the Temple in proportion as I have done, that building would have been finished before now. But I am not obliged to build Temples for the people; this is our common duty, in order that all may have the privilege to officiate for themselves and their dead. How long, Latter-day Saints, before you will believe the Gospel as it is? The Lord has declared it to be his will that his people enter into covenant, even as Enoch and his people did, which of necessity must be before we shall have the privilege of building the Centre Stake of Zion, for the power and glory of God will be there, and none but the pure in heart will be able to live and enjoy it. Go to now, with your might and with your means, and finish this Temple. Why, for what reason? The reasons are very obvious, and you understand them.

President Joseph Smith, Jun.
Teachings of the Prophet Joseph Smith, Page 182

The Temple of the Lord is in process of erection here, where the Saints will come to worship the God of their fathers, according to the order of His house and the powers of the Holy Priesthood, and will be so constructed as to enable all the functions of the Priesthood to be duly exercised, and where instructions from the Most High will be received, and from this place go forth to distant lands.

President Joseph Smith, Jun.
Teachings of the Prophet Joseph Smith, Page 224

Said that if the people had common sympathies they would rejoice that the sick could be healed; that the time had not been before that these things could be in their proper order; that the Church is not fully organized, in its proper order, and cannot be, until the Temple is completed, where places will be provided for the administration of the ordinances of the Priesthood.

President Joseph Smith, Jun.
Teachings of the Prophet Joseph Smith, Page 237

And the communications I made to this council were of things spiritual, and to be received only by the spiritual minded: and there was nothing made known to these men but what will be made known to all the Saints of the last days, so soon as they are prepared to receive, and a proper place is prepared to communicate them, even to the weakest of the Saints; therefore let the Saints be diligent in building the Temple, and all houses which they have been, or shall hereafter be, commanded of God to build; and wait their time with patience in all meekness, faith, perseverance unto the end, knowing assuredly that all these things referred to in this council are always governed by the principle of revelation. (May 4, 1842.) D.H.C. 5:1-2.

Holy Ordinances of the Temple

President Joseph Smith, Jun.
Teachings of the Prophet Joseph Smith, Page 330

But how are they to become saviors on Mount Zion? By building their temples, erecting their baptismal fonts, and going forth and receiving all the ordinances, baptisms, confirmations, washings, anointings, ordinations and sealing powers upon their heads, in behalf of all their progenitors who are dead, and redeem them that they may come forth in the first resurrection and be exalted to thrones of glory with them; and herein is the chain that binds the hearts of the fathers to the children, and the children to the fathers, which fulfills the mission of Elijah. And I would to God that this temple was now done, that we might go into it, and go to work and improve our time, and make use of the seals while they are on earth.

President Joseph Smith, Jun.
Teachings of the Prophet Joseph Smith, Page 362

The declaration this morning is, that as soon as the Temple and baptismal font are prepared, we calculate to give the Elders of Israel their washings and anointings, and attend to those last and more impressive ordinances, without which we cannot obtain celestial thrones. But there must be a holy place prepared for that purpose.*** These must, however, be a place built expressly for that purpose, and for men to be baptized for their dead. It must be built in this central place; for every man who wishes to save his father, mother, brothers, sisters and friends, must go through all the ordinances for each one of them separately, the same as for himself, from baptism to ordination, washing and anointings, and receive all the keys and powers of the Priesthood, the same as for himself.

President Brigham Young
JD 9:317 July 13, 1862 SLC

The servants of God will officiate for the dead in the temples of God which will be built. The Gospel is now preached to the spirits in prison, and when the time comes for the servants of God to officiate for them, the names of those who have received the Gospel in the spirit will be revealed by the angels of God and the spirits of just men made perfect; also the places of their birth, the age in which they lived, and everything regarding them that is necessary to be recorded on earth, and they will then be saved so as to find admittance into the presence of God, with their relatives who have officiated for them.

The Utah War

Evil Reports Against My Holy Law of Priesthood Ignite Bitter Attack of Governing Power

Orson F. Whitney
Popular History of Utah, Page 118

The trouble [Utah War] was caused by false reports of a rebellion in Utah, and the sending of Federal troops to put down the alleged uprising.***

One of the main causes of the misunderstanding was a letter written by Judge William W. Drummond to the Attorney-General of the United States, charging that the Supreme Court records at Salt Lake City had been destroyed with the direct knowledge and approval of Governor Brigham Young; that Federal officers had been grossly insulted for questioning the treasonable act; and that a condition of affairs existed calling for a change of Governors and for military aid to enable the new Executive to perform the duties of his office.

These were grave charges; but even worse were made. Judge Drummond intimated that the murder of Captain Gunnison, the death of Judge Shaver, and the killing of Secretary Babbitt had all been done by the advice and direction of the leading authorities of the "Mormon" Church; and he asserted that all who opposed those authorities, in any manner whatsoever, were harassed, insulted, and even murdered, by their orders or under their influence.

President Brigham Young
JD 5:77 July 26, 1857 SLC

What is now the news circulated throughout the United States? That Captain Gunnison was killed by Brigham Young, and that Babbitt was killed on the

Plains by Brigham Young and his Danite band. What more? That Brigham Young has killed all the men who have died between the Missouri river and California. I do not say that President Buchanan has any such idea, or the officers of the troops who are reported to be on their way here; but such are the newspaper stories. Such reports are in the bellows, and editors and politicians are blowing them out.

According to their version, I am guilty of the death of every man, woman, and child that has died between the Missouri river and the California gold mines; and they are coming here to chastise me.

Lies of Apostate and Government Agents Rebuked by Brigham Young

President Brigham Young
JD 5:56 July 19, 1857 SLC

There is another item that I will touch upon. Two weeks ago to-day, I mentioned the course of some individuals in this place who are writing slanders concerning us, stating that a man cannot live here unless he is a "Mormon," when at the same time they come here to meeting with perfect impunity. Some of them are in the meeting to-day, and are now preparing lies for their letters. A parcel of them clan together and fix up letters, and they write to the East how desperately wicked the "Mormons" are -- how they are killing each other, killing the gentiles, stealing and robbing, and what wicked, miserable creatures the "Mormons" are. And when any of them go from here, they report, "We have barely escaped with our lives: Oh! it was a very narrow escape that we made; but we did manage to get out of the place with our lives; yes, we did get away without being killed." They all safely escape to tell their lies.

They say that it is with great difficulty that they can live with the Saints, when at the same time no one has molested them during all the time they have been writing lies to stir up the wicked to destroy us. They pass and repass in our streets with the same privileges that other citizens enjoy; and there are professedly of our faith those who sympathize for them. May God Almighty let His curse rest on all such sympathizers.

President Brigham Young
JD 8:323 February 10, 1861 SLC

One of the most contemptible of characters we ever had here could swear falsely in Washington, and the Government could receive his oath, and make it a basis, with other lies, of sending an army here. William Drummond went to Washington and swore that we were treasoners, and to many palpable falsehoods; and King James could act upon that and send an army here at an expense of, probably, fifty million dollars. Says King James -- "Those lies are true." "What! receive a lie?" Yes, go and swear to a lie, and the Government can hear that and act upon it.*** What a reign is the reign of King James! It is enough to astound and throw into the shade the wisdom of all nations upon the earth!

Orson F. Whitney
History of Utah, Volume 1 Page 584

Several other letters found their way to Washington before or soon after Judge Drummond's resignation, and though some were of too late a date to have influenced the original action of the Government in sending troops to Utah, others arrived in ample time to contribute to that end, and all serve to show the feeling of hostility that inspired the movement, and shaped the policy of the administration toward the people of this Territory at that interesting and critical point in their history.***

Along with the Magraw letter, which was merely the preface to Judge

Drummond's book of blood and horror, the foregoing documents were presented by President Buchanan to Congress in 1858. Possibly it occurred to some of those astute lawyers and statesmen to enquire, after reading the charges relating to the murder of Captain Gunnison, Judge Shaver and Secretary Babbitt, what manner of men these Mormons were, to be suspected (?) of killing their best friends, and allowing their worst enemies, such as Judge Drummond, ex-mail contractor Magraw, Indian Agent Hurt and others, to say nothing of the Craigs and Kerrs, the Hockadays and Burrs, "Gentiles of Salt Lake City," to be among them, still alive, or to slip through the fingers of that awful "oath-bound organization," and escape unmolested from the Territory.***

Other Federal officials, writing from Utah, or filing their affidavits at the national capital, also contributed to stir up prejudice throughout the east against the Mormon people. Among these were Associate Justice Stiles, who had had a difficulty with several local members of the bar, and accused the Saints of intimidating his court. Indian Agent Hurt found fault with Brigham Young, as Superintendent of Indian Affairs, for his policy in relation to the red men, and intimated that the funds appropriated for them by Congress had been improperly expended. Mormon proselyting among the native tribes was represented as being highly prejudicial. Others, whose only grievance was that they hated Mormonism and all things connected with it, had complaints more or less trivial to lodge against the Mormon leader. In one of these the absurd charge was made that he opened and read all the letters that came into or went out of Utah.

It was upon such allegations as these, most of them utterly false, and the remainder grossly exaggerated, that President Buchanan, in the spring of 1857, without taking time to investigate as to their truth or falsity, decided that a rebellion existed in Utah, appointed a successor to Brigham Young as Governor of the Territory, and ordered an army to march to Salt Lake City to forcibly install and maintain in office the new Executive.

President Brigham Young
JD 5:125 August 9, 1857 SLC

Almost every man that has come from the East of late is telling you the political feelings and desires of the Government towards this people. Brother Taylor has just related that a gentleman he met on the road remarked, "What! can you 'Mormons' fight the United States? Can you contend with them? You had better take a more specific policy than you have. Do not speak about the President, nor about any of the officials." We shall talk as we please about them; for this is the right and privilege granted to us by the Constitution of the United States: and, as ministers of salvation, we shall take the liberty of telling men of their sins.

I shall take the liberty of talking as I please about the President of the United States, and I expect that I know his character better than he knows it himself.***

I wish that Hickory Jackson was now our President; for he would kick some of those rotten-hearted sneaks out, or rather order his negroes to do it. If we had a man in the chair who really was a man, and capable of magnifying his office, he would call upon his servants, and order him to kick those mean, miserable sneaks out of the presidential mansion, off from its grounds, and into the streets. But the President hearkens to the clamour around him; and, as did Pontius Pilate, in the case of Jesus Christ, has washed his hands, saying, "I am clear of the blood of those Latter-day Saints. Gentlemen, you have dictated, and I will order a soldiery and officials to Utah." It is said in the Bible, that whosoever ye yield yourselves to obey, his servants ye are. The President has yielded himself a servant to cliques and parties, and their servants he shall be. And all that has been spoken of him by brother Kimball, in the name of Jesus Christ, shall come upon him.

Do you think that we shall be called treasoners, for rebuking him in his sinful course? Yes. Talk of loyalty to Government! Hardly a man among them cares for the Government of the United States, any more than he does for the useless card that lies on the table while he is playing out his hand. They disregard the Constitution as they would any old fable in any old school book. Scarcely a member on the floor of Congress cares anything about it.***

With regard to the present contention and strife, and to our position and situation, there are few things to be considered, and there is much labour to be performed. Let the Saints live their religion; let them have faith in God, do all the good they can to the household of faith and to everybody else, and trust in God for the result; <u>for the world will not believe one truth about us. I tell you that the Government of the United States, and other governments that are acquainted with us, will not believe a single truth about us. What will they believe? Every lie that every poor, miserable, rotten-hearted curse can tell</u>. What are we to do, under these circumstances? Live our religion. Are you going to contend against the United States? No. But when

they come here to take our lives solely for our religion, be ye also ready.

Do I expect to stand still, sit still, or lie still, and tamely let them take away my life? I have told you a great many times what I have to say about that. I do not profess to be so good a man as Joseph Smith was. I do not walk under their protection nor into their prisons, as he did. And though officers should pledge me their protection, as Governor Ford pledged protection to Joseph, I would not trust them any sooner than I would a wolf with my dinner; neither do I trust in a wicked judge, nor in any evil person. I trust in my God, and in honest men and women who have the power of the Almighty upon them. What will we do? Keep the wicked off as long as we can, preach righteousness to them, and teach them the way of salvation.

Public Outcry Against Brigham Young in the United States Causes President Buchanan to Remove Him as Governor of the Territory

President Brigham Young
JD 4:41 August 31, 1856 SLC

I am still governor of this Territory, to the constant chagrin of my enemies; but I do not in the least neglect the duties of my Priesthood, nor my office as governor; and while I honor my Priesthood I will do honor to my office as governor. This is hard to be understood by the wicked, but it is true. The feelings of many are much irritated because I am here, and Congress has requested the President to inquire why I still hold the office of governor in the Territory of Utah. I can answer that question; I hold the office by appointment, and am to hold it until my successor is appointed and qualified, which has not yet been done. I shall bow to Jesus, my Governor, and under him, to brother Joseph.

Though he has gone behind the vail, and I cannot see him, he is my head, under Jesus Christ and the ancient Apostles, and I shall go ahead and build up the kingdom. But if I was now sitting in the chair of state at the White House in Washington, everything in my office would be subject to my religion. Why? Because it teaches me to deal justice and mercy to all. I am satisfied to love righteousness and be full of the Holy Ghost, while all hell yawns to destroy me, though it cannot do it.

Utah Was at Peace While Government Was at Way of War

Orson F. Whitney
History of Utah, Volume 1 Page 612

Governor Young: -- "I deny that any books of the United States have been burned. All I ask of any man is, that he tell the truth about us, pay his debts and not steal, and then he will be welcome to come or go as he likes. I have broken no law, and under the present state of affairs I will not suffer myself to be taken by any United States officer, to be killed as they killed Joseph."

George A. Smith
JD 11:181 October 8, 1865 SLC

The administration of President Buchanan brought the power of the Government to bear against us. The traitor, General A. S. Johnston, was sent with what was then called by Secretary Floyd the best appointed army that was ever fitted ont [out] by this Government since its formation. General Scott issued orders to keep the troops massed and in hand, the supply trains to be kept with the main body of the army. The newspaper press of the country asserted that this army was to cause the blood of the Elders and Saints to flow in the streets of Great Salt Lake City. The mails being stopped, and

the ordinary sources of communication closed, it was supposed the "Mormons" would be ignorant of the movements until the army came upon them like a thunder cloud. The Governorship was tendered to a number who were unwilling to come out with a formidable army, but were willing to come without. Benjamin McCullough, of Texas, declined the honor on the ground that a confirmed old bachelor ought not to interfere with polygamy. Colonel Alfred Cumming accepted the office, and his appointment was hailed with general acclamation by the enemies of Utah, as he was considered a man of desperate character, who had on one occasion compelled even Jeff. Davis to apologise. When Governor Cumming arrived here and investigated the matter, he was satisfied that the Administration had been duped, and he made official reports to Washington that the charges against the Saints were totally unfounded, and the Administration let the whole matter fizzle out, and Uncle Sam, the generous old gentleman, had to submit to his pocket being picked to the tune of about forty millions of dollars -- the cost of the Utah expedition.

President Brigham Young
JD 5:226 September 13, 1857 SLC

I have been in this kingdom a good while -- twenty-five years and upwards, and I have been driven from place to place; my brethren have been driven, my sisters have been driven; we have been scattered and peeled, and every time without any provocation upon our part, only that we were united, obedient to the laws of the land, and striving to worship God. Mobs repeatedly gathered against this people, but they never had any power to prevail until Governors issued their orders and called out a force under the letter of the law, but breaking the spirit, to hold the

"Mormons" still while infernal scamps cut their throats. I have had all that before me through the night past, and it makes me too angry to preach. Also to see that we are in a Government whose administrators are always trying to injure us, while we are constantly at the defiance of all hell to prove any just grounds for their hostility against us; and yet they are organizing their forces to come here, and protect infernal scamps who are anxious to come and kill whom they please, destroy whom they please, and finally exterminate the "Mormons."***

On the 24th of July last, a number of us went to Big Cottonwood Kanyon to pass the anniversary of our arrival into this Valley. Ten years ago the 24th of July last, a few of the Elders arrived here, and began to plough and to plant seeds, to raise food to sustain themselves. Whilst speaking to the brethren on that day, I said, inadvertently. If the people of the United States will let us alone for ten years, we will ask no odds of them; and ten years from that very day, we had a message by brothers Smoot, Stoddard, and Rockwell, that the Government had stopped the mail, and that they had ordered 2,500 troops to come here and hold the "Mormons" still, while priests, politicians, speculators, whoremongers, and every mean, filthy character that could be raked up should come here and kill off the "Mormons." I did not think about what I had said ten years ago, till I heard that the President of the United States had so unjustly ordered troops here; and then I said, when my former expression came to my mind, In the name of Israel's God, we ask no odds of them.

I do not often get angry; but when I do, I am righteously angry; and the bosom of the Almighty burns with anger towards those scoundrels; and they shall be consumed, in the name of Israel's God. We have borne enough of their oppression and hellish abuse, and we will not bear any more of it; for there is no just law requiring further forbearance on our part. And I am not going to have troops here to protect the priests and a hellish rabble in efforts to drive us from the land we possess; for the Lord does not want us to be driven, and has said, "If you will assert your rights, and keep my commandments, you shall never again be brought into bondage by your enemies."***

Well, the enquiry is, "What is the news? What is the conclusion?" It is this -- We have to trust in God. I am not in the least concerned as to the result, if we put our trust in God. The administrators of our Government have issued orders for marching troops and expending much treasure, and all predicated upon falsehoods, while every honourable man would have first made an economical and peaceful enquiry into the circumstances. And even now, every honourable man would use all his influence to avert the present unjust and entirely groundless movement against us; but Captains, Majors, Colonels, and other subordinate officers have not the power. Wicked persons, solely for the accomplishment of their unhallowed schemes, have had the power to array the Government against us, through their lying and misrepresentation; but citizens, unorganized into cliques and parties, no matter how good their intentions and wishes, have not the power to avert the blow when the Administration of our Government is arrayed against us, unless they will also unite against the few well-organized scoundrels who are plundering our treasury and fast urging our country to dissolution. We have got to protect ourselves by the strength of our God. Do not be concerned in the least with regard to all the affairs that are before you; for we shall live and grow finely, as said a certain woman, who weighed but two pounds when an infant, and was put in quart cup. Upon being asked whether she lived, "O yes," she said, "I lived and grew finely." It will also be said of the Latter-day Saints, "They lived and grew finely."***

Do not be angry. I will permit you to be as angry as I am. Do not get so angry that you cannot pray: do not allow yourselves to become so angry that you cannot feed an enemy -- even your worst enemy, if an opportunity should present itself. There is a wicked anger, and there is a righteous anger. The Lord does not suffer wicked anger to be in his heart; but there is anger in his bosom, and he will hold a controversy with the nations, and will sift them, and no power can stay his hand.

The Government of our country will go by the board through its own corruptions, and no power can save it. If we can avert the blow for another season, it is probable that our enemies will have enough to attend to at home, without worrying the Latter-day Saints. Have faith, and all will be well with us. I would like this people to have faith enough to turn away their enemies. I have prayed fervently about this matter; for it has been said that the troops would come: but I have said that, if my faith will prevent it, they shall not come.

Message of Governor Brigham Young to the Legislature

President Brigham Young
Millennial Star 20:235 December 15, 1857 SLC

The members and officers of the last Legislative Assembly, familiar with the evils visited upon the innocent by the miserably bad conduct of certain officials heretofore sent here by Government, knowing that all republican governments -- which both our General and State Governments are, in form -- are based upon the principle that the governed shall enjoy the right to elect their own officers and be guided by laws having their own consent, and, perfectly aware that, by the Constitution, residents in Territories are guaranteed that great right equally with residents in States (for Congress has not one particle more constitutional power to legislate for and officer Americans in Territories than they have to legislate for and officer Americans in States), respectfully memorialized the President and Senate to appoint officers for Utah in accordance with an accompanying list, containing the names of persons who were her first choice for the offices placed opposite those names; but, if that selection did not meet with approval, they were solicited to make the appointments from a list containing other and a larger number of names of residents, who were also the choice of the people; and if that selection was also rejected, to appoint from any part of the Union, with the simple request, in such event, that the appointees be good men. In this matter of appointment of officers, what more rights could the most tyrannical in a republican government ask a Territory to waive? Yet, up to this date, no official information concerning the action, if any, taken upon that memorial has ever reached us.

Time glided by, and travellers and newspapers began to confirm the rumour that the present Executive and a part of his Cabinet had yielded to the rabid clamour raised against Utah by lying editors, corrupt demagogues, heartless office-hunters, and the ignorant rabble, incited by numbers of the hireling clergy, and were about to send an army to Utah with the sole and avowed purpose, as published in almost every newspaper, of compelling American citizens, peacefully, loyally, and lawfully occupying American soil, to forego the dearest constitutional rights, to abandon their religion, to wallow in the mire and worship at the shrine of modern civilization and Christianity, or be expelled from the country or exterminated. Where now are constitutional rights? Who is laying the axe at the root of the tree of liberty? Who are the usurpers? Who the tyrants? Who the traitors? Most assuredly those who are madly urging measures to subvert the genius of free institutions and those principles of liberty upon which our Government is based, and to overthrow virtue, independence, justice, and true intelligence, the loss of either of which by the people, the celebrated Judge Story has wisely affirmed, would be the ruin of our Republic -- the destruction of its vitality. And ex-President James Madison, among other purposes, declared it to be the purpose of Government "to avoid the slightest interference with the rights of conscience or the functions of religion, so wisely exempted from civil jurisdiction."

Has Utah ever violated the least principle of the Constitution, or so much as broken the most insignificant constitutional enactment? No; nor have we the most distant occasion for so doing, but have ever striven to peacefully enjoy and extend those rights granted to all by a merciful Creator. But so unobtrusive and wise a course does not seem to please those who live and wish to live by office and those who make and love lies; and since those characters are numerous, and also powerful through well-disciplined organization, and since Utah has yielded right after right for the sake of peace, until

her policy has emboldened the enemies of our Union, it must needs be that President Buchanan, if he has ordered an army to Utah, as reported -- for he has not officially notified me of such a movement by his order -- has at length succumbed, either of choice or through being overcome, to the cruel and nefarious counsels of those enemies, and is endeavouring to carry out a usurpation of power which of right belongs only to the people, by appointing civil officers known to be justly objectionable to freemen, and sending a so-called army under mere colour of law, to force those officers upon us at the point of the bayonet, and to form a nucleus for the collection and protection of every gambler, cut-throat, whore-master, and scoundrel who may choose to follow in their train. Such a treasonable system of operations will never be endured, nor even countenanced, by any person possessed of the least spark of patriotism and love of constitutional liberty. The President knew, if he knew the facts in the case, as he was in duty bound to do before taking action, that the officials hitherto sent here had been invariably received and treated with all the respect their offices demanded, and that a portion of them had met with far more courtesy than elsewhere would have been extended to them or their conduct deserved; he also knew, or had the privilege of knowing, that the Memorial to the last Assembly, as already stated, respectfully informed him that Utah wished good men for officers, and that such officers would be cordially welcomed and obeyed; but that we would not again tamely endure the abuse and misrule meted by official villians, as were some who have formerly officiated here. Such being a few of the leading facts, what were the legitimate inferences to be drawn from the rumours that the President had sent a batch of officials, with an army to operate as their *posse?* That he had wilfully made the official appointments for Utah from a class other than good men, and placed himself, where tyrants often are, in the position of levying war against the very nation whose choice had made him its chief executive officer.

Fully aware, as has been justly written, that "patriotism does not consist in aiding Government in every base or stupid act it may perform, but rather in paralyzing its power when it violates vested rights, affronts insulted justice, and assumes undelegated authority," and knowing that the so-called army, reported to be on its way to Utah, was an undisguised mob, if not sent by the President of the United States, and if sent by him in the manner and for the purpose alleged in all the information permitted to reach us, was no less a mob, though in the latter event acting under colour of law, upon learning its near approach, I issued, as in constitutional duty bound, a Proclamation, expressly forbidding all bodies of armed men, under whatsoever name or by whomsoever sent, to come within the bounds of this Territory. That so-called army, or, more strictly speaking, mob, refused to obey that Proclamation, copies of which were officially furnished them, and prosecuted their march to the neighbourhood of Forts Bridger and Supply, (which were vacated and burnt upon their approach,) where it is said they intend to winter. Under these circumstances, I respectfully suggest that you take such measures as your enlightened judgment may dictate, to insure public tranquility and protect, preserve, and perpetuate inviolate those inalienable constitutional rights which have descended to us -- a rich legacy from our forefathers.

A civilized nation is one that never infringes upon the rights of its citizens, but strives to protect and make happy all within its sphere, which our Government, above all others, is obligated to accomplish, though its present course is as far from that wise and just path as the earth is from the sun. And, under the aggravated abuses that have been heaped upon us in the past, you and the whole people are my witnesses that it has more particularly fallen to my lot, and been my policy and practice to restrain rather than urge resistance to usurpation and tyranny on the part of the enemies to the Constitution and Constitutional laws, (who are also our enemies and the enemies of all republics and republicans,) until forbearance under such cruel and illegal treatment cannot well be longer exercised. No one has denied or wishes to deny the right of the Government to send its troops when, where, and as it pleases, so it is but done clearly within the authorities and limitations of the Constitution, and for the safety and welfare of the people: but when it sends them clearly without the pale of those authorities and limitations, unconstitutionally to oppress the people, as is the case in the so-called army sent to Utah, it commits a treason against itself, which commands the resistance of all good men, or freedom will depart our nation.

In compliance with a long-established custom in appointing officers not of the people's electing, which the Supreme Court of the United States would at once, in justice, decide to be unconstitutional, we have petitioned and petitioned that good men be appointed, until that hope is exhausted; and we have long enough borne the insults and outrages of lawless officials, until we are compelled, in self-defense, to assert and maintain that great constitutional right of the governed to officers of their own election and local laws of their own enactment. That the President and the counsellors, aiders and abettors of the present treasonable crusade against the peace and rights of a Territory of the United States may reconsider their course and retrace their steps, is earnestly to be desired. But, in either event, our trust and confidence are in that Being who at his pleasure rules among the armies of heaven and controls the wrath of the children of men; and most cheerfully should we be able to abide the issue.

Permit me to tender you my entire condence [confidence] that your deliberations will be distinguished by that wisdom, unanimity, and love of justice that have ever marked the counsels of our Legislative Assemblies, and the assurance of my hearty co-operation in every measure you adopt for promoting the true interest of a Territory beloved by us for its very isolation and forbidding aspect; for here, if anywhere upon this footstool of our God, have we the privilege and prospect of being able to secure and enjoy those inestimable rights of civil and religious liberty, which the beneficent Creator of all mankind has, in His mercy, made indefeasible, and perpetuate them upon a broader and firmer basis for the benefit of ourselves, of our children, and our children's children, until peace shall be restored to our distracted country.

BRIGHAM YOUNG.

The Army of Aggression of Illegal Sending Was of a Resistance to Enter the Capital City of Utah Territory by Territorial Governing Power

President Brigham Young
JD 5:210 September 6, 1857 SLC

On Friday evening, the 11th inst., two of the brethren who accompanied brothers Samuel W. Richards and George Snider from Deer Creek to 118 miles below Laramie, came in, and reported that soldiers and a heavy freight train were there encamped opposite to them and on the south side of the Platte. They could tell that they were soldiers, from the appearance of their carriages, waggons, tents, and mode of encampment. We did not learn anything very definite from these two brethren lately arrived.

Messrs. Russel and Waddle are freighting for Government, and some of their trains were scattered along to the Sweetwater. They have twenty-six waggons in each train, with a teamster and six yoke of oxen to a waggon. Some of those trains were on the Sweetwater when brother Samuel passed down, and quite a number of them are in advance of the soldiers. The brethren learned that Captain Van Vliet, Assistant Quartermaster, was coming on to purchase lumber and such things as might be needed for the army.

Last evening, brother John R. Murdock arrived direct from St. Louis. He left here with the mail on the 2nd day of July, and reached Independence in sixteen days, making by far the shortest trip on record, and in eighteen days-and-a-half from here landed in St. Louis. He tarried there till brother Horace S. Eldredge and brother Groesbeck had transacted some business, and then started up the river with a small train. On the 9th of August, brother Murdock left Atchison, K.T. Troubles were daily expected to break out in Kansas between the Republican, or Free State, and the pro-slavery parties; for which reason General Harney, with the cavalry, a portion of the infantry, and, I think, one or two companies of the Artillery, were detained there by orders from Washington, and Colonel Johnston ordered to assume the command of the army for Utah.

Some fifteen or sixteen hundred infantry started from Leavenworth; and when brother Murdock passed them, one hundred miles below Laramie, about five hundred had deserted, leaving, as he was told, about one thousand men on their way to this place. He passed a few freight trains, which were entirely deserted by the teamsters, and Russel and Waddle were not able to hire teamsters to bring those trains forward.

Brother Murdock did not think that they could get here this fall, unless we helped them in. Their teams are pretty good, but they are very much jaded. Their mule teams are in better condition, because they regularly feed them on grain.

From the time that I heard that the President of the United States had issued orders for soldiers to come here, they have had my best faith that the Lord would not let them get here. I have seen this people, when palsied with agues, fevers, and with various other diseases, hurled out of doors, driven away from their cellars full of potatoes, from their meal chests, from their cows, houses, barns, orchards, fields, and finally from their happy homes and all the comforts of life. I have seen that a good many times, and I pray that I may never see it again, unless it is absolutely necessary for the welfare and advancement of God's purposes on the earth. I want to see no more suffering. I will not use the word suffering, for I call it joy instead of sorrow, affliction, and suffering. If we live our religion and exercise faith, it is our firm belief that it is our right to so exercise our united faith that our enemies never can come here, unless the Lord in his providence sees that it will be for our good.

It is my faith and feelings that, if we live as we should live, they cannot come here; but I am decided in my opinion that, if worse comes to worst, and the Lord permits them to come upon us, I will desolate this whole Territory before I will again submit to the hellish corruption and bondage the wicked are striving to thrust upon us solely for our exercising our right of freedom of conscience.***

Orson F. Whitney
History of Utah, Volume 1 Page 631

At all events, no delay was now made in taking action calculated to convince the troops and the Government which sent them that Brigham Young and his people were in earnest, and that not without a struggle to prevent would they permit the army now east of the Wasatch Mountains to invade and occupy their valley homes. At the same time it was determined to shed no blood, to take no life if it could possibly be avoided. Such were the orders issued to the militia.***

It was a bloodless campaign that the Mormons were resolved upon, even against the armed force which they believed had been sent to kill or drive them from their homes, debauch their wives and daughters, and despoil them of all that life held dear. Moreover, the plan of that campaign had been matured in the leading councils of the Church at Salt Lake City, weeks before General Wells went to the front.

On the return of the messengers with Colonel Alexander's reply, they were invited to dine with the Lieutenant-General. During the progress of the meal he asked Major Lot Smith if he thought he could take a few men and turn back the Government supply trains that were on the way, or burn them?

"I think I can do anything that you tell me to," was the confident reply.

Pleased with the ready response, General Wells then said: "I can furnish you only a few men, but they will be sufficient, for they will seem many more to the enemy. As for provisions, none will be supplied, as you are expected to board at the expense of Uncle Sam."

Lot Smith understood the order, and the program laid out was much to his liking. Utterly devoid of fear, with a physique and a will of iron, he was admirably fitted for just such a daring and dangerous feat as the one proposed. Forty-three men were given him, Captain Horton D. Haight and Lieutenants Thomas Abbott and John Vance being his subordinate officers, and at 4 o'clock p. m. of October 3rd they set out toward Green River.

Orson F. Whitney
History of Utah, Volume 1 Page 638

Thus it was that Lot Smith burnt the Government trains. It was a daring act in itself, but not more daring than the order which directed it. If the Mormons were accused of treason before they had done anything affording the shadow of a basis for such a charge, and an army had been sent against them to suppress a rebellion which never existed, what would now be said and done in view of events that had actually taken place? But Brigham Young and his compeers were perfectly aware of the risk they were running. They had entered upon the campaign with their eyes wide open. An investigation, a hearing was what they desired. It had hitherto been denied them.***...President Buchanan, on finding that the Mormons were in earnest, and that in their efforts to maintain their rights they dared even burn Government property and paralyze for the time being the arm lifted to strike them, was finally constrained, after the first burst of indignation was over, to order an investigation into the Utah situation.

Brigham Young Meeting With Peace Commissioners June 12, 1858

President Brigham Young
History of Utah, Volume 1 Page 683

"I have listened very attentively to the Commissioners, and will say, as far as I am concerned, I thank President Buchanan for forgiving me, but I really cannot tell what I have done. I know one thing, and that is, that the people called 'Mormons' are a loyal and a law-abiding people, and have ever been. Neither President Buchanan nor any one else can contradict the statement. It is true, Lot Smith burned some wagons containing Government supplies for the army. This was an overt act, and if it is for this we are to be pardoned, I accept the pardon.

* * * * * * * * *

"What has the United States Government permitted mobs to do to us? Gentlemen, you cannot answer that question! I can, however, and so can thousands of my brethren. We have been whipped and plundered; our houses burned, our fathers, mothers, brothers, sisters and children butchered and murdered by the scores. We have been driven from our homes time and time again; but have troops ever been sent to stay or punish those mobs for their crimes? No! Have we ever received a dollar for the property we have been compelled to leave behind? Not a dollar! Let the Government treat us as we deserve; this is all we ask of them. We have always been loyal, and expect to so continue; but, *hands off!* Do not send your armed mobs into our midst. If you do, we will fight you, as the Lord lives! Do not threaten us with what the United States can do, for we ask no odds of them or their troops. We have the God of Israel -- the God of battles on our side; and let me tell you, gentlemen, we fear not your armies.

* * * * * * * * *

"Now let me say to you Peace Commissioners, we are willing those troops should come into our country, but not to stay in our city. They may pass through it, if needs be, but must not quarter less than forty miles from us.

"If you bring your troops here to disturb this people, you have got a bigger job than you or President Buchanan have any idea of. Before the troops reach here, this city will be in ashes, every tree and shrub will be cut to the ground, and every blade of grass that will burn shall be burned.

"Our wives and children will go to the canyons, and take shelter in the mountains; while their husbands and sons will fight you; and, as God lives, we will hunt you by night and by day, until your armies are wasted away. No mob can live in the homes we have built in these mountains. That's the program, gentlemen, whether you like it or not. If you want war, you can have it; but, if you wish peace, peace it is; we shall be glad of it."

President Brigham Young
JD 5:337 October 18, 1857 SLC

Should we ever be obliged to leave our houses, the decree of my heart is that there shall naught be left for our enemies but the ashes of all that will burn. [The congregation responded, "Amen."] They shall not have my house nor my furniture, as they have had hitherto.***

We have sought for peace all the day long; and I have sought for peace with the army now on our borders, and have warned them that we all most firmly believe that they are sent here solely with a view to destroy this people, though they may be ignorant of that fact. And though we may believe that they are sent by the Government of the United States, yet I, as Governor of this Territory, have no business to know any such thing until I am notified by proper authority at Washington. I have a right to treat them as a mob, just as though they had been raised and officered in Missouri and sent here expressly to destroy this people. We have been very merciful and very lenient to them. As I informed them in my unofficial letter, had they been those mobocrats who mobbed us in Missouri, they never would have seen the South Pass. We had plenty of boys on hand, and the mode of warfare they would have met with they are not acquainted with.***

Colonel Alexander preached to me a little, stating in his letter, "I warn you that the bloodshed in this contest will be upon your head." But that warning gave me no thought. But if the blood of those soldiers is shed, it will be upon the heads of their officers.***

I wish the people to hasten and gather together and secure all that they have raised in the fields; and when this little skirmish is over, I am going to instruct the people to begin to prepare for going into the mountains, also to raise their grain another year, and to secure that which we now have by putting it where our enemies cannot find it.

You want to know where you can go. I know of places enough where I can hide this people and a thousand times more, and our enemies may hunt till doomsday and not be able to find us.

I do not know but we shall call upon

the sisters to go into the fields and raise potatoes while their husbands go out to war; and if they can do that, then perhaps we will see whether they can go into the fields and raise wheat while their husbands are defending Zion. In such an operation we shall call for volunteers; we shall have no compulsion about it.***

The President of the United States, his Cabinet, the Senate, the House of Representatives, the priests of the various religious sects and their followers have joined in a crusade to waste away the last vestige of truth and righteousness from this earth, and especially from this part of it. Yes, they have joined together; and we have to maintain truth and righteousness, virtue and holiness, or they will be driven from the earth. With us, it is the kingdom of God, or nothing; and we will maintain it, or die in trying, -- though we shall not die in trying. It is comforting to many to be assured that we shall not die in trying, but we shall live in trying. We will maintain the kingdom of God, living; and if we do not maintain it, we shall be found dying not only a temporal, but also an eternal death. Then take a course to live.***

We are free. There is no yoke upon us now, and we will never put it on again. [The congregation responded, "Amen."] That is the way for every man and woman to feel.***

You hear a great many people talk about a virtuous life. If you could know what an honourable, manly, upright, virtuous life is, you might reduce it to this -- Learn the will of the Lord and do it; for he has the keys of life and death, and his mandates should be obeyed, and that is eternal life.

President Brigham Young
Millennial Star 32:577 July 25, 1870

I will just relate a little of the history of this people. When they commenced in the East the war of James Buchanan against the Latter-day Saints, they sent the flower of the army here, with the best outfit any army had ever had in this Republic up to that time. What for? To use the Saints up. The army and the hangers-on amounted to 17,000 men. We then said to the North, "give up," but did not say to the South, "keep not back." The North gave up. Every family was on the move; they marched through this city south. We calculated to march south to where our women and children could live and take care of our stock, and we would wait in the mountains, and burn everything. That was the watchword. Our tinder and every material that could be was got into the houses, so that a single match would burn every house in this city, and then continue on until they would cease to pursue us, and if they inhabited these valleys they should have them as naked as we took them. And the North did give up; they gave up willingly. They had good houses and good farms, and they were ready to cut down every green tree. You may say such a course was not necessary. It was not necessary for us to be forced to it.

President Buchanan Pardons Brigham Young

President Brigham Young
JD 11:322 February 10, 1867

We had to leave, and we have come here into these mountains, and do you think we are going to be swallowed up by our enemies? Why, they have already done their uttermost. "Could they not send a hundred thousand men here to destroy the 'Mormons?'" Yes; that is, they could try. In the winter of 1857-58, when the army was at Bridger, Col. Kane came here to see what he could do for the benefit of the people, and to caution and advise me. He was all the time fearful that I would not take the right step, and that I would do something or other that would bring upon us the ire of the nation. "Why," said he, "at one word there would be a hundred thousand men ready to come here." I replied that "I would like to see them trying it." Afterwards a calculation was made that, for men to come here, -- tarry through the winter and get back the next summer, it would require four and a half oxen to carry the food, clothing, and ammunition necessary for each man. This was more stock than they could take care of, to say nothing about fighting. I was resolved that they would find nothing here to eat, nor houses to live in, for we were determined that we would not leave a green thing, and if I had time not one adobie should be left standing on another. I was satisfied that if Col. Kane could see what I saw, he would know that the weight of such an army would be so ponderous that it would crush itself, and it could never get here. It is just so now, too.

James Buchanan did all he could do, and when he found he could do nothing, he sent a pardon here. What did he pardon us for? He was the man that had transgressed the laws, and had trampled the Constitution of the United States under his feet. We had neither transgressed against the one nor violated the other. But we did receive his pardon, you know, and when they find out they can do nothing they will be sending on their pardons again.

President Brigham Young
JD 7:56 June 27, 1858 Provo

What is the present situation of affairs? For us the clouds seem to be breaking. Probably many of you have already learned that General Johnston passed through Great Salt Lake City with his command under the strictest discipline. Not a house, fence, or side-walk has been infringed upon by any of his command. Of course, the camp-followers are not under his control; but so far as his command is concerned while passing through the city, he has carried out his promises to the letter.

Crusade Against Celestial Plural Marriage

Congress Passes an Anti-Polygamy Act -- 1862

Orson F. Whitney
History of Utah, Volume 2 Page 59

But there was also another barrier to Utah's admission [into statehood], and probably at this period it was the main objection in the minds of the majority of congressmen. It was the Mormon practice of plural marriage -- polygamy -- which the Republican party, now in power, in its original platform had coupled with slavery and stigmatized them as "twin relics of barbarism." It was rather too much to expect that the Republicans, now in the overwhelming majority in Congress, and consequently having the power to invest Utah with statehood if they so desired, would use that power in her behalf, in view of their recent declaration against polygamy, thereby placing a cudgel in the hands of their political opponents from whom they had but just succeeded in wresting the reins of national authority. Had the Mormons been willing to abandon polygamy in 1862, thus meeting the Republican party half way, it is not improbable that Utah, in view of her loyal attitude, might have been admitted into the Union; provided of course that the bug-bear of an alleged union of Church and State, of priestly influence in the politics of the Territory, had not acted as a deterrent to those who, barring these considerations, professed to be friendly to her people.

Possibly it was to help solve this problem, -- to assist the Mormons to arrive at a conclusion to forsake the plural wife practice and "be like the rest" of the nation, as to monogamy, divorce, etc., that a bill was introduced in Congress in the spring of this same year, only a few weeks after the action of the State Convention of Deseret, to punish and prevent the practice of polygamy in the Territories, and, as afterwards appeared, to disincorporate the Church of Jesus Christ of Latter-day Saints. If this hypothesis be correct, the Mormons were to receive equal rights with and be treated like the rest of American citizens, if they would put away their Mormonism and thenceforth cease to be a distinct people. General Clark, at Far West, in 1838, had made them essentially the same offer.

The bill in question was introduced in the House of Representatives on the 8th of April, 1862, by Justin S. Morrill, of Vermont. It was read twice and referred to the Committee on Territories. Being reported back on April 28th with a recommendation that it pass, the bill -- H. R. No. 391 -- was again read.***

Orson F. Whitney
History of Utah, Volume 2 Page 61

The anti-polygamy bill, having passed the House, came up in the Senate on the 3rd of June.***

The yeas and nays were ordered, and being taken, resulted -- yeas 37, nays 2.***

So the bill was passed.

The title was amended so as to read, "A bill to punish and prevent the practice of polygamy in the Territories of the United States and other places, and disapproving

and annulling certain acts of the Legislative Assembly of the Territory of Utah."***

In the House of Representatives, June 30, 1862 --

Mr. Granger, from the Committee on Enrolled Bills, reported as a truly enrolled bill an act (H. R. 391) to punish and prevent the practice of polygamy in the Territories of the United States and other places, and disapproving and annulling certain acts of the Legislative Assembly of the Territory of Utah.

President Abraham Lincoln Signs the Anti-Polygamy Act

It has often been stated that the anti-polygamy act of 1862, became law without the signature of President Lincoln. This is an error, as the following paragraph of the record already quoted from will testify:

"In the House of Representatives, July 2, 1862 --

"A message was received from the President of the United States, informing the House that he had approved and signed an act (H. R. 391) to punish and prevent the practice of polygamy in the Territories of the United States and other places, and disapproving and annulling certain acts of the Legislative Assembly of the Territory of Utah." The full text of this enactment was as follows:

The Morrill Bill

Be it enacted, etc.:

That every person having a husband or wife living, who shall marry any other person, whether married or single, in a Territory of the United States, or other place over which the United States have exclusive jurisdiction, shall, except in the cases specified in the proviso to this section, be adjudged guilty of bigamy, and, upon conviction thereof, shall be punished by a fine not exceeding five hundred dollars, and by imprisonment for a term not exceeding five years. *Provided nevertheless,* That this section shall not extend to any person by reason of any former marriage whose husband or wife by such marriage shall have been absent for five successive years without being known to such person within that time to be living; nor to any person by reason of any former marriage which shall have been dissolved by the decree of a competent court; nor to any person by reason of any former marriage which shall have been annulled or pronounced void by the sentence or decree of a competent court on the ground of nullity of the marriage contract.

And be it further enacted:

SEC. 2. That the following ordinance of the provisional government of the State of Deseret, so called, namely: "An ordinance incorporating the Church of Jesus Christ of Latter-day Saints, passed February eight, in the year eighteen hundred and fifty-one, and adopted, re-enacted, and made valid by the Governor and Legislative Assembly of the Territory of Utah, by an act passed January nineteen, in the year eighteen hundred and fifty-five, entitled "An act in relation to the compilation and revision of the laws and resolutions in force in Utah Territory, their publication, and distribution," and all other acts and parts of acts heretofore passed by the said Legislative Assembly of the Territory of Utah, which establish, support, maintain, shield, or countenance polygamy, be, and the same hereby are, disapproved and annulled: *Provided,* That this act shall be so limited and construed as not to affect or interfere with the right 'of property legally acquired under the ordinance heretofore mentioned, nor with the right' to worship God according to the dictates of conscience, 'but only to annul all acts and laws which establish, maintain, protect or countenance the practice of polygamy, evasively called spiritual marriage, however disguised by legal or ecclesiastical solemnities, sacraments, ceremonies, consecrations, or other contrivances.

And be it further enacted:

SEC. 3. That it shall not be lawful for any corporation or association for religious or charitable purposes to acquire or hold real estate in any Territory of the United States during the existence of the territorial government of a greater value than fifty thousand dollars; and all real estate acquired or held by any such corporation or association contrary to the provisions of this act shall be forfeited and escheat to the United States: *Provided,* That existing vested rights in real estate shall not be impaired by the provisions of this section.

Thus was passed the first direct Congressional enactment against the Mormon Church. As will be seen, the anti-polygamy act of 1862 remained, as predicted by Senator McDougall, a dead letter upon the statute books of the nation; only one conviction being secured under it in twenty years, and that of a man who, for test-case purposes, furnished the evidence which convicted him. That man was George Reynolds, of Salt Lake City. This law, however, was the forerunner of other acts of Congress, also directed against Mormonism, which have wrought, in these later days, great changes in Utah.

Utah Legislature Petitions Congress to Repeal the Anti-Polygamy Act

Orson F. Whitney
History of Utah, Volume 2 Page 173

In January, 1867, the Legislative Assembly memorialized Congress for the repeal of the anti-polygamy act of 1862. The reasons assigned for the request were: that according to the faith of the Latter-day Saints plurality of wives was a divine doctrine, as publicly avowed and proclaimed by the Church ten years before the passage of said act; that the doctrine had not been adopted for lustful purposes but from conscientious motives; that the enactment of the law whose repeal was desired was due, it was believed, to misrepresentation and prejudice, which the people of Utah had deplored and exerted themselves to the utmost to remove; that the Judiciary of the Territory had not tried any case under the anti-polygamy law, though repeatedly urged to do so by those who were anxious to test its constitutionality;*** The memorial stated that the Territory, as the fruit of plural marriages, had enjoyed an unexampled immunity from the vices of prostitution and its kindred evils, and for all these reasons Congress was asked to grant the prayer of the memorial, leave the people free to exercise their religion and its ordinances, and thus promote the peace and welfare of the country and frown down the insidious attempts that were being made to array the inhabitants of one section against those of another, because of differences in religious belief.***

At the same time a Representative to Congress for the State of Deseret was to be chosen, and the Constitution of the State, as amended, to be voted upon by the people.*** The amended Constitution of Deseret was adopted, and Hon. William H. Hooper was re-elected delegate to Congress, and chosen also Representative for the State of Deseret. The memorials for the repeal of the anti-polygamy act and the admission of Deseret into the Union, were soon afterwards conveyed to Washington.

The Wade Bill

Orson F. Whitney
History of Utah, Volume 2 Page 210

In this connection appropriate reference may be made to what is known as the Wade bill, which, although it never passed, was introduced and considered in Congress at the very time that militia companies from nearly all parts of the Territory were performing valiant and uncomplaining service against the savages. The bill takes its name from its parent, Senator Ben Wade, and its introduction, in June, 1866, created far less discussion than so radical a measure would have provoked during any other than the exciting times of the reconstruction period. The bill is worthy of note as embodying within itself nearly all the important items of special legislation since enacted in various Congressional laws affecting Utah affairs. It provided for the appointment by the Government of probate judges, the selection of juries and the service of process by the United States Marshal, the regulating of the marriage ceremony -- which was declared to be a civil contract -- and the recording of certificates; it declared the illegality of church divorces or marriages; required the Trustee-in-Trust of the Mormon Church to annually make a full report of all Church properties, real and personal; held acknowledgment of the marital relation in prosecutions for polygamy to be proof of cohabitation; and aimed at the entire abolition of the prevailing militia system by giving to the Governor the power to select, appoint and commission all officers, either civil or military; to organize and discipline the militia in such manner and at such times as he might direct, and to make all rules and regulations for the enrolling and mustering thereof; it further declared that "all commissions and appointments, both civil and military, heretofore made or issued, or which may be made or issued before the 1st day of January, 1867, shall cease and determine on that day, and shall have no effect or validity thereafter." As a matter of history this much notice of the sweeping measure is interesting. To comment upon it, since it went into early obscurity, would be obviously unprofitable.

Letter Written by John Taylor in Response to a Speech Given by the Vice-President of the United States

Apostle John Taylor Defends Celestial Marriage Before the Nation in Letters to the Newspapers

President John Taylor
History of Utah, Volume 2 Page 339

AMERICAN HOUSE, BOSTON, MASS.
October 20th, 1869.

To the Editor of the Deseret Evening News,

DEAR SIR: -- I have read with a great deal of interest the speech of the Hon. Schuyler Colfax, delivered in Salt Lake City, October 5th, containing strictures on our institutions, as reported in the Springfield *Republican*, wherein there is an apparent frankness and sincerity manifested. It is pleasant, always, to listen to sentiments that are bold, unaffected and outspoken; and however my views may differ -- as they most assuredly do -- from those of the Hon. Vice-President of the United States, I cannot but admire the candor and courtesy manifested in the discussion of this subject; which, though to him perplexing and difficult, is to us an important part of our religious faith.

I would not, however, here be misunderstood; I do not regard the speech of Mr. Colfax as something indifferent or meaningless. I consider that words proceeding from a gentleman occupying the honorable position of Mr. Colfax, have their due weight. His remarks, while they are courteous and polite, were evidently calmly weighed and cautiously uttered, and they carry with them a significance, which I, as a believer in Mormonism, am bound to notice; and I hope with that honesty and candor which characterize the remarks of this honorable gentleman.

Mr. Colfax remarks:

"I have no strictures to offer as to your creeds on any really religious question. Our land is a land of civil and religious liberty, and the faith of every man is a matter between himself and God alone; you have as much right to worship the Creator, through a President and Twelve Apostles of your Church organization, as I have through the ministers and elders and creed of mine; and this right I would defend for you with as much zeal as the right of any denomination throughout the land."

This certainly is magnanimous and even-handed justice, and the sentiments do honor to their author; they are sentiments that ought to be engraven on the heart of every American citizen.

He continues:

"But our country is governed by law, and no assumed revelation justifies any one in trampling on the law."

At first sight this reasoning is very plausible, and I have no doubt that Mr. Colfax was just as sincere and patriotic in the utterance of the latter as the former sentences; but with all due deference permit me to examine these words and their import.

That our country is governed by law we all admit; but when it is said that "no assumed revelation justifies any one in trampling on the law;" I should respectfully ask, what! not if it interferes with my religious faith, which you state "is a matter between God and myself alone?" Allow me, sir, here to state that the assumed revelation referred to is one of the most vital parts of our religious faith; it emanated from God and cannot be legislated away; it is part of the "Everlasting Covenant" which God has given to man. Our marriages are solemnized by proper authority; a woman is sealed unto a man for time and for eternity, by the power of which Jesus speaks, which "sealed on earth and it is sealed in heaven." With us it is "Celestial Marriage;" take this from us and you rob us of our hopes and associations in the resurrection of the just. This is not our religion? You do not see things as we do. You marry for time only, "until death does you part." We have eternal covenants, eternal unions, eternal associations. I cannot, in an article like this, enter into details, which I should be pleased on a proper occasion to do. I make these remarks to show that it is considered, by us, a part of our religious faith, which I have no doubt did you understand it as we do, you would defend, as you state, "with as much zeal as the right of every other denomination throughout the land." ***

I have, sir, written the above in consequence of some remarks which follow:

"I do not concede that the institution you have established here, and which is condemned by the law, is a question of religion."

Now, with all due deference, I do think that if Mr. Colfax had carefully examined our religious faith he would have arrived at other conclusions. In the absence of this I might ask, who constituted Mr. Colfax a judge of my religious faith? I think he has stated that "the faith of every man *is a matter between himself and God alone.*"

Mr. Colfax has a perfect right to state and feel that he does not believe in the revelation on which my religious faith is based, nor in my faith at all; but has he the right to dictate my religious faith? I think not; he does not consider it religion, but it is nevertheless mine.

If a revelation from God is not a religion, what is?

His not believing it from God makes no difference; I know it is. The Jews did not believe in Jesus but Mr. Colfax and I do; their unbelief did not alter the revelation.

Marriage has from time immemorial, among civilized nations, been considered a religious ordinance. It was so considered by the Jews. It is looked upon by the Catholic clergy as one of their sacraments. It is so treated by the Greek Church. The ministers of the Episcopal Church say, in their marriage formula, "What *God has joined together,* let not *man* put asunder;" and in some of the Protestant churches their members are disfellowshiped for marrying what are termed unbelievers. So I am in hopes, one of these times, should occasion require it, to call upon our friend, Mr. Colfax, to redeem his pledge:

"To defend for us our religious faith, with as much zeal as the right of every other denomination throughout the land." ***

But permit me here to return to the religious part of our investigations; for if our doctrines are religions, then it is confessed that Congress has no jurisdiction in this case and the argument is at an end. Mr. Webster defines religion as "*any system of faith and worship,* as the religion of the Turks, of Hindoos, of Christians." I have never been able to

look at religion in any other light. I do not think Mr. Colfax had carefully digested the subject when he said, "I do not concede that the institution you have established here, and which is condemned by law, is a question of religion."

Are we to understand by this that Mr. Colfax is created an umpire to decide upon what is religion and what is not, upon what is true religion and what is false? If so, by whom and what authority is he created judge? I am sure he has not reflected upon the bearing of this hypothesis, or he would not have made such an utterance.

According to this theory no persons ever were persecuted for their religion, there never was such a thing known. ***

You say we complain of persecution. Have we not cause to do it? Can we call our treatment by a milder term? Was it benevolence that robbed, pillaged and drove thousands of men, women and children from Missouri? Was it Christian philanthropy that after robbing, plundering, and ravaging a whole community, drove them from Illinois into the wilderness among savages?

When we fled as outcasts and exiles from the United States we went to Mexican territory. If not protected we should have been at least unmolested there. Do you think, in your treaty with Mexico, it was a very merciful providence that placed us again under your paternal guardianship? Did you know that you called upon us in our exodus from Illinois for 500 men, which were furnished while fleeing from persecution, to help you to possess that country; for which your tender mercies were exhibited by letting loose an army upon us, and you spent about forty millions of dollars to accomplish our ruin? Of course we did not suffer; "religious fanatics" cannot feel; like the eels the fishwoman was skinning, "we have got used to it." Upon what pretext was this done? Upon the false fabrications of your own officers, and which your own Governor Cumming afterward published as false. Thus the whole of this infamous proceeding was predicated upon falsehood, originating with your own officers and afterwards exposed by them. Did Government make any amends, or has it ever done it? Is it wrong to call this persecution? We have learned to our cost "that the king can do no wrong." Excuse me, sir, if I speak warmly. This people have labored under accumulated wrongs for upwards of thirty years past, still unacknowledged and unredressed. I have said nothing in the above but what I am prepared to prove. What is all this for? Polygamy? No -- that is not even pretended.

Having said so much with regard to Mr. Colfax's speech, let me now address a few words to Congress and to the nation. I hope they will not object for I too am a teacher. And first let me inquire into the law itself, enacted in 1862. The revelation on polygamy was given in 1843, nineteen years before the passage of the Congressional act. We, as a people, believe that revelation is true and came from God. This is our religious belief; and right or wrong it is still our belief; whatever opinions others may entertain it makes no difference to our religious faith. The Constitution is to protect me in my religious faith, and other persons in theirs, as I understand it. It does not prescribe a faith for me, or any one else, or authorize others to do it, not even Congress. It simply protects us all in our religious faiths. This is one of the Constitutional rights reserved by the people. Now who does not know that the law of 1862 in relation to polygamy was passed on purpose to interfere with our religious faith? This was as plainly and distinctly its object as the proclamation of Herod to kill the young children under two years old, was meant to destroy Jesus; or the law passed by Pharaoh in regard to the destruction of the Hebrew children, was meant to destroy the Israelites. If a law had been passed making it a penal offense for communities, or churches, to forbid marriage, who would not have understood that it referred to the Shaking Quakers, and to the priories, nunneries and the priesthood of the Catholic Church? This law, in its inception, progress and passage, was intended to bring us into collision with the United States, that a pretext might be found for our ruin. These are facts that no honest man will controvert. It could not have been more plain, although more honest, if it had said the Mormons shall have no more wives than one. It was a direct attack upon our religious faith. ***

Do statesmen and politicians realize what they are doing when they pass such laws? Do they know, as before stated, that resistance to the law means force, that force means an army, and that an army

means death? They may yet find something more pleasant to reflect upon than to have been the aiders and abettors of murder, to be stained with the blood of innocence, and they may try in vain to cleanse their hands of the accursed spot.

It is not the first time that presidents, kings, congresses and statesmen have tried to regulate the acts of Jehovah. Pharaoh's exterminating order about the Hebrew infants was one of acknowledged policy. They grew, they increased too fast. Perhaps the Egyptians had learned, as well as some of our eastern reformers, the art of infanticide; they may have thought that one or two children was enough and so destroyed the balance. They could not submit to let nature take its vulgar course. But in their refined and polite murders, they found themselves dwindling and decaying, and the Hebrews increasing and multiplying; and no matter how shocking it might be to their refined senses, it stood before them as a political fact, and they were in danger of being overwhelmed by the superior fecundity of the Hebrews. Something must be done; what more natural than to serve the Hebrew children as they had served their own? and this, to us and the Christian world, shocking act of brutal murder, was to them simply what they may have done among themselves; perhaps more politely *a la Madam Restelle*, but not more effectually. The circumstances are not very dissimilar. When Jesus was plotted against by Herod and the infants put to death, who could complain? *It was law*: we must submit to *law*. The Lord Jehovah, or Jesus the Savior of the world, has no right to interfere with *law*. Jesus was crucified *according to law*. Who can complain? Daniel was thrown into the den of lions strictly *according to law*. The king would have saved him, if he could; but he could not resist law. The massacre of St. Bartholomew was in accordance with *law*. The guillotine of Robespierre of France, which cut heads off by the thousand, did it according to *law*. What right had the victims to complain? But these things were done in barbarous ages. Do not let us, then, who boast of our civilization, follow their example; let us be more just, more generous, more forbearing, more magnanimous. We are told that we are living in a more enlightened age. Our morals are more pure (?) our ideas more refined and enlarged, our institutions more liberal. "Ours," says Mr. Colfax, "is a land of civil and religious liberty, and the faith of every man is a matter between himself and God alone," providing God don't shock our moral ideas by introducing something that we don't believe in. If He does let Him look out. We won't persecute, very far be that from us; but we will make our platform, pass Congressional laws and make you submit to them. We may, it is true, have to send out an army, and shed the blood of many; but what of that? It is so much more pleasant to be proscribed and killed according to the laws of the Great Republic, in the "asylum for the oppressed," than to perish ignobly by the decrees of kings, through their miserable minions, in the barbaric ages.

My mind wanders back upwards of thirty years ago, when in the State of Missouri, Mr. McBride, an old gray-haired venerable veteran of the Revolution, with feeble frame and tottering steps, cried to a Missouri patriot: "Spare my life, I am a Revolutionary soldier, I fought for liberty, would you murder me? What is my offense, I believe in God and revelation?" This frenzied disciple of a misplaced faith said, "take that, you God d---d Mormon," and with the butt of his gun he dashed his brains out, and he lay quivering there, -- his white locks clotted with his own brains and gore on that soil that he had heretofore shed his blood to redeem -- a sacrifice at the shrine of liberty! Shades of Franklin, Jefferson and Washington, were you there? Did you gaze on this deed of blood? Did you see your companion in arms thus massacred? Did you know that thousands of American citizens were robbed, disfranchised, driven, pillaged and murdered? for these things seem to be forgotten by our statesmen. Were not these murderers punished? Was not justice done to the outraged? No. They were only Mormons, and when the Chief Magistrate was applied to, he replied: "Your cause is just, but I can do nothing for you." Oh, blessed land of religious freedom! What was this for. Polygamy? No. It was our religion then, it is our religion now. Monogamy or polygamy, it makes no difference. Let me here seriously ask: have we not had more than enough blood in this land? Does the insatiate moloch still cry for more victims?

Let me here respectfully ask with all sincerity, is there not plenty of scope for the action of government

at home? What of your gambling hells? What of your gold rings, your whisky rings, your railroad rings, manipulated through the lobby into your Congressional rings? What of that great moral curse of the land, that great institution of monogamy -- *Prostitution?* What of its twin sister -- *Infanticide?* I speak to you as a friend. Know ye not that these seething infamies are corrupting and destroying your people? and that like the plague they are permeating your whole social system? that from your gilded palaces to your most filthy purlieus, they are festering and stewing and rotting? What of the thirty thousand prostitutes of New York City and the proportionate numbers of other cities, towns and villages, and their multitudinous pimps and paramours, who are, of course, all, all, honorable men! Here is ample room for the Christian, the philanthropist, and the statesman. Would it not be well to cleanse your own Augean stables? What of the blasted hopes, the tortured and crushed feelings of the thousands of your wives whose whole lives are blighted through your intrigues and lasciviousness? What of the humiliation of your sons and daughters from whom you can not hide your shame? What of the thousands of houseless and homeless children thrown ruthlessly, hopelessly and disgracefully upon the world as outcasts from society, whose fathers and mothers are alike ashamed of them and heartlessly throw them upon the public bounty, the living memorials of your infamy? What of your infanticide, with its murderous, horrid, unnatural, disgusting and damning consequences? Can you legislate for these monogamic crimes, or shall Madam Restell and her pupils continue their public murders and no redress? Shall your fair daughters, the princesses of America, ruthlessly go on in sacrificing their noble children on the altar of this Moloch -- this demon? What are we drifting to? This "bonehouse," this "powder magazine" is not in Salt Lake City, a thousand miles from your frontiers; it is in your own cities and towns, villages and homes. It carouses in your secret chambers, and flaunts in the public highway; it meets you in every corner, and besets you in every condition. Your infirmaries and hospitals are reeking with it; your sons and daughters, your wives and husbands are degraded by it. It extends from Louisiana to Minnesota, and from Maine to California. You can't hide yourselves from it; it meets you in your magazines and newspapers, and is disgustingly placarded on your walls, -- a living, breathing, loathsome, festering, damning evil. It runs through your very blood, stares out your eyes and stamps its horrid mark on your features, as indelibly as the mark of Cain; it curses your posterity, it runs riot in the land, withering, blighting, corroding and corrupting the life blood of the nation.

Ye American Statesmen, will you allow this demon to run riot in the land, and while you are speculating about a little political capital to be made out of Utah, allow your nation to be emasculated and destroyed? Is it not humiliating that these enormities should exist in your midst, and you, as statesmen, as legislators, as municipal and town authorities, as clergymen, reformers and philanthropists, acknowledge yourselves powerless to stop these damning crimes that are gnawing at the very vitals of the most magnificent nation on the earth? We can teach you a lesson on this matter, polygamists as we are. You acknowledge one wife and her children; what of your other associations unacknowledged? We acknowledge and maintain all of our wives and all of our children; we don't keep a few only, and turn the others out as outcasts, to be provided for by orphan asylums, or turned as vagabonds on the street to help increase the fearfully growing evil. Our actions are all honest, open and above board. We have no gambling halls, no drunkenness, no infanticide, no houses of assignation, no prostitutes. Our wives are not afraid of intrigues and debauchery; nor are our wives and daughters corrupted by designing and unprincipled villains. We believe in the chastity and virtue of women, and maintain them. There is not today, in the wide world, a place where female honor, virtue and chastity, are so well protected as in Utah. Would you have us, I am sure you would not, on reflection, reverse the order of God, and exchange the sobriety, the chastity, the virtue and honor of our institutions, for yours, that are so debasing, dishonorable, corrupting, defaming and destructive? We have fled from these things, and with great trouble and care have purged ourselves from your evils, do not try to legislate them upon us nor seek to engulf us in your damning vices.

You may say it is not against your purity that we contend; but against polygamy, which we consider a crying evil. Be it so. Why then, if your system is so much better, does it not bring forth better fruits? Polygamy, it would seem, is the parent of chastity, honor and virtue; Monogamy the author of vice, dishonor and corruption. But you would argue these evils are not our religion; we that are virtuous, are as much opposed to vice and corruption as you are. Then why don't you control it? We can and do. You have your Christian associations, your Young Men's associations, your Magdalen and Temperance associations, all of which are praiseworthy. Your cities and towns are full of churches, and you swarm with male and female lecturers, and ministers of all denominations. You have your press, your National and State Legislatures, your police, your municipal and town authorities, your courts, your prisons, your armies, all under the direction of Christian monogamists. You are a nation of Christians. Why are these things not stopped? You possess the moral, the religious, the civil and military power but you don't accomplish it. Is it too much to say, "Take the beam out of thine own eye and then shalt thou see clearly to remove the mote that is in thy brother's."

RESPECTFULLY, ETC.,

JOHN TAYLOR.

The Cragin and Cullom Bills -- 1870

Orson F. Whitney
History of Utah, Volume 2 Page 391

It was during the winter of 1869-70 that the measures known as the Cragin and Cullom bills were introduced into Congress.*** This was the beginning of a long series of such conspiracies by cabals of local anti-Mormons -- Federal officials and others -- with politicians at the nation's capital, to secure special Congressional legislation against the Mormon people. Here, indeed, was the virtual origin of the Utah "ring" -- child and successor of the Connor-Harding "regenerating" combination -- which obtained within the next ten years so much notoriety. The so-called "ring" was the head and front of the Gentile wing of the Liberal Party.

The sponsor of the Cragin bill was Senator Aaron H. Cragin of New Hampshire. He introduced his measure in the Senate early in December, 1869, but this, it seems, was its second presentation, it having been before Congress during the previous winter. It was a bill of forty-one sections, several more than were comprised in the Wade bill, which it resembled, though differing from it in some respects, and being deemed by the Mormons even more odious and detestable. Said the *Deseret News* of Senator Cragin's literary protege: "With the exception that it does not inflict the death penalty, no edict more thoroughly hateful and oppressive was ever concocted against the Hebrew children by Nebuchadnezzar, or the followers of Jesus by Nero."

Section ten of the bill gave the Governor the sole right to select, appoint and commission all officers of the Territory, excepting constables elected or appointed under the Territorial laws.

Section twenty-one abolished trial by jury in a certain class of cases, in that it provided that all criminal cases arising under the anti-polygamy act of 1862, "as well as all criminal cases arising under this act" -- and it was made criminal for a Mormon to solemnize marriages, to counsel or advise the practice of plural marriage, or to be present at "the ceremony of sealing" -- should be heard, tried and determined by the district courts without a jury.

Section twenty-seven virtually made the Governor of the Territory the Trustee-in-Trust of the Mormon Church; at least it required the Trustee-in-Trust to report to the Governor annually the amount, description and location of all properties and monies belonging to the Church.

Section thirty-six provided that the United States District Attorney and Marshal should attend to all Territorial business in the district courts, in lieu of the Territorial Attorney and Marshal -- which offices were abolished -- and be paid for such services out of the Territorial treasury.

Section thirty-seven provided that for the purpose of holding district courts the United States Marshal might take possession of any court house, council house, town house or other public building in Utah and furnish the same in a suitable manner for holding court, at the expense of the Territory.

Section forty took away the functions of the Legislature in relation to the jails and prisons of the Territory and bestowed them upon the Governor, who was empowered to make rules and regulations for said prisons, and appoint and remove at pleasure the wardens and other officers thereof.

Section forty-one repealed all acts or parts of acts of the United States or of Utah Territory inconsistent with this act, and made it unlawful and a misdemeanor for the Legislature of the State of Deseret to assemble, or for an election to be held for any member of said legislature or any officer under said State government.

There were many other objectionable features to the bill, but these were the most formidable. The measure *in toto* was summarized by the *News* as follows: "No American citizen who is a Mormon has any rights -- he is not a free man but a slave, to be tried, convicted, fined, imprisoned, at the will of his masters -- to be made to pay taxes, but to have those funds spent by his masters in persecuting and torturing him, and enriching them for the service -- to wear the form of man, but to have none of the privileges of manhood -- to have no right to believe the Bible, practice its precepts, follow its examples, or to worship its God."***

Mass Meeting of Mormon Women

Some time before the latter event, here in Utah was enacted a scene upon which Gentile civilization gazed with wide-eyed wonder; a mass meeting of Mormon women assembling in the Tabernacle at Salt Lake City and protesting against the passage of the Cullom bill. Three thousand of the so-called "down-trodden women of Mormondom," alleged slaves and playthings of a "polygamic hierarchy," eloquently and earnestly declaiming and resolving against the striking off of those fetters with which Christian statesmen, orators and editors insisted that they were bound.*** Strange as it may seem, the Mormon women, quite as much as the Mormon men, have upheld plurality of wives as a divine principle and conscientiously insisted upon the right of their husbands and fathers to practice it.

But to the mass meeting and its proceedings. It occurred on the 13th of January, 1870, soon after the introduction of the Cullom bill into Congress. The weather was inclement, but the Old Tabernacle, where the gathering was held, and which would comfortably seat about three thousand persons, was densely packed with ladies of all ages.***

Resolved, That we, the ladies of Salt Lake City, in mass-meeting assembled, do manifest our indignation, and protest against the bill before Congress, known as "the Cullom bill," also the one known as "the Cragin bill," and all similar bills, expressions and manifestoes.

Resolved, That we consider the above named bills foul blots on our national escutcheon -- absurd documents -- atrocious insults to the honorable executive of the United States Government, and malicious attempts to subvert the rights of civil and religious liberty.

Resolved, That we do hold sacred the constitution bequeathed us by our forefathers, and ignore, with laudable womanly jealousy, every act of those men to whom the responsibilities of government have been entrusted, which is calculated to destroy its efficiency.

Resolved, That we unitedly exercise every moral power and every right which we inherit as the daughters of American citizens, to prevent the passage of such bills, knowing that they would inevitably cast a stigma on our republican government by jeopardizing the liberty and lives of its most loyal and peaceful citizens.

Resolved, That, in our candid opinion, the presentation of the aforesaid bills indicates a manifest degeneracy of the great men of our nation; and their adoption would presage a speedy downfall and ultimate extinction of the glorious pedestal of freedom, protection, and equal rights, established by our noble ancestors.

Resolved, That we acknowledge the institutions of the Church of Jesus Christ of Latter-day Saints as the only reliable safeguard of female virtue and innocence; and the only sure protection against the fearful sin of prostitution, and its attendant evils, now prevalent abroad, and as such, we are and shall be united with our brethren in sustaining them against each and every encroachment.

Resolved, That we consider the originators of the aforesaid bills disloyal to the constitution, and unworthy of any position of trust in any office which involves the interests of our nation.

Resolved, That, in case the bills in question should pass both Houses of Congress, and become a law, by which we shall be disfranchised as a Territory, we, the ladies of Salt Lake City, shall exert all our power and influence to aid in the support of our own State government.

This meeting of "the sisters" was but the initial to many such held in various parts of the Territory during the next few days, all protesting in a similar manner against the passage of the Cullom bill.***

The Cullom Bill Passes the House of Representatives

Orson F. Whitney
History of Utah, Volume 2 Page 426

The Cullom bill, shorn of some of its repulsive features, but retaining a sufficient number of them to make it a hideous enactment, passed the House of Representatives by a vote of ninety-four to thirty-two. The parts omitted were Section 11, making the lawful wife of an accused polygamist a competent witness against him; Section 14, providing that the statute of limitations should be no bar to a prosecution; Section 30, authorizing the confiscation of the property of persons convicted; Section 31, for the temporary relief of persons reduced to destitution by the enforcement of the act, and Section 32, authorizing the employment of forty thousand volunteers to assist in its enforcement.

The news of the passage of the act by the House, being telegraphed to Utah, created a profound sensation. There was no excitement, at least none of outward exhibition -- such would not have been characteristic of the Mormon people -- but to say that a deep and widespread sentiment of indignation if not of alarm was felt throughout the community, is but to state the simple truth. Mass meetings were held all over the Territory to protest against the action of the House, and appeal to the Senate to not permit the iniquitous measure to become law.***

The Cullom Bill Dies in the Senate

Orson F. Whitney
History of Utah, Volume 2 Page 439

The result of all these movements was that the Cullom Bill, after its passage by the House of Representatives, died, like its predecessor, the Cragin Bill, in the Senate, to the infinite satisfaction of the friends of Utah everywhere, and the corresponding chagrin and disappointment of her enemies.

Brigham Young's Arrest and Imprisonment -- October 2, 1871

Orson F. Whitney
History of Utah, Volume 2 Page 589

It was the purpose, in short, to indict and try Brigham Young and other leading Mormons, not for polygamy, under the Congressional act of 1862, but for adultery, or at least lewd and lascivious cohabitation, under the laws of the Territory.

Orson F. Whitney
History of Utah, Volume 2 Page 592

It was late in the afternoon of Monday, October 2nd, 1871, that a warrant of arrest was served by U.S. Marshal Patrick upon President Brigham Young, at his residence in Salt Lake City. He was charged with lewd and lascivious cohabitation with his plural wives.*** Having been ill for several days, and at the time of his arrest being unable to leave the house, he was permitted by the kindness of the Marshal, who performed his duty in this instance in a delicate and gentlemanly manner, to remain in his own home, a deputy being left in charge of the distinguished prisoner.

Judge McKean's Remarkable Decision

Orson F. Whitney
History of Utah, Volume 2 Page 598

Finally on October 12th, [1871] Judge McKean rendered his decision, portions of which are here presented:***

It is therefore proper to say, that while the case at bar is called, *"The People versus Brigham Young"* its other and real title is, *"Federal Authority versus Polygamic Theocracy."*

The Poland Bill -- 1874

Orson F. Whitney
History of Utah, Volume 2 Page 738

On the 5th of January, 1874, Mr. Poland, of Vermont, introduced in the House a bill "relative to courts and judicial offices in the Territory of Utah." This was the nearest attempt to conform to the recommendations in the President's message, and as its provisions discriminated against the majority of the citizens of the Territory in various respects, it was vigorously opposed. The Legislature of Utah was now in session, and endeavored to ward off the proposed legislation by Congress. With this purpose in view, a memorial was unanimously adopted, denying the accusations of disloyalty made against the majority of the people of Utah and earnestly soliciting the sending of a commission of investigation, and the suspension, pending its labors and until it had rendered its report, of all action in the nature of special legislation toward this Territory.

This memorial was presented to Governor Woods for his signature, but on February 4th he returned it with a caustic veto message, accusing the legislators of the Territory of enacting improper laws. Said he: "To ask, or expect me to join you in condemning my own official acts, pronouncing them 'absolutely untrue,' and made 'with malicious intent,' is a sad commentary upon the judgment and good taste of those who ask it. That I cannot do so is certain."

The memorial, however, came before Congress, being presented by Delegate Cannon on the 16th of February. It doubtless had a measure of effect in the direction intended by the memorialists, although the House Judiciary Committee, on February 21st, expressed its opposition to the commission, and agreed to report the Poland bill. On March 2nd, Delegate Cannon introduced into the House a bill for an enabling act for the people of Utah to frame a State government.* [Footnote: This bill failed to pass, as did also one of a similar nature introduced into the House of Representatives on December 21st, 1875. The last mentioned was supported by a petition from the ladies of Utah. This bore 23,626 signatures, and in addition to the request that Utah be given statehood asked that Congress repeal the anti-polygamy law.]

Matters went along till May, with efforts for and against Utah, until, early in that month, Mr. Poland withdrew his proposed measure and presented one still further modified. This was amended and became a law on the 23rd of June. It repealed the laws of Utah respecting the Territorial Marshal and Attorney-General, and placed the powers and duties of those officers upon the United States Marshal and District Attorney. Certain judgments and decrees of the probate courts -- those already executed, and those rendered, the time to appeal from which had expired -- were confirmed, but the jurisdiction of such courts was thenceforth to be limited to the settlement of estates of decedents and to matters of guardianship and divorce. The jurisdiction of justices' of the peace was slightly extended, and the appointment, by the Territorial Supreme Court, of United States Commissioners, authorized. Certain fees to Federal officials were made payable out of the Territorial treasury. Appeals were allowed to the United States Supreme Court in bigamy and polygamy trials, as well as in cases involving capital punishment, and the drawing of grand and petit jurors was placed in the hands of the Probate Judge and the Clerk of the District Court. This gave non-Mormons equal representation on the jury list with the Mormons, though the latter were greatly in the majority in the Territory.

President Brigham Young Imprisoned for "Contempt of Court" March 1875

The Ann Eliza Case -- Brigham Young's "Nineteenth Wife" Sues for Divorce

Orson F. Whitney
History of Utah, Volume 2 Page 757

On the 28th of July, 1873, a divorce suit had been planted in the court presided over by Judge McKean. The plaintiff was Mrs. Ann Eliza Webb Young, the alleged nineteenth wife of President Brigham Young, who was made the party defendant. Besides a decree of divorce and permanent support for herself and her children, the plaintiff asked for alimony and sustenance *pendente lite*, or during the progress of the litigation.***

In answer to the complaint the defendant interposed as follows. He denied that the plaintiff was or ever had been his legal wife, though he admitted that on the 6th of April, 1868, he had married her as a plural wife according to the rites of the Church of Jesus Christ of Latter-day Saints, of which they were both members. He had been advised since their marriage, though he was not aware of it at that time, that the plaintiff had never been divorced from her former husband, James L. Dee, whom she wedded on the 10th of April, 1863. Consequently the said James L. Dee, who was living, was still her lawful husband. The defendant further alleged that on the 10th of January, 1834, at the town of Kirtland, Ohio, he had been duly and lawfully married to Mary Ann Angell, who was still living and had ever since been his lawful wife.***

On August 25th of the latter year the defendant's answer was filed, and in September following arguments were made upon the motion to grant temporary alimony and counsel fees. It was not until the 25th of February, 1875, nineteen months after the filing of the plaintiff's petition, that the question of alimony *pendente lite* was ruled upon. On that day Judge McKean gave a lengthy decision covering the point, and on the ensuing day issued an order of court conformatory thereto. He directed that the defendant pay to the plaintiff the sum of three thousand dollars to defray the expenses of prosecuting her suit, and that he also pay to her for her maintenance and the maintenance and education of her children the further sum of five hundred dollars per month, to commence from the date upon which the complaint was filed. Ten days were given the defendant in which to pay the three thousand dollars, attorney's fees, and twenty days in which to pay nine thousand five hundred dollars, accumulated alimony for the period of nineteen months. Thereafter he was to pay five hundred dollars on the first day of every month during litigation in the case. An exception was taken by the defense, and on the 8th of March, ten days after the issuance of the order, an appeal to the Supreme Court of the Territory was perfected.

At the expiration of the time within which the defendant was required to conform to that part of the decision relative to the payment of the three thousand dollars, attorney's fees, no such payment having been made, the plaintiff's counsel obtained an order of attachment requiring the defendant to come into court and show cause why he should not be punished for contempt. President Young, on the morning of the 11th of March, appeared personally and by his attorneys in the District Court and made answer accordingly. The answer, which was read by Mr. P. L. Williams, stated that the respondent had been advised by his counsel that he was by law entitled to an appeal from the decree of the 25th of February, and that pending the determination of such appeal the execution of the court's order might be stayed; that an appeal to the Supreme Court of the Territory had been taken and perfected, and that his omission and failure to comply with the said order was owing wholly to his desire to obtain the benefit of his appeal. The respondent disclaimed all intention or disposition to disregard or treat contemptuously any process of the court, and prayed that further proceedings in execution of the order relative to the payment of fees and alimony be stayed until the determination of the appeal.***

Judge McKean then wrote out and read the following order:

***It is therefore, because of the facts and premises, ordered and adjudged that defendant is guilty of disobedience to the process of the Court, and is therein guilty of contempt of Court.

And since the Court has not one rule of action where conspicuous and another where obscure persons are concerned; and since it is a fundamental principle of the Republic that all men are equal before the law; and since this Court desires to impress this great fact, this great law upon the minds of all the people of this Territory:

Now, therefore, because of the said contempt of Court, it is further ordered and adjudged, that the said Brigham Young do pay a fine of twenty-five dollars, and that he be imprisoned for the term of one day.

Done in open Court, this 11th day of March, 1875,

JAMES B. MCKEAN,
Chief Justice and Judge of the
Third District Court.

President Young Spends One Day in Prison

As soon as the reading was ended Attorney McBride requested the court to so amend the order as to cause the defendant to be imprisoned until the fees were paid. The Judge replied that he would let the future take care of itself. The three thousand dollars were paid to the plaintiff's attorneys by Mr. James Jack, President Young's chief clerk, just after the rendering of the decision.

With the calm dignity so characteristic of him, particularly in the presence of a crisis, President Young received the sentence passed upon him by Judge McKean. The same quiet demeanor which he had worn all through the proceedings ending in the indignity so ungenerously put upon him, was manifested as he arose and left the court room in custody of U.S. Deputy Marshal A. K. Smith. Entering his carriage, which had remained in waiting, the President, accompanied by his guard, was driven to his own residence, where he ate dinner, supplied himself with bedding, clothing and such other articles as he might need while in prison, and was then conveyed through a heavy snow storm to the Penitentiary. Mayor Wells, Dr. S. B. Young and Mr. William A. Rossiter accompanied the President and Deputy Marshal Smith, and remained at the Warden's house over night. Many other friends of the prisoner drove out to the Penitentiary during the afternoon, and a small host of sympathizing adherents, awaiting the hour of his deliverance, found lodgings at every available place in the vicinity. The President was at first locked in a cell -- the only one that the institution afforded -- with murderers, thieves and other convicted criminals, or men awaiting trial for alleged crimes; but this was only until better quarters could be provided for his reception. In a short time he was transferred to a room adjoining the Warden's house, where he passed the night in comparative comfort. He received from his guard all the courtesies that could consistently be granted under the circumstances. Between twelve and one o'clock next day, Friday, March 12th, -- the brief term of imprisonment having expired -- the prison gates swung open, and the freed captive, surrounded by a multitude of friends, was escorted back to the city.

The Testimony of President John Taylor Concerning President Brigham Young

President John Taylor
JD 19:138 October 14, 1877 SLC

Before the Prophet Joseph departed, he said, on one occasion, turning to the Twelve, "I roll the burden of this kingdom

on to you," and, on another occasion, he said their place was next to that of the First Presidency, and he wished them to take their place that he might attend to other duties, such as translating, etc. At the time he was taken away he was in the bloom of life and the vigor of health, and although his departure was sudden and unexpected our organization rendered it no difficult matter to decide who should assume the leadership of the Church. There was no difficulty in the matter; it was understood that the duty rested on the Twelve. Why? The revelation stated that the Twelve were to hold the keys of the kingdom in connection with the First Presidency, which were handed down under various circumstances. You will find in the history of the Prophet Joseph Smith, that this matter is made perfectly plain. He said there was no authority or power of presidency over the Twelve except the First Presidency, and where he was not there was no presidency over the Twelve. Hence President Brigham Young said, when the Prophet Joseph was taken away, "Thank God the keys of the kingdom are not taken from us," and being head of the Twelve, he assumed his position and so acted on the authority he held and according to the rules laid down. Thus there was no scattering, confusion or difficulty that might otherwise have existed if the organization of the Church had not been perfect.

President John Taylor
JD 1:229 April 8, 1853 SLC

Who have we for our ruling power? Where and how did he obtain his authority? Or how did any in this Church and kingdom obtain it? It was first obtained by a revelation from the Lord of the Universe, by the opening of the heavens, by the voice of God, and by the ministering of holy angels. It is by the voice of God and the voice of the people, that our present President obtained his authority. Many people in the world are talking about mis-rule and mis-government. If there is any form of government under the heavens where we can have legitimate rule and authority, it is among the Saints. In the first place, we have a man appointed by God, and, in the second place, by the people. This man is chosen by yourselves, and every person raises his hand to sanction the choice. Here is our President, Brigham Young, whom we made choice of yesterday, who is he? He is the legitimate ruler among this people.

President John Taylor
JD 5:189 August 30, 1857 SLC

The kingdom is put upon the shoulders of President Young and this people to carry it out, and by whom? By the Lord God -- by him who holds dominion throughout the universe; by him who created all by the word of his power; by him who said, "Let there be light, and there was light;" by him who spake, and the worlds rolled into existence. By him you received rights that are not of this world -- rights that flow from the great Eloheim.

President John Taylor
JD 5:263 September 20, 1857 SLC

Well, then, we are taught our duty to our God by our brethren. And who are our brethren? The officers and authorities of this Church -- the servants of the living God. Who is President Young? The mouthpiece of God to this Church and to the world. Has God any other? Yes, lots of them appointed by him, but he is the head.

President John Taylor
JD 7:325 October 7, 1859 SLC

When you hear a man talk against the authorities of this Church and kingdom, you may know he is sliding down hill. He does not know what spirit influences him; he is ignorant that he is in the dark; and, unless he retraces his steps quickly, he will go overboard. You may set that down as a fact all the time. Why? Because, if this is the Church and kingdom of God, and President Young is the elect of God, and his Council and the Twelve and others are the elect of God, and you seek to injure them, you run a great risk, and will be found fighting against God; for Jesus says, "He that receiveth you receiveth me, and he that receiveth me receiveth him that sent me; and he that rejecteth you rejecteth me, and he that rejecteth me rejecteth him that sent me."

President John Taylor
JD 19:123 October 7, 1877 SLC

Brigham Young needs no factitious aid to perpetuate his memory; his labors have been exhibited during the last forty-five years in his preaching, in his writing, in his counsels, in the wisdom and intelligence he has displayed, in our exodus from Nauvoo; in the building of cities throughout the length and breadth of this Territory, in his opposition to vice and his protection of virtue, purity and right. These things are well known and understood by the Latter-day Saints, and also by thousands and millions of others. But, as with his predecessor, Joseph Smith, who had to leave, while we are called upon to mourn a President dead, angels announce a President born in the eternal worlds; he has only gone to move in another state of existence.

Chapter 3

Administration of President John Taylor

Defense of the Celestial Law of Holy Union

The Celestial Law Defended as a Constitutional Religious Right

President John Taylor
JD 20:317 October 6, 1879 SLC

I was asked, "Do you believe in obeying the laws of the United States?" "Yes I do, in all except one" -- in fact I had not broken that. "What law is that?" "The law in relation to polygamy." "Well, why do you except that one?" "Because," I replied "it is at variance with the genius and spirit of our institution; because it is at variance with the Constitution of the United States; and because it is in violation of the law of God to me." The United States Supreme Court, however, since that time has made it a law of the land, that is, it has sanctioned it; it was not sanctioned at that time, that question was not then decided. We are here to-day, gathered together according to the word and law of God and the commandments of God to us. "Gather my Saints together unto me," says one of the old prophets, "those that have made a covenant with me by sacrifice." "I will take you," says another, "one of a city and two of a family, and I will bring you to Zion, and I will give you pastors according to mine heart, which shall feed you with knowledge and understanding." Now, the servants of God in these last days have been sent out as they were in former days to gather the people, and the Lord has given us this law -- the [Celestial Law] -- among other things, and I know it before God and can bear testimony of it, if nobody else knows it. I know that it came from God, and that God is its author. But there are hundreds and thousands of others who have a knowledge of the same thing; but I speak of it in this wise to testify before God, angels and men, before this nation and all other nations that it came from God. That is the reason that I speak of it, that I may bear my testimony to you and to the nations of the earth. Now, then, about the result of it; that is with God and with the people. It is for us to do the will of God; it is for the Lord to bring about the results in his own way.

George Q. Cannon
JD 20:38 July 7, 1878 SLC

What is the crime of which the people of Utah are accused? It is that of marrying women! It is not that of seducing or debauching them. All the pains and penalties inserted in bills before Congress for the punishment of the "Mormon" people are affixed to the marriage of women. This is made a crime, and because of it, it is proposed to punish men. Not one word of condemnation, nor penalty of any character, is proposed for the seducer, or the vile betrayer of female innocence;***...but the man who marries women, and maintains them honorably and virtuously, sustaining family and parental relations in all purity and sacredness, is to be disfranchised and visited with other pains and penalties!

First Place of My Union Eternal Being Required to be of Full Exalting

Joseph F. Smith
JD 20:28 July 7, 1878 SLC

Some people have supposed that the doctrine of plural marriage was a sort of superfluity, or non-essential to the salvation or exaltation of mankind. In other words, some of the Saints have said, and believe, that a man with one wife, sealed to him by the authority of the Priesthood for time and eternity, will receive an exaltation as great and glorious, if he is faithful, as he possibly could with more than one. I want here to enter my solemn protest against this idea, for I know it is false.*** The marriage of one woman to a man for time and eternity by the sealing power, according to the law of God, is a fulfillment of the celestial law of marriage in part...*** But this is only the beginning of the law, not the whole of it. Therefore, whoever has imagined that he could obtain the fullness of the blessings pertaining to this celestial law, by complying with only a portion of its conditions, has deceived himself. He cannot do it.***

Saints Encouraged to Endure the Persecutions

President John Taylor
JD 25:87 February 10, 1884 SLC

The carnal mind knows not the things of God, and is not subject to the law of God, neither can it be. They form all kinds of opinions, even, with regard to our gathering. "Why don't you stop at home as other folks do?" Some say that it is an emigration scheme gotten up to make money, and that missionaries are sent out by us to deceive the weak and the ignorant, and to gather them together that they may be made merchandise of. That is one idea. You all know how far that is true, and how far it is false. Others say that we are gathered here for licentious purposes -- to carry out polygamic ideas, to corrupt, demoralize, and trample under foot the women who come and associate with us, and to destroy their virtue; whereas you know there is not a place in the world where women are better protected and their virtue

more sacredly guarded than in Utah. They compare plural marriage to their whoredom, seductions, their social evils, and the many kinds of iniquity, corruption and rottenness that prevail among themselves. Reasoning from their own standpoint, they consider that we are a very wicked, corrupt and licentious people. But according to the statistics that we have pertaining to these matters, our immorality is twenty to forty times less than theirs here in our midst, without going any further. The crimes, iniquities and corruptions committed by the small minority of outsiders in our midst very far exceed, perhaps by twenty to thirty times, the crimes of the Latter-day Saints. This excess of crime on the part of outsiders is what might be reasonably expected; for we profess to be a better people, and we ought to be a better people than those who make no pretentions to be guided by divine revelation. Examine the records of our city jail, of the Penitentiary, of the county prisons, which have been published and are being published, and you will find a full statement in relation to these matters and the per cent of crime that exists between one and the other.***

Speaking of the doctrine of the plurality of wives, I remember talking with one of our Presidents -- I mean one of the Presidents of the United States -- on this subject in Washington, a number of years ago, as I have with others since on the same subject; but I remember some of the remarks made on that occasion. "Well," said he, after talking some little on politics, and one thing and another, "what about your polygamy?" "Mr. Pierce," said I, -- I can mention his name now as it is a thing of the past -- "it may be possible that some of us may have wrong ideas in regard to these things. We read about such a man as Abraham, who is described as 'the friend of God;' we read about such a man as David, who is described as 'a man after God's own heart:' we read about Jacob, who had twelve sons, whose names are to be written upon the twelve gates of the holy city. Who was Jacob? He was a man who had several wives, by whom he had these twelve sons. Then we read of Moses -- a man of God, a leader of Israel, and a law-giver. He told the people how they should treat their children whether by the first wife or by the second, and how all these matters were to be arranged. "Mr. Pierce," said I, "It is possible that we of the nineteenth century, have not been able to instruct the Lord very much in regard to these matters. Probably He knew just as much about them then as we do now, and that in regard to our marital laws, we have made some mistakes. "Well," said Mr. Pierce, "I cannot say." Of course he coul [could] not.

Crusade of Government Powers Against Celestial Law of Eternal Marriage During John Taylor's Administration

The George Reynolds Case October 23, 1874 -- January 6, 1879 Declared Constitutional by the United States Supreme Court

Orson F. Whitney
History of Utah, Volume 3 Page 45

The opening of the year 1879 brought with it a very important decision from the Supreme Court of the United States. It was the final decree in the celebrated Reynolds case, involving the constitutionality of the anti-polygamy law of 1862. This was the first effectual move made by the Federal Government against what the Gentiles termed "the Mormon power." Though the immediate result was not momentous in a general way, the defendant in the case and those dependent upon him being the only ones seriously affected, it nevertheless had an indirect bearing upon the fortunes of the whole Mormon community, foreshadowing as it did a radical change in the policy of the Government toward Utah, and constituting a precursor of the great crusade inaugurated under the Edmunds law.***

Ever since the enactment of the anti-polygamy law, in 1862, the Mormon people and many others had considered it unconstitutional, being violative, as they believed, of one of the cardinal principles upon which the United States Government was founded, the principle of religious liberty. This opinion was held by some of the leading statesmen and jurists of America. The reader need not be told that the Constitution, in its first amendment, declares: "Congress shall make no law respecting an establishment of religion, or prohibiting the free exercise thereof." Nor is it necessary to state to those who have followed this narrative to the present point, that at the time Congress created the law in question, plurality of wives was a portion of the Mormon religion, and had been proclaimed as such, at the seat of government, ten years previously; Apostle Orson Pratt, in the year 1852, having taken a special mission to the city of Washington for that purpose. Consequently this law was looked upon, especially by the Latter-day Saints, as unconstitutional and therefore void. They believed that such would be the decision of the court of last resort, as soon as a case involving the principle at issue should come fairly and squarely before that tribunal. So confident were they in relation to this matter that many leading Mormons, including President Young himself, repeatedly expressed the wish that a test case might be passed upon by the Supreme Court at Washington.

The local representatives of the Government, despairing of accomplishing much toward the extirpation of polygamy, as the law and public sentiment in Utah then stood, were no less desirous that such a case might be brought. In the summer of 1874 negotiations were opened between the Mormon authorities and the United States Attorney, Mr. Carey, and it was arranged that the case should be provided. Mr. Carey and his assistants were preparing at this very time to launch a series of prosecutions for polygamy against prominent Mormons, who, though it was known that they could not be legally convicted, -- their polygamous relations being of older standing than the law under which it was proposed to prosecute them, -- had nevertheless been singled out as targets for a vain though vigorous onslaught.

The District Attorney agreed that if a test case were furnished, these proceedings should all be dropped. This circumstance no doubt expedited the subsequent arrangement. It was stipulated that the defendant in the case should produce the evidence for his own indictment and conviction, and it was generally understood that the infliction of punishment in this instance would be waived. Only the first half of the arrangement was realized. The defendant in the test case, George Reynolds, supplied the evidence upon which he was convicted, but his action did not shield him from punishment; though it doubtless had the effect of mitigating the same. Such was the inception of the Reynolds case, which had its origin on the 23rd of October, 1874, when the first indictment was found therein.

Elder George Reynolds, the person selected to be the defendant in the celebrated

case which bears his name, is at the present time -- 1896 -- numbered with the general authorities of the Mormon Church, being one of the First Seven Presidents of the Seventies. At the beginning of these proceedings, however, he was not so conspicuous a character, though a man of some repute among his people in an official and literary way. He had been the private secretary of President Brigham Young. An Englishman by birth, a native of the city of London, he had been a Mormon since May, 1856, and a resident of Utah since 1865. He was thirty-two years of age and the husband of two wives when he stepped to the front to become the defendant in this *causa celebre*. His first wife, Mary Ann Tuddenham, was married to him on the 22nd of July, 1865; his second wife, Amelia Jane Schofield, on the 3rd of August, 1874. These facts were communicated to the Grand Jury of the Third District at the September term of the last named year. The result was his indictment for polygamy, or, as the law styled his offense, bigamy, on the 23rd of October. Three days later he went before the District Court, surrendered himself a prisoner and asked to be admitted to bail. According to previous agreement between U. S. Attorney Carey and the defendant's counsel, J. G. Sutherland, the bond was fixed at twenty-five hundred dollars.

The trial took place in the spring of 1875, beginning on the 31st of March and ending on the 1st of April. Judge Emerson presided, Messrs. Carey and Baskin prosecuted the case and Messrs. Sutherland, Bates and Snow defended it. The jury was composed of seven Mormons and five non-Mormons, namely, Joseph Siegel, Jesse West, George M. Ottinger, Albert W. Davis, William Naylor, DeWitt C. Thompson, Joseph Peck, S. F. Nuckolls, Samuel Bringhurst, M. B. Callahan, W. C. Morris and James McGuffy.

Among the witnesses was Mrs. Amelia J. Reynolds, the defendant's plural wife, who admitted the fact of their marriage on the 3rd of August, 1874. The ceremony, she stated, took place *** at Salt Lake City, President Daniel H. Wells officiating. The latter confirmed this statement, which was also conceded by the defense. The Judge having charged the jury, they retired to their room, but returned in about half an hour with the following verdict:

SALT LAKE CITY

April 1st, 1875.

We, the jury in the case of the People of the United States in the Territory of Utah *vs.* George Reynolds, indicted for polygamy, find a verdict of guilty, and recommend the prisoner to the mercy of the court.

SAMUEL BRINGHURST,

Foreman.

It was now discovered that the defendant, who had just been pronounced guilty, had not been arraigned before trial, and that the indictment had not been read to him. His counsel took advantage of this point, and moved an arrest of judgment and the setting aside of the verdict, preliminary to a motion for a new trial. The court granted the motion. Mr. Carey, though somewhat nonplussed, announced that he was ready to proceed immediately and re-try the case. This, however, was rendered unnecessary by the defendant, who waived the point and pleaded "Not guilty as charged in the indictment." Pending further proceedings Elder Reynolds was released in bonds of five thousand dollars. On the 10th of April the convicted man received his sentence, which was that he should be imprisoned in the Utah Penitentiary at hard labor for one year, and pay a fine of three hundred dollars. An appeal was taken to the Supreme Court of the Territory, where,

on the 19th of June, the decision of the District Court was reversed. The ground for reversal was the illegality of the Grand Jury which had found the indictment; it being composed of twenty-three instead of fifteen men, as required by law. Chief Justice Lowe by that time had arrived, and it was he, with Associate Justices Emerson and Boreman, who then composed the Supreme Court. Elder Reynolds was now released from his bonds.

During the progress and immediately after the close of the trial, the prosecution manifested considerable animus against the defendant. They even insisted that he be imprisoned pending his appeal to a higher court. Judge Emerson, however, would not yield to this demand. The reversal of the decision of the District Court served only to increase the bitterness of the prosecuting officers.

Elder Reynolds was again indicted in the fall of 1875, by a Grand Jury composed of seven Mormons and eight non-Mormons. The date of this indictment was October 30th. The witnesses upon whose testimony it was found were John and Mary Tuddenham, Daniel H. Wells, Amos K. Lucas and Arthur Pratt. The defendant was arrested on the 1st of November and was forthwith admitted to bail in the same sum as before. His second trial began on the 9th of December before Chief Justice Alexander White...*** The defendant having pleaded not guilty to the charge of bigamy, the trial began. It had become evident by this time that the U. S. Attorney, under the stress of anti-Mormon influence, had departed from his design to try the case purely as a test of the constitutionality of the law, and that it was the intention to fasten criminality upon the prisoner with a view to securing his punishment. Owing to this vindictive spirit, Mrs. Amelia J. Reynolds refused to appear as a witness, and was not found when the officers went in quest of her. The Court, however, permitted the prosecuting attorney to call the lawyers and other persons in attendance at the former trial, and accepted as evidence their testimony of what Mrs. Reynolds had stated at that time. The witnesses examined were John and Mary Tuddenham, Daniel H. Wells, Amos K. Lucas, John R. McBride, George R. Maxwell, Arthur Pratt, J. G. Sutherland, Hamilton Gamble, Orson Pratt, Sr., John Nicholson and John Sharp. The jury on the 21st of December found a verdict of guilty against the defendant, but recommended him to the mercy of the court. The judgment was that he be imprisoned at hard labor for a term of two years, and pay a fine of five hundred dollars. The defendant appealed to the Supreme Court of the Territory, where the case was heard on the 13th of June, 1876, Chief Justice Schaeffer then presiding. The decision of the lower court was unanimously affirmed.

As contemplated from the beginning an appeal was taken to the Supreme Court of the Nation, where, on the 14th of November, 1878, the case was argued, Messrs. G. W. Biddle, of Philadelphia, and Ben Sheeks, of Salt Lake City, appearing for the appellant, and Solicitor General Phillips for the Government. Two days were occupied by the arguments, and the case was then taken under advisement. The court's decision, which was unanimous, but for the non-concurrence of Associate Justice Field on a minor point, was delivered on the 6th of January, 1879. It was voiced by Chief Justice Waite. It confirmed the decisions of the lower courts, and declared constitutional the act of Congress making criminal the Mormon practice of plural marriage.

John Taylor With the Courage of Heaven

Orson F. Whitney
History of Utah, Volume 3 Page 50

A few days after the delivery of the decision a notable interview occurred between President John Taylor, the head of the Mormon Church, and Colonel O. J. Hollister, U. S. Collector of Internal Revenue for Utah, and correspondent of the New York Tribune. The meeting, which was solicited by Mr. Hollister, took place in the President's office at Salt Lake City, June 13, 1879. Besides the two principals, several prominent Mormons were present and took part in the conversation. Asked as to whether he took issue with Judge Waite's statement of the scope and effect of the amendment to the Constitution guaranteeing religious freedom, President Taylor answered in the affirmative. He then said:

PRESIDENT TAYLOR. A religious faith amounts to nothing unless we are permitted to carry it into effect. Congress and the Supreme Court are carrying out the same principles that were practised in the persecutions against the Huguenots in France, the Waldenses and Albigenses in Piedmont, the Non-conformists in England, and others who have been persecuted on account of their religion.*** They will allow us to think -- what an unspeakable privilege that is -- but they will not allow us the free exercise of that faith which the Constitution guarantees. Here is the injustice and the manifest breach of faith.

COLONEL HOLLISTER. Is it not true that marriage is the basis of society, that out of it spring the social relations, obligations and duties with which governments must necessarily concern themselves? And is it not therefore within the legitimate scope of the power of every civil government to determine whether marriage shall be polygamous or monogamous under its dominion?

PRES. T. I do not look upon it in that way. I consider that when the Constitution of the United

States was framed and adopted, those high contracting parties did positively agree that they would not interfere with religious affairs. Now, if our marital relations are not religious, what is? This ordinance of marriage was a direct revelation to us through Joseph Smith the Prophet.*** You may not know it, but I know that this is a revelation from God and a command to His people, and therefore it is my religion. I do not believe that the Supreme Court of the United States nor the Congress of the United States has any right to interfere with my religious views, and in doing it they are violating their most sacred obligations.

COL. H. My idea of religion is this: -- that man acknowledges, loves, reverences, worships and gives thanks to God; that constitutes religion. Worship may take various forms of expression, but where did it ever, how can it, take the form of marrying and raising families -- either single or plural families?

PRES. T. Mr. Hollister, are you a believer in the Bible?

MR. PENROSE. Mr. Hollister's question is answered by the Bible, which plainly says that marriage is ordained of God, etc.

PRES. T. Now, Mr. Hollister, I have so far answered your questions, will you answer mine?

COL. H. In one sense I do. I believe that part of the Bible that my reason approves of.

PRES. T. It would not be of any use arguing with you on this subject then; but as my opinions are desired for the public, I will state that I believe in the Bible, and believing in it, I believe in those principles therein set forth.

COL. H. If marriage can be legitimately called religion, what human relation or pursuit may not be so called? And if everything is religion, and the state is prohibited from interfering with it, what place is there left for the state?

* * * * * * * *

MR. P. That is easily answered. When one's religion assumes to interfere with the rights and liberties of others.

PRES. T. Whose rights do we interfere with? That is a question I was going to ask you.

COL. H. I consider that you interfere with men's rights and women's rights and children's rights.

PRES. T. How can we interfere with men's rights or with women's rights if all enter into it voluntarily?

COL. H. I think it interferes with the rights of men and women, because when a man marries a second woman, some other man must do without any.***

You believe that Mormonism will be universally received, but polygamy cannot become universal, because the sexes are born in about equal numbers. How can a principle, not of universal applicability, be philosophically sound, or sound in any sense?

MR. P. What need of going out of Utah?

COL. H. If you are going to defend polygamy as a sound philosophical principle, I don't see how you can avoid going out of Utah.

MR. P. But we only practice it as a part of our religion.

COL. H. But if it is a true principle it must be of universal applicability.

* * * * * * * *

PRES. T. These theories are too visionary and too far in the future. It is well known that there are scores of thousands of women in these United States who cannot obtain husbands and the same also in England and other Christian countries. And furthermore, we regard the plural order of marriage as being voluntary, both on the part of the man and the woman. If there should be any disparity, as you refer to -- if there should not be two wives for one man, why then he could not get them.

* * * * * * * *

COL. H. Viewed socially or philosophically, apart from all religious considerations, do you regard polygamy as worthy of perpetuation at the cost of perpetual antagonism between your people and their countrymen?

PRES. T. However we may respect the government and its institutions, I would respectfully say we are not the parties who produce this antagonism.*** Our revelation given in August,

1831, specifically states that if we keep the laws of God we need not break the laws of the land. Congress has since, by its act, placed us in antagonism to what we term an unconstitutional law, and it now becomes a question whether we should obey God or man.

COL. H. But in taking that position do you not set yourselves up as the judges of the Constitution, whereas the laws (Sec. 709 R. S.) make the Supreme Court the judge of the constitutionality of the laws of Congress?

PRES. T. Without any interpretations from the Supreme Court, I take it that the words themselves are explicit on this point. *** When the Constitution says Congress shall make no law respecting an establishment of religion or prohibiting the free exercise thereof, we take it to mean what it says. Congress, indeed, can pass laws, and the Supreme Court can sanction those laws; but while they have the power, being in the majority, the justice of those laws is another matter.

COL. H. Viewed as above, do you regard polygamy as superior to monogamy as the form or law of marriage, and if so wherein?

PRES. T. I consider it altogether superior to the law of monogamy in a great many particulars. First, I base it upon the will and command of God both in ancient and modern times; second, I base it upon the natural results of monogamy. There is in all monogamic countries, the United States not excepted, a terrible state of things arising from the practice of monogamy, infanticide and foeticide prevailing to an alarming extent. *** Polygamy protects its offspring; monogamy does not. How many are there now in Washington, New York, Chicago, Philadelphia and other cities, that make it a practice to cohabit with other women, to whom children are born, the results of their adultery, whom they do not acknowledge, but who are turned out upon the streets to become waifs in the shape of newsboys, street-sweepers, etc., outcasts and pariahs of society, augmenting also the criminal classes and the paupers, leaving other people to provide for their illicit offspring! And it is not an infrequent thing for such children, while engaged sweeping the street crossings, to ask their own fathers for a penny, the child not knowing the father nor the father the child.

COL. H. Do you consider these evils the necessary concomitants of monogamy more than of polygamy?

PRES. T. These are the results of monogamy, whether necessary or not, and these are the evils associated with it. We acknowledge our children, we acknowledge our wives; we have no mistresses. We had no prostitution here until it was introduced by monogamy, and I am now told that these other diabolical deeds are following in its train. The courts have protected these people in their wicked practices. We repudiate all such things, and hence I consider that a system that will enable a man to carry out his professions, and that will enable him to acknowledge his wife or wives and acknowledge and provide for his children and wives, is much more honorable than that principle which violates its marital relations, and, whilst hypocritically professing to be true to its pledges, recklessly violates the same and tramples upon every principle of honor, which sits down and coolly and deliberately decides how many children shall be murdered and how many shall live. The one, Mr. Hollister, is a great deal better system than the other.

*   *   *   *   *   *   *   *   *

You say you think it wise for the government to endeavor to suppress polygamy. I think they should first manifest their antagonism to the practice of infanticide and foeticide and the prevailing prostitution, and instead of prosecuting and proscribing us, they should assist us in removing these contaminating influences from our borders. Furthermore, while Great Britain is a monarchial government she can tolerate 180,000,000 of polygamists [in India] and throw around them the protecting aegis of the law, while the United States, a republican and professedly a free government, is enacting laws prosecuting and proscribing so small a number as 150,000 in her Territory.

*   *   *   *   *   *   *   *   *

Polygamy is not a crime, per se; it was the action of Congress that made polygamy a crime. As before stated, the British government allows one hundred and eighty millions of their people to practice it, and by law, protects them in it. It is very unfortunate that our republican government cannot be as generous to its provinces as a monarchial government can to its colonies.***

COL. H.   If you persist in the future as in the past in this practice, what kind of an ultimate outcome do you anticipate? Could you not consistently surrender polygamy on the ground that there is no prospect of changing the opinion and law of the country against it, and that nullification of the laws is sure to result disastrously in the end to the nullifiers?

PRES. T.   Not so much so as the nullification of the Constitution.***

MR. MUSSER.   I think the Lord could better answer that question.

COL. H.   "The Lord" is a foreign power to this government, in the sense in which you constantly refer to Him.

PRES. T.   I am afraid He is, and there lies the difficulty. When nations forsake God we cannot expect them to act wisely. In doing what they have done, they have opened the flood gates of discord to this nation which they cannot easily close. We are now proscribed, it will be others' turn next. Congress has assumed a most fearful responsibility in breaking down its Constitutional barrier.***

COL. H.   You hold, then, that your church possesses the oracles of heaven exclusively, and that the condemnation of polygamy by all Christian nations is without reason and wisdom, and contrary to the spirit of revelation?

PRES. T.   We most assuredly do.

*   *   *   *   *   *   *   *   *

COL. H.   Is not, in fact, what you call revelation, the expression of the crystallized public sentiment of your people; and if a majority of them should desire to abandon polygamy, would what is called revelation deter them from doing so?

MR. CALDER.   Mr. Colfax, when he was here, and as he was leaving, said to President Young, "Mr. Young, you say Joseph Smith had a revelation instituting polygamy; my advice to you is to get a revelation to do away with it."

COL. H.   My idea of revelation is embodied in my question. In your case I look upon it as the crystallized expression of the highest wisdom of

your people, speaking through your organ, the head of the Church.

*   *   *   *   *   *   *   *   *

PRESIDENT JOSEPH F. SMITH.   It is very unfair, Mr. Hollister, in you to even think that a people who have suffered as we have for our faith, having been driven five different times from our homes, and suffered even to martyrdom, should be insincere in our belief. Questions you have asked here repeatedly imply that we could get up revelations to suit ourselves.

*   *   *   *   *   *   *   *   *

COL. H.   What effect, on the whole, do you apprehend Chief Justice Waite's decision will have on the question?

PRES. T.   I don't know that it will have any effect, except to unite us and confirm and strengthen us in our faith.

As soon as the nature of the decision against Elder Reynolds became known, an effort was made to have the case reopened, on the ground that the sentence rendered included "hard labor," which was in excess of the law and the authority of the judge to pronounce. The Supreme Court refused to set aside the verdict and order the proceedings quashed, but on the ensuing 5th of May it issued a supplemental order to the following effect: "That this cause be and the same is hereby remanded to the said Supreme Court [of Utah Territory] with instructions to cause the sentence of the District Court to be set aside, and a new one entered on the verdict in all respects like that before imposed, except so far as it requires the imprisonment to be at hard labor." A mammoth petition, signed by over thirty-two thousand citizens of Utah, was now forwarded to Washington, setting forth the fact that the defendant's was a test case, and asking for his pardon by the Executive. President Hayes heeded not the petition.

On the 14th of June Elder Reynolds

was re-sentenced, and two days later, in custody of Deputy Marshals George A. Black and William T. Shaughnessy, set out for the State prison at Lincoln, Nebraska, whither he had been ordered by the Department of Justice. He remained at Lincoln twenty-five days -- during which time he was given the position of book-keeper of the prison -- and was then brought back to Utah.

Arriving at Salt Lake City on the 17th of July, he was at once conveyed to the Penitentiary, where he was held in confinement; serving out his full term, barring one hundred and forty-four days remitted on account of good behavior. He was kindly treated by Warden Butler and the guards, and spent much of his time in prison writing for the press and in teaching a school attended by the other convicts. His example and instructions had such a salutary effect that the warden was wont to say: "Reynolds is worth more than all the guards in keeping order among the prisoners." Repeated efforts were made to secure his pardon, Delegate Cannon doing all in his power to obtain it, and Marshal Shaughnessy also interesting himself in the prisoner's behalf; but all in vain. The President was deaf to every appeal for clemency. The captive remained in prison until January, 1881, suffering the full penalty pronounced against him, except the payment of his fine, which was remitted.

George Reynolds Case Was of a Full Destroying of the Way of Constitutional Guarantee of Religious Freedom

President Rulon Jeffs
Rulon Jeffs' Sermons 7:23 July 3, 1988 Sandy

The George Reynolds decision of 1879, when there was a deliberate case taken up to the Supreme Court of the United States, decided the issue not on the language of the Constitution of the United States, which says, "Congress shall make no law respecting the establishment of religion or prohibiting the free exercise thereof." The object of that case was the Cullom Bill passed by Congress, against the Constitution of the United States, prohibiting polygamy in the territories of the United States. And the Supreme Court upheld the constitutionality of the Cullom Bill, but they ignored the wording of the Constitution and went to the mores, or moralities of the day, saying simply that polygamy was an abomination under the morality of the day. And as far as it being a religious belief is concerned, the court said: "Yes, you can believe anything you want, but when it comes to the practice of it, if it collides with the mores of the day, we must give way to it;" and compared polygamy, practiced by the Latter-day Saints, to that of a cult, or religion which believed in human sacrifice, which they would not stand for. The one destroys life, the other brings life.

SECTION REVELATION 219

Revelation of the Lord Jesus Christ Palestine, Texas Monday, October 3, 2011

1. Thus saith the Lord to the powers of government who uphold the ruling of the Supreme Court in the George Reynolds Case of 1879, wherein the laws against my Celestial Law of Celestial Plural Marriage were upheld:

2. I, your God over all, declare you continue to not uphold my inspired rule of law, the Amendment

to the Constitution of the United States guaranteeing religious and faith freedom; even now you are of a illegal way.

3. You have allowed this evil and destructive ruling to be as a guide.

4. Now overrule that wrong court ruling; for it is not constitutional, nor just.

5. It is used wrongly by present courts, as though man's government can overrule my revealed law of Celestial Eternal and exalting power; a pure holy law of my revealing through my servant Joseph Smith; only to be lived by pure men and women in my Priesthood, and not for the world.

6. You are of a breaking of righteous principles of freedom when continuing to uphold such a misruling of unjust way.

7. I revealed my holy law to be administered by my own revelations to my Keyholder of Priesthood in each of their administrations.

8. Now let there be a repealing of this unjust ruling, to be of true freedom of religion. Amen.

Anti-Mormon Measures Introduced Into Congress -- December 1881

Orson F. Whitney
History of Utah, Volume 3 Page 165

When the Nation's law-makers met in December, [1881] a most bitter feeling prevailed against the Mormons almost universally. The Senate and House were fairly inundated with petitions from all parts, praying for speedy and effective action upon the Utah question. Early in the session several Anti-Mormon measures were introduced into both branches of Congress, among them the famous Edmunds Bill, which was destined to become law. It derived its name from Senator George F. Edmunds, of Vermont.***

President Taylor Explains the Importance of the Laws of God

President John Taylor
JD 22:229 June 26, 1881 Bountiful

Here is Brother George Reynolds, who is present, he was subject to the law. Did he fulfil the law? Yes, he did. Did he meet all its demands? Yes. And having met them, what more remains? If a law is made, and because we are conscientious before God, seeking to fulfil his law unto us, we violate such a law, and we are deprived of our liberty, by the help of God, his power and grace being with us to sustain us, we will bear the consequence. What can be asked then? We think we can fulfil the law of God and the law of man as near as they will let us; and if they wish to punish us for keeping the commandments of God, let them do it, and let them abide the consequence. And when we get through we will say, you Judge and Jury, who passed upon certain men, we have met your requirements, we now go to the Lord and say, Father, we have also met thy requirements; we could not barter away thy laws; we could not violate thy commandments, but, O God, we have been true to thee, and we have been true to our national obligations. And having done our best to promote peace, and having fulfilled the law of both God and man, we feel that we shall be justified by the Lord, and by all honorable, highminded, just and patriotic men. We are not the first who have been put to the test -- Daniel and the three Hebrew children had to pass through this ordeal, they met the consequences, as we propose doing. This was under a despotic government, but under our republican form of government, and with our free institutions, with a Constitution guaranteeing human liberty and the free exercise of religious faith, we have a right to expect a different action. But should this nation persist in violating their Constitutional guarantees, tear away the bulwarks of liberty, and trample upon the principles of freedom and human rights, that are sacred to all men, and by which all men should be governed, by and by the whole fabric will fall, and who will sustain it? We will, in the name of Israel's God. Of this the Prophet Joseph Smith prophesied long, long ago. This is the position we stand in. And if the Government of the United States can afford to oppress us, we can afford to suffer and grow strong.

Let us go to the law of God. We are here to build up Zion; and how ought we to feel?

President John Taylor
JD 11:223 April 7, 1866 SLC

Let us now go back to the action of Congress in relation to plural marriage, of which these eternal covenants are the foundation. The Lord says, "I will introduce the times of the restitution of all things; I will show you my eternal covenants, and call upon you to abide in them; I will show you how to save yourselves, your wives and children, your progenitors and posterity, and to save the earth from a curse. Congress says, if you fulfill that law we will inflict upon you pains and penalties, fines and imprisonments; in effect, we will not allow you to follow God's commands. Now, if Congress possessed the constitutional right

to do so, it would still be a high-handed outrage upon the rights of man; but when we consider that they cannot make such a law without violating the Constitution, and thus nullifying the act, what are we to think of it? Where are we drifting to. After having, with uplifted hands to heaven, sworn that they will "make no law respecting the establishment of religion, or prohibiting the free exercise thereof," to thus sacrilegiously stand between a whole community and their God, and deliberately debar them, so far as they have the power, from observing his law, do they realize what they are doing? Whence came this law on our statute books? Who constituted them our conscience keepers? Who appointed them the judge of our religious faith, or authorized them to coerce us to transgress a law that is binding and imperative on our consciences? We do not expect that Congress is acquainted with our religious faith; but, as members of the body politic, we do claim the guarantees of the Constitution and immunity from persecution on merely religious grounds.

What are we to think of a United States judge who would marry a man to another man's wife. He certainly ought to know better. We are told that she was a second wife, and, therefore, not acknowledged. Indeed, this is singular logic. If she was not a wife, then polygamy is no crime in the eyes of the law; for Congress have passed no law against whoredom. A man may have as many mistresses as he please, without transgressing any law of Congress. The act in relation to polygamy contemplates punishing a man for having more wives, not mistresses. If she was simply his mistress, then the law is of no effect; and the very fact of Congress passing such a law is the strongest possible proof, in law, of the existence of a marriage covenant, which, until that law was passed, was by them considered valid. If, then, she was not his wife, no person could be punished under that law for polygamy. If she was his wife, then the judge transgressed the law which he professionally came to maintain.

In relation to all these matters, the safe path for the Saints to take is, to do right, and, by the help of God, seek diligently and honorably to maintain the position which they hold. Are we ashamed of anything we have done in marrying wives? No. We shall not be ashamed before God and the holy angels, much less before a number of corrupt, miserable scoundrels, who are the very dregs of hell. We care nothing for their opinions, their ideas, or notions; for they do not know God, nor the principles which he has revealed. They wallow in the sink of corruption, as they would have us do; but, the Lord being our helper, we will not do it, but we will try to do right and keep the commandments of God, live our religion, and pursue a course that will secure to us the smiles and approbation of God our Father. Inasmuch as we do this He will take care of us, maintain His own cause, and sustain His people. We have a right to keep His commandments. But what would you do if the United States were to bring up an army against you on account of polygamy, or on account of any other religious subject? We would trust in God, as we always have done. Would you have no fears? None. All the fears that I am troubled with is that this people will not do right -- that they will not keep the commandments of God. If we will only faithfully live our religion, we fear no earthly power. Our safety is in God. Our religion is an eternal religion. Our covenants are eternal covenants, and we expect to maintain the principles of

our religion on the earth, and to possess them in the heavens. And if our wives and children do right, and we as fathers and husbands do right in this world, we expect to have our wives and children in eternity. Let us live in that way which will secure the approbation of God, that we, his representatives on the earth, may magnify our calling, honor Him, and maintain our integrity to the end; that we may be saved in His celestial kingdom, with our wives, and children, and brethren, from generation to generation, worlds without end. Amen.

President John Taylor
JD 25:349 October 19, 1884 Ogden

I remember some little time ago a gentleman named Mr. Pierpont (who was Attorney-General under President Grant) called upon me. I was pleased to see him, and am pleased to see all honorable gentlemen.*** After talking further with him upon the subject I said, "Now, Mr. Pierpont, you are well acquainted with all these legal affairs. Although I have yielded in this matter in order that I might not be an obstructionist, and do not wish to act as a Fenian, or a Nihilist, or a Communist, or a Kuklux, or a Regulator, or a Plug Ugly, or a Molly Maguire, yet, sir, we shall stand up for our rights and protect ourselves in every proper way, legally and constitutionally, and dispute inch by inch every step that is taken to deprive us of our rights and liberties." And we will do this in the way that I speak of. We are doing it to-day; and as you have heard it expressed on other occasions, it looks very much like as though the time was drawing near when this country will tumble to pieces; for if the people of this nation are so blind and infatuated as to trample under foot the Constitution and other safeguards provided for the liberties of man, we do not propose to assist them in their suicidal and traitorous enterprises; for we have been told by Joseph Smith that when the people of this nation would trample upon the Constitution, the Elders of this Church would rally round the flag and defend it. And it may come to that; we may be nearer to it than some of us think, for the people are not very zealous in the protection of human rights. And when legislators, governors and judges unite in seeking to tear down the temple of liberty and destroy the bulwarks of human freedom, it will be seen by all lovers of liberty, that they are playing a hazardous game and endangering the perpetuity of human rights. For it will not take long for the unthinking to follow their lead, and they may let loose an element that they never can bind again. We seem to be standing on a precipice and the tumultuous passions of men are agitated by political and party strife; the elements of discord are seething and raging as if portending a coming storm; and no man seem scompetent [seems competent] to take the helm and guide the ship of State through the fearful breakers that threaten on every hand. These are dangerous things, but it becomes our duty as good citizens to obey the law as far as practicable, and be governed by correct principles.

I had some papers read over at the General Conference, giving my views in relation to some of these matters. They have been published, but I will have one or two extracts read for your information.

President Cannon then read as follows:

The distinction being made between Polygamy and Prostitution:

1st. Congress made a law which would affect both; and cohabitation with more than one woman was made a crime whether in polygamy or out of polygamy.

2nd. The Governor turned legislator, added to this law, and inserted in a test oath to officials, the following words regarding cohabitation, "in the marriage relation;" thus plainly and definitely sanctioning prostitution, without any law of the United States, or any authority.

3rd. The United States Commissioners, also without legislation, adopted the action of the Governor, and still insisted on this interpolation, in the test oath in election matters, and placed all polygamists under this unconstitutional oath, and released prostitutes and their paramours from the obligations placed upon others.

4th. The Prosecuting Attorney has sanctioned these things, and pursued a similar course: and while he has asked all the "Mormon" grand jurors certain questions pertaining to their religious faith in the doctrines of the "Mormon" Church, and challenged them if they answered affirmatively as to their belief in polygamy, he has declined to ask other jurors whether they believed in prostitution, or whether they believed in cohabiting with more than one woman or not.

5th. Chief Justice Zane when appealed to on this question, refused to interfere, or give any other ruling.

Thus a law was first passed by Congress, which has been perverted by the administration, by all its officers, who have officiated in this Territory, and made to subserve the interests of a party who have placed in their political platform an Anti-Mormon plank; and have clearly proven that there is a combination entered into by all the officers of state officiating in this Territory, to back up this political intrigue in the interest of party, and at the sacrifice of law, equity, jurisprudence, and all the safeguards that are provided by the Constitution for the protection of human rights.

Congress cannot be condemned for these proceedings. The law as it stands on the nation's Statute Books make no such distinction, so far as the qualification of jurors are concerned, between those who cohabit with more than one woman in the marriage relation, and those who do so outside of that relation. All the rest has been aided by officials here. The law reads: "Section 5: That in any prosecution for bigamy, polygamy, or unlawful cohabitation, under any Statute of the United States, it shall be sufficient cause of challenge to any person drawn or summoned as a juryman or a talesman, first, that he is or has been living in the practice of bigamy, polygamy, or unlawful cohabitation with more than one woman, * * or second, that he believes it right for a man to have more than one living and undivorced wife at the same time, or to live in the practice of cohabiting with more than one woman." It will thus be seen that the same questions can be properly put to both classes; and such was the evident, unmistakable intention of Congress. But the Prosecuting Attorney with red-hot zeal changes all this, in his religio-political crusade against the faith of the Latter-day Saints he insists upon his right to propound the question with the Governor's interpolation super-added, whilst he entirely ignores the other side of the case; hence those who cohabit outside of the marriage relation can go scot free, without interrogation or questioning, and when attention is drawn to this perversion of the law, he asserts that he has the right to propound what questions he chooses,

and decline to ask those he has no mind to; in fact that the whole proceeding was a purely optional matter with him. Thus the whole weight of the law is unjustly and unrighteously thrown on the shoulders of those who believe and act in the marriage relation, and entirely removed from the others, who develop into the jurors, who are to indict, try and condemn the other and far more honorable class.

The People of Utah Petition Congress for a Commission of Investigation -- 1882

Orson F. Whitney
History of Utah, Volume 3 Page 180

On that very day [that the Edmunds bill passed the Senate] the Utah Legislature, which had been in session for several weeks, adopted a memorial praying Congress not to act hastily upon the extreme measures then pending before it, inimical to the people of this Territory, and asking for a commission of investigation.*** Later, another memorial, giving reasons why a commission of investigation should be sent, was drafted by a special joint committee of both branches of the Assembly, unanimously adopted and signed by the officers and members thereof, and a printed copy sent to the President of the United States, each member of his Cabinet, each Senator and Representative in Congress, and other government officials and prominent persons.

This memorial stated that for many years the people of Utah had patiently endured the misrepresentations and slanders of unscrupulous persons who had located at different times in the Territory, and who, from various unworthy motives, had formed themselves into political and religious cliques avowedly to represent the liberal and progressive element of the Territory, but really to vex and annoy the majority of the people and deprive them, if possible, of their civil, religious and political rights.***

This action of the people's representatives was supplemented by mass meetings of citizens in various parts of the Territory, and four mammoth petitions, signed respectively by men, women and the youth of both sexes, denying the falsehoods and detractions set afloat concerning them, and asking for a fair and full investigation of the charges, were prepared and sent to Washington. The signers of these petitions aggregated over sixty-five thousand souls.

Edmunds Bill Passes the Senate
February 16, 1882

Orson F. Whitney
History of Utah, Volume 3 Page 180

Doubtless many who voted for the Edmunds Bill did so from choice, being in full sympathy with the measure. There were some, however, who supported it against their inclination, fearing it would displease their constituents if they listened to the dictates of conscience and regarded their oaths to sustain the Constitution. All were more or less influenced by the terrible rush and roar of the Anti-Mormon crusade; a hurricane of hatred and bigotry, before which statesmen, usually strong-minded and courageous, bent like willows in a storm. It was Thursday, the 16th of February, when the bill passed the Senate.

The Edmunds Bill Becomes Law
March 22, 1882

Orson F. Whitney
History of Utah, Volume 3 Page 186

In the interim the Edmunds Bill, which

had passed the Senate, was "railroaded" through the House of Representatives. The entire discussion occupied only two hours; little or no opportunity was given for amendments; speeches were limited to five minutes each, and every effort was made by the friends of the bill, who were in the majority, to prevent a full and free discussion of its provisions.***

The bill passed the House by a vote of 199 to 42; 51 members not voting. On the 22nd of March it received the signature of President Arthur and became a law of the land.

Arrival of the Utah Commission --
August 1882

Orson F. Whitney
History of Utah, Volume 3 Page 207

The summer of 1882 also witnessed the arrival in Utah of the five Commissioners [Utah Commission] provided for in the Edmunds Act and recently appointed by the President of the United States.*** Those duties, as defined in the Act creating the Commission, were:

First -- To appoint officers to perform each and every duty relating to the registration of voters, the conduct of elections, the receiving or rejection of votes, the canvassing and returning of the same and the issuing of certificates or other evidence of election.

Second -- To canvass the returns of all the votes cast at elections for members of the Legislature, and issue certificates of election to those persons who, being eligible for such election, should appear to have been lawfully elected.

Third -- To continue in office until the Legislative Assembly, so elected and qualified, should make provision for filling the offices vacated by the Edmunds Act, as therein authorized.

The Test Oath, Precluding Members of the Church to Vote

Orson F. Whitney
History of Utah, Volume 3 Page 228

TERRITORY OF UTAH, ⎱
COUNTY OF . . . . ⎰ ss.

I. . . . . . ., being first duly sworn (or affirmed), depose and say that I am over twenty-one years of age, and have resided in the Territory of Utah for six months, and in the precinct of . . . . one month immediately preceding the date hereof, and (if a male) am a native born or naturalized (as the case may be) citizen of the United States and a taxpayer in this Territory, or (if a female), I am native born, or naturalized, or the wife, widow or daughter (as the case may be) of a native born or naturalized citizen of the United States; and I do further solemnly swear (or affirm) that I am not a bigamist or a polygamist; that I am not a violator of the laws of the United States prohibiting bigamy or polygamy; that I do not live or cohabit with more than one woman in the marriage relation, nor does any relation exist between me and any woman which has been entered into or continued in violation of the said laws of the United States prohibiting bigamy or polygamy; and (if a woman) that I am not the wife of a polygamist, nor have I entered into any relation with any man in violation of the laws of the United States concerning polygamy or bigamy.

Subscribed and sworn before me
this. . . . . day of. . . . ., 1882.
Registration Officer,
. . . . Precinct.

How the People of the Church Regarded the Test Oath

Orson F. Whitney
History of Utah, Volume 3 Page 231

The Mormon people did not propose to sit supinely and allow any such discrimination to daunt them. With all polygamists disfranchised they were still in the great majority in the Territory, and, unlike their opponents, had no reason to fear the result of an election, if each party was given a fair field, "a free ballot and an honest count." The First Presidency, in an address to the members of the Church, dated at Salt Lake City, August 29, 1882, animadverted upon the Commissioners and their test oath, and counseled their own followers in this wise:

It has been with feelings of profound regret that we have seen the Commissioners, men of high position and bearing honored names, take this view of the law, and frame such an oath as this to be administered unto the people, yet on the other hand, it is with unmixed satisfaction we perceive that the oath draws the line so sharply and distinctly between marriage and licentiousness. By the attempt in the construction of this oath to shield from injury those who, by their illicit connections with the other sex, might, under the provisions of the Edmunds law, be disfranchised, the Latter-day Saints, who, in all sincerity and honor, have obeyed a revelation from God, are not reduced to their degraded level.

Our counsel, then, is to the Latter-day Saints, who can truthfully take this oath, there is no reason we know of in the Gospel, or in any of the revelations of God, which prevents you from doing so. *** Very many of you can take this oath with conscientiousness and entire truthfulness, as you could even if it were in a form which many of your traducers could not take without perjury; and yet there would be no impropriety, while you do take it, in protesting against it as a gross wrong imposed upon you.

* * * * * * * * *

In regard to your political arrangements, the Territorial Central Committee is an organization that has for its object the preservation of the rights of every citizen of this Territory, without regard to party or sect. They will doubtless issue such instructions, from time to time, as circumstances demand. It is in the interest of every patriot to faithfully observe and practically carry out the suggestions that they may make.

The Anti-Polygamy Laws
Made Retroactive

The next act of the Commission was the issuance of an order prohibiting the registration of any person, male or female, who, at any time since the passage of the anti-polygamy laws of 1862 and 1882, had lived in bigamous or polygamous relations.

President Taylor Speaks of the
Edmunds Bill and the
Untruths Circulated

President John Taylor
JD 23:60 April 9, 1882 SLC

I give these statements of facts for the information of the brethren who are here from a distance; but, then, they know them as facts; that is, they know how these *soi disant* regenerators act, but many of them do not know what their civilization is here, and what is sought to be introduced among us, and the infamous statements circulated concerning us. We are ready, as I said before, to compare notes with them or the people of this or any nation at any time. And then again, we ought to be more pure and virtuous than they, for we do profess to be the Saints of the Most High God. With this view, when this Edmunds bill was being canvassed, and there was a prospect of its passing -- although we thought at first it was impossible that such a concern could pass through Congress; but when we saw the falsehoods that were being circulated, the furore that was being raised and fanned by religious fanatics and political demagogues, petitions were gotten up by the people here, one of them representing the male class, another our Relief Societies, another our young men, and another our young ladies' Improvement Societies. All of them represented that we were a virtuous people -- that polygamy was a religious institution; and the young people asserted that it had been taught to them by their parents from their youth up, and that the principles of purity, virtue, integrity and loyalty to the government of the United States had been instilled into their minds and hearts since their earliest childhood; and further, that they had been taught and understood that chastity was their greatest boon, far above jewels or wealth, and more precious than life itself. In a few days we had 165,000 [65,000] signatures, and they were forwarded to Washington. The request was that Congress would not act as the government had before -- first sent out an army and then send commissioners to inquire, but that they would send commissioners first to inquire into the facts of the case. But they did not choose to listen. In fact, there has been a great furore in the United States in relation to these matters, and that has originated to an extent through our Governor. Now I am very much averse to talking about official men; I do not like to do such things. They ought to be honorable men; the most charitable construction I could put upon his acts would be to say that his education had been sadly neglected, and that he was not acquainted with figures.

Annie Gallifant in Contempt for
Failure to Testify Against Her
Husband Before Grand Jury --
November 17th 1882

Orson F. Whitney
History of Utah, Volume 3 Page 275

A few months later occurred a sensational episode which, though isolated from the long series of raids and prosecutions that followed, was a precursor of what was approaching and gave token of some of the tactics that would be employed by the crusaders. It was the imprisonment of a young Mormon woman named Annie Gallifant. She was the alleged plural wife of John Connelly, a baker and confectioner. On the 17th of November, 1882, the young woman -- she was under twenty years of age -- was before the Grand Jury at Salt Lake City, where she was plied with questions the answers to which, it was supposed, would lead to the conviction of her reputed husband. One of the questions was a direct demand for the name of the person to whom she was married. She refused to answer, whereupon she was taken before Chief Justice Hunter, who informed her that the questions asked were proper, and that it was her duty to reply to them. Still she refused. The Judge then sentenced her to imprisonment in the Penitentiary until such time as she should be willing to answer.

The event created considerable indignation, which was not in any degree lessened when it became known that the young woman thus consigned to a felon's cell was about to become a mother. She was a frail little creature, and it was feared that a premature birth might result from the excitement attendant upon her incarceration, to be followed by the death of both mother and child.*** All fears, however, were set at rest regarding the imprisoned witness on the day following her incarceration. The Grand Jury having been discharged, she was released from custody and permitted to return to her home. Her child was born four days later. Subsequently, John Connelly, who proved to be her husband, was indicted for polygamy and in the fall of 1884 was tried and acquitted.*** [Footnote: Subsequently John Connelly was convicted of unlawful cohabitation and sent to the Penitentiary.]

Rudger Clawson's Arrest -- April 24, 1884

Orson F. Whitney
History of Utah, Volume 3 Page 278

Another year passed and then came the arrest and initial proceedings in the case of Rudger Clawson; the virtual opening, on the part of the courts, of the great anti-polygamy crusade. The defendant in this celebrated case was a son of Bishop H. B. Clawson and his second wife, Margaret Judd. He was a young man of exemplary habits, zealous for the cause in which he had been nurtured from childhood. His intrepid conduct at the time of the murder of his fellow missionary, Joseph Standing, in Georgia, has been dwelt upon. He was a firm believer in the principle of plural marriage, to which he owed his earthly origin, and had married, according to rumor, two wives. His first wife was Florence Dinwoodey, daughter of Henry Dinwoodey, the wealthy head of a large furniture establishment at Salt Lake City. His alleged plural wife was Lydia Spencer, daughter of Daniel Spencer; a name prominent in early Utah annals.

Rudger Clawson was arrested by United States Marshal Ireland on the 24th of April, 1884; the same day on which he had been indicted by the Grand Jury. Taken before U. S. Commissioner William McKay, he was placed under bonds in the sum of three thousand dollars and was then given his liberty.

Chief Justice Zane Arrives in Utah -- August 1884

Orson F. Whitney
History of Utah, Volume 3 Page 266

While all Utah was ringing with the dreadful news of the massacre of the Mormon missionaries and their friends in Tennessee, and just one day after the train bearing the bodies of the murdered Elders reached its destination, there arrived at Salt Lake City a man whose remarkable career in these parts as a representative of the Federal Government will form much of the matter of the remaining portion of this volume. That man was Hon. Charles S. Zane, late of Springfield, Illinois, who had recently been appointed Chief Justice of this Territory.

The wonderful changes following and in part flowing from Judge Zane's administration might induce in many the belief that he was an instrument of Destiny, and that he came to Utah with a special mission from the Government; a mission for which he had been carefully chosen and vested with extraordinary powers. Indeed, he was more than once styled "a mission jurist," and, like Judge McKean, whom he was supposed at one time to be ambitiously emulating, was charged with having as his object the overthrow of Mormonism as a religion.***

Judge Zane's Past Record and the Prospect Confronting Him

Judge Zane's appointment seems to have come in the ordinary course of events; no Jesuitical influence securing him the office, and no Star Chamber council at Washington instructing him how to discharge its functions. The case in a nutshell is this: The Government was determined to suppress the practice of polygamy in the Territories; a law had been passed by Congress to that end, and the Federal officials in Utah were under obligations to enforce it. A vacancy occurred in the Chief Justiceship of the Territory, and Charles S. Zane, being considered a proper man for the place, was sent to fill it. Not that the appointment came independently, without the usual

intervention of powerful friends and their influence; but it came, according to his account, without his solicitation or seeking.

The Mormon Leaders Go Into Exile

Orson F. Whitney
History of Utah, Volume 3 Page 344

The President [John Taylor] took his own counsel and retired from public view; an example speedily followed by his Counselors, the Apostles, and other leading men of the Church; with others less prominent but still liable to prosecution. From time to time the First Presidency communicated with their people by means of epistles read to them at their general conferences; but with the exception of a few intimate friends, including members of his family, who accompanied him in his secret journeyings from place to place, sharing his retirement and acting as guards or messengers for him and his fellow exiles, the Latter-day Saints never again saw President Taylor alive. The most persistent efforts were put forth for his capture, but all to no purpose. The friends whom he trusted were true, and coaxings, promises and threats were alike ineffectual in leading to his discovery. There was no traitor, or what is almost as bad, no thoughtless, mischievous gossip in the ranks of the faithful souls surrounding the venerable exile during the few sad years remaining to him.

The United States Supreme Court Upholds the Edmunds Law -- 1885

Orson F. Whitney
History of Utah, Volume 3 Page 351

It was on March 23rd of this year [1885] that the Supreme Court of the United States rendered its decision in the case of Murphy *vs.* Ramsey, the effect of which was to establish the constitutionality of the

Edmunds Law, but to nullify the test oath formulated by the Utah Commission,***

The Edmunds Law was declared constitutional; Congress having the right to enact it for the reason that the power of the Government of the United States over the national Territories was supreme.

Orson F. Whitney
History of Utah, Volume 3 Page 356

Meantime the Federal courts continued the prosecution of polygamous cases, and the United States Marshal and his deputies busied themselves in raiding the settlements and searching houses suspected of harboring men and women wanted as victims of the crusade. Early in April Marshal Ireland and several of his aids visited Logan, as did U. S. Marshal Dubois, of Idaho, and some of his subordinates; the unusual event of a general conference at that point inspiring them with the hope that some of those whom they most desired to apprehend would be found or heard of in Cache Valley at that time. They were doomed to disappointment, and returned empty-handed, and empty-headed -- so far as information of the whereabouts of the Mormon Presidency was concerned -- to their accustomed haunts in and around the capitals of their respective Territories.

Arrests of persons less notable went on, however, and well nigh the whole inter-mountain region was overrun by the emissaries of the courts, hunting with all the assiduity of sleuth-hounds, and with as little pity as would have been shown by such animals, men accused or suspected of violating the Edmunds Law. The officers, who usually traveled in squads, would suddenly pounce upon some small settlement at midnight or in "the wee sma' 'ours" [the wee small

hours] between midnight and daybreak, rudely arousing the inhabitants from slumber, sometimes by discharging firearms at hastily decamping fugitives, and spreading general terror and dismay. Delicate women, fleeing from or frightened by the marauders, received injuries from which they never recovered, and more than one death lies at the door of these heartless disturbers of the peace of innocent and unoffending citizens. Even wise and brave men lost their judgment at times, and had their courage unstrung by this hateful system of harassment; so much more difficult to deal with, since the offenders were officers of the law, than if they had been thieves and trespassers, in which event many of them would undoubtedly have bitten the dust.

President John Y. Barlow Speaks Concerning the Edmunds Act

President John Y. Barlow
John Y. Barlow's Sermons
[RTJ] 8:363 November 23, 1947 SCA

We have been out of jail for two years. Whether they will release us yet, we do not know. If they do, we will be free from that score. But what is back of it? There is a law that has been made by the legislature of this State that makes it a felony, from one to five years in the penitentiary; and if we teach the commandments of God as is laid down, why, we are subject to that law.

When the Edmunds Law was made, we either had to go for the laws of God or the laws of the land, one of the two things. Every member of the Church either had to go to the laws of God or the laws of the land. Some preferred the laws of God, and some the laws of the land. Some will say, if we live the laws of the land, we are free, so far as the law of the land is concerned. If we follow the laws of God, then we can have eternal increase. But if we follow the laws of the land, that is the end of your kingdom, you cannot have an increase. That is what the good book says.

President John Y. Barlow
John Y. Barlow's Sermons
[RTJ] 8:134 August 25, 1940 SLC

When the higher ordinances of the Gospel were given to the people by the Prophet, only two percent of the people obeyed these ordinances. Then what came? The Edmunds Law, and the people got scared and ran. Finally the Master said, "What have you done? Get up the young men and the middle-aged and go back and redeem My land."

Brothers and sisters, we are in that condition today. God has spoken, and He is going to come back here, and the people are going to redeem that land. I want to bear my testimony that God never gives any commandment unless He opens the way. It will take more than a Manifesto to ever stop the principle of Celestial Marriage.

The 1886 Revelation

Revelation of the Lord Jesus Christ Given to President John Taylor September 27, 1886

Priesthood Articles, Page 178

My son John, you have asked me concerning the New and Everlasting Covenant how far it is binding upon my people.

Thus saith the Lord: All commandments that I give must be obeyed by those calling themselves by my name unless they are revoked by me or by my authority, and how can I revoke an everlasting covenant, for I the Lord am everlasting and my everlasting covenants cannot be abrogated nor done away with, but they stand forever.

Have I not given my word in great plainness on this subject? Yet have not great numbers of my people been negligent in the observance of my law and the keeping of my commandments, and yet have I borne with them these many years; and this because of their weakness -- because of the perilous times, and furthermore, it is more pleasing to me that men should use their free agency in regard to these matters. Nevertheless, I the Lord do not change and my word and my covenants and my law do not, and as I have heretofore said by my servant Joseph: All those who would enter into my glory must and shall obey my law. And have I not commanded men that if they were Abraham's seed and would enter into my glory, they must do the works of Abraham. **I HAVE NOT REVOKED THIS LAW, NOR WILL I,** for it is everlasting, and those who will enter into my glory MUST obey the conditions thereof; even so, Amen.

The Lorin Woolley Statement

Priesthood Articles, Page 180

As further and ultimate proof of the existence of this revelation we quote a statement in extenso from Lorin C. Woolley, a bodyguard of John Taylor at the time the revelation was received, and who was given a copy of the same on the day it was written, as the statement indicates.

Statement of Lorin C. Woolley with reference to the revelation of 1886, on the subject of Celestial or plural marriage, given September 22, 1929:

There were present Lorin C. Woolley, Daniel R. Bateman, John Y. Barlow, J.

Leslie Broadbent and J. W. Musser. Prayer was offered by John Y. Barlow.

Lorin C. Woolley related the following:

While the brethren were at the Carlisle residence (in Murray) in May or June of 1886, letters began to come to President John Taylor from such men as John Sharp, Horace Eldredge, William Jennings, John T. Cain, Abraham Hatch, President Cluff and many other leading men from all over the Church, asking the leaders to do something, as the Gentiles were talking of confiscating their property in connection with the property of the Church.

These letters not only came from those who were living in the plural marriage relation, but also from prominent men who were presiding in various offices in the Church who were not living in that relation. They all urged that something be done to satisfy the Gentiles so that their property would not be confiscated.

George Q. Cannon, on his own initiative, selected a committee comprising himself, Hyrum B. Clawson, Franklin S. Richards, John T. Caine and James Jack, to get up a statement or manifesto that would meet the objections urged by the brethren above named. They met from time to time to discuss the situation. From the White home, where President Taylor and companions stopped, after leaving the Carlisle home, they came out to father's. George Q. Cannon would go and consult with the brethren of the committee, I taking him back and forth each day.

On September 26, 1886, George Q. Cannon, Hyrum B. Clawson, Franklin S. Richards, and others met with President John Taylor at my father's residence at Centerville, Davis County, Utah, and presented a document for President Taylor's consideration.

I had just got back from a three days' trip, during most of which time I had been in the saddle, and being greatly fatigued, I had retired to rest.

Between one and two o'clock P.M. Brother Bateman came and woke me up and asked me to be at my father's home, where a manifesto was to be discussed. I went there and found there were congregated Samuel Bateman, Charles H. Wilkins, L. John Nuttall, Charles Birrell, George Q. Cannon, Franklin S. Richards and Hyrum B. Clawson.

We discussed the proposed Manifesto at length, but we were unable to become united in the discussion. Finally George Q. Cannon suggested that President Taylor take the matter up with the Lord and decide the same the next day.

Brothers Clawson and Richards were taken back to Salt Lake. That evening I was called to act as guard during the first part of the night, notwithstanding the fact that I was greatly fatigued on account of the three days' trip I had just completed.

The brethren retired to bed soon after 9 o'clock. The sleeping rooms were inspected by the guards as was the custom. President Taylor's room had no outside door. The windows were heavily screened.

Some time after the brethren retired and while I was reading the Doctrine and Covenants, I was suddenly attracted to a light appearing under the door leading to President Taylor's room, and was at once startled to hear the voices of men talking there. There were three distinct voices. I was bewildered because it was my duty to keep people out of that room and evidently someone had entered without my knowing it. I made a hasty examination and found the door leading to the room bolted as usual. I then examined the outside of the house and found all the window screens intact. While examining the last window, and feeling greatly agitated, a voice spoke to me saying, "Can't you feel the Spirit? Why should you worry?"

At this I returned to my post and continued to hear the voices in the room. They were so audible that although I did not see the parties I could place their positions in the room from the sound of their voices. The three voices continued until about midnight, when one of them left, and the other two continued. One of them I recognized as President John Taylor's voice. I called Charles Birrell *[Footnote: Charles Birrell was also a bodyguard of the brethren and was to take the second shift in watching on this night.]* and we both sat up until eight o'clock the next morning.

When President Taylor came out of his room about eight o'clock of the morning of September 27, 1886, we could scarcely look at him on account of the brightness of his personage.

He stated, "Brethren, I have had a very pleasant conversation with Brother Joseph (Joseph Smith)." I said, "Boss, who is the man that was there until midnight?" He asked, "What do you know about it, Lorin?" I told him all about my experience. He said, *"Brother Lorin, that was your Lord."*

We had no breakfast, but assembled ourselves in a meeting. I forget who opened the meeting. I was called to offer the benediction. I think my father, John W. Woolley, offered the opening prayer. There were present at the meeting, in addition to President Taylor, George Q. Cannon, L. John Nuttall, John W. Woolley, Samuel Bateman, Charles Wilkins, Charles Birrell, Daniel R. Bateman, Bishop Samuel Sedden, George Earl, my mother, Julia E. Woolley, my sister, Amy Woolley, and myself. The meeting was held from about 9 o'clock in the morning until 5 in the afternoon, without intermission, being about eight hours in all.

President Taylor called the meeting to order. He had the Manifesto, that had been prepared under the direction of George Q. Cannon, read over again. He then put each person under covenant that he or she would defend the principle of Celestial or plural marriage, and that they would consecrate their lives, liberty and property to this end, and that they personally would sustain and uphold that principle.

By that time we were all filled with the Holy Ghost. President Taylor and those present occupied about three hours up to this time. After placing us under covenant, he placed his finger on the document, his person rising from the floor about a foot or eighteen inches, and with countenance animated by the Spirit of the Lord, and raising his right hand to the square, he said, "Sign that document? -- Never! I would suffer my right hand to be severed from my body first. Sanction it -- never! I would suffer my tongue to be torn from its roots in my mouth before I would sanction it!"

After that he talked for about an hour and then sat down and wrote the revelation which was given him by the Lord upon the question of Plural Marriage (the text of which revelation is given above). Then he talked to us for some time, and said, *"Some of you will be handled and ostracized and cast out from the Church by your brethren because of your faithfulness and integrity to this principle, and some of you may have to surrender your lives because of the same, but woe, woe, unto those who shall bring these troubles upon you." (Three of us were handled and ostracized for supporting and sustaining this principle.* There are only three left who were at the meeting mentioned -- Daniel R. Bateman, George Earl, and myself. So far as I know, those of them who have passed away all stood firm to the covenants entered into from that day to the day of their deaths.)

After the meeting referred to, President Taylor had L. John Nuttall write five copies of the revelation. He called five of us together: Samuel Bateman, Charles H. Wilkins, George Q. Cannon, John W. Woolley, and myself.

He then set us apart and placed us under covenant that while we lived we would see to it that no year passed by without children being born in the principle of plural marriage. We were given authority to ordain others if necessary to carry this work on, they in turn to be given authority to ordain others when necessary, under the direction of the worthy senior (by ordination), so that there should be no cessation in the work. He then gave each of us a copy of the revelation.

I am the only one of the five now living, and so far as I know all five of the brethren remained true and faithful to the covenants they entered into, and to the responsibilities placed upon them at that time.

During the eight hours we were together, and while President Taylor was talking to us, he frequently arose and stood above the floor, and his countenance and being were so enveloped by light and glory that it was difficult for us to look upon him.

He stated that the document (referring to the Manifesto) was from the lower regions. He stated that many of the things he had

told us we would forget and they would be taken from us, but that they would return to us in due time as needed, and from this fact we would know that the same was from the Lord. This has been literally fulfilled. Many of the things I forgot, but they are coming to me gradually, and those things that come to me are as clear as on the day on which they were given.

President Taylor said that the time would come when many of the Saints would apostatize because of this principle. He said "one-half of this people would apostatize over the principle for which we are now in hiding; yea, and possibly one-half of the other half" (rising off the floor while making the statement). He also said the day will come when a document similar to that (Manifesto) then under consideration would be adopted by the Church, following which "APOSTASY AND WHOREDOM would be rampant in the Church."

He said that in the time of the seventh President of this Church, the Church would go into *bondage both temporally and spiritually* and in that day (the day of bondage) the one Mighty and Strong spoken of in the 85th Section of the Doctrine and Covenants would come.

Among other things stated by President Taylor on this occasion was this, *"I would be surprised if ten per cent of those who claim to hold the Melchizedek Priesthood will remain true and faithful to the Gospel of the Lord Jesus Christ, at the time of the seventh president, and that there would be thousands that think they hold the priesthood at that time, but would not have it properly conferred upon them."*

John Taylor set the five mentioned apart and gave them authority to perform marriage ceremonies, and also to set others apart to do the same thing as long as they remained upon the earth; *and while doing so, the Prophet Joseph Smith stood by directing the proceedings. Two of us had not met the Prophet Joseph Smith in his mortal lifetime and we -- Charles H. Wilkins and myself -- were introduced to him and shook hands with him.*

(Signed) LORIN C. WOOLLEY

Excerpts from an Epistle of the First Presidency to the Church of Jesus Christ of Latter-day Saints -- April 8, 1887

The Mind and Will of the Lord,
Page 177 Address 36

Due to the question over the legality of polygamy and the desire of certain federal officials to imprison, prosecute, and/or otherwise hound church leaders into compliance with questionable civil law, many of the Brethren, notably members of the First Presidency, were forced to go underground to avoid public appearances. Unable to attend the 57th Annual General Conference of The Church of Jesus Christ of Latter-day Saints, and in lieu of what they might have said had they been able to attend, President John Taylor issued the following epistle that was read to the conference by Bishop G. F. Whitney on April 8, 1887. As a number of the Brethren were experiencing the same difficulties with the law, it was thought advisable to hold General Conference in Provo, Utah, rather than in Salt Lake City as usual.***

Millennial Star, Volume 49 Page 292

From the day of the organization of the Church of Jesus Christ of Latter-day Saints, the adversary of souls has stirred up the wicked to accomplish its destruction. Various agencies have been employed to effect this purpose. Falsehood, tradition, deep-rooted prejudice, the learning, wealth and power of Christendom, mob violence, fire, fetters, the rifle and the sword, wholesale expulsion and military force having been tried in vain, a new crusade has been inaugurated in the form of legislative and judicial tyranny, prompted by Satan and carried on by cunning adventurers and reckless fanatics.

Perhaps the most shameful and unrepublican attempt of this character was the latest scheme devised by the local conspirators. What is known as the Edmunds law -- the act of March 22, 1882 -- was hoped to be broad enough in its intended scope to secure the political control of the Territory to the anti-"Mormon" voters. A large number of both sexes were by that act deprived of the franchise. That it did not wrench the control of the Territory out of the hands of the majority of its residents, is not to be credited to the absence of such a wish and design on the part of its authors and promoters, but to the overruling providence of the Almighty. The ground which those who favored this measure seemed to take was, that it was both praiseworthy and justifiable to violate the soundest political principles, and even the Constitution itself, to take the political control of the Territory of Utah from the "Mormon" majority and concentrate it in the hands of the anti-"Mormon" minority. Having gone thus far to accomplish this end, it was scarcely to be expected they would hesitate to make other and more outrageous attempts, when they found that the Edmunds law had not answered the full purpose for which it was intended. It appears to be one of the effects which follow a departure from sound republican and constitutional principles like the enactment of such a strange piece of legislation as the Edmunds Law, that every future attempt in the same direction will be more regardless of the settled principles of political liberty than its predecessor.***

With full confidence that the dense clouds which have darkened our horizon during the past two or three years will be soon dissipated by the bright rays of the sun of righteousness, and invoking the blessings that come through patient endurance of affliction and faithful adherence to the right, upon the Saints of God in all the world, we subscribe ourselves your fellow servants in the great work of the latter days,

JOHN TAYLOR
GEORGE Q. CANNON
JOSEPH F. SMITH
First Presidency of the Church of Jesus Christ of Latter-day Saints

April, 1887.

President John Taylor Died a Double Martyr

President Leroy S. Johnson
Leroy S. Johnson's Sermons 2:506 July 16, 1972 SLC

In the days of Joseph the Prophet, He was establishing His work in the earth and He instructed the Prophet Joseph Smith daily what to do and how to set in order His house. But through the unfaithfulness of the people, Joseph was not permitted to do all that the Lord wanted him to do. If we will go into history, we will find that there were very few men who stood by the Prophet Joseph continually and faithfully without accusation about his performance. But, because of the criticism and the unstable minds of men, he was not permitted to accomplish what he would like to have done.

After the Prophet Joseph passed, we can say the same thing of Brigham Young and John Taylor -- John Taylor, especially. Why John Taylor, especially? John Taylor was with the Prophet when he was martyred; and when it became his duty to rule over the saints, what happened? He was driven into hiding. He wasn't permitted, because of the unfaithfulness of his brethren, to do the things that he would like to have done. He was permitted to accomplish some things. He was permitted to set in order a movement that later on would eventually set in order the machinery to be used in the redemption of Zion. Today this machinery is operating.

President Leroy S. Johnson
Leroy S. Johnson's Sermons 1:61
September 25, 1960 Canada

There are many ways we can improve ourselves day by day to measure up to the character of that great Being. One of the greatest responsibilities upon us today is to teach our children to become like God. If you can put into practice the things taught here, you will have a community here that will cease to worship golden calves; and they will worship our Father in Heaven. Joseph Smith tried to put this idea over; Brigham Young tried in his day; John Taylor also tried in his day, but he had to go into hiding and died a martyr because he didn't have friends enough to help him.

President Rulon Jeffs
Rulon Jeffs' Sermons 3:167 October 7, 1973 CCA

There were none closer to the Prophet than John Taylor, who once said, "I did not know who Joseph really was until that night in Carthage." And he was a witness and a testator for Joseph. All praise to his name, for he died a double martyr, going from house to house of his friends to avoid his enemies who would have destroyed him. And he was able, thus, to finish his work, the greatest part of which was in hiding.

President Rulon Jeffs
Rulon Jeffs' Sermons 5:508 Oct. 28, 1984 Sacred Grove

Jesus and Joseph came to John Taylor to see that this great work was carried on, and responsible keyholders to follow, because the Church had given up the fullness of the Gospel and rejected the Lord. There were not very many men who would give the Prophet John Taylor succor and help as he was in hiding.

President Leroy S. Johnson
Leroy S. Johnson's Sermons 4:1276 Sept. 19, 1976 SLC

Every man, woman, and child that dares to say that Joseph Smith was a Prophet of God, takes their lives in their hands when they say it. They did in Joseph's day; they did in Brigham Young's day; and they did in John Taylor's day. John Taylor even had to go into hiding because he couldn't tell the people that he knew that Joseph Smith was a Prophet and be safe and know that he would be a live man after he said the words.

President Lorin Woolley Bears Testimony of President John Taylor by John Y. Barlow Account

President John Y. Barlow
John Y. Barlow's Sermons
[RTJ 8:284] May 14, 1944 SLC

I knew Lorin Woolley, and he also told me things. I want to bear my testimony to the truth when he said that the Priesthood came on down from John Taylor, etc. Read the 90th Section of the Doctrine and Covenants, where it tells us that the keys of the Kingdom were given to Joseph Smith. Now I want you to find any other place in the Church where they say that. The keys came on down through John Taylor and the others. I was glad to hear my brother say that he got that testimony for himself. I want you to find out these things for yourselves.

Chapter 4

Administration of President John W. Woolley

SECTION REVELATION 220

Revelation of the Lord Jesus Christ
Palestine, Texas
Sunday, October 2, 2011

1. Thus saith the Lord to all peoples, that my holy servant John Taylor was called to be my Keyholder of Priesthood; which keys of power I, your Lord, only place on a man of my holy Order Eternal.

2. Thus he was faithful in all his word and labors, in upholding every word of my giving, both through the Keyholders before him, and also my will through him.

3. I, your Lord, visited him in his time of hiding from government persecuting powers; having mine holy resurrected servant, Joseph Smith, with me as the authority I sent to teach John Taylor, and Brigham Young before him.

4. John Taylor was instructed to keep my Priesthood and Celestial Law of Plural Celestial Marriage alive and increasing on earth.

5. He was shown of the coming greater prosecuting powers of the United States government against my Celestial Law.

6. He was told to set apart six men as confirmed apostles of your Lord, and place them as men of silent labor, to only promote my Celestial Law among they who would receive in sacred trust my Celestial Plural Marriage Law in full plural and holy living.

7. When the governing powers pressured the President of the Church, who was not my Keyholder of Priesthood, even Wilford Woodruff, he gave in, notwithstanding I gave my own word to him beforehand to not make any compromises to the wicked concerning my Celestial Law.

8. He lost Priesthood, and was an instrument to lead astray many of my Church; until the leaders of that organization fully opposed my Priesthood, and sought to destroy the continuation of my Celestial Plural Marriage Law from continuing on earth.

9. I called my servant John W. Woolley to be my holy and authorized Keyholder of all the sealing keys and powers of Priesthood after I took my servant John Taylor from the earth in his passing unto the spirit world, to await his resurrection.

10. John Woolley was fully pure,

faithful, and noble in fulfilling my will.

11. He was a silent witness of the apostasy of the majority of the members of that branch called the Church of Jesus Christ of Latter-day Saints, which broke itself away from my Holy Priesthood, becoming gentile and of the apostasy of rebelling against God and His Celestial Law.

12. Now learn that my true Priesthood continued through John Woolley.

13. He was of full Priesthood authority.

14. He was faithful and abided my Celestial Law.

15. He was of a power to visit often the former Prophets.

16. He could see beyond the veil, and visit with my Priesthood of the full authority as he held.

17. He was led by revelation to test the President of the Church, even Heber J. Grant; a man who fully opposed my Celestial Law when he was in the President position, and proved himself a traitor to Priesthood and my Celestial Law.

18. Thus, Heber J. Grant caused much persecution to come against my Priesthood during the days of my Keyholders of Priesthood, namely, in the times of John W. Woolley, Lorin C. Woolley, and John Y. Barlow.

19. These Keyholders, each in their time, stood faithful in continuing my Celestial Law of Plural Marriage.

20. Thus I reveal to all peoples that I, your Lord, guided my authority on earth to continue my Priesthood power and Priesthood law of Celestial Plural Marriage on earth.

21. Now learn that the Church calling itself the Church of Jesus Christ of Latter-day Saints is apostate and not of my Priesthood.

22. My true Church on earth, saith your Lord, is now of a naming to represent the upholding of all my laws of Celestial power to exalt unto eternal lives, even the Fundamentalist Church of Jesus Christ of Latter-day Saints; which Church continues as an organization of my full Priesthood authority now on earth.

23. This sacred revealing is to tell all peoples on earth I, your Lord, have continued my Church, Priesthood, and Kingdom on earth by preserving my Keyholders who lived fully my Celestial and Eternal laws of Priesthood, even my law of Celestial Plural Marriage.

24. Now learn that I, God, have done this.

25. Thus, all who speak against my Priesthood and against my Celestial Law are not of me, and shall not prosper, but shall be brought low, and be among the wicked.

26. My holy law is pure, holy,

and purifies the obedient to my law unto an exalting throne in heaven of Godhood -- they who abide the fulness of my law through the Priesthood I authorize on earth.

27. Now be of an understanding that my Priesthood and my Celestial Law is on earth, and is governed by my will and holy power.

28. All who fight against my Priesthood and my Celestial Law of Celestial Plural Marriage are against God.

29. Therefore, they shall be of a full receiving of my judgments on earth, and in the eternal judgment that shall come on all peoples hereafter.

30. Know that my Celestial Law is mine, and is eternal, and cannot be done away; but continues with my keys of Priesthood on earth, even my servant in bondage at this time.

31. He is of full keys of my eternal authority and power of thy Lord.

32. All who fight against him fight against God.

33. Therefore, repent, and know my judgments of cleansing are nigh at hand.

34. Let my servant go free to do my will.

35. I, even Jesus Christ, the God over all peoples of every time of earth's history, speaketh.

36. So shall I preserve my Priesthood and Celestial Law.

37. Now let all learn that the present persecution through prosecution is not of righteousness, but of evil; and all who thus participate shall feel my judgments of humbling.

38. Some shall be taken. Others shall be laid low of power.

39. I am God that saith my will to the persecution combination of government prosecuting and policing powers who have derided my holy law, and also to all peoples, that my holy way is not of the world, but of a Celestial eternal power and authority, not governed by earthly governing authority.

40. My law is pure. My pure people are commanded of their God to abide my law in purity.

41. Let them be freed who are in bondage, lest a more severe judgment increasingly come upon the land, saith Jesus Christ, the God over all. Amen.

SECTION REVELATION 221

Revelation of the Lord Jesus Christ
San Angelo, Texas
Monday, August 1, 2011

1. Let all know my pure way of Eternal Union Celestial power of Priesthood of my keys and authority was continued through a holy vessel of sacred worth of eternal power.

2. My holy and pure and named

and ordained servant of continuing my Keyholder power after John Taylor was of a martyr's crown Celestial; even to be of the holy and exalting power of ruling over all by my will of revealing saving truth to few in a day of falling away from truth, was John Woolley.

3. I revealed through John Taylor, September 26, 1886, my will, saith your Redeemer, Jesus Christ, to set apart five faithful apostles, to carry on my holy law of Celestial Marriage of Plural Order, who did so under my servant John Woolley; who also was a son of God, who was able to visit the heavenly powers, able to dwell in thy Lord's own presence; having my power of full sealing power to bless all of my eternal power of holy, pure way; to be my power on earth to officially continue my holy pure way of Eternal Union of Marriage Eternal; to be of a holy way of noble doing, to be of silent way under a covenant to not let any know of my holy Priesthood authority on earth save I should reveal.

4. Let him be of my noble and great ones, who, for forty-one years, was of noble way.

5. Let all now rejoice in John Woolley, and my holy way being of a continuation of every gift, power, authority, eternal keys of Melchizedek Priesthood on earth; there being only one man on earth at a time holding keys of sealing up into eternity, even being temple worker at times, when thy Lord would visit freely in holy places of my naming; even on street, in city, or in wilderness, or as I named; able to see beyond the veil to know greater truths.

6. Let his name be heralded to all my Priesthood to be preserved for an underground way of silent keeping, all remaining among generation falling away from my Holy Priesthood.

7. Let him be known as an holy vessel of pure way of life eternal.

8. He was visited often by Joseph Smith, as well as thy Savior; and was led to accomplish the way of eternal covenant of Union Celestial, while all around him were men of apostate doing away with religious way of revealing; until he continued my law in hiding until John Y. Barlow, remembering worthiness is discerning of character of all around and among falling-away members who sold their Priesthood way for naught.

9. Let it be heralding to all nations John W. Woolley is my son of loyal integrity worth of Celestial power; who visits my servant on earth, who is of the power of Union Eternal of key power of eternal Priesthood in full; now an administering power to many.

10. Let him be among my sons of holy Godhood, eternity of pure holy power in him abiding; while the branch of being as a dead branch broke off when Wilford Woodruff sold his Priesthood rights and power by a way of ceasing my Order of Celestial Plural Marriage power in his own domain, and giving way to governing powers, thus not being Keyholder of sealing power.

11. John W. Woolley continued in the key position, teaching, expounding, advancing my work eternity of blessing power of Priesthood.

12. He was and is stalwart, immovable in ordinance preserving of holy way of Eternal Power Priesthood in all things. Amen.

Testimonies Concerning the Prophet John W. Woolley

President Leroy S. Johnson
Leroy Johnson's Sermons 4:1575 June 3, 1978 Canada

All the leaders that have come to the earth and taken their place among God's people were fore-ordained before they came here. They were given enough knowledge to guide them along the way before their time of administration came.

I was almost fifty years old before the Lord put His finger on me. He said He wanted me to get prepared for another work when He called me into the Apostleship. About four or five years before that, I visited Brother John W. Woolley who was then head of the Priesthood -- God's chosen servant in the earth. He was the first to hold the presidency after John

Taylor in this line of Priesthood. My brother took me to see him, introduced me to him. I sat down on the couch after shaking hands with Brother Woolley. He looked a hole through me for a moment. I thought, "Oh, this man is going to tell me of all the trials and tribulations I have had." He startled me by saying, "Get up, young man, and come over here. I want to feel your hand again." I don't know whether I was shaking or whether I wasn't. I know I had a feeling that I was being tested. He looked me in the eye and said, "My boy, you'll do. You'll do." He told me to go and sit down, and I did. He says, "Now I know that I am among friends." And he opened up and told me of the revelation of 1886 and the eight-hour meeting.

A few years later, a meeting was held at Brother Charley Owens' home.*** Two weeks later, I met my brother, Price, again. He says, "Well, Roy, what do you think about what you were told in that meeting at Brother Owens' the other day?"

Until that time, I had been having an argument in my mind, because I was a good follower in the Church. I had held many prominent positions up until that time, presiding in the Aaronic Priesthood, in the Sunday School, and so forth. But when my brother put the question to me, I felt the fire go through me. I said, "Price, every word that those men told us was true. If you and I don't do what they told us to do, we will be swept off with the wicked." I have never varied from that testimony. That was the testimony given to me of this work -- this order of things. And it has been since I joined up with this order of the Priesthood that I have come to understand how Priesthood works, the order of things from the beginning until now.

President Leroy S. Johnson
Leroy Johnson's Sermons 4:1606 August 20, 1978 SLC

If I understand the record correctly, the Prophet John Taylor was visited by the One Mighty and Strong as well as by another party from the heavens. They instructed the Prophet John Taylor to set men apart to carry on the work of the Priesthood until the Redemption of Zion. I believe that that order that was given to the Prophet John Taylor by those two men that night was the true order of things that we have today and that this priesthood is trying to carry on. If this be the case, it has been told to us by all of the brethren from time to time that John W. Woolley was the man that was set apart to see that this work was carried on from that time.

There was, for awhile after the death of John W. Woolley, a short time that Lorin Woolley carried the load alone. But the work had to go on, so the Lord sent John Woolley to his son and he told him who to call and set apart to carry this work along. And those men were called.

President Leroy S. Johnson
Leroy Johnson's Sermons 5:27 Dec. 28, 1952 SCA

If the words of the Prophet Brigham Young are true and the Priesthood of God is out of the hands of the Church of Jesus Christ of Latter-day Saints, where is it? Where has it gone? Either it is somewhere outside of the Church, or Brigham Young is a false prophet. John W. Woolley filled a little niche in the line of Priesthood. He had to live in obscurity out of the lives of most people. There were only a few people that knew his position, and those who did find out his position had a hard time doing so. They had to be men of God and the Spirit of God would have to be upon them in order to find it out. Lorin Woolley stood alone in the capacity for some time, until the Lord came to him and told him to fill

up the quorum, or call other men to his assistance.

President John Y. Barlow
John Y. Barlow's Sermons
[RTJ] 8:216 September 3, 1942 SLC

My brothers and sisters, I have been greatly edified and built up through the remarks of my brethren. Looking over the congregation now, I am wondering how many are here that were with us a few years ago. I can see a few faces here that were with us a few years ago. When we used to go up to Uncle John Woolley's and Lorin Woolley's, they would tell us of things -- how the Savior and Joseph Smith came to their place and what He told them to do to keep this principle alive. I have heard those men testify to that many times. I have been called into their Council and told of these things -- tutored up. I used to live just a little way from Uncle Lorin Woolley, and I knew Uncle John Woolley; and I heard the neighbors say that Joseph F. Smith used to go up and visit with him. They said that Joseph F. thought a lot of him, that he went up and pled with him and pled with him. Yes, he did -- he counselled with him, but he wasn't pleading with him as they thought he was doing.

President John Y. Barlow
John Y. Barlow's Sermons
[RTJ] 8:169 May 25, 1941 SLC

My brothers and sisters, I have been greatly pleased with the testimonies that have been borne this afternoon. I know that this work is true. I know it only through the Spirit of God. When Brother Price Johnson was talking of Brother John Woolley, I thought many are the hours I have spent with him. Many things were showed to me then. We have seen many of those things literally fulfilled. I have seen these other men and know that they had the

Spirit of God upon them. The Holy Ghost is the Spirit of prophecy.

There are a great many things that I would like to say this afternoon. One is concerning the keys. Brothers and sisters, those keys were conferred upon us brethren. None asked for them. All we can do is bear our testimony to you that these things are true, and that God has set us apart to see that these things are done.

D.& C. 132

45. For I have conferred upon you the keys and power of the priesthood, wherein I restore all things, and make known unto you all things in due time.

46. And verily, verily, I say unto you, that whatsoever you seal on earth shall be sealed in heaven; and whatsoever you bind on earth, in my name and by my word, saith the Lord, it shall be eternally bound in the heavens; and whosoever sins you remit on earth shall be remitted eternally in the heavens; and whosoever sins you retain on earth shall be retained in heaven.

President John Y. Barlow
John Y. Barlow's Sermons
[RTJ] 8:330 April 1, 1945 SLC

Brethren, let us get a lineup on the Priesthood and find out what people are following the Priesthood of God. In the Doctrine and Covenants, Section 90 verse 4, it says that the oracles of God will be given through the Prophet Joseph. Find any other people that you can where the oracles were given through Joseph Smith. Can you find any others that have the line that comes from Joseph Smith to Brigham Young, from Brigham Young to John Taylor, to these men? Can you find any other line? I want to know the authority in the things I want. I have not heard of any other group that has been able to furnish an abstract deed as this group has in the line of the Priesthood. I just wanted to say these few words. We want you to get the testimony for yourselves. I had to get it for myself.

President John Y. Barlow
John Y. Barlow's Sermons
[RTJ] 8:147 December 31, 1940 SLC

In our day, when we stop to think of what has happened -- Elijah, holding all the power, came to the Prophet Joseph and gave it to him; and now here we are receiving it. Are we not blessed? Others are rejecting it.

Lorin Woolley used to keep telling us that his father, John Woolley, came to him quite a bit. I asked the Lord whether it was so, or whether it was not. Next time John Woolley came, I was in the room. He turned to me and said, "There is scarcely a man in this Church under ninety years old that is abiding this covenant." He gave me to understand that men out of the Church were abiding it, those who had been ostracized. (Lorin testified that I was there when his father came.)

Now, sisters, before Lorin died, he wanted to fill the Sanhedrin, and he told us that the Priesthood on the other side went from Canada to Mexico, and they couldn't find men to do it. What a condition. Talk about apostasy.

President John Y. Barlow
John Y. Barlow's Sermons
[RTJ] 8:364 November 23, 1947 SCA

Joseph Smith is the head of this dispensation and Joseph Smith is the One Mighty and Strong. John Woolley asked me if I knew who the One Mighty and Strong was. I said, "It is Joseph Smith." He said, "I know it, my boy, I know it. I am sure of it." Just a short time before that, he told us he expected the visit of some of the brethren. I said, "Uncle John, did they come and see you?" He said, "They sure did." The Doctrine and Covenants speaks of Joseph Smith. It speaks his name right out. The only thing we claim is this: God set us apart to see that all these laws and ordinances are kept alive.

Supreme Court Upholds Edmunds-Tucker Bill -- 1890

A Chronology of Federal Legislation on Polygamy

1890 April The United States Supreme Court sustained Edmunds-Tucker Bill, increasing the threat of total disfranchisement, wherein the Church would be dissolved and its property escheated. The Court held that "Congress may not only abrogate laws of the Territorial Legislature but it may itself legislate directly for the local government. Congress had a full and perfect right to repeal its [LDS] charter and abrogate its corporate existence." (United States Reports, Vol. 136, pp. 1-68. The late corporation of the Church of Jesus Christ of Latter-day Saints vs. United States, Nos. 1030, 1054.)

Law Against Plural Marriage in Utah

Constitution of the State of Utah 1896, Page 6

Article 3. Ordinance. The following ordinance shall be irrevocable without the consent of the United States and the people of this State: First: -- Perfect toleration of religious sentiment is guaranteed. No inhabitant of this State shall ever be molested in person or property on account of his or her mode of religious worship; but polygamous or plural marriages are forever prohibited.

Proceedings for the Confiscation of Mormon Church Property

Orson F. Whitney
History of Utah, Volume 3 Page 588

The day after the funeral of President Taylor, proceedings for the confiscation of Mormon Church property began, under the provisions of the Edmunds-Tucker Law. To this end, two suits were planted, at the instance of the United States Attorney General, in the Supreme Court of the Territory.***

Orson F. Whitney
History of Utah, Volume 3 Page 599

The Court's decision was delivered on the 5th of November. It was voiced by Chief Justice Zane and was a unanimous opinion. It sustained the position of counsel for the Government, and granted the motion for the appointment of a Receiver.

The Supreme Court of the United States Sanctions the Confiscation of Mormon Church Property -- May 1890

Orson F. Whitney
History of Utah, Volume 3 Page 740

On the 19th of May another sensation was created in Utah by the telegraphed announcement that the Supreme Court of the United States had that day rendered a decision adverse to the defendant in the great suit of the Federal Government vs. the Mormon Church; the issue in which was the confiscation of the Church property under the provisions of the Edmunds-Tucker Act. For more than a year the Court had had this case under advisement, the arguments therein having been made in January, 1889.

The Court's opinion -- voiced by Mr. Justice Bradley -- reasserted the constitutionality of the Edmunds-Tucker Act, and confirmed the decision confiscating the Mormon Church property. That Church, the Court said, was an organized rebellion, a contumacious organization, the distinguishing features of whose creed were polygamy and the absolute ecclesiastical control of its members. It wielded by its resources immense power in Utah, and employed those resources in propagating a practice offensive to civilization, and in constantly attempting to oppose, subvert and thwart the legislation of Congress and the will of the Government. Hence, Congress had the right to do as it had done. "We have carefully examined the decree, and do not find anything in it that calls for a reversal. It may perhaps require modification in some matters of detail, and for that purpose only the case is reserved for further consideration."

The Manifesto -- September 24, 1890 Plural Marriage Suspended by the Mormon Church

Orson F. Whitney
History of Utah, Volume 3 Page 743

The autumn of the year witnessed an event of supreme importance to Utah and the Mormon people. No event in the history of the Territory has caused more comment or been more prolific of results. It was the issuance by the President of the Church of Jesus Christ of Latter-day Saints and the unanimous acceptance by its members, of what is known as "The Manifesto," an official declaration in which the Mormon leader -- Wilford Woodruff -- made known his intention to submit to the laws of Congress enacted against the practice of plural marriage, and use his influence to induce his people to do the same.

Many Fall in Upholding Manifesto Against the Celestial Law

President Leroy S. Johnson
Leroy Johnson's Sermons 4:1357 March 20, 1977 SLC

And I guess one of the greatest stumbling blocks of all times was the signing of the Manifesto by President Wilford Woodruff. It caused more people to stumble and lose

their way than anything I know of. Yet, the Lord has allowed stumbling blocks to be laid in the paths of the Priesthood as well. And many of the Priesthood have fallen away because of these stumbling blocks.

President Leroy S. Johnson
Leroy Johnson's Sermons 1:211 Sept. 8, 1970 CCA

It was mentioned here today of the 1886 Revelation; and in that revelation it tells us that the way was prepared for the continuation of this Gospel through a wicked generation of people. In 1890 the Manifesto was signed by the President of the Church of Jesus Christ of Latter-day Saints; and not only did they sign away their privileges to the New and Everlasting Covenant, or the law of Plural Marriage, but they broke every other commandment that God has given. Why? Because God says: Break one of these commandments and you are guilty of the whole. Why doesn't every Latter-day Saint in the Church of Jesus Christ of Latter-day Saints back up the law of Plural Marriage and the Celestial Law in its fullness? Simply because they have signed away their rights to it.

The Priesthood in Hiding in the Days of the Persecution by the Power of Government

President John Y. Barlow
John Y. Barlow's Sermons
[RTJ] 8:321 Dec. 24, 1944 SLC

I can well remember the underground days. I can remember men hiding at our home and women being taken across. I remember Uncle John Woolley telling of a case where he went to Grantsville with a woman who gave birth to a child on the way, and he had to attend to her himself. How many of you have read the pamphlet that Ellis got out? Get it and follow up the trials and tribulations they went through.

We haven't gone through anything like that yet. What we will go through, I don't know. But I do know this -- if you are humble and prayerful, a door will be opened and we will be relieved.

Mormon Church Joins Law Enforcement in Prosecuting the Priesthood People; Presidents John and Lorin Woolley Suffer at the Hand of the Mormon Church

**Testimony of Fred M. Jessop
and Richard S. Jessop**

Threats of prosecution were made to Lorin Woolley personally. Richard Seth Jessop, a friend and close associate of John and Lorin Woolley related, that Lorin Woolley attended a stake conference in 1922 and was told by a leading church official that, "your father has not suffered enough. We intend to put that old man away for 6 months."

**April 1931 Deseret Evening News,
Conference Report**

At the April conference of 1931, President Heber J. Grant had pledged the resources of the Church and its members to the prosecution and imprisonment of all those adhering to the law of plural marriage, asking them to ratify the same by vote. He stated at this conference: "We have been, however, and we are entirely willing and anxious too that such offenders against the law of the State should be dealt with and punished as the law provides. We have been and we are willing to give such legal assistance as we legitimately can in the criminal prosecution of such cases."

Chapter 5

Administration of President Lorin C. Woolley

SECTION REVELATION 222

**Revelation of the Lord Jesus Christ
Palestine, Texas
Wednesday, October 5, 2011**

1.   Thus saith the Lord unto all peoples, that my servant Lorin C. Woolley was next Keyholder of full sealing powers and keys after his father John Woolley passed on.

2.   He stood alone bearing the apostleship for a time; I then having a quorum called by him to receive the apostleship.

3.   He was my son of witnessing his father's administration; and of witnessing the apostasy of most of my people when they persecuted my Priesthood as a Church, fighting against my Celestial Law of Celestial Plural Marriage; even that organization once of my Priesthood.

4.   He, Lorin, was of the gift of receiving my own presence.

5.   He is witness to eternal visions, visitations and visiting eternal powers Celestial while in the flesh; confirming him in knowledge of God in full exalting power.

6.   He shall yet be on earth again

as a son of full power of Priesthood holy power, in the governing of the earth during my holy reign of peace. Amen.

SECTION REVELATION 223

**Revelation of the Lord Jesus Christ
San Angelo, Texas
Monday, August 1, 2011**

1. My sole apostle on earth at a time of Priesthood in hiding was Lorin Woolley, a son of a Keyholder, and also next Keyholder of all full powers of Priesthood. He often met with thy Lord in wilderness, and in sacred temple places; was so pure, he could be of a conveying to peoples far away; to teach and bless.

2. Lorin C. Woolley continued as Keyholder, alone in apostleship holding until he was of an ordaining way of pure apostleship power upon a quorum of sons who he taught full key powers of Priesthood power; John Y. Barlow next to stand in my Keyholder position, able to also visit the Holy Priesthood on the other side of the veil.

3. He, Lorin Woolley, was a great Prophet, able to walk and

talk with me, even momentarily as needing guiding to be preserving my Priesthood on earth, now a God of eternal power.

4. Let all rejoice in the mission and pure abiding power of Priesthood I bestowed upon Lorin Woolley, a son of God of eternal power of holy power Celestial. He was witness to his father's administrating all keys of Priesthood; and of power to visit places of needing Priesthood power.

5. Let my Holy Priesthood power be of resounding joy.

6. Let all know I shall preserve my holy way unto Zion, unto full power eternal. Amen.

Testimonies Concerning the Prophet Lorin C. Woolley

President Rulon Jeffs
Rulon Jeffs' Sermons 6:330 December 14, 1986 CCA

And this is a continuation; this work and this Priesthood, which we have with us, is a continuation from that time through John W. Woolley, through Lorin C. Woolley, through John Y. Barlow, and Leroy Sunderland Johnson. The Lord set up that order of Priesthood, a continuation of it, in 1886, in contemplation of the Church leaving the Priesthood. The Church left the Priesthood and went into the wilderness and is now roaming around in darkness.

So, my dear brothers and sisters, you can see why I have to say what lies before me is awesome. But I testify to you that God is at the helm, and the work of God will continue according to His direction and His ways and His will.

President Leroy S. Johnson
Leroy S. Johnson's Sermons 4:1606 Aug. 20, 1978 SLC

There was, for awhile after the death of John W. Woolley, a short time that Lorin Woolley carried the load alone. But the work had to go on, so the Lord sent John Woolley to his son and he told him who to call and set apart to carry this work along. And those men were called.***

So, the house of God is still in order. It is going along being led and directed by the same characters that visited the Prophet Joseph Smith, Brigham Young, and John Taylor. So, we are on our way. My dear brothers and sisters, we are on our way. Let us continue our preparation, for in all ages of the world men have had to be prepared for the great and glorious work the Lord had for them to accomplish. So, this work is going on. There is no discrepancy in the leadership that we have, for we have all been called under the same spirit and are being directed by the same spirit that directed the organization of the Church of Jesus Christ of Latter-day Saints, and the setting up of the Priesthood work. And it is going to go on. It is going to continue until the way is prepared for someone else to take over.

President John Y. Barlow
John Y. Barlow's Sermons
[RTJ] 8:214 Aug. 9, 1942 SLC

I know this work is true, and I know these brethren sitting by me today have the authority that they say they have. I know that. Many of the other brethren here have been with them and know wherein they spoke it was true. When I was set apart in this work I said, "Are you doing this because I am your friend?" He [Lorin C. Woolley] said, "I had nothing to do with it whatever. God told me to set you apart."

I want to bear my testimony to you that I did go to the Lord as I was told to do, and I got my testimony. God did set these brethren apart to do this special work, and to see that these principles were kept alive. God never reveals in any day or age non-essentials. When God reveals a law, He gives it to you because it is essential.

President John Y. Barlow
John Y. Barlow's Sermons
[RTJ] 8:149 Jan. 3, 1941 SLC

Hail to the Prophet ascended to heaven. Let me tell you something here, that the Prophet Joseph has ascended to heaven, and there are times he comes down to earth. I had the privilege of seeing him come from heaven, and he told me he wanted a man, and he wanted him quick. I told the brethren that it was Brother Isaac Carling, that he was wanted on the other side. We don't know any day when the Lord will say, "We want them up there and want them quick." I have heard Brother

Lorin tell when he was very sick -- I miss him -- Lorin Woolley told Brother John, "Brother John, I make that promise to you, that you will do a great and mighty work in the Kingdom of God here on the earth;" and I want to say that every man that has been called of God by revelation is doing a great and mighty work upon this earth today.

President John Y. Barlow
John Y. Barlow's Sermons
[RTJ] 8:216 Sept. 13, 1942 SLC

When we used to go up to Uncle John Woolley's and Lorin Woolley's, they would tell us of things -- how the Savior and Joseph Smith came to their place and what he told them to do to keep this principle alive. I have heard those men testify to that many times. I have been called into their Council and told of these things -- tutored up. I used to live just a little way from Uncle Lorin Woolley, and I knew Uncle John Woolley... .

Chapter 6

Administration of President John Y. Barlow

SECTION REVELATION 224

Revelation of the Lord Jesus Christ
Palestine, Texas
Sunday, October 2, 2011

1. I, your Lord Jesus Christ, the God over all, now reveal concerning my servant John Y. Barlow; that he was my full and pure Keyholder of Priesthood after my servant Lorin C. Woolley passed on.

2. Let it be known that John Y. Barlow continued my keys of Priesthood and my Celestial Law of Celestial Plural Marriage, and all the laws of Priesthood on earth, faithfully.

3. He was imprisoned for living my Celestial Law.

4. He was faithful to the end.

5. He called twelve brethren of the apostleship to be faithful, ordaining seven of them himself by my appointing.

6. He was of the full receiving of all keys of Elijah of sealing power.

7. He was of the receiving of revelations, dreams, visitations of former Prophets, to guide him of me, saith your Lord.

8. Now receive my word:

9. John Y. Barlow continued my Priesthood and Celestial Law on earth by my word and full Priesthood authority.

10. He is of they who returneth and helps to govern the nations during my reign on earth of the Millennial Time of Peace soon at hand.

11. Now learn that the wicked persecuted John Y. Barlow unto the end, he being as a holy and pure martyr for my cause; and shall be a witness against the people of the Church of apostate persecuting power, and against governing powers of the nation, in a time of full judging of thy God upon this wicked generation. Amen.

The Prophets Speak About Persecution

President John Y. Barlow
John Y. Barlow's Sermons
[RTJ] 8:265 Feb. 6, 1944 SCA

Brigham Young said, "Be careful how you persecute this people. God will hold men responsible for every act against the Latter-day Saints."

We have been preaching to get the Spirit of God and keep it. Brothers and sisters, we are going to need it. We have got to be more humble; we have got to let the things of this world go by and bring our minds and our souls and everything under God. If we don't, we are going to be in a trap. If we do it, God will open up a door, and just as men think they have us caught,

Uncle Lorin told us, if we will exercise the right kind of faith, a door will open and we will go through.

Supposing some of us are put in jail. What difference does it make? The Prophet Joseph never was convicted in law. Why was he ever arrested? Because of the prejudice of the people. Every history that we have of the saints of God on earth is just like we are getting today. You hear them say, "Why, it is against the law of the land." Who made the laws? Men did. They aren't the laws of God. Those are the things we are looking for. When Daniel was told not to pray because it was against the law of the land, Daniel prayed just the same. It wasn't against the laws of God. They threw him into the lions' den, but he had the Spirit of God around him and those lions couldn't touch him. The Three Hebrews were cast into the fiery furnace, and the fire couldn't hurt them.

President Leroy S. Johnson
Leroy S. Johnson's Sermons 6:136 June 12, 1966 CCA

The servants of God have been trying to get before the people of the world for a number of years now, the truth of the everlasting Gospel as it was given to the Prophet Joseph Smith for the salvation of the human family. And what is the reaction? I first got acquainted with this work in 1934. Since that time, we have seen four raids come in because the people were afraid that we were going to get too strong. They tried to whip us on conspiracy to teach lewd and obscene doctrine to the people through the mails. But it didn't go. Why? Because the Lord would not let it. His doctrine is not lewd and obscene, but it pertains to the eternal salvation of man. That didn't suit them. They sent some of our men to jail. They came out with the same spirit that they had before. They would not give up. Then they tried it

again, but they did not succeed -- in 1935, and in 1941. In 1944, they took us in for conspiracy. In 1953, they came in and took all of us out. They took the men out and put them in jail, then they came in and loaded their families and took them away.

1935 Raid in
Short Creek, Arizona

President Leroy S. Johnson
Leroy S. Johnson's Sermons 4:1256 Aug. 8, 1976 CCA

...in 1934, President Barlow, Price Johnson, and Carling Spencer were arrested and brought to trial. At this time, I had already had the privilege of hearing the brethren speak and I believed what they had to say sufficient that I commenced to get on my armor and began to fight for the rights of the Priesthood. Since that time, we have gone through several other raids in which I was personally involved to some extent.

President Leroy S. Johnson
Leroy S. Johnson's Sermons 5:350 Oct. 6, 1963 SLC

...he [the prosecutor] was in Short Creek holding court over President Barlow *** [the defense] entered a demur in the case, on the ground that the warrants were based upon belief and not on knowledge. The Justice of the Peace acknowledged the demur and dismissed the case. So, while Brother Bollinger was getting his papers ready for a new arrest based on knowledge, we slipped the prisoners out of the road and put them on their way. Brother Barlow's case was dismissed entirely, so he got out of it. The other two men had to flee for their lives.

Arizona Authorities Assisted by
Mormon Church in Arrest of
President Barlow

President John Y. Barlow
December 18, 1935, Letter to the Saints, SCA

No doubt you have heard or read of the

trial and will say that in it all, the testimony showed that it was backed by those of the Church, and things that had been done in the High Councils of the stakes were taken as evidence. This is just another testimony that will stand against the leaders, and fulfills the scripture which says "They that lead thee cause thee to err and turn from the truth." We had for witness against them, a Stake president, a Bishop, and men who were born thru this Law.

Government Power Raids Priesthood in 1944 in Utah, Arizona, and Became Persecutor of Religion

President Rulon Jeffs
History of Priesthood Succession, Page 199

At six o'clock in the morning on March 7, 1944, officers arrested sixty people in three states all at the same time.***

In the course of the morning, after having been docketed in the county jail, we were taken over to the Federal Building on 4th South and Main Street to be arraigned before the U.S. magistrate. The charges were conspiracy to put into the United States mail lewd and lascivious matter, like the Truth Magazine. Our charges on the state level were conspiracy to teach the practice of plural marriage and unlawful cohabitation.

President John Y. Barlow and Fourteen Other Men Go to Prison in May 1945

History of Priesthood Succession, Page 205
[Truth 11:26]

The Supreme Court of the United States denied the petition for rehearing in the cases involving the unlawful cohabitation charges. Accordingly, the defendants appeared before Judge Van Cott on May 12, [1945], and were committed to the custody of the sheriff to carry out the sentence. Immediately, attorneys for the defendants served notice of petition for writ of habeas corpus, and they were retained in the county jail pending hearing of the petition in the court of Judge J. Allan Crockett. He heard the arguments April 14 and 15, and denied the petition for such writ.

The fifteen***have been incarcerated in the state penitentiary for an indeterminate period not to exceed five years.

The hearts of all honest and truth-loving people go out to these men and their families, who are called upon to make this sacrifice for the sake of the Gospel.

The Entity Called The Church of Jesus Christ of Latter-day Saints Assists Government

President John Y. Barlow
John Y. Barlow's Sermons
[RTJ] 8:278 April 6, 1944 SLC

The government is against us, but we do know that it is being run by those at the head of Main Street [the Mormon Church]. We know that this has all been fixed up by a man now made president of a European mission, and we do know that it was a bishop who put the law forth. Are we going to get mad? Let us let the Lord take a hand in that, and say within ourselves, "God, forgive them, for they know not what they do." Let us let the Lord take a hand in it. I do know that every man who raises a hand against these laws of God will sooner or later feel the power of God upon them. The Lord says to forgive all men, and He will forgive whom He will. If they can stand it, then we can. The only way we can get out of this is by fasting and praying to the Lord. I saw this over a year ago, and said if we would be humble and prayerful, that there would be a door open in the wall.

President John Y. Barlow
John Y. Barlow's Sermons
[RTJ] 8:334 April 7, 1946 SCA

My brothers and sisters, I cannot tell you how thankful I am. I cannot tell you how I love this people here. Yes, we knew you had prayed; we knew a lot of other things, too. We knew there were others fighting, and we knew that some were praying, and knew that God was hearing and answering prayers. The first time I went before the board of pardons, they were just as bitter as could be (I should say parole board). I went home and fasted and prayed; and in a week I went back again, and he said, "You can go and stay as long as you want to, and just let us know when you want to come back." I know that God touched their hearts.

President John Y. Barlow Goes to Prison; One Man Rule Upheld

President Rulon Jeffs
Rulon Jeffs' Sermons 7:489 February 26, 1949 SLC

The grandest example we have in this life are the sacrifices of the Lord Jesus Christ. They were many. As He made one sacrifice after another, He gained strength. But think of the power He had to go and stand with His Father, and lay hold on eternal life, brothers and sisters, after He made the last great sacrifice.

Brother Johnson and Brother John and others made the sacrifice, and don't you think that after coming out of prison, that their strength and power is greater now than it was? They now have power over their traducers, those who have striven to take their lives. How can we go before the Lord and have confidence that He will answer when we know we are doing some wrong? Let us resolve to clean up our lives. "If ye love Me, keep My commandments."

Fifteen imprisoned in 1945, John Y. Barlow front row, second from right.

President Rulon Jeffs
Rulon Jeffs' Sermons 7:525 January 1, 1950 SLC

And let no man set upon the name of any who preceded John Y. Barlow, and John Y. Barlow himself; for I would stand between him and you, if you would. I want to tell you, John Y. Barlow was a servant of God.***

No one can destroy this Priesthood or the principles of the Everlasting Gospel, and though I lay down my life for it, it will go on. It will take the best blood of this generation yet. I would consider it a privilege and honor to give mine, if it would be needed. Let us see to our knitting.

President John Y. Barlow
John Y. Barlow's Sermons
[RTJ] 8:286 May 28, 1944 SLC

2 Timothy 3

12. Yea, and all that will live godly in Christ Jesus shall suffer persecution.

Connect that up with this group that are being fought against. Find out about them. God said, I believe to Nephi, that He never commanded a people to do a work except that He opened a way to do it. Now the laws of the land come up and say if you do live the laws of God, you will be sentenced. I, among others, am being sentenced, and they want to put us in jail and make it hard for us to keep out. I do not know but what it will be a good thing for some of us. It will humble us. I do not want to go if I can get out of it, but if they do put us in, I hope the Lord will give me the strength to go on. As Brother Snow said, "Though I go to prison, God will not change the laws of marriage." This people should know by this time that Mormonism, if one of its leading principles is wrong, because it is from God, all God's laws are wrong.

Some of us know that that thing is right. We know what is coming, that we have a fight on our hands.

The whole thing is not plural marriage. It is the Priesthood of God and who has the right to it. It is not long before that stone is going to roll, and when it starts it will not stop; and as the consumptive decree will be sent out there, it will put an end to all nations. There is not any of us that needs a Prophet of God to see what is coming. It is before us.

I say to all you men and women, get behind the laws of God.

John Y. Barlow's Testimony of Celestial Plural Marriage Unto This Generation

President John Y. Barlow
John Y. Barlow's Sermons
[RTJ] 8:256 Dec. 12, 1943 SLC

Nothing less than eternal salvation will satisfy the immortal soul. We were put on this earth to live a Celestial Law. If we fail to live these commandments, then we will be thrown back. How will we feel when we think that we might have gone on? It is this law that is going to exalt us.

President John Y. Barlow
John Y. Barlow's Sermons
[RTJ] 8:156 Feb. 23, 1941 SLC

Are we obeying it? Are we keeping it? I tell you what is going to happen to us if we don't obey the voice of the Lord. President Young says the only people that will be exalted will be those that are living the Celestial Law. John Taylor said that God has given a revelation that will exalt us in the eternal worlds, and we do not intend to have it kicked out, whether in the Church or not.

President John Y. Barlow
John Y. Barlow's Sermons
[RTJ] 8:162 April 6, 1941 SLC

My brothers and sisters, I have been greatly edified by the words that have been spoken today. I heard a man say the other day, "Is it in this life that plural marriage first came into existence?" Do you expect to get into the Celestial Kingdom? That law was taught in the beginning. Adam had to live it, and he had to beget spirit children in that law before he came here to earth. That law was taught and practiced in that time as well as it is now. Then we, no doubt, understand it before we came to this life. Remember, this law, plural marriage, is not a law of the people; it is a law of the holy Priesthood. It was taught to Joseph Smith and some of his friends, and he had twenty-seven wives sealed to him before it was made known to the people. It was taught to him in 1831, but it was not until 1843 that it was made known to others. The people of the Church never accepted it until 1852, and in a special Conference here in Salt Lake, they adopted the principle, and sent Brother Orson Pratt to Washington. It was taught as a law of the Church, and in 1890, it was rejected. Then the Priesthood picked it up again and it was never rejected; and God saw that it went on and sent His Son Jesus Christ and Joseph Smith here to earth to see that this law was continued. Why? Because you and I cannot be Gods without it. There is a law irrevocably decreed upon which every blessing is predicated.

President Leroy S. Johnson and President Rulon Jeffs Bear Testimony of the Prophet John Y. Barlow

President Leroy S. Johnson
Leroy S. Johnson's Sermons 8:180 Feb. 22, 1953 SCA

The name of John Y. Barlow will someday be heralded as one of the greatest Prophets of this time, and one of the greatest leaders of this time, because he lived in a time when the Priesthood of God came out of hiding. He not only bore testimony to the truthfulness of the Priesthood, but he suffered imprisonment, he suffered persecution, and he died a martyr to the cause.

President Rulon Jeffs
Rulon Jeffs' Sermons 1:13 December 8, 1946 SCA

John Y. Barlow, the President of the Priesthood upon the earth, is the mouthpiece of God. I know it as I know I live. He, along with his co-workers, are God's servants.

President Rulon Jeffs
Rulon Jeffs' Sermons 1:21 Sept. 14, 1947 Widtsoe

I know that this is the work of God, and John Y. Barlow is the mouthpiece of God on the earth today. I know I bear the Priesthood of God, and that I am an Apostle of Jesus Christ. I can't believe that unless I believe that John Y. Barlow holds the keys of the Priesthood on earth today, because I got mine from him. Let us stand shoulder to shoulder.

Chapter 7

Administration of President Leroy S. Johnson

SECTION REVELATION 225

Revelation of the Lord Jesus Christ
Palestine, Texas
Sunday, October 2, 2011

1. I, your Lord, speak to all peoples, that my son of faithful and peaceful way, even Leroy S. Johnson, was of the full Keyholder power and authority of my Eternal Priesthood after John Y. Barlow passed on to his reward.

2. Leroy S. Johnson held keys of Priesthood from the time of John Y. Barlow's passing; I, your Lord, giving him those keys of power, to continue mine authority on earth, as also mine holy Celestial Law of Celestial Plural Marriage, and all my Priesthood laws.

3. Thus, he was also persecuted.

4. In 1953, a raid of the government came upon him and my community in Short Creek, Arizona, carrying away all women and children, even mothers with their children; the government announcing they were going to adopt out all the children, trying to destroy my Celestial Law and Priesthood.

5. I led my servant, Leroy S. Johnson, to overthrow this government attack, and to gather back all my people who were taken.

6. Thus did I overthrow this attack, and preserved my Priesthood and the Celestial Law on earth.

7. He is among the Gods in eternal power, and shall also be among the governing Celestial powers that are on earth guiding my Priesthood in Councils of full governing authority during my Millennial Reign of Peace, now soon to burst forth upon all nations.

8. He is my son of suffering power, suffering unto a full reward as a God of full power. Amen.

1928 Meeting With John W. Woolley

President Leroy S. Johnson
Leroy S. Johnson's Sermons 4:1575
June 3, 1978 Canada

I was almost fifty years old before the Lord put His finger on me. He said He wanted me to get prepared for another work when He called me into the Apostleship. About four or five years before that, I visited Brother John W. Woolley who was then head of the Priesthood -- God's chosen servant in the earth. He was the first to hold the presidency after John Taylor in this line of Priesthood. My brother took me to see him, introduced me to him. I sat down on the couch after shaking hands with Brother Woolley. He looked a hole through me for a moment. I thought, "Oh, this man is going to tell me of all the trials and tribulations I have had." He startled me by saying, "Get up, young man, and come over here. I want to feel your hand again." I don't know whether I was shaking or whether I wasn't. I know I had a feeling that I was being tested. He looked me in the eye and said, "My boy, you'll do. You'll do." He told me to go and sit down, and I did. He says, "Now I know that I am among friends." And he opened up and told me of the revelation of 1886 and the eight-hour meeting.

A few years later, a meeting was held at Brother Charley Owens' home. I heard Brother Zitting, Brother Kelsch, Brother Joseph Musser declare that John Y. Barlow held the keys of the Priesthood. I knew that Brother John W. Woolley had passed away, and that was all I had heard about it. I never saw Lorin Woolley. I never had the privilege of seeing Leslie Broadbent. Until that time, I had never met John Y. Barlow. My nephew, Isaac Carling, was the man that took me out to this meeting at Brother Owens' place. My brother, Price, was there, too. Two weeks later, I met my brother, Price, again. He says, "Well, Roy, what do you think about what you were told in that meeting at Brother Owens' the other day?"

Until that time, I had been having an argument in my mind, because I was a good follower in the Church. I had held many prominent positions up until that time, presiding in the Aaronic Priesthood, in the Sunday School, and so forth. But when my brother put the question to me, I felt the fire go through me. I said, "Price, every word that those men told us was true. If you and I don't do what they told us to do, we will be swept off with the wicked."

I have never varied from that testimony. That was the testimony given to me of this work -- this order of things. And it has been since I joined up with this order of the Priesthood that I have come to understand how Priesthood works, the order of things from the beginning until now.

I bear testimony to you that Joseph Smith was a prophet of God; and this is his work continued, and nobody elses. It is the work of Joseph Smith continued in the earth. In other words, this is the work of Jesus Christ, the Church and Kingdom of God continued in the earth; and anyone who fights against this order of things will be sloughed off, and be damned, for the Lord has said so. It does not make any difference what our relatives say, or those who are near and dear to us by the ties of nature. It is the same. If we don't keep the commandments of God as they are given to us through this order of things, we will be sloughed off and destroyed.

1953 Raid on Short Creek

What Really Happened at Short Creek, by an Eye Witness

Fred M. Jessop, December 1953
History of Priesthood Succession, Page 256
(Truth 19:193-198)

They knew the raid was coming, but plans for commemorating the advent of the coming of the pioneers had been made. They celebrated gravely and with mingled feelings. Observing the 24th, consisted of cannon salute and flag ceremony at sunrise. Men and boys were up unusually early to participate. Several World War II veterans maneuvered and gave a rifle salute as those present signified true patriotism. Among those present was one venerated by a life of honesty and candor for 84 years, his flowing beard yielded manifestly in the cool morning breeze, the performing ex-soldiers who had seen foreign action for freedoms cause, seeing this from the corner of their eye, bowed their homage in spirit to their superior patriot grandfather, standing bare-headed, slightly bent with faithfulness over so many snows, while Old Glory was drawn up to be kissed by the first rays of sunrise at the public square.

Celebration programme was for all day.

Preparations for lemonade stand, playground and entertaining facilities used up the time of well organized crews of younger men and boys. The yard had been previously raked clean of trash and anything unsightly that would mar the enjoyment of the day.

At ten o'clock people gathered from every quarter. Work had been suspended. Pickups, cars and trucks loaded with families, boys and girls cleaned up specially, all eager eyed chattering exuberantly in anticipation, unloaded at the school ground. The rig that had been dispatched to Cedar City, seventy miles distant to bring the ice cream, was the last to come, just in time for every one to be crowded into the auditorium for the program, where appropriate songs and speeches imbued the hearts of all present with genuine gratitude for pioneer sacrifices, and carefully adjusted attitudes to appropriately celebrate. The program concluded with a humble benediction and a blessing on the food. A corps of busy efficient women under the direction of the general committee had by this time prepared a dinner and facilities to serve the congregated 500 towns folk and visiting people a wholesome dinner, forty at a time, on roast chicken, mashed potatoes, green salad, corn bread, buttermilk, raisin pie and ice cream.

No one felt the burden of so fine a spread because it was beforehand planned, the expense having been taken care of from the general treasury, into which all had pooled their earnings. Men from the sawmill, timber crews, fence building crews, fruit pickers, farmers, gardeners, mechanics, and carpenters, took pride in realizing this was their treat to their great happy community family. Children frequented the lemonade stand and joined the games intermittently. All was free, activities well organized and supervised. No one was hurt, no one offended. Thoughtful people carried trays of food home to those not able to attend the dinner.***

Social relations at a pitch almost out of this world attained by careful guidance, willing and diligent practice.

Tired and happy children went to bed that evening while adolescents and grown ups gathered for the final celebration social. Despite the gravity in the minds of the oldsters over the impending possible disaster, genuine smiles were exchanged from behind beards and beneath bonnets in keeping with the theme of the pioneer character ball they were attending.

Religious -- in work and in play, devotion is never neglected. After a prayer for propriety to characterize the social co-mingling, music began, and the well practiced dancers forgot their worries in wholesome decorum. As the larger hours presented, the celebration's 'finale' was rendered by selected home talent in a chorus anthem, *"Grant us peace O Lord, and we will serve Thee"*, *"Let all who fight Thee be confounded, let the Righteous dwell in peace."* *"In all Thy holy mountains let peace abide forever, Grant Thou our prayer."* Tenors, altos, sopranos, basses, in ecstatic harmony filled the atmosphere with melody and penetrated every listening heart. Fired them with determination to stand true, to the commandments of God given to the early founders, enjoining faithful compliance upon all those seeking salvation. *Every accountable heart knew the history, when the birth of this nation guided by the hand of providence became a haven for the religiously oppressed -- knew God made obligatory the practice of ancient orders by which to seal earth to heaven -- knew that in course of time political debauchees had steered legislative enactments against the Mormon exiles. Knew that the faithless of the banished people predominated over the stalwarts, and succumbed their commonwealth to the persecutions, fearing man more than God. Knew that since that time those who braved salvation's pathway did so at the peril of infractions of the law. Knew as Jesus knew that the resurrection was beyond Gethsemane -- and resolved to accept the inevitable, yet hoping with every American corpuscle that "we hold these truths, (our God-inspired Constitution) to be self-evident, that all men are created equal, that they are endowed by their Creator with certain inalienable rights, that among these are life, liberty and the pursuit of happiness. That to secure these rights governments are instituted among men, deriving their just powers from the consent of the governed. That whenever any form of government becomes destructive of these ends, it is the right of the people to alter or abolish it, and to institute new government laying its foundations on such principles and organizing its powers in such form, as to them shall seem most likely to effect their safety and happiness."*

It was midnight......twenty-four hours elapsed......I heard the dynamite blasts that warned the townspeople that the raid was coming on, and to get up and be dressed. Saw a pickup shuttle through the village giving the call to assemble at the schoolhouse. In record time they gathered. One of the fellows hurried across lots and started the generator. The people went inside. The long converted barracks building had been carefully set for worship. Men and women took their places quickly and without comment, while the elders went to the stand, grave faced but perfectly composed, two sat and one stood at the pulpit, perfect attention was given to "Uncle Roy" a genial father by nature, solid and prophetic befitting his leadership responsibility, his steel grey eyes and vibrant voice sweetly and willingly respected, he wore an overcoat and was a little hoarse but undaunted and fearless, explained the reasons for "our calling you together." "We want to be ready when they come." He called for the chorister -- hymn books quickly whisked through the audience, then in calm unmistakable voice declared that "We will use 'Brigham's weapon, the songs of Zion," page announced, prelude ended, and the congregation again responded accurately, swelled the building with harmonic, ecstatic determination. I heard the patriarch dedicate *"this people to the Lord"*, I saw the elders beckoned outside to receive the whispered report of intercepted radio conversation of the tattler and the invaders. Breathless, heard the report and resounding admonition to *"stand true to God," "this has not come upon us because we have failed to keep God's commandments or broken any moral law, but because the Lord has found a people willing to be made an example of," "let us rid our hearts of all dis-unity or ill feelings toward one another, we are all in His hands."*

Further songs of prayer and praise were

interrupted by a runner from the hill top as he stumbled in, fatigued and gasping intelligence of the long line of blacked out police cars moaning along in the last dim light of the eclipsed moon. People moved outside into a little tight knot on the lawn.

All eyes turned toward the horizon as husbands held tight handclasps to their wives and the few children not left in the houses were huddled close and told not to cry, "we must be brave" and "God will take care of us". The low moan of the sirens and flashing red lights and sweeping spotlights moving like a stealthy serpent in upon the waiting community, filled every heart with unmistakable apprehension -- this is it!! Some one rang the bell -- the elder called "sing" and the taut nerves of the compact little group then responded to the patriotic resignation produced by "America" sung to full resounding volumes in early morning darkness. A veteran soldier led in a unison pledge of allegiance to the flag almost before it reached the top of the mast. By this time the county sheriff's car leading the cavalcade was in front of the schoolhouse. The sheriff, with a trace of tension in his voice, called out through a radio speaker, *"Stay where you are. Stay where you are."* "This is Sheriff Porter. We have warrants for your arrest. Stay where you are." No sooner had the first word sounded than the police cars bristling with artillery filled the streets, every officer covered by another officer. *Immediately the little knot on the lawn was literally corralled by armed officers with their hands only inches from their undrawn guns -- all was poised to handle a dirty mess -- BUT THERE WAS NONE. "Uncle Roy" in fearless but not unkind voice sounded out clear above the tumult, "Why have you come here? We're bothering no one. Why don't you let us alone? We're not giving up if it costs the* *blood of every man of us! Why don't you clean up your own places? You are a bunch of cowards to come so upon us." This said as he strode from officer to officer who formed the stockade. There I saw a man whom the world calls brave -- one who has braved many a hole, taken his life in his hands to take a desperado, armed with all the paraphernalia to render his prey helpless and lifeless at the quickest instant -- stand mute before that lion of the Lord [President Leroy S. Johnson] as he stood bare handed and bare headed before that officer, snatching a frightened child from her mother presenting it to the gallant officer armed to the teeth covered in the darkness with machine-guns and tear gas and scores of riflemen prepared to quell a riot, saying, "Have you the heart to take this screaming child from its mother? Have you?" I saw and heard the octogenarian [Joseph Smith Jessop] virile with the experience of a life-time of rectitude step forward, his voice booming over the foray say, "If it's blood you want take mine, I'm ready!" Saw two Korean frontlinemen standing on the perimeter declare their utter disgust at such gestapo tactics, dismayed at such a homecoming, and over a dozen other veterans identify themselves as having served in foreign theaters for freedom, asking why such preposterous un-American proceedings.*

Officers in charge all but fought back the pressmen by the hundreds, who previously invited, had come especially to cover the synthetic news; representatives of local, county and state newspapers and leading magazines from California, Denver, Chicago, New York, London and Paris, until official photographs were taken. Daylight found the little group still corralled. A few conspiring stooges were brought forth to identify the principle men and to attach names to faces now seen in the early grey light of a desecrated Sabbath day.

The well ordered chapel room was quickly converted into court chambers. Officials and henchmen smoked and littered in the Sunday School room. One adjoining room, guarded on every side, served as the jail. The line of demarkation was drawn, men were hailed into court and thus incarcerated. Women and children with none to counsel or advise them, save those who wiley sought the downfall of their homes, milled wantonly about the schoolyard forbidden to leave. (One woman sought leave to go home to her baby but was restrained; she insisted a gentleman would not detain her.)

By this time the whole town was under a type of martial law, every home had been invaded, literature, deeds, documents, books, bibles and effects taken by police, officers, investigators and welfare agents. Women and children were rounded up to attend court, charged like their husbands with conspiracy to commit rape, bigamy, adultery, white slavery, etc. Detachments from the National Guard with all the gear for occupation, set up radio station, field kitchen, road blockades, medics station, Welfare, and officers quarters.

Breakfast was hours belated, the community mercy sister entreated for the privilege to go home for bread for a delicate woman and to take nursing mothers to relief, but was denied. Men from the chow march to the field kitchen in a pasture a quartermile distant, waving smiles and greetings to their companions and anxious children, heard the governor's radio speech as he sat securely in the Capitol padded by the colossal conspiracy of aggregated press and propaganda machinery, set up for a planned political parade, droning out the news almost before it happened, promising that though the men were already enroute to the county jail, the children would be provided for and be granted "happiness of their own choosing". The children looking back, knew they were loved, wanted, planned for, yet bewildered, heard horrid threats that the bonds of their honorable fathers and virtuous mothers, ordained and approved by God, would be nullified and their homes abated, deported themselves as only well bred children can. And this because of complaints that tax money from cattle grazed on Government free used land begrudged the education of children whom God had sent -- children whose lives and calibre the State authority has not the power to produce but disconcerted to guarantee to them their freedoms.

Leave taking came. It was by dint of heroic manhood in certain humane officers that one man and a venerable old patriarch were escorted to their homes to take leave of a sick wife and change to more appropriate clothing respectively. Goodbyes were waved to singing "sisters" as the prisoners were directed into cars for the parade of "captured polygamists" to jail. Having spent that long hot July day in the Sunday School room, men had fanned themselves intermittently with hymn books -- some few they carried with them to jail, there serving to cheer the prisoners and to prompt prayers for deliverance and perhaps entertain the passers-by with the balanced harmony renditions, or to annoy the other 'criminals' downstairs, as the case may be.

For a week the occupation continued obnoxious in the erstwhile quiet little valley divested of its providers and protectors, where cattle had grazed contentedly, where evening breezes vivified the growing things that strove against the bright and burning daytime sun. Where the children's play and musical voices were now transformed to whispers and apprehension. Obnoxious for the disruption dealt the daily labors of the chore boys, and because of added anxiety to heroic mothers keeping vigil, going unrewarded of deserving sleep necessary for physical fortitude to keep inviolate the sanctity and dignity of their American homes. *Obnoxious occupation because, with all the admitted 26 months of planned prosecution, the children, not all processed through shameful juvenile hearings, were all loaded unwillingly into five large buses to be transferred to appropriate (?) homes 450 miles distant. Loyal mothers heroically refusing to be separated from their own flesh and blood would have rather submitted to extinction in these United States in preference thereof, accompanied them. From Sunday to Saturday the awful strain continued then when the few older boys left to take care that the dumb creatures (the cows) lactating, suffer not, watched the caravan make off with the political kidnap of their loving mothers and dear little brothers and sisters, stood courageously by in a downpour of rain wept graciously from heaven to cleanse the evacuated little hamlet of the stench of tobacco smoke and the more intolerable intrusion, influences of people of vile lives, prejudiced minds and evil intents, come to clean up the mess where real delinquency only existed on legal (?) documents and in the minds of bitter antagonists.* The boys fatigued from so gallant a stand for a week were soon lost in the reverie that brings all men peace. Strangely true, at this juncture the bailed out 31 men and nine childless women and grandmothers arrived home by truck. No lights shone in the village, all was quiet and still, the air was sweet and fresh from the rain. One by one the men alighted from the truck took his hat and jacket in hand, and entered in at his own gate, found overturned playthings left on the pathway, his house dark and quiet, no light shone in the window, no loving companion heard his foot falls nor welcomed him home. The rooms littered, showed a hurried leave the children's beds were all empty. His house left desolate. He was alone.

Doubtless the pen has never been touched able to describe the feelings that coursed through the heart of every man as he realized his situation. In his mind saw expectancy, as the woman in travail with the dragon before her, leering greedily in wait to devour her child as soon as it was born -- thusly his unborn given of God to be seized at its birth by the State with a ban on its heritage, his parental endowment adjudicated as naught. Mentally saw and heard infant children kneeling, lisping sweet prayers for their father, saw mothers preoccupied by the formidable prospects of piloting alone the bark of life upon which her orphaned family was thrust. *Re-echoed the Governor's boast guaranteeing 'Happiness of their own choosing', wondering what manner of sophistry had crept into places of political trust. Reviewing the past long week of experience, saw how the 'political', boisterous and bombastic all but run amuck hatefully disregarding the very basis of its origin -- the 'ecclesiastical'. Watched unhallowed polity break the rules, felonize the citizenry, kidnap community and run for a judicial touchdown, while bought-off referees wagged their impious heads and said, "how unfortunate", as half those in the grandstand rose and ignorantly cheered to the dismay and disgust of the other half. Saw by the vision of the ages, the great umpire rise and gather his principals, saw the regents summon the people and move to correct the ill-gotten score. Puzzled, fatigued, but undaunted resigned himself to God knowing that his heart harbored no malice -- smiled determinedly and wearily slept.*

FRED JESSOP.

Test on the Mormon Church, the Government, and the Priesthood

President Leroy S. Johnson
Leroy S. Johnson's Sermons 1:62
September 25, 1960 Canada

God can fight the battles better than we can. In 1953, Governor Pyle made a notorious speech to the world that he had stopped a great insurrection, wiped out a city, put the men in jail, and was going to adopt the children out so that in two years their identity would be lost. David O. McKay, on the radio, told the people that he and the Latter-day Saint Church were in full harmony with the State of Arizona and what they did.

Brigham Young said, "If the time ever comes that this Church strikes hands with the wicked, know ye then that the Priesthood is lost from them." Whether we know it or not, the Lord is giving us another chance to align ourselves with His work, or He will raise up another people. He could easily do it if you don't get on the ball and take hold of His work. The Lord may do it another way to carry off His work, but scriptures tell us that He will carry off the Kingdom. If we want to be partakers of this blessing, we must hasten. See that we don't sleep with feelings in our hearts against our neighbors, wives, or husbands. See to it that we don't harbor any feeling of enmity or jealousy or whatever and keep it.

President Leroy S. Johnson
Leroy S. Johnson's Sermons 3:1081 July 20, 1975 SLC

We will bring it down now a little closer. After a little time the Saints were driven from their homes. They had to find a new place to live, so they came to this goodly land upon which we live today thinking that they would come out of the world and be able to live and obey the laws that would save them from another great destruction. But soon after they arrived here, the leadership was lowered into carnal security; and through the promises of great wealth and great security, they gave up the Celestial Law.

I am going to bring it down now to my day -- my experiences in this work. In 1944 two great wars started. To put it in the words of the prophet Joseph W. Musser, "Today war was declared in the east, and today war was declared in the west." When war was declared by the United States against Germany in the Second World War, the same day war was declared against the Celestial Law in this goodly land in which we live. Since that time, we have been persecuted, driven, pulled out of our homes, and our wives and children have been taken out and held captive.

In 1953, that great day when the army came in and took over the city of Short Creek, it started to rain a gentle rain. The Lord told the people at that time that the heavens wept. This is not the only time that the heavens wept. You can go to the Book of Moses and find out what was done in the days of Enoch. The heavens wept. The heavens did not stop weeping in 1953 until after the enemy had accomplished its work. They took the men out and put them in jail. Then they ravaged their homes, took their wives and children, loaded them on buses and took them away. It took a week's time to accomplish all this, but they did it. When they were going out, there was so much mud on the roads that the buses had to be helped until they got to Fredonia, a distance of about forty miles, till they got on the oiled roads. So, the heavens wept because of what was taking place. Was it altogether because of what was taking place? Was it altogether because of the taking away of wives and children and men? No. It was another great test that had to be accomplished, and this was the way the Lord had of accomplishing it. He had to know again how the Church of Jesus Christ of Latter-day Saints felt toward the Celestial Law. So, this is what happened: Soon after these people landed in Phoenix, Arizona, there was a quarterly conference held in Mesa, Arizona. President David O. McKay was in that conference, and he made this statement, "I want the people to know that the Church of Jesus Christ of Latter-day Saints is in full harmony with the actions of the state of Arizona in the Short Creek episode."

President Leroy S. Johnson
Leroy S. Johnson's Sermons 4:1390 May 22, 1977 SLC

In 1944 when the government made a raid upon this order of the Priesthood, the Federal government joined in with the state and made war against this people -- this order of things. And at that time, the Church of Jesus Christ of Latter-day Saints was tried. I am going to tell you what happened at that time.

An attempt had been made prior to this to do away with the Doctrine & Covenants by printing a little book called Commandments of More Enduring Value. Some two hundred sections or parts of sections of the Doctrine & Covenants had been taken out and this little book was printed to take the place of the Doctrine & Covenants. But at that time the people rejected it. There was only one edition made and put out to the public. I have, in my possession, one of the publications which I value very dearly because it is good evidence of what took place.

At the same time, one of our Apostles was haled before the courts and the man that wrote the book -- or the revision of the Doctrine & Covenants was the star witness against him. He appeared on the witness stand and took the oath that he would tell the truth and nothing but the truth, but before he was on the stand long enough to answer any questions to amount to anything, he fell over. He was carried out and in a week or so he was laid away.

In 1953, the state of Arizona raided this order of the Priesthood and carried away the women and children. They first put the men in jail and then raided their homes while they were yet in jail, and carried their wives and children away to Phoenix, Arizona. After a week's time, the day the buses left Short Creek, Arizona, with the women and children, the men were released from prison in Kingman, Arizona, and came home -- to empty homes.

Again the Church was tried. They answered to the tune of $50,000 to assist the State in carrying away the women and children of this people. They haled nine men into court and placed them on parole for a year. They had to report to the court every month for a year for their actions. And while this was going on we were fighting for our deliverance from the hands of the enemy of righteousness. But soon after the raid was made, at a Conference in Mesa, Arizona, President David O. McKay made this remark. He said, "I want the world to know that the Church of Jesus Christ of Latter-day Saints is in full harmony with the actions of the State of Arizona in the Short Creek episode."

When I read this piece in the paper, I said to my wife, who was then in a detention home where I went to see her, I said, "This is the turning point. The key is turned now and from now on we will win the battles of the Saints." Which we did. The Lord had preserved us up to that time, and soon after that they started their adoption of the children -- or tried to. But the Lord told us where to find the necessary law to stop it. And He spoke through my mouth. He said, "In your law book there is a clause that reads something like this, 'No child can be adopted out without the consent of the parents.'" They said if it was there they would find it, and they started to work to find it. The next morning the lawyers called me in. "I want to read to you what I found. 'No child can be adopted out without the written consent of the parents.' So, we will see what happens." So, the lawyer called the Attorney General and told him to get Statute number such and such and turn to a certain page. Now read clause such and such. And our lawyer read it over the phone to him. He says, "When we meet you in court today, we are going to stand on this point of the law." There was a short hesitation and then the Attorney General said, "This case will be continued until we study the law." Our lawyer shut up his book and says, "That's it. We have won the case. You won't have to bring your children in for adoption."

However, the Governor of Arizona, at the time of the raid or before, asked J. Edgar Hoover, the head of the F.B.I., to send men to help take part in the raid. J. Edgar Hoover, before he would answer the Governor, called the Federal Judge in Phoenix and asked him for his opinion on whether or not they should take part in the raid on the Short Creek people. The Judge says, "It's my opinion that if we take part in this raid they will beat hell out of us. So let's keep out of it." So the F.B.I. kept out of it.

Establishing My "One Man Rule" Among the Church and Kingdom of God

President John Taylor
JD 6:25 November 1, 1857 SLC

If there cannot be a people anywhere found that will listen to the word of God and receive instructions from him, how can his kingdom ever be established? It is impossible? What is the first thing necessary to the establishment of his kingdom? It is to raise up a Prophet and have him declare the will of God; the next is to have people yield obedience to the word of the Lord through that Prophet. If you cannot have these, you never can establish the kingdom of God upon the earth.

What is the kingdom of God? It is God's government upon the earth and in heaven.

What is his Priesthood? It is the rule, authority, administration, if you please, of the government of God on the earth or in the heavens; for the same Priesthood that exists upon the earth exists in the heavens, and that Priesthood holds the keys of the mysteries of the revelations of God; and the legitimate head of that Priesthood, who has communion with God, is the Prophet, Seer, and Revelator to his Church and people on the earth.

When the will of God is done on earth as it is in heaven, that Priesthood will be the only legitimate ruling power under the whole heavens; for every other power and influence will be subject to it. When the millennium which we have been speaking of is introduced, all potentates, powers, and authorities -- every man, woman, and child will be in subjection to the kingdom of God; they will be under the power and dominion of the Priesthood of God: then the will of God will be done on the earth as it is done in heaven.

This places man in his true relationship to the Most High; and while others are boasting of their own intelligence, powers, authority, rule, greatness, and might, our boast, glory, might, strength, and power are in the Lord.

President Rulon Jeffs
History of Priesthood Succession, Page 313

In the fall of 1979, President Johnson became very sick. I had a visit with him. He was laying on a couch in the front room in Lincoln Street. After talking some matters over, I got up to leave, and he called me back. He said, "Brother Jeffs, I and you must establish once and for all the one man rule," according to Section 132.

President Rulon Jeffs
Rulon Jeffs' Sermons 6:258 August 10, 1986 CCA

It is my testimony to you that Leroy Sunderland Johnson was designated by John Y. Barlow to receive that position, and I have been busily engaged, since this split and this crisis that has come to this work, in trying to establish, as Brother Johnson told me I was to do; he said in the fall of 1979, "Brother Rulon, I and you must re-establish the one man rule in the holy Priesthood," referring to Section 132 verse 7. I have been busily engaged in doing just that ever since, and I hope to continue.

President Rulon Jeffs
Rulon Jeffs' Sermons 5:374 March 18, 1984 Sandy

As one of the speakers indicated here, and I have told you I think before, in late 1979, President Johnson, when I was visiting him, had confirmed some marvelous items of truth, which he confirmed to me. As I was about to leave him he said, "Brother Jeffs, I and you have the responsibility of establishing once for all the one man rule as set out in Section 132 verse 7,"*** There is only one man, the head, who is to receive revelation and commandments for the people."

Summary Teachings of President Leroy S. Johnson:

Strong Warnings of Preparation for the Redemption of Zion and the Whirlwind Judgments

President Leroy S. Johnson
Leroy S. Johnson's Sermons 7:251
September 7, 1975 Canada

We're entering into one of the greatest scenes of bloodshed the world has ever seen, so said the Prophet Joseph Smith. So great was the scene, said he, "I could not look upon it any longer. So I asked God to close the scene from before my eyes."

Zion must be redeemed. The Lord has said so. It doesn't matter what happens on this earth, Zion will be redeemed. Who is going to redeem Zion? The Lord said, "I will take the young and middle-aged and redeem Zion." We're here in the midst of the work of God. We're here to work out our salvation in fear and trembling before Him. Every man and woman that desires to be crowned with a celestial crown must be able to stand under the pressure of whatever name or nature it might be. It was hard for the Prophet to look upon the scene; it will be hard for you and me to witness it, but we are about to witness something that the world has never seen before. We have seen the bloodshed and all this and that, and men have been wiped completely off this earth, so the record tells us, but the Lord told the Prophet Joseph that never again will the Priesthood be taken from the earth.

When I read Third Nephi, I believe the words of the Savior, when He said the remnant of Jacob would walk through the Gentiles if they wouldn't repent, and tread them down, and none could deliver. "I'll throw down their strongholds, destroy their chariots, destroy their cities, their orchards," and so forth.

So it's going to be terrible, and great famines will be upon the land, but we have one thing, one thread to hang to -- and no other people have it. It is that God has said that He would protect His saints if He had to send fire from heaven to do so, and He's a man of His word. He did it when Christ visited the Nephites upon this continent. The record tells us that all the wicked were killed and only the more righteous were saved. So He has ways and means of protecting His saints. We should go down the road with our heads up and our minds clean and free from turmoil and confusion. We should have a prayer in our hearts continually to the God of heaven to protect us from the evil doer.

President Leroy S. Johnson
Leroy S. Johnson's Sermons 7:353 Feb. 12, 1984 CCA

We will see the judgments of God poured out more and more from this time forth until this part of the earth is empty of its inhabitants -- those who are not able to say, "I am clean every whit," and have the Lord call us up. So we are working under a great handicap, my dear brothers and sisters. If this people that I am speaking

to today don't hasten to lay away their sins and their wrong-doings and come clean before the Lord, they are going to find the Lord is not pleased with them, and they will have to go down with the wicked.

Now, I pray that God's blessings will be upon us, because He has granted us a few days more to clean up our lives and get down on our knees and pray night and day for deliverance as He has said. This is the time we will have to begin that practice. God bless you, amen.

President Leroy S. Johnson
Leroy S. Johnson's Sermons 4:1361 Mar. 27, 1977 CCA

Think about it, you young boys and girls. We are living in a time when we have got to be prepared -- when the Lord is trying to prepare a people that He can use, not only in the heavens but on this earth for a thousand years. And those who are partakers of that great blessing will have to be clean every whit, so says the Lord. And that means clean up our minds, clean up our bodies and keep ourselves clean and free from the destroying elements that are abroad upon the earth today, not only in the minds of the people but in the minds of our educators, our legislators, and our rulers. The whole world has rejected the Celestial Law.

We have a little pamphlet called, "The Coming Crisis and How to Meet it." The coming crisis and how to meet it is upon us. The crisis is here now. The thing we have to do is learn how to meet it, how to clean up our minds, our bodies and our determinations, not only in our thoughts but in our actions and in our everyday life. Let your light so shine that the world might wonder what is going on. Let us be prepared, everyone of us, to be counted worthy of being called upon when the time comes when our names are called, that we can come up and be counted worthy members of that great Kingdom called Zion. For Zion is the home of the pure in heart.

President Leroy S. Johnson
Leroy S. Johnson's Sermons 7:394
June 24, 1984 Canada

The Lord has said, "Stand ye in holy places and watch the arm of the Lord made manifest." The only holy places we have are our dedicated homes. The Lord is very angry with the Church of Jesus Christ of Latter-day Saints for the way it has acted and operated throughout the last hundred years or more. Since the days of Brigham Young, they have rejected the Celestial Law. Not only that -- when Wilford Woodruff signed the Manifesto, he not only signed away his rights to the Celestial Law, but he signed away his rights to the Priesthood, also. That being the case, what priesthood have they been operating under? They claim they have been operating under a priesthood. Read "The Coming Crisis and How to Meet it." It will tell you exactly who they have been serving and what has transpired in the last few years.

It is our place now to clean up our minds and get the Spirit of God and keep it, because the Spirit of God is the only protection that we will have. The scriptures tell us that there will be two working at the mill; one will be taken and the other left. Two will be working in the field; one will be taken and the other left, and so forth. This is true. We will have to have the Spirit of God upon us enough to be caught up when the judgments of God go over the earth, then we will be let down again. That is the only way the Lord can protect His people. He says He will protect His saints if He has to send fire from heaven to do so; and this, He will do.

First Two Great Commandments Must be Lived to Be Part of Zion and the Holy United Order

President Leroy S. Johnson
Leroy S. Johnson's Sermons 6:386 Nov. 16, 1969 SLC

If we labor all our days, if this Priesthood Council labors all their days and they can bring up a people that can learn to keep the two great commandments -- Love the Lord thy God with all thy heart, might, mind, and strength; and the second is like unto it, Love thy Neighbor as thyself; if we can bring a people up that can keep those two commandments, we will be ready for the United Order.

President Rulon Jeffs
Rulon Jeffs's Sermons 6:487 January 10, 1988 CCA

So let us unite. Let us be one. God will not be able to accomplish His work unless He has such a people, and I know He will have it, this people. I pray the Lord to be with us always, dear brethren and sisters. Learn to love. The first law of heaven is obedience. The first commandments to be obeyed are to love the Lord our God with all our heart, might, mind, and strength; and the second is like unto it, thou shalt love thy neighbor as thyself. If we would but carry out these two commandments, all other things would follow: unity, become one people, become a power in the hands of God to go forward and redeem Zion. The thing that I loved about Uncle Roy was his vision of preparing a people to redeem Zion.

President Leroy S. Johnson
Student Star Vol. 17, Page 384
December 29, 1963 Sunday School

The Lord cannot look upon sin in the least degree of allowance. You can't do anything evil without paying a penalty for it. We must be kind and honest to one another and not hold feelings. The first great commandment is: Love the

Lord with all your heart, might, mind, and strength, and the second one like unto it: Love your neighbor as yourself.

President Rulon Jeffs
Rulon Jeffs' Sermons 6:47 May 17, 1985 Sandy

The greatest lesson you can teach your children, my dear sisters -- and the great responsibility rests upon you, as Brigham Young said -- is to teach them obedience, obedience to the first two great commandments which covers all the rest: Thou shalt love the Lord thy God with all thy heart, might, mind, and strength, and thy neighbor as thyself. Disobedience to these two great commandments shows up in the lives of our children, and it comes and extends largely from the example of their parents.

President Rulon Jeffs Bears Testimony of the Prophet Leroy S. Johnson

President Rulon Jeffs
Rulon Jeffs' Sermons 4:390 October 8, 1978 Sandy

I testify to you that President Leroy Johnson is our Prophet, our head, the mouthpiece of God, and that he has given us continually the truths of heaven by the Spirit of revelation day in and day out, month in and month out.

President Rulon Jeffs
Rulon Jeffs' Sermons 3:28 August 6, 1972 Sandy

Now, dear brethren, you heads of families, draw near to the keyholder, as Heber, as Brigham, as John and the others drew near to Joseph, which assured them an inheritance with him in Zion. They set the glorious example. Others have followed since, and we have as our head, Leroy Johnson, our advocate with the Father, the keyholder by which we must come up to see the face of God, if we ever do. These brethren who lead us, dear brothers and sisters, these fathers in the Priesthood, are the ones by whom we must pass to see the face of Joseph, and Jesus, and Father. Talk about the love of brethren. I love the attributes of God as they exist in these my brethren -- Leroy Johnson, John Y. Barlow. These I must pass by, and the others before them, before I see Joseph, Jesus, and the white locks of Father Michael; and you must do likewise.

President Rulon Jeffs
Rulon Jeffs' Sermons 4:123 April 10, 1977 Sandy

So we have a great deal going for us, this people; and we have a true representative of the Lord Jesus Christ as our President and head -- a Christlike man, Leroy Johnson, who stands at the head of all. And we of this generation will have to account to him. He stands in the same position among us as Joseph did to the saints in his day -- the mouthpiece of God through whom all things must be revealed for the Church and Kingdom of God.

President Rulon Jeffs
Rulon Jeffs' Sermons 5:266 November 10, 1981 SLC

I know God is at the helm through this great and faithful man, Leroy S. Johnson. He is the keyholder of the holy Priesthood and of the sealing powers. He is the mouthpiece of God, and he is the fountainhead through whom the Holy Spirit of God is dispensed to the people who come under his presidency and direction. I know this by the Spirit of God, and I testify of it to you...

President Rulon Jeffs
Rulon Jeffs' Sermons 4:483 May 6, 1979 CCA

President Johnson is a man I love with all my heart, and I want to tell you why. The love of brethren transcends any other in life but the love of the chosen of God, for the chosen of God has to come in the same way as we love God. I love God because of the perfection of His attributes and character. That is what I worship in God -- the perfection of His character and attributes; and that is what I love in Roy Johnson. He is the most Christlike as any man I know, and stands in the position that God has called him to fill before he came here. Like Joseph Smith said, he was called by the Council before he came here to fill his position; and Brother Johnson is his legal successor. I say, though there are other Apostles, they come under the direction of the head, the chief Apostle, who leads us today; and that is the place I desire to be. I desire to be an advocate for him and to build him up, and we should all be doing the same thing. Why? Because he holds the keys, the means to obtain the mind and will of God; as Brigham Young said after the death of Joseph Smith, when Sidney Rigdon and others came to try and take charge. He has the means to obtain the mind and will of God for us, and all revelation must come through him for the people.

President Rulon Jeffs
Rulon Jeffs' Sermons 7:390 September 7, 1992 Sandy

Those remarks concerning President Johnson, I realize I am to carry on for him, as to the redemption of Zion.***

He said when he was in his last days there, "I want you to know that I am going to be there," at the redemption of Zion. That is what I pledged when I took over, that I was to carry on exactly as he has, build on the foundation he has laid. He is a grand and great Prophet, thirty-seven years at the helm of the Kingdom of God. Only John W. Woolley exceeded him in time, forty-one years, all that time in hiding.

He went to visit John Woolley, Uncle Roy did, a few months before he died. He and his brother Price went to visit with him, and after a very fine interview, as Uncle Roy was about to leave, Uncle John summoned him back. He took his hand and said, "My boy, you will do." I have had much the same association with Uncle Roy. As you know, he turned you all to me.

Chapter 8

Administration of President Rulon Jeffs

SECTION REVELATION 226

Revelation of the Lord Jesus Christ
Palestine, Texas
Sunday, October 2, 2011

1. I, even Jesus Christ, reveal that my servant Rulon T. Jeffs was of full Keyholder power of my giving him keys of sealing power in full, keys of the holy Eternal Union authority.

2. He continued my Holy Priesthood in fulness on earth, by my holy will guiding him.

3. He continued my Celestial Law of Celestial Plural Marriage; also my other laws of Priesthood.

4. I caused him to file Corporation Sole legal papers for the recognition of my true Church on earth to be named the Fundamentalist Church of Jesus Christ of Latter-day Saints, my continued Church under my Priesthood authority.

5. I restored my Priesthood first in the sending Peter, James, and John to Joseph Smith to receive my fulness of the Melchizedek Priesthood as an apostle of Jesus Christ; thereafter did I establish on earth again, through Priesthood, my Church on earth.

6. That Church organization rejected both my Priesthood and also my Priesthood Celestial Law of Celestial Plural Marriage.

7. Therefore, it became as a dead branch connected to my Priesthood tree of life, and broke itself off fully as they persecuted my Priesthood.

8. Thus, even now that apostate gentile organization labors, both in public and in secret labor, against my Priesthood and Celestial Law, and are not of me; though the name of their organized and legal corporation bears my name.

9. I, your Lord, reveal to all peoples that my Church of Jesus Christ of Latter-day Saints is now of the name Fundamentalist Church of Jesus Christ of Latter-day Saints, meaning my Church upholds all the fundamental laws and principles revealed through my servant Joseph Smith; none of which can be done away.

10. All my Celestial laws must be in my Church to be my Church, and must be guided by my Priesthood of full keys of Priesthood.

11. The revelations of my will always uphold my previous revealed will of eternal principles.

12. I cannot do away with a Celestial eternal law.

13. Rulon Jeffs is of full power of Priesthood, and is among they who cometh with me in the clouds of heaven at my glorious appearing.

14. He shall assist governing nations through the guiding of my Priesthood on earth by my revealing.

15. He is of full Priesthood power of Eternal Power Celestial as a witness against this now most wicked generation ever to be on earth.

16. He is a Judge in Israel. Amen.

Labor to Prepare a People of God for Zion

President Rulon Jeffs
Rulon Jeffs' Sermons 6:360 April 5, 1987 CCA

If we can go on now, dear brothers and sisters, in this great common cause to prepare a people to redeem Zion, to build a great city and the temples of the Most High God, we will realize the glorious desires of God for us, which existed also in the heart and the mind and the being of President Leroy Johnson. And I am committed, dear brothers and sisters, to carry on that work which he has so gloriously commenced and laid the foundations for us to go on down the road with him. And we are yet going to have him with us as we go down that road. The great ambition which I have, to the glory of God and the accomplishment of His purposes, with this people, is to find that group of five hundred Elders of Israel, which shall be the heart's core of the great work of the redemption of Zion, and going on that journey.

And as I have said before, dear brethren and sisters, we must have the spirit of Zion in our hearts, here and now! And regardless of whether there be those around us who don't have it, it is up to us to get it, if we want to be in that great concourse of Priesthood which will go down the road.

President Rulon Jeffs
Rulon Jeffs' Sermons 3:196 January 6, 1974 Sandy

We are being constantly reminded that this people is supposed to be prepared to redeem Zion, a people raised up out of the heart's core of the people of the Church of Jesus Christ of Latter-day Saints -- for this is what we are -- that they might become the nucleus of the great Millennium, and usher it in by redeeming Zion.

I was struck by the thought that in the redemption of Zion a people must be prepared. The Lord tried to get enough faithful men under Joseph Smith in the formation of what we call Zion's Camp to go back and redeem Zion. In calling for five hundred men, and finally settling for one hundred, who would go up under Joseph and not murmur and follow their commander, their leader, as one man under God, they could have redeemed Zion.***

This is what President Johnson and all of our Priesthood fathers have been telling the saints from Joseph on down, trying to prepare a people to redeem Zion.

In order for us to redeem Zion, if this may help us, we must first have Zion in our hearts; create a Zion in our families. Zion is not only a place. And by the way, the whole of America is Zion. The center place is Jackson County, and all of the other places will be stakes of Zion. This is the place. But Zion is also a condition, a condition of the heart and of the mind, of the spirit. Until we have Zion in our hearts, the Zion of the true and the faithful, the Zion of our God, with a pure love of Christ, charity, with knowledge, perfect faith, with justice, and mercy, and judgment, and truth -- until we are filled with these, which are the Holy Ghost, and become one, we cannot go there and accomplish that great objective of the last dispensation of the fullness of times, which has fully come.

President Rulon Jeffs
Rulon Jeffs' Sermons 7:51 August 28, 1988 CCA

What I have uppermost, as I see the will of God concerning this people, is to prepare for Zion, the redemption of Zion. That was the burden of Uncle Roy's remarks and his labors, to prepare a people. We have heard so very well here today how that preparation can be made.

Testimony of Priesthood Keyholders

President Rulon Jeffs
Rulon Jeffs' Sermons 6:106 October 6, 1985 Sandy

I am impressed more and more all of the time by the conditions under which we obtain faith, and hope, and charity -- meek and lowly of heart. I think too few of us understand the meaning of that. We are so wrapped up in our own opinions and traditions. And I would to God we all understood Priesthood. I would to God we all understood Jesus Christ when He said, "I am meek and lowly in heart." He was simply asking us to become like Him. He is our God and Savior. And Joseph Smith is the Witness of the Father and the Son, and stands in the office of the Holy Ghost as a man. The Holy Ghost is a Personage of Spirit, which centers in the Father and issues forth from Himself to His children through one man, His representative upon the earth. It has ever been so eternally, and ever will be so. What do you suppose the Lord meant in that parenthetical matter when He said, "There is never but one man upon the earth at a time upon whom this power," this sealing power, "and the keys of the holy Priesthood are conferred"?

Training on Principles of Priesthood

What Is Priesthood?

President John Taylor Millennial Star 9:321

What is Priesthood? Without circumlocution I shall as briefly answer that is the government of God, whether on the earth or in the heavens, for it is by that power, agency, or principle that all things are governed on the earth and in the heavens, and by that power that all things are upheld and sustained. It governs all things -- it directs all things -- it sustains all things -- and has to do with all things that God and truth are associated with. It is the power of God delegated to intelligences in the heavens and to men on the earth.

President Brigham Young
JD 2:139 December 3, 1854 SLC

When we talk of the celestial law which is revealed from heaven, that is, the Priesthood, we are talking about the principle of salvation, a perfect system of government, of laws and ordinances, by which we can be prepared to pass from one gate to another, and from one sentinel to another, until we go into the presence of our Father and God. This law has not always been upon the earth; and in its absence, other laws have been given to the children of men for their improvement, for their education, for their government, and to prove what they would do when left to control themselves; and what we now call tradition has grown out of these circumstances.

President Brigham Young
JD 11:249 June 17, 1866 SLC

The priesthood of the Son of God in its operations comprises the kingdom of

God, and I know of no form of expression that will better tell what that priesthood is than the language given to me by the Spirit, namely, that it is a pure system of government. If the people who subject themselves to be governed by it, will live strictly according to its pure system of laws and ordinances, they will harmonize in one, and the kingdom of God will steadily move on to the ultimate triumph of truth and the subjugation of wickedness everywhere on this earth.

President Brigham Young
JD 10:320 July 31, 1864 SLC

Our religion is founded upon the Priesthood of the Son of God -- it is incorporated within this Priesthood. We frequently hear people inquire what the Priesthood is; it is a pure and holy system of government. It is the law that governs and controls all things, and will eventually govern and control the earth and the inhabitants that dwell upon it and all things pertaining to it.

President Brigham Young
JD 7:202 July 31, 1859 SLC

The holy Priesthood is a system of laws and government that is pure and holy; and if it is adhered to by intelligent man, whom God has created a little lower than angels, it is calculated to preserve our tabernacles in eternal being; otherwise they will be resolved into native element. Nothing is calculated to satisfy the mind of an intelligent being, only to obtain principles that will preserve him in his identity, to enable him to increase in wisdom, power, knowledge, and perfection.

President John Taylor
JD 1:224 April 8, 1853 SLC

Perhaps it may be well, at this stage of my remarks, to give you a short explanation of my ideas on government, legitimacy, or Priesthood, if you please.

The question, "What is Priesthood?" has often been asked me. I answer, it is the rule and government of God, whether on earth, or in the heavens; and it is the only legitimate power, the only authority that is acknowledged by Him to rule and regulate the affairs of His kingdom. When every wrong thing shall be put right, and all usurpers shall be put down, when he whose right it is to reign shall take the dominion, then nothing but the Priesthood will bear rule; it alone will sway the sceptre of authority in heaven and on earth, for this is the legitimacy of God.

President John Taylor
JD 5:187 August 30, 1857 SLC

Some people ask, "What is Priesthood?" I answer, "It is the legitimate rule of God, whether in the heavens or on the earth;" and it is the only legitimate power that has a right to rule upon the earth; and when the will of God is done on earth as it is in the heavens, no other power will bear rule.

President John Taylor
JD 21:159 December 7, 1879 14th Ward

In doing this, among other things, he [Abraham] found he had a right to the priesthood. I need not stop to tell you what that is, you Latter-day Saints. You understand it is the rule and government of God, whether in the heavens or on the earth, and when we talk of the kingdom of God we talk of something that pertains to rule, government, authority and dominion; and that priesthood is the ruling principle that exists in the heavens or on the earth, associated with the affairs of God. Hence, we are told in the Scriptures that Christ was a priest forever after the order of Melchisedec. Then of what order was Melchisedec? A priest for ever after the order of the Son of God, for if Christ was after the order of Melchisedec, Melchisedec must have been after the order of Christ, as a necessary consequence. Very well. Now, then, in relation to that priesthood it was something that ministered in time and through eternity; it was a principle that held the keys of the mysteries of the revelations of God, and was intimately associated with the Gospel, and the Gospel, wherever it existed, was in possession of this priesthood; and it could not exist without it. It always "brought life and immortality to light."

Only One Man at a Time Holds the Keys

President Leroy S. Johnson
Leroy S. Johnson's Sermons 7:352 Feb. 12, 1984 CCA

There is only one man at a time, and that is the way it has been throughout all the history of God's dealings with people, both in this world and the world before this one, and the world before that one. Only one man at a time holds the keys and power of the sealing power, and those who act during his administration are only acting under a delegated authority.

President Rulon Jeffs
Rulon Jeffs' Sermons [LSJ] 7:302
August 17, 1982 Creston

Brothers and sisters, there is one thing that Brother Johnson has laid upon me, and that is to establish the truth of Section 132, verse 7; and there's more in this section.

(Doctrine & Covenants, Section 132:7-8)

"And verily I say unto you, that the conditions of this law are these: (Pertaining to the new and everlasting covenant which was instituted for the fullness of His glory.) *All covenants, contracts, bonds, obligations, oaths, vows, performances, connections, associations, or expectations, that are not made and entered into and sealed by the Holy Spirit of promise, of him who is anointed, both as well for time and for all eternity, and that too most holy,*

by revelation and commandment through the medium of mine anointed, whom I have appointed on the earth to hold this power (and I have appointed unto my servant Joseph to hold this power in the last days, and there is never but one on the earth at a time on whom this power and the keys of this priesthood are conferred), are of no efficacy, virtue, or force in and after the resurrection from the dead; for all contracts that are not made unto this end have an end when men are dead.

Behold, mine house is a house of order, saith the Lord God, and not a house of confusion."

These keys and powers are conferred upon one man. The keys of the power of sealing and of the Holy Priesthood are conferred upon one man. By whom? It's all right here.

(132:45) "For I (God speaking) *have conferred upon you* (speaking to Joseph) *the keys and power of the Priesthood, wherein I restored all things, and make known unto you all things in due time."* (The same is done for those who are appointed in his stead by God Himself.)

President Rulon Jeffs
Rulon Jeffs' Sermons 5:316 November 25, 1983 CCA

Brethren, can't we draw near to our head? Draw our families near with us, that we may be called together in one place to prepare a people for the redemption of Zion, under President Leroy S. Johnson, who is holding the keys of the holy Priesthood. Priesthood is God; God is Priesthood. The Holy Spirit centers in the Father, as Brigham Young told us, and from it goes throughout all of His dominions, and through this one holding those keys. He becomes the fountain head of that Holy Spirit to those under his dominion, being the mouthpiece of God to us.

President Rulon Jeffs
Rulon Jeffs' Sermons 6:298 October 19, 1986 SLC

I desire above all, as I stand before you to have you know that I am four-square, one hundred percent with President Johnson, and I want, above all things, to enjoy his confidence. I cannot think of a more devastating thing that could come to me if I were to find that I had lost his confidence. I have full confidence in him, and I love him with all my heart. I desire to obey the commandments of God which he gives to us. I know he is a Prophet of God, called at this time and anointed of the Lord to lead this people and prepare this people to redeem Zion.

I used to say he is as Enoch to us; he is as Moses. And it is my testimony that he has been raised up as one like unto Moses, as Section 103 tells us, to lead us to Zion under the Lord Jesus Christ and the Prophet Joseph Smith, who is at the elbow of President Johnson all the time. I testify to you that he is full of the Holy Ghost and has the Spirit of revelation to deliver to this people. He is the mouthpiece of God. He is the keyholder and President of the holy Priesthood. And the Holy Ghost, being the power of the Priesthood, which centers in the Father, is dispensed to us through this man and the power of the Priesthood which he has. That is how I feel about him, brothers and sisters, and the only way we are going to accomplish what he wants to accomplish -- as the Lord wants him to accomplish -- is for us to draw near unto him, and he will draw near unto us. The Lord says this, "Draw near unto me, and I will draw near unto you." But this man is a representative of God upon the earth, the greatest man on earth to guide and direct a people to come back into the presence of the Lord Jesus Christ and our Father, Michael. He has

said to us on different occasions that we have not made much progress in lo, these many years.

President Rulon Jeffs
Rulon Jeffs' Sermons 1:544 July 3, 1966 CCA

I think there is nothing more foolish or foolhardy than for a man and woman to come to this Priesthood and get blessings, the ordinances of the holy Priesthood, and then refuse to follow its counsels and dictates, becoming a law unto themselves. There is nothing more foolish. I know that all my life and light and wisdom must come from the Holy Ghost, which was administered through the power of this Priesthood through the key man, Leroy S. Johnson. I cannot get it in any other way. Heber C. Kimball spoke the truth when he said, "How will you get the Holy Ghost except through us?" speaking of Brigham and the leading brethren holding the holy Apostleship. I don't expect to get it in any other way.

The power of my Priesthood is ineffective; the power of your Priesthood, brethren, is absolutely ineffective save it be in concert, and in following the leadership and counsel and direction of President Johnson. I tell you this in the name of the Lord. I cannot see any other way to get back to Father Adam except through those whom He has called and chosen, and who administer everlasting lives through the ordinances of the holy Priesthood. There is no other way.

Purity in the Family Order of Heaven

President Rulon Jeffs
Rulon Jeffs' Sermons 7:533 February 12, 1950 SLC

Let us set a worthy example and be pure above all things. The Spirit of God cannot dwell in us unless we are living humble, pure lives, and I mean sexual purity. I mean it. The law of plural marriage is set forth by the Gods because it calls for purity, and it makes Gods and Goddesses of us.

President Rulon Jeffs
Rulon Jeffs' Sermons 4:49 November 21, 1976 Sandy

The world and the doings of satan is so full of satanic and devilish things, that we little recognize them when they are presented before us, brothers and sisters; and these things are doing terrible things to the minds of our children. The suggestive things that are thrown in advertising, even in the newspapers and magazines, all of these things are very suggestive and clutter up our minds. We must clean them up from these things and create an atmosphere in our homes where the Spirit of God can dwell. These are the things that pollute and destroy. Immorality, practices that are destructive of the very life and soul of men and women, and of children, are among us. To be pure means to be sexually pure. This is the cardinal sin in the world today, the terrible immorality that is all around us. So we must clean up in this way and abide the laws of chastity in our families and in all of our doings. We must be clean every whit.

I love the proverb in which is spoken, "Come to the Lord with clean hands and pure hearts," clean hands and pure hearts. We must present ourselves in that condition before He can bless us and own us, and before we can be one. So, a part of the process of becoming one is to clean up our minds and bodies, our hearts, and live in love together, in our families and as a people. Until we come to this point, brothers and sisters, the Lord will not own us and bless us; and I pray that we may indeed come to this condition with full purpose of heart.

President Rulon Jeffs
Rulon Jeffs' Sermons 2:402 January 17, 1971 Sandy

We obtain this, my dear brothers and sisters, by getting and keeping the Spirit of God, the Holy Ghost, if you please, which is the power of the Priesthood that administers everlasting life unto us. We cannot get it except through that channel. Sisters, I repeat again, you cannot get and keep the Spirit of God, except you keep the channel clear through your husband who bears all the Melchizedek Priesthood, without which he cannot hold you, and without which he cannot administer to his family. Authority, my dear brothers and sisters, is all -- authority from Almighty God, which He restored through Joseph the Prophet and on down till this present day, to that one man standing at the head. "Draw near to Me," God says, "and I will draw near to you." How can we draw to Him? Through His Priesthood. Draw near to your husbands, sisters. And brethren, draw near to those who administer eternal lives unto you.

The Inspiring and Exalting Nature of My Celestial Law

President Rulon Jeffs
Rulon Jeffs' Sermons 2:351 September 6, 1970 Sandy

I am impressed with the great importance of our becoming like God. This is the burden of the Gospel of Jesus Christ. This is the burden of the laws of the holy Priesthood, brothers and sisters, which are designed specifically to make us like God if we will only abide those laws. Truly, the initiatory ordinances of the Gospel are the foundation for these things -- faith, repentance, baptism by immersion, and the laying on of the hands of the Priesthood for the gift of the Holy Ghost; the reception and the magnifying of the holy Priesthood by the brethren and their wives and their children -- all of these things together, abiding in the crowning principles and laws of the Holy United Order and Celestial and Plural Marriage, the Family Order of Heaven. These laws were given to us specifically to make us like God, for it is His work and His glory to bring to pass the immortality and the eternal life of His children. It is His glory that we become like Him, that we might receive of those things that He has and is.

SECTION REVELATION 227

Revelation of the Lord Jesus Christ
Eldorado, Texas
Saturday, July 23, 2011

1.   I, your Lord, speaketh to every nation on earth; to now prepare for my power eternal of full governing power, even my Holy Priesthood, to be among you as my governing authority on earth, to be my holy power eternal dwelling among you, to be my holy representatives among your peoples; to administer my will, to make known my full Power of Union of Celestial Power of my holy Union authority.

2.   Let my power eternal be your guiding light.

3.   Let all be of my holy way; to know a governing power of my sending from the eternal power of Celestial pure holy power shall be the power of peace and holiness among all nations; to be the New Era of Union Eternal on earth; to have among all peoples my knowledge of truth, even eternal truth, that exalts

the soul unto eternal life; learning my order of pure holy union.

4.   Let it be a way of peace in every land.

5.   Let it be my order of revealing through my Holy Priesthood how to live a full law of Celestial power of my giving full way of pure holy truth unto the full way of salvation for all who receive me and my Father's power of Union Eternal.

6.   I am Son Ahman, who is Jesus Christ, the Son of my Eternal Father of redeeming and atoning power. I am Eternal; Endless and Holiness is my name.

7.   I am above all by the power of pure and holy Celestial power of the Godhood of full Priesthood power over all things.

8.   My love shines forth upon all creation, giving all things their existence.

9.   I am a full power of Eternal Godhood over Michael, who is my Son of Creation.

10. My Father is Elohim, of the Council of the Gods of Creation, Eloheim.

11. My Father is over all, and I am the God of Creation over the earth upon which you dwell, as a probationary orb of testing in a mortal condition, to see your worth of becoming of the way of Union Celestial, in eternal realms of power

of my giving to faithful sons of Priesthood holy authority; which is always my holy love extant ruling all things in a perfect way of order, peace, light eternal, and with power of increase.

12. Let my Church on earth be sanctified. Let my domain of each people in every land be ready to acknowledge me as King of kings, Lord over all peoples at my appearing in the power of Priesthood of Godhood over all.

13. Let all people now be ready to be of the knowing I am among you on earth, in Zion, unto my full work being revealed in building my governing city, even New Jerusalem on the center place in America.

14. Let it be my holy place.

15. Let the people of the nation of United States of America now prepare.

16. Let peace, purity, kindness, love of God, truth, and justice proper be your way of life; for I shall cause a great cleansing power to come forth, to prepare my land for New Jerusalem soon at hand.

17. Be ye clean and holy, that you may dwell on my holy land and perchance visit New Jerusalem unto your salvation on earth and in heaven.

18. I shall bring with me eternal knowledge, to lift up all people to a greater love for eternal truth, which comes to you by my Spirit of truth abiding in you.

19. Let all now be of pure and holy walk in the daily labor of their individual places of abiding, of working, of habitations.

20. Let my holy order of peace be my holy order among you, all nations, peoples, tongues, and all kindreds.

21. Let all now be the pure way of Celestial power.

22. My time of whirlwind judgments is at hand, to bring all peoples to the knowledge I have spoken from the heavens, and shall fulfill my word of eternal salvation, to be given at the time I appear in my glory unto my people being of a pure holy Celestial oneness.

23. Let all now be of purity, so as to abide my power and glory in a more pure way; to be ready to receive Celestial power in every land, to be governed by my Priesthood in righteousness and in truth.

24. My Priesthood is being readied to receive, to receive their Lord in honor before Him and His heavenly host coming to earth, in the pure holy power of Eternal Union; to govern the earth; to be my spokesmen unto your nation and people.

25. Violence must stop in every surviving land.

26. The spirit of murder is in most lands.

27. When I appear in my glory, I shall abolish all such evil, even to be my full judging on murder of innocence in children unborn, being destroyed by their own parents; to now be an abolished practice among all nations.

28. I shall fulfill this, my will, among every nation, kindred, tongue, and people on every land.

29. Prepare ye, prepare ye, for all of this is nigh at hand.

30. I am the Giver of all good, the Governing Power over all peoples, nations, tongues, and kindreds. Come unto me, your Lord, to gain eternal life. Amen.

Historical Attacks Against the Priesthood During the Administration of Rulon Jeffs

Lawsuit Filed in Federal Court by Apostates

President Rulon Jeffs
Rulon Jeffs' Sermons 6:468 December 13, 1987 CCA

Another assault is being made on the United Effort Plan. It is being made according to the pattern that we have in the times and life of the Prophet Joseph Smith -- by apostates. A massive lawsuit has been filed in the United States District Court in Salt Lake City. The complaint is a hundred pages long, eighty pages of complaint and twenty pages of exhibits.***

I would like to speak on the nature of this United Effort Plan. In 1942, after the United Trust operation was attempted here in Short Creek, and failed because of the selfishness and aspiring nature of some men, the United Effort Plan was brought together and formed under the inspiration of God, and brought into being on November 9, 1942, under the scrutiny and direction of President John Y. Barlow, Joseph Musser, and Leroy Johnson. They, with Brother Hammon and myself, were made Trustees in the original Trust agreement. We knew not then what God had wrought, as we are now seeing this great assault that has been made time and time again against this great document which God inspired and directed in the minds of John Y. Barlow and Joseph Musser and Leroy Johnson.***

Five days later this action was filed in court, Salt Lake District Court of the federal government. We haven't been served yet. We are having to go and get copies of the complaint ourselves to know what is going on. The press knew about it before it was even filed.***

Well, we just felt like reporting this to you, and I just want to emphasize one thing. This is a religious common-law Trust, with members. No one on United Effort land is a beneficiary under the common understanding of Trusts. Surely they could be revoked. But this is a religious Trust with members, and a religion can excommunicate its members.

President Rulon Jeffs
History of Priesthood Succession, Page 366

As everyone who has lived upon land in Colorado City and Hildale (Short Creek) knows, according to the articles, where there are transgressors or those acting inimical to the interests of the Trust, they may be removed. Everyone has understood when they built improvements upon the land that was assigned to them, housing and improvements attached to the land remain with it. And they are "tenants-at-will" of the trustees of the United Effort Plan.

President Rulon Jeffs
Rulon Jeffs' Sermons 6:491 February 7, 1988 Sandy

We are under attack. We are laboring now with the large firm of· attorneys in answering the complaint of some thirty-five plaintiffs who have attached their names to the document; which is an attack, as Brother Truman has said, against the United Effort Plan and against the Priesthood. It has been brought to my attention that the principal party engaged in getting that complaint filed and getting it together expects to see the United Effort Plan destroyed.

President Rulon Jeffs
Rulon Jeffs' Sermons 7:287 December 16, 1990 Sandy

Well, the Lord has spoken through these brethren as I have prayed for each of them, and I don't feel there is any more to add at this point except this: God Almighty is governing and is overruling in this court action. It is in His hands, as to the enemy and as to the judge. I just want to express my gratitude to the Lord for these great blessings that have come to us. There is more to go through, but God is at the helm. Let us stand as one man, and God will deliver the enemy into the hands where they belong. We are dealing with apostates. Just read what the Prophet·Joseph had to say about them. And we will make no agreements with them.

They proposed in a settlement that we give them ten-year leases, renewable and assignable. Uncle Roy said, "I want you to get discouraged and leave," and they have got to agree to leave before we can go any further. Zion must be made clean and pure. We are building a Zion where we are, dear brethren and sisters. Each of us in

our hearts must have Zion, and as a whole, one people acting as one man, preparing to live that holy order. The enemy is trying to destroy it, but God will be our "Right-hand Man".

No Compromise With the Apostates

President Rulon Jeffs
Rulon Jeffs' Sermons 7:294 February 17, 1991 Sandy

I feel impressed to talk a little about apostasy and apostates. We are having to deal with so many of them in this lawsuit, but all of the apostates are not on the lawsuit; and by the word of God, through Uncle Roy, they must leave our community. During the past two months, the opposition lawyers approached our lawyers and asked that they consider a settlement out of court. They are tired of the case. They know they don't have a case. But they started it and they have got to finish it.

Training on Keeping the Spirit of God Through the Prophet Rulon Jeffs

"Keep Sweet" Is Our Only Protection

President Rulon Jeffs
Rulon Jeffs' Sermons 7:316 May 26, 1991 CCA

The Gospel of Jesus Christ is the plan of God unto salvation. If we want our salvation we must pay a price, the price of obedience. Be sweet. "Keep sweet," as Uncle John always said, and which I can't help but repeat every day in talking to people. Keeping sweet means keeping the Holy Spirit of God. That is the grand, all-powerful influence, and power of the Gods, and by which we become like God, to have a fullness of that Holy Spirit in us. Seek for it and live by it, I pray in the name of Jesus Christ, amen.

President Rulon Jeffs
Rulon Jeffs' Sermons 7:368 December 6, 1991 Sandy

I want you all to understand the continual use of the two words "keep sweet," means keep the Holy Spirit of the Lord, until you are full of it. Only those who have it will survive the judgments of God which are about to be poured out without let or hindrance upon the earth, beginning at the House of God, where the Mormons are. I mean the Mormon Church, which is now apostate completely, and will never be set in order. We have the true and living Church of Jesus Christ of Latter-day Saints under our administration. And we add the word "Fundamentalist" in order to distinguish the true Church of Jesus Christ of Latter-day Saints from the name of the one that now is a complete gentile sectarian church. The Lord has rejected it.

President Rulon Jeffs
Rulon Jeffs' Sermons 7:385 June 7, 1992 Sandy

The Lord has surely answered my prayers, giving the messages that I wanted given here. It has been marvelous. I want you all to know I love you, and I want to save you, by the power of God. My sermon is: Keep sweet. It is a matter of life or death. The remnant spoken of will be those who are full of the Holy Ghost. May we all be there, I pray in the name of Jesus Christ, amen.

President Rulon Jeffs
Rulon Jeffs' Sermons 7:402 December 4, 1992 Sandy

Just these brief words, dear young people. I love you, and I want to save you in the Celestial Kingdom of God. So, if you will keep the grand teaching that we are trying to get over: Keep the Holy Spirit of God. KEEP SWEET! It is a matter of life or death.

You have had the teaching regarding what is required in order for us to survive the judgments, sufficient of the Holy Spirit of God that we can be lifted up and then set down after it is over. That will be the remnant which will go to redeem Zion. The wicked will be swept off from the face of this land. The wicked are they who come not unto Christ. There is only one people who comes unto Christ, and that is this people under His servant.

President Warren S. Jeffs' Testimony Concerning His Father, Rulon Jeffs

President Warren S. Jeffs
Warren S. Jeffs' Sermons December 20, 1998 Sandy

President Rulon Jeffs holds the Priesthood after the order of the Son of God, and his right-hand Man is the Lord God Himself. And on his side stand the hosts of heaven and all the Prophets who looked forward to the accomplishment of the promised work that they were given.

Upon whom do the Prophets Isaiah, Jeremiah, Moses, Abraham, Isaac, Jacob, Father Adam -- all the Prophets of old -- who do they look to, that their work will not fall to the ground unheeded? They look to this Prophet, President Rulon Jeffs, in preparing a people who can survive the great judgments and go into the Millennium establishing Zion; a people who will build a beautiful city that God Himself will visit, who can receive the ancient Prophets into their living rooms and be taught of them; a people who will meet Enoch as he descends and they rise. And in all these great events ahead, President Rulon Jeffs will be in the midst of it. He will receive the Prophet Joseph, who is the One Mighty and Strong, visiting this Prophet on earth. The Prophet Joseph, a Celestial, glorified being covered with light, will come to his legal successor, President Jeffs. He will be told by revelation who from among this people are worthy to go back and redeem Zion in the new Zion's Camp. And this Prophet, to accomplish these great events, will be renewed and restored, strengthened, taking those of his family and this people who are prepared.

I testify to you, dear brothers and sisters, this work is just beginning for the obedient. Press forward in your preparation. Success is within reach through your faith unto repentance; purifying your life so you can be filled with the Holy Spirit of God. It comes to you through your love and obedience to this Prophet, President Jeffs, and you know it. You know the evil powers are trying with their might to stop you from placing your whole confidence in the words and teachings of our Prophet. It is taking the greatest battle of faith that you have ever fought to press forward and perfect your lives as our Prophet teaches you. This is a witness that you must go forward with all of your might. Do not lighten up. Stand fast and know that God is with this Prophet.

This is my testimony to you this day, that though individuals might be taken, or fall, there will be sufficient from among this people for our Prophet to use; and they will become the nucleus of the great Millennium. Nothing can stop this work -- the work the Lord has given the Prophet Joseph and continued in the life of our Prophet, President Jeffs. Draw near and the Lord will give you this testimony, for you will be buoyed up -- lifted up in your hearts and feelings. With greater energy do all the good possible within your reach.

I yearn that we will be encouraged, that whatever we are called to go through, it will be worth it. The blessings that await that prepared people are so great. Do not

be cast down because you cannot see it all right now. This is your test of faith. Press forward and the Lord will be with you as you are with President Jeffs.

President Warren S. Jeffs
Eldorado, Texas
Thursday, July 21, 2011

A son of God of Eternal Union of full keys of sealing power of the Holy Priesthood of Melchizedek was given to my father by our Lord. Ordained an apostle in April 1945, he was an holy inspired Prophet of Priesthood truths, always perfectly loyal to the Keyholder of the Priesthood over him. He was as a little child in obeying the Prophets over him.

His love for God and the Holy Priesthood was a full love loyalty of perfect sweetness.

God chose this Prophet to finish their preparing for Zion's mission of the order of pure Priesthood principles taught and lived. His power of heavenly-empowered Priesthood power was felt. He loved the saints, suffering unto death for the Priesthood and for our Heavenly Father. He gave, of the Lord, the Godhead training, teaching who God is and how to become like Him. He was a God in humanity and is like God, and is one of the Gods of eternity under Christ our Lord, and under our Father in heaven. Let all rejoice in the Lord for Rulon Jeffs and his perfect walk before God and all men.

Having a perfect understanding of Priesthood, he was a loyal apostle to John Y. Barlow and Leroy S. Johnson, and was a full power of Priesthood keys and authority on earth over all men. The majesty of his Priesthood was felt increasingly; and he gathered a people to be taught the key to be Zion, even to keep sweet, and be filled with the Spirit of God.

John Y. Barlow said of my father, Rulon Jeffs: "You are sweet and sound." He labors now in the heavenly Kingdom with God and the Prophets in behalf of the saints whom he loved, as a guiding, perfect father, only desiring the will of God. His guiding light was to read, learn, and teach of Joseph Smith the Prophet; and was able to declare his oneness with God through Joseph Smith and the Keyholders before him, as he, with them, declared: "I have only taught what Joseph Smith taught."

Thus, the work of God through Joseph Smith was carried on through each Keyholder of Priesthood, as did my father, Rulon Jeffs. He taught us the correct understanding of Priesthood, saying -- "God is Priesthood; Priesthood is God with us and among the people." He fulfilled the Lord's directive to him by the Prophet Leroy S. Johnson, "to help establish once and for all the One Man Rule" of the Keyholder of Priesthood, even God's rule through His chosen servant on earth, who is ordained by God Himself to hold the full sealing powers of Elijah, unto the full ordinances being performed unto eternal life, by our Lord's will revealed. He and all the Keyholders were foreordained to hold the key position of Priesthood power, even before the earth was made. He is one of the sons of God, continuing on to do our Lord's will.

My testimony of Priesthood, given of me of the Lord through my father, is that correct understanding of Priesthood is: God, through His Keyholder of Priesthood, has the right to rule in every area of our lives; and we, the people of God, have the right, duty, and privilege to love to obey God through His Keyholder of Priesthood.

"He that receiveth my servants receiveth me," saith the Lord. "Obey the Priesthood of God to obey God" is his life's example of a pure and holy walk before God, and before all men. The Lord guided him and gave him revelation up to his passing moment. God and my father did and do right, is my testimony of them, which I give in the name of our Lord Jesus Christ. Amen.

Chapter 9

Administration of President Warren S. Jeffs

SECTION REVELATION 228

Revelation of the Lord Jesus Christ
Palestine, Texas
Sunday, October 2, 2011

1. I, the Lord over all people, who is God in the power of full governing, reveal to all people my holy and eternal way.

2. My Holy Priesthood of full keys of sealing power is among men on earth.

3. Let all know I have a son of Priesthood who is of my order of keys of power, to bless all who will receive me and my plan of salvation; to administer the will of God to them; to be a full power of my authority and eternal gifts of exalting power; to bless on earth that which I shall uphold eternally in heaven.

4. Thus is your Lord to soon appear, to cause all to know, even they in the world of departed spirits, as well as all on earth, of my eternal Gospel of salvation; always of my Priesthood of the Eternal Union authority of my revealing and guiding.

5. I am He who has suffered for all men; who hath conquered death; who shall resurrect all people unto a judgment of eternal and full reward for all their deeds done in the flesh while on the earth.

6. My plan is of a full authority by all Celestial and eternal power of my Godhood over all.

7. Let all come unto me through my servant Warren Jeffs, as he is called to receive my will to all peoples.

8. Now know I am giving my will to all peoples to know I am soon of a full revealing of my power of cleansing all peoples; to prepare for my holy and pure governing powers to be on earth for a thousand years; after which cometh the end of the time of this earth's preparation; to be of a complete cleansing by eternal fire, consuming all dross; to Celestialize the earth unto a power of heaven; a sea of glass as a Urim and Thummim of revealing to all who dwell on the Celestial orb, truths of all kingdoms of a lesser power, to govern those kingdoms.

9. Let all know of my revelation of the degrees of glory in my holy word called Doctrine and Covenants, even that Section 76 therein, to know of my redeeming power; to know of the degree of glory yet to be given every person

as their spirit of their keeping shall be given them in fulness; even to be as they chose on earth.

10. Let all be repenting, therefore, and be of the increase of my holy power, which is the gift of the Holy Ghost given by the laying on of hands of my Priesthood; to be the light of my power dwelling in the obedient who are of my baptized and preparing people of covenants unto eternal life.

11. Now prepare ye, all ye people of the earth, for my message of full power unto salvation; as I appear and preserve all who can receive my glorious way unto eternal life. Amen.

SECTION REVELATION 229

Thus Saith Jesus Christ, a Holy Revealing, of Evil Powers Seeking to Destroy My Celestial Power of Priesthood

Revelation of the Lord Jesus Christ Palestine, Texas Wednesday, October 12, 2011

1. Thus saith the Lord to all peoples of all nations: Having bestowed full Priesthood powers of keys of Elijah on my servant Warren Jeffs, I led him to perform sealings, and to begin a work of the Redemption of Zion mission.

2. He was led by me to find lands. He called people to my holy labor.

3. A holy house was built.

4. A people of my own order, unto my purposes being fulfilled, have now been laboring to be worthy of my presence.

5. Now learn that evil powers have combined with one another to seek to hinder or even destroy my Zion's mission.

6. A secret order was given evil revealings of lies, pure evil intent, to bring my servant Warren Jeffs into a place of harm, even in their surmisings, wanting to take life.

7. Let it be known this combination of evil is in full working, desiring to destroy him and my Priesthood.

8. Now I say, as God over all, my work shall triumph; my Priesthood shall be preserved; my Zion is increasing on earth through my will, unto New Jerusalem soon to rise; notwithstanding the evil combinings of the apostates and the government powers who have received of a similar dark spirit as apostates, when believing their lying ways of pure evil intent.

9. Thus have they lied, even in book publishings designed to turn this generation away from my holy authority.

10. Let it be known the

falsehoods now believed by government officials are no longer to be heard nor of a following; for I reveal that Dan Fischer, a wicked man who once lived Celestial Plural Union of Marriage, turned bitter, and has actively used his riches to pay the way of persecution; helping to embitter other former and now apostate members of my Priesthood to fight against my Priesthood.

11. My Priesthood, Church, and Celestial Law of Celestial Plural Union of Marriage are pure.

12. All who fight against my law of pure holy Union Celestial are of evil corrupt ways, unto the spirit of murder in their hearts.

13. This shall be truth learned as government authorities take upon themselves lies against my servant, against my Priesthood and law of pure holy way.

14. I am God. My way of Priesthood law is pure, holy, noble, godly.

15. Only they who obey my law know of the purity required to live my law in pure holy way.

16. These apostates became immoral, and lost my power, and are darkening more each day.

17. Let all heed them not.

18. They are traitors against me and my holy way.

19. Now let their own lives be examined to see they are corrupt.

20. Let governing authority be of a labor to examine these false witnesses, who only have a lying spirit, twisting truth with lying zeal, as though good is seen through unenlightened eyes as evil intent.

21. Thus, government courts, investigators, powers of legislative labor, governors, all have taken on the false way of these lying former saints, now darkened; who only look upon life through darkened minds; yielding themselves to persecute innocence unto imprisonment, robbing of lands, houses; and also seeking the virtue of my Priesthood to be destroyed, in promoting false authority, or full adulterous and Sodom sins; apostates losing all ways of pure holy living, following after the evil way inspired by Lucifer to thus harm in every way my holy people now preparing for my own power to dwell with them in New Jerusalem soon to come forth.

22. Thus, this man helped other apostates to file false charges.

23. Thus courts have been of a persecuting labor.

24. Now know my authority, though being of a way of past fearful and wondering way as great attacks came against him; yet I am with my servant, and reveal, through my grace, my own will, for I have him in my hands; and he gives my pure will to all peoples, by my pure revealing.

25. Now let him be about my full labor as my servant, to lead my Church.

26. Let all governing powers cease prosecuting work, lest my judgment of greater power come upon all who oppose my Priesthood.

27. Let judge of present labor against my servant recuse herself completely from all cases pertaining to my Church.

28. Let all witnesses be examined in their lives.

29. Let this secret combination of apostate, with governing powers, fully be of a overthrow.

30. You shall reap my full way of power of judgment if you continue thy false way. Amen.

SECTION REVELATION 37

Warning of Judgment of Pure Justice

**Revelation of the Lord Jesus Christ
Big Lake, Texas
Wednesday, March 23, 2011**

2. For how can I, the Lord, uphold you as a nation when you continue the greater evils within your borders, even the murder of unborn children, of Sodom and adultery, licentious and corrupt ways; of persecuting an innocent religious minority who abide my laws of a Celestial, eternal

nature; who persecute them to the taking of their lands and houses and hindering their advancement in my cause of Zion.***

16. Hasten to correct these evils, or you shall begin to experience workings of destruction within thine own borders in a greater manner than before; for heretofore I have been merciful upon thee when thy peoples have cried for mercy, and for the purpose of mine elect to be preserved on my land of Zion.

SECTION REVELATION 230

Motion of Jesus Christ in Court Proceedings in the Trial of My Servant

**Revelation of the Lord Jesus Christ
San Angelo, Texas
Sunday, July 31, 2011**

1. Let motion for my holy dismissing be of my doing, to be of a recusing of this judge to be of no longer a way of persecution, to have a way of no power over present doing of the attack of the power of the enemy who seek to destroy purity of my doing in full law of eternal power.

2. Let it begin with the way of the court of usual titling, with my own word to be in content of the writing to show my rule is above all

as an holy way to recuse, to allow all to know God is in the labor of this and other labor of pure way of truth, having full way of knowing what is in the heart of each person who is on my holy way of pure doing, to let them see I am the Doer of my delivering for my Order of Eternal Union of the holy noble way of my most pure way of pure abiding my law powering of pure holy labor in a full labor of my holy way being of Celestial power of my revealing truth.

3. Let all now hear my will of pure holy truth as I show my way of justice by my power of truth of Celestial light, by which I know the way to discern and judge with eternal power; a light of my holy power pertaining to court abuse of power against my Church of Jesus Christ to be my holy way of pure revealing unto the true way known of motion to be of a removal by law, having performed illegal way of using Judicial power to be of a way to be of a unjust and corrupting work against innocence of children, loss of sacred and pure trust of religious and noble revealings pertaining to holy temple, now being a defiling of your way of ruling against my call to stop such injustice, yet not heeding my will of pure holy call to be a just and righteous upholder of justice in a nation that has constitutional guarantee of religious freedom;

yet allowing my holy religious and sacred temple to be as no holy worth, not to be of government interference by right of pure principle of religion to be of greater protecting than the legal way of man; wherein my holy way is of heaven, saith Jesus Christ, the Lord of all, to Barbara Walther, present judge over case of unjust way; having allowed my holy way to be deriding before all people, even after my own will was of a giving; yet unheeded by you for no other reason than your own judging; not considering I told thee to cease this unjust and intrusive way against a holy, pure way of religion on earth, to be of salvation for all people who learn truth of my holy way of being ready for my holy coming.

4. Learn now thy transgression has been child abusing when you caused my innocent children to be carried away into the hand of your appointed and government agency people, who were of the way of taking children into evil places of their bondage from family protection, into homes of corrupt, immoral way of upbringing; to have some be abused unto loss of virtue by workers in the caretaking homes, not monitoring the moral and unholy way of such who are of the world in conduct; yet my innocent ones, thrust into way of corrupting, were touched, handled, abused, even morally in their innocent unprotecting way of

living, that my vengeance of eternal power shall be upon all such who destroy innocence, virtue, purity of morals.

5. Such was the truth of your intent to remove my holy way of life from children born and brought up in a most holy way of pure living, where prayer, moral discipline, worship of their Lord -- who now speaketh to thee; even to where I cause you to see your abuse by testimony of other caretakers of temporary helping, who later testified about abuse of the children, both mental and physical, in not allowing loving mother of each child to be the watch-care over innocence; thrust into homes of no moral training, thus exposed to corrupt ways of living, unto some being of an abusing by wicked and immoral and deceiving, lying agents of your order way of social and unholy and unjust doing.

6. I, your Lord, say to you, I shall bring to light your evil intent now, before all people, to destroy my Church on earth by allowing sacred and private trust to be heralding over all nations; as you continue to allow prosecution of unjust way to be as a desecrating of sacred law of pure holy religion of revealing from heaven, by a God of holy, pure, just way of abiding in eternal power, guiding His authority of heavenly power

to be as watchman over my law of holy power of exalting way; unto all being of a more and a greater standard of moral purity, requiring a moral way above the way of those not of my holy religious way.

7. Thus you have abused me and my Church unto a desecrating of holy and sacred religious way of exalting my people to be my elect of pure religion from heaven revealing of my giving; to now be of a greater condemning way of thy Lord than before, when I called on you to cease proceedings of unjust rulings; allowing my holy house to now be as non-religious defiling of sacred place of holy labor of Priesthood and eternal blessings administering, as unto life everlasting of my holy way of pure, noble, righteous power of eternal power.

8. I am to now recuse you from this case.

9. Let your heart be open to the way of your now being before all nations, to know you would not preserve religious freedom, nor religious sacred trust, while you could thus do a labor of just way, of noble trust of a governing power to hold sacred to all, a religious principle dear to most faiths; to not defile sacred trust of holy place of my temple; now as a defiling that cannot be undone; as you now

become a hiss and a by-word among all people, because you allowed my Church to be abandoned to ridicule unjustly, only having the intent to display my holy way before all people without any just cause, save to allow your will to be done; even when I had my Mouthpiece voice my warning of my own word declare you to Stop! Cease!, and thus be just in rulings that could be upon correct principle of keeping sacred to all peoples their religious edifices; now setting a way of defiling any religious sacred building; as though constitutional protection of religious faith and living is of no value; unto you now being an enemy to all religious and pure-faith way of worship.

10. This you did not consider as I sounded my voice and will in the proceedings before many; now heralding unjust way against sacred and religious way in every nation.

11. Hear my now judging of you as an unholy way of pure defiling of holy way; now to recuse yourself from present case; to now be of honor and step away from this abuse of power against a religious and pure faith in the Lord; who now is Judge of you, through my servant now voicing my will; to now be of honor to step away from these unjust doings, and no longer be of a judge over religious way of worship of your Lord, who shall be of a soon appearing to my Church and people of every nation who remain after my power of pure holy cleansing removes the evil off my land where my holy place shall be a refuge of pure worship of God and way of my administering my holy law of Celestial Union of holy and noble way of living, unto pure honoring sons and daughters who abide a purity of living my Celestial Marriage holy Union of my revealing.

12. Let thy mind now turn to the truth of my will; and be of an honorable way, to step away from present case and not again rule against a holy way.

13. This from your Lord who hath bought all people with the price of His own suffering, to redeem all people unto life, to be judged for deeds and desires in the flesh, unto eternal judgment and just and pure truth revealing each heart; all things being revealed unto the knowing of all peoples their hidden way, none being exempt from my eternal power of judging all people.

14. Let this be a sober way of thy thinking; to now do as I direct, even Jesus Christ now revealing thy mind, as you sat before court contemplating ruling, you were to be of a just thought of ruling in favor of religious protection; yet you allowed a fear to enter in

that my Church was not of a pure way; you thus did a private way of judging God and His revealing of laws eternal of Plural Celestial Union of my administering.

15. I fear you not, and shall show you as a worker against pure religious freedom by my own will being of a publishing to all people of your unjust way of adjudicating cases against my Church and principle of Union Eternal, thinking your court could deter practice of my faith and holy principle of eternal power of Priesthood guiding of members' lives in a way of abiding Celestial law, not of the earth, but of me, your Lord, who is Ruler over all.

16. Now sign order to recuse thyself; and allow this proceeding to stop; to now be reversed by your own doing of ruling mistrial, then recusing from case, and any other you have allowed to come against my elect, who some are suffering from thy way of court doing, in family and brotherhood ties broken as fathers and faithful, religious and principled men, imprisoned for religious motive practice, living as I, their Lord, command; thus being of thy persecuting way, need also delivering.

17. I append this, my motion, with a new will of God revealing thy work soon to be a publishing to all people; to know of thy way of unjust and unprincipled ruling in a case where you could be of a just way for religion being protecting of thy court power; now defamed by your power to extol your way before all people; yet now being of an justice defiler way.

18. This is my judging, to be of public knowing now in court assembling, to be published by my will to all people.

19. Let it now be your doing to hear this writing, to now do honor to true justice abiding way of honorable removing thyself from case now before the court.

20. Let my servant sign his name as my holy and noble authority on earth to deliver my will to all nations, peoples, tongues, kindreds, and governing powers, saith Jesus Christ, whose right it is to rule over all, who shall bring true just and holy way of governing power with Him in my appearing over all peoples as King over all the earth, God over all; who shall be as a Rewarder of pure judging to all peoples, eternal in power, pure and holy in exalting power unto salvation for all who come unto me through repenting of sin, and doing justly to all who are of the more righteous among all nations.

21. I, the Lord, have spoken. Amen.

SECTION REVELATION 231

Jesus Christ's Holy Will to Court of Unjust Way During Trial; Read in Record of Court to Tell All of My Way of Pure Holy Power Being of My Power Authority, and to Call Court to Cease Unjust Attack Against Me and My Holy Order of Pure Religion Revealed From Heaven

**Revelation of the Lord Jesus Christ
San Angelo, Texas
Thursday, August 4, 2011**

1. I your Lord who reigns over all my world of probationary and testing condition of pure holy creating power; even your Lord and God over all things, yea, He who spake, and the world was made, the God of my servant now dwelling in an unjust holding, to face thy unholy attack against all I have him perform unto my purpose of Zion being of a real place, kingdom, power, people, and ruling governing power over all nations; look at thy sin now of a heightening tower ready to fall with Babylon, the unholy way of persecuting power, now in a supposed court of law; to be of a unholy way of unjust attack in court, allowing prosecuting way to accuse me, the God over all, who is the power of you being of a power on my world of holy way of Celestial abiding, which world shall be my only way of salvation for all who have and will dwell thereon; to be of a heaven to all who live a Celestial Law; not of man, but of my revealing unto him who is Mouth on earth at this time to all people; of the way of my giving truth through revealing through authority of my holy calling; not of man's appointing, but of thy Lord, who is over all nations; who is of the authority of Godhood, who can see all in true judging of hearts to be just in holy and pure ways.

2. Let this court now be just, to cease letting my holy way of Celestial Law be as a dishonor among they of my power of governing authority be derided, mocked, as a way of accusing my holy way, thus accusing me, your Lord, of being not of noble pure way of doing.

3. I am God, and send thee my word: Cease! Do not present my holy way as a thing of naught; lest judgment come to a full measure to be cleansing powers sent to be a judging of all of my holy and pure power attending your evil intent.

4. Hear my warning as a full awakening unto repenting of your attack against pure religion Celestial, only for they of purity

of life in religious way of eternal authority of my Priesthood.

5. Let my holy way be of freedom; to have my people be of my holy way.

6. Let my word now be of an awakening to all, that I, your Lord Jesus Christ, still speak from revealing of eternal and pure holy power to all on earth, through him you have caused to be as a witness against no justice given in the way of civil governing power, misjudging a servant of my sending, as a full attack of thy doing against thy Lord and His authority of noble pure way of Celestial and Priesthood law revealed from heaven; to be my authority among men to prepare my people of Celestial power for my holy coming.

7. I am soon to fulfill my will of cleansing the land of Zion, North and South America, by whirlwind judgments.

8. Let all prepare.

9. Let court cease this attack, is the will of thy Lord Jesus Christ who now reveals your own lives are as a light now turning to darkness by thy own choosing; to be persecuting power against innocence, that standeth firm in revelations of my giving; to abide more pure and holy judging than is known to man, who are not enlightened in my Celestial way of truth. Amen.

SECTION REVELATION 232

Jesus Christ Calls on Court to Cease Unjust Proceedings, to Have Recusal Hearing for Removal of Judge of Unjust Use of Power

Revelation of the Lord Jesus Christ
San Angelo, Texas
Tuesday, August 2, 2011

1. I who reign on high speaketh to court of present judication:

2. Cease this aggression against my own true Church, which I, your Lord, have established to perform the labor of final preparing of a pure and sacred labor of my inspiring; to have upon them the requiring way of eternal purity of purpose, of faith, of the nature of Celestial Law abiding in pure Celestial performing; to be my pure religion of perfect way of holy religion; guaranteed freedom of performing religion without government intervening, according to constitutional law of guarantee of all religion of pure purpose.

3. Verily I say unto you who now are of the legal work of deriding my sacred law of pure holy way, to cause the naming of your own will as if I were subject to you whom I, the God over all, have created and give place on my own domain of my creating, to have life, the ability to prove thyself, whether each son or daughter would obey law eternal

that exalts unto salvation earned by a pure way of abiding law of pure way, in a giving of obeying to a just and holy Father of eternal power; able to exalt thee unto life and have place in my eternal domain of Celestial exalting.

4. Now receive ye my word, even from thy Lord through my servant, now being of a labor to be of a witness against this unholy way of unrighteous labor against my holy revealing of pure noble way, of my own eternal authority being of a victim of government attack because of the way of my sending my own law of Eternal Union to earth, through revelation of my own will unto him who is my Mouthpiece to the world; to receive their Lord's own mind and way unto eternal life, by abiding in Celestial revealing of my own purposes, fulfilling all required way to become a son of God in realms eternal, a daughter of holy and pure Celestial Union with a son of God who can be able to dwell in realms eternal; by living law of that Celestial and eternal way, revealing my own purposes, fulfilling the measure of thy creation, of Him who is able to exalt thy soul unto my own eternal power.

5. Let the present course of this ruling judicial power now be of a postponing of proceedings.

6. Let transcript of sessions be given time to be preparing to be presented to a recusal hearing, lest the court perform a labor of unrelenting zeal of persecution against innocent way of eternal life lived in ordinances of my holy way, requiring the obedience to Celestial, holy, pure law, to earn the reward of faithful and righteous children unto the Father over all.

7. I who reign over all speaketh: Let this proceeding stop, lest there be unjust way of thy doing that is harmful to innocent people, not having right to religious and holy law and Celestial power attending, now being of a deriding by present and unholy way; not having foundation at all to allow the presentation of the holy and sacred doing of God with a work of full intent to interfere with my holy way being the full law of a pure kingdom to rise on earth through the living of Celestial Plural Marriage, now having been of a law of eternal power from eternity; not to be done away by the prejudice of man, nor by earthly law that does not exalt the soul.

8. Let these realities awaken present judge to see the treading on my holy law is to turn to legal way of greater persecution against my holy way, even my pure way of exalting sons of God, daughters of holy and pure way, unto life eternal.

9. This from the Lord, even thy Creator, now sending His own will to present court, to know that my will shall be fulfilled in the end; whether it be by thy consent and righteous ruling in protecting religion of pure holy power of a way of my giving; or by my intervening by almighty power of judging this people of present dwelling on my land of my soon power of governing power on earth in Zion; to be my holy abode on earth as I dwell among men, to be the governing power of my holy eternal power of governing authority over all who will acknowledge me, your Lord and Governor over all, Jesus Christ, who will be my elect of the way of Celestial power eternal; to be my only way of pure holy abiding on earth for a thousand years of peace; to rule over all nations extant, in dominion of Celestial power, not allowing unjust way of religion being of a persecuting way by governing power in the way of hindering their freedom of abiding law and way eternal of my own revealing unto all lands; a holy way of pure holy doing unto my coming among my people who are of the law of Celestial pure way; even my law of Celestial Marriage, and my other holy law of the full Celestial way of Holy Order of Eternal Union of full sacred way of having all things common, a way of requiring my faithful to live pure in every way of their dwelling among my Holy City Zion; soon to be built by faithful and obedient children of my calling and empowering, to prepare for my own presence.

10. Let this court now rule in favor of postponing until recusal hearing can be properly prepared for in having court transcript preparing for review, to show unjust way of ruling against my holy Priesthood, Church, people, and Celestial Law of eternal and holy way, saith Jesus Christ, unto thy being forgiven as you do such just way; to preserve my holy way unto a full doing of holy and pure raising of a people unto thy God for salvation to be administered unto my Israel, to be gathered unto my land, Zion, even the land upon which you now dwell.

11. If thou do it not, know that innocence shall be harmed, and defiling of pure holy way become a way of government infringement on a pure holy faith of my own keeping to be a God of Creation.

12. Let all now be of the way of just and righteous judgment, to have as my will being performed; to have the nation now be of free exercise of religion in reality and in truth.

13. I, the Lord, have spoken it. Amen.

SECTION REVELATION 233

Jesus, Your Lord, Giveth His Word to Governing Power; Also My Will to My People to Prepare for My Full Power of Holy Power of Zion to Come Forth Among Nations of the Earth; Judgments Soon to Cleanse the Land

**Revelation of the Lord Jesus Christ
Eldorado, Texas
Sunday, July 24, 2011**

1. Let all now learn of their Lord, His will of my pure holy way of my full labor to redeem Zion unto New Jerusalem being built by power eternal soon to happen; to have my Church be the instrument of pure revelation on earth to know my will of Zion from heaven coming to earth; to be a pure and perfecting and, in time, lifted-up dwelling of the holy Order of Union Celestial.

2. Verily I say unto you, I called on my servant, each Priesthood Keyholder, to be as my holy will to my people who would hear my will; to teach how to become pure in all holy way and pure living; to be a people filled with my holy love in the keeping all my holy will; to love eternal, pure, holy, and exalting way of uplifting more noble laws of God that exalt unto Zion being only pure.

3. I have led my servant in each full giving of my word, even my Keyholder of full sealing key power of my Holy Priesthood; each one being of full way to seal marriage and other blessings of Celestial power sent by your God, to have the labor of sealing Celestial Marriage of holy pure abiding; unto all my people having a labor of true hope for a holy resurrection of their Lord, according to their walk in this probation of testing, to be my proving all -- who will abide Celestial Law of exalting way.

4. Thus have I sent each Prophet to lead my chosen people who would receive my holy way, by revelation and commandment from your God.

5. They are my people, sent by your Lord to build up my Church in abiding law Celestial, to earn my Zion to come forth in fulness.

6. Let all now be of my holy way, to be part of Zion soon to be on my holy way of Celestial power on earth; for I shall come in the cloud of my holy will being performed in all full power of pure eternal power.

7. Let all people learn of my holy way.

8. Let my Church be pure in all holy and inspiring, righteous, exalting, noble way of pure living.

9. Come out of Babylon to be my pure holy generation to build New City of Holiness, even Zion.

10. Let my people be free to dwell on my holy land of pure abiding,

even Zion, the land of my coming, both North and South America; for I shall cleanse the land of all wicked and corrupt and impure way of their following the carnal, sensual way of evil doing.

11. All must now be of a warned and preparing way, to be surviving my cleansing power of God's own will being done in judgment of my power of pure judging; to hold every man of his own conduct unto there being no excuse for sin, when I have sent my own will to all peoples, nations, kindreds, tongues; and holy way of living have I taught all peoples.

12. Let my Spirit be your power of holy living.

13. Pray always in your minds and hearts until my appearing, to be ready; for when I come, a setting in order shall take place, to purge all corrupt and ungodly from among them; to have full power to perfect their lives unto a Celestial way, that I may be to them a God, and they to me a pure people to be Zion, who are the pure in heart.

14. Love your God, because He is love, even with all your heart, might, mind, and strength; and love your neighbor as yourself in all holy and pure way, to be the holy people who can ask to be of a full deliverance unto my Kingdom being a preserving unto Celestial eternal

powers dwelling among them for a thousand years, while I come and go as I will.

15. I have spoken it. Great are the soon coming events just when I am to cleanse the land of Zion in full measure.

16. I am now purifying the few elect who are seeking unto me through my servant on earth at this time, who is in my hands, though held by my children of governing powers in a bondage because he only seeks to do my will to establish Zion on earth by my holy will revealing who is to be of eternal power of Celestial Union in my Church.

17. Let him go, to do my holy will, is the call of thy Lord and Redeemer.

18. Let his brethren be free, each one imprisoned by false way of using man's law to afflict my Church in marriage sent of God.

19. Let all now know I will be as a full Judge upon all powers of man.

20. Let all know I will preserve my Holy Priesthood, though tried in the sieve of persecution resulting from lying and deceiving witnesses who were of my Church, then left because they were of a non-compliance to my holy way themselves in their own personal living; turning as the dog to his vomit and the sow of cleansing to

the mire, after being cleansed by my Gospel of pure holy way.

21. Let my people be free.

22. Return their lands and houses taken by unjust rulings, inviting the open enemies of my people to dwell in my houses that were a consecration of my people unto their God, now taken and used to persecute and deprive my faithful from having all things mine in their holy, pure living of Celestial laws of my holy will revealing, to be my Zion.

23. Now awake to the day of cleansing. I am soon to sweep the wicked out of every land of every nation who continue in immoral and violent, murderous way, of sinning against life, even they who also live Sodom, as well as the murder of unborn children; which evil is corrupting the way before your Lord; having to cleanse all peoples of these evils by judgments eternal, even Celestial power of my sending the cleansing and destructive power; for you are ripened in iniquity, to be only of a condition to be removed from the land of my holy coming, who are of these evils, whether in practice, or by toleration, by assenting to such practices.

24. You then become a spiritually-dark people, seeing not your own evils of immoral way of corrupting yourselves and your habitations and families in way of ungodliness and in traditions of fighting against the way of life.

25. Cleanse yourselves and let my people live my holy pure way, by my revealing the power of my holy way of my Holy Priesthood, to administer my Celestial Law of Plural Celestial power of Union Marriage.

26. Let my people be my preserving of pure holy way of living on earth, to become my holy, pure, and enlightened vessels, who shall be sent to surviving peoples, nations, kindreds, tongues in every land and nation, that my Gospel of salvation may be my holy will being as a saving way unto eternal life.

27. I have now called upon you, the court of oppression, to be as a delivering power for my servant Warren Jeffs and his brethren, with this, my own will, being revealed as the testimony of pure eternal truth given to you and all people of the nation; which testimony is of your Lord of pure will manifest.

28. Let them be free.

29. Let all now know I am to soon reward all liars and hypocrites who have sought to destroy my people, with a judgment of their being overthrown in every way, where they who joined with them who have sought my people's destruction, I shall turn it upon their

own heads, to purge all corrupt way of following and loving a lie from the people of the land of Zion.

30. Let all nations beware.

31. I have sent my word of final warning of great judgments at hand.

32. Let no one be found against me, lest you become the unwise and be left outside my city New Jerusalem to dwell with they who have fought against Zion on earth, to no longer be a power to oppose the rise of Zion on earth.

33. Now be of a doing.

34. Let him, my servant, go, to do my will among my chosen people; and if you will be of truth, free my sons of my Holy Priesthood now unrighteously and unjustly held in bondage.

35. Let the witness of main testimony herself be examined.

36. She is a liar, a traitor to truth she once held dear, and turned from my law of Eternal Power, and is in darkness, used by prosecuting authority; willing to lie about the purity of my holy way she once said was her delight; now wallowing in sin herself of immoral way.

37. Let there be the work of witnessing of one of the law and of the profession of the police way who has had intimate way with the one who is of the chief witness against my holy law, to learn of a connection unclean pertaining to the cases of unjust imprisonment; as well as the corrupt, immoral ways of apostate witnessing.

38. Look into their lives to know they themselves are of an unclean way of immoral doing; who then accuse my pure way of unclean and evil intent; judging others according to the way of darkness within themselves.

39. Such do the wicked who once upheld my holy way as the only way to salvation in eternal life with your God, who is only holy, pure, righteous, exalting in all ways of holy power eternal; who now speaketh to present governing power to examine motive of false testifying against my pure and innocent ones, who only live my holy law of Celestial authority and pure Priesthood way by my command.

40. Now know that I shall be a deliverance unto my people.

41. I shall be as a power to reveal secret and wicked joining of the false witnesses and governing powers.

42. Let my people be free, lest my revealing shows you who prosecute and defame my holy way to be known in your corrupt way.

43. Let all now be pure before your God, who sees and knows all things, who shall reward all for how they receive my holy will; who are of the way of unbelief; who

deny eternal truths of my revealing as they sin away the day of their final preparing, as my judgments of cleansing power are soon to be upon all peoples; to prepare for my glorious coming nigh at hand, saith your Lord, even Jesus Christ, who speaketh to all peoples through my servant in this time of final warning and preparing for the whirlwind judgments I shall soon send forth. Amen.

SECTION REVELATION 234

How to Labor Instant by Instant in the Increase of the Holy Spirit, the Gifts and Powers of Enlivening Joy, Perfecting Godliness in Your Natures Through Exalting Powers in Eternal Life, Even From That God Who Created You

Revelation of the Lord Jesus Christ
Eldorado, Texas
Thursday, May 5, 2011

1. Thus saith the Lord who reigns on high, in a manner of your understanding, laboring through my servant and with Zion's mission, my inspired love-giving to you, sustaining you day by day in life unto eternal life:

2. Thus must be your living awakening within you, wherein you possess lively hope unmeasured, filling your soul with enlightening Celestial glory; for this is the reality of the increase of my heavenly light within your nature as you abide Celestial laws in the spirit of your calling; not in an empty manner, not in an empty wondering; coming alive in the reality of my Spirit burning in you, known as a gentle peace of enlivening and enlightening joy, the joy of your Lord as your guide instant by instant.

3. Repent ye of thinking you are qualifying for my mission of Zion wherein you continue in a manner having times of darkness and then light, then the darkness.

4. Thus saith the Lord, it is not so. Overcoming must take place. Thereby do you learn to dwell in the increase of my light in the joy of your Lord, Him visiting you with continual flow of exalted thoughts and desires, willing to give all in a manner only to please your God, though it take your life; knowing you have a greater hope beyond this life unto eternal life with your eternal and loving Father who dwells in eternal burnings of everlasting glory, an earth like unto that orb shining upon thee giving thee daylight, Celestial planet of governing power, for thus it is.

5. And this I reveal to your sacred keeping, you on the mission of Zion's redemption where my

Land of Holiness has upon it all things being prepared for the elect to be gathered.

6. Thus, faith is known by the continual increase of my Spirit; for this is faith, this power of the Spirit of God in action, my righteousness revealed, exercised through my giving power -- not of thy choice alone, but of the increase of thy Lord to thee, which always brings an acknowledgment of rejoicing in Him as you feel the thrill of joy, the witness of gentle peace and enlivening truth that exalts, as a witness that I am hearing and answering prayers.

7. Prayers will be answered in my time, according to my will and thy continued faithful walk before me.

8. Thus, you are my Zion as you live in the spirit of your callings, thus described in this, my revealing, some needing more explanation, and not assuming righteousness or faith or hope.

9. And my holy love extant is not an empty doing that comes and goes, as it were, in some people's lives, where they feel a darkness at times because they choose to hearken to the whisperings of a dark power, and set upon by the memory of the past, in particular, as a great weakness in Zion's mission.

10. Look not back to a dark power. When I remind thee of that which was in the past, there is a lifting-up power, enlivens your soul to remember the good.

11. And when evil is remembered, particularly personal sins or weaknesses that have been repented of, I lead thee to repent further, wherein you may be continuing in pleasure in unrighteousness in looking back, or being reminded how blessed you are at this time to continue in Zion's mission and among my Priesthood.

12. Thus I give you this detailed training of righteous living, all you on my Land of Holiness.

13. Have faith, the witness of gentle peace of enlivening and enlightening joy.

14. Be ye one on Zion's cause, is my love-giving message to you, my Zion's mission this day, called to the most holy work, sent from above from the God of Creation who reigns over thee.

15. And as the enlivening joy and enlightenment of mind of exalted and noble thoughts and feelings awakens your soul to a lifting-up above that which has troubled thee in the past, walk forward with that power, a confidence that as you thus receive, that power can continue with thee through thy continued rejoicing gratitude, never looking back in a downcast or worried or fearful way, walking hand in hand with thy Lord

through the Spirit of peace of gentle nature, that enlivening enlightening to the soul.

16. When you still hear the whisperings of darkness when my light whispers to you there is further repenting; yea, and even times required atoning, whether it be a power I send, intervening for thee, upon one of atoning authority; whether it be humbling, justice satisfied -- the loss of my Spirit, feeling a darkness, a spiritual groping, waiting for deliverance and salvation until my Spirit returns to awaken you that you cannot choose darkness -- any degree of excuse, whether it be pleasure in evil, or fearsome worry you hang on to, to no effect, troubling thy soul, receiving, in return, emptiness; thus awakening thee to further repenting needed, turning to thy God in joyous lays, lifting-up happiness when He restores His Spirit, uplifting nature into your soul.

17. Let these details of laboring in the spirit with thy Lord, Him being your very real Heavenly Father, dwelling in eternal burnings on a Celestial orb of governing power, who sees and knows all things and can read and understand your minds, thoughts, and desires of your hearts and souls, an immediate return of the result of your choice; even whispering where to repent and improve instant by instant, not having to go a long time without that light burning in you -- instant return to Him when a dark power attempts to deride and disturb your soul --

18. Take these truths into thy exertion of your mind in faith, using the gifts and powers of my Spirit, which is always a feeling of holy love extant, perfect kindness, undisturbed in nature, lowliness of heart, rejoicing in thy Lord, the Author of all good and righteous doing, all creation, and in thy individual thinking and feelings, which needs of an exalting nature increased more fully, all on Zion's mission.

19. This is my revealing. All must improve and not continue in a manner of dwelling on that which does not exalt, in a bothered or continued feeling downcast and disturbed way in your life, saith the Lord Jesus Christ, who sees and knows all things and has all power to lift thee up above the whisperings of darkness in a moment of need; yea, instant by instant, until your character is perfected in every form of godliness, revealed from my heavenly habitation, from the Father, to be called in Priesthood covenants to abide the Order of Eternal Union inspired love-giving. And I am with thee.

20. My presence comes among thee, even making known to thee heavenly powers are around thee,

angels from Celestial and eternal glory whispering to your minds: "Pray now. Do this." Heed my warning of improvement, deliverance from that which can harm, perfection needed further -- always a greater humbling to depend completely on the whispering power of salvation of my Holy Spirit, which lifts you up in the real and holy way of life that can be discerned, delicious to the soul.

21. Thus it is a gift of my giving, causing you to acknowledge thy God in all things with rejoicing gratitude, the necessary element of the prayer of faith always abiding in thee as a witness of my Spirit, that power of faith by which you labor instant by instant unto the perfecting of Zion within you.

22. And I am with you who stay constant unto me in that joyous-gratitude prayer of faith, visited at times with a testing, a lessening of that heavenly light, witnessing to you a greater need to be more fervent and diligent in my cause of Zion, and in thy further preparing in this manner I am now revealing through my servant of a needed gift of enlightenment, truth from above your understanding -- the immediate applying, adding to your immediate prayer of faith at this time, that your worrisome fears may be obliterated out of your nature concerning past sins or present weaknesses or feelings downcast, saith your Lord.

23. Be of an enlivening power among your fellows, both men and women, even children, to be of the prayer of faith extant, not abiding in a lonesome, wearied, or withdrawn manner.

24. None of you need abide a lesser light on Zion's mission, for my house of holiness dwells ready for a people to receive the ordinances of mine house, yet empty at this time, waiting the final preparing of mine elect, soon to be gathered.

25. Faith is a certainty of soul, not the wandering of the mind in wonderment, leading to doubts and fears that cause that darkening for an instant.

26. Turn unto me. The whispering is real, gentle and peaceful, enlivening with an enlightenment joy where you know I am a God at hand to whisper to the purer mind the full flow of exalted thoughts and feelings.

27. This is the Holy Spirit in your life, preparing you to be my Zion, perfecting your lives unto godliness, Godhood and Goddesshood, those who are well prepared.

28. Heed my word and holy sacred revealing, giving you the details of how to be perfected in the gifts of my Holy Spirit instant by instant.

29. You need not spend moments searching for your Lord, wondering if He is near.

30. My Spirit is extant, filling all in all through all creation, giving all creation its form, appearance, and nature.

31. Thine own creation is an organized spirit and body together, a son and daughter, each one as the offspring of God.

32. This is my revealing to you.

SECTION REVELATION 235

Declaration of My Revealed Will of Warning to the President of the United States, Along with the Proclamation to All Government Officials

**Revelation of the Lord Jesus Christ
Eldorado, Texas
Thursday, July 21, 2011**

Jesus Christ, Your Lord and King, Sendeth His Own Will to You of the Governing Power on the Land of America, and to all People of the Earth; and to Know My Holy Pure Way Is on Earth to Be a Way of Zion Soon Coming Forth -- and a Call to Let My People Go Free as My Work of Cleansing Shall Be in Full Measure Soon. Hear Ye My Will and Soon Promises to Be Fulfilled.

1. Thus saith the Lord to the people of this present and most unworthy of all people who have ever inhabited my chosen land of Zion where New Jerusalem shall be in full as the Celestial authority, to be as the governing power over all nations; who are of the power to be of pure way; who shall learn eternal way and living in Zion; unto my Church and Kingdom, even Jesus Christ, who giveth my own will to you now dwelling on my land; to yet be of a full purity and cleansing by judgments of my sending, to cleanse all wickedness from off the whole land; to prepare for New Era of holy, pure way of eternal power to govern the whole earth as a Celestial power of my giving; is as a fire of all purity and holy enlivening: I am soon to be of a pure and full labor of my full power of judgment on all people in every land.

2. Let all now hear my will: I am Son Ahman, who is Jesus Christ, the God over all the world; who shall be as a full power Celestial; to govern all nations who remain from Jerusalem of my New Order of Eternal Power, as New Era of my holy power comes to my earth, to be the holy power of my right to be your Ruler and King; to dwell among all of Zion in full power of my new way of pure giving life and holy work of Celestial Eternal Union.

3. I reveal my Celestial Law of Marriage is a most holy way, and

can only be lived by my pure people of my holy and pure Priesthood who are of obeying all my holy will; not for the wicked nor unbelieving who are not receiving of my Church and will.

4. Let all now be of the witness of my law being holy, pure, sacred, righteous; and of my giving and revealing through my Keyholder of Priesthood authority, who is my servant Warren Jeffs, being of the way of captivity for doing my way and holy will.

5. Thus is he being of a power to give my will, to make known that I am soon to purge my land of my New City of Holy Celestial Power to be the governing power over all peoples, nations, tongues, and kindreds on all lands; to have my holy will known that my love is to be of a power of eternal, holy governing; to be my full way of pure governing of you, my sons of Israel, and all peoples;

6. For I am the Holy One of the Order of Endless Power, who was God from before the earth was made; who was born on earth among men, rejected by my own, sacrificing all for my Father's will to be fulfilled, even for full salvation to be given to all who are of obeying eternal law of my revealing, unto pure dominions of eternal power in never-ending increase. I am He

who was of your needed delivering from death, all to be raised unto life in the power of the Redemption; to be as a full Order of Eternal Power. I am He who sendeth these words of warning --

7. Let my people go! to be of my holy Order of Eternal Power in living Celestial Law of pure holy way, of pure religious love-giving unto God, to do His revealed way.

8. I have decreed a famine to soon come on the land where my New City of Holy and Pure Power shall soon rise.

9. Many shall perish in the dearth that cometh.

10. Repent ye, repent ye, all of my believing and receiving people, who can be of my Church on earth, unto the purifying their lives unto becoming mine holy nation of Kings and Priests unto God, Queens and Priestesses of pure way; in living my Celestial Law of holy eternal power of Priesthood; who are to be as pure holy Saviors on Mount Zion; to be as holy pure vessels of my saving unto eternal life.

11. I shall soon send an overflowing scourge, a full cleansing of my land of new holy and pure dwelling; when only mine holy pure Israel who gather to Zion shall remain on the land.

12. I shall be your holy and pure power of redeeming power, to be

of the way of the holy pure law of Union Eternal, to be my Church of Celestial Power, to be a full order of my New Era of holy love, bringing peace to all nations; to be the pure holy vessels of holy way in eternal power; of my power unto my holy pure way being thy way, to be the people of Zion who are in the way of life in a full way of my power Celestial.

13. Such shall be my holy power on an enlightened people who obey my will, to learn ways Celestial in every way of pure holy power, the holy power of eternal full and noble way of my pure giving; to receive the full way of my holy New Era of Zion to dwell on earth.

14. Let all now be of a final way of pure holy way of living, saith your Lord and Holy Savior, even Jesus Christ, who is of the full power of pure and holy way; to be the Life of all, the Light of all; the Judge of all people unto eternal life for the more faithful of all people; and a judgment of eternal decrease and sorrow, of weeping unto everlasting regret upon those who seek the way of the fallen and unclean who seek evil; who will only be of a way of a lower gift in the eternal realm of Jehovah.

15. I am He. Come unto me. Obey my voice, saith your God to this people on earth who will not abide my law of salvation; who is now of the way of unbelief and derision against my Celestial Law, who have no desire for my holy way; who persecute my people.

16. Let my people be as a free and pure holy way, to bless all other of my Israel, and of all nations of surviving on earth; for I come and bring with me my holy way; to recompense to every man that which he has measured to his fellow man unto eternity and full measure of reward what thou hast done in the flesh, according to the light given while in the way of this earth, to have all things of a full giving as thou hast performed unto your fellow sojourners on earth.

17. With my holy way now being on earth, you know I am soon to come to mine holy pure vessels of pure way.

18. Be ye pure to be of a surviving unto Zion, the pure way to redeem all peoples, nations, tongues; and faithful obedient people who will be my holy Order of Celestial Power in my New Jerusalem.

19. Let my holy order be one in pure holy law of my revealing.

20. Let my will be read to all people in every land on earth, to know what is soon to take place on earth, even judgments of full power to cleanse all nations of the ungodly. Amen.

SECTION REVELATION 236

Revelation of the Lord Jesus Christ
Huntsville, Texas
Saturday, August 20, 2011

1. One Dan Fischer was giving bribe money to legislators in states prosecuting my servant.

2. Now trace this money, to know moneys of bribes being paid to prosecute my servant.

3. Let this now become a public outcry.

4. Let money be shown as political pressure to attack my Church.

5. Let judge of unjust way also be known as not being of honor, who would not defend religious freedoms guaranteed by Constitution of the nation.

6. Let it be shown she hath commanded this full attack from the beginning; should recuse herself, and cease such evil.

SECTION REVELATION 237

Your Lord Jesus Christ
Declareth Unjust Ruling of
Prison Sentencing

Revelation of the Lord Jesus Christ
Huntsville, Texas
Saturday, August 20, 2011

1. Thus saith the Lord to the governing power that performed work of no justice; but did a labor of destroying freedom of religion and worship, by allowing an open and notorious presenting of all lying and use of that which is preserved for religious governing, to be of a presenting before all peoples; as though my holy pure way is not holy, pure, noble, righteous, exalting, inspiring.

2. I heed you not.

3. You have only destroyed religious protection.

4. You are a fallacy of justice.

5. You shall be overruled.

6. Your determined, open, and full attack against pure holy way of my revealed religion shall soon be heralded to all as false and base.

7. All who joined with government shall be of a foundering, to know their foundation is on conspiracy of falsehood told over years of apostate lies being enhanced; until my Priesthood answers them nothing.

8. They are from the lying spirit of the devil. Money is their god. They shall fall.

SECTION REVELATION 238

Revelation of the Lord Jesus Christ
Palestine, Texas
Tuesday, October 11, 2011

1. I who is over all speaketh to the whole world, your Lord who is of the

Power of Eternity, now of a full labor to now be the holy order of Celestial authority governing all people:

2. Let all now be preparing for my holy power over all lands, to be of the full power of my Celestial holy eternal governing authority; to be your holy and Eternal Lord, King, and Redeemer; even my holy power now being revealed.

3. Let kings, rulers of nations, government over nations, be of a cleansing of all their ways of power; to be of the just way of righteous and peaceful way.

4. Let all people of the calling of my holy way be of a full purity; to dwell in my Zion. Let this be as a full holy and authorizing call, to be ready. Amen.

APPENDIX A

WARNINGS OF PREVIOUS SENDING TO LEADERS OF THE NATION

A Warning to the Nation

SECTION REVELATION 5

A Petition to the President of the United States of America

Revelation of the Lord Jesus Christ
Draper, Utah
Thursday, October 7, 2010

1. To the honorable President of the United States of America now as standing at the head of this nation:

2. I who dwells on high, even your Lord and Savior, who redeemed all mankind by the shedding of His own blood, and who is over all and has all power, send to you my word.

3. Cause that my servant who presides over my Church now be delivered by thy hand.

4. Let my servant go, that he may perform his mission to prepare my people for my coming.

5. Cause that the prosecutors now cease their attack upon my servant Warren Jeffs.

6. Cause that this nation now restore to my people the consecrated land taken from them.

7. Cause that there be remuneration given them for the loss of the homes that are occupied illegally by the enemies of my people who are in the Colorado City, Arizona and Hildale, Utah area.

8. Cause that the attack against my people in Texas be stopped.

9. I, the Lord, shall cause my judgments to be withheld as you thus perform this work.

10. Otherwise, let this nation know I am with my people, and shall sweep the wicked from off the face of the land of America.

11. Thus shall I perform my work by my almighty power.

12. This from your Lord, even Jesus Christ, who shall subdue all His enemies under His feet.

13. Even as I have spoken, so shall I fulfill. Even so. Amen.

SECTION REVELATION 35

Revelation of the Lord Jesus Christ to the Peoples of the Nation of the United States of America and to the Peoples of the Earth Through My Servant Warren Jeffs

Big Lake, Texas
Saturday, February 5, 2011

1. Thus saith the Lord unto the nation of the United States of America: I, the Lord, am soon to send the shaking of the earth in a place in thy land not known as a usual place of violent shaking, unto the loss of many lives.

2. Let it be known, I, the Lord, have sent my message to government officials to free my servant Warren Jeffs, to cause my people to receive back their lands and houses, and you heed me not.

3. Thus I shall cause a great destruction in the land of Illinois, to the loss of life and to your awakening, that when I, the Lord, speak, let my word be fulfilled, lest you become as a people only worthy to be swept off my land of Zion;

4. For verily I say unto you, this earth is mine, and I have caused my people to receive a preparation work for my glorious coming on earth to establish my Zion, and they are my people. Let them go! For you shall now feel the wrath of an Almighty God in a place of my naming in a soon-to-happen event.

5. Though you deny me, know that I, the Lord, have spoken, and I send to you my word at this time, to receive my word that I shall cause my servant on earth to deliver to thee, a message of warning, that I, the Lord, will no longer uphold thee as a nation, corrupting your way before me, having in your midst legalized murder of unborn children, thus shedding innocent

blood before the heavens, and allowing the sins of Sodom and immoral practices among you by legal consent; yet you persecute my people who abide by my will and my governing principles of purity, required of them by me.

6. No longer consider I shall preserve thy land as you continue to allow him whom I have chosen to receive and give my word to the peoples of the earth to remain in bondage; when he only is seeking to fulfill my will, saith the Lord, in preparing my people to establish on my holy land my Zion, a place of peace; which you know is among them, having illegally carried away innocent children, examining my people, knowing they are free from the corrupting influences of this wicked generation by your own examining.

7. Though you accuse them of corrupt practices and evil motives, they are my people, saith the Lord Jesus Christ, who sendeth this message to you: Let my people go! or you shall reap the whirlwind of judgments in near future sending, such as you have not seen; for I am God, and I speak from the heavens through him whom I have anointed.

8. Though he received testing, fearing for a time, yet I, the Lord, have raised him up and delivered him and am guiding him -- Now step forth and deliver my word to all peoples:

9. Repent ye! Repent ye! My day of judgments upon all the earth is at hand.

10. Send forth my word of warning to all peoples, beginning with this nation, and hereafter shall I cause a greater sounding of my warning voice, which, if you heed me not, shall be fulfilled in fulness; for I shall appear in the power of my might in the clouds of heaven, to make myself known to all peoples my right to rule; and nothing can hinder the progress of my Zion rising in fulness;

11. For though you stretch forth your hands to persecute mine elect on the earth, who have received exalted ways in pure religious motive and practice; yet you believe traitors who are themselves corrupt, partaking of a spirit of outward prosecution, condemning that which is holy because thine own hearts are corrupt before me; accusing mine elect of wicked motives who only receive my laws of Celestial Plural Marriage and my Economic Order of Heaven, a United Order of religious practice by my word, by the revelations of my will.

12. And this is my Church upon the earth, living laws that you know are of scriptural record among you; yet you condemn that which I, the Lord, have established for the salvation of the earth.

13. Verily I say unto you, let there be an immediate stop to the prosecution and governmental interference against my servant and against my people, lest you incur mine anger unto the fulfilling of what I have named, that I now send to you in a writing of your understanding.

14. And though false witnesses stand forth seeking to brand guilt upon innocence, I, the Lord, shall defend my people in a manner of deliverance to thine eternal regret and condemnation, as you stand before me in the day of judging, having lifted your hand against your God who created you.

15. Receive my word of warning, and know that I, the Lord, have spoken from the heavens at a needed time when you can respond to my word.

16. And as a testimony this is my word, I shall send forth a great storm in the land, crippling thy nation again, which I have been sending in increasing power since you allowed an unjust judge to confine my servant still, and other court actions in thy land against the holding of property where my people dwell; in that place in the Hildale, Utah and Colorado City, Arizona area, illegally, by your own laws, interfering with a religious trust by governmental intervention.

17. Now this country of the United States of America shall go down, as she does not defend innocence, religious organization of pure religious intent.

18. I, the Lord, have spoken it. Hasten to respond to my word, as I send my word again to you, lest mine anger be kindled unto the fulfilling of all my promises against a wicked generation in a manner you have not seen before.

19. This from your Lord and Savior, Jesus Christ, who hath redeemed all mankind, who will respond to my message of salvation; which shall go forth again to all surviving nations, they who will respond to my word and preserve my people who shall go among them to deliver my message of salvation in a day soon at hand.

20. And nothing can stay mine hand, saith the Lord, for all nations shall know I have spoken it.

21. And as my word is fulfilled, though the wicked among you deny me still, I shall preserve mine elect and establish my Zion

until all nations shall know I am doing my work on the earth as I have promised.

22. Receive ye my word to thy understanding, and I shall preserve thy land as you execute equity and justice, not allowing the persecution of an innocent people who are only seeking to do the will of their God -- a revelation of my giving in the law of Celestial Plural Marriage, and revelations of my giving in the Law of Consecration of Stewardships, called the Holy United Order among my people.

23. These laws are of me, saith the Lord, and are of ancient record, that record being in your hands, by my faithful apostles and patriarchs of old, by prophets and kings and rulers who lived laws of my revealing in their time, which must be lived in purity, with no corruption among them, or they cannot be my people, saith the Lord.

24. And though you condemn my law, my law shall triumph over all opposition, all opposing powers, though all the world combine; for these laws are of me.

25. My people know that they must needs abide these laws to be my people; thus, they have suffered persecution, lo, these many years, rather than surrender eternal exalting laws from their God.

26. And this is why they continue the living of my revealed eternal laws, seeking salvation of souls for themselves and all others who would come unto me through my authorized representative on earth, each in their time; yea, verily, my Prophets, upholding my law as revealed through my servant Joseph Smith, Jun., as he was instrument in mine hands to restore my Gospel of salvation and mine authority to administer my laws upon the earth; which authority continues in the person of my servant Warren Jeffs, whom I have preserved, though tried; yet he continues to receive my word.

27. And verily I say unto you, my judgments are soon to be poured forth upon all nations that forget their God, who will not heed my word and purify their lives before me, in righteous principles known to all peoples, if you corrupt your ways before me, in licentious and immoral practices that lead to the shedding of innocent blood, in most nations where murder of unborn children is allowed by legal consent; and this stench can no longer continue, for I shall stretch forth mine hand and all peoples shall know I have spoken.

28. Repent ye! Cease these evil practices immediately!

29. Change your laws that allow this evil practice, and other evil immoral practices that lead to the murder of the unborn; for you shall rise in the resurrection unto a buffeting worthy only for murderers who consent to this practice, even a whole generation upon the earth led astray by wicked men of evil practice themselves among you.

30. Thus is my word boldly given to you and sent to you in a manner of thy receiving, with no confusion involved, for this is a pure giving from the heavens unto you through my Church of Jesus Christ of Latter-day Saints upon the earth, known among you -- separating themselves from that branch that broke away from my Priesthood on the earth, to be known as upholding the original revelations and principles I revealed to my servant Joseph Smith, known as the Fundamentalist Church of Jesus Christ of Latter-day Saints, of a legal Corporation Sole among you, which I, the Lord, have now set in order, revealing the name of my servant as President of this Corporation Sole; which legal entity should be allowed by the courts to receive my consecrated lands.

31. But an unjust court illegally resolved to change the articles thereof to allow the taking away of my lands and houses belonging to me, saith the Lord, out of the hands of those appointed officers who answered you nothing because they only answer to the Lord their God for their religious responsibility before me; and you knowing the government, court, or authority in your land has no right to interfere with a religious trust of full religious intent, which I, the Lord, caused to be established to preserve my people in an organized labor, to live a law of eternal nature earning them a salvation in the Kingdom of heaven.

32. And they abide my law in a pure walk before me, which can only be administered by inspired religious leadership, not of governmental appointing.

33. And thus you have interfered in my Church; and I name this to you, O ye government officials of this nation -- Repair this, for you have sinned a sin against the God of Creation who made you, in interfering with my Church, taking away my lands and houses, consecrated by religious giving by a people baptized and confirmed as members of my Church upon the earth, and thou knowest it; and you have been convinced by apostate and wicked people who thus persecute my people, though it be by outward show of legal authority.

34. And through your own corruptions among you, then you accuse my people of wicked intent. And how can it be, when they give their all and are willing to suffer at thine hands, even imprisonment, rather than give up in their lives their religion, which I, the Lord, have commanded them that they must live to earn a place with me in the heavens?

35. I, the Lord, reveal this much to you -- that you have interfered, through your legal procedures, with the Lord your God and His work of bringing forth a righteous people to receive Him in His glory, whose only purpose in living these exalted laws is to glorify their God and bring salvation to a corrupt world; that I shall cleanse by my power as I descend in the clouds of heaven to my land of Zion; and also to my Old Jerusalem, to gather mine Israel, which promises are in sacred writings among you.

36. I now step forth and cause my servant on earth to declare my word to you:

37. Let my people go! or suffer the judgments of a just God; and in eternity, the damnation of your souls, knowing that religious freedom should be guaranteed in every nation -- which you labor for; yea, for many, save for my people; having prejudiced your minds against them as though I, the Lord your God, was not guiding my Church.

38. Now receive my word and my promise of a judgment soon to come of thy knowing, and respond; for my almighty power shall be shown as a beginning of the cleansing of my land of Zion, known to you as North America, where my New Jerusalem shall be built, and extending to South America, saith the Lord God of heaven;

39. My land of Zion, appointed by me, before thy nation ever inhabited my land, to be the place of a glorious kingdom, revealed from heaven unto an obedient and pure people on earth, which revelations have been among you since I restored my Priesthood and my revealed word through the Prophet Joseph Smith; and this generation has rejected my word.

40. And I am a God of truth and shall fulfill my word, saith the Lord God of heaven, Jehovah Christ, the God of

Abraham, and of Isaac, and of Jacob, and of mine apostles; who came to earth and suffered on the cross, that all men may be raised unto life and receive an eternal reward for their deeds and desires in the flesh.

41. And all things are known unto me, as I reveal your hearts, even this wicked generation upon my land of Zion, for you are a murderous and adulterous generation, legalizing the slaughter of innocence among you.

42. For verily I say unto you, you are like unto Herod of old, who sought to destroy my life when but a youth, in the slaughter of children in the city of my begetting through a pure virgin.

43. Thus you slaughter innocence like unto him, by legal consent, which must now be cleansed off the earth before my glorious appearing, saith the Lord God of heaven.

44. And this I reveal to you through him whom I have appointed to send my message unto all peoples.

45. Though you listen not, in the trembling of the earth, some shall begin to awake.

46. And as the storms roll forth of more violent nature in thy land, some shall begin to awaken and wonder what is taking place.

47. And now you know I have spoken it.

48. Receive ye my word; and if you heed me not, prepare for my word to be fulfilled, warning you through him whom I have appointed.

49. This is the word of the Lord thy God, who created all things, who preserves all nations in their place, until they prove themselves so corrupt before me, I cause the dissolution of the wicked; yea, they who are ripened in iniquity as you, the people on my land of Zion who persecute my Church upon the earth, have now become.

50. And though you deny my record, revealed through the Prophet Joseph Smith -- my holy record named as the Book of Mormon -- like the Jaredites and Nephites of old, ye shall be swept off my land, saith the Lord, as you continue in your corrupt ways as did they of old; who followed these same practices in their lives, until I, the Lord, could not allow it any longer.

51. This from Him who reigns on high and who shall render eternal justice upon all -- a reward of eternal life for the pure and the righteous among you, and the reward of a damnation unto suffering for the wicked; who knowingly sin away the day of grace, knowing mine own word hath been sent to all peoples as delivered by mine ancient apostles, my Gospel spreading over the earth and being restored anew through the instrumentality of Joseph Smith, my servant; who was martyred among you; whose murder is yet an event to be avenged by me, saith the Lord, upon this wicked nation; and the driving of my people, the murdering of my people since the days of the establishment of my Church upon the earth in thy land; whose innocent blood was shed, still cries from the ground for vengeance against this nation.

52. Thus shall I be justified, at thy receiving my warning, to send forth greater judgments, until justice is satisfied; for you reek in the shedding of innocent blood as a nation, allowing this great evil among you, destroying life of my sending, of perfect innocence, unable to defend themselves; for your immoral practices have led you to this murderous work which I have named before you, as worthy to only be swept off my land of Zion.

53. This is the word of the Lord. Heed my word, lest I send my judgment upon you.

54. And in a time the more wicked step forth to further hinder my work, my judgments shall be poured forth without let or hindrance, to leave the wicked neither root nor branch of an inheritance upon my land of Zion, as I, the Lord, have foretold, my word being revealed through my servants, the Prophets.

55. And like the days of Noah, only those I preserve shall remain upon my land of Zion.

56. Thus you shall know thy God hath spoken, both on earth, and as you plead for deliverance in the day you dwell in the world of departed spirits, suffering justice until you have paid the debt for your evil ways upon her, before I can raise you up to a degree of glory, according to the law you lived on earth.

57. And those who shed innocent blood commit an unpardonable sin.

58. Though they shall be raised from the dead, they shall yet suffer for their evils, resulting from immoral practices among you.

59. How can you continue this corruption, O ye people of the earth, fighting against the laws of life, your own life preserved only by my grace and power, saith the Lord your God who created you; though you deny that gift for others through interfering with the gift of life in their coming forth?

60. Such legalized murder corrupts all peoples in your land, consenting thereto by allowing it to continue among you.

61. Yet you persecute my people, who have none of these evils among them, but are careful to preserve life that I send forth, and raise up children in principles of an exalting nature; which is known among you now as you carried away my innocent children from among my people in a raid that was unjust, having broken none of your laws that are just, accusing them of being abusive to children simply because they seek to live my high and holy and pure law, required by me, the Lord your God, for eternal exaltation to be earned; which my people know as the pure religious motive in their lives, willing to suffer at the hands of injustice to abide an eternal law and earn salvation in the Kingdom of heaven.

62. Let my people go! for my Zion shall rise from among them, notwithstanding all the opposition against my Church upon the earth.

63. I, the Lord, have caused this understanding now to be given in plain language.

64. I, the Lord, have spoken it; thus shall I fulfill to the sorrow of the wicked, to the rejoicing of mine elect.

65. Though they suffer at the hands of the wicked, they shall be delivered unto eternal salvation who stay faithful to my cause of Zion.

66. Thus, I record this on this day of giving mine own word from the heavens unto this wicked nation, which shall be known yet as I send forth more of my word, until all peoples know that I am a God of power and know all things.

67. I am a just God and a merciful God also, to those who repent and remove these evils from among them.

68. Now put it on record, saith the Lord, there shall now be a shaking in the place I have named, in a manner that government officials shall know beforehand that it would be so, which shall awake a few, denied by most unto their

eternal condemnation, knowing my word, and would not heed my word.

69. And when they find more of my word has been given, they shall be among those that curse God and die, not caring for their own lives, let alone the lives of others.

70. Thus are they a murderous and a wicked and immoral generation, adulterous in nature, having pleasure in unrighteousness unto the murder of innocence.

71. And though I cause this to be on record, they heed me not until the sign of judgments, of removing the wicked from my land of Zion, takes place.

72. Then they shall know, in the world of spirits, to a degree, some of their sin; for the evil powers there will promote lies, deceiving many, until they sin away every day of grace I have granted them.

73. And thus this record on earth is being made in a time I, the Lord, have reached for this generation to repent and earn a salvation, yet they would not; which causeth the heavens to mourn; yet they shall not mourn longer; for soon my justice shall be satisfied, and there shall be a cleansing; then mercy shall reach for those who repent and come unto me for salvation, saith the Lord Jesus Christ.

74. I shall cause a soon happening that shall humble many people to their awakening, that my word is coming forth with exactness, and I fulfill my word, to humble my Priesthood people, many of whom shall hasten to prepare, knowing I have spoken unto public knowing among this nation; for thus it shall be advertised and mocked and scorned until the time of fulfilling.

75. Then some few shall heed, while others shall mock more: "What else hath he said?" they will declare.

76. And when he steps forth to deliver more, and I thus fulfill, the mocker shall mourn, many taken in the holocaust of the several judgments I shall send; yet still in the spirit world, in their choosing darkness when my light was offered them, many will continue to deny me until every opportunity of salvation is rejected.

77. And when their memory is restored of once dwelling in a Celestial world with their Eternal God, who is their Father, that is the day of weeping and wailing and gnashing of teeth of eternal disappointment, that they turned against their Father, who only loveth them; yet they would not heed every warning given.

78. Thus is the fate of the wicked who deny me, saith the Lord, put on record on earth at a time my Gospel of salvation is among them; yet they persecute my servant and my people, and decry against them falsely; though all they desire is the salvation of souls through abiding eternal laws that exalt, even those who abide these laws in a pure way before me.

79. Let go of this wicked generation, saith the Lord.

80. Seek not after it, or you will partake of this sin of consenting to murder and adultery, to Sodom and other licentious practices.

81. Such are the people raised up in honor among the wicked, even many rulers partaking of these licentious and corrupt practices, some even of murder of the unborn, which lawmakers uphold the laws.

82. Though some publicly oppose, this wicked generation allows it, and all are tainted thereby who do not actively do battle against these unjust laws.

83. Thus I, the Lord, shall reward all according to their deeds and the desires of their heart.

84. Justice shall be satisfied, my work shall triumph, my Zion is rising as I cleanse my people, and deliver this, my word, to you.

85. Let there also be this sent to those government officials in the Canadian state, a nation also corrupted before me by their own choice of murderous and adulterous and immoral practices.

86. I shall cleanse my land Zion, and nothing can stay my hand.

87. Oh, this wicked generation and unbelieving and corrupt people who will not heed even common sense of truth, for how can you murder an unborn child and think you do right? Thus shows the corruption of their nature.

88. Thus saith the Lord Jesus Christ to this most wicked generation, guilty of child murder in the destruction of the unborn, an immoral and corrupt and adulterous generation, like unto previous generations that have inhabited my land of Zion, who were swept off the land when fully ripe in iniquity -- I, the Lord, have spoken;

89. Therefore, LET MY PEOPLE GO! And no longer allow these evil practices destroy your souls; for I am a just God and shall reward every man and woman, and children of age, according to their deeds done in the flesh.

90. Thus, I give my word to this nation as a final warning; and if you do not respond to my word, saith the Lord, I shall send the judgment named to awaken you, that when I, the Lord, speak, so do I fulfill.

91. This from your Lord and Savior, the God over all the earth, even Jesus Christ, who hath all power to discern the mind and heart of each and every son and daughter sent to mine earth, for nothing is hidden from me.

92. Let there be an awakening of this wicked generation against the day that my whirlwind judgments shall be poured forth.

93. Let there be an acknowledgment of my word sent by those of governing powers of this nation, that you will thus respond to my word -- to him whom I have revealed to thee is my Mouthpiece, even your Lord Jesus Christ calling my servant Warren Jeffs to that work upon the earth, that I may know you will now fulfill my word, lest this judgment come upon you, and mine other judgments, as I have promised through the mouths of all my holy Prophets, known to thee in sacred writ.

94. This is my word to this generation: Repent ye. I, the Lord, have spoken it, and so shall I fulfill.

95. I, the Lord God, am eternal and my judgments are just. I see and know all things.

96. Let this generation be warned, by this my message sent, that my day is at hand when wickedness must be swept off my land of Zion, and my New Jerusalem shall be built, and I shall come in my glory as I have promised, and none shall remain who are unclean before me.

97. Let there be an awakening in government officials of an eternal judgment that shall come upon them from the God who made them, if they allow the continuation of these wicked practices of the destruction of innocence; of which I shall hold you eternally accountable; desiring life thyself, yet denying it, through legal consent, to unborn children, as though thou art God.

98. Let there now be an instant repeal of those laws that allow this wickedness among you, lest my judgments be hastened, having innocent blood upon your skirts, as it were; now having come up before your

God, notwithstanding your professions of justifying nature.

99. I, the Lord, shall reveal more to this generation through my servant Warren Jeffs.

100. Hearken to my word, ye rulers of nations, lest your lands be left desolate in my day of greater judgments upon the earth; for I shall be known among all nations, and my power and righteous government shall be known, for I shall reveal to all peoples my message of salvation on earth who remain.

101. And all shall hear me; for I am God, thy Redeemer, doing the will of my Father, unto the salvation of souls of those who will receive me through my Priesthood authority upon the earth; which I have restored and preserved, which Gospel of salvation has been among you, O ye people of the earth.

102. Seek unto Him who created you, and receive His message of salvation that I may own and bless you, yea, with an eternal salvation unto those who receive my Gospel through my authorized Priesthood authority among you.

103. And those who receive my Gospel of salvation on earth shall earn an eternal reward with me and with my Father; for mine atoning blood shall reach those who purify their lives in abiding the laws of my Church and Kingdom revealed among man on earth.

104. O ye people of the earth, repent ye, repent ye! My day of judgment is at hand and my word shall be fulfilled that I have spoken through the mouths of all my holy Prophets.

105. Attaint your wicked and corrupt ways. Come unto me, thy Lord and Savior. I, the Lord, have spoken it. Amen.

SECTION REVELATION 63

Fundamentalist Church of Jesus Christ of Latter-day Saints
P.O. Box 840459
Hildale, Utah 84784

Thus Saith Son Ahman, Even Jesus Christ, the God Over All Creation, to the President of the United States of America

Revelation of the Lord Jesus Christ
Eldorado, Texas
Tuesday, April 26, 2011

1. Thus saith the Lord Jesus Christ unto you, the leader of the nation of the United States of America, even the President of this nation:

2. I address you, as the God of Creation, even Jesus Christ, who gave His life for the salvation of all mankind and is able to raise all in the resurrection

and judge all for their deeds done in the flesh.

3. Righteous is my name; Endless and Eternal is my name.

4. When I speak, I fulfill.

5. I have sent to you mine own word to let my people go, and release my servant from bondage, and allow them freedom of worship in Celestial laws of my revealing.

6. I have warned this nation and the leaders of this nation by sending mine own word to overthrow those laws that allow murder of unborn children, the gross immorality of Sodom and adultery; promotion of which is allowed by legal consent, even in entertainments and music and social ways throughout your land.

7. As the leaders of this nation allow these great evils to continue, I shall bring you to judgment.

8. Thou sayest you promote peace among nations and religious freedom, the freedom of expression; yet, since the days of my servant Joseph Smith receiving my Gospel of salvation, restored from heaven to earth, upholding my word in Old and New Testament, the words of all the ancient Prophets, my people have been a driven people.

9. And government powers of this nation of the United States of America have used their civil powers to prosecute and persecute my people of my Church of Jesus Christ of Latter-day Saints; which Church has continued under my Priesthood eternal authority revealed from heaven to Prophets since Joseph Smith's time, now known among men as the Fundamentalist Church of Jesus Christ of Latter-day Saints, known as upholding all the laws of my Gospel revealed through Joseph Smith, of their Lord.

10. But I will support and sustain and preserve my people, even through great whirlwind judgments that I prophesied of, as you can read in New Testament record.

11. I refer you to Matthew 24 specifically, one of mine apostles of old who heard my word and recorded my word.

12. I send you this, my word, calling upon you who leads this nation to promote true justice and religious freedom for my people; for they are of peaceful nature and only desire the salvation of all peoples.

13. They are seeking to build my Zion, prepare for my glorious appearing;

14. And if you will heed my word, blessings shall come upon this nation; else there shall come judgments to make room for the rise of Zion on this, the American continent, which is my land of Zion where New Jerusalem shall be built, as described by John the Beloved in the Book of Revelations in New Testament record; and I refer this to your reading, knowing of my Bible record.

15. My servant on earth is in bondage through unjust laws aimed to destroy my Priesthood, Church, and Kingdom upon the earth;

16. For I am the God of eternity, and the laws of my Church are revealed from heaven and guided by your Lord; and my people in thy land, of my Church and Kingdom, have rights of religious worship and religious freedom; and my Celestial Law is pure and only promotes happiness and salvation among the pure in heart.

17. My Zion shall rise through the principles of the laws of my Church and Kingdom upon the earth, revealed from heaven.

18. You can peruse these laws in my sacred writings through Joseph Smith in Doctrine and Covenants.

19. You can read of my coming among a former people that dwelt on this land, and my prophecies to them concerning these days -- of this nation coming upon this land.

20. My record is extant and witnesses of my glorious coming, both ancient scripture and modern revelation, as is known among men.

21. And these are the motives of my Priesthood and my servant and my servants in my Church and Kingdom, who seek to live pure and eternal laws of salvation, which I require of them in this mortal existence on earth to prove worthy of an eternal salvation;

22. And this is the motive of their lives, notwithstanding the persecuting zeal of those who come against them, promoted by the lies of former members who have apostatized because their own lives were full of sin, accusing my Priesthood, Church, and Kingdom of unrighteous domain.

23. Come to understand the truth of these realities among you, and free my servants who are in bondage because of their religious beliefs and practices in obedience to my eternal laws, the revealed religion from heaven.

24. As I spoke concerning the destruction of Jerusalem and the scattering of the Jews, and thus fulfilled my word, so have I spoken concerning the judgments of God -- even of your Lord who sendeth this word to you -- upon this nation and the nations of the earth, if you continue to promote these great evils among your peoples, and allow the persecution and prosecution, which is an injustice against my Church, people, and Kingdom upon the earth.

25. And if you heed me not, you leaders of this nation of the United States of America, you shall feel the chastening hand of a just God; and all my promises and prophecies of judgments upon the gentile nations shall be fulfilled in full measure.

26. Heed my word, that the more righteous among you may be preserved; and if you do not, and the peoples of this nation oppose the rise of Zion, I must needs come out in judgment to cleanse my land of Zion.

27. I shall come in my glory to establish righteous domain, a just and equitous government of eternal power, to rule over all nations, and nothing can stay mine hand, being the God of all creation over all nations.

28. Thus I send my word to you again, according to the understanding of men, in simple language, that you may see truth revealed by your God, which truth you can understand by simple perusal of the scriptures revealed through Joseph Smith, my servant, continued on earth in my Church and Kingdom.

29. I have declared to you that if these evils continue among your people and this nation, that I have named in many messages I have sent, the judgments I have promised shall take place, for wickedness shall not reign.

30. There shall be a thousand years of peace under my righteous rule, saith Jesus Christ, the Beginning and the End, who has all power and authority and right to rule, in heaven and on earth.

31. As you see a great storm of paralyzing nature over many parts of thy nation, and also an earthquake of damaging nature and the loss of lives in a place of unusual happening, as I have named, let your heart be touched that thy God hath spoken; and when He speaks, He fulfills His word.

32. My coming in glory is nigh.

33. I send you my word through my authority of Priesthood on the earth.

34. I, the Lord, reveal to you, the leader of this nation, the formation of that which is of a secret combination among rich businessmen and some leaders of this nation, disturbed by thy policies of economic practices, using government powers, some of whom have joined with organized crime, plotting thy destruction.

35. This I reveal to you, to be careful in thy movements.

36. There are some of them determined to overthrow your influence, thinking your policies are destroying this nation in economic power, fearing that political means may not be sufficient in their power to bring another into that presidential position in future election.

37. Let there be an investigation, of careful means and ways, into the organization of business leaders of banking industry combining with the political arm that is promoting free trade, opposing thy policies of increased debt that are joined with authorities from China, to which this nation has depended on investment into treasury and other stocks to bolster this economy, which organization is of the policy of free trade without restrictions, wanting to set aside governmental restrictions to allow economic growth without government hindrance, wherein the policies of this nation presently limit some exports to nations considered in human rights violations; yet this organization desires free trade, notwithstanding the policies of this government today.

38. Look well into organized crime in Chicago connecting with rich businessmen of an organization seeking free trade, and also having made some connections with foreign powers who also seek economic benefit by changing of laws and rules, in trade and commerce, the laws of this nation, seeking to get gain thereby.

39. I, the Lord, reveal this much, that the fears of this secret combination are, they will lose their wealth if you promote certain policies in government concerning economic development.

40. I give you this, my word, saith the Lord, that you may know I see and know all things; can reveal my word and preserve life as I will.

41. I have named judgments to come upon this nation if they continue these most wicked practices of murder of unborn children, and Sodom, and the immoral wickedness that promotes these sins against innocence and against life;

42. Yet, if you will heed my word and now promote the repeal of those practices now upheld by law, I, the Lord, shall cause this nation to continue as they allow freedom of religion of my Church and Kingdom.

43. And if the leaders of this nation heed me not, my full judgment shall come to thy knowing; for I am the God of glory and fear no man, and shall come to earth in my glory to reign a thousand years in righteous dominion and government over all nations.

44. This is my word to you. Heed my word and promote principles of righteous government.

45. And thus this message is to the leaders of all bodies of government over this nation, to promote righteous principles that preserve life and purity and religious freedom.

46. I tell you these things beforehand for thy good.

47. Do not be taken in a snare by rich businessmen in promoting thy attending

a business conference in Chicago of soon naming.

48. Excuse thyself that you may be preserved, is the word of the Lord to you.

49. Promote no longer war against other nations, save for self-defense.

50. Do not be the originator of attack against any nation, that this nation may be justified before your God as you also remove these great evils I have named from among thy peoples, which are allowed by legal consent in this day.

51. I, the Lord, have spoken it. Give heed to my word, and know that I shall repay all peoples according to the measure they have measured to their fellow men, an eternal judgment, being the God over all creation, who came to earth among mortal men and suffered more than man can suffer, conquering death, hell, and the grave, to raise all peoples up in the resurrection to stand before the judgment bar of God, which tribunal shall render an eternal judgment upon all peoples -- happiness and eternal life for those who measured justice, righteousness and equity, and purity of life toward their fellow men and in their own lives; and promoting a great and eternal punishment upon those who would seek the destruction of life and of innocence, whether openly by legal means, or in private.

52. I have warned the leaders of nations to remove these great sins from among their peoples before my glorious appearing by sending forth my word.

53. And I shall be justified in cleansing the more wicked out of every nation on earth before my glorious appearing, preserving the more righteous who will receive my message of salvation and a righteous government power, even of thy Lord, on earth for a thousand years, a Millennial Reign of Peace, as I have promised.

54. My coming is nigh at hand. Let my people go, to worship me in the freedom guaranteed by the laws of thy nation, my revealed religion from heaven promoting pure and holy principles unto eternal life for those who obey my religious laws, that should be protected by the laws of thy land, yet have not been protected for many years -- legal prosecution and persecution coming against my people in many ways in this nation.

55. I send you my word to help you overcome the inward prejudice held by many lawmakers against my true Church and religion upon earth.

56. Peruse my policies of government in my recent sending of my publishing to thee, with the warnings to this nation and other nations.

57. I say to you lawmakers and government officials in this nation and in every state: My time of coming is at hand.

58. Turn to righteous principles that promote life and virtue and innocence, and protect the same, for I shall hold you accountable, saith the Lord God of heaven and over the earth.

59. Righteous and Holy is my name. Endless is my name. Eternal is my name, even Jesus Christ.

60. This earth is mine.

61. I have given man his agency to choose. Both good and evil are present before all peoples.

62. Choose to promote righteousness.

63. A heavenly power is coming to earth to govern the nations of the earth on my land of Zion, and my power shall be among them; and this is revealed in the scriptures of holy writ in thine hands.

64. I am a God of truth, and I have spoken my word through all the holy Prophets, and shall fulfill. Amen.

SECTION REVELATION 70

Fundamentalist Church of Jesus Christ of Latter-day Saints
P.O. Box 840459
Hildale, Utah 84784

Thus Saith Son Ahman, Even Jesus Christ, Your Lord and Savior Who Hath Redeemed All Mankind, Whose Right It Is to Rule Over the Heavens and the Earth, a Just God Who Sees and Knows All Things, and Shall Recompense to Every Man That Which He Has Measured to His Fellow Man, According to the Light and Knowledge They Have Received: Thus I Speak to the President of the United States of America, Now in Power, and Also to the Peoples of This Nation -- This Message of Warning of the Doctrine of Eternal Judgment Upon Thee, Even Upon All Peoples, Being the God of Eternal Power, an Eternal God Who Shall Bring All to Justice; Whose Mercy Shall Claim Those Who Repenteth in a Manner to Earn the Benefit of My Atoning Power -- Even Him, a God of Atoning and Redeeming Power, Who Suffered on the Cross and Was Raised From the Grave Unto Eternal Power to Judge All Mankind According as Their Works Are:

Revelation of the Lord Jesus Christ
Eldorado, Texas
Tuesday, May 3, 2011

1. Let there be written my word, saith the Lord, in a manner of correspondence to the leader of this nation of the United States of America, a word of warning and counsel -- even Jesus Christ, who reigneth over all, empowering this nation to be a free nation since its creation, I guiding forefathers of the revolutionary battles wherein they broke away from the mother gentile nation from which they emanated.

2. And I, your God, inspired leaders of this nation to establish the Constitution of the United States, and the Bill of Rights, as it is called, guaranteeing religious freedom, even freedom of worship in a land of plenty at that time.

3. Thus saith the Lord to those who thus murdered Osama bin Laden:

4. You have transgressed greatly, turning to murder in a manner of seeking to retaliate against one in another land, not using the government powers where he dwelt to apprehend him safely, which could have easily been accomplished had you thus stepped forth and acted on correct principles.

5. But in thy glory-seeking and in thy violent nature, yea, to the celebration of millions in thy nation, you hath murdered a man who could have been apprehended peacefully, were attempts made therein by the governing power of the nation

where he dwelt, being near the capital city and power of authority of that nation in Pakistan.

6. I, the Lord, rebuke thee for thy murderous intent, turning to violence when peaceful means, or the governing powers over that place of residence, could have been used to apprehend and take in custody one accused of crimes.

7. And if you continue this practice, your murderous intentions shall turn upon thine own peoples, and mob rule shall ensue throughout thy land; murder and rapine, robbery and violence one against another, showing thy murderous intent and nature of the people of this nation, proving to thy God you are not worthy to remain on my land of Zion, but would have to be swept clean by just, yea, by justified judgments of God, to send thee to the world of departed spirits where you transgress no more in this mortal existence of probationary testing; which I, the Lord your God, have sent all mankind to be tested, allowing good and evil to be placed before all, sending my Spirit -- which is only good, of the inspiring unto good -- to the mind and heart of every man, woman, and child who would receive and listen to what they call their conscience unto righteous works, choosing good, eschewing and casting off evil.

8. And thus all have their agency, as they come to mature years more especially, even the age of accountability; yea, even by the age of eight years old, a child knows good from evil.

9. Thus saith the Lord: As you continue in the spirit of murder of unborn children, and then become aggressive when peaceful means could be used -- I command thee to repent!

10. I am the God of Creation.

11. Cease these murderous ways.

12. Cease your military actions in nations who have not thus attacked thee.

13. I, the Lord, command thee to repent unto a bringing forth of a change of policy and intent, and even justice served upon leaders of nations, thus saith the Lord, within each nation by their lawmaking bodies, and not think that you can transgress the borders of another nation aggressively and perform murder -- thine own pride satisfied, and not correct principle of law-abiding and just ways being followed.

14. Thus I send this corresponding of mine own words to the leader of this nation, to his Cabinet, to lawmakers of high standing.

15. I reveal my word to thee: Repent of thy murderous and immoral ways, the leaders of this nation as well as the peoples of this nation, for you have offended thy God, the great numbers in millions celebrating in their hearts the murder of a soul who could have been taken peaceably, and tried before the courts in the jurisdiction appointed, and of justice, by the nation that could have apprehended him.

16. Thus saith the Lord: Let this wicked generation repent speedily, lest my cleansing process sweep them off my land of Zion and leave them neither root nor branch -- in earthquake, tornado, storm and windstorms, pestilence, hail, and famine, the overflowing scourge and desolating sickness promised this wicked generation if they repent not.

17. For I am the God that made you. You are sons and daughters of God sent to a probationary earth to be tested what you will choose.

18. And when leaders of nations choose wickedness, I, the Lord, execute

judgment upon them through righteous justice administered, even overthrowing leaders of nations, removing them from power, and, at times, sweeping the wicked of a nation off the earth, where they can further repent, if they will, in the world of departed spirits; I being a God of love, laboring for the salvation of all, whether on earth, whether they be spirits yet unborn who shall be sent to this probationary earth, preserving their lives unto those who can beget them unto correct principles, just and righteous, to earn an eternal salvation; and also among those in the world of departed spirits.

19. My Gospel message shall go to all on this earth and in the world of departed spirits, now and in the future giving.

20. And I shall be called justified as every knee bows and every tongue confesses that Jesus is the Christ, a God over all creation, and He ruleth righteously, and He hath done right toward all peoples, nations, kindreds, and tongues.

21. This shall be declared in future time as truth is revealed and all secrets are made known.

22. And thus saith the Lord to the leaders of this nation and all nations: All your secret acts and intentions of the heart shall be revealed in the Millennial Reign of Peace, in the government of God in Zion, and sent forth to the nations, and in the day of judgment when you stand before a just God in the resurrection;

23. For I am the Resurrection and the Life, and the God that shall judge thee, appointed by my Father, Elohim, even Ahman; for I am Son Ahman, to perform that work of judging all mankind.

24. Ye shall stand before me.

25. I shall unlock thy mind, which shall reveal all the secrets of thy life, and nothing hidden; and you shall be judged by a just and holy God, even your Lord and Redeemer, Jesus Christ, who speaketh these words to the leaders of this nation through mine authority on earth.

26. Thus saith your God to thee: You shall be judged, and wickedness shall be punished with that degree of buffetings and suffering requisite for justice to be satisfied upon every person who repenteth not, even a full justice;

27. For my atoning power and suffering can only be a benefit to those who repent and accept my Gospel of salvation; yea, my message of salvation I shall soon send to every nation of the earth, both before my glorious appearing, to prepare many peoples, and a greater degree after my glorious coming to New Jerusalem, which shall rise in this generation.

28. This is my revealing to you at this time of a needed message to be given to the leaders of this nation of the United States of America, for you have offended your God in following wicked and unjust and corrupt principles, even unto murder, not having placed the accused before a tribunal, which you do in your own land for any criminal thus apprehended, of general policy, save those secret combinations which the leaders of this nation have sometimes followed in destroying life secretly in murderous intent.

29. Thus have the people of this nation offended their God, in glorying in murder, which could have been avoided.

30. The wicked shall slay the wicked, even in mob violence in thy land, if you heed me not; if this spirit of glorying in the loss of life, instead of mourning when one who is wicked passes on unprepared for salvation -- thus should all peoples do, understanding the purposes of thy God of Creation over thee, in bringing thee forth

in this life of probationary and testing time to prove thy characters, whether or no you will love life and eternal principles that exalt, or transgress against the principles of life and earn a never-ending judgment of sorrow, not being exalted to be with the God who made thee.

31. And in the resurrection there shall be added to your mind the memory of having been born to a God of Creation, well-prepared; to know the purpose of this mortal life, forgetting previous existence as a test, yet having my Spirit of light and life in thee at birth, and in thy growing years, to teach you good from evil, prompting you in what you call your mental conscience unto better works.

32. I am the God of Creation whose Spirit of light and life shineth upon all creation, to give all creation its existence.

33. I am a God of love that blesseth all.

34. And as death passeth on all, sending their spirits inhabiting their mortal bodies, the body lying in the grave, the spirits going to a world of living, a place of departed spirits where my Priesthood labors to administer the message of my salvation to all of every nation, kindred, tongue, and peoples; verily, I reveal to you, murderers hath no forgiveness.

35. If you take on the spirit of that sin and consent to this evil in the conduct of any person, you shall also have the same degree of judgment according to thy crimes in the flesh -- crimes against thy God, and eternal, exalting principles; crimes against thine own knowledge; for all shall be judged according to the light they received in this mortal existence, saith the Lord God, who administers life unto eternal life to those who love and obey laws that exalt, ways to their greatest ability to understand according to the light they receive; yea, even a God who can exalt thee unto eternal life, those who

live laws of progression unto eternal life, of my message, and Priesthood, Church and Kingdom, of salvation powers that are now on the earth, preparing the way for the rise of Zion in fulness, a New Jerusalem built on the continent where the United States of America dwells at this time; and nothing can stay mine hand;

36. For I shall sweep the more wicked off the earth and preserve the more righteous unto my reign of righteousness, which shall be for a thousand years of my dwelling among men, to their knowing, in my power and glory in Zion; and the Kingdom of heaven coming forth to earth as the governing power over all nations.

37. Heed my word.

38. Repent of your murderous and immoral ways, which leads thee to a murderous way;

39. For thus are the corrupt in heart not able to govern themselves, being blinded by their own corruptions, justifying their murderous ways.

40. I, the Lord, shall bring them to justice, even in the eternal duration of time, feeling the wrath of a just God, who hath given them His Spirit in their minds and hearts as a conscience to know good from evil.

41. Let the policies of thy government cease this practice, is the command of thy Lord in this correspondence of needed message to thee. Amen.

42. Thus saith your Lord and Savior, Jesus Christ, further, to the people of the nation of the United States of America:

43. Repent ye! Repent ye! for my day of my glorious coming is nigh at hand.

44. Heed my word.

45. I have sent many warnings to the leaders of this nation, and to the peoples of this nation, of recent doing.

46. You must heed my words, lest there be upon you a greater judgment than you can bear, to leave you neither root nor branch of posterity upon the earth.

47. There are the sins of the shedding of innocent blood of unborn children legalized in this nation; the sins of corruption, of secret combinations to get gain by evil means, even of murder, upon this land and among your peoples, even among the leaders of this nation, which I, the Lord, reveal openly, and shall reveal more in a time soon to come;

48. For you cannot hide from a God who seeth all things, and is just and holy and righteous, who shall judge all men according to their deeds done in the flesh.

49. Thus saith the Lord: Let there not be a celebration of thy peoples again of any man's being murdered, yea, his death.

50. Mourn over the loss of life when they go to the world of departed spirits, not having my message of salvation, unprepared for a glorious salvation, losing the same because they would not hear my word sent forth by testimony and holy writ.

51. Let not this people of this nation again glorify themselves in murder, wherein a man whose known location in another nation could have been apprehended by the authorities of that nation and placed before a tribunal, and not taken in death.

52. Thus saith the Lord: Let this cease in your natures.

53. Violence covereth this land, even in the spirit of the people of this nation.

54. Thus saith the Lord: I am the God of peace.

55. I will sweep those off the land where thy nation resides, in every nation on that continent, yea, on the North American continent who have violence in their nature.

56. For Zion is a place of peace, and my Zion shall rise, even New Jerusalem in the Center Stake of Zion, in Jackson County, Missouri, as I have proclaimed; and nothing can stay mine hand.

57. Thus I have sent this warning to the leader and peoples of this nation to repent, and know that my coming is nigh at hand. Amen.

SECTION REVELATION 91

Fundamentalist Church of Jesus Christ of Latter-day Saints
P.O. Box 840459
Hildale, Utah 84784

Thus Saith Jesus Christ, Who Is Son Ahman, to the Leader of This Nation of the United States of America, and All the Leaders of This Nation in Their Several Governing Appointments and Powers; and Thus to the Peoples of This Nation, Mine Own Word From the Heavens; Even the God of Glory Who Speaketh Thus to Your Understandings -- A Call to Heed My Word, Even I Who Am Soon to Come in the Powers of Heaven to Dwell Among Men, a Governing Power Over All Nations of the Earth -- Hear My Words:

Revelation of the Lord Jesus Christ
Eldorado, Texas
Thursday, May 26, 2011

1. Thus saith the Lord Jesus Christ, Son Ahman, the Creator of heaven and earth, who is Jehovah Christ, the Great I AM, even the Beginning and the End, who reigns in the heavens eternal, Creator over this earth, sending forth the children of the Father to this probationary world for their time of testing, being given their agency to know good from evil, left to choose, yet being born with enough of my holy light to know good from evil from birth, yea, to be agents to themselves --

2. I who created all things speaketh from on high as one crying in the wilderness, a light that reigns over all, yet the inhabitants of the earth, dwelling in gross darkness, discern not the light that came among them in the meridian of time as the sacrifice of atoning power to conquer death and raise all in the resurrection to be judged by a just God for the deeds and desires in the flesh;

3. Yea, I speaketh, saith your Lord who created you, again, to the leader of the nation that now inhabits my land of Zion where my New Jerusalem shall be built, that you have heeded me not.

4. Though I have sent mine own word, my revealed word to thee, and have spared thy life as the God of Creation over thee, who giveth life to all who dwell upon the earth, who enlightens the mind to more noble thoughts and works; thus have I sent my words to you.

5. And you have gloried in thy doings wherein I have reproved thee and this nation, of which you, the President of the United States of America, officiate over by my grace, in that executive branch of earthly governing power, having influence over many peoples.

6. And how shalt thou stand in the day of judgment when the resurrection is brought forth in thy behalf before a just

God, knowing the word of God has been given you, warning thee to bear influence to cease the murder of innocent unborn children in this nation, and bear influence in other nations to do the same?

7. And I have reproved thee and the leaders of this nation by mine own words revealed from the heavens for thy aggressive acts toward other nations who have not attacked thee, not being justified in thine aggressions, which shall clip thy power; as I have weighed thee in the balance and found you and the leaders of this nation wanting.

8. And as I have spoken judgments against thee and this nation, if you heed me not, so shall I fulfill.

9. And you have witnessed, even by personal traveling to see the destruction of the windstorms I have sent, that I warned thee of in my previous communicating, saith the Lord Jesus Christ;

10. Thou hast seen the power of thy God humble this nation in allowing windstorms and flooding, as an example that when He speaketh, He fulfilleth His word.

11. My word is sure, unto an eternal duration of the consequence of the choices made in every man's life being returned upon them -- a just recompense of reward -- that as they measure to their fellow man, so shall I, their God, measure an eternal judgment upon each one favored to come to the age of accountability.

12. Thus saith the God of heaven: My time is at hand.

13. My chastening hand is upon this nation and upon the nations of the earth, and I have sent forth mine own word through my servant, my Mouthpiece I have appointed and ordained on earth.

14. And my word has now gone forth to the leaders of all nations to cease their wars and draw their military and armies into their own borders, to only be used for defensive needs, save I, the Lord, shall command; for in my glorious appearing, I, your Lord and King, shall be the governing power known among all nations to humble all peoples who continue in a violent nature and in murderous and immoral ways.

15. I am the God of glory who giveth and taketh life as I will; and I doeth the will of the Father, performing a work to bring forth a thousand years of peace under the reign of a governing power sent from heaven, known among men as the Kingdom of God, yea, the Kingdom of Ahman, my Father;

16. For I am Son Ahman and doeth the will of the Father in all things, to the redeeming of all mankind from the grave and judging all in the resurrection.

17. And nothing shall be hidden, and all secrets shall be revealed, and the wicked shall tremble before me, a just and holy God who must soon send forth His message of salvation to all surviving nations; for this murder of unborn children, and Sodom, and violent and unjust ways, and immoral and corrupt ways cannot stand.

18. And I have sent forth my word to be justified before the heavens to send forth the cleansing powers to sweep the more wicked out of the lands of every nation on earth, to preserve the more righteous, who shall know of my ways of Zion and of New Jerusalem, that shall be built in that Center Stake appointed, of Jackson County, Missouri; and nothing can stay mine hand.

19. I have caused you to be warned of an assassination plot among the rich of this nation. Heed my word and I shall preserve thy life, to the performing of the works of overcoming these great outward evils I have named -- of legal consent in

thy nation, upholding those evils to exist among thy people.

20. I have allowed you to know of mine own words coming forth, showing thee and the leaders of this nation, and the leaders of all nations, that I, the God of Creation, who brought forth this earth and caused the peopling thereof, am able to speak from the heavens; yet few will heed my words and accept my Gospel of salvation, having pleasure in unrighteousness;

21. Yet I, the God of glory, who am just and holy, shall reward all, and wickedness cannot reign.

22. A righteous government of heavenly power cometh to earth as I caused mine apostles in the meridian of time to preach the same; which record, known as the Bible, though it has been altered by wicked men in parts, yet it testifieth many truths of my coming, and the building of New Jerusalem, which is on the land known as North America, as I have named -- my land of Zion -- as I shall cleanse, as a whirlwind coming upon them, which example you have recently seen in the sweeping of life off certain places of thy land with the whirlwinds, of such destructive nature that should humble all peoples that the God of power and of glory speaketh.

23. Yet they heed me not, in overcoming their own evils, needing to cleanse the inside of the platter, as it were, in your own nation; for your laws are corrupt that uphold these great sins I have named, which sins shall be swept off the earth, saith the Lord Jesus Christ, out of every nation in the great judgments of a just God soon at hand.

24. And if you would seek the blessings of thy God who created thee, act on these true and correct principles to favor life, virtue and purity, honesty, lest

my judgments humble you to the dust, and thy power be so clipped, you rise not again as leaders of a nation that could have done the works of righteousness, yet only promote the justifying of thy peoples in ways opposing the plan of life established by the God who created thee; which the murder of unborn children and sodomy and adultery and immoral ways promote that sin of corruption of immoral ways that promotes the destruction of life of unborn children.

25. How canst thou not be touched by the flagrant and outward attack on the principle of life?

26. Yea, thy God speaking to the leader of this nation and all the leaders within this nation:

27. Awake! This sin of gross darkness shall blight thy soul unto an eternal damnation, you having been warned in this mortal and earthly existence by thy God sending His own word unto thine understanding, and you heed me not; I being justified now to send forth more judgments upon this nation -- earthquake, more storms of destructive nature, to thy knowing I have warned thee.

28. And as thou continuest warring against nations and supporting other nations in their wars against other nations, when those nations that are attacked by thee and thine allies, yea, thy NATO allies, not having attacked thee first, you become the aggressors in the sight of heaven and are promoting violence and war among nations, that if you do not withdraw, your violent ways shall erupt in a conflict that shall absorb nations in that prophesied war that my servant John my Beloved recorded, seeing in vision these last days before my glorious appearing, to establish peace once again upon earth among all nations, by establishing my New Jerusalem,

my Zion on my land of Zion in full power from heaven.

29. Thus I send my word again to the leaders of this nation, and I fear thee not; for thy power can only exist of governing ability by the grace of God who created thee.

30. And as I predicted, during my ministry among mine apostles, the destruction of the Jewish nation and the scattering of that people, so shall it be with this nation -- a sweeping of this nation clean who oppose my Zion and my righteous rule soon to come, by opposing my Priesthood, Church, and Kingdom upon the earth, imprisoning and persecuting my people who are established by the revelations of their God, even Jesus Christ, who speaketh these words unto thee and sendeth them to thee by my Priesthood and eternal authority now dwelling upon the earth, my people being prepared for my glorious appearing, to build my Zion, even New Jerusalem, to receive their Lord in His glory.

31. Thus my people have been a persecuted people since the days of Joseph Smith, my servant and Prophet, whom I used, saith Jesus Christ, to restore my Church, Priesthood, and Kingdom upon the earth.

32. I have sent forth my policies of governing power in my publishings, mine own word revealed from heaven, that the governing power in New Jerusalem and in Zion shall administer justice and equity, and pure and noble ways of living.

33. Study the same, correct thy laws, and remove these greater outward evils from being upheld by legal consent.

34. Warn thy people of coming judgments soon at hand -- the sea heaving beyond its bounds, great cities swallowed up in the earth, disease, the overflowing

scourge with no cure being sent forth upon this people who will not heed my word, but continue in their gross wickedness and corrupt ways.

35. Oh, that you would heed my word!

36. For the heavens weep over the wickedness now dwelling in the hearts of the children of men in this nation and in all the nations of the earth; yet I must do my will, declared from the heavens, the will of the Father, whose perfect way and will I do, saith Son Ahman.

37. And this earth shall know one thousand years of peace, my Zion the ruling city, the capital city of governing power over the earth, raised up by the visitation of the heavenly powers to earth.

38. As recorded in holy writ, verily it shall be so.

39. And because you are my children on earth, having your agency, I, your just and holy God, who loveth all, send forth the warning voice that you shall reap as you have sown.

40. And my day of greater judgments are soon at hand.

41. And I loveth the salvation of souls through righteous works, who promote life and purity of life unto their own salvation and the salvation of the generations ahead.

42. There shall not be a prolonging much further in my merciful hand of warning.

43. My judgments have begun to cleanse my land of Zion, to preserve mine elect who will heed my words.

44. Mine Israel shall be gathered from all nations under heaven unto New Jerusalem and inherit their promised lands -- both my land of Zion and that land of Old Jerusalem.

45. I shall humble this nation through a judgment they have not expected -- of

a large city mostly destroyed, which city the inhabitants thereof have continued in gross wickedness for many years, having been warned since the days of my servant Joseph Smith, yet they will not repent.

46. And I being a just God, shall fulfill my word.

47. I have allowed my servant to be in the hands of bondage, and now make known that my word is coming forth to the leaders of all nations, and to thy peoples in every nation, that you may know I, a just God, am able to speak from the heavens and deliver my word, to be justified to cleanse wickedness off the earth and preserve the more righteous, who uphold the ways of life and virtue, justice and equity.

48. With blessings unmeasured shall the more righteous be favored -- with knowledge from heaven and the blessings of a just and holy God upon them, who sees and knows all things, and nothing is hidden.

49. And verily, upon the ungodly who delight in violent ways, in murder, in immoral and in corrupt ways, sudden judgment and a sweeping off the earth shall take place.

50. And I send you my warning voice again, that I may be justified, as a just and holy God, to perform this work of cleansing the earth and my land of Zion, to prepare the way for a righteous government of heavenly power coming to earth to rule over all nations, even by their consenting, seeing the noble and exalting ways of a Celestial heavenly power, and desiring the ways of Zion in their own lives, yea, those who remain upon the earth.

51. Now heed my word:

52. If you would reap the blessings, through repentance, from thy Lord, to preserve thy peoples in more righteous ways, and to receive my Zion without obstruction, without persecuting zeal against them -- neither by prosecution nor by mob rule, as has been done against my people in days gone by, even in this nation that professed religious freedom, driving my saints from that Center Stake of Zion in Missouri, never having made reparation to my Church and my Kingdom, which testimony cometh up before the heavens, justifying thy God to clip the power of this nation and bring them low, as I have done other wicked nations in ages gone by, when they rose to the height of corruption; for this nation is ripened in iniquity to overflowing in the eyes of heaven.

53. And I have declared that this land of Zion shall be reserved for a righteous people who serve the God of the land, even Jesus Christ.

54. I am He, your Lord and Savior, that speaketh these words, which you shall know in the day of judgment and resurrection that thy God hath spoken, and shall hold thee accountable, the leader of this nation and the leaders of this nation, in the several offices and government positions, for your conduct; for the judge on earth shall be judged of a just Judge in heaven.

55. Behold the earth, the heavens, the perfection of the bringing forth of life upon earth in every form and nature, the mysteries of which are only known by a God of Creation.

56. I am He who created this earth and peoples this earth by sending forth spirits to dwell in earthly bodies, giving them their life.

57. And this gross crime of the murder of innocence, of unborn children, is the powers of darkness working on the selfish will of those of immoral nature, to have pleasure in unrighteousness and not meet

the responsibility of their own actions, thus destroying life before it is born, depriving spirits appointed this earth from the heavens to come to this earth and prove themselves, through their agency, whether or not they would choose good and eschew and cast off evil;

58. For my plan of salvation is extant, and shall reach all mankind -- past, present and future.

59. And I am the God of heaven that shall cause my Gospel of salvation to spread to every nation on earth in the day of the thousand years of peace, as I come to earth in my glory and cause my Kingdom of God, Council of Fifty, to be the ruling body over all nations, having representatives therein sufficient to maintain the rights of religious freedom and other freedoms thy God bestoweth upon His children to work out their salvation, without intrusion upon other peoples and their religious ideas and ways and tenets.

60. Therefore, know that the God of glory cometh, and hath warned the people of this nation and the leaders of this nation of greater judgments soon at hand, such that you have not witnessed before in your lifetimes nor in thine history as a nation;

61. For I have preserved this land to be a land of freedom where religion would be protected by law, yet my people have been a persecuted people by the falsehoods promoted by those of aspiring power and apostate and wicked intent, darkened by their own sins to persecute an innocent people.

62. And only by the grace of the God of heaven has my Church and Kingdom continued on earth;

63. Yea, verily, only by my grace do all nations keep their place; and all leaders of all nations shall soon be held accountable

to the God of heaven, who cometh to earth in His glory, to their knowing I have come to earth.

64. And in that accounting, justice shall be satisfied where murderous and immoral ways have been promoted to gain power and to increase in power of governing nature.

65. Great Babylon, yea, spiritual Babylon, of which this nation is a part, soon falleth; and my Zion shall rise; and I shall preserve those who can be representatives of righteous living in the Zion of our God coming forth in fulness.

66. I, the Lord, have spoken it; and as I have spoken, so shall I fulfill.

67. And though the heavens weep over this most wicked generation that has ever been on my land of Zion, I must fulfill my word; for I am a God of truth, and nothing is hidden from before mine eyes.

68. And though I have been long-suffering, I shall send my fire from heaven to purify my land of Zion of all wickedness, and raise up a more righteous generation of mine Israel, and other peoples that shall be brought to my land of Zion, and receive my message of salvation unto their eternal lives being earned, and the blessing of many souls upon the earth unto eternal life; and also, the blessing of many souls who dwell in the world of departed spirits awaiting the blessings and ordinances of salvation through the Redemption of Zion;

69. For I, the Lord, have organized this earth to fulfill the purpose of its creation, and I send forth children to earth to prove themselves.

70. And there is a day of judgment beyond this life that pertains to this life of your earthly existence, when all secrets shall be known and nothing hidden from all.

71. Thus, awake! Awake!

72. Repent ye! Repent ye! is the call of thy just God, even your Lord and Master, who ruleth over all things, soon to come in the clouds of heaven in the power of His might to visit the righteous and to sweep the wicked off this land of Zion and in many lands of the earth. Amen.

73. I who reigns on high speaketh further -- He who has all power:

74. Though no man knoweth the hour or the day of my glorious appearing, it is nigh at hand.

75. And these, my words, being sent to the leaders of this nation, and mine other words revealed to the leaders of all nations, sent forth by my Church and Kingdom upon the earth, the sending forth of my word is witness that my coming is nigh at hand, to justify thy Lord in what He must do to preserve Zion -- a city of righteousness, of peace and holiness, wherein all who dwell therein shall be called holy.

76. Let none oppose my Zion, or I shall send forth the judgments of a just God upon thee, saith the Lord to this nation and all peoples of the earth.

77. And that nation that raises their hand against my Zion shall be laid low and lose power and influence on earth;

78. For my judgments are just, and all peoples shall stand before me in the day of the resurrection and know that thy God who created thee, who redeemed thee from the grave, hath done right.

79. And the wicked shall tremble at my appearing and stand afar off.

80. How oft would I have gathered you into the arms of my redeeming love, O ye peoples of the earth, and you heed me not.

81. Yet those who mock their God shall mourn and know that He fulfilleth His word, all being accountable to a just God for the conduct through their agency on earth.

82. I, your Lord Jesus Christ, call upon the leader of this nation and those who are of influence in Congress to heed my word:

83. Be peacemakers among nations.

84. Overthrow these wicked laws that allow murder of unborn children, and of Sodom and adultery in thy land; for you are like the people in the days of Noah, with evil continually in your minds, and violence throughout thy land and in thy natures; and of a sudden, my whirlwind judgments shall come upon thee, even this nation on my land of Zion, and other nations on this land where my New Jerusalem shall rise.

85. While the governing powers are in thine hands, O ye leaders of this nation, do well.

86. Let deliverance and protection come for my people, for my servant and my servants in bondage.

87. And as my servant Daniel of old saw the destruction and upheaval of nations until Michael, mine Archangel, shall be sent to give the governing powers into the hands of my saints, there shall be unrest and overthrow of nations until only my Zion remaineth on my land of Zion.

88. War shall come to thy borders. Millions shall flee to the center of thy land and fill the mountains.

89. A great famine shall be among those who flee, and where the war taketh place on thy borders, because you heed me not.

90. How can I favor thy nation above others in continued protection if you allow these gross evils to exist among you, and allow the persecution of my Church and Kingdom upon the earth, whether by

persecuting zeal of outward prosecution of government powers against my Church and Kingdom, or whether it be persecuting zeal of a secret nature, seeking the lives of mine elect in a day of greater violence soon to come among the people of this land? -- which shall disrupt governing powers, unable to control thine own peoples, the unrest increasing, notwithstanding your supposed military might in the world today; a day when all people shall fear, when brother shall rise up against brother, mother against daughter, and daughter against mother, father against son, as I predicted, revealing these truths of coming events to mine apostles of old, which shall take place in this nation, being a nation of supposed freedom, which I have favored with great power and influence on earth; yet, if you continue in these most wicked ways, my justice and full judgment shall fall upon thee.

91. Oh, that you would heed my words and turn thy lives to righteousness, and turn thy governing powers to justice and equity.

92. You depend upon thy God who created thee for the breath of life, for health, for the preservation of all you have, for the sun that shineth, and the rains that bringeth water of life to thy crops and fields and orchards, that allows peace in thy borders and in the hearts of the children of men, mine own heavenly Spirit sent forth to touch people's minds and hearts to be of a peaceful way if they would receive the impressions of good, of kindness and peace in their souls.

93. And as I labor with the children of men, giving them their agency, I am a just God who intervenes in the lives of those who do what is right in the sight of their God.

94. And my Gospel of salvation has been published and sent to the nations of the earth lo, these many years, both in that holy writ known as Bible printing, and also in the revelations of your God, even Jesus Christ, through my servant Joseph Smith, Jun., which has been published to all peoples, nations, kindreds, and tongues.

95. And therein my word declares of my glorious appearing to preserve the righteous, who remembereth thy Lord in His ways, who rejoice in His coming and glory in His redeeming love, applying His Gospel of salvation of righteous principles, yea, eternal principles revealed from heaven to their individual lives.

96. Thus shall be the favored lot of those who heed my word.

97. In my holy love, I send forth these words of warning to the leaders of this nation of the United States of America in plain, understanding language; a God of eternal power speaking, inviting thee, the leaders of this nation and the peoples of this nation, to be of an influence of more righteous ways, and preserving my people in their freedoms to establish Zion in their midst;

98. For I shall reward all peoples according to the blessings offered, yet, through their own actions and words and desires, reject blessings that could promote life, yea, and also eternal life for those who would receive my message of salvation, saith your Lord.

99. And in my glory coming to earth, I shall heal the surviving nations and make known to them the mysteries of all ages of time; and truth shall be told concerning every nation, people, tongue of every age of time. Even so. Amen.

SECTION REVELATION 99

Fundamentalist Church of Jesus Christ of Latter-day Saints
P.O. Box 840459
Hildale, Utah 84784

Thus Saith Jesus Christ, Son Ahman, Unto the Leaders of the Nation of the United States of America, and to the Peoples Thereof, Warning and Continued Call to Prepare for Great Day of Final Judgments, Who Saith:

Revelation of the Lord Jesus Christ
Huntsville, Texas
Thursday, August 18, 2011

1. Verily, verily, thus saith the Lord, even Jesus Christ, the Great Power over all peoples; who is the power of Eternal Union of all other powers; who spake, and the world was made; who came in the day of the way of redemption; who suffered and atoned for all peoples; who hath conquered death; who is Resurrection and Life to all;

2. Verily I say to all peoples of the entire world, by the Mouthpiece of my sending: Ye are of fully ripening in iniquity.

3. Soon, yea, very soon cometh the entire cleansing I have given in many warnings, and by Isaiah, Jeremiah, and other Prophets, as testimony of my holy word being fulfilled.

4. The evil powers are as a blinding power over all mankind, though my language is given to your understanding; though you can read in a worldwide accepted language; yet you heed me not.

5. I, the Creator over all things, have not been silent.

6. I have given to national powers what must be done to survive my day of full cleansing power of whirlwind and destructive power.

7. My holy scriptures are full.

8. My time is nigh.

9. I shall burn my holy land of Zion of all evil, to prepare for a holy city to rise, even Zion, New Jerusalem; telling all peoples before what I shall do; that all may know thy God hath fulfilled His word, and shall continue to speak and fulfill.

10. Let now the storm of great power soon come to be as a full measure to humble this nation.

11. Know I held off this judgment to see if you would heed my word, in preparing for my coming; in cleansing thy evil laws of evil power, to be just; to preserve virtue, life; and also to send forth deliverance for my Mouthpiece; yet you heed me not.

12. Does not the loss of life mean anything to the rulers of this land?

13. Do they not see wickedness rules over the land -- putting innocence in prison now, even mine elders of obedient doing to Celestial Law of religion of my own revealing?

14. I am God, and all shall know my will.

15. Now cometh a shaking on thy land to humble thousands; yea, all the nation shall feel the result.

16. Let the people of my Church go free, lest I needs continue to pour out judgments on the land, like I did unto Pharaoh and the Egyptians, until they no more could oppose my right to rule.

17. I am Jehovah, even Jesus Christ, Son Ahman, the Full Governing Power of Celestial Priesthood power over the earth; yea, over the nation boasting great power on earth; yet now being but a waning power, none to console her, as nations turn from thee in the great fall of power of money system.

18. I alone have held thee in place.

19. Only I, your Lord, can preserve any of all peoples.

20. Let it be known a great heavenly body cometh, unseen by your technology; I able to blind your way until I take away the covering.

21. Know it shall be of a happening within new year's coming; an event of such magnitude, all peoples shall wonder.

22. I tell not exact time, whether one or two years of my giving a warning; yet some heavenly bodies of larger size shall soon strike the earth to the amazing thoughts of many; which shall begin to disturb the protective atmosphere layer, to cause men on earth to not be of my protecting; to suffer greater burnings on their bodies, as my servant John Beloved recorded; caused by heavenly bodies increasing to disturb the protective atmosphere layer.

23. Judgments shall be felt in the rising up of the people of Turkey, and cause many other people to falter in European stability.

24. NATO has lost credibility; has become spread far; is now an aggressive alliance.

25. Let all know I warned all of the fall of earthly powers.

26. Now know Israel shall step forth and be of an aggressive way when threatened.

27. Then shall my people know I have spoken, as I preserve the nation; though many perish because they also heed me not; do not cleanse their own peoples; nor do the peace labor I have named.

28. Libya is now a full way of aggression by countries never attacked by that nation.

29. Example of fear of aggression shall unite other nations to fight NATO nations.

30. Disunity shall absorb thee.

31. The economy of your lands shall wither. United States is a power of soon instability in own economic instability.

32. The holy law of retribution for aggression is upon her.

33. I am God. I hath spoken truth. She will not free him, my servant.

34. She shall feel my wrath soon; then shall come to pass mine elect be preserved, while the wicked shall tremble and be no more a power against Zion rising.

35. O ye people of my earth, awake to catastrophe you are bringing upon yourselves.

36. I must fulfill the purpose of this earth.

37. Your temporary ways cannot overrule the eternal purposes of a God of power.

38. You are my creation.

39. Humble thyselves, to be of a receiving of some degree of life and salvation, from your Lord, Jesus Christ, who speaketh, as a voice from the wilderness -- from the wilderness because you seeth me not; my voice being my Spirit of truth,

which toucheth every pure, honest mind with a witness of truth, in a gentle peace.

40. My holy way shall soon be known unto all peoples.

41. Receive ye my next warning; from thy God who loveth all, yet despiseth evil; to guide all here and hereafter to repentance, lest full eternal judgment cometh upon the soul who dies in their sins; to rise in never-ending sorrow for turning from me, your Redeemer; thus choosing death.

42. I am the Light, Life, Happiness, Peace, Truth, and Hope of all peoples.

43. I am your Savior, which speaketh.

44. Seek unto me through my Priesthood to receive my will; to benefit nations, peoples, individuals in soul-raising powers unto earthly and eternal salvation; through the full way of pure holy religion being my authority of heaven, now on earth.

45. Let the wicked of false testifying have one soon reveal their lying; to now show the world prosecuting power followed a scheme of lying combination of years of maturing; to imprison my servant.

46. Their falsehoods shall become a blot on their lives not able to be borne, even before all peoples.

47. Let the governing powers cause the illegal governing work of fighting a holy religion, clouded over by blinding legal and unjust attack of falsehoods, now to be a catalyst to be of a fulfilling all my will concerning my own word to leaders of this nation, and other nations.

48. I am God who lendeth you breath; who upholds all powers of every kingdom to exist; to test all; to now be judged.

49. Let all receive my will, and hasten to be repenting, lest all my full judgments of full power of pure way be sent forth, to be testimony of my almighty power to all peoples of every nation.

50. I cometh quickly. Amen.

SECTION REVELATION 100

Fundamentalist Church of Jesus Christ of Latter-day Saints
P.O. Box 840459
Hildale, Utah 84784

Thus Saith Son Ahman, Your Lord Jesus Christ, to All Peoples of the Earth Unto Your Salvation if You Heed Me, Saying Thus:

Revelation of the Lord Jesus Christ
Huntsville, Texas
Friday, August 19, 2011

1. Verily, saith your Lord, come unto me, all ye people who have the power to repent, lest sore affliction soon overtake you, in a manner you think not; in an awakening the soul from deep sleep spiritual; in bringing all to hear my way of salvation eternal, saith Jesus Christ.

2. I am your Advocate with the Father.

3. I have overcome, and sit at the right hand of the Father to bring all unto Him who will receive the message of salvation of souls.

4. Let all hear my will.

5. I am now to send a sickness upon the land of my coming, even in power upon all the earth, to be known of all peoples thy God of glory reigneth!

6. Let all now be of the order of endless and eternal lives, of the people of the promise of Israel being gathered unto Zion, as I confided in Peter, James, and John would take place in power in the days of wickedness, when I would be of the power of gathering all who have the blood of Israel of the pure seed of my holy family of the flesh, when I was on earth; with eternal power as thy Lord.

7. I was with men with the full power of Priesthood.

8. I could raise the dead, heal and bless by the power of Godhead in my own possession, of the Father, doing His will in all things.

9. Thus, am I your Advocate with the Father, to bring all unto salvation to all who heed my word unto character of God becoming your natural way, of my Spirit; through thy faith always exercised.

10. Let all be of the way of improving.

11. Let all be of truth.

12. Let all be of receiving my own way, saith the Light of all men.

13. Let my light of pure holy way enlighten thy daily walk unto overcoming evil.

14. I am only Just, Holy, True, Righteous; Governing Power; Equitous, Noble, Exalting, and the Rock of Salvation for all to build on.

15. Let all come unto me, your Lord, who saith to all nations of the earth -- come to me.

16. Be ye clean to survive my holy power of cleansing judgments upon all nations.

17. Let my love shine in you. Forgive all peoples.

18. I shall repay in a just judgment.

19. Let the Holy Priesthood be purged.

20. Let my Church be cleansed.

21. Let all now live my Gospel of peace. Amen.

SECTION REVELATION 101

Jesus Christ Speaketh to the Nation of the United States Solemn Warning Again, Mine Own Word From the Heavens, to Be Heeded Lest Judgments Follow Upon Those Who Heed Me Not, Saith the Lord, Even Son Ahman

Thus Saith the Lord Jesus Christ to the Leaders and Peoples of the United States of America, My Holy Word of Continued Warning of Final Judgments Soon at Hand, Heed My Word, Which Saith:

Revelation of the Lord Jesus Christ
Tennessee Colony, Texas
Sunday, September 25, 2011

1. I who reign on high speaketh, even Jesus Christ, through my servant on earth to the nation of the United States of America: You have transgressed and not kept my word, though I have sent mine own word unto you in sacred revealings and publishings, yea, to leaders of nations.

2. My warning voice has been sounded. I am the God of Creation which speaketh. My servant is in bondage. You yet hold him from my people.

3. My Zion shall rise, and I shall intervene in a judgment that you shall soon feel, and it shall continue until opposition is removed.

4. Thus saith the Lord to the leaders and peoples of this nation: Though my voice has been sounded often to you and sent forth, and you heed me not, I shall fulfill my word, and you shall know at the removing of those in power to their everlasting regret for not heeding my word when sent to them.

5. And I give my word to you as a witness that thy God can speak from the heavens and communicate in preparing those who will heed my word for my coming; for I shall have a people in every nation that survives to come to Zion and receive of the greater light coming forth of my revealing.

6. And I, the Lord, give to this nation and this people the warning, to be justified in the cleansing that must take place if they heed not the God who created them;

7. For I am God, Son Ahman, and I do the will of the Father, who is Ahman.

8. And thus saith the Lord: The will of the Father is being done, for you have seen increased storms, flooding, even more than you have witnessed before in areas where it has not taken place before.

9. Ye shall witness further, as I have named, until you are humbled.

10. O that you would heed my word and receive my word; and I send my word to you again, that hearts can be touched who will heed my word, both of the leaders

of this nation, of states, counties, places of governing power, and also among the population of thy people, for the cleansing shall be of such a nature that only that which can be of a purification remain.

11. I have named many places that shall be cleansed entire, and as you witness this, the memory of my word shall hearken in your souls that thy God reigneth; and if you are of the ability to repent, your hearts shall be touched.

12. Yet my word shall be fulfilled, as I spoke before I was taken upon the cross to be sacrificed, saith the Lord Jesus Christ, even that word that among the wicked in the last days, when judgments come, many would lift up their voices against me, cursing God and perishing because they would not heed my word, having their hearts set on wickedness and pleasure in unrighteousness.

13. Repent ye of the great sins I have named that are among your people, for the murder of unborn children is a stench of corruption that causeth all thy works to be of the way of ignoble shame, the very heavens seeing your works limiting the coming forth of spirits to earth, appointed to receive tabernacles and prove their worthiness before the Lord.

14. Your practice of this murder of children yet unborn shall be answered upon thy souls in the day of eternal judgment, with a suffering of soul that you would be of an assenting or agreeing to this sin and would not stop it among your peoples.

15. Your adulterous ways are the motive for this sin that must be obliterated of my judgments coming upon all who will not receive my word and change their ways from this terrible crime against innocence, purity, and life.

16. I, your God, have spoken it.

17. Let the laws be changed if you would be of a repentance, else full judgment shall come upon thy peoples, and you shall know it.

18. You have also persecuted my Church and Kingdom and allowed my leadership to be in bondage, when I have called upon thee to let my people go to their worshiping and laboring, having their houses and lands restored to them of legal appointing, being of an illegal way in removing them from their homes, who have thus been ruled against in courts of law.

19. Heed my word: Let my servant go.

20. And let there be a changing of your laws to purify thy peoples, lest there be full judgment of the removing of this nation from this land, of whirlwind nature, that I have promised in all my holy scriptures through my servants, the Prophets, whom I have sent -- in particular, Joseph Smith, Jun., in revealing my word to this generation.

21. There shall come upon the nation that inhabits this land, yea, each nation, a full judging, a cleansing, to only allow there to remain those who can endure the presence of God in Zion, New Jerusalem being built in that Center Stake appointed on the land called United States of America; that Center Stake being Jackson County, Missouri, well-appointed, and nothing can stay mine hand; for I shall claim my lands purchased by my Priesthood in former times, taken from them by mobocracy and driving and killing in the days of my servant Joseph Smith.

22. Heed my word: I shall recover what belongeth to me, and New Jerusalem shall rise, and nothing can stay mine hand.

23. Though you oppose me, and pass laws, and have thy people rise up against innocence, against my Church, I shall be

of a defending nature, and you shall know that I have preserved my people against the day of my coming in my glory, as I have promised mine apostles in the meridian of time when I was upon the earth and after I was resurrected, angels revealing to them my glorious coming in power in the clouds of heaven.

24. This is in sacred holy writ, which you can peruse.

25. My coming is soon, and there cannot be these sins and corruptions on my land where I shall appear unto an elect people who have kept Celestial laws, holy laws of eternal revealing.

26. My law is pure, and you have attacked my Law of Celestial Plural Marriage and other laws of my Priesthood as though it was of a corrupt way. It is not so.

27. My law is pure and of my governing through my revealed authority, my Priesthood, my servant on earth, not to be given to general populous among your peoples, only to those who are pure and holy.

28. Thus you have imprisoned men who are holy and pure, of pure religious motive, not desiring harm to anyone; and your prosecuting zeal is of a crime against my Priesthood, Church, and Kingdom that shall be answered upon thy people and governing powers if you heed me not.

29. Let them go, saith the Lord. Amen.

APPENDIX B

APPENDIX OF MY NEW WORD OF PURE POWER PRINTED IN THIS MY PROCLAMATION TO ALL PEOPLES ON ALL LANDS REFERENCING PAGES TO FIND MY WORD IN THIS PUBLISHING

Appendix of My New Word of Pure Power
Printed in This My Proclamation to All Peoples on All Lands
Referencing Pages to Find My Word in This Publishing

APPENDIX C

DOCUMENTS SHOWING THE LEGAL AND
RELIGIOUS ESTABLISHING AND CONTINUING
OF THE FUNDAMENTALIST CHURCH OF JESUS
CHRIST OF LATTER-DAY SAINTS AMONG MEN
ON EARTH, THY LORD ESTABLISHING HIS
CHURCH APRIL 6, 1830, THROUGH JOSEPH
SMITH, CONTINUED ON EARTH THROUGH MY
PRIESTHOOD; NOW A LEGAL ORGANIZATION
ACCORDING TO LAW OF LAND AMONG
MEN, SAITH JESUS CHRIST, YOUR LORD

149512

ARTICLES OF INCORPORATION

FOR

THE CORPORATION OF THE PRESIDENT

OF

THE FUNDAMENTALIST CHURCH OF JESUS CHRIST OF LATTER-DAY SAINTS INC.

STATE OF UTAH   )
                     : ss.
COUNTY OF SALT LAKE)

RECEIVED 1991 FEB -6 PM 3: 23

I, RULON T. JEFFS, having been duly chosen and appointed President of The Fundamentalist Church of Jesus Christ of Latter-day Saints, in conformity with the rites, regulations and discipline of said Church, being desirous of forming a corporation for the purpose of acquiring, holding and disposing of Church or religious society property, for the benefit of religion, for works of charity and for public worship, hereby make and subscribe these Articles of Incorporation for a corporation sole pursuant to the provisions of Sections 16-7-1 et seq. of the Utah Code Annotated (1953, as amended).

ARTICLE I

The name of the corporation shall be THE CORPORATION OF THE PRESIDENT OF THE FUNDAMENTALIST CHURCH OF JESUS CHRIST OF LATTER-DAY SAINTS. INC.

ARTICLE II

The object of the corporation shall be to acquire, hold, or dispose of such real and personal property as may be conveyed to or acquired by said corporation for the benefit of the members of The Fundamentalist Church of Jesus Christ of Latter-day Saints, a religious society, for the benefit of religion, for works of charity, for public worship, for the establishment of schools and for the advancement of both religious and secular education, and for all other lawful purposes necessary or incident thereto. Such real and personal property may be situated, either within the State of Utah, or elsewhere (including foreign countries), and this corporation shall have power, without any authority or authorization from the members of said Church or religious

society, to grant, sell, convey, rent, mortgage, exchange, or
otherwise deal with or dispose of any part or all of such
property.

ARTICLE III

The estimated value of property to which I hold the legal
title and which I desire to place in this corporation for the
purpose aforesaid, at the time of making these Articles, is the
sum of $568,000.

ARTICLE IV

The title of the person making these Articles of
Incorporation is "President of The Fundamentalist Church of Jesus
Christ of Latter-day Saints. *INC.*"

ARTICLE V

In the event of the death or resignation from office of the
President of The Fundamentalist Church of Jesus Christ of Latter-
day Saints, or in the event of a vacancy in that office for any
cause, the First Counselor of the First Presidency of said Church
(or in the event such First Counselor shall not then be living or
shall be disabled, the Second or next subsequent Counselor in the
First Presidency as the President shall have designated prior to
his death or disability) shall, pending installation of a
successor President of The Fundamentalist Church of Jesus Christ
of Latter-day Saints, be the corporation sole under these
articles, and the laws pursuant to which they are made, and shall
be and is authorized in his official capacity to execute in the
name of the corporation all documents or other writings necessary
to the carrying on of its purposes, business and objects, and to
do all things in the name of the corporation which the original
signer of the articles of incorporation might do; it being the
purpose of these articles that there shall be no failure in
succession in the office of such corporation sole. At the time
of signing of these Articles, the First Counselor in the First
Presidency of said Church is Parley J. Harker, and the Second
Counselor is Fred M. Jessop. The President shall have authority
to designate new counselors in the First Presidency of said
Church, or to change the office of existing counselors, as he
shall see fit.

- 2 -

ARTICLE VI

In the event of the winding up or dissolution of this corporation, after paying or adequately providing for the debts and obligations of the corporation, the remaining assets shall be distributed to a nonprofit fund, foundation or corporation, which is organized and operated exclusively for charitable, educational, or religious and/or scientific purposes.

ARTICLE VII

This corporation shall exist perpetually unless sooner dissolved by law.

DATED this 6th day of February, 1991.

Rulon T. Jeffs, President
The Fundamentalist Church of Jesus
Christ of Latter-day Saints
3611 East 9400 South

Sandy, Utah 84092

STATE OF UTAH   )
                : ss.
COUNTY OF SALT LAKE)

I hereby certify that on this 6th day of February, 1991, personally appeared before me Rulon T. Jeffs, who is known to me to be the person whose name is subscribed to the foregoing instrument as President of The Fundamentalist Church of Jesus Christ of Latter-day Saints, and duly acknowledged to me that he executed the same as such president.

Notary Public
Residing in Salt Lake City, Utah

My Commission Expires:

7/10/92

NOTARY PUBLIC
My Commission
Expires 7-10-92
PATRICIA B. BIRCH
10 Exchange Place, 11th Floor
Salt Lake City
UT 84111
STATE OF UTAH

- 3 -

CO 149512

AMENDED AND RESTATED ARTICLES OF INCORPORATION

OF

THE CORPORATION OF THE PRESIDENT

OF

THE FUNDAMENTALIST CHURCH OF JESUS CHRIST OF LATTER-DAY SAINTS

Pursuant to Utah Code Ann. § 16-7-14, The Corporation of the President of the Fundamentalist Church of Jesus Christ of Latter-day Saints, Inc., amends and restates its Articles of Incorporation to read in their entirety as follows:

ARTICLE I

The name of the corporation shall be "THE CORPORATION OF THE PRESIDENT OF THE FUNDAMENTALIST CHURCH OF JESUS CHRIST OF LATTER-DAY SAINTS."

ARTICLE II

The object of the corporation shall be to acquire, hold, or dispose of such real and personal property as may be conveyed to said corporation for the benefit of The Fundamentalist Church of Jesus Christ of Latter-Day Saints, a religious society, for the benefit of religion, for works of charity, for public worship, for the establishment of schools and for the advancement of both religious and secular education, and for all other lawful purposes necessary or incident thereto. Consequently, this corporation has not been organized for the purpose of making a profit. Such real and personal property may be situated, either within the State of Utah, or elsewhere (including foreign countries), and this corporation have power, without any authority or authorization of the members of said Church or religious society, to grant, sell, convey, rent, mortgage, exchange, or otherwise dispose of the same, or any part thereof; however this corporation is prohibited from declaring or paying dividends.

ARTICLE III

The corporate seal shall contain the words, "President FLDS Church, Corporate Seal," and an impression thereof is hereto affixed.

ARTICLE IV

In the winding up and dissolution of this Corporation, after paying or adequately providing for the debts and obligations of the Corporation, the remaining assets shall be distributed among legal entities of similar objectives, that is, to a non-profit fund, foundation or corporation, which is organized and operated exclusively for charitable, educational, religious and/or scientific purposes and which has established its tax exempt status under § 501(c)(3) (or its successor) of the Internal Revenue Code.

ARTICLE V

The estimated value of property to which I hold the legal title and which I desire to place in this corporation for the purpose aforesaid, at the time of making these Articles, is the sum of $1,000.

ARTICLE VI

The title of the person making these Articles of is "The President of The Fundamentalist Church of Jesus Christ of Latter-Day Saints."

IN WITNESS WHEREOF these Amended and Restated Articles of Incorporation are adopted by The Corporation of the President of the Fundamentalist Church of Jesus Christ of Latter-day Saints.

Rulon T. Jeffs, President and Corporation Sole

-2-

STATE OF UTAH   )
                              :ss.
COUNTY OF SALT LAKE)

       I hereby certify that on this _23_ day of December, 1997, personally appeared before me Rulon T. Jeffs, who is known to me to be the person whose name is subscribed to the foregoing instrument as President of The Fundamentalist Church of Jesus Christ of Latter-Day Saints, and duly acknowledged to me that he executed the same as such President.

                                     NOTARY PUBLIC
                                     Residing in _SALT LAKE COUNTY_

My Commission Expires:

      _8·8·78_

-3-

RECEIVED

FEB 15 2011

Utah Div. of Corp. & Comm. Code

This form must be type written or computer generated.	Date:	02/15/2011

EXPEDITE

Receipt Number: 3481449
Amount Paid: $90.00

State of Utah
Department of Commerce
Division of Corporations & Commercial Code
Corporation Registration Information Change Form

Non-Refundable Processing Fee: $15.00

Entity File Number: 1107221-0145

Entity Name: The Corporation of the President of the Fundamentalist Church of Jesus Christ of Latter-Day Saints

For each Yes button that you mark the question will appear below for you to fill out.

1). Do you want to Change the Business Purpose?   ○ Yes   ◉ No

2). Do you want to Change the Registered Agent or the Address of the Registered Agent?   ○ Yes   ◉ No

3). Do you want to Change the Principal Address of the Business Entity?   ○ Yes   ◉ No

4). Do you want to Add individuals to the Business Entity?   ◉ Yes   ○ No

4). If Yes, who do you want to Add to the Business Entity and what Position will they hold?

Name: Warren Steed Jeffs   Position: President
Address: P.O. Box 840900   City Hildale   State UT   Zip 84784
Name: Warren Steed Jeffs   Position: Corporation Sole
Address: P.O. Box 840900   City Hildale   State UT   Zip 84784

5). Do you want to Remove individuals from the Business Entity?   ○ Yes   ◉ No

6). Do you want to Change the Address of the Business Entity's Principal(s)?   ○ Yes   ◉ No

Optional Inclusion of Ownership Information: This information is not required.

Is this a female owned business?   Yes   No

Is this a minority owned business?   ○ Yes   ○ No   If yes, please specify: Select/Type the race of the owner here

Under GRAMA {63-2-201}, all registration information maintained by the Division is classified as public record. For confidentiality purposes, you may use the business entity physical address rather than the residential or private address of any individual affiliated with the entity.

Under penalties of perjury and as an authorized authority, I declare that this statement of change(s), has been examined by me and is, to the best of my knowledge and belief, true, correct and complete.

Name/Title: Warren S. Jeffs/President   Signature: _Warren S. Jeffs_   Date: 2-10-2011

Mailing/Faxing Information: www.corporations.utah.gov/contactus.html   Division's Website: www.corporations.utah.gov

(side text, rotated): 02-15-11P03:49 RCVD

MP

RECEIVED

FEB 15 2011

Utah Div. of Corp. & Comm. Code

State of Utah
Department of Commerce
Division of Corporations & Commercial Code
Heber M. Wells Building
160 East 300 South
Salt Lake City, UT 84111

CERTIFICATE

TO WHOM IT MAY CONCERN:

I, the undersigned, WARREN STEED JEFFS, have been called and sustained as the President of The Fundamentalist Church of Jesus Christ of Latter-Day Saints, and by virtue of such calling I am the corporation sole of the Corporation of the President of the Fundamentalist Church of Jesus Christ of Latter-Day Saints, organized under the laws of the State of Utah.

Entity Name: The Corporation of the President of the Fundamentalist Church of Jesus Christ of Latter-Day Saints

Entity Address: 1020 West Utah Avenue
P.O. Box 840900
Hildale, UT 84784-0900

Entity Number: 1107221-0145

IN TESTIMONY WHEREOF, I have hereunto subscribed my name this _10th_ day of February, 2011.

Warren S Jeffs
Warren Steed Jeffs

02-15-11P03:51 RCVD

Utah Business Search - Details

CORPORATION OF THE PRESIDENT OF THE FUNDAMENTALIST CHURCH OF JESUS CHRIST OF LATTER-DAY SAINTS INC.

Entity Number: 1107221-0145
Company Type: Corporation - Sole
Address: 1020 W UTAH AVE P O BOX 840900 Hildale, UT 84784
State of Origin: UT
Registered Agent: BOYD L KNUDSON
Registered Agent Address:
1020 W UTAH AVE P O BOX 840900 Hildale UT 84784

Status: Administrative Hold

Status: Administrative Hold *as of 03/31/2011*
Status Description: Hold
Employment Verification: <u>Not</u> Registered with Verify Utah

History

Registration Date: 02/06/1991
Last Renewed: N/A

Additional Information

NAICS Code: 8131 **NAICS Title:** 8131-Religious Organizations

Refine your search by:

- Search by:
- Business Name
- Number
- Executive Name
- Search Hints

Name:

Utah Business Search - Registered Principals

Registered Principals

Name	Type	City	Status
CORPORATION OF THE PRESIDENT OF THE FUNDAMENTALIST CHURCH OF JESUS CHRIST OF LATTER-DAY SAINTS INC.	Corporation	Hildale	Administrative Hold

Position	Name	Address	
President	WARREN STEED JEFFS	PO BOX 840900	Hildale UT 84784
Registered Agent	BOYD L KNUDSON	1020 W UTAH AVE	Hildale UT 84784

If you believe there may be more principals, click here to

Search by:

- Search by:
- Business Name
- Number
- Executive Name
- Search Hints

Name:

AFFIDAVIT OF BOYD L. KNUDSON
THAT THE CONGREGATIONS ASSEMBLED UPHOLD BY THE LAW OF COMMON CONSENT THE CALLING AND POSITION OF WARREN STEED JEFFS AS THE PRESIDENT OF THE FUNDAMENTALIST CHURCH OF JESUS CHRIST OF LATTER-DAY SAINTS

TO WHOM IT MAY CONCERN:

STATE OF TEXAS   )
                                  : ss.
COUNTY OF SCHLEICHER   )

1.   I, the undersigned Boyd L. Knudson, am the Official Representative and Registered Agent of The Corporation of the President of the Fundamentalist Church of Jesus Christ of Latter-day Saints which is a Corporation Sole entity as allowed by Title 16, Chapter 7 of the Utah Code with an entity number 1107221-0145 assigned by the State of Utah.

2.   I am a member in good standing of the "Church" known as the Fundamentalist Church of Jesus Christ of Latter-day Saints.

3.   I am over 18 years of age and am otherwise competent to testify to the facts set forth herein.

4.   I have personal knowledge of the matters set forth herein.

5.   On February 6, 1991, Rulon T. Jeffs organized The Corporation of the President of the Fundamentalist Church of Jesus Christ of Latter-day Saints. See attached "Exhibit A" for a "Utah Business Search - Details" verifying the entity name, number, address, registration date and registered agent. On December 26, 1997, the Amended and Restated Articles of Incorporation signed by Rulon T. Jeffs, attached hereto as "Exhibit B," were filed with the State of Utah.

6.   On April 10, 2011, I sat before a Special Conference held in Colorado City, Arizona of the Church of Jesus Christ of Latter-day Saints known as the Fundamentalist Church of Jesus Christ of Latter-day Saints and there witnessed the congregation of near 2,000 Melchizedek and Aaronic Priesthood bearers with other officers of the Church in conference assembled vote unanimously as individuals and as a congregation according to the Church law of common consent and according to the Church tenets, rites, rules

Page 1 of 2

and laws to uphold and sustain Warren Steed Jeffs as President of Priesthood, President of said Church, and Presiding Bishop of said Church.

      7.   On April 3, 2011, I sat before a General Assembly in Colorado City, Arizona of over 4,000 Church members and witnessed them individually and together as a congregation of the Church of Jesus Christ of Latter-day Saints known as the Fundamentalist Church of Jesus Christ of Latter-day Saints, according to the tenets, rites, regulations, discipline, rules and laws of said Church and according to the Church law of common consent, unanimously stand and raise their hands and voices in favor of sustaining Warren Steed Jeffs as President of Priesthood, President of said Church, and Presiding Bishop of said Church.

      8.   Warren Steed Jeffs is the President of the Fundamentalist Church of Jesus Christ of Latter-day Saints and by virtue of this office is the Corporation Sole and President of the Corporation of the President of the Fundamentalist Church of Jesus Christ of Latter-day Saints, organized under the laws of the State of Utah.

      9.   The Certificate attached hereto as "Exhibit C" signed by Warren S. Jeffs on February 10, 2011 as filed on February 15, 2011 with the State of Utah, Department of Commerce, Division of Corporations & Commercial Code in testimony that Warren Steed Jeffs is the President of The Fundamentalist Church of Jesus Christ of Latter-day Saints and is the Corporation Sole is true, correct and valid according to the rules of the Church. See attached "Exhibit D" for a "Utah Business Search - Registered Principals" verifying the President and registered agent of the Corporation Sole.

      I, Boyd L. Knudson, being first duly placed under oath by the undersigned official authorized to administer oaths under the laws of this State, do solemnly swear that the information herein is true and correct.

Boyd L. Knudson

Boyd L. Knudson

Subscribed and sworn to before me this 22nd day of July, 2011.

EDMUND LORIN BARLOW, SR
Notary Public, State of Texas
My Commission Expires
December 03, 2013

Edmund Barlow

Notary Public
Commission Expires: 12-3-2013

Page 2 of 2

SECOND EDITION OF MY HOLY WARNING TO ALL NATIONS, EVEN JESUS CHRIST

Chapter 10

Word of the Lord Jesus Christ of Continued Sacred Warning to All Peoples on Earth

The Lord Jesus Christ Sendeth This, a Holy Word to All Nations, to Know I Continue to Speak From the Heavens Through My Servant on Earth, Warren Jeffs, and That You Must Heed My Word, for I Shall Send Whirlwind Judgments if There Is the Impurity of Life Continued in Nations Who Uphold Murder of Unborn Youth and Other Evils of Immoral Way. I Loveth All the Honest in Heart Who Will Purify Their Lives, Saith the Lord. Heed My Word in This Printing. Amen.

SECTION REVELATION 239

Jesus Christ
Son Ahman

Revelation of the Lord Jesus Christ
Palestine, Texas
Tuesday, September 25, 2012

1. Thus saith God over all nation order: Be ready.

2. I cometh soon to all national order of world, to hearken to God, even your full power of nation way, my will to be thy full now hearkened order of now labor -- put all war way aside.

3. Do so now. Future is soon of my coming.

4. Care thou not for thine own life on earth, nor for eternal life with God?

5. I am He, Jesus Christ, that speaketh, He who created all nations, even world order entire.

6. Nature bespeaketh majesty of God, organized to perfecting -- all plant, animal life organized so no specie is invading on the way of procreating another.

7. Now hearken, all ye nations.

8. Receive my own word: Cease war way.

9. Soon evil land of harm to many peoples start war with hate-motive, only to do evil to all people on earth.

10. Have own control of own navy soon, so retaliating spirit ruleth not.

11. Suicide bomber way shall be beginning of naval battle of United States being attacked to provoke conflict.

12. Do not retaliate at all.

13. Do not join hastening of conflict.

14. A holy order is to forgive, then guard own nation for more aggression if of true peace. Amen.

15. Thus saith the Lord to all nations:

Go to own home day war of large order is of a happening, to fast, pray, seek unto God for end to world conflict, so I can see who is of faith, unto preserving all worthy clean people desiring God's truth order through soon-sent messenger order.

16. Now repent of violent living or evil desires so I can preserve thee, is the Lord Jesus Christ will to all nations. Amen.

17. I, your Lord, tell all nations to now make peace.

18. I am soon coming to world of thy inhabiting.

19. All people shall see me together. Amen.

Jesus Christ

SECTION REVELATION 240

Jesus Christ
Son Ahman

Thus Saith God Over All Peoples on World, a Word of Full Guiding All to Prepare Now for My Full Power Judgment Holy Power Order, Soon on Earth. Amen.

Revelation of the Lord Jesus Christ
Palestine, Texas
Tuesday, October 2, 2012

1. Thus saith the Lord God Almighty: Repent, for all flesh shall feel the full justice of an holy God. Amen.

2. Now let all people cease female abuse, child abuse.

3. Let not thy tradition rule.

4. Female order should be respected for pure way of holy living, only of full holy living in married order; not abused in any religious organization simply for male authority to show strength over womankind.

5. Let family be love-kind living, not abusive in tradition of world lust evil order. Amen.

6. Let child order be of schooling in all arts of living, to do full order guiding in youth in holy moral living by parent order.

7. Consider own youth as holy time for learning purity living, of abstinence of the connecting with other youth in the child siring order.

8. Such shall my rule over all peoples on earth be. Amen.

9. I, Christ Jesus, your God, have all in my power now; to know thy secret truths of

moral living; to judge each for sure reward of own choice of living.

10. Sacrifice selfish immoral living now; to do full order holy living; to be ready for my holy Advent on world of thy living.

11. Now be holy. Amen.

12. Tell thy family, each household leader father order, to lay aside all evil communicating with sin order; no evil movie or drug way; no evil immoral way; all learning more holy love for God in all connections with all world. Amen.

13. This is final time full warning from thy God. Amen.

14. Now send to my holy order of full Priesthood authority a letter of truth-telling of desire for salvation.

15. Do so soon as letter sending shall be soon hindered.

16. Do so to tell him, my Prophet representative, I am of thy love power, to survive holocaust of the soon war, other judgment order God-sent. Amen.

17. Now do so, so all record is on hand of all nations having received my several warning order letter order, warning of my justice upon they of all way unholy living.

18. Do no more murder of unborn child order, by the hospital physician order, nor by the pill medicine way; for both destroy life. Amen.

19. Now do this. Amen.

20. Tell the ruler in own nation to protect unborn child order by gathering to do full inquiry to lawmaker order.

21. Also do full no-using physician order who do unholy way removal of living fetus from first conception time in woman. Amen.

22. Such are guilty of murder in youth unborn in mother order; to be of full order judged as murder way in eternal judgment of God on all such.

23. Cease such, for I come.

24. I shall reward all, here on world, also in eternity order of spirit judgment; to do full order repenting here in this time on world, so I can reward you each according to works done in the flesh; also thy own heart order desire living, as though you would do such as you have lived desire for all such sin way.

25. Now do own holy repenting. Amen.

26. Now let nation in unrest, Herzegovina of the old Yugoslavic land, not be violent secret murder evil order; both public and private way; of both private doing of small criminal evil combating; also government secret murder of opposition to the way of government doing, of government order secret way assassinating opposition there. Amen.

27. I see such taking place.

28. All shall be of full way rewarded with eternal in-soul suffering way when mind is unlocked in day of my judging each. Amen.

29. Now repent also, Herzegovina, of own desire as nation, to not attack any neighbor order nation. Amen.

30. I, God, give full order warning, so all nations of Europe join not in conflict if the order of war is in Serbia nation or neighbor nation order.

31. Restrain full attack. Do so to do peace new negotiating order, lest world order join in evil extended conflict; as I, God, foresee such as was beginning area of world wars of last century.

32. Now restrain use of mass-destructive weapon evil way of mass fast life-taking weapon order, lest own nation also be annihilated by vengeance feeling

hate of other nation order of more power to destroy. Amen.

33. Now this is like a governing power over all world speaking to all national leader order; so all be restraint way doing such unholy weapon of full destruction power in single fire of weapon of nuclear or disease weapon; largest defense order national power of United States, Russia, also other European order, China and North Korea; all need to do disarming now, lest war of hate-vengeance taketh place.

34. Let leader order now do full destroying of all such person way destroying of full city order with one bomb. Amen.

35. Now tell own leader order to do so. Amen.

36. Let also religious leader order in all national order of power to bear influence on government order, hear people in nation oppose peacefully all nuclear, chemical, also disease-spreading bomb way of destroying life on earth. Amen.

Isaiah 52 (Inspired Version)

1. Awake, awake, put on thy strength, O Zion; put on thy beautiful garments, O Jerusalem, the holy city; for henceforth there shall no more come into thee the uncircumcised and the unclean.

2. Shake thyself from the dust; arise, and sit down, O Jerusalem; loose thyself from the bands of thy neck, O captive daughter of Zion.

3. For thus saith the Lord, Ye have sold yourselves for naught; and ye shall be redeemed without money.

4. For thus saith the Lord God, My people went down aforetime into Egypt to sojourn there; and the Assyrian oppressed them without cause.

5. Now therefore, what have I here, saith the Lord, that my people is taken away for naught? they that rule over them make them to howl, saith the Lord; and my name continually every day is blasphemed.

6. Therefore, my people shall know my name; yea, in that day they shall know that I am he that doth speak; behold, it is I.

7. And then shall they say, How beautiful upon the mountains are the feet of him that bringeth good tidings unto them, that publisheth peace; that bringeth good tidings unto them of good, that publisheth salvation; that saith unto Zion, Thy God reigneth!

8. Thy watchmen shall lift up the voice; with the voice together shall they sing; for they shall see eye to eye, when the Lord shall bring again Zion.

9. Break forth into joy, sing together, ye waste places of Jerusalem; for the Lord hath comforted his people, he hath redeemed Jerusalem.

10. The Lord hath made bare his holy arm in the eyes of all the nations; and all the ends of the earth shall see the salvation of our God.

11. Depart ye, depart ye, go ye out from thence, touch no unclean thing; go ye out of the midst of her; be ye clean, that bear the vessels of the Lord.

12. For ye shall not go out with haste, nor go by flight; for the Lord will go before you; and the God of Israel will be your rereward.

13. Behold, my servant shall deal prudently, he shall be exalted and extolled, and be very high.

14. As many were astonied at thee; his visage was so marred more than any man, and his form more than the sons of men;

15. So shall he gather many nations; the kings shall shut their mouths at him; for that which had not been told them shall they see; and that which they had not heard shall they consider.

SECTION REVELATION 241

Jesus Christ
Son Ahman

I, Jesus Christ, Send My Own Will to All Nations on World. Be Hearing, Telling My Exact Will to Thy People. Amen.

Revelation of the Lord Jesus Christ
Palestine, Texas
Wednesday, October 10, 2012

1. May all honor, power, glory, all majesty be of God only, in Millennial Time of Peace by all nation power of earth!

2. Glory to Him who dwelleth in everlasting burnings, Celestial power eternal, ruling all peoples, even to do His will at His pleasure by laws of eternity.

3. All nations -- hear with fear and awakening order -- I come soon!

4. I, Jesus Christ, your holy Redeemer speak, and shall be heard soon by all nation leader order, to cease war; to beat war metal into plowshares, pruning hooks for orchards; to use steel and other refined metals on weaponry as usable of only raising crops, machine way.

5. Let all turn all to peace.

6. Earth trembles as a shaking leaf in wind when I cometh.

7. Now be peace negotiating.

8. Now be peace emissary to violent neighbor nations.

9. Now be ready; for full truth of heart intent shall be answered by a just God of almighty power. Amen.

10. Now turn thy face toward Zion, also Old Jerusalem at time earth is of no stable order, as lightnings, thunder causeth all creation to be dissolved, as it were, in power almighty.

11. Now believe leader order needs do full way labor to cease, now, murder of unborn child order entire in own land. Amen.

12. Now do so, even use of contraceptive murder of life of unborn child order; for life begins at conception. Amen.

13. Now cease thy use of the earthly destruction of health, so I can use you as witness to new youth generation that tobacco, drugs of harm, evil way use of own body causeth disease, death, suffering not needed at all.

14. Do so now, so new youth grow to be of greater order health. Amen.

15. These are my own will now, saith your God.

16. Soon all shall hasten when I humble all peoples to hearken at my messaging. Amen.

17. Now let Moldova be hearing my message:

18. I see, in leader order, murder way intent, even war intent.

19. Cease such, for humbling cometh soon on thee if thou art a violent people. Amen.

20. Also let Romania not build any more bomb order, lest you be bombed to thy full way humbling by Russia in future war. Amen.

21. Let Russia remember my other previous warning -- Cease war spirit in thy heart.

22. Full way humbling cometh on thee after thy aggression labor against Europe, United States; also thy own people who suffer because communist order is Godless order.

23. I, God, fear thee not. I shall make myself known to thee by judgment, unto only new peace generation dwells in thy land. Amen.

24. Let United States on Zion land cease manufacture of both armored vehicles of land, air flying order; also all weaponry of armor-piercing ability, to show God you believe I soon cometh to do cleansing of all murder order of intent to kill other peoples by unprovoked attack because of fear other nation doeth same.

25. Now do not attack any other unattacking against thee nation, as three witness order wars are on thee of aggression not of attack against you -- Iraq, Libya, also now war in Afghanistan.

26. Now cease such, withdrawing now.

27. Only be peacemaking by thy influence.

28. Join with Russia only in peace order, not agreeing to bomb any people, as Russia watcheth in jealous violent intent as you, American nation of power, spread own military across many continent land order; soon to be surprised when own navy is helpless.

29. Let all people learn peace now.

30. I cometh, even thy God of all nations, suddenly. Amen.

31. Now come to United Nations. Call in my servant, who is unjustly held, to speak.

32. Question him only to humbly learn my will for thy own land, soon, lest full judgment cometh as a thief in the night, suddenly.

33. I shall tell thee what my will is. Amen.

34. Now come to me, all people on world.

35. Repent, repent, is God's call to all nations. Amen.

36. Now do full message thy people do receive my will written.

37. Now tell my servant you do believe my holy message to all nations.

38. Do so now, else I know you are murder order in own nation. Amen.

39. This to all leader order in power. Amen.

40. Tell all the people I cometh and to prepare.

41. This is my word from on high. Amen.

Jesus Christ, Author

SECTION REVELATION 242

Jesus Christ
Jehovah Son Ahman

I, Jesus Christ, Send My Warning to All Nations of Soon Coming to Deliver All Murder of Unborn Child Order Who Claim Such Is Legal According to Man's Law, Now Knowing God Forbids Such. Hear My Will. Amen.

Revelation of the Lord Jesus Christ
Palestine, Texas
Friday, October 19, 2012

1. Thus saith the Lord to all world, even Jesus Christ, God over heaven and earth: Repent! Repent!

2. Full holy order cleansing cometh on all who are evil intent against youth unborn order. Amen.

3. I, God, am the Life and Light of all world.

4. I give or take mortal living by covenant with my spirit order on eternal world, to grant each son or daughter to do full test passing, according to eternal way holy order of life appointed by God to each.

5. Now be no longer interfering with God's plan for all spirit children order dwelling on telestial world. Amen.

6. Do now repenting, all people of all nations.

7. Do not decrease.

8. Do full responsibility of bringing life, healthy way, forth on world, so child order is stronger than parent order.

9. Raise child order to do right.

10. Do no evil example that child order would mimic in unholy living through parent order. Amen.

11. Now also destroy all armored weapon vehicles, air power of military way that can harm other nation order, if desiring God-given preserving during time I send whirlwind judgment power on Zion land, also on all nation order, saith your God. Amen.

12. Now tell thy people in all lands on world to repent of violent way living; to make also peace with all other people by negotiating in calm peace way. Amen.

13. Let also all be no longer attacking other nation order that do not attack you direct military way. Amen.

14. I, God, am now justified to do full order holy way judgment of God sending on all nations.

15. Now do repenting.

16. Thy mortal way cannot save thee.

17. Only I, God, can do such. Amen.

18. The full warning in book is soon to be sent of all my holy revealing order, of recent order.

19. Read such with soberness. Amen.

Jesus Christ, Author

SECTION REVELATION 243

Jesus Christ
Jehovah Son Ahman

Revelation of the Lord Jesus Christ
Palestine, Texas
Thursday, October 25, 2012

1. The order of communist country of the Yugoslav former nation allied with the Russian order shall do full attack way against neighbor soon; also Russia shall come to conquer, using excuse to assist any of former order Yugoslav order nation way.

2. Do not do unholy attack is the will of your God, even Jesus Christ, to all former Yugoslav nation order, lest war spread. Amen.

Jesus Christ, Author

SECTION REVELATION 244

Jesus Christ
Son Ahman

Revelation of the Lord Jesus Christ
Palestine, Texas
Monday, November 5, 2012

1. Thus saith Jesus Christ to nation on my land of Zion, where my holy City of Righteousness shall soon rise unto all saints assisting of all time, then coming forth in power Celestial order government of eternity --

2. I speak to all world: I cometh. Amen.

3. Do holy repenting, all inhabitants on earth, lest my glory order holy power consume you. Amen.

4. Now be pure in soul, in establishing my Kingdom of purity, holiness, sanctified by my holy power of Spirit of God.

5. All receive a portion of my Celestial love at birth, then evil is given by evil power of the devil; yet my light hath power so you need simply obey voice of inspired enlightenment, through honest prayer to do my holy way in all things; then strength cometh from on high; heavenly power extant overrides evil.

6. Overcome evil of immorality.

7. Defend virtue.

8. Obey eternal principles of truth, eternal truth, that God is Father, governing power over all on world of my coming, saith Jesus Christ. Amen.

9. Now let world hear prophecy: I, Jesus Christ, God over all, cometh soon in the might of Union Eternal Holy Godhood Power, fire from heaven accompanying my coming, to melt all dross, to destroy all corruptible things.

10. Now repent to survive. Amen.

11. Nations who do as I named, also who do removal of all military of nation from all other nations back into own border order, also to destroy all armored vehicles, shall show faith in Jesus Christ, to be of survival order.

Jesus Christ, Author

SECTION REVELATION 245

Jesus Christ
Jehovah Son Ahman

Revelation of the Lord Jesus Christ
Palestine, Texas
Monday, November 5, 2012

1. The Lord speaketh to all nation order a holy word of full order commandment, to now do full honoring of God.

2. Now show faith through full acknowledging Christ your Lord hath right to rule over all earth.

3. Do so by building in capital city of each nation a holy sanctuary.

4. Let it be decorated by thy riches of no idol nor useless work, only to be of furniture of use.

5. Let it contain a writing displayed at entry of "Holiness to the Lord Jesus Christ, Our God Over All".

6. Thus shall thy people be spared, they not of murder nor of immoral living. Amen.

7. When great judgments of cleansing wicked out of all lands is happening, place twelve olive branch wreaths on twelve locations at outside entrance.

8. Do so to show the angel of judgment, sent from eternal world, thy nation submitteth to Christ's rule, else full holy cleansing cometh to thy land, saith your Lord Jesus Christ, God over all nations. Amen.

9. Let also all write to my holy order of pure Priesthood authority, my servant still in bondage, of thy full way loyalty to the Lord of all, Jesus Christ, accounting to God through His anointed Mouthpiece you build a sanctuary for Christ in peace love. Amen.

10. Let also all peoples of pure

repenting in all nations be of soon ready order for my glorious appearing, even

eternal power to be known by all who survive judgment of God. Amen.

Jesus Christ, Author

SECTION REVELATION 246

Jesus Christ
Jehovah Christ

Revelation of the Lord Jesus Christ
Palestine, Texas
Monday, November 12, 2012

1. The coming of your holy God is nigh, saith Jesus Christ; who looked upon all eternity as a God of holy redeeming power, before the world was.

2. I did holy way living from birth, led by angelic guiding;

3. My Father who was Father of my mortal tabernacle, being a Celestial God with earthly body, my mother mortal, of the holy preparing to bring to this world a Son of the Almighty God to world, He having promised all people I would redeem all mankind.

4. Now learn, all you who are heavy-laden with trials of the flesh, come unto your Lord, who offered Himself a holy sacrifice for redemption of all who are born on this world unto full order salvation.

5. I can heal you.

6. I am God over all.

7. I elevate faithful order to eternal life; sin way I judge unto eternal punishing. Amen.

8. Now do full repenting, all people on world.

9. I come. Nothing shall remain of sin way. Amen.

10. The holy God of all is first humbled to do His Father's will.

11. Do so always, not of self way at all. Amen.

12. Thus saith the Lord Jesus Christ unto all people of the nation of United States: Though you celebrate President of nation re-elected, know he is in transgressing order, not hearing my peace of my Spirit whisper correct principle; yet you as a nation uphold one in power who hath upheld murder of unborn youth order; thus I decry against all who knowing order uphold shedding of innocent blood of the most helpless dependent of all children, the unborn.

13. Now repent, for my word of warning now to all peoples on world hath been sounded.

14. And like old Babylon, Babel, other ancient peoples of great power on world, thy full power shall be taken, given to mine elect of Priesthood.

15. Thy navy shall diminish in usefulness order; thy missile power is depleted by war use; thy army is volunteer of desiring to shed blood in battle not of self-defense alone.

16. Thus I, God, do say, the power of God resteth on mine Israel, soon to go forth conquering all neighbor nations.

17. Now be of more holy way, this warning to nation of the free order defending all inalienable rights of all world; yet murder of unborn child order is on thy souls. Amen.

18. Now let President of nation be more upholding domestic defense, not of attack on faraway lands anymore.

19. Declare no war against any, save I, God, command.

20. Cleanse thy ruler order of Sodom, of adultery, of drug use, also of bribery way dishonorable ruling.

21. Now do so.

22. Investigate CIA also for secret murder way of private portion not of reporting to any to keep their secret as silent.

23. Let a full investigating happen, lest President be target of secret attack by CIA in near future.

24. John F. Kennedy was thus taken by secret CIA evil combining; other government order bowing in secret combining with rich money order in nation who felt threatened by John Kennedy's proposal to return to gold way of all money needing gold order backing to keep economic power solid. Amen.

25. Now know when leader doth not protect most helpless of all children, of unborn child order, under attack by government sanction upholding practice of legal contraceptive evil life-taking order, also abortion of even full term developed

unborn child order; behold I say unto you, all nation is of taint in mine eyes of bloodletting. Amen.

26. Repent, all people of nation. Repent, lest God power judgment order cometh to cleanse land entire way. Amen.

27. Now learn I know all things.

28. My thousand years of peace is now to begin on earth; my coming is nigh; no man knoweth the exact time, only my Father in heaven.

29. Now cleanse all. Amen.

30. Zion is soon to be only ruling governing power on entire world, as I appear in mighty power to all people, making all evil intent order of all sin way afraid.

31. Do the full repentance, is my will to all nation order of all world. Amen.

32. The war of army power on world soon cometh.

33. Entire land of Zion shall be of war.

34. Be ready. Amen.

35. Now know I shall preserve my people. Amen.

36. Tell all people of world I cometh, saith Jesus Christ, your holy Lord. Amen.

37. Now be of truth-telling of own sin, not of seeking to name other person's sin, to be holy repenting holy labor.

38. Forgive all others on earth to be forgiven of me, your God. Amen.

39. Forgiveness order is to do good, not to join evil way at all.

40. Now do own truth-telling to me, your Redeemer. Amen.

41. The holy Advent of God includeth disastrous cleansing; a holy purging of world of all murder of unborn child order; thus all people on earth shall be judged.

42. A holy power of peace shall rest upon all pure in soul to preserve them.

43. Fear cometh on evil-intending

people such that only clean pure thought living can be Celestial power receiving, unto preserving.

44. Promote peace-love-joy power extant in own life, all people on world. Amen.

45. Now repent, repent, all people of all lands on world, to survive my cleansing authority, soon to be poured out without measure, eternal power unto world becoming terrestrial more holy condition. Amen.

Jesus Christ, Author

SECTION REVELATION 247

Jesus Christ
Son Ahman

Revelation of the Lord Jesus Christ
Palestine, Texas
Friday, November 16, 2012

1. I, Jesus Christ, tell nation of Israel, I see secret murder way of plane unpiloted by satellite control, to destroy and assassinate people of no direct way to defend self in a way to show innocence of self-defending in battle.

2. Now cease use of unhallowed violence way, lest I cause thy own sin to come on you full measure. Amen.

3. Also, do not use nuclear weapon in thy possession at all, lest most of thine own people perish in retaliation attack. Amen.

Jesus Christ, Author

Chapter 11

Second Edition Continued Revealings

SECTION REVELATION 248

Fundamentalist Church of Jesus Christ of Latter-day Saints
P.O. Box 840459
Hildale, Utah 84784

Thus Saith the Lord to the Nation of Brazil, Even Son Ahman, Who Is Jesus Christ:

Revelation of the Lord Jesus Christ
Big Lake, Texas
Saturday, March 26, 2011

1. I, the Lord, now give my word concerning the nation of Brazil:

2. Corrupt art thou. Thou shalt fall.

3. You reek with corruption from within, and I shall send a judgment measured to your corruption.

4. And I send forth my word to thee:

5. There shall be a remnant of those whom you call the Aborigines.

6. They are of the House of Israel, and they shall receive that land of me, while all those of a corrupt nature shall fall, being swept off by a desolating scourge and also other judgments.

7. Thou art corrupt, and you corrupt the way of many nations by allowing your carnivals of corruption, your evils of organized crime, and great evils in your government and laws that deride against innocence, that fight against life.

8. Thus, you are corrupt before me, and I will send my judgment upon you,

that you remain not a nation to deride against your God anymore.

9. I, the Lord, send you this word; and those in your borders who can repent, let them hear my word:

10. Touch not the unclean gentile way, lest you go down with the wicked.

11. And come out of this wicked generation in the murder of unborn children, and adultery, and Sodom, and other licentious and immoral practices; for you cannot stand, saith the Lord, against a just God who seeth and knoweth all things.

12. Thus may Brazil receive my message, of a soon happening, to their embassy.

13. Though it be in this land of America, where the United States of America dwells, they shall receive my word. Amen.

14. Thus saith Jesus Christ. Amen.

SECTION REVELATION 249

Jesus Christ
Jehovah Son Ahman

I, Jesus Christ, Speak to All Nations, Holy Will of God, Even Father Over All, to Repent, to Be Holy; to Do Full Receiving Prophecy Order of Soon Happenings on World; to Know Great Truths Come Soon, Unobstructed by Prejudices of Men. Receive My Will of Holy Revealing With Solemn Hearts Into Eternity:

Revelation of the Lord Jesus Christ
Palestine, Texas
Friday, May 10, 2013

1. I, God, speak to all people on world: Now cometh season of full order destructing power from heaven --

2. Cities destroyed; nations bankrupt, in ruin; people fleeing with no place to reside in safe order; upheaval entire of the Babylon empire of all nations on world.

3. Read John my Beloved in New Testament, Book of Revelation, to now Babylon suddenly falleth, and all wicked peoples mourn.

4. Now come to me, Jesus Christ, before full judgment cometh on all world.

5. Die not in evil condition.

6. This life is for preparing for eternal life with God, not evil purposes at all, as all are accountable for sojourn on world of testing. Amen.

7. Let all rulers of all lands on world learn what they never considered.

8. Drug war in Brazil bringeth full scourging of overflowing continued sickness, millions dying suddenly.

9. Flame order burneth Albany.

10. Drought destroyeth the land of America.

11. Full war in North America soon is on land.

12. Let all call on God in now day of seeming peace, so when full order judgments cometh, you can do holy surviving.

13. Now do thy sackcloth and ashes repenting, lest full taking of all unprepared peoples is so constant, thy heart faileth all such.

14. Come, O Zion.

15. Now be only former glory of Enoch and his city, which city of holiness soon cometh from another planet in solar holy sun system.

16. Also Ten Order Tribes of Israel cometh, to also help cleanse all wicked order on Zion land.

17. Now awake, O people on North America.

18. Love of man, heart and soul, hardeneth among all peoples.

19. Now know I reject halfhearted living; part for God, other for Lucifer, who rejected all good, fled with followers to this earth from heavenly orbit.

20. Now do full holy repenting.

21. God-power can no man overthrow, saith Jesus Christ, the God over all. Amen.

22. Tell United Nations this, my will, to all resign from ambassador, your peoples, if they yet follow murder order of unborn child order.

23. Also call on thy people to rather die in earthly life, rather than taking innocence of living. Amen.

24. Holy God cometh in flaming fire, which fire shall pour forth all other judgments.

25. Christian religious orders all deny portion of prophecy of John Beloved concerning great war.

26. Now do full repenting, so I, God, can spare all honest in heart. Amen.

27. All nations, saith Jesus Christ, now cease all murder of unborn child order, or I shall. Amen.

28. Now know this is my word, not man's.

29. Repent, all peoples, lest full prophecy is upon world, to the sweeping the wicked off world. Amen.

30. Holy, holy art thou, Lord God of host! Come to rescue the truly penitent.

31. Do so before all peoples are full of element of darkness. Amen.

32. I, God, seeth and knoweth all things.

33. Nothing is hidden from me, your very souls and thoughts known to me always; for my holy power of Spirit Celestial holy order penetrates all things, gives life to all things, even you, all people on world.

34. Know my holy power is within reach to all believing; who pray, repent, and do only love-kind way toward all.

35. Be ready for full power to stop many armies in invasion of my land of Old Jerusalem after murder of all mannerism is swept off land by war, pestilence, famine, other power order of God, to cleanse all off world who love and believe a lie.

36. Now repent, all peoples on earth. Amen.

37. Let Israel repent of assassinating labor, also all nation order, saith Jesus Christ. Amen.

38. Israel must rise in defending law, not aspiring. Amen.

39. Let Syria be no more violent. Amen.

40. Also let Albania cease multiple way of secret government murderings.

41. Let all nations now be pure peace love-power of God, for I cometh soon to earth in power heavenly. Amen.

42. Now come to me, your holy Lord Redeemer, Eternal Peace Friend, to earn my approbation unto eternal life. Amen.

43. When rain mixed with fire on ground cometh, know pestilence order from heaven is on earth.

44. Prepare. Amen.

45. Also cometh parts of earth soon, to be in exact place where such left for time of preserving some on world.

46. When these portions return, then cometh wind, rain, hail, shaking of world, like a drunken man reeling to and fro, causing such wicked cities as in Nevada, in New Jersey, of gambling capitals order, for such promote all living to get gain;

47. All such shall be stopped. Amen.

48. Now come to thy God who made you, through Priesthood. Amen.

49. Let also Mormon Church, as world calls such, repent, as I shall cause Mount Olympus to fall on Salt Lake City, to make promised prophecy fulfilled, that Salt Lake

would be a lake again, Mount Olympus falling across valley in world land pressure explosion.

50. That city is my enemy now. Amen.

51. Now repent, the now fully apostate church of my name, which broke away from my Priesthood in 1890, Wilford Woodruff warned by me in 1890 to not sign agreement with hell, covenant of death as Isaiah foresaw.

52. Now know only Fundamentalist Church is my own true saving power in Priesthood on world. Amen.

53. Let this now be heard by all peoples on world. Amen.

54. He who divideth the world knoweth how to gentle way join parts to leave other parts of world untouched by judgment power.

55. Know desolating sickness is soon upon all land of Zion.

56. Overcome all immoral ways.

57. Cease unholy use of tobacco, of strong liquors; all destructive to mortal living.

58. Let also all parent order cease using the contraceptive methods to cause loss of unborn child order.

59. Also cease use of the way of immoral dressing. Amen.

60. When the people use strong drink and tobacco for vanity social living, they do harm to all future child order they do bring forth.

61. Also use of abortion physician order is sin unto death, all such being guilty on earth, guilty of murder of unborn child.

62. Now know time is short to repent.

63. Desire to promote principles of life.

64. I who hath the heavens in my power, all people order on world, again name time is soon for glorious appearing of Jesus Christ in glory holy order power.

65. Holify thy own life, thinking, desires, to please God, to stand honorable before Him who is the Life of all. Amen.

66. I, God, do full warning concerning national alliancing, NATO of Europe defending; also Pacific Ocean national alliance with South Korea; other Asian nation order: Traitor labor hath already betrayed full defending strategy in both alliancing organized, unto United States betrayed by other nation order in both locatings.

67. Thus, when defending is of full need, all military movement is already known to soon coming enemy.

68. You must not rely on other nation order for full knowing own military movement.

69. Do independent plan of own nation labor of movement order, so enemy is not of full knowing all thy military defense labor.

70. Thus is the will of God. Amen.

71. Let also England national alliance with Great Britain beware France not of full order assisting when full attack of Russian alliance cometh against most European nation order. Amen.

72. This is my will, to not be first to use any mass destructive weapon order; and only as I, God, guide.

73. Let my will be sought by all in day of full order conflict, through my servant Warren Jeffs, when you see my deliverance for my Church in now United States not of such way to deliver my holy order of Church and Priesthood from own attack of legal, illegal way; thus this nation hinders my Zion from full order rising at present, which shall result in whole nation feeling my judgment order soon.

74. Let my servant go. Let my people receive full order of my consecrated lands now under attack by governing state powers by influence of apostate lies.

75. Let my holy order of Priesthood on world be consulted before any nation goeth to war against any other nation, is the will of Jesus Christ, your God. Amen.

SECTION REVELATION 250

Jesus Christ
Jehovah Son Ahman

I, Jehovah Christ, Your Lord, Speaketh My Own Word to All People on World, to Be Answered on All Who Are of Understanding, Even Eternal Judgment in Hereafter in Full Order of Judging. Amen.

Revelation of the Lord Jesus Christ
Palestine, Texas
Wednesday, May 22, 2013

1. I, Jesus Christ, Redeemer and Holy Lord over all, speak to all nation order, even He who is Creator of world, Jehovah Christ:

2. Come unto thy God and now overthrow the way of unborn child murder by legal way consent.

3. Also, cast out of power in all nations, by peace way, ruler order who are of legal upholding murder of unborn child order.

4. Do this to be more ready for my coming, to be preserved by God through soon coming whirlwind judgments of God, justified by my holy word published to all nations. Amen.

5. Now do full holy repentance, all peoples on world of my soon Advent. Amen.

SECTION REVELATION 251

Jesus Christ
Jehovah Son Ahman

I, Jesus Christ, of the Order of Governing Authority Over All the Earth, Speak Final Full Warning Unto All Peoples, Rulers of the Nations, a Holy Call to Be of Now Hearing. Amen.

Revelation of the Lord Jesus Christ
Palestine, Texas
Thursday, May 30, 2013

1. The great Creator of heaven, world of now dwelling of the order of mortal living, my holy will to all world:

2. Sin way entire of immoral living in same gender legal marriage is of Lucifer, who enticeth way unto the order of no life increase in union of same gender, full Sodom order.

3. Let not any people legal way uphold the sin of Sodom; and be of no way living sin of no marriage Sodom life of full God judgment.

4. Let government be more labor doing of no Sodom sin among their nation. Amen.

5. Let the full order of the United Nations be of no Sodom sin in governing any other land.

6. No such practice of Sodom can have the sure gift of my blessing order. Amen.

7. Let all full order governing authority in all lands cleanse them of Sodom from way of legislating power, by law governing the powers of legislating. Amen.

8. The full way of thy military to be victory order in justified defense of own nation is to have no soldiery of sin

of Sodom at all, for such shall thy Lord overthrow. Amen.

9. The full labor to purge thy nation is to only legalize order of purity, to have a man have woman for family of child order, no union of out-of-marriage way.

10. Now be pure. Amen.

11. The order of marriage is of the Bible order of Adam having Eve for wife, unto procreating, to multiply posterity unto the purpose of world's creating.

12. The sin of Sodom is to depopulate world in sin of no increase, a full way to do the destroying life and purity of the nation.

13. Let all speedily do full holy order of repenting. Amen.

14. I, Lord of all, cometh. Amen.

15. The full way of purity includeth no adultery, also respect of living unto God, to please Him who made you.

16. No longer do Sodom nor adultery way. Amen.

17. In the full glory of heaven, I, Jesus Christ, come soon, to recompense to each, full reward for all done in mortal living.

18. Now know nothing is hidden from me.

19. Do full repenting soon, to be

surviving whirlwind judgment order; also full labor to guide child order to bettering their life unto moral living.

20. Now do so, is the will of God to all peoples on earth.

21. Let Bible history be of the reading of my full judgment on the order of nations who degraded unto sin of immoral living -- many nations destroyed after I gave my own will to kings, rulers over powerful nations -- murder of both the living order of born child order, also unborn child murder of abortion doing; all such nations of full order destroyed by judgment of God.

22. I am He of full order judging.

23. Sin of the nation order is known in heaven, on earth.

24. Cease war preparing.

25. Do full obedience to my will, to draw military into own lands, lest world conflict start in alliance order defending.

26. Let no order of mass-destructive weapon unholy murder of mass of peoples with the loss of many in nuclear order, other new weapon way of bright power energy of life-destroying; weapon of design in United States, Russia order; both to not create weapon now in planning.

27. Let such cease.

28. Do only peace labor, that I, God, can preserve thy nation, even in all lands. Amen.

29. Now do the full cleansing of own peoples, not to war against other nations.

30. No more weapon selling to small violent nation order, is the will of God. Amen.

31. Let not the way of the nation order join in aggression.

32. Let all be peace order. Amen.

33. Raise youth with only pure language of no immoral speaking in home, school, church order way, to raise them unto pure way.

34. This is my will, saith Jesus Christ, to all people on world. Amen.

SECTION REVELATION 252

Jesus Christ
Jehovah Christ Son Ahman

I, Your Holy Lord Jesus Christ, Speak Holy Will to All Peoples on World, to Make Peace. Hear My Will:

Revelation of the Lord Jesus Christ
Palestine, Texas
Friday, July 5, 2013

1. Thus speaketh the holy God over all world, even the Creator of heaven, earth; all power to govern in Millennium of Peace: I am now of full ready full order power to do full governing order, to rule righteous and holy order of full power. Amen.

2. Now be pure, all in nation now on Zion land.

3. I, Jesus Christ, now declare all to be holy if remaining, of my power.

4. Let all be subject to God power, by full way peace obedience.

5. Now come to me, your Redeemer, is the will of my word to thy having full order accounting to the Judge of all. Amen.

6. Let nation of Great Britain be of full help defending the full order of NATO confidence labor in now order, to be no order traitor to defense of Europe.

7. Now look into privacy keeping in own military command, to not be of betrayal in soon order of invading power in Europe. Amen.

8. Now call on my full order of United Holy Full Order of full world national government of Church of full authorized and pure Kingdom of God, my council of the full power to govern all nation order, to know my will.

9. Thus I, God, speak unto all government power order: Now be of acknowledging your holy God, unto the coming of Him to all nation order on world.

10. Come unto me, and have truth eternal; yea, only peace power and full holy authority of the government of Jesus Christ as thy true holy way to govern; else judgment power of the Creator over all shall be full power on earth. Amen.

11. I call on nation of the order of my soon order of Israel full gathered order now old holy land of Jerusalem of old -- Let not assassination evil and murder of the order of secret sudden and unneeded death labor against the unproved enemy you do not know are the work against thee.

12. Now be of no order in thy way to unrighteously do a way to destroy supposed leader order; to only capture accused, try and do true order full justified sure proved by law of tribunal justice.

13. I, God, call on all nation order to cease evil of the way to be a full order of illegal life-taking and harm way in the power to murder.

14. Now know God speaketh -- None can escape my judging in full knowing all order of the full truth.

15. Let governing order on all world make peace among you, lest I, God, do full holy power judging. Amen.

16. Let nation of Turkey be no longer traitor of NATO defending, to be confidence and alliance peace order, of all ability to help also United States, as the enemy is determined to overthrow national authority your now Prime Minister of the way to do own compromising.

17. Now do full way strengthening waterway to Black Sea, as called among nation order.

18. Do full way causing Istanbul to be of full order of military strength, as such is target of the order of invading, of Greece and the jealous order of yestertime enemy order of full way taking the full defending of water straits of the full Mediterranean Sea access of Black Sea.

19. Let Turkey nation be examining own loyal way of the full truth of military connecting with spy order of any order foreign nation now happening. Amen.

20. Let all nation order of nuclear weapon holding of the world entire, meet to now agree unto full destroying all nuclear order mass-destructing weapons.

21. This to be now doing, is the holy way to make peace.

22. Let all now assemble, lest world order of all lands reach no peace agreement unto full order war.

23. Let my will be unto all now

existing and developing nuclear weapon nations now do this. Amen.

24. I, God, even thy Lord and holy Redeemer, reveal Quebec shall be of full war as avenue of enemy into Canada, also New York when no army of large order defending is on locating there on river, unto a full way access by present no-army of great order in place.

25. Canada, now do full order recall from all foreign nation order, to do full ready way defending own nation.

26. Do so soon. Amen.

27. Nation of Japan, be of fulfilling my word of previous sending, lest full order of economic loss of rich order fall unto economic full collapse.

28. Let bank order do loans not unto lands where child prostituting of slave order at all.

29. Do not condone evil of child prostituting by investing in nation order that live by slave unholy forced labor of business trade order.

30. Such is the nation of Thailand, also in Myanmar, of the robbing of poor, to be child forcing unto the harm of family order.

31. Let all nation order bring the national way business of slave forced labor, to do no use of any produced items by such labor, so no nation profits or gain monetary order increase.

32. Now do this peace way, not attack of many nations, so all is of peace. Amen.

33. Tell all nation order, bank order, to now do away with this great evil of child slave forced labor, lest own nation also reveal own support of child violent way by government of full such harm. Amen.

34. I soon cometh, even thy Lord, unto all people on earth.

35. I bring all full power to rule in Celestial order power among the way of nation order on world for a Millennial order, a full way of all people of world knowing I am with Zion, a holy way on world to live on full order heavenly New Era of Peace world.

36. Let all now read Isaiah of Zion coming.

37. Do so, and be ready. Amen.

38. The God of all world also is of the order to purify all who come unto the full holy power to learn of me, a holy God of eternal holy full creating power.

39. Be of me, all nations on earth, to be full surviving judgment of God full order cleansing. Amen.

40. Let all my Church be purifying own living even as I have revealed.

41. Do not mingle with Babylon of fallen order, lest first way order power judgment cleansing remove all hypocrite lying people breaking order of covenants Celestial.

42. Now be my Zion, all my Union Eternal Holy Order. Amen.

43. Let all not of my Church repent as I have revealed my will to all peoples, of child murder order of unborn child order, of adultery, Sodom, licentiousness, all sin of full knowing wrong is done. Amen.

44. Thus saith the Lord, your Redeemer, even Jesus Christ, a full order message to nation order: Repent, repent, for my holy way is only pure order holy life living by praying always, unto the prayer of pure innocence living before me. Amen.

SECTION REVELATION 253

Jesus Christ
Jehovah Son Ahman

I, Your Lord Jesus Christ, Send Full Warning to All Peoples on Earth, This My Will to Cease Murder Order; Make Peace Now.

Revelation of the Lord Jesus Christ
Palestine, Texas
Friday, July 12, 2013

1. Thus saith Jesus Christ, Redeemer and Creator of all flesh on earth, to all peoples on world: Come to the now awakened reality God lives, and rules over all heaven and world of thy now living a life of testing, to be judged by me, Jesus Christ, Son of God, who was holy in my administrating time in the flesh; who is God of all nations.

2. Now awake to my truth of eternal order -- You cannot hide anything from me, who knoweth all hidden and false evil order, to subjugate Lucifer unto no power over souls of purity abiding godly living.

3. Now be awake to time of full holy judgments of my giving world cleansing of all murder order entire.

4. Let all cast off such in full, that you may be of survival. Amen.

5. Now be awake in mind to full revealed truth -- I, God, am of eternity power, unto power of the holy power to hold world and heaven in organizing all creation, all on earth known by my all-seeing eye, the power of Godhood atonement Holy Redeemer God power; thus nothing hidden.

6. Now let all lives be pure, to escape all power of eternity damnation of evil order.

7. Let all repent, is the call of thy Lord. Amen.

8. The full order to repent includeth atoning, even here on earth, for a way of justifying God to redeem soul of all who can repair life.

9. Murder is taking life in evil intent, often the way of violence or life-harm order in unholy order of child unborn child life-taking; whether open order to a living fetus removal unto death, or contraceptive using that does life-taking at near-time of concepting.

10. Now know all life is in my power to exist.

11. I know when murder intent was in heart of full doing, or intent to do harm unto life order.

12. Thus I, God, shall judge all flesh in ruling over all world forever, always thy Judge. Amen.

13. My holy will is to all nations to now do change of law to have no abortion labor of murder; to do prosecution of such by rule of law; to do away with the unholy murder way.

14. Let such be now. Amen.

15. Also pull all army order, military order back into own alerted need of peace

order, own national land, so all know no evil attack is coming.

16. Know I, God, send soon stop to all war, as leader order do all peace negotiating, to preserve life.

17. Do so now. Amen.

18. Let all of pure peace-loving in all world write to leader of own land, asking for negotiating order, to bring peace to all nations.

19. Let this now happen in all war-lands.

20. A holy way is to watch peace way with silent peace order surrounding all violent order, with hope they also stay of no way murder labor. Amen.

21. Surround all such military order of evil use of the way of the violent way, by millions.

22. Do so now, peace way. Amen.

23. Let United Nations cease all military labor on world entire, is my way to do peace in full order way; not to send ambassador, save of only peace.

24. Remember my order I, God, did through a man of peace in Gandhi, in nation of violent order of religion against religion; he of fasting order until violent way stopped.

25. Rather do the peace order, all leaders of nations, to not be of fear; for God shall intervene if of no evil murder secret assassinating way of harm secret order.

26. Let such cease, not hidden at all from my all-seeing eye. Amen.

27. Now learn my way to humble nation order --

28. Famine of no way to feed the order of starving order soon on world.

29. You shall all feel my power of humbling if violence order is thy way. Amen.

30. Let United States also stop aggression in all war order, now, to be full power peace order, never attacking other nation of no aggression against you.

31. Let only self-defending be of thy holy order to be no aggressive unholy order.

32. I shall humble all of aggression with no first peace offering. Amen.

33. Now do full order new leader electing if present leader is of the army using of no way justified order.

34. Let all peace call be through new elected peace-example way, now. Amen.

35. My holy order is to offer negotiating peace way.

36. Let this now do full way order peace order among all peoples, lest great world war soon happeneth; as John my Beloved saw in vision, now in Book of Revelation order, Bible, last book in my holy Bible known to all nations.

37. Repent, make peace among all nations.

38. Offer to help feed the starving in all nations.

39. There is enough and to be full no way order of death by starvation, if all cooperate now. Amen.

40. The United Nations also must stop promotion of unholy unrestricted aborting unborn child order entire, lest I, God, do full order no way use of such an unholy order of murder of unborn child order.

41. A way of purifying is to not use contraceptive unholy order.

42. Do full order legal labor in all nations to do away with all adultery, Sodom unholy living entire, so I, God, shall spare the more righteous of purity way order. Amen.

43. Now do this for your own people's sake, saith Jesus Christ.

44. A way to do the change of the evil law-upholding and protecting sin way of immoral adultery, Sodom way, is to place only those in authority in own nation of the more pure way personal living. Amen.

45. Now do full examining for purity living of all leader order.

46. I, God, shall reveal to thy people who in thy nation is of more purity living through my servant Warren Jeffs, as you send ambassador to visit with real intent to learn God's word of cleansing holy living order, no immoral, more noble-in-heart leader to be upheld by the nation.

47. I know who is honorable in truth-order. Amen.

48. When nation order seeketh peace, only I, your God, can guide.

49. Let this be known -- I of eternity knowledge cometh to establish peace on world, after murder way order in nation order is of full order way removed by my holy order judgment of whirlwind full natural order; pestilence, famine, earthquake, hail; all God-sending, until murder way is not in the nation order.

50. This from thy holy God, Jesus Christ, soon to appear in full glory order of heaven. Amen.

51. I, God, even Jesus Christ, speak to Israel nation: Do not go to war in the first provocation at all, to be of sure way justified.

52. Do defense order to degree of being attacked, after the full peace order of many attempts to make peace.

53. This from Jehovah, who is the God of Abraham. Amen.

54. Thus saith the Lord who rules over all people on world: Do full pure way peace holy order, no war nor assassinating secret murder.

55. Do only the full order peace labor, is the now full message of God to all nation order. Amen.

SECTION REVELATION 254

Jesus Christ
Jehovah Christ, Son Ahman

I, Your Holy Lord, Jesus Christ, Send My Own Will to All People on World, Unto Final Warning; to Do Awakening Unto My Full Order Holy Will Being Purity Living, Purity Peace Holy Living. Hear My Will:

Revelation of the Lord Jesus Christ
Palestine, Texas
Tuesday, July 23, 2013

1. The holy God speaketh: Do no order murder of unborn child order in all world.

2. Such is full eternity damnation unto suffer order eternal.

3. Let this go forth to all world.

4. Now do full order law holy way to do no way government legal order allowing murder of child unborn youth.

5. Be all of purity living in own living.

6. Do no murder of violent order.

7. I shall recompense full order all the full way reward order as you hath done unto all in mortal life.

8. Do no such corrupt order of slave order of young order child forcing way labor.

9. Do no way prostitution of female order, nor male order of young and adult order, lest all destroy virtue unto full judgment of my giving.

10. A holy order is to promote pure order in all nations by legal order.

11. Now do this in all lands, peoples, kindreds, nations.

12. Let United Nations Assembly vote for World Health Organization to do no use of contraceptive way to do the losing child unborn way, unto no legal order aborting, nor legal contracepting; for such is full way losing child unborn life.

13. Do this soon, is my will to all people on world, is my full word on such evil of full murder of unborn child order.

14. A holy God speaketh, even God over all creation, Jesus Christ, the Life and the Light of all nations. Amen.

15. Let the full order holy way living the way unto peace order of no nuclear order of all people on world choosing national order no such weapon order.

16. Thus do now, so I can be full pure order governing power on world soon to come, to all seeing glory Celestial order in full among Zion order in both Old Israel and in Zion land New Jerusalem order, mine abode on both order governing all nations in pure order peace holy power, eternal power holy order. Amen.

17. Tell President of both Russia, also United States, to do full negotiating to do full peace holy living, soon, so all fear of war unholy way is not in world; as both nuclear nation order are of capable full loss of life on world entire when nuclear war is of thy full power on earth.

18. Do so now; peace unto no nuclear war, all nuclear order weapon nation order; also join in full-order destroying nuclear order weapon order.

19. I have power to destroy all world with my full Godhood order; yet I control life by love power, giving all lifetime on world to test all.

20. Thy nuclear order of weapon order is not of me at all, only Luciferian order to destroy all world, is his way to take all in death.

21. Do such now, negotiating of all nuclear lands holding weapons nuclear way, doing no more weapon making.

22. Let Iran not build weapon of small nuclear order, hiding such in a planned full harm to the order of Annapolis Naval Center in a boat close offshore; such is unholy plan of Iran.

23. Do no more preparing such. Amen.

24. Let also Pakistan no longer build nuclear order weapon order, lest full use destroyeth own land entire by retaliating India land of own fault proud unholy living false way thinking that war will destroy enemy India land.

25. Such is able to destroy all opponents in full defending.

26. Do such negotiating to never use nuclear weapon order at all, is God's will now.

27. A holy God cometh.

28. Do full disarming nuclear weapon order in all world, lest my power to disarm

sudden order cleanseth such from all lands soon happening.

29. Let Israel never do nuclear order weapon use, or thou shalt be no order nation survival order until I, God, intervene in my holy power to gather peace order Israel of God defending such on world unto full prophecy fulfilling. Amen.

30. Now tell all world Christ Jesus is God over all earth, heaven order, on full earth knowing I am among my Zion holy order people, even among Israel of my full apostle holy order on Zion land; also two sons Isaiah foretold in Old Israel, called to testify Christ hath come to Israel in Old Jerusalem by apostle testimony that I came in humble holy administer order to bless all world by self-order suffering for all peoples on world, unto conquering death, unto resurrection to the full judging all in eternity after time of suffer order of wicked.

31. Now let Moslem religion order lands do full no attack against Israel, nor among each other at all.

32. Thy religion is not of Allah God, as you call me; thus I am God telling all to make holy peace now.

33. Do so now, is my most fervent call; thus no world order violence way war at time of my intervening in all lands. Amen.

34. Now let Mauritania cease living child young child murder by now stopping such doing, lest a full mountain falleth on violent order ruler who doth do murder of parent child order to subjugate people out of fear child order is taken and killed.

35. Stop now all such, lest also famine cometh on you sudden way.

36. I have spoken it. Amen.

37. Tell Sudan now is time for peace negotiation.

38. No more war.

39. Famine is on thee to humble all in Sudan.

40. Do not help Libya or other border land Ethiopia in any war labor; nor to be sudden nuclear attacked land, losing all, by China doing preserving ally of signed secret order Somalia.

41. Let China do full nuclear no nuclear weapon labor. Amen.

42. Order, in full, weapon nuclear disarming.

43. Do so, to be true peace people.

44. Let Nepal be peace holy order, China no longer enemy order unto violent labor.

45. I, God, have spoken, and hath all order recompense on China when full restoring of part of world of Prophet Peleg is on my way to restore.

46. Such shall be people I use in future to destroy China from full murder unholy labor child murder unholy murder of unborn child order.

47. Now cease force order, on parent unholy pressure way order, to use abortive way, contraceptive unholy loss of child unborn fetus order.

48. Now cease this most heinous practice; and I shall do full need population feeding sufficient, unto all world prospering under reign of Christ on the land of Zion. Amen.

49. Let island land Samoa, all population, move to a large land of Asia, in knowing island shall be no more island soon.

50. Do so now.

51. Be of full order moved; no one remain on Samoa, nor other islands of the lowland way in Asia Pacific area -- a portion of prophesy land returning, in John Beloved prophecy, cometh -- land of coming into water order, destroying

shipping of evil order Babylon, spiritual order of Babylon, among all rich people on world order, fulfilling also land of America, Zion order cometh. Amen.

52. Who can withstand God?

53. I come soon.

54. Repent, repent, of all murder way soon, is my way to establish peace on world for a thousand years.

55. Zion in old order Enoch people cometh soon, also Melchizedek and people of full Zion order returning to world -- all Zion order uniting to govern all lands in joy-peace love of God holy order -- binding satan; peace of knowing I, God, reigneth through my authority on world, even Prophet order of all years, of full order heaven coming to world to govern all people. Amen.

56. Now let this be my full order holy will, to let my servant Warren Jeffs be of the freedom to do full counseling of United Nations, soon, so I can reveal my governing holy order, God-given, God-led, God-empowering; all unto peace love joy in God holy order.

57. I soon cometh.

58. Do such now. Amen.

59. Read my holy book published to all nation order, my full order holy Bible prophecy of John in the last portion of judgment order, chapters 8, 9, 16 -- all speak of God sending star or part of world return order.

60. He saw most die who were sin way unholy living, Babylon, spiritual and earthly Babylon perishing full order, by my glory power.

61. I can tell all nation order how to overcome violent unholy order through my servant Prophet I have ordained of full Priesthood now holding, my order of full power salvation administering unto all nations, now on world since I appeared to my Prophet Joseph Smith, whose holy way is well published, as my full order Proclamation printed in Jesus Christ Book of Warning now among thee in all nation holy sent order recent time.

62. Let library order keep all my letter order of full referencing full messaging of God to all people on world.

63. Now know Warren Jeffs is missionary of pure power of eternity power Priesthood holy order to give word of God.

64. Do no harm to he of apostle order, my full Keyholder power on world, lest sudden storm of great destruction cometh on land of him dwelling.

65. Let all in nation of New Jerusalem soon building in place I design to do full order power government over all world, living among men in Celestial power.

66. Let nation now do no harm in taking holy temple from my people.

67. Let all land in Short Creek Utah, Arizona order be restored to my Church, no government unholy order do such unholy way; unto full returning; with soon governing power of full order returning all land of Canada to my people.

68. Now do so, lest mountain full order judgment falleth on all cities of thieving land of capital of state or province order, to stop such stealing by false legal order.

69. I have all power to deliver mine elect people of my holy Zion holy labor.

70. Now return my consecrated lands in full by legislature repaying all loss order soon, so I may do full preparing my order of Zion order for my coming, is the will of the Lord to all such. Amen.

71. Let also Texas return all damaging.

72. Let all they were unholy way

seizing restore such to my people, all such as was of holy record holy keeping on temple order holding.

73. Do no longer use of seizing land.

74. I shall do more for Texas way healing if legislature, governor, judge order do full releasing Prophet and other order Church sons in bondage unholy bondage held in prison.

75. Now do so; also do no more prosecution of my people who only do my way of Zion living. Amen.

SECTION REVELATION 255

Jesus Christ
Jehovah Christ, Son Ahman

I, Your Lord, Speak to All People on Earth, My Holy Love Pure Way Peace Order. Hear My Will:

Revelation of the Lord Jesus Christ
Palestine, Texas
Monday, July 29, 2013

Holy Will of God

1. Thus saith the holy God over all the creation order of all that exists, even Jesus Christ, Son Ahman, the Holy One of Israel, who hath all power unto full redemption order to raise all from grave of death unto eternal living of the salvation earned:

2. Now be holy unto full preparing by living unto God.

3. Do so now. Amen.

4. Let all nation order come to my power of holy authority, to learn my will of the order of full way to please God, so I, your God, can heal all who remain in all lands after whirlwind judgments of God, of the way to humble all unto repenting. Amen.

5. Let not the evil of child unborn murder be in land of thy order of living on world.

6. I come soon to all people of world.

7. Now do full order holy repenting, changing unto my holy will, learning to do only purity living.

8. Now do full change, not just lip-service of no repented order; of changing to more godly order of thy Lord, who speaketh, even Jesus Christ, God over all heaven order, earth order, worlds of my creating.

9. Unbelief is thy doom, entire order, if no heed given to the full order warning order. Amen.

10. Do no order of war at all.

11. Despotic nation order do full order loss of all by God-given power of full humbling soon, a holy order repenting order of change, now. Amen.

12. Let representative come to him,

my Prophet Warren Jeffs, to do full order receiving my will concerning thy nation.

13. Do so soon, as he shall soon go to safe order dwelling out of bondage. Amen.

14. Let all be no war labor of weapon order manufacturing of bomb, gun, other war weapon order, no order armored vehicle order of cannon labor.

15. Let all such be now changed to no harm ability, only self-defending; no offensive bomb order in any land shall be way you desire peace.

16. Do full no nuclear bomb in nation of full power holy order. Amen.

17. The holy God speaketh to all lands of world:

18. Now do no way war.

19. A full order of peace is to do no manufacturing weapon unholy order.

20. Now stop all making weapon of harm order. Amen.

21. Let nation of Israel be no first order unholy attack against any, so I, God, will do full holy defending.

22. Let all nations thus do. Amen.

23. All lands now do full order honesty of the holy way of no order war.

24. Let all now be peace order. Amen.

25. Let United Nation assembly be full truth order.

26. Let all nation order now truth way declare peace order, all to name all peace labor.

27. Do so now, is my way of Millennial Labor Peace Order establishing peace unto God monitoring; Zion full order holy power on all nation holy living unto God ruling by love-pure-peace-order, a holy order of sacred revealed holy order.

28. Now be only peace holy making, all to do homage unto God, even Jesus Christ, who giveth my will through him I

have as Mouthpiece for me until my own power reveals my presence on world to all surviving nations, they of pure holy living peace. Amen.

29. The holy living is now, not after I must humble all nation order.

30. Now do law upholding not of weapon making, nor of transporting weapon to battle other land.

31. Do full order negotiating so no bomb of destroying full land nuclear order can be conveyed against other land.

32. Do only peace living in land of thy dwelling. Amen.

33. Let the United States do no nuclear weapon transport by a way of nation who in anger taketh from military weapon on their jurisdiction of nation order, as was before in land of a way such did take place, yet able to have the weapon returned.

34. Let not such folly happen. Amen.

35. Let Russia do likewise. Amen.

36. Know Afghanistan shall no longer be peace as long as foreign nations are of military labor in that land.

37. Let all NATO nation order now withdraw -- if need be leave ally government there armed to defend self.

38. Do so now, so peace is declared, notwithstanding long conflict hath deprived many innocent child, woman, and male order civilian order death by misapplied order of attack by both sides of war labor.

39. Do no more military attack in Afghanistan, any foreign nation, is the will of God. Amen.

40. Let the land of my once refuge, even Egypt, do negotiating when many attack Israel, so Egypt is no war against Israel. Amen.

41. Now let all withdraw from other

lands who only desire peace, not war by thy intervening, only as defending order.

42. Now do holy living, all people on world -- no murder order of any kind; no immoral upholding by any legal way consenting in thy land; no offense of business against any land at all; only prospering other order of land not of thy governing, through peace fair trade law of all equal to buy needs for their people.

43. Such shall Zion governing order rule in full order Christ order rule on world. Amen.

44. Let Burma, Myanmar be holy employing order, no child slave unholy order; also Thailand, Singapore, other Asia economic labor, of proper pay to labor so no starvation in thy land by usury of business order, banking unholy seeking profit by usury of slave order allowed by unholy governing authority. Amen.

45. The Lord speaketh to nation of Albania: Cease secret murder of dissident order in own nation.

46. Judgment of God cometh for all murder way of the unholy power keeping way. Amen.

47. Let Mauritania repent now of all child, living child murder, so population is at pure protected living. Amen.

48. Let all nations do full no-murder living child murder way in Asia. Amen.

49. Judgment follows my word by tempest flooding nation of evil ury of child order, also of adult forc or of slavery unholy order in Asian na on of the order of prisoner for political differences order.

50. Now repent.

51. Now do holy living, even in Old World tradition of Asian lands, is God's word, to be followed soon by God-sending judgment order. Amen.

52. Let Barbados nation do no more child order killing to make population submit to governing power.

53. A soon judgment of God cometh on the land of Barbados, even new war, civil war, to the harm of many innocent people.

54. Do negotiating.

55. No more order kidnaping child order, killing they of youth to cause submitting of people to forcing discipline of military power in Barbados.

56. I, God, rule all lands and call on all to do holy kind order governing, so people in thy land, agency willing doing, do full self-discipline to maintain peace.

57. Let this nation now cease getting military help from United Nations or other world supply of arms.

58. A holy way is to not sell weapons made in thy own nation, only self-defending until I come in heavenly order governing power, saith Jesus Christ, the eternal order holy God-power of love for truth, for God. Amen.

59. Now let all nation order do negotiating, no nuclear weapon order in way of the use now to destroy all such. Amen.

60. All nation order meet soon to do this, is the Lord of all speaking to all nations of nuclear order holding now on world. Amen.

61. Let Russia cease enslaving own people in Siberian order, unholy forcing many in slave-prison order.

62. Repent, Russia leader order.

63. Plague cometh to ruling order in all nations of unholy forcing in slavery order.

64. A holy way is use United Nation order of only fair agreement order of full pay for labor if of business honorable labor.

65. I shall be Paymaster in resurrection of each soul. Amen.

66. Now do holy change, all nation order, to fair business employing labor. Amen.

67. I shall do full world government establishing Zion in God-power.

68. Do only pure living until I come. Amen.

SECTION REVELATION 256

Jesus Christ
Jehovah Christ Son Ahman

I, Your Holy God, Send Message to All Lands of Holy Order Truth Prophesying and Holy Order Cleansing Order. Be of My Full Order Peace, Holy Order Living.

Revelation of the Lord Jesus Christ
Palestine, Texas
Sunday, August 11, 2013

Holy Will of Jesus Christ

1. The Lord Jesus Christ sendeth His will to all people of land of the nation of Somalia:

2. Cease evil war now!

3. Do no more unholy piracy ship attack way of harm.

4. Do no way living the harm way of abusing women, child order in prostituting, evil force way of unholy tradition to put such in harm way living among war tribe order.

5. I shall bring judgment upon nation, of famine, pestilence, if you heed not my way to do peace order. Amen.

6. Let nation of Jordan hear my will: Do no order of gathering Moslem nation power to do harm to nation of Israel in time you join with the other Moslem order to do such alliance way to harm Israel.

7. Cease to hear Hezbollah or Hamas tribe of the Palestinian violence order of aggressive attack.

8. Do this -- only promote peace, and thy nation shall be of existing when full way pure peace cometh at my holy power order.

9. The attack against Israel must not come from thy land; else thy nation suffers full desolating attack, entire loss of all national power. Amen.

10. Let Moslem nation of Yemen hear my will, is Jesus Christ will to Yemen:

11. Let new peace order be President of Yemen relinquish dictatorial power, unto elected order representative of a congress order, to give people of nation full freedom living in religion, in civil pure representation; also women freedom of the way no abuse legal upholding way of own husband order violent force way;

child order of only peace order, not joining militant order against government of nation of Yemen. Amen.

12. Let India hear the way of more pure holy living unto no murder order tradition of burning widow of deceased husband, unholy murder by legal consent in many traditional religious way of Hindu way; to not do such henceforth. Such is Lucifer doctrine.

13. You need only pass law to preserve widow order living free way of no fear of husband dying before wife order. Amen.

14. Also do away, India, with caste order of lower untouchable caste; all same free order governing power preserving same order of no favorite order; in land ownership; in religious freedom living.

15. Such caste order is Lucifer doctrine of lower order class of poor order kept poor, like slave order to rich upper class order.

16. Let all be equal in government preserving power, so starvation of many lower class ceaseth.

17. Do so now, is the will of Jesus Christ. Amen.

18. Let nation of France learn future order if unholy way order Sodom, adultery extant living of thy nation continueth: Full order of nation of loss of identity as a world power; no order of such heinous crime of murder of unborn child order from adulterous or Sodom unholy immoral living. Such is thy dishonor before me, saith God, even Jesus Christ, unto nation of France.

19. Thy family order is of full way immoral living in all nation and is of the soon full judging of thy Lord against all unholy living. Amen.

20. Let my word be sent to all nations, saith Jesus Christ.

21. Let all nations cease murder of unborn child unholy murder order.

22. Do so now, lest my full judgment cleanse all such from nation order of legal upholding such heinous crime against life order, of now doing legal order to stop such. Amen.

23. Let soon peace order be by disarmament of all lands.

24. I, Jesus Christ, soon appeareth to all nations.

25. All flesh on world shall see me together in soon appearing on world as I do full order cleansing, so heaven order may govern remnant of all nation order as I promised in New Testament holy order holy record. Amen.

26. Now do full order communication, all nation order, unto my holy Prophet Warren Jeffs; thy labor to reveal labor to full order holy peacemaking order; also no murder of unborn youth child unborn holy order; unholy murder of unborn child order full way stopped, else my order of full judgment cometh to all nation order on world. Amen.

27. Let Australia nation cease unholy removal of child youth order at four years of age, older also, from all parent order, who do such way to not raise child order in parent-love order.

28. If child order is not raised by parent order, school governing all child order living, such becometh foundation of evil, violent or immoral order in child order.

29. Do not take child order from parent order by government order, save abuse of real family disorder happens.

30. A holy way is abolish all such policy, a fallacy of education order in land of Australia nation.

31. Also do so for Aborigine peoples,

so they raise own child order in family order. Amen.

32. Let nation of Israel hear my will: Do not do a policy of no religion conversion any longer; such hindereth freedom preservation.

33. Do so now. Let freedom to proselyte not be of a hinderment in my Israel land.

34. A holy order of truth cometh soon.

35. Do no hindering freedom of speech of peace order, nor of freedom of press of pure truth of holy religion press to train all my holy order revealed order religion, of pure order to teach my holy order of revelation. Amen.

36. I, God, speak to all communist government unholy forcing of own peoples in no religious freedom, no freedom of expression, nor of peaceful press of publishing religious order holy God-sending order:

37. Now do full freedom of such God-given freedom holy way life of freedom holy order. Amen.

38. When Zion is my full abode on world, I shall be governing order holy power over all world, soon. Amen.

39. Now prepare.

40. Only the more righteous in own land shall remain.

41. Read again Revelation Book of John my Beloved apostle order, holy will of the Lord vision of cleansing power soon to come by God doing judging.

42. I send my own word now, to be fully of the order justified to do full cleansing of all peoples.

43. Do so now, even own cleansing of murder; forcing child order to do labor, slave order labor; also full order immoral living unto prostituting women, or other order in own nation. Amen.

44. Now is time of full warning.

45. Nation order all over world are of Babylon spiritual darkness unholy order, as John Beloved foretold.

46. Now read my word through my Prophet holy book of Bible, of the very word I, Jesus Christ, delivered to Israel two thousand years ago, prophesying Jerusalem then would be destroyed, Israel scattered, temple not one stone on another -- in Matthew order testimony chapter 24. I send it with this holy word.

47. Also read Isaiah, how all nation order on world would be of my judgment in latter day of world, which is now time of my holy order of the world time of probation. Amen.

48. Let nation of Canada also do no removal of youth in early child order from parent order; for unholy removal is not of natural child raising.

49. Let school order only do educating, never full responsibility of all life of kindergarten age youth.

50. Let parent order do full child-raising in all lands on world. Amen.

51. Now do holy order preparing, all nation order.

52. I cometh soon, saith Jesus Christ, your holy order of holy power of heaven holy government holy power; the full order to rule peace policy holy order. Amen.

53. Now do only peace negotiation of full peace in all lands -- no more nuclear order weapon making at all from this time. Amen.

54. Also, withdraw military power into own land; not any in other nation order, unto full order peace in all nation order. Amen.

55. Let nation of Mexico soon do full order cleansing of the illegal bribe by drug cartel order from national, also

local government order; lest full war is of nation, to take power.

56. Let United States place army at Mexico border in all states soon; as Mexico shall erupt in unholy civil strife, to do harm to southern land of United States when economic order causeth mob order violence in own land.

57. Let this soon take place; as drug order shall raid across border up to Albuquerque, New Mexico; also Arizona, Tucson, unprotected order if no national defending in place soon; also California, San Diego area at mercy of violent invasion from Mexican drug violence unholy order.

58. Such shall do harm in full violent way, unto states bordering Mexico suffering great violent way by drug cartel power if nation of Mexico continues unholy bribe order from drug cartel unholy order. Amen.

59. Know when full war cometh, Venezuela shall help do unholy attack against United States in alliance with the communist nation order alliance now in the way of agreement in secret order.

60. They look for the time to do full attack if United States is no longer international power.

61. Withdraw from Afghanistan now; also do full NATO preparing, better order to do full defending at time economic failure, bank, oil industry failure taketh place in world in time money system confidence is full order to fail. Amen.

62. Let nation of Czech Republic, also Slovakia, same national order now separate order, not do unholy attack on each other, nor to do any way help to attack Western Europe when communist alliance attacks.

63. Let peace be thy holy way; for if you do unnecessary order to attack any other nation, you will lose all nation

power and only become tributary slave order to large communist nation, if you do any order violence labor against all other Europe order nation order.

64. Do peace order in full attack against other western nations when communist large coalition of nations unite sudden order again.

65. Do this, so own nation is only peace, no military assisting communist nation order coalition order. Amen.

66. Let nation of Chile not do unholy alliance with Asian nation, so South America is not attacked by communist Asian land. Amen.

67. Now let Germany again hear my will of full call to do away with full order allowed by law of nation to allow full naked order outward doing.

68. Such is violence inviting in soon time to happen.

69. Moral purity must be upheld by law for God to preserve thy land. Amen.

70. Let now land of former order larger portion of former Yugoslavia do holy order outlawing violence, justified now by anger or emotion way loss of personal order mental order out of simple emotion, doing violent attack on own order child, wife order.

71. Do not justify by law such violent way. Amen.

72. Also let all former Yugoslavia, now separate nation order, do full peace order, lest world order violent order be thy promoting.

73. All nations of Europe do no order full attack on Yugoslavia breakaway nation order, Serbia, Bosnia, other nation breakaway lands.

74. Do peace order negotiation. Amen.

75. Let Syria leader be no longer leader.

76. Resign, as you are violent order, for own people's sake.

77. Do so peace order soon, is Jesus Christ holy will to President, other leader order of Syria of violent order. Amen.

78. Now let Israel nation do all I have named, to clean own laws, to not allow unborn child order murder abortion of unborn child order at all, to not use contraceptive destruction of unborn order in law-way upholding, lest I, God, do not full defending at time a coalition of Moslem lands join soon against thee.

79. Do no nuclear weapon use at all, is my own will, saith Jehovah Christ. Amen.

80. Let nation of Laos do holy order peace negotiation with own people of the order of so-called rebel force in mountain land in thy nation.

81. Do so soon; also all peaceful order of all nation order.

82. Know communist order of no freedom order for the human right order of freedom of speech protected by law, freedom of religion, of news press -- all must be of lawful privilege upheld.

83. Communist order shall be full way overthrown by God order of Zion holy power of heaven, even I, your Lord and Redeemer, Jesus Christ, coming soon to world, known to all people on world. Amen.

84. Let Tibet also hear holy will of God: Allow freedom of holy expressing, of holy religious freedom upheld by law; also learn thy unholy religion that is of no order marriage order is not of God, only an unholy monastery of order not of my way to do holy order dwelling; thy way only tradition order.

85. Prepare for truth, truth eternal from God. Amen.

86. Now let land of United States on my land of Zion do full order repeal of abortion of Supreme Court ruling, an unjust evil against child unborn order, that ruling by court being not majority at time ruling made; majority of Congress nor of population; though all now guilt way for allowing murder of unborn child order.

87. Now do full order repeal.

88. Do legislative labor soon, or all are of guilt eternal judgment on lawmaking power, answered as eternal judgment on soul by God in next life order of resurrection order.

89. A holy way is to do holy living in this life, toward all; even to do full protecting of unborn child order.

90. This is will of Jesus Christ, Holy Order of Holy God Order Holy Power, Eternal Power Order, who knows even the thought order of all people on world, even motive order of honesty living, or evil intent unholy living order. Amen.

91. Let nation of Latvia, also Estonia, not join communist coalition at time of large order attack against western order unto any assisting; only do peace order. Amen.

92. Let Norway also not allow use of military when conflict of large order cometh. Amen.

93. Let Sweden repent of immoral and all law order allowing no dress of body covered, naked unholy law-allowed unholy order.

94. Let no unholy murder of unborn youth child unborn order.

95. Do no way military order with communist coalition at all. Amen.

96. Let Finland do no military joining with communist coalition at all, not even during peace time of no order conflict order. Amen.

97. Also let Denmark no longer do abortion order, nor unholy way of immoral

euthanasic suicide evil labor by legal law order.

98. Do not do any such, lest you no longer exist on world nation order; or such shall all full attack of enemy come, unto no nation identity at all, by my judgment order, saith God. Amen.

99. Let Serbia do full order peace labor with neighbor nation order, lest no more order world peace.

100. Let thy land and people be only for full order peace order. Amen.

101. Let Greece not go against Turkey land if of weakening in military, even Turkey. Amen.

102. I, Jesus Christ, am God over all nation order.

103. All shall know I have appeared on earth.

104. All shall be humbled.

105. All shall know my power only gives light, life, pure holy peace.

106. Read my book of holy will to all nations to learn how policy of Zion ruleth over all people, nations, tongues, order of nations -- a holy will of God to be of full repentance. Amen.

107. Thus is my message to all nations. Amen.

Matthew 24 (Inspired Version)
(Also in Pearl of Great Price, Joseph Smith Chapter 1)

1. And Jesus went out, and departed from the temple; and his disciples came to him for to hear him, saying, Master, show us concerning the buildings of the temple; as thou hast said; They shall be thrown down and left unto you desolate.

2. And Jesus said unto them, See ye not all these things? And do ye not understand them? Verily I say unto you, There shall not be left here upon this temple, one stone upon another, that shall not be thrown down.

3. And Jesus left them and went upon the mount of Olives.

4. And as he sat upon the mount of Olives, the disciples came unto him privately, saying, Tell us, when shall these things be which thou hast said concerning the destruction of the temple, and the Jews; and what is the sign of thy coming; and of the end of the world? (or the destruction of the wicked, which is the end of the world.)

5. And Jesus answered and said unto them, Take heed that no man deceive you.

6. For many shall come in my name, saying, I am Christ; and shall deceive many.

7. Then shall they deliver you up to be afflicted, and shall kill you; and ye shall be hated of all nations for my name's sake.

8. And then shall many be offended, and shall betray one another, and shall hate one another.

9. And many false prophets shall arise, and shall deceive many.

10. And because iniquity shall abound, the love of many shall wax cold.

11. But he that remaineth steadfast, and is not overcome, the same shall be saved.

12. When ye therefore, shall see the abomination of desolation, spoken of by Daniel the prophet, concerning the destruction of Jerusalem, then ye shall stand in the holy place. (Whoso readeth let him understand.)

13. Then let them who are in Judea, flee into the mountains.

14. Let him who is on the housetop, flee, and not return to take anything out of his house.

15. Neither let him who is in the field, return back to take his clothes.

16. And woe unto them that are with child, and unto them that give suck in those days!

17. Therefore, pray ye the Lord, that your flight be not in the winter, neither on the Sabbath day.

18. For then, in those days, shall be great tribulations on the Jews, and upon the inhabitants of Jerusalem; such as was not before sent upon Israel, of God, since the beginning of their kingdom until this time; no, nor ever shall be sent again upon Israel.

19. All things which have befallen them, are only the beginning of the sorrows which shall come upon them; and except those days should be shortened, there should none of their flesh be saved.

20. But for the elect's sake, according to the covenant, those days shall be shortened.

21. Behold these things I have spoken unto you concerning the Jews.

22. And again, after the tribulation of those days which shall come upon Jerusalem, if any man shall say unto you, Lo! here is Christ, or there; believe him not.

23. For in those days, there shall also arise false Christs, and false prophets, and shall show great signs and wonders; insomuch that, if possible, they shall deceive the very elect, who are the elect according to the covenant.

24. Behold, I speak these things unto you for the elect's sake.

25. And ye also shall hear of wars, and rumors of wars; see that ye be not troubled; for all I have told you must come to pass. But the end is not yet.

26. Behold, I have told you before, Wherefore, if they shall say unto you, Behold, he is in the desert; go not forth. Behold, he is in the secret chambers; believe it not.

27. For as the light of the morning cometh out of the east, and shineth even unto the west, and covereth the whole earth; so shall also the coming of the Son of man be.

28. And now I show unto you a parable. Behold, wheresoever the carcass is, there will the eagles be gathered together; so likewise shall mine elect be gathered from the four quarters of the earth.

29. And they shall hear of wars, and rumors of wars. Behold, I speak unto you for mine elect's sake.

30. For nation shall rise against nation, and kingdom against kingdom; there shall be famine and pestilences, and earthquakes in divers places.

31. And again, because iniquity shall abound, the love of men shall wax cold; but he that shall not be overcome, the same shall be saved.

32. And again, this gospel of the kingdom shall be preached in all the world, for a witness unto all nations, and then shall the end come, or the destruction of the wicked.

33. And again shall the abomination of desolation, spoken of by Daniel the prophet, be fulfilled.

34. And immediately after the tribulation of those days, the sun shall be darkened, and the moon shall not give her light, and the stars shall fall from heaven, and the powers of heaven shall be shaken.

35. Verily I say unto you, this

generation, in which these things shall be shown forth, shall not pass away until all I have told you shall be fulfilled.

36. Although the days will come that heaven and earth shall pass away, yet my word shall not pass away; but all shall be fulfilled.

37. And as I said before, after the tribulation of those days, and the powers of the heavens shall be shaken, then shall appear the sign of the Son of man in heaven; and then shall all the tribes of the earth mourn.

38. And they shall see the Son of man coming in the clouds of heaven, with power and great glory.

39. And whoso treasureth up my words, shall not be deceived.

40. For the Son of man shall come, and he shall send his angels before him with the great sound of a trumpet, and they shall gather together the remainder of his elect from the four winds; from one end of heaven to the other.

41. Now learn a parable of the fig tree: When its branches are yet tender, and it begins to put forth leaves, ye know that summer is nigh at hand.

42. So likewise mine elect, when they shall see all these things, they shall know that he is near, even at the doors.

43. But of that day and hour no one knoweth; no, not the angels of God in heaven, but my Father only.

44. But as it was in the days of Noah, so it shall be also at the coming of the Son of man.

45. For it shall be with them as it was in the days which were before the flood; for until the day that Noah entered into the ark, they were eating and drinking, marrying and giving in marriage, and knew not until the flood came and took them all away; so shall also the coming of the Son of man be.

46. Then shall be fulfilled that which is written, that, In the last days,

47. Two shall be in the field; the one shall be taken and the other left.

48. Two shall be grinding at the mill; the one taken and the other left.

49. And what I say unto one, I say unto all men; Watch, therefore, for ye know not at what hour your Lord doth come.

50. But know this, if the good man of the house had known in what watch the thief would come, he would have watched, and would not have suffered his house to have been broken up; but would have been ready.

51. Therefore be ye also ready; for in such an hour as ye think not, the Son of man cometh.

52. Who then is a faithful and wise servant, whom his Lord hath made ruler over his household, to give them meat in due season?

53. Blessed is that servant, whom his Lord when he cometh shall find so doing;

54. And, verily I say unto you, he shall make him ruler over all his goods.

55. But if that evil servant shall say in his heart, My Lord delayeth his coming; and shall begin to smite his fellow servants, and to eat and drink with the drunken; the Lord of that servant shall come in a day when he looketh not for him, and in an hour that he is not aware of, and shall cut him asunder, and shall appoint him his portion with the hypocrites; there shall be weeping and gnashing of teeth.

56. And thus cometh the end of the wicked according to the prophecy of Moses, saying, They should be cut off from among the people. But the end of the earth is not yet; but bye and bye.

SECTION REVELATION 257

Jesus Christ
Jehovah Christ Son Ahman

I, Jesus Christ, Do Give Holy Will of My Holy Power Unto All Nations on World; to Now Hear; to Now Tell All in the World My Holy Message.

Revelation of the Lord Jesus Christ
Palestine, Texas
Wednesday, August 21, 2013

Holy Will of God

1. I, Jesus Christ, speak unto all nations, a holy will of thy Creator unto salvation.

2. Now be holy repenting of all evil in thy living gentile fallen way of Babylon, as named in Peter, James, John Beloved, Paul and other apostle record of New Testament holy writing. Amen.

3. Let all nations hear my full saving order: My holy order is to do full holy order purity living of New Testament full teaching of repenting of all evil.

4. Adulterous, evil, immoral living leadeth to full order no salvation of murder of unborn child order.

5. Repent of own sin leading to such murder of life in mother order, father or other medical labor that destroyeth living holy child of unborn innocence order, lest God judgment in full come upon thee and all who, of a full labor upholding such evil, are of no longer repenting labor in world of the order of earthly existing. Amen.

6. Let law officials in all nations do full order holy law upholding against unborn child murder of unborn child order. Amen.

7. Let all church order also uphold my will; no more lustful nor murder sin way; of all purity living to be taught by honorable teacher of now holy order of my word in New Testament; they of honest labor to teach in own religious order, now to also be God-judged soon, if of worthy order to be in Millennial holy appearing, soon to take full power over all nations order in all world; Jesus Christ, your God over all lands, nations, kindreds, tongues, peoples on entire surviving world through judgment of God, soon in full power to be on all earth. Amen.

8. Now do holy way living.

9. Let war weapon industry be stopped.

10. They who sell weapons for gain in world weapon selling are murder order, not peace way living.

11. My doctrine is to beat sword into plowing tools, pruning hooks, for food raising; not of violent living.

12. Weapon, bullet, bomb, evil mass destruction weapon unholy evil order -- all are not of me, your God. Amen.

13. Let all nation leader order in all earth meet soon for full order stop to weapon making; to destroy all such now existing; to govern nation by peace order, by truth of my holy Gospel soon to be full

message to all surviving nation order when I do full appearing to all people on earth at once, none excepted, all seeing God together by my vision order in mind, also in person to Israel; who surviveth through purity living of Gospel of salvation of my own holy order revealed in Bible, also my word in all to do full order purity of life doing in the world order of earth living mortal in body order. Amen.

14. Let all nuclear weapon order be of all nations destroyed soon, so war of great violent order doeth not Lucifer plan of evil depopulating all lands on world.

15. I, God, shall intervene when such is doing; then my order of judgment removeth all violent living order throughout world, by my wisdom preserving more righteous of all nation order; a work of angel holy labor, as named in Bible, Luke of my Inspired Version Joseph Smith holy translation holy Bible record.

16. As it was in Noah's time, so shall it be in this, the final time of evil on earth before my power coming to govern all people on earth.

17. My order is soon to be on earth, Zion, to govern in perfect love all people on earth; Jesus Christ, your Lord and Holy Order Redeemer of all flesh speaking to all nations.

18. Few on world listen; most of evil joyful sinful living; as though I, God, am not.

19. I AM that I AM, I told Israel; no one on world of greater authority than I am, He of Jehovah name in old Bible writing, even Jesus Christ, your Redeemer Order who conquered death, the Resurrection and the Life. Amen.

20. I am of Celestial order power.

21. I, God, dwell in eternal fire Holy Ghost Spirit of God order, above brightness of sun in firmament to mortal eye, a brightness of Celestial holy exalted power.

22. I created all things, both in heaven and on world.

23. I am the Light and Life of all peoples.

24. My light is Spirit that goeth forth to all creation on world and in heaven.

25. I bring heaven order to world after full judgment of God on world cleanseth sin of murder order from all lands, murder of unborn child order eliminated entire.

26. Now do full knowing, New Era of Holy Peace holy living soon cometh by God intervening in all world.

27. A holy way is to believe I am, that I cometh soon, as New Testament holy Bible declareth.

28. This, my word, is also a holy testament to all, that I have already revealed through my Prophet Joseph Smith in Doctrine and Covenants, also Book of Mormon holy writing, my own will; to prepare for Israel people of pure living to build New Jerusalem unto me, Jesus Christ, to do holy living. Amen.

29. The holy will of thy God is of pure holy order authority of God of my holy appointed Mouth Order on world, Warren Jeffs, whom I do give holy revelation unto full salvation order to all in world who seek salvation holy order of thy Lord Jesus Christ power order.

30. Come unto me, your God, Jesus Christ, to be of saved from damning self by denying path of living holy unto pure way order holy order of God. Amen.

31. Let all my word be sacred to all order people on world.

32. Let name of Jesus Christ be honored by all people, to be survival order of God-

sent holy order cleansing of all sin way on earth, is my will to all on world. Amen.

33. The full holy living power of righteous living is by my power of prayer holy receiving.

34. I can hear all mind order in organizing order, all at one time in Godhood power.

35. Thus, nothing is of a hiding from my power; the Holy Spirit of God recording all in all; to do full judging on all in resurrection of all. Amen.

36. Thus the righteous look toward full holy reward in resurrection.

37. The wicked fear, unto the way of gnashing of teeth, trembling in full way condemnation by God over coming holy power judging of the Lord on all wicked; who tremble at my coming soon; when Babylon of all nation unholy evil way living shall be of my full overcoming soon.

38. Repent, repent, is the Lord's holy way word to all people.

39. Let leader order of all lands print this to their own language of perfect translating; also do so in this original side-by-side English language, so all have my original word in English as mailed to all church order or leader order of all lands.

40. A holy way is to mail back to my order of return address all such double side-by-side print in both thy national language of perfect accuracy with English copy, side by side, each in column next to each other language holy translating order; else let my Church organize authorized holy translation; to print in all news order in full.

41. I soon mail complete order all previous order holy new revealed warning holy word holy order to all nation order.

42. A holy way is to now make holy

acknowledging to my servant Warren Jeffs by writing you did publish accurately my now letter of full warning to thy nation as I have told in this corresponding. Amen.

43. Let all church order, all faith holy order Christian Church order, read to congregation this, my full message. Amen.

44. Now do holy order full reading of Book of Warning of Jesus Christ I sent to all nations, to all leader order in all lands. Amen.

45. The full word of God is to be ready for my glory-power appearing soon to all lands, people, nations, tongues; all to see me at same time in glory heaven-order holy power. Amen.

46. Let my people of my Church also be full holy living Celestial laws of my Holy Priesthood, Church and Kingdom now on earth, as revealed through Joseph Smith and the Prophet apostolic holy power of my holy revealed religion now named in my holy book called Warning of Jesus Christ to All Nations.

47. Included therein is my holy order revelation of the order at end of book, a holy authority named as a Proclamation of the Lord to all peoples, showing my holy way is of authority continued on world. Amen.

48. Let all people humble themselves before God; so I know how you do full repentance, by my holy will living on earth, now; no waiting after death to repent.

49. Now, in this life, is time to repair unto God; all thy evil turning unto good; to reveal to me, your God, you do feel penitent unto full order repenting while alive.

50. A holy order is to pray always unto God.

51. Do so now, is my holy will. Amen.

52. Now let leader of nation on Zion

land receive my holy revealed word: Nation is on brink of precipice of full dissolution, as evil of violence, evil of allowed by legal consent murder of unborn child order, legal consent of Sodom way unholy evil order, such as I named unto fire and brimstone order full judgment in Lot's, Abraham's time.

53. Let Bible record be sufficient order testifying my hot displeasure against adultery, Sodom way unholy living; even Lot's wife struck dead unto the soil left of salt order when looking back unholy doing of desire for Sodom glory unholy living, her own child order overcome.

54. A holy order is to not allow legal consent of same order gender legal order unholy union living by law. Amen.

55. Such governing authority complete order denieth God and my right to rule through holy guiding prayerful order to legal order doing my righteous way, if of noble holy order living no Sodom, adulterous way; of own knowing I, God, decry against all such immoral way, that always leads to murder of unborn child order, or to limit ability to bring to life child order.

56. A holy way is abstinence of all not of holy man-woman wife by law to man holy living together in principle of marriage above sin way. Amen.

57. Let all be honoring own marriage order by law.

58. My people are to live as I name; not to have governing power of man interfere religious order doing, of full religion of freedom in land of United States; also to release my Prophet soon by order of governing authority.

59. He is innocent.

60. He doeth holy will of my holy power authority on my world, by my inspiring in all government of Church.

61. No longer hold him in bondage.

62. Murder plot was of apostate order against he of full order of leader order of my Holy Priesthood since he became my Prophet order.

63. Now protect him unto full order releasing him to friend order in my Church, is my holy way to show repenting of murder order in nation of unborn child order. Amen.

64. Let all now turn to repay unto my Church all robbing by governing power, lands, houses, other remunerating for loss of the way of the way of paying for all loss by government unholy ruling order. Amen.

65. Let all court labor now do full examining -- witness of apostate order are lying; none actual witness to any accusing; people of prejudice entire against my Celestial holy religion of holy revelation, a holy order of religion of my giving to Joseph Smith before any law of evil attack on my Celestial Law of Holy Marriage to only Church members holy living order, not to world at all.

66. I, God, speak purity living.

67. My holy word is of holy way unto saving all who live pure holy religion of my pure power order of my Church.

68. Now cease holding my One Man who holds power to administer my law unto only member holy living order of my Church.

69. Lying apostate order accuseth holy way to be evil; then world of evil practice of immoral living are believing lie of apostate order who are also of evil practice of loss of all virtue in own living world way of unholy immoral allowing by legal consent.

JESUS CHRIST SON AHMAN

70. A holy way is to always confirm actual intent of witness of unholy own living in own life, to determine truth.

71. Now know the way to undo all court action against my member order is to do pardon by presidential power so no way attack against pure religious order taketh place against same order. Amen.

72. Also let all Congress repeal old law against my holy marriage order entire, from yester-order century in time government order imprisoned full way attack in 1800's time against my Church.

73. Let history show Reynolds Supreme Court ruling was the order of no religious freedom, continued to this time in nation of supposed freedom of religion.

74. A holy way is to review, using my holy order of holy writing of only truth, as was filed in Texas Supreme Order Jurisdiction, now published in my holy book of warning of Jesus Christ Warning to All Nations, also in my holy warning to all people. Amen.

75. Now do full holy repeal of unholy religious attack by prejudiced law order in yester-century time in nation.

76. Present church of my Latter-day Saint name of modern order church that did compromise against me and my holy Marriage Law of Plural Order is not my now Church on world, having full upholding repentance for unholy adultery, also forgiving false way murder of unborn child order if of religious following of false order of no true salvation; even holy order of the holy temple is changed, not of my holy original revealed holy order.

77. Now do full order study of history of apostasy of Mormon Church, by their own naming, unto all in church not of me. Amen.

78. Now do my holy way, all nations

on world: Repent, repent, is the Lord Jesus Christ holy way. Amen.

79. I, God, speak to nation of Jordan: Let no aggressive labor against nation of Israel be thy labor, lest the full loss of national identity come against all who fight against my will being Israel surviveth. Amen.

80. Let nation of Turkey assist Israel if of full justifying defending. Amen.

81. Also, let the coalition of Moslem attack cease all aggression against Israel.

82. Make peace. Amen.

83. Let all nation order of United Nations assemble to do full order negotiating, now, for peace in entire disarmament, all to be peacemaking when I, God, appear to all people. Amen.

84. Now do holy order holy living, as I, Jesus Christ, have named.

85. Do no murder order to keep power in own nation, all governing order; for I, God, shall reward all with full recompense. Amen.

86. Now receive my will to all in full order Zion coming to rule.

87. I, Jesus Christ, cometh in full glory.

88. I am full Authority to govern all people on earth, from the Governing Authority that created all.

89. I am to do full cleansing of wicked order of violent order in all lands.

90. Nothing can stay my hand.

91. Earthquake, storm of great power, as revelation of John Beloved named as start of great judgment -- first angel casting incense order to world, bringing lightning, thunder, storm of judgment -- this shall happen.

92. All remaining shall witness earth portions return -- the portion on land, one portion in sea, one portion as a star; all in chapter eight of Book of Revelation.

93. Now do full order holy living.

94. I cometh soon.

95. Judgment of my power cleanseth all nation order soon.

96. Repent, repent, is my holy will. Amen.

97. Now do homage to God.

98. Have own family do holy order fasting often, to repent.

99. Do so unto me, your God. Amen.

100. Now receive my holy way: A holy living is abstaining from all immoral living.

101. Movies of violent depicting on world should not be seen, nor they of immoral way example to all.

102. Do no reading of violence, nor evil of sport, so-called, unholy doing of violent way doing.

103. Cease doing war practice with own military as though you come near border of the nation order you shall attempt to attack in future way doing.

104. Let military only patrol border order, to have only defending thy way if attacked. Amen.

105. Now let all Africa do negotiating soon, to stop all such who invade other nation order. Amen.

106. Let all who do so receive economic sanction from all world union, voting only to use peace, no violent order to promote peace.

107. A holy way is send order of full peace representing to violent nation. Then seek my servant, to know my way to defend, after three or more labor order of peace labor. Amen.

108. Now know I speak my will from heaven to Mouthpiece on world.

109. Let he be free to do full way counsel of my giving, soon, so all nation order do no more violent living.

110. Such shall be my Zion governing order; now all nation order knowing where to learn my will in all world order now to be peace living.

111. A holy way is to have all people in thy nation pray to me, thy God, when representative is sent to counsel with God through my Prophet Warren Jeffs, always believing I am, that I can give pure holy will of God to all nation order.

112. Such is my way, even now, to all nation order, preparing all for Millennium of Pure Order Peace. Amen.

113. Let this be policy of United Nations: First offer peace three attemptings with violent nation. Then all approach me through my Prophet of the full need to know God's way to bring united peace order.

114. If you do so, I, God, shall be there to counsel. Amen.

115. Also, let nation of Russia, also China, dissolve all tie of unholy order of silent agreeing in secret compact to attack other nation order when they do full arming of own military; even now doing such. Amen.

116. World will soon know I speaketh truth of secret order military alliance of communist order.

117. Now repent soon, so all nation order is of full order peace living, unto counsel order with me, thy God, through Mouthpiece of God now on earth.

118. A holy way is to write to nation holding him in prison now, to release him, unto he coming to tell all in United Nation assembly of me, of my policy order of Millennium of Peace soon to be full order on world. Amen.

119. Let all European land only be

pure order living, to be protected of God when evil attack of aggression cometh. Amen.

120. Let Japan do full named in my former order messaging repenting, lest a full unholy way attack of the communist alliance cometh to humble thee to do only subservice to they of violent order. Amen.

121. Now be holy on entire earth, nation order. Amen.

SECTION REVELATION 258

Jesus Christ
Jehovah Christ Son Ahman

I, Jesus Christ, Do Tell Nations of All World, Soon Need to Move All People Off Island Lands Named; Also to No Way Use Mass Destructive Weapon Order. Hear My Own Will to All Nations. Amen.

Revelation of the Lord Jesus Christ
Palestine, Texas
Monday, September 2, 2013

1. Thus saith Jesus Christ, God over all nation order, who seeth all things, who hath all power to discern intent of soul in all my people now on world: I speak word of holy revealing of delivery of some on world, now in a way to know I did give holy love-warning against time of the full judgment power of God on earth of the cleansing power --

2. Now know both Polynesia island order, Micronesia island order shall be of no existing after I send full judgment God-power; all such not on surface of earth.

3. Let all now move far away to highland; also island of Fiji; also Philippine lowland island order.

4. Taiwan shall be of full loss after own order military loseth war against same nation people of the original nation order once having Taiwan as part of nation.

5. Do holy peaceful surrender; not to be of any use of mass destructing nuclear order by any. Amen.

6. Let Asia be of receiving all population of these island nations soon. Amen.

7. God hath thus spoken. Amen.

SECTION REVELATION 259

Jesus Christ
Jehovah Christ Son Ahman

I, Jesus Christ, God Over All World, Do Send My Holy Word to All Nation Order, My Will of How to Prepare for My Holy Coming Soon on World. Amen.

Revelation of the Lord Jesus Christ
Palestine, Texas
Wednesday, October 2, 2013

Holy Will of God

1. Let all nation order learn my way to do full holy repenting, saith Jesus Christ, Son Ahman, even thy God of life, light eternal, unto salvation: I am He who hath conquered death, hell, and the power order of satan entire.

2. Let faith be my power of prayer unto full confession of all sin way.

3. Now know truth, that sin is to be of willful disobeying against revealed truths.

4. Revealed truths are revelations of thy Lord Jesus Christ.

5. Revelation is inspired will of Jesus, thy God.

6. Now know there is only one Prophet holy order Mouthpiece of Jesus Christ on earth at a time.

7. All other divine authority doth seek my holy way through mine holy way of power of truth revealed.

8. Now come unto me, God, through now Mouthpiece of Jesus Christ, even my Prophet Warren Jeffs.

9. He is of my holy power, anointed of me, to do full holy truth holy will of God revealing. Amen.

10. Now tell all world to repent.

11. Do no more war preparing.

12. Give full order peace love power.

13. Do no more way to do evil of the loss of pure innocence of child holy innocent living.

14. Keep child order from evil.

15. Live family purity way of father, mother; no divorcing once youth is born, nor before of bringing child into world.

16. Now keep earthly promise of married order, no adultery nor Sodom way doing.

17. Only be of one wife, save I, God, appoint direct way through my Prophet for pure Church member of Church of my name Jesus Christ, through my revealing; as I did through Nathan of old to King David, also bringing judgment on King David, an eternal judgment unto damnation of King David when he, adulterous living, shed innocent blood of the order of full intent to do such -- to one whom he stole, a woman -- the soldier loyal to King David.

18. King David, adulterous order, killed

stolen woman's husband; Nathan sent to correct David of Old Israel ruler power.

19. Now know this is of all mankind knowing I did holy judging, even of David of Old Israel ruler authority.

20. My Church hath fulness of my Gospel of salvation through the fulness of divine heaven order authority called apostle order of my High Priesthood.

21. I, God, restored to man, through Joseph Smith, my holy order of apostle office order. Amen.

22. Tell all world to now be holy repenting order, following my new order restored through Joseph Smith, continued through a pure order of Prophet holy full Keyholding Power even after martyrdom of Joseph Smith.

23. Let nation who killed he of high power, Prophet Joseph Smith, hath yet full order of full retribution to be my God-judgment order, who did unto Joseph Smith murder order, with no justice upon murder order even to this time. Amen.

24. Nation order of all world come to me, Jesus Christ, thy God who made thee.

25. Now do so. Amen.

26. Tell all nations to come to God through cleansing out of thy way of doing all murder order.

27. Do no legal upheld murder of unborn child, holy child, innocent child holy order; of need to protect unborn youth holy order. Amen.

28. Now repent, all nation order, of war preparing; only do defense of own nation order, no aggression. Amen.

29. Let all people hear: I, Jesus Christ, come soon, to all world seeing God, Jesus Christ, Jehovah, even Son Ahman, together as a full light, holy power of governing order from heaven; soon to dwell among mankind on world. Amen.

30. For I, God, soon shall be on earth in full glory power in New Jerusalem, also appear on Mount of Olives to Judah after they are of my Priesthood order; my order of missionary converted order soon in Old Israel, as Judah gathers there in Old Israel. Amen.

31. Also lost Tribes of Israel shall be gathered, first to Zion order; then to promised land of Old Israel I promised Abraham of old, also Isaac, his son, also Jacob, Isaac's son named Israel.

32. Israel, my chosen, come to me, thy Lord Jehovah.

33. I came to mine own, and they, Israel as a nation, full way crucified Jesus Christ, their holy Messiah, causing a full order retribution upon Jewish nation of Old Israel; of loss of Old Jerusalem unto this day; when I, Jesus Christ, did full way order war victory power against all nation order; to be my nation, Israel, restored.

34. Let leader order of all nations defend Israel.

35. Let all be of peace, unto Israel preparing for my glorious coming, saith Jesus Christ, even Jehovah Christ, God over all world. Amen.

36. Jesus Christ, God over all, speaketh word to all world to be holy in deed, in thought, in all way holy as unto me, in all holy way order living.

37. Let no violence be in family order.

38. Love one another of my prayer order, praying for one another to be of happiness in doing only good.

39. Thus, do I, God, bless the people who do praying in honest holy pure inspired living.

40. A holy living is to acknowledge God in all good received. Amen.

41. Now be love of God in action, all nation holy order; all people on earth do

full order holy living, no evil intent, nor action one against another; even nation order make peace between you and all other nations.

42. Do so now, so I, Jesus Christ, can preserve all such of more pure holy living, as I, God, do cleanse all nation order soon of violent living not to be thy way at all.

43. A holy order is to be self-praying to me.

44. I hear honesty prayer holy order of no evil living of pleasure in unrighteousness.

45. A holy way is to do confession to God, then repent. Amen.

46. Let the way of all government of men power be now to do only peace-making, unto the time of the full holy order of the way to be ready for Jesus Christ's coming, even I, God, who sendeth this, my word, to all nation order.

47. Violence is of evil inspiring to bloodshed.

48. Pray. Be humble. Do no evil in own living.

49. Make true peace. Amen.

SECTION REVELATION 260

Revelation of the Lord Jesus Christ
Palestine, Texas
Sunday, September 29, 2013

Holy Word of God

1. Come to me, thy holy Lord, all on world who have been of sin way; to come to thy God through mine holy authority on world whom I have ordained unto apostolic holy authority in my Holy Priesthood. Amen.

2. Now repent, all ye people on world.

3. Be holy as I, God, am holy.

4. Let all nation order do so. Amen.

5. Jesus Christ is God.

6. He comes unto my holy apostle order, saith your God unto all world. Amen.

7. Now receive holy truth: I, God, create all in world.

8. I made heaven, earth, full universe order by my Godhood power, a light like the sun in the solar order Celestial power.

9. I reside on world of eternal fire.

10. Each of the way to know truth by my light unto the mind awakening to holy truth, is of all things to be testimony I, God, created all things.

11. Light of holy power is called the Holy Spirit; a light of knowledge, of pure peace that lifts up the mind to know truth.

12. Let prayer of full honest seeking God be thy way; and I, God, shall enlighten thy mind to know truth of eternal living.

13. This world is mine, even the orb on which all people now dwell of this earth.

14. I made sun, moon, stars, earth, all things.

15. I create man after mine own image.

16. Let truth be full order believed, that God created all full order of all things.

17. Nothing is hidden from my all-seeing mind.

18. Let all be pure holy living.

19. My power shineth on all.

20. Prayer is thy mind reaching in holy thinking honest holy desire order, unto thy God, even thy Lord, who speaketh to all people on world. Amen.

21. Now behold, Jesus Christ is God over all world. Amen.

22. Come to thy Lord unto repentance, to be received into my order of holy Church of Jesus Christ on earth.

23. Come unto me to be saved holy way living, unto full order of salvation, only through the holy Godhead of Father, even my Father Elohim; Son, even thy Lord Jesus Christ; and the Holy Ghost, even the power of my pure Spirit of God.

24. Now obey Celestial order to be of heaven order; to dwell with God forever.

25. Come to me through my authority on earth, even my apostolic order, whom I, God, ordained under the Keyholder Priesthood holy power of Prophet order.

26. Let all look to God through His Prophet ordained by Prophet order; who is now Warren Jeffs on now earth. Amen.

27. Thy Lord Jesus Christ hath only One Man at a time on earth who holds all authority to bless all people by apostle power; holding full holy key order of highest Priesthood from heaven; bestowed on him of the apostleship holy called order of my holy authority, even under hands of Holy Priesthood prior Keyholder holy Prophet.

28. Thus, I name my Key Man who dwelleth on world to all people.

29. Let all be coming to God through His authorized Prophet, a man on earth now among you, is my holy will to all. Amen.

30. Now do my way, all nation order.

31. Come to God through my Priesthood authority. Amen.

32. Let all nation order hear this before I come in majesty Celestial power of clouds of heaven, to all people on earth.

33. Come now to my Priesthood.

34. Do so, so I can receive all by my authority of power unto salvation.

35. Let all come to God by faith prayer; repentance of all thy sin way; unto holy ordinance of baptism by my authority of Priesthood on world; so I, God, can heal thee unto full order holy living on earth.

36. I bring full power, heavenly order soon to entire world.

37. This is my call, to now be holy the way I make mankind holy; by my heavenly order power.

38. A holy power of God cometh to world soon, Zion holy order.

39. Let thy faith-prayer be unto me, thy God; who heareth even thought holy thinking in all minds on world. Amen.

40. Tell all on world I, Jesus Christ, soon cometh on earth with power to govern all nation order.

41. Let this be final call to all on earth before I cleanse entire world of evil of immoral living; of sin of adultery, of Sodom; of child unborn child murder unholy evil of the destroying my unborn child order.

42. Now repent, repent, is God's own word to all on earth. Amen.

43. I, God, speak to nation of my full order of humbling, even United States: Hear full holy warning.

44. My great power comes to humble all unto Celestial holy order of cleansing all murder of all way of evil life harming innocence and life of both unborn holy order child order as well as child living order.

45. Come to full holy living, so youth is raised to pure living as unto me, your holy God. Amen.

46. Now let nation of full need of full

humbling, even Barbados of Africa land, do full change to no harm to both unborn child order, also no slave order of either child order, or women order of unholy order of illicit forced immoral order.

47. A holy way is own army be cleansed, so force by weapon use is not in military that is force unto corrupting power against all order of virtue, innocence. Amen.

48. I shall humble all nation order who do unholy force of women in illicit moral, immoral living, saith Jesus Christ. Amen.

49. I, Jesus Christ, reveal United States of America is full way fallen unto murder way thinking against me, the God who died on cross; three days after the crucifying way, was resurrected unto eternal power as God over all heaven and earth.

50. This nation allows murder of unborn child order unto legal way protecting.

51. Now change law of land so abortion, contraceptive drug, also medical removal of fetus be of no legal doing.

52. Now be truth living, all people of United States of America; that God-given power to bring to life child holy order is legal protected for unborn. Amen.

53. Let all nations on world do such in own legal law upholding by rule of law. Amen.

54. I, Jesus Christ, soon come to world as power to be full order governing power Celestial power, eternal Godhood power over all nations. Amen.

55. Also let all people on world be holy as I, God, am holy.

56. This world is mine, saith God.

57. No one is ruler save thy God, who is Jesus Christ.

58. Now repent unto full preparing for God's glory power to dwell among all lands, people, nations, tongues; all people on world knowing Jesus Christ is God. Amen.

59. Tell all people on world to hear this by leader order exact copy sending this word: Be holy, for holy God cometh on world soon to judge all. Amen.

SECTION REVELATION 261

Revelation of the Lord Jesus Christ
Palestine, Texas
Friday, August 30, 2013

Holy Word of God

1. The holy God over the nation of the future land of Zion, New Jerusalem on land of new holy order, is soon to appear.

2. There first cometh full order cleansing of all way of Babylon, even the cleansing all nation order off land who do murder order; taint not to be present at all who consent to murder of unborn child holy order; also all murder way of evil only in mind through pleasure in unrighteousness, and law way evil upholding.

3. Repent, repent, is the call of God to all. Amen.

APPENDIX REVELATION

Revelation of the Lord Jesus Christ
Palestine, Texas
Friday, September 20, 2013

1. All additions to any revelations are now of full order accurate until the Lord delivereth Mouthpiece unto personal order approval by God's own way of Keyholding authority making all truth known about the Lord Jesus Christ guiding my book, saith the Lord through my servant; to be of full order any other holy revealed word if any published revealed word was of partial publishing, or if further compiling errors exist in any published holy word.

2. Enemy holdeth my servant in bondage, not of full freedom to mail all needed correspondence; some letters not of full allowed order to be sent.

3. Thus, in soon time cometh more holy word to all people on world. Amen.

Chapter 12

Compiling Errors of First Edition
of Now Correction

Second Edition Witnessing to
Compiling Errors Being Corrected

We, the following order of witnessing order, do testify to all world these errors have been of a correcting and thus Second Edition book benefit of all peoples knowing God hath commanded an accuracy checking wherein there is a full order of purity and His word trusted by all peoples. Thus we give our names in saying accuracy hath been again holy revealed called of God to check any errors of compiling where they compared original to printed word, and this new word is of full holy order accurate. Amen.

Nov. 25, 2013

Lyle S. Jeffs

Elder in the Fundamentalist
Church of Jesus Christ of Latter-day Saints

Ben E Johnson

Nov 25, 2013

Ben E. Johnson

Elder in the Fundamentalist
Church of Jesus Christ of Latter-day Saints

Compilers Note

We, the compiler labor, do give to all world correction to all typing or misread proofing, so all is as original of holy revealing of Jesus Christ word through His servant on earth, Warren Jeffs, His Mouthpiece as His One Spokesman on earth.

Preface, verse 10

Was: ...through Keyholding authority of apostle order.

Now corrected: ...through Keyholding authority of **full** apostle order.

Table of Contents

All Section Revelation numbers are now bolded in Second Edition Table of Contents for easy referencing.

Section Revelation 172 Title, p. XXIX

Title was missed in First Edition Table of Contents, now added in Second Edition.

Jehovah Speaketh, Who Is Jesus Christ

Proclamation Table of Contents, pp. XXXIV-XLV, 551-562

Formatting of Proclamation Table of Contents has been adjusted in Second Edition.

Section Revelation 5 Heading, pp. XLIII, 560

A portion of the heading was missed in First Edition Table of Contents, now added in Second Edition.

Revelation of the Lord Jesus Christ

Section Revelation 100 Date, pp. XLIV, 561

Was: **Thursday**, August 19, 2011

Now corrected: **Friday**, August 19, 2011

Introduction, p. XLIX

In First Edition, the Introduction began on page XLVII. Due to additional pages in Second Edition Table of Contents, the Introduction now begins on page XLIX.

Introduction, verse 131, p. LIV

Was: Such are unholy **to** the sight of thy Lord entire.

Now corrected: Such are unholy **in** the sight of thy Lord entire.

Section Revelation 3:2, p. 4

Was: ...and have seen **the** wickedness in high places among the rulers of this nation;

Now corrected: ...and have seen wickedness in high places among the rulers of this nation;

Section Revelation 3:14, p. 5

Was: ...and broke away from my Priesthood authority**, and** they rejected my Celestial Law of Marriage;

Now corrected: ...and broke away from my Priesthood authority **when** they rejected my Celestial Law of Marriage;

Section Revelation 13:5, p. 19

Was: ...who have helped preserve your nation in **the** times of political and military attack.

Now corrected: ...who have helped preserve your nation in times of political and military attack.

Section Revelation 22:11, p. 25

Was: Therefore, shall the blessings of peace cause my greater **blessings**

Now corrected: Therefore, shall the blessings of peace cause my greater **blessing**

Section Revelation 23:21, pp. 26, 103

Was: ...to all the people in the borders and throughout **the** nation.

Now corrected: ...to all the people in the borders and throughout **thy** nation.

Section Revelation 24:9, p. 28

Was: My people shall yet dwell upon my **lands**

Now corrected: My people shall yet dwell upon my **land**

Section Revelation 26:15, p. 31

Was: Make peace in your western borders with other **people**

Now corrected: Make peace in your western borders with other **peoples**

Section Revelation 27:59, p. 35

Was: ...who abuse the system of government to get gain, **subjecting** the poor to suffering poverty.

Now corrected: ...who abuse the system of government to get gain, **subjugating** the poor to suffering poverty.

Section Revelation 29:2, pp. 36, 305

Was: ...of coming **desolations** upon you who continue

Now corrected: ...of coming **desolation** upon you who continue

Section Revelation 29:15, pp. 36, 305

Was: ...judgment to come of desolation of **abominable** and corrupt ways,

Now corrected: ...judgment to come of desolation of **abominatable** and corrupt ways,

Section Revelation 34:1, p. 41

The following verse was missed in First Edition, now added in Second Edition; thus changing succeeding verse numbering.

1. Cause the preamble of the Kingdom of God to read: "Holy, holy, art thou, O Lord and Ruler of all things. Thy righteous will be done.

Doctrine and Covenants Section 43:18, p. 44

Was: ...the Lord shall utter his voice out of **the** heaven;

Now corrected: ...the Lord shall utter his voice out of heaven;

Luke 17:34, p. 51

Was: ...the one shall be taken, the other left.

Now corrected: ...the one shall be taken, **and** the other left.

Luke 17:35, p. 51

Was: ...the one shall be taken, the other left.

Now corrected: ...the one shall be taken, **and** the other left.

2 Peter 3:13, p. 51

Was: ...And we look for new heavens,

Now corrected: ...And we look for **a** new heavens,

Section Revelation 35:4, pp. 61, 804

Was: ...in **the** place of my naming in a soon-to-happen event.

Now corrected: ...in **a** place of my naming in a soon-to-happen event.

Section Revelation 35:7, pp. 61, 804

Was: ...or you shall reap **a** whirlwind of judgments in near future sending,

Now corrected: ...or you shall reap **the** whirlwind of judgments in near future sending,

Section Revelation 35:26, pp. 63, 806

Was: ...though tried; **and** he continues to receive my word.

Now corrected: ...though tried; **yet** he continues to receive my word.

Section Revelation 35:29, pp. 63, 806

Was: ...**or** you shall rise in the resurrection unto a buffeting

Now corrected: ...**for** you shall rise in the resurrection unto a buffeting

Section Revelation 35:33, pp. 64, 807

Was: ...O ye **governmental** officials of this nation --

Now corrected: ...O ye **government** officials of this nation --

Section Revelation 35:35, pp. 64, 807

Was: ...bringing forth a righteous people **who** receive Him

Now corrected: ...bringing forth a righteous people **to** receive Him

Section Revelation 35:37, pp. 64, 807

Was: ...religious freedom should be guaranteed in every nation -- which you **labored** for;

Now corrected: ...religious freedom should be guaranteed in every nation -- which you **labor** for;

Section Revelation 35:41, pp. 65, 808

Was: ...legalizing **a** slaughter of innocence among you.

Now corrected: ...legalizing **the** slaughter of innocence among you.

Section Revelation 35:50, pp. 65, 808

Was: ...until I, the Lord, **did** not allow it any longer.

Now corrected: ...until I, the Lord, **could** not allow it any longer.

Section Revelation 35:51, pp. 65, 808

Was: ...and the driving of my people **and** murdering of my people since the days

Now corrected: ...and the driving of my people**, the** murdering of my people since the days

Section Revelation 35:52, pp. 66, 808

Was: ...as worthy **only to** be swept off my land of Zion.

Now corrected: ...as worthy **to only** be swept off my land of Zion.

Section Revelation 36:1, p. 69

Was: ...even Him who reigns on high, **and** has all power in heaven and on earth

and rules over all peoples **by** the power of His might:

Now corrected: ...even Him who reigns on high, **who** has all power in heaven and on earth and rules over all peoples **in** the power of His might:

Section Revelation 36:3, p. 69

Was: ...which causes all nations to reek with impure **and** unclean ways.

Now corrected: ...which causes all nations to reek with impure unclean ways.

Section Revelation 36:21, p. 70

Was: ...shall rise **and** govern the earth,

Now corrected: ...shall rise **to** govern the earth,

Section Revelation 36:45, p. 71

Was: Let there also be **an** assembly of the nations to hear my word...for nation shall rise up against nation, **of** a soon happening.

Now corrected: Let there also be assembly of the nations to hear my word...for nation shall rise up against nation **in** a soon happening.

Section Revelation 36:48-49, p. 71

Due to the word corrections, the punctuation and wording has been adjusted in the following verses.

Was: 48. Therefore, let this assembly...come among you -- **more of** my word, to be read by one appointed wherein I, the Lord, shall name.

49. **My** Mouthpiece on earth **will** deliver my word to the nation that now inhabits my land of Zion...and remember my word against a day **when** I **fulfill** my word in full.

Now corrected: 48. Therefore, let this assembly...come among you --

49. More of my word, to be read by one appointed wherein I, the Lord, shall name my Mouthpiece on earth deliver my word to the nation that now inhabits my land of Zion...and remember my word against a day where I **fulfilled** my word in full.

Section Revelation 36:66, p. 72

Was: Cause my people, **that** many ways **have** lost lands and houses because of unjust judges taking their lands from them --

Now corrected: Cause my people, **the** many ways **of** lost lands and houses because of unjust judges taking their lands from them --

Section Revelation 36:74, p. 73

Was: ...who dwells in everlasting burnings, **an** all-consuming fire

Now corrected: ...who dwells in everlasting burnings, **in** all-consuming fire

Section Revelation 36:88, p. 73

Was: Cause him who administers my word to the nation, to the peoples of all the earth, **to** go free to be among my people

Now corrected: Cause him who administers my word to the nation, to the peoples of all the earth, go free to be among my people

Section Revelation 36:133, p. 75

Was: ...of great judgment when Babylon shall fall, **and** trade and commerce **are** overthrown.

Now corrected: ...of great judgment when Babylon shall fall, **the** trade and commerce **be** overthrown.

Section Revelation 36:140, p. 75

Was: The **scourges** I shall bring upon this earth

Now corrected: The **scenes** I shall bring upon this earth

Section Revelation 36:159, p. 76

Was: ...to promote equity, virtue, and purity of life,

Now corrected: ...to promote equity **and** virtue and purity of life,

Section Revelation 36:171, p. 76

Was: ...who came in the meridian of time **and** suffered more than man can suffer, on the cross, to redeem all mankind from the grave and raise up those **that are of** noble and pure lives unto a salvation.

Now corrected: ...who came in the meridian of time, **who** suffered more than man can suffer, on the cross, to redeem all mankind from the grave and raise up those **who live** noble and pure lives unto a salvation.

Section Revelation 36:176-177, p. 77

Due to the word corrections, the punctuation and wording has been adjusted in the following verses.

Was: 176. Be diligent...**for** your conduct toward those in need**.**

177. **Bring** just and righteous principles which should be lived in every land; for if you do it not, I shall reward thee according to thy deeds in the flesh.

Now corrected: 176. Be diligent... **by** your conduct toward those in need**,** **by** just and righteous principles which should be lived in every land;

177. For if you do it not, I shall reward thee according to thy deeds in the flesh.

Section Revelation 36:185, p. 77

Was: ...continue under righteous rule **and domain** and not evil practices of fallen Babylon.

Now corrected: ...continue under righteous rule **on the land** and not evil practices of fallen Babylon.

Section Revelation 36:186, p. 77

Was: ...those who will receive, **O ye** peoples, my message of salvation.

Now corrected: ...those who will receive, **among your** peoples, my message of salvation.

Section Revelation 36:189, p. 77

Was: I, the Lord, have spoken it, thus shall I fulfill.

Now corrected: I, the Lord, have spoken it, **and** thus shall I fulfill.

Section Revelation 37:4, p. 78

Was: **Wherefore**, I, the Lord, declare unto you

Now corrected: **Therefore**, I, the Lord, declare unto you

Section Revelation 37:16, pp. 79, 780

Was: ...for heretofore I have been merciful upon thee when **my** peoples have cried for mercy,

Now corrected: ...for heretofore I have been merciful upon thee when **thy** peoples have cried for mercy,

Section Revelation 37:19, p. 79

Was: ...by preserving a people who **will receive** Celestial laws,

Now corrected: ...by preserving a people who **have received** Celestial laws,

Section Revelation 37:29, p. 80

Was: ...there shall also come forth a work of **a** greater light that shall fill the earth.

Now corrected: ...there shall also come forth a work of **the** greater light that shall fill the earth.

Section Revelation 39:34, p. 89

Was: Cease your war that is raised up one against another. **Justify** yourself in United Nations Council to humble one nation**, it** shall spread;

Now corrected: Cease your war that is raised up one against another, **justifying** yourself in United Nations Council to humble one nation**. It** shall spread;

Section Revelation 39:35, p. 89

Was: ...that **exist** in almost all nations everywhere on earth.

Now corrected: ...that **exists** in almost all nations everywhere on earth.

Section Revelation 40:25, p. 95

Was: ...and if you heed me not, you shall reap the **result** of thy choice

Now corrected: ...and if you heed me not, you shall reap the **results** of thy choice

Section Revelation 41:7, p. 99

Was: Now I, the Lord, declare **that** the European nations also repent

Now corrected: Now I, the Lord, declare**: Let** the European nations also repent

Section Revelation 41:32-33, p. 100

Due to the changes in punctuation, the wording has been adjusted in the following verses.

Was: 32. Cease these evils and purify your own peoples, **as you are**

now seeking to rule over other nations or bear influence in their lives.

33. Cleanse the inside of the platter first.

Now corrected: 32. Cease these evils and purify your own peoples.

33. As you are now seeking to rule over other nations or bear influence in their lives, cleanse the inside of the platter first.

Section Revelation 42 Date, pp. V, 102

Was: **Wednesday, March 30, 2011**

Now corrected: **Saturday, March 26, 2011**

Section Revelation 44 Date, pp. V, 108

Was: **Wednesday, March 30, 2011**

Now corrected: **Thursday, March 31, 2011**

Section Revelation 44:22, p. 109

Was: ...called Zion, that shall come upon the earth **of** my glorious appearing,

Now corrected: ...called Zion, that shall come upon the earth **at** my glorious appearing,

Section Revelation 45:1-4, p. 110

The following verses were missed in First Edition, now added in Second Edition; thus changing verse numbering; also shifting ending wording on page 110, and beginning and ending wording on pages 111-114.

1. I, the Lord Jesus Christ, speak to the nations of the earth again on a day of warning when my judgments are soon to be poured out without measure, beginning among mine elect and my people on the earth, spreading across the land of Zion and to the nations of the earth.

2. Zion shall remain. The pure in heart are Zion, who love God with an undivided heart, who have in their hearts His law burned in constant remembrance as a living fire to their righteous doing, of my giving.

3. And only they who abide a Celestial Law can be part of Zion; and Celestial means heavenly, sent from above -- the laws of a kingdom of glory, of eternal all-consuming fire, that fire being the Holy Ghost, the Spirit of God.

4. Thus saith the Lord to the nations of the earth: I am soon to come in my glory and my power, and you shall feel this power, even to consume the wicked and preserve the more righteous among you, saith Jesus Christ.

Section Revelation 45:10, p. 111

Was: **6.** ...**you** shall be filled with such unrest

Now corrected: **10.** ...**ye** shall be filled with such unrest

Section Revelation 45:53, p. 113

Was: **49.** ...that only a people in your lands uphold life **and** a more virtuous and pure walk before your God,

Now corrected: **53.** ...that only a people in your lands uphold life **in** a more virtuous and pure walk before your God,

Section Revelation 47:28, p. 117

Was: Thus it shall be on record to your knowing **unto** the future peoples in your lands,

Now corrected: Thus it shall be on record to your knowing **and to** the future peoples in your lands,

Section Revelation 47:44, p. 118

Was: ...and adultery, and immoral and corrupt ways that destroy life.

Now corrected: ...and adultery, and immoral and corrupt ways that destroy life **and virtue**.

Section Revelation 47:53, p. 118

Was: ...your wickedness **hath** come up before me;

Now corrected: ...your wickedness **has** come up before me;

Section Revelation 49:14, p. 122

Was: Repent ye, is my word to **unto** you, the nation of Italy.

Now corrected: Repent ye, is my word to you, the nation of Italy.

Section Revelation 52:18, p. 127

The following verse was missed in First Edition, now added in Second Edition as verse 18; thus changing succeeding verse numbering.

18. Preserve religious rights, preserve equitous and just laws, freedoms of my giving to all mankind to have their agency in freedom of worship and freedom of expression without bringing violence upon others.

Section Revelation 53:27, p. 129

Was: ...there shall be cleansing of the land,

Now corrected: ...there shall be **a** cleansing of the land,

Section Revelation 54:3, p. 131

Was: Let there not be **a** continuation of the wars in thy borders...with judgments that **you** shall know the God of heaven hath sent,

Now corrected: Let there not be **the** continuation of the wars in thy borders... with judgments that **ye** shall know the God of heaven hath sent,

Section Revelation 54:14, p. 132

Was: There shall be peace **and** my message of salvation sent to all peoples.

Now corrected: There shall be peace **in** my message of salvation sent to all peoples.

Section Revelation 55:4, p. 132

Was: ...and you must needs be ready to receive the proclamations of righteous **government**;

Now corrected: ...and you must needs be ready to receive the proclamations of righteous **governments**;

Section Revelation 55:16, p. 133

Was: I have suffered the pains of all men, saith **the** Lord Jesus Christ.

Now corrected: I have suffered the pains of all men, saith **your** Lord Jesus Christ.

Section Revelation 55:37, p. 134

Was: I, the Lord, have spoken it, and all **people** shall know

Now corrected: I, the Lord, have spoken it, and all **peoples** shall know

Section Revelation 56:12, p. 136

Was: **You** shall feel my wrath; and I am justified,

Now corrected: **Ye** shall feel my wrath; and I am justified,

Section Revelation 56:15, p. 136

Was: ...of representation, **of** privileges that promote happiness, rights to women.

Now corrected: ...of representation **and** privileges that promote happiness, rights to women.

Section Revelation 56:17, p. 136

Was: My **judgment** shall be upon you if you heed me not,

Now corrected: My **judgments** shall be upon you if you heed me not,

Section Revelation 57:29-30, p. 141

Due to the changes in punctuation, the wording has been adjusted in the following verses.

Was: 29. Read my words of warning...received of recent sending.

30. **T**hose nations that allow the receiving, through the mailing ability, publishings of my word, **n**ow know that thy God hath spoken from the heavens;

Now corrected: 29. Read my words of warning...received of recent sending, **t**hose nations that allow the receiving, through the mailing ability, publishings of my word.

30. **N**ow know that thy God hath spoken from the heavens.

Section Revelation 57:58, p. 142

Was: ...**You** shall be held accountable before thy God,

Now corrected: ...**Ye** shall be held accountable before thy God,

Section Revelation 57:65, p. 143

Was: ...to prepare for my glorious appearing and my righteous government to reign upon the earth

Now corrected: ...to prepare for my glorious appearing and **for** my righteous government to reign upon the earth

Section Revelation 57:82, p. 144

Was: And they were called upon by me, in receiving of my **word**,

Now corrected: And they were called upon by me, in receiving of my **words**,

Section Revelation 57:90, p. 145

Was: Thus shall it be, the cleansing **powers** so complete

Now corrected: Thus shall it be, the cleansing **power** so complete

Section Revelation 57:91, p. 145

Was: ...which world of departed spirits I visited

Now corrected: ...which world of **the** departed spirits I visited

Section Revelation 57:95, p. 145

Was: ...to receive my **word** of salvation,

Now corrected: ...to receive my **words** of salvation,

Section Revelation 58:1, p. 147

Was: ...being the Resurrection **and** the Life, speaketh.

Now corrected: ...being the Resurrection **of** the life, speaketh.

Section Revelation 58:29, p. 149

Was: ...they will have to meet the full measure of justice, even **an** eternal judgment.

Now corrected: ...they will have to meet the full measure of justice, even **in the** eternal judgment.

Section Revelation 58:55, p. 150

Was: ...great judgments will sweep millions of people **from** off the face of the earth who are more wicked,

Now corrected: ...great judgments will sweep millions of people off the face of the earth who are **the** more wicked,

Section Revelation 58:56, p. 150

Was: Oh, that you would heed my word! for I am **the** God of salvation;

Now corrected: Oh, that you would

heed my word! for I am **a** God of salvation;

Section Revelation 59:18, p. 153

Was: ...I, the Lord, dictated to him mine own word to **the** nation of Israel

Now corrected: ...I, the Lord, dictated to him mine own word to nation of Israel

Section Revelation 59:41, p. 155

Was: ...shall be a place of great warmongering, **corrupting** the nations round about into unrest.

Now corrected: ...shall be a place of great warmongering, **erupting** the nations round about into unrest.

Section Revelation 59:84, p. 157

Was: ...**for** in some lands, even under legal authority,

Now corrected: ...**where** in some lands, even under legal authority,

Section Revelation 59:114, p. 158

Was: Remember the ancient city of Nineveh, **how** Jonah was sent to preach repentance

Now corrected: Remember the ancient city of Nineveh, **that** Jonah was sent to preach repentance

Section Revelation 61:30, p. 161

Was: If the leaders of this nation uphold those of secret combination of a murderous doing among your own peoples**, that** keep in power;

Now corrected: If the leaders of this nation uphold those of secret combination of a murderous doing among your own peoples **to** keep in power,

Section Revelation 70:7, pp. 188, 330, 818

Was: ...to the mind and heart **to** every man, woman, and child

Now corrected: ...to the mind and heart **of** every man, woman, and child

Section Revelation 70:22, pp. 189, 331, 819

Was: And thus saith the Lord to leaders of this nation and all nations:

Now corrected: And thus saith the Lord to **the** leaders of this nation and all nations:

Section Revelation 70:24, pp. 189, 331, 819

Was: **You** shall stand before me.

Now corrected: **Ye** shall stand before me.

Section Revelation 70:48, pp. 191, 333, 821

Was: ...**and** who shall judge all men according to their deeds done in the flesh.

Now corrected: ...who shall judge all men according to their deeds done in the flesh.

Section Revelation 71:15, p. 193

Was: And I shall send, of necessity, **the** cleansing power **of** the earth, yea, to cleanse the more wicked out of every nation and every land of the earth; preserve the more righteous.

Now corrected: And I shall send, of necessity, **a** cleansing power **over** the earth, yea, to cleanse the more wicked out of every nation and every land of the earth**, and** preserve the more righteous.

Section Revelation 72:6, p. 194

Was: I have sent you warning,

Now corrected: I have sent you **a** warning,

Section Revelation 73:8, p. 196

Was: And though I, the Lord, may allow a humbling of other nations by **thy** hand,

Now corrected: And though I, the

Lord, may allow a humbling of other nations by **thine** hand,

Section Revelation 73:37, p. 199

Was: ...and would oppress other nations likewise if I **allow** thee to expand thy power elsewhere**,** over other nations on the earth.

Now corrected: ...and would oppress other nations likewise if I **allowed** thee to expand thy power elsewhere over other nations on the earth.

Section Revelation 74:1, pp. 200, 301

Was: ...an attack against the nation of Libya**; and** I sent you warning to cleanse the inside of the platter.

Now corrected: ...an attack against the nation of Libya**, when** I sent you warning to cleanse the inside of the platter.

Section Revelation 74:13, pp. 201, 302

Was: ...**the** murder of unborn children --

Now corrected: ...**even** murder of unborn children --

Section Revelation 75 Title, pp. IX, 203

Was: ...Yea, to Both **the** Leaders and the Peoples of This Nation,

Now corrected: ...Yea, to Both Leaders and the Peoples of This Nation,

Section Revelation 77:1, p. 208

Was: ...the Governor and Ruler **of** heaven who shall soon come to earth in His power and glory to make Himself known to the **people** of all nations,

Now corrected: ...the Governor and Ruler **in** heaven who shall soon come to earth in His power and glory to make Himself known to the **peoples** of all nations,

Section Revelation 77:5, p. 208

Was: ...I shall send upon the earth...as I have given **thy** land to the descendants of Abraham, Isaac, and Jacob,

Now corrected: ...I shall send upon **the nations of** the earth...as I have given **my** land to the descendants of Abraham, Isaac, and Jacob,

Section Revelation 77:8, p. 208

Was: ...**that** do not allow the murder of unborn children, **that** allows religious freedom in thy nation,

Now corrected: ...**but** do not allow the murder of unborn children, **but** allows religious freedom in thy nation,

Section Revelation 77:9, p. 208

Was: ...to defend thyself against foreign nations **who** shall come against thee

Now corrected: ...to defend thyself against foreign nations **that** shall come against thee

Section Revelation 79:20, p. 215

Was: ...the warning voice to the **nations** and leaders of Russia:

Now corrected: ...the warning voice to the **nation** and leaders of Russia:

Section Revelation 79:27, p. 215

Was: ...and only use your military for defensive principles and not **for** aggression at all.

Now corrected: ...and only use your military for defensive principles and not **of** aggression at all.

Section Revelation 81:2, p. 219

Was: ...wherein you have sought to get gain and bear influence and promote war **or** aspiring to power,

Now corrected: ...wherein you have

sought to get gain and bear influence and promote war **for** aspiring to power,

Section Revelation 82 Title, pp. X, 221

Was: ...Concerning Just Judgment Soon to Come Upon Thee, Yea, Upon the More Wicked Among Thee.

Now corrected: ...Concerning **a** Just Judgment Soon to Come Upon Thee, Yea, Upon the More Wicked Among Thee.

Section Revelation 82:1, p. 221

Was: I, who created all things, even Jesus Christ,

Now corrected: I, who **have** created all things, even Jesus Christ,

Section Revelation 82:22, p. 222

Was: I shall rule over all nations, **the** God of heaven coming to earth,

Now corrected: I shall rule over all nations, **a** God of heaven coming to earth,

Section Revelation 83:5-6, p. 224

Due to the word corrections, the punctuation and wording has been adjusted in the following verses.

Was: 5. The vengeance of a just God cometh upon thee**,** that I may be justified in performing this work of cleansing **thy** land and thy peoples... peoples of the earth at this time**.**

6. I am sending my word of warning,

Now corrected: 5. The vengeance of a just God cometh upon thee**.**

6. **And** that I may be justified in performing this work of cleansing **my** land and thy peoples...peoples of the earth at this time**,** I am sending my word of warning,

Section Revelation 84:24, p. 227

Was: Thus I **could** have continued my Priesthood,

Now corrected: Thus I have continued my Priesthood,

Section Revelation 85:8, p. 229

Was: ...to whom you shall join in **a** time soon to come

Now corrected: ...to whom you shall join in time soon to come

Section Revelation 86:26, p. 234

Was: Now be of full power to correct **thy** heinous crimes

Now corrected: Now be of full power to correct **these** heinous crimes

Section Revelation 86:53, p. 235

Was: Cease thy wicked **attack**,

Now corrected: Cease thy wicked **attacks**,

Section Revelation 86:56, p. 235

Was: ...who combined with lying apostate witnesses **in** evil combination with government prosecuting power,

Now corrected: ...who combined with lying apostate witnesses **of** evil combination with government prosecuting power,

Section Revelation 86:58, p. 236

Was: ...to voice **belief**, without harm coming upon them;

Now corrected: ...to voice **beliefs**, without harm coming upon them;

Section Revelation 86:67, p. 236

Was: **This** evil of unborn children being murdered,

Now corrected: **Thus,** evil of unborn children being murdered,

Section Revelation 86:131, p. 239

Was: ...unto full power **of** judgments,

Now corrected: ...unto full power judgments,

Section Revelation 86:132, p. 239

Was: Thus **I am** doing all things righteous and holy,

Now corrected: Thus **am I** doing all things righteous and holy,

Section Revelation 86:139, p. 239

Was: ...to administer eternal salvation **to** any on earth.

Now corrected: ...to administer eternal salvation **unto** any on earth.

Section Revelation 86:148, p. 240

The following verse was missed in First Edition, now added in Second Edition as verse 148; thus changing succeeding verse numbering.

148. Now let these truths go before appeals courts as my own will, saith Jesus Christ, to be of full way considered, as pure truth; sufficient to reverse all unjust court rulings against my servant and his brethren prosecuted because they live my Celestial Law, which only I, the Lord, can rightly govern.

Section Revelation 87:18, p. 242

Was: ...restricting life from coming forth through natural process **at** birth.

Now corrected: ...restricting life from coming forth through natural process **of** birth.

Section Revelation 91:1, pp. 251, 822

Was: ...**a** Creator over this earth,

Now corrected: ...Creator over this earth,

Section Revelation 91:15, pp. 252, 823

Was: ...to bring forth a thousand years of peace under **a** reign of a governing power sent from heaven,

Now corrected: ...to bring forth a thousand years of peace under **the** reign of a governing power sent from heaven,

Section Revelation 91:42, pp. 254, 825

Was: There shall not be a prolonging much further **of** my merciful hand of warning.

Now corrected: There shall not be a prolonging much further **in** my merciful hand of warning.

Section Revelation 91:49, pp. 255, 826

Was: ...**and** murder, **and** immoral and corrupt ways,

Now corrected: ...**in** murder, **in** immoral and **in** corrupt ways,

Section Revelation 91:52, pp. 255, 826

Was: ...**either** by prosecution **or** by mob rule,

Now corrected: ...**neither** by prosecution **nor** by mob rule,

Section Revelation 91:68, pp. 256, 827

Was: ...and the **blessings** of many souls upon the earth unto eternal life;

Now corrected: ...and the **blessing** of many souls upon the earth unto eternal life;

Section Revelation 91:80, pp. 257, 828

Was: How oft **I would** have gathered you

Now corrected: How oft **would I** have gathered you

Section Revelation 91:87, pp. 257, 828

Was: ...shall be sent to give the governing powers **unto** the hands of my saints,

Now corrected: ...shall be sent to give the governing powers **into** the hands of my saints,

Section Revelation 91:93, pp. 258, 829

Was: And as **they** labor with the children of men,

Now corrected: And as **I** labor with the children of men,

Section Revelation 93:20, p. 262

Was: ...wherein **was** published my policies of governing power,

Now corrected: ...wherein **is** published my policies of governing power,

Section Revelation 95:26, p. 267

Was: Prepare thy peoples at that time for my deliverance;

Now corrected: **To** prepare thy peoples at that time for my deliverance;

Section Revelation 95:35, p. 267

Was: ...well prepared to guide the nations of the earth to **a** peace and equity and justice among themselves.

Now corrected: ...well prepared to guide the nations of the earth to peace and equity and justice among themselves.

Section Revelation 97:3, pp. 273, 338

Was: ...unto the great war mine apostle John my Beloved testified of in that **new** book of New Testament recording,

Now corrected: ...unto the great war mine apostle John my Beloved testified of in that book of New Testament recording,

Section Revelation 97:22, pp. 275, 340

Was: ...**Mine** Doctrine and Covenants is mine own word,

Now corrected: ...**My** Doctrine and Covenants is mine own word,

Section Revelation 98:1, p. 279

Was: ...the First and Last, the Beginning and the End,

Now corrected: ...the First and **the** Last, the Beginning and the End,

Section Revelation 98:8, p. 279

Was: ...calling on the **deliverances** of my people

Now corrected: ...calling on the **deliverance** of my people

Section Revelation 98:13, p. 280

Was: Overthrow **these** evils I have named are in most nations **to** my previous publishings;

Now corrected: Overthrow **those** evils I have named are in most nations **in** my previous publishings;

Section Revelation 98:24, p. 280

Was: I love all, and call upon all everywhere to repent.

Now corrected: I love all, and call upon all **men** everywhere to repent.

Section Revelation 99:28, pp. 282, 831

Was: Libya is now **of** full way of aggression by countries never attacked by that nation.

Now corrected: Libya is now **a** full way of aggression by countries never attacked by that nation.

Section Revelation 99:34, pp. 282, 831

Was: ...Then come to pass mine elect be preserved,

Now corrected: ...Then **shall** come to pass mine elect be preserved,

Section Revelation 99:45, pp. 282, 832

Was: ...to now show world prosecuting power followed a scheme

Now corrected: ...to now show **the**

world prosecuting power followed a scheme

Section Revelation 99:47, pp. 282, 832

Was: Let **my** governing powers cause

Now corrected: Let **the** governing powers cause

Section Revelation 101:1, pp. 284, 834

Was: ...though I have sent mine own word **to** you in sacred revealings and publishings,

Now corrected: ...though I have sent mine own word **unto** you in sacred revealings and publishings,

Section Revelation 101:6, pp. 285, 834

Was: And I, the Lord, give to this nation and this people **a** warning,

Now corrected: And I, the Lord, give to this nation and this people **the** warning,

Section Revelation 101:9, pp. 285, 834

Was: **You** shall witness further,

Now corrected: **Ye** shall witness further,

Section Revelation 101:11, pp. 285, 835

Was: ...**a** memory of my word shall hearken in your souls

Now corrected: ...**the** memory of my word shall hearken in your souls

Section Revelation 103:3, pp. 290, 311

Was: ...and remove thy habitation of **present** and work labor staying to be inland.

Now corrected: ...and remove thy habitation of **personal** and work labor staying to be inland.

Section Revelation 103:4, pp. 290, 311

Was: ...for great and **noticeable** cities on the coast shall be swept off the land.

Now corrected: ...for great and **notable** cities on the coast shall be swept off the land.

Section Revelation 103:6, pp. 291, 311

Was: ...also volcano and earthquake take power in many **habited** and large populated places in Utah and Arizona.

Now corrected: ...also volcano and earthquake take power in many **inhabited** and large populated places in Utah and Arizona.

Section Revelation 103:19, pp. 291, 311

Was: ...yet having the greatest **criminals** of immoral ways and murderous ways among themselves,

Now corrected: ...yet having the greatest **crimes** of immoral ways and murderous ways among themselves,

Section Revelation 103:20, pp. 291, 312

Was: ...attacking other nations who never **attacked** her.

Now corrected: ...attacking other nations who never **attack** her.

Section Revelation 104:2, p. 292

Was: ...at the time enemy influence of **Palestine** Arab Moslem peoples incite unrest there.

Now corrected: ...at the time enemy influence of **Palestinian** Arab Moslem peoples incite unrest there.

Section Revelation 106:5, p. 294

Was: Let **thy** call to be ready be of a full way.

Now corrected: Let **the** call to be ready be of a full way.

Section Revelation 106:11, p. 294

Was: ...over all peoples, nations, **even** kindreds and tongues,

Now corrected: ...over all peoples, nations, kindreds and tongues,

Section Revelation 107 Title, pp. XIV, 295

Was: ...a Thousand Years of **the** Righteous Pure Way

Now corrected: ...a Thousand Years of Righteous Pure Way

Section Revelation 107:1, p. 295

Was: ...who will thus continue in **sin** of destruction of purity,

Now corrected: ...who will thus continue in **sins** of destruction of purity,

Section Revelation 103 Letterhead, p. 310

The letterhead was missed in First Edition, now added in Second Edition; thus shifting ending wording on page 310 and beginning wording on page 311.

**Fundamentalist Church of
Jesus Christ of Latter-day Saints
P.O. Box 840459
Hildale, Utah 84784**

Section Revelations 119, 5, 63, 70 Opening Word, pp. XVII, 320

Was: ...to the Members of Congress, **of** Senate and House of Representatives,

Now corrected: ...to the Members of Congress, **Both** Senate and House of Representatives,

Section Revelation 119:3, p. 321

Was: ...sent forth as the light of intelligent **thought**

Now corrected: ...sent forth as the light of intelligent **thoughts**

Section Revelation 119:4, p. 321

Was: ...who **hath** sent forth many messages through my servant on earth,

Now corrected: ...who **has** sent forth many messages through my servant on earth,

Section Revelation 119:6, p. 321

Was: ...and Him not upholding **you** in that greater **gifts** of influencing peoples of the nation and of the earth;

Now corrected: ...and Him not upholding **thee** in that greater **gift** of influencing peoples of the nation and of the earth;

Section Revelation 119:10, p. 321

Was: ...the God of glory, **have** spoken beforehand,

Now corrected: ...the God of glory, **hath** spoken beforehand,

Section Revelation 119:12, p. 321

Was: ...the **God** of innocence shall be upon thee,

Now corrected: ...the **blood** of innocence shall be upon thee,

Section Revelation 119:16, p. 322

Was: ...yea, God over all Creation giving His own name,

Now corrected: ...yea, **the** God over all Creation giving His own name,

Section Revelation 119:21, p. 322

Was: **And** I have caused my own word to be sent forth

Now corrected: I have caused my own word to be sent forth

Section Revelation 63 Letterhead, p. 324

The letterhead was missed in First Edition, now added in Second Edition.

**Fundamentalist Church of
Jesus Christ of Latter-day Saints
P.O. Box 840459
Hildale, Utah 84784**

Section Revelation 63 Title, p. 324

Formatting on title has been adjusted.

Section Revelation 70 Letterhead, p. 329

The letterhead was missed in First Edition, now added in Second Edition.

**Fundamentalist Church of
Jesus Christ of Latter-day Saints**
P.O. Box 840459
Hildale, Utah 84784

Section Revelation 125:78, p. 352

Was: ...unto full way **not** longer being on earth.

Now corrected: ...unto full way **no** longer being on earth.

Section Revelation 127:75, p. 358

Was: Let all be of pure holy intent; **no longer** of the way of pure holy laws; but of upholding wicked, corrupt, Sodom and immoral ways.

Now corrected: Let all be of pure holy intent **who are not** of the way of pure holy laws, but of upholding wicked, corrupt, Sodom and immoral ways.

Section Revelation 127:109, p. 359

Was: Some nations shall be humbled by **judgment** of my sending if they heed me not;

Now corrected: Some nations shall be humbled by **judgments** of my sending if they heed me not;

Section Revelation 128 Title, pp. XX, 360

Was: ...to Leaders of Power... **Heeding** My Will, Even Thus:

Now corrected: ...to Leaders of **National** Power...**Heed** My Will, Even Thus:

Section Revelation 128:11, p. 360

Was: **Nonetheless**, if you heed me not,

Now corrected: **Nevertheless**, if you heed me not,

Section Revelation 129:1, p. 361

Was: ...to the people of land and kingdom on earth called among **you** as Philippines:

Now corrected: ...to the people of **the** land and kingdom on earth called among **men** as Philippines:

Section Revelation 129:3, p. 361

Was: ...allowing **tradition** of European gentile nations to be of a following.

Now corrected: ...allowing **traditions** of European gentile nations to be of a following.

Section Revelation 129:15, p. 361

Was: ...even Jesus Christ, your holy **God** and Redeemer,

Now corrected: ...even Jesus Christ, your holy **Lord** and Redeemer,

Section Revelation 130:33, p. 365

Was: ...much bloodline of Lehi of Book of Mormon history,

Now corrected: ...much **of** bloodline of Lehi of Book of Mormon history,

Section Revelation 130:51, p. 366

Was: ...as **Israel** my holy Prophet saw and recorded concerning triumph of Israel in the latter days.

Now corrected: ...as **Isaiah** my holy Prophet saw and recorded concerning triumph of Israel in the latter days.

Section Revelation 130:59, p. 366

Was: ...and **Prophets** of old;

Now corrected: ...and **Prophet** of old;

Section Revelation 130:118, p. 369

Was: ...and the other nation of power to humble the nation **of** my land of Zion,

Now corrected: ...and the other nation

of power to humble the nation **on** my land of Zion,

Section Revelation 130:123, p. 369

Was: ...yea, **of** full Celestial new governing

Now corrected: ...yea, **a** full Celestial new governing

Section Revelation 130:138, p. 369

Was: ...yet having **not** religious authority among them from me,

Now corrected: ...yet having **no** religious authority among them from me,

Section Revelation 130:141, p. 370

Was: **This,** my warning, includeth my invitation to be receiving my truth,

Now corrected: **Thus** my warning includeth my invitation to be receiving my truth,

Section Revelations 131-132 Opening Word, pp. XXI, 371

Was: ...Now to Be an Announcing of No Further Jurisdiction of Court in the **Persecution** of My Representative;

Now corrected: ...Now to Be an Announcing of No Further Jurisdiction of Court in the **Prosecution** of My Representative;

Section Revelation 132 Letter Closing, p. 372

The letter closing was missed in First Edition, now added in Second Edition.

**The Lord Jesus Christ
Author**

Section Revelation 134:26, p. 376

Was: Now be of full power to correct **thy** heinous crimes

Now corrected: Now be of full power to correct **these** heinous crimes

Section Revelation 134:53, p. 377

Was: Cease thy wicked **attack,**

Now corrected: Cease thy wicked **attacks,**

Section Revelation 134:56, p. 377

Was: ...who combined with lying apostate witnesses **in** evil combination with government prosecuting power,

Now corrected: ...who combined with lying apostate witnesses **of** evil combination with government prosecuting power,

Section Revelation 134:58, p. 378

Was: ...to voice **belief,** without harm coming upon them;

Now corrected: ...to voice **beliefs,** without harm coming upon them;

Section Revelation 134:67, p. 378

Was: **This** evil of unborn children being murdered,

Now corrected: **Thus,** evil of unborn children being murdered,

Section Revelation 134:131, p. 381

Was: ...unto full power **of** judgments,

Now corrected: ...unto full power judgments,

Section Revelation 134:132, p. 381

Was: Thus **I am** doing all things righteous and holy,

Now corrected: Thus **am I** doing all things righteous and holy,

Section Revelation 134:139, p. 381

Was: ...to administer eternal salvation **to** any on earth.

Now corrected: ...to administer eternal salvation **unto** any on earth.

Section Revelation 134:148, p. 382

The following verse was missed in First Edition, now added in Second Edition as verse 148; thus changing succeeding verse numbering.

148. Now let these truths go before appeals courts as my own will, saith Jesus Christ, to be of full way considered, as pure truth; sufficient to reverse all unjust court rulings against my servant and his brethren prosecuted because they live my Celestial Law, which only I, the Lord, can rightly govern.

Section Revelation 137:9, p. 384

Was: ...who is of full authority to cleanse ungodly way of unborn **children** murder,

Now corrected: ...who is of full authority to cleanse ungodly way of unborn **child** murder,

Section Revelation 138:12, p. 385

Was: From among your own **peoples** cometh unrest...for I will not allow you of the **America** land to continue in pleasure in unholy wicked way;

Now corrected: From among your own **people** cometh unrest...for I will not allow you of the **American** land to continue in pleasure in unholy wicked way;

Section Revelation 138:34, p. 386

Was: ...cease life-corrupting way;

Now corrected: ...cease **such** life-corrupting way;

Section Revelation 138:40, p. 387

Was: ...as **storms** shall be of damaging electrical system

Now corrected: ...as **storm** shall be of damaging electrical system

Section Revelation 140:27, p. 390

Was: ...to remove the wicked by full **judgment** of war,

Now corrected: ...to remove the wicked by full **judgments** of war,

Section Revelation 140:30, p. 390

Was: ...a full sin unto eternal death of **the** spirit

Now corrected: ...a full sin unto eternal death of **thy** spirit

Section Revelation 141:6, p. 392

Was: ...throughout the population in **certain** wicked places on earth.

Now corrected: ...throughout the population in **some** wicked places on earth.

Section Revelation 141:10, p. 392

Was: ...other tribes gathering to that former land of **my** possessing,

Now corrected: ...other tribes gathering to that former land of **their** possessing,

Section Revelation 141:13, p. 392

Was: ...even declaring **more** windstorms and earthquakes,

Now corrected: ...even declaring **new** windstorms and earthquakes,

Section Revelation 141:14, p. 392

Was: ...lifting them **above** the earth, if needs be by power of Celestial power.

Now corrected: ...lifting them **up off** the earth, if needs be, by power of Celestial power.

Section Revelation 143:2, p. 396

Was: I, who am of **the** full Godhood power over world,

Now corrected: I, who am of full Godhood power over world,

Section Revelation 146:37, p. 401

Was: If **they** heed me not,

Now corrected: If **thou** heed me not,

Section Revelation 147:18, p. 405

Was: ...as prophesied by my holy apostle of the **writing** in holy order of my New Testament

Now corrected: ...as prophesied by my holy apostle of the **writ** in holy order of my New Testament

Section Revelation 147:28, p. 406

Was: **Nations** of the way of my New Era holy way,

Now corrected: **Nation** of the way of my New Era holy way,

Section Revelation 149:63, p. 410

Was: ...in all **religions** of pure way teaching.

Now corrected: ...in all **religion** of pure way teaching.

Section Revelation 150 Title, pp. XXIV, 412

Was: ...Let All Awake to Reality of Holy Power

Now corrected: ...Let All Awake to Reality of **My** Holy Power

Section Revelation 150:46, p. 414

Was: Be **prompting** life way

Now corrected: Be **promoting** life way

Section Revelation 150:70, p. 414

Was: **Thus** is my holy word to all peoples,

Now corrected: **This** is my holy word to all peoples,

Section Revelation 150:89, p. 415

Was: ...to be of a full way delivered from death, hell, **and** the devil,

Now corrected: ...to be of a full way delivered from death, hell, the devil,

Section Revelation 150:114, p. 416

Was: I have caused Joseph Smith to retranslate **the** Bible,

Now corrected: I have caused Joseph Smith to retranslate **my** Bible,

Section Revelation 151:9, p. 418

Was: Receive my warnings, all of **legislature** power,

Now corrected: Receive my warnings, all of **legislative** power,

Section Revelation 153:8, p. 420

Was: ...which considers murder of whom you will as a national interest of **prosecution**.

Now corrected: ...which considers murder of whom you will as a national interest of **preservation**.

Section Revelation 155:1, p. 422

Was: ...have spoken**, and the** whirlwind judgment nature soon at hand.

Now corrected: ...have spoken **of a** whirlwind judgment nature soon at hand.

Section Revelation 156:15, p. 423

Was: ...by abiding Celestial Law of probationary pure holy governing **Godhead** law of my Eternal Order;

Now corrected: ...by abiding Celestial Law of probationary pure holy governing **Godhood** law of my Eternal Order;

Section Revelation 156:51, p. 425

Was: ...that God speaketh in this day,

Now corrected: ...that God speaketh in this **thy** day,

Section Revelation 158 Title, pp. XXVI, 431

Was: ...Unto a Judging **All** a Full

Eternal Order Power Judging, of a Just God,

Now corrected: ...Unto a Judging, a Full Eternal Order Power Judging of a Just God,

Section Revelation 158:64, p. 433

Was: ...all of the way of truth-loving order, **or** governing power.

Now corrected: ...all of the way of truth-loving order **of** governing power.

Section Revelation 158:92, p. 434

Was: ...to have **holy** peace in thy soul,

Now corrected: ...to have **only** peace in thy soul,

Section Revelation 158:95, p. 434

Was: ...to all who come to **die,** by my Holy Priesthood power authority on earth.

Now corrected: ...to all who come to **me** by my Holy Priesthood power authority on earth.

Section Revelation 159:59, p. 438

Was: ...to accounting **in** eternal judgment of full justice power.

Now corrected: ...to accounting**; an** eternal judgment of full justice power.

Section Revelation 159:77, p. 439

Was: Nation of evil shall be humbled by my power of full **judgment** of cleansing order;

Now corrected: Nation of evil shall be humbled by my power of full **judgments** of cleansing order;

Section Revelation 159:80, p. 439

Was: ...as I send **judgments** to be of my way of my coming among all nations.

Now corrected: ...as I send **judgment**

to be of my way of my coming among all nations.

Section Revelation 159:113, p. 440

Was: ...on land **of** professing freedom;

Now corrected: ...on land professing freedom;

Section Revelation 159:134, p. 441

Was: ...let them go by my appeal to Supreme Court of that state,

Now corrected: ...let them go by my appeal to **the** Supreme Court of that state,

Section Revelation 159:144, p. 441

Was: ...full way power of **delivering** unto innocence.

Now corrected: ...full way power of **delivery** unto innocence.

Section Revelation 159:147, p. 441

Was: Pass **laws** for religion to be of free way in all lands,

Now corrected: Pass **law** for religion to be of free way in all lands,

Section Revelations 160-161 Opening Word, pp. XXVI, 443

Was: ...Live Unto Righteous Holy Way**,** to Be **of** Surviving My Judgment on All Wicked Corrupt Peoples;

Now corrected: ...Live Unto Righteous Holy Way to Be Surviving My Judgment on All Wicked Corrupt Peoples;

Section Revelation 160:29, p. 445

Was: I **am** able to reveal truth in all cases of judging

Now corrected: I able to reveal truth in all cases of judging

Section Revelation 160:30, p. 445

Was: ...of all involved in any **cause** of misconduct.

Now corrected: ...of all involved in any **case** of misconduct.

Section Revelation 160:34, p. 445

Was: ...as all shall **know** by my power eternal order of governing order on earth;

Now corrected: ...as all shall **be known** by my power eternal order of governing order on earth;

Section Revelation 160:58, p. 446

Was: ...all at once suddenly of **the** knowledge,

Now corrected: ...all at once suddenly of **my** knowledge,

Section Revelation 161:28, p. 448

Was: ...of my **unholy** condemning them of immoral way

Now corrected: ...of my condemning them of immoral way

Section Revelation 161:76, p. 450

Was: ...**then** to be used by government prosecution order

Now corrected: ...**they** to be used by government prosecution order

Section Revelation 161:100, p. 451

Was: ...of the way of **Godhood** order over this world.

Now corrected: ...of the way of **Godhead** order over this world.

Section Revelation 161:111, p. 452

Was: Let all not be of unbelieving on earth;

Now corrected: Let all not be of unbelieving **way** on earth;

Section Revelations 162-163 Opening Word, pp. XXVII, 453

The following portion was missed in First Edition, now added in Second Edition.

Let All Take Heed to Be of Eternal Wise Order. Hear My Will of the Order of Eternal Power:

Section Revelation 162:17, p. 454

Was: ...on the way of **nation** no longer of trust

Now corrected: ...on the way of **nations** no longer of trust

Section Revelation 162:18, p. 454

Was: ...personal business way debt or **peoples** of personal debt;

Now corrected: ...personal business way debt or **people** of personal debt;

Section Revelation 163:3-4, p. 459

Due to the word corrections, the punctuation and wording has been adjusted in the following verses.

Was: 3. ...murderers in thy God's eyes, **an Eternal Judge.**

4. **You** shall meet thy Lord in shame,

Now corrected: 3. ...murderers in thy God's eyes.

4. **In eternal judgment** you shall meet thy Lord in shame,

Section Revelation 163:5, p. 459

Was: ...that this sin must be answered by thine own suffering, **an** eternal judgment of a just God;

Now corrected: ...that this sin must be answered by thine own suffering **in** eternal judgment of a just God;

Section Revelation 163:9, p. 459

Was: ...where you heed not thy **love-**Lord message given.

Now corrected: ...where you heed not thy Lord message given.

Section Revelation 165:28, p. 465

Was: ...cleansing off **earth's** more wicked out of all lands,

Now corrected: ...cleansing off **earth** more wicked out of all lands,

Section Revelation 165:40, p. 465

Was: ...leaving thee and **the** people in thy land of desolate way,

Now corrected: ...leaving thee and **thy** people in thy land of desolate way,

Section Revelation 165:90, p. 468

Was: ...Millennial Reign of **h**oly peace **o**rder; love **order** and of truth prevailing.

Now corrected: ...Millennial Reign of **H**oly **P**eace **O**rder, love **of God** and of truth prevailing.

Section Revelation 165:99-100, p. 469

Wording and punctuation for the following verses has been adjusted.

Was: 99. ...holy revealed order word **n**ow.

100. **B**e holy governing way order,

Now corrected: 99. ...holy revealed order word.

100. **N**ow **b**e holy governing way order,

Section Revelation 165:120, p. 470

Was: Let all such apostate enemies; whom shall be of full judgment in day of my coming to earth.

Now corrected: Let all such apostate enemies, **lying to court, taking Priesthood lands, be of full knowing** they **shall be they** whom shall be of full judgment in day of my coming to earth.

Due to the words that were missed in First Edition, now added in Second Edition, the ending wording on page 470 and beginning wording on page 471 has shifted.

Section Revelation 166:34, p. 474

Was: I will witness peace to **an** honest heart

Now corrected: I will witness peace to **any** honest heart

Section Revelation 167:20, p. 477

Was: ...of the order of pure holy way order of heavenly order **coming** to world

Now corrected: ...of the order of pure holy way order of heavenly order **come** to world

Section Revelation 171:6, p. 486

Was: ...the order of conquering way to harm other nation power order

Now corrected: ...the order of conquering **in** way to harm other nation power order

Section Revelation 171:12, p. 486

Was: A way to cleanse nation is **individually** labor

Now corrected: A way to cleanse nation is **individual** labor

Section Revelation 172 Title, p. 487

Placement of title has been adjusted in Second Edition.

Section Revelation 172:13, p. 488

Was: ...on pure principle of constitutional freedom **guaranteed** of religion.

Now corrected: ...on pure principle

of constitutional freedom **guarantee** of religion.

Section Revelation 173:8, p. 490

Was: ...who are living **more** pure holy lives.

Now corrected: ...who are living **moral** pure holy lives.

Section Revelation 173:27, p. 491

Was: ...governing bodies **of** officials

Now corrected: ...governing bodies **or** officials

Section Revelation 177 Title, pp. XXX, 499

Was: ...to All Peoples on **Order** of Earth You Now Dwell Upon,

Now corrected: ...to All Peoples on **Orb** of Earth You Now Dwell Upon,

Section Revelation 178:17, p. 502

Was: ...Rid yourselves of **a** heinous crime

Now corrected: ...Rid yourselves of heinous crime

Section Revelation 178:31, p. 503

Was: ...**yes**, of an eternity of loss of life for they of evil of murder,

Now corrected: ...**yea**, of an eternity of loss of life for they of evil of murder,

Section Revelation 178:33, p. 503

Was: ...you put my **servant** in prison;

Now corrected: ...you put my **servants** in prison;

Section Revelation 178:49, p. 503

Was: ...is thy Lord Jesus **Christ's** own word to this generation,

Now corrected: ...is thy Lord Jesus **Christ** own word to this generation,

Section Revelation 178:52, p. 504

Was: ...to govern all peoples **repenting** on earth.

Now corrected: ...to govern all peoples **remaining** on earth.

Section Revelation 178:69, p. 504

Was: Look at acquired **communicating** of such that has China in admiration power

Now corrected: Look at acquired **communicatings** of such that has China in admiration power

Section Revelation 178:99, p. 506

Was: ...for the way of **"amen"** shall not save you,

Now corrected: ...for the way of **men** shall not save you,

Section Revelation 178:103, p. 506

Was: ...wicked **peoples** removed by judgment of God,

Now corrected: ...wicked **people** removed by judgment of God,

Section Revelation 179:6, p. 508

Was: ...the order of shipping **any** cargo freight source from land of Pakistan... order of danger **for** government of United States;

Now corrected: ...the order of shipping **off** cargo freight source from land of Pakistan...order of danger **to** government of United States;

Section Revelation 179:12, p. 509

Was: ...encasement **top** disassembled portion of nuclear weapon,

Now corrected: ...encasement **for** disassembled portion of nuclear weapon,

Section Revelation 179:14, p. 509

Was: Now know source was of other Islamic nation **of** Pakistan;

Now corrected: Now know source was of other Islamic nation **to** Pakistan;

Section Revelation 180:3, p. 512

Was: **The** earthly weapons are of no defense

Now corrected: **Thy** earthly weapons are of no defense

Section Revelation 180:20, p. 512

Was: ...broken off from Catholic **connections** are also not holy

Now corrected: ...broken off from Catholic **connection** are also not holy

Section Revelation 180:21, p. 512

Was: All **are** not of principle of now revelation from God;

Now corrected: All not of principle of now revelation from God;

Section Revelation 181:15, p. 516

Was: ...to send food, clothing to North Korea to **keep** their order of poor of the way of humanitarian good done;

Now corrected: ...to send food, clothing to North Korea to **feed** their order of poor, of the way of humanitarian good done;

Section Revelation 183:12, p. 520

Was: ...after knowing such is of **guilt** order.

Now corrected: ...after knowing such is of **guilty** order.

Section Revelation 185:2, p. 522

Was: ...as combined nation order shall attack all sides of thy now border order.

Now corrected: ...as combined nation

order shall attack **from** all sides of thy now border order.

Section Revelation 190:33, p. 528

Was: Let thy youth in all nation order be of **thy** way to respect life

Now corrected: Let thy youth in all nation order be of **the** way to respect life

Appendix Footer, pp. 539-541

Was: **Chapter 9**

Now corrected: **Appendix**

Section Revelation 200:8, p. 540

Was: Now cleanse out all in thy **nations** of murder of unborn child order.

Now corrected: Now cleanse out all in thy **nation** of murder of unborn child order.

Section Revelation 200:10, p. 540

Was: Now do full **obedience** to Jesus Christ,

Now corrected: Now do full **obeisance** to Jesus Christ,

Section Revelation 204:1, p. 547

Was: ...**with** many tasks of government interference against my holy revealed religion,

Now corrected: ...**in the** many tasks of government interference against my holy revealed religion,

Section Revelation 205:2, p. 548

Was: ...my chosen people, **to** live the law of holy pure intent,

Now corrected: ...my chosen people **who** live the law of holy pure intent,

Section Revelation 205:17, p. 549

Was: Let my word be conveyed to governing power on **the** land of my coming,

Now corrected: Let my word be conveyed to governing power on **my** land of my coming,

Section Revelation 205:40, p. 550

Was: ...as is guaranteed by the law of original power of full religious freedom.

Now corrected: ...as is guaranteed by the law of original power of **the** full religious freedom.

Section Revelation 207:20, p. 577

Was: Let all now acknowledge **my** having the right to rule

Now corrected: Let all now acknowledge **me** having the right to rule

Section Revelation 209:1, p. 579

Was: **It is** my holy will concerning Celestial Law

Now corrected: **In** my holy will concerning Celestial Law

Section Revelation 210:2, p. 584

Was: I sent the Keyholders of keys and **power** to deliver to my One Man

Now corrected: I sent the Keyholders of keys and **powers** to deliver to my One Man

Section Revelation 213:2, p. 630

Was: ...in raising up nation **free of** religious exercise

Now corrected: ...in raising up nation **of free** religious exercise

Section Revelation 213:20, p. 631

Was: ...even **endow** my pure holy way being known to all people.

Now corrected: ...even my pure holy way being known to all people.

Section Revelation 213:28, p. 632

Was: Let it be **of** law in the land by constitutional preserving power...to be

my authority of law above the changing law of **many**,

Now corrected: Let it be **a** law in the land by constitutional preserving power...to be my authority of law above the changing law of **man**,

Section Revelation 215:25, p. 645

Was: ...holding the sealing power of Elijah in full Priesthood power **and** all people;

Now corrected: ...holding the sealing power of Elijah in full Priesthood power **over** all people;

Section Revelation 221:2, p. 732

Was: ...ordained servant of continuing my Keyholder power**,** John Taylor,

Now corrected: ...ordained servant of continuing my Keyholder power **after** John Taylor

Section Revelation 221:3, p. 732

Was: ...who was able to visit the heavenly **power**...save I **shall** reveal.

Now corrected: ...who was able to visit the heavenly **powers**...save I **should** reveal.

Section Revelation 221:8, p. 732

Was: ...until he continued my law in hiding **unto** John Y. Barlow,

Now corrected: ...until he continued my law in hiding **until** John Y. Barlow,

Section Revelation 222:2, p. 739

Was: ...I then having quorum called by him

Now corrected: ...I then having **a** quorum called by him

Section Revelation 222:3, p. 739

Was: ...Law of Celestial Plural

Marriages; even that **origination** once of my Priesthood.

Now corrected: ...Law of Celestial Plural **Marriage**; even that **organization** once of my Priesthood.

Section Revelation 227:11, p. 771

Was: ...light **eternally**, and with power of increase.

Now corrected: ...light **eternal**, and with power of increase.

Section Revelation 230:16, p. 784

Was: ...I, their Lord, command; being of thy persecuting way, need also delivering.

Now corrected: ...I, their Lord, command; **thus** being of thy persecuting way, need also delivering.

Section Revelation 233:23, p. 791

Was: ...even they who also **love** Sodom...even Celestial power of my sending the cleansing and destructive **powers**;

Now corrected: ...even they who also **live** Sodom...even Celestial power of my sending the cleansing and destructive **power**;

Section Revelation 233:41, p. 792

Was: ...wicked joining of the false **witness** and governing powers.

Now corrected: ...wicked joining of the false **witnesses** and governing powers.

Section Revelation 236, p. 800

Verse numbering began with 4 in First Edition, now corrected to begin with 1 in Second Edition.

Section Revelation 236:5, p. 800

Was: 8. ...by Constitution of nation.

Now corrected: 5. ...by Constitution of **the** nation.

Section Revelation 5, p. 803

The comprising note in First Edition did not pertain to this Section Revelation and was removed in Second Edition.

Proclamation Appendix B, pp. 838-841

Formatting has been adjusted in Second Edition.

Section Revelation 218 Title, p. 839

The title was not listed in First Edition Appendix B, now added in Second Edition.

Law of Eternal Marriage Made Known to All People as a Holy Way of Pure Holy Law of Exaltation

Third Court of Appeals Filing, p. 949

In the filed document, the Zip Code should have been 76936.

Third Court of Appeals Filing, p. 959

In the filed document, Exhibit 1 should have been listed as a Letter to the 51ˢᵗ Judicial District Court of Schleicher County, Texas.

Supreme Court of Texas Filing, p. 962

In the filed document, the misplaced comma in verse 8 should have been directly after the word "read".

Section Revelation 159:46, p. 437

Section 132 of Doctrine and Covenants, written by Joseph Smith in behalf of the Lord on Celestial Plural Marriage, was of compiling error not included in original mailing and was to have been printed with Section Revelation 159; now found in this book to fulfill the word of the Lord.

Doctrine and Covenants, Section 132

Revelation of the Lord Jesus Christ
Given to President Joseph Smith, Jun.
Nauvoo, Illinois
Recorded July 12, 1843

1. Verily, thus saith the Lord unto you my servant Joseph, that inasmuch as you have inquired of my hand to know and understand wherein I, the Lord, justified my servants Abraham, Isaac, and Jacob, as also Moses, David and Solomon, my servants, as touching the principle and doctrine of their having many wives and concubines --

2. Behold, and lo, I am the Lord thy God, and will answer thee as touching this matter.

3. Therefore, prepare thy heart to receive and obey the instructions which I am about to give unto you; for all those who have this law revealed unto them must obey the same.

4. For behold, I reveal unto you a new and an everlasting covenant; and if ye abide not that covenant, then are ye damned; for no one can reject this covenant and be permitted to enter into my glory.

5. For all who will have a blessing at my hands shall abide the law which was appointed for that blessing, and the conditions thereof, as were instituted from before the foundation of the world.

6. And as pertaining to the new and everlasting covenant, it was instituted for the fulness of my glory; and he that receiveth a fulness thereof must and shall abide the law, or he shall be damned, saith the Lord God.

7. And verily I say unto you, that the conditions of this law are these: All covenants, contracts, bonds, obligations, oaths, vows, performances, connections, associations, or expectations, that are not made and entered into and sealed by the Holy Spirit of promise, of him who is anointed, both as well for time and for all eternity, and that too most holy, by revelation and commandment through the medium of mine anointed, whom I have appointed on the earth to hold this power (and I have appointed unto my servant Joseph to hold this power in the last days, and there is never but one on the earth at a time on whom this power and the keys of this priesthood are conferred), are of no efficacy, virtue, or force in and after the resurrection from the dead; for all contracts that are not made unto this end have an end when men are dead.

8. Behold, mine house is a house of order, saith the Lord God, and not a house of confusion.

9. Will I accept of an offering, saith the Lord, that is not made in my name?

10. Or will I receive at your hands that which I have not appointed?

11. And will I appoint unto you, saith the Lord, except it be by law, even as I and my Father ordained unto you, before the world was?

12. I am the Lord thy God; and I give unto you this commandment -- that no man shall come unto the Father but by me or by my word, which is my law, saith the Lord.

13. And everything that is in the world,

whether it be ordained of men, by thrones, or principalities, or powers, or things of name, whatsoever they may be, that are not by me or by my word, saith the Lord, shall be thrown down, and shall not remain after men are dead, neither in nor after the resurrection, saith the Lord your God.

14. For whatsoever things remain are by me; and whatsoever things are not by me shall be shaken and destroyed.

15. Therefore, if a man marry him a wife in the world, and he marry her not by me nor by my word, and he covenant with her so long as he is in the world and she with him, their covenant and marriage are not of force when they are dead, and when they are out of the world; therefore, they are not bound by any law when they are out of the world.

16. Therefore, when they are out of the world they neither marry nor are given in marriage; but are appointed angels in heaven, which angels are ministering servants, to minister for those who are worthy of a far more, and an exceeding, and an eternal weight of glory.

17. For these angels did not abide my law; therefore, they cannot be enlarged, but remain separately and singly, without exaltation, in their saved condition, to all eternity; and from henceforth are not gods, but are angels of God forever and ever.

18. And again, verily I say unto you, if a man marry a wife, and make a covenant with her for time and for all eternity, if that covenant is not by me or by my word, which is my law, and is not sealed by the Holy Spirit of promise, through him who I have anointed and appointed unto this power, then it is not valid neither of force when they are out of the world, because they are not joined by me, saith the Lord, neither by my word; when they are out of the world it cannot be received there, because the angels and the gods are appointed there, by whom they cannot pass; they cannot, therefore, inherit my glory; for my house is a house of order, saith the Lord God.

19. And again, verily I say unto you, if a man marry a wife by my word, which is my law, and by the new and everlasting covenant, and it is sealed unto them by the Holy Spirit of promise, by him who is anointed, unto whom I have appointed this power and the keys of this priesthood; and it shall be said unto them -- Ye shall come forth in the first resurrection; and if it be after the first resurrection, in the next resurrection; and shall inherit thrones, kingdoms, principalities, and powers, dominions, all heights and depths -- then shall it be written in the Lamb's Book of Life, that he shall commit no murder whereby to shed innocent blood, and if ye abide in my covenant, and commit no murder whereby to shed innocent blood, it shall be done unto them in all things whatsoever my servant hath put upon them, in time, and through all eternity; and shall be of full force when they are out of the world; and they shall pass by the angels, and the gods, which are set there, to their exaltation and glory in all things, as hath been sealed upon their heads, which glory shall be a fulness and a continuation of the seeds forever and ever.

20. Then shall they be gods, because they have no end; therefore shall they be from everlasting to everlasting, because they continue; then shall they be above all, because all things are subject unto them. Then shall they be gods, because they have all power and the angels are subject unto them.

21. Verily, verily, I say unto you, except ye abide my law ye cannot attain to this glory.

22. For strait is the gate, and narrow

the way that leadeth unto the exaltation and continuation of the lives, and few there be that find it, because ye receive me not in the world neither do ye know me.

23. But if ye receive me in the world, then shall ye know me, and shall receive your exaltation; that where I am ye shall be also.

24. This is eternal lives -- to know the only wise and true God, and Jesus Christ, whom he hath sent. I am he. Receive ye, therefore, my law.

25. Broad is the gate, and wide the way that leadeth to the deaths; and many there are that go in thereat, because they receive me not, neither do they abide in my law.

26. Verily, verily, I say unto you, if a man marry a wife according to my word, and they are sealed by the Holy Spirit of promise, according to mine appointment, and he or she shall commit any sin or transgression of the new and everlasting covenant whatever, and all manner of blasphemies, and if they commit no murder wherein they shed innocent blood, yet they shall come forth in the first resurrection, and enter into their exaltation; but they shall be destroyed in the flesh, and shall be delivered unto the buffetings of Satan unto the day of redemption, saith the Lord God.

27. The blasphemy against the Holy Ghost, which shall not be forgiven in the world nor out of the world, is in that ye commit murder wherein ye shed innocent blood, and assent unto my death, after ye have received my new and everlasting covenant, saith the Lord God; and he that abideth not this law can in nowise enter into my glory, but shall be damned, saith the Lord.

28. I am the Lord thy God, and will give unto thee the law of my Holy Priesthood, as was ordained by me and my Father before the world was.

29. Abraham received all things, whatsoever he received, by revelation and commandment, by my word, saith the Lord, and hath entered into his exaltation and sitteth upon his throne.

30. Abraham received promises concerning his seed, and of the fruit of his loins -- from whose loins ye are, namely, my servant Joseph -- which were to continue so long as they were in the world; and as touching Abraham and his seed, out of the world they should continue; both in the world and out of the world should they continue as innumerable as the stars; or, if ye were to count the sand upon the seashore ye could not number them.

31. This promise is yours also, because ye are of Abraham, and the promise was made unto Abraham; and by this law is the continuation of the works of my Father, wherein he glorifieth himself.

32. Go ye, therefore, and do the works of Abraham; enter ye into my law and ye shall be saved.

33. But if ye enter not into my law ye cannot receive the promise of my Father, which he made unto Abraham.

34. God commanded Abraham, and Sarah gave Hagar to Abraham to wife. And why did she do it? Because this was the law; and from Hagar sprang many people. This, therefore, was fulfilling, among other things, the promises.

35. Was Abraham, therefore, under condemnation? Verily I say unto you, Nay; for I, the Lord, commanded it.

36. Abraham was commanded to offer his son Isaac; nevertheless, it was written: Thou shalt not kill. Abraham, however, did not refuse, and it was accounted unto him for righteousness.

37. Abraham received concubines, and they bore him children; and it was accounted unto him for righteousness, because they were given unto him, and he abode in my law; as Isaac also and Jacob did none other things than that which they were commanded; and because they did none other things than that which they were commanded, they have entered into their exaltation, according to the promises, and sit upon thrones, and are not angels but are gods.

38. David also received many wives and concubines, and also Solomon and Moses my servants, as also many others of my servants, from the beginning of creation until this time; and in nothing did they sin save in those things which they received not of me.

39. David's wives and concubines were given unto him of me, by the hand of Nathan, my servant, and others of the prophets who had the keys of this power; and in none of these things did he sin against me save in the case of Uriah and his wife; and, therefore he hath fallen from his exaltation, and received his portion; and he shall not inherit them out of the world, for I gave them unto another, saith the Lord.

40. I am the Lord thy God, and I gave unto thee, my servant Joseph, an appointment, and restore all things. Ask what ye will, and it shall be given unto you according to my word.

41. And as ye have asked concerning adultery, verily, verily, I say unto you, if a man receiveth a wife in the new and everlasting covenant, and if she be with another man, and I have not appointed unto her by the holy anointing, she hath committed adultery and shall be destroyed.

42. If she be not in the new and everlasting covenant, and she be with another man, she has committed adultery.

43. And if her husband be with another woman, and he was under a vow, he hath broken his vow and hath committed adultery.

44. And if she hath not committed adultery, but is innocent and hath not broken her vow, and she knoweth it, and I reveal it unto you, my servant Joseph, then shall you have power, by the power of my Holy Priesthood, to take her and give her unto him that hath not committed adultery but hath been faithful; for he shall be made ruler over many.

45. For I have conferred upon you the keys and power of the priesthood, wherein I restore all things, and make known unto you all things in due time.

46. And verily, verily, I say unto you, that whatsoever you seal on earth shall be sealed in heaven; and whatsoever you bind on earth, in my name and by my word, saith the Lord, it shall be eternally bound in the heavens; and whosesoever sins you remit on earth shall be remitted eternally in the heavens; and whosesoever sins you retain on earth shall be retained in heaven.

47. And again, verily I say, whomsoever you bless I will bless, and whomsoever you curse I will curse, saith the Lord; for I, the Lord, am thy God.

48. And again, verily I say unto you, my servant Joseph, that whatsoever you give on earth, and to whomsoever you give any one on earth, by my word and according to my law, it shall be visited with blessings and not cursings, and with my power, saith the Lord, and shall be without condemnation on earth and in heaven.

49. For I am the Lord thy God, and will be with thee even unto the end of the world, and through all eternity; for verily I

seal upon you your exaltation, and prepare a throne for you in the kingdom of my Father, with Abraham your father.

50. Behold, I have seen your sacrifices, and will forgive all your sins; I have seen your sacrifices in obedience to that which I have told you. Go, therefore, and I make a way for your escape, as I accepted the offering of Abraham of his son Isaac.

51. Verily, I say unto you: A commandment I give unto mine handmaid, Emma Smith, your wife, whom I have given unto you, that she stay herself and partake not of that which I commanded you to offer unto her; for I did it, saith the Lord, to prove you all, as I did Abraham, and that I might require an offering at your hand, by covenant and sacrifice.

52. And let mine handmaid, Emma Smith, receive all those that have been given unto my servant Joseph, and who are virtuous and pure before me; and those who are not pure, and have said they were pure, shall be destroyed, saith the Lord God.

53. For I am the Lord thy God, and ye shall obey my voice; and I give unto my servant Joseph that he shall be made ruler over many things; for he hath been faithful over a few things, and from henceforth I will strengthen him.

54. And I command mine handmaid, Emma Smith, to abide and cleave unto my servant Joseph, and to none else. But if she will not abide this commandment she shall be destroyed, saith the Lord; for I am the Lord thy God, and will destroy her if she abide not in my law.

55. But if she will not abide this commandment, then shall my servant Joseph do all things for her, even as he hath said; and I will bless him and multiply him and give unto him an hundred-fold in this world, of fathers and mothers, brothers and sisters, houses and lands, wives and children, and crowns of eternal lives in the eternal worlds.

56. And again, verily I say, let mine handmaid forgive my servant Joseph his trespasses; and then shall she be forgiven her trespasses, wherein she has trespassed against me; and I, the Lord thy God, will bless her, and multiply her, and make her heart to rejoice.

57. And again, I say, let not my servant Joseph put his property out of his hands, lest an enemy come and destroy him; for Satan seeketh to destroy; for I am the Lord thy God, and he is my servant; and behold, and lo, I am with him, as I was with Abraham, thy father, even unto his exaltation and glory.

58. Now, as touching the law of the priesthood, there are many things pertaining thereunto.

59. Verily, if a man be called of my Father, as was Aaron, by mine own voice, and by the voice of him that sent me, and I have endowed him with the keys of the power of this priesthood, if he do anything in my name, and according to my law and by my word, he will not commit sin, and I will justify him.

60. Let no one, therefore, set on my servant Joseph; for I will justify him; for he shall do the sacrifice which I require at his hands for his transgressions, saith the Lord your God.

61. And again, as pertaining to the law of the priesthood -- if any man espouse a virgin, and desire to espouse another, and the first give her consent, and if he espouse the second, and they are virgins, and have vowed to no other man, then is he justified; he cannot commit adultery for they are given unto him; for he cannot commit

adultery with that that belongeth unto him and to no one else.

62. And if he have ten virgins given unto him by this law, he cannot commit adultery, for they belong to him, and they are given unto him; therefore is he justified.

63. But if one or either of the ten virgins, after she is espoused, shall be with another man, she has committed adultery, and shall be destroyed; for they are given unto him to multiply and replenish the earth, according to my commandment, and to fulfil the promise which was given by my Father before the foundation of the world, and for their exaltation in the eternal worlds, that they may bear the souls of men; for herein is the work of my Father continued, that he may be glorified.

64. And again, verily, verily, I say unto you, if any man have a wife, who holds the keys of this power, and he teaches unto her the law of my priesthood, as pertaining to these things, then shall she believe and administer unto him, or she shall be destroyed, saith the Lord your God; for I will destroy her; for I will magnify my name upon all those who receive and abide in my law.

65. Therefore, it shall be lawful in me, if she receive not this law, for him to receive all things whatsoever I, the Lord his God, will give unto him, because she did not believe and administer unto him according to my word; and she then becomes the transgressor; and he is exempt from the law of Sarah, who administered unto Abraham according to the law when I commanded Abraham to take Hagar to wife.

66. And now, as pertaining to this law, verily, verily, I say unto you, I will reveal more unto you, hereafter; therefore, let this suffice for the present. Behold, I am Alpha and Omega. Amen.

JESUS CHRIST SON AHMAN

CAUSE NOS. 990, 997, 1017, 1061

STATE OF TEXAS	§	**IN THE DISTRICT COURT**
VS.	§	**51ST JUDICIAL DISTRICT**
WARREN STEED JEFFS	§	**SCHLEICHER COUNTY, TEXAS**

AMENDED COVERSHEET ONLY

NOT PRO SE / FILED DECEMBER 27, 2011 AT 10:23 AM

Fundamentalist Church of Jesus Christ of Latter-day Saints
P.O. Box 840459
Hildale, Utah 84784

Jesus Christ, Even God Over All, Saith:

Thus Saith Son Ahman, Even Jesus Your Lord, to Present Court, That Is Not of Authority to Judge and Confine My People, Being No Authority Over Religion of Constitution Guarantee of Preserving Religious Freedom; Yet You Now Are of a Full Way of Persecuting Power Against My Innocent Obeying Order of Holy Eternal Priesthood; Hear My Own Message to Thee, Now to Be an Announcing of No Further Jurisdiction of Court in the Persecution of My Representative; of Full Authority to Administer My Celestial Law Unto Pure Noble Sons, Unto My Holy Way Celestial Preparing for My Own Coming Among Men:

Revelation of the Lord Jesus Christ Given to President Warren S. Jeffs

Palestine, Texas
Monday, October 24, 2011

1. Verily, thus saith the Lord, even Son Ahman, unto court of persecution against my Church, of the way of not being of pure ruling; using governing power unjustly; even unto a wrong ruling of penalizing my Priesthood power of my own eternal power on earth unto bondage keeping, as it were, for a life sentencing --

2. I, your Lord, have seen the conspiring and evil combining, in mind and word also now in full way of fulfilling, to put my holy servant in prison unto a full lifetime.

3. Let all now know I shall be my full administrating justice on all of the power of dark intent, who have judged my holy way to be of evil, when my appointed servant and Keyholder of the full power of Eternal Power of thy God on earth, only has done my holy appointed guiding, ordaining, administering, of a holy Celestial Law; not to be interfered with by earthly and civil governing powers; my Order being of full religious protecting by Constitution guarantee; thus you have been told by my own will sent to you of thy full sin.

4. Now reverse all rulings of unjust, and now imprisoning way.

5. Now let my servant be free.

6. I shall have all be of an accounting, unto Eternal Judgment, saith your God. Amen.

Revelation of the Lord Jesus Christ
Given to President Warren S. Jeffs

Palestine, Texas
Thursday, October 13, 2011

1. I, even Jesus Christ, speak to the present judge over court proceedings against my servant Warren Jeffs: I cause him to no longer be of an answering of your unjust and corrupt and unauthorized rulings; as I, the Lord, even Jesus Christ, am above all, and my law is religious and of me, a heavenly power over all creation.

2. Your judging is not based on truth.

3. I cause him to not answer to the court.

4. Let thy rulings against him cease.

5. I shall soon lay a heavy hand on all who fight against my Priesthood and Church, saith the Lord.

6. Now know I am God, even above all, and court of persecution shall be of a ceasing in my way of eternal power taking a hand if you will continue unjust way. Amen.

The Lord Jesus Christ
Author

_____

President Warren S. Jeffs, President of Church of Jesus Christ
Representative of our Lord and God who is Jesus Christ

Kingdom of Zion
2420 CR 300
Eldorado, Texas 76936

Jesus Christ, Even Jehovah, God Over All Creation

Thus I Have Redeemed My People. I Am Now Their Holy King Of the Kingdom of Ahman of the Domain of Son Ahman. Amen.

Thus saith the Lord to appeals court in consideration of appeal number 03-11-00568-CR:

Revelation of the Lord Jesus Christ Given to President Warren S. Jeffs

Palestine, Texas
Saturday, November 12, 2011

1. I, Jesus Christ, over all, even God over all, speak to appeals court:

2. Let my servant and his brethren in prison go free.

3. Reverse unjust court's rulings.

4. Do not uphold unjust way.

5. My religion of my own revealing has constitutional protection of freedom of religion.

6. Now be of just power.

7. Receive my holy will.

8. My word is truth.

9. I am now of full power to reverse all courts.

10. Be ready to do justly on following cause numbers:

    51st Judicial District Court Cause No. 990

    51st Judicial District Court Cause No. 997

    51st Judicial District Court Cause No. 1017

    51st Judicial District Court Cause No. 1061

11. I, your Lord, am soon to drive all evil from my land of Zion, even America.

12. I shall be of full way of cleansing.

13. Now deal justly, and order case dismissed; reversing unjust life sentence on foundation truth my religion of my own giving among men is not being protected by law of constitutional freedom. Amen.

14. Hear now my revealing in thy souls.

15. Let my own appeal document of my own revealing touch truth-loving hearts. Amen.

Kingdom of Zion
2420 CR 300
Eldorado, Texas 7636

Jesus Christ, Even Jehovah, God Over All Creation

Thus I Have Redeemed My People. I Am Now Their Holy King of the Kingdom of Ahman of the Domain of Son Ahman. Amen.

Thus saith your Lord Jesus Christ, the Holy Power of Redeeming Power for all mankind of all nations, of all ages of time, to all nations, peoples, kindreds, tongues, and governing powers; my own word in great plainness to all peoples, of my own coming; of great whirl-wind judgments of the pure way of my holy love justifying judgments of Eternity Power; thus giving mine own word to all peoples on earth; a word of eternal importance to all now on the earth, to be of full receiving my own will concerning all peoples on earth; also to teach truth of pure way of judging, of holy way of my eternal law of holy Marriage Union of Eternal Union of Plural Celestial Marriage of my holy power authorizing select few to thus live; not to be of interference by any not of my own authority of Holy Eternal Priest-hood of my sending; thus saith the Lord to this now generation on the earth, my own will to all; both of the governing powers of all nations; also their peoples. Hear thou my holy message given by my holy servant on earth as my Mouthpiece, though in bondage; to be in the hands of all peoples, to know of my soon labor of cleansing all lands of more wicked, to preserve the more righteous; yea, hear my own word given through my own power, to my holy servant Warren Jeffs; though suffering in prison; yet of my order of pure Priesthood of holy calling to give my own will to all peoples, by my power, who will receive my word.

Revelation of the Lord Jesus Christ
Given to President Warren S. Jeffs

Palestine, Texas
Monday, December 12, 2011

1. Let all peoples be of a listening; to be of full pure receiving; to have my own will manifest unto the way of pure holy eternal truth being sent to all nations on earth.

2. Let now my holy will be known.

3. Let all render honor, obeying, and pure holy living unto your Holy Redeemer, even I who speaketh, Jesus Christ, who is of eternity unto eternity in full Godhood power over all peoples, both on earth; also departed spirits who are of salvation unto my Priesthood eternal power among all nations of the way of teaching my plan of eternal salvation to all, past, and now on the earth in the flesh.

4. Now receive my final power-word warning:

Page 1

5. You are only of the earth; I am of Eternal Power Celestial over all creation.

6. Now be of full obeying my will, to repent, lest sudden eternal holy power full judgments cometh on all nations.

7. Let all be humble.

8. Let all be ready.

9. I soon cometh in holy power of heavenly governing holy authority, to rule on earth for a thousand years with the heavenly hosts, come with my holy authority to be among all peoples, a Millennial Reign of Peace; pure governing power Celestial.

10. Thus I send mine own will to all -- Repent, and be of pure living Celestial way of holy power; a government of pure knowing all things, nothing secret.

11. Verily I say unto all nations -- be ye ready.

12. Make peace, both among thine own peoples and with all other peoples of every land, kindred, tongue; yea, be of my peace-loving forgiveness; for I, God, am the Judge of all peoples, with eternal knowledge Celestial to be my power of knowing all things, nothing hidden.

13. Therefore, fear ye, all ye wicked peoples who are not of belief of my power eternal Celestial; for you shall be of a sudden awaking unto fear when my hand of eternal holy way is stretched forth in judgments of eternal power, such as earthquake, tornado, the sea heaving beyond its bounds unto many swept away; yea, the desolating sickness, the overflowing pestilence of new diseases, of insects, animals, of crops destroyed, famine -- all to humble all people who will not give heed to my holy will, the God of all the earth, even Son Ahman, who is Jesus Christ, the Righteous Judge, the Holy Governor, your Eternal Ruler as King over all peoples.

14. Let now my published Proclamation be of full giving, even to all thy peoples; now of full mailing to libraries all over the world in all nations.

15. Let my other revealings of holy word of my sending, published to all, warning all of my soon power of cleansing; let these go to all thy peoples, having been mailed to the libraries of the earth; so common, and high, and they of power way can read my holy revealing of events of judgments soon to happen on earth; to cleanse off the face of the earth the more wicked; to preserve the more righteous.

16. Let my word cause all to be of sober way, to change from wickedness of violent way, of immoral, murder of unborn children way of living, and be more holy and pure of motive also of living.

17. Let all be more of peace.

18. I soon come to be of a revealing all secrets, past, present, and many eternal future happenings of God's dealings with the nations.

19. Let all now be receiving my holy will. Amen.

20. Let all peoples now give heed.

21. Let my holy power be upon thee through prayer; through noble, humble forgiving all; for the love-peace kindness toward all.

22. Let my holy peace dwell in thy heart, each one, by choosing my holy power Celestial; by receiving my holy Gospel; by knowing all thy works cannot establish peace without God and His eternal power. Amen.

23. Let also all peoples dwell in holy peace of my governing power I send among you when

I come; to have Zion my Capital Governing Authority; to have Old Jerusalem a governing power; for my people Israel shall be gathered from among all nations under heaven.

24. Read Isaiah in Old Testament.

25. He telleth thee mine own will concerning Israel being my Holy Priesthood Celestial authority, to rule all nations under thy Lord and His Celestial power extant, over all the world.

26. Now be of full power to correct thy heinous crimes upheld by your national laws in many lands, the murder of unborn children, some full term, of soon delivery, murdered by legal consent.

27. Thus it is among all peoples -- lustful immoral ways cause many to shed innocent blood, thus becoming nations of murder of innocent, and of unholy doing against innocence.

28. Let all be of my way to uphold virtue, purity of living as honorable, to provide for the raising of children in peace, in a virtuous way; not of hindering the bringing forth of life.

29. Let all cease this most eternal damning sin.

30. Let all know I cometh to bring to an end these horrible evils on earth, to provide new peoples sent by my power Celestial to earth.

31. Let all be my people of pure motive of virtue and life-giving way; to protect unborn children.

32. I shall provide thy peoples with sufficient, to provide food, raiment, housing; all life-needed elements to give to all born on earth; to govern in peace; for the nations on earth shall prosper unto the plenteous gifts of life without covetous way; which leadeth to war and violence among nations, and among peoples of nations one against another.

33. My rule is sure, and true, and of peace, of righteous holy way of living.

34. Come unto me, your Lord.

35. Your earthly governing powers cannot exalt any to eternal life.

36. Only I, your Holy Redeemer, can bring salvation eternal to all who live eternal pure holy way of my holy power of the heavenly powers come to earth.

37. I send you my new publishing of final warning to all nations.

38. Let this be a final word, before whirlwind eternal power judgments cometh on all nations; more especially on my land of Zion, even North and South America, soon to happen;

39. For my holy warning is my justification to sweep the wicked off my land Zion, and from all lands who heed me not, but continue in the sins of spiritual Babylon, which shall fully be removed from the nations, even the corrupt unholy people that inhabit all lands, who have fallen into temptation as entire nations corrupt themselves before the Lord, saith He, even Jesus Christ, who shall recompense to all people the measure they measured to their fellow man on earth; unto a full judgment hereafter;

40. For you are each a son or daughter of God, sent to earth by my power, to be of full way proving thy life, whether you would choose evil or good; the good being of me and my eternal plan of salvation, even the Gospel of life unto eternal life.

41. I am Eternal, my power is eternal.

42. I see all things.

43. Tremble, all ye nations, at my power soon to be fully felt as I remove the righteous unto safety, and the wicked slay the wicked in wars; also, by my eternal power, swift judgments

need to come in order that the wicked do not slay all mine elect who can be of my holy Zion; a chosen pure holy people; my holy people who will receive me and my Gospel in full power Celestial.

44. Let these eternal truths touch honest hearts and minds everywhere.

45. Let only my holy way be thy way, saith God over all, your Lord and Just Holy King; yea, King of kings and Lord of lords. Amen.

46. I, your Lord, now reveal through my servant on earth my holy will, even him whom I have preserved to cause my holy will to go forth before my glorious appearing, to justify thy God to send full cleansing powers to the whole earth, soon to take place.

47. I have him in mine hands. Harm him not.

48. Be of a more sure way of preserving his life while in hands of the present governing powers on my land of my soon coming; for evil and unholy people are seeking to be of a full way removing him from the earth.

49. I, your Lord, tell you of governing powers this truth, so he may be of protecting to do my will.

50. Hinder not my will from coming to all people, lest a swift judgment cometh.

51. I am God.

52. I have all peoples in mine holy hands of eternal power.

53. Cease thy wicked attack, ye government authorities in the United States of America, against my people and my Church.

54. Do not be of the way like they who crucified your Lord, believing false witnessing against my servant and my people on earth.

55. Let all my servants in bondage go free.

56. Merril Jessop, an aged ailing pure holy man of my Church, of eternal holy way of pure holy living, is now also unjustly held in prison by an unjust court; an evil tribunal who combined with lying apostate witnesses in evil combination with government prosecuting power, to put innocent and obeying sons of my Priesthood authority behind the prison walls.

57. Now let them all go free, lest the nation prove only to be of the way of persecuting innocence; destroying life of unborn children; of taking away my people's homes by court unjust rulings in the way of false witnesses believed; a holy Church under government attack, not protected in religious practice in a land boasting of religious freedom; yet denying my people freedom to live my holy religion revealed from heaven by your Lord, through the instrumentality of my holy Prophet Joseph Smith in previous century in thy nation of the United States.

58. Behold my Proclamation recently mailed to all nations, to all leaders of nations, to governing authorities in every state in thy nation of the United States; yea, to all religious societies and libraries -- all receiving my own holy will of pure truth; telling all of my holy religion being of persecuted way since Joseph Smith's time; he also suffering a martyr's death in a nation of supposed freedom; leaders not willing to step forth and protect an unpopular people; who, at many instances, aided in the drivings, persecutions, and prosecuting labor lo, these many years, yea, even one hundred and eighty years since my Church was organized in the nation of constitutional guarantee of religious freedom, of pure freedom, to voice belief, without harm coming upon them; yet you protect not my people and my Church, because you claim

they are law-breaking people for living my holy Eternal Union Marriage Law of Celestial Plural Holy Union.

59. Let my people be free to live my holy law, lest judgments come in full way, to you no longer being a power to oppose me and my Zion, to no longer be a land of persecution, to no longer be a people of pure government of freedom powers, because leaders do not uphold constitutional law.

60. Let this truth be heeded by judges, President, Congress, all branches of governing power on thy land.

61. Let Canada be warned to not persecute my holy law and Church among you.

62. I shall turn on your own heads pure judgment of thy own intent against my people and Church; to humble all with the war soon coming on thy own land; verily it shall be so.

63. Let all be preparing for thy God to intervene, by correcting thyselves, thy rulers, thy evil ways now no longer followed.

64. Thy pride as a nation is of over-towering height, soon to fall by my power eternal.

65. Let all beware.

66. Let all become more pure, more holy, more of upholding virtue and innocence, of preserving life, even of unborn children.

67. This evil of unborn children being murdered, even by government consent, bringeth a judgment of a just God of Creation on all peoples.

68. This causes you to be nations of murdering way.

69. Thus it is. Amen.

70. Let this be my final full way of pure truth, telling all peoples to repent, to aid my servant to go free, to allow my Church freedom of religion, as guaranteed to all religions by governing pure principled powers of the nation on my holy land of Zion; a New Jerusalem soon to rise without opposition, because I, your God, provide full power of deliverance, and no one can stay my hand.

71. You are all my creations.

72. Nothing can stay my hand from taking whom I will in death.

73. Let all beware, lest you corrupt the way before yourselves, bringing eternal damnation upon you, even a punishment of suffering for sins of thy knowing.

74. Now my own will has been made known to all nations.

75. Let this be thy now full awakening to eternity truth, that all will have to answer for deeds and desires done on the earth, before a just and holy God, who has all things pure, holy, noble, righteous in His power, to judge a pure, holy, noble righteous way, all peoples of all generations.

76. Now receive this, my holy will, to let my servant Warren Jeffs, also Merril Jessop and their innocent brethren in prison, in a country now proving no religious free way is in thy land; to be of a letting go unto freedom, unto my right to rule; even more so than the rule of man's governing power.

77. Let pure religion alone, ye rulers and judges.

78. Let my holy religion be full free to live Celestial laws of pure holy revealed pure holy laws

only pertaining to those of my Church, who seek to live those eternal laws, who only are of peace, pure way of living.

79. The lies of apostates are believed by wicked powers in power, and by people of juries who listen.

80. Let it now be of truth telling: The false witnesses are of lying way; they once having been of truth living the very eternal laws of holy religion, then turned therefrom because of their own corrupt way.

81. Thus it is now. They are guilty of now being unjust persecuting power using governing powers in way of prosecuting power to harm my people of my Church.

82. No victims are harmed, thus not being a victim; yet courts sentence innocent men to full lifetime sentence in prison for only living their holy religion, is the pure truth.

83. I, Jesus Christ, am the Author of this holy religion.

84. I am the God of Abraham, Isaac, and Jacob, mine Israel.

85. They also lived these eternal ways.

86. Now this nation seeks to hinder my people from earning full Celestial power salvation.

87. How can you be justified when I, God, have commanded them to live this holy eternal law, which can only be guided and governed by your Lord, through His appointed and ordained holy authority on earth.

88. This earth is mine, saith the Lord.

89. Believe principles of pure truth; that marriage is of pure religion, since the time I put Adam and Eve together to people the earth; a religious principle eternal.

90. You are breaking thine own national laws when you hinder a religion from obeying righteous holy way.

91. Let this be a full reversing; these unjust laws against my holy law Celestial Union Law of Marriage, a holy law of my revealing, of my holy authority being full authority to bless unions to be eternal; all of me, even your Lord.

92. This is my holy way to call on all powers of governing to be of protecting religious freedom in the nation of guarantee of religious freedom.

93. Now heed my word.

94. I shall soon sweep this unholy, most wicked generation off my land of Zion with the besom of whirlwind judgments, soon of full power.

95. Thy people have seen me send tornados of full destructive power show to all complete judgment, nothing but rubble remaining.

96. How can your puny arm of flesh withstand my almighty power?

97. The whirlwind power is an ensample of all my cleansing powers eternal.

98. Let all see this life of earthly existence is temporary, and of my power to tell length of living on earth for every individual.

99. Now be repenting unto more pure works.

100. Let all be of holy way.

101. Let all be pure in heart, that my holy people can be also of an example of Zion, my own holy power on earth from heaven, come to redeem all mankind of all ages of time.

102. Let this truth tell all I can administer eternal life gifts, even to people of past ages and nations now as organized spirit people awaiting the holy resurrection, by first receiving eternal blessings of my own revealing to my authority on earth, who is worthy for blessings Celestial, unto eternal lives.

103. Thus, thy God is Just, Eternal, Holy, Pure, Noble, Righteous, Peace and Pure Way of Eternal Power of Governing Way over all nations.

104. Thus, I have now given full way justification to let my servant and my servants in prison house go free; also to let my people of my holy revealed religion on earth be of full free way.

105. Let all now be warned: Those places of prosecuting zeal against my holy religion shall be of no power to do so again.

106. Let them cease such unholy way of persecuting innocent people, when thy nation reeks in the blood of innocence of murder of unborn children through adultery and Sodom rampant on the land among all other peoples and religions.

107. Now cleanse thine own households of thine own begetting, of thy schools and governing powers; thy laws of corrupt way allowing immoral way to go unchecked; yet my innocent people are imprisoned for pure way of living; no crime, no corrupt way, no evil way among those who are of my Celestial Law, who are holy in practice of my holy law of my own holy power among them, judging each person who is of full way receiving my Celestial Law, unfettered by evil powers, governing powers and persecuting powers; to be of full freedom of religious living their only motive.

108. Now be of truth: Prosecutors lie. Witnesses lie.

109. My people go to prison because of lies told and believed in court of unjust way.

110. I caused my own word to be read in open court, telling these truths when my servant stood alone to voice the truth of unjust way of court proceedings, of the power to stop religious pure holy way being of ignoble attack in open court, defiling sacredness of my holy religion.

111. Thus, court shall be of full receiving my judging of eternal power in day to come, when all shall stand before me, even your Holy Redeemer, to be judged.

112. All shall know unobstructed truth then, when they stand before a just holy God to be of full way power to render true justice.

113. Let all be careful how they are of a way of believing lying court and prosecuting power; for my law is only holy, pure, noble, and of Celestial power; not of man, nor of the world; only to be of full way holy knowledge to obedient sons and daughters to my eternal law of Celestial Plural Union Marriage; my own way in heaven.

114. Thus I revealed this to my servant Joseph Smith over one hundred seventy years ago.

115. Let this truth be told: My law is of pure religious motive, no evil intent nor practice.

116. All must be pure to live my law, to be of receiving my Celestial Law and gifts of happiness therein.

117. This truth apostate lying witnesses know, who themselves sinned against my holy Celestial Law, to follow practices of immoral way of this wicked generation.

118. You who dwell in corrupting ways and unholy practices set up yourselves as judges of the

most holy pure way of living my Celestial Law of eternal exalting authority for obedient sons and daughters.

119. Now receive my full warning.

120. My coming is soon to take place.

121. I shall reward all for deeds and desires done in the flesh on earth.

122. You cannot escape my all-seeing eye.

123. I know all things.

124. I am to bring all to full power judging of their individual lives.

125. Be ye pure, to stand before a holy God, to be of happiness on earth, and hereafter, in eternal world of glory, my heaven coming to earth to build New Jerusalem, my Zion, prophesied of by all holy Prophets of my sending; whose record is in Bible to thy easy reading; which gift I preserved through mine Israel; a people soon to be gathered to Zion, notwithstanding all opposition.

126. Be ye ready.

127. Great changes on my land of my holy New Jerusalem, on the surface thereof, soon cometh; even present cities, many to be of full cleansing, to be without inhabitant; yea, great and notable cities now on my land of Zion shall be sunk in the earth, or covered by mountains; or sunk in the sea; some destroyed by my eternal fire; some of the destruction by war, mob rule rising in many places; leaders of governing power without power to govern; armies left desolate; places of more wicked way destroyed in full.

128. Such shall be where they of full hatred against my holy law of Celestial Eternal Union of my Eternal Order of Marriage of Plural living in holy order of pure noble way; yea, those who thus seek to destroy my holy law and authority shall be of full receiving of my judgment.

129. Let all these truths settle on the mind of each; even to awake all people unto full way power to repent; unto my holy way becoming the way of salvation to all honest in heart everywhere.

130. Let this be my holy word eternal, to be of full weight on each who is of this present generation, to be of full authority to judge all; yea, all now on my land of Zion having within reach my holy word; both my word of generations past in Bible recording, also my word in Book of . Mormon, Doctrine and Covenants, Pearl of Great Price; now my new published word mailed of recent time to all peoples in all nations.

131. Thus I am doing my work of pure holy justice, unto full power of judgments, being the God of Creation, whose right it is to rule.

132. Thus I am doing all things righteous and holy, to be of full power justified to render full judgment here and hereafter.

133. Be ye pure. Be ye clean in morals.

134. No one need destroy themselves.

135. All can choose to do good, and eschew evil, even now.

136. Let all religions be of truth.

137. Let all tell truth, they receive not mine own revealed word for thy Lord unto the people of their religious group or order.

138. None can name my will; only my holy power attending my Mouthpiece.

139. Let all be of truth; they have not authority from God to administer eternal salvation to any on earth.

140. Such was the first revealing to my holy servant Joseph Smith, Jun., in 1820, when God, the Father, and His Only Begotten Son, Jesus Christ, appeared to him in a sacred grove, after he was of full faith.

141. I gave him my eternal authority called Priesthood.

142. I caused him to know of Celestial Plural Eternal Union of pure living marriage, a most holy law requiring purity of living entire.

143. Let this most wicked generation be of receiving truth: You of corrupt way persecute my pure way of pure revealed holy way of my Church.

144. Now cease thy folly.

145. Your laws against my Celestial Law of Eternal Union Marriage of Celestial Plural Union are unjust from the beginning.

146. Congress and President in each time of passing these unjust rulings of man's law were purposeful attacks against my holy law and religion.

147. I am of full way power to set all right; even by removing from the earth all wicked and evil-practicing immoral people; to preserve mine elect who do abide my holy law in full way Celestial power. Amen.

148. Let also this be published to all peoples in every land and nation, to learn truth of my glorious coming as both a Holy Redeemer, also the Righteous Judge over all peoples; soon to send, before my coming in full power glory eternal Celestial authority, full judgments of cleansing power on all nations; which promise I gave in the New Testament, even in Matthew 24; also in Doctrine and Covenants, also in my holy true book called Book of Mormon; all telling same truth of my coming; first sending whirlwind judgments.

149. Let all know I am God who speaketh, who tells only truth; who is of full power Celestial to do all as I have spoken.

150. Now receive my word.

151. Obey my will, to abide the day of my coming. Amen.

Revelation of the Lord Jesus Christ Given to President Warren S. Jeffs

Palestine, Texas
Tuesday, November 8, 2011

1. I, your Lord Jesus Christ, speak to appeals court, my own will, to have true justice administered; to have unjust imprisonment of my servant reversed, he of free way; also to release my other servants in the unjust holding in prison who only obey my will in abiding Celestial Law of my holy Order Eternal.

2. Now receive my own word; also appendix of my own will of Proclamation to governing powers as testimony of my own right to rule over all nations; thus court of prosecuting power

is of no jurisdiction in cases brought before court; also unjust ruling to cause no religious protection.

3. Let appeals court now consider my will:

Revelation of the Lord Jesus Christ
Given to President Warren S. Jeffs

Palestine, Texas
Thursday, October 13, 2011

1. I, even Jesus Christ, speak to the present judge over court proceedings against my servant Warren Jeffs: I cause him to no longer be of an answering of your unjust and corrupt and unauthorized rulings; as I, the Lord, even Jesus Christ, am above all, and my law is religious and of me, a heavenly power over all creation.

2. Your judging is not based on truth.

3. I cause him to not answer to the court.

4. Let thy rulings against him cease.

5. I shall soon lay a heavy hand on all who fight against my Priesthood and Church, saith the Lord.

6. Now know I am God, even above all, and court of persecution shall be of a ceasing in my way of eternal power taking a hand if you will continue unjust way. Amen.

> Holy Power Celestial of the Domain of Ahman in my own Kingdom Son Ahman

In behalf of Jesus Christ, Warren Jeffs is to sign for court to know I represent our Lord.

_____

President Warren S. Jeffs, President of Church of Jesus Christ
Servant of Jesus Christ